D0301705

HERIOT-WATT UNIVERSITY LIBRARY

WITHDRAWN

TRANSPORT PHENOMENA
A Unified Approach

McGraw-Hill Chemical Engineering Series

Editorial Advisory Board

James J. Carberry, *Professor of Chemical Engineering, University of Notre Dame*
James R. Fair, *Professor of Chemical Engineering, University of Texas, Austin*
William P. Schowalter, *Professor of Chemical Engineering, Princeton University*
Matthew Tirrell, *Professor of Chemical Engineering, University of Minnesota*
James Wei, *Professor of Chemical Engineering, Massachusetts Institute of Technology*

Max S. Peters, *Emeritus Professor of Chemical Engineering, University of Colorado*

BUILDING THE LITERATURE OF A PROFESSION

Fifteen prominent chemical engineers first met in New York more than 60 years ago to plan a continuing literature for their rapidly growing profession. From industry came such pioneer practitioners as Leo H. Baekeland, Arthur D. Little, Charles L. Reese, John V. N. Dorr, M. C. Whitaker, and R. S. McBride. From the universities came such eminent educators as William H. Walker, Alfred H. White, D. D. Jackson, J. H. James, Warren K. Lewis, and Harry A. Curtis. H. C. Parmelee, then editor of *Chemical and Metallurgical Engineering,* served as chairman and was joined subsequently by S. D. Kirkpatrick as consulting editor.

After several meetings, this committee submitted its report to the McGraw-Hill Book Company in September 1925. In the report were detailed specifications for a correlated series of more than a dozen texts and reference books which have since become the McGraw-Hill Series in Chemical Engineering and which became the cornerstone of the chemical engineering curriculum.

From this beginning there has evolved a series of texts surpassing by far the scope and longevity envisioned by the founding Editorial Board. The McGraw-Hill Series in Chemical Engineering stands as a unique historical record of the development of chemical engineering education and practice. In the series one finds the milestones of the subject's evolution: industrial chemistry, stoichiometry, unit operations and processes, thermodynamics, kinetics, and transfer operations.

Chemical engineering is a dynamic profession, and its literature continues to evolve. McGraw-Hill and its consulting editors remain committed to a publishing policy that will serve, and indeed lead, the needs of the chemical engineering profession during the years to come.

THE SERIES

Bailey and Ollis: *Biochemical Engineering Fundamentals*
Bennett and Myers: *Momentum, Heat, and Mass Transfer*
Beveridge and Schechter: *Optimization: Theory and Practice*
Brodkey and Hershey: *Transport Phenomena: A Unified Approach*
Carberry: *Chemical and Catalytic Reaction Engineering*
Coughanowr and Koppel: *Process Systems Analysis and Control*
Edgar and Himmelblau: *Optimization of Chemical Processes*
Fahien: *Fundamentals of Transport Phenomena*
Finlayson: *Nonlinear Analysis in Chemical Engineering*
Gates, Katzer, and Schuit: *Chemistry of Catalytic Processes*
Holland: *Fundamentals of Multicomponent Distillation*
Holland and Liapis: *Computer Methods for Solving Dynamic Separation Problems*
Katz, Cornell, Kobayashi, Poettmann, Vary, Elenbaas, and Weinaug:
  Handbook of Natural Gas Engineering
King: *Separation Processes*
Luyben: *Process Modeling, Simulation, and Control for Chemical Engineers*
McCabe, Smith, J. C., and Harriott: *Unit Operations of Chemical Engineering*
Mickley, Sherwood, and Reed: *Applied Mathematics in Chemical Engineering*
Nelson: *Petroleum Refinery Engineering*
Perry and Chilton (Editors): *Chemical Engineers' Handbook*
Peters: *Elementary Chemical Engineering*
Peters and Timmerhaus: *Plant Design and Economics for Chemical Engineers*
Probstein and Hicks: *Synthetic Fuels*
Reid, Prausnitz, and Sherwood: *The Properties of Gases and Liquids*
Resnick: *Process Analysis and Design for Chemical Engineers*
Satterfield: *Heterogeneous Catalysis in Practice*
Sherwood, Pigford, and Wilke: *Mass Transfer*
Smith, B. D.: *Design of Equilibrium Stage Processes*
Smith, J. M.: *Chemical Engineering Kinetics*
Smith, J. M., and Van Ness: *Introduction to Chemical Engineering Thermodynamics*
Treybal: *Mass Transfer Operations*
Valle-Riestra: *Project Evolution in the Chemical Process Industries*
Van Ness and Abbott: *Classical Thermodynamics of Nonelectrolyte Solutions:*
  With Applications to Phase Equilibria
Van Winkle: *Distillation*
Volk: *Applied Statistics for Engineers*
Walas: *Reaction Kinetics for Chemical Engineers*
Wei, Russell, and Swartzlander: *The Structure of the Chemical Processing Industries*
Whitwell and Toner: *Conservation of Mass and Energy*

TRANSPORT PHENOMENA
A Unified Approach

Robert S. Brodkey

The Ohio State University

Harry C. Hershey

The Ohio State University

McGraw-Hill Book Company

New York   St. Louis   San Francisco   Auckland   Bogotá   Hamburg
London   Madrid   Mexico   Milan   Montreal   New Delhi   Panama
Paris   São Paulo   Singapore   Sydney   Tokyo   Toronto

25-65936oy

This book was set in Times Roman.
The editor was B. J. Clark;
the production supervisor was Denise L. Puryear;
the cover designer was Stephanie Blumenthal.
Project supervision was done by Universities Press, Belfast.
R. R. Donnelley & Sons Company was printer and binder.

TRANSPORT PHENOMENA
A Unified Approach

Copyright © 1988 by McGraw-Hill, Inc. All rights reserved. Printed in the United
States of America. Except as permitted under the United States Copyright Act of 1976,
no part of this publication may be reproduced or distributed in any form or by any
means, or stored in a data base or retrieval system, without the prior written permission
of the publisher.

234567890 DOC DOC 8921098

ISBN 0-07-007963-3

Library of Congress Cataloging-in-Publication Data

Brodkey, Robert S.
   Transport phenomena.

   (McGraw-Hill chemical engineering series)
   Bibliography: p.
   Includes index.
   1. Transport theory.   I. Hershey, Harry C.
II. Title.   III. Series
TP156.T7B76   1988   660.2'842   86-34414
ISBN 0-07-007963-3

CONTENTS

Part II   Applications of Transport Phenomena

Part III Transport Property

Appendixes

PREFACE

After publication of the pioneering book *Transport Phenomena* by Bird, Stewart, and Lightfoot in 1960, educators everywhere recognized that the previous "unit operations–unit processes" organization of material for the curricula of chemical engineers was inadequate for modern engineering education. Many schools found that the 1960 book was suitable for graduate courses and an excellent reference, but too difficult for most undergraduates, especially if the course was offered early in the curriculum. Others followed this pioneering effort by writing simpler versions.

This book was designed to provide an integrated treatment of the three areas of transport: momentum, heat, and mass. The similarities and the differences of the three transports are clearly stated at a level suitable for second-semester sophomores and first-semester juniors in engineering or the other sciences where the mathematics requirement is similar. Many of the basic equations are mathematically identical, when expressed in terms of the generalized flux and property variables. This identity helps the student understand transport phenomena and forms the basis for the organization of the material here. A typical curriculum teaches momentum transfer before heat and mass because a complete treatment of these latter two is not possible without a prior discussion of fluid dynamics. This text allows heat transfer, which is encountered daily by everyone and easily visualized, to explain by analogy momentum transfer, which is not easily visualized or understood by neophytes. Transport is rapidly becoming more widely used in most branches of engineering, and this text provides all engineering disciplines with a readable and otherwise useful treatment of this difficult subject. In most of the other books on this subject, these topics are covered separately.

We believe that this text provides a solid foundation for engineering design and research. At the same time, some interesting and important problems are solved. A study of transport phenomena does not replace unit operations, but understanding of transport phenomena provides deeper insight into the fundamental processes occurring in the unit operations. The engineer who masters the material in this text will be better able to analyze the unit operations he or she encounters.

McGraw-Hill and the authors would like to express their thanks for the many useful comments and suggestions provided by colleagues who reviewed this text during the course of its development, especially Charles E. Hamrin, Jr., University of Kentucky; Richard W. Mead, University of New Mexico; Robert Powell, University of California-Davis; and James Wei, Massachusetts Institute of Technology.

Finally, the authors owe much thanks to many who have helped over the years with this project. A partial list (in alphabetical order) includes F. Bavarian, A. M. Cameron, J. F. Davis, L. Economikos, L. S. Fan, L. Fishler, K. S. Knaebel, S. G. Nychas, J. Y. Oldshue, C. E. Patch, A. Syverson, G. B. Tatterson, J. L. Zakin, and the many typists who have helped with this effort, especially Pat Osborn.

Robert S. Brodkey
Harry C. Hershey

TO THE INSTRUCTOR

This text covers transport phenomena in an integrated manner. It is our opinion that a solid understanding of fluid mechanics is essential to understanding and solving problems in heat and mass transport. Hence, all topics suitable for a course in undergraduate fluid mechanics are covered in detail. This text introduces the basic equations of heat and mass transfer as well. This text also covers heat and mass transport applications that are in the transport phenomena area. It does not cover topics that are traditionally taught as unit operations. It is expected that the students will purchase a unit operations book for course work and reference beyond our coverage.

After the introductory chapter, the basic equations of molecular transport are covered first, then the general property balance, followed by the combination of the balance and molecular transport. The topic of convection is in Chapter 5. Our treatment is especially strong in discerning the differences between transport problems with flow but no net convective flux, and those with a net convective flux. Chapter 5 also contains a lengthy section on the fundamentals of mass transport phenomena. Chapter 6 on turbulent flow provides a thorough discussion of modern turbulence theory. There are also two chapters (7 and 8) on methods of analysis—integral methods and dimensional and modeling approaches. Dimensional analysis is applied to agitation in Chapter 9. The remaining chapters contain advanced applications. Chapters 10 and 11 cover transport in ducts. Flow past immersed bodies and fluidization are discussed in Chapter 12. Chapter 13 covers unsteady-state transport phenomena. Chapter 14 covers the estimation of the transport properties μ, k, and D_{AB}; this chapter can be covered in conjunction with Chapter 2, or anything thereafter, as the instructor wishes. Chapter 15 on non-Newtonian phenomena is unique in that this important topic is largely ignored in other texts. This chapter also can be covered whenever the instructor wishes; at Ohio State, we have found that our students cannot really appreciate non-Newtonian flow until they understand Newtonian flow. Hence, we teach Chapter 15 in conjunction with Chapter 10. If the instructor desires to cover only the laminar aspects of non-Newtonianism, the appropriate material from Chapter 15 could be taught much earlier in the course. The appendix is in five parts: properties of materials, mechanical characteristics of piping and tubing, conversion tables, vector mathematics, and a list of computer programs.

Taken as a whole, this text covers the area of fluid mechanics thoroughly. The basic equations of change are in the early chapters. Laminar flow solutions are found in both Chapters 4 and 5 on molecular and convective transport. The sections on agitation, turbulence, and fluidization contain the most modern concepts and procedures. Fluid statics is covered in Chapter 7 on integral methods, where it arises naturally from the general integral balance equations. Advanced topics include discussions of design of complex piping systems, the boundary layer, ideal flow, flow past immersed bodies such as spheres and cylinders, fluidization, packed beds, banks of tubes, and non-Newtonian fluids. The inclusion of an entire chapter on non-Newtonian transport phenomena is an indication of the importance of this subject to chemical engineers; non-Newtonian fluids are encountered daily in our lives, as well as being common in industry. The engineer needs some familiarity with this area.

The topics of heat and mass transfer are covered only to the extent that transport phenomena can be applied. Excellent books exist for these topics, especially for heat transfer, for which our colleagues in mechanical engineering have written well-conceived textbooks. In 1984 and 1985, three major books on mass transfer were published. Because heat and momentum transport are so closely linked, a weakness of many heat transfer texts lies in their limited treatment of the fluid mechanics topics needed for heat-exchanger design. Our integrated approach is intended to explain fully the coupled nature of heat and momentum transport. The heat transport and momentum transport equations are presented together for laminar applications, turbulent flow, flow past immersed bodies, fluidized beds, etc. Similarly, the basic equations for mass transport are integrated with those for heat and momentum. Chapter 5 discusses mass transport phenomena in detail, including the additional complexities inherent in mass diffusion. The presentation is in a clear fashion that undergraduates can understand, especially the reasons why the mass diffusion equations as simplified for gases do not strictly apply to liquid systems. The basic principle of diffusion in solids is also covered; this topic is important in catalysis, and other areas as well. The unsteady-state chapter combines heat and mass transfer and includes the modern numerical methods as the Crank–Nicolson.

Our text is expected to serve widely as a reference. Hence, more material and more detail have been included than undergraduates can usually assimilate. At the Ohio State University, this text is used for a 4-credit-hour, one-quarter course, in transport phenomena which is offered to sophomores who have completed differential equations, freshman chemistry, stoichiometry, and two quarters of physics. In our course, the material in Chapters 1 to 8 is covered in detail. The topics of agitation (Chapter 9) is covered rapidly. The design material in Chapters 10 and 12 occupy the last part of the course. Chapter 15 on non-Newtonian phenomena is covered briefly after Chapter 10 on fluid flow in ducts. Our thermodynamics course, usually taken later or concurrently, emphasizes the applications of the first law to flow problems. Note that this material is in Chapter 7 in our text and in Chapter 2 in *Introduction to Chemical Engineering Thermodynamics* by Smith and Van Ness. Fluid statics is also covered at the start of the thermodynamics course. At Ohio State, a second course in transport focuses entirely on heat transfer; that course covers Chapter 11 in detail plus, of course, much more. That second course requires the students to purchase a specialized heat transfer text (usually a mechanical engineering series) in order to cover the specialized topics in heat transfer, such as radiation, boiling, and condensation.

Further topics in mass transfer can be taught in an additional course or courses that combine discussions of mass transfer with unit operations not previously covered, such as absorption, distillation, drying, evaporation, and filtration. The basic material for mass diffusion is in Section 5.3; most of the material presented is not covered in the traditional unit operations texts. Again, the analogy with heat and momentum assists the student in understanding the difficult concepts in mass diffusion.

In solving the example problems, we used a computer or a hand-held calculator. Calculations with these retain many digits in order to reduce truncation errors. The example problems in this text make no serious effort to ascertain the correct number of significant digits for every final answer, inasmuch as the purpose of the examples is to illustrate the method of calculation. The instructor should point out from time to time the probable accuracy of final answers, especially when the physical constants (such as mass diffusivity) are not usually known accurately or approximate methods of solution are used. Also, many of the example problems and homework problems in this text have been in use at Ohio State for more than 20 years. Hence, their origins are obscure. We sincerely apologize if we have inadvertently used problems that originated with someone else.

A book on transport phenomena always encounters nomenclature problems, because the three areas of transport developed independently in the early days. A problem of more recent vintage is the decision of the American Institute of Physics to switch the viscosity notation from μ to η. Chemical Engineers have used μ from the beginning; this text will also use μ, although the instructor may wish to point out that the other symbol is also recommended by some.

Finally, there are some excellent films available, which illustrate most of the important topics in fluid mechanics. The Encyclopaedia Britannica Educational Corporation, 425 North Michigan Avenue, Chicago, IL, 60611 has available for purchase or loan twenty-two 16-mm films and a hundred thirty-three 8-mm film loops as a part of their fluid mechanics program. At the Ohio State University, we use the 8-mm loops, which are shown with a small portable projector and lend themselves easily to informal discussion. These film loops are referenced by number at the appropriate locations in the text.

Robert S. Brodkey
Harry C. Hershey

TRANSPORT PHENOMENA
A Unified Approach

PART

I

BASIC
CONCEPTS
IN TRANSPORT
PHENOMENA

CHAPTER
1

INTRODUCTION TO TRANSPORT PHENOMENA

NOMENCLATURE

A	Area (m^2, ft^2)
a	Acceleration ($m\,s^{-2}$, $ft\,s^{-2}$)
C_A	Concentration of species A ($kmol\,m^{-3}$, $lb\,mol\,ft^{-3}$)
F	Force (N, lb_f)
g_c	Gravitational conversion constant ($32.174\,lb_m\,lb_f^{-1}\,ft\,s^{-2}$)
m	Mass (kg, lb_m)
n	Number of moles of gas (kmol, lb mol)
p	Pressure (kPa, atm, $lb_f\,in.^{-2}$)
R	Gas constant, see Appendix, Table C.1
T	Temperature (K, °R, °C, °F)
V	Volume (m^3, ft^3)
x	Unknown in algebraic equation
y	Unknown in algebraic equation
z	Unknown in algebraic equation
τ	Shear stress ($N\,m^{-2}$, $lb_f\,ft^{-2}$)

This chapter provides a brief introduction to the material to be covered in detail in subsequent chapters. First, a brief historical perspective of the role of transport phenomena in the solution of engineering problems is discussed.

Then some fundamental concepts from physics, chemistry, and mathematics are presented.

1.1 TRANSPORT PHENOMENA AND UNIT OPERATIONS

The pioneering work *Principles of Chemical Engineering* was published in 1923 under the authorship of Walker, Lewis, and McAdams [W1]. This book was the first to emphasize the concept of unit operations as a fundamental approach to physical separations such as distillation, evaporation, drying, etc. This was the era when the profession of chemical engineering matured into a separate area, no longer the province of the industrial chemist. The study of unit operations such as distillation is predicated on the idea that similarities in equipment and fundamentals exist regardless of the process. In other words, the principles of distillation apply equally to the separation of liquid oxygen from liquid nitrogen as well as to the thousands of other distillations routinely carried out in industries around the world. The study of transport phenomena is undertaken because this topic is the basis for most of the unit operations. In simple terms, transport phenomena comprise three topics: heat transfer, mass transfer, and momentum transfer (fluid flow). In many of the unit operations (such as distillation), all three transport phenomena (i.e., fluid flow, heat transfer, and mass transfer) occur, often simultaneously. The concepts presented in transport phenomena underly the empirical procedures that are used in the design of unit operations. Empiricism is required because the exact equations cannot be solved.

1.2 EQUILIBRIUM AND RATE PROCESSES

Many problems can conveniently be divided into two classifications: equilibrium and nonequilibrium. Under conditions of nonequilibrium, one or more variables change with time. The rates of these changes are of much interest, naturally. A typical engineer-scientist reading this book will be involved with four types of rate processes: rate of heat transfer, rate of mass transfer, rate of momentum transfer, and rate of reaction. The first three of these are the subject of this text. The fourth, rate of reaction, will not be covered in any detail, except for the inclusion of the appropriate terms in the general equations and in a few elementary examples.

Equilibrium processes. The science of thermodynamics deals mainly with systems in equilibrium. Consider Fig. 1.1 which shows a gas composed of 50 mole percent nitrogen and 50 mole percent oxygen enclosed in a tank at a pressure of 2 atm at 300 K. Let this gas be surrounded by ambient air at the same temperature. After an appropriately long time, the gas inside the tank is at physical equilibrium. Its temperature is the same as that of the surrounding

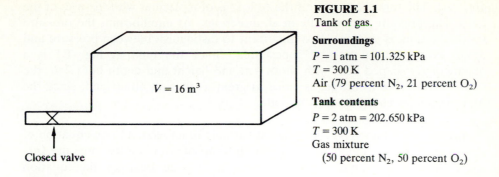

FIGURE 1.1
Tank of gas.

Surroundings
$P = 1$ atm $= 101.325$ kPa
$T = 300$ K
Air (79 percent N_2, 21 percent O_2)

Tank contents
$P = 2$ atm $= 202.650$ kPa
$T = 300$ K
Gas mixture
    (50 percent N_2, 50 percent O_2)

gas, 300 K. Inside the tank, there will be no concentration gradients. The science of chemistry tells us that this gas will not be in chemical equilibrium. Although oxygen and nitrogen can form a series of compounds, such as N_2O, NO, NO_2, and N_2O_5, in actuality none of these is formed in the present system because the rate of reaction is essentially zero. If the gas in the tank were pure nitrogen, then there would be complete equilibrium inside the tank, i.e., physical (often called mechanical) and chemical equilibrium.

Rate processes. When nonequilibrium processes are considered, the system under consideration progresses in a manner such as to approach equilibrium. All such rate processes are characterized by a driving force. The rate of transport is proportional to the driving force. The topic will be discussed thoroughly in Chapter 2.

1.3 FUNDAMENTAL VARIABLES AND UNITS

Temperature. Interestingly, temperature (T) can be defined only in the empirical sense as a relative measure of "hotness" [D1, M1]. The temperature scales in present use are defined with only one fixed point, the triple point of water, 273.16 K. Temperature scales are based on changes in properties of materials with temperature. The change of resistivity of a solid such as platinum or the change of volume of a liquid such as mercury is easily measured as a function of temperature, and therefore can be used as an indication of temperature. Temperature units are Kelvin (K), Celsius (°C), Fahrenheit (°F), and Rankine (°R). The reader already knows how to convert from one to the other. Temperature is one of the most important quantities in a system. Temperature manifests itself in the motions of the molecules: the higher the temperature, the higher are the velocities of the molecules. Almost all properties are strongly dependent on temperature. The rate processes are likewise functions of temperature.

Pressure. The pressure in the tank in Fig. 1.1 has units of force (F) per unit area (A). The force is a result of the collisions of molecules with the wall of the tank. The pressure acts equally in all directions. At equilibrium, the pressure inside the tank is uniform. It is important to distinguish between pressure and force. Force equals pressure times area. Since the tank in Fig. 1.1 is a rectangularly shaped box, with width 4 m and height and depth both 2 m, the total force on the front face is twice as great as that on either end, since the front area is twice the area of an end.

Volume. The volume (V) is the easiest variable to understand. An equation of state expresses the volume of a material in terms of temperature, pressure (p), and composition or total number of moles (n). For an ideal gas, the equation of state is

$$pV = nRT \tag{1.1}$$

where R is the gas constant (see Appendix, Table C.1).

Concentration. The concentration of species A (C_A) has units of moles (or mass) per volume. The following example illustrates concentration.

> **Example 1.1.** Calculate the concentration of nitrogen in the tank in Fig. 1.1, assuming that the ideal gas law holds. The answer is to be in lb mol ft^{-3}.
>
> **Answer.** The total volume of the tank is given as 0.01283 m^3, which in English units is 0.4531 ft^3 (using the conversion 35.316 ft^3 = 1 m^3 from the Appendix, Table C.18). The total number of pound moles is found from Eq. (1.1):
>
> $$n = (pV)/(RT) = (2)(0.4531)/[(0.73)(300)(1.8)] \frac{(\text{atm})(\text{ft}^3)}{\dfrac{(\text{atm})(\text{ft}^3)}{(\text{lb mol})(°\text{R})}(°\text{R})}$$
>
> $$= 2.299 \times 10^{-3} \text{ lb mol} \tag{i}$$
>
> where the gas constant R is from Table C.1. The temperature in K is multiplied by 1.8 to convert to °R. Since the mole fraction of N_2 is 0.5, then the amount of N_2 in the tank is 1.149×10^{-3} lb mol. Therefore the concentration is
>
> $$C_A = (1.149 \times 10^{-3})/(0.4531) \text{ (lb mol)}/(\text{ft}^3) = 2.54 \times 10^{-3} \text{ lb mol ft}^{-3} \tag{ii}$$

Shear stress. The shear stress (τ) is also a force per area, as is pressure. The shear stress may have components in any or all directions in contrast to pressure which acts in a direction normal to a surface. For now, let us consider a simple view of shear stress, Fig. 1.2. A block with an area of 2 m^2 is imbedded in a concrete floor. A force of 5 newtons is impressed against the side of a second block that is glued to the bottom block. The shear stress on the glue is 5 N per 2 m^2, or 2.5 N m^{-2}. The pressure on the glue is atmospheric pressure plus the weight of the block (due to gravity) divided by the area.

Flux. A flux is a certain quantity per unit area per unit time. Answers to

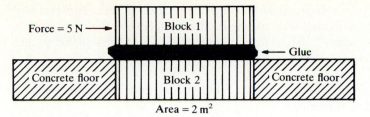

FIGURE 1.2
Shear stress and pressure.

problems in heat transfer are often expressed in units of Btu, cal, or J. Therefore, a heat flux may have units of $J\,m^{-2}\,s^{-1}$. Similarly, a mass flux may have units of $kg\,m^{-2}\,s^{-1}$.

Phases. In a simple view of matter, there are three states: solid, liquid, and gas. Any given system contains only one gas phase, but may possess several solid or liquid phases. For example, if a small amount of crude oil is added to a container half filled with water, then at equilibrium there are two liquid phases, water on the bottom and hydrocarbon floating on top, plus a vapor phase consisting of air, water molecules, and hydrocarbon molecules. Transport phenomena often occur in systems where several phases are present. Naturally, solutions of such problems are more complicated than solutions of single-phase problems.

Units. Engineers must be familiar with all systems of units. The abundance of tables in the literature that use English or CGS units requires all of us to be reasonably familiar with all systems of units. This text will use SI units (Système International d'Unités), as well as the traditional English system with units such as Btu, pound force (lb_f), and pound mass (lb_m).

In the SI system, mass in kilograms (kg), length in meters (m), time in seconds (s), and temperature in kelvins (K) are taken as basic units. Many other units are derived from these. In practice, some of the SI units are quite cumbersome. For example, the SI unit for pressure is the pascal (Pa), which is defined as $N\,m^{-2}$. One atmosphere is 101 325 Pa; obviously the use of the SI system is clumsy here. Some authors use the bar, which is 100 kPa or 0.986 923 atm. But one can argue that the bar is no more fundamental a unit than the atmosphere.

Another point of confusion in the use of SI units is in the definition of the mole. The basic SI unit is mol, which is defined as the amount of a species whose mass in grams is numerically equal to its molecular weight (also called its molar mass, symbol M). Thus 1 mol of a molecular substance always contains Avogadro's Number of molecules. Since most tables present molecular weights in units of $g\,mol^{-1}$, this SI unit is the same as the old "g-mole" unit. Since the SI unit of mass is the kilogram, many authors prefer the kmol unit (1000 mol) as the most practical for tables of properties, etc. This text will use kmol, as well as lb mol. For example, the molecular weight of CO_2 is approximately $44 \, kg \, kmol^{-1}$. Therefore, 1 kmol of CO_2 contains 44 000 g, and 1 lb mol of CO_2 contains $44 \, lb_m$.

Force. The relationship between force and mass may be expressed by Newton's second law of motion:

$$F = ma \tag{1.2}$$

where a is the acceleration. A conversion factor g_c is sometimes included to make Eq. (1.2) dimensionally consistent:

$$F = ma/g_c \tag{1.3}$$

Early authors called g_c the gravitational conversion constant or the standard gravitational constant. The origin of this nomenclature lies in the fact that the definition of the pound force (lb_f) in the English system of units is the force necessary to accelerate one pound mass (lb_m) in a standard gravitational field on earth. Thus in the English system, the constant g_c has the value $32.1740 \, lb_m \, lb_f^{-1} \, ft \, s^{-2}$. In spite of this origin, g_c is a conversion constant having the same value on the moon and everywhere else in the universe.[1]

In the SI system, two viewpoints of the role of g_c are prevalent. The unit of force is a derived unit from Eq. (1.2), i.e., $kg \, m \, s^{-2}$, which has been named the newton (N) in honor of Sir Isaac Newton. One view is that g_c equals $1.0 \, kg \, m \, N^{-1} \, s^{-2}$. A second interpretation is that g_c is really unity and dimensionless, since $1 \, N$ is identical to $1 \, kg \, m \, s^{-2}$. This text takes the latter view, and therefore g_c will be omitted from equations in the future.

Numerous example problems with English units have been included, in order to illustrate the proper use of g_c. Note that in the CGS system, the gram-force unit (analogous to the lb_f) is almost never used and, since the dyne is defined as $g \, cm \, s^{-2}$, when F is expressed in dynes, g_c is again unity and dimensionless.

Many equations in transport phenomena involve both lb_m and lb_f if English units are used. The reader must always be very careful to use consistent and correct units in all problems. Also, there are some unusual mass and force units in the English system, such as the slug ($lb_f \, s^2 \, ft^{-1}$), and the poundal ($lb_m \, ft \, s^{-2}$). Each of these is defined via Eq. (1.2). These will be ignored in this text.

---

[1] The acceleration due to gravity is approximately $32.174 \, ft \, s^{-2}$ here on earth. It is this value that changes from location to location. Its equivalent is $9.80665 \, m \, s^{-2}$ in the SI system or $980.665 \, cm \, s^{-2}$ in the CGS system.

1.4 THE ROLE OF INTERMOLECULAR FORCES

Intermolecular forces are responsible for the behavior of matter in the world around us. The balance between attractive (long-range) forces and repulsive (short-range) forces is responsible for the existence of the gas, the liquid, and the solid phases. Liquids and solids exist at the lower temperatures, at which the kinetic energy of the molecules is less than at higher temperatures at which only the gas phase can be present.

Intermolecular forces are also responsible for the transport phenomena. The basic equations for momentum, heat, and mass can be derived directly from the Boltzmann equation of statistical mechanics. This derivation is extremely complex [H1]. Any effort at an exact solution gives results so simplistic as to have no direct use in the solution of engineering problems. Instead, the following chapters will introduce transport phenomena via both empirical laws such as Newton's law of viscosity, and fundamental laws such as conservation of mass, momentum, and energy. The empirical nature of these laws obscures their molecular origin. The reader should always keep in mind that intermolecular forces are responsible for the phenomena at hand but that the exact equations are too difficult to solve.

1.5 SIMPLE BALANCES

Material balances. Perhaps most fundamental of the physical laws is the conservation of mass. The classic reference is in Chapter 7 of the text by Hougen, Watson, and Ragatz [H2], although more modern books are used today. The idea of conservation of mass is simple: the total mass entering (IN) must equal the total mass leaving (OUT)—unless there is generation, depletion, or accumulation. Generation or depletion might come from a nuclear reaction. For example, uranium-238 can decay upon emission of an α particle into thorium-234. An example of accumulation is the simple filling of a tank. The reader of this text is expected to be familiar with these types of balances, at least in a general manner.

> **Example 1.2.** The waste acid from a nitrating process contains 15 percent HNO_3, 45 percent H_2SO_4, and 40 percent H_2O by weight. This acid must be concentrated to 25 percent HNO_3, 50 percent H_2SO_4, and 25 percent H_2O. Available are concentrated solutions of acid in water, one of 95 percent H_2SO_4 and the other of 85 percent HNO_3. If 1500 kg of final product is required, find the mass of each concentrated solution to be added.
>
> **Answer.** In this problem, there is no accumulation or generation. The solution requires an overall mass balance, plus balances of two of the species—water, HNO_3, or H_2SO_4. All concentrations are known. All weight percentages are converted to weight fractions by dividing by 100. The convenient basis is to

consider 1500 kg of product. Convenient variables are as follows:

Let x = kg concentrated H_2SO_4, 5 percent H_2O

Let y = kg concentrated HNO_3, 15 percent H_2O

Let z = kg of waste acid before concentration.

Overall balance (IN = OUT)

$$x + y + z = 1500 \tag{i}$$

Water balance (H_2O IN = H_2O OUT)

$$0.05x + 0.15y + 0.40z = (1500)(0.25) \tag{ii}$$

H_2SO_4 balance (H_2SO_4 IN = H_2SO_4 OUT)

$$0.95x + 0.00y + 0.45z = (1500)(0.50) \tag{iii}$$

HNO_3 balance (HNO_3 IN = HNO_3 OUT)

$$0.00x + 0.85y + 0.15z = (1500)(0.25) \tag{iv}$$

Since the summation of Eqs. (ii), (iii), and (iv) results in Eq. (i), only three of Eqs. (i) through (iv) are independent. Arbitrarily, Eq. (iv) will not be used. Now Eqs. (i) through (iii) constitute three equations in three unknowns. Solution is by elimination of variables. First, Eq. (i) is solved for z and the results are substituted into Eqs. (ii) and (iii):

$$0.05x + 0.15y + (0.40)(1500 - x - y) = 375 \tag{v}$$

$$0.95x + (0.45)(1500 - x - y) = 750 \tag{vi}$$

Simplifying these:

$$0.35x + 0.25y = 225 \tag{vii}$$

$$0.50x - 0.45y = 75 \tag{viii}$$

Equation (viii) is multiplied by 2 and rearranged to

$$x = 150 + 0.90y \tag{ix}$$

This equation is substituted into Eq. (vii) and the result is solved for y. Then:

$$(0.35)(150 + 0.90y) + 0.25y = 225 \tag{x}$$

$$y = \frac{225 - (0.35)(150)}{(0.35)(0.90) + 0.25} = 305 \tag{xi}$$

From Eq. (xi), the amount of concentrated HNO_3 is 305 kg. From Eq. (ix), x, the amount of concentrated H_2SO_4, is 425 kg. The amount of waste acid is 770 kg [from Eq. (i)].

Energy balances. The principle of the energy balance is similar to the mass balance: IN equals OUT, if there is no accumulation or generation. However, in practice energy balances involve several more concepts not yet introduced. These will be explained thoroughly in Chapter 7 on Integral Methods. Briefly, either the first law of thermodynamics or the mechanical energy balance is needed in order to provide the correct relationship of the many terms in the energy balance: molecular (internal) energy, potential energy, kinetic energy, radiant energy, electrical energy, magnetic energy, chemical reaction effects, heat supplied from external sources, and work done.

A further consideration of Example 1.2 illustrates some of the complexities of the energy balance. Suppose in that example all three streams (waste, concentrated HNO_3, and concentrated H_2SO_4) were at 25°C. What would be the final temperature upon mixing? The answer requires knowledge of the "heat of mixing". When the concentrated acids are added to the waste stream, there will be a substantial temperature rise, owing to the large heats of mixing in this system.

PROBLEMS

1.1. If g equals 9.8 m s^{-2}, find the weight of a 20 kg object in units of: (a) N; (b) lb_f

1.2. The heat capacity of carbon dioxide gas at very low pressure is expressed by the equation

$$c_p = 10.57 + 0.0021T - (2.06 \times 10^5)T^{-2}$$

where c_p has units of $\text{cal mol}^{-1}\text{K}^{-1}$ and T is in K. What are the units of the constant of value 2.06×10^5?

1.3. Pure sulfur is burned with air at the rate of $400 \text{ lb}_m \text{ h}^{-1}$ of sulfur. The outlet gas is 10 percent O_2.
 (a) Find the number of lb mol of SO_2 produced per hour.
 (b) Find the number of ft^3h^{-1} of air required if the entering air is at 1 atm pressure and 100°F.

1.4. A waste acid stream (to be designated as stream W) contains 4 percent HNO_3, 20 percent H_2SO_4, and the rest water, by weight. A ton of acid of concentration 21 percent HNO_3 and 35 percent H_2SO_4 is required. Available are concentrated acid solutions as follows: stream A (92 percent H_2SO_4, 8 percent H_2O); stream B (81 percent HNO_3, 2 percent H_2SO_4, and 17 percent H_2O). Find the number of pounds of each concentrated solution to be added to make 1 ton of product.

1.5. Wet green lumber containing 12.5 percent moisture is fed continuously to a drying oven at a rate of 10 ton h^{-1}. The drying oven consists of two kilns, operated in series. From the first kiln the "partially dried" lumber is fed to a second. Tests on the second show that the final dried lumber leaving contains 4.0 percent moisture. Also, $650 \text{ lb}_m \text{ h}^{-1}$ of moisture are removed from the entering lumber in the second kiln.
 (a) Find the $\text{lb}_m \text{ h}^{-1}$ of "dried" lumber exiting from the second kiln.
 (b) Find the $\text{lb}_m \text{ h}^{-1}$ of water removed in the first kiln.
 (c) What is the percentage moisture in the "partially dried" lumber exiting from the first kiln?

1.6. Zinc is to be extracted from a roasted ore. All zinc is present as $ZnSO_4$. Roasted ore of the following composition is obtained: $ZnSO_4$ 18 percent; gangue 75 percent; moisture 7 percent. The roasted ore at a rate of 25 ton h^{-1} is extracted with pure water. The resulting solution containing 12 percent $ZnSO_4$ represents a 100 percent recovery of the $ZnSO_4$. One ton of inert gangue will carry with it 2 tons of solution. Calculate the $\text{lb}_m \text{ h}^{-1}$ of water required.

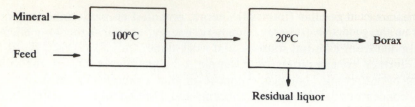

FIGURE 1.3
Process flow diagram for production of borax (Problem 1.8).

1.7. Peat as dug from the ground contains 88 percent moisture, 8.05 percent volatile combustible matter, 3.18 percent fixed carbon, and 0.77 percent ash. For use as a domestic fuel, the peat is dried until it contains 10 percent moisture. The cost of drying is 9 cents per 100 lb$_m$ water removed, and the cost of mining the peat is $7.58 per ton. Find the cost of processing 1 ton of dried peat.

1.8. Borax ($Na_2B_4O_7 \cdot 10H_2O$) is produced from a mineral containing 85 percent $Na_2B_4O_7 \cdot 4H_2O$ by dissolving in water under pressure at 100°C, filtering, and crystallizing at 20°C. The flow sheet for the process is shown in Fig. 1.3. The mineral is fed along with the water into a vessel at 100°C. When all the $Na_2B_4O_7 \cdot 4H_2O$ is dissolved, the solution passes to a second vessel where the temperature is lowered to 20°C. The borax is then filtered, leaving a residual liquor. The solubility of anhydrous sodium tetraborate is 52.5 parts per 100 parts water (by weight) at 100°C, and 3.9 parts per 100 at 20°C. For 1000 kg of borax produced, calculate the following:
(a) number of kg of mineral required
(b) number of kg of water used
(c) number of kg of residual liquor produced

1.9. Methanol is synthesized from carbon monoxide and hydrogen according to the reaction

$$CO + 2H_2 \rightarrow CH_3OH$$

The feed stream to a methanol plant consists of 250 kmol h^{-1} CO, 625 kmol h^{-1} H$_2$, and 50 kmol h^{-1} N$_2$. The process flow diagram for this process is shown in Fig. 1.4. The gross feed enters a reactor where the conversion per pass is 50 percent. The gross product stream enters a condenser where all the methanol is removed.

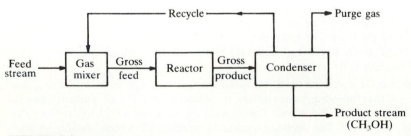

FIGURE 1.4
Process flow diagram for synthesis of methanol (Problem 1.9).

The unreacted gases are recycled to the gas mixer located just before the reactor. From the condenser, there is a purge stream which removes the inert nitrogen, plus some valuable CO and H_2. The concentrations in the purge stream are identical to those in the recycle line. If the ratio of moles of feed gas to moles of purge gas is 3.5, find the flow rate ($kmol\ h^{-1}$) of all components in all streams.

REFERENCES

D1. Denbigh, K.: *The Principles of Chemical Equilibrium,* 3d ed., Cambridge University Press, Cambridge, 1971.

H1. Hirschfelder, J. O., C. F. Curtiss, and R. B. Bird: *Molecular Theory of Gases and Liquids,* April 1967 printing, Wiley, New York, 1954.

H2. Hougen, O. A., K. M. Watson, and R. A. Ragatz: *Chemical Process Principles. Part 1 Material and Energy Balances,* 2d ed., Wiley, New York, 1954.

M1. Moore, W. J.: *Physical Chemistry,* 4th ed., Prentice-Hall, Englewood Cliffs, NJ, 1972.

W1. Walker, W. H., W. K. Lewis, and W. H. McAdams: *Principles of Chemical Engineering,* McGraw-Hill, New York, 1923.

CHAPTER 2

MOLECULAR TRANSPORT MECHANISMS

NOMENCLATURE

A	Area (m^2, ft^2)
A	Empirical constant in viscosity correlation, Eq. (2.52) ($kg\,m^{-1}\,s^{-1}$ or $N\,m^{-2}\,s$, $lb_m\,ft^{-1}\,s^{-1}$, $lb_f\,ft^{-2}\,s$)
A	Species A: A_1 and A_2 are species A at locations 1 and 2
B	Species B; subscripts 1 and 2 represent locations
B	Empirical constant in viscosity correlation, Eq. (2.52) (units same as RT)
C	Concentration ($kmol\,m^{-3}$, $lb\,mol\,ft^{-3}$); C_A and C_B are concentrations of species A and B; C_T is total concentration
c_p	Heat capacity at constant pressure ($kJ\,kg^{-1}\,K^{-1}$, $Btu\,lb_m^{-1}\,°F^{-1}$); c_v is heat capacity at constant volume
D	Diffusion coefficient (mass diffusivity) ($m^2\,s^{-1}$, $ft^2\,s^{-1}$); D_{AB} is diffusion coefficient for A in a mixture of A plus B; D_0 is diffusion coefficient at base temperature T_0 and pressure p_0
d	Diameter (m, ft)
e	Base of natural logarithm, 2.718 281 8. . .
F	Force (N, lb_f)
g	Acceleration due to gravitational field ($m\,s^{-2}$, $ft\,s^{-2}$)

g_c	Gravitational conversion constant ($32.174 \text{ lb}_m \text{ lb}_f^{-1} \text{ ft s}^{-2}$)
$\boldsymbol{i}$	Unit vector in x direction
J_A/A	Molar flux vector in Fick's law, Eq. (2.4), defined with respect to a plane of no net volume flow ($\text{kmol m}^{-2} \text{s}^{-1}$, $\text{lb mol ft}^{-2} \text{s}^{-1}$); subscripts A or B are for flux of species A or B; called J_A^v/A in Chapter 5
$(j_A/A)_x$	Mass flux of species A in the x direction, defined with respect to a plane of no net volume flow ($\text{kg m}^{-2} \text{s}^{-1}$, $\text{lb}_m \text{ft}^{-2} \text{s}^{-1}$)
$\boldsymbol{j}$	Unit vector in y direction
$\boldsymbol{k}$	Unit vector in z direction
k	Thermal conductivity ($\text{W m}^{-1} \text{K}^{-1}$ or $\text{J m}^{-1} \text{K}^{-1} \text{s}^{-1}$, $\text{Btu ft}^{-1} {}^\circ\text{R}^{-1} \text{s}^{-1}$)
L	Length (m, ft)
M_A	Molecular weight (molar mass) of species A (kg kmol^{-1}, $\text{lb}_m \text{ lb mol}^{-1}$)
m	Mass (kg, lb_m)
N_A	Molar flow vector for species A, defined with respect to fixed coordinates (kmol s^{-1}, lb mol s^{-1}); subscripts A or B are for species A or B; $(N_A/A)_x$ is the flux of species A in the x direction; N_B/A is the flux of species B
$\boldsymbol{n}$	Mass flow vector, equal to molar flow N times molecular weight M (kg s^{-1}, $\text{lb}_m \text{s}^{-1}$)
n	Number of moles of gas (kmol, lb mol)
p	Pressure (kPa, atm, $\text{lb}_f \text{in.}^{-2}$); p_0 is reference pressure at T_0; $\bar{p}_A$ is partial pressure of species A, Eq. (2.38)
q	Energy (heat) flow vector (J s^{-1}, Btu s^{-1})
R	Gas constant; see Appendix, Table C.1, for values
T	Temperature (K, ${}^\circ\text{R}$, ${}^\circ\text{C}$, ${}^\circ\text{F}$); T_0 is reference temperature for correlations; T_1 and T_2 are temperatures at locations 1 and 2
$^\text{T}$	Superscript meaning transpose of a tensor or matrix
t	Time (s); subscripts: t_0 is initial time; t_1 and t_2 are intermediate times, t_∞ is steady-state time
U	Velocity vector (m s^{-1}, ft s^{-1}); U is magnitude of U; U_x, U_y, U_z are components in directions x, y, z
V	Volume (m^3, ft^3)
x	Rectangular (Cartesian) coordinate
x_A	Mole fraction of species A in liquid in Problem 2.17
y	Rectangular (Cartesian) coordinate
y_A	Mole fraction of species A in gas, dimensionless
z	Rectangular (Cartesian) coordinate
α	Thermal diffusivity ($\text{m}^2 \text{s}^{-1}$, $\text{ft}^2 \text{s}^{-1}$), defined by Eq. (2.10)
β	Angle in Problem 2.21
Δ	Difference, state 2 minus state 1; e.g. ΔT means $T_2 - T_1$, the value of the temperature at location 2 minus the value at location 1

δ — Generalized diffusivity ($m^2\,s^{-1}$, $ft^2\,s^{-1}$)

μ — Viscosity ($kg\,m^{-1}\,s^{-1}$ or $N\,m^{-2}\,s$, $lb_m\,ft^{-1}\,s^{-1}$, cP)

ν — Kinematic viscosity (momentum diffusivity) ($m^2\,s^{-1}$, $ft^2\,s^{-1}$)

ρ — Density ($kg\,m^{-3}$, $lb_m\,ft^{-3}$); subscripts refer to species

$\mathbf{\Psi}$ — Generalized flux vector (e.g., units for heat flux are $J\,m^{-2}\,s^{-1}$ or $W\,m^{-2}$, $Btu\,ft^{-2}\,s^{-1}$; see Table 2.1 for more details); Ψ_x, Ψ_y, Ψ_z are components in directions x, y, z

ψ — Generalized concentration of property (e.g., units for concentration of heat are $J\,m^{-3}$ or $Btu\,ft^{-3}$; see Table 2.1 for more details)

τ — Momentum flux (or shear stress) tensor ($N\,m^{-2}$, $lb_f\,ft^{-2}$); τ_{xy}, τ_{yx}, etc. are components of the momentum flux tensor, where subscripts refer to direction of momentum transfer and direction of velocity

$\mathbf{\nabla}$ — Vector operator del, defined by Eq. (2.16) (m^{-1}, ft^{-1})

$\mathbf{\nabla}U$ — Shear rate tensor, defined by Eq. (2.41) (s^{-1})

$(\mathbf{\nabla}U)^T$ — Transpose of shear rate tensor, defined by Eq. (2.42)

In Chapter 1, the role of intermolecular forces was briefly introduced. The discussion concluded that the exact equations for the rate processes could not be solved for most engineering problems. The empirical approach usually separates transport into two major divisions: transport by turbulent mechanisms and transport by molecular means, with or without convection. Turbulent flow will be introduced in Chapter 6. This chapter treats the equations and mechanisms of molecular transport. Molecular transport may occur in solids, liquids, gases, or mixtures thereof. The simplest example of molecular transport is the conduction of heat from a high-temperature region to a low-temperature region through a rod, as shown in Fig. 2.1(a). If one end of a rod at ambient temperature is held firmly while the other end is thrust into a roaring fire, heat is transferred to the hand-held end of the rod from the end in the fire by molecular transport. The hot molecules in the fire have more energy than the adjacent cooler molecules of the rod. As the molecules collide, energy is transferred from the hotter molecules to the cooler molecules. The process is repeated millions of times until the rod is too hot to hold. The difference in temperature (temperature of the hot fire minus hand temperature) is the driving force for the heat transfer. For mass transport, the situation is more complicated because there must be at least two species present. Consider two identical flasks joined through a valve as shown in Fig. 2.1(b). Let one flask be filled with pure nitrogen, the other with pure oxygen, both at the same pressure and temperature. If the valve in the middle is opened, oxygen will diffuse into the nitrogen side and nitrogen into the oxygen side until each flask contains 50 percent nitrogen and 50 percent oxygen. Concentration is the driving force.

Of the three types of molecular transport, momentum transfer is the most difficult to explain briefly and concisely. First, the basic equation relates shear stress (introduced in Chapter 1) and velocity gradient. The velocity of each

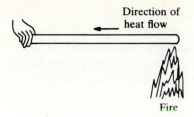

Direction of
heat flow

Fire

(*a*) Molecular heat transfer

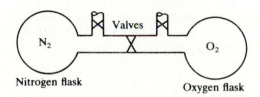

Valves

N$_2$

O$_2$

Nitrogen flask

Oxygen flask

(*b*) Molecular mass transfer

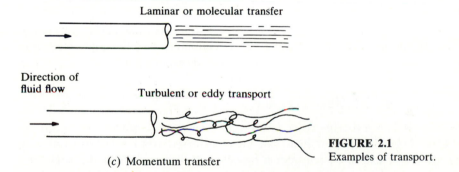

Laminar or molecular transfer

Direction of
fluid flow

Turbulent or eddy transport

FIGURE 2.1
Examples of transport.

(*c*) Momentum transfer

molecule in the fluid changes from point to point in many flow problems. Mathematically the velocity gradient is $\partial U_x/\partial y$, the rate of change of the velocity in the x direction (U_x) with respect to the y direction. In the last two paragraphs describing heat and mass transfer, the reader easily visualized what was being transferred and the nature of the driving force. In the case of momentum transfer, momentum flux (τ) is being transferred, and the velocity gradient ($\partial U_x/\partial y$) is the driving force; both of these are difficult to visualize and will be discussed further.

Fluid flow is a simple example of momentum transfer. The driving force for fluid flow is a pressure difference. For example, when the valve in a drinking fountain is opened, the water flows out in a jet because the water pressure inside the fountain is much higher than the atmospheric pressure into which the jet discharges. Figure 2.1(*c*) shows a simple example of the flow of a fluid (gas or liquid) in a pipe. A pump or fan may force the fluid through the pipe. If a very small pump or fan is used (thus creating only a small pressure drop), the flow in the pipe will be relatively slow and will be laminar. If there is a large pressure drop, the flow in the pipe will be much larger and probably turbulent. Let Fig. 2.1(c) represent smoke-filled air being blown through the pipe. In the laminar case (molecular transport), the fluid issues from the pipe in a smooth, ordered fashion. In the turbulent case, the fluid motion is chaotic with blocks of molecules (called eddies) moving in all directions.

In summary, the molecular mechanisms involve transport of heat by conduction, of mass by molecular diffusion, and of momentum as occurs in laminar fluid flow. A limited analogy among these three transport phenomena can be used to help gain better insight into the processes of the transfer. However, care must be taken not to carry the analogy too far, and its limitations will be indicated as our development proceeds.

2.1   THE ANALOGY

It is common to formulate a general rate equation as

$$(\text{RATE}) = (\text{DRIVING FORCE})/(\text{RESISTANCE}) \qquad (2.1)$$

In Eq. (2.1), as the driving force increases, the rate increases. Also the larger the resistance, the smaller is the rate. Common sense verifies Eq. (2.1), and it is useful to begin discussion of the transport analogy with a simple example from our experience of heat transfer in the world around us.

2.1.1   The Case for Heat Transfer

In heat transfer, the driving force is the temperature difference. Our intuition and experience tells us that heat can be transferred from a hot region to a colder area. For example, consider a block of copper, in which the sides are insulated so that heat conduction occurs only in one direction, the x direction. At this point, it may be helpful for the reader to draw a picture of the block on a piece of scratch paper. Let the initial temperature of the block be 273.15 K (0°C). Next to your drawing of the block, plot a temperature profile, i.e., T versus x. Note that initially for all values of x, T is constant and equal to 273.15 K. Label this curve "$t = t_0$".

Now a temperature difference is established by placing the copper block on top of a block of ice and by immersing the top of the block in steam so that the top temperature is instantaneously raised to 373.15 K. Let us draw a second picture of the block and a second temperature profile, this time with the temperature at the hot end equal to 373.15 K. Elsewhere, the block is still at 273.15 K. Since this is the very first instant of time for the experiment, there has been no time allowed for the temperature below the upper surface to be raised. However, shortly after commencing the experiment, the temperature begins to rise in the areas below the upper surface. At this point a third temperature profile must be drawn—a curved shape from 273.15 to 373.15 K. Label this curve "$t = t_1$". This curve is shaped like a parabola, but its exact nature is a complex solution of the unsteady-state problem (to be covered in Chapter 13).

At some later time t_2, the temperature profile will still be curved. However, the profile will be flatter and more nearly a straight line. Finally, when time equals infinity ($t = t_\infty$, steady-state), the profile will become a straight line.

These temperature profiles have been plotted together in Fig. 2.2. The linear temperature gradient in Fig. 2.2 is an experimental observation and, provided enough time is allowed, the linear temperature distribution is observed as long as the temperatures at the bottom and the top are maintained at the same preset values. The observation is attributed to Fourier, and the equation given below is named after him. The readers' attention is drawn to the fact that once steady-state is achieved ($t = t_\infty$), the temperature profile in the block is invariant with further increase in time. The system is therefore said to be at steady-state. The heat from the steam is conducted down the temperature gradient to the bottom where it is absorbed by the ice and causes melting. The heat being transferred per unit time and unit area, or what is called the heat flux, is directly proportional to the difference between the temperatures and inversely proportional to the distance; this is the temperature gradient ($\partial T / \partial x$). The proportionality is shown by the equation in the figure and is

$$(q/A)_x = -k(\partial T / \partial x) \tag{2.2}$$

where q is the amount of heat transferred per unit time, A is the area, and the subscript x on the flux term denotes that in Eq. (2.2) the heat flux is considered in the x direction only. The proportionality constant k is called the thermal conductivity. It varies from material to material over a wide range, as will be discussed later. For now, only this one-dimensional case will be treated; multidimentional cases will be introduced in Section 2.2. Partial derivatives were used in Eq. (2.2), rather than total derivatives because more than one direction may be involved.

The minus sign in Eq. (2.2) is required because the heat flows from hot to cold. In Fig. 2.2, the plot of T versus x shows that the gradient or derivative ($\partial T / \partial x$) is positive. Common sense tells us that the heat will flow from the top of the block (373.15 K) to the bottom (273.15 K). Hence the heat flux $(q/A)_x$ is in the negative direction, and Eq. (2.2) requires the minus sign. Note that the direction of $(q/A)_x$ is labeled in Fig. 2.2.

The quantity q is the rate of heat transfer, and has typical units $J\,s^{-1}$ or $Btu\,h^{-1}$. Therefore, if Eq. (2.2) were to be rearranged into the form of the generalized rate equation, Eq. (2.1), the results would be

$$\text{rate} = q$$

$$\text{resistance} = \partial x / (kA) \tag{2.3}$$

$$\text{driving force} = \partial T$$

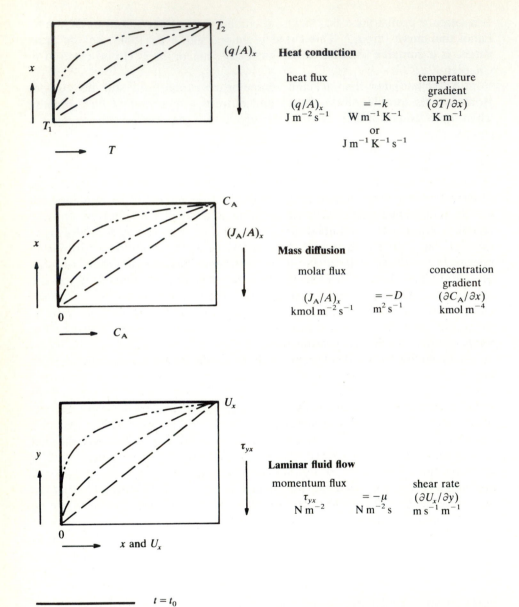

Heat conduction

heat flux		temperature gradient
$(q/A)_x$	$= -k$	$(\partial T/\partial x)$
$\mathrm{J\,m^{-2}\,s^{-1}}$	$\mathrm{W\,m^{-1}\,K^{-1}}$	$\mathrm{K\,m^{-1}}$
	or	
	$\mathrm{J\,m^{-1}\,K^{-1}\,s^{-1}}$	

Mass diffusion

molar flux		concentration gradient
$(J_A/A)_x$	$= -D$	$(\partial C_A/\partial x)$
$\mathrm{kmol\,m^{-2}\,s^{-1}}$	$\mathrm{m^2\,s^{-1}}$	$\mathrm{kmol\,m^{-4}}$

Laminar fluid flow

momentum flux		shear rate
τ_{yx}	$= -\mu$	$(\partial U_x/\partial y)$
$\mathrm{N\,m^{-2}}$	$\mathrm{N\,m^{-2}\,s}$	$\mathrm{m\,s^{-1}\,m^{-1}}$

$t = t_0$

$t = t_1$

$t = t_2$

$t = t_\infty$

FIGURE 2.2
The analogy of the transport phenomena (SI units are shown below the quantities in the equations).

It is often useful to cast Eq. (2.2) into its "resistance" form, especially when heat conduction through a wall is combined with heat transfer to and from fluids on either side. Such advanced problems are in later chapters.

The profiles in Fig. 2.2 for $t = t_1$ and $t = t_2$ are for the case of "unsteady-state" heat transfer. The temperature at any location x in the block is increasing as time passes from the start to steady-state. Calculation of unsteady-state profiles will be given in Chapter 13.

2.1.2   The Case for Mass Transfer

A gaseous material in a box is taken as the mass transfer example. Let us suggest that by some magical means, possibly chemical, the concentration at the bottom is maintained at zero level. At the top there will have to be a source of the material maintained at a higher level denoted by C_A, which has units of moles per volume. At the instant of starting the experiment, the concentration distribution is given by the line marked $t = t_0$. Not enough time has been allowed for any of the material to diffuse into the box. However, at some later time t_1, material has diffused towards the bottom and the concentration gradient as shown in Fig. 2.2 is formed. A little later in time at $t = t_2$, the gradient will look like that shown. If enough time is allowed, a linear gradient will form as denoted by $t = t_\infty$.

The similarity of mass transfer to heat transfer is apparent. The curves in Fig. 2.2 for various times are nearly the same, and one might suspect that the equations are similar also. Let the molar flux $(J_A/A)_x$ be the moles of species A being transferred per unit time per unit area with respect to a plane across which there is no net volume flow.[1] Experimentally it is observed that the molar flux $(J_A/A)_x$ at steady-state (and constant temperature and pressure) is proportional to the difference in concentration and inversely proportional to distance from boundary to boundary. The difference in concentration of species A divided by the difference in length for a differential element of the box is called the concentration gradient. The concentration gradient is denoted by $(\partial C_A/\partial x)$. The equation which represents the experimental observation at steady-state is

$$(J_A/A)_x = -D(\partial C_A/\partial x) \qquad \begin{cases} (T = \text{constant}) \\ (p = \text{constant}) \end{cases} \qquad (2.4)$$

Again, the subscript x denotes mass transfer in the x direction only. The proportionality constant D is called the diffusion coefficient. Less commonly, D is referred to as the molecular mass diffusivity or just mass diffusivity.

---

[1] Most other authors denote this flux as J_A or J_A^v. Our convention of the flux as $(J_A/A)_x$ is justified to emphasize the analogy being developed in Fig. 2.2 and to assist in solving problems where the area is not constant (Chapter 4).

Equation (2.4) is named after Fick who suggested it in 1855. In Fick's law, the flux of A, $(J_A/A)_x$, occurs with respect to a plane across which there is no net volume flow (cf. Section 2.3). The added complication of a net volume flow is considered in detail in Chapter 5.

2.1.3 The Case for Momentum Transfer

As the final example, consider a fluid maintained between parallel plates, as illustrated in the bottom picture of Fig. 2.2. The lower plate remains motionless, and a force is applied to the top plane to maintain it at a velocity U. Because of the internal frictional resistance in the fluid and the friction between the fluid and the plate, the fluid between the plates begins to move with the top plate. For the same reasons, the fluid in contact with the lower plate which is not moving remains stationary. This is an experimental observation and is called the no-slip condition at the boundary. It is, however, true even for such non-wetting materials as mercury in contact with glass.[2]

Figure 2.3 shows the coordinate system that is usually used for momentum transfer. Note the change from the simple, one-direction coordinate in Fig. 2.2. In Fig. 2.3, it is necessary to have two coordinates: x (the direction of the velocity U_x) and y (the direction for the change in U_x and the direction of momentum transfer).[3]

At the instant of starting the upper plate into motion, there has been no

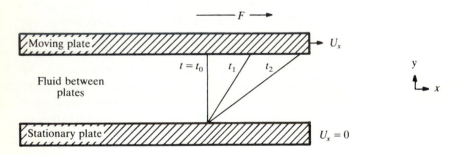

FIGURE 2.3
The no-slip boundary condition. A force F is needed everywhere along the plate to hold it stationary.

---

[2] The fluid dynamics film loop, FM6, dramatically illustrates the no-slip condition. See page xix for details.

[3] The convention of x as the direction of flow and y as the direction of momentum transfer, as used here, was established in the early literature.

time allowed for the fluid to be accelerated and the velocity gradient is given by the curve marked $t = t_0$ in Fig. 2.2. At a larger value of t, some of the fluid is pulled along with the plate. As time progresses, more and more fluid is drawn along with the plate until at a very long length of time, denoted by $t = t_\infty$, a linear velocity gradient develops.

Let the force on the top plate in Fig. 2.3 be of magnitude F and let the area of the plate be A. The ratio F/A is commonly called the shear stress, which is equal in magnitude to the momentum flux τ. For the steady-state case $(t = t_\infty)$ where the flow is laminar between the moving plate and the stationary plate, it is experimentally observed that

$$F/A = \tau_{yx} = -\mu(\partial U_x/\partial y) \tag{2.5}$$

Equation (2.5) is Newton's law of viscosity, where the proportionality constant μ is the viscosity of the fluid. Typical units of μ are $\mathrm{kg\,m^{-1}\,s^{-1}}$ ($\mathrm{N\,m^{-2}\,s}$) in SI, or $\mathrm{lb_m\,ft^{-1}\,s^{-1}}$ ($\mathrm{lb_f\,ft^{-2}\,s}$) in the English system. At steady-state, the velocity gradient $\partial U_x/\partial y$ is constant, the viscosity μ is constant and, since A is constant, F must also be constant or the same everywhere. The sign of F depends on the coordinate system being used, and may be equal in sign or opposite in sign to the momentum flux τ. Regardless, the velocity gradient is always opposite in sign to the momentum flux. Physically, the momentum flux is the transfer of momentum through the fluid from the region of high velocity to the region of low velocity. The force F will not be considered further until Chapter 7.

In Eq. (2.5), the double subscript on the shear stress, i.e., τ_{yx}, implies that there must be other components of the shear stress (see Section 2.4). For now, the part being considered is the transfer in the y direction as a result of an x velocity component; note that the x velocity component changes magnitude as y increases or decreases. Convention dictates that the first subscript (y) refers to the direction of momentum transfer, and that the subscript (x) refers to the direction of the velocity; thus τ_{yx} is used in Eq. (2.5) and Fig. 2.3.

The similarity of Newton's law, Eq. (2.5), to the laws of Fourier and Fick is readily apparent. In the case of Fourier's law, the example was a hand-held rod in a fire. If the temperature of the fire increases, the temperature gradient $\partial T/\partial x$ also increases, and therefore the heat flux increases. This simple experiment is easy to visualize. The mass transfer example in Fig. 2.1(b) is just as easy to understand. However, in Fig. 2.1(c), the reader can easily visualize a fluid in motion, but not a shear stress or momentum transfer. Hence a detailed explanation of momentum transfer is required.

In the case of both the mass and the heat transfer, a quantity was being transferred per unit time per unit area. The case of momentum transfer is the same. The definition of momentum is mass times velocity. In the following unit analysis, the momentum flux (also called shear stress) τ_{yx} is shown to be equivalent to a force per unit area:

$$\tau_{yx} = \frac{(\text{mass})(\text{velocity})}{(\text{time})(\text{area})} = \frac{F}{A} \tag{2.6}$$

SI units

$$\frac{(\text{kg})(\text{m s}^{-1})}{(\text{s})(\text{m}^2)} = \frac{(\text{kg})(\text{m})}{(\text{s}^2)(\text{m}^2)} = \text{N m}^{-2}$$

English units (τ_{yx}/g_c)

$$\frac{(\text{lb}_m)(\text{ft s}^{-1})}{(\text{s})(\text{ft}^2)(\text{lb}_m \, \text{lb}_f^{-1} \, \text{ft s}^{-2})} = \text{lb}_f \, \text{ft}^{-2}$$

In the above equation using SI units, velocity has units of m s^{-1}, and one newton is one kg m s^{-2}. Thus, both the shear stress and the product of velocity times mass per area per time are clearly shown in Eq. (2.6) to be force per area. Therefore, the shear stress, which was previously defined as force per area in Chapter 1, is indeed a momentum flux, as proven by Eq. (2.6).

Momentum transfer is easier to visualize in Fig. 2.3 than in Fig. 2.1(*c*). At steady-state, when the top plate is pulled in the *x* direction with force *F*, there must be the same force on the bottom plate—equal and in the opposite direction. Thus, the momentum of the top plate is transferred via the fluid to the bottom plate.

Momentum transfer is not experienced in the same sense as heat being transferred along a rod from the fire to a hand. To illustrate the existence of momentum transfer, let us use as an example a deck of playing cards. When the cards are sitting on the table and they are new, one can, with a simple flick of the thumb, cause the topmost card to fly from the deck. There is little interaction between the cards and they fly off one by one. After a few hours of card playing and in particular on a warm and humid night, if the experiment is repeated, one will find that a number of cards will move, and the deck will fan out. Yet all that has been done is to push the top card. What has happened? The top card has a mass and, because it has been given a velocity, it has momentum. In the first experiment, little of this momentum was transferred to the card below. But in the latter experiment, a considerable amount of the momentum was transferred because the frictional resistance between the cards caused an interaction. In effect, by pushing the top card, one has induced a momentum in the card below: the card has a mass and has been given a velocity. Looking at the third card, the same thing has happened but somewhat less, and so forth. Momentum, mass times velocity, has been transferred from the top card all the way down the deck. In the analogous case, as in Fig. 2.3, the fluid during laminar fluid flow can be pictured as lying in layers, i.e., laminae. Moving the top layer transfers momentum from the top layer to the next and so forth. The fact that momentum is first applied only to the top and that subsequently momentum appears below is indicative of momentum transfer. The momentum, mass times velocity, has been transferred from the top layer to layers lying further down in the fluid.

An important manifestation of transfer of momentum is in the pumping of fluids. As a result of flow in pipes, tubes, ducts or channels, a pressure drop or loss occurs when momentum is transferred from fluid to wall. In the design of flow systems, this pressure loss determines the size of pump or compressor needed to maintain the desired flow.

2.1.4 The Analogous Forms

Three analogous equations (often called constitutive relations) have been introduced: Fourier's law for heat transfer, Eq. (2.2), Fick's law for mass transfer, Eq. (2.4), and Newton's law for momentum transfer, Eq. (2.5). In each of the foregoing equations, a minus sign has been used in the proportionality. This was not arbitrary, for in each case the flux is transported down the corresponding gradient. For example, the heat is transferred from the higher to the lower temperature. In the direction from our hand to the fire, the temperature increases so that the temperature gradient from the hand to the fire is positive, but the heat goes from the fire to our hand. Thus, the flux of heat is transferred from the higher to the lower temperature and down the temperature gradient. The same is true for the concentration gradient and molar flux.

Fluid mechanics developed as a subject earlier than heat or mass transfer. Momentum transfer is a modern way to look at fluid mechanics. For momentum transfer, momentum is transferred from the high-velocity region to the low and thus the negative sign is required in Eq. (2.5). However, in earlier days, before the momentum transport concept and the analogy, a positive sign was used in Eq. (2.5). Since momentum transfer and its direction were not of concern, it did not matter what sign was used, as long as the use was consistent. There are some textbooks today which do not concern themselves with transport phenomena concepts and still retain the use of a positive sign in Eq. (2.5).

The three empirical laws [Eqs. (2.2), (2.4), and (2.5)] established by observation many years ago are useful only when point properties are involved. Thus when the properties cannot be regarded as continuous these equations do not apply. Simply stated, the laws of Fourier, Fick, and Newton apply only to a continuum. The three proportionality constants in these equations are three fundamental properties. The first, k, is the thermal conductivity; the second, D, is the diffusion coefficient (the mass diffusivity); and the third, μ, is the viscosity (also called the molecular or dynamic viscosity).

The analogy is of much more recent origin. The three equations (Eqs. (2.2), (2.4), and (2.5)) are quite similar. Each involves a flux term, a proportionality constant, and a gradient of some measurable parameter. However, the equations are not exactly in their analogous forms. A general one-dimensional flux equation is

$$\Psi_x = -\delta(\partial \psi / \partial x) \tag{2.7}$$

where Ψ_x is the flux in the x direction of whatever is going to be transferred per unit time per unit area, δ is the proportionality constant, which this book will refer to as the diffusivity, and finally $\partial \psi / \partial x$ is the derivative (gradient) of the concentration of property ψ. The quantity ψ is the concentration of whatever it is that is transferred in the units of the item to be transferred per unit volume. In order to apply Eq. (2.7), each transport equation must be in the appropriate form. Inspection of Eqs. (2.2) and (2.5) shows this not to be the case. For example, the temperature in Eq. (2.2) is in units of degrees and is not a quantity per volume. Also, as a result of our coordinate selection in Fig. 2.2, the derivative $\partial \psi / \partial x$ must be changed to $\partial \psi / \partial y$ in the case of momentum. Nevertheless, it is a simple matter to convert the equations to their mathematically analogous forms.

Heat transfer. In the case of heat conduction, q is being transferred; its units are joules (or cal or Btu) per unit time. The term ψ, which is the concentration of property, must have the units of $J\,m^{-3}$, which is not consistent with any of the terms in Eqs. (2.2) or (2.3). The following illustrates how to convert temperature driving force (∂T) into the heat contained in the body $(J\,m^{-3})$. First, the property that is associated with the heat content of a body is the heat capacity c_p, typical units $J\,kg^{-1}\,K^{-1}$. Therefore, the product of $(c_p T)$ may have units of $J\,kg^{-1}$. To convert the term ∂T to units of $J\,m^{-3}$, the density ρ must also be included:

$$
\begin{array}{cccc}
T & \rho & c_p & = & \rho c_p T \\
\end{array}
$$

units: (2.8)

$$
\begin{array}{cccc}
K & kg\,m^{-3} & J\,kg^{-1}\,K^{-1} & = & J\,m^{-3}
\end{array}
$$

The term $\rho c_p T$ is the concentration of heat and has units of $J\,m^{-3}$. Now, Eq. (2.2) is converted into its analogous form by multiplying the right-hand side by the fraction $\rho c_p / \rho c_p$:

$$(q/A)_x = -[k/(\rho c_p)][\partial(\rho c_p T)/\partial x] = -\alpha[\partial(\rho c_p T)/\partial x] \tag{2.9}$$

Mathematically, there was an additional assumption in Eq. (2.9), namely that the product ρc_p is constant, in order to arrive at the term $\partial(\rho c_p T)/\partial x$. The group $k/(\rho c_p)$ is often represented by α (units $m^2\,s^{-1}$) and is called the thermal diffusivity; i.e.,

$$\alpha = \frac{k}{\rho c_p} \tag{2.10}$$

Mass transfer. In Fick's law, Eq. (2.4), the mass transfer flux $(J_A/A)_x$ is in units of $kmol\,m^{-2}\,s^{-1}$, and the concentration C_A is in units of $kmol\,m^{-3}$. Therefore, the equation is already in its analogous form. The proportionality constant D is the diffusion coefficient or mass diffusivity in units of $m^2\,s^{-1}$.

Momentum transfer. The momentum equation, Newton's law, must be treated in a manner similar to that for the heat. The left-hand side of Eq. (2.5) is in the form of a flux. In order to obtain the concentration of momentum that is being transferred, the density is multiplied by U_x. The units of ρU_x are $\text{kg m}^{-2}\text{s}^{-1}$ or $\text{N m}^{-3}\text{s}$. After multiplying Eq. (2.5) by (ρ/ρ) and rearranging, the result is

$$\tau_{yx} = F/A = -[\mu/\rho][\partial(\rho U_x)/\partial y] = -v[\partial(\rho U_x)/\partial y] \qquad (2.11)$$

The proportionality constant μ is the molecular viscosity. When μ is divided by the density ρ, the result is called the kinematic viscosity v (or sometimes the momentum diffusivity):

$$v = \mu/\rho \qquad (2.12)$$

In Eq. (2.11) the density ρ has been assumed constant in order to form the term $\partial(\rho U_x)/\partial y$.

Summary. The one-dimensional transport equations are now in their analogous form and are reviewed in Table 2.1. One must emphasize that Eq. (2.7) is a mathematical analogy as applied to the three transport phenomena. The equations are the same from the mathematical standpoint. With a given set of boundary conditions, a solution for one is a solution for all; the only difference is in the symbols representing the various terms. This mathematical analogy in no way means that the physical mechanisms occurring in the three cases are in any way the same. The mechanisms are totally different. For the heat conduction example, the heat is conducted from the fire towards our hand through energy transfer mechanisms which are dependent upon the material contained in the rod. In metals, the rapid migration of an energy-containing "electron gas" is the primary energy transfer mechanism. Mass transfer often involves at least two materials, one material being transferred by relative motion through the other. In the latter case, the molecules move from one

TABLE 2.1
The one-dimensional transport equations in their analogous forms

Transport	Flux	Flux units (SI)	Diffusivity	Gradient of the concentration of property	Equation no.
General	Ψ_x		δ	$\partial\psi/\partial x$	(2.7)
Heat	$(q/A)_x$	$\text{J m}^{-2}\text{s}^{-1}$	α	$\partial(\rho c_p T)/\partial x$	(2.9)
Mass	$(J_A/A)_x$	$\text{kmol m}^{-2}\text{s}^{-1}$	D	$\partial C_A/\partial x$	(2.4)
Momentum	τ_{yx}	N m^{-2} or $\text{kg m}^{-1}\text{s}^{-2}$	v	$\partial(\rho U_x)/\partial y$	(2.11)
Units		$@@\,\text{m}^{-2}\text{s}^{-1}$	m^2s^{-1}	$@@\,\text{m}^{-3}\text{m}^{-1}$	

In the row for units, the symbol (@@) stands for whatever is being transferred. It can be joules (J) for the case of heat transfer, kilomoles for the case of mass transfer, or momentum (in units of kg m s^{-1} or its equivalent N s).

place to another, whereas in heat transfer through a solid rod the molecules are relatively stationary. Momentum transfer involves a combination of mechanisms which, for the most part, are different from those of the other transports. Thus, let us emphasize again that our analogy is mathematical in nature. However, even this mathematical analogy is not completely adequate. Each of the transports has its own complications, and these will be discussed in future sections.

The following examples illustrate the use of the basic transport laws.

Example 2.1. Calculate the steady-state heat flux across a copper block 10 cm thick, one side of which is maintained at 0°C and the other at 100°C (see Fig. 2.4). The thermal conductivity can be assumed constant at 380 W m^{-1} K^{-1}.

Answer. The physical situation is that given by the steady-state curve of Fig. 2.2, and the controlling equation is Eq. (2.2). The area through which the heat is being transferred is constant, and there is only one direction of transfer, the x direction. First, the variables in Eq. (2.2) are separated:

$$\int_{x_1}^{x_2} (q/A)_x \, dx = -k \int_{T_1}^{T_2} dT \tag{i}$$

This equation can be easily integrated if the heat flux $(q/A)_x$ is constant. At steady-state, it is obvious that all the heat (q) that enters at face 2 must leave at face 1, if there is no internal generation. Since the area is constant, then it follows that the flux is constant. In Section 4.1.1, it will be proved that $(q/A)_x$ is constant for this geometry. After integration, Eq. (i) becomes

$$(q/A)_x(x_2 - x_1) = -k(T_2 - T_1) \tag{ii}$$

The quantities ΔT and Δx are

$$\Delta T = T_2 - T_1 = 100 - 0 = 100 \deg \text{C} = 100 \deg \text{K} \tag{iii}$$

$$\Delta x = x_2 - x_1 = 10 \text{ cm} = 0.1 \text{ m} \tag{iv}$$

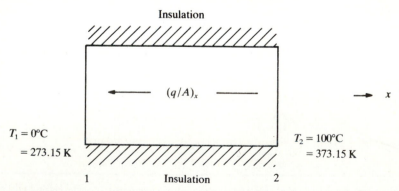

FIGURE 2.4
Heat transfer across a block.

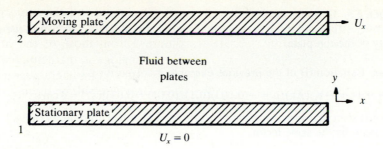

FIGURE 2.5
The moving plate problem.

These are substituted into Eq. (ii):

$$(q/A)_2 = -(380)(100)/(0.1) = -3.8 \times 10^5 \text{ W m}^{-2} \qquad \text{(v)}$$

or in alternate units:

$$(q/A)_2 = -3.8 \times 10^5 \text{ J m}^{-2} \text{s}^{-1} = -9.1 \text{ cal cm}^{-2} \text{s}^{-1} \qquad \text{(vi)}$$

The temperature increases from 1 to 2; the minus sign indicates the heat flux is opposite to this; i.e., from 2 to 1.

Example 2.2. Two parallel plates are 10 cm apart. The bottom plate is stationary. The fluid between the plates is water which has a viscosity of 1 centipoise. Calculate the momentum flux and force per unit area necessary to maintain a plate in motion at a velocity of 30 cm s^{-1}.

Answer. Figure 2.5 illustrates this example, and Eq. (2.5) applies:

$$\tau_{yx} = F/A = -\mu(\partial U_x/\partial y) \qquad (2.5)$$

It will be proved later that τ_{yx} is a constant for this problem. If so, the variables in Eq. (2.5) may be separated and integrated, as shown in the previous two examples for heat and mass. The result is

$$\tau_{yx}(\Delta y) = -\mu(\Delta U_x) \qquad \text{(i)}$$

The quantity $\Delta U_x/\Delta y$ for the moving plate problem is called the shear rate:

$$\Delta U_x/\Delta y = \partial U_x/\partial y = (0.3)/(0.1) = 3 \text{ s}^{-1} \qquad \text{(ii)}$$

Viscosity conversions are in Table C.17:

$$\mu = 1 \text{ cP} = 0.01 \text{ poise} = 0.001 \text{ kg m}^{-1}\text{s}^{-1} \qquad \text{(iii)}$$

Using this information in Eq. (2.5) gives the momentum flux τ_{yx}:

$$\tau_{yx} = -(0.001)(3) = -0.003 \text{ kg m}^{-1}\text{s}^{-2} = -0.003 \text{ N m}^{-2} \qquad \text{(iv)}$$

The minus sign indicates the momentum is transferred in the minus y direction (down in Fig. 2.5); note that the shear stress (F/A) at the top plate is the same in magnitude as the momentum flux, but of opposite sign.

Example 2.3. Consider the apparatus in Fig. 2.5. If water is replaced with a fluid of viscosity 10 cP, and if the momentum flux remains at 0.003 N m^{-2}, find the new velocity of the top plate.

Answer. Equation (i) of the previous example is solved for ΔU_x:

$$\Delta U_x = -\tau_{yx}(\Delta y)/\mu = -(0.003)(0.1)/(0.01) = 0.03 \text{ m s}^{-1} = 3 \text{ cm s}^{-1} \qquad \text{(i)}$$

Thus, it is seen that increasing the viscosity by a factor of 10 reduces the velocity of the plate by the same factor.

2.2 HEAT TRANSFER

The transfer of heat can be found throughout industrial processing. Heat must be removed when it is generated in compressions or in chemical reactions such as found in process reactors, power plants using chemical combustion or nuclear sources, etc. Heat or other energy must be provided in purification processes and is often needed in mass transfer operations such as drying and distillation. The conservation of heat in plants is important because heat loss is costly; thus, in large plants one finds extensive use of heat exchangers, which are pieces of equipment to remove heat from one stream and transfer it to a second stream. One aspect common to all three transport phenomena is the three-dimensional nature of the world. All previous equations have been valid for transfer in one direction only. Suppose a camper held one end of a copper rod in the shape of a wide "L" in a fire and the other in his hand. Our experience tells us that his hand would get burned. The flow of heat would not travel just in one coordinate direction, but would travel around the bend in the rod. The conclusion from this experiment is that the heat flux, and the temperature gradient as well, are vector quantities.[4] Fourier's law is

$$(q/A)_x = -k(\partial T/\partial x) \qquad (2.2)$$

Equation (2.2) is actually only the x component of the general three-dimensional equation. The other two components are:

$$y \text{ component:} \qquad (q/A)_y = -k(\partial T/\partial y) \qquad (2.13)$$

$$z \text{ component:} \qquad (q/A)_z = -k(\partial T/\partial z) \qquad (2.14)$$

These components can be added as any components of a vector and result in

$$(q/A) = -k[i(\partial T/\partial x) + j(\partial T/\partial y) + k(\partial T/\partial z)]$$

or

$$(q/A) = -k\nabla T \qquad (2.15)$$

---

[4] For those not familiar with vectors from their calculus courses, a brief tutorial should be covered here before going further. Physics film loops VK 1 through VK 6 can be of considerable help at this point.

where (q/A) is a vector quantity. Also i, j, and k are the unit vectors in the x, y, and z directions, respectively, and ∇ (del) is an operator which may operate on any scalar. Using T as an example, the term ∇T is:

$$\nabla T = i(\partial T/\partial x) + j(\partial T/\partial y) + k(\partial T/\partial z) \tag{2.16}$$

In Eq. (2.15) it has been assumed that the thermal conductivity is the same in each direction, i.e., it is isotropic. If the material is anisotropic, a reasonable approximation is

$$(q/A) = -[ik_x(\partial T/\partial x) + jk_y(\partial T/\partial y) + kk_z(\partial T/\partial z)] \tag{2.17}$$

where k_x, k_y, and k_z are the thermal conductivities in the three directions. Anisotropic conduction can occur in wood, films, fibers, and certain crystalline materials. In wood, differences are observed if the conduction is with or across the grain. The solution of differential equations such as Eq. (2.17) is relatively simple for the one-dimensional case, but can be quite complex for two- or three-dimensional problems. The general vector form can be derived in a similar manner, but also can be written down by inspection and the use of our analogy; i.e.,

$$\Psi = -\delta \nabla \psi \tag{2.18}$$

Example 2.4. Compare the rates of heat transfer across a sample of white pine wood when the transfer is across the grain and when it is parallel to the grain.

Answer. The thermal conductivity of this sample can be found in standard references, such as *Perry's Chemical Engineers' Handbook* [P1]. For white pine
  Across the grain:

$$k = 0.087 \, \text{Btu h}^{-1} \, \text{ft}^{-1} \, °\text{F}^{-1} \tag{i}$$

  Parallel to the grain:

$$k = 0.20 \, \text{Btu h}^{-1} \, \text{ft}^{-1} \, °\text{F}^{-1} \tag{ii}$$

For a given area and temperature gradient, the relative rates of heat transfer are given by the thermal conductivities (Eq. 2.17); thus, white pine wood conducts heat 2.3 times faster $(0.20/0.087 = 2.3)$ parallel to the grain than across. Note that one need not convert to SI units, as clearly all the conversion factors cancel out.

Example 2.5. A glass rod of diameter 1.3 mm is 1 m long. One end is maintained at the normal boiling point of toluene, 110.6°C. The other end is affixed to a block of ice. The thermal conduction along the rod is at steady-state. The heat of fusion of ice is 79.7 cal g^{-1}. The thermal conductivity of glass in SI units is 0.86 W m^{-1} K^{-1} (Equivalent units are J m^{-1} s^{-1} K^{-1} and J m^{-2} s^{-1} (K^{-1} m).) Assume no heat is lost from the exposed surface of the rod. Find:

(a) the amount of heat transferred in joules per second;
(b) the number of grams of ice that melt in 30 minutes.

Answer. This problem is a one-dimensional heat conduction problem, and Eq.

(2.2) applies

$$(q/A)_x = -k(\partial T/\partial x) \tag{2.2}$$

At steady-state, $(q/A)_x$ is constant. Thus, Eq. (ii) from Example 2.1 follows:

$$(q/A)_x(\Delta x) = -k\,\Delta T \tag{i}$$

where ΔT is the temperature difference along the rod and Δx is the total length of the path of conduction. Ice melts at 0°C. Now the quantities ΔT, Δx, and the heat flux are

$$\Delta T = T_2 - T_1 = 110.6 - 0 = 110.6 \deg C = 110.6 \deg K \tag{ii}$$

$$\Delta x = x_2 - x_1 = 1 \, \text{m} \tag{iii}$$

$$(q/A)_x = -k(\Delta T)/(\Delta x) = -(0.86)(110.6)/1 = -95.1 \, \text{J m}^{-2}\,\text{s}^{-1} \tag{iv}$$

The $+x$ coordinate has been selected from T_1 to T_2, i.e., in the direction of the increase in temperature. Thus, the flux must be negative. The area of the rod in m^2 is

$$A = \pi d^2/4 = \pi(0.0013)^2/4 = 1.327 \times 10^{-6} \, \text{m}^2 \tag{v}$$

The heat flow is flux times area:

$$q_x = (q/A)_x(A) = (-95.1)(1.327 \times 10^{-6}) = -1.26 \times 10^{-4} \, \text{J s}^{-1} \tag{vi}$$

The heat of fusion of ice is

$$(79.7 \, \text{cal g}^{-1})(4.184 \, \text{J cal}^{-1}) = 333.5 \, \text{J g}^{-1} \tag{vii}$$

By making the appropriate unit equation, the ice melted in grams per 30 minutes equals q times 60 seconds per minute times 30 minutes divided by the heat of fusion:

$$\frac{(1.26 \times 10^{-4})(30)(60)}{(333.5)}\left(\frac{(\text{J s}^{-1})(\text{min})(\text{s min}^{-1})}{(\text{J g}^{-1})}\right) = 6.8 \times 10^{-4} \, \text{g of ice melted} \tag{viii}$$

2.3 MASS TRANSFER

Like heat transfer, mass transfer is also described by a vector equation in three dimensions. Fick's law becomes

$$(J_A/A) = -D\nabla C_A \qquad \begin{cases} (T = \text{constant}) \\ (p = \text{constant}) \end{cases} \tag{2.19}$$

where

$$\nabla C_A = i(\partial C_A/\partial x) + j(\partial C_A/\partial y) + k(\partial C_A/\partial z) \tag{2.20}$$

In Eq. (2.19), the diffusion coefficient D has been assumed not to vary in any of the three coordinate directions. Equation (2.19) is obtained by analogy from Eq. (2.15) or from Eq. (2.18). However, even in one dimension, the mass transfer analysis has an additional complexity which does not exist for the corresponding heat transfer case. Let us return to our example, the two flasks of nitrogen and oxygen in which the diffusion of two components is occurring.

Whenever a particular molecule of this mixture diffuses, it must diffuse through other molecules; consequently, in almost every practical example there are at least two components present and possibly more. In many chemical engineering operations, separation of molecules is paramount, and mass transfer is the process that effects the separation.

Mass transfer in industrial equipment often occurs between two streams, one of which is being enriched by mass transfer at the expense of the second. For example, in distillation the rising vapor contacts the descending liquid with the more volatile components being transferred from the liquid to the gas, which results in an enriched overhead product of the more volatile materials. Production of brandy is a tasty example. Such mass transfer operations are usually classified as being unsteady-state or steady-state and batchwise or continuous. Drying is an unsteady-state batchwise operation. Evaporation of water in a cooling tower is a steady-state continuous operation. Successive washing of a solid containing a soluble salt by water is a batchwise operation. The distillation system described above is often done as a continuous operation, but can also be done batchwise. A gas absorption column is another continuous-contact operation where the gas rises as bubbles through a descending liquid. Equations (2.4) and (2.19) are for the diffusion of the component A. Let us call the second component B, and let us say that A is diffusing through a mixture of A plus B. There are two possibilities for B: B may diffuse or it may not. The case of B nondiffusing is called "diffusion through a stagnant film of B" (see Section 5.3.3). If B diffuses, then there must be another equation for the diffusion of the B component; i.e., for the x direction:

$$(J_B/A)_x = -D(\partial C_B/\partial x) \qquad \begin{cases} (T = \text{constant}) \\ (p = \text{constant}) \end{cases} \qquad (2.21)$$

For the three-dimensional case:

$$(J_B/A) = -D\nabla C_B \qquad \begin{cases} (T = \text{constant}) \\ (p = \text{constant}) \end{cases} \qquad (2.22)$$

Equations (2.4), (2.19), (2.21) and (2.22) all contain the diffusion coefficient D, thus implying that D is identical in all these equations. This assumption is true only for a system of two ideal gases. The approximation is often reasonable for real gases; however, for liquids, the diffusion coefficient in Eq. (2.19) does not equal the diffusion coefficient in Eq. (2.22). If the system is binary, Eqs. (2.4), (2.19), (2.21), and (2.22) in more general form require that the quantity D be replaced with D_{AB} (the diffusion coefficient of component A diffusing through a mixture of A plus B) or with D_{BA} (the diffusion coefficient of component B diffusing through A + B). When it is important to distinguish between D_{AB} and D_{BA}, the appropriate subscripts will be used. Diffusion with three or more components is extremely complex, and will be discussed briefly in Section 5.3.7.

Diffusion may occur in solids, liquids, or gases. In this section, the case of

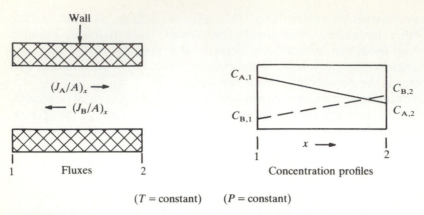

(T = constant)   (P = constant)

FIGURE 2.6
One-dimensional, two-component equimolar counter diffusion.

binary diffusion between two ideal gases under conditions of constant temperature and pressure will be considered. A more general treatment is given in Chapter 5.

Notation. Figure 2.6 represents a typical case of steady-state diffusion between points 1 and 2 under conditions of constant temperature and pressure. Let both species A and B be ideal gases. A typical problem of interest to engineers is to calculate the rate of movement of gases A and B through the apparatus in Fig. 2.6. Since the apparatus is fixed in space, the rates of movement of A and B must be determined relative to fixed coordinates, not relative to the volume velocity, as in the term $(J_A/A)_x$. Let N_A be the moles of A that pass by an arbitrary location x in Fig. 2.6; let N_B be the moles of B that pass by the same location. The quantities N_A and N_B are termed the molar flow rates, typical units (kmol s^{-1}); these are vectors as well. Often, it is convenient to define a molar flux $(N_A/A)_x$ that is the flux of A with respect to fixed coordinates. In all problems in this chapter, the flux $(J_A/A)_x$ equals the flux $(N_A/A)_x$.[5]

Equimolar counter diffusion. Figure 2.6 shows two gases that are diffusing under conditions of constant temperature and pressure. Since both gases are at

---

[5] In most engineering processes involving mass transfer, there is a volume flow rate caused by a difference in pressure. In this chapter, $(J_A/A)_x$ is the molar flux with respect to a plane of no volume flow. Fick's law, which is presented in terms of the flux $(J_A/A)_x$, applies in a coordinate system that moves exactly with that volume flow. Naturally, it is more useful to solve problems with respect to fixed coordinates, i.e., with respect to the boundaries represented by the walls of the apparatus. Then it is necessary to calculate the flux $(N_A/A)_x$, not the flux $(J_A/A)_x$. In Chapter 2, all mass transfer problems have been selected so there is no net volume flow; then these two fluxes are equal. Unfortunately, the mass transfer literature has introduced other fluxes as well. A complete discussion is in Chapter 5.

the same pressure, it follows from the ideal gas law that as a molecule of gas A traverses from left to right in Fig. 2.6 that molecule must be replaced with a molecule of B in order to maintain a constant pressure. Since at any arbitrary location x the number of molecules is always constant, there can be no volume flow. Such a diffusion is called "equimolar counter diffusion". Then for equimolar counter diffusion:

$$N_A = -N_B \tag{2.23}$$

The minus sign in Eq. (2.23) is required because B diffuses in the minus x direction. Since the diffusional area in the apparatus in Fig. 2.6 is constant, then the fluxes of A and B are equal in magnitude and opposite in sign:

$$(N_A/A)_x = -(N_B/A)_x \tag{2.24}$$

Since there is no volume flow in Fig. 2.6 under conditions of constant pressure and temperature, the flux with respect to stationary coordinates equals the flux with respect to the volume velocity:

$$(N_A/A)_x = (J_A/A)_x = -D_{AB}(\partial C_A/\partial x) \tag{2.25}$$

$$(N_B/A)_x = (J_B/A)_x = -D_{BA}(\partial C_B/\partial x) \tag{2.26}$$

$$(T = \text{constant}) \qquad (P = \text{constant}) \qquad (\text{Ideal gas})$$

In conclusion, Fick's law applies directly to the example in Fig. 2.6 if the three restrictions noted above apply. Note that gas A is being supplied at face 1 at the same rate as it is being diffused and removed at face 2. Likewise, gas B is diffusing in the same manner but in the minus x direction (hence the term counter). As many moles are being put in as are being taken out; the total concentration C_T remains constant since the pressure is maintained constant in the system:

$$C_T = C_A + C_B = \text{constant} \tag{2.27}$$

When Eq. (2.27) is differentiated with respect to x, the result is

$$\partial C_T/\partial x = \partial C_A/\partial x + \partial C_B/\partial x = 0 \tag{2.28}$$

or

$$\partial C_A/\partial x = -(\partial C_B/\partial x) \tag{2.29}$$

Combining Eqs. (2.24) through (2.29) results in

$$D_{AB} = D_{BA} \tag{2.30}$$

Equation (2.30) is restricted to the binary diffusion of ideal gases at constant temperature and pressure.

Mass flux. A mass flux is defined simply as the mass per area per time. It is common practice to define two new fluxes similar to the molar fluxes already introduced:

$$(j_A/A)_x = [(J_A/A)_x](M_A) \tag{2.31}$$

$$(n_A/A)_x = [(N_A/A)_x](M_A) \tag{2.32}$$

where M_A is the molecular weight. The flux $(j_A/A)_x$ is the mass flux of A with respect to a plane of no net volume velocity; typical units are $(\text{kg m}^{-2} \text{s}^{-1})$. The flux $(n_A/A)_x$ is the mass flux with respect to fixed coordinates in the same units; then the mass flow rate is n_A; units are (kg s^{-1}).

The corresponding driving force for mass transfer is the mass concentration of A. The mass concentration is the density ρ_A, typical units (kg m^{-3}). The density and concentration are related by

$$\rho_A = C_A M_A \tag{2.33}$$

When Eqs. (2.31) and (2.33) are substituted into Fick's law, the result is

$$(j_A/A)_x = -D(\partial \rho_A / \partial x) \qquad \begin{cases} (T = \text{constant}) \\ (p = \text{constant}) \end{cases} \tag{2.34}$$

where the diffusion coefficient D in Eq. (2.34) is identical to that in the previous equations. Equation (2.34) is another expression of Fick's law. Both Eqs. (2.4) and (2.34) are restricted to constant temperature, constant pressure, and no net volume flow.

Equation (2.34) is seen to be in the analogous form of Eq. (2.18), with

$$\Psi_x = (j_A/A)_x \tag{2.35}$$

$$\psi = \rho_A \tag{2.36}$$

Partial pressure. Under many conditions the ideal gas law is a reasonable assumption:

$$pV = nRT \tag{1.1}$$

Using Eq. (1.1), the concentration can be expressed as

$$C_A = n/V = \bar{p}_A/(RT) \tag{2.37}$$

where $\bar{p}_A$ is the partial pressure of A:

$$\bar{p}_A = y_A p_{\text{total}} \tag{2.38}$$

In Eq. (2.38), y_A is the mole fraction of A in the gas phase and p_{total} (or p) is the total pressure. When Eq. (2.37) is combined with Eq. (2.19), one obtains

$$(J_A/A) = -[D/(RT)][\nabla \bar{p}_A] \qquad \begin{cases} (T = \text{constant}) \\ (p = \text{constant}) \end{cases} \tag{2.39}$$

where the flux is now in terms of the partial pressure of A.

The following examples illustrate the application of Fick's law to a problem in molecular diffusion and the use of Eqs. (2.37) through (2.39).

Example 2.6. Two gas streams, CO_2 and air, are flowing in the same direction in a channel. The channel is divided into equal volumes by a piece of iron 4 cm thick (see Fig. 2.7). At the plane A–A, there is a hole 1.2 cm in diameter drilled in the iron so that CO_2 diffuses from left to right and air from right to left. At the plane

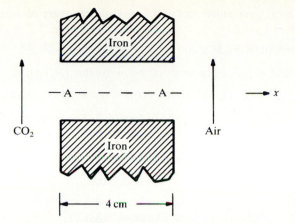

FIGURE 2.7
Flow system for diffusion.

A–A, both gases are at a pressure of 2 atm and a temperature of 20°C. Upstream of the hole both gases are pure. Under the conditions given, the concentration of CO_2 equals 0.083 kmol m^{-3}, i.e., the concentration of CO_2 on the left at the point A. At the right-hand side of the hole, the concentration of CO_2 in air may be assumed to be zero because air is flowing rapidly past the hole. The diffusion coefficient of CO_2 in air is 1.56×10^{-3} m^2 s^{-1}.
(a) Find the molar flux of CO_2.
(b) Find the number of pounds of CO_2 that pass through the hole in the iron in one hour.

Answer. The CO_2 diffuses through the hole in the iron at steady-state if the flow rates of CO_2 and air are constant. Since both gases are at the same temperature and pressure, Eq. (2.25) applies:

$$(N_A/A)_x = (J_A/A)_x = -D_{AB}(\partial C_A/\partial x) \qquad (2.25)$$

The concentration of CO_2 at the air end of the hole is zero ($C_A = 0$) as indicated in the statement of the problem. The characteristics of the hole are

$$L = 4\,\text{cm} = 0.04\,\text{m}$$
$$d = 1.2\,\text{cm} = 0.012\,\text{m} \qquad \text{(i)}$$
$$A = \pi d^2/4 = 1.131 \times 10^{-4}\,\text{m}^2$$

At steady-state, the molar flux $(N_A/A)_x$ must be constant in the hole throughout its length because all the CO_2 entering from the left exits into the air stream. Hence Eq. (2.25) rearranges to

$$[(N_A/A)/D]\,dx = -dC_A \qquad \text{(ii)}$$

where $(N_A/A)/D$ is constant and D_{AB} has been replaced by D. Integrating Eq. (ii) from point 1 (pure CO_2) to point 2 (length 0.04 m) yields

$$[(N_A/A)/(D)]\int_{0.0}^{0.04} dx = -\int_{0.083}^{0.0} dC_A = \int_{0.0}^{0.083} dC_A \qquad \text{(iii)}$$

or

$$[(N_A/A)/(D)][0.04] = 0.083 \qquad \text{(iv)}$$

Since $D = 1.56 \times 10^{-3}\,\text{m}^2\,\text{s}^{-1}$, the molar flux with respect to stationary coordinates (i.e., the apparatus) is

$$(N_A/A)_x = [0.083/(0.04)][1.56 \times 10^{-3}] = 3.237 \times 10^{-3}\,\text{kmol m}^{-2}\,\text{s}^{-1} \qquad \text{(v)}$$

For part (b), the mass flux expressed in terms of the molar flux $(N_A/A)_x$ is

$$(n_A/A)_x = [(N_A/A)_x](M_A) \qquad (2.32)$$

where M_A is the molecular weight of CO_2, 44.01 kg mol^{-1}. The mass flow is the mass flux times the area:

$$
\begin{aligned}
n_A &= (n_A/A)_x A = [(N_A/A)_x](M_A)(A) \\
&= \frac{(3.237 \times 10^{-3})(1.131 \times 10^{-4})(44.01)(3600)}{0.4539} \\
&\quad \times \left(\frac{(\text{kmol m}^{-2}\,\text{s}^{-1})(\text{m}^2)(\text{kg kmol}^{-1})(\text{s h}^{-1})}{(\text{kg lb}_m^{-1})} \right) \\
&= 0.128\,\text{lb}_m\,\text{h}^{-1} \qquad\qquad\qquad\qquad\qquad\qquad\qquad\qquad \text{(vi)}
\end{aligned}
$$

The mass flow is positive because the CO_2 flows from right to left.

Example 2.7. Air and carbon dioxide are mixed together in a simple "T" pipe. Air at 3 atm pressure and 30°C enters one end of the "T" at a flow rate of 2 kmol min^{-1}. Carbon dioxide at 3 atm pressure and 30°C enters the other end of the "T" at a flow rate of 4 kmol min^{-1}. The two gas streams exit from the middle of the "T", still at 3 atm and 30°C.
(a) Calculate the concentration of CO_2 entering in kg m^{-3}.
(b) Calculate the concentration of N_2 entering in the air stream in lb mol ft^{-3}.
(c) Calculate the concentration of CO_2 exiting in mol cm^{-3}.
(d) Calculate the concentration of O_2 exiting in kmol m^{-3}.

Answer. The molecular weight of CO_2 is 44.01. The temperature is

$$T = 30 + 273.15 = 303.15\,\text{K} \qquad (i)$$

For gases, concentration may have units of moles per volume, n/V. From the ideal gas law

$$C_A = n/V = \bar{p}_A/(RT) \qquad (2.37)$$

where $\bar{p}_A$ is the partial pressure of component A, Eq. (2.38). For a pure gas, such as the CO_2 entering, y_A is one and $\bar{p}_A$ equals p_{total}, 3 atm.
Part (a). From Table C.1, the value of the gas constant is 8.2057×10^{-2} atm m^3 kmol^{-1} K^{-1}. Using Eq. (2.37) above, the concentration is calculated:

$$C_{CO_2} = \frac{3}{(0.082057)(303.15)} \left(\frac{(\text{atm})}{(\text{atm m}^3\,\text{kmol}^{-1}\,\text{K}^{-1})(\text{K})} \right) = 0.121\,\text{kmol m}^{-3} \qquad \text{(ii)}$$

which is equivalent to $(0.121)(44.01)$ or 5.31 kg m^{-3}. Note that the concentration is independent of the flow rate for the pure material.
Part (b). Air is 79 mole percent nitrogen and 21 mole percent oxygen. Therefore,

the mole fraction of nitrogen is 0.79 and from Eq. (2.37):

$$\bar{p}_{N_2} = (0.79)(3) = 2.37 \text{ atm} \qquad \text{(iii)}$$

From Table C.1, the gas constant is $0.7302 \text{ atm ft}^3 \text{ lb mol}^{-1}{}^{\circ}\text{R}^{-1}$. The temperature must be in °R:

$$T = (303.15)(1.8) \text{ K}({}^{\circ}\text{R/K}) = 545.7{}^{\circ}\text{R} \qquad \text{(iv)}$$

From Eq. (2.37):

$$C_{N_2} = \bar{p}_{N_2}/(RT) = 2.37/[(0.7302)(545.7)] = 5.95 \times 10^{-3} \text{ lb mol ft}^{-3} \qquad \text{(v)}$$

Part (c). The exiting stream composition must be calculated. The appropriate basis is one minute. In one minute, 2 kmol of air enter the tee and are mixed with 4 kmol of CO_2. Hence the total is 6 kmol, and

$$\text{kmol } CO_2 = 4$$
$$\text{kmol } O_2 = (2)(0.21) = 0.42 \qquad \text{(vi)}$$
$$\text{kmol } N_2 = (2)(0.79) = 1.58$$

The mole fractions (y) in the vapor phase are:

$$y_{CO_2} = 4/6 = 0.667$$
$$y_{O_2} = 0.42/6 = 0.07 \qquad \text{(vii)}$$
$$y_{N_2} = 1.58/6 = 0.263$$

As a check, these sum to 1.000; the sum of the mole fractions in any phase always sums to unity. The calculation now proceeds as in part (b):

$$R = 82.057 \text{ atm cm}^3 \text{ mol}^{-1} \text{ K}^{-1}$$
$$\bar{p}_{CO_2} = p_{total} y_{CO_2} = (3)(0.667) = 2 \text{ atm} \qquad \text{(viii)}$$
$$C_{CO_2} = \bar{p}_{CO_2}/(RT) = 2/[(82.057)(303.15)] = 8.04 \times 10^{-5} \text{ mol cm}^{-3}$$

Part (d). The mole fraction of O_2 in the exit stream was found to be 0.07 in part (c). The calculation proceeds as in part (b):

$$R = 8.3143 \text{ kPa m}^3 \text{ kmol}^{-1} \text{ K}^{-1}$$
$$\bar{p}_{O_2} = (3)(0.07) = (0.21 \text{ atm})(101.325 \text{ kPa atm}^{-1}) = 21.28 \text{ kPa} \qquad \text{(ix)}$$
$$C_{O_2} = \bar{p}_{O_2}/(RT) = (21.28)/[(8.3143)(303.15)] = 8.44 \times 10^{-3} \text{ kmol m}^{-3}$$

Example 2.8. A tank containing 15 mole percent of CO_2 in air is connected to a second tank containing only air. The connection line is 5 cm in diameter and 30 cm long, as shown in Fig. 2.8. Both tanks are at 1 atm pressure and at 298.15 K. The volume of each tank is very large compared to the volume of gas in the 30-cm connection line so that concentration changes in each tank are negligible for a very long time after the beginning of the experiment. The diffusion coefficient of CO_2 in air at 1 atm and 25°C is $0.164 \times 10^{-4} \text{ m}^2 \text{ s}^{-1}$. Calculate the initial rate of mass transfer of the CO_2. Is the air transferred?

Answer. Assume that both gases are ideal. The diffusional transfer is equimolar counter diffusion, and Eq. (2.25) applies:

$$(N_A/A)_x = (J_A/A)_x = -D_{AB}(\partial C_A/\partial x) \qquad \text{(2.25)}$$

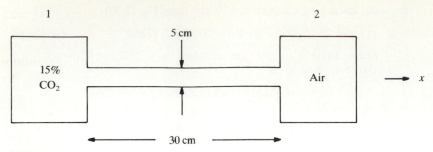

FIGURE 2.8
Mass transfer system.

Equations (2.25) and (2.39) can be combined as follows:

$$(N_A/A)_x = -[D/(RT)][d\bar{p}_A/dx] = -[D/(RT)][\Delta\bar{p}_A/\Delta x] \tag{i}$$

where $(N_A/A)_x$ is the flux with respect to the apparatus in Fig. 2.8.

The initial rate is that under the conditions given in the problem statement above. After the diffusion has progressed, the rate will decrease as the concentration in the two tanks equalizes. For the case under consideration:

$$\Delta x = 30 - 0 = 30 \text{ cm} = 0.3 \text{ m} \tag{ii}$$

$$A = \pi d^2/4 = (3.1416)(5)^2/4 = 19.6 \text{ cm}^2 = 1.96 \times 10^{-3} \text{ m}^2 \tag{iii}$$

$$R = 8.314 \times 10^3 \text{ N m kmol}^{-1} \text{ K}^{-1} \tag{iv}$$

$$\Delta\bar{p}_A = \bar{p}_2 - \bar{p}_1 = 0 - (0.15)(p) = (-0.15)(1) = -0.150 \text{ atm}$$
$$= -1.52 \times 10^4 \text{ N m}^{-2} \tag{v}$$

Equation (i) is solved for the molar flow rate, and the above values substituted:

$$N_A = -\frac{DA}{RT}\frac{\Delta\bar{p}_A}{\Delta x}$$

$$= -\left(\frac{(1.64 \times 10^{-5})(1.96 \times 10^{-3})}{(8.314 \times 10^3)(298.15)}\right)\left(\frac{-1.52 \times 10^4}{0.3}\right)$$

$$\times \left(\frac{(m^2 s^{-1})(m^2)}{(N \text{ m kmol}^{-1} \text{ K}^{-1})(K)}\right)\left(\frac{N \text{ m}^{-2}}{(m)}\right)$$

$$= +6.57 \times 10^{-10} \text{ kmol s}^{-1} \tag{vi}$$

The plus sign indicates that the diffusion is from 1 to 2 (to the right) in Fig. 2.8. In order for the pressure to remain at 1 atm, a diffusion of air must occur which is in the opposite direction and equal to 6.57×10^{-10} kmol s^{-1}.

2.4   MOMENTUM TRANSFER

Momentum transfer or fluid dynamics is a part of nearly every process in the chemical industry. Often heat and mass transfer occur in association with moving streams, and thus it is necessary to have some understanding of the fluid flow before one can really understand the other superimposed operations. Examples of fluid dynamics problems typically encountered are pressure drop in systems so as to determine pumping requirements, flow rate measurements and control, flow over immersed bodies and through porous media, motions of solid particles in fluids (e.g., smoke), heat or mass transfer between flowing streams, and the motions of drops and bubbles.

Temperature and mass are scalar quantities. The gradients of these (∇T or ∇C_A) and the flux terms (q/A or J_A/A or N_A/A) are vectors. In marked contrast, the velocity itself is a vector, and the gradient of this (∇U) is a second-order tensor.[6]

Correspondingly, the momentum flux or shear stress is also a second-order tensor. Instead of a simple vector equation as in Eqs. (2.15) or (2.19), the momentum equation in three dimensions is a tensor relation, which for an incompressible fluid is

$$\tau = -\mu[\nabla U + (\nabla U)^{\mathrm{T}}] \qquad (2.40)$$

Equation (2.40) shows that the stress tensor τ is a function of the shear rate tensor ∇U and its transpose $(\nabla U)^{\mathrm{T}}$. Additional discussion of Eq. (2.40) can be found elsewhere [B2, B3]. Because of this extreme complexity, let us dwell longer on this tensorial nature of the momentum transfer equation.

Velocity, which is a vector quantity, has three components. Any one of these components can vary in three directions. Consequently, there are three components taken three ways, or nine possible terms. In the form of an array, these terms are

$$\nabla U = \begin{pmatrix} \partial U_x/\partial x & \partial U_y/\partial x & \partial U_z/\partial x \\ \partial U_x/\partial y & \partial U_y/\partial y & \partial U_z/\partial y \\ \partial U_x/\partial z & \partial U_y/\partial z & \partial U_z/\partial z \end{pmatrix} \qquad (2.41)$$

Equation (2.41) is, of course, in the most general form; in most problems, many of the components will be identically zero. The transpose tensor $(\nabla U)^{\mathrm{T}}$ is just Eq. (2.41) with the rows and columns exchanged:

$$(\nabla U)^{\mathrm{T}} = \begin{pmatrix} \partial U_x/\partial x & \partial U_x/\partial y & \partial U_x/\partial z \\ \partial U_y/\partial x & \partial U_y/\partial y & \partial U_y/\partial z \\ \partial U_z/\partial x & \partial U_z/\partial y & \partial U_z/\partial z \end{pmatrix} \qquad (2.42)$$

---

[6] Tensors will be discussed only in a very superficial manner in this text. Tensors, like matrices, find most of their use in engineering as "shorthand" for writing complex equations in a simple form. The tensorial representation being developed here is really shorthand for nine equations. The material in this section is by no means simple or complete, and the student is to be warned that he or she should not expect to have a full understanding without work beyond this text. It is hoped, though, that this brief introduction will provide an idea as to this complexity and some of the physics involved in momentum transfer.

Since Eq. (2.40) must be homogeneous, the left-hand side must also be a second-order tensor, i.e.,

$$\boldsymbol{\tau} = \begin{pmatrix} \tau_{xx} & \tau_{xy} & \tau_{xz} \\ \tau_{yx} & \tau_{yy} & \tau_{yz} \\ \tau_{zx} & \tau_{zy} & \tau_{zz} \end{pmatrix} \tag{2.43}$$

Each row of the tensor has three terms. In the first row of Eq. (2.43) there is one normal stress τ_{xx} and two tangential stresses, τ_{xy} and τ_{xz}. The three normal stresses in Eq. (2.43) (the diagonal elements) act in the x, y, and z directions, and each is the force per unit area on a plane perpendicular to the direction in which it acts.

As already indicated, Eq. (2.40) is a shorthand representation for nine equations. Several of these are[7]

$$\tau_{xx} = -\mu(\partial U_x/\partial x + \partial U_x/\partial x) = -2\mu(\partial U_x/\partial x) \tag{2.44}$$

$$\tau_{yx} = -\mu[(\partial U_x/\partial y) + (\partial U_y/\partial x)] \tag{2.45}$$

$$\tau_{xy} = -\mu[(\partial U_y/\partial x) + (\partial U_x/\partial y)] \tag{2.46}$$

For the one-dimensional problem of Eq. (2.5), U_x varies in the y direction only, and both U_y and U_z are zero. Thus, most derivatives in ∇U are zero:

$$\partial U_x/\partial x = \partial U_x/\partial z = 0 \tag{2.47}$$

$$\partial U_y/\partial x = \partial U_y/\partial y = \partial U_z/\partial z = 0 \tag{2.48}$$

$$\partial U_z/\partial z = \partial U_z/\partial y = \partial U_z/\partial z = 0 \tag{2.49}$$

From the nine equations represented in shorthand by Eq. (2.40) only two equations remain, Eqs. (2.45) and (2.46), both of which are identical to Eq. (2.5) since $\partial U_y/\partial x$ is zero and τ_{xy} equals τ_{yx}. It therefore follows that for the one-dimensional problem where Eq. (2.5) is valid, there are only two non-zero shear stress terms, which are τ_{yx} and τ_{xy}.

The physical interpretation of $\boldsymbol{\tau}$ is complicated by the fact that $\boldsymbol{\tau}$ is commonly used both as a momentum flux and as a shear stress (F/A). Hence, $\boldsymbol{\tau}$ in Eq. (2.43) is commonly called the stress tensor. Figure 2.9 considers the shear stresses τ_{xx}, τ_{xy}, and τ_{xz} at a point in space, Fig. 2.9(a). Figure 2.9(b) shows a typical experiment that might generate τ_{xy}, i.e., a flat plate moving with velocity U_{plate} in the y direction. This plate causes a velocity gradient so that U_y in the fluid is a function of x. There is a momentum flux τ_{xy} that acts in the x direction on the yz plane, shown as shaded in Fig. 2.9(a).

The shear stress, on the other hand, is in the y direction as a result of a

---

[7] The ordering of subscripts comes from writing Newton's equation (2.5) as $\tau_{yx} = -\mu(\partial/\partial y)(U_x)$, i.e., the y (momentum transfer direction) precedes x (velocity direction).

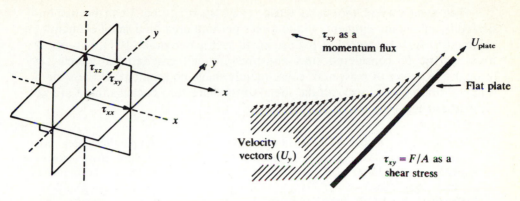

(a) Stress tensor on the yz plane   (b) The xy component as a momentum flux

FIGURE 2.9
The momentum flux τ_{xy}.

force **F** (not shown) in the y direction that is needed to pull the plate with velocity U_{plate}. It is admittedly confusing when the same symbol τ_{xy} is used to denote the momentum flux and the shear stress, especially when they are equal in magnitude but in differing directions.

Figure 2.10 shows the momentum flux and the shear stress for a flat plate moving in the x direction. The momentum flux τ_{yx} acts on the xy plane, shown as shaded in Fig. 2.10(a). The shear stress τ_{yx} acts in the x direction. Note that the terms τ_{xx}, τ_{yx}, and τ_{zx} all act in the same x direction and are coincident. They are also the flux of x momentum in the three directions x, y, and z.

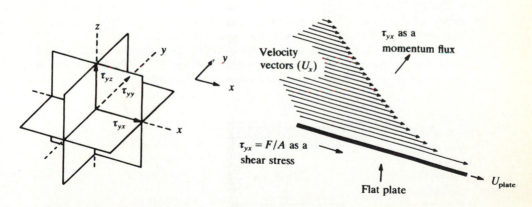

(a) Stress tensor on the xz plane   (b) The yx component as a momentum flux

FIGURE 2.10
The momentum flux τ_{yx}.

The symmetry of the stress tensor (i.e., $\tau_{yx} = \tau_{xy}$, etc.) can be demonstrated by taking the moments of the forces per unit area on a small element of volume ($dx\,dy\,dz$) centered at the origin. In such a derivation [C1], only shear stresses need be considered since the pressure and gravitational effects act through the center of mass and, consequently, have no moment. If the system is at equilibrium or at rest, all the shear stresses are zero because there are no velocity gradients [by Eq. (2.40)].

Example 2.9. Toluene is contained between two identical and parallel plates each of area $5.0\,\text{m}^2$. The top plate is pulled in the minus x direction by a force of $0.083\,\text{N}$ at a velocity of $0.3\,\text{m}\,\text{s}^{-1}$. The bottom plate is pulled in the opposite direction by a force of $0.027\,\text{N}$ at a velocity of $0.1\,\text{m}\,\text{s}^{-1}$, as shown in Fig. 2.11. The plates are 10 mm apart. Calculate the viscosity of toluene in centipoise.

Answer. Since the plates are parallel, the flow is one-dimensional, and Eq. (2.5) applies

$$\tau_{yx} = F/A = -\mu(\partial U_x/\partial y) \tag{2.5}$$

Since for this problem F, A, and μ are all constants, Eq. (2.5) integrates to

$$F/A = -\mu(\Delta U_x/\Delta y) \tag{i}$$

$$\Delta U_x = U_{x,2} - U_{x,1} = -0.3 - 0.1 = -0.4\,\text{m}\,\text{s}^{-1} \tag{ii}$$

$$\Delta y = y_2 - y_1 = 10\,\text{mm} = 0.01\,\text{m} \tag{iii}$$

Therefore, the velocity gradient is

$$\Delta U_x/\Delta y = (-0.4)/(10^{-2}) = -40\,\text{s}^{-1} \tag{iv}$$

The shear stress is force divided by area. Logically, if the bottom plate were stationary, then the force would be 0.083 N. If the force on the bottom plate were in the same direction as the force on the top plate, it follows that the force available in the shear stress term would be diminished. In fact if the force on the bottom plate were equal in magnitude and direction to the force on the top plate, both plates would move in the same direction and with the same velocity. The fluid between, at steady-state, would not move with respect to the plates and the shear stress in the fluid would be zero. For the problem of Fig. 2.11 the force on the bottom plate acts in the opposite direction from the force on the top plate and

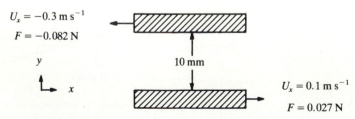

$U_x = -0.3\,\text{m}\,\text{s}^{-1}$

$F = -0.082\,\text{N}$

y

x

10 mm

$U_x = 0.1\,\text{m}\,\text{s}^{-1}$

$F = 0.027\,\text{N}$

FIGURE 2.11
Parallel plate system.

thus increases the shear stress in the fluid. Therefore, the momentum flux is

$$\tau_{yx} = F/A = [0.083 - (-0.027)]/5.0 = 0.022 \text{ N m}^{-2} \tag{v}$$

Note that it is easy to confuse the sign when the problem is given in terms of the forces on the flat plates. Perhaps it is best to refer to Eq. (2.5). In this problem, since $\partial U_x/\partial y$ is negative, then τ_{yx} must be positive.

Equation (2.5) can be solved for the viscosity

$$\mu = \tau_{yx}/(-dU_x/dy) = (0.022)/(40)(\text{N m}^{-2})/(\text{s}^{-1})$$
$$= 5.5 \times 10^{-4} \text{ N s m}^{-2} \tag{vi}$$

Since one newton (N) is one kg m s^{-2}, the viscosity in cP is

$$\mu = 5.5 \times 10^{-4} \text{ kg m}^{-1} \text{s}^{-1} = 5.5 \times 10^{-3} \text{ poise} = 0.55 \text{ cP} \tag{vii}$$

Example 2.10. An incompressible fluid flows between two large plates in the x direction at steady-state. The bottom plate is flat. The top plate is divided into two flat plates by a reducer plate set at an angle to the bottom plate. The fluid flows in a 2-cm wide channel at the inlet, then into the reducer section, and out a 1-cm-wide channel (see Fig. 2.12). The flow is laminar throughout the channel. In the reducer, which of the nine components of the velocity tensor ∇U and the stress tensor τ are non-zero?

Answer. Since both plates are large and flow is in the x and y directions only, the velocity in the z direction (perpendicular to the plane of the paper in Fig. 2.12) will be zero as will all derivatives of U_z:

$$\partial U_z/\partial x = \partial U_z/\partial y = \partial U_z/\partial z = 0 \tag{i}$$

In the reducer the incompressible fluid must accelerate because the area is being reduced while the mass entering the reducer equals the mass exiting. Since the fluid is accelerating in the x direction:

$$\partial U_x/\partial x \neq 0 \tag{ii}$$

The velocity U_x is a function of y everywhere between the plates (zero at both

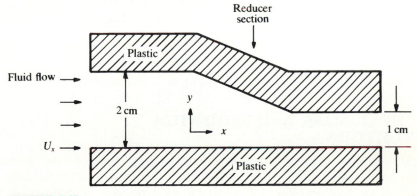

FIGURE 2.12
Convergent plate system.

walls, finite and variable in between):

$$\partial U_x / \partial y \neq 0 \tag{iii}$$

Furthermore, the fluid must flow in the minus y direction as well as the positive x direction in order to squeeze into the 1-cm-wide channel. The velocity U_y will vary in the x direction as well as in the y direction:

$$\partial U_y / \partial x \neq 0 \neq \partial U_y / \partial y \tag{iv}$$

Since the plates are large, there is no variation of any velocity with the z direction, thus

$$\partial U_x / \partial z = 0 = \partial U_y / \partial z \tag{v}$$

In conclusion, for the two-dimensional flow in the reducer, there are four non-zero derivatives in ∇U: $\partial U_x / \partial x$, $\partial U_x / \partial y$, $\partial U_y / \partial x$, and $\partial U_y / \partial y$.

To find the non-zero shear stress terms, each shear stress is written in terms of the velocity derivative, as done in Eq. (2.44) through (2.46). The normal stresses are

$$\tau_{xx} = -2\mu(\partial U_x / \partial x) \neq 0$$
$$\tau_{yy} = -2\mu(\partial U_y / \partial y) \neq 0 \tag{vi}$$
$$\tau_{zz} = -2\mu(\partial U_z / \partial z) = 0$$

The other six shear stresses are for the x direction:

$$\tau_{xy} = -\mu[(\partial U_y / \partial x) + (\partial U_x / \partial y)] \neq 0$$
$$\tau_{xz} = -\mu[(\partial U_z / \partial x) + (\partial U_x / \partial z)] = 0 \tag{vii}$$

For the y direction:

$$\tau_{yx} = -\mu[(\partial U_x / \partial y) + (\partial U_y / \partial x)] \neq 0$$
$$\tau_{yz} = -\mu[(\partial U_z / \partial y) + (\partial U_y / \partial z)] = 0 \tag{viii}$$

For the z direction:

$$\tau_{zx} = -\mu[(\partial U_x / \partial z) + (\partial U_z / \partial x)] = 0$$
$$\tau_{zy} = -\mu[(\partial U_y / \partial z) + (\partial U_z / \partial y)] = 0 \tag{ix}$$

Hence, there are four non-zero shear stress terms in the reducer, i.e., τ_{xx}, τ_{yy}, τ_{xy}, and τ_{yx}. Note the symmetry of the stress tensor:

$$\tau_{xy} = \tau_{yx} \qquad \tau_{xz} = \tau_{zx} \qquad \text{etc.} \tag{x}$$

The stress tensor is always symmetrical under normal conditions.

2.5 HEAT, MASS, AND MOMENTUM DIFFUSIVITIES

In the previous sections a mathematical analogy between the molecular transports has been developed. The analogy is mathematical in the sense that Eq. (2.9) for heat transfer, Eq. (2.4) for mass transfer, and Eq. (2.11) for momentum transfer (fluid flow) have the same form. Therefore, these three differential equations have similar solutions for an identical set of boundary conditions. The mechanisms for molecular transfer are obviously not the same: molecular diffusion commonly occurs in multicomponent mixtures with a concentration gradient as the driving force; momentum transfer occurs perpendicular to the direction of flow (the direction of the pressure drop, i.e. the driving force that causes the flow); heat transfer by molecular transport (conduction) in solids does not involve flow or relative motion of the molecules at all.

Fourier's law, Eq. (2.2), Fick's law, Eq. (2.4) and Newton's law, Eq. (2.5) are all empirical. The respective constants in these three equations have different units:

(1) thermal conductivity, k: units of $W\,m^{-1}\,K^{-1}$
(2) diffusion coefficient, D: units of $m^2\,s^{-1}$
(3) viscosity, μ: units of $kg\,m^{-1}\,s^{-1}$

In developing the analogous equations, these three empirical constants were modified (see Table 2.1) in order to equate the flux Ψ_x with the concentration gradient, $\partial\psi/\partial x$:

$$\Psi_x = -\delta(\partial\psi/x) \qquad (2.7)$$

where δ is the general diffusivity which can be the thermal diffusivity for heat transfer (α), the diffusion coefficient (mass diffusivity) for mass transfer (D), or the kinematic viscosity (momentum diffusivity) for momentum transfer or fluid flow (v). In this form, the proportionality constant, δ (α, D, or v), has the same units ($m^2\,s^{-1}$).

The empirical constants (k, D, and μ) are material constants which vary widely from material to material. Furthermore, these three constants vary with changes in temperature, pressure, and, in the case of D, concentration. Generally, it is necessary to find the individual properties (k, ρ, c_p, and μ) in order to compute the diffusivities. Tabulations and/or correlations of thermal diffusivity α and momentum diffusivity (kinematic viscosity) v are rarely directly available; these are normally computed from k, ρ, c_p, and μ. Table 2.2 provides some experimentally determined transport properties for a variety of systems. More complete tabulations are available [P1, R1]. Methods of predicting the transport properties are discussed in Chapter 14.

2.5.1 Thermal Conductivity

Two properties of materials which are important in heat transfer are the thermal conductivity and thermal diffusivity. The thermal conductivity has been defined in Eq. (2.2) and its use illustrated in Examples 2.1, 2.4, and 2.5. Some typical values of the thermal conductivity are given in Table 2.2.

As with the other transport properties, the thermal conductivity of gases

TABLE 2.2
The transport properties

	Gases at low pressures (approximately 1 bar)[a,b,f]			
	Viscosity		**Thermal conductivity**	
	Temperature, K	$\mu \times 10^6$, N s m^{-2}	Temperature, K	k, W m^{-1} K^{-1}
Air				
	273.15	17.2	273.15	0.0241
	280.00	17.5	280.00	0.0247
	300.00	18.5	300.00	0.0261
	350.00	20.8	350.00	0.0297
	400.00	22.9	400.00	0.0331
Ammonia				
			213	0.0164
	273.15	93.3	273.15	0.0221
	373.15	131	373.15	0.0320
	673.15	251		
Carbon dioxide				
	303.15	151	300	0.0167
	373.65	181		
	473.25	219	473.15	0.0283
Ethanol				
	383.15	111	375	0.0222
	423.15	123	401	0.0249
	473.15	137		
	573.15	165		
Sulfur dioxide				
	283.15	120	273.15	0.0083
	373.15	163		
	773.15	315		
	1173.15	432		
Water				
	373.15	12.0	373.15	0.0248

(See page 50 for footnotes)

may be predicted more accurately than the thermal conductivity of liquids or solids. In gases the energy is carried by the molecules themselves, and our ability to describe statistically the molecular motion in gases is good. In liquids and solids other mechanisms are operative. Since heat transfer by conduction is effected by transfer of energy through molecular collisions, it follows that the thermal conductivity in liquids and solids is much greater than in gases. For example, in Table 2.2 for water vapor at 0°C, k equals 0.0228 W m^{-1} K^{-1}, whereas for liquid water at 0°C, k equals 0.561 W m^{-1} K^{-1}, which is a factor of 24.6 greater.

TABLE 2.2
The transport properties (continued)

Diffusion coefficients of binary gases at atmospheric pressure[c]		
Gas pair	Temperature, K	$D \times 10^4$, $m^2 s^{-1}$
H_2–CO_2	298.0	0.646
D_2–air	296.8	0.565
He–N_2	323.2	0.766
He–N_2	413.2	1.20
He–N_2	600	2.40
He–N_2	900	4.76
He–N_2	1200	7.74
He–propanol	423.2	0.676
O_2–H_2O	308.1	0.282
O_2–H_2O	352.4	0.352
O_2–benzene	311.3	0.101
Freon-12-benzene	298.2	0.0385
Air–CO_2	293.0	0.165
Air–water	298.2	0.260
Air–ethanol	298.2	0.135

TABLE 2.2
The transport properties (continued)

	Liquids at saturation pressures[a,b,f]			
	Viscosity		Thermal conductivity	
	Temperature, K	$\mu \times 10^3$, $N s m^{-2}$	Temperature, K	k, $W m^{-1} K^{-1}$
Carbon tetrachloride				
	273.15	1.369	273.15	0.107
	303.15	0.856	293.15	0.103
	343.15	0.534		
	373.15	0.404		
Ethanol				
	273.15	1.770	293.15	0.165
	313.15	0.826	313.15	0.152
	348.15	0.465	347	0.135
Toluene				
	293.15	0.587		
	303.15	0.550	303.15	0.145
	330.15	0.380		
Water				
	273.15	1.750	273.15	0.569
	290.00	1.080	290.00	0.598
	300.00	0.855	300.00	0.613
	373.15	0.279	373.15	0.680

TABLE 2.2
The transport properties (continued)

Diffusion Coefficient[b]			
Solute (at infinite dilution)	**Solvent**	**Temperature, K**	**$D \times 10^{10}$, $m^2\,s^{-1}$**
n-Propanol	Water	288.15	8.7
Ethanol	Water	283.15	8.4
Ethanol	Water	283.15	10.0
Ethanol	Water	298.15	12.4
Oxygen	Water	298.15	24.0
Methanol	Water	288.15	12.6
Water	Ethanol	298.15	12.4
Iodine	Hexane	298.15	41.5[a]

TABLE 2.2
The transport properties (continued)

Solids					
Thermal conductivity of selected solids at 300 K[a]		Diffusion coefficient of species A in a solid[d,e]			
Material	**k, $W\,m^{-1}\,K^{-1}$**	**Species A**	**Solid**	**Temperature, K**	**D, $m^2\,s^{-1}$**
Steel	45	Hydrogen	Silicon	1473	2.1×10^{-8}
Copper	398	Copper	Silicon	1473	1.5×10^{-9}
Silver	424	Carbon	Silicon	1473	3.3×10^{-15}
Aluminum	273	Phosphorus	Silicon	1473	2.4×10^{-16}
Drywall	0.17	Germanium	Silicon	1473	5.2×10^{-18}
Glass fiber	0.036	Gold	Silver	1033	3.6×10^{-14}
Brick	0.72	Carbon	Steel	1273	2.0×10^{-11}
Corkboard	0.43	Nitrogen	Steel	1273	1.3×10^{-11}
Plywood	0.12				

[a] From reference P1.
[b] From reference R1.
[c] From reference F1.
[d] From reference B1.
[e] From reference S1.
[f] From Appendix A.

2.5.2 Diffusion Coefficient

The diffusion coefficient, as defined in Eq. (2.4), is in one sense the simplest of the diffusivities in that other properties are not involved; however, it is the most difficult to measure and correlate. The complexity arises from the fact that according to Fick's law the diffusion coefficient D must be measured in an experiment where there is no net volume velocity. Also, the diffusion coefficient is small in magnitude; therefore, experimental errors are magnified in relation to the actual value of D. Some typical values are given in Table 2.2. Other tabulations are available [G1, P1, R1]. In general, the diffusion coefficient of binary mixtures increases with temperature, but not linearly, and decreases with pressure. The diffusion in gas systems depends upon gas molecules moving from one point to another. Since at higher temperatures the molecules have a higher kinetic energy, they move further and faster; consequently, the diffusion coefficient increases with temperature as just stated. When the pressure is increased, there are more molecules in the system and collisions between molecules increase; consequently, molecular motion is retarded, and the diffusivity decreases with pressure. By the same token, there are large differences between the diffusivities in gases and those in liquids and solids as is observed in Table 2.2. Also, the difference among the diffusion coefficients in solids is 26 orders of magnitude! In silicon, copper diffuses at a rate 10^9 times faster than germanium at 1200°C [S1].

There are a number of equations available for estimating the diffusion coefficient of gases [P1, R1]. These will be covered in Chapter 14, along with a discussion of diffusion coefficients in liquids and solids. For gases, the pressure and temperature dependence can be expressed as:

$$D = D_0 \frac{p_0}{p} \left(\frac{T}{T_0}\right)^n \tag{2.50}$$

where D_0 is known at T_0 and p_0, and the exponent n varies between 1.75 and 2.0 over a range of normal temperatures and pressures. Usually, the value of n is closer to the 1.75 value than to the higher figure. As long as the pressure is less than approximately 5 atm, there is no concentration dependence of the diffusion coefficient. Details are elsewhere (M1).

Example 2.11. Predict the diffusion coefficient of water vapor in air at 2 atm and 75°C, if the diffusion coefficient is 0.219×10^{-4} m² s⁻¹ at 1 atm and 0°C. Assume n is 1.75.

Answer. The value of n to be used in Eq. (2.50) is 1.75. Then

$$D_0 = 0.219 \times 10^{-4} \text{ m}^2 \text{ s}^{-1} \qquad (T_0 = 273.15 \text{ K}, \ p_0 = 1.0 \text{ atm}) \tag{i}$$

$$T = 273.15 + 75 = 348.15 \text{ K} \qquad (p = 2.0 \text{ atm}) \tag{ii}$$

$$D = D_0 \frac{p_0}{p} \left(\frac{T}{T_0}\right)^n = (0.219 \times 10^{-4}) \left(\frac{1.0}{2.0}\right) \left(\frac{348.15}{273.15}\right)^{1.75}$$

$$= 0.167 \times 10^{-4} \text{ m}^2 \text{ s}^{-1} \tag{iii}$$

2.5.3 Viscosity

Most pure (single-component) materials obey Newton's law of viscosity at conditions commonly encountered in practical problems:

$$\tau_{yx} = -\mu(\partial U_x/\partial y) \tag{2.51}$$

Table 2.2 contains some typical values of viscosity. Extensive tables and charts are available in various handbooks [G2, L1, P1]. In Chapter 14 we review the theory of viscosity and discuss methods of prediction. In general, the viscosity of gases increases with temperature at low pressures, while that of liquids usually decreases. The reason for the difference in the temperature dependence lies in the differences in the mechanisms by which momentum is transferred. For gases at low pressures, it can be shown that the expected variation with temperature is the square root of temperature in absolute units, if the molecules are rigid spheres. Actually, the observed dependency is from about 0.6 power of temperature to the first power of temperature. The viscosity of gases is independent of pressure in the low-pressure region up to ten times atmospheric pressure. Of course, the kinematic viscosity of gases is quite dependent on both temperature and pressure change through the effect of these on the gas density. For liquids, the theories are far less developed. However, an approximate empirical observation for the temperature dependency of liquids is

$$\mu = Ae^{B/(RT)} \tag{2.52}$$

where A and B are empirical constants in this equation. Equation (2.52) can be used with viscosity data (minimum two points) for interpolation or modest extrapolation. Because of the incompressibility of liquids, their viscosities are relatively independent of pressure.

There is an important class of materials that do not obey Newton's law when the shear rate is varied in an experiment. These fluids are called non-Newtonian. There are many non-Newtonian materials that one encounters in chemical processing. Common examples include multigrade motor oils, greases, elastomers, many emulsions, oil well drilling muds, clay suspensions, concrete mixes, toothpaste, milkshakes and other foodstuffs, and some medicines. If the material has a very high molecular weight (in the order of thousands), as do polymer melts, such a material will also be non-Newtonian. Non-Newtonian materials will be discussed in detail in Chapter 15.

Example 2.12. Estimate the viscosity of air and of water at 53°C.

Answer. For air (a gas), a simple solution is to plot the data as given in Table 2.2, and read the value at 53 °C (326.15 K). It is expected that the viscosity of gases will follow this approximate equation:

$$\mu = AT^B \tag{i}$$

or after taking logarithms

$$\ln \mu = \ln A + B \ln T \tag{ii}$$

Therefore, the data should be plotted on log–log graph paper or as $\ln \mu$ versus $\ln T$.

Another solution is to use Eq. (ii) to interpolate between the values in Table 2.2. For air at 40°C (313.15 K) and 74°C (347.15 K), the substitution into

Eq. (ii) yields two equations in two unknowns (A and B):

$$\ln(1.91 \times 10^{-5}) = \ln A + B \ln(313.15) \tag{iii}$$

$$\ln(2.10 \times 10^{-5}) = \ln A + B \ln(347.15) \tag{iv}$$

Solving these simultaneously yields

$$B = 0.92005$$
$$A = 9.656 \times 10^{-8}\,\mathrm{N\,s\,m^{-2}} \tag{v}$$

At 326.15 K from Eq. (i)

$$\mu = 9.656 \times 10^{-8}(326.15)^{0.92005} = 1.98 \times 10^{-5}\,\mathrm{N\,s\,m^{-2}} = 0.0198\,\mathrm{cP} \tag{vi}$$

For water, Eq. (2.52) applies. A similar calculation using data from Appendix A.1 at 325 K and 330 K yields

$$B/R = 1646 \qquad A = 3.336 \times 10^{-8}\,\mathrm{N\,s\,m^{-2}} \tag{vii}$$

Thus, from Eq. (2.52):

$$\mu(T = 53°C) = 3.336 \times 10^{-8} \exp(1646/326.15) = 5.19 \times 10^{-4}\,\mathrm{N\,s\,m^{-2}}$$
$$= 0.519\,\mathrm{cP} \tag{viii}$$

These can be compared to handbook values of 0.0196 and 0.523 cP respectively at 53°C.

2.6 A COMPARISON OF THE TRANSPORTS

At the beginning of this chapter a set of analogous equations for heat, mass, and momentum transfer was developed. These equations, based on the laws of Fourier, Fick, and Newton, apply only in a continuum, i.e., in applications where all properties are continuous. It was emphasized that this was a mathematical analogy and that the fundamental physical processes of the transfers were quite different. In the three previous sections, the mathematical analogy has been demolished in the sense that the equations are by no means identical. In its more complicated form, heat transfer is described by a vector equation as is mass transfer. However, mass transfer involves at least two equations, since there must be equations for each of the species present. Finally, it has been demonstrated that the momentum transfer is described by a second-order tensor equation and, in the most general case, there are nine component equations. Nevertheless, any given single component of these equations is of the same mathematical form as those in mass and heat transfer.

Let us return to the case of the diffusion between flasks [see Fig. 2.1(*b*)] and try to picture our analogy in physical terms. Further, let us restrict our view to a very dilute gas. For mass transfer, in order to move a molecule from one flask to the other through the connecting tube, that molecule must be moved physically. For one such molecule, the movement is shown by the dotted line in Fig. 2.13. If the molecule should strike another molecule or the

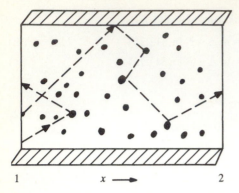

FIGURE 2.13
Mass transfer mechanism.

1   x ⟶   2

container wall during its transfer, it may not arrive at the other side; this situation is indicated by the dashed line. In this crude dilute gas experiment, a molecule has a difficult, tortuous path in order to be transferred from one side of the vessel to the other. This process of diffusion by random molecular collisions is called a "random walk" process, and it can be observed in the Brownian movement in suspensions [B1]. The mass diffusion process may be contrasted to the transfer of energy of the molecule as indicated in Fig. 2.14. As in the case of mass transfer, every time a molecule is moved, its temperature is transferred with it. However, there is another mechanism which contributes even more to the transfer of heat. This mechanism is analogous to the transfer of energy encountered in playing pool, and it is shown by the dashed line in Fig. 2.14. There are both migration and collision mechanisms for the transfer of the energy or temperature. Thus, in relatively dense systems, the thermal diffusivity is greater than the mass diffusivity. The same is true for the momentum transfer case for which there are still other mechanisms as a result of its tensorial nature. To provide a simple comparison, the

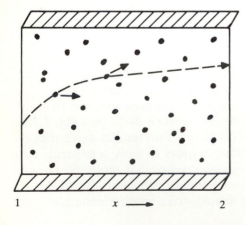

FIGURE 2.14
Heat transfer mechanism.

1   x ⟶   2

transport properties for liquid water at 0°C are compared:

$$D = 1.36 \times 10^{-9} \, \text{m}^2 \, \text{s}^{-1}$$
$$\alpha = 142 \times 10^{-9} \, \text{m}^2 \, \text{s}^{-1} \tag{2.53}$$
$$\nu = 1800 \times 10^{-9} \, \text{m}^2 \, \text{s}^{-1}$$

It is fortunate that, from an experimental standpoint, the various mechanisms are described by the same equation. Equation (2.53) shows that the various diffusivities, of mass, of momentum, and of heat, are not equal. If only one mechanism had been controlling all three phenomena, then these diffusivities would be equal.

Finally, all problems with a numerical solution in this chapter can be solved only because the flux is constant and due to one of the fundamental laws discussed. More complex problems will be forthcoming in following chapters.

PROBLEMS

2.1. What is meant by the analogy between mass transfer, momentum transfer, and heat transfer?

2.2. Write the three molecular transport equations and discuss the meaning of, and units for, each term in the equations.

2.3. The ratio of momentum diffusivity to heat diffusivity and the ratio of momentum diffusivity to mass diffusivity form two dimensionless ratios. Discuss the meaning of these ratios.

2.4. What are the analogous terms for heat, mass, and momentum transfer? Discuss!

2.5. Give a physical interpretation of equimolar counter diffusion.

2.6. Mass transfer has a complication that does not exist in heat transfer. Discuss!

2.7. Momentum transfer has a complication that does not exist in either mass or heat transfer. Discuss!

2.8. Consider a flat plate that is submersed in a fluid and is moving at velocity U_{plate} which is entirely in the z direction. Prepare a figure similar to Fig. 2.10 for this example.

2.9. In the discussion of Fig. 2.10, it is pointed out that τ_{xx}, τ_{yx}, and τ_{zx} all act in the same x direction and are coincident. Find the coincident shear stresses in the y and z directions.

2.10. Find the thermal conductivity (in $\text{W} \, \text{m}^{-1} \, \text{K}^{-1}$) and thermal diffusivity ($\text{m}^2 \, \text{s}^{-1}$) for a new insulating material for which the following information has been determined:

Test sample: $\frac{1}{2}$ in. by 1 ft square
ΔT across sample: 5°F
Heat flow: 24 Btu in a 10 h test at steady-state
Sample density: $0.15 \, \text{g} \, \text{cm}^{-3}$
Sample heat capacity: $0.3 \, \text{kcal} \, \text{kg}^{-1} \, \text{K}^{-1}$

2.11. The heat input to a cold box is to be reduced by adding extruded polystyrene sheets ($\rho = 55 \, \text{kg} \, \text{m}^{-3}$, $k = 0.027 \, \text{W} \, \text{m}^{-1} \, \text{K}^{-1}$, $c_p = 1.21 \, \text{kJ} \, \text{kg}^{-1} \, \text{K}^{-1}$) to all sides.

The box is 3 ft on a side and all sides are in contact with air. When the box is placed in a constant-temperature room which is maintained at 70°F, the heat loss is 40 000 Btu h^{-1}. It is desired to reduce this by a factor of 100 while maintaining the inside temperature at $-30°F$. Find the appropriate insulation thickness in inches.

2.12. A house wall consists of $\frac{1}{2}$ in. drywall, $3\frac{5}{8}$ in. glass fiber insulation, and an outside brick wall, 4-in. thick. Assume that there is perfect contact between each layer. The thermal conductivities of drywall, glass fiber, and brick are 0.17, 0.036, and 0.72 W m^{-1} K^{-1}, respectively. The inside temperature of the house is 70°F; the outside air temperature (no wind present) is 0°F.
  (a) Find the heat flux in Btu ft^{-2} h^{-1}.
  (b) Find the temperature (K) at the junction between the drywall and the glass fiber insulation.
  (c) Find the location (in inches from the inside surface of the drywall) where moisture freezes.

2.13. Two cylinders of different materials are brought into contact as shown in Fig. 2.15. Cylinder 1 is 2 m long with cross sectional area of 0.03 m^2 and thermal conductivity 0.7 W m^{-1} K^{-1}. Cylinder 2 is 3 m long with cross sectional area of 0.04 m^2 and thermal conductivity 1.2 W m^{-1} K^{-1}. The temperatures at each end of the apparatus are 280 (T_1) and 310 K (T_3), as shown in Fig. 2.15. Find the temperature T_2 at the point where the two cylinders are joined.

2.14. Two cylinders of different materials are brought into contact as shown in Fig. 2.15. Cylinder 1 is 2 m long with cross sectional area of 0.03 m^2 and thermal conductivity 0.7 W m^{-1} K^{-1}. Cylinder 2 is 3 m long with cross sectional area of 0.04 m^2 and unknown thermal conductivity. The temperatures at each end of the apparatus are 280 (T_1) and 310 K (T_3), as shown in Fig. 2.15. If the temperature at the point of juncture is 300 K, find the thermal conductivity of cylinder 2. Your solution contains an assumption not discussed in Chapter 2. What is it?

2.15. A conditioning room has an atmosphere of air with a 30 mole percent CO_2 concentration. Outside of the room, the concentration of CO_2 is very small; however, there is a hole in the wall. The pressure is 1 atm and the temperature is 25°C. Under these conditions, the diffusivity of CO_2 in air is 0.164×10^{-4} m^2 s^{-1}.

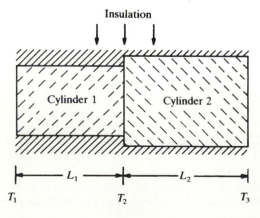

FIGURE 2.15
Heat transfer in adjoining cylinders
(Problems 2.13 and 2.14).

The hole is 10 cm in diameter, and the wall is 30 cm thick. Determine
(a) the amount of CO_2 that exits the room (kmol h^{-1})
(b) the amount of air that enters the room (kg h^{-1})

2.16. In Problem 2.15, the loss over a long period is considered to be excessive. Unfortunately, for other reasons, the hole cannot be reduced below 4 cm in diameter, but it is still desired to reduce the loss by a factor of 10. Design something to reduce the loss by a factor of 10, if the diameter of the hole is reduced by a factor of 2.5.

2.17. A distillation column separates alcohol A and alcohol B at 1 atm and 372 K. At a particular location in the column, the liquid phase and gas phase contain 30 mole percent A and 40 mole percent A, respectively. Assuming that the resistance to mass transfer is a gas-phase film of thickness 0.3 mm, calculate the molar flux of A from the liquid to the gas phase. The following information is required:

$$D = 5.4 \times 10^{-6} \, \text{m}^2 \, \text{s}^{-1}$$

$$\bar{p}_A = y_A p = H_A x_A; \text{ Henry's law constant } H_A = 0.7056 \text{ atm.}$$

2.18. Two horizontal plates are placed 5 cm apart. The space is filled with a high-viscosity lubricating oil (100 poise). The bottom plate is stationary and the upper plate moves at a velocity of $+0.8 \, \text{m s}^{-1}$. Considering an area of $0.01 \, \text{m}^2$ located far from any edges find the force (in units of newtons), the shear stress, and the momentum flux (N m^{-2}).

2.19. In Problem 2.18, convert the velocity to ft s^{-1}, the distance between plates to ft, the area to ft^2, and the viscosity to lb$_m$ ft^{-1} s^{-1}. Then find the force on the plate in lb$_f$. Do you prefer the English or the SI system and why?

2.20. A possible design for a parallel plate viscometer consists of a vertical, rectangular box with a centrally located plate inside. The fluid to be tested is placed in the box and the force necessary to remove the plate at a fixed speed is measured. The unit is shown in Fig. 2.16. Calculate the viscosity in cP for the following conditions: the weight of the plate is negligible; the plate is located equidistant between the walls; clearance between plate and each wall is 0.5 cm; total area of plate immersed at instant of reading is 70 cm^2 on a side; when the plate is moved at a velocity of 1 cm s^{-1}, the force required is 5.6×10^{-4} N; end effects are negligible.

2.21. When a film of liquid flows down an inclined plate, it can be shown that the stress

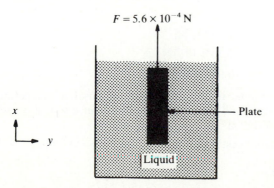

$F = 5.6 \times 10^{-4} \, \text{N}$

Plate

Liquid

FIGURE 2.16
Plate viscometer (Problem 2.20).

developed due to gravity is

$$\tau_{yx} = \rho g y \cos \beta$$

where the x coordinate is aligned with the direction of flow and the y coordinate begins at the surface of the film and is positive in the direction towards the plate. The angle β is the angle between the surface and the vertical.

(a) Determine the velocity distribution (U as a function of y) in the film if the film thickness is L.

(b) Find the maximum velocity and the value of y at which it occurs.

2.22. Three parallel flat plates are separated by two fluids. Plate 1 (on the bottom) is at rest. Water, viscosity 0.8007 cP at 30°C, lies between plates 1 and 2. Toluene, viscosity 0.5179 cP at 30°C, lies between plates 2 and 3. The distance between each pair of plates is 10 cm. Plate 3 moves at 3 m s^{-1}. Find:

(a) the velocity of plate 2 at steady-state

(b) the force per unit area on plate 3 required to maintain the 3 m s^{-1} velocity

2.23. The thermal conductivity of a solid is approximated by

$$k = A + BT$$

where A is a positive constant and B may be positive or negative. Consider Fig. 2.4 and Example 2.1; sketch the temperature profile corresponding to $B < 0$, $B = 0$, and $B > 0$.

2.24. Estimate the thermal conductivity of gold at 500 K from the data below.

T, K	200	400	600	800	1000
k, $\text{W m}^{-1}\text{K}^{-1}$	323	311	298	284	270

2.25. Estimate the thermal conductivity of silicon carbide at 1300 K from the data below.

T, K	1000	1200	1500
k, $\text{W m}^{-1}\text{K}^{-1}$	87	58	30

2.26. The kinetic theory of gases predicts that the thermal conductivity of a gas equals the product of the heat capacity at constant volume times the viscosity; this theory also predicts that the viscosity varies as the square root of temperature and is independent of pressure. For CO_2 at 1 atm and 273.15 K, the following data are available:

$$c_v = 0.640 \text{ kJ kg}^{-1}\text{K}^{-1}$$
$$\mu = 1.38 \times 10^{-5} \text{ N s m}^{-2}$$
$$k = 0.01435 \text{ W g}^{-1}\text{K}^{-1}$$

Assuming that c_v is proportional to the first power of absolute temperature, estimate k at 300 K and 1 atm. Find the percent error of your estimate based on the literature value of $0.01655 \text{ W m}^{-1}\text{K}^{-1}$.

2.27. Use the data in the Appendix to estimate for air at 348.15 K and 2 atm:

(a) the viscosity

(b) the thermal conductivity

(c) the kinematic viscosity

(d) the thermal diffusivity

2.28. Use the data in the Appendix to estimate for water at 348.15 K and 1 atm:

(a) the viscosity

(b) the thermal conductivity

(c) the kinematic viscosity

(d) the thermal diffusivity

2.29. The diffusion coefficient of air–carbon dioxide at 1 atm and 276.2 K is $0.142 \times 10^{-4}\,m^2\,s^{-1}$. Estimate the diffusion coefficient at 3 atm and 320 K.

REFERENCES

B1. Barrer, R. M.: *Diffusion in and through Solids,* Cambridge University Press, Cambridge, 1951.

B2. Bird, R. B., W. E. Stewart and E. N. Lightfoot: *Transport Phenomena,* Wiley, New York, 1960.

B3. Brodkey, R. S.: *The Phenomena of Fluid Motions,* Addison-Wesley, Reading, MA, 1967. [Fourth printing available from The Ohio State University Bookstores, Columbus, Ohio 43210.]

C1. Cox, R. T.: *Statistical Mechanics of Irreversible Change,* Johns Hopkins Press, Baltimore, 1955, pp. 10, 29–32.

F1. Fuller, E. N., P. D. Schettler and J. C. Giddings: *Ind. Eng. Chem.* **58**(5): 18 (1966) and **58**(8): 81 (1966).

G1. Geankoplis, C. J.: *Mass Transport Phenomena,* Geankoplis, Minneapolis, MN, 1972.

G2. Gray, D. E.: *American Institute of Physics Handbook,* 3d ed., 1982 printing, McGraw-Hill, New York, 1972.

L1. Lange, N. A.: *Lange's Handbook of Chemistry,* 13th ed., J. A. Dean (ed.), McGraw-Hill, New York, 1985.

M1. Marrero, T. R., and E. A. Mason: *J. Phys. Chem. Ref. Data* **1:** 3 (1972).

P1. Perry, R. H., and D. W. Green: *Perry's Chemical Engineers' Handbook,* 6th ed., McGraw-Hill, New York, 1984.

R1. Reid, R. C., J. M. Prausnitz and T. K. Sherwood: *The Properties of Gases and Liquids,* 3d ed., McGraw-Hill, New York, 1977.

S1. Sharma, B. L.: *Diffusion in Semiconductors,* Trans Tech Publications, Adolf-Ey-Str. 1d, D-3392 Clausthal-Zellerfeld, W. Germany, 1970.

CHAPTER 3

THE GENERAL PROPERTY BALANCE

NOMENCLATURE

A Area (m^2, ft^2)

A   Species A; A_1 and A_2 are species A at locations 1 and 2

B   Species B; subscripts 1 and 2 represent locations

C Concentration (kmol m^{-3}, lb mol ft^{-3}); C_A, C_B, C_i are concentrations of species A, B, i; C_T is total concentration

C C_1, C_2, C_3, $C(x, y)$, $C(y, z)$ are integration constants, evaluated from given boundary conditions

c   Subscript denoting flux contribution due to convection

c_p Heat capacity at constant pressure (kJ kg^{-1} K^{-1}, Btu lb_m^{-1} $°F^{-1}$)

D Diffusion coefficient (mass diffusivity) (m^2 s^{-1}, ft^2 s^{-1})

F Force (N, lb_f); subscripts refer to force in coordinate directions; also F is the force vector with components in coordinate directions

i Unit vector in x direction

J_A/A Molar flux vector in Fick's law, Eq. (2.4), defined with respect to a plane of no net volume flow (kmol m^{-2} s^{-1}, lb mol ft^{-2} s^{-1}); subscripts A or B are for flux of species A or B; called J_A^v/A in Chapter 5

j_A/A Mass flux vector of species A, defined with respect to a plane of no net volume flow (kg m^{-2} s^{-1}, lb_m ft^{-2} s^{-1})

j	Unit vector in y direction
k	Unit vector in z direction
k	Thermal conductivity (W m^{-1} K^{-1} or J m^{-1} K^{-1} s^{-1}, Btu ft^{-1} °R^{-1} s^{-1})
m	Mass (kg, lb$_m$)
m	subscript denoting contribution due to molecular transport
n	number of moles (kmol, lb mol)
n	number of components in a mixture
p	Pressure (kPa, atm, lb$_f$ in.$^{-2}$)
Q	Volume rate of flow (ft^3 s^{-1})
q	Energy (heat) flow vector (W, J s^{-1}, Btu s^{-1})
S	Cross sectional area (m^2, ft^2)
T	Temperature (K, °R, °C, °F); T_1 and T_2 are temperatures at locations 1 and 2
t	Time (s)
U	Velocity vector (m s^{-1}, ft s^{-1}); U is magnitude of U; U_x, U_y, U_z are components in directions x, y, z; U is the mass average velocity [see Eq. (3.22)], whereas U^* is molar average velocity [see Eq. (3.23)]
V	Volume (m^3, ft^3)
w	Mass flow rate (kg s^{-1}, lb$_m$ s^{-1})
x	Rectangular (Cartesian) coordinate
y	Rectangular (Cartesian) coordinate
z	Rectangular (Cartesian) coordinate
α	Thermal diffusivity (m^2 s^{-1}, ft^2 s^{-1})
Δ	Difference, state 2 minus state 1; e.g., ΔT means $T_2 - T_1$
δ	Generalized diffusivity (m^2 s^{-1}, ft^2 s^{-1})
μ	Viscosity (kg m^{-1} s^{-1} or N m^{-2} s, lb$_m$ ft^{-1} s^{-1}, cP)
ν	Kinematic viscosity (momentum diffusivity) (m^2 s^{-1}, ft^2 s^{-1})
ρ	Density (kg m^{-3}, lb$_m$ ft^{-3}); subscripts refer to species
$\boldsymbol{\Psi}$	Generalized flux vector (e.g., units for heat flux are J m^{-2} s^{-1} or W m^{-2}, Btu ft^{-2} s^{-1}; see Table 2.1); Ψ_x, Ψ_y, Ψ_z are components in directions x, y, z; $\Psi_{x,m}$ or $\boldsymbol{\Psi}_m$ is flux due to molecular transport; $\Psi_{x,c}$ or $\boldsymbol{\Psi}_c$ is flux due to convection
ψ	Generalized concentration of property (e.g., units for concentration of heat are J m^{-3}, Btu ft^{-3}; see Table 3.1 for complete listing)
$\dot{\psi}_G$	Rate of generation of heat or mass or momentum in a unit volume (e.g., for heat, units are J m^{-3} s^{-1}, Btu ft^{-3} s^{-1})
$\boldsymbol{\tau}$	Momentum flux (or shear stress) tensor (N m^{-2}, lb$_f$ ft^{-2}); τ_{xy}, τ_{yx}, etc., are components of the momentum flux tensor, where subscripts refer to direction of momentum transfer and direction of velocity
∇	Vector operator del, defined by Eqs. (2.16) or (3.45) (m^{-1}, ft^{-1})
∇^2	Laplacian operator, defined in Eq. (3.64) (m^{-2}, ft^{-2})

The conservation laws of mass, energy, and momentum are the most widely applicable laws in our universe. Many practical problems can be solved by application of these laws either alone or in combination. The conservation of energy forms the basis for the first law of thermodynamics, a separate subject in itself. Einstein's theory of relativity relates mass to energy, but the relation becomes important only under conditions encountered in some nuclear engineering applications. In the case of nuclear fission, a small amount of mass is converted into a large quantity of energy. However, neither relativity nor nuclear fission plays a very important role in most applications of the laws of conservation. In this chapter, the laws of conservation of mass, energy, and momentum will be expressed in an analogous fashion. The resultant generalized equation is called the general property balance.

3.1   THE BALANCE OR CONSERVATION CONCEPT

Conservation of energy, conservation of mass, and conservation of momentum are mathematically analogous; a discussion of one applies equally to the others. Let us select conservation of energy to discuss in detail. Further, let us consider one-dimensional conservation. A simple volume is illustrated in Fig. 3.1. Heat enters from the left and exits to the right. The inlet and outlet areas need not be equal, but the input and output must occur only in the x direction. No transfer of any kind occurs in the y direction or z direction. The problem we are considering is described as a one-directional transfer problem. Also, the specific shape of the inlet and outlet areas is unimportant. They can be pictured as circles. Since there is no heat gained or lost through the sides of the cylinder, the volume in Fig. 3.1 may be considered as a hole in a piece of insulation. There are four types of terms to be considered:

1. INPUT   The input is the amount of heat that enters the volume (V) in a given period of time. Let us say that the heat enters through face 1 in the x direction only.

2. OUTPUT   The amount of heat that exits the volume through the outlet face 2 in the same period of time is the output. The output is also restricted to the x direction.

3. GENERATION   It is possible for heat to be generated in the

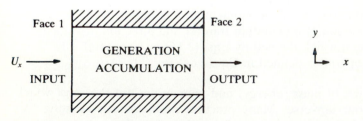

FIGURE 3.1
A volume V with INPUT and OUTPUT.

volume during the period of time. A common mechanism for heat generation is by means of chemical reaction. Absorption of heat by chemical or other means is simply negative generation or depletion.

4. ACCUMULATION   If the heat transfer is not occurring under steady-state conditions, the temperature in the volume between faces 1 and 2 may increase or decrease in the period of time (i.e., be positive or negative). At steady-state, the accumulation term is always zero.

These four concepts (INPUT, OUTPUT, GENERATION, AND ACCUMULATION) are sufficient to describe the heat balance for the volume in Fig. 3.1. For steady-state conditions the total rate of heat input into the system plus the rate at which heat is generated within the system must equal the total rate at which heat is removed; otherwise heat accumulates. The law of conservation of energy (or mass or momentum) says

$$\text{INPUT} + \text{GENERATION} = \text{OUTPUT} + \text{ACCUMULATION} \qquad (3.1)$$

In other words: what goes in (INPUT) plus what is made there (GENERATION) must come out (OUTPUT), or must stay (ACCUMULATION). At this point a further comment on the GENERATION term is required. Some authors separate this term into two parts: generation and depletion. A more prevalent viewpoint is that depletion is simply negative generation. Equation (3.1) is the general property balance. It was discussed in terms of heat transfer, but it applies to conservation of mass and momentum by analogous reasoning. In its present form, Eq. (3.1) is not particularly useful, since it is not in mathematical terms.

In the preceding chapter, the concept of a flux (Ψ) and property concentration (ψ) were introduced and found to be useful in presenting the analogy between transfer of heat, mass, and momentum. Table 2.1 provided a summary of the various analogous forms. In each case, ψ was related to the flux, Ψ, by a transport equation. Thus, the concentration of property ψ is conserved and represented in the general property balance. For heat or energy transfer, ψ is $\rho c_p T$; for mass transfer, ψ is the total mass per unit volume (ρ) or the concentration of any individual species in mass units (ρ_A) or in molar units (C_A); for momentum transfer, ψ can be ρU_x, ρU_y, or ρU_z, depending on the direction being considered. The various properties are summarized in Table 3.1.

As shown, the four concepts of INPUT, OUTPUT, GENERATION, and ACCUMULATION are sufficient to make a balance on the volume in Fig. 3.1. Remember that, in the present analysis, the input and output may occur only in the x direction and that no transfer occurs in the y or z directions. Let us first consider the INPUT and OUTPUT, then GENERATION, and finally ACCUMULATION.

TABLE 3.1.
Complete list of Ψ, ψ, and δ for use in the general property balance

Transport in the balance	Flux	Flux units (SI)	Diffusivity, $m^2 s^{-1}$	Concentration of property ψ	Units of ψ
Heat	q/A	$J\,m^{-2}\,s^{-1}$	α	$\rho c_p T$	$J\,m^{-3}$
Mass	J_A/A	$kmol\,m^{-2}\,s^{-1}$	D	C_A	$kmol\,m^{-3}$
	j_A/A	$kg\,m^{-2}\,s^{-1}$	D	ρ_A	$kg\,m^{-3}$
Total mass	—	—	—	ρ	$kg\,m^{-3}$
Momentum					
x direction	τ	$N\,m^{-2}$	v	ρU_x	$kg\,m^{-2}\,s^{-1}$
y direction	τ	$N\,m^{-2}$	v	ρU_y	$kg\,m^{-2}\,s^{-1}$
z direction	τ	$N\,m^{-2}$	v	ρU_z	$kg\,m^{-2}\,s^{-1}$

3.1.1 Input–Output Balance

The INPUT is related to the flux of the property being transferred. The concentration of property is ψ, and its flux in the x direction is Ψ_x. The flux Ψ_x is the total amount of property transferred per area per time, regardless of the mechanism of transfer. The units of Ψ_x are (property $m^{-2}\,s^{-1}$), as shown in Table 3.1. The rate of transferred material (property s^{-1}) is simply the flux times the area $(\Psi_x A)_1$. The same reasoning can be applied to the OUTPUT to give $(\Psi_x A)_2$. As an example of flux times area, in heat transfer, the flux in the x direction is $(q/A)_x$ in units of $J\,m^{-2}\,s^{-1}$. The amount of the property transferred per unit time for heat transfer is $(q/A)_x(A)$, which equals q_x and has units of $J\,s^{-1}$.

As an example of how the flux may be used in a balance such as in Eq. (3.1), consider the number of people transported into and out of a room. Let us assume that the people enter by a door (area about $2\,m^2$) and leave through a window (area about $1\,m^2$). If more people come into the room per hour than leave per hour, then there will be an accumulation. In a long enough period of time, there may even be a generation (positive through births or negative through deaths). Note that even without accumulation or generation, the fluxes in and out need not be equal. Suppose the number of people per time coming in equals the number of people per time going out. If there is no accumulation or generation, the input people flux (number of people per unit area per unit time) is one-half the output people flux because of the differences in the areas.

Substitution of the input and output terms into Eq. (3.1) gives

$$(\Psi_x A)_1 + \text{GENERATION} = (\Psi_x A)_2 + \text{ACCUMULATION} \qquad (3.2)$$

It is important to emphasize that the terms in Eqs. (3.1) and (3.2) are rates, i.e., the property per second transferred in, transferred out, generated or accumulated. The flux Ψ_x represents a flux that may be caused by molecular transport, by convection, or by some other means. A common application of Eq. (3.2) is the case in which generation and accumulation are zero and the area is constant throughout the volume. Under these conditions the area can be canceled from the input and output terms in Eq. (3.2). As a result of the conditions imposed, the flux is uniformly constant throughout the volume:

$$(\Psi_x)_1 = (\Psi_x)_2 = (\Psi_x)_{\text{all }x} = \text{constant} \tag{3.3}$$

The example problems of Chapter 2 involved applications of these conditions, for which the flux Ψ_x is related to the property concentration ψ through Eq. (2.7).

3.1.2 Generation

The generation of the property occurs by mechanisms other than transport. The generation sometimes depends on the flux Ψ_x or the property concentration ψ. Since generation is not a transport, an arbitrary symbol $\dot{\psi}_G$ will be used to represent the rate of generation of heat, mass, or momentum in a unit of volume. Clearly, the generation term must be consistent with the other terms in Eqs. (3.1) or (3.2) as far as units are concerned. Each term in Eqs. (3.1) or (3.2) has the units of property per second.

Because generation of a specific chemical species by a chemical reaction is a common phenomenon, let us consider mass generation. Equations (3.1) or (3.2) can be applied to problems in mass transfer, i.e., a balance on a specific species of mass. In Fig. 3.1, the amount of the specific species under consideration generated by chemical reaction is related to the total volume since, if the volume were doubled, the amount of the species generated would be doubled. Thus, the logical unit of $\dot{\psi}_G$ is the property per unit volume per unit time, which is $\text{kmol m}^{-3}\,\text{s}^{-1}$ for mass transfer. The dot $(\cdot)$ in the symbol $\dot{\psi}_G$ emphasizes that a rate is being considered, i.e., a variation with time.

To express the generation term in Eqs. (3.1) or (3.2) in units of kg s^{-1} or kmol s^{-1}, the rate of generation $\dot{\psi}_G$ is multiplied by the volume (V) as shown in Fig. 3.1, i.e.,

$$\text{GENERATION} = (\dot{\psi}_G)(V) \tag{3.4}$$

Equations (3.4) and (3.2) may be combined:

$$(\Psi_x A)_1 + (\dot{\psi}_G)(V) = (\Psi_x A)_2 + \text{ACCUMULATION} \tag{3.5}$$

Equation (3.5) is, of course, restricted to the one-directional transport case.

> **Example 3.1.** Consider the copper block shown in Fig. 2.4. This block corresponds to the volume of Fig. 3.1 with a length of 10 cm. Face 2 is maintained at 100°C. The thermal conductivity is $380\ \text{W m}^{-1}\,\text{K}^{-1}$. Let the area of face 1 and of face 2 be $6\ \text{cm}^2$ $(0.0006\ \text{m}^2)$.
> (a) Find the heat flux if face 1 is maintained at 0°C.
> (b) If the same flux as in part (a) enters at face 2, find the flux at face 1 if there is now a uniform generation within the volume of $1.5 \times 10^6\ \text{J m}^{-3}\,\text{s}^{-1}$.

Answer. For part (a), the conditions of this problem correspond to Eq. (3.3):

$$\Psi_x = \text{constant} \tag{3.3}$$

Equation (2.2), Fourier's law, is used to find the flux:

$$(q/A)_x = -k(\partial T/\partial x) \tag{2.2}$$

After separating variables in Eq. (2.2) and integrating both sides, the flux is found from

$$(q/A)_x = -k(\Delta T/\Delta x) = -3.8 \times 10^5 \, \text{J m}^{-2}\,\text{s}^{-1} \tag{i}$$

Details of this calculation are in Example 2.1.

For part (b), the area is $0.0006 \, \text{m}^2$. The volume is the area times the length $(0.1 \, \text{m})$:

$$V = (A)(\Delta x) = (0.0006)(0.1) = 6 \times 10^{-5} \, \text{m}^3 \tag{ii}$$

Equation (3.5) with no accumulation, and with the known terms inserted, is

$$(\Psi_x)_1(0.0006) + (1.5 \times 10^6)(6 \times 10^{-5}) = (-3.8 \times 10^5)(0.0006) \tag{iii}$$

The above equation is solved for Ψ_x; the flux at face 1 is

$$(\Psi_x)_1 = -5.3 \times 10^5 \, \text{J m}^{-2}\,\text{s}^{-1} \tag{iv}$$

Note that the positive generation term increases the amount of heat transferred through face 1. The minus sign in Eq. (iv) indicates that the heat flux is from right to left (negative x direction). Also, q_x and thus $(q/A)_x$ are not the same at faces 1 and 2, and thus dT/dx must change with x by Eq. (2.2). The balance equation has not been expressed in a convenient differential form in order to evaluate T_1 at face 1 and throughout the block. Example 3.2 in the next section will illustrate how to find the temperature profile.

3.1.3 Accumulation

Accumulation occurs when the concentration of property ψ increases or decreases in the volume V in Fig. 3.1 with progression in time. Problems in which the accumulation is non-zero are termed unsteady-state. Conversely, if there is no change with time, the problem is said to be at steady-state. The nature of the accumulation term is similar to that of the generation term just discussed. The rate of accumulation of ψ is $\partial \psi/\partial t$, in the units of property per volume per time. The total balance requires that the total amount of ψ accumulated be proportional to the total volume so that

$$\text{ACCUMULATION} = (\partial \psi/\partial t)(V) \tag{3.6}$$

The sign of the derivative $\partial \psi/\partial t$ indicates whether the concentration of property is increasing or decreasing with time in Eq. (3.6). Equation (3.6) can be combined with Eq. (3.5) to give

$$(\Psi_x A)_1 + (\dot{\psi}_G)(V) = (\Psi_x A)_2 + (\partial \psi/\partial t)(V) \tag{3.7}$$

Equation (3.7) is the general property balance in mathematical terms, although the equation is restricted to the one-directional case of Fig. 3.1. The restriction is easily removed, as will be shown later.

3.1.4 The Balance Equation in Differential Form

Equation (3.7) is most useful in differential form. When combined with expressions for the flux, Eq. (3.7) can be integrated to give useful results. The equation can be rearranged to

$$\partial \psi / \partial t - \dot{\psi}_G = -[(\Psi_x A)_2 - (\Psi_x A)_1]/V \qquad (3.8)$$

Now consider a differential volume ΔV of length Δx as shown in Fig. 3.2. The differential volume in the figure is the volume between x_1 and x_2, and can be expressed as

$$\Delta V = (Ax)_2 - (Ax)_1 \qquad (3.9)$$

Replacing V in Eq. (3.8) with ΔV gives

$$\partial \psi / \partial t - \dot{\psi}_G = -[(\Psi_x A)_2 - (\Psi_x A)_1]/\Delta V \qquad (3.10)$$

The limit of $(\Psi_x A)_2$ minus $(\Psi_x A)_1$, divided by ΔV, as ΔV approaches zero is the definition of the derivative:

$$\lim_{\Delta V \to 0} \frac{(\Psi_x A)_2 - (\Psi_x A)_1}{\Delta V} = \frac{\Delta(\Psi_x A)}{\Delta V} = \frac{\partial(\Psi_x A)}{\partial V} \qquad (3.11)$$

Using Eq. (3.11) in Eq. (3.10) gives the one-dimensional balance equation in differential form:

$$\partial \psi / \partial t - \dot{\psi}_G = -\partial(\Psi_x A)/\partial V \qquad (3.12)$$

From Eq. (3.9), it follows that dV equals $d(Ax)$. Thus, Eq. (3.12) may be recast into

$$\partial \psi / \partial t - \dot{\psi}_G = -\partial(\Psi_x A)/\partial(Ax) \qquad (3.13)$$

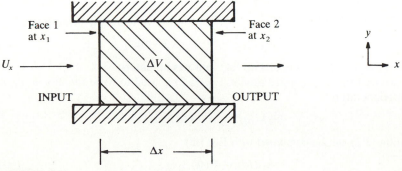

FIGURE 3.2
A differential volume of length Δx.

If the area is constant, it can be canceled out on the right-hand side of Eq. (3.13):

$$\partial \psi / \partial t - \dot{\psi}_G = -(\partial \Psi_x / \partial x) \tag{3.14}$$

Equation (3.14) is restricted to one-directional transfer in a constant area system. In Eq. (3.14) the term Ψ_x is the total flux. Equation (3.14) is not yet in a form suitable for easy problem-solving because both the concentration of property ψ and the flux Ψ_x are included. In the next section Ψ_x will be written in terms of ψ.

Example 3.2. For the copper block in Example 3.1, find the temperature profile if face 2 is at 100°C, the flux through face 2 is $-3.8 \times 10^5 \, \mathrm{J \, m^{-2} \, s^{-1}}$, and there is uniform generation in the volume of $1.5 \times 10^6 \, \mathrm{J \, m^{-3} \, s^{-1}}$. Assume steady-state conditions.

Answer. The problem is one of steady-state; therefore, the accumulation is zero. Since the area perpendicular to the heat flow is constant throughout the block represented in Fig. 3.1, Eq. (3.14) applies with the time derivative equal to zero:

$$- \dot{\psi}_G = -(d\Psi_x / dx) \tag{i}$$

where total derivatives are now used since dx is the only differential in Eq. (i). Separation of variables gives

$$\dot{\psi}_G \, dx = d\Psi_x \tag{ii}$$

Since $\dot{\psi}_G$ is constant, Eq. (ii) can be integrated to

$$(\dot{\psi}_G)(x) = \Psi_x + C_1 \tag{iii}$$

Let x be zero at face 1, then x equals 10 cm or 0.1 m at face 2. The boundary condition to evaluate C_1 is

$$\Psi_x \text{ (at } x = 0.1 \text{ m)} = -3.8 \times 10^5 \, \mathrm{J \, m^{-2} \, s^{-1}} \tag{iv}$$

Inserting these into Eq. (iii) along with the value of the generation and evaluating C_1 gives

$$C_1 = (1.5 \times 10^6)(0.1) - (-3.8 \times 10^5) = 5.3 \times 10^5 \, \mathrm{J \, m^{-2} \, s^{-1}} \tag{v}$$

From Eqs. (iii) and (v), the flux at any point in the volume may be calculated:

$$\Psi_x = (1.5 \times 10^6)(x) - 5.3 \times 10^5 \tag{vi}$$

where Ψ_x is $(q/A)_x$ in units of $\mathrm{J \, m^{-2} \, s^{-1}}$ and x is in meters.

To find the temperature profile, Eq. (2.2) is used to write the flux in terms of the temperature

$$\Psi_x = (q/A)_x = -k(dT/dx) \tag{2.2}$$

Equation (2.2) can be combined with Eq. (iii):

$$- k(dT/dx) = (\dot{\psi}_G)(x) - C_1 \tag{vii}$$

Note that Eq. (2.2) also could have been combined with Eq. (vi) in terms of the actual values of this problem. The variables in Eq. (vii) are again separated and the resulting equation is integrated to give

$$-kT = (\dot{\psi}_G)(x^2)/2 - (C_1)(x) + C_2 \tag{viii}$$

The constant of integration C_2 can be evaluated from the boundary condition

$$T(x = 0.1 \text{ m}) = 100°C = 373.15 \text{ K} \tag{ix}$$

which gives for C_2

$$C_2 = -(380)(373.15) - (1.5 \times 10^6)(0.1)^2/2 + (5.3 \times 10^5)(0.1)$$
$$= -9.63 \times 10^4 \text{ J m}^{-1} \text{s}^{-1} \tag{x}$$

Now all the constants in Eq. (viii) are known. The temperature profile can then be obtained from Eq. (viii) with the constants being inserted and by dividing through by $(-k)$:

$$T = (-1.974 \times 10^3)(x^2) + (1.395 \times 10^3)(x) + 253.41 \tag{xi}$$

where T is in units of kelvins.

It is interesting to compare the temperature at face 1 in this example with that obtained in the preceding example, part (a), where there was no generation. The flux entering the block through face 2 is identical in both examples. With no generation, the temperature at face 1 is 0°C. With generation, the temperature is 253.4 K or −19.74°C, as determined from Eq. (xi).

Example 3.3. For the copper block in Example 3.2, let the heat flow at face 1 be -270 J s^{-1}. At face 2 the heat flow is -228 J s^{-1}. The generation is the same as in Example 3.2: $1.5 \times 10^6 \text{ J m}^{-3} \text{s}^{-1}$. The heat capacity of copper is 0.093 cal $\text{g}^{-1} \text{K}^{-1}$ and the specific gravity is 8.91.
(a) Find the rate of accumulation.
(b) Find the equation for the temperature profile, and determine the temperature at face 1 after 1 min, if at the start face 2 is at 100°C.

Answer. The solution to part (a) is easy if Eq. (3.1) is used. The volume of the block was found in Example 3.1 to be $6 \times 10^{-5} \text{ m}^3$. By Eq. (3.4):

$$\text{GENERATION} = (\dot{\psi}_G)(V) = (1.5 \times 10^6)(6 \times 10^{-5}) = 90 \text{ J s}^{-1} \tag{i}$$

In Fig. 3.1 the input is the heat flow in at face 1, and the output is the heat flow out at face 2. This *convention* must be maintained; if the *actual* heat flow is reversed in a specific problem, this will be signified by the sign on the flow. Using Eq. (3.1) with each term known:

$$\text{ACCUMULATION} = \text{INPUT} + \text{GENERATION} - \text{OUTPUT} \tag{3.1}$$
$$\text{ACCUMULATION} = -270 \quad + \quad 90 \quad - (-228)$$
$$= 48 \text{ J s}^{-1}$$

In this problem the rate of accumulation is constant because the input flux, the output flux, and the generation are all constant.

In part (b), the equation for the temperature profile will be found. On a unit volume basis, from Eq. (3.6), one can obtain

$$\partial \psi / \partial t = 48/V = 48/(6 \times 10^{-5}) = 8 \times 10^5 \text{ J m}^{-3} \text{s}^{-1} \tag{ii}$$

However, it is more instructive to solve this example through the use of Eq. (3.14):

$$\partial \psi / \partial t - \dot{\psi}_G = -(\partial \Psi_x / \partial x) \tag{3.14}$$

Solution of the more difficult problems to be discussed in Chapter 4 must begin with differential equations such as Eq. (3.14). By setting ψ equal to $\rho c_p T$ (from Table 3.1), Eq. (3.14) becomes

$$\partial(\rho c_p T) / \partial t - \dot{\psi}_G = -(\partial \Psi_x / \partial x) \tag{iii}$$

The variables are separated in Eq. (iii) and the resulting equation is integrated:

$$[\partial(\rho c_p T) / \partial t - \dot{\psi}_G](x) = -\Psi_x + C_1 \tag{iv}$$

Note that the term $[\partial(\rho c_p T) / \partial t - \dot{\psi}_G]$ is a constant in this problem. The heat flow q_x is converted into a flux by dividing q_x by the area $(0.0006 \, \text{m}^2)$ perpendicular to the direction of the flux; i.e.,

$$\Psi_{x,1} = -270/0.0006 = -4.5 \times 10^5 \, \text{J m}^{-2} \, \text{s}^{-1} \tag{v}$$

$$\Psi_{x,2} = -228/0.0006 = -3.8 \times 10^5 \, \text{J m}^{-2} \, \text{s}^{-1} \tag{vi}$$

The constant of integration C_1 in Eq. (iv) is evaluated from the following boundary condition:

$$\Psi_{x,1}(x = 0) = -4.5 \times 10^5 \, \text{J m}^{-2} \, \text{s}^{-1} \tag{vii}$$

Using Eq. (vii) in Eq. (iv) gives for C_1:

$$C_1 = \Psi_{x,1} + [\partial(\rho c_p T) / \partial t - \dot{\psi}_G](0) = -4.5 \times 10^5 \, \text{J m}^{-2} \, \text{s}^{-1} \tag{viii}$$

The rate of accumulation is found from the second boundary condition:

$$\Psi_{x,2}(x = 0.1 \, \text{m}) = -3.8 \times 10^5 \, \text{J m}^{-2} \, \text{s}^{-1} \tag{ix}$$

Through use of Eq. (iv) and Eq. (viii), one obtains

$$[\partial(\rho c_p T) / \partial t - 1.5 \times 10^6](0.1) = -(-3.8 \times 10^5) - 4.5 \times 10^5 \tag{x}$$

Solving for the accumulation gives

$$\partial(\rho c_p T) / \partial t = (3.8 \times 10^5 - 4.5 \times 10^5)/0.1 + 1.5 \times 10^6 = 8.0 \times 10^5 \, \text{J m}^{-3} \, \text{s}^{-1} \tag{xi}$$

This answer is, of course, the same as was obtained from Eq. (3.1) in part (a).

To find the temperature profile for part (b), the procedure follows that in Example 3.2. First, Eq. (iv) is written with all the constants included:

$$[\partial(\rho c_p T) / \partial t - \dot{\psi}_G](x) = -\Psi_x + C_1 \tag{iv}$$

$$(8.0 \times 10^5 - 1.5 \times 10^6)(x) = -\Psi_x - 4.5 \times 10^5 \tag{xii}$$

$$4.5 \times 10^5 - (7 \times 10^5)(x) = -\Psi_x \tag{xiii}$$

Equation (2.2) is

$$\Psi_x = (q/A)_x = -k(\partial T / \partial x) \tag{2.2}$$

Equations (xii) and (2.2) can be combined as follows:

$$4.5 \times 10^5 - (7 \times 10^5)(x) = k(\partial T / \partial x) \tag{xiv}$$

Upon separation of variables and integration, Eq. (xiv) becomes

$$kT = -(7 \times 10^5)(x^2)/2 + (4.5 \times 10^5)(x) + C_2 \qquad \text{(xv)}$$

The constant in Eq. (xv) may not be evaluated until the temperature at face 2 ($x = 0.1$ m) is expressed as a function of time. First, the density and heat capacity of copper are converted to the appropriate units:

$$\rho = 8.91 \text{ g cm}^{-3} = 8.91 \times 10^3 \text{ kg m}^{-3}$$

$$c_p = 0.093 \text{ cal g}^{-1} \text{ K}^{-1} = (0.093 \text{ cal g}^{-1} \text{ K}^{-1})(4.1840 \text{ J cal}^{-1})(10^3 \text{ g kg}^{-1})$$
$$= 389 \text{ J kg}^{-1} \text{ K}^{-1} \qquad \text{(xvi)}$$
$$k = 380 \text{ W m}^{-1} \text{ K}^{-1}$$

The variables in Eq. (xi) can be separated and the equation integrated. The result is

$$\rho c_p T = (8.0 \times 10^5)(t) + C_3 \qquad \text{(xvii)}$$

The boundary condition needed to evaluate C_3 is

$$T \ (t = 0 \text{ and } x = 0.1) = 100°C = 373.15 \text{ K} \qquad \text{(xviii)}$$

The constant, from Eq. (xvii), is

$$C_3 = (8.91 \times 10^3)(389)(373.15) = 1.293 \times 10^9 \text{ J m}^{-3} \qquad \text{(xix)}$$

To find the relationship between T and t at $x = 0.1$ m, Eqs. (xvii) and (xix) are combined and solved for T. After the use of algebra, the result is

$$T = 0.231t + 373.15 \qquad \text{(xx)}$$

where T is in units of kelvins. Now Eq. (xx) is used to evaluate C_2 in Eq. (xv). Of course, C_2 will be a function of time. The boundary condition is given by Eq. (xx) which applies to the position $x = 0.1$ m for any time. Combining Eq. (xx) with Eq. (xv) gives, when solved for C_2:

$$C_2 = (k)(0.231t + 373.15) + (3.5 \times 10^5)(x^2) - (4.5 \times 10^5)(x)$$
$$= 87.7t + 1.418 \times 10^5 + (3.5 \times 10^5)(0.1)^2 - (4.5 \times 10^5)(0.1)$$
$$= 87.7t + 1.00297 \times 10^5 \qquad \text{(xxi)}$$

Substituting Eq. (xxi) into Eq. (xv) gives the temperature profile as a function of both x and t:

$$kT = -(3.5 \times 10^5)(x^2) + (4.5 \times 10^5)(x) + 87.7t + 1.00297 \times 10^5$$

or since $k = 380 \text{ W m}^{-1} \text{ K}^{-1}$

$$T = -(921)(x^2) + (1184)(x) + 0.231t + 263.9 \qquad \text{(xxii)}$$

At face 1, $x = 0$, and at 1 min (60 s), Eq. (xxii) can be used to determine the temperature:

$$T = (0.231)(60) + 263.9 = 277.7 \text{ K} = 4.65°C \qquad \text{(xxiii)}$$

In the same period of time, the temperature at face 2 will have changed and can be determined from Eq. (xx) or from Eq. (xxii):

$$T = -(921)(0.1)^2 + (1184)(0.1) + (0.231)(60) + 263.9$$
$$= 387.0 \text{ K} = 113.8°C \qquad \text{(xxiv)}$$

3.2 THE ONE-DIRECTIONAL BALANCE EQUATION INCLUDING MOLECULAR AND CONVECTIVE TRANSPORT

The general balance equation for heat, mass, or momentum transfer, Eq. (3.12), is complete for the one-directional transfer case as written in terms of ψ and Ψ_x. However, more useful forms of the equation would contain either ψ or Ψ_x, but not both. The flux in Eq. (3.12) was included as a consequence of the input and output contributions to the general balance. Considering Fig. (3.1) again, the flux that enters through face 1 and that which leaves through face 2 may occur by several mechanisms. The two mechanisms general to all transports are molecular transport (as covered in Chapter 2) and convection:

$$\Psi_x = \Psi_{x,m} + \Psi_{x,c} \tag{3.15}$$

where $\Psi_{x,m}$ is the contribution due to molecular transport as discussed in Chapter 2 and $\Psi_{x,c}$ is the contribution due to convection. In the case of heat transfer, a third mechanism, radiation, exists:

$$(q/A)_x = (q/A)_{x,m} + (q/A)_{x,c} + (q/A)_{x,\,\text{radiation}} \tag{3.16}$$

The flux contributions due to molecular transport and due to convection will be considered in turn.

3.2.1 Molecular Transport

In Chapter 2, the flux $\Psi_{x,m}$ was related to the concentration of property ψ by the empirical laws of Fourier, Fick, and Newton. The general equation is

$$\Psi_m = -\delta \nabla \psi \tag{2.18}$$

where the subscript m has been added to emphasize that in Chapter 2 only molecular transport was included. Likewise, for the one-directional, one-dimensional case as in Fig. 3.1:

$$\Psi_{x,m} = -\delta(\partial\psi/\partial x) \tag{2.7}$$

The definitions of δ, $\Psi_{x,m}$, and ψ for heat, mass, or momentum transfer are given in Tables 2.1 and 3.1.

3.2.2 Convection[1]

A property can also be carried into and out of a volume by a flow mechanism. Convection is the bulk flow of a fluid due to the external influences such as a pressure difference or the force of gravity. The pressure difference may be a

---

[1] The term conveyance is sometimes used instead of the term convection.

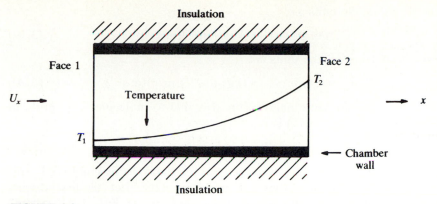

FIGURE 3.3
Heat transfer with conduction, convection, and generation.

result of a density difference, as for the case of air in a room heated with radiators. The radiator is supplied with hot water or steam from a furnace. At the radiator surface, the room air is heated; its density decreases, and the air rises toward the ceiling. Thus the air at the radiator surface is continually replaced and convection currents are set up. In a solid there is no convection possible and thus no flux contribution due to convection.

A flux may consist of both a molecular and a convection contribution, each occurring simultaneously. This situation can be visualized by referring to Fig. 3.3, in which a fluid enters a chamber with a temperature T_1 and velocity U_x. If the chamber is subjected to, for example, a strong microwave field (as in a microwave oven), then heat can be generated within the volume.

Because of the generation, the temperature at the outlet in Fig. 3.3 is higher than the temperature at the inlet. Thus, by Fourier's law, heat will be conducted by molecular transport from the right to the left, against the flow. Heat will be removed from the volume only by the hot fluid flowing out (convection mechanism). Of course, heat is also being carried in by the flow at the inlet since the inlet stream has a finite temperature. In other words, if the contents of the volume are at steady-state, the net convected heat plus the net conducted heat must balance exactly the heat generated within the volume. Whether by the convection or the conduction mechanism, the net heat is output minus input. In Fig. 3.3, if the temperatures were high enough, one might also have a contribution from radiative effects.

The convection flux $\Psi_{x,c}$ is associated with the property being convected and the flow velocity. When the velocity is zero, there is no convective contribution. The correct form is simply the property concentration times the velocity:

$$\Psi_{x,c} = (\text{property concentration})(\text{velocity}) \qquad (3.17)$$

For heat transfer, the units are

$$\mathrm{J\,m^{-2}\,s^{-1}} = (\mathrm{J\,m^{-3}})(\mathrm{m\,s^{-1}}) \qquad (3.18)$$

For mass transfer, the units are

$$kmol\ m^{-2}\ s^{-1} = (kmol\ m^{-3})(m\ s^{-1}) \tag{3.19}$$

For momentum transfer, the units are

$$N\ m^{-2} = kg\ m^{-1}\ s^{-2} = (kg)(m\ s^{-1})(m^{-3})(m\ s^{-1}) \tag{3.20}$$

Note that $\Psi_{x,c}$ has the same units as the flux due to molecular transport. In mathematical terms, Eq. (3.17) is

$$\Psi_{x,c} = \psi U_x \tag{3.21}$$

where U_x is the average velocity of the property ψ that is being convected. This velocity U_x takes different forms for each property. Let us first discuss momentum transfer in the absence of mass transfer. In Fig. 3.4 a volume $(1\ m^3)$ of fluid of density ρ is convected with velocity U_x through a unit area $(1\ m^2)$ in unit time $(1\ s)$. The density determines the mass contained in that volume. The velocity of the mass that is convected with that volume is called the mass average velocity, which is defined mathematically for a mixture of n components as

$$U = \sum_{i=1}^{n} (\rho_i U_i) \Big/ \sum_{i=1}^{n} \rho_i \tag{3.22}$$

where U_i is the velocity of species i and ρ_i is its density.

In this problem, each cubic meter of volume is associated with a certain amount of momentum, e.g., ρU_x (units of which are $kg\ m^{-2}\ s^{-1}$). Recall that the amount of momentum is equal to the mass in the volume times the velocity of that mass (i.e., the mass average velocity). In one second, one unit of volume $(1\ m^3)$ is convected past the one-square-meter area. This one unit of volume contains $(\psi \cdot 1)$ amount of the property per unit time and unit area (the flux of the property) and is numerically equal to ψ. If the velocity were doubled, so that two units of volume were convected in unit time, the flux would be twice as large. Thus, Eq. (3.21) is seen to be in appropriate form.

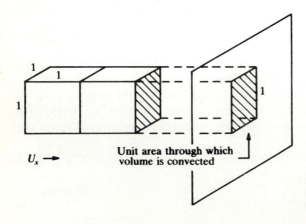

$U_x \longrightarrow$

Unit area through which
volume is convected

FIGURE 3.4
Convection of a unit volume
(dimensions in meters).

For heat transfer with no mass transfer, the concentration of property ψ is the concentration of heat in J m^{-3}, and the same reasoning applies. In mass transfer, the velocity U_x is as depicted in Fig. 3.4 for the case of one component (species A) undergoing mass transfer. For the most general case of a convection flux coupled to molecular fluxes in both positive and negative directions, U_x must be selected on the same basis as the property ψ in Eq. (3.21). If ψ is taken as ρ_A in kg m^{-3}, then U_x is the mass average velocity of species A, denoted by U_x or U, and is the same velocity as that defined by Eq. (3.22). If ψ is taken as C_A in kmol m^{-3}, then the velocity in Eq. (3.21) is the molar average velocity of the species (denoted by U_x^*), which is defined in general as

$$U^* = \sum_{i=1}^{n} (C_i U_i) \Big/ \sum_{i=1}^{n} C_i \tag{3.23}$$

where U_i is the same species velocity that appeared in Eq. (3.22) and C_i is the concentration of species i. The difference between molar average and mass average velocity will be discussed fully in Chapter 5. This difference is not often of practical importance in solving problems in science and engineering. For homogeneous systems, there is no difference between the mass average velocity U and the molar average velocity U^*.

The total flux is the sum of the contributing fluxes which, in one-directional flow, is given by Eq. (3.15). Combining Eq. (3.15) with Eq. (2.7) and Eq. (3.21), the total flux is

$$\Psi_x = \Psi_{x,\mathrm{m}} + \Psi_{x,\mathrm{c}} = -\delta(\partial\psi/\partial x) + \psi U_x \tag{3.24}$$
$$\text{molecular} \qquad \text{convective}$$

Keep in mind that for heat transfer a third mechanism, radiation, exists.

Taking the partial derivative of Eq. (3.24) with respect to x gives

$$\frac{\partial\Psi_x}{\partial x} = \frac{\partial(\Psi_{x,\mathrm{m}} + \Psi_{x,\mathrm{c}})}{\partial x} = \frac{\partial}{\partial x}\left(-\delta\frac{\partial\psi}{\partial x}\right) + \frac{\partial(\psi U_x)}{\partial x} \tag{3.25}$$

Equation (3.25) can be combined with Eq. (3.14) to give the general equation for one-directional transfer in a constant area system in terms of the concentration of property only:

$$\frac{\partial\psi}{\partial t} - \dot\psi_{\mathrm{G}} = -\frac{\partial}{\partial x}\left(-\delta\frac{\partial\psi}{\partial x}\right) - \frac{\partial(\psi U_x)}{\partial x} \tag{3.26}$$

If δ is constant, Eq. (3.26) reduces to

$$\frac{\partial\psi}{\partial t} - \dot\psi_{\mathrm{G}} = \delta\frac{\partial^2\psi}{\partial x^2} - \frac{\partial(\psi U_x)}{\partial x} \tag{3.27}$$
$$\text{ACC} \quad \text{GEN} \quad \text{MOLEC} \qquad \text{CONV}$$

Equation (3.26) is the general property balance equation for the concentration of property ψ. The assumptions of one-directional transfer and constant area apply. In the case of heat transfer, there may be a radiation contribution at high temperatures. It must be emphasized that the equation is for one-directional transfer only, and there can be no contributions, either by molecular or convective means, from the y or z directions. For these, a three-dimensional treatment is necessary and will be considered in the next section.

Equations (3.26) and (3.27) are commonly presented in the following rearranged form:

$$\frac{\partial \psi}{\partial t} + \frac{\partial (\psi U_x)}{\partial x} = \dot{\psi}_G + \frac{\partial}{\partial x}\left(\delta \frac{\partial \psi}{\partial x}\right) \tag{3.28}$$

In Eq. (3.28), ψ is the concentration of property per unit volume being conserved, in other words, any one of the seven entries in Table 3.1. For example, consider heat transfer with no radiation for which Eq. (3.28) reduces to

$$\frac{\partial (\rho c_p T)}{\partial t} + \frac{\partial (\rho c_p T U_x)}{\partial x} = \dot{\psi}_G + \frac{\partial}{\partial x}\left(\alpha \frac{\partial (\rho c_p T)}{\partial x}\right) \tag{3.29}$$

since, from Table 3.1, ψ is $\rho c_p T$ and δ is α or $k/(\rho c_p)$. For constant k, ρ, and c_p, this equation becomes

$$\frac{\partial T}{\partial t} + \frac{\partial (T U_x)}{\partial x} = \frac{\dot{\psi}_G}{\rho c_p} + \alpha \frac{\partial^2 T}{\partial x^2} \tag{3.30}$$

For mass transfer, Eq. (3.28) becomes

$$\frac{\partial \rho_A}{\partial t} + \frac{\partial (\rho_A U_x)}{\partial x} = \dot{\psi}_G + \frac{\partial}{\partial x}\left(D \frac{\partial \rho_A}{\partial x}\right) \qquad \begin{cases} (T = \text{constant}) \\ (p = \text{constant}) \end{cases} \tag{3.31}$$

when ψ is expressed in terms of mass units. For ψ in terms of molar units, Eq. (3.28) becomes

$$\frac{\partial C_A}{\partial t} + \frac{\partial (C_A U_x^*)}{\partial x} = \dot{\psi}_G + \frac{\partial}{\partial x}\left(D \frac{\partial C_A}{\partial x}\right) \qquad \begin{cases} (T = \text{constant}) \\ (p = \text{constant}) \end{cases} \tag{3.32}$$

where U_x^* has been used because the property is concentration of moles and the velocity is now a molar average velocity [defined by Eq. (3.23)]. For momentum transfer in the x direction with constant μ and ρ [therefore ν by Eq. (2.12)], one obtains

$$\frac{\partial U_x}{\partial t} + \frac{\partial (U_x^2)}{\partial x} = \frac{\dot{\psi}_G}{\rho} + \nu \frac{\partial^2 U_x}{\partial x^2} \tag{3.33}$$

Actually the second term on the left-hand side of Eq. (3.33) is zero, as will be shown in Section 3.4.

If the area were variable rather than constant, as assumed in Eq. (3.14), then Eq. (3.24) would have to be multiplied by the variable area, differentiated, and then combined with Eq. (3.12). The equation parallel to

Eq. (3.28) for the case of variable area is

$$\frac{\partial \psi}{\partial t} + \frac{\partial (A\psi U_x)}{\partial V} = \dot{\psi}_G + \frac{\partial}{\partial V}\left(A\delta\frac{\partial \psi}{\partial x}\right) \tag{3.34}$$

As will be illustrated in Chapter 4, one-directional transfer problems with a variable area can be treated by use of this equation.

3.3 THE THREE-DIMENSIONAL BALANCE EQUATION

In a volume in space, the generation and accumulation terms were seen to apply to the volume as a whole, as discussed in Sections 3.1.2 and 3.1.3. Thus in the general balance equation (3.1) the form of these two terms is unchanged whether the discussion is for three-dimensional or for one-dimensional transfer. The balance in each direction contributes to the accumulation and each directional effect can be added. In other words, the input and output terms may have contributions from one, two, or three directions.

Consider the volume in Fig. 3.5, a parallelepiped of dimensions dx, dy, and dz. The volume of the parallelepiped is the product of these dimensions:

$$dV = (dx)(dy)(dz) \tag{3.35}$$

The generation from Eq. (3.4) in the parallelepiped is

$$\text{GENERATION} = \dot{\psi}_G \, dV = [\dot{\psi}_G][(dx)(dy)(dz)] \tag{3.36}$$

From Eq. (3.6), the accumulation in the cube is

$$\text{ACCUMULATION} = (\partial\psi/\partial t)(dV) = (\partial\psi/\partial t)[(dx)(dy)(dz)] \tag{3.37}$$

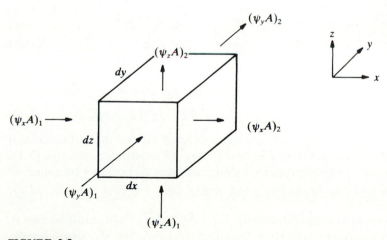

FIGURE 3.5
The balance on a cube.

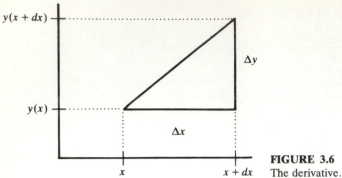

FIGURE 3.6
The derivative.

For the two faces perpendicular to the x axis, the area is $(dy)(dz)$, and so on for the other pairs of faces in Fig. 3.5. Thus, the input is the sum of the total flux in each direction times the appropriate area:

$$\text{INPUT} = (\Psi_x)_1(dy)(dz) + (\Psi_y)_1(dx)(dz) + (\Psi_z)_1(dx)(dy) \qquad (3.38)$$

Similarly, for the output one obtains

$$\text{OUTPUT} = (\Psi_x)_2(dy)(dz) + (\Psi_y)_2(dx)(dz) + (\Psi_z)_2(dx)(dy) \qquad (3.39)$$

Next, the basic definition of the derivative is reviewed with the aid of Fig. 3.6. The definition of the derivative dy/dx is the limit of $\Delta y/\Delta x$ as Δx approaches zero. Thus, the value of y at location $x + dx$, i.e., $y(x + dx)$, equals the value of $y(x)$ plus the derivative times Δx. In other words, the derivative times Δx is really Δy. Applying this result to Ψ_x at the face $x + dx$, the result is

$$(\Psi_x)_2 = (\Psi_x)_{x+dx} = (\Psi_x)_x + (\partial \Psi_x/\partial x)\, dx \qquad (3.40)$$

Similarly for the y and z directions:

$$(\Psi_y)_2 = (\Psi_y)_{y+dy} = (\Psi_y)_y + (\partial \Psi_y/\partial y)\, dy \qquad (3.41)$$

$$(\Psi_z)_2 = (\Psi_z)_{z+dz} = (\Psi_z)_z + (\partial \Psi_z/\partial z)\, dz \qquad (3.42)$$

The above three equations are substituted into Eq. (3.39):

$$\text{OUTPUT} = (\Psi_x)_x(dy)(dz) + (\Psi_y)_y(dx)(dz) + (\Psi_z)_z(dx)(dy)$$
$$+ (\partial \Psi_x/\partial x + \partial \Psi_y/\partial y + \partial \Psi_z/\partial z)[(dx)(dy)(dz)] \qquad (3.43)$$

Now every term in Eq. (3.1) has been defined for the three-dimensional case. Equations (3.36), (3.37), (3.38), and (3.43) are substituted into Eq. (3.1). After canceling, the general property balance in three dimensions becomes

$$\partial \psi/\partial t = -(\partial \Psi_x/\partial x + \partial \Psi_y/\partial y + \partial \Psi_z/\partial z) + \dot{\psi}_G \qquad (3.44)$$

As stated previously in conjunction with Eq. (3.12), Eq. (3.44) must be cast in terms of the property concentration ψ rather than the flux Ψ_x. Considerable simplification is possible by the introduction of the operator ∇. The ∇ operator was introduced previously in Eq. (2.16). The operator may be applied to a scalar such as temperature or concentration:

$$\nabla T = \boldsymbol{i}(\partial T/\partial x) + \boldsymbol{j}(\partial T/\partial y) + \boldsymbol{k}(\partial T/\partial z) \tag{2.16}$$

$$\nabla C_A = \boldsymbol{i}(\partial C_A/\partial x) + \boldsymbol{j}(\partial C_A/\partial y) + \boldsymbol{k}(\partial C_A/\partial z) \tag{3.45}$$

where once again $\boldsymbol{i}$, $\boldsymbol{j}$, and $\boldsymbol{k}$ are the unit vectors in the x, y, and z directions. The term ∇T is called the gradient of T. The operator can be pictured as a "short-hand" notation for the string of unit vectors and partial derivatives as shown above.

The operator ∇ may be also applied to a vector such as the flux $\boldsymbol{\Psi}$. The flux vector in rectangular coordinates is

$$\boldsymbol{\Psi} = \boldsymbol{i}\Psi_x + \boldsymbol{j}\Psi_y + \boldsymbol{k}\Psi_z \tag{3.46}$$

The application of the operator ∇ to a vector is called the divergence of that vector, or more simply the dot product; for rectangular coordinates:

$$(\nabla \cdot \boldsymbol{\Psi}) = \partial\Psi_x/\partial x + \partial\Psi_y/\partial y + \partial\Psi_z/\partial z \tag{3.47}$$

which when combined with Eq. (3.44) gives

$$\partial\psi/\partial t = -(\nabla \cdot \boldsymbol{\Psi}) + \dot{\psi}_G \tag{3.48}$$

Equation (3.44) and Eq. (3.48) are identical, but, Eq. (3.48) is a more compact way of writing the expression.

As a further example, consider the convective flux of Eq. (3.21), but as a vector, i.e.,

$$\boldsymbol{\Psi}_c = \psi U \tag{3.49}$$

If the same operation is done on the convective flux, one obtains

$$(\nabla \cdot \psi U) = \partial(\psi U_x)/\partial x + \partial(\psi U_y)/\partial y + \partial(\psi U_z)/\partial z \tag{3.50}$$

This can be expanded by use of the general relation

$$\partial(xy) = x\,\partial y + y\,\partial x \tag{3.51}$$

The result is

$$(\nabla \cdot \psi U) = \psi\left(\frac{\partial U_x}{\partial x} + \frac{\partial U_y}{\partial y} + \frac{\partial U_z}{\partial z}\right) + U_x\frac{\partial\psi}{\partial x} + U_y\frac{\partial\psi}{\partial y} + U_z\frac{\partial\psi}{\partial z} \tag{3.52}$$

Equation (3.52) is written in terms of the ∇ operator. The product $(U \cdot \nabla)$ operating on ψ is

$$(U \cdot \nabla)\psi = U_x\frac{\partial\psi}{\partial x} + U_y\frac{\partial\psi}{\partial y} + U_z\frac{\partial\psi}{\partial z} \tag{3.53}$$

The right-hand side of Eq. (3.53) is seen to be the last three terms in Eq. (3.52). Similarly,

$$\psi(\nabla \cdot U) = \psi\left(\frac{\partial U_x}{\partial x} + \frac{\partial U_y}{\partial y} + \frac{\partial U_z}{\partial z}\right) \tag{3.54}$$

where $(\nabla \cdot U)$ is of the same form as $(\nabla \cdot \Psi)$, shown in Eq. (3.47). The last two equations can be used to simplify Eq. (3.52):

$$(\nabla \cdot \psi U) = \psi(\nabla \cdot U) + (U \cdot \nabla)\psi \tag{3.55}$$

Equation (3.55) means the same as Eq. (3.50) and Eq.(3.52); yet it is much simpler to write.

The product $(\nabla \cdot \psi U)$ is called the divergence of ψU or the dot product of ∇ and ψU; the resulting product is a scalar. Note that the gradient (a vector ∇ times a scalar such as T) yields a vector. As will be seen in Chapter 5, the operator ∇ has a further advantage in that it may be expressed in curvilinear coordinates. This will be helpful when the balance equations must be expressed in alternate coordinate systems.

In Eq. (3.24), the flux was presented as the sum of molecular and convective terms. For the three-dimensional problem, the corresponding vector equation is

$$\Psi = \Psi_m + \Psi_c \tag{3.56}$$

The divergence of the flux is

$$(\nabla \cdot \Psi) = (\nabla \cdot \Psi_m) + (\nabla \cdot \Psi_c) \tag{3.57}$$

The flux due to molecular transport is given by Eq. (2.18) and the flux due to convection by Eq. (3.49). When these equations are substituted into Eq. (3.57), the result is

$$(\nabla \cdot \Psi) = (\nabla \cdot \delta\nabla\psi) + (\nabla \cdot \psi U) \tag{3.58}$$

Equation (3.58) can now be combined with Eq. (3.48) to give the three-dimensional property balance:

$$\partial\psi/\partial t = (\nabla \cdot \delta\nabla\psi) - (\nabla \cdot \psi U) + \dot{\psi}_G \tag{3.59}$$

This equation can be expanded by use of Eq. (3.55) and rearranged into a more common form:

$$\underset{\text{ACC}}{\partial\psi/\partial t} + \underset{\text{CONV}}{(U \cdot \nabla)\psi} = \underset{\text{GEN}}{\dot{\psi}_G} + \underset{\text{MOLEC}}{(\nabla \cdot \delta\nabla\psi)} - \underset{\text{CONV}}{\psi(\nabla \cdot U)} \tag{3.60}$$

The reason for the two convection terms in Eq. (3.60) will become clear in Section 3.5. If the diffusivity is constant, a further simplification is possible:

$$(\nabla \cdot \delta\nabla\psi) = \delta(\nabla \cdot \nabla\psi) \tag{3.61}$$

Inserting this equation into Eq. (3.60):

$$\partial\psi/\partial t + (U \cdot \nabla)\psi = \dot{\psi}_G + \delta(\nabla \cdot \nabla\psi) - \psi(\nabla \cdot U) \tag{3.62}$$

The term $(\nabla \cdot \nabla\psi)$ can be easily presented in rectangular coordinates by using Eq. (3.47); i.e.

$$(\nabla \cdot \nabla \psi) = \left[\nabla \cdot \left(i\frac{\partial \psi}{\partial x} + j\frac{\partial \psi}{\partial y} + k\frac{\partial \psi}{\partial z} \right) \right] = \frac{\partial}{\partial x}\frac{\partial \psi}{\partial x} + \frac{\partial}{\partial y}\frac{\partial \psi}{\partial y} + \frac{\partial}{\partial z}\frac{\partial \psi}{\partial z}$$

$$= \frac{\partial^2 \psi}{\partial x^2} + \frac{\partial^2 \psi}{\partial y^2} + \frac{\partial^2 \psi}{\partial z^2} \tag{3.63}$$

The dot product $(\nabla \cdot \nabla)$, operating on a scalar occurs so often that it is given a special symbol ∇^2, and a special name, the Laplacian operator:

$$\nabla^2 \psi = \frac{\partial^2 \psi}{\partial x^2} + \frac{\partial^2 \psi}{\partial y^2} + \frac{\partial^2 \psi}{\partial z^2} \tag{3.64}$$

The general heat or mass balance is easily obtained from Eq. (3.60) by the appropriate substitution for ψ from Table 3.1. For heat transfer the equation is

$$\partial(\rho c_p T)/\partial t + (U \cdot \nabla)(\rho c_p T) = \dot{\psi}_G + [\nabla \cdot \alpha\nabla(\rho c_p T)] - (\rho c_p T)(\nabla \cdot U) \tag{3.65}$$

For mass transfer the result in terms of mass concentration is

$$\partial\rho_A/\partial t + (U \cdot \nabla)\rho_A = \dot{\psi}_G + (\nabla \cdot D\nabla\rho_A) - (\rho_A)(\nabla \cdot U) \tag{3.66}$$

In terms of molar concentration, the equation is

$$\partial C_A/\partial t + (U^* \cdot \nabla)C_A = \dot{\psi}_G + (\nabla \cdot D\nabla C_A) - (C_A)(\nabla \cdot U^*) \tag{3.67}$$

The momentum transfer balance is complicated by the fact that ψ is a vector composed of three components: ρU_x, ρU_y, and ρU_z. However, the proper equations for rectangular coordinates can be obtained by simply considering each component separately as a scalar term. For example, the x component of momentum is ρU_x, which is substituted for ψ in Eq. (3.60):

$$\partial(\rho U_x)/\partial t + (U \cdot \nabla)(\rho U_x) = \dot{\psi}_G + [\nabla \cdot v\nabla(\rho U_x)] - (\rho U_x)(\nabla \cdot U) \tag{3.68}$$

The equations for the y and z components are similarly obtained.

Example 3.4. Obtain the three-dimensional equation for heat transfer in vector notation and show the form that can be obtained for constant properties. Also, express this equation completely in rectangular notation.

Answer. The vector equation is obtained by replacing ψ with $\rho c_p T$ and δ with α in Eq. (3.60). The resulting equation is Eq. (3.65):

$$\partial(\rho c_p T)/\partial t + (U \cdot \nabla)(\rho c_p T) = \dot{\psi}_G + [\nabla \cdot \alpha\nabla(\rho c_p T)] - (\rho c_p T)(\nabla \cdot U) \tag{3.65}$$

For constant properties ρ, c_p, k, and thus α, Eq. (3.65) reduces to

$$\partial T/\partial t + (U \cdot \nabla)T = \dot{\psi}_G/(\rho c_p) + \alpha(\nabla^2 T) - T(\nabla \cdot U) \tag{i}$$

The expression in rectangular (Cartesian) coordinates may be obtained from Eqs.

(i), (3.53), (3.54), and (3.64):

$$\frac{\partial T}{\partial t} + U_x \frac{\partial T}{\partial x} + U_y \frac{\partial T}{\partial y} + U_z \frac{\partial T}{\partial z} = \frac{\dot{\psi}_G}{\rho c_p} + \alpha \left(\frac{\partial^2 T}{\partial x^2} + \frac{\partial^2 T}{\partial y^2} + \frac{\partial^2 T}{\partial z^2} \right)$$

$$- T \left(\frac{\partial U_x}{\partial x} + \frac{\partial U_y}{\partial y} + \frac{\partial U_z}{\partial z} \right) \qquad \text{(ii)}$$

3.4 THE CONTINUITY EQUATION

As indicated earlier, one of the most important properties conserved in a system is the total mass. Naturally, the total mass is the total amount of all materials in the system. The total mass must be distinguished from the amount (or concentration) of some individual species that can diffuse in and out of the system. In heat or momentum transfer problems it is vital to account for the mass in or out, even if a single-component system is present or if the composition is invariant in a multiple-component system (such as air). Let us assume that no mass is manufactured or lost by nuclear means (i.e., no generation), then the mass balance becomes

$$\text{INPUT} = \text{OUTPUT} + \text{ACCUMULATION} \qquad (3.69)$$

For a single component system, there can be no diffusional contribution to the flux, hence Eq. (3.59) reduces to

$$\partial \psi / \partial t + (\boldsymbol{\nabla} \cdot \psi \boldsymbol{U}) = 0 \qquad (3.70)$$

where the concentration of property ψ is now the total mass per volume and is the density ρ:

$$\partial \rho / \partial t + (\boldsymbol{\nabla} \cdot \rho \boldsymbol{U}) = 0 \qquad (3.71)$$

Equation (3.71) is the "Equation of Continuity", a general mass balance that holds in all problems with no net generation of mass by nuclear means and with no mass transfer.

In the presence of mass transfer, Eq. (3.71) sometimes applies under the following restriction. In Eq. (3.71) there is no net molecular contribution to mass transfer. Therefore, Eq. (3.71) applies if the mass transfer contributes nothing to the overall mass balance. Equation (3.21) defined the convective contribution of property in the overall balance in terms of the average velocity of that property. If there is no net mass diffusion relative to that velocity, which is the mass average velocity $\boldsymbol{U}$, then Eq. (3.71) applies equally to mass transfer problems as well as to heat and momentum transfer.

Using the identity of Eq. (3.55) with ρ replacing ψ, Eq. (3.71) becomes

$$\partial \rho / \partial t + (\boldsymbol{U} \cdot \boldsymbol{\nabla}) \rho = -(\rho)(\boldsymbol{\nabla} \cdot \boldsymbol{U}) \qquad (3.72)$$

The equation of continuity can be simplified under conditions of steady flow or constant density or both. Under steady-state conditions, the time derivative is zero and Eq. (3.71) reduces to

$$(\nabla \cdot \rho U) = \frac{\partial(\rho U_x)}{\partial x} + \frac{\partial(\rho U_y)}{\partial y} + \frac{\partial(\rho U_z)}{\partial z} = 0 \qquad (3.73)$$

In many engineering problems, the density can be assumed constant, i.e. the flow is incompressible. The assumption of incompressibility is true even for gas flows when the changes in pressure are modest. If the density is constant, then Eq. (3.71) reduces to

$$(\nabla \cdot U) = \partial U_x/\partial x + \partial U_y/\partial y + \partial U_z/\partial z = 0 \qquad (3.74)$$

since ρ is in general not zero.

Equation (3.74) is extremely important and has wide application. It should also be emphasized that Eq. (3.74) is true for any constant density system; it is not necessary to assume steady-state, since $\partial \rho/\partial t$ must be zero if the density is constant. This means, for example, that the correct form of the continuity equation for an unsteady-state fluid flow problem, such as blood flow from the heart, is still described by Eq. (3.74).

It is possible to express the equation of continuity on a molar basis. Equation (3.70) expresses the conservation of moles if there is no change in the number of moles throughout the system. Remember that Eq. (3.70) is restricted to no net diffusion relative to the velocity of the property. Here the property is the total molar concentration C_T, and the corresponding average velocity in Eq. (3.70) must be the molar average velocity U^*. Equation (3.70) becomes

$$\partial C_T/\partial t + (\nabla \cdot C_T U^*) = 0 \qquad (3.75)$$

At steady-state and constant overall molar concentration, Eq. (3.75) reduces to

$$(\nabla \cdot U^*) = 0 \qquad (3.76)$$

Equation (3.76) is not as useful as Eq. (3.74) because more problems involve constant density than involve constant concentration.

Example 3.5. A flow in rectangular coordinates is given by

$$U = i(x^3 y) + j(2yx^2 z) \qquad (i)$$

Is this flow compressible?

Answer. If the flow is incompressible, then $(\nabla \cdot U)$ will be zero as required by Eq. (3.74). The components of the velocity vector from Eq. (i) are

$$U_x = x^3 y \qquad U_y = 2yx^2 x \qquad U_z = 0 \qquad (ii)$$

Thus

$$\partial U_x/\partial x = 3x^2 y \qquad \partial U_y/\partial y = 2x^2 z \qquad \partial U_z/\partial z = 0 \qquad (iii)$$

These derivatives are substituted into Eq. (3.74):

$$(\nabla \cdot U) = \partial U_x/\partial x + \partial U_y/\partial y + \partial U_z/\partial z = 0 = 3x^2 y + 2x^2 z = (x^2)(3y + 2z) \quad (iv)$$

The dot product $(\nabla \cdot U)$ is zero at the plane $(x = 0)$. It is also zero along the plane

$$3y + 2z = 0 \tag{v}$$

or

$$y = (-2z)/3 \tag{vi}$$

Therefore, this flow is compressible because the dot product $(\nabla \cdot U)$ is not zero throughout the entire flow field.

Example 3.6. An incompressible flow at steady-state in rectangular coordinates is given by the vector components

$$U_x = x^3 y \qquad U_y = 2yx^2 z \tag{i}$$

and U_z is unknown. Find U_z.

Answer. Equation (i) above for U_x and U_y contains two of the components of the velocity given in the previous example. If the flow is incompressible, then Eq. (3.74) holds. Using the derivatives in Eq. (iii) from the previous example gives

$$(\nabla \cdot U) = 3x^2 y + 2x^2 z + \partial U_z / \partial z = 0 \tag{ii}$$

After separating variables, Eq. (ii) becomes

$$\partial U_z = -(3x^2 y + 2x^2 z) \, \partial z \tag{iii}$$

Next, this equation is integrated:

$$U_z = -3x^2 yz - x^2 z^2 + C(x, y) \tag{iv}$$

The term $(-x^2 z)$ can be factored out of the first two terms in Eq. (iv). Then the z component of velocity U_z becomes

$$U_z = (-x^2 z)(3y + z) + C(x, y) \tag{v}$$

Note that $C(x, y)$ is a constant of integration to be determined from the boundary conditions and may be a function of x and y; it cannot be determined from the information given in this problem. Hence, the final answer will express the vector U as follows:

$$U = i(x^3 y) + j(2yx^2 z) + k[(-x^2 z)(3y + z) + C(x, y)] \tag{vi}$$

The flow is incompressible for all values of x, y, z, and $C(x, y)$.

Example 3.7. Does the velocity in a one-directional incompressible flow in rectangular (Cartesian) coordinates change with the direction of flow?

Answer. For incompressible flow in rectangular coordinates, Eq. (3.74) holds

$$(\nabla \cdot U) = \partial U_x / \partial x + \partial U_y / \partial y + \partial U_z / \partial z = 0 \tag{3.74}$$

Now if a one-directional flow is in the x direction, U_y and U_z must be zero

$$U_y = U_z = 0 \tag{i}$$

Therefore

$$\partial U_y / \partial y = \partial U_z / \partial z = 0 \tag{ii}$$

and from Eq. (3.74)

$$\partial U_x / \partial x = 0 \qquad \text{(iii)}$$

Integration of Eq. (iii) yields

$$U_x = C(y, z) \qquad \text{(iv)}$$

Therefore U_x does not change in the direction of the flow, the x direction, since $C(y, z)$ can only vary in the y or z directions. The importance of this result must be emphasized again. The continuity equation demands that in a one-dimensional incompressible flow, the velocity cannot change in the direction of flow for any reason.

3.5 THE GENERAL PROPERTY BALANCE FOR AN INCOMPRESSIBLE FLUID

In most applications in this text, the fluid in the system may be assumed incompressible, which means constant density with respect to time and position. Equation (3.60) is the general property balance equation:

$$\partial \psi / \partial t + (\boldsymbol{U} \cdot \boldsymbol{\nabla}) \psi = \dot{\psi}_G + (\boldsymbol{\nabla} \cdot \delta \boldsymbol{\nabla} \psi) - (\psi)(\boldsymbol{\nabla} \cdot \boldsymbol{U}) \qquad (3.60)$$

If the flow is incompressible then the last term on the right-hand side is zero by Eq. (3.74), and Eq. (3.60) reduces to

$$\partial \psi / \partial t + (\boldsymbol{U} \cdot \boldsymbol{\nabla}) \psi = \dot{\psi}_G + (\boldsymbol{\nabla} \cdot \delta \boldsymbol{\nabla} \psi) \qquad (3.77)$$
$$\quad \text{ACC} \qquad \text{CONV} \quad \text{GEN} \quad \text{MOLEC}$$

If the transport coefficient δ can be considered constant, then Eq. (3.77) reduces further:

$$\partial \psi / \partial t + (\boldsymbol{U} \cdot \boldsymbol{\nabla}) \psi = \dot{\psi}_G + \delta \, \nabla^2 \psi \qquad (3.78)$$

where ∇^2 is the Laplacian operator, Eq. (3.64).

Equation (3.78) is the starting point for almost all transport phenomena problems. If the density and diffusivity are allowed to vary, the corresponding equations, such as Eq. (3.60) and Eq. (3.77), are frequently too complicated for exact solution. From this chapter, the reader is expected to know how to write down the general balance equation for any property being conserved by finding the appropriate values of ψ and δ in Table 3.1 and plugging those values into Eq. (3.78), Eq. (3.60), or Eq. (3.77). Solutions of the resulting equations will be discussed in the subsequent chapters. In Chapter 4, the general balance equation will be applied to problems where the total flux, Eq. (3.56), consists of the molecular transport contribution only. In Chapter 5, the general balance equation will be applied to problems where the total flux is the sum of molecular plus convective contributions and where the flow is relatively slow. In Chapter 6 the flows under consideration will be at high velocities where turbulent conditions prevail. In Chapter 13, these equations will be applied to unsteady-state problems.

Example 3.8. Obtain the equation for x direction momentum for a general momentum transfer problem that can have velocities in all three directions. Show the equation for (a) compressible flow and (b) incompressible flow in both vector notation and in rectangular coordinates.

Answer. (a) For the x direction of momentum, the property ψ is replaced with ρU_x and δ with v (which is μ/ρ) from Table 3.1. Equation (3.60) in vector form for compressible flow is

$$\partial(\rho U_x)/\partial t + (\boldsymbol{U} \cdot \boldsymbol{\nabla})(\rho U_x) = \dot{\psi}_G + [\boldsymbol{\nabla} \cdot v\boldsymbol{\nabla}(\rho U_x)] - (\rho U_x)(\boldsymbol{\nabla} \cdot \boldsymbol{U}) \qquad \text{(i)}$$

If the density is constant, then the divergence of $\boldsymbol{U}$ is zero by Eq. (3.74), and Eq. (i) reduces to

$$\partial U_x/\partial t + (\boldsymbol{U} \cdot \boldsymbol{\nabla})U_x = \dot{\psi}_G/\rho + (\boldsymbol{\nabla} \cdot v\boldsymbol{\nabla}U_x) \qquad \text{(ii)}$$

Note that Eq. (ii) has been simplified by division by ρ. This equation also could have been directly obtained from Eq. (3.77). Now if v is also constant, one obtains from Eq. (ii) or Eq. (3.78):

$$\partial U_x/\partial t + (\boldsymbol{U} \cdot \boldsymbol{\nabla})U_x = \dot{\psi}_G/\rho + v(\nabla^2 U_x) \qquad \text{(iii)}$$

In rectangular coordinates, as one example, Eq. (iii) with the help of the expressions for $(\boldsymbol{U} \cdot \boldsymbol{\nabla})\psi$ and $\nabla^2 \psi$ as given in Eqs. (3.53) and (3.64), respectively, becomes

$$\frac{\partial U_x}{\partial t} + U_x\frac{\partial U_x}{\partial x} + U_y\frac{\partial U_x}{\partial y} + U_z\frac{\partial U_x}{\partial z} = \frac{\dot{\psi}_G}{\rho} + v\left(\frac{\partial^2 U_x}{\partial x^2} + \frac{\partial^2 U_x}{\partial y^2} + \frac{\partial^2 U_x}{\partial z^2}\right) \qquad \text{(iv)}$$

If v were not constant, then Eq. (ii) would have to be expanded and, if ρ were also not constant, then Eq. (i) would have to be expanded.

Example 3.9. Obtain the equation for mass transfer for a two-dimensional flow in the x and y directions when the density and diffusion coefficient can be considered constant and when there is no chemical reaction.

Answer. For constant-density problems, the property ψ is conveniently taken as ρ_A. Note that there must be at least two components in order to have a mass transfer problem. From the statement of the problem, the following are true:

$$\boldsymbol{U} = iU_x + jU_y \qquad \psi = \rho_A \qquad \delta = D \qquad \dot{\psi}_G = 0 \qquad \text{(i)}$$

Equation (3.78) with the substitutions from Eq. (i) becomes

$$\partial\rho_A/\partial t + (\boldsymbol{U} \cdot \boldsymbol{\nabla})\rho_A = D(\nabla^2 \rho_A) \qquad \text{(ii)}$$

The second term on the left is obtained from Eq. (3.53):

$$(\boldsymbol{U} \cdot \boldsymbol{\nabla})\rho_A = U_x\frac{\partial\rho_A}{\partial x} + U_y\frac{\partial\rho_A}{\partial y} \qquad \text{(iii)}$$

In Eq. (3.53), U_z for this problem is zero since there is no variation in the z direction for a two-dimensional flow. The Laplacian of ρ_A is given by Eq. (3.64):

$$\nabla^2 \rho_A = \frac{\partial^2 \rho_A}{\partial x^2} + \frac{\partial^2 \rho_A}{\partial y^2} \qquad \text{(iv)}$$

where again the last term in Eq. (3.64) is zero. Equation (3.78), in rectangular coordinates, becomes

$$\frac{\partial \rho_A}{\partial t} + U_x \frac{\partial \rho_A}{\partial x} + U_y \frac{\partial \rho_A}{\partial y} = D \left(\frac{\partial^2 \rho_A}{\partial x^2} + \frac{\partial^2 \rho_A}{\partial y^2} \right) \qquad \text{(v)}$$

3.6 SUMMARY

The basic idea in this chapter is that mass, energy, and momentum must be conserved. The law of conservation says that INPUT plus GENERATION yields OUTPUT plus ACCUMULATION. This law was developed in a general mathematical form as Eq. (3.60):

$$\partial \psi / \partial t + (U \cdot \nabla) \psi = \dot{\psi}_G + (\nabla \cdot \delta \nabla \psi) - \psi (\nabla \cdot U) \qquad \text{(3.60)}$$
$$\text{ACC} \qquad \text{CONV} \qquad \text{GEN} \qquad \text{MOLEC} \qquad \text{CONV}$$

This equation is the starting point for the solution of many problems, as will be illustrated in subsequent chapters. Also, there are some important simplifications of Eq. (3.60). The first of these is the "Equation of Continuity", which arises when the concentration of property ψ equals density ρ and there is no generation of mass:

$$\partial \rho / \partial t + [\nabla \cdot (\rho U)] = 0 \qquad \text{(3.71)}$$

An important simplification of Eq. (3.71) is the case of incompressible flow (constant density) where

$$(\nabla \cdot U) = 0 \qquad \text{(3.74)}$$

Equation (3.74) is often applicable because the assumption of constant density is reasonable in many problems. For example, liquid systems are almost always at constant density, even when there are changes in composition, temperature, etc. Note that steady-state need not be assumed with regard to Eq. (3.74). Equation (3.74) is valid as long as the density is constant with changes in position and in time.

The constant density case arises so often that Eq. (3.60) is simplified for this assumption. If the transport coefficient is also constant, then

$$\partial \psi / \partial t + (U \cdot \nabla) \psi = \dot{\psi}_G + \delta (\nabla^2 \psi) \qquad \text{(3.78)}$$

The reader must understand the derivations of these four equations, what each term means, and how to begin problem solving with these equations by eliminating the terms that are zero.

PROBLEMS

3.1. Consider a rectangular piece of iron ($k = 80.2 \text{ W m}^{-1} \text{K}^{-1}$, $\rho = 7870 \text{ kg m}^{-3}$, $c_p = 447 \text{ J kg}^{-1} \text{K}^{-1}$), insulated in both y and z directions; the distance between face 1 and face 2 (cf. Fig. 3.1) is 1.5 m; the other dimensions of the rectangle are

0.5 m and 0.02 m. An electric current is passed through the iron, thus generating $4.0\,\mathrm{J\,s^{-1}}$, while the fluxes at faces 1 and 2 are held constant at $-2941\,\mathrm{J\,m^{-2}\,s^{-1}}$ and $-2643\,\mathrm{J\,m^{-2}\,s^{-1}}$, respectively. At time zero, the temperature of face 2 is 320 K.
(a) Find the rate of accumulation in $\mathrm{J\,s^{-1}}$.
(b) Find the equation for the temperature profile and determine the temperature at face 1 at time zero and after $10^4\,\mathrm{s}$.

3.2. Show that the velocity U satisfies the Equation of Continuity at every point except the origin for a fluid of constant density.

$$U = i\frac{4x}{x^2 + y^2} + j\frac{4y}{x^2 + y^2}$$

3.3. Does the velocity U satisfy the law of mass conservation for incompressible flow?

$$U = i(5x) + j(5y) + k(-10z)$$

3.4. A certain two-dimensional shear flow near a wall has the velocity component U_x. Derive from the Equation of Continuity the velocity component $U_y(x, y)$ assuming that $U_y = 0$ at the wall, $y = 0$. The equation for U_x is:

$$U_x = U\left(\frac{2y}{ax} - \frac{y^2}{a^2 x^2}\right)$$

where U and a are constants.

3.5. Given two incompressible-flow components U_x and U_y, find the most general form of the third component $U_z(x, y, z)$ that satisfies the Equation of Continuity.

$$U_x = xy^2 + x^2 z \qquad U_y = y^2 z$$

3.6. Determine whether U satisfies the Equation of Continuity for a steady-state, incompressible flow:

$$U = i(2xy) + j(x - z) + k(y - 2xy)$$

3.7. A fluid flows into a channel through an entrance (as in Fig. 2.12) in such a way that its velocity distribution is uniform across the opening to the entrance. From this point the velocity profile changes gradually downstream, to that for fully developed flow, such as a parabolic profile for laminar flow. Using the Equation of Continuity:
(a) Show whether there is a y component of velocity in the entrance region.
(b) Show whether there is a y component of velocity in the fully-developed region where the velocity U_x is not a function of x, which is the direction of flow down the channel.

3.8. Consider the flow of a fluid in a pipe. Define the cross sectional area of the pipe as S ($\mathrm{m^2}$); the velocity is U ($\mathrm{m\,s^{-1}}$); the volume flow rate is Q ($\mathrm{m^3\,s^{-1}}$); the mass flow rate is w ($\mathrm{kg\,s^{-1}}$); the density ρ of the fluid is constant. Show that:
(a) $w = Q\rho$.
(b) $w = \rho SU$

3.9. Water (density $995\,\mathrm{kg\,m^{-3}}$) enters one end of a perforated, round pipe of diameter 0.3 m and length 2.0 m with an average velocity of $8.0\,\mathrm{m\,s^{-1}}$. Water discharges from the pipe in two places: the opposite end from the inlet and from the perforations in the walls of the pipe. The discharge velocity can be approximated by a linear velocity profile, as shown in Fig. 3.7, the equation for

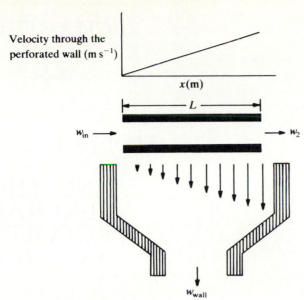

FIGURE 3.7
Velocity through a perforated pipe wall.

which can be found from the following boundary conditions:

$$U \ (x = 0) = 0 \qquad U \ (x = L) = 0.4U_2$$

where U_2 is the velocity of water exiting the pipe in the x direction and w_2 is the corresponding mass flow rate. Using the equations in Problem 3.8:
(a) Find the mass flow rate (kg s^{-1}) of water exiting the pipe in the x direction.
(b) Find the mass flow rate (kg s^{-1}) of water exiting through the perforated wall.

3.10. Repeat Problem 3.9 for the same boundary conditions, but assume that the velocity profile is parabolic (i.e., follows the equation $U = C_1 x^2$).

3.11. Repeat Problem 3.9, but assume that the velocity profile is parabolic as

$$U = C_1 + C_2 x^2$$

Also, let the discharge velocity through the perforated pipe wall be subject to the following boundary conditions:

$$U \ (x = 0) = 0.6U_2 \qquad U \ (x = L) = 0.1U_2$$

MOLECULAR TRANSPORT AND THE GENERAL PROPERTY BALANCE

NOMENCLATURE

A Area (m^2, ft^2); subscripts denote direction normal to coordinate, e.g., A_r is area normal to radius (area of a cylinder)

A   Species A; A_1 and A_2 are species A at locations 1 and 2

B   Species B; subscripts 1 and 2 represent locations

C Concentration ($kmol\, m^{-3}$, $lb\, mol\, ft^{-3}$); C_A, C_B, C_i are concentrations of species A, B, i; C_T is total concentration; $C_{A,1}$ and $C_{A,2}$ are concentrations at locations 1 and 2

C $C(x, y)$, C_1, and C_2 are constants of integration

$\dot{C}_G$ Rate of generation of mass ($kmol\, m^{-3}\, s^{-1}$, $lb\, mol\, ft^{-3}\, s^{-1}$)

c   Subscript denoting flux contribution due to convection

c_p Heat capacity at constant pressure ($kJ\, kg^{-1}\, K^{-1}$, $Btu\, lb_m^{-1}\, °F^{-1}$)

D Diffusion coefficient (mass diffusivity) ($m^2\, s^{-1}$, $ft^2\, s^{-1}$)

d Diameter (m, ft); d_o is diameter of a tube or pipe

F Force (N, lb_f); subscripts denote components in coordinate direction; F_g is the force due to a gravitational field

g Acceleration due to a gravitational field ($m\, s^{-2}$, $ft\, s^{-2}$); also, $\boldsymbol{g}$ is the gravitational vector, Eq. (4.49)

g_c Gravitational conversion constant (32.174 $lb_m\, lb_f^{-1}\, ft\, s^{-2}$)

i	Unit vector in x direction
$\mathbf{J}_A/A$	Molar flux vector in Fick's law, Eq. (2.4), defined with respect to a plane of no net volume flow ($kmol\,m^{-2}\,s^{-1}$, $lb\,mol\,ft^{-2}\,s^{-1}$); subscripts A or B are for flux of species A or B; called $\mathbf{J}_A^v/A$ in Chapter 5
$\mathbf{j}_A/A$	Mass flux vector of species A, defined with respect to a plane of no net volume flow ($kg\,m^{-2}\,s^{-1}$, $lb_m\,ft^{-2}\,s^{-1}$)
$\mathbf{j}$	Unit vector in y direction
$\mathbf{k}$	Unit vector in z direction
k	Thermal conductivity ($W\,m^{-1}\,K^{-1}$ or $J\,m^{-1}\,K^{-1}\,s^{-1}$, $Btu\,ft^{-1}$ $°R^{-1}\,s^{-1}$); k_m is mean thermal conductivity over the range of integration
k_n	Specific reaction rate constant of order n, as given in Eq. (4.105)
L	Length (m, ft)
$\dot{M}_G$	rate of generation of momentum in a unit volume ($kg\,m^{-2}\,s^{-2}$, $N\,m^{-3}$, $lb_m\,ft^{-2}\,s^{-2}$, $lb_f\,ft^{-3}$)
m	Mass (kg, lb_m)
m	Subscript denoting contribution due to molecular transport
$\mathbf{N}_A$	Molar flow vector for species A, defined with respect to fixed coordinates ($kmol\,s^{-1}$, $lb\,mol\,s^{-1}$); if written not as a vector, then N is subscripted for direction of transfer
$\mathbf{n}_A$	Mass flow vector for species A, equal to molar flow $\mathbf{N}_A$ times molecular weight ($kg\,s^{-1}$ $lb_m\,s^{-1}$)
n	Order of reaction in Eq. (4.105)
p	Pressure (kPa, atm, $lb_f\,in.^{-2}$); $\bar{p}_A$ is partial pressure of species A, Eq. (2.38)
Q	Volume rate of flow ($m^3\,s^{-1}$, $ft^3\,s^{-1}$); also subscript denoting torque
$\mathbf{q}$	Energy (heat) flow vector ($J\,s^{-1}$, $Btu\,s^{-1}$)
R	Gas constant, see Table C.1 for values
r	Cylindrical coordinate
r	Radius (m, ft); in heat transfer, r_i is radius of inside tube wall and r_o is radius of outside tube wall; in momentum transfer, the convention is to designate r_o (and d_o) as the radius (and diameter) of the tube through which the fluid is flowing (i.e., the inside radius)
S	Area perpendicular to the direction of the velocity vector $\mathbf{U}$
T	Temperature (K, $°R$, $°C$, $°F$); T_1 and T_2 are temperatures at locations 1 and 2; T_w is temperature of the wall or surface; $T_{\mathcal{C}}$ is temperature at the center line
$\dot{T}_G$	Rate of generation of heat ($J\,m^{-3}\,s^{-1}$, $Btu\,ft^{-3}\,s^{-1}$)
t	Time (s)
$\mathbf{U}$	Velocity vector ($m\,s^{-1}$, $ft\,s^{-1}$); U is the magnitude of $\mathbf{U}$; U_x, U_y, U_z, U_θ, U_r are components in directions x, y, z, θ, r; $\mathbf{U}$ is the mass average velocity [Eq. (3.22)], whereas $\mathbf{U}^*$ is molar average velocity [Eq. (3.23)]
V	Volume (m^3, ft^3)
x	Rectangular (Cartesian) coordinate; x_o is thickness of laminar film

y	Rectangular (Cartesian) coordinate; $(2y_o)$ is distance between two parallel plates
z	Rectangular (Cartesian) coordinate
α	Thermal diffusivity $(m^2\,s^{-1}, ft^2\,s^{-1})$
β	Constant used in Problem 4-16
Δ	Difference, state 2 minus state 1; e.g., ΔT means $T_2 - T_1$
δ	Generalized diffusivity $(m^2\,s^{-1}, ft^2\,s^{-1})$
θ	Angle, curvilinear coordinate direction
μ	Viscosity $(kg\,m^{-1}\,s^{-1}$ or $N\,m^{-2}\,s$, $lb_m\,ft^{-1}\,s^{-1}$, cP)
ν	Kinematic viscosity (momentum diffusivity) $(m^2\,s^{-1}, ft^2\,s^{-1})$
π	Ratio of circumference of a circle to its diameter $(3.141\,592\,65\ldots)$
ρ	Density $(kg\,m^{-3}, lb_m\,ft^{-3})$; subscripts refer to species
$\dot{\rho}_G$	Rate of generation of mass $(kg\,m^{-3}\,s^{-1}, lb_m\,ft^{-3}\,s^{-1})$
τ	Momentum flux (or shear stress) tensor $(N\,m^{-2}, lb_f\,ft^{-2})$; τ_{xy}, τ_{yx}, etc., are components of the momentum flux tensor, where subscripts refer to direction of momentum transfer and direction of velocity
$\boldsymbol{\Psi}$	Generalized flux vector (e.g., units for heat flux are $J\,m^{-2}\,s^{-1}$ or $W\,m^{-2}$; see Table 3.1 for complete listing); Ψ_x, Ψ_y, Ψ_z, Ψ_r are components in directions x, y, z, r; $\Psi_{x,m}$ or $\boldsymbol{\Psi}_m$ is flux due to molecular transport; $\Psi_{x,c}$ or $\boldsymbol{\Psi}_c$ is flux due to convection
ψ	Generalized concentration of property (e.g., units for concentration of heat are $J\,m^{-3}$, $Btu\,ft^{-3}$; see Table 3.1 for complete listing)
$\dot{\psi}_G$	Generalized rate of generation of heat or mass or momentum in a unit volume (see Table 4.2 for units)
∇	Vector operator del, defined by Eq. (2.16) or Eq. (3.45) (m^{-1}, ft^{-1})

In the preceding chapter the general property balance was developed for both one-directional transfer and for the more general three-dimensional case. In this chapter specific applications of the balance to molecular transport will be discussed. In the problems considered in this chapter, it will be found that the convective contributions are zero even though in several cases there is flow. Chapter 5 will cover non-zero convective contributions.

This chapter will treat a number of molecular transport problems by using the general property balance. The simplest problems are one-directional and involve only input and output, i.e., no generation and also no accumulation because of steady-state conditions. First, constant area will be treated, then variable area problems. Next, generation will be added but still the problems will be at steady-state so that there is no accumulation.

In Chapter 2 the molecular transport equations were developed. To review briefly, the general flux $\boldsymbol{\Psi}$ and the concentration of the property being transferred ψ were useful to present the analogy among heat, mass, and momentum transfers. Table 4.1 reviews the terms with an emphasis on the units involved. Table 4.1 will be needed often in the material to follow. In a limited one-directional form, the same information was presented in Table 2.1.

TABLE 4.1
Definitions and units for Ψ and ψ

	Flux	Diffusivity	Concentration of property ψ	Units of (ψV) SI	English
General	Ψ	δ	ψ		
Heat	q/A	α	$\rho c_p T$	J	Btu
Mass	J_A/A	D	C_A	kmol	lb mol
	N_A/A	D	C_A	kmol	lb mol
	n_A/A	D	ρ_A	kg	lb_m
Momentum	τ	ν	ρU	$kg\ m\ s^{-1}$	$lb_m\ ft\ s^{-1}$
				or	or
				N s	$lb_f\ s$

Note: the basic transport equation is

$$\Psi = -\delta\nabla\psi = -\delta[i(\partial\psi/\partial x) + j(\partial\psi/\partial y) + k(\partial\psi/\partial z)] \qquad (2.18)$$

4.1 STEADY TRANSPORT IN ONE DIRECTION INVOLVING INPUT–OUTPUT WITH NO GENERATION

As shown in Chapter 3, if there is no accumulation and no generation, then a balance on a volume such as shown in Fig. 3.1 yields

$$(\Psi_x A)_1 = (\Psi_x A)_2 \qquad (4.1)$$

This equation is Eq. (3.2) with the appropriate terms equated to zero. If the area is constant, then A cancels from both sides of Eq. (4.1):

$$(\Psi_x)_1 = (\Psi_x)_2 = (\Psi_x)_{\text{all}\ x} = \text{constant} \qquad (3.3)$$

Equation (3.3) states that for constant area and no generation or accumulation, the flux is uniformly constant throughout the volume. Equation (4.1) may also be generalized to the following:

$$(\Psi_x A)_1 = (\Psi_x A)_2 = (\Psi_x A)_{\text{all}\ x} = \text{constant} \qquad (4.2)$$

For variable area and no generation or accumulation, Eq. (4.2) states that the product of flux times area is uniformly constant throughout the volume. This equation is the starting point for many solutions to one-directional molecular transport problems.

The net result given by Eq. (4.2), when applied to heat transfer, is

$$(\Psi A)_x = (q/A)_x (A_x) = q_x = \text{constant} \qquad (4.3)$$

For mass transfer, Eq. (4.2) becomes

$$(\Psi A)_x = (J_A/A)_x (A_x) = J_{A,x} = \text{constant} \qquad (4.4)$$

The analogous equation for momentum transfer is more complex because there are two coordinate directions to be considered (see Fig. 2.2), and the momentum transfer is perpendicular to the flow velocity or the force. The result is

$$(\Psi A)_y = (\tau_{yx} A_y) = (F_x/A_y)A_y = F_x = \text{constant} \tag{4.5}$$

The total flux is the sum of the molecular and convective contributions:

$$\Psi_x = \Psi_{x,m} + \Psi_{x,c} \tag{3.15}$$

The discussion in this chapter will be restricted to problems where the net convective flux $\Psi_{x,c}$ is zero. The reader already knows that in problems of heat conduction through a solid there is no net convective flux, since in Section 3.2.2 convection was defined as the bulk flow of a fluid due to the external influences of a pressure difference or a force of gravity. In Chapter 5, it will be shown that the term $\Psi_{x,c}$ is also zero for a variety of other problems, such as one-directional laminar pipe flow.

For the case of $\Psi_{x,c}$ equal to zero, Eq. (2.7) is used to replace $\Psi_{x,m}$ in Eq. (3.15):

$$\Psi_x = \Psi_{x,m} = -\delta(d\psi/dx) \tag{4.6}$$

Equation (4.6) is combined with Eq. (4.2):

$$(\Psi_m A)_x = \text{constant} = -\delta A_x(d\psi/dx) \tag{4.7}$$

Since $(\Psi_m A)_x$ is constant for all values of x, the variables in Eq. (4.7) are separable. After separation, the result in integral form is

$$(\Psi_m A)_x \int_{x_1}^{x_2} \frac{dx}{A_x} = -\int_{\psi_1}^{\psi_2} \delta \, d\psi \tag{4.8}$$

where the product $(\Psi_m A)_x$ is taken outside the integral because it is constant for all x.

Equation (4.8) is general for one-directional, molecular transport with no generation or accumulation. For heat transfer, $(\Psi_m A)_x$ is q_x from Eq. (4.3).[1] Using the values of ψ and δ from Table 3.1 or 4.1, Eq. (4.8) becomes

$$(q/A)_x (A_x) \int_{x_1}^{x_2} \frac{dx}{A_x} = -\int_{\rho c_p T_1}^{\rho c_p T_2} \alpha \, d(\rho c_p T) \tag{4.9}$$

Reviewing, the definition of the thermal diffusivity α is

$$\alpha = \frac{k}{\rho c_p} \tag{2.10}$$

The right-hand side of Eq. (4.9) may be simplified considerably for constant ρ

---

[1] Note that in the rest of this chapter the subscript m will not be carried through even though only molecular transfer is being considered.

and c_p. After canceling, Eq. (4.9) becomes

$$q_x \int_{x_1}^{x_2} \frac{dx}{A_x} = -\int_{T_1}^{T_2} k \, dT \tag{4.10}$$

where the limits of integration are now from x_1 and T_1 to x_2 and T_2.

With the appropriate substitutions from Tables 3.1 or 4.1, a corresponding relation exists for mass transfer:

$$N_{A,x} \int_{x_1}^{x_2} \frac{dx}{A_x} = -\int_{C_{A,1}}^{C_{A,2}} D \, dC_A \tag{4.11}$$

where N_A equals J_A for the case of no convective (volume) flow, as discussed in Section 2.3.

Again, momentum transfer is more complicated because the flow direction differs from the transport direction; it will be discussed separately in Section 4.2.2. The general equation, Eq. (4.8), and its specific forms, Eq. (4.10) and Eq. (4.11), apply for one-directional, steady-state transfer with no generation, no accumulation, and no net convective flux.

4.1.1 Constant Area Transport

For most of the sample problems in Chapter 2, the material properties (k, μ, ρ, D) were assumed constant so that the right-hand side of Eq. (4.8), Eq. (4.10), or Eq. (4.11) could be easily integrated. If A_x is constant, then the left-hand side can also be easily integrated. Under these conditions, Eq. (4.10) for heat transfer integrates to

$$q_x(x_2 - x_1) = -kA_x(T_2 - T_1) \tag{4.12}$$

Using the following definitions:

$$\Delta x = x_2 - x_1 \tag{4.13}$$
$$\Delta T = T_2 - T_1 \tag{4.14}$$

Eq. (4.12) becomes

$$(q/A)_x = -k(\Delta T / \Delta x) \tag{4.15}$$

Equation (4.15) confirms the results already intuitively used in Fig. 2.2; i.e., the temperature gradient dT/dx, which here is $\Delta T/\Delta x$, is constant. Note that both $(q/A)_x$ and k are constant in Eq. (4.15). A constant gradient $\Delta T/\Delta x$ in Eq. (4.15) corresponds to a linear temperature gradient in Eq. (4.10) for one-directional, steady-state heat transfer problems with constant area and no generation, no radiation, and no net convective flux.

4.1.2 Variable Area Transport

Input–output transport in one-directional problems with variable area most often occurs in cylindrical or spherical geometries. Especially important are problems in cylindrical coordinates such as the flow of fluid in a circular pipe or heat transfer through a pipe wall. Up to this point in the discussion, only rectangular (Cartesian) coordinates have been considered. In Chapter 5, the complete equations for both cylindrical and spherical coordinates will be presented, but for now the discussion will be limited to transfer in the radial direction only. In such cases, the area through which transport occurs varies with radius.

The empirical laws of heat transfer (Fourier's), mass transfer (Fick's) and momentum transfer (Newton's) for one-directional transfer along a radius are

$$(q/A)_r = -k(dT/dr) \tag{4.16}$$

$$(J_A/A)_r = -D(dC_A/dr) \tag{4.17}$$

$$\tau_{rz} = -\mu(dU_z/dr) \tag{4.18}$$

These equations can be written in the following analogous form:

$$\Psi_r = -\delta(d\psi/dr) \tag{4.19}$$

where r is the distance from the origin in the radial direction.

The reader is no doubt familiar with cylindrical coordinates, in which the rectangular coordinates x and y are expressed in terms of radius r and the angle θ:

$$\cos \theta = \frac{x}{r} \tag{4.20}$$

In cylindrical coordinates, the most general problem will have terms in all three directions, Ψ_r, Ψ_θ, and Ψ_z. For one-directional transfer in a geometry where cylindrical coordinates are appropriate (e.g., heat transfer in the r direction through the wall of a tube), both Ψ_z and Ψ_θ are zero.

Equation (4.18) for the shear stress τ_{rz} assumes that there is no angular velocity U_θ. Angular velocity, measured in radians per second, introduces some complexity into the problem, and this will be covered in Chapter 5. Equations (4.16) through (4.19) are often required for use in systems in which cylindrical coordinates simplify the boundary conditions so that a solution to some given problem is possible. Similar equations exist for spherical coordinates, with r being the coordinate along the radius of the sphere.

For one-directional transfer along the radius, Eq. (4.19) is substituted into Eq. (4.2):

$$(\Psi A)_r = \text{constant} = -(\delta A_r)(d\psi/dr) \tag{4.21}$$

Again, the product $(\Psi A)_r$ is constant for all values of r except at the origin $(r = 0)$, which is a singular point. The variables in Eq. (4.21) are separated and integrated with the result

$$(\Psi A)_r \int_{r_1}^{r_2} \frac{dr}{A_r} = -\int_{\psi_1}^{\psi_2} \delta \, d\psi \tag{4.22}$$

From Table 4.1, the appropriate substitutions for ψ and δ are made. The resulting equations for heat and mass transfer are

$$\text{Heat:} \qquad q_r \int_{r_1}^{r_2} \frac{dr}{A_r} = -\int_{T_1}^{T_2} k \, dT \qquad (4.23)$$

$$\text{Mass:} \qquad N_{A,r} \int_{r_1}^{r_2} \frac{dr}{A_r} = -\int_{C_{A,1}}^{C_{A,2}} D \, dC_A \qquad (4.24)$$

These two equations are for heat and mass transport along a radius only, at steady-state and with no generation or convection. Note that the transport is still one-directional (the radial direction).

Figure 4.1 shows the geometry for heat or mass transfer through a pipe wall in the radial direction. The area term in Eq. (4.22) is A_r, the area through which the property is being transferred. That area at any distance r is the distance around (i.e., the circumference, $2\pi r$) times the distance in the z direction, L:

$$A_r = 2\pi r L \qquad (4.25)$$

Note that A_r varies as r changes. Unfortunately, the transport area is often confused with the inside area perpendicular to the direction of fluid flow (S) in Fig. 4.1(c), since the inside of the tube usually contains a fluid in heat or mass

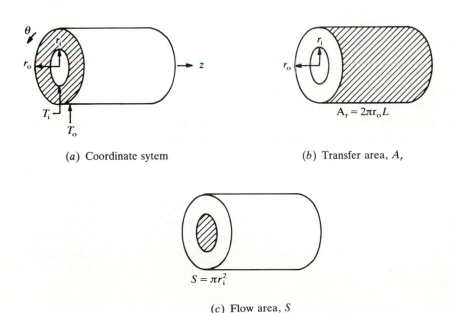

(a) Coordinate sytem

(b) Transfer area, A_r

$A_r = 2\pi r_o L$

$S = \pi r_i^2$

(c) Flow area, S

FIGURE 4.1
Heat or mass transfer through a pipe wall.

transfer problems. Example 4.1 will emphasize the seriousness of confusing A_r with the inside area ($S = \pi r_i^2$).

If simple symmetry exists, heat or mass transfer through a pipe wall is a one-dimensional transfer problem as described by Eq. (4.22), Eq. (4.23), or Eq. (4.24), and as shown in Fig. 4.1(b). An appropriate set of boundary conditions specifies the skin temperatures or concentrations at both the inside wall r_i and the outside wall r_o of the tube. There is no variation of T or C_A with the θ coordinate if the tube is uniformly manufactured. In many problems the length L is chosen so that the inside skin temperature T_1 or concentration $C_{A,1}$ and outside skin conditions do not vary with changes in z.

For simplicity, the discussion following will deal with heat transfer, because it is more commonly encountered in this geometry than is mass transfer.[2] The area of heat transfer A_r, given by Eq. (4.25), is substituted into Eq. (4.23):

$$q_r \int_{r_1}^{r_2} \frac{dr}{2\pi r L} = -\int_{T_1}^{T_2} k \, dT \tag{4.26}$$

After integration, the result is

$$q_r \ln \frac{r_2}{r_1} = -(2\pi L k_m)(T_2 - T_1) \tag{4.27}$$

If the two temperatures T_2 and T_1 are fairly close, it is common to replace k with the average value k_m. If k is a known function of T, then the right-hand side of Eq. (4.26) can be integrated analytically or graphically.

Historically, in heat transfer work authors have preferred to use the following form of Eq. (4.15):

$$(q/A)_r = -k_m(\Delta T/\Delta r) = q_r/A_m \tag{4.28}$$

For application to the problem of heat transfer through a tube wall, the appropriate area term A_m depends on the geometry under consideration. The actual form of the area term in Eq. (4.28) is obtained by comparing Eqs. (4.27) and (4.28). Equating the heat flux terms gives the area as

$$A_m = \frac{(2\pi L)(r_2 - r_1)}{\ln(r_2/r_1)} = A_{lm} \tag{4.29}$$

The quantity A_{lm} is called the log-mean area. Reference to it is often made in the literature; hence one should know what the log-mean area is, and how it is derived. However, in this text, and in general, any problem encountered should be analyzed from fundamentals by integrating with the appropriate

---

[2] There are practical examples of mass transfer through a tube wall. For instance, helium diffuses rapidly through glass. Hence, the helium present in many natural gas wells may be separated from natural gas by the radial diffusion through glass tubes.

boundary conditions. Such an approach has the advantage of avoiding misuse (or forgetfulness of the source and meaning) of the log-mean area. The derivation of Eq. (4.29) clearly shows that Eq. (4.29) applies only for the transfer across a pipe or tube wall. The mean area does not in any way depend on the type of flux or the property being transferred. The mean area is a geometrical term and will vary with the geometry being considered.

The following examples illustrate the importance of careful consideration of boundary conditions.

Example 4.1. A worker desired to measure the thermal conductivity of piping used in a processing system. A small sample of pipe, shown in Fig. 4.2, was insulated both inside and outside. The worker then maintained the top edge of the pipe at 10°C and the bottom edge at the temperature at which ice melts. He determined that 3.2 Btu h^{-1} was transferred from top to bottom by measuring the amount of ice that melted in a given time under steady-state conditions. The pipe was 2-inch schedule 40 pipe, 5 inches long. From Appendix B, Table B.1, the following data are available:

inside diameter: 2.067 in.
wall thickness: 0.154 in.
wall sectional area of metal: 1.075 in.^{2}

Determine the thermal conductivity. What would be the error if the log-mean area were incorrectly used?

Answer. In this problem heat transfer is in the z direction only because the pipe is insulated in the r direction. In the z direction the pipe area is constant:

$$A_z = (1.075)(1/144)(\text{in.}^2)(\text{ft}^2\,\text{in.}^{-2}) = 7.46 \times 10^{-3}\,\text{ft}^2 \qquad \text{(i)}$$

The length of transfer in the z direction [which corresponds to Δx in Eq. (4.13)] is

$$\Delta z = 5/12 = 0.4167\,\text{ft} \qquad \text{(ii)}$$

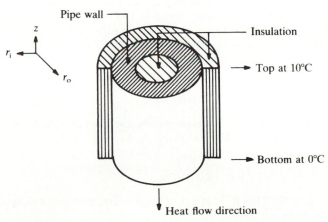

FIGURE 4.2
Pipe test sample.

Note that the heat transferred q is now -3.2 Btu h^{-1}; the minus sign indicates that heat flows from top to bottom (warm to cold). The temperature difference is from Eq. (4.14)

$$\Delta T = 10 - 0 = 10°C = 18°F \qquad \text{(iii)}$$

Equation (4.15) applies to this problem except that heat transfer is in the z direction. Replacing x with z, Eq. (4.15) becomes

$$(q/A)_z = -k(\Delta T/\Delta z) \qquad \text{(iv)}$$

Since the data were obtained in engineering units, these will be used. Solving Eq. (iv) for k and substituting:

$$k = \frac{(q/A)_z}{(\Delta T/\Delta z)} = -\frac{(-3.2)/(7.46 \times 10^{-3})}{(18)/(0.4167)} = 9.92 \text{ Btu h}^{-1}\text{ ft}^{-1}\text{ °F}^{-1}$$

$$= 17.17 \text{ W m}^{-1}\text{ K}^{-1} \qquad \text{(v)}$$

The use of A_{lm} is incorrect in the geometry of Fig. 4.2. The log-mean area [Eq. (4.29)] for a section of the pipe 5 in. long is

$$A_{lm} = \frac{(2\pi)(0.154/12)(5/12)}{\ln(2.375/2.067)} = 0.242 \text{ ft}^2 \qquad \text{(vi)}$$

The miscalculated k is

$$k_{incorrect} = k_{correct}(A_{correct}/A_{incorrect})$$
$$= (9.92)(7.46 \times 10^{-3}/0.242) = 0.306 \text{ Btu h}^{-1}\text{ ft}^{-1}\text{ °F}^{-1} = 0.529 \text{ W m}^{-1}\text{ K}^{-1} \qquad \text{(vii)}$$

The error is a factor of 32.4.

Example 4.2. Calculate the heat loss from a 2-inch, schedule 40 pipe if the inside skin temperature is maintained at 10°C and the outside skin temperature is maintained at 0°C.

Answer. The data for a 2-inch, schedule 40 pipe are given in Example 4.1. Note that this problem involves heat transfer between 10°C and 0°C with a piece of pipe just as in Example 4.1. But there is an important difference: in this problem, heat transfer is in the r direction. Solution of Example 4.2 therefore involves the derivation of Eq. (4.27) as done previously:

$$q_r = -k_m \frac{2\pi L}{\ln(r_2/r_1)} \Delta T \qquad \text{(4.27)}$$

The value of k_m from the previous problem will be used to calculate the heat loss per unit length of pipe (1 m):

$$q_r = -(17.17)\frac{(2\pi)(1)}{\ln(1.1875/1.0335)}(-10) = 7767 \text{ W} \qquad \text{(i)}$$

In English units, q_r is 8080 Btu h^{-1} for 1 ft of length. The plus sign indicates that the heat flow is radially out from the center.

Example 4.3. Solve Example 4.2 by the log-mean area concept.

Answer. Equations (4.28) and (4.29) define the concept:

$$q_r/A_{lm} = -k_m(\Delta T/\Delta r) \tag{4.28}$$

The log-mean area was determined in Example 4.1 as 0.242 ft^2 for a 5-in. length of pipe which is $(0.242)(12/5)$ or 0.581 ft^2 for a 1-ft length. Thus,

$$q_r = -(9.92)(0.581)\frac{(-10)(1.8)}{(0.154/12)}\left(\frac{\text{Btu}}{\text{h ft}^2 \, (°\text{F ft}^{-1})} \, \text{ft}^2 \frac{°\text{F}}{\text{ft}}\right)$$

$$= +8079 \text{ Btu h}^{-1} \tag{i}$$

In SI units, the log-mean area is 0.177 m^2 per meter of length and

$$q_r = -(17.17)(0.177)\frac{(-10)}{(0.154)(0.0254)}\left(\frac{\text{W}}{\text{m K}}\text{m}^2\frac{\text{K}}{\text{m}}\right) = +7767 \text{ W} \tag{ii}$$

Of course, the results of Examples (4.2) and (4.3) must be the same.

The preceding discussion on variable-area one-directional transfer problems emphasized heat transfer, which is more commonly encountered in this geometry. However, analogous equations for mass transfer exist and are solved similarly. The next example illustrates a problem in mass transfer through a variable area.

Example 4.4. Determine the mass transfer rate for the conical section shown in Fig. 4.3. The concentratiion of CO_2 in air is 30 mole per cent at the 10 cm opening, and 3 mole per cent at the 5 cm opening. For this mixture, the diffusion coefficient is $0.164 \text{ cm}^2 \text{ s}^{-1}$. The gas is at 1 atm and 25°C (298.15 K) everywhere. The section is 30 cm thick. Neglect any possible two-dimensional effects.

Answer. Since diffusion takes place at constant temperature and pressure, J_A equals N_A, as discussed in conjunction with Eq. (2.25) and in Example 2.6.

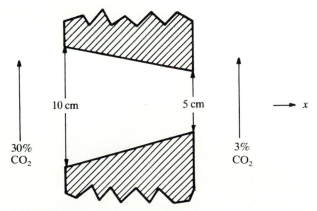

10 cm   5 cm $\longrightarrow x$

30%
CO_2

3%
CO_2

FIGURE 4.3
A conical section for mass transfer.

Equation (4.11) is

$$N_{A,x} \int_{x_1}^{x_2} \frac{dx}{A_x} = -\int_{C_{A,1}}^{C_{A,2}} D \, dC_A \tag{4.11}$$

In Section 2.3, the concentration was calculated from the partial pressure and temperature. Equation (4.11) may be cast in terms of the partial pressure $\bar{p}_A$ from Eq. (2.37):

$$C_A = \frac{\bar{p}_A}{RT} \tag{2.37}$$

Naturally, Eq. (2.37) applies for gases only. The derivative of Eq. (2.37) at constant temperature is

$$dC_A = \frac{d\bar{p}_A}{RT} \tag{i}$$

Then Eq. (i) is substituted into Eq. (4.11):

$$N_{A,x} \int_{x_1}^{x_2} \frac{dx}{A_x} = -\frac{D}{RT} \int_{\bar{p}_{A,1}}^{\bar{p}_{A,2}} d\bar{p}_A \tag{ii}$$

The area for mass transfer is circular:

$$A_x = \pi d^2 / 4 \tag{iii}$$

The area A_x decreases as x goes from 0 to 30 cm. The variation of the diameter with x is linear:

$$d = 10 - \frac{x}{6} \tag{iv}$$

where d and x are in units of centimeters. This equation and Eq. (iii) are inserted into Eq. (ii):

$$N_{A,x} \int_{x_1}^{x_2} \frac{dx}{(\pi/4)[10 - (x/6)]^2} = -\frac{D}{RT} \int_{\bar{p}_{A,1}}^{\bar{p}_{A,2}} d\bar{p}_A \tag{v}$$

Integrating:

$$(N_{A,x}) \frac{4}{\pi} \frac{(6)}{[10 - (x/6)]} \Big|_0^{30} = (N_{A,x}) \frac{24}{\pi} \left(\frac{1}{5} - \frac{1}{10}\right) = (N_{A,x}) \frac{2.4}{\pi}$$

$$= -\frac{D}{RT}(\bar{p}_{A,2} - \bar{p}_{A,1}) \tag{vi}$$

Thus

$$N_{A,x} = -\frac{\pi}{2.4} \frac{D}{RT}(\bar{p}_{A,2} - \bar{p}_{A,1}) = -\frac{\pi}{2.4} \frac{(0.164)}{(82.057)(298.15)}(0.03 - 0.3)$$

$$\times \left(\frac{\text{cm}^2 \, \text{s}^{-1}}{(\text{cm}^3 \, \text{atm} \, \text{mol}^{-1} \, \text{K}^{-1})\text{K}} \text{atm}\right)$$

$$= +2.37 \times 10^{-6} \, \text{mol s}^{-1} = +8.53 \times 10^{-3} \, \text{mol h}^{-1} \tag{vii}$$

The plus sign indicates diffusion to the right.

4.2 STEADY-STATE TRANSPORT WITH GENERATION

As discussed in Section 3.1.2, at steady-state there may be a generation or depletion of the property of interest. For example, there can be generation of heat or its removal through chemical reaction. There can be heat generation through electrical means or nuclear reactions. Individual species can be produced or depleted through chemical or nuclear reaction. For momentum transfer, a generation term appears as a result of external forces (pressure drop, drag on surfaces, etc.). Table 4.2 provides the symbols and units used for generation terms. The generation will be constant in many cases but will vary in others. Generation may often be a function of position in the system and of temperature. In such cases the solution of transport problems can be complicated by this variation.

For one-directional transfer at steady-state, Eq. (3.12) reduces to

$$\partial(\Psi_x A) = \dot{\psi}_G \, \partial V \tag{4.30}$$

Let us not assume constant area; therefore, in Eq. (4.30), the proper variation of area must be used. Furthermore, let us consider only molecular transport so that Ψ_x is given by

$$\Psi_x = -\delta(\partial\psi/\partial x) \tag{2.7}$$

Combining Eqs. (4.30) and (2.7):

$$-\partial[(\delta A)(\partial\psi/\partial x)] = \dot{\psi}_G \, \partial V \tag{4.31}$$

For a system in which transfer is in the radial direction, Eq. (4.31) becomes

$$-\partial[(\delta A)(\partial\psi/\partial r)] = \dot{\psi}_G \, \partial V \tag{4.32}$$

In summary, Eq. (4.31) or Eq. (4.32) is the starting point for solving steady-state problems for molecular transport only and with variable area and generation included. It is useful to discuss constant generation of heat and of mass together because the final equations are very similar. Momentum transfer will be discussed separately because of the complication of convection.

TABLE 4.2
The generation term

Application	Symbol	SI units	English units
General	$\dot{\psi}_G$		
Heat	$\dot{T}_G$	$J\,m^{-3}\,s^{-1}$ or $W\,m^{-3}$	$Btu\,ft^{-3}\,s^{-1}$
Mass	$\dot{C}_{A,G}$	$kmol\,m^{-3}\,s^{-1}$	$lb\,mol\,ft^{-3}\,s^{-1}$
	$\dot{\rho}_{A,G}$	$kg\,m^{-3}\,s^{-1}$	$lb_m\,ft^{-3}\,s^{-1}$
Momentum	$\dot{M}_G$	$kg\,m^{-2}\,s^{-2}$ or $N\,m^{-3}$	$lb_m\,ft^{-2}\,s^{-1}$ or $lb_f\,ft^{-3}$

4.2.1 Heat or Mass Transport with Constant Generation

Again, only one-directional problems will be considered. In order to solve Eq. (4.31) or Eq. (4.32), the thermal conductivity, area of transfer, and the generation term must be known before integration. In the following discussion, the thermal conductivity and generation terms will be assumed constant. For example, let us determine the temperature distribution in a wire with electrical heat generation. Figure 4.4 shows a wire of length L with mean thermal conductivity k_m. Let the temperature at the wall be T_w and the temperature at the center line ($r = 0$) be $T_{\mathcal{C}}$. The area for transfer is the surface area of the cylinder [i.e., as given in Eq. (4.25)] and not the cross sectional area; the surface area is

$$A_r = 2\pi r L \tag{4.25}$$

The volume is given by

$$V = \pi r^2 L \tag{4.33}$$

From this equation, the differential volume is

$$dV = 2\pi r L \, dr \tag{4.34}$$

The basic equation that leads to the variation of T with r is Eq. (4.32). With ψ and δ for heat transfer taken from Tables 3.1 or 4.1 and the generation from Table 4.2, Eq. (4.32) becomes

$$-\partial\{(\alpha A_r)[\partial(\rho c_p T)/\partial r]\} = \dot{T}_G \, \partial V \tag{4.35}$$

As shown in conjunction with Eq. (4.10), the assumption of constant (ρc_p) results in simplification of Eq. (4.35) to

$$-\partial[(k A_r)(\partial T/\partial r)] = \dot{T}_G \, \partial V \tag{4.36}$$

The differential volume from Eq. (4.34) and the area from Eq. (4.25) are

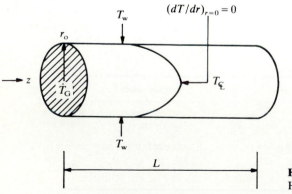

FIGURE 4.4
Heated wire geometry.

substituted into Eq. (4.36):

$$-d[(kr)(dT/dr)] = (\dot{T}_G)r\, dr \tag{4.37}$$

This equation is integrated once:

$$-(kr)(dT/dr) = (\dot{T}_G/2)(r^2) + C_1 \tag{4.38}$$

Note that at this step, the thermal conductivity k need not be constant, as it is inside the differential during the integration. The constant of integration C_1 is zero for this problem. There are two ways to prove this. The first is to realize that the temperature in Fig. 4.4 will be symmetric about the center line of the conduit, i.e., $T(r)$ is independent of the coordinate θ. While T varies with r, the slope dT/dr also must vary with r and furthermore must be a continuous function (i.e., either a maximum or a minimum at the center line, $r = 0$). Under these restrictions, the slope or gradient dT/dr at the center line will be zero. Then by inspection of Eq. (4.38), the constant C_1 is seen to be zero.

The second way to prove C_1 to be zero is to integrate Eq. (4.38) a second time and apply the known boundary conditions. This procedure will be detailed in Example 4.6, as well as in Section 4.2.4.

Equation (4.38) with C_1 equal to zero is

$$dT/dr = -[\dot{T}_G/(2k)]r \tag{4.39}$$

The equation is integrated again by separation of variables:

$$T = -[\dot{T}_G/(4k_m)]r^2 + C_2 \tag{4.40}$$

where at this step the thermal conductivity has been assumed constant at an average value k_m. The constant of integration C_2 can be evaluated at the surface where the temperature is designated as T_w at $r = r_o$ (the wire radius):

$$C_2 = T_w + \dot{T}_G r_o^2/(4k_m) \tag{4.41}$$

Equation (4.41) is inserted into Eq. (4.40):

$$T - T_w = [\dot{T}_G/(4k_m)](r_o^2 - r^2) \tag{4.42}$$

Example 4.5. Calculate the temperature distribution in the steel wire (1-inch O.D.) of Fig. 4.4 if electrical current generates heat at the rate of $2 \times 10^7\,\mathrm{J\,m^{-3}\,s^{-1}}$. The outside surface of the wire is maintained at 30°C. For steel wire, the mean conductivity is $17.3\,\mathrm{W\,m^{-1}\,K^{-1}}$.

Answer. For this problem

$$r_o = 0.5\,\mathrm{in.} = 0.0127\,\mathrm{m} \qquad \dot{T}_G = 2 \times 10^7\,\mathrm{J\,m^{-3}\,s^{-1}} \qquad T_w = 30°C \tag{i}$$

Equation (4.42) describes the temperature distribution for this problem:

$$T = T_w + \frac{\dot{T}_G}{4k_m}(r_o^2 - r^2) \tag{4.42}$$

Substituting:

$$T = 30 + \frac{2 \times 10^7}{(4)(17.3)} [(0.0127)^2 - r^2] = 30 + 46.6 - (2.89 \times 10^5)(r^2)$$

$$= 76.6 - (2.89 \times 10^5)(r^2) \tag{ii}$$

where r is in meters and T is in °C. At the center line ($r = 0$), the maximum temperature is 76.6°C. At the outside, the temperature reduces to the boundary condition value of 30°C. The distribution is parabolic between these limits.

The problem just considered was one in which the temperature distribution was symmetrical about the axis of symmetry. In such cases the constant of integration can be evaluated directly. However, there are problems in which this constant cannot be determined, and one must carry it through the second integration. After the second integration, two boundary conditions can be used for the determination of the two constants of integration by the solution of a pair of simultaneous equations. The following example illustrates this point for the problem of heat transfer in a slab, the two faces of which are maintained at different temperatures.

Example 4.6. Obtain the temperature distribution for the slab shown below in which there is a uniform heat generation. The slab in Fig. 4.5 is assumed to be large in both y and z directions so that any boundary effects may be neglected.

Answer. The basic equation for this problem comes from Eq. (4.31); again Table 3.1 is used to replace ψ and δ for heat transfer. Upon assumption of constant physical properties ρ and c_p, Eq. (4.31) reduces to

$$-d[(kA_x)(dT/dx)] = \dot{T}_G \, dV \tag{i}$$

The area of transfer is constant. The volume is the area times the distance:

$$V = A_x x \tag{ii}$$

or in differential form, for constant area:

$$dV = A_x \, dx \tag{iii}$$

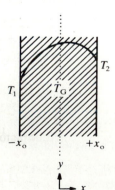

y
x

FIGURE 4.5
Heat transfer across a slab with generation.

Equation (iii) is used to eliminate dV in Eq. (i):

$$-d[(kA_x)(dT/dx)] = \dot{T}_G A_x\, dx \qquad (iv)$$

The area term can be canceled from both sides of Eq. (iv), since the transfer area is constant in Fig. 4.5. At this point, it is also convenient to assume that the slab has a constant thermal conductivity k_m as discussed before. Then Eq. (iv) can be integrated:

$$dT/dx = -(\dot{T}_G/k_m)(x) + C_1 \qquad (v)$$

The problem is not symmetric. Although dT/dx might be zero somewhere, it is not known where, so C_1 cannot be determined. However, Eq. (v) can be integrated again:

$$T = -[\dot{T}_G/(2k_m)](x^2) + C_1(x) + C_2 \qquad (vi)$$

There are two boundary conditions that can be used to determine the two constants of integration. These are

$$T(x = -x_o) = T_1$$
$$T(x = +x_o) = T_2 \qquad (vii)$$

These are substituted into Eq. (vi) to give two equations in two unknowns:

$$T_1 = -[\dot{T}_G/(2k_m)](x_o^2) - C_1(x_o) + C_2$$
$$T_2 = -[\dot{T}_G/(2k_m)](x_o^2) + C_1(x_o) + C_2 \qquad (viii)$$

The two equations can be solved for C_1 and C_2:

$$C_1 = -(T_1 - T_2)/(2x_o) = (T_2 - T_1)/(2x_o) \qquad (ix)$$
$$C_2 = [\dot{T}_G/(2k_m)](x_o^2) + (T_1 + T_2)/2 \qquad (x)$$

Combining these into Eq. (vi) gives

$$T = [\dot{T}_G/(2k_m)](x_o^2 - x^2) + \tfrac{1}{2}(T_2 - T_1)(x/x_o) + \tfrac{1}{2}(T_1 + T_2) \qquad (xi)$$

At $x = x_o$, T in Eq. (xi) reduces to T_2 and at $x = -x_o$, it reduces to T_1, both of which are the given boundary conditions, Eq. (vii). One can determine the maximum temperature point from Eqs. (v) and (ix):

$$dT/dx = 0 = -(\dot{T}_G/k_m)(x) + (T_2 - T_1)/(2x_o) \qquad (xii)$$

Solving for x:

$$x_{max} = [k_m/(2\dot{T}_G x_o)](T_2 - T_1) \qquad (xiii)$$

When $T_2 = T_1$, x_{max} is zero; i.e., the temperature profile is symmetric about the center line with maximum temperature at $x = 0$, as already shown in Example 4.5. For the unsymmetrical distribution problem, Eq. (xi) applies. An example of such a problem is a steel wire pressed into a narrow wide slab with the conditions of Example 4.5 and with

$$T_1 = 30°C \qquad \text{and} \qquad T_2 = 85°C \qquad (xiv)$$

Thus from Eq. (xi)

$$T = \left(\frac{(2 \times 10)^7}{(2)(17.3)}\right)[(0.0127)^2 - x^2] + \frac{(55)(x)}{(2)(0.0127)} + (115/2)$$

$$= 93.2 - (5.78 \times 10^5)(x^2) + (2165.4)(x) + 57.5$$

$$= 150.7 - (5.78 \times 10^5)(x^2) + (2165.4)(x) \tag{xv}$$

In Eq. (xv), x is in meters. At $x = x_o$, T equals 85°C and at $x = -x_o$, T becomes 30°C, which are the given boundary conditions. The temperature at the center is 150.7°C, but this is not the maximum. The maximum point is given by Eq. (xiii):

$$x_{max} = \frac{(17.3)(55)}{(2)(4 \times 10^7)(0.0127)} = +0.94 \times 10^{-3} \, m \tag{xvi}$$

The plus sign means x_{max} is to the right of the center line. From Eq. (xv), this temperature is

$$T_{max} = 150.7 - 0.51 + 2.03 = 152.2°C \tag{xvii}$$

Although no mass transfer problems have been presented in this section, the solution to problems of mass transfer in solids with constant generation is basically the same as just outlined. However, a complication arises because the rate of generation in mass transport problems (i.e., the rate of reaction) generally depends on concentration; hence, it is rarely permissible to assume $\dot{C}_{A,G}$ for generation of moles of species A as constant. Variable generation is discussed in Section 4.2.5. Also, the more common problems in mass transfer involve convection, which is not considered in the heat transfer problems of this section.

4.2.2 Momentum Transfer with Generation at Steady-State

In Chapter 2, momentum was introduced as the product of mass times velocity. Momentum in a fluid can be created by a boundary moving with respect to a second boundary, as seen in Example 2.9. In such an example, there is no generation of momentum within the fluid; the moving plate in Fig. 2.13 imparts momentum to the fluid as a result of the no-slip-at-the-wall condition and the fluid viscosity.

Industrial problems in fluid transport do not often involve a moving boundary. Instead, the fluid flows in a pipe or similar conduit, propelled by a pressure gradient or by the force of gravity. Thus, there are two mechanisms for the generation of momentum: pressure gradients and force fields. Gravity is by far the most commonly encountered force field, and all subsequent discussion in this book will be limited to pressure gradients and gravitational fields.

To derive the form of the momentum generation term, it is necessary to reconsider the simple volume in Fig. 3.1. Let there be a pressure gradient

$\Delta p/L$ where

$$\Delta p = p_2 - p_1 \qquad (4.43)$$

If the flow of fluid is in the $+x$ direction, the pressure difference Δp must be negative because p_1 must be greater than p_2 to cause a positive U_x. Newton's second law of motion states that the sum of all the forces on a body equals the mass times the acceleration. Under conditions of steady-state one-directional flow, there is no acceleration; hence the sum of the forces equals zero. One force, acting in the x direction on the faces 1 and 2, is that associated with the pressure. The product pS, where S is the cross sectional area shown in Fig. 4.1(c), is a force term since the pressure is the total force divided by the area:

$$p = F/S \qquad (4.44)$$

Another force acting on the volume in the x direction is that associated with the momentum transfer shown in Eq. (4.5). A balance of these forces gives

$$\tau_{yx} A_y = S(-\Delta p) \qquad (4.45)$$

The minus sign is required since Δp is negative for $p_1 > p_2$. For the case of $p_1 > p_2$, there is a force in the $+x$ direction. Note that the x direction force associated with the shear stress τ_{yx} is a result of momentum transfer in the y direction through an area A_y. In the specific set of coordinates in use here, the area S is equivalent to A_x.

The nature of the term $S(-\Delta p)$ can be obtained from a rate of momentum balance, but a simple one-dimensional balance is inadequate since there is more than one direction to be considered. A comparison of Eq. (4.45) with a steady-state version (zero accumulation) of a three-dimensional counterpart to Eq. (3.2) suggests that

$$\text{GENERATION} = S(-\Delta p) \qquad (4.46)$$

Now, by Eq. (3.4):

$$\text{GENERATION} = \dot{\psi}_G V = \dot{M}_G V \qquad (3.4)$$

where the $\dot{M}_G$ term is defined in Table 4.2. The volume is the length times the constant flow area:

$$V = S \, \Delta x \qquad (4.47)$$

Thus, from the above equations, one obtains

$$\dot{M}_G = (S)(-\Delta p)/V = (S)(-\Delta p)/(S \, \Delta x) = -\Delta p/\Delta x \qquad (4.48)$$

where Δp is given in Eq. (4.43). For a differential element, $\Delta p/\Delta x$ becomes dp/dx.

The analysis in terms of the rate of momentum transfer suggests that the negative of the pressure gradient is the generation of momentum, $\dot{M}_G$. In this brief analysis, it has been assumed that the only molecular momentum transfer term is τ_{yx} and that there is no net contribution as a result of convection; both of these assumptions are true for the constant-area case. This latter point will be shown later in this section.

A gravitational field may also generate momentum. The most general treatment is to assume that gravity is a vector with a component acting in each direction in an arbitrarily oriented rectangular coordinate system:

$$\mathbf{g} = \mathbf{i}g_x + \mathbf{j}g_y + \mathbf{k}g_z \qquad (4.49)$$

where g_x is the component of gravity in the x direction and similarly for g_y and g_z. For coordinates aligned with the earth, g_x and g_y are zero, and g_z, the vertical component, is the local acceleration due to the earth's gravitational field. This quantity varies slightly from location to location on earth. At Columbus, Ohio

$$g_z = -9.80089 \text{ m s}^{-2} \qquad (4.50)$$

Gravity causes an acceleration; hence the force due to gravity on an element is mass times acceleration, by Newton's second law of motion. Mass is density times total volume, so the force due to gravity on the volume is

$$\mathbf{F}_{\mathrm{g}} = \rho V \mathbf{g} = \rho S \, \Delta z \, \mathbf{g} \qquad (4.51)$$

If only the gravitational force in the z direction is included in the force balance and a vertical orientation (z) is considered (see Fig. 4.6), then Eq. (4.45) becomes

$$\tau_{xz} A_x = -S \, \Delta p + \rho S \, \Delta z \, g_z \qquad (4.52)$$

Since the volume is now $S \, \Delta z$, Eq. (4.48) takes the form

$$\dot{M}_{\mathrm{G}} = -\Delta p / \Delta z + \rho g_z \qquad (4.53)$$

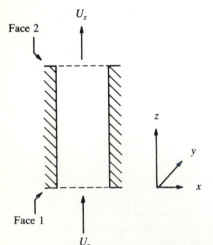

FIGURE 4.6
A vertically oriented flow system with gravity.

TABLE 4.3
The generation term for momentum transport in rectangular coordinates

Direction	Pressure term	Gravity term
x	$-dp/dx$	ρg_x
y	$-dp/dy$	ρg_y
z	$-dp/dz$	ρg_z

Again, Eqs. (4.52) and (4.53) are for one-directional, constant-area flow. The quantity g_z will be positive or negative depending on whether it acts in the positive or negative z-direction. For the vertical flow depicted in Fig. 4.6, the flow is upward in the $+z$ direction with $p_1 > p_2$. Thus, the first term will be positive. Gravity acts oppositely to the flow, and the second term will be negative because of the sign on g_z as given in Eq. (4.50). Should there be components of the gravitational force in two or more directions because of the orientation of the coordinate system, Eq. (4.53) becomes

$$\dot{M}_G = -\nabla p + \rho g \tag{4.54}$$

Since most fluid flow problems involve non-zero pressure gradients $\Delta p/L$, Eq. (4.53) or Eq. (4.54) will find frequent application. Table 4.3 summarizes the components for $\dot{M}_G$. Note that each term in Eq. (4.53) or Eq. (4.54) has units N m^{-3} or, equivalently, $\text{kg m}^{-2}\text{s}^{-2}$.

In this section, discussion has been limited to one-directional, constant-area transfer. For fluid flow, the further restriction of constant density (i.e., incompressible fluid) is added. In general, all liquids (and many gases too) may be considered incompressible in flow problems without appreciable error. For the steady flow of an incompressible fluid, the term $(\nabla \cdot U)$ is zero as shown in Section 3.4:

$$(\nabla \cdot U) = \frac{\partial U_x}{\partial x} + \frac{\partial U_y}{\partial y} + \frac{\partial U_z}{\partial z} = 0 \tag{3.74}$$

For one-directional flow in the z direction only, U_x and U_y are zero, and from Eq. (3.74):

$$\frac{\partial U_z}{\partial z} = 0 \tag{4.55}$$

Thus,

$$U_z = \text{constant} = C(x, y) \tag{4.56}$$

A complete discussion of the last two equations is given in Example 3.7.

In Section 3.5, it was shown that for an incompressible fluid

$$\frac{\partial \psi}{\partial t} + (U \cdot \nabla)\psi = \dot{\psi}_G + (\nabla \cdot \delta \nabla \psi) \tag{3.77}$$

The first term of Eq. (3.77) is zero at steady-rate. The second term is expanded in Eq. (3.53). After substituting ρU_z for ψ from Table 3.1 and using the incompressibility condition of constant density, Eq. (3.53) becomes

$$(\boldsymbol{U} \cdot \boldsymbol{\nabla})\psi = (\boldsymbol{U} \cdot \boldsymbol{\nabla})(\rho U_z) = \rho(\boldsymbol{U} \cdot \boldsymbol{\nabla})U_z = \rho\left(U_x \frac{\partial U_z}{\partial x} + U_y \frac{\partial U_z}{\partial y} + U_z \frac{\partial U_z}{\partial z} \right) \quad (4.57)$$

In Eq. (4.57), the first two terms of the expansion are zero because U_x and U_y are zero for one-directional flow in the z direction. The last term is likewise zero because the gradient of the z velocity in the z direction is zero by Eq. (4.55). In other words, there is no net convective flux in the steady-state, one-directional, constant-area flow of an incompressible fluid. Even though in all momentum transport problems with fixed boundaries there is convection, there is no net convective flux of momentum for the reasons just stated. All momentum transfer is by molecular transport. Thus, Eq. (4.30) applies

$$\partial(\Psi_x A) = \dot{\psi}_G \, \partial V \quad (4.30)$$

Since the flux occurs by molecular transport only, Eq. (4.31) or Eq. (4.32) applies as well. For a system where momentum transfer is in the radial direction, Eq. (4.32), with the appropriate substitutions for ψ, δ, and $\dot{\psi}_G$, becomes

$$-\partial\{(\nu A_r)[\partial(\rho U_z)/\partial r]\} = \dot{M}_G \, \partial V \quad (4.58)$$

or, for constant density, through use of the definition of ν in Eq. (2.12):

$$-\partial[(\mu A_r)(\partial U_z/\partial r)] = \dot{M}_G \, \partial V \quad (4.59)$$

For a system in which momentum transfer is in the y direction as a result of a flow in the x direction, Eq. (4.31) with the appropriate substitution is

$$-\partial[(\mu A_y)(\partial U_x/\partial y)] = \dot{M}_G \, \partial V \quad (4.60)$$

Equation (4.59) or Eq. (4.60) applies to the steady-state, one-directional, constant-area flow of an incompressible fluid. Equation (4.59) is analogous to Eq. (4.36), which was applied to heat transfer in a wire with generation. When the appropriate substitutions are made in Eq. (4.30) for momentum transfer in a constant area, one-directional flow, the result is

$$\partial(\tau_{yx} A_y) = \dot{M}_G \, \partial V \quad (4.61)$$

Integrating:

$$\tau_{yx} A_y = S(-\Delta p) = \dot{M}_G V \quad (4.62)$$

where the term $S(-\Delta p)$ comes from the force balance of a horizontal flow, Eq. (4.45). Note that Eq. (4.62), when $\Delta p/\Delta x$ is substituted for $\dot{M}_G$, becomes Eq. (4.48). Thus, the brief analysis given in the derivation of Eq. (4.48) is confirmed.

4.2.3 Laminar Flow in a Tube

Tube flow is the most important laminar flow problem because circular conduits contain the most volume for the least amount of construction material. Also, circular tubes have the easiest geometry to manufacture, and in them friction losses are least. Let us consider the laminar flow of a fluid in a tube or pipe, at some distance from the inlet so that there are no entrance effects. The problem is shown in Fig. 4.7. The area and volume terms for momentum transport in the r direction are given by Eq. (4.25) and Eq. (4.33), respectively. These terms are identical to those used in the analogous heat transfer case shown in Fig. 4.4.

Velocity distribution. Substituting Eq. (4.25) and Eq. (4.33) into Eq. (4.59), the answer is

$$-d\left(2\pi\mu r L \frac{dU_z}{dr}\right) = \dot{M}_G 2\pi r L\, dr \tag{4.63}$$

with $\dot{M}_G$ given by Eq. (4.53) if the flow is vertical. Equation (4.63) applies to the tube flow problem because for a uniformly manufactured tube there will be no velocity in either the r direction or the θ-direction:

$$U_r = U_\theta = 0 \tag{4.64}$$

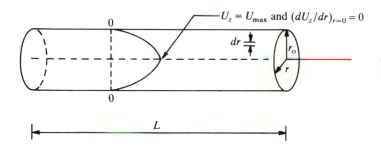

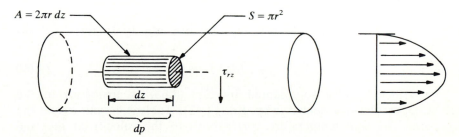

FIGURE 4.7
Laminar flow in the pipe geometry.

Momentum will be transferred from the fluid to the tube wall in the r direction only.

Five assumptions are involved in arriving at a solution to Eq. (4.63) for the tube flow problem:

1. Steady-state [Equation (4.63) includes this assumption.]
2. No entrance or exit effects [as expressed by Eq. (4.64)]
3. Constant molecular viscosity (no change with shear stress or shear rate)
4. Constant density [as assumed in obtaining Eq. (4.63)]
5. Laminar flow.

As a result of assumption (3), the viscosity is taken outside the partial derivative in Eq. (4.63). After canceling and rearranging, Eq. (4.63) integrates to the following:

$$r(dU_z/\partial r) = -[\dot{M}_G/(2\mu)]r^2 + C_1 \tag{4.65}$$

At the center line in Fig. 4.7 ($r = 0$), the velocity gradient dU_z/dr must be zero. The argument for this assertion is the same as that for the constant C_1 in Eq. (4.38) for the heat generation problem. The velocity U_z is a smooth and continuous function of r. Since U_z is symmetric, then $\partial U_z/\partial r$ is zero at the center line of the pipe. Thus, the constant C_1 is zero because in Eq. (4.65) the radius r is zero at the center line. With C_1 zero, Eq. (4.65) is divided by r and integrated again:

$$U_z = -[\dot{M}_G/(4\mu)]r^2 + C_2 \tag{4.66}$$

The velocity U_z is zero at the wall, where $r = r_o$, because of the no-slip condition when a fluid contacts a solid boundary; thus, C_2 is found from Eq. (4.66) at $r = r_o$:

$$C_2 = [\dot{M}_G/(4\mu)]r_o^2 \tag{4.67}$$

The final velocity profile equation is obtained from Eq. (4.66) and Eq. (4.67) as

$$U_z = [\dot{M}_G/(4\mu)](r_o^2 - r^2) \tag{4.68}$$

where, if both pressure and gravity act to cause flow, $\dot{M}_G$ from Table 4.3 in the z direction is

$$\dot{M}_G = -(dp/dz) + \rho g_z \tag{4.69}$$

The velocity profile represented by Eq. (4.68) is analogous to the temperature profile in a heated wire, Eq. (4.42). Table 4.4 summarizes the comparison. The wall temperature corresponds to the velocity at the wall which is zero as seen in the table. The derivations of the two equations are also similar.

TABLE 4.4
Comparison of velocity profile in a tube with temperature in a wire

Eq. (4.42)	Eq. (4.68)	
T	U_z	
T_w	$U_z = 0$	(at wall)
k_m	μ	
$\dot{T}_G$	$\dot{M}_G = -dp/dz$	

For a horizontal tube, g_z is zero, and Eq. (4.68) and Eq. (4.69) become

$$U_z = -\frac{(dp/dz)}{4\mu}(r_o^2 - r^2) \tag{4.70}$$

Since U_z, μ, r, and r_o are all constant with changes in p or z, Eq. (4.70) can be integrated according to the boundary conditions:

$$p\,(z = 0) = p_1 \qquad p\,(z = L) = p_2 \tag{4.71}$$

These are used to replace dp/dz:

$$U_z = \left(\frac{-\Delta p}{4\mu L}\right)(r_o^2 - r^2) \tag{4.72}$$

The velocity profile of fluid flowing in a horizontal tube (under the five assumptions listed previously) is given by Eq. (4.72). A plot is shown in Fig. 4.8. At the center line ($r = 0$), the velocity reaches a maximum, and the slope (dU_z/dr) is zero; i.e., at $r = 0$

$$U_{z,\,max} = \frac{(r_o^2)(-\Delta p)}{4\mu L} \tag{4.73}$$

If Eq. (4.72) is differentiated with respect to r, then at the center line the

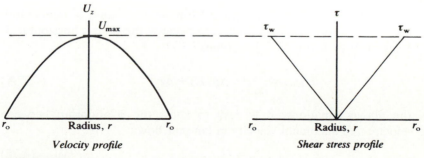

Velocity profile   *Shear stress profile*

FIGURE 4.8
Laminar flow in a tube.

velocity gradient $(\partial U_z/\partial r)$ is zero. The velocity profile is often written in terms of $U_{z,\,max}$. By algebraic manipulation of Eq. (4.72) and Eq. (4.73), one obtains

$$\frac{U_z}{U_{z,\,max}} = 1 - \frac{r^2}{r_o^2}. \tag{4.74}$$

Hagen–Poiseuille law. The volume flow rate Q is the product of velocity times area. Since both U_z and the area are functions of the radius r, U_z must be integrated over the area. The appropriate area is

$$S = \int_0^{2\pi} \int_0^{r_o} r\,dr\,d\theta = \int_0^{r_o} 2\pi r\,dr = \pi r_o^2 \tag{4.75}$$

A similar integration yields the volume flow rate:

$$Q = \int_0^{2\pi} \int_0^{r_o} U_r r\,dr\,d\theta = \int_0^{r_o} U_z 2\pi r\,dr$$

$$= \int_0^{2\pi} \int_0^{r_o} [(-\Delta p)/(4\mu L)](r_o^2 - r^2) r\,dr\,d\theta$$

$$= [(-\Delta p)/(8\mu L)](\pi r_o^4) \tag{4.76}$$

Equation (4.76) is the well-known Hagen–Poiseuille law, named after the two scientists who independently discovered it between 1839 and 1841. The law was experimentally established from the observation that the flow rate was proportional to both the pressure difference and the fourth power of the capillary radius and inversely proportional to the length. Actually, the workers were interested in the medical application of blood flow in capillaries. As it turns out, it was quite fortunate that they did not select whole blood as their experimental fluid, because it is now known that whole blood is non-Newtonian and does not obey Newton's law of viscosity.

The average velocity $U_{z,\,ave}$ is the volume rate of flow divided by the area

$$U_{z,\,ave} = \frac{Q}{S} = \frac{(r_o^2)(-\Delta p)}{8\mu L} = \frac{(d_o^2)(-\Delta p)}{32\mu L} \tag{4.77}$$

The derivation of Eq. (4.77) uses Eq. (4.69) for the generation of momentum in the z direction, but the gravity term is zero because the tube is horizontal. If the tube is vertical, then Eq. (4.77) becomes

$$U_{z,ave} = \frac{r_o^2}{8\mu} [(-\Delta p/L) + \rho g_z] \tag{4.77A}$$

In the above equations, it is easy to show the relationship between average velocity and maximum velocity in laminar flow:

$$U_{z,\,ave} = U_{z,\,max}/2 \tag{4.78}$$

The equations for velocity and velocity profile in laminar pipe flow are summarized in Table 4.5.

TABLE 4.5
Equations for laminar pipe flow

Hagen–Poiseuille law

$$Q = [(-\Delta p)/(8\mu L)](\pi r_o^4) \tag{4.76}$$

Velocity and velocity profile

$$U_z = \left(\frac{-\Delta p}{4\mu L}\right)(r_o^2 - r^2) \tag{4.72}$$

$$U_{z,\,max} = \frac{(r_o^2)(-\Delta p)}{4\mu L} \tag{4.73}$$

$$\frac{U_z}{U_{z,\,max}} = 1 - \frac{r^2}{r_o^2} \tag{4.74}$$

$$U_{z,\,ave} = \frac{Q}{S} = \frac{(r_o^2)(-\Delta p)}{8\mu L} = \frac{(d_o^2)(-\Delta p)}{32\mu L} \tag{4.77}$$

$$U_{z,\,ave} = U_{z,\,max}/2 \tag{4.78}$$

Shear stress

$$\tau_{rz} = \frac{r(-\Delta p)}{2L} \tag{4.79}$$

$$\tau_w = \tau_{rz,\,wall} = \frac{r_o(-\Delta p)}{2L} = \frac{d_o(-\Delta p)}{4L} \tag{4.80}$$

$$\frac{\tau_{rz}}{\tau_w} = \frac{r}{r_o} \tag{4.81}$$

$$\tau_w = -\mu \left(\frac{\partial U_z}{\partial r}\right)_{wall} \tag{4.82}$$

$$\tau_w = \frac{r_o(-\Delta p)}{2L} = \mu\left(\frac{4U_{z,\,ave}}{r_o}\right) = \mu\left(\frac{8U_{z,\,ave}}{d_o}\right) = \mu\left(\frac{4Q}{\pi r_o^3}\right) \tag{4.83}$$

Shear rate at the wall

$$\left(\frac{\partial U_z}{\partial r}\right)_{wall} = \frac{4Q}{\pi r_o^3} = \frac{4U_{z,\,ave}}{r_o} = \frac{8U_{z,\,ave}}{d_o} \tag{4.84}$$

Shear stress. The shear stress can be established from the force balance given as Eq. (4.45). For pipe flow, the areas involved are shown in Fig. 4.7 and are given by Eq. (4.25) and Eq. (4.33). Equation (4.45) becomes for cylindrical coordinates:

$$\tau_{rz} = \frac{S(-\Delta p)}{A_r} = \frac{\pi r^2(-\Delta p)}{2\pi rL} = \frac{r(-\Delta p)}{2L} \tag{4.79}$$

The latter form is included to remind the reader that the pressure difference Δp (which is $p_2 - p_1$) is negative, and as a result the shear stress τ_{rz} is positive.

At the wall ($r = r_o$), Eq. (4.79) becomes

$$\tau_w = \tau_{rz,\,wall} = \frac{r_o(-\Delta p)}{2L} = \frac{d_o(-\Delta p)}{4L} \tag{4.80}$$

The shear stress is seen to be zero at the tube center line, maximum and equal to $r_o(-\Delta p)/(2L)$ at the wall, and varying linearly with r in between:

$$\frac{\tau_{rz}}{\tau_w} = \frac{r}{r_o} \tag{4.81}$$

where Eq. (4.81) comes from dividing Eq. (4.79) by Eq. (4.80). Figure 4.8 also shows τ as a function of r, as given by Eq. (4.81).

The Hagen–Poiseuille law, Eq. (4.76), is often expressed in a useful form involving the shear stress at the wall, Eq. (4.80). Newton's law of viscosity, Eq. (4.18), applied at the wall, is

$$\tau_w = -\mu \left(\frac{\partial U_z}{\partial r} \right)_{wall} \tag{4.82}$$

The Hagen–Poiseuille law can be rearranged into a similar form. Equation (4.77) can be solved for $r_o(-\Delta p)/(2L)$:

$$\tau_w = \frac{r_o(-\Delta p)}{2L} = \mu \left(\frac{4U_{z,\,ave}}{r_o} \right) = \mu \left(\frac{8U_{z,\,ave}}{d_o} \right) = \mu \left(\frac{4Q}{\pi r_o^3} \right) \tag{4.83}$$

The term $-(dU_z/dr)_{wall}$ is called the shear rate at the wall. As shown in Fig. 4.8, the wall shear rate is the maximum shear rate in pipe flow. Comparison of Eqs. (4.82) and (4.83) yields several useful expressions for the wall shear rate:

$$\left(\frac{\partial U_z}{\partial r} \right)_{wall} = \frac{4Q}{\pi r_o^3} = \frac{4U_{z,\,ave}}{r_o} = \frac{8U_{z,\,ave}}{d_o} \tag{4.84}$$

Equation (4.83) is used to determine whether a particular fluid obeys Newton's law. The fluid is made to flow in a tube in laminar flow. Usually, it is best to use a small-diameter tube, called a capillary, because Eq. (4.76) shows that for a constant-volume flow the pressure drop increases with the fourth power of diameter. Hence, a tube with a small diameter will yield a large Δp that can be measured more accurately than a small Δp. If, for different values of Q, the viscosity μ as measured experimentally is not the same, then the fluid is said to be non-Newtonian. Chapter 15 considers non-Newtonian fluids in detail.

Example 4.7. A capillary viscometer, shown in Fig. 4.9, contains a tube 100 cm long and 0.2 cm in diameter. A pressure reading of 145 psig in the fluid reservoir causes a flow of 360 cm³ h⁻¹. The fluid's specific gravity is 1.1. In the analysis of this viscometer, the possible problems associated with end effects, viscous heating

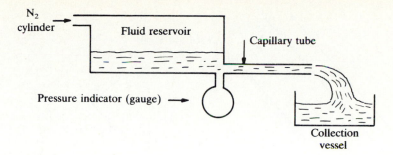

FIGURE 4.9
Horizontal capillary viscometer.

effect, and turbulence are to be neglected (see ref. B1 for more information on these). Assume the flow is laminar and determine the viscosity of the fluid.

Answer. The SI system of units will be used. The radius is 0.1 cm or 10^{-3} m. The length is 1 m. The flow rate is

$$Q = 360 \text{ cm}^3 \text{ h}^{-1} = 0.1 \text{ cm}^3 \text{ s}^{-1} = 10^{-7} \text{ m}^3 \text{ s}^{-1} \tag{i}$$

Since a pressure of 1 atm equals 14.696 psia or $1.01325 \times 10^5 \text{ N m}^{-2}$:

$$(-\Delta p) = (145)(1.01325 \times 10^5)/(14.696) \text{ [(psia)(N m}^{-2})/\text{psia]}$$
$$= 10^6 \text{ N m}^{-2} = 10^6 \text{ Pa} \tag{ii}$$

The density of the fluid equals the specific gravity times the density of water at some reference temperature. If no reference temperature is specified, 4°C is used, at which the density of water is 1.0000 g cm^{-3} or 1000 kg m^{-3}:

$$\rho = (1.1)(1000.0) = 1100 \text{ kg m}^{-3} \tag{iii}$$

Since Q is known, Eq. (4.83) is solved for μ:

$$\mu = \frac{r_o(-\Delta p)(\pi r_o^3)}{(4Q)(2L)} = \frac{(10^{-3})(-10^6)(\pi)(10^{-3})^3}{(4)(10^{-7})(2)(1)} \left(\frac{(m)(N \text{ m}^{-2})(m^3)}{(m^3 \text{ s}^{-1})(m)} \right)$$
$$= 3.927 \text{ N s m}^{-2} \tag{iv}$$

Viscosity is commonly reported in poise or centipoise:

$$\mu = 3.927 \text{ N s m}^{-2} = 39.27 \text{ poise} = 3927 \text{ cP} \tag{v}$$

4.2.4 Laminar Flow Between Parallel Plates

Consider Fig. 4.10, which depicts two parallel plates a distance $2y_o$ apart. The plates make an angle θ with respect to the vertical. Fluid flow between the plates in the x direction in Fig. 4.10 is caused by both gravity and a pressure gradient. Momentum is transferred from the moving fluid to the stationary walls in the y direction. It is desired to know the shear stress distribution and the velocity profile between the plates. The solution to the parallel plate

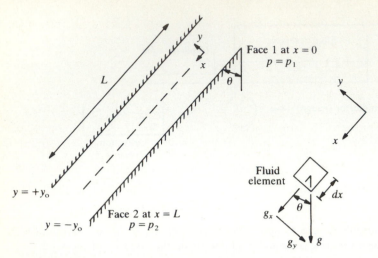

FIGURE 4.10
Laminar flow between parallel plates with gravity.

problem is very similar to that for the problem of heat generation in a slab, Example 4.6; the solution to the tube flow problem is also similar. First, it is always important to align the coordinate axis with the flow so that

$$U_y = U_z = 0 \tag{4.85}$$

Therefore only U_x is non-zero. The components of the force due to gravity are also shown in Fig. 4.10. Note that because of the coordinate system selected, the force of gravity has components in both the x and y directions.

The parallel plate problem is usually solved with the following assumptions:

1. Steady-state
2. Plates infinitely large in the z direction
3. Constant molecular viscosity μ (no change with shear rate or shear stress)
4. Constant density
5. Laminar flow

Equation (4.60) applies:

$$-\partial[(\mu A_y)(\partial U_x/\partial y)] = \dot{M}_G \, \partial V \tag{4.60}$$

The area of transfer is constant with changes in y. The volume is the area times distance

$$V = A_y y \tag{4.86}$$

or in differential form

$$dV = A_y \, dy \tag{4.87}$$

The last two equations are inserted into Eq. (4.60), and A_y cancels from both sides since it is constant. The resulting equation is integrated once:

$$-\mu(dU_x/dy) = \dot{M}_G y + C_1 \qquad (4.88)$$

From the analogy with the tube flow problem it may be surmised that dU_x/dy is zero at $y = 0$, which means C_1 is zero. But it is more rigorous to carry C_1 through the next integration and evaluate it afterwards, as done in Example 4.6. Upon a second integration, Eq. (4.88) becomes

$$-\mu U_x = (\dot{M}_G/2)(y^2) + C_1 y + C_2 \qquad (4.89)$$

The velocity of the fluid is zero at each plate. In mathematical form, the boundary conditions for the parallel plate problem are

$$U_x(y = \pm y_o) = 0 \qquad (4.90)$$

These are substituted into Eq. (4.89) to give two equations in two unknowns

$$0 = (\dot{M}_G/2)(y_o^2) + C_1 y_0 + C_2 \qquad (4.91)$$
$$0 = (\dot{M}_G/2)(y_o^2) - C_1 y_0 + C_2 \qquad (4.92)$$

First, these two equations are added and the result solved for C_2:

$$C_2 = -\dot{M}_G y_o^2/2 \qquad (4.93)$$

Then C_2 from Eq. (4.93) is inserted into either Eq. (4.91) or Eq. (4.92) and the result solved for C_1:

$$C_1 = \frac{\dot{M}_G y_o^2/2 - \dot{M}_G y_o^2/2}{y_o} = 0 \qquad (4.94)$$

As predicted after Eq. (4.88), the constant C_1 is zero, and as a result the velocity gradient dU_x/dy is zero at $y = 0$. The velocity profile for the parallel plate problem is obtained from Eqs. (4.89), (4.93), and (4.94):

$$U_x = [\dot{M}_G/(2\mu)](y_o^2 - y^2) = [\dot{M}_G y_o^2/(2\mu)][1 - (y/y_o)^2] \qquad (4.95)$$

Equation (4.95) is very similar to Eq. (xi) in Example 4.6 for the temperature distribution in a slab, if $T_1 = T_2 = 0$. This boundary condition corresponds to zero velocity at the wall.

Next, the generation of momentum $\dot{M}_G$ will be evaluated for the problem in Fig. 4.10. Let us consider the gravity term. There is a component of gravity in both x and y directions as shown in Fig. 4.10. If θ is the angle of each plate with the vertical, then

$$g_x = g \cos \theta \qquad (4.96)$$
$$g_y = -g \sin \theta \qquad (4.97)$$

Of these, only g_x causes flow. Thus from Table 4.3:

$$\dot{M}_G = -(dp/dx) + \rho g_x = -(dp/dx) + \rho g \cos \theta \qquad (4.98)$$

Equation (4.98) is used to replace $\dot{M}_G$ in Eq. (4.95):

$$U_x = \frac{-(dp/dx) + \rho g \cos \theta}{2\mu} (y_o^2 - y^2) \tag{4.99}$$

Since none of the variables in Eq. (4.99) varies or depends upon either p or x, dp may be easily separated from dx and integrated according to the boundary conditions in Eq. (4.71) and shown in Fig. 4.10. The result is

$$U_x = \frac{(-\Delta p)/L + \rho g \cos \theta}{2\mu} (y_o^2 - y^2) \tag{4.100}$$

The velocity is maximum at $y = 0$:

$$U_{x, \max} = [(-\Delta p)/L + \rho g \cos \theta][y_o^2/(2\mu)] \tag{4.101}$$

The dimensionless velocity $U_x/U_{x, \max}$ is found by dividing Eq. (4.100) by Eq. (4.101):

$$U_x/U_{x, \max} = 1 - (y/y_o)^2 \tag{4.102}$$

This equation is analogous to Eq. (4.74) for $U_z/U_{z, \max}$ in a tube. The average velocity is found by integrating U_x over the cross sectional area to obtain the volume rate of flow and then dividing by the area. The answer is similar to Eqs. (4.76) and (4.77):

$$Q = \int_{-y_o}^{y_o} U_x \, dy = \left(\frac{-\Delta p}{L} + \rho g \cos \theta\right) \frac{2y_o^3}{3\mu} \tag{4.103}$$

Equation (4.103) applies for a unit distance in the z direction. If there had been variation in the z direction, then integration over that direction would also have been necessary. The average velocity $U_{x, \text{ave}}$ is found from the quotient Q/S. When Eq. (4.103) is divided by the flow area S, the result is

$$U_{x, \text{ave}} = \frac{Q}{S} = \left(\frac{-\Delta p}{L} + \rho g \cos \theta\right) \frac{y_o^3}{3\mu} \tag{4.104}$$

Note that the area S equals $2y_o$ for unit distance in the z direction, and this result was used to obtain the last equation. The average to maximum velocity ratio from Eqs. (4.101) and (4.104) is

$$U_{x, \text{ave}} = \tfrac{2}{3} U_{x, \max} \tag{4.105}$$

Recall that for pipe flow the factor was $\tfrac{1}{2}$.

Shear stress. The equations for shear stress in the parallel plate geometry are similar to those in Table 4.5 for laminar pipe flow. Following the development for Eq. (4.79), the shear stress is

$$\tau_{yx} = \frac{S(-\Delta p) + \rho S L g \cos \theta}{A_y} \tag{4.106}$$

Again for unit distance in z direction, the flow area S is $2y$, the momentum transfer area A_y is $2L$, and the volume is $2yL$; thus Eq. (4.106) becomes

$$\tau_{yx} = \frac{(2y)(-\Delta p) + (2yL\rho g)(\cos\theta)}{2L} = \frac{y(-\Delta p)}{L} + (y\rho g)(\cos\theta) \quad (4.107)$$

Note that the shear stress is linear in y; for pipe flow, the shear stress was linear in r.

Figure 4.8 shows the velocity and shear stress distribution for the pipe problem; the forms of the plots for the plate problem and the pipe problem are similar except that the shear stress in the parallel plate problem switches sign between the location $y = -y_o$ and $y = +y_o$. Remember that the equations just presented are subject to the five assumptions listed after Eq. (4.85).

In conclusion, the solution to the problem of laminar flow between parallel plates has been shown to be similar to that for heat transfer in a slab with uniform generation, if the faces of the slab are maintained at zero (equivalent to zero velocity at the walls). The shapes of the plots of shear stress and velocity are identical with those in the tube flow problem.

Example 4.8. Consider Fig. 4.11 in which a fluid of constant ρ and μ is flowing between parallel plates. The bottom plate is at rest. The top plate is moving at a constant velocity U_o. Prepare a graph of y versus U_x/U_o for various pressure gradients.

Answer. Equation (4.60) is the equation for steady-state flow in the x direction only. Equation (4.60) is integrated appropriately to obtain Eq. (4.89):

$$-\mu U_x = (\dot{M}_G/2)y^2 + C_1 y + C_2 \quad (4.89)$$

The boundary conditions for this problem are

$$U_x(y = +y_o) = U_o \qquad U_x(y = -y_o) = 0 \quad (i)$$

The boundary conditions are substituted into Eq. (4.89) to yield two equations in two unknowns (C_1 and C_2):

$$-\mu U_o = (\dot{M}_G/2)y_o^2 + C_1 y_o + C_2 \quad (ii)$$

$$0 = (\dot{M}_G/2)y_o^2 - C_1 y_o + C_2 \quad (iii)$$

After adding these two equations, the constant C_1 is eliminated, and C_2 is

$$C_2 = -(\mu U_o/2) - (\dot{M}_G/2)y_o^2 \quad (iv)$$

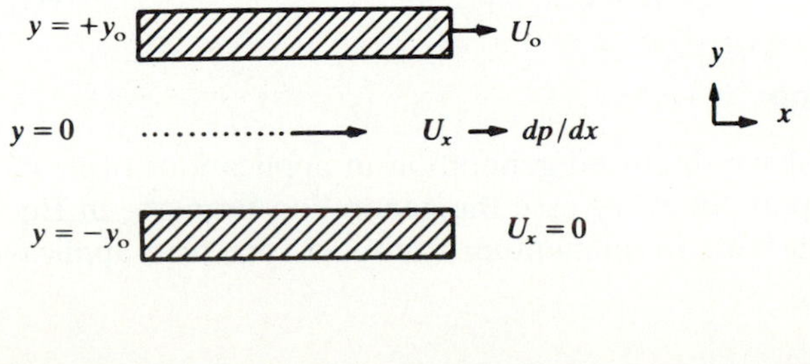

FIGURE 4.11
Flow between two parallel flat plates (Couette flow).

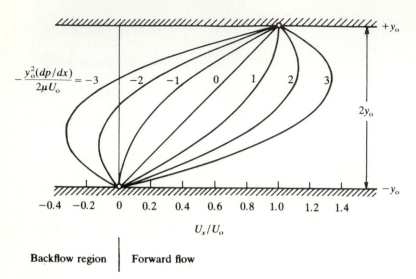

U_x/U_o

Backflow region | Forward flow

FIGURE 4.12
Couette flow between two parallel flat plates. (*Adapted from Schlichting, "Boundary Layer Theory", 7th ed., p. 85, McGraw-Hill, N.Y. 1979. By permission.*)

The constant C_2 is substituted into either Eq. (ii) or Eq. (iii) to find C_1:

$$C_1 = -\mu U_o/(2y_o) \tag{v}$$

From Eq. (4.89) and the values of the constants, the final result is

$$U_x = (U_o/2)(1 + y/y_o) + [\dot{M}_G y_o^2/(2\mu)][1 - (y/y_o)^2] \tag{vi}$$

where $\dot{M}_G$ is the pressure gradient

$$\dot{M}_G = -dp/dx \tag{vii}$$

The solution is shown in Fig. 4.12. For the case of $dp/dx = 0$, the velocity is linear across the fluid. This case is called simple Couette flow. For a negative pressure drop, the velocity is positive everywhere, and for a pressure increase, the velocity can become negative, i.e., a backflow [S1]. The point of reversal is that point at which $dU_x/dy = 0$ at $y = -y_o$. From Eq. (vi), this occurs when

$$dp/dx = U_o\mu/(2y_o^2) \tag{viii}$$

4.2.5 Variable Generation

The preceding four sections have discussed generation in applications of heat, mass, and momentum transport. In every case the generation term $\dot{\psi}_G$ in Eq. (4.31) or Eq. (4.32) was constant. In momentum transport, practical applications usually involve a constant pressure gradient. Gravity, the other contribution to momentum generation as seen in Table 4.3, is always constant for a specific location on this planet. Thus $\dot{M}_G$ is safely assumed constant, as it was previously in the steady-state generation problems.

In heat transfer, the generation term may be a weak function of temperature. For example in the electric wire problem, if the voltage is kept constant, then the power input varies with temperature because the resistance of the wire is a function of temperature. With the aid of modern instrumentation, the power input could easily be kept constant by continually varying the voltage.

In mass transfer with generation, variable generation is the rule rather than the exception in most problems. Suppose species A is initially present. For the depletion or generation of an individual species in a chemical reaction, a general expression for $\dot{C}_{A,G}$ is

$$\dot{C}_{A,G} = -k_n C_A^n \tag{4.108}$$

assuming that the rate of the reverse reaction is negligible. The exponent n is called the order of reaction; n is usually 1, 2, or 3, although it may be a fraction. Both k_n and n are determined empirically. If there are three species present, A, B, and F, all of which react, then

$$\dot{C}_{A,G} = -k_n (C_A)^{n_1} (C_B)^{n_2} (C_F)^{n_3} \tag{4.109}$$

Equation (4.108) assumes that there is no reverse reaction.

For illustrative purposes consider that the Eq. (4.32) in cylindrical coordinates applies to a problem with variable mass generation. After substituting for ψ and δ from Table 3.1, Eq. (4.32) for mass transport is

$$-D\, d[r(\partial C_A/\partial r)] = \dot{C}_{A,G} r\, dr \tag{4.110}$$

Let $\dot{C}_{A,G}$ be given by Eq. (4.108); substitution of $\dot{C}_{A,G}$ from Eq. (4.108) into Eq. (4.110) yields

$$d[r(dC_A/dr)] = (k_n/D)(rC_A^n)\, dr \tag{4.111}$$

which cannot be easily integrated, except for $n = 1$, but can be rearranged to

$$d^2C_A/dr^2 + (1/r)(dC_A/dr) - (k_n/D)C_A^n = 0 \tag{4.112}$$

For $n = 2$ the solution is in terms of Bessel functions; for other values, an analog computer solution or numerical solution is best.

Solutions to mass transport problems such as these are considered under the topic "kinetics". The reader should refer to texts on kinetics for an in-depth treatment of this subject.

4.3 CONCLUDING REMARKS

This chapter has considered at length several important transport problems in which there was only molecular transport. All these problems involved one-directional transfer. A procedure was given to handle easily one-directional transport through a variable area.

The generation term was discussed in detail. In momentum transport it was shown that an incompressible fluid in a one-directional flow must flow in a constant-cross-sectional area conduit. Further, in such a problem there is no net convective flux, even though there must be convection in most practical fluid flow problems. The generation term in fluid flow was shown to be equal to the negative pressure gradient plus the gravity term.

Not discussed so far are problems in unsteady-state molecular transport; in these, the concentration of property ψ varies with both time and position. The resulting equations, even with the simplification of no net convective flux, are partial differential equations. Solution of partial differential equations is primarily mathematical and not very instructive in understanding and applying the balance concept; discussion of this topic will be delayed until Chapter 13.

PROBLEMS

4.1. What are the dangers of the log-mean area concept?

4.2. Why is the Hagen–Poiseuille law important?

4.3. A liquid metal transfer pipe (1 inch outside diameter, 10 ft long) carries mercury, which transfers heat from a nuclear reactor to a heat exchanger. The heat loss from this 10-ft line is minimized by using an insulation, 8-inches thick. Find the heat transfer (Btu h^{-1}) through the insulation, if the temperature on the pipe side is 1000 K and the temperature on the outside is 300 K. The thermal conductivity for the insulation is $k = 0.120 + 4.5 \times 10^{-5} T$, where T is in °F, and k in Btu h^{-1} ft^{-1} °F^{-1}.

4.4. Find the error in the heat loss in Problem 4.3 if (a) the log-mean is used and (b) an arithmetic mean is used.

4.5. Derive the equation for the mean area of a hollow sphere.

4.6. A copper plug has been installed in an insulated wall. The shape of the plug is shown in Fig. 4.13 and is in the form of a truncated cone. The temperature T_1 is

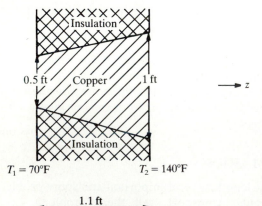

FIGURE 4.13
Copper plug in an insulated wall.

$70°F$; the temperature T_2 is $140°F$. Find q in $J\,s^{-1}$ and in $Btu\,h^{-1}$. Neglect any two-dimensional effects.

4.7. Determine the heat loss for Problem 4.6 if the temperature difference is reversed.

4.8. It is desired to reduce the CO_2 transfer in Example 4.4. The shape of the hole must be maintained, but the diameter can be reduced by a factor of 3. Find the new diffusion rate in $kmol\,s^{-1}$.

4.9. A piece of porous glass tubing is used as a diffusion cell to measure the diffusion coefficient of an air–gas mixture. The inside diameter and outside diameter of the cell are 1 mm and 4 mm respectively. It was found that with a difference in mole fraction of 10 percent at $25°C$ and 1 atm pressure, the molar flow rate was $4.0 \times 10^{-6}\,mol\,s^{-1}$ per centimeter of length. Find the diffusion coefficient in $m^2\,s^{-1}$.

4.10. Heat is generated within a spherical catalyst particle because of chemical reaction. The particle is 8 mm in diameter, has thermal conductivity of $0.003\,cal\,cm^{-1}\,s^{-1}\,K^{-1}$, and has a surface temperature of $300°C$. The generation of heat decreases linearly towards the center of the particle because of the decrease in the amount of material that reacts (longer diffusion path). The generation is given by $[(67.5)(r/r_o)]\,cal\,s^{-1}\,cm^{-3}$. Assume that the generation of heat is exactly balanced by the loss of heat at the surface. Determine the temperature distribution and more particularly the maximum temperature. The catalyst tends to lose activity above $700°C$; is this temperature exceeded?

4.11. In Problem 4.10, it was stated that the catalyst tends to lose activity above $700°C$. If the activity were reversible (i.e., if the catalyst would regain its activity when the temperature again dropped below $700°C$), describe what you think would happen if the generation were doubled in Problem 4.10. Locate the region (in terms of r/r_o) of maximum temperature.

4.12. Nuclear reactor elements can be in the form of long thin slabs, 0.5 cm thick. One side is at $100°C$ (boiling water) and the other side is in contact with a liquid metal at $175°C$. The thermal conductivity is $50\,Btu\,ft^{-1}\,h^{-1}\,°F^{-1}$, and the heat generation is $10^9\,Btu\,ft^{-3}\,h^{-1}$. Determine the maximum temperature reached under these conditions. The elements are expected to fail at $1100°F$. What is the temperature at the center line of the element? What is the temperature distribution, T as a function of x?

4.13. Water at $30°C$ flows through a horizontal pipe (1 inch inside diameter), in which the pressure drop is to be limited to $0.015\,lb_f\,ft^{-2}$ per foot of length. This low pressure per foot is imposed by the excessively long line involved. Calculate the volume flow rate ($ft^3\,s^{-1}$), the mass flow rate ($lb_m\,s^{-1}$), the average and maximum velocities ($ft\,s^{-1}$), and the velocity distribution U_z as a function of r.

4.14. Derive the velocity distribution for the flow of a Newtonian fluid in an annulus; your answer will be an equation for U_z as a function of pressure drop $(-dp/dz)$, viscosity, r, r_1 (the radius of the small tube), and r_2 (the radius of the large tube). Then find the average velocity $U_{z,ave}$ by integrating this equation across the flow area [cf. Eq. (4.76)]. Determine also the point at which the maximum velocity occurs. Finally, note the limiting form of velocity in the velocity distribution equation as r_1 approaches zero.

4.15. Consider Fig. 14.11, in which water at 330 K is contained between two parallel plates (separated by 0.02 m), one of which is moving. Let the system in Fig. 14.11

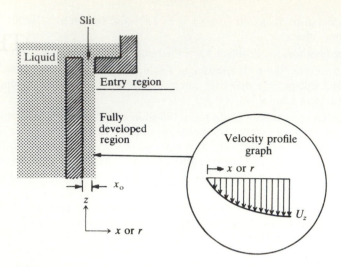

FIGURE 4.14
Thin film flow on the outside of a solid surface.

be rotated so that the plates and the flow are in the vertical (y) direction. The velocity of the moving plate U_y is maintained constant at $5.0 \, \text{m s}^{-1}$, and gravity (in the $-y$ direction) is $9.8 \, \text{m s}^{-2}$. Neglecting all end effects, compute the pressure gradient in N m^{-3} required to obtain a velocity of $6.0 \, \text{m s}^{-1}$ at the midpoint between plates.

4.16. In a gas absorption experiment, a viscous fluid flows down a flat plate in a thin film, as shown in Fig. 4.14. Gravity is the driving force causing the flow. The film of liquid is of thickness x_o after a fully-developed velocity profile has been established. Find the velocity distribution in the falling film, neglecting entrance effects; neglect any interaction between gas and liquid; express your answer in terms of g_z.

4.17. Suppose Fig. 4.14 depicts a tube of radius r_o; let a viscous fluid flow upward through the center of the tube and then downward through the slit. In the fully-developed region, the distance from the tube center line to the outside of the laminar film is βr_o, and the difference between βr_o and r_o is x_o. Find an equation for the velocity distribution of the fluid flowing uniformly down the outside of the tube in terms of βr_o.

REFERENCES

B1. Brodkey, R. S.: *The Phenomena of Fluid Motions,* Addison-Wesley, Reading, MA, 1967. [Fourth printing available from The Ohio State University Bookstores, Columbus, Ohio 43210.]

S1. Schlichting, H.: *Boundary Layer Theory,* 7th ed., McGraw-Hill, New York, 1979.

TRANSPORT WITH A NET CONVECTIVE FLUX

NOMENCLATURE

A	Area (m^2, ft^2); subscripts denote direction normal to coordinate, e.g., A_r is area normal to radius (area of the surface of a cylinder)
A	Species A; A_1 and A_2 are species A at locations 1 and 2
B	Species B; subscripts 1 and 2 represent locations
C	Concentration ($kmol\,m^{-3}$, $lb\,mol\,ft^{-3}$); C_A, C_B, C_i are concentrations of species A, B, i; C_T is total concentration; $C_{A,1}$ and $C_{A,2}$ are concentrations at locations 1 and 2
C	C_1 and C_2 are constants of integration
C	Species C
$\dot{C}_G$	Rate of generation of mass ($kmol\,m^{-3}\,s^{-1}$, $lb\,mol\,ft^{-3}\,s^{-1}$); other subscripts refer to species
c	Subscript denoting flux contribution due to convection
c_p	Heat capacity at constant pressure ($kJ\,kg^{-1}\,K^{-1}$, $Btu\,lb_m^{-1}\,°F^{-1}$)
D	Diffusion coefficient (mass diffusivity) ($m^2\,s^{-1}$, $ft^2\,s^{-1}$); D_{AB} is diffusion coefficient for A diffusing through A + B; D_{BA} is for B diffusing through A + B; D^v is diffusion coefficient based on volume average velocity; D_A^* is intradiffusion (tracer) diffusion coefficient; D_{AA} is self-diffusion coefficient of A in pure A; $D_{AB}^°$ is

	coefficient of A in essentially pure B; D_{KA} is Knudsen diffusion coefficient, Eqs. (5.78) and (5.79)
$D\psi/Dt$	Substantial derivative of ψ, defined by Eq. (5.16)
d	Diameter (m, ft); d_o is diameter of a tube or pipe
F	Force vector (N, lb_f); subscripts denote components in coordinate direction; F_g is the force due to a gravitational field
g	Acceleration due to a gravitational field (m s^{-2}, ft s^{-2}); also, g is the gravitational vector, Eq. (4.49)
g_c	Gravitational conversion constant (32.174 $lb_m\,lb_f^{-1}\,ft\,s^{-2}$)
i	Unit vector in x direction; i_r, i_θ, i_ϕ are unit vectors in the subscript directions
J_A/A	Molar flux (kmol m^{-2} s^{-1}, lb mol ft^{-2} s^{-1}); subscript A is for species A; superscripts * and v refer to molar flux with respect to the molar average velocity U^* and volume average velocity U^v
j_A/A	Mass flux (kg m^{-2} s^{-1}, lb_m ft^{-2} s^{-1}); subscript A refers to species A; superscripts * and v refer to molar flux with respect to the molar average velocity U^* and volume average velocity U^v
j	Unit vector in y direction
k	Unit vector in z direction
k	Thermal conductivity (W m^{-1} K^{-1} or J m^{-1} K^{-1} s^{-1}, Btu ft^{-1} °R^{-1} s^{-1}); k_m is mean thermal conductivity over the range of integration
L	Length (m, ft)
M_i	Molecular weight (molar mass) of species i (kg kmol^{-1}, lb_m lb mol^{-1})
$\dot{M}_G$	Rate of generation of momentum in a unit volume (kg m^{-2} s^{-2}, N m^{-3}, lb_m ft^{-2} s^{-2}, lb_f ft^{-3})
m	Mass (kg, lb_m)
m	Subscript denoting contribution due to molecular transport
N	Molar flow vector, defined with respect to fixed coordinates (kmol s^{-1}, lb mol s^{-1}); subscripts A or B are for species A or B; if written not as a vector, then N is subscripted for direction of transfer; N_T is total net molar flow due to all species present
N_{Kn}	Knudsen number, defined as (λ/d_o), dimensionless
n	Mass flow vector, equal to molar flow N times molecular weight M (kg s^{-1}, lb_m s^{-1})
n	Order of reaction in Eq. (4.108)
P'	Permeability constant, defined by Eq. (5.73)
p	Pressure (kPa, atm, lb_f in.$^{-2}$); $\bar{p}_A$ is partial pressure of species A, Eq. (2.38)
Q	Volume rate of flow (ft^3 s^{-1}); also subscript denoting torque
q	Energy (heat) flow vector (J s^{-1}, Btu s^{-1})
R	Gas constant, see Appendix, Table C.1
r	Cylindrical coordinate (m, ft)
r	Radius, (m, ft); r_o is value of r at the tube wall (the distance from

the center of the tube to the wall of the tube); in heat transfer, r_i is radius of inside tube wall, r_o is radius of outside tube wall

S — Area perpendicular to the direction of the velocity vector U (m^2, ft^2)

T — Temperature (K, °R, °C, °F); T_1 and T_2 are temperatures at locations 1 and 2; T_w is temperature of the wall or surface; T_∞ is temperature in open channel

T — Subscript denoting total; C_T is total concentration

$T_{Q,i}$ — Torque at inner wall in a Couette viscometer (N m, ft lb$_f$)

$\dot{T}_G$ — Rate of generation of heat (J m^{-3} s^{-1}, Btu ft^{-3} s^{-1})

t — Time (s)

U — Velocity vector (m s^{-1}, ft s^{-1}); U is magnitude of U; U_x, U_y, U_z, U_θ, U_r, U_ϕ are components in directions x, y, z, θ, r, ϕ; U is the mass average velocity [cf. Eq. (3.22)]; U^* is molar average velocity [cf. Eq. (3.23)]; U^v is volume average velocity [cf. Eq. (5.24)]; U_∞ is velocity in open channel (free stream velocity);

V — Volume (m^3, ft^3); $\bar{V}_i$ is partial molar volume of species i

v — Superscript denoting volume; U^v is volume average velocity, Eq. (5.24)

w_A — Mass fraction of species A; also, w is the mass flow rate (kg s^{-1}, lb$_m$ s^{-1})

x — Rectangular (Cartesian) coordinate

x_A — Mole fraction of species A in a solid or liquid (dimensionless)

y — Rectangular (Cartesian) coordinate; ($2y_o$) is distance between two parallel plates

y_A — Mole fraction of species A in a gas (dimensionless); $y_{A,1}$ and $y_{A,2}$ are concentrations at locations 1 and 2

z — Rectangular (Cartesian) coordinate

α — Thermal diffusivity (m^2 s^{-1}, ft^2 s^{-1})

Δ — Difference, state 2 minus state 1; e.g., $(-\Delta p)$ means $p_1 - p_2$

δ — Generalized diffusivity (m^2 s^{-1}, ft^2 s^{-1})

θ — Angle, curvilinear coordinate direction

λ_A — Mean-free-path (m, ft); cf. Eq. (5.74)

μ — Viscosity (kg m^{-1} s^{-1} or N m^{-2} s, lb$_m$ ft^{-1} s^{-1}, cP)

v — Kinematic viscosity (momentum diffusivity) (m^2 s^{-1}, ft^2 s^{-1})

π — Ratio of circumference of a circle to its diameter (3.141 592 65. . .)

ρ — Density (kg m^{-3}, lb$_m$ ft^{-3}); subscripts refer to species

$\dot{\rho}_G$ — Rate of generation of mass (kg m^{-3} s^{-1}, lb$_m$ ft^{-3} s^{-1}); subscripts refer to species

τ — Momentum flux (or shear stress) tensor (N m^{-2}, lb$_f$ ft^{-2}); τ_{xy}, τ_{yx}, etc., are components of the shear stress tensor, where subscripts refer to direction of momentum transfer and direction of velocity

ϕ — Spherical coordinate (rad)

Ψ — Generalized flux vector (e.g., units for heat flux are J m^{-2} s^{-1} or W m^{-2}, Btu ft^{-2} s^{-1}; see Tables 2.1 and 4.1 for more details); Ψ_x,

Ψ_y, Ψ_z are components in directions x, y, z; $\Psi_{x,m}$ or $\boldsymbol{\Psi}_m$ is flux due to molecular transport; $\Psi_{x,c}$ or $\boldsymbol{\Psi}_c$ is flux due to convection

ψ Generalized concentration of property (e.g., units for concentration of heat are $J\,m^{-3}$, $Btu\,ft^{-3}$; see Table 3.1 for complete listing)

$\dot{\psi}_G$ Generalized rate of generation of heat, mass, or momentum in a unit volume (see Table 4.2 for units; e.g., for heat, units are $J\,m^{-3}\,s^{-1}$, $Btu\,ft^{-3}\,s^{-1}$)

ω Angular velocity, velocity of rotation in a Couette or plate-and-cone viscometer (s^{-1})

$\boldsymbol{\nabla}$ Vector operator del, defined by Eqs. (2.16) or (3.45) (m^{-1}, ft^{-1})

∇^2 Laplacian operator, defined in Eq. (3.64) (m^{-2}, ft^{-2})

$\boldsymbol{\nabla}U$ Shear rate tensor, defined by Eq. (2.41)

$(\boldsymbol{\nabla}U)^{\mathrm{T}}$ Transpose of shear rate tensor, defined by Eq. (2.42)

In Chapter 3, the general equations were derived for the conservation of a property. In Chapter 4, these equations were applied to problems for which the net convective flux was zero. In one case, momentum transfer in a pipe (laminar flow), the net convective flux of momentum was zero even though there was a flow of fluid. In this chapter, problems that involve the convection term will be discussed. The complete equations for rectangular (Cartesian) and curvilinear (cylindrical and spherical) coordinates will be presented.

Convection is the bulk flow of a fluid due to the external influences of a pressure difference or a force field such as gravity. In Section 3.2.2, convection as just defined was represented by the convection flow flux $\Psi_{x,c}$. The convection flux is always zero if there is no net velocity in the fluid or solid. However, mass transfer may induce a velocity and therefore a non-zero convection flux. The mass transfer effect may or may not be superimposed on a bulk flow caused by external influences. Both cases will be considered in this chapter.

5.1 CONVECTIVE FLUX CAUSED BY FORCED CONVECTION

A convective flux contribution to the transfer of a property by forced convection must involve a flow velocity. There are situations where there is no convective flux even though there is a velocity. For example, momentum transfer as a result of incompressible laminar flow in a channel or pipe is an important case that was considered in Chapter 4. Reviewing briefly, if the fluid

FIGURE 5.1
One-directional laminar pipe flow of an incompressible fluid.

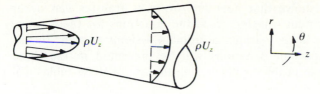

FIGURE 5.2
A two-directional flow.

is incompressible and flows in a one-directional parallel flow, the amount of momentum carried into an element of the pipe at any given position 1 is equal to that carried out at position 2 (see Fig. 5.1), as discussed in Section 4.2.2. For the flow shown in Fig. 5.1, the change in momentum due to convection is zero, but there is a momentum flux down the velocity gradient to the wall in the r direction, perpendicular to the direction of the flow. If the flow in Fig. 5.1 is laminar, then the momentum flux in the r direction occurs by a molecular mechanism, as discussed in Section 4.2.3.

The flow shown in Fig. 5.2 is two-dimensional because there are non-zero velocity components in the z and r directions, but U_θ is zero. Figure 5.2 may be visualized as a pipe with an increasing circular cross section (like a megaphone used by a cheerleader at a football game). In this case, there must be a net convective flux of momentum in both the r and z directions because the velocities in both directions at point 2 are different from the velocities at point 1 (by the conservation of mass). There is, of course, molecular transfer in these directions, but by symmetry there is no transfer of any kind in the θ direction.

Figure 5.3 represents laminar flow with heat transfer through walls into the flowing fluid. From Table 4.1, the concentration of property ψ for heat is $\rho c_p T$. If heat is added through the wall, then T_2 will be greater than T_1, and $\rho c_p T_2$ will be greater than $\rho c_p T_1$. Thus, there will be a net convective flux of heat. A systematic approach is needed to solve problems such as illustrated in Figs. 5.2 and 5.3.

The selection of the coordinate system is arbitrary. The object is to select that system which makes the problem simplest. For example, one could use rectangular coordinates, but then all three components of the velocity are non-zero in the conical section in Fig. 5.2. Clearly a solution in cylindrical coordinates is simpler. Hence, the momentum equations of Chapter 3 must be readily available in cylindrical and spherical as well as rectangular coordinates.

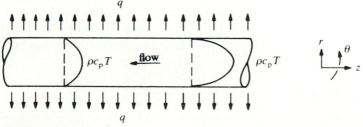

FIGURE 5.3
Laminar flow with heat transfer.

The problem in Fig. 5.3 shows that heat and/or mass transfer can occur simultaneously with momentum transfer; thus, the equations for these transfers must also be available in the various coordinate systems as well. In this chapter, tables of the important equations will be presented in the three coordinate systems. Example problems illustrating the use of these tables will follow.

5.1.1   The Balance Equation

The balance equation was developed in Chapter 3 to relate the concentration of property ψ to the flux $\boldsymbol{\Psi}$. The four types of terms (INPUT, OUTPUT, GENERATION, and ACCUMULATION) were considered in turn, and the most general form of the general balance was shown to be

$$\partial\psi/\partial t = (\boldsymbol{\nabla}\cdot\delta\boldsymbol{\nabla}\psi) - (\boldsymbol{\nabla}\cdot\psi\boldsymbol{U}) + \dot\psi_{\mathrm{G}} \tag{3.59}$$

In expanded form, Eq. (3.59) became

$$\partial\psi/\partial t + (\boldsymbol{U}\cdot\boldsymbol{\nabla})\psi = \dot\psi_{\mathrm{G}} + (\boldsymbol{\nabla}\cdot\delta\boldsymbol{\nabla}\psi) - \psi(\boldsymbol{\nabla}\cdot\boldsymbol{U}) \tag{3.60}$$
$$\quad\text{ACC}\qquad\text{CONV}\qquad\text{GEN}\quad\text{MOLEC}\qquad\text{CONV}$$

The nature of each term is written under Eq. (3.60) for emphasis.

In Section 3.4 it was shown that an important consequence of the continuity equation (conservation of mass) for problems of constant density is Eq. (3.74):

$$(\boldsymbol{\nabla}\cdot\boldsymbol{U}) = \partial U_x/\partial x + \partial U_y/\partial y + \partial U_z/\partial z = 0 \tag{3.74}$$

Hence, the last term in Eq. (3.60) is zero for an incompressible fluid, and Eq. (3.60) reduces to

$$\partial\psi/\partial t + (\boldsymbol{U}\cdot\boldsymbol{\nabla})\psi = \dot\psi_{\mathrm{G}} + (\boldsymbol{\nabla}\cdot\delta\boldsymbol{\nabla}\psi) \tag{3.77}$$

If the transport coefficient δ is constant, Eq. (3.77) becomes

$$\partial\psi/\partial t + (\boldsymbol{U}\cdot\boldsymbol{\nabla})\psi = \dot\psi_{\mathrm{G}} + \delta(\nabla^2\psi) \tag{3.78}$$
$$\quad\text{ACC}\qquad\text{CONV}\qquad\text{GEN}\quad\text{MOLEC}$$

Equation (3.78) is restricted to problems of constant density and constant coefficient δ. This equation is the starting point for solving practically all transport phenomena problems. If the density and the transport coefficient are allowed to vary, Eq. (3.60) applies. However, Eq. (3.60) is even more complicated than Eq. (3.78), and thus there are few exact solutions. For each problem to be solved, each term in Eq. (3.78) must be investigated to determine if that term is zero or non-zero. Tables to be presented subsequently will assist in this task.

5.1.2   Coordinate Systems

The balance equations in rectangular coordinates were presented in detail in Chapter 3. The property concentration, diffusivity, and generation forms from

Tables 3.1 and 4.2 are substituted into the vector equations just discussed. Then it is necessary to eliminate the operators by the appropriate equations, such as those in Eqs. (3.53) and (3.64). Several such example problems were solved in Chapter 3. But, as seen in Chapter 4, some problems may be better solved in cylindrical or spherical coordinate systems (curvilinear systems). Extension of the ∇ operator and of other vector operations to curvilinear coordinates is tedious, and only the results will be given in this text.

The need for vector shorthand notation such as $(\nabla \cdot U)$, $(U \cdot \nabla)\psi$, $\nabla^2 \psi$, etc., was amply demonstrated in Chapter 3. Table 5.1 provides these quantities and several other useful ones in curvilinear coordinates as well as in rectangular coordinates. It must be emphasized that the concentration of property ψ is a scalar quantity; for rectangular coordinates ψ can be the rectangular vector components: ρU_x, ρU_y, or ρU_z. For curvilinear coordinate systems, if ψ is a vector (such as ρU), the forms given in Table 5.1 for $(U \cdot \nabla)\psi$ and $\nabla^2 \psi$ cannot be used. For these two operations, additional terms are introduced and will be discussed more fully in Section 5.1.6 on the momentum balance. Of course, in curvilinear coordinates, the forms as given in Table 5.1 can be used as long as the ψ is a scalar.

5.1.3 Relationship Between Shear Stress and Shear Rate

Newton's law of viscosity, Eq. (2.5), which is

$$\tau_{yx} = -\mu(\partial U_x / \partial y) \qquad (2.5)$$

originated from experimental observations. The shear stress (or momentum flux) τ_{yx} is proportional to the velocity gradient for a simple laminar parallel flow. The law was also presented for one-directional molecular transport along a radius:

$$\tau_{rz} = -\mu(dU_z / dr) \qquad (4.18)$$

These simple forms are correct as given. But for flows in two or three directions the relationship between shear stress and velocity gradient is more complex. A more general tensor form for an incompressible fluid was previously given as

$$\tau = -\mu[\nabla U + (\nabla U)^T] \qquad (2.40)$$

and was illustrated for rectangular coordinates in Section 2.4 and particularly in Example 2.10. An additional term $(2\mu/3)(\nabla \cdot U)$ exists and contributes only if the subscripts on τ are the same and if the flow is compressible [B3]. Table 5.2 summarizes in several coordinate systems the relationships between the shear stress and velocity gradient. Included in Table 5.2 is the compressibility effect that gives rise to additional terms in the normal (xx, yy, or zz) components. Clearly, these terms are zero if the flow is incompressible $[(\nabla \cdot U) = 0]$.

TABLE 5.1
Vector expansions in rectangular and curvilinear coordinates

Rectangular coordinates	Cylindrical coordinates	Spherical coordinates
$\nabla\psi = i\dfrac{\partial\psi}{\partial x} + j\dfrac{\partial\psi}{\partial y} + k\dfrac{\partial\psi}{\partial z}$	$\nabla\psi = i_r\dfrac{\partial\psi}{\partial r} + i_\theta\dfrac{1}{r}\dfrac{\partial\psi}{\partial\theta} + i_z\dfrac{\partial\psi}{\partial z}$	$\nabla\psi = i_r\dfrac{\partial\psi}{\partial r} + i_\theta\dfrac{1}{r}\dfrac{\partial\psi}{\partial\theta} + i_\phi\dfrac{1}{r\sin\theta}\dfrac{\partial\psi}{\partial\phi}$
$\nabla^2\psi = \dfrac{\partial^2\psi}{\partial x^2} + \dfrac{\partial^2\psi}{\partial y^2} + \dfrac{\partial^2\psi}{\partial z^2}$	$\nabla^2\psi = \dfrac{\partial^2\psi}{\partial r^2} + \dfrac{1}{r}\dfrac{\partial\psi}{\partial r} + \dfrac{1}{r^2}\dfrac{\partial^2\psi}{\partial\theta^2} + \dfrac{\partial^2\psi}{\partial z^2}$	$\nabla^2\psi = \dfrac{1}{r^2}\dfrac{\partial}{\partial r}\left(r^2\dfrac{\partial\psi}{\partial r}\right) + \dfrac{1}{r^2\sin\theta}\dfrac{\partial}{\partial\theta}\left(\sin\theta\dfrac{\partial\psi}{\partial\theta}\right) + \dfrac{1}{r^2\sin^2\theta}\dfrac{\partial^2\psi}{\partial\phi^2}$
$(U\cdot\nabla)\psi = U_x\dfrac{\partial\psi}{\partial x} + U_y\dfrac{\partial\psi}{\partial y} + U_z\dfrac{\partial\psi}{\partial z}$	$(U\cdot\nabla)\psi = U_r\dfrac{\partial\psi}{\partial r} + \dfrac{U_\theta}{r}\dfrac{\partial\psi}{\partial\theta} + U_z\dfrac{\partial\psi}{\partial z}$	$(U\cdot\nabla)\psi = U_r\dfrac{\partial\psi}{\partial r} + \dfrac{U_\theta}{r}\dfrac{\partial\psi}{\partial\theta} + \dfrac{U_\phi}{r\sin\theta}\dfrac{\partial\psi}{\partial\phi}$
$(\nabla\cdot U) = \dfrac{\partial U_x}{\partial x} + \dfrac{\partial U_y}{\partial y} + \dfrac{\partial U_z}{\partial z}$	$(\nabla\cdot U) = \dfrac{1}{r}\dfrac{\partial(rU_r)}{\partial r} + \dfrac{1}{r}\dfrac{\partial U_\theta}{\partial\theta} + \dfrac{\partial U_z}{\partial z}$	$(\nabla\cdot U) = \dfrac{1}{r^2}\dfrac{\partial}{\partial r}(r^2 U_r) + \dfrac{1}{r\sin\theta}\dfrac{\partial}{\partial\theta}(U_\theta\sin\theta) + \dfrac{1}{r\sin\theta}\dfrac{\partial U_\phi}{\partial\phi}$
$(\nabla\cdot\delta\nabla\psi) = \dfrac{\partial}{\partial x}\left(\delta\dfrac{\partial\psi}{\partial x}\right) + \dfrac{\partial}{\partial y}\left(\delta\dfrac{\partial\psi}{\partial y}\right)$ $+ \dfrac{\partial}{\partial z}\left(\delta\dfrac{\partial\psi}{\partial z}\right)$	$(\nabla\cdot\delta\nabla\psi) = \dfrac{1}{r}\dfrac{\partial}{\partial r}\left(r\delta\dfrac{\partial\psi}{\partial r}\right)$ $+ \dfrac{1}{r^2}\dfrac{\partial}{\partial\theta}\left(\delta\dfrac{\partial\psi}{\partial\theta}\right) + \dfrac{\partial}{\partial z}\left(\delta\dfrac{\partial\psi}{\partial z}\right)$	$(\nabla\cdot\delta\nabla\psi) = \dfrac{1}{r^2}\dfrac{\partial}{\partial r}\left(r^2\delta\dfrac{\partial\psi}{\partial r}\right) + \dfrac{1}{r^2\sin\theta}\dfrac{\partial}{\partial\theta}\left(\delta\sin\theta\dfrac{\partial\psi}{\partial\theta}\right)$ $+ \dfrac{1}{r^2\sin^2\theta}\dfrac{\partial}{\partial\phi}\left(\delta\dfrac{\partial\psi}{\partial\phi}\right)$

Note: The quantity ψ represents the scalar concentration of property, which is C_A for mass transfer or $(\rho c_p T)$ for heat transfer. For momentum transfer, ψ represents the rectangular vector components $(\rho U_x, \rho U_y,$ or $\rho U_z)$ when ψ is substituted for in the rectangular coordinate column. It is incorrect to substitute the rectangular vector components for ψ in the cylindrical or spherical column. Also, the quantities i_r, i_θ, i_ϕ, etc., represent the unit vectors in the subscript direction.

TABLE 5.2
Shear stress–velocity gradient relationships for constant viscosity

Rectangular coordinates

$$\tau_{xx} = -2\mu(\partial U_x/\partial x) + (2\mu/3)(\nabla \cdot U) \tag{A}$$

$$\tau_{yy} = -2\mu(\partial U_y/\partial y) + (2\mu/3)(\nabla \cdot U) \tag{B}$$

$$\tau_{zz} = -2\mu(\partial U_z/\partial z) + (2\mu/3)(\nabla \cdot U) \tag{C}$$

$$\tau_{xy} = \tau_{yx} = -\mu[(\partial U_x/\partial y) + (\partial U_y/\partial x)] \tag{D}$$

$$\tau_{yz} = \tau_{zy} = -\mu[(\partial U_y/\partial z) + (\partial U_z/\partial y)] \tag{E}$$

$$\tau_{xz} = \tau_{zx} = -\mu[(\partial U_x/\partial z) + (\partial U_z/\partial x)] \tag{F}$$

Cylindrical coordinates

$$\tau_{rr} = -2\mu(\partial U_r/\partial r) + (2\mu/3)(\nabla \cdot U) \tag{G}$$

$$\tau_{\theta\theta} = -2\mu\left[\frac{1}{r}\left(\frac{\partial U_\theta}{\partial\theta}\right) + \frac{U_r}{r}\right] + (2\mu/3)(\nabla \cdot U) \tag{H}$$

$$\tau_{zz} = -2\mu(\partial U_z/\partial z) + (2\mu/3)(\nabla \cdot U) \tag{I}$$

$$\tau_{r\theta} = \tau_{\theta r} = -\mu\left[r\frac{\partial}{\partial r}(U_\theta/r) + \frac{1}{r}\left(\frac{\partial U_r}{\partial\theta}\right)\right] \tag{J}$$

$$\tau_{\theta z} = \tau_{z\theta} = -\mu\left[\left(\frac{\partial U_\theta}{\partial z}\right) + \frac{1}{r}\left(\frac{\partial U_z}{\partial\theta}\right)\right] \tag{K}$$

$$\tau_{rz} = \tau_{zr} = -\mu[(\partial U_r/\partial z) + (\partial U_z/\partial r)] \tag{L}$$

Spherical coordinates

$$\tau_{rr} = -2\mu(\partial U_r/\partial r) + (2\mu/3)(\nabla \cdot U) \tag{M}$$

$$\tau_{\theta\theta} = -2\mu\left[\frac{1}{r}\left(\frac{\partial U_\theta}{\partial\theta}\right) + \frac{U_r}{r}\right] + (2\mu/3)(\nabla \cdot U) \tag{N}$$

$$\tau_{\phi\phi} = -2\mu\left[\frac{1}{r\sin\theta}\frac{\partial U_\phi}{\partial\phi} + \frac{U_r}{r} + (U_\theta/r)(\cot\theta)\right] + (2\mu/3)(\nabla \cdot U) \tag{O}$$

$$\tau_{r\theta} = \tau_{\theta r} = -\mu\left[r\frac{\partial}{\partial r}(U_\theta/r) + \frac{1}{r}\left(\frac{\partial U_r}{\partial\theta}\right)\right] \tag{P}$$

$$\tau_{\theta\phi} = \tau_{\phi\theta} = -\mu\left[\frac{\sin\theta}{r}\frac{\partial}{\partial\theta}\left(\frac{U_\phi}{\sin\theta}\right) + \frac{1}{r\sin\theta}\frac{\partial U_\theta}{\partial\phi}\right] \tag{Q}$$

$$\tau_{r\phi} = \tau_{\phi r} = -\mu\left[\frac{1}{r\sin\theta}\frac{\partial U_r}{\partial\phi} + r\frac{\partial}{\partial r}(U_\phi/r)\right] \tag{R}$$

Use of Table 5.2 is illustrated by considering incompressible laminar flow in a tube, as shown in Fig. 4.7. The first step in applying Table 5.2 is to choose the coordinate system; cylindrical coordinates are the logical choice. Next the various terms are examined in order to eliminate the zero terms. Flow in a tube is one-directional, so

$$U_r = 0 = U_\theta \tag{5.1}$$

If U_r and U_θ are zero, then all derivatives of these are zero. The velocity in the

z-direction is a function of tube radius and independent of z and θ:

$$U_z = f(r) \tag{5.2}$$

From Eq. (5.2) the derivative of U_z with respect to z or θ is zero, but the derivative of U_z with respect to r is non-zero. Referring to Table 5.2, since $(\nabla \cdot U)$ is 0, τ_{rr} is zero from Eq. (G):

$$\tau_{rr} = -2\mu(\partial U_r/\partial r) + (2\mu/3)(\nabla \cdot U) = 0 \tag{5.3}$$

Similarly

$$\tau_{\theta\theta} = \tau_{zz} = \tau_{r\theta} = \tau_{\theta r} = \tau_{\theta z} = \tau_{z\theta} = 0 \tag{5.4}$$

Only Eq. (L) in Table 5.2 has a non-trivial result:

$$\tau_{rz} = \tau_{zr} = -\mu(\partial U_z/\partial r) \tag{5.5}$$

This result extends Eq. (4.18) to show that τ_{zr} equals τ_{rz} for laminar tube flow.

Example 5.1. Find the relations between shear stress and shear rate in a fluid of constant density and viscosity that flows in a tube of expanding diameter, as in Fig. 5.2.

Answer. The flow is incompressible (constant density) so that $(\nabla \cdot U)$ is 0. Cylindrical coordinates are chosen. There is no velocity in the θ-direction, i.e.,

$$U_\theta = 0 \tag{i}$$

All derivatives with respect to θ are likewise zero. Both U_z and U_r are non-zero and vary with both r and z, but not with θ. Hence, Eqs. (G) through (L) become

$$\tau_{rr} = -2\mu(\partial U_r/\partial r) \tag{ii}$$

$$\tau_{\theta\theta} = -2\mu U_r/r \tag{iii}$$

$$\tau_{zz} = -2\mu(\partial U_z/\partial z) \tag{iv}$$

$$\tau_{r\theta} = \tau_{\theta r} = 0 \tag{v}$$

$$\tau_{\theta z} = \tau_{z\theta} = 0 \tag{vi}$$

$$\tau_{rz} = \tau_{zr} = -\mu[(\partial U_r/\partial z) + (\partial U_z/\partial r)] \tag{vii}$$

A flow such as in Fig. 5.2 is called decelerating if the flow is left to right. Note that all three normal stresses $(\tau_{rr}, \tau_{\theta\theta}, \tau_{zz})$ are non-zero, whereas in the one-directional tube flow of Fig. 4.7 or Fig. 5.1, all three were zero as shown by Eqs. (5.3) and (5.4).

5.1.4   The Continuity Equation

The continuity equation expresses mathematically the law of the conservation of mass:

$$\partial\rho/\partial t + (\nabla \cdot \rho U) = 0 \tag{3.71}$$

where ρ is the density of the fluid under consideration. Equation (3.71) applies

TABLE 5.3
The continuity equation

General equation $\quad \dfrac{\partial \rho}{\partial t} + (\nabla \cdot \rho U) = 0$ $\hfill$ (3.71)

Rectangular coordinates

$$\frac{\partial \rho}{\partial t} + \frac{\partial(\rho U_x)}{\partial x} + \frac{\partial(\rho U_y)}{\partial y} + \frac{\partial(\rho U_z)}{\partial z} = 0 \qquad (A)$$

Cylindrical coordinates

$$\frac{\partial \rho}{\partial t} + \frac{1}{r}\frac{\partial(\rho r U_r)}{\partial r} + \frac{1}{r}\frac{\partial(\rho U_\theta)}{\partial \theta} + \frac{\partial(\rho U_z)}{\partial z} = 0 \qquad (B)$$

Spherical coordinates

$$\frac{\partial \rho}{\partial t} + \frac{1}{r^2}\frac{\partial(\rho r^2 U_r)}{\partial r} + \frac{1}{r \sin \theta}\frac{\partial}{\partial \theta}(\rho U_\theta \sin \theta)$$

$$+ \frac{1}{r \sin \theta}\frac{\partial}{\partial \phi}(\rho U_\phi) = 0 \qquad (C)$$

For steady-state, incompressible fluid $(\nabla \cdot U) = 0$ $\hfill$ (3.74)

Rectangular coordinates

$$\frac{\partial U_x}{\partial x} + \frac{\partial U_y}{\partial y} + \frac{\partial U_z}{\partial z} = 0 \qquad (D)$$

Cylindrical coordinates

$$\frac{1}{r}\frac{\partial(r U_r)}{\partial r} + \frac{1}{r}\frac{\partial U_\theta}{\partial \theta} + \frac{\partial U_z}{\partial z} = 0 \qquad (E)$$

Spherical coordinates

$$\frac{1}{r^2}\frac{\partial(r^2 U_r)}{\partial r} + \frac{1}{r \sin \theta}\frac{\partial}{\partial \theta}(U_\theta \sin \theta) + \frac{1}{r \sin \theta}\frac{\partial U_\phi}{\partial \phi} = 0 \qquad (F)$$

---

for the fluid as a whole at a given point; i.e., it does not apply to individual species in the mixture. For steady-state problems, $\partial \rho / \partial t$ is zero [see Eq. (3.73)]. For an incompressible fluid at steady-state or unsteady-state, Eq. (3.71) reduces to Eq. (3.74). Both Eq. (3.71) and Eq. (3.74) are expanded in the three coordinate systems in Table 5.3. Note that the fourth line in Table 5.1 was used for the terms in Table 5.3. The use of Table 5.3 is illustrated in Example 5.2, which follows. Table 5.3 may be used to solve Examples 3.5, 3.6, and 3.7 as well.

Example 5.2. A flow in cylindrical coordinates is given by

$$U = i_r r^3 \theta + i_\theta 2r^2 \theta z \qquad (i)$$

Is this flow compressible?

Answer. If the flow is incompressible, then $(\nabla \cdot U)$ will be zero as required by Eq. (E) from Table 5.3

$$(\nabla \cdot U) = (1/r)[\partial(r U_r)/\partial r] + (1/r)(\partial U_\theta / \partial \theta) + \partial U_z / \partial z = 0 \qquad (E)$$

The velocity in cylindrical coordinates is

$$U = i_r U_r + i_\theta U_\theta + i_z U_z \tag{ii}$$

Thus, from the problem statement:

$$U_r = r^3 \theta \tag{iii}$$

$$U_\theta = 2r^2 \theta z \tag{iv}$$

$$U_z = 0 \tag{v}$$

The derivatives required in Eq. (E) are found from Eq. (iii) through Eq. (v):

$$\partial(rU_r)/\partial r = \partial(r^4 \theta)/\partial r = 4r^3 \theta \tag{vi}$$

$$\partial U_\theta/\partial \theta = \partial(2r^2 \theta z)/\partial \theta = 2r^2 z \tag{vii}$$

$$\partial U_z/\partial z = 0 \tag{viii}$$

Now Eqs. (vi) though Eq. (viii) are inserted into $(\boldsymbol{\nabla} \cdot \boldsymbol{U})$ given by Eq. (E) above:

$$(\boldsymbol{\nabla} \cdot \boldsymbol{U}) = (1/r)(4r^3 \theta) + (1/r)(2r^2 z) + 0 = 4r^2 \theta + 2rz \tag{ix}$$

Equation (ix) is seen to be zero only at $r = 0$ or along the surface

$$2\theta r = -z \tag{x}$$

Clearly the flow is compressible.

The general mass balance for species A, also called the continuity equation for species A, is given by Eq. (3.66), and after substituting $\dot{\rho}_{A,G}$ for $\dot{\psi}_G$, Eq. (3.55) becomes

$$\tag{5.6}$$

$$\partial \rho_A/\partial t + (\boldsymbol{U} \cdot \boldsymbol{\nabla})\rho_A = \dot{\rho}_{A,G} + (\boldsymbol{\nabla} \cdot D\boldsymbol{\nabla}\rho_A) - (\rho_A)(\boldsymbol{\nabla} \cdot \boldsymbol{U})$$
$$\quad\text{ACC}\qquad\text{CONV}\qquad\quad\text{GEN}\qquad\text{MOLEC}\qquad\quad\text{CONV}$$

where D is the diffusion coefficient of species A diffusing through the rest of the mixture. Below the equation is written the nature of each term. Exact solutions to Eq. (5.6) must contend with several subtle problems due to the presence of mass transfer; for instance, the average molecular weight might vary with position (as well as D) owing to mass transfer. Another problem occurs in diffusion in liquid systems, where the total concentration and density change as a result of mass diffusion. Lastly, $\boldsymbol{U}$ in Eq. (5.6) is the mass average velocity [cf. Eq. (3.22)]; therefore, the molecular term must also be based on the mass average velocity.

For an incompressible fluid, $(\boldsymbol{\nabla} \cdot \boldsymbol{U})$ is zero [Eq. (3.74)], and the last term in Eq. (5.6) is dropped. For a binary system, an analogous equation exists for the other species present, B. For an incompressible fluid, diffusion of B is governed by

$$\partial \rho_B/\partial t + (\boldsymbol{U} \cdot \boldsymbol{\nabla})\rho_B = \dot{\rho}_{B,G} + (\boldsymbol{\nabla} \cdot D\boldsymbol{\nabla}\rho_B) \tag{5.7}$$

where $\dot{\rho}_{B,G}$ is generation of species B by chemical reaction, and D here is the diffusion coefficient of species B through the rest of the mixture (again based on the mass average velocity). For mass transfer to occur, there must be at least two components present, or identifiable. An example is self-diffusion, which is the mass transfer of one isotope of a material through a different isotope or isotopes of the same material.

For a binary system, the conservation of mass yields three equations: Eq. (3.71), the overall balance; Eq.(5.6), the conservation of species A; and Eq. (5.7), the conservation of species B. However, only two of these are independent; the third can be obtained from the other two. Any two of these equations may be used to solve a binary mass transfer problem. Similarly, for a ternary system a total of four continuity equations may be written, the overall equation and one for each of the three components, but only three are independent because the sum of the individual masses of each species must equal the total mass of the system. Diffusion in systems with three or more components is a much more difficult problem than indicated by this discussion, since the various diffusion coefficients are coupled and depend on the fluxes as well [C2, L1]. For a ternary system, there are four distinct diffusion coefficients [R1]. In systems with three or more components, there are little data and no satisfactory correlations for diffusion coefficients. This topic will be mentioned briefly in Section 5.3.5. Additional reading is available [B2, B3, C2, H1, H2, L1, R1, T3].

Equation (5.6) can be expressed in terms of molar concentration by dividing by the molecular weight of species A:

$$\partial C_A/\partial t + (\boldsymbol{U} \cdot \boldsymbol{\nabla})C_A = \dot{C}_{A,G} + (\boldsymbol{\nabla} \cdot D\boldsymbol{\nabla}C_A) - (C_A)(\boldsymbol{\nabla} \cdot \boldsymbol{U}) \qquad (5.8)$$

where the last term is zero for an incompressible fluid. This equation can be contrasted to Eq. (3.67) written directly in terms of the molar concentration. After substitution for ψ_G from Table 4.2, Eq. (3.67) is

$$\partial C_A/\partial t + (\boldsymbol{U}^* \cdot \boldsymbol{\nabla})C_A = \dot{C}_{A,G} + (\boldsymbol{\nabla} \cdot D\boldsymbol{\nabla}C_A) - (C_A)(\boldsymbol{\nabla} \cdot \boldsymbol{U}^*) \qquad (5.9)$$

In this form Eq. (5.9) is not particularly useful since $(\boldsymbol{\nabla} \cdot \boldsymbol{U}^*)$ is not equal to zero in most problems, as discussed in Chapter 3 in conjunction with Eq. (3.76). Equation (5.8) is preferred, since in a mass transfer problem in a flowing system the same mass average velocity $\boldsymbol{U}$ appears in the overall continuity equation, the equation for an individual species, and in the momentum balance equations. Table 5.4 summarizes in several coordinate systems the continuity equation for species A in an incompressible medium, Eq. (5.8).

Mass transfer problems may be solved in terms of concentration [i.e., Eq. (5.6)] or in terms of the flux vector N_A/A, which in rectangular coordinates is:

$$N_A/A = \boldsymbol{i}(N_A/A)_x + \boldsymbol{j}(N_A/A)_y + \boldsymbol{k}(N_A/A)_z \qquad (5.10)$$

The flux vector $\boldsymbol{\Psi}$ was introduced in Eq. (3.56) for three-dimensional flow and contains both the molecular and convective contributions. The flux vector may be N_A/A or q/A. The general property balance in terms of $\boldsymbol{\Psi}$ is Eq. (3.48),

TABLE 5.4
The continuity equation for species A

General equation

$$\frac{\partial C_A}{\partial t} + (U \cdot \nabla)C_A = \dot{C}_{A,G} + (\nabla \cdot D\nabla C_A) - (C_A)(\nabla \cdot U) \qquad (5.8)$$

Incompressible media, rectangular coordinates

$$\frac{\partial C_A}{\partial t} + U_x \frac{\partial C_A}{\partial x} + U_y \frac{\partial C_A}{\partial y} + U_z \frac{\partial C_A}{\partial z} = \dot{C}_{A,G} + \frac{\partial}{\partial x}\left(D\frac{\partial C_A}{\partial x}\right) + \frac{\partial}{\partial y}\left(D\frac{\partial C_A}{\partial y}\right) + \frac{\partial}{\partial z}\left(D\frac{\partial C_A}{\partial z}\right) \quad (A)$$

Incompressible media, cylindrical coordinates

$$\frac{\partial C_A}{\partial t} + U_r \frac{\partial C_A}{\partial r} + \frac{U_\theta}{r}\frac{\partial C_A}{\partial \theta} + U_z \frac{\partial C_A}{\partial z} = \dot{C}_{A,G} + \frac{1}{r}\frac{\partial}{\partial r}\left(rD\frac{\partial C_A}{\partial r}\right) + \frac{1}{r^2}\frac{\partial}{\partial \theta}\left(D\frac{\partial C_A}{\partial \theta}\right) + \frac{\partial}{\partial z}\left(D\frac{\partial C_A}{\partial z}\right) \quad (B)$$

Incompressible media, spherical coordinates

$$\frac{\partial C_A}{\partial t} + U_r \frac{\partial C_A}{\partial r} + \frac{U_\theta}{r}\frac{\partial C_A}{\partial \theta} + \frac{U_\phi}{r \sin\theta}\frac{\partial C_A}{\partial \phi} = \dot{C}_{A,G} + \frac{1}{r^2}\frac{\partial}{\partial r}\left(r^2 D\frac{\partial C_A}{\partial r}\right)$$

$$+ \frac{1}{r^2 \sin\theta}\frac{\partial}{\partial \theta}\left(D \sin\theta \frac{\partial C_A}{\partial \theta}\right) + \frac{1}{r^2 \sin^2\theta}\frac{\partial}{\partial \phi}\left(D\frac{\partial C_A}{\partial \phi}\right) \qquad (C)$$

Note that D is the diffusion coefficient of species A in the mixture.

which after substitution for mass transfer becomes

Molar units

$$\partial C_A/\partial t = -[\nabla \cdot (N_A/A)] + \dot{C}_{A,G} \qquad (5.11)$$
$$\quad\; \text{ACC} \qquad\qquad \text{FLUX} \qquad \text{GEN}$$

Mass units

$$\partial \rho_A/\partial t = -[\nabla \cdot (n_A/A)] + \dot{\rho}_{A,G} \qquad (5.12)$$

Equation (5.11) expands easily in curvilinear coordinates by using the fourth line of Table 5.1, with U replaced by N_A/A. Similar equations can be written in terms of ρ_A and n_A/A. The results are given in Table 5.5, the continuity equation for species A in terms of the molar flux. No further simplification results for the case of an incompressible media.

5.1.5 The Energy Balance

The general heat (or energy) balance was presented in Chapter 3 as Eq. (3.65). After substitution for $\dot{\psi}_G$ from Table 4.2, Eq. (3.65) becomes

$$\partial(\rho c_p T)/\partial t + (U \cdot \nabla)(\rho c_p T) = \dot{T}_G + [\nabla \cdot \alpha\nabla(\rho c_p T)] - (\rho c_p T)(\nabla \cdot U) \quad (5.13)$$
$$\quad \text{ACC} \qquad\qquad \text{CONV} \qquad\quad \text{GEN} \qquad \text{MOLEC} \qquad\qquad \text{CONV}$$

Once again, the nature of each term has been included beneath the equation. For an incompressible fluid, the last term is zero as a consequence of Eq. (3.74). Using Table 5.1, Eq. (5.13) can be expanded routinely for various

TABLE 5.5
The continuity equation for species A in terms of the molar flux

General equation

$$\frac{\partial C_A}{\partial t} = -(\boldsymbol{\nabla} \cdot N_A/A) + \dot{C}_{A,G} \tag{5.11}$$

Rectangular coordinates

$$\frac{\partial C_A}{\partial t} = -\left(\frac{\partial (N_A/A)_x}{\partial x} + \frac{\partial (N_A/A)_y}{\partial y} + \frac{\partial (N_A/A)_z}{\partial z}\right) + \dot{C}_{A,G} \tag{A}$$

Cylindrical coordinates

$$\frac{\partial C_A}{\partial t} = -\left(\frac{1}{r}\frac{\partial}{\partial r}[r(N_A/A)_r] + \frac{1}{r}\frac{\partial}{\partial \theta}(N_A/A)_\theta + \frac{\partial}{\partial z}(N_A/A)_z\right) + \dot{C}_{A,G} \tag{B}$$

Spherical coordinates

$$\frac{\partial C_A}{\partial t} = -\left(\frac{1}{r^2}\frac{\partial}{\partial r}[r^2(N_A/A)_r] + \frac{1}{r\sin\theta}\frac{\partial}{\partial \theta}[(N_A/A)_\theta \sin\theta] + \frac{1}{r\sin\theta}\frac{\partial}{\partial \phi}(N_A/A)_\phi\right) + \dot{C}_{A,G} \tag{C}$$

coordinate systems; the incompressible form of Eq. (5.13) in several coordinate systems is presented in Table 5.6. Note that the generation term must also account for the generation of heat by viscous dissipation. In systems with large velocity gradients or with fluids of very high viscosity (such as molten polymers), the viscous dissipation term may be significant [B3]. Thus, generation of heat may occur by several mechanisms such as viscous dissipation, presence of fields (electric, magnetic, microwave), chemical reaction, and nuclear reaction.

TABLE 5.6
The energy equation

General equation

$$\frac{\partial (\rho c_p T)}{\partial t} + (\boldsymbol{U} \cdot \boldsymbol{\nabla})(\rho c_p T) = \dot{T}_G + [\boldsymbol{\nabla} \cdot \alpha \boldsymbol{\nabla}(\rho c_p T)] - (\rho c_p T)(\boldsymbol{\nabla} \cdot \boldsymbol{U}) \tag{5.13}$$

Incompressible media, rectangular coordinates

$$\frac{\partial T}{\partial t} + U_x \frac{\partial T}{\partial x} + U_y \frac{\partial T}{\partial y} + U_z \frac{\partial T}{\partial z} = \frac{\dot{T}_G}{\rho c_p} + \frac{\partial}{\partial x}\left(\alpha \frac{\partial T}{\partial x}\right) + \frac{\partial}{\partial y}\left(\alpha \frac{dT}{dy}\right) + \frac{\partial}{\partial z}\left(\alpha \frac{\partial T}{\partial z}\right) \tag{A}$$

Incompressible media, cylindrical coordinates

$$\frac{\partial T}{\partial t} + U_r \frac{\partial T}{\partial r} + \frac{U_\theta}{r}\frac{\partial T}{\partial \theta} + U_z \frac{\partial T}{\partial z} = \frac{\dot{T}_G}{\rho c_p} + \frac{1}{r}\frac{\partial}{\partial r}\left(r\alpha \frac{\partial T}{\partial r}\right) + \frac{1}{r^2}\frac{\partial}{\partial \theta}\left(\alpha \frac{\partial T}{\partial \theta}\right) + \frac{\partial}{\partial z}\left(\alpha \frac{\partial T}{\partial z}\right) \tag{B}$$

Incompressible media, spherical coordinates

$$\frac{\partial T}{\partial t} + U_r \frac{\partial T}{\partial r} + \frac{U_\theta}{r}\frac{\partial T}{\partial \theta} + \frac{U_\phi}{r\sin\theta}\frac{\partial T}{\partial \phi} = \frac{\dot{T}_G}{\rho c_p} + \frac{1}{r^2}\frac{\partial}{\partial r}\left(r^2\alpha \frac{\partial T}{\partial r}\right)$$

$$+ \frac{1}{r^2 \sin\theta}\frac{\partial}{\partial \theta}\left(\alpha \sin\theta \frac{\partial T}{\partial \theta}\right) + \frac{1}{r^2 \sin^2\theta}\frac{\partial}{\partial \phi}\left(\alpha \frac{\partial T}{\partial \phi}\right) \tag{C}$$

Equation (5.13) and Table 5.6 are often inadequate for many problems. Suppose, for example, one must design a gas compressor system with a heat exchanger, which pressurizes the gas and removes the heat in order to keep the gas reasonably cool. Equation (5.13) provides no insight into the terms necessary for such a design. These complexities will be considered in later chapters; Chapter 7 deals with the mechanical engineering equation, useful in compressor design.

Example problems using some of these tables follow. It is important for the reader to be able to apply the tables in Chapter 5 to problems that are encountered. Admittedly, the equations in these tables are lengthy, boring to contemplate, and confusing initially. However, these equations describe "the real world" and must be mastered. The procedure for problem-solving is:

1. Make a drawing that represents the problem.
2. From the problem statement, determine if the flow is incompressible $[(\boldsymbol{\nabla} \cdot \boldsymbol{U}) = 0]$ and which physical properties (ρ, k, μ, D, etc.) may be considered as constant.
3. Identify the coordinate system that best describes the transport occurring.
4. Determine which velocity components (U_x, U_y, U_z, U_r, U_θ, U_ϕ) are zero.
5. Determine which velocity gradients ($\partial U_z / \partial z$, etc.) are zero.
6. Write the applicable differential equations from the tables in Chapter 5, eliminating all the zero terms.
7. Determine the boundary conditions from the statement of the problem.
8. If the number of variables exceeds the number of equations, it is necessary to formulate additional constitutive equations from kinetics, stoichiometry, physical properties, etc., until the number of equations equals the number of unknowns.
9. Integrate the equations analytically or numerically and obtain the solution.

Example 5.3. Consider the problem in Fig. 2.4 from Example 2.1. A copper block is subjected to a temperature difference across the face at $x = 0$ and at $x = 10$ cm. All other faces are insulated. Derive the differential equation to be solved using Table 5.6.

Answer. Rectangular coordinates are chosen; the thermal transfer is in the x direction. Since the copper is a solid in Example 2.1, all velocities are zero in this problem. Thus

$$U_x = U_y = U_z = 0 \qquad \qquad \text{(i)}$$

Equation (A) of Table 5.6 applies with the following terms being zero for the reasons given

$$\partial T / \partial t = 0 \qquad \qquad \text{(steady-state)} \qquad \qquad \text{(ii)}$$

$$\dot{T}_G = 0 \qquad \qquad \text{(no generation of any kind)} \qquad \qquad \text{(iii)}$$

$$\partial T / \partial y = 0 = \partial T / \partial z \qquad \text{(temperature varies only in the } x \text{ direction)} \qquad \text{(iv)}$$

Thus, Eq. (A) has only one non-zero term for this problem

$$0 = \frac{\partial}{\partial x}\left(\alpha \frac{dT}{dx}\right) \tag{v}$$

This equation integrates to

$$C_1 = \alpha \frac{dT}{dx} \tag{vi}$$

where C_1 is a constant of integration and where ordinary differentials are used because the variation is only with x. Equation (2.10) is

$$\alpha = \frac{k}{\rho c_p} \tag{2.10}$$

This is used to replace α in Eq. (vi). For constant density and heat capacity, Eq. (vi) becomes

$$C_2 = \frac{k \, dT}{dx} \tag{vii}$$

where C_2 is a new constant equal to $(C_1 \rho c_p)$. Equation (vii) is integrated between the limits

$$x \ (T = T_1) = x_1$$
$$x \ (T = T_2) = x_2 \tag{viii}$$

The result is

$$C_2(x_2 - x_1) = k(T_2 - T_1) \tag{ix}$$

Comparison of Eq. (ix) with Eq. (ii) in Example 2.1 shows that

$$C_2 = (q/A)_x \tag{x}$$

Thus, it is shown that for the conditions of this problem, the flux $(q/A)_x$ is constant with changes in x.

Example 5.4. Figure 5.3 illustrates a typical problem in laminar flow with heat transfer. Let the tube be of uniform cross sectional area so that the flow is one-directional. From Table 5.6 set up the differential equation that describes the temperature profile if the flow is steady-state and incompressible.

Answer. Cylindrical coordinates are chosen to describe the temperature distribution in the pipe, Eq. (B). Only U_z is non-zero:

$$U_r = U_\theta = 0 \tag{i}$$

Since the flow is at steady-state

$$\partial T / \partial t = 0 \tag{ii}$$

The temperature will vary with r and z, but not with the θ-direction. As is typical for applications involving a gaseous fluid, or even water and oil, there is no generation of heat by viscous or other means:

$$\dot{T}_G = 0 \tag{iii}$$

Substituting the above relations into Eq. (B) in Table 5.6:

$$U_z \frac{\partial T}{\partial z} = \frac{1}{r} \frac{\partial}{\partial r}\left(r\alpha \frac{\partial T}{\partial r}\right) + \frac{\partial}{\partial z}\left(\alpha \frac{\partial T}{\partial z}\right) \tag{iv}$$

Equation (iv) is a second-order partial differential equation that describes exactly the temperature profile in laminar heat transfer. Further assumptions are necessary to solve this equation subject to typical boundary conditions. In Example 5.6 this specific problem will be discussed further.

5.1.6   The Navier–Stokes Equation

The balance equation for momentum transport is most often applied when the density and viscosity are assumed constant. Equation (3.78) is for constant density and constant transport property δ. The equation was given earlier in this chapter. After substitution from Tables 4.1 and 4.2 and from Eq. (4.54), Eq. (3.78) becomes

$$\partial(\rho U)/\partial t + (U \cdot \nabla)(\rho U) = -\nabla p + \rho g + v[\nabla^2 (\rho U)] \tag{5.14}$$

or after dividing by ρ:

$$\partial U/\partial t + (U \cdot \nabla)U = -(1/\rho)\nabla p + g + v(\nabla^2 U) \tag{5.15}$$

Equation (3.78) is a scalar equation when applied to heat transfer, mass transfer, or the overall conservation of mass. In contrast, Eqs. (5.14) and (5.15) are vector equations; i.e., they represent three equations each. Equation (5.15) is called the Navier–Stokes equation after the men who first derived the equation in the 1820s.

In rectangular coordinates there is an equation for each of the x, y, and z directions. Each one of these component equations can be obtained directly from Eq. (3.78) by considering each component separately as a scalar term. Following this procedure, Eq. (3.68) for the x component of momentum was obtained from the full balance equation [Eq. (3.60)]. In Example 3.8 the procedure was illustrated further.

For curvilinear coordinates, there is no simple way to reduce the vector equation (5.15) to its component equations analogous to the case for rectangular coordinates. The rotational nature of curvilinear coordinate systems precludes a simple reduction. It is instructive to consider why the momentum balance equations are more complex in curvilinear coordinates than in rectangular. A rigorous mathematical treatment can show that additional terms exist in curvilinear coordinate systems [B3, B4]. Considera- tion of a simple experiment leads to insight into the source of these additional terms. Consider a weight tied to a string. The string is attached to a shaft rotating at a constant angular velocity. At steady-state, the velocity com- ponents in the r and z directions are zero; the only non-zero momentum contribution is in the θ direction. However, a force balance (such as was made in Section 4.2.2) on the weight must take into consideration the centripetal

TABLE 5.7
The Navier–Stokes equations for fluids of constant ρ and μ

Navier–Stokes equation in vector form (rectangular coordinates only)

$$\partial U/\partial t + (U \cdot \nabla)U = -(1/\rho)\nabla p + g + v(\nabla^2 U) \qquad (5.15)$$

Rectangular coordinates

x component:
$$\frac{\partial U_x}{\partial t} + U_x\frac{\partial U_x}{\partial x} + U_y\frac{\partial U_x}{\partial y} + U_z\frac{\partial U_x}{\partial z} = -\frac{1}{\rho}\left(\frac{\partial p}{\partial x}\right) + g_x + v\left(\frac{\partial^2 U_x}{\partial x^2} + \frac{\partial^2 U_x}{\partial y^2} + \frac{\partial^2 U_x}{\partial z^2}\right) \qquad (A)$$

y component:
$$\frac{\partial U_y}{\partial t} + U_x\frac{\partial U_y}{\partial x} + U_y\frac{\partial U_y}{\partial y} + U_z\frac{\partial U_y}{\partial z} = -\frac{1}{\rho}\left(\frac{\partial p}{\partial y}\right) + g_y + v\left(\frac{\partial^2 U_y}{\partial x^2} + \frac{\partial^2 U_y}{\partial y^2} + \frac{\partial^2 U_y}{\partial z^2}\right) \qquad (B)$$

z component:
$$\frac{\partial U_z}{\partial t} + U_x\frac{\partial U_z}{\partial x} + U_y\frac{\partial U_z}{\partial y} + U_z\frac{\partial U_z}{\partial z} = -\frac{1}{\rho}\left(\frac{\partial p}{\partial z}\right) + g_z + v\left(\frac{\partial^2 U_z}{\partial x^2} + \frac{\partial^2 U_z}{\partial y^2} + \frac{\partial^2 U_z}{\partial z^2}\right) \qquad (C)$$

Cylindrical coordinates

r component:
$$\frac{\partial U_r}{\partial t} + U_r\frac{\partial U_r}{\partial r} + \frac{U_\theta}{r}\frac{\partial U_r}{\partial \theta} + U_z\frac{\partial U_r}{\partial z} - \frac{U_\theta^2}{r}$$
$$= -\frac{1}{\rho}\left(\frac{\partial p}{\partial r}\right) + g_r + v\frac{\partial^2 U_r}{\partial r^2} + \frac{v}{r}\frac{\partial U_r}{\partial r} - v\left(\frac{U_r}{r^2}\right) + \frac{v}{r^2}\frac{\partial^2 U_r}{\partial \theta^2} - \frac{2v}{r^2}\frac{\partial U_\theta}{\partial \theta} + v\frac{\partial^2 U_r}{\partial z^2} \qquad (D)$$

θ component:
$$\frac{\partial U_\theta}{\partial t} + U_r\frac{\partial U_\theta}{\partial r} + \frac{U_\theta}{r}\frac{\partial U_\theta}{\partial \theta} + U_z\frac{\partial U_\theta}{\partial z} + \frac{U_r U_\theta}{r}$$
$$= -\frac{1}{\rho r}\frac{\partial p}{\partial \theta} + g_\theta + v\frac{\partial^2 U_\theta}{\partial r^2} + \frac{v}{r}\frac{\partial U_\theta}{\partial r} - v\left(\frac{U_\theta}{r^2}\right) + \frac{v}{r^2}\frac{\partial^2 U_\theta}{\partial \theta^2} + \frac{2v}{r^2}\frac{\partial U_r}{\partial \theta} + v\frac{\partial^2 U_\theta}{\partial z^2} \qquad (E)$$

z component:
$$\frac{\partial U_z}{\partial t} + U_r\frac{\partial U_z}{\partial r} + \frac{U_\theta}{r}\frac{\partial u_z}{\partial \theta} + U_z\frac{\partial U_z}{\partial z}$$
$$= -\frac{1}{\rho}\frac{\partial p}{\partial z} + g_z + v\frac{\partial^2 U_z}{\partial r^2} + \frac{v}{r}\frac{\partial U_z}{\partial r} + \frac{v}{r^2}\frac{\partial^2 U_z}{\partial \theta^2} + v\frac{\partial^2 U_z}{\partial z^2} \qquad (F)$$

Spherical coordinates

r component:
$$\frac{\partial U_r}{\partial t} + U_r\frac{\partial U_r}{\partial r} + \frac{U_\theta}{r}\frac{\partial U_r}{\partial \theta} + \left(\frac{U_\phi}{r\sin\theta}\right)\frac{\partial U_r}{\partial \phi} - \frac{U_\theta^2}{r} - \frac{U_\phi^2}{r} = -\frac{1}{\rho}\frac{\partial p}{\partial r} + g_r + \frac{v}{r^2}\left(\frac{\partial}{\partial r}\left(r^2\frac{\partial U_r}{\partial r}\right)\right)$$
$$+ \left(\frac{v}{r^2\sin\theta}\right)\left(\frac{\partial}{\partial \theta}\left(\sin\theta\frac{\partial U_r}{\partial \theta}\right)\right) + \left(\frac{v}{r^2\sin^2\theta}\right)\left(\frac{\partial^2 U_r}{\partial \phi^2}\right) - \frac{2vU_r}{r^2}$$
$$- \frac{2v}{r^2}\frac{\partial U_\theta}{\partial \theta} - \frac{2vU_\theta}{r^2}\cot\theta - \left(\frac{2v}{r^2\sin\theta}\right)\frac{\partial U_\phi}{\partial \phi} \qquad (G)$$

θ component:
$$\frac{\partial U_\theta}{\partial t} + U_r\frac{\partial U_\theta}{\partial r} + \frac{U_\theta}{r}\frac{\partial U_\theta}{\partial \theta} + \left(\frac{U_\phi}{r\sin\theta}\right)\left(\frac{\partial U_\theta}{\partial \phi}\right) + \frac{U_r U_\theta}{r} - \frac{U_\phi^2}{r}\cot\theta$$
$$= -\frac{1}{\rho r}\frac{\partial p}{\partial \theta} + g_\theta + \frac{v}{r^2}\left(\frac{\partial}{\partial r}\left(r^2\frac{\partial U_\theta}{\partial r}\right)\right) + \left(\frac{v}{r^2\sin\theta}\right)\left(\frac{\partial}{\partial \theta}\left(\sin\theta\frac{\partial U_\theta}{\partial \theta}\right)\right) + \left(\frac{v}{r^2\sin^2\theta}\right)\frac{\partial^2 U_\theta}{\partial^2 \phi}$$
$$+ \frac{2v}{r^2}\frac{\partial U_r}{\partial \theta} - \left(\frac{vU_\theta}{r^2\sin^2\theta}\right) - \left(\frac{(2v)\cos\theta}{r^2\sin^2\theta}\right)\frac{\partial U_\phi}{\partial \phi} \qquad (H)$$

ϕ component:
$$\frac{\partial U_\phi}{\partial t} + U_r\frac{\partial U_\phi}{\partial r} + \frac{U_\theta}{r}\frac{\partial U_\phi}{\partial \theta} + \left(\frac{U_\phi}{r\sin\theta}\right)\frac{\partial U_\phi}{\partial \phi} + \frac{U_r U_\phi}{r} + \frac{U_\theta U_\phi}{r}\cot\theta$$
$$= -\left(\frac{1}{\rho r\sin\theta}\right)\frac{\partial p}{\partial \phi} + g_\phi + \frac{v}{r^2}\left(\frac{\partial}{\partial r}\left(r^2\frac{\partial U_\phi}{\partial r}\right)\right) + \left(\frac{v}{r^2\sin\theta}\right)\left(\frac{\partial}{\partial \theta}\left(\sin\theta\frac{\partial U_\phi}{\partial \theta}\right)\right)$$
$$+ \left(\frac{v}{r^2\sin^2\theta}\right)\frac{\partial^2 U_\phi}{\partial \phi^2} - \left(\frac{vU_\phi}{r^2\sin^2\theta}\right) + \left(\frac{2v}{r^2\sin\theta}\right)\frac{\partial U_r}{\partial \phi} + \left(\frac{2v\cos\theta}{r^2\sin^2\theta}\right)\frac{\partial U_\theta}{\partial \phi} \qquad (I)$$

force exerted by the string which counteracts the centrifugal force due to the mass of the rotating weight. A second force whose existence is similarly proven is the Coriolis force. The Coriolis force is an effective force in the θ direction that appears when a mass moves in both the r and θ directions. A fluid mechanics problem involving Coriolis forces is the problem of flow near a rotating disk in a large tank.

Contributions from such forces as the centripetal and Coriolis forces are the source of the additional terms that appear in the momentum balance equation in curvilinear coordinates. The final results are given in Table 5.7 for the various coordinate systems. Note that on the left-hand side of each equation in curvilinear coordinates the form for $(U \cdot \nabla)U$ from Table 5.1 appears in addition to the extra terms. On the right-hand side, the form for $\nabla^2 U$ from Table 5.1 appears in addition to the extra terms. For rectangular coordinates there are no additional terms.

Application of the Navier–Stokes equation to problems requires first the selection of the most appropriate coordinate system. Then every term in each component equation must be investigated to determine whether it is zero or non-zero. Naturally most terms must be zero in order for an exact mathematical solution to exist. The following four examples illustrate the many practical problems that can be solved by using Eq. (5.15), the Navier–Stokes equation.

Example 5.5. Determine the velocity distribution for the steady-state, laminar, incompressible flow of a fluid in a pipe. The flow configuration is horizontal.

Answer. The problem is best expressed in cylindrical coordinates as shown in Fig. 5.1 or Fig. 4.7. From Table 5.7, Eqs. (D), (E), and (F) apply. The flow is one-directional (z direction), so that U_z is non-zero and

$$U_r = U_\theta = 0 \tag{i}$$

If the pipe is perfectly round, i.e., circular in cross section, U_z is symmetric in the r and θ directions. By symmetry, all derivatives with respect to θ are zero. The fluid velocity U_z is zero at the wall and a maximum at the tube center line. Thus, $\partial U_z / \partial r$ is finite and non-zero.

The continuity equation for this problem, Eq. (E) in Table 5.3, is

$$(1/r)[\partial(rU_r)/\partial r] + (1/r)(\partial U_\theta / \partial \theta) + \partial U_z / \partial z = 0 \tag{ii}$$

As a consequence of Eq. (i), the first two terms in Eq. (ii) are zero; hence

$$\partial U_z / \partial z = 0 \tag{iii}$$

After integrating once, Eq. (iii) becomes

$$U_z = \text{constant} \tag{iv}$$

where the constant or U_z can vary with r, but not with z. Thus, by the use of the continuity equation [Eq. (ii)] for an incompressible one-directional pipe flow, the velocity in the flow direction is invariant in that direction as was previously proved for rectangular coordinates in Example 3.7.

In Eq. (D), for the r component of the Navier–Stokes equation, the entire left-hand side is zero as a result of Eq. (i). Similarly the right-hand side reduces to

$$-(1/\rho)(\partial p/\partial r) + g_r = 0 \tag{v}$$

where g_r is the component of the gravitational force acting in the r direction. The usual assumption in the horizontal tube problem is that the effect of g_r is very small compared to the force causing the flow; thus g_r is taken as zero and $\partial p/\partial r$ is zero as well by Eq. (v). This assumption is equivalent to neglecting the hydrostatic pressure as a result of g_r, when compared to the dynamic pressure giving rise to the flow (e.g., the pressure provided by a pump). The total pressure is the sum of the hydrostatic and dynamic pressures. For the horizontal pipe problem, the Navier–Stokes equation is exact if the dynamic pressure is used.

In Eq. (E) for the θ component of the Navier–Stokes equation, all terms are likewise zero as a consequence of Eq. (i). Equation (F) for the z component has non-zero terms. For steady-state

$$\frac{\partial U_z}{\partial t} = 0 \tag{vi}$$

By continuity, as just shown

$$\frac{\partial U_z}{\partial z} = 0 \tag{iii}$$

The gravity component g_z in the horizontal direction is zero. Since U_z varies with r, but not with θ or z, Eq. (F) reduces to

$$0 = -\frac{1}{\rho}\frac{\partial p}{\partial z} + \nu\left(\frac{\partial^2 U_z}{\partial r^2} + \frac{1}{r}\frac{\partial U_z}{\partial r}\right) \tag{vii}$$

Equation (v) was used to prove that the pressure is independent of radius. Symmetry considerations show that the pressure is not a function of θ; thus, the pressure is a function only of the z direction. By the force balance resulting in Eq. (4.80), dp/dz must be constant and is given by

$$\frac{\partial p}{\partial z} = \frac{\Delta p}{L} \tag{viii}$$

The derivative of a product is given by Eq. (3.51). Thus

$$\frac{\partial}{\partial r}\left(r\frac{\partial U_z}{\partial r}\right) = r\frac{\partial^2 U_z}{\partial r^2} + \frac{\partial U_z}{\partial r} = r\left(\frac{\partial^2 U_z}{\partial r^2} + \frac{1}{r}\frac{\partial U_z}{\partial r}\right) \tag{ix}$$

The kinematic viscosity ν is related to the molecular viscosity μ by

$$\nu = \frac{\mu}{\rho} \tag{2.12}$$

Using Eqs. 2.12, (viii), and (ix), Eq. (vii) becomes

$$\frac{\mu}{r}\left[\frac{\partial}{\partial r}\left(r\frac{\partial U_z}{\partial r}\right)\right] = \frac{\partial p}{\partial z} = \frac{\Delta p}{L} \tag{x}$$

Separation of variables results in

$$\mu\, d\left[r\frac{\partial U_z}{dr}\right] = \frac{\Delta p}{L}r\,dr \tag{xi}$$

where the partial derivatives have been replaced by total derivatives, since the only variation is with r. Integrating:

$$\mu r \frac{dU_z}{dr} = \frac{\Delta p}{L} r^2/2 + C_1 \tag{xii}$$

The constant of integration can be determined from the center line boundary condition. At the center line $r = 0$ and $dU_z/dr = 0$ from symmetry; thus C_1 equals 0, and Eq. (xii) reduces to

$$\mu \frac{dU_z}{dr} = \frac{\Delta p}{L} \frac{r}{2} \tag{xiii}$$

Further integration gives

$$U_z = \frac{(\Delta p/L) r^2}{2\mu} + C_2 \tag{xiv}$$

The second constant of integration is determined from the wall condition:

$$U_z (r = r_o) = 0 \tag{xv}$$

From Eqs. (xiv) and (xv), the constant C_2 is

$$C_2 = \frac{(-\Delta p)/L}{4\mu} r_o^2 \tag{xvi}$$

Combining Eq. (xvi) with Eq. (xiv) gives the final result as

$$U_z = \frac{(-\Delta p)/L}{4\mu} (r_o^2 - r^2) \tag{xvii}$$

This answer is the same as Eq. (4.72), previously derived for laminar flow.

Example 5.6. Consider laminar heat transfer in a tube. Begin with Eq. (4.72) for velocity profie and Eq. (iv) in Example 5.4 and develop an equation to describe the variation of temperature with radius. Assume no viscous dissipation, no heat generation, constant physical properties, and a fully developed temperature profile ($\Delta T/L =$ constant). Figure 5.3 applies; in heat transfer, the inside radius of the tube is r_i.

Answer. The energy equation, Eq. (B) of Table 5.6, in cylindrical coordinates was simplified in Example 5.4; the result was a differential equation describing the variation of T with r. The answer from Eq. (iv) in that example (for constant α) is

$$U_z \frac{\partial T}{\partial z} = \alpha \left[\frac{1}{r} \frac{\partial}{\partial r} \left(r \frac{\partial T}{\partial r} \right) + \frac{\partial^2 T}{\partial z^2} \right] \tag{i}$$

The variation of the velocity U_z with r is given by the Navier–Stokes equation, which simplified to Eq. (x) in Example 5.5:

$$\frac{\mu}{r} \left[\frac{\partial}{\partial r} \left(r \frac{\partial U_z}{\partial r} \right) \right] = \frac{\Delta p}{L} \tag{ii}$$

Equation (ii) is said to be coupled to Eq. (i) because U_z appears in both equations, and the final solution for U_z must satisfy both differential equations and all applicable boundary conditions as well. Every problem in mass or heat transport with convection results in coupled differential equations. Exact solutions are usually not possible, but a reasonably good solution is sometimes attainable if the equations can be decoupled, i.e., solved independently as Eq. (ii) was in Example 5.5.

Let us assume that the temperature change in this problem is relatively small. Then the physical properties may be assumed constant with little error. If the density and viscosity (the property most sensitive to temperature changes) are constant, then the fact that heat transfer is occurring will have no effect on the momentum transfer. Under these conditions, Eq. (ii) is no longer coupled to Eq. (i). Measurement of the velocity profile will prove or disprove the validity of this assumption. If the equations can be decoupled, the velocity profile is given by the solution to Example 5.5:

$$U_z = \frac{(-\Delta p)/L}{4\mu}(r_i^2 - r^2) \tag{iii}$$

where r_i is the inside tube diameter. Equations (i) and (iii) can be combined:

$$\frac{\alpha}{r}\left[\frac{\partial}{\partial r}\left(r\frac{\partial T}{\partial r}\right)\right] + \alpha\frac{\partial^2 T}{\partial z^2} + \frac{\Delta p/L}{4\mu}(r_i^2 - r^2)\frac{\partial T}{\partial z} = 0 \tag{iv}$$

Equation (iv) is a most complex equation to solve without more assumptions. For the special case of flow far away from the entrance to the pipe and the beginning of the heat transfer section, the temperature profile will be fully developed, i.e., the following slope is constant:

$$\partial T/\partial z = \Delta T/L = \text{constant} \tag{v}$$

If Eq. (v) is integrated, the result states that T is a linear function of z. If Eq. (v) is differentiated, the result is

$$\frac{\partial^2 T}{\partial z^2} = 0 \tag{vi}$$

Note that T is a function of both r and z. The above equations are next used to simplify Eq. (iv):

$$\frac{\alpha}{r}\left[\frac{\partial}{\partial r}\left(r\frac{\partial T}{\partial r}\right)\right] + \frac{(\Delta p/L)(\Delta T/L)}{4\mu}(r_i^2 - r^2) = 0 \tag{vii}$$

where both $\Delta p/L$ and $\Delta T/L$ are constants. Ordinary differentials can be used since the only variation of T is with r. Separation of variables and integration yields

$$r\frac{dT}{dr} = -\frac{(\Delta p/L)(\Delta T/L)}{4\mu\alpha}\left(\frac{r_i^2 r^2}{2} - \frac{r^4}{4}\right) + C_1 \tag{viii}$$

The center line boundary condition is

$$\frac{dT}{dr}(r = 0) = 0 \tag{ix}$$

Therefore, C_1 is zero, and Eq. (viii) becomes

$$\frac{dT}{dr} = -\frac{(\Delta p/L)(\Delta T/L)}{4\mu\alpha}\left(\frac{r_i^2 r}{2} - \frac{r^3}{4}\right) \tag{x}$$

This equation must satisfy the second boundary condition of Eq. (v), the derivation of which will be covered in Chapter 11. Equation (x) is integrated again:

$$T = -\frac{(\Delta p/L)(\Delta T/L)}{4\mu\alpha}\left(\frac{r_i^2 r^2}{4} - \frac{r^4}{16}\right) + C_2 \tag{xi}$$

A useful equation is obtained from Eq. (xi) by eliminating C_2 in favor of the temperature at the wall T_w:

$$T\,(r = r_i) = T_w \tag{xii}$$

Using this boundary condition, Eq. (xi) becomes

$$T_w = -\frac{(\Delta p/L)(\Delta T/L)}{4\mu\alpha}\left(\frac{r_i^4}{4} - \frac{r_i^4}{16}\right) + C_2 = -\frac{(\Delta p/L)(\Delta T/L)}{4\mu\alpha}\frac{3r_i^4}{16} + C_2 \tag{xiii}$$

Equation (xiii) is subtracted from Eq. (xi):

$$T - T_w = -\frac{(\Delta p/L)(\Delta T/L)}{4\mu\alpha}\left(\frac{r_i^2 r^2}{4} - \frac{r^4}{16} - \frac{3r_i^4}{16}\right)$$

$$= -\frac{(\Delta p/L)(\Delta T/L)}{4\mu\alpha}(r_i^4)\left(\frac{1}{4}\frac{r^2}{r_i^2} - \frac{1}{16}\frac{r^4}{r_i^4} - \frac{3}{16}\right) \tag{xiv}$$

Equation (xiv) expresses the temperature as a function of radius for heat transfer between a pipe wall and a fluid in laminar flow. The most important assumption in the derivation of Eq. (xiv) is that the gradient $\Delta T/L$ is constant. This assumption is equivalent to assuming constant heat rate (q_w) at the wall, as will be proved in Chapter 11. Also in that chapter it will be shown that T_w is not constant, but varies down the pipe when $\Delta T/L$ and q_w are constant. Note also that this derivation eliminates C_2 from the final equation.

A useful form of Eq. (xiv) replaces $\Delta p/L$ with the average velocity, which in Chapter 4 was shown to equal half the center line velocity $U_{z,\,max}$. From Eq. (4.73) or Eq. (iii) evaluated at $r = 0$:

$$\frac{-\Delta p}{L} = \frac{4U_{z,\,max}}{r_i^2} = \frac{8U_{z,\,ave}}{r_i^2} \tag{xv}$$

Then Eq. (xiv) becomes

$$T - T_w = \frac{U_{z,\,ave}}{\alpha}\frac{\Delta T}{L}(r_i^2)\left(\frac{1}{2}\frac{r^2}{r_i^2} - \frac{1}{8}\frac{r^4}{r_i^4} - \frac{3}{8}\right) \tag{xvi}$$

Over a good part of the cross section, the fourth-power term $(r/r_i)^4$ is small compared to the other term, and the distribution has a parabolic shape. At the center line ($r = 0$), the maximum (or minimum) temperature equals

$$T_{r=0} = T_w - \frac{3}{8}\frac{U_{z,\,ave}}{\alpha}\frac{\Delta T}{L}r_i^2 = C_2 \tag{xvii}$$

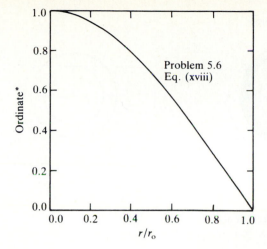

FIGURE 5.4

Temperature distribution for laminar pipe flow with constant heat flux at the wall.

$$*\text{Ordinate} = \frac{8}{3} \frac{T_w - T}{(U_{z,\,ave}/\alpha)(\Delta T/L)(r_i^2)}$$

Note that from Eq. (xi) $T_{r=0}$ equals C_2. Figure 5.4 shows the temperature distribution (Eq. (xvi)) in a non-dimensional form:

$$\frac{8}{3} \frac{T_w - T}{(U_{z,\,ave}/\alpha)(\Delta T/L)(r_i^2)} = 1 - \frac{4}{3}\frac{r^2}{r_i^2} + \frac{1}{3}\frac{r^4}{r_i^4} \qquad \text{(xviii)}$$

Recall that the following assumptions were made in order to arrive at Eqs. (xiv), (xvii), and (xviii):

1. The properties c_p and k are constant and independent of temperature if temperature changes are small; also ρ and μ are likewise constant so that momentum transfer (i.e., the velocity profile) is unaffected by heat transfer.
2. The temperature profile is fully established, and the gradient $\Delta T/L$ is constant [cf. Eq. (v)], i.e., constant wall flux q_w.
3. Laminar flow exists.
4. The velocity profile is fully established when the fluid enters the heat transfer section of the tube.
5. The final equations are valid far from the entrance to the heat transfer section so that Eq. (v) is satisfied.

Example 5.7. Solve the Couette flow problem shown in Fig. 5.5. This geometry is often used for viscosity measurements. The fluid is placed in the gap between the outer and inner cylinders. The outer cylinder is rotated at a constant speed ω, which is low enough that the flow is laminar. A torque is measured at the inner cylinder by means of a calibrated spring. The apparatus is designed so that there are no end effects.

Answer. The Couette flow is interesting because the flow is in the θ direction only, so that

$$U_r = U_z = 0 \qquad \text{(i)}$$

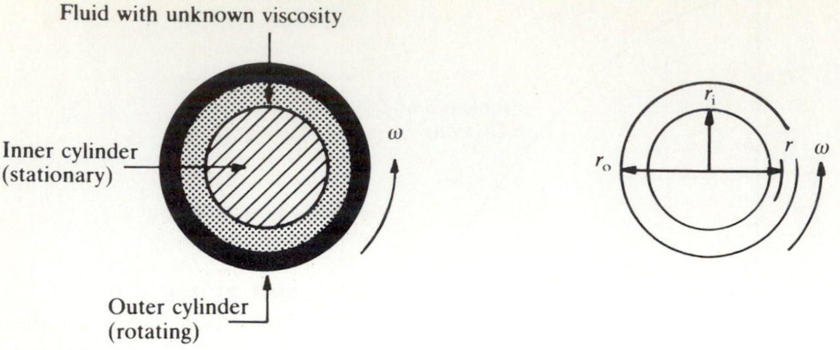

Fluid with unknown viscosity

Inner cylinder
(stationary)

ω

Outer cylinder
(rotating)

r_i

r_o

r ω

FIGURE 5.5
Flow between concentric cylinders (Couette flow).

and of course all derivatives of U_r and U_z are zero. The logical choice of coordinates is cylindrical. The angular velocity is carefully controlled so that steady-state prevails:

$$\frac{\partial U_\theta}{\partial t} = 0 \tag{ii}$$

The viscometer is long enough in the z-direction so that end effects are negligible; thus

$$\frac{\partial U_\theta}{\partial z} = 0 \tag{iii}$$

If the viscometer is manufactured carefully so that the cylinders are concentric, then the flow will be symmetric

$$\frac{\partial U_\theta}{\partial \theta} = 0 \tag{iv}$$

Equation (iv) also follows from the continuity equation (E) of Table 5.3. The viscometer configuration is such that gravity acts only in the z direction so that

$$g_r = 0 = g_\theta \tag{v}$$

The value of g_z at Columbus, Ohio, is

$$g_z = 9.80089 \text{ m s}^{-2} \tag{4.50}$$

The Navier–Stokes equations for cylindrical coordinates are Eqs. (D), (E), and (F) in Table 5.7. Equation (D) for the r component becomes

$$\frac{-U_\theta^2}{r} = -\frac{1}{\rho}\frac{\partial p}{\partial r} \tag{vi}$$

Equation (E) for the θ component is

$$0 = \frac{\partial^2 U_\theta}{\partial r^2} + \frac{1}{r}\frac{\partial U_\theta}{\partial r} - U_\theta/r^2 \tag{vii}$$

Equation (F) for the z component is

$$0 = -\frac{1}{\rho}\frac{\partial p}{\partial z} + g_z \tag{viii}$$

Equation (viii) shows that the vertical pressure drop is due only to gravity acting on the fluid mass:

$$\frac{\partial p}{\partial z} = \rho g_z \tag{ix}$$

The equation for the θ velocity, Eq. (vii), does not involve a convective contribution. It is an exact differential and can be written as

$$\frac{d}{dr}\left(\frac{1}{r}\frac{d(rU_\theta)}{dr}\right) = 0 \tag{x}$$

where the partial derivatives are replaced by total derivatives, since all variation in this problem is in a single direction r. Equation (x) can be verified by use of the derivative of a product given by Eq. (3.51), which was used similarly for Eq. (ix) in Example 5.5. After integration, Eq. (x) becomes

$$\frac{1}{r}\frac{d(rU_\theta)}{dr} = C_1 \tag{xi}$$

Integrating again:

$$rU_\theta = C_1(r^2/2) + C_2 \tag{xii}$$

The two boundary conditions are

$$U_\theta\,(r = r_i) = 0 \qquad U_\theta\,(r = r_o) = \omega r_o \tag{xiii}$$

where ω is the velocity of rotation of the outer cylinder. Substitution of the boundary conditions into Eq. (xii) results in two equations in two unknowns:

$$0 = C_1 r_i^2/2 + C_2 \qquad \omega r_o^2 = C_1 r_o^2/2 + C_2 \tag{xiv}$$

These equations are solved for C_1 and C_2:

$$C_1 = 2\omega r_o^2/(r_o^2 - r_i^2)$$
$$C_2 = -\omega(r_o^2 r_i^2)/(r_o^2 - r_i^2) \tag{xv}$$

Equations (xii) and (xv) are now combined to give the velocity distribution:

$$U_\theta = \frac{\omega r_o^2}{r_o^2 - r_i^2}\left(r - \frac{r_i^2}{r}\right) \tag{xvi}$$

or

$$U_\theta = \frac{\omega r_o^2}{r}\frac{(r^2 - r_i^2)}{(r_o^2 - r_i^2)} \tag{xvii}$$

Note that Eq. (xvii) satisfies the boundary conditions in Eq. (xiii).

With U_θ now given by Eq. (xvii), the radial pressure distribution can be determined from Eq. (vi). Note that there is a convective contribution; i.e., the centrifugal force balanced by the radial pressure gradient. From Eqs. (vi) and (xvii), the radial pressure gradient is

$$\frac{\partial p}{\partial r} = \frac{\rho \omega^2 r_o^4}{r^3} \frac{(r^2 - r_i^2)^2}{(r_o^2 - r_i^2)^2} \tag{xviii}$$

The appropriate boundary conditions for this equation are: at $r = r_i$, $\partial p / \partial r = 0$ and at $r = r_o$, $\partial p / \partial r = \rho \omega^2 r_o$. Equation (xviii) may be integrated with respect to r to give the pressure distribution across the flow, but this integration is of no interest in operating the viscometer and will be left to the discretion of the reader. The pressure distribution is highly nonlinear owing to the U_θ^2 term.

As discussed earlier, in the Couette viscometer, the angular velocity ω and force F on the inner cylinder are measured. If A is the area of the inside cylinder contacted by the fluid, then the wall shear stress at $r = r_i$ is

$$\tau_{r\theta} = F/A \tag{xix}$$

where $\tau_{r\theta}$ is the θ momentum transferred in the r direction. Note that this equation is very similar to Eq. (2.6). From Table 5.2, Eq. (J) is the equation for $\tau_{r\theta}$:

$$\tau_{r\theta} = -\mu \left(r \frac{\partial}{\partial r} (U_\theta / r) + \frac{1}{r} \frac{\partial U_r}{\partial \theta} \right) \tag{xx}$$

For this problem, the term $\partial U_r / \partial \theta$ is zero, and Eq. (xx) reduces to

$$\tau_{r\theta} = -\mu r \frac{d(U_\theta / r)}{dr} \tag{xxi}$$

Combining Eqs. (xvi) and (xxi) at $r = r_i$ gives

$$(\tau_{r\theta})_i = -\mu \frac{2\omega r_o^2}{r_o^2 - r_i^2} \tag{xxii}$$

The shear stress $(\tau_{r\theta})_i$ can be related to the torque $T_{Q,i}$ as follows:

$$T_{Q,i} = F r_i \tag{xxiii}$$

and

$$(\tau_{r\theta})_i = -F/A = -F/(2\pi r_i L) \tag{xxiv}$$

where L is the length of the cylinder. Combining Eqs. (xxii) through (xxiv):

$$\frac{T_{Q,i}}{2\pi r_i^2 L} = \mu \frac{2\omega r_o^2}{r_o^2 - r_i^2}$$

or

$$\mu = \frac{T_{Q,i}}{4\pi r_i^2 L} \left(\frac{r_o^2 - r_i^2}{\omega r_o^2} \right) \tag{xxv}$$

Clearly, a knowledge of the rotation rate ω and the torque at the inner wall $T_{Q,i}$ plus the geometry (r_i, r_o, and L) is required to establish the viscosity.

An interesting extension of this problem is consideration of the heating effects in the viscometer. The heating comes from viscous dissipation within the fluid. If appreciable, the viscosity will vary because of its temperature dependence. The velocity equation then becomes coupled to the energy equation through the dependence of viscosity upon temperature. Such solutions have been reviewed by Fredrickson [F1] and Brodkey [B4].

5.1.7 The Boundary Layer

Whenever a fluid is forced to flow along a solid surface (boundary), a boundary layer is formed as a result of the fluid velocity being zero at the surface. Recall Fig. 2.3, in which the no-slip boundary condition was illustrated for a fluid contained between two parallel plates, one being stationary. In the fluid mechanics literature, the boundary layer is defined as that portion of fluid whose velocity profile is appreciably affected (say, by greater than one percent) by the presence of a solid surface. Figure 5.6 illustrates this definition. The velocity of the fluid at some distance from the plate is called the free stream velocity U_∞; the fluid with velocity U_∞ is not in the boundary layer. Fluid with velocity U_x, where U_x is less than 99 percent of U_∞, is in the boundary layer. A detailed discussion on the boundary layer will be delayed until Chapter 12. However, for now some of the basic principles of the flow itself will be discussed so that the governing equations can be obtained.

The classical boundary layer problem is the flow over a flat plate, as illustrated in Fig. 5.6. The experiment is designed so that the velocity profile of the fluid approaching the leading edge of the plate is flat. As the fluid passes along the flat plate, the influence of viscosity between molecules at rest at the solid boundary surface and molecules in the bulk flow causes the velocity to decrease in the neighborhood of the boundary. The dotted line in Fig. 5.6 marks the edge of the boundary layer, where the velocity is 99 per cent of the free stream velocity U_∞. The example that follows illustrates the equations necessary for the mathematical analysis of the flat plate problem.

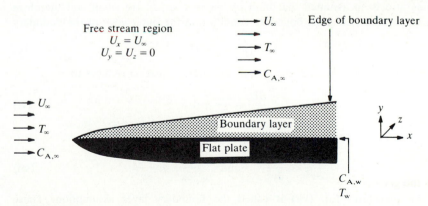

FIGURE 5.6
Boundary layer flow past a flat plate.

Example 5.8. An incompressible fluid flows in laminar flow past a flat plate. Assume that the plate is able to transfer heat and mass as well as momentum to the fluid. Find the non-zero terms in the appropriate balance equations. Figure 5.6 shows the geometry of system.

Answer. The flat plate experiment is perhaps the simplest explanation of boundary layer flows because there is only one surface under consideration. The fluid approaches the plate at uniform velocity U_∞, temperature T_∞, and concentration $C_{A,\infty}$. Flow is in the x direction. The z direction is perpendicular to the paper in Fig. 5.6, and there are no changes of any kind taking place in that direction. When the fluid reaches the front or leading edge of the plate $(x = 0)$, the velocity profile must change because of the boundary condition of no slip:

$$U_x = U_y = 0 \qquad (y = 0) \tag{i}$$

The velocity must be zero at any solid surface as Eq. (i) states. As x increases, the boundary layer thickness δ increases. The fluid whose velocity has decreased must go somewhere. It moves outward and gives rise to a small but finite velocity U_y. Inside the boundary layer, therefore, the local velocity is a function of both x and y. Outside the boundary layer, the velocity is constant and equal to the free stream velocity U_∞. Clearly, both the x and y directions must be considered, but the z direction can be ignored as discussed previously. Thus

$$U_z = 0 \qquad \frac{\partial U_x}{\partial z} = \frac{\partial U_y}{\partial z} = 0 \tag{ii}$$

However, the remaining four partial derivatives of U_x and U_y are non-zero ($\partial U_x/\partial x$, $\partial U_x/\partial y$, $\partial U_y/\partial x$, and $\partial U_y/\partial y$). Equations (A) and (B) from Table 5.7 for steady-state apply, and by using Eq. (ii) they reduce to

$$U_x \frac{\partial U_x}{\partial x} + U_y \frac{\partial U_x}{\partial y} = v\left(\frac{\partial^2 U_x}{\partial x^2} + \frac{\partial^2 U_x}{\partial y^2}\right) \tag{iii}$$

$$U_x \frac{\partial U_y}{\partial x} + U_y \frac{\partial U_y}{\partial y} = v\left(\frac{\partial^2 U_y}{\partial x^2} + \frac{\partial^2 U_y}{\partial y^2}\right) \tag{iv}$$

It has also been assumed that both dp/dx and dp/dy are small and therefore negligible. The additional boundary condition at the outer edge of the boundary layer is

$$U_x \,(y = \infty) = U_\infty \tag{v}$$

From Eq. (D) in Table 5.3, the overall continuity equation reduces to

$$\frac{\partial U_x}{\partial x} + \frac{\partial U_y}{\partial y} = 0 \tag{vi}$$

It will be assumed that δ (and consequently y) are small, so that

$$\frac{\partial^2 U_x}{\partial x^2} \ll \frac{\partial^2 U_x}{\partial y^2} \qquad \text{and} \qquad \frac{\partial^2 U_y}{\partial x^2} \ll \frac{\partial^2 U_y}{\partial y^2} \tag{vii}$$

In the literature, Eq. (vii) is called the boundary layer assumption. These approximations are valid only for fairly high velocities in laminar flow (see Chapter 12 for more details [B4]). After invoking the boundary layer assumption,

Eqs. (iii) and (iv) reduce to

$$U_x \frac{\partial U_x}{\partial x} + U_y \frac{\partial U_x}{\partial y} = v \frac{\partial^2 U_x}{\partial y^2} \tag{viii}$$

$$U_x \frac{\partial U_y}{\partial x} + U_y \frac{\partial U_y}{\partial y} = v \frac{\partial^2 U_y}{\partial y^2} \tag{ix}$$

These equations, plus the continuity equation, are the starting point for the boundary layer analysis. However, Eq. (ix) need not be used since Eq. (viii) and the continuity equation (vi) are enough to define the system and allow a solution for U_x and U_y.

   If the flat plate is maintained at a uniform temperature T_o which is different from the free stream temperature T_∞, then another equation must be added to those above. The energy equation (A) from Table 5.6 for steady-state, no generation, and constant properties reduces to

$$U_x \frac{\partial T}{\partial x} + U_y \frac{\partial T}{\partial y} = \alpha \left(\frac{\partial^2 T}{\partial x^2} + \frac{\partial^2 T}{\partial y^2} \right) \tag{x}$$

where dissipation has been neglected. The boundary layer approximation for heat transfer is $\partial^2 T / \partial x^2 \ll \partial^2 T / \partial y^2$. Equation (x) then simplifies to

$$U_x \frac{\partial T}{\partial x} + U_y \frac{\partial T}{\partial y} = \alpha \frac{\partial^2 T}{\partial y^2} \tag{xi}$$

   In order to solve the heat and momentum transfer problems together, Eqs. (vi), (viii), and (xi) must be solved simultaneously for U_x, U_y, and T as a function of x and y for given values of the momentum and thermal diffusivities and the given boundary conditions. Note that the temperature changes have been assumed small enough so that the physical properties can be considered constant. Even so, the "coupled" set of equations are a formidable task to solve.

   Mass transfer may also be present in the problem. For example, if the plate were porous, or perhaps soluble in the fluid passing over it, so that a constant concentration $C_{A,o}$ could be maintained at the surface, then there would be a mass boundary layer formed on the plate as a result of mass transfer to or from the plate. The assumptions to be invoked have already been discussed. The mass transfer case is analogous to the heat transfer case, which resulted in Eq. (xi). The final equation is

$$U_x \frac{\partial C_A}{\partial x} + U_y \frac{\partial C_A}{\partial y} = D \left(\frac{\partial^2 C_A}{\partial x^2} + \frac{\partial^2 C_A}{\partial y^2} \right) \tag{xii}$$

This equation can also be obtained from Eq. (A) in Table 5.4. The boundary layer approximation for the mass transfer problem is

$$\frac{\partial^2 C_A}{\partial x^2} \ll \frac{\partial^2 C_A}{\partial y^2} \tag{xiii}$$

Thus

$$U_x \frac{\partial C_A}{\partial x} + U_y \frac{\partial C_A}{\partial y} = D \frac{\partial^2 C_A}{\partial y^2} \tag{xiv}$$

Equation (xiv) applies for constant D and no chemical reactions to produce or remove C_A. If the transfer is equimolar, which implies no induced velocity as a result of mass transfer, then U_x and U_y are the forced convection velocities as solved for from the momentum equations. If, however, the transfer is not equimolar, then there will be additional terms associated with an induced velocity (cf., Section 5.3.1).

In summary, for the problem of a laminar boundary layer over a flat plate with no heat or mass transfer, both Eqs. (vi) and (viii) must be solved simultaneously. If either heat transfer or mass transfer occurs in addition, then three differential equations [Eqs. (vi), (viii), and either (xi) or (xiv)] must be solved simultaneously. If all possibilities (heat, mass, and momentum) occur, then all four equations [(vi), (viii), (xi), and (xiv)] must solved simultaneously.

No attempt will be made to solve these equations here as the mathematics are quite involved. The point to be appreciated by the reader is that the general equations presented in this chapter form the basis of solution to practically all laminar flow engineering problems. The nine-step procedure for problem solution was summarized in Section 5.1.5. Briefly, the applicable differential equations are to be selected from the tables in Chapter 5. Then the zero terms are identified in order to simplify those equations so that a solution of some kind will be possible. Solution of the most common of these problems is available in the technical literature, as well as in Chapter 12.

5.2   CONVECTED COORDINATES

Visualize a situation in which an observer is moving exactly with an element of fluid in a simple flow such as in Fig. 5.3. The problem is easiest to visualize if there is no appreciable velocity profile, as exists in the middle of a wide river. For example, an observer in a canoe floating down a lazy river is being convected with the flow. The element of fluid is convected at some velocity U, but from the viewpoint of the observer there is no velocity. The velocity U is relative to stationary coordinates (the river bank). Analytical solutions to reasonably complex problems are sometimes possible if a coordinate system convected with the flow is chosen.

The generalized balance equation for incompressible fluids with constant properties is:

$$\frac{\partial \psi}{\partial t} + (\boldsymbol{U} \cdot \boldsymbol{\nabla})\psi = \dot{\psi}_G + \delta(\nabla^2 \psi) \tag{3.78}$$

In a coordinate system convected with $\boldsymbol{U}$, there will be no contribution from convection. Hence, a new derivative, given the symbol $D\psi/Dt$ and called the substantial derivative, is defined mathematically as

$$\frac{D\psi}{Dt} = \frac{\partial \psi}{\partial t} + (\boldsymbol{U} \cdot \boldsymbol{\nabla})\psi \tag{5.16}$$

This substantial derivative has the property of being zero for a steady-state problem with no net velocity vector relative to the position of the observer. Equation (5.16) is combined with Eq. (3.78) to give the balance equation in terms of the substantial derivative:

$$\frac{D\psi}{Dt} = \dot{\psi}_G + \delta(\nabla^2 \psi) \tag{5.17}$$

The substantial derivative is particularly convenient in simplifying the continuity equation, Eq. (3.71):

$$D\rho/Dt = -\rho(\nabla \cdot U) \tag{5.18}$$

Equation (5.17) is identical to Eq. (3.78) with U zero except for the derivative notation. A solution in terms of "D" would be the same as a solution in terms of "∂" if there were no velocity in the latter case; i.e., the result that the moving observer sees is the same the stationary observer sees with no velocity. Problems of this nature were solved in Chapter 4, where in each case $(U \cdot \nabla)\psi$ was zero, either as a result of no velocity or as a result of the derivatives being zero, as in the case of laminar fluid flow.

The defining equation for the substantial derivative, Eq. (5.16), can be used to express the various forms of the general property balance in terms of this derivative. The Navier–Stokes equation, Eq. (5.15), is often found in terms of the substantial derivative [B3, B4]. The heat transfer literature makes little use of convected coordinates. In mass tranfer, there are several choices for convected coordinate systems; these will be covered in the following section.

5.3 MASS DIFFUSION PHENOMENA

In Section 5.1 it was shown that there can be a momentum flux due to convection as caused by a pressure gradient or other force. It is also possible to have mass transfer occurring simultaneously with momentum transfer. For example, if the pipe in Fig. 5.3 were made of a soluble material, then as the fluid flowed through the pipe there would be mass transfer between the wall and fluid. The bulk flow in such an experiment is caused by a pressure gradient. Sometimes a bulk flow can also be caused by mass transfer even when there is no measurable pressure gradient. Of course, contributions to the bulk flow may involve both momentum transfer and mass transfer mechanisms. Both of these cases will be considered in this section.

Mass diffusion is the most complex of the three transports because there are several useful choices for the frame of reference in mathematically describing the mass flux. The presentation of mass diffusion in the presence of forced convection begins with this topic.

5.3.1 Mass Fluxes in Stationary and Convected Coordinates

There are at least eight fluxes that have been introduced at one time or another. These are distinguished by two parameters. First, the frame of reference can be with respect to fixed coordinates or with respect to one of the velocities to be discussed in this section. Secondly, the flux can be on a molar or a mass basis. The most important flux, N_A/A, introduced in Chapter 2, is the number of moles of component A per unit time moving through the area A, relative to stationary coordinates. Also introduced in Chapter 2 was n_A/A which is the mass flux relative to stationary coordinates. The flux N_A/A is sufficient for most problems; other fluxes will be introduced briefly in order to point out their significance and to assist the reader in understanding the literature. The other fluxes are especially important in calculating diffusion coefficients from experimental data.

Convective flux. Equation (3.15) equated the total flux with the flux due to molecular transport plus the flux due to convection:

$$\Psi_x = \Psi_{x,m} + \Psi_{x,c} \tag{3.15}$$

where the convective flux $\Psi_{x,c}$ is

$$\Psi_{x,c} = \psi U_x \tag{3.21}$$

The velocity U_x in Eq. (3.21) is the average velocity of whatever property is being convected. For one-directional flow in the x direction, the total mass flux convected is

$$(n_T/A)_{x,c} = \rho U_x \tag{5.19}$$

In this equation, appropriate units for $(n_T/A)_{x,c}$ are $(\text{kg m}^{-2}\,\text{s}^{-1})$, for ρ (kg m^{-3}), and for U_x (m s^{-1}). The velocity in Eq. (5.19) is the velocity of the mass being convected through the area A, as shown in Fig. 3.4.

At this point, it is desirable to change the notation in order to avoid confusion and to be consistent with the presentations of other authors in mass transfer. From this point on in Chapter 5, let the diffusion be in the z direction in order to avoid conflict with x_A (mole fraction of species A in the solid or liquid phase) and y_A (mole fraction of A in the gas phase). For a mixture of n components, U_z is the z component of U, the mass average velocity vector, which was defined rigorously as

$$U = \sum_{i=1}^{n} (\rho_i U_i) \Big/ \sum_{i=1}^{n} \rho_i \tag{3.22}$$

where ρ_i is the density of species i and U_i is the velocity vector of species i. The velocity U_i is commonly called the species velocity.

The species velocity U_i is the velocity of species i with respect to stationary coordinates by any and all mechanisms. The species velocity of A, U_A, is found by realizing that Eq. (3.21) can be written to relate U_A to the total flux of species A convected:

$$(N_A/A)_c = C_A U_A = (\rho_A/M_A)U_A \tag{5.20}$$

where $(N_A/A)_c$ is the molar flux based on stationary coordinates and

$$\rho_A = C_A M_A \tag{2.33}$$

If Eq. (5.20) is multiplied by the molecular weight M_A, then the mass flux $(n_A/A)_c$ (units of which are $kg\,m^{-2}\,s^{-1}$) appears:

$$(n_A/A)_c = \rho_A U_A \tag{5.21}$$

where the mass flux $(n_A/A)_c$ is based on stationary coordinates and is also defined as

$$(n_A/A)_c = (N_A/A)_c (M_A) \tag{5.22}$$

For a fluid mixture, it is possible that one or more species of the mixture are diffusing in addition to being convected by a flow which is caused by some external force such as a pressure drop or gravity. In this case there are three average velocities to be considered: the mass average velocity, the molar average velocity, and the volume or nondiffusional average velocity. The mass average velocity is given by Eq. (3.22). The molar average velocity appears in the equation for the total molar flux, N_T/A (units $kmol\,m^{-2}\,s^{-1}$), which comes from applying Eq. (3.21) for the case of total moles being convected:

$$(N_T/A)_x = C_T U_z^* \tag{5.23}$$

where U_z^* is the z component of the molar average velocity U^*. Recall that U^* is the velocity of the molecules being convected through the area A, as shown in Fig. 3.4. The molar average velocity has already been defined rigorously as

$$U^* = \sum_{i=1}^{n} (C_i U_i) \Big/ \sum_{i=1}^{n} C_i \tag{3.23}$$

where U_i is again the species velocity of component i. Note that the species velocity is a unique quantity, independent of mass units or molar units. The species velocity U_i appears in both Eqs. (3.22) and (3.23).

The volume average velocity U^v is defined as

$$U^v = \sum_{i=1}^{n} (\rho_i U_i)(\bar{V}_i/M_i) = \sum_{i=1}^{n} C_i U_i \bar{V}_i = \sum_{i=1}^{n} (N_i/A)\bar{V}_i \tag{5.24}$$

where $\bar{V}_i$ is the partial molar volume[1] of species i and M_i is its molecular weight. The velocity given by Eq. (5.24) is also the velocity of any and all nondiffusing components. These nondiffusing components must move at the velocity of the volume in Fig. 3.4.

---

[1] The partial molar volume is computed from density–composition data. See any standard thermodynamics text for more details [S1].

If there is no diffusion, all three average velocities are exactly equal:

$$U = U^* = U^v \tag{5.25}$$

Of course, flows of single components cannot involve mass diffusion and Eq. (5.25) applies.

Induced velocity. As implied, a concentration gradient for species i superimposed on a bulk flow causes a net velocity of species i relative to the volume average velocity; in other words, the species velocity U_i does not equal U^v. In this case, all three average velocities (mass, molar, volume) may be different, as will be illustrated by Example 5.11. Naturally, it is possible to design an experiment in which the volume average velocity is zero. In the presence of mass diffusion with zero volume average velocity, there is normally a non-zero mass average velocity and a non-zero molar average velocity as a consequence of the three velocities differing. Therefore, the conclusion is that mass transfer induces a net convective flux. Similarly, a bulk flow can be caused by mass transfer even when there is no measurable pressure gradient. Of course, contributions to the bulk flow may involve both momentum transfer and mass transfer mechanisms.

Experimentally it is possible to measure all three velocities. The mass average velocity is found through various momentum-measuring devices such as a Pitot tube, which is discussed in Chapters 7 and 10. The molar average velocity is found by somehow counting molecules passing through a plane perpendicular to the flow. The volume velocity can be measured by introducing an additional component such as a tracer particle or other nondiffusing species and by measuring its velocity. Because of the complexity with these three "average" velocities, it may be advantageous to consider the velocity of species i relative to the mass or molar average velocity.

As a consequence of Eq. (3.15), the total flux is always the sum of the flux due to molecular transfer (i.e., Fick's law) and the flux due to convection. The above discussion has shown that the velocity U_z in Eq. (3.21) is the average velocity of whatever property is being convected, and that velocity is not, in general, equal to the volume average velocity. In other words, there can exist in a multicomponent mixture a nondiffusing species whose species velocity (with respect to fixed coordinates) is zero; furthermore, there could be and often is a net molar or mass average velocity due to mass diffusion alone when the volume average velocity is zero.

In order to compute the mass flux due to convection, it is helpful to define the "mass diffusion velocity" and the "molar diffusion velocity":

$$U_i - U = \text{diffusion velocity of } i \text{ with respect to } U \tag{5.26}$$

$$U_i - U^* = \text{diffusion velocity of } i \text{ with respect to } U^* \tag{5.27}$$

A diffusion velocity relative to the volume velocity also exists, but since Eqs. (5.8) and (5.9) are in terms of either mass average or molar average velocity, it is not included here.

TABLE 5.8
Fluxes for binary systems (*After Bird et al.*, 1960.)

Reference system	Molar flux	Mass flux
Fixed coordinates	$N_A/A = C_A U_A$	$n_A/A = \rho_A U_A$
Molar average velocity	$J_A^*/A = C_A(U_A - U^*)$	$j_A^*/A = \rho_A(U_A - U^*)$
Mass average velocity	$J_A/A = C_A(U_A - U)$	$j_A/A = \rho_A(U_A - U)$
Volume average velocity	$J_A^v/A = C_A(U_A - U^v)$	$j_A^v/A = \rho_A(U_A - U^v)$

Notation. Fluxes are likewise defined on a mass or molar or volume basis, with the choice of stationary coordinates, coordinates relative to U, coordinates relative to U^*, or coordinates relative to U^v. The notation in the literature unfortunately differs in practically every article or book. This text will adopt notation similar to that in Bird, Stewart, and Lightfoot [B3],[2] namely that N_A/A and n_A/A are with respect to fixed coordinates and J_A/A and j_A/A are with respect to mass, molar, or volume velocities. The quantities J_A and j_A are superscripted to indicate the frame of reference, as shown in Table 5.8. No superscript refers to mass velocity (in order to be consistent with the heat and mass transfer equations), while the superscripts $*$ and v refer to molar and volume velocity, respectively.

Table 5.8 summarizes the various fluxes. For example, for component A, the mass and molar fluxes relative to stationary coordinates have been discussed previously:

$$\text{Molar flux:} \quad N_A/A = C_A U_A \qquad (5.20)$$

$$\text{Mass flux:} \quad n_A/A = \rho_A U_A \qquad (5.21)$$

The mass and molar fluxes relative to the mass average velocity U are

$$\text{Molar flux:} \quad J_A/A = C_A(U_A - U) \qquad (5.28)$$

$$\text{Mass flux:} \quad j_A/A = \rho_A(U_A - U) \qquad (5.29)$$

where J and j are relative to moving coordinates (here, the mass average velocity) and N and n are relative to stationary coordinates.

Of the eight fluxes, N_A/A is probably the most useful in design because process equipment design is primarily concerned with the size of equipment. In this regard, N_A/A must always be determined. Other fluxes are useful in

---

[2] In Bird, Stewart, and Lightfoot [B3], and most other texts, the area is not explicitly noted; in other words, the molar flux is called N_A, J_A^*, J_A^v, or J_A and not N_A/A, J_A^*/A, J_A^v/A, or J_A/A as done here. The units for the flux are moles (or mass) per unit time per unit area regardless of the symbol or symbols used. The motivation for including the area in this text lies in clarity of presentation for those being exposed to mass transfer for the first time, and an emphasis that in equations such as Eq. (5.11), and in examples such as Example 4.4, the area may vary.

determining diffusion coefficients and in other applications [H1, T3]. The relationships among the fluxes are detailed elsewhere [B3, C2, H1].

Example 5.9 illustrates the numerical difference among three average velocities and shows how, since the molar average velocity differs from the volume average velocity, it is possible for mass diffusion to cause a bulk flow.

Example 5.9. In Fig. 5.7 is a cubic volume which is 1 cm on each side and is being convected at $1 \, \text{cm s}^{-1}$ in the z direction. In the volume at steady-state are 2 mol of A (molecular weight 2), 3 mol of B (molecular weight 3) and 4 mol of C (molecular weight 4). Superimposed on the flow is un-equimolar counter diffusion. Molecules of A diffuse in the +z direction at a rate of $2 \, \text{mol s}^{-1}$; molecules of B diffuses in the opposite direction at a rate of $1 \, \text{mol s}^{-1}$. Find U_z and U_z^*.

Answer. In this problem, the z subscript will be dropped for simplicity. First, from the problem statement the volume velocity or bulk velocity is given as $1 \, \text{cm s}^{-1}$; also, there must be nine moles total in the $1 \, \text{cm}^3$ volume. On a mass basis, moles times molecular weight yields grams:

$$(2 \, \text{mol of A})(2) = 4 \, \text{g of A}$$
$$(3 \, \text{mol of B})(3) = 9 \, \text{g of B}$$
$$\underline{(4 \, \text{mol of C})(4) = 16 \, \text{g of C}}$$
$$\text{Total} = 29 \, \text{g cm}^{-3}$$

At steady-state there is no accumulation. Across any face perpendicular to the flow direction, the total flux of each component equals the diffusion flux plus the convection flux [from Eq. (3.15)]. For each component of the mixture:

$$N_A/A = 2 \, \text{mol cm}^{-2} \, \text{s}^{-1} \text{ diffusing} + 2 \, \text{mol cm}^{-2} \, \text{s}^{-1} \text{ convected} = 4 \, \text{mol cm}^{-2} \, \text{s}^{-1} \quad \text{(i)}$$

$$N_B/A = -1 \, \text{mol cm}^{-2} \, \text{s}^{-1} \text{ diffusing} + 3 \, \text{mol cm}^{-2} \, \text{s}^{-1} \text{ convected} = 2 \, \text{mol cm}^{-2} \, \text{s}^{-1} \quad \text{(ii)}$$

$$N_C/A = 0 \, \text{mol cm}^{-2} \, \text{s}^{-1} \text{ diffusing} + 4 \, \text{mol cm}^{-2} \, \text{s}^{-1} \text{ convected} = 4 \, \text{mol cm}^{-2} \, \text{s}^{-1} \quad \text{(iii)}$$

The total flux is found from the sum of these:

$$N_T/A = N_A/A + N_B/A + N_C/A = 10 \, \text{mol cm}^{-2} \, \text{s}^{-1} \quad \text{(iv)}$$

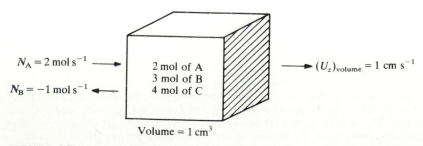

$N_A = 2 \, \text{mol s}^{-1}$ 2 mol of A $(U_z)_{\text{volume}} = 1 \, \text{cm s}^{-1}$
3 mol of B
$N_B = -1 \, \text{mol s}^{-1}$ 4 mol of C

Volume = $1 \, \text{cm}^3$

FIGURE 5.7
Convected volume for Examples 5.9 and 5.10.

On a mass basis, these correspond to

$$n_A/A = 4\,\text{g cm}^{-2}\,\text{s}^{-1} \text{ diffusing} + 4\,\text{g cm}^{-2}\,\text{s}^{-1} \text{ convected} = 8\,\text{g cm}^{-2}\,\text{s}^{-1} \qquad \text{(v)}$$

$$n_B/A = -3\,\text{g cm}^{-2}\,\text{s}^{-1} \text{ diffusing} + 9\,\text{g cm}^{-2}\,\text{s}^{-1} \text{ convected} = 6\,\text{g cm}^{-2}\,\text{s}^{-1} \qquad \text{(vi)}$$

$$n_C/A = 0\,\text{g cm}^{-2}\,\text{s}^{-1} \text{ diffusing} + 16\,\text{g cm}^{-2}\,\text{s}^{-1} \text{ convected} = 16\,\text{g cm}^{-2}\,\text{s}^{-1} \qquad \text{(vii)}$$

The total mass flux is the sum of these:

$$n_T/A = n_A/A + n_B/A + n_C/A = 30\,\text{g cm}^{-2}\,\text{s}^{-1} \qquad \text{(viii)}$$

Concentrations are expressed on a molar basis:

$$C_A = 2/1 = 2\,\text{mol cm}^{-3} \qquad \text{(ix)}$$

$$C_B = 3/1 = 3\,\text{mol cm}^{-3} \qquad \text{(x)}$$

$$C_C = 4/1 = 4\,\text{mol cm}^{-3} \qquad \text{(xi)}$$

$$C_T = \sum_i C_i = C_A + C_B + C_C = 9\,\text{mol cm}^{-3} \qquad \text{(xii)}$$

Densities are on a mass basis:

$$\rho_A = (2)(2)/1 = 4\,\text{g cm}^{-3} \qquad \text{(xiii)}$$

$$\rho_B = (3)(3)/1 = 9\,\text{g cm}^{-3} \qquad \text{(xiv)}$$

$$\rho_C = (4)(4)/1 = 16\,\text{g cm}^{-3} \qquad \text{(xv)}$$

$$\rho = \sum_i \rho_i = \rho_A + \rho_B + \rho_C = 29\,\text{g cm}^{-3} \qquad \text{(xvi)}$$

The species velocity is found from Eq. (5.20):

$$U_A = (N_A/A)/C_A = 4/2 = 2\,\text{cm s}^{-1} \qquad \text{(xvii)}$$

$$U_B = 2/3 = 2/3\,\text{cm s}^{-1} \qquad \text{(xviii)}$$

$$U_C = 4/4 = 1\,\text{cm s}^{-1} \qquad \text{(xix)}$$

Exactly the same result is obtained from Eq. (5.21):

$$U_A = (n_A/A)/\rho_A = 8/4 = 2\,\text{cm s}^{-1} \qquad \text{(xx)}$$

$$U_B = (n_B/A)/\rho_B = 6/9 = 2/3\,\text{cm s}^{-1} \qquad \text{(xxi)}$$

$$U_C = (n_C/A)/\rho_C = 16/16 = 1\,\text{cm s}^{-1} \qquad \text{(xxii)}$$

The species velocity of the nondiffusing species C is $1\,\text{cm s}^{-1}$, i.e., exactly the same as the given volume velocity, U_z^v. The nondiffusing material is carried with the volume.

The mass average velocity follows from the z component of Eq. (3.22):

$$U_z = \frac{\sum_i \rho_i U_i}{\sum_i \rho_i} = \frac{(4)(2) + (9)(2/3) + (16)(1)}{4 + 9 + 16} = 30/29\,\text{cm s}^{-1}$$

$$= 1.034\,\text{cm s}^{-1} \qquad \text{(xxiii)}$$

The same result can be obtained from Eq. (5.19) by using Eqs. (viii) and (xvi):

$$U_z = \frac{(n_T/A)_x}{\rho} = 30/29 = 1.034\,\text{cm s}^{-1} \qquad \text{(xxiv)}$$

The molar average velocity follows from the z component of Eq. (3.23):

$$U_z^* = \frac{\Sigma_i (C_i U_i)}{\Sigma_i C_i} = \frac{(2)(2) + (3)(2/3) + (4)(1)}{9} = 10/9 \text{ cm s}^{-1}$$

$$= 1.11 \text{ cm s}^{-1} \qquad \text{(xxv)}$$

Again, the same result can be obtained from Eq. (5.23):

$$U_z^* = \frac{N_T/A}{C_T} = 10/9 = 1.11 \text{ cm s}^{-1} \qquad \text{(xxvi)}$$

For this example, both U_z^* and U_z are slightly greater than the volume velocity of 1 cm s^{-1}, because there is a net molar and mass diffusion in the positive direction. Had the net diffusion been negative, then U_z^* and U_z would have been less than U_z^v. Clearly, for equimolar counter diffusion, U_z^* would be the same as U_z^v and for equimass counter diffusion, U_z would equal U_z^v. Finally, since the three velocities differ, it is entirely possible for mass diffusion to induce a net volume velocity.

5.3.2   Total Flux and Fick's Law

So far in Section 5.3, the total mass flux of species A (i.e., any of the eight quantities in Table 5.8) has been shown to be the sum of the molecular diffusion flux plus the convective diffusion flux [cf. Eq. (3.15)]. As a result, the experimental techniques to measure the diffusion coefficient D are usually designed so that the total flux due to convection is zero. In Chapter 2, Fick's law was introduced as

$$(J_A/A)_x = -D(\partial C_A/\partial x) \qquad (2.4)$$

In actuality, this equation is restricted to the diffusion of species A across a plane of no net volume flow.

Let us further consider this equation in the z direction, because it will be desirable to introduce x_A and x_B as mole fractions:

$$x_A = C_A/C_T \qquad (5.30)$$

$$x_B = C_B/C_T = 1 - x_A \qquad (5.31)$$

$$(J_A/A)_z = -D(\partial C_A/\partial z). \qquad (5.32)$$

where C_T is the total concentration of all species. Equation (5.32) is Fick's law for species A in the z direction, again restricted to a plane of no net volume flow.

The total molar flux of species A in the z direction is

$$(N_A/A)_z = (J_A/A)_{z,m} + (N_A/A)_{z,c} \qquad (5.33)$$

Recall that the notation N_A/A is with respect to fixed axes; therefore, all concentrations must be measured with respect to fixed axes. To measure D experimentally, it is necessary to design an experiment in which the convective flux $(N_A/A)_{z,c}$ is zero. Then the total flux $(N_A/A)_z$ reduces to the molecular flux $(J_A/A)_{z,m}$, which contains the diffusion coefficient.

TABLE 5.9
Fick's law for binary systems ($\nabla p = 0 = \nabla T$)

Molar flux	Mass flux
$J_A^v/A = -D\nabla C_A$	$j_A^v/A = -D\nabla\rho_A$
$J_A^*/A = -C_T D\nabla x_A$	$j_A^*/A = -\rho D\nabla w_A$
$J_A^*/A = -\left(\dfrac{\rho^2}{C_T M_A M_B}\right)D\nabla w_A$	$j_A^*/A = -\left(\dfrac{C_T^2 M_A M_B}{\rho}\right)D\nabla x_A$
$N_A/A = -C_T D\nabla x_A + x_A(N_A/A + N_B/A)$	$n_A/A = -\rho D\nabla w_A + w_T(n_A/A + n_B/A)$

Note: For constant pressure, $\nabla p = 0$; for constant temperature, $\nabla T = 0$.

Fick's law. A complication to Fick's law arises because it is possible and often desirable to use driving forces other than concentration in Eq. (5.32); these driving forces include the mole fraction x_A or y_A, the mass fraction w_A, and the volume fraction, although for chemical engineers the mole fraction x_A or y_A is by far the most useful. Each driving force can gives rise to a modification of Fick's law. At this point, it is possible to introduce a different diffusion coefficient, each with its own frame of reference and units, for each driving force. A better approach is to keep the units of the diffusion coefficient as area per unit time and to use flux expressions with consistent diffusion coefficients in the most convenient frame of reference. Table 5.9 summarizes the forms of Fick's law for binary systems. The various fluxes were defined earlier in Table 5.8; note that J/A and N/A refer to molar fluxes, whereas j/A and n/A refer to mass fluxes. Cross-definitions, such as the mass flux with respect to the molar average velocity, are not used in this text; accordingly, the notation is simplified so as to identify readily which flux is being represented: J_A^v/A with respect to volume average velocity, J_A^*/A with respect to molar average velocity, and J_A/A with respect to mass average velocity. It is important to emphasize that D is identical in each equation in Table 5.9. Note the restriction of constant temperature and pressure for each relation in Table 5.9; in practice, there is always a small temperature or pressure gradient, but this is neglected. A complete discussion of this table follows.

Total flux. The total flux is the diffusion contribution plus the convection contribution [cf. Eq. (5.33)], as well as the sum of the individual fluxes; for a binary system, the total flux is

$$N_T/A = N_A/A + N_B/A \tag{5.34}$$

where N_T/A is the total mass flux vector, N_A/A is given by Eq. (5.10), and N_B/A is of similar form.

To find the total molar flux in terms of mole fraction, the derivation begins with the equation for J_A^*/A from Table 5.8:

$$J_A^*/A = C_A(U_A - U^*) \tag{5.35}$$

Using Eq. (5.20) to replace $C_A U_A$ and Eq. (3.23) as the definition of U^*, the above equation becomes

$$N_A/A = J_A^*/A + C_A U^* = J_A^*/A + (C_A/C_T)(C_A U_A + C_B U_B) \qquad (5.36)$$

Using Eq. (5.20) again, plus the corresponding equation for species B and the definition of mole fraction, Eq. (5.36) becomes

$$N_A/A = J_A^*/A + x_A(N_A/A + N_B/A) \qquad (5.37)$$

where

$$J_A^*/A = -C_T D \nabla x_A \qquad (5.38)$$

In one dimension, these equations are

$$(N_A/A)_z = -C_T D(\partial x_A/\partial z) + x_A[(N_A/A)_z + (N_B/A)_z] \qquad (5.39)$$

$$\underset{\substack{\text{TOTAL} \\ \text{FLUX}}}{} \qquad \underset{\substack{\text{DIFFUSIONAL} \\ \text{FLUX}}}{} \qquad \underset{\substack{\text{CONVECTIVE} \\ \text{FLUX}}}{}$$

$$J_{A,z}^*/A = -C_T D(\partial x_A/\partial z) \qquad (\nabla p = 0 = \nabla T) \qquad (5.40)$$

Equation (5.39) is extremely useful, and therefore is included in vector form in Table 5.9. Note the simplicity of the convective flux term; it states in mathematical terms that the convective flux of species A is the total flux of all molecules times the mole fraction of A. The principal assumptions in Eq. (5.39) are those of steady-state, constant temperature, constant pressure, and a binary mixture.

A similar derivation leads to an equivalent expression in terms of the concentration gradient and the convection (in terms of the product of species concentration and flux):

$$(N_A/A)_z = -D(\partial C_A/\partial z) + C_A[\bar{V}_A(N_A/A)_z + \bar{V}_B(N_B/A)_z] \qquad (5.41)$$

where the convective flux of species A is the last term in the above equation:

$$(N_A/A)_{z,c} = C_A[\bar{V}_A(N_A/A)_z + \bar{V}_B(N_B/A)_z] \qquad (5.42)$$

Fick's law was originally proposed as Eq. (2.4). A comparison of Eqs. (2.4) and (5.41) shows that the original Fick's law was valid only for the case of fixed volume, i.e., zero convective flux with respect to the volume average velocity. Note also that Eq. (2.4) is valid only for $\nabla p = 0 = \nabla T$.

Equations (5.37) through (5.40) are based on the molar average velocity and are often the most convenient to use. Since the diffusion coefficient D in all equations presented thus far is identical to those in Table 5.9, the diffusion coefficient can be determined using Eq. (2.4) in experiments where the convective flux term in Eq. (5.41) is zero. Note that for a binary system [R1]:

$$(J_A^v/A)\bar{V}_A + (J_B^v/A)\bar{V}_B = 0 \qquad (5.43)$$

Also, it can be shown that

$$J_A^v/A = \frac{\bar{V}_B}{V}(J_A^*/A) \qquad \text{and} \qquad J_B^v/A = \frac{\bar{V}_A}{V}(J_B^*/A) \qquad (5.44)$$

Note that for ideal gases, the partial and molar volumes are identical, and Eq. (5.44) shows that the flux with respect to the volume average velocity equals the flux with respect to the molar average velocity. Other relationships between the fluxes in Tables 5.8 and 5.9 are available [B3, C2, H1]. These are often more confusing than helpful, however; the reader should convert any given problem into concentration or mole fraction driving forces and use the fluxes given previously.

Example 5.10. Calculate the fluxes for the problem of Example 5.9.

Answer. The stationary fluxes were found in Example 5.9 in order to find the species velocities:

$$n_A/A = 8 \text{ g cm}^{-2}\text{s}^{-1} \tag{i}$$

$$n_B/A = 6 \text{ g cm}^{-2}\text{s}^{-1} \tag{ii}$$

$$n_C/A = 16 \text{ g cm}^{-2}\text{s}^{-1} \tag{iii}$$

$$N_A/A = 4 \text{ mol cm}^{-2}\text{s}^{-1} \tag{iv}$$

$$N_B/A = 2 \text{ mol cm}^{-2}\text{s}^{-1} \tag{v}$$

$$N_C/A = 4 \text{ mol cm}^{-2}\text{s}^{-1} \tag{vi}$$

The fluxes relative to the mass average velocity are found by substituting into Eq. (5.28) and Eq. (5.29):

$$J_A/A = C_A(U_A - U) \tag{5.28}$$

$$J_A/A = (2)(2 - 30/29) = 1.9310 \text{ mol cm}^{-2}\text{s}^{-1} \tag{vii}$$

$$J_B/A = (3)(2/3 - 30/29) = -1.1034 \text{ mol cm}^{-2}\text{s}^{-1} \tag{viii}$$

$$J_C/A = (4)(1 - 30/29) = -0.1379 \text{ mol cm}^{-2}\text{s}^{-1} \tag{ix}$$

$$j_A/A = \rho_A(U_A - U) \tag{5.29}$$

$$j_A/A = (4)(2 - 30/29) = 3.8621 \text{ g cm}^{-2}\text{s}^{-1} \tag{x}$$

$$j_B/A = (9)(2/3 - 30/29) = -3.3103 \text{ g cm}^{-2}\text{s}^{-1} \tag{xi}$$

$$j_C/A = (16)(1 - 30/29) = -0.5517 \text{ g cm}^{-2}\text{s}^{-1} \tag{xii}$$

The fluxes relative to the molar average velocity are found from the molar average equations in Table 5.8:

$$J_A^*/A = C_A(U_A - U^*) \tag{5.35}$$

$$J_A^*/A = (2)(2 - 10/9) = 1.7778 \text{ mol cm}^{-2}\text{s}^{-1} \tag{xiii}$$

$$J_B^*/A = (3)(2/3 - 10/9) = -1.3333 \text{ mol cm}^{-2}\text{s}^{-1} \tag{xiv}$$

$$J_C^*/A = (4)(1 - 10/9) = -0.4444 \text{ mol cm}^{-2}\text{s}^{-1} \tag{xv}$$

$$j_A^*/A = \rho_A(U_A - U^*) \tag{xvi}$$

$$j_A^*/A = (4)(2 - 10/9) = 3.5556 \text{ g cm}^{-2}\text{s}^{-1} \tag{xvii}$$

$$j_B^*/A = (9)(2/3 - 10/9) = -4.0000 \text{ g cm}^{-2}\text{s}^{-1} \tag{xviii}$$

$$j_C^*/A = (16)(1 - 10/9) = -1.7778 \text{ g cm}^{-2}\text{s}^{-1} \tag{xix}$$

The fluxes relative to the volume average velocity are found from the volume average equations in Table 5.8:

$$J_A^v/A = C_A(U_A - U^v) \tag{xx}$$

$$J_A^v/A = (2)(2-1) = 2 \text{ mol cm}^{-2} \text{ s}^{-1} \tag{xxi}$$

$$J_B^v/A = (3)(2/3-1) = -1 \text{ mol cm}^{-2} \text{ s}^{-1} \tag{xxii}$$

$$J_C^v/A = (4)(1-1) = 0 \tag{xxiii}$$

$$j_A^v/A = \rho_A(U_A - U^v) \tag{xxiv}$$

$$j_A^v/A = (4)(2-1) = 4 \text{ g cm}^{-2} \text{ s}^{-1} \tag{xxv}$$

$$j_B^v/A = (9)(2/3-1) = -3 \text{ g cm}^{-2} \text{ s}^{-1} \tag{xxvi}$$

$$j_C^v/A = (16)(1-1) = 0 \tag{xxvii}$$

Note that the flux J_C^v/A is zero because species C is nondiffusing. Likewise, the fluxes J_A^v/A and J_B^v/A are equal to the values given in the problem statement of Example 5.9; the rates of molecular diffusion were with respect to the reference volume.

5.3.3 Binary Mass Diffusion in Gases

Mass diffusion in a gas due to the presence of a concentration gradient can be separated into three categories: equimolar counter diffusion, diffusion through a stagnant film, and unequimolar counter diffusion. In this section, each will be considered in turn, after the basic equations are presented. Equation (3.67) or Eq. (5.9) applies to all the aforementioned cases:

$$\partial C_A/\partial t + (U^* \cdot \nabla)C_A = \dot{C}_{A,G} + (\nabla \cdot D\nabla C_A) - (C_A)(\nabla \cdot U^*) \tag{5.9}$$

Discussion of Eq. (5.9) will proceed with the following conditions:

1. Steady-state: $\partial C_A/\partial t = 0$.
2. No generation: $\dot{C}_{A,G} = 0$.
3. Binary mixture.
4. Constant diffusion coefficient: $D = D_{AB} = D_{BA}$. This condition is true for ideal gases and other fluids under certain frames of reference; also, $\partial D/\partial x = \partial D/\partial y = \partial D/\partial z = 0$.
5. Constant total concentration C_T; this condition, together with condition (2), indicates that $(\nabla \cdot U^*) = 0$ from Eq. (3.76) (also true for ideal gases and a good approximation for real gases).
6. No pumping or external force field present to generate convection by momentum transfer mechanisms.
7. Constant temperature and pressure.

Under these restrictions, Eq. (5.9) simplifies to

$$(U^* \cdot \nabla)C_A = D(\nabla^2 C_A) \tag{5.45}$$

If the problem is further restricted to a one-dimensional case (the z direction), Eq. (5.45) reduces to

$$U_z^* \frac{\partial C_A}{\partial z} = D \frac{\partial^2 C_A}{\partial z^2} \tag{5.46}$$

In this equation, ordinary differentials may also be used since variation is only with the z direction. Partial derivatives have been retained, however, to emphasize that the mass transfer flux N_A/A and the concentration gradient are vectors or vector components. This equation is consistent with the previous development. Using the same procedure introduced earlier when Eq. (5.35) was transformed into Eq. (5.39), Eq. (5.46) becomes

$$\frac{(N_A/A)_z + (N_B/A)_z}{C_T} \frac{\partial C_A}{\partial z} = D \frac{\partial^2 C_A}{\partial z^2} \tag{5.47}$$

This equation can be integrated once to yield

$$\frac{C_A}{C_T}[(N_A/A)_z + (N_B/A)_z] = D \frac{\partial C_A}{\partial z} + C_1 \tag{5.48}$$

A comparison of Eqs. (5.39) and (5.48) indicates that the constant of integration C_1 must equal the total flux of species A. The derivative $\partial C_A/\partial z$ for constant total concentration is

$$\frac{\partial C_A}{\partial z} = \frac{\partial}{\partial z}(y_A C_T) = C_T \frac{\partial y_A}{\partial z} \tag{5.49}$$

where the mole fractions in the gas phase y_A and y_B are defined as

$$y_A = C_A/C_T = \bar{p}_A/p \tag{5.50}$$

$$y_B = C_B/C_T = \bar{p}_B/p = 1 - y_A \tag{5.51}$$

From either Eq. (5.39) or a combination of Eqs. (5.48) and (5.49), the final equation for diffusion in the gas phase is

$$(N_A/A)_z = -C_T D \frac{\partial y_A}{\partial z} + y_A[(N_A/A)_z + (N_B/A)_z] \tag{5.52}$$

Equation (5.52) will be solved for three cases: equimolar counter diffusion, diffusion through a stagnant film, and unequimolar counter diffusion.

Equimolar counter diffusion. In Chapter 2, equimolar counter diffusion was defined as

$$N_A = -N_B \tag{2.23}$$

Consequently, for equimolar counter diffusion the total bulk flow N_T equals zero, and Eq.(5.52) reduces to

$$(N_A/A)_z = -C_T D \frac{\partial y_A}{\partial z} \tag{5.53}$$

Equation (5.53) can be integrated between locations 1 and 2 (for constant area):

$$(N_A/A)_z = -C_T D \frac{\Delta y_A}{\Delta z} = -C_T D \left(\frac{y_{A,2} - y_{A,1}}{z_2 - z_1} \right) \tag{5.54}$$

where $y_{A,1}$ is the mole fraction of A at location z_1 and $y_{A,2}$ is the mole fraction of A at location z_2. Similarly, for component B in equimolar counter diffusion:

$$(N_B/A)_z = -C_T D \frac{\Delta y_B}{\Delta z} = -C_T D \frac{y_{B,2} - y_{B,1}}{z_2 - z_1} \tag{5.55}$$

Since y_A is $1 - y_B$, for equimolar counter diffusion the concentration gradients are equal in magnitude and opposite in sign:

$$\frac{\Delta y_A}{\Delta z} = -\frac{\Delta y_B}{\Delta z} = \frac{dy_A}{dz} = -\frac{dy_B}{dz} \tag{5.56}$$

This equation can also be proved from Eq. (2.24) and Eqs. (5.54) and (5.55).

In Chapter 2, Example 2.2 illustrated an application of Eq. (5.54). If the area is not constant, then the area variation must be accounted for. In Chapter 4, Example 4.4 illustrated the additional complexity introduced in variable-area problems. Equation (5.54) can be easily expressed in terms of partial pressures, as was done for the solution in both Examples 2.8 and 4.4. Assuming an ideal gas, the total concentration is

$$C_T = \frac{p}{RT} \tag{5.57}$$

Using Eqs. (5.50) and (5.57), Eq. (5.54) becomes

$$(N_A/A)_z = -\frac{D}{RT} \frac{\Delta \bar{p}_A}{\Delta z} = -\frac{D}{RT} \frac{\bar{p}_{A,2} - \bar{p}_{A,1}}{z_2 - z_1} \tag{5.58}$$

In equimolar counter diffusion involving two components, concentration (or partial pressure) varies linearly with distance, as the preceding equations indicate. Figure 5.8 shows the profile of partial pressure versus distance for the equimolar case. Example 5.9 demonstrates once again how to apply the preceding equations. Equimolar counter diffusion is a commonly occurring mass transfer process in gases. As an example, it can often be assumed that equimolar counter diffusion occurs in distillation operations. Although there is no net transfer of number of moles [cf. Eq. (2.23)] in equimolar counter

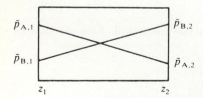

FIGURE 5.8
Pressure–distance profile in equimolar counter diffusion.

diffusion, there will be a net transfer of mass if the molecular weight of A differs from the molecular weight of B.

Diffusion through a stagnant film. It is possible for one component to diffuse through other molecules that are not diffusing. If component B is nondiffusing and the six assumptions listed before Eq. (5.45) apply, then N_B is zero by definition:

$$N_B = 0 \tag{5.59}$$

The equation above constitutes the definition of diffusion through a stagnant film. Note that a truly stagnant film does not really exist, owing to small pressure and temperature gradients, etc.

Equation (5.52) for the transfer of species A by all mechanisms can be simplified with the assistance of Eq. (5.59):

$$(N_A/A)_z = -C_T D(\partial y_A/\partial z) + y_A(N_A/A)_z \tag{5.60}$$

This equation rearranges to

$$(N_A/A)_z = \frac{-C_T D}{1 - y_A} \frac{\partial y_A}{\partial z} \tag{5.61}$$

Equation (5.61) is similar to Fick's law for equimolar counter diffusion [Eq. (5.53)], but with the additional factor $1/(1 - y_A)$, which must always be greater than one for any finite y_A. Thus, there is an enhancement of the transfer of component A because of the bulk flow that is caused by the motion of A and B. This induced velocity in the direction of diffusion carries with it component A, which then adds to that transferred by the diffusion process.

A simple example of diffusion through a stagnant film occurs when a mixture of CO_2 and N_2 is passed across the surface of a sodium hydroxide solution. Carbon dioxide is very soluble in aqueous sodium hydroxide and is absorbed, whereas the nitrogen is not absorbed appreciably. Thus, CO_2 diffuses from the bulk stream through a thin, almost stagnant layer to the liquid surface, and N_2 does not diffuse. The N_2 is the stagnant component.

Equation (5.61) can be integrated for constant area and diffusion coefficient by separation of variables. The boundary conditions are the same as used in obtaining Eq. (5.54). For diffusion of species A through a stagnant film, the result is

$$(N_A/A)_z = \frac{C_T D}{z_2 - z_1} \ln \frac{1 - y_{A,2}}{1 - y_{A,1}} = \frac{C_T D}{z_2 - z_1} \ln \frac{y_{B,2}}{y_{B,1}} \tag{5.62}$$

where $y_{A,1}$ and $y_{A,2}$ are the mole fractions at locations x_1 and x_2, respectively. Equation (5.62) can also be expressed in terms of partial pressure:

$$(N_A/A)_z = \frac{Dp}{RT(z_2 - z_1)} \ln \frac{p - \bar{p}_{A,2}}{p - \bar{p}_{A,1}} = \frac{Dp}{RT(z_2 - z_1)} \ln \left(\frac{\bar{p}_{B,2}}{\bar{p}_{B,1}}\right) \tag{5.63}$$

where p is the total pressure. The partial pressure–distance profile is nonlinear

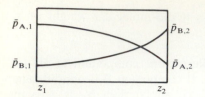

FIGURE 5.9
Pressure–distance profile in diffusion through a stagnant film of species B.

for the $(N_B = 0)$ case, as shown in Fig. 5.9. Note that in Fig. 5.9 the nonlinearity is exaggerated, compared to typical curves encountered in practical problems; in fact, in practical problems a straight line is often a reasonable approximation. It must be emphasized that there is a net bulk flow of moles (and mass) from the region of high concentration of A to the region of low concentration. This transfer is induced by the diffusion of component A. Diffusion though a stagnant film is important in many industrial operations, including gas absorption, leaching, and extraction.

Mass diffusion through a stagnant film may be compared to the example of the moving sidewalk. The velocity of the moving sidewalk is the convection velocity. A person (species B) walking in the opposite direction at the same speed is stationary with respect to fixed coordinates (i.e., N_B is zero). A second person (species A) walking in the same direction as the moving sidewalk moves at higher velocity than the sidewalk. The net transfer of A (i.e., N_A) is enhanced.

Example 5.11. A tube 1 cm in inside diameter that is 20 cm long is filled with CO_2 and H_2 at 2 atm total pressure at 0°C. The diffusion coefficient of the CO_2–H_2 system under these conditions is $0.275 \text{ cm}^2 \text{ s}^{-1}$. If the partial pressure of CO_2 is 1.5 atm at one end and 0.5 atm at the other end, find the rate of diffusion for (a) steady-state equimolar counter diffusion and (b) steady-state diffusion of CO_2 through stagnant H_2.

Answer. For the equimolar case $(N_A/A = -N_B/A)$, Fick's law in the form of Eq. (5.53) applies. The most convenient equations for gaseous systems involve partial pressure terms:

$$(N_A/A)_z = -\frac{D}{RT}\frac{\Delta \bar{p}_A}{\Delta z} = -\frac{D}{RT}\left(\frac{\bar{p}_{A,2} - \bar{p}_{A,1}}{z_2 - z_1}\right) \tag{5.58}$$

The conditions of the problem are:

$$T = 0°C = 273.15 \text{ K}$$

$$\bar{p}_{A,2} = 1.5 \text{ atm} \qquad \bar{p}_{A,1} = 0.5 \text{ atm}$$

$$z_2 = 20 \text{ cm} \qquad z_1 = 0 \text{ cm} \tag{i}$$

$$p = 2 \text{ atm}$$

$$A = \pi d^2/4 = (\pi)(1)^2/4 = 0.7854 \text{ cm}^2$$

From Table C.1:

$$R = 0.082\,057 \text{ atm m}^3 \text{ kmol}^{-1} \text{ K}^{-1} \tag{ii}$$

For part (a), substitution of these values into Eq. (5.58) yields

$$(N_A)_z = \frac{-(0.275)(1.5-0.5)(0.7854)}{(0.082\,057)(10^2)^3(273.15)(20)}\left(\frac{(\text{cm}^2\,\text{s}^{-1})(\text{atm})(\text{cm}^2)}{(\text{atm m}^3\,\text{kmol}^{-1}\,\text{K}^{-1})(\text{cm m}^{-1})^3(\text{K})(\text{cm})}\right)$$

$$= -4.82 \times 10^{-10}\,\text{kmol s}^{-1} \qquad\qquad\qquad\qquad\qquad\qquad (\text{iii})$$

Note that the negative sign indicates diffusion from point 2 to point 1.

Next, part (b) will be solved. For diffusion through a stagnant film, Eq. (5.63) applies:

$$(N_A/A)_z = \frac{Dp}{RT(z_2-z_1)}\ln\frac{p-\bar{p}_{A,2}}{p-\bar{p}_{A,1}} = \frac{Dp}{RT(z_2-z_1)}\ln\left(\frac{\bar{p}_{B,2}}{\bar{p}_{B,1}}\right) \qquad (5.63)$$

This equation is solved for N_A, and the answer is

$$(N_A)_z = -\frac{(0.275)(2)(0.7854)}{(0.082\,057)(10^2)^3(273.15)(20)}\ln\left(\frac{2.0-1.5}{2.0-0.5}\right)$$

$$\times\left(\frac{(\text{cm}^2\,\text{s}^{-1})(\text{atm})(\text{cm}^2)}{(\text{atm m}^3\,\text{kmol}^{-1}\,\text{K}^{-1})(\text{cm m}^{-1})^3(\text{K})(\text{cm})}\right)$$

$$= -9.637 \times 10^{-10}\ln(0.5/1.5) = -1.06 \times 10^{-9}\,\text{kmol s}^{-1} \qquad (\text{iv})$$

The induced velocity increases the net transport of A by the ratio of 10.6×10^{-10} to 4.82×10^{-10} or 2.2 times. This increase is equivalent to 120 percent.

Counter diffusion with non-zero fluxes. The most important diffusion problems are the equimolar and stagnant film cases; however, other situations occur for which the number of moles transferred in one direction are different from in the other and neither is zero. For the same general restrictions, Eq. (5.52) still applies, but the physical situation is different. For example, consider Fig. 5.10 in which a chemical reaction at the surface of a catalyst occurs. The catalyst accelerates the rate of reaction of A to B while remaining unchanged in any way. The reaction on the surface of the catalyst is

$$A \rightarrow 2B \qquad\qquad\qquad\qquad\qquad\qquad (5.64)$$

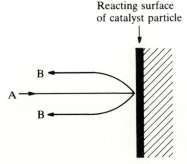

Reacting surface
of catalyst particle

Reaction on surface is A ⟶ 2B

FIGURE 5.10
Diffusion and chemical reaction.

In Fig. 5.10, molecules of A diffuse to the surface, but for each molecule A reaching the surface two molecules of B form and diffuse away from the surface. The diffusion rate of B is twice that of A, but in the negative direction. There are two moles of B leaving this surface for every mole of A arriving. Consequently, the following holds:

$$N_B = -2N_A \tag{5.65}$$

Equation (5.65) is substituted into the general steady-state, mass transfer equation, Eq. (5.52). The rate of transfer of A to the surface is

$$(N_A/A)_z = -C_T D \frac{\partial y_A}{\partial z} + y_A[(N_A/A)_z - 2(N_A/A)_z] \tag{5.66}$$

This equation, when solved for $(N_A/A)_z$, becomes

$$(N_A/A)_z = \frac{C_T D}{1 + y_A} \frac{\partial y_A}{\partial z} \tag{5.67}$$

Equation (5.67) can be integrated between points 1 and 2:

$$(N_A/A)_z = -\frac{C_T D}{z_2 - z_1} \ln \frac{1 + y_{A,2}}{1 + y_{A,1}} \tag{5.68}$$

Equation (5.68) implies the existence of a hypothetical "film" of thickness $(z_2 - z_1)$, through which diffusion occurs. This film does not exist in reality, but experience shows that modeling of real mass transfer processes is often successful with a similar approach. More details are given in Section 6.3.

Equations (5.67) and (5.68) can be compared with the stagnant diffusion case given by Eqs. (5.61) and (5.62). For the present case, the diffusion of component A is reduced because of the net induced flux counter to the diffusion of component A. The result will be valid only if the generation of B at the catalyst surface occurs so rapidly that two molecules of B leave the surface at essentially the same time A arrives. Under such conditions, the rate of reaction is said to be diffusion-controlled, and consideration of diffusion rates will be paramount in designing the reactor. The opposite case often occurs, namely, that the rate of reaction is slow compared to the rate of diffusion. Solution of such problems is beyond the scope of transport phenomena.

Example 5.12. Repeat Example 5.11, this time assuming that N_B is $0.75N_A$ in magnitude.

Answer. The basic equation for counter diffusion with non-zero fluxes is Eq. (5.52):

$$(N_A/A)_z = -C_T D \frac{\partial y_A}{\partial z} + y_A[(N_A/A)_z + (N_B/A)_z] \tag{5.52}$$

For the sake of generality, let N_B be expressed in terms of N_A as follows:

$$N_B = -kN_A \tag{i}$$

where $k = 1$ for equimolar counter diffusion, 0 for diffusion through a stagnant film, 2 for the example in Fig. 5.10, and 0.75 for this example. Upon substitution of Eq. (i) in Eq. (5.52), the answer is

$$(N_A/A)_z \, dz = -\frac{C_T D \, dy_A}{1 - y_A + ky_A} = -\frac{C_T D \, dy_A}{1 - y_A(1 - k)} \tag{ii}$$

where the partial derivatives are replaced by total derivatives because the molar flux is in the z direction only.

Equation (ii) can be expressed in terms of the partial pressure, using the definitions in Eqs. (5.50) and (5.57):

$$(N_A/A)_z \, dz = -\frac{(D/RT) \, d\bar{p}_A}{1 - (\bar{p}_A/p)(1 - k)} \tag{iii}$$

For the conditions of the problem as given:

$$T = 273.15 \text{ K}$$

$$\bar{p}_{A,2} = 1.5 \text{ atm} \qquad \bar{p}_{A,1} = 0.5 \text{ atm}$$

$$z_2 = 20 \text{ cm} \qquad z_1 = 0 \text{ cm}$$

$$p = 2 \text{ atm} \tag{iv}$$

$$A = \pi d^2/4 = (\pi)(1)^2/4 = 0.7854 \text{ cm}^2$$

$$R = 0.082057 \text{ atm m}^3 \text{ kmol}^{-1} \text{ K}^{-1}$$

Integration of Eq. (iii) with the above boundary conditions results in

$$(N_A/A)_z = -\frac{D}{RT(z_2 - z_1)} \ln \frac{1 - (\bar{p}_{A,2}/p)(1 - k)}{1 - (\bar{p}_{A,1}/p)(1 - k)} \tag{v}$$

Note that Eq. (v) is incorrect if k equals unity [see Eq. (5.54)]. If k is zero (diffusion through a stagnant film), then Eq. (v) reduces to Eq. (5.63). In this example, k equals 0.75, and the flux is

$$(N_A/A)_z = \frac{(0.275)(2)(0.7854)}{(0.082057)(10^2)^3(273.15)(20)} \ln \left(\frac{1.0 - (1.5/2.0)(1 - 0.75)}{1.0 - (0.5/2.0)(1 - 0.75)} \right)$$

$$= 9.636 \times 10^{-10} \ln 0.8667 = -1.38 \times 10^{-10} \text{ kmol s}^{-1} \tag{vi}$$

Note that this answer is larger than the rate for equimolar counter diffusion but smaller than the rate for diffusion through a stagnant film. Sometimes the rate for diffusion through a stagnant film can be considered as an "upper bound", if k lies between zero and one.

5.3.4 Binary Mass Diffusion in Liquids

Mass diffusion in liquids is important to many industrial separation processes such as distillation and extraction. Often, the largest resistance to overall mass transfer is in the liquid phase. In Chapter 2, it was pointed out that the diffusion coefficients in liquid systems are very low when compared to gas systems. For example, the diffusion coefficient for air diffusing in liquid water at 293.15 K has been reported as $2.5 \times 10^{-9} \text{ m}^2 \text{ s}^{-1}$, whereas the diffusion coefficient for the gas-phase air + water system at 313.15 K and 1 atm is

$2.88 \times 10^{-5} \, \text{m}^2 \, \text{s}^{-1}$ [S2]. Hence, the low rates of diffusion in the liquid phase make small effects, such as the volume change upon mixing, very important; the presence of a concentration gradient causes mass diffusion, but that rate may be equally dependent upon other factors.

Equations (5.39) and (5.40) are valid for liquid systems as written; however, in order to integrate Eq. (5.39) exactly, both D and C_T must be constant, and neither are. The total concentration varies in general because of the volume change just cited. This effect is often highly significant in view of the low rates of diffusion common in liquid systems.

It is possible to relate the diffusion coefficient in Eqs. (5.39) and (5.40) to the coefficient that can be experimentally measured with respect to a cell-fixed reference frame. Tyrrell and Harris [T3] show that the difference between the two coefficients depends on the absolute value of C_A, the concentration gradient $\partial C_A / \partial z$, and the quantity $\partial \bar{V}_A / \partial z$. Hence, for dilute solutions $(C_A \to 0)$, or for small concentration gradients, or for partial molar volume independent of concentration, the difference between diffusion coefficients is negligible. Otherwise, some complex corrections are required.

Diffusion through a stagnant film. Equation (5.39) can be integrated approximately by assuming some average value of D and C_T. Generally, the total concentration is calculated by the linear average between locations 1 and 2:

$$C_T \approx \frac{\rho_1/M_1 + \rho_2/M_2}{2} \tag{5.69}$$

where M is molecular weight. Since N_B equals zero, the integration yields an equation similar to that obtained for gases [cf. Eq. (5.62)]:

$$(N_A/A)_z = \frac{C_T D}{z_2 - z_1} \ln \frac{1 - x_{A,2}}{1 - x_{A,1}} = \frac{C_T D}{z_2 - z_1} \ln \left(\frac{x_{B,2}}{x_{B,1}} \right) \tag{5.70}$$

Un-equimolar counter diffusion. In the case of diffusion in gases, it was possible to obtain useful solutions for both equimolar and unequimolar counter diffusion. The equimolar counter diffusion case almost never occurs in liquid diffusion because of the concentration dependence of D and $\bar{V}_i$. The unequimolar case occurs, but any type of a solution similar to Eq. (5.68) or Eq. (v) in Example 5.12 is of doubtful value, since the product $C_T D$ varies.

5.3.5   Diffusion in Solids

This section provides a brief overview of diffusion in solids. A more complete treatment can be found elsewhere [B1, G1]. The most important chemical engineering problems where species diffuse in solids are those of unsteady-state (covered in Chapter 13).

Diffusion coefficients in solids are much less than those in gases and range from slightly less than those in liquids to very small, as indicated in Section

2.5.2. Diffusion in solids often occurs in conjunction with adsorption and chemisorption phenomena. Metallurgists have been interested in solid diffusion because of its importance in such problems as degassing of metals and graphite, carburization, nitriding and phosphorizing of steel, and desulfurization of steel [B1]. An example of diffusion coupled with adsorption is the sulfur–iron system. It has been suggested that sulfur diffuses in iron by an alternate dissociation and formation of sulfides, rather than by interpenetration or by place change.

There have been many studies of the interdiffusion of metals. For instance, it was known before 1900 that at 300°C gold diffuses more rapidly through lead than does sodium chloride through water at 18°C [R2]. Radioactive tracers are convenient in following interdiffusion in metals. Diffusion in polymers is another active research area [C1]. The presence of vapors or gases sometimes alters the internal structure and external dimensions of a polymer solid. Diffusion in polymers is of interest in the drying and dyeing of textiles, in the air or water permeability of paint films and packaging materials, and in the migration of plasticizers.

Diffusion in solids may be divided into two classes: structure-insensitive and structure-sensitive diffusion [T2]. Structure-insensitive diffusion refers to the case in which the solute is dissolved so as to form a homogeneous solution. An example is the interdiffusion of metals, where the solute is part of the solid structure. The copper–zinc system behaves in this manner, as does the lead–gold system. In contrast, structure-sensitive diffusion occurs in the case of liquids and gases flowing through the interstices and capillary passages in a solid; an example is the diffusive flow of fluids through sintered metal, such as that used in catalysts.

For structure-insensitive diffusion, the recommended equation for diffusion in solids is Fick's law in a fixed volume, which in the z direction is

$$(J_A/A)_z = -D \frac{\partial C_A}{\partial z} \tag{5.32}$$

where the bulk flow term included in Eq. (5.41) and similar equations is always neglected, even if bulk flow is present [G1]. In essence, any contribution to mass transport due to bulk flow is considered to be part of the diffusion coefficient. Integration of this equation between locations 1 and 2 is trivial (cf. Example 2.6). If diffusion occurs through a cylinder wall, then Fick's law is converted to transport in the r direction:

$$\frac{N_{A,r}}{2\pi r L} = -D \frac{\partial C_A}{\partial r} \tag{5.71}$$

where the area A is $(2\pi r L)$ and L is the length of the diffusion area. This equation is integrated with the result

$$N_A = \frac{2\pi D L}{\ln(r_2/r_1)} (C_{A,1} - C_{A,2}) \tag{5.72}$$

5.3.6 Diffusion Due to a Pressure Gradient

Structure-sensitive diffusion may occur in porous media, such as beds of granular solids, oil-bearing rock formations, and sintered metals. Diffusion occurs because of a pressure gradient, in contrast to Eq. (5.32). Thus, viscous flow may be present as a result of the pressure gradient, in addition to the diffusive flow. The relative importance of these separate mechanisms depends on the physical structure of the solid and the nature of the solute.

In porous media, transport of species A can be by molecular diffusion, induced flow, and/or by forced flow; it is not possible to separate the individual contributions and treat flow through porous media in the fundamental manner presented in this chapter. Normally, a lumped or combined empirical approach is required, as will be considered in Chapter 12. Here, a few brief comments are provided to put the subject in proper perspective.

Often, the resistance of porous media to the passage of fluids is given in terms of a permeability constant P', which is defined by

$$P' = \frac{Q/S}{-dp/dz} \tag{5.73}$$

where Q is the volume of fluid at standard conditions diffusing per unit time through the cross sectional area S under the pressure gradient $(-dp/dz)$. Equation (5.73) is also a form of the well-known Darcy's law for viscous flow through porous media [P1]. Whether viscous flow or diffusive flow is present, the permeability constant must be determined experimentally.

For the case of gas flowing through porous media, there are strong differences between diffusive flow and viscous flow that allow the mechanism of a particular experiment to be determined. The easiest is to measure the variation in P' with temperature. The variables in the laminar flow equations [cf. Eq. (4.76), the Hagen–Poiseuille law] are weak functions of temperature; thus, viscous flow shows only a slight temperature effect, while the diffusion coefficient is a strong function of temperature.

In fundamental studies of catalysis, diffusion in porous solids is very important; four types of diffusion will be discussed next: ordinary (molecular) diffusion, Knudsen diffusion, transition diffusion, and surface diffusion. Surface diffusion occurs when molecules are adsorbed on a solid surface and subsequently transported by diffusion from the region of high concentration to the region of low concentration. Ordinary diffusion is governed by Fick's law and the equations and principles presented earlier; it occurs when the mean-free-path of the molecules of the gas is small in comparison to the diameter of the pores. The mean-free-path is the average distance a molecule travels before it collides with a surface or with another molecule. From the kinetic theory of gases, the mean-free path-is

$$\lambda_A = 32 \frac{\mu_A}{p} \left(\frac{RT}{2\pi M_A} \right)^{1/2} \tag{5.74}$$

where λ_A is the mean-free-path (m), μ_A is viscosity ($kg\,m^{-1}\,s^{-1}$), p is total pressure (Pa), R is the gas constant (cf. Table C.1), T is in K, and M_A is the molecular weight of A.

Knudsen diffusion. The Knudsen flow regime [K2] occurs when the Knudsen number, N_{Kn}, is of the order of 100 or greater [G1]. The Knudsen number is

$$N_{Kn} = \frac{\lambda_A}{d_o} \qquad (5.75)$$

where d_o is the diameter of the tube or pore in a porous solid. The equation for Knudsen flow in a long capillary tube is [L2]

$$w_A = \frac{d_o^3}{6} \left(\frac{2\pi M_A}{RT}\right)^{1/2} \left(\frac{-\Delta \bar{p}_A}{L}\right) \qquad N_{Kn} > 10 \qquad (5.76)$$

where w_A is the mass flow rate ($kg\,s^{-1}$) and the term ($\Delta \bar{p}_A$) is the difference in the partial pressure of A in the length L. The assumptions for Eq. (5.76) are reviewed elsewhere [B1, K1, L1]. In the region ($10 \le N_{Kn} \le 100$), the error using Eq. (5.76) can be as great as 10 percent [G1]. Of course, Knudsen diffusion can occur in tubing if the pressure is very low. It is possible to have Knudsen diffusion with a single component if a means exists to create and maintain a difference in partial pressure. It is also possible to have Knudsen diffusion at constant total pressure, if a partial pressure difference exists.

In Knudsen diffusion, the mean-free-path of the molecule is of the order of the system size; the gas molecules collide with the walls, rather than with each other. Because the boundary is interacting with individual molecules, a colliding molecule may bounce off in any direction (i.e., at a random angle). In Knudsen diffusion, there are not enough molecules present for the temperature to be meaningful (although the solid has temperature), nor are there enough molecules to have any interactions between molecules, such as would be necessary to have viscous effects. In laminar flow of a gas (governed by the Hagen–Poiseuille law), the presence of the large number of molecules, all colliding with one another as well as colliding with the walls, results in viscous effects that completely negate Knudsen diffusion.

It is interesting to compare the Knudsen flow equation, Eq. (5.76), with the Hagen–Poiseuille equation, Eq. (4.76), which for the laminar flow of an ideal gas can be written as

$$w_A = \frac{\pi d_o^4}{128\mu} \frac{pM_A}{RT} \left(\frac{-\Delta p}{L}\right) \qquad N_{Kn} \le 10^{-2} \qquad (5.77)$$

The mass flow rate in laminar flow depends on d_o^4, whereas in Knudsen flow the dependence is d_o^3. Also, Knudsen diffusion is independent of the total pressure and viscosity, in contrast to Eq. (5.77).

A Knudsen diffusion coefficient D_{KA} can be defined by the following equation:

$$(N_A/A)_z = -D_{KA}\frac{dC_A}{dz} = -\frac{D_{KA}}{RT}\frac{d\bar{p}_A}{dz} = \frac{D_{KA}p}{RTL}(y_{A,1} - y_{A,2}) \tag{5.78}$$

where the Knudsen diffusion coefficient is

$$D_{KA} = 48.5d_o\left(\frac{T}{M_A}\right)^{1/2} \tag{5.79}$$

Equations (5.78) and (5.79) predict that if two species are diffusing in Knudsen flow the flux ratios will be inversely proportional to the square root of the molecular weight. This result is the same as predicted by the well-known Graham's law of diffusion [G2], first proposed in 1831 [M1]:

$$N_A/N_B = (M_B/M_A)^{1/2} \tag{5.80}$$

This equation applies to equal-pressure counter diffusion,[3] which is not usually of engineering interest; it can be shown that Eq. (5.80) also applies to Knudsen diffusion, as well as to transition diffusion and effusion of gases into a vacuum, although the mechanisms and governing equations of each of these are entirely different [D1, M1]. As a point of interest, equimolar counter diffusion of real gases does not take place at constant pressure. If the experiment begins at constant pressure, the presence of equimolar counter diffusion causes a small but measurable pressure gradient [M1]. Graham's law does not hold for equimolar counter diffusion. Diffusion through a stagnant film also does not take place at constant pressure.

Transition. As might be expected, in the transition region between Knudsen diffusion and Poiseuille flow, flow occurs by both mechanisms. Rothfeld [R3] showed that the transition region covers a 1000-fold range of Knudsen numbers. Geankoplis presents equations for the transition region [G1]:

$$\beta = 1 + \frac{(N_A/A)_z}{(N_B/A)_z} \tag{5.81}$$

$$(N_A/A)_z = \frac{Dp}{\beta RTL}\ln\frac{1 - \beta y_{A,2} + D/D_{KA}}{1 - \beta y_{A,1} + D/D_{KA}} \qquad 10^{-2} \le N_{Kn} \le 10 \tag{5.82}$$

In the region $10^{-2} \le N_{Kn} \le 10^{-1}$, the error using Eq. (5.82) is no greater than 10 percent [G1]. Note that these equations are not particularly useful, because the ratio of fluxes (related to β) must be known before Eq. (5.82) can be solved for the flux of A.

Example 5.13. A stainless-steel tubing is 1.6×10^{-3} m in inside diameter and 4 m long. One end is evacuated. Calculate the pressure in the other end in order for

---

[3] See Mason and Kronstadt [M1] for details.

the Knudsen number to be 10. The gas inside is of molecular weight 92, viscosity $6.5 \times 10^{-4}\,\mathrm{kg\,m^{-1}\,s^{-1}}$, and temperature 300 K.

Answer. Since the Knudsen number is given, Eq. (5.75) is solved for the mean-free-path:

$$\lambda_A = N_{Kn} d_o = (10)(1.6 \times 10^{-3}) = 1.6 \times 10^{-2}\,\mathrm{m} \tag{i}$$

Equation (5.74) is used to calculate the pressure from the mean-free-path:

$$\lambda_A = 32 \frac{\mu_A}{p} \left(\frac{RT}{2\pi M_A}\right)^{1/2} \tag{5.74}$$

$$p = (32)\left(\frac{6.5 \times 10^{-4}}{1.6 \times 10^{-2}}\right)\left(\frac{(8314)(300)}{(2\pi)(92)}\right)^{1/2}\left(\frac{\mathrm{kg\,m^{-1}\,s^{-2}}}{\mathrm{m}}\right)\left(\frac{(\mathrm{kg\,m^2\,s^{-2}\,kmol^{-1}\,K^{-1}})(K)}{\mathrm{kg\,kmol^{-1}}}\right)^{1/2}$$

$$\tag{ii}$$

$$= 85.39\,\mathrm{kg\,m^{-1}\,s^{-2}} = 85.39\,\mathrm{Pa} = \frac{85.39}{1.01325 \times 10^5}\left(\frac{\mathrm{Pa}}{\mathrm{Pa\,atm^{-1}}}\right) = 8.43 \times 10^{-4}\,\mathrm{atm}$$

$$\tag{iii}$$

where R is $8314\,\mathrm{kPa\,m^3\,kmol^{-1}\,K^{-1}}$ (or $\mathrm{kg\,m^2\,s^{-2}\,kmol^{-1}\,K^{-1}}$) in SI units (cf. Table C.1). The value of 10 for the Knudsen number is on the border between Knudsen diffusion and transition flow.

Molecular effusion. Effusion is the passage of free molecules through a small aperture in a thin plate into a vacuum. The mean-free-path of the gas in the pressurized compartment is small compared with the size of the compartment; in other words, gas–gas collisions are favored. However, the mean-free-path of the gas is large compared with the diameter of the hole in the plate; the thickness of the plate is small compared with the diameter of the hole. Effusive flow differs from Knudsen flow in that the length of the capillary is very short. The equation governing effusive flow is [L1]

$$w_A = \frac{\pi d_o^2}{4}(-\Delta p)\left(\frac{M_A}{2\pi RT}\right)^{1/2} \tag{5.83}$$

According to the kinetic theory and Eq. (5.83), molecules in effusive flow must pass through the hole at the same flow rate as their flow across a cross sectional area of equal size located anywhere else in the flow. Further, since the plate is very thin, there exists a very small chance of a molecular collision inside the hole.

Another experiment in effusion consists of two compartments of unequal pressure. In this case, molecules will pass through the hole in either direction. However, the net transfer will be from the high-pressure side to the low-pressure side. By analogy with Knudsen diffusion, there are three regions of flow through an aperture in a plate: effusive flow, orifice flow (see Section 10.4.1), and a transition region where both types are important. There also exists a transition from the case of an infinitely long capillary (Knudsen flow) to the case of the very thin plate (effusive flow); this has not been investigated extensively.

Both effusive flow and Knudsen flow might be used for separation of gaseous species of differing molecular weights, were it not for the fact that the low pressures and small diameters required for the proper range of Knudsen number would result in impractically low flow rates. However, of more interest is that in many industrial catalysts the diffusion mechanism is governed by both Knudsen and molecular (Fickian) diffusion (i.e., the transition region [R3, W1]). Also related are flows through porous plates, refractories, and sandstone [B1]. Finally, note that the equations of change, such as Eqs. (5.6) through (5.12) and those in Tables 5.4 and 5.5, do not apply to rarefied gases. These aforementioned equations assume a continuum, which is not justified when considering molecular collisions and the mean-free-path.

5.3.7 Diffusion with Three or More Components

Equations for diffusion in multicomponent (three or more) systems may be generalized from the treatment presented earlier, and are available elsewhere [H2, T3]. Solutions have been worked out for several cases of steady-state molecular diffusion in multicomponent systems. Unfortunately, there have been relatively few measurements of multicomponent diffusion coefficients. Also, there appears to be no reliable method of predicting these coefficients. In general, the diffusion coefficients in multicomponent systems are strongly concentration-dependent. As a result, specific solutions to steady-state molecular diffusion problems with three or more components are not likely to be of practical value to engineers. Multicomponent diffusion can sometimes be treated by considering two or more components as a single system, e.g., an air–water system. In this instance, an "effective" diffusion coefficient is used with success.

In spite of the intractability of multicomponent diffusion in general, there are many industrial examples of multicomponent mass transfer. Toor [T1] pointed out three phenomena occurring in multicomponent diffusion in gas mixtures that are of practical significance. The first is that the rate of diffusion of a species may be zero even though the concentration gradient of that species is not zero. This is called a diffusion barrier. Secondly, there may be osmotic diffusion, in which the rate of diffusion of a species is not zero even though its concentration gradient is zero. Lastly, there may be reverse diffusion, in which a component diffuses against the gradient of its concentration. Under the right set of circumstances, such phenomena might be observable in industrial equipment.

5.4 LESS COMMON TYPES OF MASS AND THERMAL TRANSPORT

For heat transfer and mass transfer, the most important driving forces for transport are temperature gradient and concentration gradient, respectively.

However, other mechanisms exist and will be discussed briefly here. From a rigorous standpoint, a general presentation of the conservation equation must include terms representing these effects. The tables presented earlier in this chapter have not included these effects, which are usually negligible.

5.4.1 Heat Transport

For heat transport the energy flux vector may, in general, be composed of five contributions:

$$q/A = q^{(T)}/A + q^{(C)}/A + q^{(d)}/A + q^{(p)}/A + q^{(r)}/A \tag{5.84}$$

In Eq. (5.84) the first contribution is that expressed by Fourier's law: ordinary heat conduction due to a temperature gradient (see Table 4.1):

$$q^{(T)}/A = -\alpha[\nabla(\rho c_p T)] = -k(\nabla T) \tag{5.85}$$

The second contribution is the convective contribution, which is the heat being convected by the mass average velocity. By analogy with Eq. (3.21), this term is

$$q^{(C)}/A = (\rho c_p T)(U) \tag{5.86}$$

In most practical heat transfer problems the conduction and convection terms dominate.

The third contribution is the energy flux due to the fact that all species diffusing with respect to the mass average velocity carry with them a certain amount of intrinsic energy, the sum of which may or may not be zero with respect to U [B3].

The fourth contribution is the energy flux associated with a superimposed concentration gradient. This effect is also known as the "diffusion-thermo effect" or the "DuFour effect". The energy flux associated with the DuFour effect is quite small, and no general expression has ever been developed [B3].

The last contribution is the radiation flux. The general equation for radiation is the Stefan–Boltzmann equation [cf. Eq. (11.1)], which is discussed in detail in heat transfer texts [M2]. Radiation is important at the elevated temperatures encountered in equipment such as furnaces.

5.4.2 Mass Transport

For mass transport the mass flux vector may in general be composed of five contributions. One contribution is mass transport by convection, Eq. (3.21), which is eliminated if coordinates relative to the mass average velocity are considered. Then

$$j_A/A = j_A^{(x)}/A + j_A^{(p)}/A + j_A^{(F)}/A + j_A^{(T)}/A \tag{5.87}$$

In Eq. (5.87) the first contribution is that expressed by Fick's law: ordinary mass diffusion due to a concentration gradient.

The second contribution to the mass flux is mass transport due to pressure diffusion. Under ordinary conditions, pressure diffusion through some sort of barrier such as a plastic tube wall, a rubber tube wall, or a clay pipe wall results in separation. The separation efficiency of such a process depends on relative molecular weights. For example, pressure diffusion is the mechanism used for separation of the isotope ^{235}U from ^{238}U. This process is called the gaseous diffusion process. Uranium is converted to the volatile hexafluoride. Pressure diffusion has also been used for laboratory-scale separations. Naturally, pressure diffusion is limited in practice to gases.

The third contribution to the mass flux is mass transport due to external forces. For example, ions in solution may diffuse as a result of the presence of an electrical field. Recently, many countries have sponsored research projects in which the isotopes of uranium hexafluoride are separated by gas centrifuges, in which the heavier gas $^{238}UF_6$ is preferentially separated from $^{235}UF_6$ at high speeds of rotation.

The last contribution to the mass flux vector is the mass transport by thermal diffusion. Thermal diffusion, sometimes identified with the name Soret, is a reciprocal process when compared to the DuFour effect. A concentration gradient causes a small heat flux; a temperature gradient causes a mass flux. Mass flux by thermal diffusion is usually a very small contribution if fluxes by other mechanisms are present. Thermal diffusion is a practical, although expensive, way of separating isotopes [B3]. The Clusius–Dickel column produces very high temperature gradients and may be used in stages to effect separations.

The four contributions to the mass flux vector in Eq. (5.87) can all be important in effecting separations of various types. Separations employing pressure diffusion, external forces, and thermal diffusion are used only when other less expensive separation methods fail.

5.5 SUMMARY

Chapter 5 is the last of the introductory chapters covering the theory and the applications of the transport of heat, mass, and momentum with either laminar flow or zero flow. This chapter accomplishes three main goals. First, it covers in detail the application of the equations in Chapters 2, 3, and 4 to three-dimensional problems, especially where curvilinear coordinates (cylindrical and spherical) are required. Secondly, it introduces in detail the nomenclature, equations, and assumptions that are required in the study of mass diffusion. Lastly, it covers some specialized and not too commonly encountered phenomena. One example is mass transfer, in which a net convective flux is induced by mass transfer in the absence of a pressure gradient. Other specialized phenomena include Knudsen diffusion, effusion, multicomponent mass diffusion, the DuFour effect in heat transfer and the flux contributions due to pressure diffusion, thermal diffusion (Soret effect), and centrifugal forces.

Chapter 5 begins with a review of convection. Convection is defined as the bulk flow of a fluid due to external influences, such as a pressure difference or a force field such as gravity. In order to convert equations from Chapters 2 to 4 into curvilinear coordinates, it is necessary to have the common vector expansions, such as $\nabla^2 \psi$, in all three coordinate systems. The reader must cover in detail and master the material on the three-dimensional balance equations in the three coordinate systems. The balance equations in their most general forms are used as the starting point for solution of common problems. These equations are simplified by omitting the terms that are zero or negligible. This chapter emphasizes the formulation of the appropriate equations and the identification of the terms that are zero or negligible.

If the density and viscosity of a fluid may be assumed constant, then these simplifications to the momentum balance result in the well-known Navier–Stokes equation, Eq. (5.15). In rectangular (Cartesian) coordinates, there is an equation for each coordinate, as given in Table 5.7. The equations in curvilinear coordinates, also given in Table 5.7, are even more complex. The terms for the centripetal and Coriolis forces arise in the balance equations in curvilinear coordinates as a result of the mathematics of transforming rectangular coordinates into curvilinear ones. The Navier–Stokes equations are complex, even after the simplifications of constant density and viscosity. However, four example problems are included to illustrate the many practical problems that the Navier–Stokes equations can be used to solve.

The boundary layer concept is also introduced in this chapter by applying the Navier–Stokes equations to the flow past a flat plate. The Navier–Stokes equations are simplified for this example. A full discussion of the boundary layer is delayed until Chapter 12.

Section 5.3 deals with mass diffusion and the complexity in this subject caused by convection. Mass transfer is unique in that mass transfer itself can contribute a convective flux. Section 5.4 discusses less common types of heat and mass transport.

PROBLEMS

5.1. Discuss the meaning of each term of Eqs. (3.59), (3.60), (3.74), and (3.77). These equations are given at the beginning of this chapter.

5.2. Discuss the term $(U \cdot \nabla)U$. Consider its source, meaning, etc. What happens to this term if the view is changed to that of an element moving with the stream?

5.3. The equations used with this chapter very rapidly become too complex to solve. What suggestion could you make for some kind of solution to these more complex problems? For example, consider the flow over a sphere in which the important equations are given as Eqs. (D), (E) and (F) in Table 5.7.

5.4. Three derivatives have been considered in this chapter (d, ∂, D). Discuss these in terms of their physical meaning.

5.5. The total and partial derivatives of temperature with respect to time are zero at steady-state. Is the substantial derivative always zero at steady-state?

5.6. Set up the differential equations for fluid flow along a porous flat plate with a suction velocity of U_o and a uniform flow U_∞, which is the free stream velocity. Assume steady-state.

5.7. The normal shear stresses are τ_{xx}, τ_{yy}, and τ_{zz}. Show that the sum of these must be zero using a generalized form of Eq. (5.3):

$$\tau_{ii} = -2\mu \frac{\partial U_i}{\partial x_i} + \frac{2}{3}\mu(\nabla \cdot U)$$

for $i = x$, y, or z and $x_i = x$, y, or z.

5.8. The plate-and-cone viscometer, shown in Fig. 5.11, is used to measure the viscosity of non-Newtonian fluids. Assume this viscometer is to be used for a Newtonian fluid. The plate (on the bottom) rotates an angular velocity of ω (direction ϕ). The angle (direction θ) between the plate and the cone (which is stationary) is uniform as shown in the figure. The flow is maintained laminar by keeping the angular velocity small. Find the equations to describe this experiment, indicating which terms are zero and why. Also, give the boundary conditions necessary to solve the system of equations, but do not solve.

5.9. Fluid flows at steady-state between two inclined plates, as shown in Fig. 5.12. The plates are kept at constant temperature T_w, which is greater than T_o, the temperature of the entering fluid. Set up the differential equations that describe the temperature distribution, as well as the boundary conditions.

5.10. Set up the differential equation for equimolar counter diffusion (mass transfer) between parallel plates with a forced flow in the x direction.

5.11. Obtain the equation for the case of the steady-state diffusion in a slab that is completely uniform in the z direction if the rate of reaction is first-order.

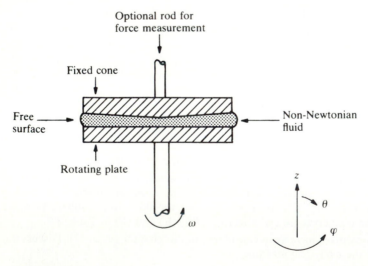

FIGURE 5.11
Plate-and-cone viscometer.

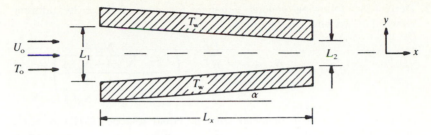

FIGURE 5.12
Heat transfer during flow between converging plates.

5.12. A fluid is flowing down a cylindrical tube whose walls are soluble in the fluid. Obtain the equation for the variation of concentration of the wall material with distance. Assume steady-state conditions and no chemical reaction. The velocity profile is flat (plug flow) and equal to a constant U over the entire length and radius of the tube. It is not necessary to solve the resulting equation, but rather indicate simplifying assumptions that might be made in order to obtain an ordinary differential equation.

5.13. Discuss and compare equimolar counter diffusion and diffusion through a stationary gas.

5.14. A drop is suspended in an atmosphere of air. The drop's radius is r_1. What is the integrated equation for the mass transfer of the fluid from the spherical shape?

5.15. Find the equation for the flux of A that diffuses in an equimolar diffusion system from the surface of a sphere r_i through a distance of Δr.

5.16. Find the equation for the flux of A that diffuses from the surface of a circular tube of radius r_o and length L for a distance Δr:
(a) if the diffusion is equimolar.
(b) if the diffusion is through a stagnant film.

5.17. Water is at the bottom of a can 4 inches in diameter and 1 ft high. The ambient temperature is 77°F and the pressure is 1 atm. There is a slight wind across the top of the can, which maintains a water concentration of zero. The wind is not strong enough to disturb the air in the can. Calculate the rate of loss of water from the can in $lb_m\ s^{-1}$ at steady-state when the water is 2 in. deep.

5.18. A spherical drop of compound B is surrounded by fluid A. Component B is nondiffusing, but does react with fluid A to form product P according to the reactions below. Find the integrated equation for the molar flow of P for each case:
(a) $A + B = P$;
(b) $A + B = 2P$;
(c) $2A + B = 3P$;

5.19. Prove D_{AB} equals D_{BA} for an ideal gas. Is this true for a diffusion in a binary liquid system? Why, or why not?

5.20. For an ideal gas, prove that the molar volume equals the partial molar volume of each component present.

5.21. Beginning with Eq. (5.46), derive Eq. (5.47).

5.22. Derive the following general equation for mass transfer by diffusion and convection. Assume constant area.

$$N_A/A = \frac{N_A/A}{N_A/A + N_B/A} \frac{\frac{Dp}{RT}}{z_2 - z_1} \ln\left(\frac{y_{A,2} - \frac{N_A/A}{N_A/A + N_B/A}}{y_{A,1} - \frac{N_A/A}{N_A/A + N_B/A}}\right) \tag{i}$$

5.23. A circular tank 3 m in diameter contains liquid toluene (C_7H_8) at 31.8°C, for which the vapor pressure is 0.0526 atm. When this tank is open to the atmosphere, diffusion may be assumed to be occurring through a film 0.001 m thick. Assume the concentration of toluene on the ambient side equals zero. The diffusion coefficient of toluene in air at 30°C is $0.88 \times 10^{-5} \, m^2 \, s^{-1}$. Find the loss of toluene in kilograms per day.

5.24. It is desired to extract methanol from a methanol–water solution. Assume that the water is insoluble in the extracting solution, that all mass transfer takes place by diffusion of methanol through a thin film of thickness 0.005 m and that the concentration of methanol on the water side is 15 percent by weight and on the other side 6 percent; assume the diffusion coefficient is $16 \times 10^{-10} \, m^2 \, s^{-1}$. Find the steady-state flux with respect to fixed axes if the pure component densities are $990 \, kg \, m^{-3}$ for water and $800 \, kg \, m^{-3}$ for methanol. Assume that the volume change upon mixing is zero.

5.25. A mixture of air (A) and carbon dioxide (B) at 0°C is diffusing through a capillary of diameter $10^{-6} \, m$ and 2 m long. Assume that it is possible to have the inlet concentration of carbon dioxide at 50 mole percent and the outlet at 0 mole percent. The molecular diffusion coefficient is $1.4 \times 10^{-5} \, m^2 \, s^{-1}$ at 1 atm. The viscosity of CO_2 at 0°C is 0.013 cP; assume for air that the value at 1 atm from Table A.2 in the Appendix applies.

(a) Calculate all six ratios of molecular diffusion coefficient to Knudsen diffusion coefficient at total pressures of 0.030, 3.0, and 300 atm.

(b) At total pressures of 0.030, 3.0, and 300 atm, find the mass flow rate of CO_2 in $kg \, s^{-1}$. HINT: for the transition region, you may assume Graham's law in order to find β; for the Fickian region, the total pressure is constant.

5.26. Consider the volume in Fig. 5.7 for the following system: convected velocity of the volume (1 m on each side) is $2 \, m \, s^{-1}$; species A is nitrogen (N_2), concentration $0.2 \, kmol \, m^{-3}$; species B is carbon dioxide, concentration $0.1 \, kmol \, m^{-3}$; species C is water vapor, concentration $0.3 \, kmol \, m^{-3}$. The nitrogen is not diffusing; however, carbon dioxide diffuses in the $-z$ direction at a rate of $0.6 \, kmol \, s^{-1}$, and water vapor diffuses in the $+z$ direction at a rate of $0.8 \, kmol \, s^{-1}$. Find U_z and U_z^*.

5.27. For the data in Problem 5.26, find all fluxes defined in this chapter.

5.28. Calculate the mean-free-path of:

(a) air at 25°C and 1 atm;

(b) helium (viscosity $1.348 \times 10^{-5} \, kg \, m^{-1} \, s^{-1}$) at 0°C and 0.001 atm;

(c) carbon dioxide (viscosity $22 \times 10^{-6} \, kg \, m^{-1} \, s^{-1}$) at 200°C and 0.1 atm.

5.29. Pure nitrogen is diffusing through a capillary tube 50 μm in diameter and 0.1 m long at 0°C under a pressure difference of 2×10^{-6} atm. At the inlet, the absolute pressure is 2×10^{-6} atm and the viscosity is 0.016 cP.

(a) Calculate the flow regime.

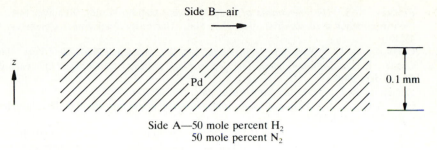

Side B—air

z

Pd

0.1 mm

Side A—50 mole percent H_2
50 mole percent N_2

FIGURE 5.13
Diffusion of hydrogen through a palladium membrane.

(b) Calculate the flow rate in $kg\,s^{-1}$
(c) If a one to one mole ratio of hydrogen to nitrogen is originally present at the capillary inlet, calculate the outlet composition in mole percent at the outlet.

5.30. It is desired to separate helium (viscosity $1.348 \times 10^{-5}\,kg\,m^{-1}\,s^{-1}$) from methane (viscosity $1.030 \times 10^{-5}\,kg\,m^{-1}\,s^{-1}$) using a thin Pyrex glass wall as a diffusional barrier. The inlet stream contains 2 mole percent He at 0°C and 1 atm. The thin Pyrex glass may be approximated by an effusive barrier model, with a diameter of 35 Å, negligible length, and 10^8 pores per m^2. The pressure drop for diffusion is 0.5 atm.
(a) Calculate the Knudsen number (high-pressure side only).
(b) Calculate the mass flux ($kg\,m^{-2}\,s^{-1}$) of He through the barrier.
(c) Find the steady-state He composition in the low-pressure chamber.
(d) Find the cross sectional area in m^2 necessary to remove 1 kmol of He per hour.

5.31. A thin metallic membrane of palladium (0.1 mm thick) is permeable to the diffusion of hydrogen only. On side A of the membrane, as shown in Fig. 5.13, is a mixture of 50 mole percent hydrogen and the rest nitrogen; on side B, air flows at high velocity in order to maintain the concentration of hydrogen as zero. At 293 K and 1 atm, the diffusion coefficient of the hydrogen–nitrogen system is $7.63 \times 10^{-5}\,m^2\,s^{-1}$. Let the apparatus be operated at 313 K and 1 atm pressure, at which it can be assumed that the resistance to mass transfer in the gas phase occurs through a hypothetical film of thickness 1.0 mm, immediately adjacent to side A. Further, it is known that the concentration of hydrogen on side A of the membrane (between the solid and the film) is 20 mole percent. Calculate:
(a) the flux ($kmol\,m^{-2}\,s^{-1}$) of hydrogen through the Pd membrane;
(b) the diffusion coefficient of hydrogen through the Pd membrane.

REFERENCES

B1. Barrer, R. M.: *Diffusion in and through Solids*, Cambridge University Press, Cambridge, 1951.
B2. Bird, R. B.: in *Advances in Chemical Engineering*, vol. 1, T. B. Drew and J. W. Hoopes (eds.), Academic Press, New York, 1956.
B3. Bird, R. B., W. E. Stewart, and E. N. Lightfoot: *Transport Phenomena*, Wiley, New York, 1960.

B4. Brodkey, R. S.: *The Phenomena of Fluid Motions,* Addison-Wesley, Reading, MA, 1967. [Fourth printing available from the Ohio State University Bookstores, Columbus, Ohio 43210.]

C1. Crank, J., and G. S. Park, eds. *Diffusion in Polymers,* Academic Press, New York, 1968.

C2. Cussler, E. L.: *Diffusion: Mass Transfer in Fluid Systems,* Cambridge University Press, Cambridge, 1984.

D1. Dullien, F. A. L., and D. S. Scott: *Chem. Eng. Sci.* **17:** 771 (1962).

F1. Fredrickson, A. G.: *Principles and Applications of Rheology,* Prentice-Hall, Englewood Cliffs, NJ, 1964, p. 173.

G1. Geankoplis, C. J.: *Mass Transport Phenomena,* 5th printing, 1982. [Distributed and sold by Ohio State University Bookstores, Columbus, Ohio, 43210.]

G2. Glasstone, S.: *Textbook of Physical Chemistry,* 2d ed., Van Nostrand, Princeton, NJ, 1946. Nostrand, Princeton, NJ.

H1. Hines, A. L., and R. N. Maddox: *Mass Transfer: Fundamentals and Applications,* Prentice-Hall, Englewood Cliffs, NJ, 1985.

H2. Hirschfelder, J. O., C. F. Curtiss, and R. B. Bird: *Molecular Theory of Gases and Liquids,* 4th printing April, 1967, Wiley, New York, 1954.

K1. Kennard, E. H.: *Kinetic Theory of Gases,* McGraw-Hill, New York, 1938.

K2. Knudsen, M.: *Ann. Physik* **28:** 75 (1909).

L1. Lightfoot, E. N., and E. L. Cussler: *Chemical Engineering Progress Symposium Series* No. 58, **61:** 66 (1965).

L2. Loeb, L. B.: *The Kinetic Theory of Gases,* 2d ed., McGraw-Hill, New York, 1934.

M1. Mason, E. A., and B. Kronstadt: *J. Chem. Educ.* **44:** 740 (1967).

M2. McAdams, W. H.: *Heat Transmission,* 3d ed., McGraw-Hill, New York, 1954.

P1. Perry, R. H., and D. W. Green: *Perry's Chemical Engineers' Handbook,* 6th ed., McGraw-Hill, New York, 1984.

R1. Reid, R. C., J. M. Prausnitz, and T. K. Sherwood: *The Properties of Gases and Liquids,* 3d ed., McGraw-Hill, New York, 1977.

R2. Roberts-Austen, W. C.: *Philos. Trans. Roc. Soc. (London)* **A187:** 383 (1896).

R3. Rothfeld, L. B.: *AIChE J.* **9:** 19 (1963).

S1. Sandler, S. I.: *Chemical and Engineering Thermodynamics,* Wiley, New York, 1977, p. 295.

S2. Sherwood, T. K., R. L. Pigford, and C. R. Wilke: *Mass Transfer,* McGraw-Hill, New York, 1975.

T1. Toor, H. L.: *AIChE J.* **3:** 198 (1957).

T2. Treybal, R. E.: *Mass-Transfer Operations,* 3d ed., McGraw-Hill, New York, 1980.

T3. Tyrrell, H. J. V., and K. R. Harris: *Diffusion in Liquids,* Butterworths, London, 1984.

W1. Wakao, N., and J. M. Smith: *Chem. Eng. Sci.* **17:** 825 (1962).

CHAPTER
6

TURBULENT
FLOW

NOMENCLATURE

A	Species A; A_1 and A_2 are species A at locations 1 and 2
A	Constant in velocity profile equation
A	Example quantity to be averaged in Reynolds rules of averaging
a	Empirical constant in Pai's equations; subscripts 1, 2; see Eq. (6.113)
B	Empirical constant in the logarithmic velocity distribution, Eq. (6.77)
B	Example quantity to be averaged in Reynolds rules of averaging
C	Instantaneous concentration (kmol m^{-3}, lb mol ft^{-3}); C_A, C_B, C_i are concentrations of species A, B, i; $C_{A,1}$ and $C_{A,2}$ are concentrations at locations 1 and 2; $\bar{C}_{A,w}$ is time-averaged concentration of species A at the wall; $C_{A,\text{ave}}$ is bulk concentration of species A
C	Constant of integration
c_p	Heat capacity at constant pressure (kJ kg^{-1} K^{-1}, Btu lb$_m^{-1}$ °F^{-1}); other subscripts defined as used
D	Diffusion coefficient (mass diffusivity) (m^2 s^{-1}, ft^2 s^{-1})
d	Diameter (m, ft); d_o is inside diameter of pipe, as used in fluid flow
E	Eddy diffusivity (m^2 s^{-1}, ft^2 s^{-1}); E_τ, E_M, E_H are eddy diffusivities of momentum, mass, and heat, respectively
E	Voltage

e	Pipe roughness (m, ft); see Table 10.2 for more details
e	Base of natural logarithms (2.718 281 8. . .)
f	Fanning friction factor, Eq. (6.89)
$\boldsymbol{g}$	Vector representing the acceleration due to a gravitational or other field (m s^{-2}, ft s^{-2})
g_c	Gravitational conversion constant (32.174 lb$_m$ ft lb$_f^{-1}$ s^{-2})
h	Heat transfer coefficient, defined by Eq. (6.86) (W m^{-2} K^{-1}, Btu ft^{-2} h^{-1} °F^{-1})
I	Number of intervals during integration
I_x	Intensity of turbulence, defined by Eq. (6.31)
$\boldsymbol{i}$	Unit vector in x direction
$\boldsymbol{j}$	Unit vector in y direction
$\boldsymbol{k}$	Unit vector in z direction
k	Thermal conductivity (W m^{-1} K^{-1} or J m^{-1} K^{-1} s^{-1}, Btu ft^{-1} °R^{-1} s^{-1})
k_c'	Equimolar mass transfer coefficient, defined by Eq. (6.87) [kmol m^{-2} s^{-1} (kmol m^{-3})$^{-1}$, lb mol ft^{-2} s^{-1} (lb mol ft^{-3})$^{-1}$]
k_n	Specific reaction rate constant in Eq. (4.108) or Eq. (6.45)
L	Length (m, ft)
l	Prandtl mixing length, cf. Eq. (6.69)
m	Integer parameter in Pai's equation, Eq. (6.113)
$\boldsymbol{N}$	Molar flow vector, defined with respect to fixed coordinates (kmol s^{-1}, lb mol s^{-1}); subscripts A or B are for species A or B; if written not as a vector, then N is subscripted for direction of transfer
N	Number of points to compute the average
N_{Re}	Reynolds number, Eq. (6.1) or Eq. (6.2), $d_o U_{z,\,ave}\,\rho/\mu$ for pipe flow
n	Order of reaction, Eq. (4.108) or Eq. (6.45)
n	Constant in Eq. (6.99)
p	Pressure (kPa, atm, lb$_f$ in.$^{-2}$)
$\boldsymbol{q}$	Energy (heat) flow vector (J s^{-1}, Btu s^{-1}); subscripts denote components in coordinate directions
r	Cylindrical coordinate (m, ft)
r	Radius (m, ft); r_o is value of r at the tube wall
s	Parameter in Pai's equation, Eq. (6.117)
T	Instantaneous temperature (K, °R, °C, °F); T_1 and T_2 are temperatures at locations 1 and 2; T_w is temperature of the wall or surface; T_∞ is temperature in open channel; T_{ave} or T_b is bulk temperature, Eq. (11.31)
T	Total time
t	Time (s); t_c is contact time in Eq. (6.101)
$\boldsymbol{U}$	Instantaneous velocity vector (m s^{-1}, ft s^{-1}); U is magnitude of $\boldsymbol{U}$; U_x, U_y, U_z, U_θ, U_r, U_ϕ are components in directions x, y, z, θ, r, ϕ; U^* is friction velocity, Eq. (6.53); $U_{z,\,ave}$ is mean velocity in z direction; $\bar{U}_z$ is time-averaged velocity in z direction; U_x' is instantaneous velocity fluctuation in x direction; U_∞ is velocity in open channel (free stream velocity); U^+ is dimensionless time-averaged velocity, Eq. (6.78), $\bar{U}_z/U^*$

w	Subscript denoting wall
x	Rectangular (Cartesian) coordinate
x	Distance from leading edge of a flat plate (m, ft)
y	Rectangular (Cartesian) coordinate; ($2y_o$) is distance between two parallel plates
y	Distance from the wall, $r_o - r$ (m, ft)
y^+	Dimensionless distance from the wall, Eq. (6.79), $yU^*\rho/\mu$
z	Rectangular (Cartesian) coordinate
α	Thermal diffusivity ($m^2 s^{-1}$, $ft^2 s^{-1}$)
Δ	Difference, state 2 minus state 1; e.g., ΔT means $T_2 - T_1$
δ	Generalized diffusivity ($m^2 s^{-1}$, $ft^2 s^{-1}$)
ε	Eddy viscosity, Eq. (6.62) (units the same as for μ)
θ	Curvilinear coordinate direction
μ	Viscosity ($kg\,m^{-1}\,s^{-1}$ or $N\,m^{-2}\,s$, $lb_m\,ft^{-1}\,s^{-1}$, cP); μ_w is viscosity at wall
ν	Kinematic viscosity (momentum diffusivity) ($m^2 s^{-1}$, $ft^2 s^{-1}$)
κ	Empirical constant in several correlations in Chapter 6
ξ	Generalized transport coefficients associated with h, f, k_c', Eq. (6.90); also, ξ_H, ξ_τ, ξ_M refer to generalized coefficient for heat, momentum, and mass, respectively
π	Ratio of circumference of a circle to its diameter (3.141 592 65...)
ρ	Density ($kg\,m^{-3}$, $lb_m\,ft^{-3}$); subscripts refer to species
τ	Momentum flux (or shear stress) tensor ($N\,m^{-2}$, $lb_f\,ft^{-2}$); τ_{xy}, τ_{yx}, etc., are components of the momentum flux tensor, where subscripts refer to direction of momentum transfer and direction of velocity; τ_L is laminar-like contribution; τ_T is turbulent contribution; τ_w is shear stress at the wall
$\boldsymbol{\Psi}$	Generalized flux vector (e.g., units for heat flux are $J\,m^{-2}\,s^{-1}$ or $W\,m^{-2}$, $Btu\,ft^{-2}\,s^{-1}$; see Tables 2.1 and 3.1 for more details); Ψ_x, Ψ_y, Ψ_z are components in directions x, y, z; $\Psi_{x,m}$ or $\boldsymbol{\Psi}_m$ is flux due to molecular transport; $\Psi_{x,c}$ or $\boldsymbol{\Psi}_c$ is flux due to convection
ψ	Generalized concentration of property (e.g., units for concentration of heat are $J\,m^{-3}$, $Btu\,ft^{-3}$; see Table 3.1 for complete listing)
$\dot{\psi}_G$	Generalized rate of generation of energy or mass or momentum in a unit volume (see Table 4.2 for units; e.g., for heat, units are $J\,m^{-3}\,s^{-1}$, $Btu\,ft^{-3}\,s^{-1}$)
∇	Vector operator del, defined by Eq. (2.16) or Eq. (3.45) (m^{-1}, ft^{-1})
∇^2	Laplacian operator, defined by Eq. (3.64) (m^{-2}, ft^{-2})

Note

The overbar denotes time average ($\bar{U}$, $\bar{C}_A$, $\bar{T}$, etc.); the prime denotes fluctuation with respect to the mean (U', T', etc.)

In Section 2.1.3, a phenomenological description of momentum transfer in fluid flow was given using the metaphor of a deck of playing cards. Such a flow between parallel plates, one stationary and one moving, as in Fig. 2.3, is called laminar or streamline flow. Laminar flow predominates at low flow rates in such pressure-driven flows as that between parallel plates or in a circular tube or pipe. At high flow rates the streamlines represented by the playing cards metaphor are destroyed by small groups of fluid that are called eddies. These eddies move in all directions, not just in the direction of bulk motion. Naturally, there is a transition region between laminar and turbulent flow. This chapter contains a detailed description of the physical nature of transitional and turbulent flow.

The general balance equation [Eq. (3.60)] applies in all flows—laminar, transitional, or turbulent. The Navier–Stokes equation for constant density (i.e., incompressible fluid) and for constant viscosity is

$$\partial U / \partial t + (U \cdot \nabla)U = -(1/\rho)(\nabla p) + g + \nu(\nabla^2 U) \tag{5.15}$$

Equation (5.15) was derived from the general property balance [Eq. (3.60)] with the appropriate substitutions for momentum transfer. Equation (5.15) can be applied to any incompressible fluid flow field. However, problems solved in the preceding chapters were laminar in nature. The complexities of applying Eq. (5.15) to turbulent flow will be discussed in the following sections.

6.1   TRANSITIONAL AND TURBULENT FLOW

The physical nature of transitional and turbulent flow is best illustrated by describing the results of some flow visualization experiments, which have been remarkably useful in studying turbulent flows. The earliest technique to observe the nature of the flow was to inject a thin stream of dye into the flow and observe the dye stream as it moved with the bulk motion. Alternative and more recent experiments involve adding very small particles as flow markers and taking photographs. Also, the use of small hydrogen bubbles formed by electrolysis in the flow has proved successful. Brodkey, Hershey, and coworkers [C2, N3, P7] used high-speed cinematography to obtain motion pictures with stereoscopic flow visualization. These experiments, which allowed observation of three-dimensional motions using both particle flow markers and dye injection, have been in part responsible for the present-day understanding of turbulent flows.

6.1.1   The Reynolds Experiment

The 1883 experiments of Reynolds [R1] were the first to illustrate the differences between laminar and turbulent flow. In Reynolds' experiments (see Fig. 6.1), a fluid initially at rest in a tank was allowed to flow through a glass pipe. A thin stream of dye was injected at a point in the tank, and the motion of the dye was observed as it moved into the pipe and downstream with the fluid. At low velocities, the dye moved in a straight line along the tube,

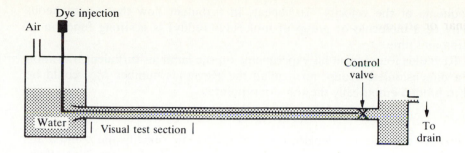

DYE INJECTION RESULTS

FIGURE 6.1
The Reynolds experiment.

indicating laminar flow. As the velocity was increased, the dye line became thinner and began a wave-like or sinuous motion. A further increase in the velocity caused the dye line to break up into segments, or what are pictured as turbulent eddies.[1] Reynolds' results are summarized as follows: as the flow velocity is increased, a transition between laminar and turbulent flow occurs, and at higher velocities the flow becomes fully turbulent.

In a one-dimensional flow, such as flow through a pipe, turbulent eddies often move in directions oblique to the bulk flow velocity vector. The local velocity vector associated with an eddy of fluid will have non-zero components in the r, θ, and z directions. This local velocity vector is called the instantaneous velocity. The flow on the average moves only in the axial direction, while instantaneously the velocity vector of a particle of fluid can be in any direction. Note also that there is no net flow in the radial direction, since the pipe has no holes in its wall and there is no generation of mass. But there is an instantaneous velocity component in the radial direction at any instant in time. This radial component is zero only when averaged over a long period of time. Thus, at any given instant in time, there can be three

---

[1] Fluid dynamics film loops FM-1, FM-8, FM-25, FM-32, and FM-147 can be used to assist the reader in visualizing laminar, transitional, and turbulent flows.

components of the velocity. To repeat, in turbulent flow the instantaneous velocity of a molecule or group of molecules (eddy) is a strong function of position and time.

Reynolds found from his experiments on the laminar–turbulent transition that a dimensionless group, now called the Reynolds number N_{Re}, could be used to predict empirically the transition point:

$$N_{Re} = LU\rho/\mu \qquad (6.1)$$

where L is a characteristic length, U is a charactersitic velocity and ρ and μ are the fluid density and viscosity, respectively. Specifically, for pipe flow, Reynolds found

$$N_{Re} = d_o U_{z, ave}\rho/\mu \qquad (6.2)$$

where d_o is the pipe diameter and $U_{z, ave}$ is the average velocity across the pipe. For laminar flow, $U_{z, ave}$ is given by Eq. (4.77). In the SI system of units, d_o has units of meters, $U_{z, ave}$ has units of m s^{-1}, and ρ units of kg m^{-3}. Hence, the net units of the product $d_o U_{z, ave}\rho$ are kg m^{-1} s^{-1}. Since kg m^{-1} s^{-1} are the units of μ, the Reynolds number is seen to be dimensionless.

The transition to turbulent flow occurs when the shear stress (momentum flux) or shear rate at the wall in the flow becomes so large that the layer-like laminar flow is no longer possible or stable. Then eddies are formed which effect the higher transfer of momentum found in turbulent flow. The point where laminar flow no longer exists in a pipe is known as the "critical Reynolds number". When experimenters have taken elaborate precautions to still the fluid in the tank and to eliminate any disturbance at the entrance to the pipe, critical Reynolds numbers as high as 40 000 have been obtained. Although the critical Reynolds number depends rather markedly on the geometry and the conditions of the system, the critical Reynolds number is typically 2100 for a pipe flow system with a highly disturbed entry. Above a Reynolds number of 10 000 in most flow systems that are in commercial installations, the flow is fully turbulent.

Example 6.1. Water flows in a 2-inch schedule 40 pipe, at a rate of 50 gallons per minute (gpm). The actual inside diameter of commercial piping can be determined from Table B.1 in the Appendix. If the temperature is 86°F, determine whether the flow is laminar, turbulent, or transitional. At 86°F, the viscosity of water is 0.8007 cP, and the density of water is 0.99568 g cm^{-3}.

Answer. From Table B.1, a 2-inch schedule 40 pipe has an inside diameter of 2.067 in. and a flow area of 0.02330 ft^2. The solution can be accomplished in any set of units; the English system of units will be used for this example. The following conversions are needed:

$$1\,\text{g cm}^{-3} = 62.43\,\text{lb}_m\,\text{ft}^{-3}$$
$$7.48\,\text{gal} = 1\,\text{ft}^3 \qquad (i)$$
$$1\,\text{cP} = 6.72 \times 10^{-4}\,\text{lb}_m\,\text{ft}^{-1}\,\text{s}^{-1}$$

The velocity of water in the pipe is found by converting the gallons per minute to cubic feet and dividing by the cross sectional (flow) area:

$$U_{z,\,ave} = \frac{50}{(60)(7.48)(0.0233)} \left(\frac{(\text{gal min}^{-1})}{(\text{s min}^{-1})(\text{gal ft}^{-3})(\text{ft}^2)} \right) = 4.78 \text{ ft s}^{-1} \qquad \text{(ii)}$$

The properties of water converted to the proper units are

$$\rho = (0.99568)(62.43)[(\text{g cm}^{-3})(\text{lb}_m \text{ ft}^{-3})/(\text{g cm}^{-3})] = 62.16 \text{ lb}_m \text{ ft}^{-3}$$
$$\mu = (0.8007)(6.72 \times 10^{-4})[(\text{cP})(\text{lb}_m \text{ ft}^{-1} \text{s}^{-1})/(\text{cP})]$$
$$= 5.381 \times 10^{-4} \text{ lb}_m \text{ ft}^{-1} \text{s}^{-1} \qquad \text{(iii)}$$

The Reynolds number is calculated from Eq. (6.2):

$$N_{Re} = \frac{d_o U_{z,\,ave} \rho}{\mu} = \frac{(2.067/12)(4.78)(62.16)}{5.381 \times 10^{-4}} \left(\frac{(\text{ft})(\text{ft s}^{-1})(\text{lb}_m \text{ ft}^{-3})}{\text{lb}_m \text{ ft}^{-1} \text{s}^{-1}} \right)$$
$$N_{Re} = 95\,100 \qquad \text{(iv)}$$

Hence, the flow is turbulent. Note also that N_{Re} is dimensionless.

6.1.2 Transitional Flow

The Reynolds experiment indicated a transitional region in tube flow as seen in Fig. 6.1. Equations (4.82) and (4.83) show that the slope of the velocity profile at the wall $(dU_z/dr)_w$ in laminar pipe flow is proportional to the pressure drop. As the pressure drop is increased in a given pipe such as in Fig. 6.1, the velocity profile at the wall becomes steeper and steeper. A simplistic picture of the transition is that a disturbance such as a bit of roughness in the pipe, a pulse in the flow caused by a pump or valve, or a vibration in the system can trigger the transition. The velocity profile given by Eq. (4.72) breaks down, and turbulent eddies form.

Tube flow is actually a special case of a more general flow termed boundary layer flow. The laminar boundary layer over a solid flat surface (boundary) was discussed in Section 5.1.7 and illustrated in Fig. 5.6. The boundary layer forms as a result of the no-slip-at-the-wall boundary condition, which was illustrated in Fig. 2.3. The experiment is designed so that the velocity profile approaching the leading edge of the plate is flat, as is shown to the left in Fig. 6.2. The free stream fluid approaches the leading edge at a velocity U_∞. Adjacent to the leading edge of the plate, the flow in the boundary layer is laminar. However, as the fluid progresses along the plate and the boundary layer becomes larger (thicker), the flow becomes unstable and a transition to turbulent flow begins. Example 5.8 considered the laminar flow along a flat plate. For the flat plate, the Reynolds number corresponding to the form of Eq. (6.1) is

$$N_{Re,x} = x U_\infty \rho / \mu \qquad \text{(6.3)}$$

where x is the distance from the leading edge of the plate in Fig. 6.2.

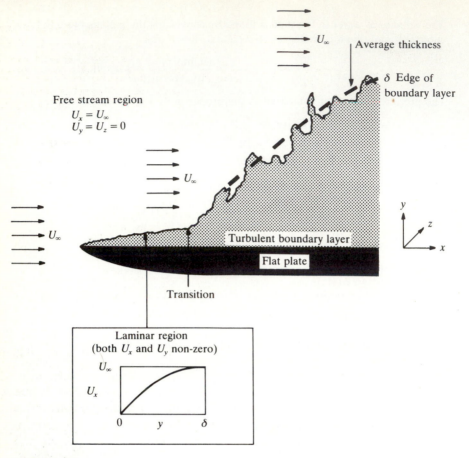

FIGURE 6.2
The boundary layer.

The exact point of transition in the boundary layer adjacent to a flat plate is itself unstable and will tend to vary randomly with time over a small range of x values. For flow past a flat plate, transition occurs at a Reynolds number $xU_\infty\rho/\mu$ in the range of 5×10^5 to 5×10^6. If the leading edge of the flat plate is made rough, then the laminar boundary layer can be "tripped" to become turbulent immediately. Also influencing the location of the transition is the shape of the leading edge of the plate and the degree of turbulence in the free stream where the velocity is U_∞.

Example 6.2. Calculate the location along a flat plate (Fig. 6.2) where transition would be expected to occur for a free stream velocity of 4.78 ft s^{-1} for water at 86°F.

Answer. The appropriate Reynolds number is

$$N_{\mathrm{Re},x} = xU_\infty\rho/\mu \qquad (6.3)$$

This equation is solved for x. The lower limit of 5×10^5 for the transition Reynolds number range is substituted along with the properties of water as cited in Example 6.1:

$$x = \frac{N_{\mathrm{Re},x}\mu}{U_\infty \rho} = \frac{(5 \times 10^5)(5.381 \times 10^{-4})}{(4.78)(62.16)}\left(\frac{(\mathrm{lb_m\,ft^{-1}\,s^{-1}})}{(\mathrm{ft\,s^{-1}})(\mathrm{lb_m\,ft^{-3}})}\right) = 0.91\ \mathrm{ft}$$

(i)

Thus, the transition could start at about 0.9 ft. The Reynolds number at the upper end of the transition range is 5×10^6. The value of x at this location is ten times the value in Eq. (i), or 9.1 ft.

A transition from laminar flow occurs in all types of flows. For each geometry there will be a critical Reynolds number of the general form as given by Eq. (6.1). Sometimes the transition can be from one specific form of laminar flow to another well-defined laminar flow. A good example of this phenomenon is the Taylor instability [T1],[2] in which the flow between concentric cylinders (considered in Example 5.7) undergoes a transition to a complex vortex motion superimposed on the basic flow. A photograph of this motion is shown in Fig. 6.3. There are further transitions at still higher Reynolds numbers, and finally there is a transition to turbulent flow.

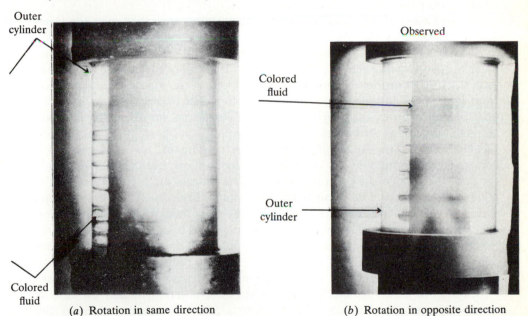

(a) Rotation in same direction   (b) Rotation in opposite direction

FIGURE 6.3
Taylor instability for inner cylinder in rotation and outer cylinder at rest. (*From Taylor, Phil. Trans. Roy. Soc. (London)* **A223**, *289 (1923). By permission.*)

---

[2] Film loop FM-31 illustrates this type of transition.

TABLE 6.1
Characteristic length for the Reynolds number

Symbol for length	Flow	Description
d_o	pipe	inside diameter
x	past flat plate	distance from leading edge
δ	past flat plate	the boundary layer thickness
L_o	between parallel plates	separation distance between the plates
d_o	past sphere or cylinder	diameter of sphere or cylinder

All laminar boundary layer and related flows undergo transition to turbulence. Typical flows with transitions are flow past a plate as just discussed, flow between parallel plates, flow inside a pipe, and flow over a sphere or a long cylinder. The definition of the characteristic length L in Eq. (6.1) for each of these flows is given in Table 6.1. Flow in ducts will be discussed in detail in Chapter 10. Flow over a sphere or a long cylinder is generally labeled as "flow past immersed bodies"; this will be discussed in Chapter 12.

The nature of the transition has been carefully researched over the years and is still an active research area. In terms of the changes in the flow, the idea of a critical Reynolds number is much too simplistic and fails to explain the mechanistic changes such as the presence or absence of turbulence. A further discussion of transition is warranted to explain these ideas.[3] The transition from laminar to turbulent flow occurs in the region where the flow becomes unstable and forms local turbulent spots. The spots spread to replace the laminar flow with turbulent eddies, providing the final, fully developed turbulent flow. This transition is essentially continuous; i.e., the process is composed of a number of developing steps and is not a sudden, single catastrophic change. In general, the transition process for the flow over a flat plate can be pictured as occurring in four steps: first, small two-dimensional waves are formed and amplified; secondly, the two-dimensional waves develop into finite three-dimensional waves and are amplified by nonlinear interactions; thirdly, turbulent spots form as localized points at the fronts of the three-dimensional waves; and finally, the turbulent spots propagate to fill the entire flow field with turbulence, at which point the flow is said to be fully turbulent.

For pipe flow, the mechanism is somewhat different in that the flow is stable to small disturbances and it takes a finite disturbance to start the transition. Slugs of turbulence form along the pipe, and the flow looks much like an alternating sequence of laminar and turbulent parts. The turbulent

---

[3] See film loops FM-23, FM-92, and FM-148.

regions grow as the flow progresses down the pipe. When the turbulent regions occupy the entire flow, the fluid is in the fully developed turbulent flow regime.

A very small, electrically-heated wire or film can be used to measure the instantaneous velocity in a flowing fluid stream. This hot-wire or hot-film anemometer senses temperature changes that are caused by changes in flow velocity. The wire or film is electrically heated so that its temperature is above the temperature of the fluid. Thus, the fluid passing over the surface of the probe cools the film; the amount of cooling is related to the instantaneous velocity by a complex 4th-power relationship. The electronics of the system detect the temperature changes in the film that occur when the velocity over the sensing element changes. A typical sensing element for one of these devices is shown in Fig. 6.4. A hot-wire anemometer is used in gas flows, whereas the hot-film anemometer is best for liquids, for which mechanical stresses due to higher densities cause a high failure rate with hot-wire probes.

A more recent technique, laser anemometry, combines the visual and electronic approaches. A laser beam is sent into the flow, and the scattered light from small tracer particles is measured. The small tracer particles cause a shift in the frequency of the light (called the Doppler effect), which can be measured and related to the velocity of the particles.

The hot-wire or hot-film anemometer quantifies the qualitative results found by Reynolds and others. If such a probe is placed in a pipe flow stream and the velocity of the flow is increased by steps until some high steady-state flow rate is obtained, a trace similar to that in Fig. 6.5 will be obtained. At low velocities, the flow remains steady and is laminar in nature. As the velocity is further increased, a transition region occurs. In the transition region, the flow is seen to be laminar part of the time and turbulent the rest of the time. As the flow rate is further increased, the turbulence occurs continuously, and the flow is said to be fully turbulent. When the flow rate is increased further, the

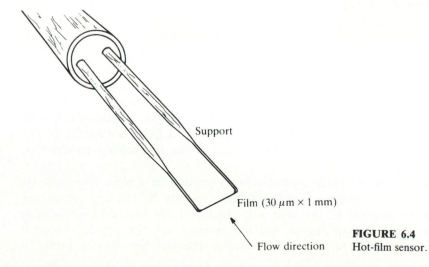

Support

Film (30 μm × 1 mm)

Flow direction

FIGURE 6.4
Hot-film sensor.

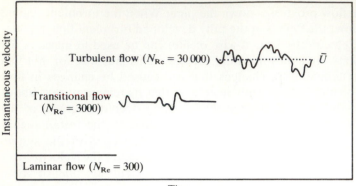

FIGURE 6.5
The instantaneous velocity.

turbulent trace from the anemometer shows larger amplitudes of velocity fluctuations and a broader range of frequencies.

6.1.3 Fully Developed Turbulent Flow

Most industrial flows are turbulent. In turbulent flow in a pipe there is a bulk flow in the z direction only. In the turbulent region of Fig. 6.5, it is seen that the average velocity is constant, but the velocity of individual fluid elements or eddies varies about the time average as previously mentioned. Both the time-averaged velocity and the instantaneous velocity may be measured by a hot-wire or hot-film anemometer. The instantaneous velocity in the z direction in the pipe is denoted by U_z and is a function of both time and position across the pipe. At any one point in the flow, a time-averaged velocity can be obtained by

$$\bar{U}_z = \frac{1}{T} \int_0^T U_z \, dt \tag{6.4}$$

where the overbar on $\bar{U}_z$ denotes time-average and T is the total time over which the average is taken. This velocity in a steady flow is a function only of position within the pipe. If the time-averaged velocity is integrated over the pipe radius, then the bulk velocity $U_{z,\,\text{ave}}$ is obtained. This procedure is exactly the same as was done for laminar flow in using Eq. (4.75) to obtain Eq. (4.77). Note that $U_{z,\,\text{ave}}$ is the velocity usually used in the Reynolds number, Eqs. (6.1) and (6.2).

Figure 6.6 shows three typical velocity profiles in a pipe. The axes are "normalized" by plotting a dimensionless velocity $\bar{U}_z / \bar{U}_{z,\,\text{max}}$ versus the dimensionless position in the pipe r/r_o. Included are two average velocity profiles in the turbulent region and the laminar velocity profile, which is obviously independent of Reynolds number. The laminar velocity profile is

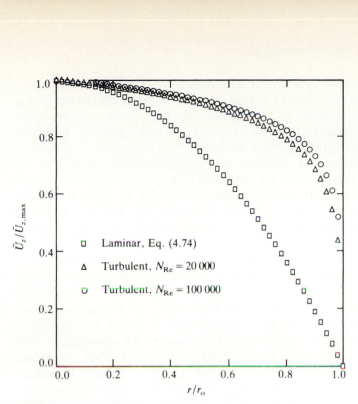

FIGURE 6.6
Turbulent velocity profile for water in a 1-in pipe.

given by Eq. (4.74):

$$U_z/U_{z,\,max} = 1 - (r/r_o)^2 \qquad (4.74)$$

where U_z is the velocity at any given radius r, $U_{z,\,max}$ is the velocity at the pipe center line ($r = 0$), and r_o is the pipe radius. Note that in this equation U_z is used and not $\bar{U}_z$. For laminar flow, there are no fluctuations about the mean so that $\bar{U}_z$ is exactly the same as U_z. The dimensionless form of the plot in Fig. 6.6 allows for easy comparisons among the three curves.

It is instructive to discuss the Reynolds number effect in the profiles shown in Fig. 6.6. The velocity profile in turbulent flow is considerably flatter in the center core region than that observed in laminar flow. Similarly, the profile in turbulent flow is much steeper in the wall region ($r \rightarrow r_o$). This steeper velocity gradient near the wall creates a zone of high instantaneous shear stress, which is a key factor in the production of turbulent eddies. Note also in Fig. 6.6 that the velocity profile at the higher Reynolds number is flatter in the core region and steeper in the wall region than that at the low Reynolds number (20 000). Keep in mind that the turbulent profiles in Fig. 6.6 are average velocities. At any given instant in time, the instantaneous velocity profile will be much different.[4]

---

[4] Film loops FM-89, FM-134, and FM-135 can be used to illustrate the cross-stream mixing that gives rise to the flatter turbulent profiles and also to illustrate instantaneous velocity profiles.

Most turbulent flows of practical importance occur during "shear flow". Shear flow is defined as a flow of a fluid in which there is a gradient in the mean velocity. The motions in such flows are not totally random since measurements have shown that the velocity in one direction is highly correlated with the velocity in another direction.

In spite of a century of research, many aspects of turbulent flow are poorly understood. Fully developed turbulent flow is currently being extensively studied by visual and other experimental means in order to further understand the mechanisms involved. Visual studies [C2, K1, N3, P7] have shown that turbulent eddies are much less random in nature than previously thought and that turbulent events occur in an organized sequence. The occurrence of the sequence of these events is random so that the flow is not periodic in the sense of a sine wave. For purposes of this discussion a turbulent event is an acceleration, a deceleration, a rotation or vortex, or a constant velocity that is experienced by a relatively large cluster of molecules which is called an "eddy". The size of an eddy ranges from a fraction of a millimeter to the order of the characteristic dimensions of the system. All molecules of fluid within an eddy follow the same general fluid motions and share a common fate. Which event is actually the start of the turbulent cycle is not clear. Therefore, this discussion will begin with a fluid eddy moving near the wall of a pipe where the flow is fully turbulent. In a local region not far removed from the wall, the flow decelerates and shows almost no velocity gradient. From the center core region, a large eddy structure at a relatively high rate of speed comes into the wall region at an angle oblique to the pipe axis and begins to interact with the low-speed fluid. This process is called a sweep. As shear forces build up, an ejection occurs in which the low-speed fluid accelerates rapidly away from the wall region.

Figure 6.7 depicts the series of events in the boundary layer flow past a flat plate. The ordinate in this figure is the distance (y) normal to the plane of the surface. Figure 6.7(a) shows the flow and the camera both moving in the $-x$ direction. The high-speed front crossing the whole boundary layer is also moving in the $-x$ direction. As the high-speed front contacts the decelerated fluid in the wall region, a rotation results in the transverse vortex as shown. This vortex increases in size as time elapses, as shown in the successive figures. In Fig. 6.7(b), the vortex has increased in size from that in Fig. 6.7(a); furthermore, it has moved away from the wall and has caused a bulge in the boundary layer edge, as shown. In Fig. 6.7(c), the ejection is labeled; note that the bulge in the boundary layer has increased to the point where a large inflow has formed in front of the transverse vortex. In Figs. 6.7(d) and 6.7(e), the end of the first ejection is shown, plus the beginning of a new cycle some distance behind the first.

The picture of turbulent flow just described suggests that transfer from the wall region to the center core primarily involves acceleration and ejection events. As an eddy accelerates away from the wall, a second eddy must fill the space behind the first. This sequence has to be important when considering

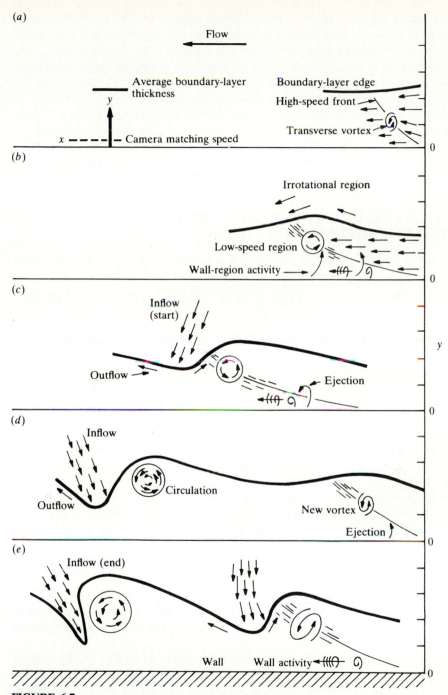

FIGURE 6.7
Sketch of the progession of the flow. (*From Praturi and Brodkey, A Stereoscopic Visual Study of Coherent Structures in Turbulent Shear Flow, J. Fluid Mech.* **89,** 251 (1978). *By permission.*)

heat and mass transfer. Heat or mass transfer from a wall to the bulk fluid in turbulent flow occurs by a combination of molecular transport and convective transport. In turbulent flow, the convective mechanism predominates. The eddy that is swept away from the wall probably accounts for a significant portion of the heat or mass transfer. Farther out in the flow, the fluid from the wall region merges with the fluid of different temperature or concentration.

The sequence of events in turbulent flow is quite complex and not fully understood at this juncture. This complexity precludes the development of anything but simple models as an attempt to describe turbulent shear flow. Even though a complete description is lacking, a great deal has been done that can be used by the engineer in the design of turbulent flow systems.

6.2 THE EQUATIONS FOR TRANSPORT UNDER TURBULENT CONDITIONS

The general property balance equation was previously presented in the most general form as Eq. (3.60):

$$\partial \psi / \partial t + (U \cdot \nabla)\psi = \dot{\psi}_G + (\nabla \cdot \delta \nabla \psi) - \psi(\nabla \cdot U) \qquad (3.60)$$

$$\text{ACC} \qquad \text{CONV} \qquad \text{GEN} \quad \text{MOLEC} \qquad \text{CONV}$$

This equation is valid for turbulent flow, provided it is applied to the instantaneous values of all quantities being considered. At this point the reader may question why equations heretofore used to solve laminar problems apply in turbulent flows as well. In the earlier chapters the balance equations were formulated generally and included all known mechanisms of transfer. An assumption of a laminar flow regime was not made in the derivations. Turbulent flow introduces no new transport mechanisms. As just discussed, convective transfer dominates in turbulent transport over molecular transfer, but both mechanisms contribute and are in Eq. (3.60) and subsequent equations. The derivation does assume that the fluid is a continuous medium rather than composed of discrete molecules. In laminar flow under normal conditions for gases and for liquids, the fluid can be considered continuous. For this assumption, as has been seen, the equations can be solved under restricted conditions.

In the case of turbulent flow, the assumption of a continuum is valid because it is known that the smallest scales of turbulence are still orders of magnitude larger in size than molecules. Within a given lump of turbulent fluid or eddy, the medium is continuous, the flow is laminar-like, and the molecular transport equations apply at each local point, i.e., to the instantaneous value at that local point.

The relegation of the concentration of property ψ in Eq. (3.60) only to instantaneous or local values turns out to be a serious barrier to the use of the balance equations in solving practical problems. Design of systems involving heat, mass, or momentum transfer generally requires knowledge of the time-averaged values of ψ and U. The instantaneous values of ψ and U are

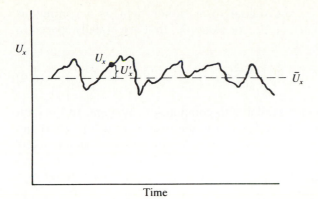

FIGURE 6.8
Instantaneous velocity in turbulent flow.

always fluctuating and are therefore often less useful. As suggested in Figs. 6.1 and 6.5, the instantaneous property values vary to such a degree that little information can be obtained by a direct application of the basic equations, and thus some modification is necessary. It is necessary to use a statistical average and a measure of the deviation from that average.

Figure 6.8 is a sketch of a typical trace of the instantaneous velocity U_x as a function of time in a fully developed turbulent flow (like that in Fig. 6.5). The instantaneous point velocity U_x is denoted by the solid line. Again, the long time-average of all the U_x values is denoted with a dashed line marked $\bar{U}_x$. The difference between the average and the instantaneous value is the x direction velocity fluctuation U'_x:

$$U'_x = U_x - \bar{U}_x \tag{6.5}$$

Equation (6.5) is solved for U_x:

$$U_x = \bar{U}_x + U'_x \tag{6.6}$$

where the prime superscript is used to denote the velocity fluctuation about the mean $\bar{U}_x$. Now the instantaneous velocity U_x is represented as a sum of the mean value $\bar{U}_x$ and a superimposed fluctuation U'_x about the mean. In terms of vectors, this concept can be expressed in terms of the vector velocity:

$$U = iU_x + jU_y + kU_z \tag{6.7}$$

where U is a point velocity. If the time-average is the true average of this velocity, then the instantaneous velocity can be written as the sum of its average velocity and the instantaneous deviation from that average; i.e.

$$U = \bar{U} + U' \tag{6.8}$$

where $\bar{U}$ is the mean velocity at the point and U' is the relative motion as a superimposed fluctuation on the mean.

The mean at a point is determined from Eq. (6.4) by integration over a total period of time T that must be large enough so that a statistically representative sample occurs in the period T. In modern turbulence research the data are obtained in discrete digital form rather than as a continuous signal. In such cases, the values of U_x, for example, that are equally spaced in time are summed and averaged, i.e.,

$$\bar{U}_x = \frac{1}{N} \sum_{1}^{N} U_x \qquad (6.9)$$

where N is the number of points available to compute the average. In the limit of a large data set there will be no difference in the results from Eqs. (6.4) and (6.9). Since such data are often taken with hot-film or hot-wire anemometers or with laser-Doppler anemometers, these averages are obtained electronically, and the average velocities in question are simply read from a meter or a computer printout.

Example 6.3. Calculate the mean velocity for the flow data in Table 6.2.

TABLE 6.2
Instantaneous velocity data

t, s	Index i	U_x, m s^{-1}	U_y, m s^{-1}	U_z, m s^{-1}
0.00	1	3.84	0.43	0.19
0.01	2	3.50	0.21	0.16
0.02	3	3.80	0.18	0.17
0.03	4	3.60	0.30	0.13
0.04	5	4.20	0.36	0.09
0.05	6	4.00	0.28	0.10
0.06	7	3.00	0.35	0.16
0.07	8	3.20	0.27	0.15
0.08	9	3.40	0.21	0.13
0.09	10	3.00	0.22	0.18
0.10	11	3.50	0.23	0.17
0.11	12	4.30	0.36	0.18
0.12	13	3.80	0.35	0.17

Answer. Since the velocity in the x direction is the largest, it appears that these data were gathered from a channel or a flow past a flat plate, as in Figs. 6.2 and 6.7. The time-averaged velocity in the z direction is given by Eq. (6.4):

$$\bar{U}_z = \frac{1}{T} \int_0^T U_z \, dt \qquad (6.4)$$

Similarly for the x and y directions:

$$\bar{U}_x = \frac{1}{T} \int_0^T U_x \, dt \qquad (i)$$

$$\bar{U}_y = \frac{1}{T} \int_0^T U_y \, dt \qquad (ii)$$

where T is 0.12 s for this example. There are 13 data points for each component of velocity in Table 6.2. This number is insufficient to use the discrete sample equation, Eq. (6.9).

It is possible to plot the given data in the form of velocity versus time and evaluate the time-averaged velocities graphically by measuring the area under the curves. In Table 6.2, the time interval between each of the 13 points is constant and equal to 0.01 s. Let the increment in time be Δt and the number of intervals in time be I so that

$$\Delta t = 0.01 \text{ s} \qquad I = 12 \tag{iii}$$

Then the limit T in Eqs. (6.4), (i), and (ii) is

$$T = I\,\Delta t = 0.12 \text{ s} \tag{iv}$$

Instead of preparing three graphs, it is convenient to solve this example by performing a numerical integration, since the data are evenly spaced in the abscissa. One possibility is to use Simpson's rule, which is described in standard textbooks on numerical analysis and in handbooks [P4]. However, the simplest method is the trapezoid rule, which will be demonstrated here. Consider the first two points for the x direction in Table 6.2:

$$
\begin{aligned}
t &= 0.00 \qquad U_x = 3.84 \text{ m s}^{-1} \\
t &= 0.01 \qquad U_x = 3.50 \text{ m s}^{-1}
\end{aligned}
\tag{v}
$$

Let y denote the ordinate and x the abscissa. The trapezoid rule finds the average height in the interval as the mean of the two values:

$$y_{\text{ave}} = (3.84 + 3.50)/2 = 3.67 \text{ m s}^{-1} \tag{vi}$$

The area contribution is the area of the rectangle formed by y_{ave} and Δt:

$$\text{AREA} = (y_{\text{ave}})(\Delta t) = (3.67)(0.01) = 0.0367 \text{ m} \tag{vii}$$

The trapezoid rule repeats this calculation for all $N-1$ intervals, where N is the total number of points, 13 for this example. Using the index i, which goes from 1 to 13, as shown in Table 6.2, the generalized formula for the trapezoid rule is

$$\text{AREA} = \frac{\Delta x}{2}\left(y_1 + y_N + 2\sum_{i=2}^{N-1} y_i\right) \tag{viii}$$

When Eq. (viii) is applied to this problem, it becomes

$$\text{AREA} = \frac{\Delta t}{2}\left(U_1 + U_{13} + 2\sum_{i=2}^{12} U_i\right) \tag{ix}$$

Equation (ix) is applied to each of Eqs. (6.4), (i), and (ii):

$$\bar{U}_x = \frac{\text{AREA}}{T} = \left(\frac{1}{0.12}\right)\left(\frac{0.01}{2}\right)[3.84 + 3.80 + (2)(3.50 + 3.80 + 3.60 + \cdots + 4.30)]$$

$$= 3.61 \text{ m s}^{-1} \tag{x}$$

Similarly

$$\bar{U}_y = 0.28 \text{ m s}^{-1} \tag{xi}$$

$$\bar{U}_z = 0.15 \text{ m s}^{-1}. \tag{xii}$$

The magnitude of any vector is the square root of the sum of the squares of the components in each direction:

$$\bar{U} = (\bar{U}_x^2 + \bar{U}_y^2 + \bar{U}_z^2)^{1/2}$$
$$= [(3.61)^2 + (0.28)^2 + (0.15)^2]^{1/2} = 3.624 \text{ m s}^{-1} \qquad \text{(xiii)}$$

Because of the low magnitude of $\bar{U}_y$ and $\bar{U}_z$, the direction of the velocity vector is very close to the x axis. The cosine of the angle between $\bar{U}$ and the x axis is $\bar{U}_x/\bar{U}$.

In the solution just presented, the simplest type of numerical integration was used to obtain the average velocities from the small sample of 13 points. As a matter of curiosity, let us compute these averages from Eq. (6.9):

$$\bar{U}_x = \frac{1}{N} \sum_{}^{N} U_x$$

$$= (1/13)(3.84 + 3.50 + 3.80 + 3.60 + \cdots + 3.80) = 3.626 \text{ m s}^{-1} \qquad \text{(xiv)}$$

This answer differs only 0.4 percent from that obtained in Eq. (x). This agreement is deemed fortuitous. Repeating the calculation for the y and z components of velocity, the approximations from Eq. (6.9) as applied to each direction are

$$\bar{U}_y = (1/13)(0.43 + \cdots + 0.35) = 3.75/13 = 0.289 \text{ m s}^{-1} \qquad \text{(xv)}$$
$$\bar{U}_z = (1/13)(0.19 + \cdots + 0.17) = 1.98/13 = 0.152 \text{ m s}^{-1} \qquad \text{(xvi)}$$

These answers vary from those in Eqs. (xi) and (xii) by only 3.0 percent and 1.5 percent, respectively.

6.2.1   Reynolds Rules of Averaging

When the important equations of Chapters 3 and 5 are applied to time-averaged values of ψ and U, some complex terms arise. As a result, the nomenclature becomes complex. For example, it is often necessary to take the average of a quantity already averaged. Let us denote the average of the average with a double bar superscript, e.g., $\bar{\bar{A}}$.

Another consideration is that if any fluctuating quantity (e.g., U') is time-averaged, that average must be zero as a consequence of its definition [cf. Eq. (6.6)]. However, if any quantity such as U' is squared before it is averaged (e.g., $\overline{U_x'^2}$), that average will be non-zero because each value of $U_x'^2$ is never less than zero. Also if the product of two fluctuating components is averaged (e.g., $\overline{U_x'U_y'}$), that average can be non-zero as well. Note the notation used in this case.

Because these averages are so important in turbulent theory, Reynolds formulated certain rules of approximation in the calculation of averages. These will not be discussed fully here but will be presented with the assumption that they do apply to the turbulence problem. The rules are:

1. Quantities which have already been averaged may be considered as constants in subsequent averaging:

$$\bar{\bar{A}} = \bar{A} \tag{6.10}$$

$$\overline{\bar{A}B} = \bar{A}\bar{B} \tag{6.11}$$

2. Averaging obeys the distributive law:

$$\overline{A + B} = \bar{A} + \bar{B} \tag{6.12}$$

3. Derivatives of quantities obey the averaging law:

$$\overline{\partial A/\partial x} = \partial \bar{A}/\partial x \tag{6.13}$$

An important consequence of these rules is evident from the following treatment of the average of the product AB, where the A and the B are instantaneous quantities, each composed as the sum of a mean and a fluctuating value [cf. Eq. (6.6) for U_x]:

$$\overline{AB} = \overline{(\bar{A} + A')(\bar{B} + B')} = \overline{\bar{A}\bar{B}} + \overline{A'\bar{B}} + \overline{\bar{A}B'} + \overline{A'B'} = \bar{A}\bar{B} + \overline{A'B'} \tag{6.14}$$

where the terms $\overline{A'\bar{B}}$ and $\overline{\bar{A}B'}$ are zero for the reasons discussed at the beginning of this section. The application of the Reynolds rules in Eq. (6.14) shows that upon averaging any product of instantaneous quantities a meaningful term $\bar{A}\bar{B}$ is recovered that contains the averages of the two quantities; however, in addition, an unwanted term appears, i.e., the average of the product of the fluctuations of those two quantities. It will be shown shortly that this average of the product of fluctuations cannot be eliminated in the analysis of turbulent flow.

The product of a vector A times a vector B is a second-order tensor and involves nine terms.[5] For example, the product UU produces nine terms; note that U was defined in Eq. (6.7). If U is the instantaneous velocity and is replaced [via Eq. (6.8)] by the sum of the mean velocity plus the fluctuation U', then the product UU will contain nine terms of fluctuation products, as well as nine terms of average products:

$$\overline{UU} = \bar{U}\bar{U} + \overline{U'U'} \tag{6.15}$$

where each term is a second-order tensor and is a representation of an array of nine elements. Equation (6.15) is the vector counterpart of Eq. (6.14). Several examples of the elements of Eq. (6.15), taken term by term, are

$$\overline{U_x U_x} = \overline{U_x^2} = \bar{U}_x \bar{U}_x + \overline{U_x'^2} \tag{6.16}$$

$$\overline{U_x U_y} = \bar{U}_x \bar{U}_y + \overline{U_x' U_y'} \tag{6.17}$$

The other seven products follow similarly.

---

[5] For a brief discussion of tensors, see Section 2.4 and especially Eqs. (2.40) through (2.46).

At the beginning of this section, it was stated that the time average of any fluctuating component is zero. This conclusion is logical when Eq. (6.8) is examined:

$$U = \bar{U} + U' \tag{6.8}$$

After all, the average velocity $\bar{U}$ is found by averaging U. It is easy to prove that $\overline{U'}$ is zero by applying Reynolds rules to Eq. (6.8):

$$\bar{U} = \bar{\bar{U}} + \overline{U'} \tag{6.18}$$

Since the first rule is that the average of an average is the average [cf. Eq. (6.10)], this equation becomes

$$\bar{U} = \bar{U} + \overline{U'} \tag{6.19}$$

or

$$\overline{U'} = 0 \tag{6.20}$$

The quantity $\overline{U'}$ is a vector, and clearly each part must be zero in order to satisfy Eq. (6.20):

$$\overline{U'_x} = \overline{U'_y} = \overline{U'_z} = 0 \tag{6.21}$$

Even though $\overline{U'_x}$ and $\overline{U'_y}$ are zero, the quantity $\overline{U'_x U'_y}$ will not be zero in the general case. Similarly, the quantity $\overline{U'_x U'_x}$, or $\overline{U'^2_x}$, is non-zero and must always be positive as well. The quantities $\overline{U'^2_x}$, $\overline{U'^2_y}$, and $\overline{U'^2_z}$ must often be computed for turbulent flows. The equation for $\overline{U'^2_x}$, sometimes called the mean square of U'_x, is

$$\overline{U'^2_x} = \frac{1}{T} \int_0^T (U'_x)^2 \, dt = \frac{1}{T} \int_0^T (U_x - \bar{U}_x)^2 \, dt \tag{6.22}$$

where U'_x is replaced with its definition, Eq. (6.5). This equation is similar to Eq. (6.4), which defined the mean of U_z. For equally spaced digital data, Eq. (6.22) is approximated by

$$\overline{U'^2_x} = \frac{1}{N} \sum^N (U'_x)^2 = \frac{1}{N} \sum^N (U_x - \bar{U}_x)^2 \tag{6.23}$$

Again, N is the number of points available to compute $\bar{U}_x$ and therefore $\overline{U'^2_x}$. The equations for the other two components in the y and z directions are analogous to Eqs. (6.22) and (6.23).

Since the property ψ in Eq. (3.60) refers to the instantaneous value at any point of time, it follows that

$$\psi = \bar{\psi} + \psi' \tag{6.24}$$

In heat or mass transfer in a turbulent flow field, not only is there a distribution of velocities but a distribution of fluctuating temperatures or concentrations as well. The following equations based on Eq. (6.24) may be written:

$$\rho c_p T = c_p(\bar{\rho}\bar{T} + \bar{\rho}T' + \rho'\bar{T} + \rho'T') \qquad (6.25)$$

$$C_A = \bar{C}_A + C'_A \qquad (6.26)$$

$$\rho = \bar{\rho} + \rho' \qquad (6.27)$$

In Eq. (6.25), c_p has been assumed constant; the product (ρT) is first expanded as illustrated in Eq. (6.24) and the product $(\bar{\rho}\bar{T})$ simplified as illustrated in Eq. (6.14). Rigorous solutions of turbulent heat or mass transfer problems must consider random fluctuation of ρ, T, or C_A as well as the velocity. Of course, for incompressible flow with constant properties, there are no fluctuations in ρ or c_p, and Eq. (6.25) simplifies considerably:

$$\rho c_p T = \rho c_p(\bar{T} + T') \qquad (6.28)$$

   A familiar analogy to the mean and fluctuation velocities can be found in electrical power applications. In the United States, electric lights, clocks, televisions, etc., are powered by electricity at 115 volts and 60 hertz (cycles per second). In this case, the average voltage $\bar{E}$ is zero, and the instantaneous voltage (E) is identical to the fluctuation in voltage (E'). Clearly, this is a special application of the analysis just presented for turbulence. Figure 6.9 shows a typical sine wave electrical signal. The current alternates in direction, and 115 volts corresponds to the root-mean-square (r.m.s.) voltage. The mean square of a quantity is computed by integrating its square over a period of time T [see Eq. (6.22) for the mean square of U'_x]. The root-mean-square is simply the square root of the mean square. In turbulence, the concept of mean square is applied to fluctuations about a mean quantity. In the study of a.c. electricity, where $\bar{E}$ is zero, the r.m.s. voltage is defined by

$$\sqrt{\overline{E^2}} = \sqrt{\overline{E'^2}} = \left(\frac{1}{T}\int_0^T (E')^2\, dt\right)^{1/2} \qquad (6.29)$$

For a pure sine wave:

$$\sqrt{\overline{E^2}} = \sqrt{\overline{E'^2}} = 0.707 E_{max} \qquad (6.30)$$

The term $\overline{E'^2}$ is similar to $\overline{U'^2_x}$, which appears in Eqs. (6.16) and (6.22).

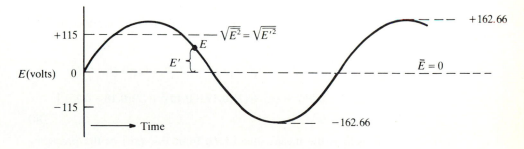

FIGURE 6.9
A sine wave electrical signal.

Note that direct current (d.c.) has a non-zero $\bar{E}$; direct current is used in some electrical systems and in low-voltage applications. The r.m.s. voltage about the mean in d.c. circuits is ideally zero because the voltage is held constant and there is no fluctuation about the mean, i.e., E' is zero.

The mean square concept as expressed by Eq. (6.22) may be applied to any of the fluctuating variables cited in Eqs. (6.14) through (6.28). The fluctuating velocities are also used to compute the intensities of turbulence. The intensity of turbulence is defined as the ratio of the r.m.s. value of the fluctuating component to the magnitude of the velocity vector, expressed as a percentage:

$$I_x = \frac{100\sqrt{\overline{U'^2_x}}}{U} \tag{6.31}$$

The equations for y and z components are similar. All intensities are, of course, zero in laminar flow, up to 10–15 percent in turbulent pipe flow and as much as 100 percent in a mixing vessel near the impeller.

Example 6.4. For the data of Example 6.3, calculate the three r.m.s. values of the fluctuating velocities, the corresponding intensities of turbulence, and the cross turbulence term $\overline{U'_x U'_y}$. Express the cross term as a ratio to the r.m.s. values.

Answer. Equation (6.22) gives the mean squared value $\overline{U'^2_x}$, and the r.m.s. value is the square root. The z component of velocity will be illustrated; Eq. (6.22) for the z component becomes

$$\overline{U'^2_z} = \frac{1}{T}\int_0^T (U'_z)^2 \, dt = \frac{1}{T}\int_0^T (U_z - \bar{U}_z)^2 \, dt \tag{i}$$

The trapezoid rule as given by Eq. (viii) in Example 6.3 will be used to evaluate the integral in Eq. (i):

$$\overline{U'^2_z} = \frac{1}{T}\int_0^T (U_z - \bar{U}_z)^2 \, dt$$

$$= \frac{1}{T}\frac{\Delta t}{2}\left[(U_z - \bar{U}_z)_1^2 + (U_z - \bar{U}_z)_N^2 + 2\sum_{i=2}^{12} (U_z - \bar{U}_z)_i^2\right] \tag{ii}$$

For T and Δt equal to 0.12 s and 0.01 s respectively, the mean square velocity in the z direction is

$$\overline{U'^2_z} = \left(\frac{1}{0.12}\right)\left(\frac{0.01}{2}\right)[(0.19 - 0.15)^2 + (0.17 - 0.15)^2 + (2)(0.16 - 0.15)^2$$

$$+ (2)(0.17 - 0.15)^2 + \cdots + (2)(0.17 - 0.15)^2 + (2)(0.18 - 0.15)^2]$$

$$= 8.917 \times 10^{-4} \, \text{m}^2 \, \text{s}^{-2} \tag{iii}$$

where the value 0.15 is the mean value of U_z from Eq. (xii) of the preceding example. The r.m.s. value is obtained from Eq. (iii) by taking the square root:

$$\sqrt{\overline{U'^2_z}} = \sqrt{8.917 \times 10^{-4}} = 0.02986 \, \text{m s}^{-1} \tag{iv}$$

Equation (6.16) relates the mean square velocity to the square of the mean plus the mean of the square of the fluctuating velocity; for the z direction, Eq. (6.16) becomes

$$\overline{U_z^2} = (\bar{U}_z)^2 + \overline{U_z'^2} \tag{v}$$

After substituting in the numbers and taking the square root, the r.m.s. value of the instantaneous z velocity is

$$\sqrt{\overline{U_z^2}} = \sqrt{(0.15)^2 + 8.917 \times 10^{-4}} = 0.1529 \text{ m s}^{-1} \tag{vi}$$

Note that the result in Eq. (iv) is the r.m.s. value of the fluctuating velocity as is commonly reported for turbulence data, while Eq. (vi) is the r.m.s. value of the instantaneous velocity (of less interest).

It is also possible to evaluate $\overline{U_z^2}$ directly through use of the following equation:

$$\overline{U_z^2} = \frac{1}{T} \int_0^T U_z^2 \, dt \tag{vii}$$

Applying the trapezoid rule to Eq. (vii) results in

$$\overline{U_z^2} = \frac{1}{T} \frac{\Delta t}{2} \left[(U_z)_1^2 + (U_z)_N^2 + 2 \sum_{i=2}^{N-1} (U_z)_i^2 \right]$$

$$= \left(\frac{1}{0.12} \right) \left(\frac{0.01}{2} \right) \{ (0.19)^2 + (0.17)^2 + (2)[(0.16)^2 + \cdots + (0.18)^2] \}$$

$$= 2.807 \times 10^{-3} / 0.12 = 0.02340 \text{ m}^2 \text{ s}^{-2} \tag{viii}$$

The r.m.s. value is

$$\sqrt{\overline{U_z^2}} = \sqrt{0.02340} = 0.1529 \text{ m s}^{-1} \tag{ix}$$

This answer agrees with that in Eq. (vi) because the equations used are mathematically identical.

The r.m.s. values of the fluctuating velocities can also be calculated from Eq. (6.23), which is recommended for large samples. Equation (6.23) for the mean square velocity in the z direction is

$$\overline{U_z'^2} = \frac{1}{N} \sum^N (U_z')^2 = \frac{1}{N} \sum^N (U_z - \bar{U}_z)^2 \tag{x}$$

Using this equation, the mean square fluctuating z velocity is

$$\overline{U_z'^2} = \left(\frac{1}{13} \right) [(0.19 - 0.1523)^2 + \cdots + (0.17 - 0.1523)^2]$$

$$= 8.947 \times 10^{-4} \text{ m}^2 \text{ s}^{-2} \tag{xi}$$

The corresponding r.m.s. value is

$$\sqrt{\overline{U_z'^2}} = \sqrt{8.947 \times 10^{-4}} = 0.02991 \text{ m s}^{-1} \tag{xii}$$

Agreement between Eqs. (iv) and (xii) is excellent. It is more common to find that the error in the fluctuating velocity exceeds that in the mean velocity, because errors are compounded as a result of subtracting the mean from the instantaneous velocity.

The answer in Eq. (xii) can be used in calculations similar to those in Eqs. (v) through (ix). Using Eq. (v):

$$\overline{U_z^2} = (\bar{U}_z)^2 + \overline{U_z'^2} = (0.1523)^2 + 8.947 \times 10^{-4} = 0.02409 \text{ m}^2 \text{ s}^{-2} \qquad \text{(xiii)}$$

The r.m.s. value is

$$\sqrt{\overline{U_z^2}} = \sqrt{0.02409} = 0.1552 \text{ m s}^{-1} \qquad \text{(xiv)}$$

This answer compares with that in Eq. (ix) by 1.5 percent.

The intensity of turbulence in the z direction may be obtained from applying Eq. (6.31) to the z direction:

$$I_z = 100\sqrt{\overline{U_z'^2}}/U = (100)(0.02986)/(3.626) = 0.82 \text{ percent} \qquad \text{(xv)}$$

where 3.626 m s^{-1} is the magnitude of the velocity [Eq. (xiv) of Example 6.3]. Similarly for the x and y directions:

$$\sqrt{\overline{U_x^2}} = 3.63 \text{ m s}^{-1} \qquad \text{(xvi)}$$

$$\sqrt{\overline{U_x'^2}} = 0.41 \text{ m s}^{-1} \qquad \text{(xvii)}$$

$$I_x = 11.37 \text{ percent} \qquad \text{(xviii)}$$

$$\sqrt{\overline{U_y^2}} = 0.288 \text{ m s}^{-1} \qquad \text{(xix)}$$

$$\sqrt{\overline{U_y'^2}} = 0.069 \text{ m s}^{-1} \qquad \text{(xx)}$$

$$I_y = 1.92 \text{ percent} \qquad \text{(xxi)}$$

Computation of the quantity $\overline{U_x'U_y'}$ is more tedious. First, Eq. (6.8) is used to obtain U_x' and U_y' at each instant in time; the product of these is then integrated as before. For example, for time zero:

$$U_x' = 3.84 - 3.61 = 0.23 \text{ m s}^{-1} \qquad \text{(xxii)}$$

$$U_y' = 0.43 - 0.28 = 0.15 \text{ m s}^{-1} \qquad \text{(xxiii)}$$

$$U_x'U_y' = (0.23)(0.15) = 0.0345 \text{ m}^2 \text{ s}^{-2} \qquad \text{(xxiv)}$$

These calculations are repeated for the remaining points. The average is obtained from

$$\overline{U_x'U_y'} = \frac{1}{T} \int_0^T (U_x'U_y') \, dt = 0.01108 \text{ m}^2 \text{ s}^{-2} \qquad \text{(xxv)}$$

The ratio requested can then be calculated as

$$\overline{U_x'U_y'}/(\sqrt{\overline{U_x'^2}} \sqrt{\overline{U_y'^2}}) = (0.01108)/[(0.41)(0.069)] = 0.39 \qquad \text{(xxvi)}$$

6.2.2 Reynolds Equations for Incompressible Turbulent Flow

Equation (3.78) is the general property balance for constant density and constant transport coefficient δ:

$$\partial\psi/\partial t + (U \cdot \nabla)\psi = \dot{\psi}_G + \delta(\nabla^2 \psi) \qquad \text{(3.78)}$$

This equation can be applied to turbulence with the instantaneous vector velocity given by Eq. (6.8) and the instantaneous property given by Eq. (6.24). Substitution of Eqs. (6.8) and (6.24) into Eq. (3.78) yields an equation that involves average and fluctuating components:

$$\partial \bar{\psi} / \partial t + \partial \psi' / \partial t + (\bar{U} \cdot \nabla) \bar{\psi} + (\bar{U} \cdot \nabla) \psi' + (U' \cdot \nabla) \bar{\psi} + (U' \cdot \nabla) \psi'$$
$$= \overline{\dot{\psi}_G} + \dot{\psi}_G' + \delta(\nabla^2 \bar{\psi}) + \delta(\nabla^2 \psi') \tag{6.32}$$

If this equation is averaged by applying Reynolds rules of averaging, the following equation is obtained, after considerable manipulation:

$$\partial \bar{\psi} / \partial t + (\bar{U} \cdot \nabla) \bar{\psi} + \overline{(U' \cdot \nabla) \psi'} = \overline{\dot{\psi}_G} + \delta(\nabla^2 \bar{\psi}) \tag{6.33}$$

Again, without showing the details of the mathematics, this equation can be rearranged to

$$\partial \bar{\psi} / \partial t + (\bar{U} \cdot \nabla) \bar{\psi} = \overline{\dot{\psi}_G} + \delta(\nabla^2 \bar{\psi}) - [\nabla \cdot (\overline{U' \psi'})] \tag{6.34}$$

Note that this equation has the same form as the original equation, Eq. (3.78), except that average properties now appear in place of point properties, and an additional term is included that is associated with the fluctuations. Equation (6.34) cannot be solved, even with the assumptions of constant density and δ already made, for there are more unknowns than there are available equations. It should be noted that Eq. (3.78) is determinate in the sense that there are as many equations as unknowns. Equation (3.78) cannot be solved analytically because of the complexity of the instantaneous velocities and properties. It is clear that one pays quite a penalty for the use of averages, i.e., more unknowns than equations.

Since neither Eq. (3.78) nor Eq. (6.34) may be solved analytically, the possibility of solving Eq. (3.78) by direct numerical means may be considered [B7]. Such a solution bypasses the last term in Eq. (6.34), which was introduced through Reynolds rules of averages and the presence of which results in more unknowns than equations. Such an approach encounters the difficulty that instantaneous U and ψ in Eq. (3.78) fluctuate in three dimensions even for a turbulent flow in one direction, as in a pipe. Thus, the numerical solution is inherently three-dimensional. Turbulent eddies range in size from a fraction of a millimeter to those approximating the size of the system (i.e., a meter). This range can be of order of 1000 in any one direction. A solution space to be solved numerically would therefore comprise a cube 1000 units on each side or a numerical mesh of $(1000)^3$, which is 10^9 and is indeed a large number. Thus, a full direct numerical solution has yet to be accomplished, and the use of averages cannot yet be abandoned.

Over the years a tremendous amount of work has been focused on Reynolds' rules of averaging and the resultant Eq. (6.34). In most practical applications, only the average quantities ($\bar{U}$, $\bar{T}$, $\bar{C}_A$, or $\bar{\rho}$) can be easily measured. For example, a thermometer or thermocouple in a pipe line measures $\bar{T}$. Examination of Eq. (6.34) shows that it contains only one term with instantaneous fluctuations, $[\nabla \cdot (\overline{U' \psi'})]$, whereas in Eq. (3.78) every term contains instantaneous properties.

The nature of Eq. (6.34) can be seen more clearly if some of the equations for transport are written out in detail. To repeat, both the density and the transport coefficient are assumed constant in the following equations. The x component equation for momentum is found by substituting for ψ and ψ' in Eq. (6.34):

$$\rho\frac{\partial \bar{U}_x}{\partial t} + \rho(\bar{U}\cdot\boldsymbol{\nabla})\bar{U}_x$$

$$= -\frac{\partial \bar{p}}{\partial x} + \mu(\nabla^2\,\bar{U}_x) - (\rho)\left(\frac{\partial}{\partial x}\,(\overline{U_x'^2}) + \frac{\partial}{\partial y}\,(\overline{U_x'U_y'}) + \frac{\partial}{\partial z}\,(\overline{U_x'U_z'})\right) \quad (6.35)$$

where the operation $(\bar{U}\cdot\boldsymbol{\nabla})$ from Table 5.1 is in this case

$$(\bar{U}\cdot\boldsymbol{\nabla})\bar{U}_x = \bar{U}_x\frac{\partial \bar{U}_x}{\partial x} + \bar{U}_y\frac{\partial \bar{U}_x}{\partial y} + \bar{U}_z\frac{\partial \bar{U}_x}{\partial z} \quad (6.36)$$

Also, from the same table the term $\nabla^2\,\bar{U}_x$ is

$$\nabla^2\,\bar{U}_x = \frac{\partial^2\bar{U}_x}{\partial x^2} + \frac{\partial^2\bar{U}_x}{\partial y^2} + \frac{\partial^2\bar{U}_x}{\partial z^2} \quad (6.37)$$

The term $[\boldsymbol{\nabla}\cdot(\overline{U'\psi'})]$ is of the form $(\boldsymbol{\nabla}\cdot\bar{A})$, which from Table 5.1 is

$$(\boldsymbol{\nabla}\cdot\bar{A}) = \frac{\partial \bar{A}_x}{\partial x} + \frac{\partial \bar{A}_y}{\partial y} + \frac{\partial \bar{A}_z}{\partial z} \quad (6.38)$$

Thus, the term $[\boldsymbol{\nabla}\cdot(\overline{U'\psi'})]$ becomes

$$[\boldsymbol{\nabla}\cdot(\overline{U'\psi'})] = \frac{\partial}{\partial x}\,(\overline{U_x'\psi'}) + \frac{\partial}{\partial y}\,(\overline{U_y'\psi'}) + \frac{\partial}{\partial z}\,(\overline{U_z'\psi'}) \quad (6.39)$$

The x component of momentum is found from Eq. (6.39) with ψ equal to $\rho\bar{U}_x$ and ψ' equal to $\rho U_x'$:

$$\rho[\boldsymbol{\nabla}\cdot(\overline{U'U_x'})] = \rho\left(\frac{\partial}{\partial x}\,(\overline{U_x'^2}) + \frac{\partial}{\partial y}\,(\overline{U_y'U_x'}) + \frac{\partial}{\partial z}\,(\overline{U_z'U_x'})\right) \quad (6.40)$$

The equations for the y and z components of momentum also follow from Eq. (6.34):

$$\rho\frac{\partial \bar{U}_y}{\partial t} + \rho(\bar{U}\cdot\boldsymbol{\nabla})\bar{U}_y$$

$$= -\frac{\partial \bar{p}}{\partial y} + \mu(\nabla^2\,\bar{U}_y) - \rho\left(\frac{\partial}{\partial x}\,(\overline{U_x'U_y'}) + \frac{\partial}{\partial y}\,(\overline{U_y'^2}) + \frac{\partial}{\partial z}\,(\overline{U_y'U_z'})\right) \quad (6.41)$$

$$\rho\frac{\partial \bar{U}_z}{\partial t} + \rho(\bar{U}\cdot\boldsymbol{\nabla})\bar{U}_z$$

$$= -\frac{\partial \bar{p}}{\partial z} + \mu(\nabla^2\,\bar{U}_z) - \rho\left(\frac{\partial}{\partial x}\,(\overline{U_x'U_z'}) + \frac{\partial}{\partial y}\,(\overline{U_y'U_z'}) + \frac{\partial}{\partial z}\,(\overline{U_z'^2})\right) \quad (6.42)$$

The equation for heat transport is

$$\rho c_{\mathrm{p}} \frac{\partial \bar{T}}{\partial t} + \rho c_{\mathrm{p}}(\bar{U} \cdot \nabla)\bar{T}$$

$$= \bar{\dot{T}}_{\mathrm{G}} + k(\nabla^2 \bar{T}) - \rho c_{\mathrm{p}}\left(\frac{\partial}{\partial x}(\overline{U'_x T'}) + \frac{\partial}{\partial y}(\overline{U'_y T'}) + \frac{\partial}{\partial z}(\overline{U'_z T'})\right) \quad (6.43)$$

The equation for mass transport is

$$\frac{\partial \bar{C}_{\mathrm{A}}}{\partial t} + (\bar{U} \cdot \nabla)\bar{C}_{\mathrm{A}} = \bar{\dot{C}}_{\mathrm{A,G}} + D(\nabla^2 \bar{C}_{\mathrm{A}}) - \frac{\partial}{\partial x}(\overline{U'_x C'_{\mathrm{A}}}) - \frac{\partial}{\partial y}(\overline{U'_y C'_{\mathrm{A}}}) - \frac{\partial}{\partial z}(\overline{U'_z C'_{\mathrm{A}}})$$

$$(6.44)$$

The mass generation term might involve a contribution from a chemical reaction such as

$$\bar{\dot{C}}_{\mathrm{A,G}} = -k_n\overline{C_{\mathrm{A}}^n} \quad (6.45)$$

which for $n = 1$ is $k_1\bar{C}_{\mathrm{A}}$ and for $n = 2$ is $k_2(\bar{C}_{\mathrm{A}}^2 + \overline{C'^2_{\mathrm{A}}})$.

The overall mass balance equation (continuity) can also be worked out in a similar manner. Equation (3.71) reduces to

$$\partial \bar{\rho}/\partial t = -[\nabla \cdot (\bar{\rho}\bar{U})] - [\nabla \cdot (\overline{\rho' U'})] \quad (6.46)$$

If the flow is incompressible, Eq. (6.46) reduces to

$$(\nabla \cdot \bar{U}) = 0 \quad (6.47)$$

This result is similar to Eq. (3.74), but now applies to the mean velocity. By use of Eq. (6.8), it can be easily shown that

$$(\nabla \cdot U') = 0 \quad (6.48)$$

A comparison of any of these equations [Eqs. (6.35), (6.41), and (6.42)] with the corresponding laminar flow equations of Chapter 5 shows the difference to be the appearance of time-averaged terms and the additional term involving fluctuating quantities. These nine additional terms are called the Reynolds stresses. Equations (6.35), (6.41) and (6.42) are commonly called the Reynolds equations for turbulent flow with constant density and transport coefficients.

6.2.3 Reynolds Stresses

Nine terms can be obtained by multiplying the density by $[\nabla \cdot (\overline{U' \psi'})]$, which is the last term in Eq. (6.34) with $(\rho U')$ substituted for ψ'. These terms are called the Reynolds stresses. Specifically, the Reynolds stress tensor is $\rho(\overline{U'U'})$, which has nine components, as seen from inspection of Eqs. (6.35), (6.41) and (6.42). When completely written out, the Reynolds stress tensor is

$$\rho(\overline{U'U'}) = \rho \begin{pmatrix} \overline{U'^2_x} & \overline{U'_x U'_y} & \overline{U'_x U'_z} \\ \overline{U'_y U'_x} & \overline{U'^2_y} & \overline{U'_y U'_z} \\ \overline{U'_z U'_x} & \overline{U'_z U'_y} & \overline{U'^2_z} \end{pmatrix} \quad (6.49)$$

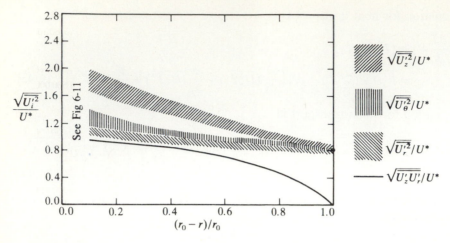

FIGURE 6.10
Turbulent stresses for pipe flow. (*From Laufer, NACA Report 1174 (1954). By permission.*)

Each element on the right-hand side of Eq. (6.49) is called a Reynolds stress because those terms arise from the Reynolds rules of averaging. Less commonly, those terms are called eddy stresses or turbulent stresses. There are nine Reynolds stresses in total, six of which are different, since $\overline{U'_z U'_x}$ equals $\overline{U'_x U'_z}$ and so on; the tensor on the right-hand side of Eq. (6.49) is said to be symmetrical. Four of these fluctuating velocity elements in Eq. (6.49) were calculated in Example 6.4 for the data of Example 6.3. The Reynolds stresses are obtained by multiplying the velocity terms by the density.

The velocity components of the normal Reynolds stresses $\rho \overline{U'^2_x}$, $\rho \overline{U'^2_y}$, $\rho \overline{U'^2_z}$ can be measured with the hot-wire or hot-film anemometer shown in Fig. 6.4; however, a more complex multi-element probe must be used for the cross stress measurements. The instantaneous output from the unit in Fig. 6.4 can be directed into a root-mean-square meter to measure $\sqrt{\overline{U'^2_x}}$. In Fig. 6.10, these terms are plotted as a function of dimensionless distance for pipe flow. The normalizing velocity U^* and the dimensionless distance y^+ used in Fig. 6.10 will be explained in the next section.[6] Reynolds stresses are also often plotted as a fraction of the maximum center line velocity. There is some variation of the Reynolds stresses with Reynolds number, but these are not shown in the figure except as a range of the values reported in the literature. Near the center of the pipe the effect of Reynolds number is quite small. For the region close to the wall, which is the region of most interest for turbulent transport phenomena, Fig. 6.11 shows that, as expected, the fluctuating terms go to zero. For the area near the wall, the effect of Reynolds number is large and is shown in Fig. 6.11. A review and summary is available [B6].

---

[6] See Eq. (6.53) for U^* and Eq. (6.79) for y^+.

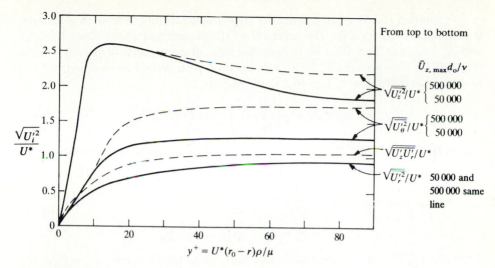

From top to bottom

$\bar{U}_{z,\text{max}} d_o / \nu$

$\sqrt{\overline{U_z'^2}}/U^* \begin{cases} 500\,000 \\ 50\,000 \end{cases}$

$\sqrt{\overline{U_\theta'^2}}/U^* \begin{cases} 500\,000 \\ 50\,000 \end{cases}$

$\sqrt{\overline{U_z' U_r'}}/U^*$

$\sqrt{\overline{U_r'^2}}/U^*$ 50 000 and 500 000 same line

FIGURE 6.11
Turbulent stresses near the wall of a pipe; $(r_o - r)/r_o < 0.1$. (*From Laufer, NACA Report 1174 (1954). By permission.*)

6.2.4 Turbulent Flow in Channels and Pipes

Typical coordinates used for a channel are shown in Fig. 6.12(a). A channel is formed by two parallel plates, infinitely large in the z direction so that the partial derivative of any variable, such as the time-averaged velocity, with respect to z is zero. The time-averaged velocity is also constant in the x direction if the density is constant. To prove this, one need only repeat Example 3.7, this time using the continuity equation for turbulent flow as given in Eq. (6.47). Since the equations used differ only in the overbar, the final results will be the same, but will apply to the time-averaged velocity.

The velocity profile in a channel varies from zero velocity at the wall to the maximum velocity at the center line. Here y is the distance from the center line, in contrast to the flat plate problem in Fig. 6.2 for which y is the distance from the flat plate surface.

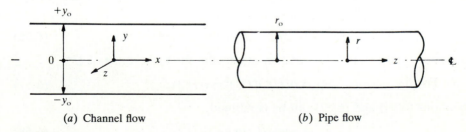

(*a*) Channel flow   (*b*) Pipe flow

FIGURE 6.12
Coordinate systems for flow in channels and pipes.

Equation (6.35) when applied to steady-state turbulent flow in a channel is simplified considerably. The term $(\bar{U} \cdot \nabla)\bar{U}_x$ is seen to be zero since both $\bar{U}_y$ and $\bar{U}_z$ are zero and $\partial\bar{U}_x/\partial x$ is zero because of continuity, Eq. (6.47). The terms $\partial(\overline{U_z'^2})/\partial x$ and $\partial(\overline{U_x'U_z'})/\partial z$ will both be zero when the average is for a long time period. Hence, Eq. (6.35) reduces to

$$0 = -d\bar{p}/dx + \mu\left(\frac{d^2}{dy^2}\bar{U}_x\right) - \rho\left(\frac{d}{dy}(\overline{U_x'U_y'})\right) \tag{6.50}$$

In Eq. (6.50), ordinary differentials can be used since $(d\bar{p}/dx)$ is a constant and the only variation is with y. The appropriate boundary conditions are

$$\bar{U}_x(y = \pm y_o) = 0$$
$$\overline{U_x'U_y'}(y = \pm y_o) = 0 \tag{6.51}$$
$$p(x = 0) = p_1 \qquad p(x = L) = p_2$$

Equation (6.50) can be integrated once and rearranged to yield

$$\rho(y/y_o)(U^*)^2 = -\mu(d\bar{U}_x/dy) + \rho(\overline{U_x'U_y'}) \tag{6.52}$$

where the friction velocity U^* is defined by

$$(U^*)^2 = \tau_w/\rho = (y_o/\rho)[(-\Delta p)/L] \tag{6.53}$$

The wall shear stress τ_w was discussed in detail in Chapter 4 [see Eq. (4.80)]. Note that the friction velocity has units of length per time. The friction velocity U^* used here should not be confused with the molar velocity U^* given in Eq. (3.23).

The equation corresponding to Eq. (6.52) in cylindrical coordinates for pipe flow is

$$\rho(r/r_o)(U^*)^2 = -\mu(d\bar{U}_z/dr) + \rho(\overline{U_r'U_z'}) \tag{6.54}$$

where the coordinate system is in Fig. 6.12(b). The friction velocity for pipe flow is

$$(U^*)^2 = \frac{\tau_w}{\rho} = \frac{(r_o/2)[(-\Delta p)/L]}{\rho} \tag{6.55}$$

where τ_w is from Eq. (4.80). The shear stress was shown to be linear in Eq. (4.81):

$$\tau_{rz} = (r/2)[(-\Delta p)/L] = (r/r_o)\tau_w \tag{6.56}$$

Equations (6.55) and (6.56) yield an expression for τ_w in terms of U^*:

$$\tau_{rz} = \rho(r/r_o)(U^*)^2 = (r/r_o)\tau_w \tag{6.57}$$

Equations (6.54) and (6.57) can be combined:

$$\tau_{rz} = -\mu(d\bar{U}_z/dr) + \rho(\overline{U_r'U_z'}) \tag{6.58}$$

The shear stress τ_{rz} in Eq. (6.58) contains one term that looks identical to

Newton's law of viscosity, Eq. (2.5), except that U_x is replaced with $\bar{U}_z$. On this basis, it is possible to consider that τ_{rz} contains a laminar-like contribution (henceforth to be called τ_L) and a turbulent contribution (denoted as τ_T):

$$\tau_{rz} = \tau_L + \tau_T \tag{6.59}$$

where

$$\tau_L = -\mu(d\bar{U}_z/dr) \tag{6.60}$$

$$\tau_T = \rho(\overline{U_r'U_z'}) \tag{6.61}$$

Note that Eq. (6.60) is the same as the defining equation for viscosity, Eq. (4.18), but with the time-averaged velocity being used. This idea of a laminar contribution and a turbulent contribution will be carried forward in the next sections.

The only restriction on Eq. (6.54) for pipe flow is constant physical properties. Unfortunately there are still two unknowns in the one equation, Eq. (6.58), i.e., $\bar{U}_z$ and $\overline{U_r'U_z'}$. A second equation relating $\bar{U}_z$ and $\overline{U_r'U_z'}$ does not exist. There is no solution that yields both the variation of $\bar{U}_z$ with r and the quantity $\overline{U_r'U_z'}$.

The dilemma of having more unknowns than equations is fundamental and insurmountable when analyzing problems in turbulent flow. Practical problems require average properties such as $\bar{U}_z$; Reynolds rules are required to introduce average properties into Eq. (3.60) or (3.78); Reynolds rules introduce terms such as the Reynolds stresses; no new equations are available to relate the new terms to the average property, so no solution exists. This inability to solve exactly for the variables of the turbulent flow system constitutes one of the major problems of turbulence.

There are ways of generating additional equations; however, even more unknowns are always introduced in the process. Accordingly, approximate solutions or correlations make some reasonable assumptions about one of the unknown terms so that a solution is possible. Often a simple mechanism for the turbulence is assumed. Then the nature of the Reynolds stress is known, and the form of the velocity distribution is derived therefrom.

6.3 TURBULENCE MODELS

The problem of having more unknowns than equations is called the "closure problem of turbulence". This section will cover some of the earlier and well-known attempts at closure. More modern theories will also be presented.

6.3.1 The Boussinesq Theory

In the last section, Eq. (6.59) separated the shear stress into a laminar-like contribution and a turbulent contribution. Boussinesq's idea [B4] was to express Eq. (6.61) in a form similar to the laminar shear stress–shear rate equation, Eq. (6.60) or Eq. (4.18):

$$\tau_T = \rho(\overline{U_r'U_z'}) = -\varepsilon(\partial \bar{U}_z/\partial r) \tag{6.62}$$

In Eq. (6.62), the term $\partial \bar{U}_z/\partial r$, which is the slope of the velocity profile in the pipe or channel, is the shear rate, and ε is called the eddy viscosity. Note that ε is defined very similarly to μ. Combining Eqs. (6.62) with (6.58) and using the linear variation of shear stress of Eq. (6.57) gives

$$\tau_{rz} = \rho(r/r_o)(U^*)^2 = -(\mu + \varepsilon)(d\bar{U}_z/dr) \tag{6.63}$$

The eddy diffusivity of momentum E_τ is defined as follows:

$$E_\tau = \frac{\varepsilon}{\rho} \tag{6.64}$$

Then Eq. (6.63) becomes

$$\tau_{rz} = \rho(r/r_o)(U^*)^2 = -(\nu + E_\tau)\frac{d}{dr}(\rho \bar{U}_z) \tag{6.65}$$

Equation (6.65) can be converted to a dimensionless form involving the ratio of the eddy diffusivity of momentum to the kinematic viscosity:

$$E_\tau/\nu = \frac{-(r/r_o)(U^*)^2}{\nu(d\bar{U}_z/dr)} - 1 \tag{6.66}$$

Equation (6.66) applies for the case of constant density. Example 6.5 illustrates the use of Eq. (6.66) in conjunction with some velocity profile data.

Equation (6.65) does not solve the closure problem as there are still two unknowns and only one equation. The velocity is still unknown, and now ε or E_τ has replaced $\overline{U_r'U_z'}$ as an unknown. The eddy viscosity ε is associated with the turbulent contribution to the shear stress; it is calculated from the gradient of the mean velocity $\partial \bar{U}_z/\partial r$ after subtracting the laminar contribution to the shear stress. The eddy viscosity is also known as the turbulent coefficient or exchange coefficient.

The molecular coefficient of viscosity μ is defined in laminar flow by Eq. (4.18). It is independent of the Reynolds number, the flow geometry, the position in the fluid, and, for Newtonian materials, the shear rate. The eddy viscosity, on the other hand, is dependent on all of these.

The concept of eddy diffusivity of momentum is easily extended to the transfer of heat and mass:

$$(q/A)_r = -(\alpha + E_H)\frac{d}{dr}(\rho c_p \bar{T}) \tag{6.67}$$

$$(N_A/A)_r = -(D + E_M)(d\bar{C}_A/dr) \tag{6.68}$$

where E_H and E_M are the eddy thermal diffusivity and the eddy mass diffusivity, respectively. Note that E_H and E_M can have three components, one for each coordinate direction; the eddy diffusivity of momentum E_τ may have as many components as there are Reynolds stresses, i.e., nine according to Eq. (6.49).

The concept of eddy transfer has been applied to many engineering problems involving heat and mass transfer in turbulent flow. Generally, the method is not the most satisfactory, and a great deal of caution must be exercised so that improper assumptions will not be made. For example, the eddy viscosity values are constant as an exception rather than as a rule, and in any practical case the various eddy diffusivities are not equal to each other. Nevertheless, the use of the eddy viscosity concept is one of the most powerful practical tools available for treating turbulent flow problems, and consequently it will be considered further. If the assumption is made that the various eddy diffusivities are equal to each other and that the molecular properties are known, there is a possibility of solving certain mass and heat transfer problems. Although the assumption is only approximate over most of the turbulent flow and probably quite invalid in the vicinity of the wall, it is in many cases the only method available for even an approximate solution. An example of the method will be given near the end of this chapter when further necessary information on the turbulent velocity distribution has been developed.

6.3.2 The Prandtl Mixing Length

The concept of eddy viscosity replaced one unknown, the Reynolds stress, with another. The dependence of the eddy viscosity on the variables of the system must still be established for the eddy viscosity to be useful.

The early researchers usually formulated some mechanistic picture of the turbulence. One of these theories was that of Prandtl who expressed the eddy stress in terms of the mean velocity by means of a length that is characteristic of the degree of the turbulence. Prandtl called his new variable the mixing length, symbol l, which he characterized as the length of the path of a mass of fluid before it loses its individuality by mixing with its neighbors. This mixing length is analogous to the concept of the mean-free-path of the kinetic theory of gases. The difference between laminar flow and turbulent flow is explained as the difference between the exchange of individual molecules between layers and the exchange of whole groups of molecules. Prandtl's theory assumes that the momentum of a group of particles or fluid mass in one layer is transferred to another layer.

In Fig. 6.13, a mass of fluid is assumed to have a velocity $\bar{U}_{z,1}$ in a stream. A velocity exists in the direction perpendicular to the flow, which displaces this mass of fluid a distance l in the radial direction. The change in velocity is the difference between the velocity at the point of origin and that at its new position which is approximately given by $l(d\bar{U}_z/dr)$. The fluctuation U_z' experienced at the new point is this difference; i.e.,

$$U_z' = l\frac{d\bar{U}_z}{dr} \tag{6.69}$$

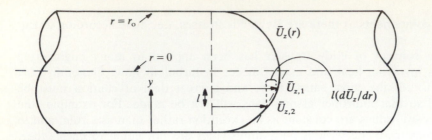

FIGURE 6.13
Mixing length for flow in a pipe.

The motion at right angles to this, U_r', must be of the same order because of the assumed momentum conservation, and is taken to be equal to U_z':

$$U_r' = l \frac{d\bar{U}_z}{dr} \tag{6.70}$$

Thus, the eddy stress is written as

$$\rho \overline{U_r' U_z'} = \rho l^2 \left(\frac{d\bar{U}_z}{dr} \right)^2 \tag{6.71}$$

The partially integrated Reynolds equation (6.54) can be combined with the expression obtained from the mixing length concept:

$$\tau_{rz} = \rho \frac{r}{r_o} (U^*)^2 = -\mu \frac{d\bar{U}_z}{dr} + \rho l^2 \left(\frac{d\bar{U}_z}{dr} \right)^2 \tag{6.72}$$

Equation (6.72) was solved by Prandtl assuming that the mixing length is directly proportional to the distance from the wall. In addition, Prandtl assumed that the shear stress was constant and equal to the wall value over the region of the flow being considered, and further that the viscous contribution was negligible. Thus, for fully developed turbulent flow the assumptions are as follows.

1. In the region being considered, the turbulent effects are much larger than the viscous effects. Thus, the term $\mu(d\bar{U}_z/dr)$ in Eq. (6.72) can be neglected.
2. In the region being considered, the stress τ_{rz} can be taken as τ_w. In other words r equals r_o.

These two assumptions are rather extreme, and Prandtl's mixing length theory is justly criticized on this basis. However, the final results support the assumptions and Eq. (6.72) has been greatly simplified; the densities cancel and after taking square roots, the result is

$$U^* = l \frac{d\bar{U}_z}{dr} \tag{6.73}$$

The third assumption is that the mixing length is proportional to the distance from the wall (y)

$$l = \kappa y \tag{6.74}$$

where κ is a universal constant and

$$y = r_o - r \tag{6.75}$$

Equation (6.75) is used to change the variable of integration from r to y, and it follows easily that

$$\bar{U}_z / U^* = \frac{1}{\kappa} \ln y + C \tag{6.76}$$

Equation (6.76) is the logarithmic velocity distribution for turbulent flow and is usually written as

$$U^+ = \frac{1}{\kappa} \ln y^+ + B \tag{6.77}$$

where the dimensionless velocity U^+ and dimensionless distance y^+ are defined by

$$U^+ = \frac{\bar{U}_z}{U^*} \tag{6.78}$$

$$y^+ = \frac{yU^*}{\nu} = \frac{yU^*\rho}{\mu} \tag{6.79}$$

The difference between Eqs. (6.76) and (6.77) is in the definition of the constant of integration; otherwise, the equations are the same. The two constants κ and B must be determined from the data obtained by measurements of the velocity distribution in the turbulent flow. Equation (6.77) has proved useful in correlating velocity profile data and will be referred to later in the appropriate section.

In the region very near the wall, Prandtl assumed that the fluid motion was greatly influenced by the wall through viscous forces. In this region, often called the viscous sublayer, it is the turbulence effects that are negligible and Prandtl's first assumption of negligible viscous effects must be modified. Thus, in this region he assumed that the first term $-\mu(d\bar{U}_z/dr)$ in Eq. (6.54) was important and that the second term $\rho \overline{U'_r U'_z}$ involving the Reynolds stress could be neglected. Prandtl also assumed that r/r_o is unity in the near-wall region. After changing the variable of integration by use of Eq. (6.75), Eq. (6.54) becomes

$$\rho(U^*)^2 = -\mu \frac{d\bar{U}_z}{dr} = \mu \frac{d\bar{U}_z}{dy} \tag{6.80}$$

Equation (6.80) can be integrated with the boundary condition of zero velocity at the wall:

$$\rho(U^*)^2 = \frac{\mu \bar{U}_z}{y} \tag{6.81}$$

This equation can be rearranged to

$$\frac{\bar{U}_z}{U^*} = \frac{yU^*}{\nu} \tag{6.82}$$

or in terms of the dimensionless variables:

$$U^+ = y^+ \tag{6.83}$$

Thus, very near the wall, Eq. (6.83) is valid; away from the wall, Eq. (6.77) is valid. As will be shown later by the available data, Eq. (6.83) is valid between $y^+ = 0$ and $y^+ = 5$.

Example 6.5. Figure 6.6 plotted $\bar{U}_z/\bar{U}_{z,\,max}$ versus r/r_o for three Reynolds numbers. Using the points at N_{Re} equal to 100 000, prepare a graph of E_τ/ν versus $(1 - r/r_o)$. The following information is available:

$$\bar{U}_{z,\,max}/U^* = 24.83 \tag{i}$$
$$r_o U^*/\nu = 2372 \tag{ii}$$

Answer. Eq. (6.66) is used to find E_τ/ν:

$$\frac{E_\tau}{\nu} = \frac{-(r/r_o)(U^*)^2}{\nu(d\bar{U}_z/dr)} - 1 \tag{6.66}$$

The slope of the data in Fig. 6.6 is

$$\text{SLOPE} = -\frac{r_o}{\bar{U}_{z,\,max}} \frac{d\bar{U}_z}{dr} \tag{iii}$$

Combining Eqs. (6.66) and (iii) gives

$$\frac{E_\tau}{\nu} = \frac{r_o U^*/\nu}{\bar{U}_{z,\,max}/U^*} \frac{r/r_o}{\text{SLOPE}} - 1 \tag{iv}$$

Using Eqs. (i) and (ii), Eq. (iv) simplifies to

$$E_\tau/\nu = 95.5 \frac{r/r_o}{\text{SLOPE}} - 1 \tag{v}$$

To calculate the eddy viscosity ratio E_τ/ν, the term SLOPE [cf. Eq. (iii)] is determined from Fig. 6.6 at a Reynolds number of 100 000 by using a ruler to draw a tangent at each point given in Table 6.3. That answer and r/r_o allow calculation of E_τ/ν from Eq. (v). The results are tabulated in Table 6.4.

Examination of Fig. 6.6 indicates that it is practically impossible to obtain an accurate slope of the velocity profile near the center line. At the center line, Eq. (v) becomes indeterminate because both the numerator r/r_o and denominator SLOPE are zero. Therefore, the eddy viscosity is undefined. Moreover, it is

TABLE 6.3
The velocity distribution

$(1-r/r_o)$	$\bar{U}_z/\bar{U}_{z,\,max}$	$(1-r/r_o)$	$\bar{U}_z/\bar{U}_{z,\,max}$
0.00	0.00	0.50	0.93
0.025	0.63	0.60	0.95
0.05	0.70	0.70	0.97
0.10	0.77	0.80	0.98
0.20	0.84	0.90	0.99
0.30	0.88	1.00	1.00
0.40	0.91		

impossible to obtain meaningful values of E_τ in the center region. In this region where the slope approaches zero, even very precise data will yield slopes with unacceptable scatter when differentiated. An alternative is to model the experimental data. In Table 6.3, the four points between y/r_o of 0.7 and 1.0 form a straight line—clearly an unrealistic model. Equation (6.77) is commonly used to predict velocity profiles in turbulent flow. The chief limitation of Eq. (6.77) is that it does not predict a zero slope at the center line (an unrealistic prediction). In Table 6.4, a model in the form of Eq. (6.77) was used, but the slope at the point $r/r_o = 0.04$ is much too large.

In summary, an accurate representation of the eddy viscosity is in doubt in the center region of the pipe. Popular models of the velocity profile yield widely varying slopes in the center region. Figure 6.14 presents a graph of the eddy viscosity ratio versus dimensionless radius, using Eq. (6.77) to represent the center region of the pipe.

TABLE 6.4
Calculations for the eddy viscosity ratio, E_τ/ν

r/r_o	$\bar{U}_z/\bar{U}_{z,\,max}$	SLOPE	E_τ/ν
0.000	1.000	0.000	Indeterminate
0.040	0.997	0.105	35.4
0.100	0.991	0.112	84.4
0.200	0.981	0.126	150.8
0.300	0.967	0.144	198.2
0.400	0.951	0.168	226.6
0.500	0.930	0.201	236.1
0.600	0.904	0.252	226.6
0.700	0.870	0.336	198.2
0.800	0.819	0.503	150.8
0.900	0.730	1.007	84.4
0.960	0.609	2.517	35.4
1.000	0.0	94.59	0.0

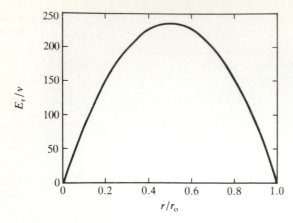

FIGURE 6.14
Eddy viscosity ratio (E_τ/v) versus dimensionless radius.

6.3.3 Analogies

Another approach in analyzing turbulent transport data is to assume that the basic mechanism of transfer is the same for heat, mass, and momentum. Equation (6.66) expressed the eddy diffusivity of momentum in terms of the slope of the velocity profile, which is reasonably well-known from equations such as Eq. (6.77) and (6.83). The simplest analogy is to equate the eddy diffusivity to the eddy heat and mass diffusivities:

$$E_\tau = E_H = E_M \qquad (6.84)$$

Then Eqs. (6.67) and (6.68) can be easily integrated and solved with the appropriate boundary conditions. This approach assumes that the mechanism of turbulent transfer of heat or mass is by eddy motion and and that this mechanism is exactly the same as that for momentum. The assumption of equal eddy properties is one analogy between the mechanisms of heat, mass, and momentum transfer.

> **Example 6.6.** Show how the analogy of equal eddy properties may be used to estimate the temperature distribution in water flowing in a heated pipe. Assume for this problem that $\bar{T}$ is a function only of radius and not of coordinates z or θ.
>
> **Answer.** The equation for temperature distribution will be derived from Eq. (6.67), which after separation of variables is
>
> $$\frac{dr}{\alpha + E_H} = -[(\rho c_p)/(q/A)_r]\, d\bar{T} \qquad (i)$$
>
> From Eq. (6.56):
>
> $$\tau_{rz} = \frac{r}{r_o}\, \tau_w \qquad (6.56)$$
>
> It is assumed that in general
>
> $$\Psi_r = \frac{r}{r_o}(\Psi_w) \qquad (ii)$$

For heat transfer,[7] Eq. (ii) becomes

$$(q/A)_r = \frac{r}{r_o}(q/A)_{r,w} \tag{iii}$$

Eq. (i) becomes

$$\int_r^{r_o} \frac{r\,dr}{(r_o)(\alpha + E_H)} = -\frac{\rho c_p}{(q/A)_{r,w}} \int_{\bar{T}}^{\bar{T}_w} d\bar{T} \tag{iv}$$

Upon integration of the right-hand side, Eq. (iv) is

$$\bar{T} - \bar{T}_w = \frac{(q/A)_{r,w}}{\rho c_p} \int_r^{r_o} \frac{r\,dr}{(r_o)(\alpha + E_H)} \tag{v}$$

where α is constant $[k/(\rho c_p)]$ and E_H depends on the Reynolds number as well as the radius. Equation (6.84) is used to replace E_H in Eq. (v):

$$\bar{T} - \bar{T}_w = \frac{(q/A)_{r,w}}{\rho c_p} \int_r^{r_o} \frac{r\,dr}{(r_o)(\alpha + E_\tau)} \tag{vi}$$

The right-hand side of Eq. (vi) can be determined for a given set of $\bar{T}_w$, $(q/A)_{r,w}$, ρ, c_p, α, and E_τ values such as those given in Table 6.4. However, Table 6.4 includes too few data points in the wall area to allow an accurate integration of Eq. (vi). A much better procedure is to use Eq. (6.66) to evaluate E_τ as a function of radius, with the slope $d\bar{U}_z/dr$ determined from an empirical correlation. Such a solution will be detailed in Example 6.8.

The basic equations defining the eddy diffusivities were given as Eqs. (6.65) through (6.68). The general equation which encompasses these is

$$\Psi_r = -(\delta + E)(\partial \psi/\partial r) \tag{6.85}$$

where E is E_τ, E_H, or E_M. In Eq. (6.85) the variables Ψ, δ, and ψ are defined as usual.

In many practical problems, the transfer at the wall is the main item to be predicted; thus, simplified forms are often used in place of Eq. (6.85). For heat transfer, the empirical equation is defined as

$$(q/A)_{r,w} = h(\bar{T}_w - T_{ave}) \tag{6.86}$$

where h is called the heat transfer coefficient and may have units of $(\text{J m}^{-1}\,\text{s}^{-1}\,\text{K}^{-1})$. For mass transfer, the empirical equation is

$$(N_A/A)_{r,w} = k'_c(\bar{C}_{A,w} - C_{A,ave}) \tag{6.87}$$

where k'_c is the mass transfer coefficient and may have units of $[(\text{kmol m}^{-2}\,\text{s}^{-1})(\text{kmol m}^{-3})^{-1}]$. For momentum transfer, the empirical equation

---

[7] Equation (iii) is approximately correct for heat transfer under the conditions of this problem: steady-state conditions, constant wall heat flux, and a location far away from the entrance.

takes the form:

$$\tau_w = \tau_{rz,w} = \tfrac{1}{2}\rho U^2_{z,\text{ave}} f \tag{6.88}$$

where f is the Fanning friction factor:

$$f = \frac{\tau_w}{\tfrac{1}{2}\rho U^2_{z,\text{ave}}} = \frac{(d_o/4)(-d\bar{p}/dz)}{\tfrac{1}{2}\rho U^2_{z,\text{ave}}} = \frac{\dfrac{d_o(-\Delta p)}{4L}}{\tfrac{1}{2}\rho U^2_{z,\text{ave}}} \tag{6.89}$$

where $(-\Delta p/L)$ is the pressure drop per unit length. Note that the friction factor is dimensionless, in contrast to h and k_c'. A more detailed discussion of the friction factor will be given in Section 6.5.

The empirical coefficients h, k_c', and f are determined from correlations of vast amounts of experimental data. The general form of these empirical equations is

$$\Psi_{r,w} = \xi(\bar{\psi}_w - \psi_{\text{ave}}) \tag{6.90}$$

For heat transfer:

$$\xi_H = h/(\rho c_p) \tag{6.91}$$

where ψ is defined as $\rho c_p \bar{T}$ for constant properties (ρc_p). For mass transfer:

$$\xi_M = k_c' \tag{6.92}$$

For momentum transfer:

$$\xi_\tau = -\frac{\tau_w}{\rho U_{z,\text{ave}}} = f U_{z,\text{ave}}/2 \tag{6.93}$$

If the transfer coefficients ξ are equated, the Reynolds analogy is found:

$$\xi_\tau = \xi_H = \xi_M \tag{6.94}$$

Equation (6.94) is the Reynolds analogy [R2], which for heat transfer is

$$h/(\rho c_p) = f U_{z,\text{ave}}/2 \tag{6.95}$$

For mass transfer, the Reynolds analogy predicts

$$k_c'/U_{z,\text{ave}} = f/2 \tag{6.96}$$

This analogy is reasonably valid for gas systems but should not be considered for liquid systems. The development of this analogy is similar to the development of the transport equations in laminar systems. Other analogies are in the literature. All of these involve a high degree of empiricism in order to correlate heat and mass transfer coefficients and friction factors with the important variables. Further discussion of the analogies is delayed until Chapter 11.

6.3.4 Film and Penetration Theories

In contrast to the analogies that say nothing about the mechanism except that it is the same for all three transfers, another approach is to model the specific fluid motions that occur in the flow. These motions are very important in the mechanism of heat or mass transfer under flow conditions. Actually, one such model of turbulence has been already presented, at least for a part of the turbulent flow; that is, the Prandtl mixing length picture of Fig. 6.14 with the resulting analytical expression for the velocity distribution with the two empirical constants given by Eq. (6.77). Such attempts at modeling specific motions in turbulent flow are still at the frontiers of science. Perhaps as more insight into the mechanism of turbulence is gained, better models will be proposed than exist presently.

The simplest model is the film theory based on Prandtl's mixing length, the development of which is largely due to Lewis and Whitman [L1, L2, W1]. In the film theory, it is assumed that the total resistance to heat or mass transfer is the same as the resistance of a "hypothetical laminar layer" of finite thickness adjacent to the wall to or from which the transfer is occurring. It is sometimes assumed that the effective film thickness of this layer is equal to the thickness of the "viscous sublayer" where Eq. (6.83) applies. Based on the actual velocity distribution data to be discussed later, this thickness corresponds to a y^+ of 5. For equimolar counter diffusion, Fick's law can be integrated over the arbitrary, effective small distance Δy_F with the assumption of a linear concentration gradient:

$$\left(\frac{N_A}{A}\right)_y = -D\,\frac{\bar{C}_{A,w} - C_{A,\,ave}}{\Delta y_F} \tag{6.97}$$

where Δy_F is the distance necessary to make the concentration at the outer limit on the integration equal to the average bulk concentration as shown in Fig. 6.15. If Eqs. (6.87) and (6.97) are compared, one sees that the mass transfer coefficient k_c' is effectively $(D/\Delta y_F)$. Unfortunately, Δy_F is unknown, although it could be taken as that distance equivalent to a y^+ of 5. If Δy_F is taken as a constant at this or any value, the film theory predicts a first-order dependence of the mass transfer coefficient on diffusion coefficient. Experi-

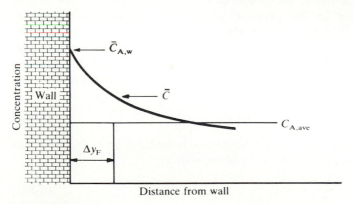

FIGURE 6.15
Film theory for mass transfer at the wall.

mentally, a D^n dependence is observed where n may vary from almost zero to about 0.9 [T5]. Probably the most serious shortcoming of the film theory is the observation, cited earlier, that the mechanism of turbulent flow in contact with a wall (the viscous sublayer region) simply does not involve a laminar sublayer and that disturbances actually occur right at the wall.

Recognizing the extreme importance of a small amount of eddy motion near the wall, many authors have attempted to determine empirically the eddy diffusivity in this region. The theory given by Eq. (6.68) is most often used with the assumption that the eddy diffusivity for turbulence and mass are the same [Eq. (6.84)]. Murphree [M4] made the assumption that the eddy viscosity is proportional to y^3 and derived a corresponding equation for a nondimensional form of the mass transfer coefficient. Lin, Moulton, and Putnam [L3], who made interferometric measurements of concentration profiles in turbulent flow, inferred that the eddy diffusivity of mass is predicted by

$$E_M = v(y^+/14.5)^3 \tag{6.98}$$

Using this eddy diffusivity, they derived an expression for the nondimensional form of the mass transfer coefficient and by use of Eq. (6.84) inferred the nature of the velocity profile. Deissler [D2] proposed that

$$E_\tau = E_M = (n^2 \bar{U}_x y)[1 - \exp(-n^2 \bar{U}_x y/v)] \tag{6.99}$$

where $n = 0.124$. Notter and Sleicher [N2] confirmed the third power dependency by an empirical analysis of the available high Prandtl ($c_p \mu/k$) and Schmidt ($\mu/\rho D$) number data for heat and mass transfer at a wall. On the other hand, Shaw and Hanratty [S1] more recently obtained new data that indicated a 3.38 power dependency of E_M or E_τ on y. Their data imply that any simple model that would give rise to integer values cannot be correct. Fractional powers might result from the nonlinear terms in Eq. (6.44), and these would have to be modeled as well.

The penetration theory, introduced by Higbie [H4], represents an entirely new approach to the prediction of mass transfer coefficients. Higbie was interested neither in the problem of turbulent mass transfer nor in solid–liquid contact. Higbie predicted the mass transfer between gas bubbles and a liquid, both of which were in laminar flow and in contact for short periods of time. Even so, his approach has wide application. Higbie assumed that the liquid could be considered as a semi-infinite medium and represented the transfer by the unsteady-state equation:

$$\partial \bar{C}_A/\partial t = D(\partial^2 \bar{C}_A/\partial y^2) \tag{6.100}$$

This equation can be solved with certain specific boundary conditions and then used to calculate the mass transfer rate at the wall as

$$\left(\frac{N_A}{A}\right)_{y,w} = 2\left(\frac{D}{\pi t_c}\right)^{1/2}(\bar{C}_A - C_{A,\,ave}) \tag{6.101}$$

where t_c is the contact time of the fluid element with the wall. When Eq.

(6.101) is compared to Eq. (6.87), a 0.5 dependency of the mass transfer coefficient on the diffusion coefficient is obtained. Later investigators showed that the experimentally observed exponent may be around 0.5 for very short contact times, but in general may vary from nearly zero to as high as 0.9 as discussed earlier [T5]. The derivation of the penetration theory required some unrealistic assumptions such as equimolar counter diffusion, laminar flow, and no gas phase resistance. Still, it represented considerable improvement upon the older film theory.

Danckwerts [D1] extended Higbie's work by assuming that fluid elements in contact with the wall are randomly replaced by fluid elements that have the bulk stream composition. The penetration theory postulated that every element was removed at the mass transfer surface when it reached an age of t_c. On the other hand, Danckwerts' surface renewal theory suggested that there should be no correlation between the age of a fluid element and its chance of being replaced. When the fluid element was at the wall, mass transfer occurred according to the prediction of Higbie's theory. Further modifications and criticisms have been suggested by Hanratty [H1], Toor and Marchello [T4], Perlmutter [P3], Harriott [H2], Ruckenstein [R4], Koppel, Patel, and Holmes [K2] and Thomas and Fan [T2, T3]. One of the most realistic models yet proposed along these lines is the one suggested by Harriott [H2]. In this model, Harriott assumes that fluid elements penetrate wallward with random frequencies to random depths. Eddies which penetrate to $y = H$ are assumed to sweep out all material between $y = H$ and $y = \infty$. During the interval between the arrival of eddies, the concentration is assumed to obey the unsteady-state solution by Higbie. The model contains three adjustable parameters that are varied so as to fit experimental data. The mass transfer coefficient varies with the 0.5 power for high diffusion rates (gases) and the dependency increases as the diffusion rate decreases. The chief criticism of Harriott's approach is that it neglects all eddy transport between penetrations. Further modifications were considered by Thomas and Fan [T2, T3] and Macleod and Ponton [M1]. Bullin and Dukler [B8] introduced an efficient means of performing the necessary numerical calculations.

Models have also been based on the concept of an unsteady state flow over a flat plate. In this model, the flow field (velocity distribution) is thought to develop in a manner similar to laminar flow over a flat plate (a solution that is based on the principles of Chapter 5). At some point in time (t), the boundary layer is swept away from the plate and a new one starts to form. Einstein and Li [E2] introduced the concept and Ruckenstein [R5], Black [B1, B2] and Meek and Baer [M2, M3] elaborated. Pinczewski and Sideman [P5] combined many features of the previous models using as a basis the visual studies of Corino and Brodkey [C2]. They solved their model equations using only hydrodynamic data rather than mass or heat transfer information. It must be emphasized here that this and all previous models deal only with the mean concentrations and not with fluctuating components which are also of importance.

Several investigators [B7, B9, C1] presented a stochastic model of turbulent diffusion. In models of this type, the unaveraged mass transfer equation [e.g., Eq. (3.63)] is solved, but with considerable restriction, in order to reduce the numerical problem to one that can be managed on today's computers.

6.4 THE VELOCITY DISTRIBUTION

The Prandtl mixing length theory was introduced in Section 6.3.2. It resulted in a logarithmic velocity distribution [Eq. (6.77)] for the flow away from the wall and in a simple linear velocity distribution [Eq. (6.83)] near the wall. Equation (6.77) does well in correlating the data for a y^+ value greater than 30, while Eq. (6.83) is valid for a y^+ less than 5. The values of the constants that have been found to provide the best fit to the data in the turbulent core for Eq. (6.77) are $\kappa = 0.4$ and $B = 5.5$ and the final form of the equation is

$$U^+ = 2.5 \ln y^+ + 5.5 \qquad y^+ \geq 30 \tag{6.102}$$

Between the two limits represented by Eq. (6.102) and Eq. (6.83), Eq. (6.77) can also be used but with different constants than are used in Eq. (6.102). Although historically the three regions have been described as a "laminar sublayer", "buffer zone", and "turbulent core", it has turned out that these are poor descriptions of the actual mechanism.[8] It has been discovered by detailed visual studies that the wall region is not laminar and the descriptive term "viscous sublayer" is more appropriate. The region that has been called the buffer zone is really the region in which the turbulent velocity fluctuations are generated. The term "generation region" is far more satisfactory than "buffer zone".

The velocity distribution equations for smooth tubes, channels, and most of the boundary layer arising from Prandtl's theory are known as the "universal velocity distribution" equations. Summarizing, these are:

Viscous sublayer

$$U^+ = y^+ \qquad\qquad y^+ \leq 5 \tag{6.83}$$

Generation zone

$$U^+ = 5.0 \ln y^+ - 3.05 \qquad 5 < y^+ < 30 \tag{6.103}$$

Turbulent core

$$U^+ = 2.5 \ln y^+ + 5.5 \qquad 30 \leq y^+ \tag{6.102}$$

In Fig. 6.16, a semi-logarithmic plot of U^+ versus y^+ shows the three equations and two sets of experimental data. One set was measured in a pipe at a Reynolds number of 43 400 [B6] and the other in a channel flow for a low Reynolds number [E1]. These equations are appropriate only for fully

---

[8] Film loop FM-2 shows the character of the flow in the different regions for the boundary layer.

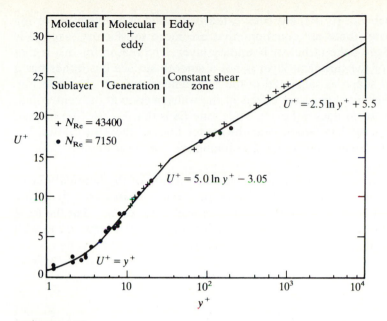

FIGURE 6.16
Universal turbulent velocity distribution.

developed velocity profiles, i.e., reasonably far from any entrance effects. It is surprising that Eq. [6.102] applies almost all the way to the center line of a pipe because the form of this equation originates from Prandtl's mixing length theory. Recall that Prandtl assumed τ_{rz} to be equal to τ_w throughout the profile; in reality, the ratio τ_{rz}/τ_w equals r/r_o. Clearly, Prandtl's assumption is unreasonable but successful. The equations shown in Fig. 6.16 adequately represent the velocity distribution over most of the flow cross section. As previously mentioned, Eq. (6.102) does not meet the boundary condition at the center line where the profile is flat. Equation (6.102) does not allow the velocity gradient $d\bar{U}_z/dr$ to be zero at the center line, as it must be (see Fig. 6.6).

Another problem with these three correlating equations is that the derivative is discontinuous at the juncture point of $y^+ = 30$, whereas the experimental data present a smooth continuous curve without discontinuities at the juncture point. The curve is continuous in its first derivative at $y^+ = 5$, as can be verified by differentiation of Eqs. (6.83) and (6.103). Unfortunately, correlations that satisfy both the boundary conditions at the wall and center line and present a smooth distribution curve have proved elusive. Equation (6.99) was an attempt to eliminate one of the juncture points, but such efforts have not been sufficiently successful to gain wide acceptance. A more complete discussion of alternate representations for a velocity distribution can be found elsewhere [B2, K3]. Here, only a brief review of some of the efforts will be given.

Even though Eq. (6.102) has been extensively used in problems involving the turbulent core, there are equations that are more satisfactory, especially for the outer edge of the turbulent boundary layer. The reason for this is that the outer edge of the turbulent layer is not a smooth surface but rather has a highly contorted shape as suggested in the two-dimensional cut shown in Fig. 6.2. In pipe and channel flows the effects of the walls overlap at the center line, and the same problem does not exist. Thus, one finds that Eq. (6.102) is quite good for the velocity distribution near the center line for these two flows, but of course does not meet the center line boundary condition of zero slope as previously noted.

Von Karman's [V2] approach for the outer region of the boundary layer was to consider the similarity of local flow patterns. He assumed, first, that viscosity is important only in the vicinity of the wall, and second, that the local flow pattern is statistically similar in the neighborhood of every point, with only the time and length scales variable. The ratio between derivative terms has the dimension of length and is taken to be proportional to the mixing length. Thus

$$\frac{(d\bar{U}_x/dy)_1}{(d^2\bar{U}_x/dy^2)_1} = \frac{(d\bar{U}_x/dy)_2}{(d^2\bar{U}_x/dy^2)_2} = \frac{l}{\kappa} \tag{6.104}$$

where κ is a universal constant. When Eqs. (6.71) and (6.104) are combined, the result is

$$\tau_{yx} = \rho\kappa^2 \frac{(d\bar{U}_x/dy)^4}{(d^2\bar{U}_x/dy^2)^2} \tag{6.105}$$

Von Karman combined this equation with Eq. (6.57) and integrated it with the proper boundary conditions to obtain the velocity defect law, which takes the form:

$$\frac{\bar{U}_{x,\max} - \bar{U}_x}{U^*} = f\left(\frac{y_o - y}{y_o}\right) \tag{6.106}$$

where f denotes some arbitrary function, not yet defined. Von Karman next applied Eq. (6.106) to pipe flow. Without going into the details of the integration, but noting that the boundary condition of the maximum velocity at the center line is used, the final resulting equation for pipe flow is

$$\frac{\bar{U}_{z,\max} - \bar{U}_z}{U^*} = -\frac{1}{\kappa}[\ln(1 - (r/r_o)^{1/2}) + (r/r_o)^{1/2}] \tag{6.107}$$

Equation (6.107) differs very little from the corresponding Prandtl equation, which is obtained by integrating Eq. (6.76) and using the center line boundary condition:

$$\frac{\bar{U}_{z,\max} - \bar{U}_z}{U^*} = -\frac{1}{\kappa}\ln[1 - r/r_o] \tag{6.108}$$

The best values for κ are 0.36 and 0.4 for Eqs. (6.107) and (6.108), respectively. These values are based on the experimental work of Nikuradse [N1] and are valid from the center line to about 85 percent of the distance to the wall [R3].

A simple parabolic form of the velocity defect law can often be used over limited ranges:

$$\frac{\bar{U}_{z,\,max} - \bar{U}_z}{U^*} = A(r/r_o)^2 \tag{6.109}$$

The velocity profiles in terms of the velocity defect laws are compared with experimental data in Fig. 6.17.

Prandtl [P6] presented an approximation for the turbulent core region, based on the well-known Blasius friction-factor equation [B3] [to be presented in Eq. (6.133)]. The approximation is known as the 1/7 power law:

$$\bar{U}_z/\bar{U}_{z,\,max} = (y/r_o)^{1/7} \tag{6.110}$$

This equation is surprisingly accurate in representing velocity profiles in spite of the simplicity and the omission of any Reynolds number dependency.

Van Driest [V1] suggested a correlation for velocity profile by modifying the Prandtl mixing length:

$$l^+ = (\kappa y^+)[1 - \exp(-y^+/A)] \tag{6.111}$$

Equation (6.111), which contains two arbitrary constants, was suggested by the

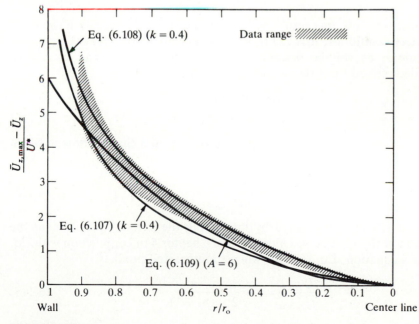

FIGURE 6.17
Velocity defect plot.

theory of damping in a fluid when a simple harmonic oscillation is set up by a plate. For the asymptotic solution $y_o^+ \to \infty$, U^+ is obtained from Eqs. (6.72) and (6.111):

$$U^+ = 2\int_0^{y^+} \frac{dy^+}{C+1} \tag{6.112}$$

$$C^2 = 1 + 4(\kappa y^+)^2[1 - \exp(-y^+/A)]^2$$

This equation fits the data quite well with κ of 0.4 and A of 36; however, it does require numerical integration for its solution and it cannot satisfy the boundary condition of the slope at the center line. This latter failure is a consequence of using the asymptotic solution rather than the complete solution.

Pai [P1, P2] developed a complete solution to the Reynolds equation [Eqs. (6.52) or (6.54)] for pipe and channel flows, by assuming the velocity profile to be of the form:

$$\frac{\bar{U}_x}{\bar{U}_{x,\,\text{max}}} = 1 + a_1\left(\frac{y}{y_o}\right)^2 + a_2\left(\frac{y}{y_o}\right)^{2m} \tag{6.113}$$

where y is now measured from the center line. For pipe flow, r/r_o replaces y/y_o, and z replaces x. The equation becomes

$$\frac{\bar{U}_z}{\bar{U}_{z,\,\text{max}}} = 1 + a_1\left(\frac{r}{r_o}\right)^2 + a_2\left(\frac{r}{r_o}\right)^{2m} \tag{6.114}$$

The simplicity of Pai's final result, added to the fact that his equation can meet the boundary conditions, makes his method very attractive. However, it also has limitations, as will be discussed shortly. The terms a_1 and a_2 can be uniquely determined from the boundary conditions:

$$a_1 = (s - m)/(m - 1) \tag{6.115}$$

$$a_2 = (1 - s)/(m - 1) \tag{6.116}$$

where m is an integer (in order to apply Eq. (6.113) to a channel flow in which y can be negative) and

$$s = \frac{(U^*)^2 r_o}{2v\bar{U}_{z,\,\text{max}}} \tag{6.117}$$

The average velocity is obtained by integrating the velocity profile over the cross section of the pipe as was illustrated in Chapter 4 in conjunction with Eq. (4.77). Pai's equation, Eq. (6.114), when so integrated predicts

$$\frac{\bar{U}_{z,\,\text{ave}}}{\bar{U}_{z,\,\text{max}}} = 1 + \frac{a_1}{2} + \frac{a_2}{(m + 1)} \tag{6.118}$$

The term m is a parameter which is expected to be a unique function of the Reynolds number. A computation of literature data for $U_{z,\,\text{ave}}/\bar{U}_{z,\,\text{max}}$ and U^*

by Brodkey [B5] showed that the parameter m can be expressed as the whole integer closest to the value given by

$$m = -0.617 + (8.211 \times 10^{-3})(N_{Re})^{0.786} \qquad (6.119)$$

The quantity s, as defined in Eq. (6.117), can also be correlated in terms of the Reynolds number [B5]:

Laminar flow
$$s = 1 \qquad\qquad N_{Re} < 2040 \qquad (6.120)$$

Transitional flow
$$s = 2.417 \times 10^{-12}(N_{Re})^{3.51} \qquad 2040 \le N_{Re} \le 2800 \qquad (6.121)$$

Turbulent flow
$$s = 0.585 + (3.172 \times 10^{-3})(N_{Re})^{0.833} \qquad 2800 < N_{Re} \qquad (6.122)$$

Although the correlation for s extends beyond a Reynolds number of 100 000, the use of Pai's equations does not; above $N_{Re} = 100\,000$, there is a serious error in the predicted profile in the vicinity of $y^+ = 75$. Above and below this region the fit is reasonably good. Therefore, above a N_{Re} of 100 000, Eqs. (6.83), (6.103), and (6.102) are recommended.

The most common velocity profile problem is to obtain the profile for a flow in a tube of known dimensions with a fluid of known properties at a specific Reynolds number. The procedure to compute the profile using Pai's method is:

1. Compute the average velocity $U_{z,\,ave}$ from Eq. (6.2) or from the experimental data.
2. Compute s and m from Eqs. (6.119) through (6.122). Round off m to an integer.
3. Compute a_1 and a_2 from Eqs. (6.115) and (6.116).
4. Compute $\bar{U}_{z,\,max}$ from Eq. (6.118).
5. Compute the velocity profile from Eq. (6.114). Note that the term $(r/r_o)^{2m}$ will be very small away from the wall and will cause computer errors due to underflow wherever r/r_o decreases below 0.07, depending on the particular computer being used.

If Eq. (6.120) for the laminar flow region is substituted into Eqs. (6.115) and (6.116), then a_1 is -1 and a_2 is zero. Hence for laminar flow Eq. (6.114) reduces to Eq. (4.74), the theoretical laminar flow profile. Pai's approach correctly predicts all the boundary conditions as well in the turbulent region. But these equations are limited to Reynolds numbers of 100 000 or less, and the extreme degree of empiricism in Eqs. (6.119) through (6.122) is evident. Nevertheless, Pai's equations yield a smooth profile with no discontinuities in slopes. Pai's equations also provide an estimate of the velocity profile in the transition region. Other velocity profile correlations may be found in the literature, and undoubtedly more will be suggested in the future. It may be hoped that some day there will be formulated a simple, completely smooth representation with a minimum of constants, or parameters, that meets all boundary conditions.

All of the previously cited equations for velocity distribution have two major limitations. First, as briefly mentioned, the equations apply only for fully developed turbulent flow. When flow first enters a pipe, there is an "entry" region where the velocity profile is changing shape and the turbulence is not fully developed. The entry region is usually defined as the region up to the point where the center line velocity achieves 99 percent of its final value. Usually one is interested in the value of this entry length and in the excess pressure drop associated with the acceleration in the entry region. Since these are quite specific practical problems, the topic will be further considered in Chapter 12. Secondly, all the equations apply only for smooth walls; roughness was not considered in any way. Roughness is very important in pressure drop calculations and as such will also be considered later. As far as the roughness effect on the velocity distribution is concerned, the following brief discussion will introduce the subject.

For rough pipe, as most commercial pipe is, some modification is necessary. If the Reynolds number were large, the laminar sublayer would be small and roughness would be controlling. On the other hand, if the Reynolds number were low and the sublayer relatively large, then the roughness would be buried in the sublayer, and the pipe would act if it were smooth. In either case, the velocity distribution of Eq. (6.77) would be approximately valid, but the boundary conditions would be changed. For a rough surface, the outer edge of the sublayer is considered proportional to e, the average depth of the roughness. With this new assumption, Eq. (6.77) becomes

$$U^+ = \frac{1}{\kappa} \ln \frac{y}{e} + B\left(\frac{eU^*}{\nu}\right) \tag{6.123}$$

The value of κ is the same; the new constant B will depend on the degree of roughness. For pipe made completely rough with sand particles, and in which roughness is the controlling factor, Nikuradse determined the value of B to be 8.5. The surface is completely rough if the parameter eU^*/ν is greater than 100; if less than 5, the roughness is negligible, and the wall acts if it were smooth [B6, K3].

Example 6.7. Calculate the velocity distribution by the various methods available for the flow of cyclohexane at 2.778 ft s^{-1} (0.8467 m s^{-1}) and 25°C in a 2-inch I.D. smooth tube. The friction factor was measured and found to be 0.00570. At the given temperature, the density of cyclohexane is 0.7749 g cm^{-3} (774.9 kg m^{-3}), and the viscosity is 0.8892 cP (8.892 × 10^{-4} kg m^{-1} s^{-1}).

Answer. Either the SI or the engineering system of units is in common usage for this type of calculation. This solution will use the SI system. The diameter in SI units is 0.0508 m. The first step is to compute the Reynolds number from Eq.

(6.2):

$$N_{Re} = d_o U_{z,\,ave}\rho/\mu = (0.0508)(0.8467)(774.9)/(8.892 \times 10^{-4})$$
$$\times\,[(m)(m\,s^{-1})(kg\,m^{-3})/(kg\,m^{-1}\,s^{-1})] = 37\,483 = 3.75 \times 10^4 \qquad (i)$$

A Reynolds number of 37 500 indicates that the flow is fully turbulent. The wall shear stress is obtained from Eq. (6.88):

$$\tau_w = \tfrac{1}{2}\rho U^2_{z,\,ave}f$$
$$= (1/2)(774.9)(0.8467)^2(0.00570)\,[(kg\,m^{-3})(m\,s^{-1})^2]$$
$$= 1.583\,kg\,m^{-1}\,s^{-2} = 1.583\,N\,m^{-2} \qquad (ii)$$

The friction velocity is obtained from Eq. (6.53) and Eq. (ii):

$$U^* = \sqrt{\tau_w/\rho} = \sqrt{(1.583)/(774.9)}\,\left(\sqrt{(kg\,m^{-1}\,s^{-2})/(kg\,m^{-3})}\right)$$
$$= 0.04520\,m\,s^{-1} = 0.1483\,ft\,s^{-1} \qquad (iii)$$

Universal velocity distribution. For purposes of illustration, values of y of 0.001, 0.02, and 1.0 inches will be chosen. First, y^+ is computed from Eq. (6.79):

$$y^+ = \frac{yU^*\rho}{\mu} \qquad (6.79)$$

For the three selected values of y and fluid properties as in Eq. (i), the values of y^+ are

For $y = 0.001$ in. (2.54×10^{-5} m):

$$y^+ = (2.54 \times 10^{-5})(0.04520)(774.9)/(8.892 \times 10^{-4})$$
$$\times\,[(m)(m\,s^{-1})(kg\,m^{-3})/(kg\,m^{-1}\,s^{-1})] = 1.00$$

For $y = 0.02$ in.: $\qquad\qquad\qquad y' = 20.0 \qquad\qquad\qquad\qquad (iv)$

For $y = 1.0$ in.: $\qquad\qquad\qquad y^+ = 1000$

Note that y^+ is dimensionless. At $y = 0.001$ in., the location is well within the viscous sublayer, and Eq. (6.83) applies

$$U^+ = y^+ \qquad (6.83)$$

At $y = 0.001$ in., U^+ is equal to 1.0, and $\bar{U}_z$ is found from Eq. (6.78):

$$\bar{U}_z = U^*U^+ = (0.04520)(1.0) = 0.04520\,m\,s^{-1} = 0.148\,ft\,s^{-1} \qquad (v)$$

At $y = 0.02$ in., the location is within the generation region $5 \le y^+ \le 30$, where Eq. (6.103) applies:

$$U^+ = 5.0\ln(20) - 3.05 = 11.929 \qquad (vi)$$

Using Eq. (6.78), the value of $\bar{U}_z$ is

$$\bar{U}_z = (0.04520)(11.929) = 0.5392\,m\,s^{-1} = 1.77\,ft\,s^{-1} \qquad (vii)$$

At $y = 1.0$ in., the location is at the center line in the turbulent core, and Eq. (6.102) is appropriate:

$$U^+ = 2.5\ln(1000) + 5.5 = 22.77 \qquad (viii)$$

Using the definition of U^+, $\bar{U}_z$ is

$$\bar{U}_z = \bar{U}_{z,\,max} = (0.04520)(22.77) = 1.029 \text{ m s}^{-1} = 3.38 \text{ ft s}^{-1} \tag{ix}$$

In a similar manner, as many points as desired can be calculated in order to obtain the complete velocity distribution (see Table 6.3). For example, at y equal to 0.9 in., y^+ is 900, and from Eqs. (6.102) and (6.78) $\bar{U}_z$ is 1.017 m s^{-1}. The ratio $\bar{U}_z/\bar{U}_{z,\,max}$ is 0.988. This value will be compared with the results from other correlations.

Velocity defect laws. The velocity defect laws do not permit estimation of $\bar{U}_{z,\,max}$; in fact, it must be known or estimated from some other source in order to determine the velocity distribution. Generally, the defect laws are used in conjunction with the universal velocity distribution equations so that the maximum velocity is determined from Eq. (6.102) at the center line. Clearly, the use of the defect laws will contain any error involved in estimation of the center line velocity. To illustrate the use of the defect laws, let us calculate the velocity at 0.9 inches from the wall. First, the von Karman equation, Eq. (6.107), with the value of 0.36 substituted for κ, is

$$\frac{\bar{U}_{z,\,max} - \bar{U}_z}{U^*} = -(1.0/0.36)[\ln(1 - \sqrt{r/r_o}) + \sqrt{r/r_o}] \tag{6.107}$$

The value of 0.1 is substituted for r/r_o into the above:

$$\bar{U}_{z,\,max} - \bar{U}_z = -(U^*)(1/0.36)[\ln(1 - \sqrt{0.1}) + \sqrt{0.1}] \tag{x}$$

This equation can be rearranged so the ratio $\bar{U}_z/\bar{U}_{z,\,max}$ is obtained. Since U^* is 0.04520 m s^{-1}, the result is

$$\bar{U}_z/\bar{U}_{z,\,max} = 1 - (0.04520)(0.1775)/\bar{U}_{z,\,max} \tag{xi}$$

Using the maximum velocity as calculated from the universal velocity distribution, $\bar{U}_{z,\,max} = 1.029$ m s^{-1}, the velocity ratio from Eq. (xi) is

$$\bar{U}_z/\bar{U}_{z,\,max} = 1 + (0.04520)(-0.1775)/(1.029) = 0.992 \tag{xii}$$

Note that this answer is not sensitive to the value of $\bar{U}_{z,\,max}$. This ratio compares with 0.988 from the universal velocity distribution alone.

Prandtl's equation, Eq. (6.108), rearranges to

$$\bar{U}_z/\bar{U}_{z,\,max} = 1 + (U^*/\bar{U}_{z,\,max})(1/\kappa)[\ln(1 - r/r_o)] \tag{xiii}$$

At $r/r_o = 0.1$, with the same values of U^* and $\bar{U}_{z,\,max}$ as in Eq. (xii) and with $\kappa = 0.4$ as suggested, Prandtl's equation predicts $\bar{U}_z/\bar{U}_{z,\,max}$ to be 0.988. As expected, the result from Prandtl's equation verifies that from the universal velocity distribution, from which it was obtained. The simple parabolic velocity equation, Eq. (6.109), can also be used, but the constant A is unknown; however, this constant is determined by the Pai approach, and thus the comparison will be covered under the Pai equations.

Power law. The 1/7 power law is simple to use. For the same location of 0.9 inches from the wall, the result from Eq. (6.110) is:

$$\bar{U}_z/\bar{U}_{z,\,max} = (0.9)^{1/7} = 0.985 \tag{xiv}$$

The maximum possible deviation among all of the last three results is less than

1 percent, which is usually well within the experimental error of measurement of the velocity.

Pai's equations. This calculation follows the outline in the discussion of Pai's equations. The average velocity is given, and the Reynolds number was previously computed as 37 483. Thus, the flow is fully turbulent; the parameter s is computed from Eq. (6.122):

$$s = 0.585 + (3.172 \times 10^{-3})(37\,483)^{0.833} = 21.066 \qquad \text{(xv)}$$

The parameter m is obtained from Eq. (6.119):

$$m = -0.617 + (8.211 \times 10^{-3})(37\,483)^{0.786} = 31.70 \cong 32 \qquad \text{(xvi)}$$

Thus, from Eqs. (6.115) and (6.116):

$$a_1 = -0.3527 \qquad \text{(xvii)}$$

and

$$a_2 = -0.6473 \qquad \text{(xviii)}$$

Equation (6.118) is used to obtain perhaps the best possible estimate of $\bar{U}_{z,\,\text{max}}$:

$$\bar{U}_{z,\,\text{max}} = (0.8467)/[1.0 + (-0.3527)/(2) + (-0.6473)/(32 + 1)]$$
$$= 1.053 \text{ m s}^{-1} = 3.455 \text{ ft s}^{-1} \qquad \text{(xix)}$$

As will be seen, this estimate of $\bar{U}_{z,\,\text{max}}$ is sometimes more reliable than that from the universal velocity equations [Eq. (ix)]. With the values of both $\bar{U}_{z,\,\text{max}}$ and the parameters now determined, the velocity predicted from Pai's equations can be calculated from Eq. (6.114): For y of 0.001 inch

$$\bar{U}_z = (1.053)[1 - (0.3527)(0.999)^2 - (0.6473)(0.999)^{64}]$$
$$= 0.04302 \text{ m s}^{-1} = 0.141 \text{ ft s}^{-1} \qquad \text{(xx)}$$

This prediction can be compared to 0.0452 m s^{-1}, which was computed from the universal velocity distribution, Eq. (v) (a 5 percent difference).

Similar calculations for $y = 0.02$ in. give a value of 0.5092 m s^{-1} for $\bar{U}_z$, based on Pai's equations. This number can be compared to 0.5392 m s^{-1} from Eq. (vii) (the universal velocity distribution), or less than 6 percent difference. The last term in Eq. (xx) contributes significantly to the final answer; however, when r/r_o becomes small enough, the last term becomes negligible since it is raised to the power $2m$. When r/r_o equals 0.92, the last term $(a_2)(r/r_o)^{2m}$ is about one percent of the value of the term $(a_1)(r/r_o)^2$. Thus, the last term can be neglected whenever r/r_o is less than 0.92. For this region in the pipe, the Pai equation, Eq. (6.114), reduces to the velocity defect, Eq. (6.109), with A given by a_1 of Pai's theory. At the center line of the pipe, $y = 1.0$ in., and the radius is zero. Hence, $\bar{U}_z$ becomes $\bar{U}_{z,\,\text{max}}$, which is 1.053 m s^{-1} as calculated from Eq. (xix). The various calculations are further compared in Table 6.5 with tabulations of $\bar{U}_z/\bar{U}_{z,\,\text{max}}$ at selected values of y^+. A set of experimental measurements [H3] under the same conditions is included. There are only two correlations that provide an estimate of $\bar{U}_{z,\,\text{max}}$. The value from the universal velocity distribution, Eq. (6.102), was 1.029 m s^{-1}, whereas Pai's equation predicted 1.053 m s^{-1}. The experimental value is 1.045 m s^{-1} [H3], and so for this case the prediction from Pai's method is somewhat better than that from the universal velocity distribution, Eq. (6.102). A check of the standard deviation from the experimental data shows that all of the

TABLE 6.5
Comparison of calculated velocity profiles with experimental data

			The ratio $\bar{U}_z/\bar{U}_{z,\text{max}}$			
r/r_0	y^+	Experimental data (H4)	Universal Velocity Distribution[a]	Von Karman defect law[b]	1/7 power[c]	Pai[d]
0.999	1.0	—	0.044	—	0.373	0.041
0.98	20.0	0.557	0.524	—	0.572	0.484
0.97	30.0	0.596	0.615	—	0.606	0.576
0.95	50.0	0.633	0.671	—	0.652	0.657
0.90	100	0.701	0.747	—	0.720	0.714
0.70	300	0.830	0.868	0.881	0.842	0.827
0.50	500	0.887	0.924	0.936	0.906	0.912
0.30	700	0.945	0.961	0.970	0.950	0.968
0.20	800	0.973	0.976	0.982	0.969	0.986
0.10	900	0.988	0.988	0.992	0.995	0.996
0.05	950	0.992	0.994	0.996	0.993	0.999

Notes: [a] Eqs. (6.83), (6.102), or (6.103). [b] Eq. (6.107). [c] Eq. (6.110). [d] Eq. (6.114).

correlations are within 3 percent. Noteworthy are the excellent predictions from the 1/7 power law, of Eq. (6.110), which is within 1 percent. This simple and unsophisticated equation often performs as well as the equations that are more tedious to use. Note also that the comparisons in Table 6.5 do not reflect the errors introduced through the estimation of the maximum velocity, $\bar{U}_{z,\text{max}}$. This quantity is difficult to estimate accurately, and as just stated, only two of the correlations presented allow any estimate whatsoever.

Example 6.8. Estimate the temperature distribution in water as it flows through a heated pipe of radius 5 cm at a Reynolds number of 120 000. The wall temperature is 40°C, and the heat flux at the wall is 1.7×10^4 W m^{-2}. The friction factor is 0.0045. Use the analogy proposed in Example 6.6.

Answer. This problem will be worked by assuming that the eddy diffusivity of momentum E_τ equals the eddy heat diffusivity E_H. If the details of this example are fully understood, it will be easy to apply a more sophisticated analogy to this or any other problem. The following properties of water are required:

$$c_p = 1.0 \text{ cal g}^{-1}\text{K}^{-1} = 4184 \text{ J kg}^{-1}\text{K}^{-1}$$

$$\rho = 1.0 \text{ g cm}^{-3} = 1000 \text{ kg m}^{-3}$$

$$k = 0.628 \text{ W m}^{-1}\text{K}^{-1} \tag{i}$$

$$\nu = \mu/\rho = 0.01 \text{ cm}^2\text{ s}^{-1} = 1.0 \times 10^{-6} \text{ m}^2\text{ s}^{-1}$$

$$\alpha = \frac{k}{\rho c_p} = \frac{(0.628)(1)}{(1000)(4184)} \left(\frac{(\text{W m}^{-1}\text{K}^{-1})(\text{J W}^{-1}\text{s}^{-1})}{(\text{kg m}^{-3})(\text{J kg}^{-1}\text{K}^{-1})} \right) = 1.501 \times 10^{-7} \text{ m}^2\text{ s}^{-1}$$

The temperature at any point in the fluid is given by Eq. (vi) in Example 6.6, which is

$$\bar{T} = \bar{T}_w - \frac{(q/A)_{r,w}}{\rho c_p} \int_r^{r_o} \frac{r \, dr}{(r_o)(\alpha + E_\tau)} \tag{ii}$$

In Eq. (ii), $\bar{T}$ is the temperature at location r, and E_τ is obtained by rearranging Eq. (6.66):

$$E_\tau = -(r/r_o)(U^*)^2/(d\bar{U}_z/dr) - \nu \tag{iii}$$

The slope of the velocity profile $d\bar{U}_z/dr$ may be obtained from any suitable correlation. The universal velocity distribution is perhaps the most generally accepted of the equations for the velocity profile in a pipe, and it will be used here:

Viscous sublayer: $\qquad U^+ = y^+$ $\hfill$ (6.83)

Generation region: $\qquad U^+ = 5.0 \ln y^+ - 3.05$ $\hfill$ (6.103)

Turbulent region: $\qquad U^+ = 2.5 \ln y^+ + 5.5$ $\hfill$ (6.102)

Equations (6.75), (6.78), and (6.79) are used to replace U^+, y^+ and y. The equation for the viscous sublayer becomes

$$\bar{U}_z = U^* y^+ = \frac{(U^*)^2 y}{\nu} = \frac{(U^*)^2}{\nu}(r_o - r) \tag{iv}$$

The equations for the other regions follow similarly. Summarizing:

Viscous sublayer: $\qquad \bar{U}_z = r_o(U^*)^2/\nu - r(U^*)^2/\nu$ $\hfill$ (v)

Generation region: $\qquad \bar{U}_z = (U^*)[5.0 \ln[(r_o - r)(U^*)/\nu] - 3.05]$ $\hfill$ (vi)

Turbulent region: $\qquad \bar{U}_z = (U^*)[2.5 \ln[(r_o - r)(U^*)/\nu] + 5.5]$ $\hfill$ (vii)

From these equations, the appropriate slopes are

Viscous sublayer: $\qquad d\bar{U}_z/dr = -(U^*)^2/\nu$ $\hfill$ (viii)

Generation region: $\qquad d\bar{U}_z/dr = \dfrac{(-5.0)(U^*)}{r_o - r} = -5.0 U^*/y$ $\hfill$ (ix)

Turbulent region: $\qquad d\bar{U}_z/dr = \dfrac{(-2.5)(U^*)}{r_o - r} = -2.5 U^*/y$ $\hfill$ (x)

These slopes are substituted into Eq. (iii) to obtain the eddy diffusivity of momentum for the generation and turbulent regions. However, for the viscous region, Eq. (6.83) was derived by Prandtl by assuming that the Reynolds stress (in other words E_τ) in Eq. (6.54) was zero. Hence, if Eq. (6.83) is assumed to apply very close to the wall, then E_τ must be taken as zero in the region $0 \le y^+ \le 5.0$. Under this stipulation, Eq. (ii) can be integrated analytically as follows:

$$\bar{T} = \bar{T}_w - \frac{(q/A)_{r,w}(r^2)}{(\rho c_p)(2 r_o \alpha)} \Big|_r^{r_o}$$

$$\bar{T} = \bar{T}_w - \frac{(q/A)_{r,w}}{(\rho c_p)(2 r_o \alpha)}(r_o^2 - r^2) \tag{xi}$$

Equation (xi) will serve as a check on the forthcoming calculation [which will integrate Eq. (ii) numerically] at y^+ equal to 5.0. Next, the ratio $(q/A)_{r,w}/(\rho c_p)$, which appears in Eqs. (ii) and (xi), will be determined:

$$\frac{(q/A)_{r,w}}{\rho c_p} = \frac{(1.7 \times 10^4)(1)}{(1000)(4184)} \left(\frac{(\text{W m}^{-2})(\text{J W}^{-1}\text{s}^{-1})}{(\text{kg m}^{-3})(\text{J kg}^{-1}\text{K}^{-1})} \right)$$

$$= 4.063 \times 10^{-3}\,\text{m K s}^{-1} \qquad \text{(xii)}$$

The average velocity is available from rearranging Eq. (6.2):

$$U_{z,\,\text{ave}} = N_{\text{Re}} v/d_o = (1.2 \times 10^5)(1 \times 10^{-6})/[(2)(0.05)][(\text{m}^2\,\text{s}^{-1})/(\text{m})]$$

$$= 1.2\,\text{m s}^{-1} = 3.94\,\text{ft s}^{-1} \qquad \text{(xiii)}$$

The friction velocity is found from Eqs. (6.55) and (6.88):

$$U^* = U_{z,\,\text{ave}} \sqrt{f/2} = (1.2)(0.0045/2)^{1/2} = 0.05692\,\text{m s}^{-1} \qquad \text{(xiv)}$$

The viscous sublayer equation, Eq. (6.83), applies up to the location $y^+ = 5.0$. Using Eq. (6.79), the value of y at this location is

$$y = y^+ v/U^* = (5.0)(1 \times 10^{-6})/(0.05692)[(\text{m}^2\,\text{s}^{-1})/(\text{m s}^{-1})]$$

$$= 8.784 \times 10^{-5}\,\text{m} = 8.784 \times 10^{-3}\,\text{cm} \qquad \text{(xv)}$$

This value corresponds to a radius of 4.9912 cm. Similarly, Eq. (6.103) applies from $y^+ = 5$ to $y^+ = 30$ (a radius of 4.473 cm), and Eq. (6.102) applies from this point to the center line.

The calculation henceforth is straightforward but tedious. The procedure is

1. Select r.
2. Locate the appropriate region (viscous, generation, or turbulent) according to the previously calculated bounds.
3. Find the slope from Eqs. (viii), (ix), or (x), according to the appropriate region as found in (2).
4. Compute E_r from Eq. (iii) (zero for the viscous region).
5. Repeat steps (1) through (4) for all points between r and r_o.
6. Integrate Eq. (ii) graphically or numerically and compute the temperature that corresponds to the r selected in step (1).
7. Repeat steps (1) through (6) for all r.

For purposes of illustration, the integration in step 6 will be performed using Simpson's rule, as discussed in standard references in numerical analysis and in handbooks [P4]. Using the nomenclature of Example 6.3,[9] the generalized

---

[9] Equation (xvi) evaluated the integral of $y\,dx$ for evenly spaced intervals of x, i.e., Δx. Any analytical function can be cast into a form appropriate for Simpson's rule; experimentally determined functions of arbitrary spacing are not suitable. In Simpson's rule, the number of points must be odd; therefore, the index i goes from 0 to N, where N is the number of intervals, always an even number.

```
C         EXAMPLE 6-8. NOTE ALL INPUT DATA HAVE SAME UNITS AS GIVEN IN
C             PROBLEM STATEMENT. ALL FURTHER CALCULATIONS ARE IN S.I.
      DIMENSION FX(102)
      DATA CP,RHO,VISKM/1.0,1.0,0.01/
      DATA CON/0.628/
      DATA RADIUS,TWALL,HFLUX/5.0,40.0,1.7E+04/
      DATA RE,FF/120000.,0.0045/
      DATA A1,A2,A3/100.,4.184,1000./
    2 FORMAT(1H0/1H0,4X,4HY(M),5X,10HRADIUS(CM),3X,10HSLOPE(1/S),3X,
     1 12HALPHA(M*M/S),3X,15HEDDY VIS(M*M/S),2X,14HTEMPERATURE(C)/1H )
    3 FORMAT(E12.5,F10.5,E15.5,E14.5,E16.5,F14.2)
    4 FORMAT(1H0/11H0END OF JOB)
    5 FORMAT(31H0FOR THE TUBE, THE RADIUS(CM)IS,E35.5/19X,15HWALL TEMP(C
     1) IS,F32.2/19X,20HHEAT FLUX(W/M**2) IS,E27.5)
    6 FORMAT(33H0FOR THE FLUID,THE REYNOLDS NO IS,F33.1/19X,
     1 26HFANNING FRICTION FACTOR IS,E21.5/19X,26HKINEMATIC VIS-MU(M*M/S
     2) IS,E21.5/19X,35HTHERMAL DIFFUSIVITY-ALPHA(M*M/S) IS,E12.5)
    7 FORMAT(1H0/39H0VISCOUS SUBLAYER REGION FROM RADIUS OF,E12.5,2X,
     1  4HM TO,E12.5,4H  M.)
    8 FORMAT(1H0/33H0GENERATION REGION FROM RADIUS OF,E12.5,6H  M TO,
     1 E12.5,4H  M.)
    9 FORMAT(1H0/30H0TURBULENT CORE FROM RADIUS OF,E12.5,21H  M TO THE C
     1ENTERLINE)
   10 FORMAT(29H0THE AVERAGE VELOCITY(M/S) IS,F11.5/30H THE FRICTION VEL
     1OCITY(M/S) IS,F10.5)
   11 FORMAT(1H )
      IO=7
      WRITE(IO,5) RADIUS,TWALL,HFLUX
C         FROM THIS POINT, ONLY SI UNITS ARE USED - J,M,S,KG
      CP=CP * A2 * A3
      RHO=RHO * A1**3 / A3
      VIS=VISKM / A1**2
      RCM=RADIUS
      RADIUS=RADIUS / A1
      D=RADIUS + RADIUS
      ALPHA=CON / (RHO * CP)
      WRITE(IO,6) RE,FF,VIS,ALPHA
      B1=HFLUX / (RHO * CP)
      UAVG=RE * VIS / D
      USTAR=UAVG * SQRT (FF * 0.5)
      WRITE (IO,10) UAVG,USTAR
      NINT=100
      SLOPEV=USTAR**2 / (-VIS)
      B2= USTAR**2 / (-RADIUS)
      T=TWALL
      Y=0.0
      AREAT=0.0
      SLOPE=SLOPEV
      DO 100 IGO=1,3
      GO TO(30,40,50),IGO
C         VISCOUS REGION
   30 YLOW=0.0
      YPLUS=5.0
   32 YHI=YPLUS * VIS / USTAR
   33 H=(YHI - YLOW) / FLOAT(NINT)
      RUP=RADIUS - YLOW
      RLO=RADIUS - YHI
      GO TO(55,61,63),IGO
C         GENERATION OR TRANSITION REGION
   40 YLOW=YHI
      YPLUS=30.
      GO TO 32
C         TURBULENT CORE
   50 YLOW=YHI
      YHI=RADIUS
      GO TO 33
```

FIGURE 6.18

Program for Example 6.8

```
   55 WRITE (IO,7)RLO,RUP
      GO TO 65
   61 WRITE (IO,8) RLO,RUP
      GO TO 65
   63 WRITE (IO,9) RUP
C        LOAD THE ORDINATES IN FX FOR NUMERICAL INTEGRATION BY SIMPSONS
   65 Y=YLOW
      CALL EDDYV(EDDY,Y,B2,VIS,SLOPE,RADIUS,R,RCM,USTAR,IGO)
      FX(1)=R / (RADIUS * (ALPHA + EDDY))
      WRITE(IO,2)
      WRITE (IO,3) Y,RCM,SLOPE,ALPHA,EDDY,T
      Y=YLOW + H
      CALL EDDYV(EDDY,Y,B2,VIS,SLOPE,RADIUS,R,RCM,USTAR,IGO)
      FX(2)=R / (RADIUS * (ALPHA + EDDY))
      WRITE (IO,3) Y,RCM,SLOPE,ALPHA,EDDY
      WRITE (IO,11)
      DO 80 I=2,NINT
      Y=YLOW + H * FLOAT(I)
      CALL EDDYV(EDDY,Y,B2,VIS,SLOPE,RADIUS,R,RCM,USTAR,IGO)
      FX(I+1)=R / (RADIUS * (ALPHA + EDDY))
      CALL SMPSN (AREA,FX,H,I)
      T=TWALL - B1 * (AREA + AREAT)
   80 WRITE (IO,3) Y,RCM,SLOPE,ALPHA,EDDY,T
  100 AREAT=AREAT + AREA
      WRITE (IO,4)
      STOP
      END
      SUBROUTINE EDDYV(EDDY,Y,B2,VIS,SLOPE,RADIUS,R,RCM,USTAR,IGO)
C        THIS SUBROUTINE COMPUTES THE EDDY VISCOSITY (EDDY, UNITS M**2/
C        S) ASSUMING THE VEL PROFILE FOLLOWS THE UNIVERSAL VELOCITY
C        DISTRIBUTION. IGO TRANSFERS CALCULATIONS TO CORRECT REGION.
C        NOTE THAT FOR VISCOUS REGION SLOPE IS COMPUTED IN MAIN PGM.
      R=RADIUS - Y
      RCM=R * 100.
      GO TO (12,20,30),IGO
C        VISCOUS REGION
   12 EDDY= 0.0
      RETURN
C        GENERATION OR TRANSITION REGION
   20 SLOPE=(-5.0) / Y * USTAR
      GO TO 40
C        TURBULENT CORE
   30 SLOPE=(-2.5) / Y * USTAR
   40 EDDY= B2 * R / SLOPE - VIS
      RETURN
      END
C ........................SUBROUTINE SMPSN........................
C
C DESCRIPTION - SMPSN FINDS THE INTEGRAL(AREA UNDER THE CURVE) OF F(X)
C               VERSUS X, WHERE THE INDEPENDENT VARIABLE X IS SUBDIVIDED
C               INTO EVENLY SPACED INCREMENTS. SIMPSONS RULE
C               IS USED IF THE NUMBER OF INCREMENTS IS EVEN. IF THE
C               NUMBER IS ODD, THEN NEWTONS 3/8 FORMULA(A CUBIC),
C               IS USED FOR THE FIRST THREE
C               INTERVALS, AND SIMPSONS RULE FOR THE REMAINDER OF THE
C               INTERVALS.
C
C CALLING PARAMETERS
C       AREA  - VALUE OF THE INTEGRAL RETURNED BY SMPSN
C       FX    - VECTOR OF TABULATED F(X)
C               NOTE THAT NINC+1 VALUES ARE REQUIRED
C       H     - SPACING IN THE X DIRECTION
C       NINC  - NUMBER OF INTERVALS OF X BETWEEN XO AND XN. NINC MUST BE
C               TWO OR GREATER.
C
```

FIGURE 6.18
(Continued)

```
      SUBROUTINE SMPSN(AREA,FX,H,NINC)
      DIMENSION FX(1)
    2 FORMAT(1H0/40H0*****ERROR IN SUBROUTINE SMPSN. NINC IS,I5,22H, WHI
     1CH IS NOT ALLOWED/51H0CONTROL RETURNED TO CALLING PROGRAM WITH ARE
     2A = 0./1H0)
      IO=6
      AREA=0.0
      IF(NINC-2) 10,12,15
   10 WRITE(IO,2)NINC
      RETURN
C
C     FOR NINC=2
C
   12 J=1
C
C     SIMPSONS 3 POINT FORMULA
C
   13 AREA=H/3.*(FX(J)+4.*FX(J+1)+FX(J+2))+AREA
      RETURN
   15 IF(NINC-4) 16,20,19
C
C     FOR NINC=3
C
   16 J=1
C
C     NEWTONS 3/8 RULE FOR NINC ODD
C
   17 AREA=3.*H/8.*(FX(1)+3.*(FX(2)+FX(3))+FX(4))
      GO TO(29,21,36),J
   19 IF(2*(NINC/2)-NINC) 30,20,30
C
C     NINC IS EVEN
C
   20 K=2
C
C     SIMPSONS RULE
C
   21 SUM4=0.0
      SUM2=0.0
      N=NINC-2
      DO 26 I=K,N,2
      SUM4=SUM4+FX(I)
   26 SUM2=SUM2+FX(I+1)
      SUM4=SUM4+FX(N+2)
      AREA=H/3.*(FX(K-1)+4.*SUM4+2.*SUM2+FX(N+3))+AREA
   29 RETURN
C
C     NINC IS ODD. NEWTONS 3/8 RULE COMPUTES AREA OF FIRST THREE
C         INTERVALS. SIMPSONS RULE COMPUTES THE REST. IF NINC=5, SPECIAL
C         CASE.
C
   30 IF(NINC-5) 31,34,31
   31 K=5
      J=2
      GO TO 17
   34 J=3
      GO TO 17
   36 J=4
      GO TO 13
      END
```

FIGURE 6.18
(Continued)

formula for Simpson's rule is

$$\text{AREA} = (\Delta x/3)\left[y_0 + y_N + 4 \sum_{i=1,3,5,\ldots} y_i + 2 \sum_{i=2,4,6,\ldots} y_i\right] \qquad \text{(xvi)}$$

where y_i represents the ordinate evaluated at index i. Note that Simpson's rule, Eq. (xvi), is restricted to an odd number of points, i.e., N must be even. Also, Eq. (xvi) represents a second-order approximation to the function being integrated numerically, i.e., it fits three points exactly with a parabola. A computer program is listed in Fig. 6.18. This program integrates Eq. (ii) numerically with 100 intervals for each of the three regions. The subroutine SMPSN will also handle N odd by resorting to Newton's three-eighths rule for the first three intervals. The results are plotted in Fig. 6.19. Note that most of the temperature drop is in the wall region. In the wall region, the conduction mechanism accounts for all the heat transfer.

At $y^+ = 5$, the radius equals 0.049912 m. From Eq. (xi), the temperature at this point is

$$\bar{T} = \bar{T}_w - \left(\frac{(4.063 \times 10^{-3})}{(2)(0.05)(1.501 \times 10^{-7})}\right)[(0.05)^2 - (0.049912)^2]$$

$$= 40.0 - 2.38 = 37.62°C \qquad \text{(xvii)}$$

The results of the numerical integration for the viscous region verify the answer of 37.62°C exactly. At $y^+ = 5.0$, the velocity profile for the generation region, Eq. (6.103), gives a negative E_τ, which is an unreasonable result. Note that Eq. (6.103) has been adjusted so that its slope at $y^+ = 5.0$ equals that of the slope of Eq. (6.83). Therefore, Eq. (6.103) should not be applied at this location because of Prandtl's assumption of zero Reynolds stress. At $y^+ = 5.0$, E_τ is zero. Similarly at the center line, a negative E_τ is found because Eq. (6.102) does not predict a zero velocity gradient at this point. Obviously, a major deficiency of Eq. (6.102)

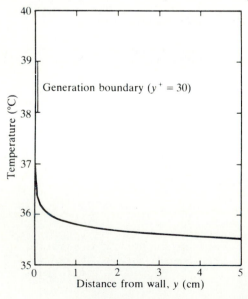

FIGURE 6.19
Temperature distribution in turbulent flow.

is the fact that its predictions do not result in a zero velocity gradient at the center of a pipe, an obvious expectation because of symmetry.

6.5 THE FRICTION FACTOR

The Fanning friction factor f was introduced in Eq. (6.89) as a nondimensional ratio of the wall shear stress τ_w to the kinetic energy of the flow, $\frac{1}{2}\rho U^2_{z,\,ave}$. As such, the friction factor can be pictured as a relative measure of the frictional losses in a system. The Fanning friction factor[10] as given in Eq. (6.89) is

$$f = \frac{\tau_w}{\frac{1}{2}\rho U^2_{z,\,ave}} = \frac{(d_o/4)(-d\bar{p}/dz)}{\frac{1}{2}\rho U^2_{z,\,ave}} = \frac{\dfrac{d_o(-\Delta p)}{4L}}{\frac{1}{2}\rho U^2_{z,\,ave}} \tag{6.89}$$

For laminar flow, the combination of Eqs. (4.77), Eq. (6.2), and (6.89) results in an equation that is easy to remember:

$$f = 16/(d_o U_{z,\,ave}\rho/\mu) = 16/N_{Re} \tag{6.124}$$

For turbulent flow, the definition of friction factor and the definition of friction velocity [Eq. (6.55)] result in the following simple expression:

$$U^* = U_{z,\,ave}\sqrt{f/2} \tag{6.125}$$

The friction factor can be predicted from the velocity profile. However, as has been emphasized previously, all the velocity profile equations proposed to date are subject to a number of serious limitations. Since this approach does provide a useful form for correlation purposes, one possibility is to start with the universal velocity distribution equation, Eq. (6.76), and integrate across the flow cross section to obtain the average velocity. The result expressed as a velocity defect is

$$\frac{\bar{U}_{z,\,max} - U_{z,\,ave}}{U^*} = \frac{3}{2\kappa} = 3.75 \tag{6.126}$$

Equation (6.126) has been confirmed experimentally, although there is considerable scatter in the data. The equation is usually referred to as Stanton's law. Equation (6.126) can be combined with Eq. (6.125) and rearranged:

$$\frac{U_{z,\,ave}}{U^*} = \frac{\bar{U}_{z,\,max}}{U^*} - \frac{3}{2\kappa} = \sqrt{\frac{2}{f}} \tag{6.127}$$

---

[10] Alternative friction factors that are various multiples of f as defined in Eq. (6.89) have been used in the literature. For example, in common usage is the Darcy or Weisbach friction factor, which is four times larger than the Fanning friction factor presented here. Since the same symbol is often used, the reader must always check the exact definition when using other texts, graphs, and tables in order to avoid any serious errors.

At the center line, the velocity can be estimated from the universal velocity distribution equation, Eq. (6.102), which in Example 6.7 was shown to estimate the center line velocity reasonably well. Equation (6.77), which is the generalized form of Eq. (6.102), can be written in terms of $\bar{U}_{z,\,max}$:

$$\frac{\bar{U}_{z,\,max}}{U^*} = (1/\kappa)\ln y_o^+ + B \tag{6.128}$$

where y_o^+ is the value of y^+ at the center line. Combining Eqs. (6.127) and (6.128), the result is

$$\sqrt{2/f} = (1/\kappa)\ln y_o^+ + B - 3/(2\kappa) \tag{6.129}$$

The y_o^+ in Eq. (6.129) can be eliminated by using its definition and Eq. (6.125) as follows:

$$y_o^+ = U^* r_o/\nu = (U^*/U_{z,\,ave})(U_{z,\,ave})(r_o/\nu)(2)(1/2)$$
$$= (1/2)(\sqrt{f/2})(N_{Re}) = (\sqrt{f/8})(N_{Re}) \tag{6.130}$$

The above, with Eq. (6.129), yields

$$\sqrt{2/f} = (1/\kappa)\ln[N_{Re}\sqrt{f/8}] + B - 3/(2\kappa) \tag{6.131}$$

Equation (6.131) provides the best form for correlating friction factors. Von Karman first derived Eq. (6.131), and Nikuradse [N1] used this form and modified the constants slightly to correlate his extensive data:

$$1/\sqrt{f} = 4.0\log_{10}(N_{Re}\sqrt{f}) - 0.4 \tag{6.132}$$

Equation (6.132), often called the Von Karman correlation, is valid to a Reynolds number of 3 200 000 for turbulent flow of fluids in smooth tubes. It is superior to any other correlation now in existence, although simpler correlations such as that of Blasius [B3] have been proposed:

$$f = 0.079(N_{Re})^{-1/4} \tag{6.133}$$

The Blasius equation approximates Eq. (6.132) up to a Reynolds number of 100 000 and can be used for quick estimates. This equation is the basis for the 1/7 power law of velocity, previously presented as Eq. (6.110).

Figure 6.20 shows a plot of friction factor versus Reynolds number. Note that the slope of Eq. (6.124) is −1 on a log–log plot for the laminar region. No equation or line exists for the transition region because the data are not reproducible from one experimental apparatus to another. Equation (6.132) is plotted in the turbulent region. Figure 10.3 is recommended for actual design calculations because it is larger in size and therefore more accurate to read.

Example 6.9. Crude oil with specific gravity 0.84 is pumped at 2000 bbl/day (barrels per day) through 2000 ft of steel pipe under a pressure drop of 80 psi. The pipe is 2 inches in diameter and schedule 40 in wall thickness. Compute the Fanning friction factor.

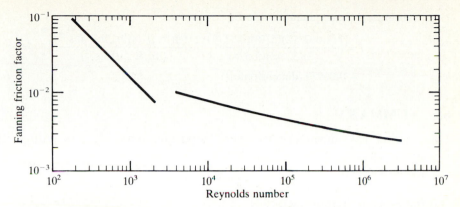

FIGURE 6.20
Friction factor versus Reynolds number for pipe flow.

Answer. Since all the information is given in engineering units, those units will be used in this solution. This problem requires conversion of each variable in Eq. (6.89) into a consistent set of units so that f will be dimensionless. After slight rearrangement, Eq. (6.89) is

$$f = \frac{(d_o/2)(-d\bar{p}/dz)}{\rho U_{z,\,ave}^2} \tag{i}$$

If the units of pressure drop are to be $lb_f\,ft^{-2}$, then the units for Eq. (i) as written must be

$$f[=]\left(\frac{(ft)(lb_f\,ft^{-2})(ft^{-1})}{(lb_m\,ft^{-3})(ft^2\,s^{-2})}\right) = lb_f\,lb_m^{-1}\,ft^{-1}\,s^2 \tag{ii}$$

Thus, to make Eq. (i) dimensionless with pressure in units of $lb_f\,ft^{-2}$, the equation must be multiplied by the gravitational conversion constant g_c:

$$g_c = 32.174\,lb_m\,lb_f^{-1}\,ft\,s^{-2} \tag{iii}$$

From Example 6.1 or Table B.1, the diameter for 2-in., schedule 40 pipe is 2.067 in., and the cross sectional flow area is $0.02330\,ft^2$. The pressure drop is

$$(-d\bar{p}/dz) = (80)(144)/(2000)\,[(lb_f\,in.^{-2})(in.^2\,ft^{-2})(ft^{-1})]$$
$$= 5.76\,lb_f\,ft^{-3} \tag{iv}$$

The velocity is computed by dividing the value for the flow rate by the area. One barrel (bbl) is equal to 42 US gallons, and 7.48 gallons is equal to $1.0\,ft^3$:

$$U_{z,\,ave} = (2000)(1/24)(1/3600)(42)(1/7.48)(1/0.02330)$$
$$\times\,[(bbl\,day^{-1})(day\,h^{-1})(h\,s^{-1})(gal\,bbl^{-1})(ft^3\,gal^{-1})(ft^{-2})]$$
$$= 5.578\,ft\,s^{-1} \tag{v}$$

The density is the specific gravity times the density of water:

$$\rho = (0.84)(62.4) = 52.42\,lb_m\,ft^{-3} \tag{vi}$$

Substituting these quantities into Eq. (i) gives

$$f = \left(\frac{(2.067/12)(5.76)(32.174)}{(2)(52.42)(5.578)^2}\right)\left(\frac{(\text{ft})(\text{lb}_f\,\text{ft}^{-3})(\text{lb}_m\,\text{lb}_f^{-1}\,\text{ft}\,\text{s}^{-2})}{(\text{lb}_m\,\text{ft}^{-3})(\text{ft}^2\,\text{s}^{-2})}\right)$$

$$= 0.00979 \text{ (dimensionless)} \tag{vii}$$

6.6 SUMMARY

This chapter has introduced two very important dimensionless groups: the Reynolds number, which for pipe flow is

$$N_{Re} = d_o U_{z,\,ave}\rho/\mu \tag{6.2}$$

and the Fanning friction factor:

$$f = \frac{\tau_w}{\frac{1}{2}\rho U_{z,\,ave}^2} = \frac{(d_o/4)(-d\bar{p}/dz)}{\frac{1}{2}\rho U_{z,\,ave}^2} = \frac{\dfrac{d_o(-\Delta p)}{4L}}{\frac{1}{2}\rho U_{z,\,ave}^2} \tag{6.89}$$

The magnitude of the Reynolds number is the criterion used for predicting whether the flow is laminar, turbulent, or in the transitional region. For pipes, the laminar region extends up to a Reynolds number of approximately 2100. In laminar flow, the fluid moves in straight lines along the pipe axis. There are no groups of fluid that move in the r or θ direction. For the laminar region, the pressure drop equations of Chapter 4 may be rearranged into

$$f = 16/N_{Re} \tag{6.124}$$

The velocity profile in the laminar region in pipe flow is parabolic in shape:

$$U_z/U_{z,\,max} = 1 - (r/r_o)^2 \tag{4.74}$$

The turbulent region is characterized by high flow rates. It is also the region in which most common applications of fluid mechanics are found. In turbulent flow, there are eddies of fluid moving in all three coordinate directions, even though the bulk flow may be in only one direction. There will be instantaneous values of velocity (and sometimes of temperature and concentration) that differ significantly from the mean values. It is important to understand the difference between transitional and turbulent flow, both in a pipe and along a solid surface such as a flat plate. Although turbulent eddies appear to be random in nature, the reader must understand that nonrandom series of events do take place in turbulent flow; these are summarized in Fig. 6.7.

This chapter has presented and discussed the equations that apply in turbulent flow. The conclusion was that there were no exact solutions. Averaging of the instantaneous values of velocity, etc., and subsequent loss of information were covered thoroughly. In view of this dilemma, several classical models of turbulence were discussed, including Boussinesq's theory, the Prandtl mixing length, the film and penetration theories, and the simple analogies such as that of Reynolds.

Finally, correlations of velocity profiles in turbulent flow were discussed in some detail. Although the turbulence models were useful in representing velocity profiles, empirical correlations are in widespread use today. Basically, all existing correlations of velocity profiles in turbulent flow are deficient in some way, but most do an adequate job of prediction, as shown in Example 6.7. The universal velocity distribution is perhaps the most generally accepted of the equations for the velocity profile in a pipe:

Viscous sublayer: $\qquad U^+ = y^+$ $\qquad\qquad\qquad\qquad\qquad\qquad$ (6.83)

Generation region: $\qquad U^+ = 5.0 \ln y^+ - 3.05$ $\qquad\qquad\qquad$ (6.103)

Turbulent region: $\qquad U^+ = 2.5 \ln y^+ + 5.5$ $\qquad\qquad\qquad$ (6.102)

In turbulent flow, the friction factor must also be correlated empirically. For flow in smooth tubes, the most accurate correlation is that of von Karman:

$$1/\sqrt{f} = 4.0 \log_{10} (N_{Re}\sqrt{f}) - 0.4 \qquad\qquad (6.132)$$

PROBLEMS

6.1. When the equations of motion are time-averaged for turbulent flow, what additional terms are introduced?

6.2. What are the assumptions involved in Eq. (6.34)?

6.3. In the vicinity of the wall there is a specific form for the velocity distribution that does not involve empirical constants. Derive this and discuss its limitations.

6.4. What are the limitations of the eddy viscosity concept?

6.5. For pipe flow a student measures the laminar–turbulent transition at a Reynolds number of 2300. Is this result of general validity? Discuss.

6.6. What are the limitations of the Prandtl mixing length concept? Do you think turbulence corresponds to this mechanistic picture? Give your reasons for this answer.

6.7. What is the problem in estimating the eddy viscosity at the center line in pipe flow?

6.8. Discuss the turbulent velocity profile in general terms from the most ideal representation to the least desirable.

6.9. List the advantages and limitations of using Pai's equations (Eq. (6.114), ff.) to represent the turbulent velocity distribution.

6.10. In terms of the eddy viscosity concept, discuss the mechanism of the transfer of mass, heat, and momentum.

6.11. Water is flowing in a 3-in. schedule 80 pipe at a flow rate of 40 gpm at 320 K. Determine if the flow is laminar, transitional, or turbulent. Use Tables A.1 and B.1 in the Appendix.

6.12. Water ($\rho = 1000 \text{ kg m}^{-3}$) flows in a pipe of diameter $2a$. At some distance from the wall, a hot-film anemometer yields the data below. Calculate the Reynolds stress τ_T.

t, s	U'_z, m s^{-1}	U'_r, m s^{-1}
0.1	4.0	1.0
0.2	1.0	−4.0
0.3	6.0	0.0
0.4	0.0	5.0
0.5	0.0	−3.0
0.6	−3.0	0.0
0.7	−5.0	2.0
0.8	2.0	−5.0
0.9	5.0	0.0

6.13. Using the universal velocity distribution, calculate the eddy viscosity ε at a distance $(d_o/4)$ from the wall of a 3-in. schedule 40 pipe for a steady-state water flow at 15°C if the Reynolds number is 9.0×10^4 and the friction factor is 4.56×10^{-3}. Use SI units throughout your calculation.

6.14. Equation (6.110), the 1/7 power law, is simple to use and surprisingly accurate in spite of its lack of theoretical basis.
  (a) Using the integral in Eq. (4.76), calculate the volumetric flow rate based on Eq. (6.110).
  (b) Find the distance from the wall where $\bar{U}_z$ equals $U_{z,\,ave}$.
  (c) Find the slope $d\bar{U}_z/dr$ as a function of r. Discuss whether the resulting equation is reasonable throughout $0 \le y \le r_o$.

6.15. Find an approximate expression using Eq. (6.73) for the mixing length distribution for a turbulent flow that is described by the 1/7 power law, Eq. (6.110).

6.16. For the 1/7 power law, Eq. (6.110), derive an equation in terms of y/r_o for (a) $\varepsilon/(\rho U^* r_o)$ and (b) $(E_\tau + v)/(U^* r_o)$. For each, locate the maximum.

6.17. For the universal velocity distribution of Eq. (6.102), derive an equation in terms of y/r_o for (a) $\varepsilon/(\rho U^* r_o)$ and (b) $(E_\tau + v)/(U^* r_o)$. For each, locate the maximum.

6.18. For the velocity distribution given by Pai's equations (Eq. (6.114), ff.), derive an equation in terms of r/r_o for (a) $\varepsilon/(\rho U^* r_o)$ and (b) $(E_\tau + v)/(U^* r_o)$. For each, locate the maximum.

6.19. How does the group $\varepsilon/(\rho U^* r_o)$ vary with Reynolds number at a given position, if the universal velocity distribution, Eq. (6.102), applies?

6.20. Find an approximate expression for the mixing length distribution for a turbulent flow that is described by the universal velocity distribution, Eq. (6.102).

6.21. Beginning with Eq. (6.72), the general expression for the Prandtl mixing length l for pipe flow, determine whether the dimensionless Prandtl mixing length (l/r_o) is a function of Reynolds number in the turbulent core. Assume that Eq. (6.102) applies.

6.22. Repeat Problem 6.17 without assuming $\tau = \tau_w$ as did Prandtl.

6.23. The hot-film probe in Figure 6.4 is to be used for measurements near the wall in a pipe flow of water. It is desired to gain information about the viscous sublayer. Criticize the experiment and justify your criticism.

6.24. Determine the velocity distribution and eddy viscosity distribution using the universal plot (U^+, y^+) when a fluid of density 1300 kg m^{-3} and kinematic viscosity 2.0×10^{-6} m^2 s^{-1} flows in a smooth pipe whose I.D. is 6 in. The pressure drop causing the flow is 1000 lb$_f$ ft^{-2}, and the pipe is 100 ft long. Do all calculations in the English system of units.

6.25. Water at 20°C flows in a 4-in. schedule 40 pipe at a Reynolds number of 55 000. Determine the velocity distribution and eddy viscosity distribution using Pai's equations. Work in English units.

6.26. Determine the velocity distribution and eddy viscosity distribution using the universal plot (U^+, y^+) when air at 20°C and 1 atm pressure flows in a 3-in. schedule 40 pipe. The velocity at the center line $\bar{U}_{z, \max}$ is $120\,\text{ft s}^{-1}$. Do all calculations in the SI system of units.

6.27. Determine the velocity distribution and eddy viscosity distribution using Pai's equations for the flow of air at 20°C and 1 atm at $16\,\text{m s}^{-1}$ average velocity in a 3-inch schedule 40 pipe. Work in SI units.

6.28. Use Pai's equations to compute the ratio $U_{z, \text{ave}}/\bar{U}_{z, \max}$ for laminar flow.

6.29. Find the error in the friction factor predicted from the Blasius correlation as compared to that from the von Karman equation at Reynolds numbers of 20 000 and 100 000. Also, find the error at a Reynolds number of 10^6, where the Blasius correlation is not satisfactory.

REFERENCES

B1. Black, T. J.: *A.I.A.A.*, Preprint No. 68–42, 1968.
B2. Black, T. J.: in *Viscous Drag Reduction*, C. S. Wells (ed.), Plenum, New York, 1969, p. 383.
B3. Blasius, H.: *Mitt. Forschungsarbeit, VDI* **131**: 1 (1913).
B4. Boussinesq, T. V.: *Mem. Pres. Par. Div. Sav., Paris* **23**: 46 (1877).
B5. Brodkey, R. S.: *AIChE J.* **9**: 448 (1963).
B6. Brodkey, R. S.: *The Phenomena of Fluid Motions*, Addison-Wesley, Reading, Mass, 1967. [Fourth printing available from The Ohio State University Bookstores, Columbus, Ohio 43210.]
B7. Brodkey, R. S., K. N. McKelvey, H. C. Hershey, and S. G. Nychas: *Int. J. Heat Mass Transfer* **21**: 593 (1978).
B8. Bullin, J. A., and A. E. Dukler: *Chem. Eng. Sci.* **27**: 439 (1972).
B9. Bullin, J. A., and A. E. Dukler: *Environ. Sci. Techol.* **8**: 156 (1974).
C1. Campbell, J. A., and T. J. Hanratty: *AIChE J.* **28**: 988 (1982); **29**: 215, 221 (1983).
C2. Corino, E. R., and R. S. Brodkey: *J. Fluid Mech.* **37**: 1 (1969).
D1. Danckwerts, P. V.: *Ind. Eng. Chem.* **43**: 1460 (1951).
D2. Deissler, R. G.: *NACA Report 1210* (1955).
E1. Eckelmann, H.: *J. Fluid Mech.* **65**: 439 (1974).
E2. Einstein, H. A., and H. Li: *Proc. Am. Soc. Civil Engrs.* **82** (EM2): paper 945 (1956).
H1. Hanratty, T. J.: *AIChE J.* **2**: 359 (1956).
H2. Harriott, P.: *Chem. Eng. Sci.* **17**: 149 (1962).
H3. Hershey, H. C.: *Drag Reduction in Newtonian Polymer Solutions*, Ph.D. Thesis (Chem. Eng.), University of Missouri (Rolla), 1965.
H4. Higbie, R.: *Trans. AIChE.* **31**: 365 (1935).
K1. Kim, H. T., S. J. Kline and W. C. Reynolds: *J. Fluid Mech.* **50**: 133 (1971).
K2. Koppel, L. B., R. D. Patel and J. T. Holmes: *AIChE J.* **12**: 941, 947 (1966).
K3. Knudsen, J. G., and D. L. Katz: *Fluid Dynamics and Heat Transfer*, McGraw-Hill, New York, 1958.
L1. Lewis, W. K.: *Ind. Eng. Chem.* **8**: 825 (1916).
L2. Lewis, W. K., and W. G. Whitman: *Ind. Eng. Chem.* **16**: 1215 (1924).
L3. Lin, C. S., R. W. Moulton, and G. L. Putnam: *Ind. Eng. Chem.* **45**: 636 (1953).
M1. Macleod, N., and J. W. Ponton: *Chem. Eng. Sci.* **32**: 483 (1977).
M2. Meek, R. L., and A. D. Baer: *AIChE J.* **16**: 841 (1970).
M3. Meek, R. L., and A. D. Baer: *Int. J. Heat Mass Trans.* **16**: 1385 (1973).
M4. Murphree, E. V.: *Ind. Eng. Chem.* **24**: 726 (1932).

N1. Nikuradse, J.: *VDI-Forschungshelf,* No. 356 (1932).

N2. Notter, R. H., and C. A. Sleicher: *Chem. Eng. Sci.* **26:** 161 (1971).

N3. Nychas, S. G., H. C. Hershey, and R. S. Brodkey: *J. Fluid Mech.* **61:** 513 (1973).

P1. Pai, S. I.: *J. Appl. Mech.* **20:** 109 (1953).

P2. Pai, S. I.: *J. Franklin Inst.* **256:** 337 (1953).

P3. Perlmutter, D. D.: *Chem. Eng. Sci.* **16:** 287 (1961).

P4. Perry, R. H., and D. W. Green: *Perry's Chemical Engineers' Handbook,* 6th ed., McGraw-Hill, New York, 1984.

P5. Pinczewski, W. V., and S. Sideman: *Chem. Eng. Sci.* **29:** 1969 (1974).

P6. Prandtl, L.: *Ergeb. Aerodyn. Versuchanstalt, Goettingen* **3:** 1 (1927).

P7. Praturi, A. K., and R. S. Brodkey: *J. Fluid Mech.* **89:** 251 (1978).

R1. Reynolds, O.: *Phil. Trans. Roy. Soc. (London)* **A174:** 935 (1883).

R2. Reynolds, O.: *Proc. Manchester Lit. Phil. Soc.* **14:** 7 (1874); see paper 14 in "Papers on Mechanical and Physical Subjects" Vol. I, by O. Reynolds, Cambridge Univ. Press, Cambridge, 1900, p. 81.

R3. Ross, D.: *Turbulent Flow in Smooth Pipes, A Reanalysis of Nikuradse's Experiments,* N.O.R.D. Report No. 7958–246, Pennsylvania State University, College Park, PA, 1952.

R4. Ruckenstein, E.: *Chem. Eng. Sci.* **18:** 233 (1963).

R5. Ruckenstein, E.: *Chem. Eng. Sci.* **22:** 474 (1967).

S1. Shaw, D. A., and T. J. Hanratty, *AIChE J.* **23:** 28 (1977).

T1. Taylor, G. I.: *Phil. Trans. Roy. Soc. (London)* **A223:** 289 (1923).

T2. Thomas, L. C., and L. T. Fan: *Ind. Eng. Chem. Fundam.* **10:** 135 (1971).

T3. Thomas, L. C.: *Chem. Eng. Sci.* **26:** 1271 (1971).

T4. Toor, H. L., and J. M. Marchello: *AIChE J.* **4:** 97 (1958).

T5. Treybal, R. E.: *Mass Transfer Operations,* 3rd ed., McGraw-Hill, New York, 1980.

V1. Van Driest, E. R.: *J. Aeronaut. Sci.* **23:** 1007 (1956).

V2. Von Karman, T.: *J. Aeronaut. Sci.* **1:** 1 (1934).

W1. Whitman, W. G.: *Chem. Metall. Eng.* **29** (4): 146 (July 23, 1923).

INTEGRAL METHODS OF ANALYSIS

NOMENCLATURE

A   Species A; A_1 and A_2 are species A at locations 1 and 2

A   Area for heat transfer (m^2, ft^2)

A_i Projected area of the elbow in Fig. 7.5; subscripts refer to direction and location

C   Concentration (kmol m^{-3}, lb mol ft^{-3}); C_A, C_B, C_i are concentrations of species A, B, i; C_T is total concentration; $C_{A,1}$ and $C_{A,2}$ are concentrations at locations 1 and 2; $\bar{C}_{A,w}$ is time-average concentration of species A at the wall; $\bar{C}_{A, ave}$ is bulk average concentration of species A

c_p Heat capacity at constant pressure (kJ kg^{-1} K^{-1}, Btu lb$_m^{-1}$ °F^{-1}); other subscripts defined as used

c_v Heat capacity at constant volume (kJ kg^{-1} K^{-1})

d Diameter (m, ft); d_o is inside diameter of pipe, as used in fluid flow

e Base of natural logarithms (2.718 281 8 . . .)

E   Total energy of system (J kg^{-1}, Btu lb$_m^{-1}$)

$\dot{E}$ Time rate of change of energy (J s^{-1}, Btu s^{-1})

F   Force (N, lb$_f$); $\boldsymbol{F}$ is vector; various subscripts defined as used

F' Energy loss due to fluid friction between walls and fluid (J, Btu)

f	Fanning friction factor, Eq. (6.89)
g	Vector representing the acceleration due to a gravitational or other field (m s^{-2}, ft s^{-2})
g_c	Gravitational conversion constant (32.174 lb$_m$ lb$_f^{-1}$ ft s^{-2})
H	Initial height of fluid in Fig. 7.2
H	Enthalpy of system (J, Btu); subscripts denote location
h	Height of a fluid in a tank (m, ft)
i	Unit vector in the x direction
M	Molecular weight (molar mass) (kg kmol^{-1}, lb$_m$ lb mol^{-1})
$\dot{M}$	Time rate of change of mass in the volume V (kg s^{-1}, lb$_m$ s^{-1})
m	Mass (kg, lb$_m$)
N	Normal vector, perpendicular to the surface S
n	Power in Eq. (7.9)
n	Number of moles (or the mass) of the system (mol, lb mol)
p	Pressure (kPa, atm, lb$_f$ in.$^{-2}$); p is always absolute pressure unless otherwise stated
$\dot{P}$	Time rate of change of momentum (N, lb$_f$); if written not as a vector, then $\dot{P}$ is subscripted for direction of transfer
Q	Volume flow rate (m^3 s^{-1}, ft^3 s^{-1})
Q	Heat added to system (J, Btu)
q	Energy (heat) flow vector (J s^{-1}, Btu s^{-1}); subscripts denote components in coordinate directions
R	Gas constant; see Appendix, Table C1 for values
R_A	Generation of species A by chemical reaction
R_{slant}	Manometer reading of a slant tube manometer (m, ft)
r	Cylindrical coordinate (m, ft)
r	Radius (m, ft); r_o is value of r at the tube wall
S	Area perpendicular to the direction of the velocity vector U; S_1 or S_2 are areas at locations 1 or 2; also used as a subscript to denote the integral over a surface
T	Temperature (K, °R, °C, °F); T_1 and T_2 are temperatures at locations 1 and 2; T_w is temperature of the wall or surface; T_∞ is temperature in an open channel; T_{ave} or T_b is bulk temperature, Eq. (11.31)
t	Time (s); t_c is contact time in Eq. (6.101)
U	Internal energy of the system (J, Btu); subscripts denote location
U	Velocity vector (m s^{-1}, ft s^{-1}); U is magnitude of U; U_x, U_y, U_z, U_θ, U_r, U_ϕ are components in directions x, y, z, θ, r, ϕ; U^* is friction velocity, Eq. (6.53); $U_{z,ave}$ or U_{ave} is mean velocity in z direction
V	Volume (m^3, ft^3); also used as a subscript to denote volume integral
$\mathcal{V}$	Displaced volume
v	Molar volume of a gas, RT/p (m^3 kmol^{-1}, ft^3 lb mol^{-1})
W	Total work done by the system (J, Btu); W_s is shaft work from a piece of equipment such as a pump, compressor, or turbine
w	Mass flow rate (kg s^{-1}, lb$_m$ s^{-1}); subscripts denote location
w	Subscript denoting wall

x	Rectangular (Cartesian) coordinate
y	Rectangular (Cartesian) coordinate
z	Rectangular (Cartesian) coordinate
α	The ratio $(U_{ave}^3)/(U^3)_{ave}$, Eq. (7.54)
α	Angle between i and U; also angle of slant manometer leg
β	The ratio $(U_{ave}^2)/(U^2)_{ave}$, Eq. (7.24)
γ	The ratio of heat capacities, c_p/c_v
Δ	Difference, state 2 minus state 1; e.g., ΔT means $T_2 - T_1$
η	Pump efficiency
θ	Curvilinear coordinate direction
θ	Angle between U and N [see Eq. (7.3)]
μ	Viscosity ($\text{kg m}^{-1}\text{s}^{-1}$ or $\text{N m}^{-2}\text{s}$, $\text{lb}_m \text{ft}^{-1}\text{s}^{-1}$, cP); μ_w is viscosity at wall
ν	Kinematic viscosity (momentum diffusivity) (m^2s^{-1}, ft^2s^{-1})
ξ	Generalized transport coefficients associated with h, f, k_c', Eq. (6.90); also, ξ_H, ξ_τ, ξ_M refer to generalized coefficients for heat, momentum, and mass, respectively
π	Ratio of circumference of a circle to its diameter (3.141 592 65. . .)
ρ	Density (kg m^{-3}, $\text{lb}_m \text{ft}^{-3}$); ρ_f and ρ_m are the densities of process fluid and manometer fluid, respectively
$\boldsymbol{\Psi}$	Generalized flux vector (e.g., units for heat flux are $\text{J m}^{-2}\text{s}^{-1}$ or W m^{-2}, $\text{Btu ft}^{-2}\text{s}^{-1}$; see Tables 2.1 and 3.1 for more details); Ψ_x, Ψ_y, Ψ_z are components in directions x, y, z; $\Psi_{x,m}$ or $\boldsymbol{\Psi}_m$ is flux due to molecular transport, $\Psi_{x,c}$ or $\boldsymbol{\Psi}_c$ is flux due to convection; $\boldsymbol{\Psi}_o$ is flux by mechanisms other than convection or molecular transport
ψ	Generalized concentration of property (e.g., units for concentration of heat are J m^{-3}, Btu ft^{-3}; see Table 3.1 for complete listing)
$\dot{\psi}_G$	Generalized rate of generation of energy or mass or momentum in a unit volume (see Table 4.2 for units; e.g., for heat, units are $\text{J m}^{-3}\text{s}^{-1}$, $\text{Btu ft}^{-3}\text{s}^{-1}$)
∇	Vector operator del, defined by Eq. (2.16) or Eq. (3.45) (m^{-1}, ft^{-1})

Note

The overbar for time average, as used in Chapter 6, is largely discarded in this and subsequent chapters because time-average properties, not instantaneous properties, are considered. As a result, the notation is considerably simplified.

In the previous chapters, detailed balances to quantify the conservation of a property (energy, mass, moles, and momentum) have been made on a differential element in the system. After simplification of the overall balance equations, the result was integrated in order to obtain the velocity, temperature, and concentration distributions for specific geometries and boundary conditions. For many cases, such detailed information is not necessary and, in fact, is impossible to obtain because of the complexity of the equations and the nature of the boundary conditions. The complexity of the system is often due to the presence of a turbulent flow in a complex flow geometry, together with heat and/or mass transfer. Much of the complexity can be eliminated if the principle of conservation of property is applied to the system on an integral (overall or macro) basis rather than on a differential (micro) basis. Balance equations can be applied over a finite volume of the system, thereby obtaining the overall balance of mass, momentum, and energy. A limited application of this approach (for a simple one-dimensional system) is given in Chapter 3. In developing Eq. (3.7), a balance was used on a finite volume but, as noted there, the interest was more in developing a differential equation [see Eq. (3.14), the one-directional balance equation]. Since the overall balance equations to be presented in this chapter represent an integration over a volume, they can give no information as to conditions inside the system. However, these equations will give the relationship between the variables at the inlet and outlet of the volume, and often this type of information is more useful than the conditions inside the system. Since the details of the flow are not needed in the analysis, the equations apply equally well for both turbulent and laminar flow. However, the nature of the flow will have an effect at both the entrance and the exit. There are four equations of this type to be considered: the overall balances of mass, momentum, energy, and mechanical energy. This chapter begins with a general overall balance on a finite volume.

7.1   THE GENERAL INTEGRAL BALANCE EQUATION

The balance, or conservation, concept presented in Section 3.1 is valid whether the volume is small (differential) or large (finite or integral). Thus, it would be well for the reader to reread that section so that the development to follow can be put into proper perspective. The balance equation given as Eq. (3.1) is repeated here:

$$\text{INPUT} + \text{GENERATION} = \text{OUTPUT} + \text{ACCUMULATION} \quad (3.1)$$

which can be rearranged to:

$$\text{ACCUMULATION} = -(\text{OUTPUT} - \text{INPUT}) + \text{GENERATION} \quad (7.1)$$

Equation (7.1) simply says that the property will accumulate if there is more flowing in than out when no property is generated within the volume. The individual terms have all been defined in Section 3.1. The approach here is to integrate the terms for accumulation and generation that are occurring within the volume; the integration must encompass the entire volume. For the input–output terms that account for transport through the surfaces of the system, the integration must be over the surface through which the transport is occurring.

Three transport modes must be included in the input–output balance: that due to convection (cf. Chapter 5), that due to molecular transport (cf. Chapter 4), and that by other means not involving the actual flow or molecular transport, such as heat transferred by the mechanism of radiation. In terms of the general property and the flux of that property, the equation can be expressed as

$$\int_V \frac{\partial \psi}{\partial t}\, dV = -\oint_S (\psi U \cdot dS) - \oint_S (\Psi_m \cdot dS) - \oint_S (\Psi_o \cdot dS) + \int_V \dot{\psi}_G\, dV \quad (7.2)$$

ACCUMULATION	INPUT–OUTPUT	GENERATION
	BY	
	CONVECTION MOLECULAR	OTHER
	TRANSPORT TRANSPORT	MEANS

where the meaning of each term is beneath the equation. Here the area dS is a vector quantity with direction N, where N is the normal vector perpendicular to the surface. The accumulation and generation terms are unchanged from the presentations in the earlier chapters. They must be integrated over the volume. The fluxes for the input–output balance are the convective flux, Eq. (3.49), the molecular flux, Eq. (2.18), and the flux Ψ_o, which is the flux by mechanisms other than convection or molecular transport. All these fluxes must be integrated over the surfaces involved in the inputs and outputs. The convection term in Eq. (7.2) can be modified by using the definition of the dot product $(U \cdot dS)$:

$$\int_V \frac{\partial \psi}{\partial t}\, dV = -\oint_S (\psi U)(\cos \theta)\, dS - \oint_S (\Psi_m \cdot dS)$$

$$-\oint_S (\Psi_o \cdot dS) + \int_V \dot{\psi}_G\, dV \quad (7.3)$$

where the angle θ is between the velocity vector U and the normal vector N (perpendicular to the area through which the transfer is occurring). The term $(\psi U)(\cos \theta)\, dS$ arises from the definition of a dot product: the magnitude ψU times the magnitude dS times the cosine of the angle θ. Note that U is the scalar magnitude of the vector U. Equation (7.3) contains both dS and dS; these are related by $(N\, dS = dS)$.

Figure 7.1 shows a typical system in which a fluid flows into a process through surface 1 and out through surface 2. At each surface the normal vector is directed away from the interior of the system. Commonly the surfaces 1 and 2 will be perpendicular to the velocity vector, in which case the angle θ in Eq. (7.3) is π radians at the entrance and zero radians at the exit. Thus, the cosines of θ will be -1 and 1, respectively, as is seen in Fig. 7.1(a). Note that $\cos \theta$ times dS is the projection of the surface in the direction of the velocity vector as shown in Fig. 7.1(b). Such a correction was not necessary in the case of the differential balance because all transport areas were in coordinate directions, as shown in Fig. 3.5. Note also in Eq. (7.3) that the symbol $\oint_S$ denotes the surface integral over the entire surface area. Naturally, flow enters and exits the volume only through the pair of areas S_1 and S_2, so the rest of the system contributes zero to the value of the surface integral.

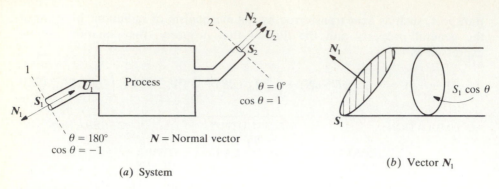

FIGURE 7.1
System for integral mass balance.

7.1.1   The Integral Mass Balance

Equation (7.3) will be considered now for conservation of overall mass. The first term of Eq. (7.3), as applied to the overall mass, becomes the time rate of change of mass integrated throughout the volume. The entire first term will now be replaced by a single symbol $\dot{M}$. The second term in Eq. (7.3) is the gain or loss of mass per unit volume (ρ) from the volume by convection as a result of the velocity U. If it is assumed that equimolar counter diffusion occurs ($N_A = -N_B$), there is no net mass flux due to molecular transport (i.e., $\Psi_m = 0$), and the third term is zero. If no miscellaneous mechanisms exist in the integral mass balance ($\Psi_o = 0$), the fourth term is zero. The generation term ($\dot{\psi}_G$) is zero regardless of the presence of any chemical reaction; $\dot{\psi}_G$ is non-zero only in problems where there is a nuclear reaction that converts mass into energy. If both Ψ_m and Ψ_o are zero, Eq. (7.3) reduces to

$$\dot{M} = -\oint_S (\rho U)(\cos\theta)\, dS \tag{7.4}$$

Equation (7.4) is the *unsteady-state overall mass balance*.

In Figure 7.1, the fluid enters at 1 and leaves at 2; the surfaces across the flow are selected so that they are perpendicular to the lines of flow. For this system, Eq. (7.4) becomes

$$\dot{M} = -\int_{S_1} (\rho U)(\cos\theta)\, dS - \int_{S_2} (\rho U)(\cos\theta)\, dS \tag{7.5}$$

At S_1 the angle between N_1 and U_1 is 180°, and $\cos\theta$ equals -1; at S_2 the angle between N_2 and U_2 is 0°, and $\cos\theta$ equals $+1$. Then Eq. (7.5) reduces to

$$\dot{M} = \int_{S_1} (\rho U)\, dS - \int_{S_2} (\rho U)\, dS \tag{7.6}$$

Often, the product ρU may assume an average value across the surface, so when Eq. (7.6) is integrated, a useful result is

$$\dot{M} = \rho_1 U_{1,\,\text{ave}} S_1 - \rho_2 U_{2,\,\text{ave}} S_2 \tag{7.7}$$

where $U_{1,\,\text{ave}}$ and $U_{2,\,\text{ave}}$ are the average (bulk) velocities at positions 1 and 2, respectively. In each case, the velocity U_{ave} is the average over the cross section at the point in question. The average velocity U_{ave} is defined in general as

$$U_{\text{ave}} = \frac{\oint (U \cdot dS)}{\oint dS} \tag{7.8}$$

When Eq. (7.8) is applied to pipe flow, it is often advantageous to define a quantity $(U^n)_{\text{ave}}$, which is U raised to a general power n and then averaged:

$$(U^n)_{\text{ave}} = \frac{\int_0^{2\pi} \int_0^{r_0} (U^n) r\, dr\, d\theta}{\int_0^{2\pi} \int_0^{r_0} r\, dr\, d\theta} \tag{7.9}$$

For a circular pipe, the denominator is simply the area, πr_0^2.

    For turbulent flow, U is replaced by $\bar{U}$, where $\bar{U}$ is the time mean of the instantaneous velocity vector U. This time mean must not be confused with the average across the pipe given by Eq. (7.8). The replacement of U by $\bar{U}$ in effect neglects the flow associated with the deviations from the mean. The exact analysis for turbulent flow follows from the insertion of Eq. (6.8), given below, into Eq. (7.9):

$$U = \bar{U} + U' \tag{6.8}$$

Recall that U' is the deviation from the mean. If Eq. (6.8) is time-averaged, then by definition $\overline{U'}$ is equal to zero. For the mass balance in which $n = 1$, the approximation is without error. For n other than 1, these averages are not zero, i.e., $\overline{(U')^2} \neq 0$, but in practice the error is small, and the more exact analysis is usually impossible to carry out. Henceforth, the instantaneous values of U, C_A, T, etc., will not be not used; the overbar notation on these quantities will be dropped. The notation without the overbar will now signify the time-average values.

    If the densities are asssumed constant or equal to some average value across the cross section, the mass flow rate w (typical units of kg s^{-1}) is in general

$$w = \rho U_{\text{ave}} S \tag{7.10}$$

Since the term $\dot{M}$ is the time rate of change of mass in the system, it follows that

$$\dot{M} = w_1 - w_2 \tag{7.11}$$

For steady-state, $\dot{M}$ is zero and

$$w = w_1 = w_2 \tag{7.12}$$

or

$$w = \rho_1 U_{1,\,\text{ave}} S_1 = \rho_2 U_{2,\,\text{ave}} S_2 \tag{7.13}$$

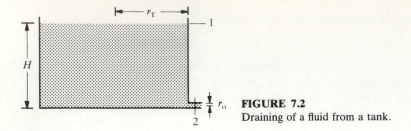

FIGURE 7.2
Draining of a fluid from a tank.

Example 7.1. A tank of radius r_T is filled to a height H with a liquid of density ρ, as shown in Fig. 7.2. The fluid drains from the bottom of the tank through a hole with a radius of r_o. The flow velocity at the exit is approximated by Torricelli's law:

$$U_{ave}^2 = 2gh \tag{i}$$

where h is the instantaneous height. What is the total time required to empty the tank?

Answer. Equation (7.11) applies. Since nothing enters the system

$$w_1 = 0 \tag{ii}$$

The mass flow exiting is the density times the velocity times the flow area (πr_o^2), Eq. (7.10):

$$w_2 = \rho U_{2,\,ave}(\pi r_o^2) \tag{iii}$$

After substituting Torricelli's law, this equation becomes

$$w_2 = (\rho)(\pi r_o^2)(2gh)^{1/2} \tag{iv}$$

Since the term $\dot{M}$ has units of mass per second, the following unit equation is valid:

$$\dot{M} = d(\rho \pi r_T^2 h)/dt \tag{v}$$

where $\pi r_T^2 h$ is the volume of fluid in the tank at any given h. Equations (ii), (iv), and (v) are combined with Eq. (7.11):

$$d(\rho \pi r_T^2 h)/dt = 0 - (\pi r_o^2 \rho)(2gh)^{1/2} \tag{vi}$$

which rearranges to

$$\frac{dh}{h^{1/2}} = -\frac{r_o^2}{r_T^2}(2g)^{1/2}\, dt \tag{vii}$$

The following boundary conditions apply:

$$h(t=0) = H$$
$$h(t=t_{total}) = 0 \tag{viii}$$

Equation (vii) is integrated with these boundary conditions to give the total time of emptying, t_{total}:

$$t_{total} = \frac{r_T^2}{r_o^2}\left(\frac{2H}{g}\right)^{1/2} \tag{ix}$$

Example 7.2. A tank of inside diameter 4 m and with a water level of 2 m is to be emptied by draining through a 3 cm exit hole. How long will it take to remove one-half of the contents? How long will it take to empty the tank?

Answer. This problem is solved by integrating Eq. (vii) in the previous example with the general boundary conditions:

$$h(t = 0) = H$$
$$h(t = t) = h \tag{i}$$

The answer is

$$h^{1/2} = H^{1/2} - \frac{r_o^2}{r_T^2} \left(\frac{g}{2}\right)^{1/2} t \tag{ii}$$

The original height H is 2 m, h is 1 m, r_o is given as 3 cm or 0.03 m, and r_T is 2 m. Substituting these into Eq. (ii), the result is

$$(1.0)^{1/2} = (2.0)^{1/2} - (0.03/2.0)^2 (9.80665/2)^{1/2} t \tag{iii}$$

where $g = 9.80665$ m s^{-2}. The time t to reach a height of 1 m is found from Eq. (iii):

$$t = 830.9 \text{ s} = 13.8 \text{ min} \tag{iv}$$

The time to completely empty the tank is found from Eq. (ix) of the previous example:

$$t_{total} = \frac{r_T^2}{r_o^2} \left(\frac{2H}{g}\right)^{1/2} = (2.0/0.03)^2 [(2)(2)/(9.80665)]^{1/2}$$

$$= 2838.5 \text{ s} = 47.3 \text{ min} \tag{v}$$

The calculated times are too long to be practical for commercial applications. Either one must pump the fluid out at a greater rate than can be obtained by Torricelli's law or one must enlarge the exit hole. The hole size to empty the tank in 10 min can be calculated from Eq. (ix) of the previous example:

$$r_o^2 = (r_T^2)(2H/g)^{1/2}/(t_{total}) = (2.0)^2 [(2)(2)/(9.80665)]^{1/2}/[(10)(60)]$$

$$= 0.004\,258 \text{ m}^2 \tag{vi}$$

or

$$r_o = 0.065 \text{ m} = 6.5 \text{ cm} \tag{vii}$$

This answer is quite reasonable for a large tank as given in this problem.

7.1.2 The Integral Balance on an Individual Species

The concentration of species A can be substituted for the property ψ in Eq. (7.3) to produce an equation similar to Eq. (7.7):

$$\dot{M}_A = C_{A,1} U_{1,\,ave} S_1 - C_{A,2} U_{2,\,ave} S_2 + R_A \tag{7.14}$$

The term R_A represents the generation of species A by chemical reaction. For no chemical reaction, the term R_A is zero. For steady-state (no chemical reaction) both R_A and $\dot{M}_A$ are zero, and Eq. (7.14) shows that the mass or number of moles of species A entering equals the mass or moles of species A leaving.

It is easiest to solve mass balance problems with chemical reaction on a mole basis. The procedures are relatively straightforward, and there are several books that contain sections on mass balances [F1, H1, S2]. The topic is usually referred to as stoichiometry. Example 7.3 is presented as an example that involves the combustion of coal.

Example 7.3. A coal hydrogasification plant normally converts coal into a hydrocarbon gas that is subsequently processed into useful organic compounds. However, owing to restricted capacity in the plant it is sometimes necessary to use the output gas as a furnace fuel. In this particular case, the fuel is burned with 40 percent excess air in a multistage furnace system that gives essentially 100 percent conversion and no CO formation. Calculate the flue (exit) gas composition. The fuel gas composition in mole per cent is

H_2	N_2	CO	H_2S	C_2H_4	C_2H_6	CH_4	CO_2
24	0.5	5.9	1.5	0.1	1.0	64	3.0

Answer. As a basis, let us select 100 moles of fuel gas. Then the percentages above are the actual moles of each compound in the feed stream. Solution of this problem follows easily, if the amount of oxygen required for complete combustion (called the theoretical oxygen) is computed. The possible chemical reactions are

$$H_2 + \tfrac{1}{2}O_2 = H_2O \tag{i}$$
$$CO + \tfrac{1}{2}O_2 = CO_2 \tag{ii}$$
$$H_2S + \tfrac{3}{2}O_2 = SO_2 + H_2O \tag{iii}$$
$$C_2H_4 + 3O_2 = 2CO_2 + 2H_2O \tag{iv}$$
$$C_2H_6 + \tfrac{7}{2}O_2 = 2CO_2 + 3H_2O \tag{v}$$
$$CH_4 + 2O_2 = CO_2 + 2H_2O \tag{vi}$$

The nitrogen is assumed to be inert at the combustion temperature. The CO_2 in the feed is also assumed not to change. The theoretical O_2 required is:

$$12.00 \text{ moles } O_2 \text{ required for 24 moles } H_2$$
$$2.95 \text{ moles } O_2 \text{ required for 5.9 moles CO}$$
$$2.25 \text{ moles } O_2 \text{ required for 1.5 moles } H_2S$$
$$0.30 \text{ moles } O_2 \text{ required for 0.1 moles } C_2H_4$$
$$3.50 \text{ moles } O_2 \text{ required for 1.0 moles } C_2H_6$$
$$128.00 \text{ moles } O_2 \text{ required for 64 moles } CH_4$$

$$\overline{149.00 \text{ total moles theoretical } O_2 \text{ required}}$$

Since the fuel gas is burned with 40 percent excess, the actual oxygen supplied is 1.4 times the 149 moles, or 208.6 moles. The nitrogen is found from a nitrogen balance, i.e., the nitrogen input equals nitrogen output in the exit stream (the flue gas). There are two sources of nitrogen: 0.5 moles N_2 in the fuel gas and a large quantity in the air, which is 79 percent N_2 and 21 percent O_2. The calculation proceeds as follows:

$$\text{total moles air} \qquad = 208.6 \text{ moles } O_2/0.21 = 993.3 \qquad\qquad \text{(vii)}$$

$$\text{total moles } N_2 \qquad = (993.3)(0.79) = 784.7 \qquad\qquad\qquad \text{(viii)}$$

$$\text{moles of } N_2 \text{ in flue gas} = 784.7 + 0.5 = 785.2 \qquad\qquad\qquad \text{(ix)}$$

$$\text{moles of } O_2 \text{ in flue gas} = (\text{moles in air}) - (\text{moles reacted})$$

$$= 208.6 - 149 = 59.6 \qquad\qquad\qquad\qquad\qquad \text{(x)}$$

Water, carbon dioxide, and sulfur dioxide are found by making the appropriate balance using the chemical reactions. The calculations follow.

H_2O and CO_2 balance. Using the reactions in Eqs. (i) through (vi):

24 moles H_2O and   0 moles CO_2 formed for 24 moles H_2 reacted

0 moles H_2O and 5.9 moles CO_2 formed for 5.9 moles CO reacted

0.2 moles H_2O and 0.2 moles CO_2 formed for 0.1 moles C_2H_4 reacted

3.0 moles H_2O and 2.0 moles CO_2 formed for 1.0 moles C_2H_6 reacted

128 moles H_2O and 64 moles CO_2 formed for 64 moles CH_4 reacted

---

156.7 total moles H_2O and 72.1 total moles CO_2 formed

The total CO_2 formed is 72.1 moles, which when added to the three moles in the fuel gas gives a total of 75.1 moles of CO_2. The total H_2O is 156.7 moles.

SO_2 balance. From the 1.5 moles of H_2S in the fuel gas, 1.5 moles of SO_2 are formed and exit in the flue gas.

At this point, the moles of each of the five gases in the flue gas have been computed on the basis of 100 moles of fuel. The compositions are found by dividing the moles of each gas by the total moles. The final composition of the flue gas is

gas	N_2	O_2	H_2O	CO_2	SO_2
moles	785.2	59.6	156.7	75.1	1.5
mole percent	72.8	5.5	14.5	7.0	0.1

7.1.3   The Integral Momentum Balance

The momentum balance is obtained by substitution of ρU for the concentration of property ψ, as found in Table 4.1. Note that ψ is a vector, since ρU is substituted. Each term in Eq. (7.3) will be considered in turn. Figure 7.3 shows

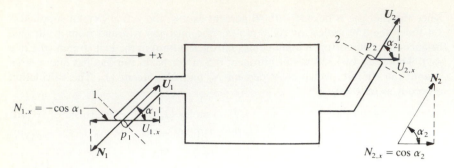

FIGURE 7.3
System for integral momentum balance.

the general system for an integral momentum balance. The time rate of change of momentum after the accumulation term is integrated over the system volume is called $\dot{\boldsymbol{P}}$:

$$\dot{\boldsymbol{P}} = \int_V \frac{\partial \psi}{\partial t}\, dV = \int_V \frac{\partial (\rho \boldsymbol{U})}{\partial t}\, dV \tag{7.15}$$

Note that $\dot{\boldsymbol{P}}$ has units of property per second, which is a force unit such as newtons. Thus each term in Eq. (7.3) as applied to momentum will have the units of force.

The second term in Eq. (7.3) is separated into two integrals, as was done in deriving Eq. (7.5). Since $\cos \theta$ is either -1 or 1, the second term becomes

$$-\oint_S (\rho \boldsymbol{U}\boldsymbol{U})(\cos \theta)\, dS = \int_{S_1} (\rho \boldsymbol{U}\boldsymbol{U})\, dS - \int_{S_2} (\rho \boldsymbol{U}\boldsymbol{U})\, dS \tag{7.16}$$

Again, it has been assumed that there is no flow through surfaces other than S_1 and S_2 and that the flow is perpendicular to these surfaces.

The third term in Eq. (7.3) arises from the input–output flux by molecular transport. There are three contributions to this term. The internal surfaces of the system in Fig. 7.3 are stationary. The moving fluid transfers momentum to these walls. The viscous drag (sometimes termed skin friction) is the largest contribution to the molecular input–output flux and is included in a term denoted as $\boldsymbol{F}_{\text{drag}}$. In this analysis, $\boldsymbol{F}_{\text{drag}}$ is the force of the fluid on the solid. The units of $\boldsymbol{F}_{\text{drag}}$ are force, such as newtons.

The second contribution to the flux by molecular transport is from the pressure at the inlet and outlet of the system:

$$-\int_{S_1+S_2} p\boldsymbol{N}\, dS = -\int_{S_1} p\boldsymbol{N}\, dS - \int_{S_2} p\boldsymbol{N}\, dS \tag{7.17}$$

The pressure p is a scalar quantity. In Eq. (7.17) the quantity $p\boldsymbol{N}$ is a vector acting normal to the surfaces S_1 and S_2. The pressure term also contributes a pressure drag (sometimes called form drag) on the internal surfaces of the system, which is included in F_{drag}. All pressures in Eq. (7.17) are absolute, a key point often confused in discussing this equation.

The third contribution to the flux by molecular transport is associated with the viscous forces at the inlet and outlet of the system volume. This contribution is usually neglected. Then the third term in Eq. (7.3) becomes

$$\oint_S (\boldsymbol{\Psi}_m \cdot d\boldsymbol{S}) = -\int_{S_1} (p\boldsymbol{N}) \, dS - \int_{S_2} (p\boldsymbol{N}) \, dS - \boldsymbol{F}_{drag} \tag{7.18}$$

In this equation, the flux $\boldsymbol{\Psi}_m$ is the shear stress $\boldsymbol{\tau}$, which is a tensor; the dot product of $\boldsymbol{\Psi}_m$ with $d\boldsymbol{S}$ is a vector, as is every term in Eq. (7.18).

The fourth term in Eq. (7.3) is zero because other means of momentum transport do not exist. The fifth term, the generation of momentum, is caused by the action of external forces on the fluid, such as the force of gravity. Such effects are denoted as $\boldsymbol{F}_{ext}$. If gravity alone is to be considered, then $\boldsymbol{F}_{ext}$ equals $\boldsymbol{F}_g$, and Eq. (4.51) applies:

$$\boldsymbol{F}_g = \rho V \boldsymbol{g} \tag{4.51}$$

The overall momentum balance is the result of substituting the five preceding equations into Eq. (7.3):

$$\dot{\boldsymbol{P}} = \int_{S_1} (\rho \boldsymbol{U}\boldsymbol{U}) \, dS - \int_{S_2} (\rho \boldsymbol{U}\boldsymbol{U}) \, dS - \int_{S_1} (p\boldsymbol{N}) \, dS - \int_{S_2} (p\boldsymbol{N}) \, dS - \boldsymbol{F}_{drag} + \boldsymbol{F}_{ext}$$

$$\tag{7.19}$$

After performing the integrations, as for the mass balance, Eq. (7.19) becomes

$$\dot{\boldsymbol{P}} = \rho_1 (\boldsymbol{U}\boldsymbol{U})_{1,\,ave} S_1 - \rho_2 (\boldsymbol{U}\boldsymbol{U})_{2,\,ave} S_2 - p_1 \boldsymbol{N}_1 S_1 - p_2 \boldsymbol{N}_2 S_2 - \boldsymbol{F}_{drag} + \boldsymbol{F}_{ext} \tag{7.20}$$

The first difference in Eq. (7.20) can be expressed in terms of the mass flow rate w [from Eqs. (7.12) and (7.13)] in order to eliminate the product ρS. Then Eq. (7.20) becomes

$$\dot{\boldsymbol{P}} = \frac{(\boldsymbol{U}\boldsymbol{U})_{1,\,ave}}{U_{1,\,ave}} w_1 - \frac{(\boldsymbol{U}\boldsymbol{U})_{2,\,ave}}{U_{2,\,ave}} w_2 - p_1 \boldsymbol{N}_1 S_1 - p_2 \boldsymbol{N}_2 S_2 - \boldsymbol{F}_{drag} + \boldsymbol{F}_{ext} \tag{7.21}$$

where again p_1 and p_2 are absolute pressures.

Equation (7.21) is a vector equation that must be resolved into its component parts before being used. For example, let us reconsider the system of Fig. 7.3, in which the angle θ is the angle between the velocity vector for the flowing fluid and the normal vector to the area of the control volume (see Fig. 7.1). The angle α is the angle between the unit vector in the x direction and the velocity vector. For the x direction, the following are true from Fig. 7.3:

$$U_{1,x} = U_1 \cos \alpha_1 \qquad\qquad U_{2,x} = U_2 \cos \alpha_2$$

$$N_{1,x} = \cos(180 - \alpha_1) = -\cos \alpha_1 \qquad N_{2,x} = \cos \alpha_2 \tag{7.22}$$

Thus, Eq. (7.21) becomes

$$\dot{P}_x = \frac{(U_1^2)_{\text{ave}}}{U_{1,\,\text{ave}}} w_1 \cos \alpha_1 - \frac{(U_2^2)_{\text{ave}}}{U_{2,\,\text{ave}}} w_2 \cos \alpha_2 + p_1 S_1 \cos \alpha_1$$

$$- p_2 S_2 \cos \alpha_2 - F_{\text{drag},\,x} + F_{\text{ext},\,x} \qquad (7.23)$$

For the y component (or the z component), the cosines become sines: otherwise, the equations are the same.

Quite often the term $(U^2)_{\text{ave}}/U_{\text{ave}}$ is replaced by U_{ave}/β, where

$$\beta = \frac{(U_{\text{ave}})^2}{(U^2)_{\text{ave}}} \qquad (7.24)$$

If the velocity entering the control volume in Fig. 7.3 is constant everywhere across area S_1, then β is unity at the entrance because U_{ave} equals U for a flat profile (i.e., plug flow). The same would apply for the exit stream if the profile were flat. Naturally, plug flow represents an idealized case. There is always a velocity profile in a real fluid with non-zero viscosity, beginning with zero velocity at a solid–fluid interface. If the velocity profile is known, then the numerator and denominator can be evaluated separately using Eqs. (7.8) and (7.9) and β can be determined. Although β is usually assumed to be unity, it has been evaluated for a number of flows:

Turbulent flow	$0.95 \le \beta \le 0.99$	(7.25)
Laminar flow	$\beta = \frac{3}{4}$	(7.26)

In the general case, β at the inlet of the volume as in Fig. 7.3 does not necessarily equal β at the outlet. However, this degree of rigor is rarely required for most problems, and the assumption of β equal to unity is often satisfactory.

Force balance and Newton's second law. Inspection of Eq. (7.21) shows that the last four terms are forces, while the first three terms involve momentum changes:

$$\dot{P} = \frac{(UU)_{1,\,\text{ave}}}{U_{1,\,\text{ave}}} w_1 - \frac{(UU)_{2,\,\text{ave}}}{U_{2,\,\text{ave}}} w_2 - p_1 N_1 S_1 - p_2 N_2 S_2 - F_{\text{drag}} + F_{\text{ext}} \quad (7.21)$$

In this equation, the terms $(-p_1 N_1 S_1)$ and $(-p_2 N_2 S_2)$ are vector forces, associated with the absolute pressure acting in a direction perpendicular to each surface S_1 and S_2. Let us call these two pressure forces F_{press}:

$$F_{\text{press}} = -p_1 N_1 S_1 - p_2 N_2 S_2 \qquad (7.27)$$

With this definition, the definition of β [Eq. (7.24)], and the definition of Δ (state 2 minus state 1), Eq. (7.21) becomes

$$\sum F = F_{\text{press}} - F_{\text{drag}} + F_{\text{ext}} = \dot{P} + \Delta(wU/\beta) \qquad (7.28)$$

The left-hand side of Eq. (7.28) is the sum of three forces. Equation (7.28) equates these to the sum of two momentum changes: $\dot{P}$ is the time rate of change of momentum, and the term $\Delta(wU/\beta)$ is the change in momentum between points 2 and 1, i.e., the convection of momentum into and out of the volume.

Newton's second law of motion can be expressed as

$$\sum F = \dot{P} = d(mU)/dt \tag{7.29}$$

where the term $d(mU)/dt$ is the total time rate of change of momentum at a point. In Eq. (7.29) convection is not explicity expressed. However, the convection term can be obtained if the total time derivative is replaced by the substantial derivative, Eq. (5.52). The result is a differential relationship similar to Eq. (7.28) that contains convection. At steady-state, the flow rate is constant, and all derivatives with respect to time, including $\dot{P}$, are zero. For this case, Eq. (7.28) becomes

$$\sum F = F_{\text{press}} - F_{\text{drag}} + F_{\text{ext}} = \Delta(wU/\beta) \tag{7.30}$$

In other words, at steady-state the sum of the forces is not equal to zero as Eq. (7.29) implies because the velocity vector may change from state 1 to state 2 as a result of a change in flow area, a change in direction, and/or a change in fluid density. Equation (7.30) clearly shows that at steady-state the convection of momentum balances the sum of the forces.

Equations (7.15) through (7.28) comprise a rather complex application of the general property balance concept to momentum. This application has the advantage of clearly indicating the nature of convection and the source and reason for the β correction factor and the other terms in the equation. In contrast, Eq. (7.29), Newton's law, tends to bypass these important concepts.

Equation (7.30) is the basis for making a force balance on a free body; a free body is the widely used term for a control volume in which all forces act *on* the body. The pressure force F_{press} can be determined from Eq. (7.27). The magnitude of F_{press} in any direction is the pressure times the projected area (from S_1 and S_2 only) in that direction, and its sign can easily be determined by common sense, rather than resorting to the normal vectors as used in Eq. (7.27). When a fluid is contained within a solid boundary, such as a nozzle, the walls of the solid exert forces on the body, i.e., F_{ext}. The normal and shear stresses counterbalance F_{ext} [S5]. A complete discussion of pressure forces is available elsewhere [D1, S5].

The concept of gauge pressure greatly simplifies the solution to some common momentum balance problems, as will be illustrated by Example 7.6. The gauge pressure is the pressure relative to the atmospheric pressure p_{atm}:

$$p_{\text{gauge}} = p_{\text{absolute}} - p_{\text{atm}} \tag{7.31}$$

As a final point when engineering units are employed in the momentum and force balance equations, the units lb_m and lb_f will both appear. The conversion factor g_c will be needed in the denominator of the right-hand side of Eq. (7.30), as can be verified by checking units in the equation. Example 7.4 illustrates the use of Eq. (7.21), the momentum balance equation, and Examples 7.5 and 7.6 illustrate the force balance on a free body that Eq. (7.30) suggests.

Example 7.4. Water flows at a rate of $10 \, ft^3 \, s^{-1}$ through a horizontal 60° reducing elbow, as shown in Fig. 7.4. The inlet absolute pressure is 100 psia, and the outlet absolute pressure is 29.0 psia. The inlet and outlet diameters are 6 in. and 4 in., respectively. Find the force exerted by the elbow on the fluid.

Answer. The force to be found here is F_{ext}, as given by Eq. (7.21):

$$\dot{P} = \frac{(UU)_{1, \text{ave}}}{U_{1, \text{ave}}} w_1 - \frac{(UU)_{2, \text{ave}}}{U_{2, \text{ave}}} w_2 - p_1 N_1 S_1 - p_2 N_2 S_2 - F_{\text{drag}} + F_{\text{ext}} \quad (7.21)$$

Since the problem is presented in engineering units, those will be used in this solution. The areas S_1 and S_2 are

$$S_1 = \pi d_1^2/4 = (3.14159)(6.0/12.0)^2/(4) = 0.1963 \, ft^2$$
$$S_2 = \pi d_2^2/4 = (3.14159)(4.0/12.0)^2/(4) = 0.0873 \, ft^2 \quad (i)$$

The velocities $U_{1, \text{ave}}$ and $U_{2, \text{ave}}$ are determined from the volumetric flow rate divided by area:

$$U_{1, \text{ave}} = Q/S_1 = (10)/(0.1963)[(ft^3 \, s^{-1})(ft^{-2})] = 50.93 \, ft \, s^{-1}$$
$$U_{2, \text{ave}} = Q/S_2 = (10)/(0.0873)[(ft^3 \, s^{-1})(ft^{-2})] = 114.6 \, ft \, s^{-1} \quad (ii)$$

Next, the Reynolds number of the flow will be checked in order to determine if the quantity β can be assumed unity. For water, the viscosity and density in English units are $6.72 \times 10^{-4} \, lb_m \, ft^{-1} \, s^{-1}$ and $62.4 \, lb_m \, ft^{-3}$, respectively. Thus, at

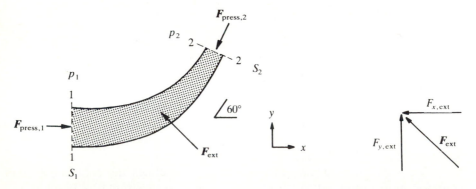

(a) Fluid inside elbow   (b) Resultant forces on elbow

FIGURE 7.4
Momentum balance on the fluid in a reducing elbow.

the inlet:

$$N_{Re} = d_o U_{ave} \rho / \mu = (6.0/12.0)(50.93)(62.4)/(6.72 \times 10^{-4}) = 2.4 \times 10^6 \qquad \text{(iii)}$$

Similarly, the outlet Reynolds number is even greater, 3.6×10^6. Thus, the assumption of $\beta = 1$ is valid:

$$(U^2)_{ave}/U_{ave} = U_{ave} \qquad \text{(iv)}$$

For this problem, there is no time rate of change of momentum because of steady-state:

$$\dot{P} = 0 \qquad \text{(v)}$$

The mass flow entering equals the mass flow exiting; these are found from Eq. (7.10) and Eq. (i) or from the product of density times volume flow rate:

$$w_1 = w_2 = \rho U_{ave} S = \rho Q = (62.4)(10) = 624 \text{ lb}_m \text{ s}^{-1} \qquad \text{(vi)}$$

The drag on the walls F_{drag} will be neglected because the length of fluid travel is short (see Chapter 10 for details). Equation (7.21) [or its restatement, Eq. (7.23)] both contain F_{ext}, which is the external force acting on the fluid inside the walls of the elbow and between surfaces S_1 and S_2. In other words, F_{ext} will be exerted by the elbow *on* the fluid. The quantity F_{ext} has a component in the z direction from gravity and in the x and y directions from the elbow. In Eq. (7.21), the normal vector N_1 acts in the negative x direction, at an angle of 180° from the x axis; N_2 acts obliquely at an angle of 60°. Since $\cos 180° = -\cos 0°$, Eq. (7.21) becomes Eq. (7.23), which with the reductions and simplifications already discussed is

$$0 = (w/g_c)[(U_{1,\,ave})(\cos \alpha_1) - (U_{2,\,ave})(\cos \alpha_2)] + p_1 S_1 \cos \alpha_1$$
$$- p_2 S_2 \cos \alpha_2 + F_{ext,\,x} \qquad \text{(vii)}$$

The angles α_1 and α_2 are zero and 60°, respectively. After substituting all values and solving Eq. (vii) for $F_{ext,\,x}$, the result is

$$F_{ext,\,x} = -(624/32.174)[(50.9)(\cos 0) - (114.6)(\cos 60)]$$
$$- (100)(144)(0.1963)(\cos 0) + (29.0)(144)(0.0873)(\cos 60)$$
$$= 123.5 - 2645.2 = -2522 \text{ lb}_f \qquad \text{(viii)}$$

where the absolute pressures have been converted to units of $\text{lb}_f \text{ ft}^{-2}$. The equation equivalent to Eq. (7.23) or Eq. (vii) for the y direction is

$$F_{ext,\,y} = -(624/32.174)[(50.9)(\sin 0) - (114.6)(\sin 60)]$$
$$- (100)(144)(0.1963)(\sin 0) + (29.0)(144)(0.0873)(\sin 60)$$
$$= 1924.8 + 315.6 = 2240 \text{ lb}_f \qquad \text{(ix)}$$

The forces $F_{ext,\,x}$ and $F_{ext,\,y}$ are the forces exerted *on* the fluid by the elbow. Equations (viii) and (ix) indicate that $F_{ext,\,x}$ acts to the left and $F_{ext,\,y}$ acts in the positive y direction, as shown in Fig. 7.4(*b*). Note that this elbow is horizontal, and gravity acts in the z direction in Fig. 7.4. If the elbow were rotated, then another force must be included in Eq. (7.21) or Eq. (7.30):

$$F_{gravity} = -\rho V g \qquad \text{(x)}$$

where ρV is the mass of the control volume in units of kg or lb_m.

Example 7.5. Repeat Example 7.4 using the force balance concept given by Eq. (7.30).

Answer. A force balance solution to this problem begins with Eq. (7.30):

$$\sum F = F_{\text{press}} - F_{\text{drag}} + F_{\text{ext}} = \Delta(wU/\beta) \qquad (7.30)$$

The free body under consideration is the fluid inside the elbow shown in Fig. 7.4(a). All forces acting on the free body must be considered. Here F_{drag} is zero, and β is one, as explained in Example 7.4. The change in momentum is easily computed for each direction, using information from Example 7.4:

$$w\,\Delta U_x = w(U_{x,2} - U_{x,1})$$
$$= (624/32.174)[(114.6)(\cos 60) - (50.9)(\cos 0)] = 123.5\ \text{lb}_\text{f} \qquad (i)$$
$$w\,\Delta U_y = w(U_{y,2} - U_{y,1}) = (624/32.174)[(114.6)(\sin 60) - 0] = 1924.7\ \text{lb}_\text{f} \qquad (ii)$$

The remaining term in Eq. (7.30) to be found is F_{press}. The force balance approach to this problem differs from the momentum balance approach in that the momentum balance assigned the direction to the velocity vector N, whereas in the force balance as applied to oblique or curved surfaces the pressure force is determined by the projected area in each coordinate direction. The pressure force can be computed from Eq. (7.27):

$$F_{\text{press}} = -p_1 N_1 S_1 - p_2 N_2 S_2 \qquad (7.27)$$

If the numbers as found in Example 7.4 are inserted, the components of F_{press} are

$$F_{\text{press},x} = -(100)(144)(0.1963)(\cos 180) - (29.0)(144)(0.0873)(\cos 60)$$
$$= 2645\ \text{lb}_\text{f} \qquad (iii)$$
$$F_{\text{press},y} = -(100)(144)(0.1963)(\sin 180) - (29.0)(144)(0.0873)(\sin 60)$$
$$= -315.6\ \text{lb}_\text{f} \qquad (iv)$$

In Eq. (7.27), the product (NS) is the projected area. This quantity may be determined without resort to vectors. From inspection of Fig. 7.4, the pressure force at location 1 in the x direction is the pressure p_1 times the projected area, simply S_1, and the sign must be positive since the pressure acts on the free body in the positive x direction:

$$F_{\text{press},x,1} = p_1 S_1 = (100.0)(144)(0.1963) = 2827.4\ \text{lb}_\text{f} \qquad (v)$$

Since there is no projected area in the y direction at location 1, $F_{\text{press},y,1}$ is zero. Similarly, the pressure force at location 2 in the x direction is the pressure p_2 times the projected area:

$$S_{2,x} = S_2 \cos \alpha_2 = (0.0873)(\cos 60) = 0.04363\ \text{ft}^2 \qquad (vi)$$
$$F_{\text{press},x,2} = -p_2 S_{2,x} = -(29.0)(144)(0.04363) = -182.2\ \text{lb}_\text{f} \qquad (vii)$$

The sign in Eq. (vii) is determined by inspection of Fig. 7.4; the pressure force on the free body is acting in the negative x direction at location 2. The net pressure force is

$$F_{\text{press},x} = F_{\text{press},x,1} + F_{\text{press},x,2} = 2827.4 - 182.2 = 2645\ \text{lb}_\text{f} \qquad (viii)$$

Note that this answer is the same as found in Eq. (iii). When all numbers are inserted into Eq. (7.30), $F_{\text{ext},x}$ is

$$F_{\text{ext},x} = 123.5 - 2645.2 = -2522 \text{ lb}_f \tag{ix}$$

This answer is the same as was obtained in Eq. (viii) of Example 7.4.

For the y direction, the calculation of the pressure force using the free body concept proceeds similarly. Inserting the numbers in the appropriate equation, the force in the y direction is

$$F_{\text{ext},y} = 1924.8 + 315.6 = 2240 \text{ lb}_f \tag{x}$$

The force exerted by the elbow on the fluid is the resolution of $F_{\text{ext},x}$ and $F_{\text{ext},y}$:

$$F_{\text{ext}} = (F^2_{\text{ext},x} + F^2_{\text{ext},y})^{1/2} = [(-2522)^2 + (2240)^2]^{1/2} = 3373 \text{ lb}_f \tag{xi}$$

$$\alpha = \arcsin (F_{\text{ext},y}/F_{\text{ext}}) = 180 - 41.6 = 138.4° \tag{xii}$$

The force has a magnitude of 3373 lb$_f$ and a direction of 138.4° from the positive x direction (in the second quadrant).

Example 7.6. The elbow in Fig. 7.4 is secured by flanges at either end. Calculate the force exerted by the bolts on the flanges. Let the atmospheric pressure be 14.7 psi.

Answer. Figure 7.5(a) shows the 60° reducing elbow previously considered in Fig. 7.4. In this problem the free body to which Eq. (7.30) will be applied is the elbow plus the fluid inside.[1] The elbow is naturally stationary, but the fluid inside is moving. Now F_{ext} is the force exerted by the bolts on the flanges. The solution

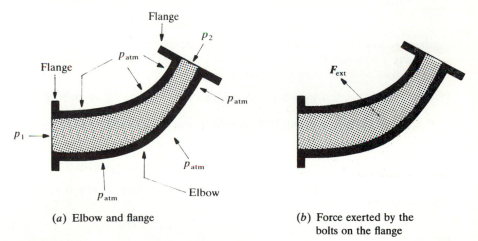

(a) Elbow and flange

(b) Force exerted by the bolts on the flange

FIGURE 7.5
Atmospheric pressure distribution on a reducing elbow.

---

[1] Recall that only the fluid was considered as the control volume or free body in the previous two examples, 7.4 and 7.5.

will show that this F_{ext} is *not* equal to the force exerted by the elbow on the fluid, as found in the preceding two example problems. The solution begins with the force balance:

$$\sum F = F_{press} - F_{drag} + F_{ext} = \Delta(wU/\beta) \tag{7.30}$$

In this problem, the pressure force due to the atmosphere must be considered, as shown in Fig. 7.5(a). The pressure force due to the atmosphere F_{atm} acts on all exposed surfaces of the elbow. The pressure force on surfaces S_1 and S_2 is given by Eq. (7.27), which already includes the atmospheric pressure. Let A_1 be the total area projected by the elbow (including S_1 and S_2) in the x direction. Obviously, A_1 as projected in the positive x direction equals A_1 as projected in the negative x direction. This key point allows the atmospheric contribution to F_{ext} to cancel in all directions as will be shown shortly. The basic equation for pressure force, Eq. (7.27), must have additional terms:

$$F_{press} = -p_1 N_1 S_1 - p_2 N_2 S_2 + F_{atm} \tag{i}$$

Rather than use Eq. (i), perhaps it is easier to consider the pressure forces acting on the free body in Fig. 7.5(a). Recall from Eq. (7.31) that the gauge pressure is related to p_1 and p_2 by:

$$p_1 = p_{1, gauge} + p_{atm} \tag{ii}$$

$$p_2 = p_{2, gauge} + p_{atm} \tag{iii}$$

In order to simplify notation, let us consider only the pressure forces in the x direction and drop the subscript x. The pressure force acting in the positive x direction F_+ is $(p_1 S_1)$ plus the atmospheric pressure acting on the area projected in the negative direction, which is $(A_1 - S_1)$:

$$F_+ = p_{1, gauge} S_1 + p_{atm} S_1 + p_{atm}(A_1 - S_1) \tag{iv}$$

where p_1 has been replaced via Eq. (ii). Next, the pressure force acting in the negative x direction F_- is $p_2 S_2 \cos 60$ plus the atmospheric pressure acting on the area projected in the positive direction $(A_1 - S_2 \cos 60°)$:

$$F_- = (p_{2, gauge} S_2)(\cos 60) + (p_{atm} S_2)(\cos 60) + p_{atm}[A_1 - (S_2)(\cos 60)] \tag{v}$$

The net pressure force acting in the x direction is the sum of F_+ and F_-:

$$F_{press, x} = F_+ + F_- = p_{1, gauge} S_1 - (p_{2, gauge} S_2)(\cos 60)$$
$$+ (p_{atm})[S_1 + A_1 - S_1 - (S_2)(\cos 60) - A_1 + (S_2)(\cos 60)] \tag{vi}$$

where p_2 has been replaced using Eq. (iii). In Eq. (vi), the p_{atm} term is identically zero, and the result is

$$F_{press, x} = p_{1, gauge} S_1 - (p_{2, gauge} S_2)(\cos 60) \tag{vii}$$

or in vector form:

$$F_{press} = -p_{1, gauge} N_1 S_1 - p_{2, gauge} N_2 S_2 \tag{viii}$$

This equation is an extremely useful and general equation that can be generally applied to the computation of the forces necessary to design supports in all types of elbows, bends, valves, etc.

Equations (ii) and (iii) are used to find the gauge pressures:

$$p_{\text{gauge}, 1} = p_1 - p_{\text{atm}} = 100.0 - 14.7 = 85.3 \text{ psig} \tag{ix}$$

$$p_{\text{gauge}, 2} = p_2 - p_{\text{atm}} = 29.0 - 14.7 = 14.3 \text{ psig} \tag{x}$$

The pressure force in the x direction is computed from Eq. (vii):

$$F_{\text{press}, x} = (85.3)(144)(0.1963) - (14.3)(144)(0.0873)(\cos 60)$$
$$= 2322.0 \text{ lb}_f \tag{xi}$$

The derivation of Eq. (vii) was for the x direction. Obviously, the derivation is easily generalized for all directions, and thus Eq. (viii) was presented. The equation for the y direction corresponding to Eq. (vii) is

$$F_{\text{press}, y} = (p_{1, \text{gauge}} S_1)(\sin 0) - (p_{2, \text{gauge}} S_2)(\sin 60) \tag{xii}$$

Inserting the appropriate numbers, $F_{\text{press}, y}$ is

$$F_{\text{press}, y} = (85.3)(144)(0) - (14.3)(144)(\sin 60) = -155.6 \text{ lb}_f \tag{xiii}$$

Using the pressure forces from the last two equations and the assumptions and numbers from Example 7.5, the external forces are

$$F_{\text{ext}, x} = 123.5 - 2322.0 = -2200 \text{ lb}_f \tag{xiv}$$

$$F_{\text{ext}, y} = 1927.7 + 155.6 = 2083 \text{ lb}_f \tag{xv}$$

In conclusion, the atmospheric pressure forces cancel on a solid body, even when that body contains a fluid that enters at a pressure p_1 and exits at p_2. When the free body is taken as the solid plus the fluid inside, the atmospheric contribution to F_{ext} cancels in all directions, and F_{press} must be calculated from Eq. (viii):

$$F_{\text{press}} = -p_{1, \text{gauge}} N_1 S_1 - p_{2, \text{gauge}} N_2 S_2 \tag{viii}$$

Then F_{ext} becomes the force necessary to hold the solid in place and is the key quantity in the determination of the thickness of the material of construction—the bolts, etc. Note that the resultant force and angle found in this problem differ from those obtained in Example 7.5. For this problem

$$F_{\text{ext}} = (F_{\text{ext}, x}^2 + F_{\text{ext}, y}^2)^{1/2} = [(-2200)^2 + (2083)^2]^{1/2} = 3030 \text{ lb}_f \tag{xvi}$$

$$\alpha = \arcsin (F_{\text{ext}, y}/F_{\text{ext}}) = 180 - 43.4 = 136.6° \tag{xvii}$$

Also, there is a force on the elbow in the z direction owing to the weight of the elbow plus the weight of the fluid inside.

Cancellation of the atmospheric pressure terms becomes obvious if one considers the elbow without flow. With no flow, the pressures at locations 1 and 2 are 1 atm; in other words, the elbow is lying at rest, totally surrounded by atmospheric pressure. Obviously, the elbow will be stationary. The conclusion is that the forces due to atmospheric pressure must balance one another; if the forces were unbalanced, Newton's second law of motion would require that there be an acceleration.

7.1.4   The Integral Energy Balance

A complete discussion of energy balances requires a thorough background in thermodynamics as well as in transport phenomena. In this section a brief introduction to the first law of thermodynamics will be presented in order to introduce and explain the concepts of heat, work, and internal energy.

Equation (7.3) can be used to obtain an energy balance upon substitution of the concentration of heat, $\rho c_p T$, for the property ψ. The resulting equation is of limited value because the first three terms in the final equation are negligible for most problems. The last two terms are often of little use because they are too general in nature for specific use. Instead, what is needed is not a balance on the concentration of heat, but rather a balance on the concentration of the total energy in the system. Such a balance will be formulated from the first law of thermodynamics and alternately from Eq. (7.3).

Figure 7.6 depicts a boundary of a system of arbitrary shape. The surroundings are the entire universe with the exclusion of the system. One statement of the first law of thermodynamics is that the total energy of the universe (i.e., system plus surroundings) is constant. It follows that the change in the total energy in the system equals the negative of the change in the total energy of the surroundings. This statement is an expression of a simple energy balance:

CHANGE IN TOTAL ENERGY OF SYSTEM

$\qquad$ = −CHANGE IN TOTAL ENERGY OF SURROUNDINGS   (7.32)

In Fig. 7.6, the heat added to the system from the surroundings is positive in sign and Q in magnitude; the work done by the system on the surroundings is positive and of magnitude W. The units of Q and W are simply those of energy (joules) as given in Table C.19. In Fig. 7.6, it is very important to realize that Q and W represent the energy changes in the surroundings. Allowing for the sign convention, therefore, Eq. (7.32) becomes

CHANGE IN TOTAL ENERGY OF SYSTEM $= Q - W$ (7.33)

where W is the total work, all kinds, passing across the boundary in Fig. 7.6. Equation (7.33) is a statement of the first law of thermodynamics.

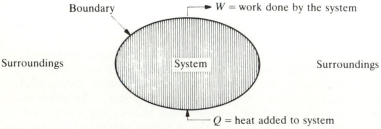

FIGURE 7.6
Boundary of a system for the first law of thermodynamics.

In Eq. (7.33) and subsequent equations, the thermodynamic sign convention will be used exclusively, namely, work done by the system is positive and heat added to the system is positive. Sometimes the opposite convention with regard to work only is found, in which case the reader must substitute $(-W)$ for W. When consulting other references, one must always determine which sign convention for the work is being used. For a more complete discussion of the first law, the reader is referred to reference books in physics [S1], physical chemistry [G1, K2, W1], or engineering [B1, S3, S4]. Note that the first law amounts to an overall energy balance on the universe.

The system of Fig. 7.6 does not have any components that involve flow. Many problems correspond to this case, which is commonly called a nonflow process, and Eq. (7.33) becomes:

$$(\Delta u)_{system} = u_2 - u_1 = Q - W \tag{7.34}$$

where u is the internal energy of the system [B1, G1, K2, S1, S3, S4, W1]. The internal energy is energy stored in the molecules of the system and is composed of contributions from the velocities of the atomic particles (kinetic energy) plus contributions from the attractive and repulsive forces in each atom (potential energy). The internal energy is a strong function of temperature:

$$(\Delta u)_{constant\ volume} = (u_2 - u_1)_V = n \int c_v \, dT \tag{7.35}$$

where c_v is the heat capacity at constant volume and n is the number of moles (or the mass) of the system. Note that in Eq. (7.35) the quantities n, c_v, and T must be in consistent units, so Δu may be expressed in units of energy. The enthalpy H is related to u by the defining relation:

$$H = u + \frac{p}{\rho} \tag{7.36}$$

or

$$\Delta H = H_2 - H_1 = \Delta u + \Delta \left(\frac{p}{\rho} \right) \tag{7.37}$$

In this equation, the term $\Delta(p/\rho)$ is

$$\Delta \left(\frac{p}{\rho} \right) = \frac{p_2}{\rho_2} - \frac{p_1}{\rho_1} \tag{7.38}$$

Note that the quantity p/ρ has units of energy and might require an appropriate conversion factor in order to be summed with u in Eq. (7.36). Enthalpy is also a strong function of temperature. It can be shown that for a reversible constant pressure process:

$$\Delta H = H_2 - H_1 = n \int c_p \, dT \tag{7.39}$$

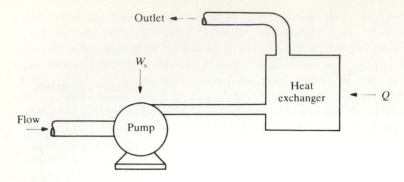

FIGURE 7.7
A flow system for the first law of thermodynamics.

where c_p is the heat capacity at constant pressure. Solutions to nonflow problems are outside the scope of transport phenomena, and the reader is referred elsewhere for a detailed discussion [G1, K2, S1, S3, S4, W1].

It is often necessary to extend Eq. (7.33) to a flow process such as that shown in Fig. 7.7. The total energy of a flowing system now consists of three contributions:

CHANGE IN TOTAL ENERGY OF SYSTEM

= CHANGE IN INTERNAL ENERGY

+ CHANGE IN KINETIC ENERGY

+ CHANGE IN POTENTIAL ENERGY $\qquad$ (7.40)

Let the total energy be denoted by E; the internal energy is U. The kinetic energy is of the form $\frac{1}{2}U^2$ (where U is velocity), and the potential energy is gz, where z is the vertical direction parallel to **g**. The units of these terms may be energy, energy per unit time, or energy per unit mass. For a change in total energy, dE, on a differential basis, these three contributions are

$$d\text{E} = d\text{U} + U\,dU + g\,dz \qquad (7.41)$$

where each term is energy per unit mass, $J\,kg^{-1}$ or its equivalent, $m^2\,s^{-2}$.

A flow system of general interest, such as that in Fig. 7.7, consists of a heat exchanger and a piece of machinery which either extracts work from the system or does work on the system. In addition, the system in Fig. 7.7 undergoes both an elevation change and a velocity change between the inlet and the outlet. The system is at steady-state. The equations to describe this flow process may be set forth either on a unit time basis or on a unit mass basis. Either is perfectly general, and the ease of solution to any particular problem is the criterion for choosing one or the other.

For the system in Fig. 7.7, the changes in total energy E are considered at the inlet and the outlet; Eq. (7.41) is substituted into Eq. (7.33) after the appropriate integrations to yield

$$\Delta u + \int_{U \text{ at } S_1}^{U \text{ at } S_2} U \, dU + g \, \Delta z = Q - W \tag{7.42}$$

where again W is the total work. The first law of thermodynamics, as applied to the system in Fig. 7.7, fails to provide sufficient information to integrate the kinetic energy term in Eq. (7.42):

$$\Delta(\text{KINETIC ENERGY}) = \int_{U \text{ at } S_1}^{U \text{ at } S_2} U \, dU \tag{7.43}$$

As discussed in conjunction with Eq. (7.24), all real problems involve a velocity profile. For the approximation of plug flow along a streamline and for a unit mass basis, Eq. (7.43) integrates easily as follows:

$$\Delta(\text{KINETIC ENERGY}) = (U_2^2 - U_1^2)/2 \tag{7.44}$$

The exact term is determined only through consideration of Eq. (7.3), as will be done shortly.

Equation (7.42) is combined with Eq. (7.37), the definition of enthalpy, and applied to the flow system in Fig. 7.7. Details of this derivation can be found elsewhere [S3]. The resulting equation, which is the basis for much design work on flow systems involving temperature changes in the process fluid, is

$$\Delta H + \Delta(\text{KINETIC ENERGY}) + wg \, \Delta z = Q - W_s \tag{7.45}$$

where W_s is the shaft work. Note that the units of each term in Eq. (7.45) are energy per unit time, since w appears explicitly in the potential energy term and therefore must also be included in the kinetic energy term. For the flow system in Fig. 7.7, the total work W appearing in Eq. (7.42) consists of three contributions: force-times-distance work, shear work, and shaft work (which will be explained shortly). The force-times-distance work appears as a pressure-times-volume term [S3], which is finally combined with Δu in Eq. (7.37) so that ΔH appears in Eq. (7.45). The shear work is negligible. The shaft work is associated with a piece of machinery, as seen in Fig. 7.7. The system can do shaft work when a gas or liquid flows through a turbine. The flowing fluid strikes blades connected to a shaft. The pressure energy in the fluid is converted to mechanical energy in order to turn the shaft. Likewise, shaft work is done on the system by a pump, in the case of a liquid system, or by a compressor or fan if the system is a gas.

The heat transferred to or from the system in Fig. 7.7 is Q, the duty or load in the heat exchanger as shown. The units of Q, ΔH, and W_s in Eq. (7.45) are energy per unit time ($J \, s^{-1}$), whereas the units of Q, Δu, and W in Eq. (7.34) for nonflow systems are simply those of energy (J). The units of Q, Δu and W in Eq. (7.42) are energy per unit mass ($J \, kg^{-1}$).

Many texts in fluid mechanics introduce a special set of symbols to differentiate the two cases of units as applied to the first law: energy per time and energy per mass. The differing symbols are more confusing than helpful. In any case, the reader must check units carefully and use appropriate conversion factors, particularly in using Eq. (7.45) and subsequent equations, in order to make terms such as $wg \, \Delta z$ compatible with Q, etc.

There are two important simplifications of Eq. (7.45). The first is for problems where both Q and W_s are zero. Then Eq. (7.45) reduces to

$$\Delta H + \Delta(\text{KINETIC ENERGY}) + wg \, \Delta z = 0 \tag{7.46}$$

A common application is the case in which density is constant and the fluid is isothermal. For both gases and liquids under isothermal conditions, the change in internal energy ΔU as a result of pressure changes is very small and may be assumed zero. Therefore ΔH reduces to $\Delta p / \rho$, as seen in Eq. (7.37). If this simplification and Eq. (7.44) are substituted into Eq. (7.46), the result is

$$\frac{\Delta p}{\rho} + \frac{U_2^2 - U_1^2}{2} + wg \, \Delta z = 0 \tag{7.47}$$

Equation (7.47) is a simplified form of the well-known Bernoulli balance. Note that Eq. (7.47) is presented on a unit mass basis. Again the kinetic energy term is valid only for problems with no velocity profile (plug flow). This equation and the more exact forms of the Bernoulli balance will be discussed in much detail later in this chapter.

When Eq. (7.45) is applied to systems in which there are large temperature changes, ΔH will be so large that the potential and kinetic energy terms are negligible. Then Eq. (7.45) reduces to

$$\Delta H = Q - W_s \tag{7.48}$$

Equation (7.48) corresponds to the most common situations and will be used frequently to solve flow problems where the first law is required.

A balance equation for the total energy in the system can be derived in general form if the concentration of energy, ρE, is substituted for the property ψ in Eq. (7.3):

$$\int_V (\partial \psi / \partial t) \, dV = -\oint_S (\psi U)(\cos \theta) \, dS - \oint_S (\mathbf{\Psi}_m \cdot d\mathbf{S})$$
$$- \oint_S (\mathbf{\Psi}_o \cdot d\mathbf{S}) + \int_V \dot{\psi}_G \, dV \tag{7.3}$$

Note that E is on a unit mass basis (J kg^{-1}) so that ρE is energy per unit volume (J m^{-3}). The first term in Eq. (7.3), after substitution of ρE for ψ in this derivation, becomes the time rate of change of energy $\dot{E}$ (units of which are J s^{-1}). The units of every term in Eq. (7.3), after substitution of ρE for ψ, are now J s^{-1}. The second term is

$$\oint_S (\rho E U)(\cos \theta) \, dS = \int_{S_1} (\rho E U) \, dS - \int_{S_2} (\rho E U) \, dS \tag{7.49}$$

since there is no flow through surfaces other than the areas S_1 and S_2, which are taken perpendicular to the lines of flow. The third term (input–output by molecular transport) is associated with the net energy flux (q/A, units of $J\,m^{-2}\,s^{-1}$) entering the system through its entire surface (units of m^2). When integrated, the third term becomes a flux times an area, equivalent to a time rate of change of energy by heat flow, and is denoted by Q (units of $J\,s^{-1}$ for a flow system). The fourth term represents the transport of energy by other methods, i.e., work that is positive if done by the system. The work consists of shear work, shaft work (W_s), and pressure–volume work over the inlet and outlet. The contribution of shear work is generally neglected. The fifth term, the generation of energy, can be neglected unless electrical or nuclear contributions exist. The energy associated with chemical reaction is included as a change in the internal energy U which is a part of the total energy. Combination of these considerations into Eq. (7.3) results in

$$\dot{E} = \int_{S_1} (\rho E U)\, dS - \int_{S_2} (\rho E U)\, dS + Q - W_s + \int_{S_1} (pU)\, dS - \int_{S_2} (pU)\, dS \quad (7.50)$$

Equation (7.41) is used to eliminate E in Eq. (7.50). After performing all integrations, the result is

$$\dot{E} = \rho_1 U_1 U_{1,\,\text{ave}} S_1 - \rho_2 U_2 U_{2,\,\text{ave}} S_2 + \tfrac{1}{2}[\rho_1 (U_1^3)_{\text{ave}} S_1 - \rho_2 (U_2^3)_{\text{ave}} S_2]$$
$$+ g\rho_1 z_1 U_{1,\,\text{ave}} S_1 - g\rho_2 z_2 U_{2,\,\text{ave}} S_2 + Q - W_s + p_1 U_{1,\,\text{ave}} S_1 - p_2 U_{2,\,\text{ave}} S_2 \quad (7.51)$$

In terms of the mass flow rate w [Eq. (7.10)], Eq. (7.51) becomes

$$\dot{E} = U_1 w_1 - U_2 w_2 + \frac{1}{2}\left(\frac{(U_1^3)_{\text{ave}}}{U_{1,\,\text{ave}}} w_1 - \frac{(U_2^3)_{\text{ave}}}{U_{2,\,\text{ave}}} w_2\right) + gz_1 w_1 - gz_2 w_2$$
$$+ Q - W_s + p_1 w_1/\rho_1 - p_2 w_2/\rho_2 \quad (7.52)$$

Each term of the balance equation [Eq. (7.50) through Eq. (7.52)] is in units of energy per unit time. For steady-state $\dot{E}$ is zero, and w_1 equals w_2 and can be replaced by w. Equation (7.37) is used to introduce ΔH into Eq. (7.52), and the result in terms of differences is

$$\Delta H + w\Delta\left(\frac{(U^3)_{\text{ave}}}{2U_{\text{ave}}}\right) + wg\,\Delta z = Q - W_s \quad (7.53)$$

Equation (7.53) is the overall energy balance. Note the similarity between this equation and Eq. (7.45) as derived from the first law of thermodynamics. Each term is identical with the exception of the kinetic energy term. The kinetic energy term in Eq. (7.53) is now exact. Thermodynamics gives no hint whatsoever as to the correct kinetic energy term. That can be deduced only via the property balance with the total concentration of energy. Yet Eq. (7.53) cannot be derived without thermodynamics. The first law states that work and heat are related to energy, and thus it was appropriate to introduce Q and W into the energy balance. For a nonflow process, the terms involving flow, change of height, and pressure are identically zero, and Eq. (7.53) can be simplified to Eq. (7.34), the most basic equation for the first law.

Equation (7.53) is useful for design of flow systems, as discussed earlier. The term $(U^3)_{ave}/(2U_{ave})$ can be replaced by $U^2_{ave}/(2\alpha)$, where the kinetic energy correction term α is defined as

$$\alpha = \frac{(U_{ave})^3}{(U^3)_{ave}} \tag{7.54}$$

The correct kinetic energy term for Eq. (7.45) is now

$$\Delta(\text{KINETIC ENERGY}) = \frac{w}{2}\left(\frac{U^2_{2,\,ave}}{\alpha_2} - \frac{U^2_{1,\,ave}}{\alpha_1}\right) \tag{7.55}$$

and Eq. (7.53) becomes

$$\Delta H + \frac{w}{2}\left(\frac{U^2_{2,\,ave}}{\alpha_2} - \frac{U^2_{1,ave}}{\alpha_1}\right) + wg\,\Delta z = Q - W_s \tag{7.56}$$

While α is usually assumed to be unity, it has been evaluated for a number of flows. Figure 7.8 is a plot of α versus N_{Re} for pipe flow [K1]. Note that for laminar flows $\alpha = \frac{1}{2}$, whereas for turbulent flows $\alpha = 0.88$ at low N_{Re} and approaches 0.96 as the velocity profile flattens out at high N_{Re}. The kinetic energy correction term α is analogous to the momentum correction term, β,

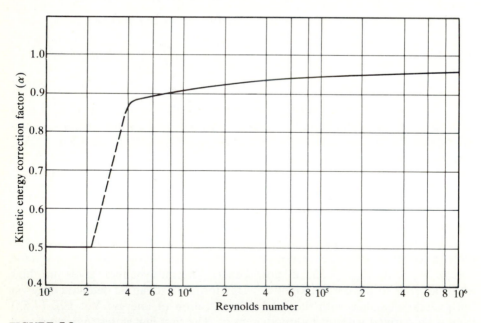

FIGURE 7.8
Kinetic energy correction factor as a function of Reynolds number for pipe flow. (*From Kays, Trans. ASME* **72**, *1067 (1950). By permission of ASME.*)

Eq. (7.24). The kinetic energy correction factor is illustrated in Example 7.7. The use of the energy equation itself is in Example 7.8.

Example 7.7. Calculate the kinetic energy correction term for the flow of water between parallel plates in Fig. 7.9 when one wall moves at unit velocity.

Answer. The correction factor α is evaluated from Eq. (7.54) where $(U^n)_{ave}$ is from Eq. (7.9). From Fig. 4.12 with no pressure drop, it is evident that the velocity profile follows the equation:

$$\frac{U_x}{U_o} = \frac{y}{y_o} \tag{i}$$

where U_o is $1\,\mathrm{m\,s^{-1}}$ for this problem and y is defined as in Fig. 7.9 (differently from that in Fig. 4.12). For this simple flow, a convenient flow area extends y_o units in the y direction and one unit in the z direction. Then in Eq. (7.9) the denominator is y_o, and the equation, when transformed to rectangular coordinates, becomes

$$(U^n)_{ave} = \frac{1}{y_o} \int_0^{y_o} U^n\, dy \tag{ii}$$

To find $U_{x,\,ave}$, the power n is one, and Eq. (ii) becomes

$$U_{x,\,ave} = \frac{1}{y_o^2}\frac{y^2}{2}\Big|_0^{y_o} = \tfrac{1}{2} \tag{iii}$$

To find $(U_x^3)_{ave}$, the power n is three, and Eq. (ii) becomes

$$(U_x^3)_{ave} = \frac{1}{y_o^4}\frac{y^4}{4}\Big|_0^{y_o} = \tfrac{1}{4} \tag{iv}$$

Therefore,

$$\alpha = U_{ave,\,x}^3/(U_x^3)_{ave} = (\tfrac{1}{2})^3/(\tfrac{1}{4}) = \tfrac{1}{2} \tag{v}$$

Note that the kinetic correction term α has the same final value for laminar pipe flow as it has for laminar flow between parallel plates.

Example 7.8. A vertical pipe of $7\,\mathrm{cm}$ inside diameter and length $7\,\mathrm{m}$ is used in a heat exchanger to heat a $0.03\,\mathrm{m^3\,s^{-1}}$ water flow from $25°\mathrm{C}$ to $45°\mathrm{C}$. Let the

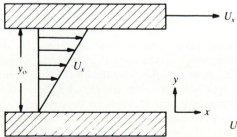

FIGURE 7.9
Flow between parallel plates with one wall in motion.

acceleration due to gravity be 9.81 m s^{-2}. The pressure loss due to friction is $4 \times 10^4 \text{ N m}^{-2}$. Find the duty (heat load) needed to accomplish the heat exchange. The water enters at the top.

Answer. The problem is one of steady-state flow, and hence Eqs. (7.53) or (7.56) apply. Since the exchanger is vertical, the potential energy term is non-zero. In problems of this nature, the error in assuming water to be incompressible is negligible. The mass flow rate w is given by

$$w = \rho U_{ave} S \tag{7.10}$$

Since for this problem w, ρ, and S are all constant, U_{ave} is also constant, which makes the kinetic energy term zero [cf. Eq. (7.55)]. Also, since there is no pump or turbine, W_s is zero. Equation (7.53) now reduces to

$$\Delta_H + wg \, \Delta z = Q \tag{i}$$

The mass flow rate is the volume flow times the density:

$$w = (0.03)(1000)[(\text{m}^3 \text{ s}^{-1})(\text{kg m}^{-3})] = 30 \text{ kg s}^{-1} \tag{ii}$$

where the density of water is 1.0 g cm^{-3} or 1000 kg m^{-3}. Also, the heat capacity of water is $1.0 \text{ cal g}^{-1} \, {}^\circ\text{C}^{-1}$ or $4184 \text{ J kg}^{-1} \text{ K}^{-1}$. Thus, Δ_H from Eq. (7.39) is

$$\Delta_H = nc_P \int_{25+273.15}^{45+273.15} dT = (30)(4184)(45-25)[(\text{kg s}^{-1})(\text{J kg}^{-1} \text{ K}^{-1})(\text{K})]$$

$$= 2.510 \times 10^6 \text{ J s}^{-1} \tag{iii}$$

The potential energy term turns out to be negligible as previously predicted in conjunction with the derivation of Eq. (7.48). The term Δz is -7 m. Thus, the potential energy term is

$$wg \, \Delta z = (30)(9.81)(-7)[(\text{kg s}^{-1})(\text{m s}^{-2})(\text{m})] = -2060 \text{ kg m}^2 \text{ s}^{-3} \tag{iv}$$

The following conversion is needed:

$$1 \text{ J} = 1 \text{ kg m}^2 \text{ s}^{-2} \tag{v}$$

Thus, the potential energy in SI units is -2060 J s^{-1}. Equation (i) provides the duty on the heat exchanger:

$$Q = 2.510 \times 10^6 - 2060 = 2.508 \times 10^6 \text{ J s}^{-1} \tag{vi}$$

Note that the potential energy term was less than 0.1 percent of the total contribution in this problem, in which the temperature rise was only 20°C. If there had been a density change, then the kinetic energy term could have been determined, but it would be several orders smaller yet. If the diameter of the pipe at the outlet differs from that at the inlet, then in some problems the kinetic energy must be calculated. The procedure is to compute the Reynolds numbers at the inlet and outlet, find α_1 and α_2 from Fig. 7.8, and finally the kinetic energy term from Eq. (7.55). As a first approximation, the α's may be assumed to be unity in order to see if the kinetic energy term is likely to be significant. If so, then the Reynolds numbers may be determined and the exact values computed.

7.1.5 The Mechanical Energy Balance and the Engineering Bernoulli Equation

The mechanical energy balance equation, an alternate form of the general conservation of energy, is often in a more convenient form for problem solving. The integral energy balance in its most general form is Eq. (7.53) or Eq. (7.56). These equations and their simplifications, such as Eq. (7.47) and (7.48), are particularly useful in problems when the term Q is significant. In contrast, the mechanical energy balance is often advantageous because, as will be seen, that equation does not involve thermal terms such as heat, internal energy, or enthalpy.

A rigorous derivation of the mechanical energy balance equation requires the use of tensors, is quite lengthy, and is beyond the scope of this text [B2]. The mechanical energy balance equation is simple in concept and in application, but difficult to derive. In differential form, on a unit mass basis, the equation [B2, S3, W2] is

$$(1/\rho)\, dp + g\, dz + U\, dU + dF' + dW_s = 0 \qquad (7.57)$$

Volume–pressure:	$(1/\rho)\, dp$
Potential energy:	$g\, dz$
Kinetic energy:	$U\, dU$
Friction:	dF'
Shaft work:	dW_s

where the nature of each term is summarized below the equation. Note that dF' is the energy contribution due to friction between the fluid and its environment. Equation (7.57) applies under the following limitations:

1. A unit of mass flows through a control volume, such as in Fig. 7.1, that is stationary in space.
2. The flow is at steady-state.
3. There are no energy terms to be considered save the five denoted in Eq. (7.57).

The mechanical energy balance arises from a consideration of the conservation of momentum and the laws of thermodynamics. If a momentum term such as mU is scalar-multiplied by the velocity vector U, the result is a term of the form of mass times velocity squared, which is an energy term. The scalar multiplication is necessary since momentum and velocity are vector quantities and energy is a scalar. The derivation proceeds by taking the scalar product between the velocity vector and the momentum balance equation. The momentum balance has previously been accomplished by substituting ρU for ψ in the general property balance equation. This substitution resulted in the

Navier–Stokes equation as given in Eq. (5.15). The derivation of the mechanical energy balance uses as the starting point an earlier form of the equation in terms of the flux vector. Recall that the general flux equation is

$$\boldsymbol{\Psi} = -\delta \boldsymbol{\nabla} \psi \tag{2.18}$$

Rather than using this equation in the derivation, the momentum flux tensor $\boldsymbol{\tau}$ is retained. The derivation for the mechanical energy balance utilizes Eq. (5.15), the equation above, and Eq. (4.54) for the generation term. The resulting equation is

$$\rho(\partial \boldsymbol{U}/\partial t) + \rho(\boldsymbol{U} \cdot \boldsymbol{\nabla})\boldsymbol{U} = -\boldsymbol{\nabla}p + \rho\boldsymbol{g} - (\boldsymbol{\nabla} \cdot \boldsymbol{\tau}) \tag{7.58}$$

Equation (7.58) is then scalar-multiplied by the velocity vector:

$$\rho[\boldsymbol{U} \cdot (\partial \boldsymbol{U}/\partial t)] + \rho[\boldsymbol{U} \cdot (\boldsymbol{U} \cdot \boldsymbol{\nabla})\boldsymbol{U}] = -(\boldsymbol{U} \cdot \boldsymbol{\nabla})p + \rho(\boldsymbol{U} \cdot \boldsymbol{g}) - [\boldsymbol{U} \cdot (\boldsymbol{\nabla} \cdot \boldsymbol{\tau})] \tag{7.59}$$

After performing the indicated mathematical operations, a scalar equation with 45 terms is obtained. The complexity of the derivation is not only in determining these terms, but also in knowing how to rearrange the terms and how to make the appropriate simplifying assumptions that are necessary to arrive at Eq. (7.57).

Equation (7.56) applies equally as well as Eq. (7.57) or an integrated form of this. The reader must choose the more convenient of the two to solve any given problem at hand. In spite of the similarity between the two equations, Eq. (7.57) does not follow from Eq. (7.56) directly. To solve any general problem, five principles or laws are involved:

1. Conservation of mass
2. Conservation of energy
3. Conservation of momentum
4. Equivalence of work and energy and their relationship to heat (the first law of thermodynamics)
5. Inability to convert energy entirely into work without rejecting part of energy input to the surroundings as heat (second law of thermodynamics)

All five principles apply at all times, both to differential volumes and integral control volumes. Furthermore, the resulting equations are often coupled in such a manner that a term appearing in, say, both the energy balance and the first law is precisely defined only by one—in this case the energy balance. Such an example is the kinetic energy term presented in Eq. (7.55).

The mechanical energy balance arises as a consequence of princples (2), (3), and (4) above. In fact, it may be substituted for the first law, principle (4), and therefore may be included as one of the five basic laws. However, since the conservation of energy, the conservation of momentum, the first law, and the mechanical energy balance are interrelated, only three of the four are independent equations and can be invoked in any single instance.

An integrated form of Eq. (7.57) will be more useful for problem solving than the present differential form. By analogy with the energy equation, the appropriate kinetic energy term is given by Eq. (7.55). The potential energy term is restricted so that the elevation change dz is relative to the change of the center of mass. The term comprising volume $1/\rho$ times dp must be integrated from entrance to the exit through the control volume. This integration requires knowledge of the actual pressure versus volume relation that exists in the mass of fluid as it travels through the system. The integrated form of Eq. (7.57) is

$$\int_{p_1}^{p_2} \frac{dp}{\rho} + g(z_2 - z_1) + \frac{1}{2}\left(\frac{U_{2,\,\text{ave}}^2}{\alpha_2} - \frac{U_{1,\,\text{ave}}^2}{\alpha_1}\right) + F' + W_s = 0 \qquad (7.60)$$

where the first integral must be left in general form. If the density is constant, the mechanical energy balance equation becomes

$$\frac{p_2 - p_1}{\rho} + g(z_2 - z_1) + \frac{1}{2}\left(\frac{U_{2,\,\text{ave}}^2}{\alpha_2} - \frac{U_{1,\,\text{ave}}^2}{\alpha_1}\right) + F' + W_s = 0 \qquad (7.61)$$

Equations (7.60) and (7.61) can sometimes be utilized in situations in which the fluid is incompressible and friction and shaft work are both zero. Under these conditions, Eq. (7.61) reduces to

$$\frac{p_2 - p_1}{\rho} + g(z_2 - z_1) + \frac{1}{2}\left(\frac{U_{2,\,\text{ave}}^2}{\alpha_2} - \frac{U_{1,\,\text{ave}}^2}{\alpha_1}\right) = 0 \qquad (7.62)$$

or more simply

$$\frac{\Delta p}{\rho} + g\,\Delta z + \Delta\left(\frac{U_{\text{ave}}^2}{2\alpha}\right) = 0 \qquad (7.63)$$

Equation (7.63) is often called the "engineering Bernoulli equation"; the classical derivation by Bernoulli yields a similar equation in differential form with the assumptions of flow along a streamline ($\alpha = 1$), zero viscosity ($F' = 0$), incompressible fluid ($\rho = $ constant), and no shaft work ($W_s = 0$).

The energy equations [Eq. (7.53), Eq. (7.56), and Eqs. (7.60) through (7.63)] apply only to a continuum where functions such as velocity, pressure, and density are continuous point functions. They do not apply across a solid–fluid boundary or a fluid–fluid boundary such as the interface between two immiscible liquids.

The mechanical engineering balance equations give approximate or exact answers to many important problems. All liquids may be assumed incompressible in most circumstances, and in many gas flows the incompressible fluid assumption is warranted as well. In a short section of pipe, the friction losses are often insignificant. Lastly, there are many situations in which the fluid is not flowing at all; in these the kinetic energy and friction terms are zero. These latter problems are studied under the general topic of fluid statics and will be covered in the next section. The following group of problems was selected to illustrate the mechanical energy balance and the more limited engineering Bernoulli equation. The simple Bernouli balance problems will be considered first. As pointed out previously, most of the equations in this section require careful scrutiny of units, since g_c will have to be added if the engineering system involving lb_m and lb_f is used. Example 7.11 is a good example of this. In Problems 7.13 and 7.14, g_c is again added where needed to keep the units on each term consistent. In SI units, each term is usually in units of $m^2 s^{-2}$, and in engineering units, each term is usually in units of $ft\, lb_f\, lb_m^{-1}$.

Example 7.9. Derive Torricelli's law, Eq. (i) of Example 7.1.

Answer. Torricelli's law related the velocity of discharge to the elevation of fluid in a tank, as depicted in Fig. 7.2. Here, the liquid is assumed incompressible. The friction loss is assumed to be negligible so that Eq. (7.62) can be used:

$$\frac{p_2 - p_1}{\rho} + g(z_2 - z_1) + \frac{1}{2}\left(\frac{U_{2,\,ave}^2}{\alpha_2} - \frac{U_{1,\,ave}^2}{\alpha_1}\right) = 0 \tag{7.62}$$

Following the nomenclature of Example 7.1, the difference $z_1 - z_2$ is h:

$$z_2 - z_1 = -h \tag{i}$$

Since the pressure on the top of the liquid is the same as the pressure of the fluid issuing from the drain, p_2 in the first term in Eq. (7.62) equals p_1, and that term is zero. Equation (7.13) relates the velocity exiting through the drain to the velocity with which the liquid level in the tank drops by equating the mass flow rate at point 1 with the mass flow rate that exits at the bottom at point 2. For constant density Eq. (7.13) becomes

$$U_{1,\,ave}S_1 = U_{2,\,ave}S_2 \tag{ii}$$

or in terms of diameters if both tank and drain are circular:

$$\frac{U_{1,\,ave}}{U_{2,\,ave}} = \left(\frac{d_2}{d_1}\right)^2 \tag{iii}$$

It is reasonable to assume that the diameter of the tank, d_1, is many times larger than the diameter of the drain, d_2, so that the ratio of diameters in Eq. (iii) is approximately zero. Then for a flat velocity profile ($\alpha_2 = 1$) the only non-zero terms left in Eq. (7.62) are

$$\tfrac{1}{2}U_{2,\,ave}^2 + g(-h) = 0 \tag{iv}$$

or

$$U_{2,\,ave}^2 = 2gh \tag{v}$$

This is Eq. (i) in Example 7.1. Note that for an outlet with a small diameter, the flow might be laminar and $\alpha = \tfrac{1}{2}$. Torricelli's law is significantly in error for this case.

Example 7.10. A hose of diameter 3 cm is used to drain a tank filled with water. The hose is draped over the side of the tank so that the water is siphoned out. The acceleration due to gravity is $9.784\, m\, s^{-2}$. If the hose discharge is $1\, m$ below the surface of the water, estimate the mass flow rate in $kg\, s^{-1}$.

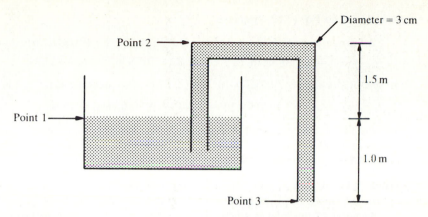

FIGURE 7.10
Siphon.

Answer. Figure 7.10 shows a siphon. A siphon implies a continuous liquid leg from the water in the tank up the siphon to point 2, the highest elevation, and down to the discharge at point 3. If frictional forces are neglected, the engineering Bernoulli equation, Eq. (7.62), applies. It is convenient to write the balance between point 1 and point 3, since the pressures at these locations are equal. Hence, Eq. (7.62) reduces to

$$\frac{1}{2}\left(\frac{U_{3,\,ave}^2}{\alpha_3} - \frac{U_{1,\,ave}^2}{\alpha_1}\right) + g\,\Delta z = 0 \qquad\text{(i)}$$

It is reasonable to assume that $\alpha_1 = \alpha_3 = 1$. Since the diameter of the tank far exceeds the diameter of the hose, the velocity at point 1 must be negligible when compared to the velocity at point 3, the hose discharge (see Example 7.9). Thus, the discharge velocity from Eq. (i) is

$$U_{3,\,ave} = (-2g\,\Delta z)^{1/2} \qquad\text{(ii)}$$

Equation (ii) is essentially the same as Eq. (v) of the preceding example, and will be used to find $U_{3,\,ave}$, with the change in elevation being 1.0 m:

$$U_{3,\,ave} = [(-2)(9.784)(-1)]^{1/2} = 4.42 \text{ m s}^{-1} \qquad\text{(iii)}$$

The density of water is approximately 1.0 g cm^{-3} or 1000 kg m^{-3}. The discharge diameter is 0.03 m. The mass flow is velocity times density times area [Eq. (7.10)]:

$$w = \rho U_{3,\,ave} S_3 = (1000)(4.42)(\pi/4)(0.03)^2[(\text{kg m}^{-3})(\text{m s}^{-1})(\text{m}^2)]$$

$$= 3.13 \text{ kg s}^{-1} \qquad\text{(iv)}$$

The minimum pressure in the siphon tube is at point 2. Before the result of 3.13 kg s^{-1} is accepted as the final value, the pressure at point 2 must be calculated in order to see if the water might boil at this point. Equation (7.62) again applies. Again, U_1 is negligible; α_2 is assumed to be unity. In the siphon of constant cross section, U_2 is the same as U_3. The height for the potential energy term is 1.5 m. So Eq. (7.62) becomes

$$\Delta p = p_2 - p_1 = \rho(U_2^2/2 + g\,\Delta z) = -(1000)[(4.42)^2/2 + (9.784)(1.5)]$$
$$= -2.446 \times 10^4 \text{ kg m}^{-1}\text{s}^{-2} = -2.446 \times 10^4 \text{ N m}^{-2} = -24.46 \text{ kPa} \qquad \text{(v)}$$

Atmospheric pressure is $1.01325 \times 10^5 \text{ N m}^{-2}$. Thus, the pressure at point 2 is

$$p_2 = p_1 + \Delta p = 1.01325 \times 10^5 - 0.2446 \times 10^5 = 0.7686 \times 10^5 \text{ N m}^{-2} \qquad \text{(vi)}$$

At normal room temperature (20°C or 293.15 K), the vapor pressure of water (Table A.1) is 0.02336 bar, or $0.02336 \times 10^5 \text{ N m}^{-2}$. Thus, the siphon can operate since the pressure p_2 is greater than the value at which the fluid boils.

Example 7.11. A venturi is used in a trichloroethylene line to measure the flow rate. The difference in pressure between the inlet and the throat is 4.2 psia. The inside diameter of the inlet is 1.049 in. The diameter of the throat is 0.6 in. The specific gravity of the process fluid is 1.45. Find the flow rate in kg s^{-1}.

Answer. Figure 7.11 is a schematic of a venturi meter. A venturi meter consists of an inlet section with a pressure tap, a converging portion where the flow accelerates, a throat section of constant diameter with a second pressure tap, and a gradually diverging section that expands to the original pipe diameter to minimize friction losses. A venturi meter is relatively short in length, and friction losses are negligible if the meter is carefully manufactured.

The engineering Bernoulli equation, Eq. (7.62), applies. If the meter is not horizontal, any elevation changes will be included in the pressure readings. Again, the velocity profile is assumed to be flat so α is unity. Hence, Eq. (7.62) reduces to

$$\frac{\Delta p}{\rho} + \tfrac{1}{2}(U_{2,\,\text{ave}}^2 - U_{1,\,\text{ave}}^2) = 0 \qquad \text{(i)}$$

The density of the fluid is its specific gravity times the density of water:

$$\rho = (1.45)(62.4) \text{ lb}_m \text{ ft}^{-3} = 90.48 \text{ lb}_m \text{ ft}^{-3} \qquad \text{(ii)}$$

The mass flow rate at the inlet equals that at the throat. The velocities at these points are related through Eq. (7.13). Since the fluid is incompressible, the

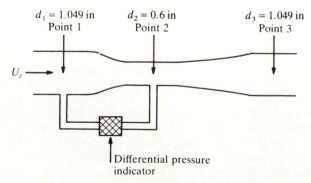

$d_1 = 1.049$ in $d_2 = 0.6$ in $d_3 = 1.049$ in
Point 1   Point 2   Point 3

$U_z \longrightarrow$

Differential pressure indicator

FIGURE 7.11
Venturi meter.

densities cancel, and Eq. (7.13) becomes

$$U_{1, \text{ave}}S_1 = U_{2, \text{ave}}S_2 \tag{iii}$$

or

$$U_{1, \text{ave}} = U_{2, \text{ave}}(S_2/S_1) = U_{2, \text{ave}}(d_2^2/d_1^2) = U_{2, \text{ave}}(0.6/1.049)^2$$
$$= 0.3272U_{2, \text{ave}} \tag{iv}$$

Substituting Eq. (iv) into Eq. (i) yields

$$(-\Delta p/\rho) = \tfrac{1}{2}[U_{2, \text{ave}}^2 - (0.3272)^2 U_{2, \text{ave}}^2] = 0.4465U_{2, \text{ave}}^2 \tag{v}$$

or

$$U_{2, \text{ave}} = (1.497)(-\Delta p/\rho)^{1/2} \tag{vi}$$

In Eq. (vi), the units of $\Delta p/\rho$ determine the units of $U_{2, \text{ave}}$. Since the preceding examples have been worked in SI units, this problem will be worked in engineering units where the gravitational conversion constant g_c is needed in order to balance units. In engineering units, Eq. (7.62) must be modified by introducing g_c into the kinetic energy and the potential energy terms.

Since the pressure drop Δp is defined as $(p_2 - p_1)$, the term $(-\Delta p)$ equals 4.2 psi since p_1 is greater than p_2. First, Δp is converted to units of $\mathrm{lb_f\ ft^{-2}}$:

$$-\Delta p = (4.2)(144)[(\mathrm{lb_f\ in.^{-2}})(\mathrm{in.^2\ ft^{-2}})] = 604.8\ \mathrm{lb_f\ ft^{-2}} \tag{vii}$$

The throat velocity is found from Eq. (vi):

$$U_{2, \text{ave}} = (1.497)(604.8/90.48)^{1/2}\,[(\mathrm{lb_f\ ft^{-2}})(\mathrm{lb_m^{-1}})(\mathrm{ft^3})]^{1/2}$$
$$= 3.869\,[(\mathrm{ft\ lb_f})(\mathrm{lb_m^{-1}})]^{1/2} \tag{viii}$$

Clearly these are not the units of velocity and g_c must be introduced. Since g_c is $32.174\ \mathrm{lb_m\ lb_f^{-1}\ ft\ s^{-2}}$, Eq. (viii) must be modified by multiplying by g_c inside the brackets: i.e.,

$$U_{2, \text{ave}} = (3.869)(32.174)^{1/2}\,[(\mathrm{ft\ lb_f})(\mathrm{lb_m^{-1}})]^{1/2}[(\mathrm{lb_m\ lb_f^{-1}\ ft\ s^{-2}})]^{1/2}$$
$$= 21.95\ \mathrm{ft\ s^{-1}} \tag{ix}$$

The mass flow is given by Eq. (7.10):

$$w = \rho U_{2, \text{ave}}S = (90.48)(21.95)[(\pi)(0.6/12.0)^2/(4)]\,[(\mathrm{lb_m\ ft^{-3}})(\mathrm{ft\ s^{-1}})(\mathrm{ft^2})]$$
$$= 3.90\ \mathrm{lb_m\ s^{-1}} \tag{x}$$

or in SI units:

$$w = (3.90)/(2.20462)\,[(\mathrm{lb_m\ s^{-1}})(\mathrm{kg\ lb_m^{-1}})] = 1.77\ \mathrm{kg\ s^{-1}} \tag{xi}$$

Example 7.12. Calculate the temperature rise for the water in Fig. 7.12 where water discharges at a rate of 50 gallons per minute from a pipe 1 inch in diameter and drops 5 feet into a large tank. The acceleration of gravity is $32.1\ \mathrm{ft\ s^{-2}}$.

Answer. This problem will be solved in engineering units in order again to illustrate the use of g_c. Since a temperature change is being calculated, the energy balance equation, Eq. (7.56), will be applied directly. For this problem there is no shaft work W_s. Furthermore, the time required for the water to fall the 5 feet

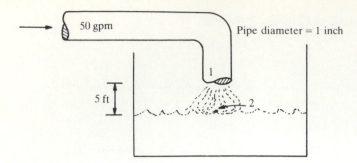

FIGURE 7.12
Discharge pipe for Example 7.12.

is assumed to be very short, so that the amount of heat Q transferred between the ambient air and the water stream is negligible. With these assumptions, Eq. (7.56) reduces to

$$\Delta H + (w/2)[(U_{2,\,ave}^2/\alpha_2) - (U_{1,\,ave}^2/\alpha_1)] + wg\,\Delta z = 0 \tag{i}$$

When the units are checked, it is found that g_c will have to be introduced into the denominator of the 2nd and 3rd items. The cross sectional area of the pipe is

$$S_1 = (\pi)(1/12)^2/(4) = 5.454 \times 10^{-3}\,\text{ft}^2 \tag{ii}$$

The velocity of water at the receiving tank, U_2, can be taken as zero. The velocity of discharge U_1 and the mass flow rate w are found from the volume rate Q, the flow area S_1, and Eq. (7.13):

$$Q = (50)/[(7.48)(60)][(\text{gpm})(\text{gal}^{-1}\,\text{ft}^3)(\text{s}^{-1}\,\text{min})] = 0.1114\,\text{ft}^3\,\text{s}^{-1} \tag{iii}$$

$$U_{1,\,ave} = Q/S_1 = (0.1114)/(5.454 \times 10^{-3})[(\text{ft}^3\,\text{s}^{-1})(\text{ft}^{-2})] = 20.43\,\text{ft}\,\text{s}^{-1} \tag{iv}$$

$$w = \rho U_{1,\,ave}S_1 = \rho Q = (62.4)(20.43)(5.454 \times 10^{-3})[(\text{lb}_m\,\text{ft}^{-3})(\text{ft}\,\text{s}^{-1})(\text{ft}^2)]$$
$$= 6.952\,\text{lb}_m\,\text{s}^{-1} \tag{v}$$

In Eq. (i), α_1 will be assumed to be unity. From the problem statement, Δz is -5 feet. Equation (i) is solved for ΔH and the appropriate numbers substituted, including g_c:

$$\Delta H = -\{(6.952)/[(2)(32.174)]\}[0 - (20.43)^2] - (6.952)(32.1/32.174)(-5)$$
$$= 79.76\,\text{ft}\,\text{lb}_f\,\text{s}^{-1} \tag{vi}$$

The units on each term should be checked to verify the results. The acceleration due to gravity g is given as $32.1\,\text{ft}\,\text{s}^{-2}$ and changes from place to place over the earth's surface and in the universe, whereas g_c is a conversion constant, the same everywhere. It is customary to express ΔH in units of Btu:

$$\Delta H = (79.79)/(778)\,[(\text{ft}\,\text{lb}_f\,\text{s}^{-1})(\text{Btu}\,\text{ft}^{-1}\,\text{lb}_f^{-1})] = 0.103\,\text{Btu}\,\text{s}^{-1} \tag{vii}$$

The temperature rise is found from Eq. (7.39) with w replacing n:

$$\Delta T = \Delta H/(wc_p) = (0.103)/[(6.952)(1.0)][(\text{Btu}\,\text{s}^{-1})(\text{lb}_m^{-1}\,\text{s})(\text{Btu}^{-1}\,\text{lb}_m\,\,^\circ\text{F})]$$
$$= 0.01475\,^\circ\text{F} \tag{viii}$$

Common sense tells us that the temperature rise will be quite small in this case, and the answer reflects that viewpoint.

Example 7.13. It is desired to design a pump to deliver water from a holding tank at atmospheric pressure to a process at 100 psig at a flow rate of 100 gpm. The process is located 30 feet higher than the holding tank. The acceleration of gravity is 32.1 ft s^{-2}. The specific volume of water is 0.0161 ft^3 lb$_m^{-1}$, and the density is the reciprocal: 62.11 lb$_m$ ft^{-3}. Calculate the horsepower required if the centrifugal pump is 77 percent efficient and if fluid friction is negligible.

Answer. Equation (7.61) is appropriate:

$$\frac{p_2 - p_1}{\rho} + g(z_2 - z_1) + \frac{1}{2}\left(\frac{U_{2,\text{ave}}^2}{\alpha_2} - \frac{U_{1,\text{ave}}^2}{\alpha_1}\right) + F' + W_s = 0 \qquad (7.61)$$

The kinetic energy term is usually negligible in problems in which the heat transfer and/or the shaft work is significant. The fluid friction F' is negligible according to the statement of the problem. The pressure of the water at the tank is atmospheric, or in other words the gauge pressure is zero. Again Δp must be in units of lb$_f$ ft^{-2}. The pressure term in Eq. (7.61) becomes

$$\frac{\Delta p}{\rho} = (0.0161)(100 - 0)(144)[(\text{ft}^3\,\text{lb}_m^{-1})(\text{lb}_f\,\text{in.}^{-2})(\text{in.}^2\,\text{ft}^{-2})]$$

$$= 231.84 \text{ ft lb}_f \text{ lb}_m^{-1} \qquad (i)$$

The potential energy term is

$$(\Delta z)(g/g_c) = (30)(32.1/32.174)[(\text{ft})(\text{ft s}^{-2})(\text{lb}_m^{-1}\,\text{lb}_f\,\text{ft}^{-1}\,\text{s}^2)]$$

$$= 29.93 \text{ ft lb}_f \text{ lb}_m^{-1} \qquad (ii)$$

where once again g_c has been added to adjust units. Equations (i) and (ii) are substituted into Eq. (7.61) to find the shaft work W_s:

$$W_s = -231.84 - 29.93 = -261.77 \text{ ft lb}_f \text{ lb}_m^{-1} \qquad (iii)$$

This work is the energy delivered to the fluid by the pump in order to raise 1 lb$_m$ of water from atmospheric pressure to 100 psig at an elevation 30 ft higher. An actual pump will require more energy input than it can deliver as output because of losses due to mechanical friction, turbulence, and so on. If the work found in Eq. (iii) is termed theoretical work, then a pump efficiency may be defined as the ratio of theoretical work to actual work required:

$$\eta_{\text{pump}} = \frac{W_{s,\text{theoretical}}}{W_{s,\text{actual}}} \qquad (iv)$$

Thus, the actual work is

$$W_{s,\text{actual}} = W_{s,\text{theoretical}}/\eta_{\text{pump}} = -261.77/0.77 = -340.0 \text{ ft lb}_f \text{ lb}_m^{-1} \qquad (v)$$

The mass flow is found from the product of the volume flow rate and the density:

$$w = \dot{Q}\rho = (100)(62.11)/[(7.48)(60)]\,[(\text{gpm})(\text{lb}_m\,\text{ft}^{-3})(\text{ft}^3\,\text{gal}^{-1})(\text{min s}^{-1})]$$

$$= 13.84 \text{ lb}_m \text{ s}^{-1} \qquad (vi)$$

The answers from Eqs. (v) and (vi) are combined to find the actual shaft work that must be delivered by an electric motor, or whatever, to the pump:

$$W_{s, \text{actual}} = -(340.0)(13.84) \left[(\text{ft lb}_f \text{ lb}_m^{-1})(\text{lb}_m \text{ s}^{-1}) \right]$$
$$= -4705 \text{ ft lb}_f \text{ s}^{-1} \tag{vii}$$

The following conversions are useful in converting ft lb$_f$ s^{-1} to horsepower (hp):

$$1 \text{ Btu} = 778 \text{ ft lb}_f \tag{viii}$$

$$1 \text{ hp} = 0.7070 \text{ Btu s}^{-1} \tag{ix}$$

Thus, the required horsepower is

$$\text{Power} = \frac{4705}{(778)(0.7070)} \left(\frac{(\text{ft lb}_f \text{ s}^{-1})}{(\text{ft lb}_f \text{ Btu}^{-1})(\text{Btu s}^{-1} \text{ hp}^{-1})} \right) = 8.55 \text{ hp} \tag{x}$$

Example 7.14. Nitrogen at 5 atm and 450 K expands through a turbine to a final pressure of 0.75 atm. It is known that at all times during this expansion the relationship between the pressure of nitrogen and its density follows

$$p(1/\rho)^\gamma = \text{constant} \tag{i}$$

where γ for nitrogen is the ratio of c_p to c_v, and is equal to 1.4. In Eq. (i) the constant has units such that the equation is dimensionally homogeneous. Assume the ideal gas law holds. Find the shaft work done by the system in J kmol^{-1}.

Answer. The mechanical energy balance with variable density applies here:

$$\int_{p_1}^{p_2} \frac{dp}{\rho} + g(z_2 - z_1) + \frac{1}{2} \left(\frac{U_{2, \text{ave}}^2}{\alpha_2} - \frac{U_{1, \text{ave}}^2}{\alpha_1} \right) + F' + W_s = 0 \tag{7.60}$$

In Eq. (7.60), the kinetic energy, potential energy, and fluid friction terms are neglected because of the large value of W_s, so that Eq. (7.60) reduces to

$$-\int \frac{dp}{\rho} = W_s \tag{ii}$$

Equation (i) is solved for $1/\rho$:

$$1/\rho = (\text{constant})^{1/\gamma} p^{-1/\gamma} \tag{iii}$$

and the result substituted into Eq. (ii):

$$W_s = -\text{constant}^{1/\gamma} \int p^{-1/\gamma} \, dp \tag{iv}$$

This equation is integrated from the inlet pressure p_1 to the outlet pressure p_2:

$$W_s = -\frac{\text{constant}^{1/\gamma}}{1 - 1/\gamma} (p_2^{1-1/\gamma} - p_1^{1-1/\gamma}) \tag{v}$$

The following identities are useful:

$$1 - 1/\gamma = (\gamma - 1)/\gamma \tag{vi}$$

and from Eq. (i):

$$\text{constant}^{1/\gamma} = p_1^{1/\gamma}(1/\rho_1) \tag{vii}$$

These are used to rewrite Eq. (v) as follows:

$$W_s = -\frac{\gamma}{\gamma - 1}\frac{p_1^{1/\gamma}}{\rho_1}(p_2^{1-1/\gamma} - p_1^{1-1/\gamma})$$

$$= -\frac{\gamma}{\gamma - 1}\left(\frac{p_1^{1/\gamma}p_2^{1-1/\gamma}}{\rho_1} - \frac{p_1}{\rho_1}\right) \tag{viii}$$

The product of p_1 to an exponent and p_2 to another exponent in Eq. (viii) can be simplified if it is multiplied by the term $p_1^{1-1/\gamma}/p_1^{1-1/\gamma}$, which is unity. The result is

$$\frac{p_1^{1/\gamma}\{p_2^{1-1/\gamma}\}}{\rho_1}\frac{p_1^{1-1/\gamma}}{p_1^{1-1/\gamma}} = \frac{p_1}{\rho_1}\left(\frac{p_2}{p_1}\right)^{1-1/\gamma} \tag{ix}$$

When Eqs. (viii) and (ix) are combined, the equation for work becomes:

$$W_s = -\frac{\gamma}{\gamma - 1}\frac{p_1}{\rho_1}\left[\left(\frac{p_2}{p_1}\right)^{1-1/\gamma} - 1\right] = -\frac{\gamma}{\gamma - 1}\frac{p_1}{\rho_1}\left[\left(\frac{p_2}{p_1}\right)^{(\gamma-1)/\gamma} - 1\right] \tag{x}$$

Equation (x) is useful in estimating the work of compression. The assumptions implicit in the use of the path of Eq. (i) are: ideal gas, no frictional losses, no heat losses, and constant ratio of c_p to c_v. If frictional losses are considered, Eq. (7.56) is often a more useful starting point, and enthalpy data for the real gas will be required to evaluate W_s.

Equation (x) requires the quotient p_1/ρ_1. This term provides the work units, and so it is convenient to choose the value of the gas constant in units of J or Btu (see Table C.1):

$$p_1/\rho_1 = RT = (8314)(450)\ [(\text{J kmol}^{-1}\text{K}^{-1})(\text{K})] = 3.741 \times 10^6\ \text{J kmol}^{-1} \tag{xi}$$

Now, all quantities in Eq. (x) are known and the shaft work of the gas as it expands through the turbine and transmits its molecular energy to the rotating blades is

$$W_s = -\left(\frac{1.4}{0.4}\right)(3.741 \times 10^6)\left[\left(\frac{0.75}{5.0}\right)^{(0.4/1.4)} - 1.0\right]\text{J kmol}^{-1}$$

$$= 5.48 \times 10^6\ \text{J kmol}^{-1} \tag{xii}$$

7.2 FLUID STATICS

In fluid statics, stationary fluids with zero velocity are considered. If there is no velocity gradient, then by Newton's law, Eq. (2.5), there is no shear stress in the fluid, and the fluid is in an equilibrium state. These problems are sufficiently complex in their own right to warrant special discussion. Three topics will be discussed in this text: manometers, buoyant forces, and variation of pressure with depth.

7.2.1 Manometers

A manometer is a device for measuring pressure by reading one or a pair of fluid elevations. The simplest type of manometer is the U-tube manometer shown in Fig. 7.13(a). Such a manometer can be connected to the pressure

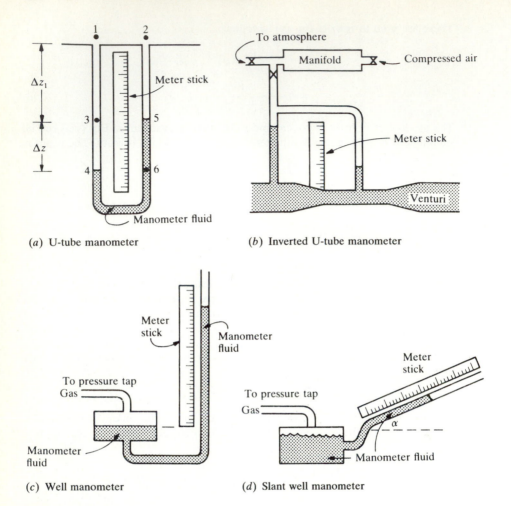

(a) U-tube manometer

(b) Inverted U-tube manometer

(c) Well manometer

(d) Slant well manometer

FIGURE 7.13
Manometers.

taps of a venturi meter, Fig. 7.11. The purpose of such a manometer is to read the pressure difference in the venturi, $p_2 - p_1$.[2] Under steady-state conditions, there is no movement of fluid in the manometer lines. If there is no movement, the kinetic energy change, shaft work, and frictional loss are all zero, and Eq. (7.61) or the Bernoulli equation, Eq. (7.63), reduces to

$$\Delta p / \rho + g \, \Delta z = 0 \qquad (7.64)$$

However, as discussed previously, Eq. (7.63) is restricted to a continuum; in

---

[2] Film loops FM-15, FM-16, FM-35, and FM-36 offer other examples.

Fig. 7.13(a) there is not a continuum but rather an abrupt change at the interface where the process fluid and the manometer fluid meet. A satisfactory relation is obtained by considering that points 4 and 6 in Fig. 7.13(a) are at the same elevation. Since the manometer fluid makes a continuous leg between points 4 and 6, the pressure at 4 equals the pressure at 6:

$$p_4 = p_6 \tag{7.65}$$

If the pressure at point 4 does not equal the pressure at point 6, there will be flow in the manometer leg.

Pressure is transmitted without change across interfaces such as those at points 4 and 6. Furthermore, the pressure at point 4 is greater than that at point 1 owing to the weight of the fluid between points 1 and 4. Since this leg is a continuous liquid phase composed of process fluid of density ρ_A, Eq. (7.64) applies:

$$p_4 - p_1 = \rho_A g(\Delta z_1 + \Delta z) \tag{7.66}$$

or

$$p_4 = p_1 + \rho_A g \, \Delta z_1 + \rho_A g \, \Delta z \tag{7.67}$$

Equation (7.64) also applies for the column of manometer fluid of density ρ_m in the leg between points 5 and 6:

$$p_6 = p_5 + \rho_m g \, \Delta z \tag{7.68}$$

and for the column of process fluid between points 2 and 5:

$$p_5 = p_2 + \rho_A g \, \Delta z_1 \tag{7.69}$$

Equations (7.68) and (7.69) are added as follows:

$$p_6 = p_2 + \rho_m g \, \Delta z + \rho_A g \, \Delta z_1 \tag{7.70}$$

Equation (7.67) is substituted into Eq. (7.65) along with Eq. (7.70). After completing the algebra, the pressure drop $p_1 - p_2$ becomes

$$p_1 - p_2 = (\rho_m - \rho_A)g \, \Delta z \tag{7.71}$$

Note that the pressure drop is independent of the distance Δz_1 from location 1 or 2 to the manometer fluid. There must be continuous fluid legs from pressure tap to manometer fluid, with no gas bubbles if fluid A is a liquid.

Equation (7.71) is the general equation for all manometers, since Δz is vertical height. In the case of the U-tube manometer, the manometer legs are positioned vertically; the manometer reading comes from noting the location of the manometer fluid meniscus in each leg with respect to the scale, usually a meter stick, as shown in Fig. 7.13(a). The low-pressure reading is subtracted from the high-pressure reading to yield Δz. The area of each manometer tube does not enter into Eq. (7.71). An error is introduced if small diameter tubes of unequal area are used in a U-tube manometer. Capillary rise or depression may lead to serious error if the manometer tube diameter is $\frac{1}{4}$ inch or less. In practice, manometer tubing is $\frac{3}{8}$ inch O.D. or greater, and the capillary correction is negligible.

The derivation of Eq. (7.71) from Eq. (7.64) points to the general procedure for deriving the appropriate equation for any manometer problem. This procedure is to apply Eq. (7.64) stepwise from some point in the system at which pressures are equal [Eq. (7.65)]. Equation (7.64) points out the equivalence between pressure and height (or head) of liquid. This equation can be used to show that 760 mm of mercury (Hg) or 29.92 inches Hg corresponds to 1 atm. Using Fig. 7.13(a), the general procedure is illustrated by realizing that the pressure at point 4 is the pressure at point 1 plus that due to the head of liquid between point 1 and 4:

$$p_1 + \rho_A g(\Delta z_1 + \Delta z) = p_4 \tag{7.72}$$

where $\Delta z_1 + \Delta z$ is the total height and ρ_A is the density of the process fluid.

The pressure at point 4 is equal to that at point 6 by Eq. (7.65). For the entire manometer leg, the heads on the low-pressure leg can be subtraced from the left-hand side of Eq. (7.72) to obtain p_2:

$$p_1 + \rho_A g(\Delta z_1 + \Delta z) - \rho_m g \, \Delta z - \rho_A g \, \Delta z_1 = p_2 \tag{7.73}$$

Equation (7.73) reduces to

$$\Delta p = p_2 - p_1 = (\rho_A - \rho_m)g \, \Delta z \tag{7.74}$$

This equation is the same as Eq. (7.71).

One problem with the simple U-tube manometer, such as shown in Fig. 7.13(a), is that the range of measurable pressures is limited. In Eq. (7.71), there are only two variables to manipulate, Δz, the height of the tubing, and ρ_m, the density of the manometer fluid. If one is interested in measuring large pressure differences, physical space limitations and the strength of the material of construction limit Δz. The greatest pressure drop may be read with mercury as the manometer fluid, since mercury is the most dense liquid at room temperatures. Accurate readings at low pressure differences are obtained either by minimizing the difference $\rho_m - \rho_A$ or by somehow modifying the apparatus so as to measure a small Δz accurately.

Liquid process fluid. Obviously the process fluid and the manometer fluid must be immiscible. For large pressure differences, space limitations usually dictate that the term $\rho_m - \rho_A$ in Eq. (7.71) be made as large as possible so the reading Δz is reasonable.

For small pressure differences, it is sometimes possible to find a manometer fluid that is immiscible with the process fluid and slightly more dense. If the term $\rho_m - \rho_A$ is small, then Δz can be read with considerable accuracy. Such fluids are available commercially for aqueous-type process fluids. Another possibility is to use the process fluid itself as manometer fluid. Such a manometer is the inverted U-tube in Fig. 7.13(b). Air is used as the fluid in the top of the manometer. Equation (7.71) still applies with

$$\rho_m - \rho_A \cong \rho_m \tag{7.75}$$

The air at the top in Fig. 7.13(b) is compressed by the two liquid columns; the pressure is approximately the pressure at the downstream tap less that due to the height of the low-pressure leg above the pressure tap. The tee at the top of the inverted manometer is required to adjust the amount of air present in order to keep the reading on the scale. The line from the top of the tee leads through a valve to a small manifold that can be evacuated to the atmosphere or pressurized by a source of compressed air. Manipulation of the three values surrounding the manifold allows air to be introduced or withdrawn from the U-tube manometer so as to place the readings at the desired location on the scale. Three valves allow finer control and less chance of manometer fluid escaping out the atmospheric vent than a two-valve arrangement.

It is possible to increase the accuracy of reading the manometer legs, especially in research equipment, by using such instruments as cathetometers. A typical cathetometer has a telescope-like optical system with a crosshair that is attached to a vernier scale and can be read to within 0.02 mm.

Gas process fluid. When the process fluid is a gas, the approximation in Eq. (7.75) holds. Eq. (7.71) then becomes

$$p_1 - p_2 = \rho_m g \, \Delta z \tag{7.76}$$

The manometer usually contains mercury for large pressure differences or water for small pressure differences. A common variation of the U-tube manometer is the well manometer, Fig. 7.13(c), in which the area of the high-pressure leg (i.e., the well) is very large compared with that of the low-pressure leg. When the well manometer is used to read gauge (and not differential) pressure, the low-pressure leg is open to the atmosphere.

Consider the well manometer shown in Fig. 7.13(c) with both pressure taps disconnected. Fluid is added to the well, and the meter stick is adjusted until the meniscus is at the zero mark. Now the line is connected to a source of high pressure. The high pressure causes manometer fluid to exit from the well into the tube. The mass of fluid entering the tube is given by density times volume, where the volume is area times height:

$$\text{Mass in tube} = \rho_m A_{tube}(\Delta z)_{tube} \tag{7.77}$$

The mass that left the well is

$$\text{Mass from well} = \rho_m A_{well}(\Delta z)_{well} \tag{7.78}$$

This mass equals the mass in the tube above the zero mark. Equations (7.77) and (7.78) are equated and the density canceled from both sides. The result is

$$A_{tube}(\Delta z)_{tube} = A_{well}(\Delta z)_{well} \tag{7.79}$$

where the total height of manometer fluid, Δz in Eq. (7.71) or Eq. (7.76), is

$$\Delta z = (\Delta z)_{\text{tube}} + (\Delta z)_{\text{well}} \qquad (7.80)$$

In a typical well, the area of the well is about 100 cm^2, whereas the area of the tube is about 1.25 cm^2. Hence

$$\frac{(\Delta z)_{\text{tube}}}{(\Delta z)_{\text{well}}} = \frac{A_{\text{well}}}{A_{\text{tube}}} \cong 80 \qquad (7.81)$$

So for every centimeter the well drops, the tube rises 80 cm. In practice the scale on a well manometer, instead of being a true meter stick as used in the U-tube and inverted manometers, is a scale calibrated to correct for $(\Delta z)_{\text{well}}$ and to read Δz directly. Hence the principal advantage of a well manometer is that there is only one leg to read and that the pressure tap is located at the well, which is at the base of the manometer.

Many types of micromanometers are available to measure low pressures in gas flows. These all work on the principle of measuring the small Δz very accurately. The simplest low-pressure manometer is the slant leg type, which may be a U-tube or a well-type as shown in Fig. 7.13(d). In the slant well manometer, the tube makes a small angle α with the horizontal. If the manometer is zeroed properly with both ends open to the atmosphere, then let R_{slant} be the reading when a pressure is applied to the well. This reading is the actual length (perhaps measured in centimeters) the manometer fluid has moved up the slant leg as a result of the applied pressure. Now Eq. (7.71) or Eq. (7.76) applies; Δz is the vertical distance the manometer fluid moves, which is related to R_{slant} by

$$\sin \alpha = \Delta z / R_{\text{slant}} \qquad (7.82)$$

Hence, the pressure drop for a slant well manometer in terms of R_{slant} is

$$p_1 - p_2 = (\rho_{\text{m}} - \rho_{\text{A}}) g R_{\text{slant}} \sin \alpha \qquad (7.83)$$

Most slant manometers are used for gas service, and the slant leg is open to the atmosphere so that the manometer reads gauge pressure.

Traps. It is easy for manometer fluids to be blown out of the manometer into the atmosphere or into the process via the low-pressure line, either through equipment malfunction or operator negligence. Mercury, a common mano-meter fluid for high pressure readings, is extremely hazardous to humans; clearly, any mercury manometer should be trapped. If a pressure difference is suddenly applied, a column of manometer fluid may escape owing to its own momentum, even though the pressure applied may be within the range of the manometer. For liquid systems, a trap also serves to eliminate gas bubbles from the manometer lines.

A typical manometer trap, shown in Fig. 7.14, consists of a cross-like cavity, located near the top of a U-tube manometer and at the highest point in

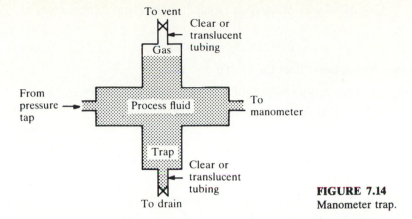

To vent

Clear or translucent tubing

Gas

From pressure tap

Process fluid

To manometer

Trap

Clear or translucent tubing

To drain

FIGURE 7.14
Manometer trap.

the manometer tubing system. The top of the trap is equipped with a clear or translucent section, such as nylon tubing, in order to observe the gas–liquid interface. The trap portion is large enough to contain all the manometer fluid, which in case of accident may be drained out of the bottom.

Example 7.15. Gas flows through a venturi meter such as depicted in Fig. 7.11. The pressure drop across the venturi is read with a U-tube manometer, whose reading is 15 cm. The manometer fluid is mercury, specific gravity 13.45. All temperatures are 25°C. The gas pressures in the manometer lines are all approximately atmospheric. Find the pressure drop across the venturi. The acceleration due to gravity is 980.7 cm s^{-2} (9.807 m s^{-2}).

Answer. The basic equation for any manometer calculation is Eq. (7.71):

$$p_1 - p_2 = (\rho_m - \rho_A)g \, \Delta z \tag{7.71}$$

The density of air can be estimated from the ideal gas law [cf. Eq. (1.1)]:

$$\rho_A = \frac{pM}{RT} = \frac{1}{C_A} \tag{i}$$

where M is the molecular weight of air, 29 kg kmol^{-1}. For Eq. (i):

$$T = 25°C = 298.15 \text{ K}$$

$$R = 82.057 \text{ atm cm}^3 \text{ mol}^{-1} \text{ K}^{-1} = 8.314 \text{ kPa m}^3 \text{ kmol}^{-1} \text{ K}^{-1} \tag{ii}$$

$$p = 1 \text{ atm} = 101.325 \text{ kPa}$$

The density of a gas, which is the reciprocal of the concentration as found in Example 1.1, is now calculated from Eq. (i):

$$\rho_A = [(29)(101.325)]/[(8.314)(298.15)] \left(\frac{(\text{kg kmol}^{-1})(\text{kPa})}{(\text{kPa m}^3 \text{ kmol}^{-1} \text{ K}^{-1})(\text{K})} \right)$$

$$= 1.185 \text{ kg m}^{-3} \tag{iii}$$

Specific gravity is defined as the ratio of the density of the material to the density of water. Taking the density of water as $1\,\mathrm{g\,cm}^{-3}$ or $1000\,\mathrm{kg\,m}^{-3}$, the density of mercury is

$$\rho_m = (1000)(13.45) = 13\,450\,\mathrm{kg\,m}^{-3} \qquad\qquad \text{(iv)}$$

The pressure drop is found from Eq. (7.71):

$$\Delta p = -(13\,450 - 1.19)(9.807)(15)(0.01)\,[(\mathrm{kg\,m}^{-3})(\mathrm{m\,s}^{-2})(\mathrm{cm})(\mathrm{m\,cm}^{-1})]$$
$$= -1.98 \times 10^4\,\mathrm{kg\,m}^{-1}\,\mathrm{s}^{-2} = -1.98 \times 10^4\,\mathrm{N\,m}^{-2}$$
$$= -413\,\mathrm{lb_f\,ft}^{-2} = -2.87\,\mathrm{psi} \qquad\qquad \text{(v)}$$

The minus sign means the upstream pressure p_1 is greater than p_2, i.e., there is a pressure drop. Note the density of air is negligible, less than 0.01 percent that of mercury, and would still be negligible if the manometer fluid were water or some other liquid. Thus, Eq. (7.75) and Eq (7.76) are shown to be correct.

Example 7.16. Rework Example 7.15, this time using engineering units.

Answer. As discussed in Examples 7.11 and 7.12, the gravitational conversion constant g_c is required in Eq. (7.71) in order to balance units when we are using the engineering system. When g_c is appropriately placed in the denominator, the ratio g/g_c appears and has the net units of $\mathrm{lb_f\,lb_m^{-1}}$. The ratio is often numerically equal to unity for all practical purposes. The reading Δz in feet is

$$\Delta z = (15)/[(2.54)(12)]\,[(\mathrm{cm})(\mathrm{in.\,cm}^{-1})(\mathrm{ft\,in.}^{-1})] = 0.4921\,\mathrm{ft} \qquad\qquad \text{(i)}$$

Equation (i) of Example 7.15 is used to estimate the density of air. In English units, the conditions are

$$T = 25°\mathrm{C} = 298.15\,\mathrm{K} = 536.67°\mathrm{R}$$
$$R = 10.73\,\mathrm{lb_f\,in.}^{-2}\,\mathrm{ft}^3\,\mathrm{lb\,mol}^{-1}°\mathrm{R}^{-1}$$
$$p = 14.696\,\mathrm{lb_f\,in.}^{-2} \qquad\qquad \text{(ii)}$$
$$g = (9.807)(3.2808)\,[(\mathrm{m\,s}^{-2})(\mathrm{ft\,m}^{-1})] = 32.175\,\mathrm{ft\,s}^{-2}$$
$$g/g_c = 32.175/32.174 = 1.00004\,\mathrm{lb_f\,lb_m^{-1}}$$

Then the density of air is

$$\rho_A = (29)(14.696)/[(10.73)(536.67)]\left(\frac{(\mathrm{lb_m\,lb\,mol}^{-1})(\mathrm{lb_f\,in.}^{-2})}{(\mathrm{lb_f\,in.}^{-2}\,\mathrm{ft}^3\,\mathrm{lb\,mol}^{-1}°\mathrm{R}^{-1})(°\mathrm{R})}\right)$$
$$= 0.074\,\mathrm{lb_m\,ft}^{-3} \qquad\qquad \text{(iii)}$$

Using $62.4\,\mathrm{lb_m\,ft}^{-3}$ as the density of water, the density of mercury is

$$\rho_m = (13.45)(62.4) = 839.28\,\mathrm{lb_m\,ft}^{-3} \qquad\qquad \text{(iiia)}$$

The pressure drop $(-\Delta p)$ is found from Eq (7.71):

$$p_1 - p_2 = (839.28 - 0.074)(32.175/32.174)(0.4921)\,[(\mathrm{lb_m\,ft}^{-3})(\mathrm{lb_f\,lb_m^{-1}})\,(\mathrm{ft})]$$
$$= 413.0\,\mathrm{lb_f\,ft}^{-2} \qquad\qquad \text{(iv)}$$

or in units of psi:

$$p_1 - p_2 = 413.0/144\,[(\mathrm{lb_f\,ft}^{-2})(\mathrm{ft}^2\,\mathrm{in.}^{-2})] = 2.87\,\mathrm{psi} \qquad\qquad \text{(v)}$$

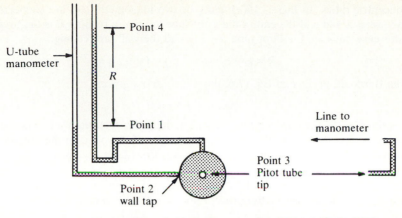

(a) Pipe cross section at wall tap (end view)   (b) Pitot tube (side view)

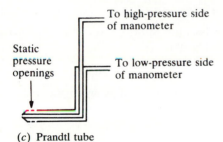

(c) Prandtl tube

FIGURE 7.15
Pressure tap and Pitot tube for measuring flow velocity.

Example 7.17. Obtain the equations for a pressure tap and Pitot[3] tube
(Fig. 7.15). Summarize the assumptions made.[4] A pressure tap is made by drilling
a hole through the tube wall with no burrs on the inside. Generally, some type of
coupling is brazed over the tap so that connections can be made to a pressure
measuring device. A Pitot tube is a hollow tube of small diameter inserted into
the flow so the tip is exactly parallel to the flow axis. Lines from the pressure tap
and the Pitot tube are connected to a pressure-measuring device such as a
manometer, as shown in Fig. 7.15(a) and Fig. 7.15(b).

Answer. The pressure tap is always located at the same point in the flow as the
end of the Pitot tube. Figure 7.15(b) shows a side view of the Pitot tube. Figure
7.15(c) shows a Prandtl tube, which is similar to a Pitot tube except the Pitot port
and the pressure tap are located on a single assembly constructed of two

---

[3] After the inventor, Henri de Pitot (1695–1771).
[4] Film loops FM-33, FM-37, and FM-38 illustrate the various pressures that are important in this
experiment.

concentric tubes. In Figs. 7.15(a) and (b), two manometer legs are connected to the pressure tap and the end of the Pitot tube, so that a reading R is the pressure difference between the Pitot tube reading and the wall tap reading:

$$R = z_4 - z_1 = (z_4 - z_3) - (z_1 - z_2) \tag{i}$$

The Bernoulli balance of Eq. (7.62) or Eq. (7.64) applies:

$$\Delta p / \rho + g \, \Delta z = 0 \tag{7.64}$$

Considering the pressure tap first, point 2 is the pressure at the wall, which is also the static pressure across the entire cross section of the pipe. In the pressure leg from the tap to the top of the manometer leg, Eq. (7.64) becomes

$$p_2 = p_1 + \rho_f g (z_1 - z_2) \tag{ii}$$

where ρ_f is the density of the process fluid which also serves as the manometer fluid in this case.

For the Pitot tube, the pressure at the tip of the tube, p_3, is

$$p_3 = p_4 + \rho_f g (z_4 - z_3) \tag{iii}$$

Since p_1 and p_4 are both equal to the pressure of the atmosphere, Eqs. (ii) and (iii) can be rearranged so these can be equated:

$$p_3 - p_2 = \rho_f g [(z_4 - z_3) - (z_1 - z_2)] = \rho_f g R \tag{iv}$$

Next, a Bernoulli balance is made in the fluid between the wall (zero velocity) and the center of the tube or the location of the Pitot tube. The Bernoulli equation is

$$\frac{p_2 - p_1}{\rho} + g(z_2 - z_1) + \frac{1}{2} \left(\frac{U_{2,\text{ave}}^2}{\alpha_2} - \frac{U_{1,\text{ave}}^2}{\alpha_1} \right) = 0 \tag{7.62}$$

Since the system is horizontal, the potential energy term disappears, and Eq. (7.62) as applied to points 2 and 3 reduces to

$$\frac{p_3 - p_2}{\rho_f} = \frac{1}{2\alpha} (U_3^2 - 0) \tag{v}$$

or after substituting Eq. (iv):

$$U_3^2 = 2\alpha g R \tag{vi}$$

Usually α is taken as unity, in which case, Eq. (vi) becomes

$$U_3 = (2gR)^{1/2} \tag{vii}$$

The assumptions in Eq. (vii) are that the velocity profile is flat (an excellent assumption for a small-diameter Pitot tube), that there are no tip effects due to the wall of the probe, and that the flow can be considered incompressible, isothermal, and without heat exchange, shaft work or frictional losses. Furthermore, in obtaining Eqs. (7.49), from which Eqs. (7.55) and (7.62) were derived, it was assumed that the $\cos \theta$ term was unity, which means that the velocity vector must be perpendicular to the Pitot opening at point 3. Because of this assumption about the velocity term, a significant error is introduced unless the velocity profile is perpendicular to the tube entrance. Specially designed multiport

Pitot tubes are sometimes used to eliminate the problem that arises when the Pitot opening is not exactly perpendicular to the velocity vector. However, it is recommended that the classic design be used and great care taken to align the Pitot probe properly.

If the shape of the velocity profile and the geometry of the Pitot tube are known, then the factor α can be computed, instead of making the assumption of unity. For laminar flow, the correction may be large. For turbulent flow, however, the profile is relatively flat, and little or no correction is necessary if the Pitot probe is of small diameter.

Example 7.18. A well manometer as depicted in Fig. 7.16 is filled with mercury so that the mercury level reaches 0 on the meter stick when both legs are open to the atmosphere. The cross sectional area of the manometer tubing is 0.049 in.^{2}, and the cross sectional area of the well is 15.5 in^2. A pressure vessel filled with water is located so that its pressure tap is 45 cm above the zero mark on the meter stick. This tap is connected to the well so that there are no air bubbles in the line; the water displaces all air in the manometer well. If the water pressure forces the mercury column to a reading of 70 cm on the meter stick, find the pressure at the vessel pressure tap. Let $g = 32.174$ ft s^{-2}.

Answer. Since this manometer is being operated with water on top of the manometer fluid in the well leg and air on top of the fluid in the other leg, none of the previously derived equations applies without further considerations. Solution of this problem is reached by first calculating the pressure at the water–mercury interface and thereafter finding the tap pressure.

With air on both sides of the manometer fluid, the height of mercury is at the zero mark on the meter stick. At the final conditions, however, the mercury level drops below the zero elevation in the well. Solution of the problem requires computation of this drop $(\Delta z)_{\text{well}}$. The volume of mercury leaving the well equals

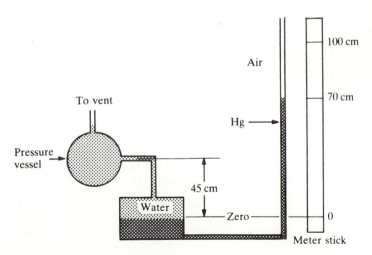

FIGURE 7.16
Well manometer in Example 7.18.

the volume in the tube when the reading is 70 cm:

$$V_{\text{Hg, well}} = V_{\text{Hg, tube}} \qquad \text{(i)}$$

or from Eq. (7.79):

$$(\Delta z)_{\text{well}} A_{\text{well}} = (\Delta z)_{\text{tube}} A_{\text{tube}} \qquad (7.79)$$

or:

$$(\Delta z)_{\text{well}} = (\Delta z)_{\text{tube}} (A_{\text{tube}}/A_{\text{well}}) = (70)(0.049)/(15.5)$$

$$= 0.2213 \text{ cm} \qquad \text{(ii)}$$

Note that the areas are used as a ratio, and it is unnecessary to convert units.

Let the water–mercury interface be a datum point. The pressure at this elevation is that exerted by the column of mercury, which is 70.2213 cm long. Equation (7.64) is the basic equation that is used to find the pressure exerted by a column of fluid:

$$\Delta p/\rho + g\,\Delta z = 0 \qquad (7.64)$$

This equation, as applied to the manometer fluid of density ρ_m and with g_c added, becomes

$$(\Delta p)_{\text{Hg}} = -\rho_m (g/g_c)\,\Delta z$$

$$= -(13.45)(62.4)\left(\frac{32.174}{32.174}\right)\left(\frac{70.2213}{(2.54)(12)}\right) \; [(\text{lb}_m \text{ ft}^{-3})(\text{lb}_f \text{ lb}_m^{-1})(\text{ft})]$$

$$= -1934 \text{ lb}_f \text{ ft}^{-2} \qquad \text{(iii)}$$

The pressure at the tap will be the pressure at the interface, as given by Eq. (iii), less the contribution of the water leg, which is 45.2213 cm long:

$$(\Delta p)_{\text{tap}} = (\Delta p)_{\text{Hg}} - \left(-(\rho_{\text{H}_2\text{O}})\frac{g}{g_c}(\Delta z)_{\text{H}_2\text{O}}\right)$$

$$= -1934 + (62.4)(1)\left(\frac{45.2213}{(2.54)(12)}\right) = -1841 \text{ lb}_f \text{ ft}^{-2} = -12.79 \text{ psi} \qquad \text{(iv)}$$

The pressure tap is 12.79 psi above atmospheric, since Δp is negative and therefore p_1 is greater than p_2.

7.2.2   Buoyant Forces

A body submerged or floating in a static fluid has a net upward force exerted on it by the fluid. This buoyant force F_B is equal to the weight of the fluid displaced. The principle of buoyancy dates from the time of Archimedes in the 3d century BC [W3]. If V is the displaced volume, then

$$F_B = ma = \rho_f V g \qquad (7.84)$$

where ρ_f is the density of the fluid displaced; $\rho_f V$ is thus the displaced mass, and g is the gravitational acceleration.

Naturally, the buoyant force F_B has no horizontal component; it always acts through the centroid of the volume (the center of buoyancy). Note that

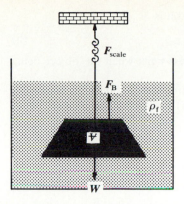

FIGURE 7.17
Free body diagram of submerged solid.

Eq. (7.84) says that every body present in the atmosphere is subject to a buoyant force from the surrounding air. The buoyancy of air may be important when weighing objects very accurately, because the object is often less dense than the weights on the balance. The buoyant force due to air must be considered when weighing to a tenth of a milligram. Consider Fig. 7.17, in which a solid body of volume V is suspended in a fluid of density ρ_f by a thin string. Three forces act upon this body: the force of gravity F_W (W for weight), the buoyant force F_B, and the force on the string as measured by the deflection of a spring (F_{scale}). Newton's second law, Eq. (7.29), applies with the acceleration zero because the body is at rest:

$$\sum F = F_{scale} + F_B - F_W = 0 \tag{7.85}$$

If Eqs. (7.84) and (7.85) are combined, the result is

$$F_{scale} + \rho_f V g - F_W = 0 \tag{7.86}$$

Equation (7.86) is the basic problem-solving equation relating buoyant forces to weight. Two applications of this equation follow.

Example 7.19. A person brings a coin into a local coin shop, where he represents that the coin is pure gold. The numismatist's pan balance shows that the coin weighs 53.32 g in air (barometer 749 Torr at 21°C) and 50.22 g in water. Is the coin gold?

Answer. Equation (7.86) applies, but there are two unknowns in this example: the volume of the sample V and its density ρ. The readings from the pan balance are actually in grams as a force, because of the method of determination, i.e., a force balance. Furthermore, Eq. (7.86) is a force equation that must be converted to a mass basis in order to solve this problem. Force and mass are related through Newton's second law, Eq. (7.29), with the acceleration being that of gravity:

$$F = mg \tag{i}$$

Substituting this equation into Eq. (7.86), the result is

$$g(m_{\text{scale}} + \rho_f \mathcal{V}) = m_{\text{true}} g \tag{ii}$$

where m_{scale} is the reading of the balance in mass units when the object being weighed is in a fluid of density ρ_f.

Now the mass of any object in a vacuum (*in vacuo*) is the true mass m_{true} and is invariant. To solve Example 7.19, Eq. (ii) is applied twice to each fluid, water ($\rho_{\text{H}_2\text{O}}$) and air ($\rho_{\text{air}}$):

$$m_{\text{air}} + \rho_{\text{air}} \mathcal{V} = m_{\text{true}} \tag{iii}$$

$$m_{\text{H}_2\text{O}} + \rho_{\text{H}_2\text{O}} \mathcal{V} = m_{\text{true}} \tag{iv}$$

Equating these, the volume of the object is

$$\mathcal{V} = \frac{m_{\text{air}} - m_{\text{H}_2\text{O}}}{\rho_{\text{H}_2\text{O}} - \rho_{\text{air}}} \tag{v}$$

The density of water is 0.998 g cm^{-3} at 21°C. The density of air may be estimated from the ideal gas law as follows:

$$p = 749/760 \, [(\text{Torr})(\text{atm Torr}^{-1})] = 0.9855 \text{ atm} \tag{vi}$$

$$T = 21°\text{C} = 21 + 273.15 = 294.15 \text{ K} \tag{vii}$$

$$v = RT/p = (82.06)(294.15)/(0.9855) = 24\,490 \text{ cm}^3 \text{ mol}^{-1} \tag{viii}$$

$$\rho_{\text{air}} = \frac{M}{v} = \frac{29}{24490} \left(\frac{(\text{g mol}^{-1})}{(\text{cm}^3 \text{ mol}^{-1})} \right) = 0.001184 \text{ g cm}^{-3} \tag{ix}$$

In the above, the value of the gas constant R is from Table C.1, v is the molar volume of air, and M is the molecular weight from Table A.2, 29 g mol^{-1}. The volume of the coin may now be found from Eq. (v):

$$\mathcal{V} = \frac{53.32 - 50.22}{0.998 - 0.001184} = 3.11 \text{ cm}^3 \tag{x}$$

The density of the coin is

$$\rho = \text{mass/volume} = 53.32/3.11 = 17.14 \text{ g cm}^{-3} \tag{xi}$$

Consulting a handbook it is seen that this result is the correct density for gold.

Example 7.20. In an experiment to find the heat of combustion of a piece of oak, a small sample is found to exactly balance 6.7348 g of brass weights in a pan balance. The density of oak is $38 \text{ lb}_{\text{m}} \text{ ft}^{-3}$, and of brass is $534 \text{ lb}_{\text{m}} \text{ ft}^{-3}$. Make the appropriate buoyancy correction to find the true mass of the wood if the temperature is 21°C and the barometer reads 749 Torr.

Answer. Since two systems of units are mixed in this problem, let us pick the CGS system. First, the densities of oak and brass are converted to CGS units:

$$\rho_{\text{oak}} = (38) \left(\frac{1.0}{62.4} \right) \left(\frac{(\text{lb}_{\text{m}} \text{ ft}^{-3})(\text{g cm}^{-3})}{(\text{lb}_{\text{m}} \text{ ft}^{-3})} \right) = 0.6090 \text{ g cm}^{-3}$$

$$\rho_{\text{brass}} = 534/62.4 = 8.5577 \text{ g cm}^{-3} \tag{i}$$

Equation (7.86) applies. After conversion to a mass basis, as done in deriving Eq. (ii) in the previous example, the equation can be expressed as

$$m_{scale} = m_{true} - \rho_f V \tag{ii}$$

If the piece of oak balances the brass weights, then F_{scale} for the oak equals F_{scale} for the brass. Equating these forces and converting to mass via Eq. (ii), the result is

$$m_{scale} = m_{oak} - \rho_{air} V_{oak} = m_{brass} - \rho_{air} V_{brass} \tag{iii}$$

The volume of oak equals the true mass divided by density; for oak and brass:

$$V_{oak} = m_{oak}/\rho_{oak} \tag{iv}$$

$$V_{brass} = m_{brass}/\rho_{brass} \tag{v}$$

Combining Eqs. (iii), (iv), and (v) yields the equation required to calculate the buoyancy correction:

$$m_{oak} = m_{brass}\left(\frac{1 - \rho_{air}/\rho_{brass}}{1 - \rho_{air}/\rho_{oak}}\right) \tag{vi}$$

The density of air was found in the previous example:

$$\rho_{air} = 0.001184 \text{ g cm}^{-3} \tag{vii}$$

Substituting the known quantities into Eq. (vi) yields

$$m_{oak} = (6.7348)\left(\frac{1 - (0.001184)/(8.5577)}{1 - (0.001184)/(0.6090)}\right) = 6.7470 \text{ g} \tag{viii}$$

The numbers from the above calculation show that buoyancy correction is 12.2 mg and must be made when claiming a weighing accuracy of 0.1 mg.

7.2.3 Variation of Pressure with Depth

Equations to describe the variation of pressure with depth in a static fluid are derived by considering a differential element such as the one in Fig. 4.7 with no flow. The derivation follows the force balance developed in Section 4.2.1, but in differential form. The result is a limited form of the mechanical energy balance equation, Eq. (7.57), with the kinetic energy, fluid friction, and shaft work terms all zero:

$$\frac{dp}{\rho} + g \, dz = 0 \tag{7.87}$$

This equation is the same as Eq. (7.64) but in differential form.

There are two important cases in which Eq. (7.87) is applied. For an incompressible fluid such as a liquid, the density ρ is constant, and Eq. (7.87) is integrated directly to find

$$\Delta p = \rho g h \tag{7.88}$$

where h is measured vertically downward from the air–liquid interface. This is, of course, the same as Eq. (7.64) with Δz replaced with $(-h)$ and is the basis for the analysis of manometers, as already presented.

The second case considers a gas in which the pressure varies. The simplest case involves an isothermal gas that obeys the ideal gas law:

$$\rho = \frac{M}{v} = \frac{Mp}{RT} \tag{7.89}$$

where M is the molecular weight of the fluid and v is the molar volume. Equation (7.89) is substituted into Eq. (7.87) and the variables separated:

$$\frac{dp}{p} = -g \frac{M}{RT} dz \tag{7.90}$$

This equation is integrated according to the following limits:

$$p\,(z = 0) = p_0 \qquad p\,(z = \Delta z) = p \tag{7.91}$$

and the answer is

$$\ln(p/p_0) = -g \frac{M}{RT} \Delta z \tag{7.92}$$

or

$$p = p_0 e^{-gM\,\Delta z/(RT)} \tag{7.93}$$

Equation (7.93) is valid for the assumptions mentioned above. If Δz is small, e.g., 50 ft, then the pressure variation is negligible as is seen in the following example.

Example 7.21. Calculate the pressure 50 ft above a beach in Fort Lauderdale if the temperature both on the beach and in the air is 30°C and the pressure at the beach level is exactly 760 Torr.

Answer. Since temperature is constant, Eq. (7.93) applies. As an example, the English system of units will be used, in which the potential energy term $g\,\Delta z$ has units of $\text{ft lb}_f\,\text{lb}_m^{-1}$. Let R be $1544\,\text{ft lb}_f\,\text{lb mol}^{-1}\,°R^{-1}$, as found in Table C.1. The temperature must be in Rankine degrees:

$$T = 30°C = 303.15\,\text{K} = 545.67°R \tag{i}$$

and M for air is equal to $29\,\text{lb}_m\,\text{lb mol}^{-1}$. Note that since engineering units are being used, g_c will have to be introduced in the exponent of Eq. (7.93) in order to obtain the correct units; i.e.,

$$\frac{g}{g_c} \frac{M}{RT} \Delta z\,[=](\text{lb}_f\,\text{lb}_m^{-1})\left(\frac{(\text{lb}_m\,\text{lb mol}^{-1})(\text{ft})}{(\text{ft lb}_f\,\text{lb mol}^{-1}\,°R^{-1})(°R)}\right) \tag{ii}$$

This equation is now dimensionless. If $g = 9.807\,\text{m s}^{-1}$, then the ratio g/g_c can be taken as unity (see Example 7.16), so that Eq. (7.93) becomes

$$p = 760\exp\{(-50)(29)/[(1545)(545.67)]\} = (760)(0.99828) = 758.7\,\text{Torr} \tag{iii}$$

Thus, the pressure decrease for an elevation of 50 ft is very small.

If Eq. (7.93) is applied to large changes in elevation, such as those encountered by an airliner, then the assumption of constant temperature is very poor. If the variation of temperature with elevation is known, Eq. (7.90) may be integrated analytically or numerically. The simplest model is to assume that the temperature decreases linearly with elevation:

$$T = T_0 + \beta z \tag{7.94}$$

where β may be assumed to be approximately constant $(-0.00357 \,°\text{F ft}^{-1})$ up to the stratosphere (about 6–15 miles above the earth's surface). Substitution of Eq. (7.94) into Eq. (7.90) yields

$$\frac{dp}{p} = -\frac{gM}{R}\frac{dz}{T_0 + \beta z} \tag{7.95}$$

If this equation is integrated with the limits of Eq. (7.91), the answer is

$$\ln(p/p_0) = \frac{gM}{R\beta} \ln \frac{T_0}{T_0 + \beta \,\Delta z} \tag{7.96}$$

More complicated models of the temperature profile may require numerical integration.

Example 7.22. Calculate the pressure and temperature 25 000 ft above a beach in Fort Lauderdale if the air temperature is 30°C and the pressure at beach level is exactly 760 Torr.

Answer. Equation (7.96) can be used. Since a change of 1 deg F is a change of 1 deg R, the constant β may be written as

$$\beta = -0.00357 \,°\text{F ft}^{-1} = -0.00357 \,°\text{R ft}^{-1} \tag{i}$$

All other terms in Eq. (7.96) were determined in the previous example problem. Equation (7.96) is exponentiated and the substitutions made:

$$p = 760 \exp\left[\left(\frac{29}{(1545)(-0.00357)}\right) \ln \left(\frac{545.67}{545.67 - (0.00357)(25000)}\right)\right]$$

$$= 760 \exp(-0.939) = 297.16 \text{ Torr} \tag{ii}$$

The temperature at 25 000 ft is calculated from Eq. (7.94):

$$T = 545.67 - (0.00357)(25000) = 456.42°\text{R} = -3.25°\text{F} \tag{iii}$$

Note that Mount Everest is more than 29 000 ft above sea level; hence the pressure is even lower at that location.

7.3 RECAPITULATION

In this chapter are the detailed balances on a finite volume, rather than on a differential volume, as was done in the early chapters. The resulting equations are extremely useful. The basic equation is Eq. (7.3):

$$\int_V (\partial \psi / \partial t)\, dV = -\oint_S (\psi U)(\cos \theta)\, dS - \oint_S (\mathbf{\Psi}_m \cdot d\mathbf{S})$$

$$- \oint_S (\mathbf{\Psi}_o \cdot d\mathbf{S}) + \int_V \dot{\psi}_G\, dV \tag{7.3}$$

The appropriate quantities for $\mathbf{\Psi}$, ψ, and $\dot{\psi}_G$ are substituted into Eq. (7.3) to obtain the integral equations of mass, momentum, and heat. The integral mass balance problems are usually covered in courses and texts on stoichiometry. The integral momentum balance can be used to compute the forces a fluid exerts on a solid body, such as on a bend in a pipe. These two balances are easy to formulate, easy to understand, and quite useful, especially the integral mass balance. However, the energy balance is much more complex. In fact, the energy balance is an important link between transport phenomena and thermodynamics, a complete subject in itself. Complexity aside, the resulting energy equations are very powerful and must be studied in detail.

Substitution of $\rho c_p T$ for ψ in Eq. (7.3) is unsatisfactory because the resulting terms in the equation are too general for specific use. There are three other approaches to the energy balance that are quite satisfactory. The first of these is the first law of thermodynamics:

$$(\Delta U)_{system} = Q - W \tag{7.34}$$

where Q and W are the heat and work associated with changes in the surroundings. The second approach is to substitute ρE, the energy per unit mass, for the concentration of property ψ in Eq. (7.3). The resulting equations are used in conjunction with the first law of thermodynamics to obtain the overall energy balance, Eq. (7.56):

$$\Delta H + \frac{w}{2} \left(\frac{U_{2,\,ave}^2}{\alpha_2} - \frac{U_{1,\,ave}^2}{\alpha_1} \right) + wg\, \Delta z = Q - W_s \tag{7.56}$$

It is interesting to note that thermodynamics provides no clue whatsoever as to the nature of the kinetic energy term in Eq. (7.56). The terms with α arise only from the integration of Eq. (7.3).

Alternately, a modified form of the Navier–Stokes equation [Eq. (7.58)] can be used to make a balance on the concentration of total energy in the system. The basic concept is that when a momentum term such as mU is scalar-multiplied by the velocity vector U, the result is an energy term. After a lengthy and complex derivation, the result is the mechanical energy balance, which can be expressed in differential form as follows:

$$\frac{1}{\rho} dp + g\, dz + U\, dU + dF' + dW_s = 0 \tag{7.57}$$

These two conservation of energy equations [Eqs. (7.56) and (7.57)] are really complementary in that one or the other may be used, but not both together.

The choice is based on the nature of the problem. Generally problems in which heat and work are involved together with significant temperature changes dictate that Eq. (7.56) be used, whereas, if there is no Q, then often the mechanical energy balance is more useful.

These two conservation of energy equations are widely used for design. For example, Eq. (7.57) is the principal equation for the approximate sizing of pumps and compressors, as well as turbines, although other equations in thermodynamics are used for exact calculations. Other applications include the rate at which a tank drains, the rate at which a siphon transfers liquid, the output from flow-measuring devices such as venturis and Pitot tubes, and the temperature rise due to changes in elevation.

An important simplification to Eq. (7.57) results in the engineering Bernoulli balance:

$$\frac{\Delta p}{\rho} + g\,\Delta z + \Delta\left(\frac{U_{\text{ave}}^2}{2\alpha}\right) = 0 \qquad (7.63)$$

This equation, with the kinetic energy term zero, is the basis for the subject of fluid statics; see Section 7.2. The reader is advised to study this section closely, because the principles and applications contained therein are often encountered.

PROBLEMS

7.1. Why are the integral methods used at times, rather than a complete solution for the velocity distribution?

7.2. Discuss the meaning of each term of Eq. (7.3).

7.3. Explain why the cosine appears in the convection term in Eq. (7.3).

7.4. The term β is called the momentum correction factor. Discuss.

7.5. What is the relation between Eqs. (7.21) and (7.29)?

7.6. Discuss the meaning of the various terms U, E, H.

7.7. What is the meaning of each term in Eq. (7.52) and in Eq. (7.56)?

7.8. The term α is called the kinetic energy correction factor. Discuss.

7.9. Discuss the meaning of each term in Eq. (7.61), the mechanical energy balance.

7.10. Tabulate the assumptions that have been invoked in deriving the Pitot tube equation in Example 7.17, $U_z = (2gR)^{1/2}$.

7.11. A funnel without a stem is allowed to drain. Determine the time required to empty the funel, if the exit velocity is given by

$$U_{\text{ave}}^2 = 2gh$$

where h is the height of fluid in the funnel, H is the original height, r_{H} is the radius at H, and r_{o} is the radius of the funnel drain. Hint: the volume of a cone is $(\pi r^2 h/3)$; assume $r(h=0) = 0$.

7.12. A funnel with a long vertical stem of radius r_{o} and length L is allowed to drain. Determine the time required to empty the funnel; let h be the height of fluid in the funnel, H the original height, and r_H the radius at H. Assume that the flow is laminar and that there are no losses in the funnel. Neglect the time to drain the stem. Hint: the volume of a cone is $\pi r^2 h/3$; assume $r(h = 0) = 0$.

7.13. Determine the time required to remove half of the contents of the tank of Example 7.1, if a horizontal length of pipe with radius r_o and length L is attached to the drain. Assume all the losses are in the pipe and that the flow is laminar.

7.14. A line has an expanding section that changes the diameter from 3 inches to 6 inches. Water (viscosity 1.0 cP and specific gravity 1.0) is flowing at $0.5 \, \text{ft}^3 \, \text{s}^{-1}$, and the pressure is 45 psia at the upstream end. Find the pressure (psia) at the downstream end. Use English units.

7.15. In Problem 7.14, the expanding section has an angle of 45°. If the inlet pressure is 40 psia, the inlet velocity is $12.22 \, \text{ft} \, \text{s}^{-1}$, and the outlet pressure is 40.94 psia, find (a) the resultant force on the fluid; (b) the resultant force holding the fitting in place. Do all work in English units.

7.16. In Problem 7.14, the flow direction is reversed (flow through a reducer). Find (a) the pressure (psia) at the downstream end; (b) the resultant force on the fluid; (c) the resultant force holding the fitting in place. Do all work in English units.

7.17. Water (viscosity 1.0 cP and specific gravity 1.0) flows through an expanding bend that turns the fluid 120°. The upstream inside diameter is 3 inches, and the pressure at this point is 80 psia. The downstream inside diameter is 5 inches. The flow is $2 \, \text{ft}^3 \, \text{s}^{-1}$. Neglecting the energy loss within the elbow, find the downstream pressure (psia). Use English units throughout.

7.18. Water (viscosity 1.0 cP and specific gravity 1.0) flows through an expanding bend that turns the fluid 120°. The upstream inside diameter is 3 inches, and the pressure at this point is 10.0 psig. The downstream inside diameter is 5 inches, and the pressure is 19.7 psig. The flow is $2 \, \text{ft}^3 \, \text{s}^{-1}$. Find (a) the resultant force on the fluid; (b) the resultant force holding the fitting in place. Do all work in English units.

7.19. Water at 295 K is flowing at $1 \, \text{m} \, \text{s}^{-1}$ in turbulent flow in a pipe whose internal diameter is 10 cm. The fluid enters a U-shaped bend such that the direction of flow of the exiting fluid is 180° from that of the entering fluid. The absolute pressure of the entering fluid is 2.2 atm; the pressure of the exiting fluid is 2.0 atm. Find (a) the resultant force on the fluid; (b) the resultant force holding the fitting in place. Do all work in SI units.

7.20. A jet of water at 290 K, 1 inch in diameter, strikes a fixed vane that deflects the jet 90° from its original direction. The jet velocity is $25 \, \text{ft} \, \text{s}^{-1}$. Find (a) the resultant force on the fluid; (b) the resultant force holding the vane in place. Do all work in English units.

7.21. A two-dimensional jet of fluid, which flows at a rate of $Q \, \text{m}^3 \, \text{s}^{-1}$, strikes a plate at an angle θ. Find the split of the flow (i.e., Q_1 and Q_2, where Q_2 is in the direction $U \cos \theta$). Hint: neglect the drag force and use a coordinate system where the y-axis is parallel to the plate. If there is no drag force, then there is no deceleration of the fluid.

7.22. Determine the total or stagnation pressure for the flow of air at 100 miles per hour, if the air is at atmospheric pressure and has a density of $0.08 \, \text{lb}_m \, \text{ft}^{-3}$. Do all work in English units.

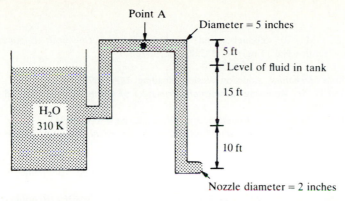

FIGURE 7.18
Siphon for Problem 7.23.

7.23. Determine the rate of flow ($kg\,s^{-1}$) of water at 310 K through the siphon in Fig. 7.18. Neglect all losses. Let g equal $9.75\,m\,s^{-2}$. Work in SI units.

7.24. Find the pressure (psia) at point A in Problem 7.23. Let atmospheric pressure be 14.4 psia. Can the system operate? Why or why not?

7.25. A tank contains both water and oil. The water and oil are immiscible, and specific gravity of the water is 1.0 and of the oil is 0.8. If the fluid layers are each 5 m in depth and contained in the tank shown in Fig. 7.2, determine the rate of discharge Q if the internal diameter of the drain and tank are 5 cm and 5 m respectively. Let g equal $9.8\,m\,s^{-2}$. Work in SI units.

7.26. Find the flow rate in $m^3\,s^{-1}$ in Problem 7.23 if the losses are $5.0\,ft\,lb_f\,lb_m^{-1}$. Work in SI units.

7.27. Find the flow rate in $m^3\,s^{-1}$ in Problem 7.25 if a length of line, of internal diameter 5 cm and losses $5\,ft\,lb_f\,lb_m^{-1}$, is attached to the exit. Neglect entrance effects. Work in SI units.

7.28. A Pitot tube is schematically pictured in Fig. 7.15. Calculate the pressure difference (in units of inches of water, psi, and kPa) obtained from a manometer connected to a Pitot tube that is located at the center line of a 2-inch schedule 40 pipe (see Table B.1), through which water at 290 K is flowing at a Reynolds number of 10^5. Let the acceleration due to gravity be $32.21\,ft\,s^{-2}$. Convert all numbers to SI and work in that system of units.

7.29. A chemist brings the following data to you. Find the *in vacuo* mass of the salt solution. Use SI units throughout.

Density of brass weights:	$8400\,kg\,m^{-3}$
Density of salt solution:	$1100\,kg\,m^{-3}$
Density of pyrex beaker:	$2500\,kg\,m^{-3}$
Grams of brass weights used to tare beaker:	$57.952\,g$
Grams of brass weights used for beaker plus salt solution:	$143.859\,g$
Atmospheric conditions during measurements:	pressure $= 742$ Torr
	temperature $= 22°C$

REFERENCES

B1. Balzhiser, R. E., M. R. Samuels, and J. D. Eliassen: *Chemical Engineering Thermodynamics,* Prentice-Hall, Englewood Cliffs, NJ, 1972.

B2. Bird, R. B.: *Chem. Eng. Sci.* **6:** 123 (1957).

D1. de Nevers, N.: *Fluid Mechanics,* Addision-Wesley, Reading, MA, 1970.

F1. Felder, R. M., and R. W. Rousseau: *Elementary Principles of Chemical Processes,* 2d ed., Wiley, New York, 1986.

G1. Glasstone, S.: *Thermodynamics for Chemists,* Van Nostrand, New York, 1947.

H1. Himmelblau, D. M.: *Basic Principles and Calculations in Chemical Engineering,* 4th ed., Prentice-Hall, Englewood Cliffs, NJ, 1982.

K1. Kays, W. M.: *Trans. ASME* **72:** 1067 (1950).

K2. Klotz, I. M., and R. M. Rosenberg: *Chemical Thermodynamics,* 4th ed., Benjamin, Menlo Park, CA, 1986.

S1. Sears, F. W.: *An Introduction to Thermodynamics,* 3d ed., Addison-Wesley, Reading, MA, 1975.

S2. Shaheen, E. I.: *Basic Practice of Chemical Engineering,* 2d ed., International Institute of Technology, Joplin, MO, 1983.

S3. Smith, J. M., and H. C. Van Ness: *Introduction to Chemical Engineering Thermodynamics,* 4d ed., McGraw-Hill, New York, 1987.

S4. Sonntag, R. E., and G. J. Van Wylen: *Introduction to Thermodynamics*: *Classical and Statistical,* 2d ed., Wiley, New York, 1982.

S5. Shames, I. H.: *Mechanics of Fluids,* 2d ed., McGraw-Hill, New York, 1982.

W1. Wall, F. T.: *Chemical Thermodynamics,* 3d ed., Freeman, San Francisco, CA, 1974.

W2. Whitaker, S.: *Introduction to Fluid Mechanics,* Prentice-Hall, Englewood Cliffs, NJ, 1968.

W3. *Ibid.,* p. 53.

METHODS OF
ANALYSIS

NOMENCLATURE

A   Species A

a Exponent

b Exponent

C Concentration (kmol m^{-3}, lb mol ft^{-3}); C_A, C_B, C_i are concentrations of species A, B, i

$\dot{C}_G$ Rate of generation of mass (kmol m^{-3} s^{-1}, lb mol ft^{-3} s^{-1})

c Exponent

c Velocity of sound in Problem 8.11 (m s^{-1})

c_p Heat capacity at constant pressure (kJ kg^{-1} K^{-1}, Btu lb$_m^{-1}$ °F^{-1})

D Diffusion coefficient (mass diffusivity) (m^2 s^{-1}, ft^2 s^{-1})

d Diameter or characteristic dimension (m, ft); d_o is inside diameter of pipe, as used in fluid flow; d_p is particle diameter

d Exponent

e Pipe roughness (m, ft); see Table 10.2 for more details

e Exponent

F Force or drag force (N, lb$_f$); F_μ, F_ρ, F_σ, and F_g represent viscous, inertial, surface, and gravitational forces, respectively, in Example 8.6

f Fanning friction factor, Eq. (6.89)

f	Exponent
G	Mass average velocity, ρU (kg m^{-2} s^{-1}, lb$_m$ ft^{-2} s^{-1})
$\mathbf{g}$	Vector representing the acceleration due to a gravitational or other field (m s^{-2}, ft s^{-2}); g is scalar magnitude of gravity, cf. Eq. (8.26)
g	Exponent
g_c	Gravitational conversion constant (32.174 lb$_m$ lb$_f^{-1}$ ft s^{-2})
h	Heat transfer coefficient, defined by Eq. (6.86) (W m^{-2} K^{-1}, Btu ft^{-2} h^{-1} °F^{-1})
h	A linear dimension (m, ft)
I	Sound intensity
j	Number of dimensions in Eq. (8.36)
k	Thermal conductivity (W m^{-1} K^{-1} or J m^{-1} K^{-1} s^{-1}, Btu ft^{-1} °R^{-1} s^{-1})
k	Number of dimensionless groups in the Buckingham-Pi method, Eq. (8.36)
k_c'	Equimolar mass transfer coefficient, defined by Eq. (6.87) [kmol m^{-2} s^{-1} (kmol m^{-3})$^{-1}$, lb mol ft^{-2} s^{-1} (lb mol ft^{-3})$^{-1}$]
k_n	Specific reaction rate constant in Eq. (4.108) or Eq. (6.45)
L	Length (m, ft); L is used as a characteristic length
L	Basic unit in dimensional analysis, length (m)
M	Basic unit in dimensional analysis, mass (kg)
$\dot{M}_G$	Rate of generation of momentum (kg m^{-2} s^{-2}, N m^{-3}, lb$_m$ ft^{-2} s^{-2}, lb$_f$ ft^{-3})
N	N represents a dimensionless number or group; Table 8.1 lists all dimensionless numbers in this text
N	Rate of rotation of impeller in Problem 8.12 (s^{-1})
n	Number of variables identified for analysis in Eq. (8.36)
n	Order of reaction, Eq. (4.108) or Eq. (6.45)
P	Power in Problem 8.12 (W)
p	Pressure (kPa, atm, lb$_f$ in.$^{-2}$)
Q	Volume rate of flow (m^3 s^{-1}, ft^3 s^{-1})
Q	Representation of variables identified for analysis; see Eq. (8.40)
q	Energy (heat) flow (J s^{-1}, Btu s^{-1})
s	Distance, cf. Eq. (8.26)
T	Temperature (K, °R, °C, °F)
T	Basic unit in dimensional analysis, temperature (K)
$\dot{T}_G$	Rate of generation of heat (J m^{-3} s^{-1}, Btu ft^{-3} s^{-1})
t	Time, cf. Eq. (8.26); $t_{relaxation}$ is the relaxation (or characteristic) time of the fluid; $t_{process}$ is the characteristic time of the process
U	Velocity (m s^{-1}, ft s^{-1}); U is used as a characteristic velocity
w	Subscript denoting wall
w	Weir width in Problem 8.13
x	Rectangular (Cartesian) coordinate
α	Thermal diffusivity (m^2 s^{-1}, ft^2 s^{-1})
α	Constant in Eq. (8.32); also α' is the reciprocal of α
β	Coefficient of expansion (K^{-1}, °R^{-1})

Δ	Difference, state 2 minus state 1; ΔT means $T_2 - T_1$
δ	Generalized diffusivity ($\text{m}^2\,\text{s}^{-1}$, $\text{ft}^2\,\text{s}^{-1}$)
η	Efficiency of removal in Problem 8.17 (dimensionless)
Θ	Basic unit in dimensional analysis, time (s)
μ	Viscosity ($\text{kg}\,\text{m}^{-1}\,\text{s}^{-1}$ or $\text{N}\,\text{m}^{-2}\,\text{s}$, $\text{lb}_{\text{m}}\,\text{ft}^{-1}\,\text{s}^{-1}$, cP); μ_w is viscosity at wall
ν	Kinematic viscosity (momentum diffusivity) ($\text{m}^2\,\text{s}^{-1}$, $\text{ft}^2\,\text{s}^{-1}$)
ξ	Generalized transport coefficients associated with h, f, k'_c, Eq. (6.90)
Π	Dimensionless groups in the pi theorem
π	Ratio of circumference of a circle to its diameter ($3.141\,592\,65\ldots$)
ρ	Density ($\text{kg}\,\text{m}^{-3}$, $\text{lb}_{\text{m}}\,\text{ft}^{-3}$); subscripts refer to species
σ	Surface tension ($\text{kg}\,\text{s}^{-2}$ or $\text{N}\,\text{m}^{-1}$, $\text{lb}_{\text{m}}\,\text{s}^{-2}$ or $\text{lb}_{\text{f}}\,\text{ft}^{-1}$)
τ	Momentum flux (or shear stress) tensor ($\text{N}\,\text{m}^{-2}$, $\text{lb}_{\text{f}}\,\text{ft}^{-2}$); τ_{xy}, τ_{yx}, etc., are components of the momentum flux tensor, where subscripts refer to direction of momentum transfer and direction of velocity; τ_w is shear stress at the wall
$\boldsymbol{\Psi}$	Generalized flux vector (e.g., units for heat flux are $\text{J}\,\text{m}^{-2}\,\text{s}^{-1}$ or $\text{W}\,\text{m}^{-2}$, $\text{Btu}\,\text{ft}^{-2}\,\text{s}^{-1}$; see Tables 2.1 and 3.1 for more details)
ψ	Generalized concentration of property (e.g., units for concentration of heat are $\text{J}\,\text{m}^{-3}$, $\text{Btu}\,\text{ft}^{-3}$; see Table 3.1 for complete listing)
$\dot{\psi}_{\text{G}}$	Generalized rate of generation of energy or mass or momentum in a unit volume (see Table 4.2 for units; e.g., for heat, units are $\text{J}\,\text{m}^{-3}\,\text{s}^{-1}$, $\text{Btu}\,\text{ft}^{-3}\,\text{s}^{-1}$)
$\boldsymbol{\nabla}$	Vector operator del, defined by Eq. (2.16) or Eq. (3.45) (m^{-1}, ft^{-1})
∇^2	Laplacian operator, defined by Eq. (3.64) (m^{-2}, ft^{-2})

The equations of the transport phenomena in laminar or turbulent flow as presented in the preceding chapters are, in general, so complex that in most practical cases exact solutions are impossible. In these situations relationships between variables must be established empirically rather than analytically. If there are many variables, as usually is the case, the resulting correlations in terms of any one variable are hopelessly complex; however, if variables are grouped in a logical manner, the correlations are considerably simplified. Experience has shown that dimensionless groups of variables are the most useful in correlating experimental data. This chapter will present general methods of analysis that establish dimensionless groups of variables such as the Reynolds number and friction factor that were discussed in Chapter 6.

The first step in dimensional analysis is to establish all the variables (such as velocity, tube diameter, density, viscosity, etc.) necessary to describe the transport phenomena being considered. When the governing differential equation is known, then obviously all the significant variables are present in that equation, which is then inspected and rearranged in the appropriate form. Sometimes the significant variables are discovered by deductive reasoning or experience with the process. Once all the variables are established, the dimensionless groups can be determined. The number of dimensionless groups is always less than the number of variables. Thus, the number of experiments to establish a correlation between dimensionless groups is correspondingly less than if each variable were considered in turn.

The use of dimensionless groups, also called numbers in engineering, is widespread, and because of this several extensive lists have been compiled. One [B1] lists the name of each group, the formula, significance, area of use (fluid mechanics, heat transfer, mass transfer, and chemical reactions), and source.

8.1 INSPECTION OF THE BASIC DIFFERENTIAL EQUATIONS

The general property balance for incompressible conditions and constant properties is Eq. (3.78):

$$\partial \psi / \partial t + (U \cdot \nabla)\psi = \dot{\psi}_G + \delta(\nabla^2 \psi) \tag{3.78}$$

Obviously each term in this equation has the same dimensions, regardless of which concentration of property is substituted for ψ. Therefore, the ratio between the various terms must be dimensionless and form some sort of dimensionless number or group.

A good starting point for dimensional analysis is to take the ratio of the convection term $(U \cdot \nabla)\psi$ to the molecular transport term $\delta(\nabla^2 \psi)$. As seen in Eq. (2.16), the operator ∇ is of the form $\partial / \partial x$ and must have units of reciprocal length. Let us replace the operator ∇ with $1/L$ (a reciprocal characteristic distance) and the velocity vector U with U, a characteristic velocity. Then the ratio of the terms $(U \cdot \nabla)\psi$ and $\delta(\nabla^2 \psi)$ in Eq. (3.78) becomes

$$\frac{(U \cdot \nabla)\psi}{\delta(\nabla^2 \psi)} = \frac{U\psi/L}{\delta\psi/L^2} = \frac{UL}{\delta} \tag{8.1}$$

The term UL/δ, where U and L are generalized in concept to signifiy a velocity and a length appropriate to the experiment, represents the ratio of the convection transport to the molecular transfer. This very important dimensionless number will be considered in turn for heat, mass, and momentum.

For momentum transfer, the diffusivity δ equals the kinematic viscosity v so that the term UL/δ becomes the Reynolds number, Eq. (6.1). With the definition of kinematic viscosity [cf. Eq. (2.12)], Eq. (8.1) becomes

$$N_{\text{Re}} = \frac{UL}{v} = \frac{LU\rho}{\mu} \tag{8.2}$$

The Reynolds number is the ratio of the convection to the molecular momentum transport; it is also often referred to as the ratio of the inertial to viscous forces. A low value of the Reynolds number means viscous forces (molecular transfer) are large when compared to inertial forces (convective transfer). This analysis is certainly consistent with the discussion on transition in Section 6.1.2.

The term UL/δ is equally important in heat transfer applications. When δ is replaced with the thermal diffusivity, Eq. (2.10), the term UL/δ becomes the Peclet number:

$$N_{\text{Pe}} = \frac{UL}{\alpha} = \frac{UL\rho c_{\text{p}}}{k} \tag{8.3}$$

The Peclet number is the ratio of the heat transported by convection to that transported by conduction. The Peclet number when divided by the Reynolds number results in the Prandtl number:

$$N_{\text{Pr}} = \frac{\nu}{\alpha} = \frac{c_{\text{p}}\mu}{k} \tag{8.4}$$

The Prandtl number depends only on the fluid properties.

A similar substitution $(\delta = D)$ for the case of mass transfer yields the mass transfer Peclet number:

$$N_{\text{Pe, mass}} = \frac{UL}{D} \tag{8.5}$$

The mass transfer Peclet number is the ratio of convective mass transfer to molecular mass transfer. If the Peclet number is divided by the Reynolds number, just as in the case of heat transfer, one obtains the Schmidt number:

$$N_{\text{Sc}} = \frac{\nu}{D} = \frac{\mu}{\rho D} \tag{8.6}$$

The Schmidt number is the ratio of momentum diffusivity to mass diffusivity; it is analogous to the Prandtl number and contains only fluid properties.

These five dimensionless numbers (N_{Re}, N_{Pe}, $N_{\text{Pe, mass}}$, N_{Pr}, and N_{Sc}) are of great importance in momentum, heat, and mass transfer. The first three represent the ratios of the convection to molecular transport of the property in question, and the remaining two involve the ratios of the diffusivities between pairs of the three transports. The ratio in N_{Pr} or in N_{Sc} is a measure of the relative magnitude of one transport to the other.

A similar analysis can be done between the terms $(\boldsymbol{U} \cdot \boldsymbol{\nabla})\psi$ and $\dot{\psi}_{\text{G}}$ of Eq. (3.78):

$$\frac{(\boldsymbol{U} \cdot \boldsymbol{\nabla})\psi}{\dot{\psi}_{\text{G}}} = \frac{U\psi/L}{\dot{\psi}_{\text{G}}} = \frac{U\psi}{L\dot{\psi}_{\text{G}}} \tag{8.7}$$

Thus, the term $(U\psi)/(L\dot{\psi}_{\text{G}})$ is a second important generalized dimensionless number. It represents the ratio of convection to generation.

For momentum transfer, the generation term is given by Eq. (4.54):

$$\dot{\boldsymbol{M}}_{\text{G}} = -\boldsymbol{\nabla}p + \rho\boldsymbol{g} \tag{4.54}$$

Since there are two terms in Eq. (4.54), there will be two dimensionless numbers formed. The first of these is the Euler[1] number:

$$\frac{U\psi}{L\dot{\psi}_G} = \frac{U\rho U}{L\dot{M}_G} = \frac{U\rho U}{L(p/L)} = \frac{\rho U^2}{p} = \frac{1}{N_{Eu}}$$

or

$$N_{Eu} = \frac{p}{\rho U^2} \tag{8.8}$$

Note that in this equation dp/dx was replaced with the simpler form p/L. The Euler number is the ratio of pressure to inertial forces or of momentum generated from pressure effects to momentum transfer by convection. The number is associated with the friction factor (Eq. 6.89), which will be considered in more detail in Chapter 10.

The second dimensionless number obtained from the ratio of the convection to generation terms in momentum transport yields

$$\frac{U\rho U}{L\dot{M}_G} = \frac{\rho U^2}{L\dot{M}_G} \tag{8.9}$$

which if restricted to the effect of gravity (ρg) gives the Froude number:

$$N_{Fr} = \frac{\rho U^2}{L\rho g} = \frac{U^2}{Lg} \tag{8.10}$$

The Froude number is the ratio of the convection to gravitational factors, and it is often referred to as the ratio of inertial to gravitational forces.

In the case of heat transfer, the term $(U\psi)/(L\dot{\psi}_G)$ becomes $(U\rho c_p T)/(L\dot{T}_G)$. In Chapter 4 the generation of heat was treated as a general term usually initiated from the outside; however, heat can be generated internally in the system owing to viscous dissipation, which for the one-dimensional case is

$$\dot{T}_G = -\tau_{yx}\frac{dU_x}{dy} = \mu(dU_x/dy)^2 \tag{8.11}$$

From a dimensional standpoint, this is equivalent to $\mu U^2/L^2$, and when combined with the term $(U\psi)/(L\dot{\psi}_G)$ Eq. (8.11) becomes

$$\frac{U\rho c_p T}{L\dot{T}_G} = \frac{U\rho c_p TL^2}{L\mu U^2} = \frac{\rho c_p TL}{\mu U} \tag{8.12}$$

This equation expresses the ratio of the heat transported by convection to that produced by viscous dissipation in the system. If Eq. (8.12) is divided into the

---

[1] Euler is pronounced as "oil-er".

Peclet number [Eq. (8.3)], the result is the Brinkman number:

$$N_{Br} = \frac{UL\rho c_p/k}{(\rho c_p TL)/(\mu U)} = \frac{\mu U^2}{kT} \tag{8.13}$$

The Brinkman number is the ratio of the heat produced by viscous dissipation to that transported by molecular conduction. The Brinkman number can also be obtained directly from the ratio between $\dot{\psi}_G$ and $\delta(\nabla^2 \psi)$:

$$\frac{\dot{\psi}_G}{\delta(\nabla^2 \psi)} = \frac{\dot{\psi}_G}{\delta\psi/L^2} = \frac{L^2\dot{\psi}_G}{\delta\psi} = \frac{L^2(\mu U^2/L^2)}{\alpha\rho c_p T} = \frac{\mu U^2}{kT} = N_{Br} \tag{8.14}$$

A high Brinkman number implies that heat produced by viscous dissipation is not easily conducted away.

In the case of mass transfer, the term $(U\psi)/(L\dot{\psi}_G)$ becomes $(UC_A)/(L\dot{C}_{A,G})$ where the rate of reaction $\dot{C}_{A,G}$ is given by Eq. (4.108):

$$\dot{C}_{A,G} = -k_n C_A^n \tag{4.108}$$

with n being the order of reaction and k_n the reaction rate constant. Equation (4.108) is used to replace $\dot{C}_{A,G}$, and the reciprocal is known as the first Damkohler number:

$$N_{Dm1} = \frac{Lk_n C_A^{n-1}}{U} \tag{8.15}$$

The first Damkohler number is the ratio of the chemical reaction rate to the rate of mass transfer by convection. Another dimensionless number, the second Damkohler number is formed by multiplying the first Damkohler number, Eq. (8.15), by the mass transfer Peclet number, Eq. (8.5), so as to eliminate velocity:

$$N_{Dm2} = \frac{L^2 k_n C_A^{n-1}}{D} \tag{8.16}$$

The second Damkohler number is the ratio of the chemical reaction rate to the rate of mass transfer by molecular diffusion. There are other Damkohler numbers in the literature [B1].

Finally, when a free surface is present, surface forces may be important. A good example is the surface force which must be overcome during the breakup of drops. The dimensionless ratio of inertial to surface forces is the Weber number:

$$N_{We} = \frac{U^2 L\rho}{\sigma} \tag{8.17}$$

where σ is the surface tension in units of $kg\,s^{-2}$ or $N\,m^{-1}$. If the gravitational conversion constant g_c is included in the denominator of Eq. (8.17), then the surface tension σ has units of $lb_f\,ft^{-1}$.

In many cases with turbulent flow, the general balance equation, Eq.

(3.78), is replaced by the transfer equation given in general terms as Eq. (6.90) and repeated here:

$$\Psi_{r,w} = \xi(\bar{\psi}_w - \psi_{ave}) \tag{6.90}$$

Any transfer of flux Ψ at the wall must necessarily be by molecular means, since the no-slip boundary condition means zero velocity. In addition, the transfer must be in the direction normal to the wall; i.e., only the radial component (not $\partial\psi/\partial\theta$ or $\partial\psi/\partial z$) can cause a flux towards or away from the wall:

$$\Psi_{r,w} = -\delta(\partial\bar{\psi}/\partial r)_w \tag{8.18}$$

Equating Eqs. (6.90) and (8.18) gives

$$\xi(\bar{\psi}_w - \psi_{ave}) = -\delta(\partial\bar{\psi}/\partial r)_w \tag{8.19}$$

A dimensionless group is formed by dividing one side of Eq. (8.19) by the other

$$\frac{\xi(\bar{\psi}_w - \psi_{ave})}{\delta(\partial\bar{\psi}/\partial r)_w} = \frac{\xi\psi}{\delta\psi/L} = \frac{\xi L}{\delta} \tag{8.20}$$

The term $\xi L/\delta$ represents the ratio of total transfer by all mechanisms (including turbulence) to molecular transfer, a concept discussed in great detail in conjunction with eddy viscosity in Section 6.3.

For heat transfer the term $\xi L/\delta$ becomes the Nusselt number with the aid of Eqs. (6.91) and (2.10):

$$\xi L/\delta = \xi_H L/\alpha = \frac{(h/\rho c_p)(L)}{k/(\rho c_p)} = \frac{hL}{k} = N_{Nu} \tag{8.21}$$

where again L is a characteristic length. The Nusselt number is the ratio of convective heat transfer to molecular heat transfer. It is widely used in the correlation of heat transfer data. In pipe flow, the characteristic length L becomes the inside pipe diameter d_o.

For mass transfer, the corresponding number derived from Eq. (8.20) is the Sherwood number:

$$N_{Sh} = \frac{k_c' L}{D} \tag{8.22}$$

The Sherwood number (also called the Nusselt number for mass transfer) is equally important in mass transfer correlations. If Eq. (6.93) for the fluid flow transfer coefficient is substituted into the group $\xi L/\delta$, the result is

$$\frac{(fU/2)L}{v} = \frac{UL}{v}\frac{f}{2} = N_{Re}\frac{f}{2} \tag{8.23}$$

where f is the Fanning friction factor, Eq. (6.89). Equation (8.23) yields no new dimensionless groups. Note the similarity between Eq. (8.23) and the von Karman correlation equation for turbulent friction factors, Eq. (6.132).

Other dimensionless numbers can be generated at will, since any combination of one or more dimensionless numbers results in a new dimensionless number. Thus, it is common to find in the literature other numbers that may simply be the square roots of some of those cited here or other simple combinations. One of the most important of these for heat transfer is the Stanton number:

$$N_{St} = \frac{N_{Nu}}{N_{Re}N_{Pr}} = \frac{Lh/k}{(LU\rho/\mu)(c_p\mu/k)} = \frac{h}{\rho c_p U} \tag{8.24}$$

One final number of importance in heat transfer by natural convection is the Grashof number:

$$N_{Gr} = \frac{L^3\rho^2 g\beta\Delta T}{\mu^2} \tag{8.25}$$

The Grashof number is obtained by dimensional analysis, as the reader may verify for himself or herself in Problem 8.16 at the end of this chapter. The term β is the coefficient of expansion or thermal fluid expansion; the units of β are reciprocal temperature difference.

The various dimensionless groups just introduced are summarized in Table 8.1. Included are other groups that are sometimes encountered. Complete lists are available elsewhere [B1, L1, M1, P1].

8.2   DIMENSIONAL ANALYSIS

The first step in dimensional analysis is to establish all the variables; the second step is to arrange these in dimensionless groups. The various procedures for the second step of dimensional analysis are mathematically rigorous [L1]. Furthermore, these procedures are easily double-checked by inspection of units in the final result. Great care must be taken to include all the variables in the analysis, for there is no way to prove whether or not all the variables have been included. The validity of those variables that are important must be decided on the basis of considerable experimental knowledge. Gross errors in the final dimensionless numbers result either when extraneous variables are included or when important variables are omitted.

Dimensional analysis is based on the requirement of dimensional homogeneity, which must exist between variables descriptive of a given system. A minimum number of fundamental dimensions or units is used, and all other dimensions are related to these. Dimensional analysis can be used without a knowledge of the controlling equations, so long as all governing variables are included in the analysis. The selection of a set of fundamental units is arbitrary. A convenient set includes length, time, mass, and temperature. In the SI system of units, the basic units are length (L) in meters, mass (M) in kilograms, time (Θ) in seconds, temperature (T) in kelvins, electric current in amperes, light intensity in candela, and molecular substance in

TABLE 8.1
Summary of dimensionless numbers

(A) General number: UL/δ

Symbol	Name	Variables	Eq. No.	Description or usage
General number		UL/δ	(8.1)	convective to molecular transport
N_{Re}	Reynolds	$UL\rho/\mu$	(8.2)	inertial to viscous forces or convective to molecular momentum transfer
N_{Pe}	Peclet	$UL\rho c_p/k$	(8.3)	convective to molecular conductive heat transfer
N_{Pr}	Prandtl	$c_p\mu/k$	(8.4)	momentum to thermal diffusivity
$N_{Pe,\,mass}$	Peclet, mass	UL/D	(8.5)	convective to molecular mass transfer
N_{Sc}	Schmidt	$\mu/(\rho D)$	(8.6)	momentum to mass diffusivity
N_{Le}	Lewis	$k/(\rho c_p D)$	—	thermal to mass diffusivity; also, ratio of Schmidt to Prandtl number

(B) General number: $(U\psi)/(L\dot{\psi}_G)$

Symbol	Name	Variables	Eq. No.	Description or usage
General number		$(U\psi)/(L\dot{\psi}_G)$	(8.7)	convective transport to generation
N_{Eu}	Euler	$p/(\rho U^2)$	(8.8)	pressure to inertial forces or momentum generation to convective momentum transfer
N_{Fr}	Froude	$U^2/(Lg)$	(8.10)	inertial to gravitational forces or convective momentum transfer to gravitational momentum transfer
—	—	$(\rho c_p TL)/(\mu U)$	(8.12)	convective heat transfer to viscous dissipation heat generation

N_{Br}	Brinkman	$(\mu U^2)/(kT)$	(8.13)	viscous dissipation heat generation to molecular conductive heat transfer
N_{Dm1}	Damkohler 1	$L k_n C_A^{n-1}/U$	(8.15)	chemical reaction generation to convective mass transfer
N_{Dm2}	Damkohler 2	$L^2 k_n C_A^{n-1}/D$	(8.16)	chemical reaction generation to molecular diffusion mass transfer
N_{We}	Weber	$U^2 L\rho/\sigma$	(8.17)	inertial to surface forces

(C) General number:* $\xi L/\delta$

General number		$\xi L/\delta$	(8.20)	total transfer to molecular transfer
N_{Nu}	Nusselt	hL/k	(8.21)	total heat transfer to molecular heat transfer
N_{Sh}	Sherwood	$k'_\xi L/D$	(8.22)	total mass transfer to molecular mass transfer
f	Fanning friction factor	$\tau_w/(\rho U^2/2)$ $= [(d_o \Delta p)/(4L)]/(\rho U^2/2)$	(6.89)	shear stress at the wall to the kinetic energy of flow
N_{St}	Stanton	$h/(\rho c_p U)$	(8.24)	total heat transferred to total heat capacity: $N_{St}=N_{Nu}/(N_{Re}N_{Pr})$
$N_{St,\,mass}$	Stanton	$k_{L,\,ave}/U_{z,\,ave}$	(11.81)	$N_{St,\,mass}=N_{Sh}/(N_{Re}N_{Sc})$

(D) Miscellaneous numbers†

N_{Ar}	Archimedes	$(\rho_p - \rho)(\rho g d_p^3)/\mu^2$	(12.89)	fluidization
N_{Bi}	Biot	hL/k	(13.16)	unsteady-state heat conduction
N_b	blend	Nt	(9.10)	agitation
j_H	Colburn heat	$(N_{St})(N_{Pr})^{2/3}$	(11.79)	Colburn factor for heat transfer analogy
j_M	Colburn mass	$(N_{St,\,mass})(N_{Sc})^{2/3}$	(11.81)	Colburn factor for mass transfer: $f/2 = j_H = j_M$

* The groups f, N_{St}, and $N_{St,\,mass}$ are derived from the general number $\xi L/\delta$.
† There are several symbols in this table that are not used elsewhere in the text. See references at the end of the chapter for more details [B1, L1, M1, P1].

TABLE 8.1 (Continued)
Summary of dimensionless numbers

(D) Miscellaneous numbers (Continued)

Symbol	Name	Variables	Eq. No.	Description or usage
N_{co}	condensation	$(h/k)[\mu^2/(\rho^2 g)]^{1/3}$	—	condensation
N_{Dn}	Dean	$N_{Re}(d_o/d_c)^{1/2}$	(10.20)	flow in curved tubes
N_{De}	Deborah	$t_{fluid}/t_{process}$	(15.18)	flow of elastic fluids
C_D	drag coefficient	$2F/(\rho U^2 A)$	(12.15)	flow past immersed bodies
N_{Fo}	Fourier	$\alpha t/L^2$	—	nondimensional time parameter
N_{Gr}	Graetz	$(w c_p)/(kL)$	—	heat transfer, laminar forced convection
N_{Gr}	Grashof	$(L^3 \rho^2 g \beta)(\Delta T)/\mu^2$	(8.25)	Reynolds number times the ratio of buoyancy force to viscous force (natural convection heat transfer)
N_{Kn}	Knudsen	λ/L	(5.75)	flow of gases at low pressure
N_{Ma}	Mach	U/c	—	flow above the speed of sound
N_{po}	power	$P/(\rho N^3 d_i^5)$	(9.8)	agitation
N_p	pumping	$Q/(ND^3)$	(9.11)	agitation
N_{Sl}	Strouhal	$f'L/U$	—	periodic flows
N_{VK}	von Karman	$N_{Re}(f)^{0.5}$	(10.13)	eliminates velocity in correlations for Δp

kmol. For most problems of interest in the transport phenomena, the basic units involve only $LM\Theta T$, and these are the simplest to use. All other derived units are expressed in terms of these basic units. Other units may be added if desired; e.g., the force (F) in newtons.

8.2.1 Rayleigh Method of Analysis

There are several essentially equivalent procedures that can be used to determine dimensionless numbers. One of the most straightforward is the Rayleigh method, which will be illustrated by a simple example. A great number of experiments have measured both the time and distance of fall of various objects in a vacuum under the influence of gravity. Experimental knowledge has indicated that the distance of fall, time of fall, and gravity are the only variables of importance. These are summarized in Table 8.2.

Let each variable $(s, t,$ and $g)$ be raised to an as-yet-unknown power, a, b, and c, respectively. If all the variables raised to the appropriate power are multiplied together and placed on the left-hand side of the equation, then this grouping of variables must be equal to a constant that will have no dimensions:

$$s^a t^b g^c = \text{constant} \tag{8.26}$$

If the dimensions raised to the power indicated in the previous equation are substituted, the result is

$$L^a \Theta^b L^c \Theta^{-2c} = \text{dimensionless} \tag{8.27}$$

If this equation is to have no dimensions on the left-hand side, then the sum of the power on any given dimension must be zero; therefore

$$
\begin{aligned}
L: & \quad a + c = 0 \\
\Theta: & \quad b - 2c = 0
\end{aligned}
\tag{8.28}
$$

There are in these two equations three unknowns, which correspond to the original three variables being considered. The solution to Eq. (8.28) requires that either a, b, or c be arbitrarily assigned. For example, one method is to select a single variable and write the other two in terms of it. The obvious choice in Eq. (8.28) is c, since neither a nor b appears in both equations. Then

$$
\begin{aligned}
a &= -c \\
b &= 2c
\end{aligned}
\tag{8.29}
$$

TABLE 8.2
Variables in a gravity experiment

Symbol	Exponent	Name	SI Units	Dimensions
s	a	distance	m	L
t	b	time	s	Θ
g	c	gravity	$m\,s^{-2}$	$L\theta^{-2}$

which when combined with Eq. (8.26) gives

$$s^{-c}t^{2c}g^c = \text{constant} \tag{8.30}$$

The constant in Eq. (8.30) is dimensionless because a, b, and c in Eq. (8.28) were so chosen. If both sides of Eq. (8.30) are raised to the reciprocal c power, the resulting constant, now called α', is also dimensionless:

$$t^2g/s = \alpha' \tag{8.31}$$

or

$$s = \alpha g t^2 \tag{8.32}$$

where α is the reciprocal of α'. Equation (8.32) is recognized as the result obtained by Galileo.

The solution leading up to Eq. (8.32) is equivalent to assigning a value of 1 to c. Then from Eq. (8.29) a is -1 and b is 2. The dimensionless group in Eq. (8.31) results. If c were assigned a value of 2, then the dimensionless group t^4g^2/s^2 is obtained. In this simple problem there were three variables and two independent equations, Eq. (8.29). Therefore, it follows that one dimensionless group can be formed. In general, the number of dimensionless numbers or groupings of variables that are required equals the number of variables considered less the number of *independent* equations available. At this point, the word independent is stressed; later in this chapter, an example will be given where not all the equations [obtained here as Eq. (8.28)] are independent.

Equation (8.32) is correct only if the object were dropped in a vacuum. If Galileo had dropped a feather and a steel ball from the Leaning Tower of Pisa, the results would not follow Eq. (8.32). If the vacuum restrictions mentioned at the beginning of the example were removed, the list of variables is greatly expanded to include such things as the drag of the air and the weight and shape of the object. This point illustrates the danger in omitting important variables from consideration when using dimensional analysis. From physics, the proportionality constant α in Eq. (8.32) is exactly $\frac{1}{2}$. Dimensional analysis finds the single dimensionless number that relates the three variables, but cannot establish the value of the constant α or whether c should be assigned one or two, or whatever.

A simple variation of the Rayleigh procedure is to write Eq. (8.26) as

$$s = \alpha t^a g^b \tag{8.33}$$

where α is a dimensionless proportionality constant. Equation (8.27) becomes

$$L = \alpha \Theta^a (L\Theta^{-2})^b \tag{8.34}$$

Equation (8.28) becomes

$$\begin{aligned} L: &\quad 1 = b \\ \Theta: &\quad 0 = a - 2b \end{aligned} \tag{8.35}$$

Solving these gives $b = 1$ and $a = 2$. For this alternate procedure, the number of dimensionless numbers is 1 plus the difference between the number of unknowns and the independent equations available; i.e., $1 + 2 - 2 = 1$. Placing these values back into Eq. (8.33) gives Eq. (8.32):

$$s = \alpha g t^2 \qquad (8.32)$$

Either procedure is satisfactory; the same result is always obtained.

Practically all problems have more variables than the three in the Galileo experiment. In this relatively unique example, the actual form of the equation was established. Because there is only one dimensionless number, the power is known. Of much more practical interest are those problems using or involving many more variables; as an example of this, the problem of the flow of fluid in a pipe is used in the next example. Afterwards, an example suggested by McAdams [M1] will be worked by the alternate procedure [Eq. (8.33)].

Example 8.1. The flow of fluid in a pipe has been studied experimentally, and it has been determined that the variables of importance are the following: velocity, pressure drop, density, viscosity, diameter, length, and roughness of the wall. Determine the necessary dimensionless numbers.

Answer. A tabulation of the variables is in Table 8.3. Each variable in Table 8.3 is raised to an exponent, as was done previously in Eq. (8.26). The product of these will be dimensionless if the exponents a through g are chosen according to the Rayleigh procedure. First, the following product is formed:

$$U^a p^b \rho^c \mu^d d_o^e L^f e^g = \text{constant} \qquad (i)$$

Dimensions from Table 8.3 are substituted into Eq. (i), in a manner similar to that used in obtaining Eq. (8.28):

$$L^a \Theta^{-a} M^b L^{-b} \Theta^{-2b} M^c L^{-3c} M^d L^{-d} \Theta^{-d} L^e L^f L^g = \text{dimensionless} \qquad (ii)$$

Equation (ii) will be dimensionless only if the sum of the power on any given dimension is zero:

$$L: \qquad a - b - 3c - d + e + f + g = 0 \qquad (iii)$$

$$M: \qquad b + c + d = 0 \qquad (iv)$$

$$\Theta: \qquad -a - 2b - d = 0 \qquad (v)$$

TABLE 8.3
Variables in pipe flow

Symbol	Exponent	Name	SI Units	Dimensions
U	a	velocity	m s^{-1}	$L\Theta^{-1}$
p	b	pressure	$\text{kg m}^{-1}\text{s}^{-2}$ (N m^{-2})	$ML^{-1}\Theta^{-2}$
ρ	c	density	kg m^{-3}	ML^{-3}
μ	d	viscosity	$\text{kg m}^{-1}\text{s}^{-1}$	$ML^{-1}\Theta^{-1}$
d_o	e	diameter	m	L
L	f	length	m	L
e	g	roughness	m	L

There are seven unknowns (a through g) and three equations, a fact which suggests that four groups are needed. Equations (iii) through (v) can be solved in terms of any four of the unknowns. Any of the unknown variables that is selected will appear only once. Let us select b, d, f, and g. Equation (v) can be solved for a:

$$a = -2b - d \tag{vi}$$

From Eq. (iv):

$$c = -b - d \tag{vii}$$

From Eq. (iii):

$$
\begin{aligned}
e &= -a + b + 3c + d - f - g \\
&= 2b + d + b - 3b - 3d + d - f - g \\
&= -d - f - g
\end{aligned}
\tag{viii}
$$

All the powers are now evaluated, and Eq. (i) becomes

$$p^b U^{-2b-d} \rho^{-b-d} \mu^d d_o^{-d-f-g} L^f e^g = \text{constant} \tag{ix}$$

In Eq. (ix), the variables are grouped according to exponent:

$$\left(\frac{p}{U^2 \rho}\right)^b \left(\frac{\mu}{U \rho d_o}\right)^d \left(\frac{L}{d_o}\right)^f \left(\frac{e}{d_o}\right)^g = \text{constant} \tag{x}$$

The first group of variables is the Euler number, the second is the reciprocal of the Reynolds number, and the third and fourth are geometric ratios. These and other numbers are summarized in Table 8.1. Dimensional analysis provides no further clues to the application of Eq. (x). Experimental data are required to establish the powers or the value of the constant. In practice, it turns out that f equals $-b$, so that the first and third groups can be combined:

$$\frac{p d_o}{U^2 \rho L} = 2f \tag{xi}$$

where f in this equation is the Fanning friction factor, Eq. (6.89), and is not to be confused with the use of f as one of the exponents. It must be emphasized that the combination of groups b and f is based on experimental evidence and not on dimensional analysis.

Example 8.2. The heat transfer coefficient h has been found to depend on the velocity, density, heat capacity, viscosity, thermal conductivity, and diameter of a rod in a specific experiment. Determine the necessary dimensionless numbers.

Answer. A tabulation of the variables is given in Table 8.4.

A common variation of the Rayleigh method will be illustrated here; this solution uses one less exponent than in Example 8.1. The units of h can be obtained from the defiining equation:

$$(q/A)_w = h(\bar{T}_w - T_{\text{ave}}) \tag{6.86}$$

Equation (6.86) rearranges to the following:

$$h = \frac{(q/A)_w}{(\bar{T}_w - T_{\text{ave}})} \left(\frac{\text{J m}^{-2}\,\text{s}^{-1}}{\text{K}}\right) = \text{J s}^{-1}\,\text{m}^{-2}\,\text{K}^{-1} \tag{i}$$

TABLE 8.4
Variables for the heat transfer coefficient

Symbol	Exponent	Name	SI Units	Dimensions
h	—	heat transfer coefficient	$J s^{-1} m^{-2} K^{-1}$ or $kg s^{-3} K^{-1}$	$M\Theta^{-3}T^{-1}$
U	a	velocity	$m s^{-1}$	$L\Theta^{-1}$
ρ	b	density	$kg m^{-3}$	ML^{-3}
c_p	c	heat capacity	$J kg^{-1} K^{-1}$ or $m^2 s^{-2} K^{-1}$	$L^2\Theta^{-2}T^{-1}$
μ	d	viscosity	$kg m^{-1} s^{-1}$	$ML^{-1}\Theta^{-1}$
k	e	thermal conductivity	$J s^{-1} m^{-1} K^{-1}$ or $kg m s^{-3} K^{-1}$	$ML\Theta^{-3}T^{-1}$
d_o	f	diameter	m	L

Now, one joule (J) is one $kg\,m^2\,s^{-2}$; therefore the units of h are

$$h [=] J s^{-1} m^{-2} K^{-1} = (kg\,m^2\,s^{-2})(s^{-1}\,m^{-2}\,K^{-1}) = kg\,s^{-3}\,K^{-1} \tag{ii}$$

For heat capacity the units are

$$c_p [=] J\,kg^{-1}\,K^{-1} = (kg\,m^2\,s^{-2})(kg^{-1}\,K^{-1}) = m^2\,s^{-2}\,K^{-1} \tag{iii}$$

For thermal conductivity, the units are found from Fourier's law:

$$(q/A)_x = -k\frac{\partial T}{\partial x} \tag{iv}$$

The result is

$$k [=] (J\,m^{-2}\,s^{-1})(m\,K^{-1}) = kg\,m\,s^{-3}\,K^{-1} \tag{v}$$

Now that the units have been established for all quantities in Table 8.4, the solution of this problem follows the development of Eq. (8.33)ff. The heat transfer coefficient is given by the following general expression:

$$h = \alpha U^a \rho^b c_p^c \mu^d k^e d_o^f \tag{vi}$$

Next, the units are substituted into the above:

$$M\Theta^{-3}T^{-1} = \alpha(L\Theta^{-1})^a(ML^{-3})^b(L^2\Theta^{-2}T^{-1})^c(ML^{-1}\Theta^{-1})^d(ML\Theta^{-3}T^{-1})^e(L)^f \tag{vii}$$

The exponents on each unit are collected as follows:

$$L: \qquad 0 = a - 3b + 2c - d + e + f \tag{viii}$$

$$M: \qquad 1 = b + d + e \tag{ix}$$

$$\Theta: \qquad -3 = -a - 2c - d - 3e \tag{x}$$

$$T: \qquad -1 = -c - e \tag{xi}$$

These four equations contain six unknowns, and for this procedure the number of groups is $(1 + 6 - 4)$ or three dimensionless groups of variables, if all four equations are independent. Let us proceed to solve in terms of a and c, which will then appear only once. Recall that two exponents are sufficient to eliminate the other exponents since there are six exponents and four equations $(6-4)$. The exponent e is eliminated using Eq. (xi):

$$e = 1 - c \tag{xii}$$

From Eq. (x):

$$d = 3 - a - 2c - 3e = 3 - a - 2c - 3 + 3c = c - a \tag{xiii}$$

From Eq. (ix):

$$b = 1 - d - e = 1 - c + a - 1 + c = a \tag{xiv}$$

From Eq. (viii):

$$f = -a + 3b - 2c + d - e = -a + 3a - 2c + c - a - 1 + c = a - 1 \tag{xv}$$

When all of these results are substituted into Eq. (vi), the result is

$$h = \alpha U^a \rho^a c_p^c \mu^c \mu^{-a} k k^{-c} d_o^a d_o^{-1} \tag{xvi}$$

Equation (xvi) rearranges as follows:

$$h d_o / k = \alpha (d_o U \rho / \mu)^a (c_p \mu / k)^c \tag{xvii}$$

In terms of the dimensionless numbers of Table 8.1, Eq. (xvii) becomes

$$N_{\text{Nu}} = \alpha N_{\text{Re}}^a N_{\text{Pr}}^c \tag{xviii}$$

Example 8.3. Repeat Example 8.2 with the density and velocity combined into the mass average velocity, since in Eq. (xvii) of Example 8.2 the product ρU occurs, which is the mass average velocity G.

Answer. A tabulation of the variables is given in Table 8.5.

Here the original Rayleigh procedure is used. The equations are

$$h^a G^b c_p^c \mu^d k^e d_o^f = \text{constant} \tag{i}$$

TABLE 8.5
Variables for Example 8.3

Symbol	Exponent	Name	SI Units	Dimensions
h	a	heat transfer coefficient	$\text{J s}^{-1}\,\text{m}^{-2}\,\text{K}^{-1}$ or $\text{kg s}^{-3}\,\text{K}^{-1}$	$M\Theta^{-3}T^{-1}$
G	b	mass average velocity	$\text{kg m}^{-2}\,\text{s}^{-1}$	$ML^{-2}\Theta^{-1}$
c_p	c	heat capacity	$\text{J kg}^{-1}\,\text{K}^{-1}$ or $\text{m}^2\,\text{s}^{-2}\,\text{K}^{-1}$	$L^2\Theta^{-2}T^{-1}$
μ	d	viscosity	$\text{kg m}^{-1}\,\text{s}^{-1}$	$ML^{-1}\Theta^{-1}$
k	e	thermal conductivity	$\text{J s}^{-1}\,\text{m}^{-1}\,\text{K}^{-1}$ or $\text{kg m s}^{-3}\,\text{K}^{-1}$	$ML\Theta^{-3}T^{-1}$
d_o	f	diameter	m	L

and

$$M^a\Theta^{-3a}T^{-a}M^bL^{-2b}\Theta^{-b}L^{2c}\Theta^{-2c}T^{-c}M^dL^{-d}\Theta^{-d}M^eL^e\Theta^{-3e}T^{-e}L^f = \text{dimensionless}$$

(ii)

Therefore:

$$M: \qquad a + b + d + e = 0 \tag{iii}$$

$$\Theta: \qquad -3a - b - 2c - d - 3e = 0 \tag{iv}$$

$$L: \qquad -2b + 2c - d + e + f = 0 \tag{v}$$

$$T: \qquad -a - c - e = 0 \tag{vi}$$

The number of dimensionless groups of variables appears to be $6 - 4$ or 2 by this procedure. Let us proceed on this basis, and solve in terms of a and c. Beginning with Eq. (vi), the exponent e is

$$e = -a - c \tag{vii}$$

From Eq. (iii):

$$b + d = -a - e = -a + a + c = c \tag{viii}$$

From Eq. (iv):

$$b + d = -3a - 2c - 3e = -3a - 2c + 3a + 3c = c \tag{ix}$$

Note that Eqs. (viii) and (ix) are identical and therefore so are Eqs. (iii) and (iv). These are clearly not independent, and one must be eliminated in the analysis.

In the correct solution to this problem, there are three independent equations. Equation (iv) will be eliminated. Thus, the final result will be in terms of three dimensionless groups of variables. Let us now solve in terms of a, b, and c. Equation (vii) still is valid. Equation (iii) or (viii) can be rearranged as

$$d = -b + c \tag{x}$$

Now, Eq. (v) gives

$$f = 2b - 2c + d - e = 2b - 2c - b + c + a + c = b + a \tag{xi}$$

All powers are now evaluated, and Eq. (i) becomes

$$\left(\frac{hd_o}{k}\right)^a \left(\frac{Gd_o}{\mu}\right)^b \left(\frac{c_p\mu}{k}\right)^c = \text{constant} \tag{xii}$$

or

$$N_{Nu}^a N_{Re}^b N_{Pr}^c = \text{constant} \tag{xiii}$$

This equation is equivalent to the last equation in the preceding example. It is very important to ascertain the number of independent equations correctly, as this example illustrates.

Sometimes a solution by dimensional analysis is not possible. If G were to replace ρ and U in Example 8.1, no solution would exist, because ρ and U do not always occur together.

Example 8.4. Repeat Example 8.1 with G replacing ρ and U.

Answer. A tabulation of the variables is given in Table 8.6.

TABLE 8.6
Variables for Example 8.4

Symbol	Exponent	Name	SI Units	Dimensions
G	a	mass average velocity	$\mathrm{kg\,m^{-2}\,s^{-1}}$	$ML^{-2}\Theta^{-1}$
p	b	pressure	$\mathrm{kg\,m^{-1}\,s^{-2}}$ $(\mathrm{N\,m^{-2}})$	$ML^{-1}\Theta^{-2}$
μ	c	viscosity	$\mathrm{kg\,m^{-1}\,s^{-1}}$	$ML^{-1}\Theta^{-1}$
d_o	d	diameter	m	L
L	e	length	m	L
e	f	roughness	m	L

The same procedure will be followed as in Example 8.1:

$$L: \quad -2a - b - c + d + e + f = 0 \tag{i}$$

$$M: \quad a + b + c = 0 \tag{ii}$$

$$\Theta: \quad -a - 2b - c = 0 \tag{iii}$$

From Eq. (ii):

$$a + c = -b \tag{iv}$$

From Eq. (iii):

$$a + c = -2b \tag{v}$$

Equations (iv) and (v) are clearly inconsistent. The correct conclusion is that the required dimensionless numbers cannot be obtained.

8.2.2   Buckingham Method

The Buckingham method, sometimes called the Buckingham pi theorem [L1] or the pi theorem [M1], is still another procedure to accomplish the same result of obtaining a proper set of dimensionless numbers. The so-called "pi theorem" states that the number of dimensionless groups obtained (k) is in general equal to the difference between the number of variables identified for analysis (n) and the number of dimensions (j):

$$k = n - j \tag{8.36}$$

Actually, the pi theorem is an extension of the discussion that follows Eq. (8.32). In the paragraph following Eq. (8.32) it was pointed out that the number of dimensionless groups equals the number of variables less the number of independent equations. Examples 8.1 and 8.2 illustrate that the number of independent equations usually equals the number of dimensions; hence the pi theorem follows directly. The exception to the pi theorem is a problem such as Example 8.3, in which the number of dimensionless groups exceeds the difference between the number of variables and the number of dimensions, since the exponent equations for M and Θ were identical and not independent. In such a case:

$$k > n - j \tag{8.37}$$

The Buckingham method is usually restricted to geometrically similar systems. Let $Q_1 \ldots Q_n$ be the n variables identified for analysis. Let Π_i be the symbol for each dimensionless number composed of $Q_1 \ldots Q_n$ variables. These dimensionless numbers may be combined in a general way so that the functional relationship is dimensionally homogeneous:

$$f(\Pi_1 \ldots \Pi_k) = 0 \tag{8.38}$$

Such a dimensionless equation was illustrated in Example 8.1 by Eq. (x):

$$\left(\frac{p}{U^2\rho}\right)^b \left(\frac{\mu}{U\rho d_o}\right)^d \left(\frac{L}{d_o}\right)^f \left(\frac{e}{d_o}\right)^g = \text{constant} \tag{8.39}$$

Now each dimensionless group in Eq. (8.38) must consist of

$$\Pi_1 = Q_1^{a_1} Q_2^{b_1} \ldots Q_j^{j_1} Q_{j+1}$$
$$\Pi_2 = Q_1^{a_2} Q_2^{b_2} \ldots Q_j^{j_2} Q_{j+2}$$
$$\vdots$$
$$\Pi_k = Q_1^{a_k} Q_2^{b_k} \ldots Q_j^{j_k} Q_{j+k} \tag{8.40}$$

where the exponents on the variables are chosen so each Π_i is dimensionless, as was done in the Rayleigh method.

The following example illustrates the Buckingham method for the heat transfer problem previously investigated.

Example 8.5. Solve Example 8.2 by the Buckingham method.

Answer. A tabulation of the variables and units is given in Table 8.4 in Example 8.2 and will not be repeated here. In this problem

$$h = f(U, \rho, c_p, \mu, k, d_o) \tag{i}$$

In Table 8.4, four dimensions are noted, L, M, Θ, and T, which suggest four possible equations. Therefore j is 4, n is 7, and from Eq. (8.36) k is 3. Thus, the pi theorem states that three dimensionless groups, Π_1, Π_2, and Π_3 are required. Equation (8.38) becomes

$$f(\Pi_1, \Pi_2, \Pi_3) = 0 \tag{ii}$$

if all four possible equations are independent.

The next step in the Buckingham method is to examine Table 8.4 to locate j variables, which when taken together contain all the fundamental dimensions. Sometimes there are more than j variables available, in which case the selection of those to appear in each dimensionless group is arbitrary. From Table 8.4, d_o, μ, ρ and k are selected to appear in all Π_i. Now according to Eq. (8.40), each Π_i is a combination of these variables plus one other from the remaining three (h,

c_p, and U); i.e.

$$\Pi_1 = d_o^a \mu^b \rho^c k^d h^e \tag{iii}$$

$$\Pi_2 = d_o^a \mu^b \rho^c k^d c_p^e \tag{iv}$$

$$\Pi_3 = d_o^a \mu^b \rho^c k^d U^e \tag{v}$$

At this point the solution proceeds like the Rayleigh method described previously. Dimensions from Table 8.4 are substituted into each of Eq. (iii) through Eq. (v). For Π_1, Eq. (iii) becomes

$$L^a M^b L^{-b} \Theta^{-b} M^c L^{-3c} M^d L^d \Theta^{-3d} T^{-d} M^e \Theta^{-3e} T^{-e} = \text{dimensionless} \tag{vi}$$

The equations are

$$L: \qquad 0 = a - b - 3c + d \tag{vii}$$

$$\Theta: \qquad 0 = -b - 3d - 3e \tag{viii}$$

$$M: \qquad 0 = b + c + d + e \tag{ix}$$

$$T: \qquad 0 = -d - e \tag{x}$$

These equations can be solved in terms of e. From Eq. (x)

$$d = -e \tag{xi}$$

From Eq. (viii):

$$b = -3d - 3e = 3e - 3e = 0 \tag{xii}$$

From Eq. (ix):

$$c = -b - d - e = e - e = 0 \tag{xiii}$$

From Eq. (vii):

$$a = b + 3c - d = -d = e \tag{xiv}$$

Thus

$$\Pi_1 = (hd_o/k)^e \tag{xv}$$

or from Eq. (8.21) for the Nusselt number:

$$\Pi_1 = (hd_o/k)^e = N_{Nu}^e \tag{xvi}$$

as obtained in Example 8.2.

The procedure is repeated for the next two Π's. The algebra in the Buckingham method is quite easy as only the last four units in Eq. (vi) change. The equations for Π_2 become

$$L: \qquad 0 = a - b - 3c + d + 2e \tag{xvii}$$

$$\Theta: \qquad 0 = -b - 3d - 2e \tag{xviii}$$

$$M: \qquad 0 = b + c + d \tag{xix}$$

$$T: \qquad 0 = -d - e \tag{xx}$$

Note that in these equations only the e terms change. Solving these in terms of e

gives

$$d = -e$$
$$b = -3d - 2e = 3e - 2e = e$$
$$c = -b - d = -e + e = 0 \tag{xxi}$$
$$a = b + 3c - d - 2e = e + e - 2e = 0$$

Thus

$$\Pi_2 = \left(\frac{c_p\mu}{k}\right)^e = N_{Pr}^e \tag{xxii}$$

For Π_3, one obtains

$$
\begin{array}{lll}
L: & 0 = a - b - 3c + d + e \\
\Theta: & 0 = -b - 3d - e \\
M: & 0 = b + c + d \\
T: & 0 = -d
\end{array}
\tag{xxiii}
$$

Solving these in terms of e gives

$$d = 0$$
$$b = -3d - e = -e$$
$$c = -b - d = -b = e \tag{xxiv}$$
$$a = b + 3c - d - e = -e + 3e - e = e$$

Thus

$$\Pi_3 = \left(\frac{d_o U\rho}{\mu}\right)^e = N_{Re}^e \tag{xxv}$$

Exactly the same result is obtained by the Rayleigh method as by the Buckingham method. Note that the selection of j variables to appear in each Π_i was not as crucial as it might have first appeared. In Π_1, both b and c were zero, and neither μ nor ρ appeared in the Nusselt number. Likewise, Π_2 dropped out d_o and ρ; Π_3 did not include k. However, the four variables selected must include all dimensions, or the method fails.

The Buckingham method is easily applied to Example 8.3 where the pi theorem does not hold, i.e., Eq. (8.37) where k will be 3, not 2. When k is first incorrectly chosen to be 2, as was done in Example 8.3, solution of the exponent equations will result in identical equations for two of the exponents. At this point the analysis will be repeated for $k = 3$, and the correct solution obtained.

Since the Rayleigh method and the Buckingham method are both mathematically rigorous and provide identical results with approximately the same amount of labor, selection of one method over the other is strictly a matter of personal preference. In fact, only one really needs to be mastered. Perhaps the Buckingham method is more confusing because of the selection of the j variables (four in the case of Example 8.5) which are to appear in each dimensionless group.

8.2.3   Completeness of Sets

Another means of obtaining the dimensionless numbers is by inspection and a knowledge of Table 8.1. For example, based on the results of Example 8.2 or Example 8.5, one might guess that h and k could go together as well as c_p and k (based on all of these having the units of joules in them). From Table 8.1, one would select

$$N_{Nu} = hd_o/k \quad \text{and} \quad N_{Pr} = c_p\mu/k \tag{8.41}$$

The variables that are left involve velocity and density, and one thinks of the Reynolds number:

$$N_{Re} = d_o U\rho/\mu \tag{6.2}$$

These three certainly are possible dimensionless numbers, but further analysis is required to see if these form a complete set. A complete set of dimensionless numbers is one in which a number outside the set can be expressed as a product of numbers in the set, but no number in the set can be identically expressed by means of other numbers in the set.

Clearly Eq. (6.2) cannot be obtained from any combination of the numbers in Eq. (8.41), since these do not contain the density or the velocity. Likewise, N_{Pr} cannot be obtained from either N_{Nu} or N_{Re}, since c_p is not contained in the latter two. The same reasoning holds for N_{Nu} from N_{Pr} and N_{Re}, as neither of these contains the heat transfer coefficient h. Since three groups were required, and these are three independent groups containing all the variables, they must be a complete set. This procedure will work for a reasonably small set of variables, but one should be cautious in using it for complex problems. Remember, the Rayleigh and Buckingham dimensional analysis methods will always work if a solution exists.

The following problem illustrates another procedure for testing for completeness of a set of dimensionless numbers.

Example 8.6. The important variables in a two-phase gas–liquid system were found to be velocity, gravity, length, and system properties: density, viscosity, and surface tension. Suggest a set of dimensionless numbers and test the set for completeness.

Answer. The variables are given in Table 8.7. There are six unknowns and three dimensions. So by the pi theorem, Eq. (8.36), three groups are required. Either by dimensional analysis or simply by inspection, three groups that can be used are

$$N_{Re} = LU\rho/\mu$$
$$N_{Fr} = U^2/(Lg) \tag{i}$$
$$N_{We} = U^2L\rho/\sigma$$

These three dimensionless numbers contain all the variables. These numbers may also be expressed as a ratio of forces. The following forces may be defined [L1]:

TABLE 8.7
Variables for two-phase flow problem

Symbol	Exponent	Name	SI Units	Dimensions
U	a	velocity	m s^{-1}	$L\Theta^{-1}$
g	b	gravity	m s^{-2}	$L\Theta^{-2}$
L	c	length	m	L
ρ	d	density	kg m^{-3}	ML^{-3}
μ	e	viscosity	kg m^{-1} s^{-1}	$ML^{-1}\Theta^{-1}$
σ	f	surface tension	kg s^{-2}	$M\Theta^{-2}$

Viscous forces: $\qquad F_\mu = \mu LU \,[(\text{kg m}^{-1}\,\text{s}^{-1})(\text{m})(\text{m s}^{-1})]$ (ii)

Inertial forces: $\qquad F_\rho = \rho U^2 L^2 \,[(\text{kg m}^{-3})(\text{m}^2\,\text{s}^{-2})(\text{m}^2)]$ (iii)

Surface forces: $\qquad F_\sigma = \sigma L \,[(\text{kg s}^{-2})(\text{m})]$ (iv)

Gravitational forces: $\quad F_g = \rho g L^3 \,[(\text{kg m}^{-3})(\text{m s}^{-2})(\text{m}^3)]$ (v)

Each dimensionless group in Eq. (i) represents a ratio of a pair of the forces in the above equations:

$$N_{\text{Re}} = \frac{F_\rho}{F_\mu} = \frac{\rho U^2 L^2}{\mu LU} = \frac{LU\rho}{\mu} \qquad\qquad \text{(vi)}$$

$$N_{\text{Fr}} = \frac{F_\rho}{F_g} = \frac{\rho U^2 L^2}{\rho g L^3} = \frac{U^2}{Lg} \qquad\qquad \text{(vii)}$$

$$N_{\text{We}} = \frac{F_\rho}{F_\sigma} = \frac{\rho U^2 L^2}{\sigma L} = \frac{U^2 L\rho}{\sigma} \qquad\qquad \text{(viii)}$$

The four forces in Eqs. (ii) through (v) are represented as vertices of a tetrahedron, as shown in Fig. 8.1(a), with six possible connecting lines. A complete set can be made up of three lines (one for each group) which do not form a triangle. One must be able to go from one point to another by one path only for the set to be complete. The set of Eq. (i) is complete and noted in the

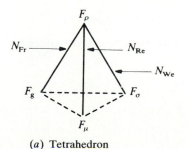

(a) Tetrahedron

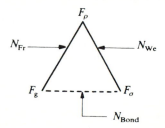

(b) Triangle (set not complete)

FIGURE 8.1
Representation of forces in two-phase flow.

figure by the solid lines. The lines connecting the forces in Fig. 8.1(a) can be associated with the ratios in Eqs. (vi) through (viii) and are labeled accordingly. Another possible set is

$$N_{Fr} = U^2/(Lg)$$
$$N_{We} = U^2 L \rho / \sigma \qquad \text{(ix)}$$
$$N_{Bond} = L^2 \rho g / \sigma$$

The Bond number is the ratio of gravitational to surface forces:

$$N_{Bond} = \frac{F_g}{F_\sigma} = \frac{\rho g L^3}{\sigma L} = \frac{L^2 \rho g}{\sigma} \qquad \text{(x)}$$

The four forces are plotted again in Fig. 8.1(b) and the dimensionless groups labeled. This set is not complete. These three numbers form a triangle, as shown in Fig. 8.1(b), because the Bond number is the ratio of N_{We} to N_{Fr}.

Example 8.7. An investigator has proposed the following dimensionless number for an application in two phase flow (e.g., flow of suspended solids in water in a pipe):

$$N_{Re} = LU\rho/\mu$$
$$N_{Fr} = U^2/(Lg)$$
$$N_{We} = U^2 L \rho / \sigma \qquad \text{(i)}$$
$$N_{property} = (\rho \sigma^3)/(g \mu^4)$$

Determine whether these numbers are all independent.

Answer. Note that $N_{property}$ contains only variables that are already included in the other three groups. Hence, a figure such as Fig. 8.1(b) will show that the four numbers N_{Re}, N_{Fr}, N_{We}, and $N_{property}$ lie in the same plane, and hence these are not independent.

Another solution is to find the exponents on the following equation:

$$N_{property} = N_{Re}^a N_{Fr}^b N_{We}^c \qquad \text{(ii)}$$

The exponents in Eq. (ii) are easily found by inserting the correct variables from Eq. (i):

$$\rho \sigma^3 g^{-1} \mu^{-4} = (LU\rho\mu^{-1})^a (U^2 L^{-1} g^{-1})^b (U^2 L \rho \sigma^{-1})^c \qquad \text{(iii)}$$

If the above equation is to be valid, then there must be unique values for a, b, and c. From the exponents on σ:

$$3 = -c \qquad \text{(iv)}$$

or

$$c = -3 \qquad \text{(v)}$$

From the exponents on ρ:

$$1 = a + c \qquad \text{(vi)}$$

or

$$a = 4 \qquad \text{(vii)}$$

From the exponents on g:

$$-1 = -b \qquad (viii)$$

or

$$b = 1 \qquad (ix)$$

Therefore, $N_{property}$ in terms of the other three numbers is:

$$N_{property} = (N_{Re})^4 (N_{Fr})(N_{We})^{-3} \qquad (x)$$

Clearly, the four numbers cannot be independent, since $N_{property}$ is an exact function of the other three, as shown by Eq. (x).

8.3 MODELING

In modeling, the idea is to make some tests or experiments on a small scale in such a fashion that the results for a large scale may be accurately predicted. An ideal setup would be to keep all of the dimensionless numbers constant between the model and the full-scale system.[2] However, in modeling it is impossible to keep these numbers constant. Attempts to keep these numbers constant often require test fluids with impossible combinations of properties, e.g., a fluid with the density of mercury and the viscosity of air. Consequently, limited modeling methods are developed for each specific case. In modeling, one always attempts to maintain geometric similarity. A model and a larger unit are geometrically similar if all dimensions in the model are proportional to the dimensions in the larger unit by the same ratio. Retaining geometric similarity is an obvious necessity. For example, it is illogical to test a model of a large airplane in which the model has a full-size body and wings one-tenth of the final size. Modeling also requires kinematic similarity. Suppose two geometrically similar systems I and II are established in which kinematic similarity is required. Then the three components of velocity in the three coordinate directions $(U_x, U_y, \text{and } U_z)$ are related:

$$U_{x,I}/U_{y,I} = U_{x,II}/U_{y,II}$$
$$U_{x,I}/U_{z,I} = U_{x,II}/U_{z,II} \qquad (8.42)$$

Also, for kinematic similarity the velocity gradients must be the same at every dimensionless location in systems I and II.

A third similarity is dynamic similarity, or Reynolds modeling. Dynamic similarity considers the viscous forces, inertial forces, and frictional forces as well as the distribution of shear stresses (and therefore shear rates) and normal forces. For example, let the ratio of inertial force to viscous force and the ratio

---

[2] Film loop FM-26 illustrates the desirability of being able to use laboratory models.

of inertial force to frictional force be maintained:

$$\frac{\text{INERTIAL FORCE}_{\text{I}}}{\text{VISCOUS FORCE}_{\text{I}}} = \frac{\text{INERTIAL FORCE}_{\text{II}}}{\text{VISCOUS FORCE}_{\text{II}}}$$

$$\frac{\text{INERTIAL FORCE}_{\text{I}}}{\text{FRICTIONAL FORCE}_{\text{I}}} = \frac{\text{INERTIAL FORCE}_{\text{II}}}{\text{FRICTIONAL FORCE}_{\text{II}}}$$

(8.43)

Reynolds modeling is very successful when applied to the case of the flow of fluids in smooth pipes. It is not successful when applied to the agitation of liquids (Chapter 9).

Other types of similarity, such as static, thermal, and chemical, are discussed elsewhere [B1]. Modeling with dimensionless groups has been successful in many areas, such as with rivers and harbors, with cavitation in pumps, and for thermal and chemical reaction systems. In each case geometric similarity is maintained. Usually the similarity required by one dimensionless number is of most importance. The effects of other factors are often successfully neglected. The importance of modeling will be illustrated further in later chapters.

Example 8.8. A new pipe material is to be used in some new plant construction, but there is not enough information available to allow an exact design because of the noncircular cross sectional area of the pipe. Assume the pipe is smooth. Consider modeling if a sample is available that is 1/10 the size considered for the plant.

Answer. From the results of Example 8.1, if the pressure drop or Euler number is to remain the same, one must maintain as constant the following three dimensionless groups: the Reynolds number, the length to diameter ratio L/d_o, and the relative roughness e/d_o. Thus, the test model should have the same values for these three dimensionless numbers as the full-scale model. If the pipe is smooth, the roughness e is essentially zero; therefore, e/d_o remains constant (zero) for any diameter. The modeling will henceforth be based on the premise of keeping constant the Reynolds number and the ratio L/d_o. If d_o is to be reduced by 1/10, then L must be likewise reduced to maintain the ratio L/d_o constant. The Reynolds number is

$$N_{\text{Re}} = d_o U \rho / \mu$$

(6.2)

The Reynolds number will be constant when d_o is reduced by 1/10 if any of the following changes take place:
(a) increase in U by a factor of 10
(b) increase in ρ by a factor of 10
(c) decrease in μ by a factor of 10
Of course, a combination of these changes is also feasible. Usually it is easier to increase U rather than to use a different fluid.

PROBLEMS

8.1. Discuss the purpose and limitations of dimensional analysis.

8.2. Section 8.1 considered the inspection of the basic differential equations. Discuss the advantages and limitations of this approach.

8.3. Discuss the mechanistic meaning of the generalized dimensionless numbers:
(a) UL/δ
(b) $(U\psi)/(L\dot{\psi}_G)$

8.4. What is meant by a complete set of dimensionless numbers?

8.5. Put Eqs. (3.65), (4.77), and (4.112) into dimensionless form by using the dimensionless numbers listed in Table 8.1.

8.6. Determine the dimensionless numbers for the noise produced in a mixing tank if the noise depends on the sound intensity (I, in units of power per unit area), density (ρ), viscosity (μ), propeller tip velocity (U), diameter of propeller (d), and diameter of tank (h).

8.7. The unsteady-state heat transfer from a slab depends on the heat source ($\dot{T}_G$), surface heat transfer coefficient (h), time (t), thermal diffusivity (α), thermal conductivity (k), temperature (T), reference temperature (T_o), and the system dimension (L). Determine the dimensionless numbers, which must include the group T/T_o.

8.8. The velocity of flow (U) through a flow-measuring nozzle has been determined to be a function of diameter of pipe (d), density (ρ), diameter of nozzle (a), viscosity (μ), and pressure drop (Δp). Determine the dimensionless numbers.

8.9. A system depends on the velocity of flow (U), gravity (g), surface tension (σ), two dimensions of the system (L, d), density (ρ), viscosity (μ), and pressure drop (Δp). Determine the dimensionless numbers.

8.10. Obtain the dimensionless numbers for the concentric cylinder problem that is described by Eq. (xxv) in Example 5.7.

8.11. The drag force (F) on certain bodies at high speed is thought to be controlled by the characteristic length (L), the approach velocity (U), gravity (g), density (ρ), viscosity (μ), surface tension (σ), and the velocity of sound (c). Determine the dimensionless numbers.

8.12. The power (P) from a rotating impeller in a mixer is a function of the rate of rotation of the impeller (N, in units of rpm), impeller diameter (d), gravity (g), density (ρ), and viscosity (μ). Determine the dimensionless numbers.

8.13. A weir is a flow-measuring device used in open channel flow. The flow rate (Q) depends upon the weir width (w), the depth of fluid above the bottom of the weir (h), viscosity (μ), surface tension (σ), density (ρ), and gravity (g). Determine the dimensionless numbers.

8.14. The heat transfer coefficient for an annular flow (h) depends on the thermal conductivity (k), heat capacity (c_p), density (ρ), viscosity (μ), velocity of flow (U), characteristic dimension (d), and gap thickness (δ). Determine the dimensionless numbers.

8.15. The mass transfer coefficient (k_c') depends on the diffusivity (D), density (ρ), viscosity (μ), velocity of flow (U), and characteristic dimension (d). Determine the dimensionless numbers.

8.16. In natural convection heat transfer, the heat transfer coefficient (h) depends upon the fluid thermal expansion (β, in units of K^{-1}), density (ρ), viscosity (μ), heat capacity (c_p), characteristic dimension of the system (d), thermal conductivity of the fluid (k), gravity (g), and the temperature difference between the fluid and the body (ΔT). Determine the necessary dimensionless numbers. Explain why your answer can be reduced to the three groups usually given in the literature (N_{Gr}, N_{Pr}, and N_{Nu}).

8.17. The deposition of fine particles (η, efficiency of removal) in filter separators is dependent upon the particle diameter (d_p), particle density (ρ_p), diffusivity of particle (D), terminal velocity of particle (U_t), filter fiber diameter (d), gas velocity (U), density (ρ), and viscosity (μ). Determine the dimensionless numbers for this operation.

8.18. The surface of a metallic sphere is coated with a special liquid by suspending the sphere with a thin wire in a liquid bath. After an appropriate time, the sphere is withdrawn from the liquid; a thin coating of liquid remains on the surface. List the six (or more) important variables that must be considered for this experiment and the dimensions of each. Make a table of SI units and dimensions.

REFERENCES

B1. Boucher, D. F., and G. E. Alves: *Chem. Eng. Progr.* **55**(9): 55–64 (1959).

L1. Langhaar, H. L.: *Dimensional Analysis and Theory of Models,* Wiley, New York, 1951.

M1. McAdams, W. H.: *Heat Transmission,* 3d ed., McGraw-Hill, New York, 1954.

P1. Perry, R. H., and D. W. Green: *Perry's Chemical Engineers' Handbook,* 6th ed., McGraw-Hill, New York, 1984.

PART
II

APPLICATIONS OF TRANSPORT PHENOMENA

CHAPTER 9

AGITATION[1]

NOMENCLATURE

A Area (m², ft²); A_p is area projected perpendicular to the velocity vector

a Exponent used in dimensional analysis and in scale-up equations

B Baffle width (m, ft)

b Exponent used in dimensional analysis

C Distance from tank bottom to impeller center line (m, ft)

C_D Drag coefficient, used for flow past immersed bodies

C_f Conversion factor in torque equation, Eq. (9.6); values of C_f are given in Table 9.2

c Exponent used in dimensional analysis

c_p Heat capacity at constant pressure (kJ kg^{-1} K^{-1}, Btu lb$_m^{-1}$ °F^{-1})

D Impeller diameter (m, ft)

D_L Liquid phase diffusion coefficient (mass diffusivity) (m² s^{-1}, ft² s^{-1})

[1] The authors wish to acknowledge Dr. Gary B. Tatterson, Department of Mechanical Engineering, Texas A & M University, College Station, TX 77843, who assisted the authors in the preparation of this chapter.

d — Exponent used in dimensional analysis

e — Exponent used in dimensional analysis

F — Force exerted by a fluid on an immersed solid (N, lb_f)

f — Fanning friction factor, defined in Eq. (6.89)

f — Exponent used in dimensional analysis

g — Exponent used in dimensional analysis

$\mathbf{g}$ — Vector representing the acceleration due to a gravitational or other field ($m\,s^{-2}$, $ft\,s^{-2}$)

g_c — Gravitational conversion constant ($32.174\,lb_m\,lb_f^{-1}\,ft\,s^{-2}$)

h — Heat transfer coefficient, defined by Eq. (6.86) ($W\,m^{-2}\,K^{-1}$, $Btu\,ft^{-2}\,h^{-1}\,°F^{-1}$)

I_x — Intensity of turbulence, defined by Eq. (6.31)

i — Exponent used in dimensional analysis

j — Exponent used in dimensional analysis

k — Thermal conductivity ($W\,m^{-1}\,K^{-1}$ or $J\,m^{-1}\,K^{-1}\,s^{-1}$, $Btu\,ft^{-1}\,°R^{-1}\,s^{-1}$)

k — Empirical constant in several equations and correlations; used with subscripts $1, \ldots, 9$

k_c' — Equimolar mass transfer coefficient, defined by Eq. (6.87) [$kmol\,m^{-2}\,s^{-1}\,(kmol\,m^{-3})^{-1}$, $lb\,mol\,ft^{-2}\,s^{-1}\,(lb\,mol\,ft^{-3})^{-1}$]

k_L — Liquid phase mass transfer coefficient [$kmol\,m^{-2}\,s^{-1}\,(kmol\,m^{-3})^{-1}$, $lb\,mol\,ft^{-2}\,s^{-1}\,(lb\,mol\,ft^{-3})^{-1}$]; cf. Table 9.2

L — Basic unit in dimensional analysis; length (m)

M — Basic unit in dimensional analysis; mass (kg)

m — Exponent used in dimensional analysis

N — Impeller speed (rpm or s^{-1}); N_1 is speed of small unit; N_2 is speed of large unit

N — N represents dimensionless number or group; Table 9.3 lists those for agitation

n — Exponent used in dimensional analysis

n — Speed scale-up exponent, Eq. (9.31)

P — Power ($J\,s^{-1}$, $ft\,lb_f\,s^{-1}$)

p — Exponent used in dimensional analysis

Q — Volume flow rate ($m^3\,s^{-1}$, $ft^3\,s^{-1}$)

R — Scale factor, defined as D_2/D_1, etc.; cf. Eqs. (9.25) and (9.27); R_f is scale factor between bench unit and plant unit in Example 9.4

s — Scale-up exponent based on power per unit volume in Eq. (9.28)

T — Basic unit in dimensional analysis; temperature (K)

T — Tank diameter (m, ft)

T_q — Torque (N m, $ft\,lb_f$ or $in.\,lb_f$)

t — Time (s)

$\mathbf{U}$ — Velocity vector ($m\,s^{-1}$, $ft\,s^{-1}$); U is magnitude of $\mathbf{U}$; $\bar{U}_z$ is time-averaged velocity in z direction; U_x' is instantaneous velocity fluctuation in x direction; U_t is the impeller tip speed, Eq. (9.7); $U_{t,1}$ and $U_{t,2}$ are impeller tip speeds in units 1 and 2

V — Volume (m^3, ft^3)

W	Width of impeller (m, ft)
w	Subscript denoting wall
x	Scale-up exponent based on torque per unit volume in Eq. (9.29)
y	Exponent in Eq. (9.23)
Z	Depth of fluid in tank (m, ft)
δ	Generalized diffusivity ($m^2\,s^{-1}$, $ft^2\,s^{-1}$)
Θ	Basic unit in dimensional analysis; time (s)
θ	Blend time (s)
μ	Viscosity ($kg\,m^{-1}\,s^{-1}$ or $N\,m^{-2}\,s$, $lb_m\,ft^{-1}\,s^{-1}$, cP); μ_w is viscosity at wall
Π	Dimensionless groups in pi theorem
π	Ratio of circumference of a circle to its diameter (3.141 592 65 . . .)
ρ	Density ($kg\,m^{-3}$, $lb_m\,ft^{-3}$)
σ	Surface tension ($kg\,s^{-2}$ or $N\,m^{-1}$, $lb_m\,s^{-2}$ or $lb_f\,ft^{-1}$)
ψ	Generalized concentration of property (e.g., units for concentration of heat are $J\,m^{-3}$, $Btu\,ft^{-3}$; see Table 3.1 for complete listing)
$\dot{\psi}_G$	Generalized rate of generation of energy or mass or momentum in a unit volume (see Table 4.2 for units; e.g., for heat, units are $J\,m^{-3}\,s^{-1}$, $Btu\,ft^{-3}\,s^{-1}$)
∇	Vector operator del, defined by Eq. (2.16) or Eq. (3.45) (m^{-1}, ft^{-1})

The first eight chapters in this text introduced the basic equations of transport along with the various methods to analyze these equations. The remaining chapters will be devoted, in the main, to applying these equations and methods to important problems of a practical nature. At this point, the ordering of topics not yet covered is arbitrary, as any of several important areas may be covered first. Agitation logically follows the discussions of dimensional analysis and similarity ratios (especially geometric and kinematic) in Chapter 8. The topic of agitation perhaps illustrates best the use of dimensionless groups and similarity for analysis and design. Many agitation problems commonly encountered in engineering involve turbulent flow, although applications in polymer processing constitute an important example of laminar flow. The complexities of turbulent flow have been detailed in Chapter 6. Agitation constitutes an excellent example of fluid flow occurring in various combinations with heat transfer, mass transfer, chemical reaction, and preparation of mixtures.

The terms "agitation", "mixing", and "dispersion" have different meanings. Agitation is the process of providing bulk motion to a liquid, thus aiding mixing and dispersion. To explain the terms mixing and dispersion, it is helpful to begin with the definition of the word "mixture". A useful definition of the word "mixture" is a complex of two or more ingredients that do not bear a fixed proportion to one another and retain their separate identity no matter how thoroughly the ingredients are commingled. In its most general sense, the word "mixing" is used to mean any blending into one mass. As a consequence of these definitions, the process of mixing begins with two or more materials, each distinct from one another in one or more properties such as composition, density, or temperature. Complete mixing occurs if the final mass has reached the maximum possible state of uniformity; the process of molecular diffusion proceeds until all temperature, pressure, and concentration gradients have been eliminated and until no further chemical reaction is possible. Unfortunately, in the literature the words "blending", "mixing", and "dispersion" have been freely interchanged in their usage and intended meanings. In this chapter, more precise definitions will be offered.

In the literature on agitation, dispersion is defined as the combination of two materials into a final product in which there are still two separate materials. Examples of dispersion processes are suspending of solids, dispersing of gases in liquids, and mixing of immiscible liquids such as are encountered in emulsions and in liquid–liquid extraction. As can be seen from the examples, in dispersion the starting materials are separated into smaller-sized groups and scattered among each other on a scale that is large when compared to molecular dimensions. The process of molecular diffusion is not present, or is present only to a minor extent, in dispersion.

Another way to consider mixing and dispersion is to realize that in the preparation of a completely homogeneous mixture, such as pure water and pure ethanol being combined in equal proportions, the first step in the process is to disperse one material in the second by some means (such as agitation). If there is no agitation, the homogeneous mixture will be achieved by the process of interdiffusion of the water and ethanol molecules, which will take a long time. If agitation is present, the eddies formed by turbulence from the agitation unit will speed up the diffusional process. However, diffusion will still be necessary in order to reach the final homogeneous state. Two other examples of complete mixing are the dissolution of solids in a liquid phase and heat transfer between two commingling streams containing the same liquid at different temperatures. Heat transfer is a mixing process, since molecules of high kinetic energy interact with those of low energy. The result is a fluid at some intermediate temperature. Mixing is very important in processes in chemical reactions, because there must be contact for a reaction between molecules to occur. Molecular diffusion is required, since the scale of the molecules is many orders of magnitude smaller than the smallest fluid elements that can be formed by turbulence or by mechanical means.

In summary, agitation produces motion in the process fluid. This motion is responsible for the desired process result, which may include mixing, blending, dissolution, heat transfer, dispersion of liquids and gases into liquids, solid suspension, and crystal growth. The purpose of this chapter is to discuss agitation and show how to design a large-scale agitation unit using the principles of Chapter 8.

9.1 INTRODUCTION TO AGITATION

Agitation of liquids is usually accomplished in a container equipped with an impeller such as a propeller, paddle, or turbine. The impeller is inserted into the liquid and rotated in such a manner as to cause both bulk motion and fine-scale eddies in the fluid. Mechanical energy is required to rotate the impeller, which in turn transmits this energy to the fluid. The mechanism of transmission is similar to that in the parallel-plate problem of Fig. 2.3, in which the moving top plate transmits velocity to the fluid nearby by the effect of viscosity. In agitation, the impeller is rotating, the sides and bottom of the tank are stationary, and the resultant velocity gradients cause mixing and dispersion.

No doubt agitation of liquids has been practiced since early mankind made the first liquid containers. The general property balance equation from Chapter 3 is

$$\partial\psi/\partial t + (\boldsymbol{U}\cdot\boldsymbol{\nabla})\psi = \dot\psi_G + (\boldsymbol{\nabla}\cdot\delta\boldsymbol{\nabla}\psi) - \psi(\boldsymbol{\nabla}\cdot\boldsymbol{U}) \qquad (3.60)$$

where the last term is zero for an incompressible fluid, as is usually the case in agitation. Obviously, application of this or any similar equation inside an agitation vessel is highly complex. In the first place, the flow is three-dimensional, and the initial and boundary conditions are not usually known. Often heat, mass, and momentum transfer must all be considered simultaneously. Moreover, in the case of agitation of liquids of low viscosity, such as water and hydrocarbons, the flow is highly turbulent, with intensities of turbulence ranging from near zero in dead zones to as much as 100 percent or greater near the impeller. Recall that the intensity of turbulence is defined in Eq. (6.31) as

$$I_x = 100\sqrt{\overline{U_x'^2}}/U \qquad (6.31)$$

With no quantitative solution to the general property balance possible, dimensional analysis approaches have been tried and found to be quite successful.

Agitation in a process generally accomplishes physical changes, chemical changes, and/or increased rates of transport. These may occur simultaneously or singly. An example of a physical change is the increase in the surface area of a solid. An example of a chemical change is the occurrence of chemical reactions; agitation assists in bringing the reactants (or reactants and catalyst) together in order for the reaction to occur. Agitation promotes high rates of heat transport. Also, agitation can increase the rate of mass transfer when mixing a miscible solute (or other material) in a liquid solvent. If the solute consists of solid crystals, then agitation is typically responsible for producing and maintaining the maximum possible concentration driving force between the solid interface and the solution. The solute may be a liquid or a gas as well. Agitation often disperses an insoluble material throughout the liquid; a common example is the case of pigments such as TiO_2 being dispersed in paint. Agitation may disperse a gas in the form of small bubbles throughout the liquid for purposes of absorption or gas–liquid reaction. In batch chemical reactors, agitation often serves the double duty of maintaining high concentration gradients and moving the fluid over a heat transfer surface so as to control the reactor temperature. In the case of a highly exothermic reaction or the production of a heat-sensitive material, temperature control and proper heat transfer may be quite important.

9.2 EQUIPMENT

Agitation equipment usually consists of a tank to hold the liquid, one or more impellers to provide the shear flow, a motor or some other means to drive the impeller, and usually wall baffles, the installation of which permits higher power input. Wall baffles are longitudinal strips attached to the inside walls of the tank. Figure 9.1 shows an agitation tank with the sides and bottom surrounded by a "jacket" that contains a fluid to provide the necessary heat transfer. Obviously, some applications, such as those involving a chemical reaction, will require a jacket while others will not. A tank with a sloping or dished bottom is often recommended, although tanks whose bottom and sides form a right angle are also commonly used. A tank with a dished bottom is often specified for suspension of solids. Some tanks have coils of tubing surrounding the impeller to transfer heat in or out of the vessel, but a jacketed vessel is easier to clean and provides better mixing. Fabrication of jacketed vessels is very routine for equipment manufacturers.

The literature on agitation uses its own nomenclature, and the definitions of those symbols are not consistent with the definitions of the same symbols as used in the earlier chapters. The biggest change in nomenclature involves the physical dimensions of the agitation unit. For the unit in Fig. 9.1, the following

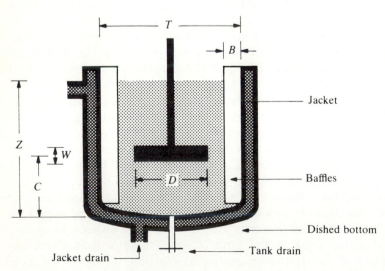

FIGURE 9.1
Agitation tank with baffles, jacket, and dished bottom.

definitions are in common usage:

B   Width of each baffle
C   Distance from tank bottom to impeller center line
D   Impeller diameter
T   Inside diameter of tank
W   Width of impeller
Z   Depth of fluid in the tank

These definitions are labeled in Fig. 9.1.

     Impeller design has a strong impact on the agitation characteristics and the energy requirement. Figure 9.2 illustrates some common impeller designs for both turbulent and laminar flow; note that the design is strongly dependent on whether the application is laminar or turbulent. The laminar impellers are usually as large as the tank itself. Since laminar flow does not transport momentum as well as turbulent flow, laminar flow impellers must be large to effect the desired physical, chemical, and transport results throughout the tank.

     Figure 9.3 shows the gross flow patterns for four important types of impellers in agitation equipment. Turbines with pitched blades and marine propellers cause axial flow patterns in baffled tanks, as shown in Fig. 9.3(a). These turbines and propellers are often used for suspension of solids because the flow patterns result in the solids being swept off the bottom of the vessel where they might otherwise settle. Impellers with vertical flat blades produce flow patterns that are radial, as shown in Figs. 9.3(b) and 9.3(c). The anchor and helix impellers in Fig. 9.2(b) are for liquids of very high viscosity, e.g., $20 \, \text{kg} \, \text{m}^{-1} \, \text{s}^{-1}$ (20 000 cP) or above. In these liquids, the agitation process is under laminar flow conditions, and unusual impeller shapes, such as the anchor, a helical ribbon, the screw impeller, or some other similar shape are most satisfactory. Many non-Newtonian solutions, usually having a high viscosity, are agitated with these types of impellers. The anchor, for example, primarily removes the fluid next to the heat transfer surface so that fresh fluid of differing temperature replaces the old fluid. The flow pattern in Fig. 9.3(d) is basically tangential, as shown. The impeller speed is low owing to its large diameter and mechanical constraints. There is no room for baffles, nor is there a need for them.

     The motor required for agitation is sized from the power requirements. Most alternating current motors operate at speeds of 1750 rpm or 1150 rpm. For many applications, a lower speed is desired from the standpoint of operating efficiency and cost. Gear drives provide speed reduction and tend to be rated according to the torque requirements. Thus accurate determination of torque is important, particularly since gear drives are expensive relative to other components in the mixing system.

     For general mixing, the most common impeller used is probably the six-blade disked turbine impeller, as shown in Fig. 9.2(a)(1). This impeller is often called the Rushton impeller, named after J. H. Rushton, an early pioneer in the field of agitation [R2, R3]. Flow patterns behind and around the

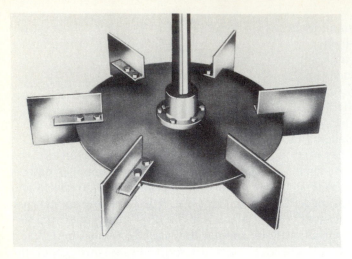

(1) Disk-blade turbine

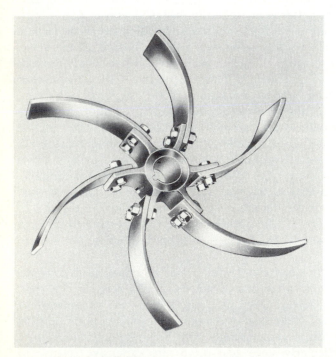

(2) Curved-blade turbine

FIGURE 9.2
Some common impeller designs. (*Courtesy of Mixing Equipment Company.*)

(*a*) Impellers for turbulent flow

(3) Open-blade fluid foil axial impeller

(4) Turbine impeller with 45° pitched blades, open style

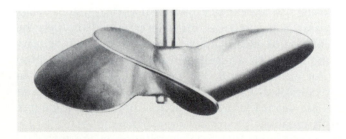

(5) Three-blade propellor

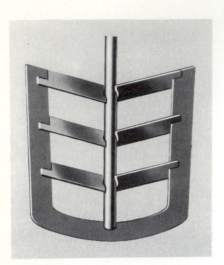

(1) Anchor

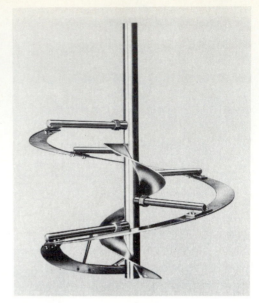

(2) Helix

(*b*) Impellers for laminar flow

FIGURE 9.2 (*Continued*)

impeller have been the object of considerable research using flow visualization techniques and other methods. In the vicinity of the impeller, complex eddy systems and high-speed jets have been observed. Whenever a fluid element travels in a circular motion, that motion is termed a vortex. In agitation, the term vortex is used to describe two major flow phenomena: (1) vortex systems near the impeller blades; and (2) the vortex formed in the center of an unbaffled tank. The first of these is associated with the local turbulent flow, as shown in Figure 9.4(*a*), in which a disk-style impeller discharges a high volume of flow in the radial direction [T2]. In the figure, the blade is moving into the paper, and the fluid in front of the blade is forced over the blade at a high speed. When the fluid passes over the blade, it attempts to re-attach itself to the back of the blade, causing the appearance of a dual vortex system. Thus the vortices form in the wake of the impeller blade as it passed through the fluid and shed from the rear side of each blade as a result of the high velocity of flow over and around the blade. As a result of these vortices, the Rushton impeller is often selected for gas dispersion. For the pitched-blade turbine in Fig. 9.4(*b*), the turbulent vortices are similar to those occurring on wings of aircraft [T1]. More studies are needed in order to help in obtaining an indepth understanding of vortices in agitation.

Almost all industrial applications that involve agitation in the turbulent region require the installation of baffles in the tank. Without baffles, a center

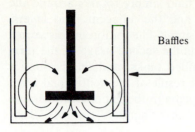

(a) Pitched-blade turbulent or propeller—axial flow

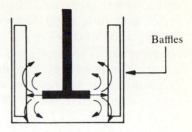

(b) Flat-blade turbine—radial flow

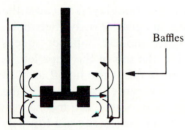

(c) Flat-blade paddle—radial flow

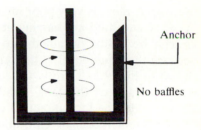

(d) Anchor—tangential flow

FIGURE 9.3
Agitation flow regimes. (*Adapted from Philadelphia Mixers, division of Philadelphia Gear Corporation, with permission.*)

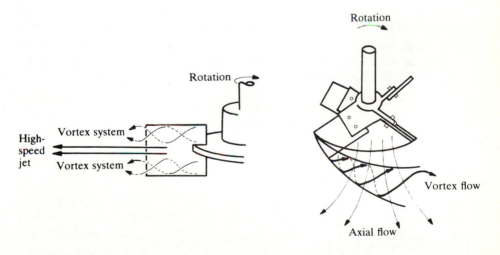

(a) Disk style turbine

(b) Pitched-blade turbine

FIGURE 9.4
Flow systems and turbulent vortices. (*Reprinted from Food Technol.* **35**(5): 65 (1981). *Copyright © by Institute of Food Technologists. By permission.*)

vortex forms, as shown in Figure 9.5, and the fluid simply rotates around the vessel with little shear between the impeller and the adjacent fluid layers. Stirring a cup of coffee or tea with a spoon is a simple illustration of this vortex phenomenon. This large-scale motion represents the second usage of the term vortex. The power input is much less in unbaffled tanks, and this is often a disadvantage in mixing. The vortex forms as a result of the centrifugal force field as expressed in the $(U \cdot \nabla)U$ term that appears in the general momentum balance equation. In Table 5.7 for the Navier–Stokes equation [Eq. (5.15)] the centrifugal force term is U_θ^2/r in Eq. (D).

The vortex phenomenon shown in Fig. 9.5 is usually not desired in mixing operations, for several reasons. First, although the fluid moves around the vessel, there is very poor mixing between adjacent fluid layers because the impeller and fluid are moving at nearly the same angular velocity. Secondly, air can be easily entrained into the liquid even at modest impeller speeds because the liquid level at the center can fall below the top of the impeller, as shown in Fig. 9.5. Thirdly, the formation of a vortex raises the liquid level at the top edge of the tank significantly, which may cause spillage. On the positive side, the formation of a center vortex can be desirable as a mechanism of solid submergence in applications where suspensions or slurries are formed.

The design of baffles is based on experimental data that show that four equispaced baffles provide reasonable performance. For center-mounted impellers, the ratio of baffle width B to tank diameter D should be 1/12 for turbine or paddle agitation and 1/18 for propellers to maximize power input. In large tanks, there may be surface baffles to break up large surface waves, as well as other internal baffles.

Figures 9.1, 9.3, and 9.5 show the impeller to be centrally mounted. There are other options, including side-entering propellers, multiple impellers on the same shaft, off-center mounting, and multiple impellers mounted separately around the tank, each with its own drive motor and gear drive. Design details for these latter cases are described elsewhere [N1, O1].

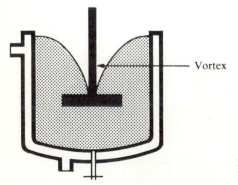

— Vortex

FIGURE 9.5
Vortex formation in an unbaffled tank.

9.3 GEOMETRIC SIMILARITY AND SCALE-UP

The most accurate approach to the design of a plant-scale agitation unit is to obtain data from an appropriate experiment in a plant-scale apparatus. Unfortunately, this approach is usually not possible for new processes, and data must be taken in laboratory-scale equipment. Naturally, the closer the size of the laboratory vessel is to that of the actual process, the more reliable the scale-up will be. Often, it is impossible to fulfil this requirement, and the design must proceed with data from a small-scale unit only.

Scale-up in agitation follows the modeling principles outlined in Section 8.3. First, geometric similarity is maintained. Figure 9.6 considers two agitators, one laboratory-scale and one plant-scale. For exact geometric similarity between units, the following ratios are satisfied:

$$C_1/T_1 = C_2/T_2 \qquad Z_1/T_1 = Z_2/T_2$$
$$D_1/T_1 = D_2/T_2 \qquad B_1/T_1 = B_2/T_2 \qquad (9.1)$$
$$W_1/D_1 = W_2/D_2$$

If these ratios are not held constant, techniques of scale-up require correction factors of uncertain magnitude. The most important ratios are discussed in more detail in the following paragraphs.

D/T ratio. Normally the D/T ratio is set at 1/3 [B1] for turbulent flow regimes. It is important that this ratio be maintained constant during scale-up. This ratio may be varied in the range:

$$0.2 \le D/T \le 0.5 \qquad \text{Turbulent flow} \qquad (9.2)$$
$$0.7 \le D/T \le 1.0 \qquad \text{Laminar flow} \qquad (9.3)$$

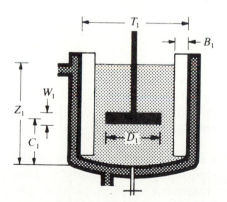

(*a*) Laboratory agitator

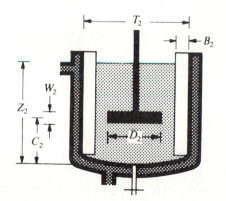

(*b*) Plant-scale agitator

FIGURE 9.6
Principal dimensions in scale-up.

In a qualitative sense, as D/T approaches 0.2, the purchase price of the unit is relatively low, and high shear is produced with high power input and high operating costs. As D/T approaches 0.5, the operating costs decrease, but the low power requirement produces low shear [V1].

Z/T ratio. This ratio describes the fluid level in the tank. Normally, this ratio is unity, although the ratio Z/T can range from 0.5 to 1.0. This ratio has little bearing on the power consumption. Changes in Z/T can change flow patterns in the tank. But if Z/T exceeds 1, there may be dead zones in the tank, which can be eliminated with the addition of more impellers.

Baffles. The design of baffles is based upon maximizing power input to the fluid. The normal ratio is

$$B/T = 1/12 \qquad (9.4)$$

with four baffles being spaced equidistantly apart along the wall.

Bottom clearance. The bottom of the impeller is located a distance C from the bottom of the tank. The normal range for C/T is

$$0.1 \le C/T \le 0.4 \qquad (9.5)$$

However, the most common value of C/T is 1/3 [B1]. Normally C/T will approach the lower limit if a low level of mixing is desired or if off-bottom suspension of solids is desired.

Impellers. Scale-up must be accomplished with geometrically similar impellers [T2]. The important considerations are the number of blades, the pitch of the blades, the ratio of blade height to tank diameter, and the ratio of impeller diameter to tank diameter.

9.4 DESIGN VARIABLES

In addition to the six dimensions in Fig. 9.6, other important variables are fluid properties (viscosity μ, density ρ, surface or interfacial tension σ, thermal conductivity k, heat capacity c_p), and impeller rotational speed N [units of s^{-1} or rpm (revolutions per minute) or rps (revolutions per second)]. These variables are used to calculate the power P and the torque T_q.

Power. The principal operating cost for an agitation unit is the cost of the power. In turbulent flow, the power P is proportional to the density ρ of the liquid, to the third power of the impeller rotational speed N and the fifth power of impeller diameter D, as shown in Table 9.1 [P2]. In laminar flow, the power P is proportional to viscosity μ, to the rotational speed N squared, and to the third power of impeller diameter D.

TABLE 9.1
Design variables in agitation

Symbol	Item	Turbulent equation*	Laminar equation*
P	Power	$k_1\rho N^3 D^5$	$k_2\mu N^2 D^3$
V	Tank volume	$k_3 T^3$	$k_3 T^3$
P/V	Power per unit volume	$k_4 N^3 D^5/T^3 = (k_4 N^3 D^2)(D/T)^3$	$k_5\mu N^2 D^3/T^3 = k_5\mu N^2 (D/T)^3$
T_q	Torque	$P/N = k_6\rho N^2 D^5$	$k_7\mu N D^3$
T_q/V	Torque per unit volume	$k_8\rho N^2 D^5/T^3 = k_8\rho N^2 D^2 (D/T)^3$	$k_9\mu N D^3/T^3 = k_9\mu N(D/T)^3$
U_t	Tip speed	πND	πND

* The k_i's are proportionality constants.

Torque. The basic definition of torque is force times distance or power times time:

$$T_q = \frac{P}{2\pi N} = \frac{P}{N}C_f \qquad (9.6)$$

In Eq. (9.6), the impeller speed was multiplied by the quantity 2π to form the angular velocity of rotation $2\pi N$. Table 9.2 provides the values of the conversion factor C_f, as defined in Eq. (9.6), for the three most commonly encountered units of torque, which are N m, in. lb_f, and ft lb_f. Note that the units of torque are identical to the units of work and energy.

The torque greatly affects the purchase price of the agitation unit. Not only is the gear drive sized according to torque, but the size of the shaft and the weight of the impeller depends on torque as well. Since the torque T_q is proportional to the power divided by impeller rotational speed, as seen in Eq. (9.6), the quantity T_q/V is proportional to D/T to the third power, as was the power per unit volume. The quantity D/T is constant when geometric similarity is maintained; hence, Eq. (9.6) emphasizes the importance of geometric similarity in scale-up.

TABLE 9.2
Value of the conversion factor C_f for torque in Eq. (9.6)

Units of T_q	Units of P	Units of N	Conversion factor C_f in Eq. (9.6)
N m (J)	W (J s^{-1})	rps	$1/(2\pi)$
in. lb_f	hp	rps	1050.4
in. lb_f	hp	rpm	63 025
ft lb_f	hp	rps	87.535

Impeller tip speed. The tip speed of the impeller, given the symbol U_t, is an important variable:

$$U_t = \pi N D \tag{9.7}$$

Note that the rotational speed N in Eq. (9.7) and subsequent equations is expressed in units of s^{-1}, not in radians per time. When N is in units of s^{-1}, the angular velocity is $2\pi N$, and the tip speed is the angular velocity times the radius of the impeller, or $\pi N D$.

The torque per unit volume can be written in terms of the tip speed. Using the turbulent flow equation for T_q/V in Table 9.1, Eq. (9.7) can be substituted, with the result

$$T_q/V = k_8 \rho N^2 D^2 (D/T)^3 = k_{10}(\rho U_t^2)(D/T)^3 \tag{9.8}$$

Therefore, when geometric similarity is maintained in scale-up in turbulent flow, the torque per unit volume becomes proportional to the square of the tip speed.

9.5 DIMENSIONLESS NUMBERS

There are at least ten dimensionless numbers associated with agitation accompanied by heat and mass transfer. These are summarized in Table 9.3. Six of these are of sufficient importance to warrant individual discussion.

TABLE 9.3
Dimensionless numbers in agitation

Name	Symbol	Definition	Comments
Blend	N_b	$N\theta$	Related to uniform mixing or blending
Froude	N_{Fr}	N^2D/g	Correlates with N_{Re} and N_{po} for unbaffled systems [R2], also important in addition of powders to liquids in agitated tanks
Nusselt	N_{Nu}	hT/k	Heat transfer to an agitation unit (jacketed or otherwise)
Power	N_{po}	$P/(\rho N^3 D^5)$	Constant in baffled systems if $N_{Re} > 10\,000$
Prandtl	N_{Pr}	$c_p\mu/k$	Fluid properties for heat transfer correlation
Pumping	N_p	$Q/(ND^3)$	Related to impeller pumping capacities
Reynolds*	N_{Re}	$D^2N\rho/\mu$	Laminar flow if $N_{Re} < 10$; turbulent flow if $N_{Re} > 10\,000$
Schmidt†	N_{Sc}	$\mu/(\rho D_L)$	Fluid properties for mass transfer correlation
Sherwood†	N_{Sh}	$k_L T/D_L$	Mass transfer between solute and solvent in an agitation unit
Weber*	N_{We}	$N^2D^3\rho/\sigma$	Related to surface behavior for two-phase systems

* This number is based on the impeller.

† The symbols D_L and k_L represent the liquid-phase mass diffusion coefficient and the liquid-phase mass transfer coefficient, respectively, where k_L is similar to k_c' in Eq. (6.87), except that the driving force is in accordance with the requirements of the mass transfer under consideration.

Reynolds number. In the defining equation for Reynolds number [Eq. (6.1)], the characteristic velocity is the tip speed, Eq. (9.7). Therefore, the Reynolds number for agitation is

$$N_{\text{Re}} = D^2 N \rho / \mu \qquad (9.9)$$

This Reynolds number is sometimes referred to as the impeller Reynolds number.

In agitation, there are three flow regions, laminar, transitional, and turbulent, just as discussed in Chapter 6 for pipe flow. For a given agitation unit, when N is slowly increased from zero a laminar flow regime exists initially. The region where laminar flow ends and fully turbulent flow begins is still under investigation. A large transitional region extends from $N_{\text{Re}} = 10$ to $N_{\text{Re}} = 10^3$ (or higher, depending on the choice of impeller [B1, P2]). In this range of Reynolds numbers, vortex systems near the impeller (not the surface vortex) begin to form. At high Reynolds numbers, the power number tends to be independent of impeller Reynolds number and dependent only on the geometry of the impeller, as will be discussed later. Note also that since the ratio D/T is usually constant and equal to 1/3 upon scale-up, the impeller Reynolds number increases with the square of the vessel size for the same rotational speed N.

Power number. The power number is defined as

$$N_{\text{po}} = P / (\rho N^3 D^5) \qquad (9.10)$$

where the power P has units of $\text{ft lb}_f \, \text{s}^{-1}$ or hp or J s^{-1}. The power number correlates well with Reynolds number for baffled systems [B2], as shown in Fig. 9.7.

An interesting result seen in Fig. 9.7 is that the power number is constant and independent of the Reynolds number in baffled systems above a Reynolds number of 10^3–10^4, depending on the impeller:

$$N_{\text{po}} = \frac{P}{\rho N^3 D^5} = \text{constant} \qquad (9.11)$$

Bates *et al.* [B1] found that for the six-blade turbine impeller [cf. Fig. 9.2(a,1)] the constant in Eq. (9.11) is equal to 4.8 at high Reynolds numbers. Note that the disk style of construction (curve 1 in Fig. 9.7) takes approximately 25 percent more power than a flat-blade style (curve 2). Turbines with pitched blades consume considerably less power, but their flow patterns are different, as shown by the flow patterns in Fig. 9.3. Figure 9.7 is useful for predicting the power in scale-up, but other factors come into play when it is desired to perform the same mixing at minimum cost. From Eq. (9.11) it is noted that at high Reynolds numbers (i.e., constant N_{po} and D) the power consumption increases as the cube of the speed.

The power number and other important dimensionless groups may be deduced from dimensional analysis, as will be illustrated shortly in Example

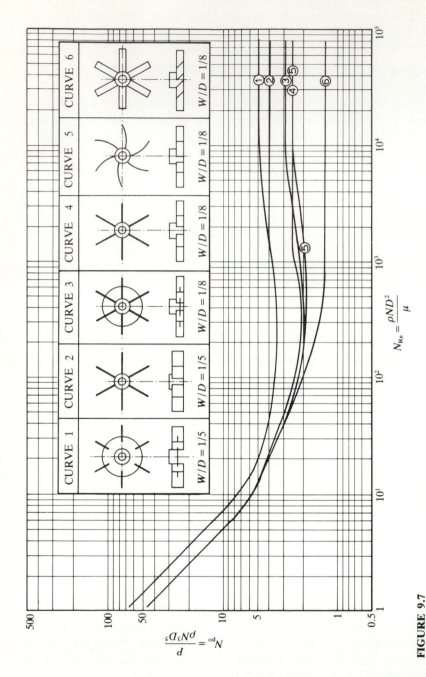

FIGURE 9.7
Turbine power correlation for baffled vessels. (*From Bates, Fondy, and Fenic, in Mixing Theory and Practice, vol. 1, Uhl and Gray, ed., Academic Press, New York, 1960. By permission.*)

9.1. An alternate treatment is to derive the form of the power number from a consideration of the forces acting on a flat plate (such as the blade of an impeller) as a result of its passage through a fluid. The shear stress at the wall is force per area:

$$\tau_{yx} = \frac{(\text{mass})(\text{velocity})}{(\text{time})(\text{area})} = \frac{F}{A} \qquad (2.6)$$

The Fanning friction factor f relates the shear stress at the wall to an inertial term in the turbulent flow in tubes:

$$f = \frac{\tau_w}{\frac{1}{2}\rho U^2_{z,\,\text{ave}}} = \frac{(d_o/4)(-d\bar{p}/dz)}{\frac{1}{2}\rho U^2_{z,\,\text{ave}}} = \frac{\dfrac{d_o(-\Delta p)}{4L}}{\frac{1}{2}\rho U^2_{z,\,\text{ave}}} \qquad (6.89)$$

Combining Eqs. (2.6) and (6.89), for turbulent flow, the force F (which the fluid exerts on the impeller blade) is proportional to the projected area A_p, the density ρ, and the velocity U squared:[2]

$$F \propto \rho A_p U^2 \qquad (9.12)$$

The basic definition of power is a force times a distance divided by a time. Replacing distance divided by time with velocity, the result is

$$P \propto FU \qquad (9.13)$$

Substitution of F from Eq. (9.12) into the above equation yields

$$P \propto \rho A_p U^3 \qquad (9.14)$$

The velocity in this equation can be replaced by N and D via Eq. (9.7). Also, when geometric similarity is maintained upon scale-up, the projected area is proportional to the impeller diameter squared. Then Eq. (9.4) becomes

$$P \propto \rho N^3 D^5 \qquad (9.15)$$

This equation is very close to Eq. (9.11). If the proportionality is removed and a constant inserted, the result rearranges to Eq. (9.11), i.e., the power number is a constant.

For laminar flow, the Hagen–Poiseuille equation for tubes, Eq. (4.76), is conveniently expressed as

$$f = 16/N_{\text{Re}} \qquad (6.124)$$

---

[2] The forces exerted by a fluid on a solid body are more properly treated in Chapter 12, "Transport Past Immersed Bodies". In Chapter 12, the drag coefficient C_D is the force per area divided by the quantity $(\rho U^2/2)$. The drag coefficient and Fanning friction factor are similar, the former being used for immersed bodies and the latter for flow through conduits. Consideration of C_D also leads to Eq. (9.12).

The Reynolds number is replaced with Eq. (9.9); then the result is combined with Eqs. (6.89) and (9.12):

$$F/(A_p \rho U^2) \propto \mu/(ND^2 \rho) \tag{9.16}$$

In this equation, the area is assumed to be proportional to the square of D; thus, the A_p term cancels the D^2 term, and the density cancels as well:

$$F \propto \mu U^2/N \tag{9.17}$$

If Eq. (9.7) is used to replace U in Eq. (9.17), and the speed is canceled from numerator and denominator, Eq. (9.17) becomes

$$F \propto \mu UD \tag{9.18}$$

This equation is also elegantly derived from the classic Stokes' equation for creeping flow past a sphere.[3] The final equation is obtained as before, using Eqs. (9.18), (9.7), and (9.13):

$$P \propto \mu N^2 D^3 \tag{9.19}$$

This treatment of power shows the origin of the power number, the origin of the entries for power in Table 9.1, and the consistency of the empirically determined curves in Fig. 9.7 with other areas in fluid mechanics, such as flow through a circular conduit.

Froude number. The Froude number, introduced previously in Table 8.1, is defined as follows for agitation:

$$N_{Fr} = N^2 D/g \tag{9.20}$$

This number includes the gravitational forces and is used to account for the effect of surface behavior (e.g., the center vortex) on the power number. Hence, the Froude number is included in correlations of N_{Re} and N_{po} for unbaffled systems [R2]. In baffled systems, there is no center vortex formed, and therefore the curves in Fig. 9.7 are independent of the Froude number.

Blend number. The blend number is

$$N_b = N\theta \tag{9.21}$$

where θ is the blend time in seconds. The blend time θ is a measure of the time required for mixing miscible liquids or gases uniformly throughout the agitator tank volume. If the blend number is constant, then the blend time is proportional to the reciprocal of impeller speed. Correlations indicate that the blend number is constant for both laminar and turbulent mixing; however, the value of the constant is different for the two regimes.

---

[3] Stokes' law is covered in Section 12.2.2.

Pumping number. The pumping number N_p relates the impeller pumping rate Q (i.e., the volumetric flow rate through the impeller area per unit time) to the speed and size of the impeller:

$$N_p = \frac{Q}{ND^3} \qquad (9.22)$$

An expanded pumping number has proved more useful:

$$N_p = \frac{Q(D/T)^y}{ND^3} \qquad (9.23)$$

where y is approximately 0.5. This number contains the very important D/T ratio which must be kept constant during scale-up. The pumping number correlates pumping capacities of different impellers with different vessel geometries.

Weber number. The Weber number was introduced as Eq. (8.17) and relates inertial to surface forces. The impeller Weber number for agitation is

$$N_{We} = N^2 D^3 \rho / \sigma \qquad (9.24)$$

Because of the importance of both inertial and surface forces in many dispersion operations, the Weber number is obviously important. However, it may be just as reasonable to use characteristic velocities or lengths other than those of the impeller. For instance, a tank Weber number or a drop Weber number may be useful. In Eq. (9.24), the characteristic velocity is the impeller tip velocity, Eq. (9.7), and the impeller diameter D.

Some of the more important dimensionless numbers in agitation may be deduced from dimensional analysis, as shown in Examples 9.1 and 9.2. Use of these dimensionless numbers for scale-up of agitation units will be illustrated in subsequent examples.

Example 9.1. From a survey of the literature on agitation, it has been established that the important variables are the rotational speed (N), impeller diameter (D), tank diameter (T), power input (P), and fluid properties of density (ρ) and viscosity (μ). Although other variables may be important, perform a dimensional analysis for these six variables.

Answer. Table 9.4 summarizes the six variables. Here the original Rayleigh procedure is used. The equations are

$$N^a D^b T^c P^d \rho^e \mu^f = \text{constant} \qquad (i)$$

and

$$\Theta^{-a} L^b L^c M^d L^{2d} \Theta^{-3d} M^e L^{-3e} M^f L^{-f} \Theta^{-f} = \text{dimensionless} \qquad (ii)$$

The three equations are

L:	$b + c + 2d - 3e - f = 0$	(iii)
M:	$d + e + f = 0$	(iv)
Θ:	$-a - 3d - f = 0$	(v)

TABLE 9.4
Variables for agitation, Example 9.1

Symbol	Exponent	Name	SI Units	Dimensions
N	a	rotational speed	s^{-1}	Θ^{-1}
D	b	impeller diameter	m	L
T	c	tank diameter	m	L
P	d	power	$kg\,m^2\,s^{-3}$	$ML^2\Theta^{-3}$
ρ	e	density	$kg\,m^{-3}$	ML^{-3}
μ	f	viscosity	$kg\,m^{-1}\,s^{-1}$	$ML^{-1}\Theta^{-1}$

There are six unknowns and three equations. Thus, the number of dimensionless groups of variables is $6 - 3$, or 3. Examining Eqs. (iii) through (v), the variables a and b or c appear once. Experience tells us that b and c cannot both be eliminated because Eq. (iii) can be used for one or the other but not both; so b is arbitrarily chosen. The next best candidate for elimination is e. The three variables to be eliminated (a, b and e) can be expressed in terms of c, d, and f by using the three equations above:

$$a = -3d - f \tag{vi}$$

$$e = -d - f \tag{vii}$$

$$b = -c - 2d + 3e + f = -c - 2d - 3d - 3f + f = -c - 5d - 2f \tag{viii}$$

Using all these results in Eq. (i) gives

$$N^{-3d-f}D^{-c-5d-2f}T^cP^d\rho^{-d-f}\mu^f = \text{constant} \tag{ix}$$

Rearranging Eq. (ix):

$$\left(\frac{T}{D}\right)^c \left(\frac{P}{N^3D^5\rho}\right)^d \left(\frac{\mu}{ND^2\rho}\right)^f = \text{constant} \tag{x}$$

Each of these dimensionless numbers has been introduced previously. The first is the reciprocal of D/T, perhaps the most important geometric ratio. The second ratio is the power number, Eq. (9.10), and the third is the reciprocal of the impeller Reynolds number, Eq. (9.9). Thus, Eq. (x) becomes

$$N_{\text{po}} = k_1(D/T)^c(N_{\text{Re}})^f \tag{xi}$$

where k_1 is an empirical constant. Note that c and f assume different values from those in Eq. (x). Equation (xi) applies for baffled tank systems as shown in Fig. 9.6. However, Eq. (xi) is insufficient for scale-up, as will be shown subsequently.

Example 9.2. Uhl [U1] correlated heat transfer data in agitated, jacketed vessels with the variables listed in Table 9.5. Develop the dimensionless groups suitable for a correlation.

Answer. The exponents in Table 9.5 were chosen to avoid confusion as much as possible. A complete explanation of the dimensions of k, c_p, and h is given in Example 8.2. The Rayleigh procedure as explained in Chapter 8 will be used; the

TABLE 9.5
Variables for heat transfer in agitated vessels, Example 9.2

Symbol	Exponent	Name	SI Units	Dimensions
ρ	d	density	kg m^{-3}	ML^{-3}
μ	e	viscosity	$\text{kg m}^{-1}\,\text{s}^{-1}$	$ML^{-1}\Theta^{-1}$
μ_w	f	wall viscosity	$\text{kg m}^{-1}\,\text{s}^{-1}$	$ML^{-1}\Theta^{-1}$
k	g	thermal conductivity	$\text{kg m s}^{-3}\,\text{K}^{-1}$	$ML\Theta^{-3}T^{-1}$
c_p	i	heat capacity	$\text{m}^2\,\text{s}^{-2}\,\text{K}^{-1}$	$L^2\Theta^{-2}T^{-1}$
h	j	heat transfer coefficient	$\text{kg s}^{-3}\,\text{K}^{-1}$	$M\Theta^{-3}T^{-1}$
N	m	rotational speed	s^{-1}	Θ^{-1}
D	n	impeller diameter	m	L
T	p	tank diameter	m	L

equations are

$$\rho^d \mu^e \mu_w^f k^g c_p^i h^j N^m D^n T^p = \text{constant} \tag{i}$$

and

$$M^d L^{-3d} M^e L^{-e} \Theta^{-e} M^f L^{-f} \Theta^{-f} M^g L^g \Theta^{-3g} T^{-g} L^{2i} \Theta^{-2i} T^{-i} M^j \Theta^{-3j} T^{-j} \Theta^{-m} L^n L^p$$
$$= \text{dimensionless} \tag{ii}$$

The four equations representing each dimension are

$$\Theta: \quad -e - f - 3g - 2i - 3j - m = 0 \tag{iii}$$

$$L: \quad -3d - e - f + g + 2i + n + p = 0 \tag{iv}$$

$$M: \quad d + e + f + g + j = 0 \tag{v}$$

$$T: \quad -g - i - j = 0 \tag{vi}$$

There are nine unknowns and four equations. Thus, five groups will be produced. In the above four equations, either n or p may be eliminated, and n is chosen arbitrarily. Also, m from Eq. (iii) and g from Eq. (vi) are easy to eliminate:

$$g = -i - j \tag{vii}$$

$$d = -e - f - g - j = -e - f + i + j - j = -e - f + i \tag{viii}$$

$$m = -e - f - 3g - 2i - 3j = -e - f + 3i + 3j - 2i - 3j$$
$$= -e - f + i \tag{ix}$$

$$n = -p + 3d + e + f - g - 2i = -p - 3e - 3f + 3i + e + f + i + j - 2i$$
$$= -p - 2e - 2f + 2i + j \tag{x}$$

Using all three results in Eq. (i) gives

$$N^{-e-f+i} D^{-2e-2f+2i+j-p} T^p \rho^{-e-f+i} \mu^e \mu_w^f k^{-i-j} c_p^i h^j = \text{constant} \tag{xi}$$

Next, the variables are grouped by similar exponent:

$$(D^{-p} T^p)(N^{-e} D^{-2e} \rho^{-e} \mu^e)(N^{-f} D^{-2f} \rho^{-f} \mu_w^f)(N^i D^{2i} \rho^i k^{-i} c_p^i)(D^j k^{-j} h^j) = \text{constant} \tag{xii}$$

This equation is rearranged as follows:

$$(D/T)^{-p}(ND^2\rho/\mu)^{-e}[\mu_w/(ND^2\rho)]^f(ND^2\rho c_p/k)^i(hD/k)^j = \text{constant} \quad \text{(xiii)}$$

The following may be substituted for each group:

$$\Pi_1 = D/T \qquad\qquad\qquad \Pi_4 = ND^2\rho c_p/k$$
$$\Pi_2 = N_{Re} = ND^2\rho/\mu \qquad \Pi_5 = hD/k \qquad\qquad\qquad \text{(xiv)}$$
$$\Pi_3 = \mu_w/(ND^2\rho)$$

These groups are now substituted into Eq. (xiii):

$$\Pi_1^{-p}\Pi_2^{-e}\Pi_3^f\Pi_4^i\Pi_5^j = \text{constant} \quad \text{(xv)}$$

These five dimensionless groups are all valid, but experience and common sense dictate some changes. The first group is the familiar geometric ratio encountered previously. The second group is the impeller Reynolds number, Eq. (9.9). The third group also looks like a Reynolds number, but the wall viscosity does not belong with the impeller variables N and D. In fact, groups Π_3, Π_4, and Π_5 are actually combinations of some other, more commonly encountered groups; a viable correlation will be obtained only if these three groups are modified. Let us consider Π_5 first. In Π_5, h is heat transfer coefficient at the wall of the tank. The area of the tank for heat transfer is

$$A_{\text{heat}} = \pi TZ \quad \text{(xvi)}$$

where T and Z are dimensions of the tank as shown in Fig. 9.6. If Π_5 is divided by Π_1, then a new dimensionless group with T replacing D is formed. The group is the important Nusselt number for heat transfer in an agitated, jacketed vessel:

$$N_{Nu} = \Pi_5/\Pi_1 = hT/k \quad \text{(xvii)}$$

The alteration of groups Π_3 and Π_4 is also required. In the case of Π_3, the wall viscosity was added to the list of variables in Table 9.4 because experimental data showed that the heat transfer coefficient was altered whenever the wall viscosity μ_w differed from the bulk fluid viscosity μ. If the group Π_3 is multiplied by N_{Re} from Eq. (9.9), which is also Π_2, a more reasonable dimensionless group μ_w/μ is obtained:

$$\Pi_3 N_{Re} = \mu_w/\mu \quad \text{(xviii)}$$

In group Π_4, the ratio c_p/k is found. This ratio also appears in the Prandtl number, Eq. (8.4), which has been found to be highly significant in heat transfer correlations. The Prandtl number is obtained by dividing Π_4 by Π_2, the Reynolds number:

$$\Pi_4/\Pi_2 = N_{Pr} = c_p\mu/k \quad \text{(xix)}$$

The Prandtl number depends only on fluid properties and is a much more reasonable dimensionless group for data correlation than Π_4, which combines too many diverse variables.

The final correlating equation is found by including in Eq. (xv) the modifications represented by Eqs. (xvii) to (xix):

$$(D/T)^{-p}(N_{Re})^{-e}[(\mu_w/\mu)^f/(N_{Re}^f)](N_{Pr}^i N_{Re}^i)[(N_{Nu}^j)(D/T)^j] = \text{constant} \quad \text{(xx)}$$

Equation (xx) is rearranged to the usual form for heat transfer correlations:

$$N_{Nu} = k_1 N_{Re}^a N_{Pr}^b (\mu/\mu_w)^c (D/T)^d \quad \text{(xxi)}$$

TABLE 9.6
Heat transfer to jacketed walls*

Impeller type	Constants in Eq. (xxii)				Range of N_{Re}	Comments
	k_2	a	b	c		
Paddle	0.40	2/3	1/3	0.14	$300-6 \times 10^5$	k_2 ranges from 0.36 to 0.40
Paddle	0.415	2/3	1/3	0.24	20–4000	baffled and unbaffled
Two curved-blade turbines						
	0.60	2/3	1/3	0.14	$2000-8 \times 10^5$	
Pitched-blade turbine						
	0.44	2/3	1/3	0.24	80–200	low position $C = 4$ inches
	0.53	2/3	1/3	0.24	20–120	intermediate position, $C = 11$ inches
Disk flat-blade turbine						
	0.54	2/3	1/3	0.14	$40-3 \times 10^5$	unbaffled
	0.74	2/3	1/3	0.14	$300-3 \times 10^5$	1, 2, or 4 baffles

* From reference [U1], p. 284, by permission.

Note that the exponents a, b, c, and d are algebraic combinations of e, f, i, j, and p so as to make Eq. (xxi) compatible with Eq. (xx). Under the restriction of constant D/T, and in terms of the variables rather than the groups, Eq. (xxi) is

$$hT/k = k_2(D^2N\rho/\mu)^a(c_p\mu/k)^b(\mu/\mu_w)^c \qquad \text{(xxii)}$$

This procedure in modifying the results of dimensional analysis to obtain reasonable and common dimensionless groups is often followed. Dimensional analysis and experience dictate how to multiply one group by some other in order to arrive at such common groups as N_{Pr} or N_{Nu}. Equation (xxii) has proved satisfactory in correlating N_{Nu} as shown in Table 9.6 from Uhl [U1]. Dimensional analysis emphasizes the importance of the restriction of constant D/T.

There is a correlation in the literature [D1] that includes the D/T term as well as a Z/T ratio. The group Z/T can also be predicted through dimensional analysis, if the variable Z is included in the list in Table 9.5. The correlation for jacket Nusselt number in the turbine agitation of a jacketed tank is

$$hT/k = (0.85)(D^2N\rho/\mu)^{0.66}(c_p\mu/k)^{0.33}(Z/T)^{-0.56}(D/T)^{0.13}(\mu/\mu_w)^{0.14} \quad \text{(xxiii)}$$

9.6 SCALE-UP

Scale-up (or scale-down) in agitation systems is a fairly complicated topic. Many complex problems exist, such as mixing of highly non-Newtonian fluids and of three or more phases (multiphase processing). Not much is known about these; hence, a conservative approach to design and scale-up is recommended, in addition to consultations with equipment manufacturers and other qualified personnel. The objective in the design of agitators during scale-up is to obtain the same (or similar) process result in the large unit as was demonstrated in the small unit. This is relatively a difficult task [O2], although the necessity occurs so often that the procedures for simple systems are well-understood.

Geometric similarity. Maintaining geometric similarity during scale-up allows definition of a single scale factor R, which is equal to any of the ratios between dimensions of agitators (a) and (b) in Fig. 9.6:

$$R = D_2/D_1 = T_2/T_1 = W_2/W_1 = Z_2/Z_1 = C_2/C_1 = B_2/B_1 \qquad (9.25)$$

where the subscript 2 represents the large agitator and 1 represents the small unit. The tank volume is the tank area $\pi T^2/4$ times the height Z. Since the ratio Z/T is constant for scale-up [see Eq. (9.1)] and Z usually equals T, the volume is proportional to T cubed:

$$V = \pi T^3/4 \qquad (9.26)$$

Then the scale factor in terms of volume is

$$R = T_2/T_1 = (V_2/V_1)^{1/3} \qquad (9.27)$$

In general, geometric similarity is desirable. In Section 9.6.5, a class of problems will be discussed in which it is neither useful nor required to maintain similarity.

Size. The size of the agitation unit is determined from considerations beyond the scope of this chapter. However, the most important considerations are the throughput in the process and the processing time (which is similar to the time constants encountered in process control). For instance, if there is a chemical reaction in the tank, then the size of the tank will be dictated by the desired flow rate of product and the kinetics of the reaction or the reaction time. If the agitation unit is to disperse a solid in a liquid, then again the size of the tank will be determined by the desired rates of flow of solid and liquid and the length of time required to disperse the solids.

9.6.1   Scale-up Procedures for Turbulent Flow with Three or More Test Volumes

In general process studies, the most reliable scale-up is obtained by performing agitation experiments in vessels of several sizes. From these results, scale-up trends are obtained which can be extrapolated to the final vessel size. The smallest test equipment recommended [P2] is a tank about 1 ft in diameter that holds 5–10 gallons. Normally, a second tank about 2 ft in diameter is also used. Each tank is capable of operating at two volumes, so that a total of four runs can be made—at volumes of 5, 10, 45, and 90 gallons. Each tank should be equipped with a variable-speed drive and a dynamometer to measure the power input accurately. It is necessary to vary the speed of the impeller until satisfactory process results are obtained.

When appropriate performance has been achieved in each volume, there are two procedures for scale-up in common use. The data are expressed as P/V, T_q/V, and V. Then two plots are prepared: $\log(P/V)$ versus $\log V$ and $\log(T_q/V)$ versus $\log V$. Whichever of these looks most linear is then extrapolated to the volume of the final vessel. These procedures correspond to the following equations:

$$(P/V)_2 = (P/V)_1(T_2/T_1)^s = (P/V)_1 R^s \tag{9.28}$$

$$(T_q/V)_2 = (T_q/V)_1(T_2/T_1)^x = (T_q/V)_1 R^x \tag{9.29}$$

In these equations, s and x are the scale-up exponents for power per unit volume and torque per unit volume, respectively, and R is the scale factor, defined in Eqs. (9.25) and (9.27). The subscripts 1 and 2 correspond to vessels of different size. It is possible that the data will not fall on a straight line in either plot. Then a least-squares analysis is recommended to obtain the final scale-up, using Eq. (9.29). The scale-up using a plot of $\log(P/V)$ versus $\log V$ is an excellent design procedure, and it is often used in industry [P2].

9.6.2 Scale-up Procedures for Turbulent Flow with Two Test Volumes

If only two volumes were tested, then there would be no point in preparing graphs, as suggested in the previous section. A simple scale-up equation, suggested by Rautzen, Corpstein, and Dickey [R1], is

$$N_2 = N_1 \left(\frac{D_1}{D_2}\right)^n = N_1 \left(\frac{1}{R}\right)^n \tag{9.30}$$

where n is the speed scale-up exponent. The above equation can be solved directly for n:

$$n = \frac{\ln(N_1/N_2)}{\ln(D_2/D_1)} \tag{9.31}$$

In this scale-up procedure, the diameter of the impeller for the process vessel (D_3) is determined from Eq. (9.25), assuming geometric similarity. Equation (9.30) is used to determine the speed of the agitator in the process vessel (N_3). The power requirement can be found from Eq. (9.11) or Fig. 9.7 after determination of V_3, D_3, and N_3. Similarly, the torque requirement can be determined from Eq. (9.6) or Eq. (9.8). This calculation is illustrated in Example 9.4, which follows shortly.

When only two volumes are available for scale-up tests, the design engineer has no estimate of the error of the experiments and no estimate of the accuracy of n from Eq. (9.31). The overall design is extremely sensitive to small changes in the value of n. In the case of four test volumes, if one were erroneous, the recommended graphs would clearly show one data point to be inconsistent with the rest. Hence, the procedure outlined in Section 9.6.1 is recommended.

In Eqs. (9.28), (9.29), and (9.30) there are three scale-up exponents: s, x, and n. From two experiments, all three exponents can be calculated, but they will not be independent. In other words, each of the three equations predicts the same values of P, T_q, and N for the vessel being designed [P2, T2]. This point will be further illustrated in the next section and in Example 9.4.

9.6.3 Scale-up Procedures for Turbulent Flow with a Single Test Volume

Sometimes it is necessary (although highly undesirable) to design and scale-up a process unit based on an experiment performed in a single unit at a single volume. Any of Eqs. (9.28), (9.29), or (9.30), each with its own scale-up exponent, may be chosen, although identical results will be obtained because the equations are not independent. The success in scale-up with a single test volume lies in correctly choosing the appropriate value of the scale-up exponent. Note that none of the following scale-up procedures corresponds to constant Reynolds number [O3].

Criteria for scale-up. The purpose of scale-up is to obtain in a plant-size agitation unit the same process results as were obtained in a small-scale unit. Much of the old literature in chemical engineering suggests that scale-up can be accomplished while keeping the ratio of power per unit volume constant from the small unit to the large unit. More sophisticated approaches [C1, P1, R1, V1] take account of the fact that different applications in mixing require different ratios to be maintained constant. The ratios to be suggested are all based on appropriate correlations and explicitly stated scale-up criteria [P2].

There are many types of criteria and procedures for scale-up. These can be separated into two distinct classes: physical uniformity and equal kinetic and/or transport conditions. A partial list can be found in Penney [P1]. Five common procedures for turbulent flow are listed below:

1. *Equal liquid motion.* Kinematic similarity will be maintained; in other words, the velocities in the large-scale unit will everywhere be approximately equal to those in corresponding locations in the small-scale unit. This scale-up approach is suggested for processes that are termed "flow sensitive" [C1]; here constant torque per unit volume is maintained. Also, it will be shown that constant torque per unit volume is identical to maintaining a constant tip velocity U_t.

2. *Equal solids suspension.* The level of solids suspension is maintained approximately constant upon scale-up. This approach is also fairly common.

3. *Equal mass transfer.* Mass transfer includes dissolving of solids or gases or

mass transfer between two liquid phases. Equal rates of mass transfer are maintained during scale-up.

4. *Equal surface behavior.* The surface of the liquid during agitation remains the same. The vortex shape (or lack thereof) will be unchanged. The shape of the surface of the liquid is important when dry solids added to the surface are dispersed. This type of scale-up, also called equal Froude number, is less commonly encountered.

5. *Equal blend time.* Equal blend time is the limiting case at the opposite end from equal liquid motion. It is rarely practical to duplicate in a large unit of, say, 10 000 gal the fast blend times (in the order of seconds) in a gallon-size unit.

There are other criteria in the literature, but these are of lesser importance. For example, in the 1940s, equal apparent superficial velocity was maintained, but this procedure is outdated today [C1]. The apparent superficial velocity is found by dividing the volumetric flow rate that the impeller produces by the tank area.

The criterion for scale-up should be clearly stated. Sometimes it is clear to the design engineer what scale-up criterion to use. For example, if fast processing is required, then equal blend time will be chosen, and so on. Often, however, it is unclear which of these to select for a given process. Furthermore, complicated processes could fall under several different scale-up procedures.

Constant torque per unit volume. Scale-up based on a torque per unit volume criterion is a recommended procedure [C1, V1] because torque is the variable that most directly correlates with initial cost. Also, when the ratio T_q/V is maintained, equal liquid motion is accomplished, which will do the same job of agitation at the corresponding points in the small and large units [V1]. In Eq. (9.29), the exponent x is zero for this case:

$$\frac{(T_q/V)_2}{(T_q/V)_1} = 1 \tag{9.32}$$

The assumption of constant torque per unit volume is identical to assuming constant tip speed in scale-up. If Eq. (9.8) or T_q/V from Table 9.1 is substituted into Eq. (9.32), under conditions of constant density and geometric similarity the following is obtained:

$$\frac{(T_q/V)_2}{(T_q/V)_1} = \frac{N_2^2 D_2^2}{N_1^2 D_1^2} = \frac{U_{t,2}^2}{U_{t,1}^2} = 1 \tag{9.33}$$

Equation (9.33) shows that the tip speed U_t is the same in both volume 1 and volume 2 for constant torque per unit volume. Equation (9.33) can be also be used to calculate the exponent n in Eq. (9.30):

$$N_2^2 D_2^2 = N_1^2 D_1^2 \quad \text{or} \quad N_2 = N_1 \left(\frac{D_1}{D_2}\right)^1 = N_1 \left(\frac{1}{R}\right)^n \tag{9.34}$$

Equation (9.34) shows that when the torque per volume exponent x is zero, the speed exponent n equals 1.0.

Equation (9.6) relates torque to power and speed. This equation can also be used to find the power per volume exponent s when x is zero:

$$T_q = \frac{P}{2\pi N} = \frac{P}{N} C_f \tag{9.6}$$

Equation (9.6) is substituted into Eq. (9.32):

$$\frac{(T_q/V)_2}{(T_q/V)_1} = \frac{P_2/(N_2 V_2)}{P_1/(N_1 V_1)} = \frac{P_2/V_2}{P_1/V_1} \frac{N_1}{N_2}$$

$$= \frac{P_2/V_2}{P_1/V_1} \frac{D_2}{D_1} = \frac{P_2/V_2}{P_1/V_1} R^1 = 1 \tag{9.35}$$

This equation can be rearranged and the result compared with Eq. (9.28). The result shows that the power per volume exponent s equals -1.0. Summarizing, for constant torque per volume or tip speed:

$$n = \quad 1.0$$
$$s = -1.0 \tag{9.36}$$
$$x = \quad 0.0$$

Table 9.7 contains the values of the three scale-up exponents for all five criteria listed previously [P2, T2]. When the design engineer is in a quandary as to which criterion in Table 9.7 to use, many authors recommend scale-up be accomplished with constant tip speed [C1, V1], because the torque per unit volume is maintained constant, equal liquid motion is approximately maintained (kinematic similarity), and experience with "flow-velocity-sensitive" applications has been favorable. Connolly and Winter [C1] recommend this criterion for many mixing operations, including suspending solids.

TABLE 9.7
Scale-up exponents for turbulent flow

Most important scale-up criterion	Value of s for Eq. (9.28)	Value of x for Eq. (9.29)	Value of n for Eq. (9.30)
(1) Equal fluid motion	−1.0	0.0	1.0
(2) Equal solids suspension	−0.55	0.5	3/4
(3) Equal mass transfer	0.0	2/3	2/3
(4) Equal surface	0.45	1.0	0.5
(5) Equal blend time	2.0	2.0	0.0

Constant power per unit volume. Under conditions of constant power per unit volume upon scale-up, equal bubble or drop diameter is maintained [P2]. Inspection of Eq. (9.28) shows that the exponent s is zero for this case:

$$\frac{(P/V)_2}{(P/V)_1} = 1 \tag{9.37}$$

The values of n and x for this criterion are found in the same manner as those in Eq. (9.36). Returning to Table 9.1, power per unit volume is proportional to the speed cubed and the diameter squared (under geometric similarity):

$$\frac{P}{V} \propto N^3 D^2 \tag{9.38}$$

Substituting this result into Eq. (9.37), the relation between speed and diameter is

$$N_1^3 D_1^3 = N_2^3 D_2^3 \quad \text{or} \quad N_2 = N_1 \left(\frac{D_1}{D_2}\right)^{2/3} \tag{9.39}$$

Comparison of Eq. (9.39) with Eq. (9.30) yields

$$N_2 = N_1 \left(\frac{D_1}{D_2}\right)^n = N_1 \left(\frac{1}{R}\right)^{2/3} \tag{9.40}$$

Thus, n for this scale-up procedure is $\frac{2}{3}$. Similarly, it is easy to show that x also equals $\frac{2}{3}$:

$$\begin{align} n &= 2/3 \\ s &= 0.0 \\ x &= 2/3 \end{align} \tag{9.41}$$

These results are shown in Table 9.7 under the heading of equal mass transfer [R1]. This criterion is also called "equal dispersion" [V1].

Equal blend time. Under the criteria of equal blend time and constant blend number N_b, the impeller speed remains constant upon scale-up:

$$N_1 = N_2 \tag{9.42}$$

Following the previous derivations, the scale-up exponents are

$$\begin{align} n &= 0.0 \\ s &= 2.0 \\ x &= 2.0 \end{align} \tag{9.43}$$

Compared to the other values of the exponents in Table 9.7, the values in Eq. (9.43) represent the opposite extremes from criterion (1)—equal fluid motion. The criterion represented by Eq. (9.43) is rarely used because the power to be specified upon scale-up is usually too large. Equation (9.28) with $s = 2.0$ becomes

$$P_2/P_1 = (V_2/V_1)R^2 = R^5 \qquad (9.44)$$

Thus, for constant blend time, the power increases as the fifth power of the tank diameter [cf. Eq. (9.11), from which the same result can easily be obtained]. It is rarely practical to require the fast blend times obtained in a small unit in a plant-sized vessel.

Example 9.3. An agitation unit consists of a 9-inch diameter, four-bladed, 45° pitched-bladed turbine impeller in a tank that is 30 inches in diameter and has four baffles. The unit is filled to a height of 30 inches with a fluid of viscosity 10 cP and specific gravity 1.1. The agitator operates at a speed of 300 rpm. Calculate the power per unit volume and the torque per unit volume if the ratio C/T is 0.3.

Answer. Figure 9.6 or literature sources will be used to find the power. The diameter of the impeller and the volume of the tank [from Eq. (9.26)] are

$$D = 9/12 = 0.75 \text{ ft} \qquad (i)$$

$$V = \pi T^3/4 = \pi(30/12)^3/4 = 12.27 \text{ ft}^3 = 91.79 \text{ gal} \qquad (ii)$$

where 7.48 gal equals 1 ft³. The fluid viscosity and density in engineering units are

$$\mu = (10)(6.72 \times 10^{-4}) \left[(cP)(lb_m \text{ ft}^{-1} \text{ s}^{-1} \text{ cP}^{-1}) \right]$$

$$= 6.72 \times 10^{-3} \text{ lb}_m \text{ ft}^{-1} \text{ s}^{-1} \qquad (iii)$$

$$\rho = (1.1)(62.4) = 68.64 \text{ lb}_m \text{ ft}^{-3} \qquad (iv)$$

The impeller speed is

$$N = 300/60 \left[(\text{rev min}^{-1})(\text{min s}^{-1}) \right] = 5.0 \text{ s}^{-1} \qquad (v)$$

The Reynolds number for agitation from Eq. (9.9) is:

$$N_{Re} = D^2 N\rho/\mu$$

$$= (0.75)^2(5.0)(68.64)/(0.00672) \left(\frac{(\text{ft}^2)(\text{s}^{-1})(lb_m \text{ ft}^{-3})}{lb_m \text{ ft}^{-1} \text{ s}^{-1}} \right) = 2.87 \times 10^4 \qquad (vi)$$

Therefore, the agitator operates in the turbulent region. Curve 6 for a six-bladed pitched-blade turbine shows a power number of 1.37. From the literature [V1], the power number for this agitator equals 1.62. Equation (9.11) is the definition of the power number; solving for P, the answer is

$$P = N_{po}(\rho N^3 D^5) = (1.62)(68.64)(5.0)^3(0.75)^5 [(lb_m \text{ ft}^{-3})(\text{s}^{-1})^3(\text{ft})^5]$$

$$= 3298 \text{ lb}_m \text{ ft}^2 \text{ s}^{-3} \qquad (vii)$$

To convert P to units of horsepower, the gravitational conversion factor g_c will be needed in the denominator of Eq. (vii):

$$P = N_{po}(\rho N^3 D^5)/g_c = (3298)/(32.174)[(lb_m \text{ ft}^2 \text{ s}^{-3})(lb_f \text{ lb}_m^{-1} \text{ ft}^{-1} \text{ s}^2)]$$

$$= 102.5 \text{ ft lb}_f \text{ s}^{-1}$$

$$= 102.5/550[(\text{ft lb}_f \text{ s}^{-1})(\text{hp s ft}^{-1} \text{ lb}_f^{-1})]$$

$$= 0.1864 \text{ hp} \qquad (viii)$$

The torque is found from Eq. (9.6), using the value of C_f from Table 9.2:

$$T_q = (P/N)(C_f) = [(0.1864)/(300)](63\,025) = 39.16 \text{ in. lb}_f \qquad \text{(ix)}$$

The power per unit volume and the torque per unit volume can be found either in units of gallons or ft³:

$$P/V = 0.1864/12.27 = 1.52 \times 10^{-2} \text{ hp ft}^{-3} = 2.02 \times 10^{-3} \text{ hp gal}^{-1} \qquad \text{(x)}$$

$$T_q/V = 39.16/12.27 = 3.19 \text{ in. lb}_f \text{ ft}^{-3} = 0.427 \text{ in. lb}_f \text{ gal}^{-1} \qquad \text{(xi)}$$

Example 9.4. An engineer has the task of designing a reactor of capacity 12 000 gal to agitate the material in the previous example. She is able to obtain equal process results in the following geometrically similar units under the conditions given in Table 9.8.

Answer. Both test units as described in Table 9.8 operate in the turbulent range. Three scale-up equations have been presented in this chapter and will be compared in the following design. The important equations are

$$R = T_2/T_1 = (V_2/V_1)^{1/3} \qquad (9.27)$$

$$(P/V)_2 = (P/V)_1(T_2/T_1)^s = (P/V)_1 R^s \qquad (9.28)$$

$$(T_q/V)_2 = (T_q/V)_1(T_2/T_1)^x = (T_q/V)_1 R^x \qquad (9.29)$$

$$N_2 = N_1(D_1/D_2)^n = N_1(1/R)^n \qquad (9.30)$$

$$n = [\ln(N_1/N_2)]/[\ln(D_2/D_1)] \qquad (9.31)$$

Speed scale-up. Following the procedure outlined in Section 9.6.2, the value of R is found from Eq. (9.27) and the value of n from Eq. (9.31):

$$R = T_{\text{pilot}}/T_{\text{lab}} = 30/10 = 3 \qquad \text{(i)}$$

$$n = [\ln(690/271)]/[\ln(3/1)] = 0.8507 \qquad \text{(ii)}$$

TABLE 9.8
Results of tests for Example 9.4

Description	Laboratory unit	Pilot plant unit
Vessel diameter, inches	10	30
Impeller diameter, ft	0.25	0.75
Impeller type—four-bladed, 45° pitched-bladed turbine impeller		
	YES	YES
Z/T	1.0	1.0
T/B	12	12
Number of baffles	4	4
Speed, rpm	690	271
Reynolds number	7342	2.595×10^4
Volume of unit, gal	3.40	91.79
Power, hp	9.33×10^{-3}	0.1374
Torque, in. lb$_f$	0.8525	31.95
P/V, hp gal^{-1}	2.744×10^{-3}	1.497×10^{-3}
T_q/V, in. lb$_f$ gal^{-1}	0.2507	0.3481

Let the subscript 3 denote the 12 000-gal reactor. Arbitrarily, let us scale-up from the pilot plant unit. The tank diameter and that scale factor (R_f) is

$$V = 12\,000/7.48[(\text{gal})(\text{ft}^3\,\text{gal}^{-1})] = 1604\,\text{ft}^3 \qquad \text{(iii)}$$

$$T = (4V/\pi)^{1/3} = 12.69\,\text{ft} \qquad \text{(iv)}$$

$$R_f = T_2/T_1 = 12.69/[(30)/(12)] = 5.075 \qquad \text{(v)}$$

Equation (9.30) is used to find the impeller speed in the reactor:

$$N_3 = N_2(D_2/D_3)^n = N_2(1/R_f)^n = (271)(1/5.075)^{0.8507} = 68.05\,\text{rpm} \qquad \text{(vi)}$$

The reactor impeller diameter is calculated from R_f, assuming geometric similarity:

$$D_3 = D_2R_f = (0.75)(5.075) = 3.806\,\text{ft} \qquad \text{(vii)}$$

Using Eq. (9.11) for constant power number [or Eq. (9.15) or Table 9.1], it is seen that the power is proportional to speed cubed and diameter to the fifth power, for constant density. Hence

$$P_3 = P_2\left(\frac{N_3^3 D_3^5}{N_2^3 D_2^5}\right) = P_2(N_3/N_2)^3 R^5 = (0.1374)(68.05/271)^3(5.075)^5 = 7.32\,\text{hp} \quad \text{(viii)}$$

The torque can be found from Eq. (9.6) and Table 9.2:

$$T_q = (P/N)(C_f) = [(7.33)/(68.07)](63\,025) = 6789\,\text{inch lb}_f \qquad \text{(ix)}$$

At this point, the design is complete. A standard-size impeller would be chosen, as well as a standard-size motor (7.5 hp or 10 hp). It is instructive to use Eqs. (9.28) and (9.29) and see whether the above results are confirmed.

Power per unit volume. Equation (9.28) is used for this procedure. The solution begins with the determination of the scale-up exponent s:

$$s = \frac{\ln[(P/V)_{\text{pilot}}/(P/V)_{\text{lab}}]}{\ln R}$$

$$= \{\ln[(1.497 \times 10^{-3})/(2.744 \times 10^{-3})]\}/(\ln 3) = -0.5516 \qquad \text{(x)}$$

Now Eq. (9.28) becomes

$$(P/V)_3 = (P/V)_2 R_f^{-0.5516} \qquad \text{(xi)}$$

This equation is the general scale-up equation, based on the power per unit volume procedure. To find the power in the 12 000-gal reactor, the numbers are inserted:

$$P_3 = V_3(P/V)_2 R_f^s = (12\,000)(1.497 \times 10^{-3})(5.075)^{-0.5516} = 7.33\,\text{hp} \qquad \text{(xii)}$$

The impeller speed in the 12 000-gal reactor can be determined by several methods. One possibility is to compute the power number for both the laboratory unit and the pilot plant unit from Eq. (9.11). The answers should agree to within experimental error, and they do. For illustration, the power number in the pilot plant unit is

$$N_{po} = \frac{Pg_c}{\rho N^3 D^5}$$

$$= \frac{(0.1374)(550)(32.174)}{(68.64)(271/60)^3(0.75)^5} \left(\frac{(hp)(ft\ lb_f\ hp^{-1}\ s^{-1})(lb_m\ lb_f^{-1}\ ft\ s^{-2})}{(lb_m\ ft^{-3})(s^{-1})^3(ft)^5} \right)$$

$$= 1.62 \tag{xiii}$$

This value is the same as used in Example 9.3 [V1]. Since the power number is constant in the turbulent region when the agitation unit is properly baffled, as is this unit, Eq. (xiii) can be used to solve for the speed of the impeller in the 12 000-gal reactor:

$$\frac{P_2 g_c}{\rho N_2^3 D_2^5} = \frac{P_1 g_c}{\rho N_1^3 D_1^5} \tag{xiv}$$

Solving Eq. (xiv) for N_2 and inserting the numbers:

$$N_2 = N_1 \left(\frac{P_2}{P_1} \right)^{1/3} \left(\frac{D_1}{D_2} \right)^{5/3} = (271) \left(\frac{7.33}{0.1374} \right)^{1/3} \left(\frac{0.75}{3.806} \right)^{5/3} = 68.07\ \text{rpm} \tag{xv}$$

The torque can be found from Eq. (9.6) and Table 9.2 as before [cf. Eq. (ix)]. The answers obtained here agree within roundoff error with those from the speed scale-up section.

Torque per unit volume. Equation (9.29) will be used for this procedure; the identical answers will be obtained. Equation (9.29) is solved for the scale-up exponent x. Inserting the numbers, x is

$$x = \ln[(T_q/V)_{\text{pilot}}/(T_q/V)_{\text{lab}}]/(\ln R)$$

$$= \{\ln[(0.3481)/(0.2507)]\}/(\ln 3) = 0.2988 \tag{xvi}$$

Now Eq. (9.29) becomes

$$(T_q/V)_3 = (T_q/V)_2 R_f^{0.2988} \tag{xvii}$$

This equation is the general scale-up equation, based on the torque per unit volume procedure. Proceeding with the solution, Eq. (xvii) is solved for the torque in the 12 000-gal reactor and the numbers inserted:

$$T_{q,3} = V_3 (T_q/V)_2 R^{0.2988}$$

$$= (12\ 000)(0.3481)(5.075)^{0.2988} = 6787\ \text{in. lb}_f \tag{xviii}$$

Thus, the answer in Eq. (xviii) from the torque per unit volume procedure is the same (within roundoff error) as obtained earlier. Therefore the speed and power will be unchanged also from the earlier answers.

Summary. If there had been three or more sets of test data, each in reactors of different size, then a graph of $\log(P/V)$ versus $\log V$ or $\log(T_q/V)$ versus $\log V$ would have been prepared and extrapolated to the final volume. If there are only two sets of test data (as in this example), any of the three scale-up equations [Eqs. (9.28), (9.29), or (9.30)] produces the same results as the others.

Example 9.5. Suppose the pilot plant data in Table 9.8 never existed. Use the laboratory data only from Example 9.4 to design the 12 000-gal reactor.

Answer. Any of Eqs. (9.28), (9.29), or (9.30) may be used, since they are equivalent, as shown in the previous example. In this example, the scale-up exponent must be determined from Table 9.7. The scale-up exponent n may vary from 0 to 1.0 in the speed equation:

$$N_2 = N_1(D_1/D_2)^n = N_1(1/R)^n \qquad (9.30)$$

Since power is proportional to speed cubed, the larger the value of n in Eq. (9.30) the smaller will be the predicted power requirement. The value of n most likely lies between 0.5 and 1.0, but no basis for choosing a value of n exists. Therefore the design engineer is certainly gambling if data on only one size are used as the basis for scale-up. In this problem, the scale factor R is

$$R = D_2/D_1 = 3.806/0.25 = 15.23 \qquad (i)$$

where the impeller diameter D_1 is taken from Table 9.8 and the agitator diameter of the reactor is taken from Eq. (vii) in Example 9.4. Table 9.9 summarizes the results for values of n ranging from 0.5 to 1.0. The speed is calculated from Eq. (9.30). The power is calculated as follows. Equation (9.11) for this example (turbulent flow) is

$$N_{po} = P/(\rho N^3 D^5) = \text{constant} \qquad (9.11)$$

Applying this equation to unit 2 (the 12 000-gal reactor) and unit 1 (the laboratory unit), the following is obtained:

$$P_2 = P_1 \left(\frac{N_2}{N_1}\right)^3 \left(\frac{D_2}{D_1}\right)^5 \qquad (ii)$$

When Eqs. (9.30) and (i) are substituted into Eq. (ii), the following is obtained:

$$P_2 = P_1 R^{(5-3n)} \qquad (iii)$$

This equation was used to compute the power for each value of n. The torque follows directly from Eq. (9.6) and is not included.

The conventional wisdom is to scale up with Eq. (9.32), or equivalently Eq. (9.36), using a value of n equal to 1, which is a criterion of constant tip speed, constant torque per unit volume, and equal fluid motion. Table 9.9 shows that such a criterion would require a 2-hp motor, whereas in Example 9.4 need for a

TABLE 9.9
Power and speed versus scale-up exponent n

n	N, rpm	P, hp
0.5	177	129
0.6	135	57
0.7	103	25
0.8	78	11
0.9	60	5
1.0	45	2

7.33-hp motor was predicted. This problem clearly indicates the sensitivity of the design calculations to the scale-up exponent n (or x or s). Tests in several volumes are clearly warranted for a reasonably reliable design. Table 9.9 has "narrowed" the range of possible power requirements to between 2 and 129 hp!

9.6.4 Scale-up Procedure for Laminar Flow

In laminar agitation, experimental data confirm that the power number and impeller Reynolds number are related by

$$N_{po} = \frac{k_1}{N_{Re}} \tag{9.45}$$

where k_1 is 75 for curves 1 and 2 and 50 for curves 3, 4, 5, and 6 in Fig. 9.7. The proportionality between power and the variables N and D may be found by substituting the definition of N_{Re} [Eq. (9.9)] and N_{po} [Eq. (9.10)] into Eq. (9.45) and rearranging:

$$\left(\frac{P}{\rho N^3 D^5}\right)\left(\frac{D^2 N\rho}{\mu}\right) = k_1 \tag{9.34}$$

or

$$P \propto \mu N^2 D^3 \tag{9.19}$$

Recall that this equation was also deduced from the equation for the laminar flow of a Newtonian fluid such as water or air in a straight pipe.

Scale-up in laminar flow is carried out exactly as recommended for turbulent flow. Equal process results should be obtained in vessels of several sizes. The data are reduced in order to make plots of $\log(P/V)$ or $\log(T_q/V)$ versus $\log V$, which are extrapolated to the plant-size unit. If only one or two sizes of units are available for a test run, any of the three scale-up equations presented previously may be used [Eqs. (9.28), (9.29), or (9.30)].

Design with a single test unit. Again, it is undesirable to design a process unit based on an experiment performed in a single volume. The ranges of scale-up exponents for laminar flow exceed those in the turbulent flow case. Nevertheless, Table 9.10 presents the scale-up exponents for some typical cases

TABLE 9.10
Laminar flow scale-up using Eq. (9.28)

Criterion	Exponent s
(1) Equal heat transfer per unit volume	8
(2) Equal heat transfer coefficients	2
(3) Equal blend time	0
(4) Equal tip speed	−2
(5) Equal impeller Reynolds number	−4

[P1, P2, T2]. These are easily worked out, using the same procedures as illustrated previously for the turbulent flow cases.

9.6.5 Scale-up Without Geometric Similarity

The scale-up procedures detailed in the preceding sections are valid for many agitation applications. These methods, all of which involve geometric scale-up, are applicable when the process is governed by a single factor, such as equal liquid motion. When there are two or more factors that must be controlled, then it is often necessary to deviate from the concepts presented; in particular, it is often desirable to deliberately vary certain geometric ratios, instead of maintaining similarity [O2, O3].

As an example of nongeometric scale-up, consider the conflicting requirements of a shear-sensitive material being produced in a reactor. Suppose the desired product is capable of further reaction to produce an undesirable side-product. This process will be hard to scale up because as the vessel size increases, the angular velocity ω decreases, but the tip speed U_t increases; the increased tip speed causes increased amounts of shear degradation of the product. If the speed of the impeller is further reduced to compensate for the increased degradation, the product will be retained in the agitation vessel for a longer time in the large unit, as compared with that in a small unit. Hence, there will be more opportunity for the product to react and produce the undesirable side-product. To design and operate such a complex agitation process, it is necessary to build either a full-size unit or a large pilot unit and then perform tests until the desired operating results are achieved in the full-size unit.

Oldshue [O3] compared the operating variables in a large unit with those in a small unit. Summarizing briefly, he pointed out that the larger vessel has a longer blend time (owing to too high pumping capacity in the small unit), a higher maximum shear rate (owing to higher tip speed), a lower average shear rate (owing to a lower operating speed), and thus a greater range of shear rates [O3]. Clearly, for complex processes, scale-up is hampered by the uncontrollable changes in the aforementioned process variables. In the example of the shear-sensitive product, too much blend time was as undesirable as too high a rate of shear. When more than one variable is of importance, as in this case, nongeometric scale-up is often required. Controlling geometric similarity and one other scale-up parameter will not suffice.

The reader must identify those applications that may potentially require nongeometric scale-up. Each of these must be considered on an individual basis. Further diffusion is beyond the scope of this chapter, as these constitute some of the most difficult problems in agitation [R1].

9.7 SUMMARY

This chapter has provided a short overview of the subject of agitation. Three scale-up equations have been presented in this chapter. The important equations are

$$R = T_2/T_1 = (V_2/V_1)^{1/3} \tag{9.27}$$

$$(P/V)_2 = (P/V)_1(T_2/T_1)^s = (P/V)_1 R^s \tag{9.28}$$

$$(T_q/V)_2 = (T_q/V)_1(T_2/T_1)^x = (T_q/V)_1 R^x \tag{9.29}$$

$$N_2 = N_1(D_1/D_2)^n = N_1(1/R)^n \tag{9.30}$$

Agitation provides an excellent example of the use of dimensionless variables and scale-up using geometric and sometimes kinematic similarity. Reliable design is obtained through tests performed in agitation vessels of various sizes that are geometrically similar. Scale-up procedures using at least four different volumes are recommended. The practicing engineer who only occasionally needs to handle agitation problems is advised to consult qualified individuals in the field, as well as equipment manufacturers.

PROBLEMS

9.1. An agitation unit consists of an 8-in. diameter disk impeller (curve 3 in Fig. 9.7). The ratio D/T is 0.3, the ratio Z/T is 1.0, and the tank is properly baffled. The impeller operates at 420 rpm. The fluid viscosity and specific gravity are 3 cP and 1.25, respectively. Calculate the Reynolds number, the power number, and the quantities P/V and T_q/V. Use English units.

9.2. Repeat Problem 9.1 using SI units.

9.3. Suppose variables for heat transfer in agitation units are correlated with 10 variables as follows: ρ, μ, μ_w, k, c_p, h, N, D, T, Z. Perform a dimensional analysis to obtain a useful equation suitable for correlation of actual data.

9.4. One reliable method of scaling up agitation units for a processing application is to maintain constant the torque per unit volume. It is desired to increase the tank diameter of a baffled unit by a factor of 6. The large unit will be geometrically similar to the small unit. Both operate in the high-Reynolds-number region. Determine the sizes ratios between the new unit and old unit for
(a) tank diameter
(b) impeller
(c) horsepower
(d) torque

9.5. A six-bladed disk-style turbine impeller (curve 1 in Fig. 9.7) is located in a baffled tank 5 ft in diameter that is filled with a 60 percent sucrose solution of specific gravity 1.29 and viscosity 55 cP at 23°C. The design of the turbine, baffles, etc., follows the normally accepted practice. The tank is filled to a depth of 5 ft. The turbine operates at 100 rpm. Find the torque (in. lb$_f$) and horsepower required for this unit. Also find the values for B and C in feet. Use English units.

9.6. A company owns two test units as described in Table 9.11. It is desired to build a 14 000-gal reactor containing a fluid of viscosity 4 cP and specific gravity 1.3. Tests are performed, and equal process results are obtained as follows:
Laboratory unit: $N = 750$ rpm; $P = 0.10$ hp
Pilot plant unit: $N = 370$ rpm; $P = 0.40$ hp
Find the horsepower, the torque, the speed and the impeller diameter for the 14 000-gal reactor.

TABLE 9.11
Test units for scale-up

Description	Laboratory unit	Pilot plant unit
Vessel diameter, inches	12	24
Ratio Z/T	1.0	1.0
Ratio D/T	0.3	0.3
Impeller type: disk style, flat blade turbine (6 blades)		

9.7. An agitation unit is being designed to handle a latex of viscosity 1200 cP, thermal conductivity 0.610 W m^{-1} K^{-1}, and density 48 lb$_m$ ft^{-3}. The tank is to be 3 ft in diameter, 3 ft high, and with D/T equal to 1/3. Suppose a 12 hp motor is available to drive the impeller at any speed; let the overall efficiency of the motor, drive train, etc., be 75 percent. Compute the speed (rpm), Reynolds number, and torque (in. lb$_f$) to operate a six-bladed turbine with no pitch in a baffled tank. Let the ratio W/D be 0.125 so that curve 4 applies.

9.8. In Problem 9.7, estimate a heat transfer coefficient from Table 9.6 if the Prandtl number of the fluid is 8.0. Compute the driving force in °F between bulk liquid temperature and the tank wall if the following equation applies (where Q is in Btu h^{-1})

$$Q = hA_{heat}\Delta t$$

Is this driving force a reasonable number to remove the equivalent of 9 hp of heat through the walls of a jacketed vessel? Note that all power added through the agitation shaft is transferred to the fluid by the impeller so that the temperature of the fluid rises unless the heat can be removed through the heat transfer area.

9.9. Consider the two units in Table 9.11. In this problem, a polymer is being prepared in a solution whose viscosity is 2.0×10^4 cP and density 50 lb$_m$ ft^{-3}. Tests are performed, and equal process results are obtained as follows:
Laboratory unit: $N = 600$ rpm; $P = 0.17$ hp
Pilot plant unit: $N = 360$ rpm; $P = 0.43$ hp
Find the horsepower, the torque, the impeller speed, and the impeller diameter for a 12 000-gal reactor.

9.10. Consider laminar flow scale-up. Using Table 9.10, determine the scale-up exponents n and r for all five cases listed.

REFERENCES

B1. Bates, R. L., P. L. Fondy, and R. R. Corpstein: *Ind. Eng. Chem. Process Design Develop.* **2:** 310 (1963).

B2. Bates, R. L., P. L. Fondy, and J. G. Fenic: in *Mixing Theory and Practice*, vol. 1, V. W. Uhl and J. B. Gray (eds.), Academic Press, New York, 1966, ch. 3.

C1. Connolly, J. R., and R. L. Winter: *Chem. Eng. Progr.* **65**(8): 70 (1969).

D1. Dickey, D. S., and R. W. Hicks: *Chem. Eng.* **83**(3): 93 (1976).

N1. Nagata, S.: *Mixing: Principles and Applications*, Halsted Press, Kodansha, Tokyo and Wiley, New York, 1975.

O1. Oldshue, J. Y.: *Fluid Mixing Technology,* Chemical Engineering, McGraw-Hill, New York, 1983.

O2. Oldshue, J. Y.: *Scale-up of Unique Industrial Fluid Mixing Processes,* paper 7 at the 5th European Conference on Mixing, Wurzburg, West Germany: 10–12 June 1985.

O3. Oldshue, J. Y.: in *Mixing of Liquids by Mechanical Agitation,* J. J. Ulbrecht and G. K. Patterson (eds.), Gordon and Breach, New York, 1985, ch. 9.

P1. Penney, W. R.: *Chem. Eng.* **78**(7): 86 (1971).

P2. Penney, W. R., and G. B. Tatterson, *Food Technol.* **37**(2): 62 (1983).

R1. Rautzen, R. R., R. R. Corpstein, and D. S. Dickey: *Chem. Eng.* **83**(23): 119 (1976).

R2. Rushton, J. H., E. W. Costich, and H. J. Everett: *Chem. Eng. Progr.* **46:** 395, 467 (1950).

R3. Rushton, J. H.: *Chem. Eng. Progr.* **47:** 485 (1951).

T1. Tatterson, G. B., H. S. Yuan, and R. S. Brodkey: *Chem. Eng. Sci.* **35:** 1369 (1980).

T2. Tatterson, G. B.: *Food Technol.* **35**(5): 65 (1981).

U1. Uhl, V. W.: in *Mixing Theory and Practice,* vol. 1, V. W. Uhl and J. B. Gray (eds.), Academic Press, New York, 1966, ch. 5, pp. 284–317.

V1. Von Essen, J. A.: *Liquid Mixing: Scale-up Procedures.* Lecture notes, *Liquid Mixing* course, The Center for Professional Advancement, East Brunswick, NJ, July 28, 1980. [Address: Philadelphia Mixers Div., Philadelphia Gear Corp., King of Prussia, PA.]

CHAPTER 10

FLUID
FLOW
IN DUCTS

NOMENCLATURE

A	Species A
A	Area of transfer (m^2, ft^2)
a	Empirical constant in Pai's equations; subscripts 1, 2; see Eq. (6.113)
a	Constant in design of nozzle or venturi, Eq. (10.71)
B_s	Empirical parameter in Fig. 10.4 and Eq. (10.8)
b	Constant in design of nozzle or venturi, Eq. (10.72)
C	Instantaneous concentration $(kmol\,m^{-3}, lb\,mol\,ft^{-3})$; C_A, C_B, C_i are concentrations of species A, B, i; $\bar{C}_{A,w}$ is time-averaged concentration of species A at the wall; $C_{A,ave}$ is bulk average concentration of species A
C	Chezy coefficient in Eq. (10.51)
C_o	Orifice (or nozzle or venturi) coefficient, cf. Eq. (10.63); also, C_1, C_2, and C_3 are similar coefficients as used in derivations
c_p	Heat capacity at constant pressure $(kJ\,kg^{-1}\,K^{-1}, Btu\,lb_m^{-1}\,{}^\circ F^{-1})$
c_v	Heat capacity at constant volume $(kJ\,kg^{-1}\,K^{-1}, Btu\,lb_m^{-1}\,{}^\circ F^{-1})$
d	Diameter (m, ft); d_o is inside diameter of pipe, as used in fluid flow; d_c is coil diameter in Eq. (10.19); d_e is equivalent diameter, Eq. (10.44)

e	Pipe roughness (m, ft); see Fig. 10.1 and Table 10.2 for more details
e	Base of natural logarithms (2.718 281 8. . .)
F	Frictional loss term in Eq. (7.61), the mechanical energy balance ($m^2 s^{-2}$, ft $lb_f lb_m^{-1}$); F' is the original term in Eq. (7.61); F_{loss} is the frictional loss term due to expansion or contraction [Eq. (10.22) or Eq. (10.32)]; F_{pipe} and $F_{fittings}$ are losses in pipes and fittings, respectively
F	Force in rotameter derivation; F_G is gravitational force, Eq. (10.74); F_B is buoyancy force, Eq. (10.75); F_D is drag force, Eqs. (10.76) and (10.77)
f	Fanning friction factor, Eq. (6.89)
f	f_i or f_{i+1} is the ith or $(i+1)$th iteration in Newton's method in Example 10.2
f	Subscript denoting rotameter float
$\boldsymbol{g}$	Vector representing the acceleration due to a gravitational or other field (m s^{-2}, ft s^{-2})
g	Function in Example 10.2 whose root is to be located; $g'(f)$ is the derivative of $g(f)$ where f is the friction factor root to be located
g_c	Gravitational conversion constant (32.174 lb_m lb_f^{-1} ft s^{-2})
h	Heat transfer coefficient, defined by Eq. (6.86) (W $m^{-2} K^{-1}$, Btu ft^{-2} h^{-1} °F^{-1})
h	Height in a triangular duct (m, ft)
$\boldsymbol{i}$	Unit vector in the x direction
K'	Empirical constant in non-Newtonian viscosity equation, Eq. (10.5)
k	Ratio of c_p to c_v for gases, Eq. (10.69)
k	Loss coefficient, cf. Eq. (10.40); k_e is expansion loss coefficient in Eq. (10.22); k_c is contraction loss coefficient; $k_{fittings}$ is sum of all loss coefficients of fittings [cf. Eq. (10.40)]
k	Thermal conductivity (W $m^{-1} K^{-1}$ or J $m^{-1} K^{-1} s^{-1}$, Btu ft^{-1} °R^{-1} s^{-1})
k_c'	Equimolar mass transfer coefficient, defined by Eq. (6.87) [kmol $m^{-2} s^{-1}$ (kmol m^{-3})$^{-1}$, lb mol ft^{-2} s^{-1} (lb mol ft^{-3})$^{-1}$]
L	Length (m, ft); L_e is equivalent length of pipe [feet or meters of straight pipe necessary to produce the same pressure drop as the fittings—cf. Eq. (10.42)]; L_p is wetted perimeter in definition of hydraulic radius, Eq. (10.45)
m	Integer parameter in Pai's equation, Eq. (6.113)
m_f	Mass of rotameter float, Eq. (10.74)
N	Number of velocity heads, Eq. (10.16)
N	Total points in velocity profile determination in Eq. (10.87)
N_A	Molar flow defined with respect to fixed coordinates (kmol s^{-1}, lb mol s^{-1}); subscript r, w means molar flow in the r direction at the wall
N_{Dn}	Dean number in Eq. (10.20), defined as $N_{Re}(d_o/d_c)^{1/2}$
N_{Re}	Reynolds number, Eq. (6.1) or Eq. (6.2), $d_o U_{z,\,ave}\rho/\mu$ for pipe flow
N_{VK}	von Karman number, Eq. (10.13)

n	Roughness factor in Eq. (10.51)
n	Index in Eq. (10.87)
n'	Empirical constant in non-Newtonian viscosity equation, Eq. (10.5)
p	Pressure (kPa, atm, $lb_f in.^{-2}$)
Q	Volume rate of flow ($m^3 s^{-1}$, $ft^3 s^{-1}$)
q	Energy (heat) flow vector ($J s^{-1}$, $Btu s^{-1}$); subscripts denote components in coordinate directions
r	Cylindrical coordinate (m, ft)
r	Radius (m, ft); r_o is value of r at the tube wall; r_H is the hydraulic radius, Eq. (10.45)
r	Pressure ratio in design of gas orifice meters, Eq. (10.68)
S	Area of a pipe or tube that is perpendicular to the z direction (i.e., the flow or cross sectional area) (m^2, ft^2); cf. Eq. (7.10); S_f is area of a rotameter float in the direction perpendicular to the flow (the projected area)
T	Instantaneous temperature (K, °R, °C, °F); $\bar{T}_w$ is time-averaged temperature of the wall or surface; T_{ave} or T_b is time-averaged or bulk temperature, Eq. (11.31)
T	Total time
t	Temperature in °C in Eq. (i) of Example 10.1
U	Instantaneous velocity vector ($m s^{-1}$, $ft s^{-1}$); U is magnitude of U; U_x, U_y, U_z, U_θ, U_r, U_ϕ are components in directions x, y, z, θ, r, ϕ; $U_{z, ave}$ and $U_{z, max}$ are mean velocity and maximum velocity in z direction, respectively; U_b, U_1, U_2, or U_3 is time-averaged velocity in z direction at locations b, 1, 2, or 3; U^* is the friction velocity, Eq. (6.53)
V_f	Volume of rotameter float in Eq. (10.74) ff.
W_s	Shaft work done by the system in the mechanical energy balance, Eq. (7.61) (J, Btu)
w	Mass rate of flow ($kg s^{-1}$, $lb_m s^{-1}$); cf. Eq. (7.10)
w	Subscript denoting wall
X	Correlation variable in Eq. (10.20), defined as the log of the Dean number
Y	Expansion factor in the design of gas orifices, Eq. (10.67)
z	Rectangular (Cartesian) coordinate
z	Height in potential energy term in the mechanical energy balance, Eq. (7.61) and Eq. (10.39)
α	The ratio of the average velocity cubed to the average of the cube of the instantaneous velocity, Eq. (7.54), as used in the mechanical energy balance, Eq. (7.61) and in Example 10.17
β	The ratio of the average velocity squared to the average of the square of the instantaneous velocity, Eq. (7.24); this ratio appears in the momentum balance equation, Eq. (7.23)
β	The ratio of orifice diameter to pipe diameter, Eq. (10.62)
Δ	Difference, state 2 minus state 1; e.g., Δp means $p_2 - p_1$

η Efficiency of a pump, defined as the theoretical power divided by the actual power

κ Empirical constant in Eq. (10.8), usually equal to 0.4

μ Viscosity ($\text{kg m}^{-1}\text{s}^{-1}$ or $\text{N m}^{-2}\text{s}$, $\text{lb}_m\,\text{ft}^{-1}\text{s}^{-1}$, cP); μ_w is viscosity at wall

π Ratio of circumference of a circle to its diameter (3.141 592 65. . .)

ρ Density (kg m^{-3}, $\text{lb}_m\,\text{ft}^{-3}$); ρ_f is density of float; ρ_A is density of the process fluid

τ Momentum flux (or shear stress) tensor (N m^{-2}, $\text{lb}_f\,\text{ft}^{-2}$); τ_{xy}, τ_{yx}, etc., are components of the momentum flux tensor, where subscripts refer to direction of momentum transfer and direction of velocity; τ_w is shear stress at the wall

Transport in ducts is one of the most important areas of study for engineers. A consideration of fluid transport through piping systems is a first step in this study. Generally, the fluid flow problem must be solved before any progress can take place on the problems of heat and mass transport. Most common applications involve fluids in turbulent flow. Chapter 6 emphasized the difficulties in arriving at exact solutions to turbulent flow problems, even in the absence of heat and mass transfer. Hence, the methods of analysis to be presented in this chapter will be empirical and will utilize the dimensionless numbers of Chapter 8. In this respect, the presentation here is much like that of Chapter 9 on agitation.

The most basic design of a duct is the pipe or tube. Design of piping systems will be covered in considerable detail. These methods are easily extended to ducts of other shapes through the introduction of an equivalent pipe diameter.

Finally, a section on measurements during transport is included. After design and building of duct systems, one often needs to make measurements of the transport variables to ascertain whether or not the system is performing properly. Furthermore, methods of measurements during transport are excellent illustrations of the principles of transport covered so far.

10.1   REVIEW

This section begins with the exact solutions to isothermal laminar tube flow problems from Chapter 4 and reviews turbulent flow conditions, first mentioned in Chapter 6.

10.1.1   Laminar Pipe Flow

In laminar pipe flow, the fluid elements move in the z direction only; as a result there are no components of velocity in the r and θ directions. Most laminar flows normally occur at Reynolds numbers of 2100 or less, although it is possible to have laminar flow at much higher Reynolds numbers; however, it is relatively easy to initiate the transition to turbulence by vibrations, rough spots in the tube, etc. The laminar flow problem is solved under the five assumptions listed just before Eq. (4.65). Generation of momentum arises from the applied pressure difference and the acceleration due to gravity. If the tube is horizontal, then the velocity U_z is related to pressure difference and radius by Eq. (4.72):

$$U_z = \frac{-\Delta p}{4\mu L}(r_o^2 - r^2) \tag{4.72}$$

or

$$\frac{U_z}{U_{z,\,max}} = 1 - \left(\frac{r}{r_o}\right)^2 \tag{4.74}$$

and

$$Q = \frac{-\Delta p}{8\mu L}\pi r_o^4 \tag{4.76}$$

where Q is the volume rate of flow and

$$U_{z,\,ave} = \frac{-\Delta p\,(r_o^2)}{8\mu L} = \tfrac{1}{2}U_{z,\,max} \tag{10.1}$$

Table 4.5 summarizes the equations for laminar flow.

The pressure difference term is conveniently included in the dimensionless group f, the Fanning friction factor of Eq. (6.89). The friction factor was introduced in Chapter 6 and is seen to occur naturally in Example 8.1 from a dimensional analysis of the flow of a fluid in a pipe. Equation (6.89) can be written as

$$f = \frac{\tau_w}{\tfrac{1}{2}\rho U_{z,\,ave}^2} = \frac{(d_o/4)(-\Delta p/L)}{\tfrac{1}{2}\rho U_{z,\,ave}^2} \tag{10.2}$$

where τ_w is the shear stress at the wall and $-\Delta p/L$ is the pressure drop per unit length. From Eq. (4.80) and Eq. (6.88), the wall shear stress can be expressed as

$$\tau_w = \frac{d_o(-\Delta p)}{4L} = \tfrac{1}{2}\rho U_{z,\,ave}^2 f \tag{10.3}$$

As discussed in Chapter 4, the shear stress τ_{rz} is zero at the pipe center line and a maximum at the wall:

$$\frac{\tau_{rz}}{\tau_w} = \frac{r}{r_o} \tag{4.81}$$

Equations (4.77) and (6.89) and the definition of the Reynolds number [Eq. (6.2)] can be combined to give the relationship

$$f = 16/(d_o U_{z,\,ave}\rho/\mu) = 16/N_{Re} \qquad N_{Re} \leq 2100 \tag{6.124}$$

Equations (10.2) and (6.124) are easily manipulated into the following form, useful in capillary viscometer experiments:

$$\tau_w = \frac{d_o(-\Delta p)}{4L} = \mu \frac{8U_{z,\,ave}}{d_o} \tag{10.4}$$

where the quantity $8U_{z,\,ave}/d_o$ is equal to the shear rate at the wall in a Newtonian fluid, $(\partial U_z/\partial r)_w$:

$$\left(\frac{\partial U_z}{\partial r}\right)_{wall} = \frac{4Q}{\pi r_o^3} = \frac{4U_{z,\,ave}}{r_o} = \frac{8U_{z,\,ave}}{d_o} \tag{4.84}$$

Equation (10.4) is useful because the pressure drop is isolated on the left-hand side and the velocity is on the other side. In the capillary viscometer, the pressure drop and the flow rate are measured; the velocity is computed from the flow rate through Eq. (7.10):

$$w = \rho U_{z,\,ave} S \tag{7.10}$$

where S is the inside area of the capillary in the direction perpendicular to the flow. Hence, by measuring Δp and w, the viscosity μ is computed using Eqs. (7.10) and (10.4).

Equation (10.4) can be generalized for non-Newtonian fluids whose viscosity varies with shear rate and/or shear history:

$$\tau_w = K'\left(\frac{8U_{z,\,ave}}{d_o}\right)^{n'} \tag{10.5}$$

where K' and n' are empirical constants. A more extensive discussion of non-Newtonian fluids will be given in Chapter 15.

Example 10.1. Hershey [H1] determined the viscosity of toluene at 30°C in a capillary viscometer with a 0.03254-in. diameter tube. A flow rate of 28.36 $cm^3\ min^{-1}$ yielded a pressure drop of 0.9364 psi per foot. Compute the viscosity in cP.

Answer. The International Critical Tables gives the following equation for the density of toluene [I1]:

$$\rho = 0.88412 - 0.92248 \times 10^{-3}t \tag{i}$$

where ρ is in units of $g\ cm^{-3}$ and t is in °C. Either Eqs. (6.124) or (10.4) can be used to find the viscosity if the flow is laminar, but Eq. (10.4) is more convenient. The pressure drop can be converted to SI units by the conversions in the Appendix, Table C.15:

$$\Delta p/L = (-0.9364)(2.2631 \times 10^4) = -2.119 \times 10^4\ kg\ m^{-2}\ s^{-2} \tag{ii}$$

The negative sign is required since Δp must be negative to cause a flow through the capillary tube ($p_2 < p_1$). The other quantities are also converted to SI:

$$d_o = 0.03254\ in. = 0.08265\ cm = 8.265 \times 10^{-4}\ m \tag{iii}$$

$$Q = 28.36\ cm^3\ min^{-1} = 4.727 \times 10^{-7}\ m^3\ s^{-1} \tag{iv}$$

From Eq. (i), the density at 30°C is:

$$\rho = 0.88412 - 0.92248 \times 10^{-3}t = 0.8564 \text{ g cm}^{-3} = 856.4 \text{ kg m}^{-3} \qquad \text{(v)}$$

The cross sectional flow area S is

$$S = \pi d_o^2/4 = 5.365 \times 10^{-7} \text{ m}^2 \qquad \text{(vi)}$$

The velocity in the tube is

$$U_{z,\text{ave}} = Q/S = 4.727 \times 10^{-7}/5.365 \times 10^{-7} = 0.8810 \text{ m s}^{-1} \qquad \text{(vii)}$$

The shear stress at the wall is found from Eq. (10.4):

$$\tau_w = d_o(-\Delta p)/(4L) = (d_o/4)(-\Delta p/L)$$
$$= (8.265 \times 10^{-4}/4)(2.119 \times 10^4)\,[(\text{m})(\text{kg m}^{-2}\text{ s}^{-2})] = 4.379 \text{ kg m}^{-1}\text{ s}^{-2} \qquad \text{(viii)}$$

The shear rate at the wall for a Newtonian fluid is

$$8U_{z,\text{ave}}/d_o = (8)(0.8810)/(8.265 \times 10^{-4}) = 8527 \text{ s}^{-1} \qquad \text{(ix)}$$

Next, Eq. (10.4) is solved for the viscosity and the numbers are inserted:

$$\mu = \tau_w/(8U_{z,\text{ave}}/d_o) = 4.379/8527 = 5.135 \times 10^{-4} \text{ kg m}^{-1}\text{ s}^{-1} = 0.5135 \text{ cP} \qquad \text{(x)}$$

Finally, it is important to check the Reynolds number to make sure Eq. (10.4) applies. From Eq. (6.2):

$$N_{\text{Re}} = d_o U_{z,\text{ave}} \rho/\mu$$
$$= (8.265 \times 10^{-4})(0.8810)(856.4)/(5.135 \times 10^{-4})$$
$$\times [(\text{m})(\text{m s}^{-1})(\text{kg m}^{-3})/(\text{kg m}^{-1}\text{ s}^{-1})]$$
$$= 1214 \qquad \text{(xi)}$$

The flow is well within the laminar region, and Eq. (10.4) is valid.

10.1.2 Turbulent Pipe Flow

In processing equipment, with the desire for high throughput, turbulent flow conditions often prevail, and thus constitute the main emphasis for this chapter. Chapter 6 contains the discussion of turbulent flow in which the Reynolds equations were presented. It was indicated that, in general, these equations cannot be solved because they have more unknowns than equations. Thus, pressure drop and profiles of temperature and concentration must be predicted from empirical correlations. The earliest correlation was that of Blasius [B2]:

$$f = 0.079(N_{\text{Re}})^{-1/4} \qquad (6.133)$$

This equation is approximately correct up to a Reynolds number of 10^5. The von Karman correlation, Eq. (6.132), is more accurate and easy to use with today's technology in computing:

$$1/(f)^{1/2} = 4.0 \log_{10}[N_{\text{Re}}(f)^{1/2}] - 0.4 \qquad 3000 \le N_{\text{Re}} \le 3.2 \times 10^6 \quad (6.132)$$

This equation applies for fully turbulent flow of Newtonian fluids in smooth tubes.

The turbulent flow equations for heat and mass cannot be solved analytically to yield equations for any of the profiles, either instantaneous or time-averaged. Empirical coefficients, called heat and mass transfer coefficients (h and k'_c, respectively), were defined previously in order to proceed with equipment designs:

$$(q/A)_{r,w} = h(\bar{T}_w - T_{ave}) \qquad (6.86)$$

$$(N_A/A)_{r,w} = k'_c(\bar{C}_{A,w} - C_{A,\,ave}) \qquad (6.87)$$

In later parts of this book, these coefficients will be correlated as functions of fluid properties and flow variables, just as Eqs. (6.124) and (6.132) give the friction factor as a function of the Reynolds number for laminar flow and turbulent flow, respectively. More specifically, use will be made of the Nusselt, Sherwood, and Stanton numbers that can be found in Table 8.1.

Finally, it should be re-emphasized that the transition from laminar to turbulent flow is ill-defined. Consider a fluid flowing through a tube in laminar flow. If the flow rate is increased sufficiently, a transition to turbulent flow will begin. The Reynolds number of 2100 is often quoted as the upper limit of the laminar region. Section 6.1.2 discusses transitional flow in some detail. Above a Reynolds number of 10 000 the flow is almost always fully turbulent. If conditions include a low-viscosity fluid in a system with lots of vibration from pumps, etc., then the flow is probably fully turbulent at a Reynolds number of 4000–5000.

> **Example 10.2.** It is desired to operate the viscometer in Example 10.1 in the turbulent region. Compute the pressure drop for the same 0.03254-in. tube at a Reynolds number of 13 700 using toluene at 30°C. Consider that the ratio L/d_o is 744 for the tube.
>
> **Answer.** Since each term in the Reynolds number of the previous example, except the velocity, remains the same, the new velocity can be obtained by a simple ratio:
>
> $$U_{z,\,ave} = U_{z,\,ave,\,old}(N_{Re}/N_{Re,\,old}) = (0.8810)(13\,700)/(1214)$$
>
> $$= 9.94 \text{ m s}^{-1} \qquad (i)$$
>
> Next, Eq. (6.132) must be solved by trial and error for the friction factor f:
>
> $$1/(f)^{1/2} = 4.0 \log_{10}[N_{Re}(f)^{1/2}] - 0.4 \qquad (6.132)$$
>
> The root of this equation can be found by any of the common root-finding methods, such as Newton's method [P2], which is particularly convenient when an analytic derivative is easily found. Experience with Eq. (6.132) indicates that a general computer program should start at a value of friction factor of 0.005. However, for hand calculations, as in this example, Fig. 6.19 provides a better guess, approximately 0.007. The root of Eq. (6.132) occurs when the function

TABLE 10.1
Calculation of friction factor by Newton's method from Eq. (6.132) at $N_{Re} = 13\,700$

Iteration	f_i	$g(f)$	$g'(f)$	f_{i+1}
1	0.007 000	−0.1152	977.82	0.007 118
2	0.007 118	−0.0014	954.66	0.007 119
3	0.007 119	1.83×10^{-5}	954.37	0.007 119

$g(f)$ is zero:

$$g(f) = 4.0 \log_{10} [N_{Re}(f)^{1/2}] - 0.4 - 1/(f)^{1/2} = 0 \tag{ii}$$

The derivative of this function is called $g'(f)$:

$$g'(f) = (2.0)(0.4342945/f) + (0.5)(f)^{-3/2} \tag{iii}$$

Newton's method, in the nomenclature of this problem, is

$$f_{i+1} = f_i - g(f_i)/g'(f_i) \tag{iv}$$

Table 10.1 summarizes the results of Newton's method as applied to the root of Eq. (ii) at a Reynolds number of 13 700. Convergence is very quick as a result of the combined efficiency of the method and the close initial guess. The friction factor from Eq. (6.132) at a Reynolds number of 13 700 is 0.007 119.

The pressure drop is easily calculated in SI units, using Eq. (10.3):

$$\tau_w = \frac{d_o(-\Delta p)}{4L} = \tfrac{1}{2}\rho U^2_{z,\,ave} f \tag{10.3}$$

First, the numbers from Example 10.1 and this problem are inserted to find τ_w:

$$\tau_w = \tfrac{1}{2}\rho U^2_{z,\,ave} f$$
$$= (1/2)(856.4)(9.94)^2(0.007\,119)$$
$$= 301.1 \text{ kg m}^{-1} \text{s}^{-2} = 301.1 \text{ N m}^{-2} \tag{v}$$

Then, Eq. (10.3) is solved for the pressure drop:

$$-\Delta p = (\tau_w)(4)(L/d_o) = (301.1)(4)(744) = 8.961 \times 10^5 \text{ N m}^{-2} = 896.1 \text{ kPa} \tag{vi}$$

where L/d_o is 744 as stated in the problem.

This problem is solved with more difficulty in English units. First, all quantities must be converted to English units:

$$d_o = 0.03254/12 = 2.712 \times 10^{-3} \text{ ft}$$
$$U_{z,\,ave} = 9.94/0.3048 = 32.61 \text{ ft s}^{-1} \tag{vii}$$
$$\rho = (856.4)(62.4/1000) = 53.44 \text{ lb}_m \text{ ft}^{-3}$$

Equation (10.3) requires the gravitational conversion constant g_c:

$$\tau_w = d_o(-\Delta p)/(4L) = [(\rho U^2_{z,\,ave})/(2g_c)](f) \tag{viii}$$

This equation is solved for $-\Delta p$ and the numbers inserted:

$$-\Delta p = (2)(\rho U_{z,\,\text{ave}}^2 f)(L/d_o)/(g_c)$$

$$= (2)(53.44)(32.61)^2(0.007\,119)(744)/(32.174)\,\frac{(\text{lb}_m\,\text{ft}^{-3})(\text{ft}^2\,\text{s}^{-2})}{\text{lb}_m\,\text{lb}_f^{-1}\,\text{ft}\,\text{s}^{-2}}$$

$$= 18\,710\,\text{lb}_f\,\text{ft}^{-2} = 130\,\text{psi} \tag{ix}$$

A pressure drop of 130 psi on a tube of length 2.017 ft $[(0.03254)(744)/(12)]$ is high and shows the impracticality of flows at high Reynolds number in small tubes.

10.2 PIPING SYSTEMS

Equation (6.132), as repeated in the preceding section, and Fig. 6.19 (the friction factor as a function of Reynolds number) are adequate for turbulent flow of fluids in smooth pipes. However, the methods for design in smooth round pipes must be extended to more complex systems. Innumerable experiments on a wide variety of systems for fluid flow have been performed in the past for evaluation of the friction factor. To try to tabulate all of these would be impracticable and not very convenient for use by engineers. Applicable, however, are the concepts developed so far in this text, namely the use of dimensionless correlations based on dimensional analysis or inspection of the governing differential equations. In this section, the detailed working equations and correlations for isothermal fluid transport will be presented together with a number of sample problems to illustrate their applications.

The correlations for pressure drop (the friction factor) and their applications to practical fluid flow problems are relatively simple and straightforward; however, there are some precautions, minor problems, and extensions that the reader should be aware of in order to apply the results.

10.2.1 Roughness

The roughness of the pipe wall is a factor of importance in turbulent flow. The pipe roughness e may be defined as shown in Fig. 10.1(a). In practice, the roughness e is not measured visually because the surface of commercial pipe contains smooth areas and rough areas. The determination of e will be covered later. The roughness was one of the variables correlated in Example 8.1, and in that problem the dimensionless group e/d_o was formed. This group is sometimes called the relative roughness.

Moody [M3] prepared a plot of the group e/d_o versus pipe diameter for a number of materials; this plot is given elsewhere [B3, C3, F2, K1, P2]. Many design engineers find so many uncertainties in other aspects of piping design that they use a typical value of e, as tabulated in Table 10.2. Most installations use commercial steel pipe, the roughness of which is seen to be 1.5×10^{-4} ft $(4.572 \times 10^{-5}\,\text{m})$.

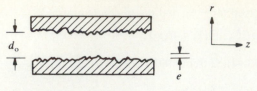

(a) Cross section of a pipe with rough walls

(b) Laminar flow

(c) Turbulent flow

FIGURE 10.1
Pipe roughness.

It is interesting to note the manner in which the relative roughness e/d_o is established. Nikuradse [N1] determined the pressure drop in artificially roughened pipes. He used several sizes of pipe, all initially smooth, and glued sand grains of constant size to the interior so that the values of the relative roughness for the different pipes were well characterized. By selection of the size of the sand grains, he was able to have as many as three pipes differing in

TABLE 10.2
Values of absolute roughness for various materials*

	Roughness	
Material	**e, m**	**e, ft**
Drawn tubing	1.524×10^{-6}	5×10^{-6}
Commercial steel, wrought iron, or welded steel pipe	4.572×10^{-5}	1.5×10^{-4}
Asphalted cast iron	1.219×10^{-4}	4×10^{-4}
Galvanized iron	1.525×10^{-4}	5×10^{-4}
Cast iron	2.591×10^{-4}	8.5×10^{-4}
Wood stave	1.829×10^{-4} to 9.144×10^{-4}	6×10^{-4} to 3×10^{-3}
Concrete	3.048×10^{-4} to 3.048×10^{-3}	10^{-3} to 10^{-2}
Riveted steel	9.144×10^{-4} to 9.144×10^{-3}	3×10^{-3} to 3×10^{-2}

* An adaptation of the original from Moody, *Trans. ASME* **66**: 671 (1944); *Mech. Eng.* **69**: 1005 (1947). By permission of ASME.

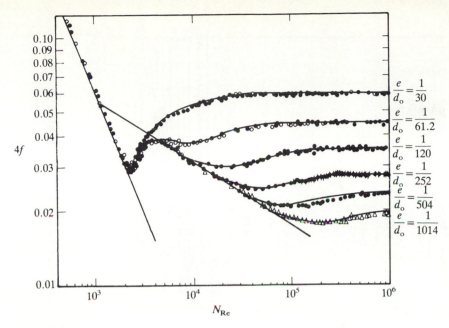

FIGURE 10.2
Sand-roughened pipe flow data of Nikuradse. (*From Schlichting, Boundary Layer Theory, 7th ed., p. 617, McGraw-Hill, New York, 1979. By permission.*)

diameter but with identical relative roughness values. He showed that the friction factor was a function of the Reynolds number and the relative roughness together, as can be clearly seen from a plot of his data. Figure 10.2 is a plot of Nikuradse' data in the form of friction factor versus Reynolds number. In laminar flow, the experimental data in Fig. 10.2 show that the dimensionless group e/d_o has no effect on either the velocity profile or Eqs. (6.124) and (10.4). In the first place, laminar flow is inherently stable, and disturbances decay and disappear. In the qualitative sense, the roughness is essentially buried in the laminar flow as suggested by Fig. 10.1(b). In turbulent flow the viscous sublayer, which is extremely small as established in Chapter 6, is of the same order or smaller than the size of the roughness e. As a result, the roughness has an effect upon the velocity gradient at the wall, which is related to the wall shear stress, upon which the pressure drop depends. Figure 10.1(c) shows the case for turbulent flow. For simplicity, the influence of roughness on the friction factor was not shown in Fig. 6.19, but a more complete plot to be shown shortly will include the group e/d_o. If the group e/d_o is not of significance for a given pipe, that pipe is said to be hydraulically smooth.

It is difficult to determine the relative roughness by direct visual measurements because the roughness is not uniform in commercial pipe. The common procedure is to measure the friction factor as a function of Reynolds number for a given commercial pipe and establish the relative roughness e/d_o

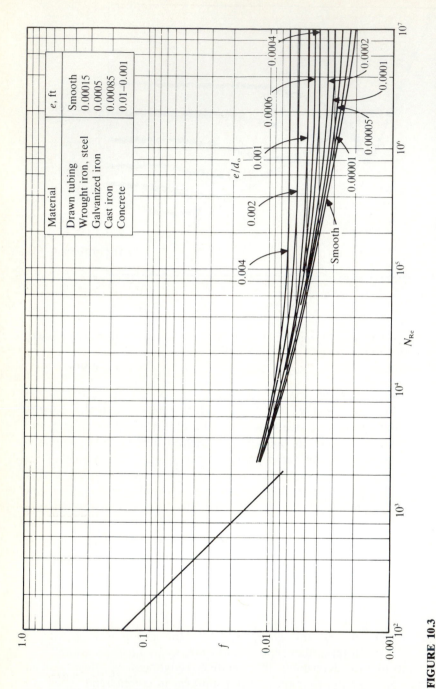

FIGURE 10.3

Friction factor versus Reynolds number for rough pipes. (*From McCabe, Smith, and Harriott, Unit Operations of Chemical Engineering, 4th ed., p. 88, McGraw-Hill, New York, 1985. By permission.*)

by comparing the measurements with the correct line in Fig. 10.2 or Fig. 10.3 (to be presented shortly).

10.2.2 Pressure Drop in Rough Pipes

The most common representation of friction factor is to present the logarithm of friction factor versus the logarithm of Reynolds number with the relative roughness e/d_o as a further parameter. This plot is shown in Fig. 10.3 and is sometimes called the Stanton plot or the Moody plot [M3]. Note that Fig. 10.3 contains the Fanning friction factor, widely used by chemical engineers because that dimensionless group is the shear stress at the wall divided by a kinetic energy term [cf. Eqs. (6.89) and (10.2)]. Another friction factor, sometimes called the Darcy–Weisbach friction factor, is four times larger and is given in some of the fluid mechanics literature. The reader can always determine which friction factor is being used by examining the equation for laminar flow, Eq. (6.124): if the constant is 16, the Fanning friction factor is used; if the constant is 64, the Darcy–Weissbach friction factor is used. Unfortunately, many authors have confused the two and intermingled both in their equations and figures. The reader must always check the accuracy of other references.

As can be seen in Fig. 10.3, for a given relative roughness, the friction factor becomes constant and independent of Reynolds number at high flow rates. Nikuradse [N1] proposed the following correlation in this region:

$$1/(f)^{1/2} = -4.0 \log_{10} \frac{e}{d_o} + 2.28 \qquad \frac{1}{(e/d_o)N_{Re}(f)^{1/2}} < 0.01 \qquad (10.6)$$

The curves in the region where f varies with N_{Re} were successfully correlated by Colebrook [C2]:

$$1/(f)^{1/2} = -4.0 \log_{10}\{[e/(3.7d_o)] + [1.255/(N_{Re}(f)^{1/2})]\} \qquad (10.7)$$

This equation is restricted to the region between the von Karman line (Eq. (6.132) for smooth tubes) and the zone where the friction factor is independent of N_{Re} (i.e., where Eq. (10.6) applies).

Equation (10.7) for rough pipe is a modification of the von Karman equation for smooth pipe, Eq. (6.132). An alternate representation for sand-roughened pipe data is the equation upon which Eq. (6.132) is based, i.e., Eq. (6.129). An empirical modification of Eq. (6.129) can be obtained by replacing y_o^+ with r_o/e:

$$\left(\frac{2}{f}\right)^{1/2} = \frac{1}{\kappa} \ln \frac{r_o}{e} + B_s - \frac{3}{2\kappa} \qquad (10.8)$$

where B_s is given in Fig. 10.4 and κ is usually 0.4. The subscript s is used to denote data for flow in sand-roughened pipes. Equation (10.8) simplifies to

$$1/(f)^{1/2} = 4.0[\log_{10}(r_o/e)] + B_s/(2)^{1/2} - 2.53 \qquad (10.9)$$

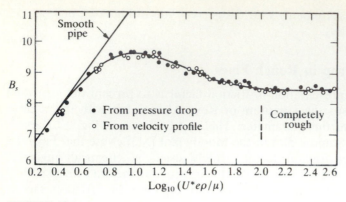

FIGURE 10.4
Sand roughness data and the constant B_s. (*From Schlichting, Boundary Layer Theory, 7th ed., p. 620, McGraw-Hill, New York, 1979. By permission.*)

where the constants have been modified slightly to improve the fit to the data. Many authors divide Fig. 10.3, the Moody chart, into three or more regions: (1) the laminar where Eqs. (6.124) and (10.4) apply; (2) a "fully turbulent" where Eq. (10.6) applies; and (3) a "transition" where the lines of constant e/d_o in Fig. 10.3 are curved and Eq. (10.7) applies. However, these designations are at variance with the nature of transitional and turbulent flow as presented in Chapter 6 and thus will be avoided in this text.

If the friction factor is constant and Eq. (10.6) applies, then for a given pipe the pressure drop should be proportional to the square of the velocity (flow rate):

$$\Delta p \propto U_{z, \text{ave}}^2 \qquad \text{(rough pipe, large } N_{\text{Re}}) \tag{10.10}$$

In hydraulically smooth tubes, the exponent is more nearly 1.75:

$$\Delta p \propto U_{z, \text{ave}}^{1.75} \qquad \text{(smooth pipe, turbulent flow)} \tag{10.11}$$

This result can be verified from the Blasius equation, Eq. (6.133), since the friction factor contains Δp to the first power and velocity to the second power (The exponent 1.75 equals 2.0 minus 0.25.). In laminar flow, the pressure drop is proportional to the first power of velocity, as can be derived easily from Eq. (10.4).

If the flow is transitional, as described in Chapter 6, the exact friction factor cannot be predicted. However, Fig. 10.3 may be used to establish limits. In the transitional region, for rough or smooth pipes, the following is true

$$0.0075 \le f \le 0.02 \qquad 2100 < N_{\text{Re}} < 4000 \tag{10.12}$$

Example 10.3. Calculate the pressure drop in a pipe of 6-cm inside diameter for water flowing at 1 m min^{-1} over a length of 300 m. The pipe is commercial steel. For water, assume the density to be 1000 kg m^{-3} and the viscosity 1.0 cP.

Answer. It is first necessary to determine the Reynolds number to see if the flow is laminar, transitional, or turbulent. From Eq. (6.2), with 1 cP equal to 1×10^{-3} kg m^{-1} s^{-1}, the velocity (1/60) m s^{-1}, and the diameter 0.06 m:

$$N_{Re} = d_o U_{ave} \rho / \mu = (0.06)(1/60)(1000)/(10^{-3}) \left(\frac{(m)(m\ s^{-1})(kg\ m^{-3})}{kg\ m^{-1}\ s^{-1}} \right)$$

$$= 1000 \qquad\qquad (i)$$

Therefore the flow is laminar. Either Eq. (6.124) or Eq. (10.4) can be used. From Eq. (6.124):

$$f = 16/N_{Re} = 0.016 \qquad\qquad (ii)$$

Equation (10.2) is solved for the pressure drop, and the numbers in SI units are inserted:

$$-\Delta p = (4f)(L/d_o)(\rho U_{ave}^2/2) = (4f/2)(L/d_o)(\rho U_{ave}^2)$$
$$= (4/2)(0.016)(300/0.06)(1000)(1/60)^2 \ [(m\ m^{-1})(kg\ m^{-3})(m^2\ s^{-2})]$$
$$= 44.4 \text{ kg m}^{-1}\text{s}^{-2} = 44.4 \text{ N m}^{-2} = 0.0444 \text{ kPa} = 6.45 \times 10^{-3} \text{ psi} \qquad (iii)$$

This result could also have been calculated from Eq. (4.77) or Eq. (10.4).

Example 10.4. Repeat the previous example for Reynolds numbers of 10 000 and 100 000. Contrast smooth pipe with commercial steel pipe and cast iron pipe.

Answer. The result in Example 10.3 applies for all kinds of pipe and will be included in the comparison of results. First the relative roughness e/d_o will be computed, using the data from Table 10.1:

Commercial steel pipe: $e/d_o = 4.572 \times 10^{-5}/0.06 = 0.000\ 762$ (i)

Cast iron pipe: $e/d_o = 2.591 \times 10^{-4}/0.06 = 0.00432$ (ii)

At Reynolds numbers of 10^4 and 10^5, the flow is fully turbulent. Figure 10.3 will be used to estimate f, instead of one of the more tedious equations [Eqs. (6.132), (10.6), (10.7), (10.9)]:

For smooth pipe:

$$N_{Re} = 10^4 \qquad f = 0.0076 \qquad\qquad (iii)$$
$$N_{Re} = 10^5 \qquad f = 0.0045 \qquad\qquad (iv)$$

For commercial steel pipe:

$$N_{Re} = 10^4 \qquad f = 0.008 \qquad\qquad (v)$$
$$N_{Re} = 10^5 \qquad f = 0.0053 \qquad\qquad (vi)$$

For cast iron pipe:

$$N_{Re} = 10^4 \qquad f = 0.009 \qquad\qquad (vii)$$
$$N_{Re} = 10^5 \qquad f = 0.0073 \qquad\qquad (viii)$$

The velocities for Reynolds numbers of 10^4 and 10^5 are found by solving Eq. (6.2)

TABLE 10.3
Comparison of pressure drops in a 0.06 m pipe

N_{Re}	Smooth	Commercial steel	Cast iron
		Δp (psi) for $L = 300$ m	
10^3	0.0064	0.0064	0.0064
10^4	0.31	0.32	0.36
10^5	18.1	21.4	29.4

for velocity:

$$U_{ave} = N_{Re}[\mu/(d_o\rho)]$$
$$= [(10^4)(10^{-3})]/[(0.06)(10^3)] \, [(kg \, m^{-1} \, s^{-1})(m^{-1})(kg^{-1} \, m^3)]$$
$$U_{ave} = 1/6 \, m \, s^{-1} \qquad (for \, N_{Re} = 10^4) \tag{ix}$$
$$U_{ave} = 10/6 \, m \, s^{-1} \qquad (for \, N_{Re} = 10^5) \tag{x}$$

The calculation of pressure drop follows that in Eq. (iii) in Example 10.3:

$$-\Delta p = (4f)(L/d_o)(\rho U_{ave}^2/2) = (4f/2)(L/d_o)(\rho U_{ave}^2) \tag{xi}$$

The results of the pressure drop calculations are in Table 10.3.

It is interesting to compare the results in Table 10.3 with a "quick-and-dirty" estimate from Eq. (10.10) or Eq. (10.11). One way to make a comparison is to generalize either equation with an unknown exponent:

$$\Delta p \propto U_{ave}^n \tag{xii}$$

If Eq. (xii) is applied to the data in Table 10.3, it is possible to solve for the exponent n:

$$(\Delta p)_2/(\Delta p)_1 = (U_{ave, \, 2}/U_{ave, \, 1})^n \tag{xiii}$$
$$n = \{\ln[(\Delta p)_2/(\Delta p)_1]\}/[\ln(U_{ave, \, 2}/U_{ave, \, 1})] \tag{xiv}$$

Using Eq. (xiv), the exponent n is computed from the results at Reynolds numbers of 10^4 and 10^5:

$$n = 1.76 \qquad (for \, a \, smooth \, pipe) \tag{xv}$$
$$n = 1.82 \qquad (for \, a \, commercial \, steel \, pipe) \tag{xvi}$$
$$n = 1.91 \qquad (for \, a \, cast \, iron \, pipe) \tag{xvii}$$

Note that the velocity ratio is the same as the ratio of Reynolds numbers (10:1) for all three tubes. The above results confirm the Blasius prediction of the exponent n, Eq. (10.11), for a smooth pipe or tube. For the rough pipes, the Reynolds numbers are not high enough for the friction factor to be independent of Reynolds number; hence the exponent did not quite reach 2.0, which is the prediction of Eq. (10.10).

10.2.3 von Karman Number

The von Karman number is the product of the Reynolds number and the square root of the friction factor:

$$N_{VK} = N_{Re}(f)^{1/2} = (d_o \rho / \mu)[d_o(-\Delta p)/(2L\rho)]^{1/2} \qquad (10.13)$$

This dimensionless number does not contain the velocity, but is determined from the pipe dimensions, fluid properties, and pressure drop. Recall that this group has appeared in many previous equations, including Eqs. (6.132) and (10.7), and in the criterion of applicability in Eq. (10.6). Hence, in problems in which the flow is the only variable to be determined, computation of the von Karman number saves a solution by trial and error. However, the trial and error is relatively simple and usually takes only a few steps. To avoid the trial and error solution an alternate plot to Fig. 10.3 is used in which the group f, $1/(f)^{1/2}$, or $(f)^{1/2}$ is plotted versus N_{VK} with relative roughness as a third parameter. This useful plot is shown in Fig. 10.5 as f versus N_{VK}. A typical problem will be solved first by the trial and error approach and then with the assistance of Fig. 10.5. Obviously, the von Karman line, Eq. (6.132), becomes a straight line if $(f)^{-1/2}$ is plotted against the von Karman number. An equivalent form of N_{VK} in terms of $d_o U^* \rho / \mu$ can be obtained from Eqs. (10.13) and (6.130).

Example 10.5. A commercial steel pipeline 300 m long and of inside diameter 0.06 m is to carry water. A pump is available that can supply pressures up to 147 kPa. Find the maximum flow velocity by trial and error. Use the fluid properties from Example 10.3.

Answer. The relative roughness for this pipe was computed in Example 10.4 in Eq. (i). This and other values from Example 10.4 are

$$e/d_o = 0.000\,762$$
$$\rho = 1000 \text{ kg m}^{-3} \qquad (i)$$
$$\mu = 1 \text{ cp} = 0.001 \text{ kg m}^{-1} \text{s}^{-1}$$

The solution to this problem requires first a guess of the friction factor, then computation of the velocity and the Reynolds number, and evaluation of the friction factor corresponding to N_{Re} and e/d_o from Fig. 10.3 until convergence is obtained. Equation (10.3), which is a rearrangement of the defining equation for f, is

$$\tau_w = \frac{d_o(-\Delta p)}{4L} = \tfrac{1}{2}\rho U_{z,\,ave}^2 f \qquad (10.3)$$

The wall shear stress is a constant for this problem:

$$\tau_w = d_o(-\Delta p)/(4L) = [-(0.06)(-1.47 \times 10^5)]/[(4)(300)] \, [(\text{m})(\text{N m}^{-2})/(\text{m})]$$
$$= 7.35 \text{ N m}^{-2} = 7.35 \text{ Pa} = 7.35 \text{ kg m}^{-1} \text{s}^{-2} \qquad (ii)$$

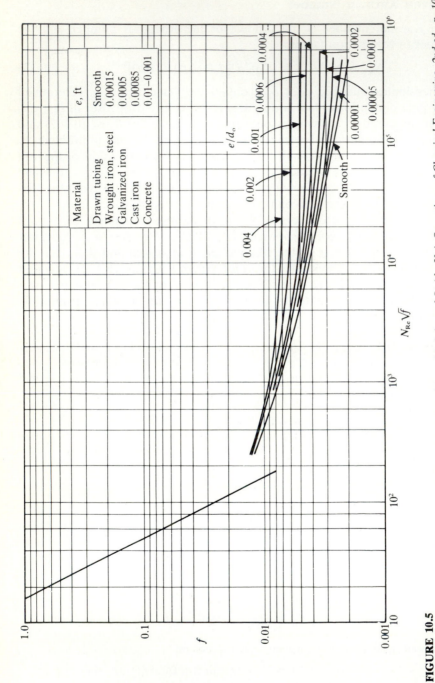

FIGURE 10.5
The friction factor as a function of the von Karman number. (*From McCabe and Smith, Unit Operations of Chemical Engineering, 2nd ed., p. 107, McGraw-Hill, New York, 1967. By permission.*)

where 1 pascal (Pa) is $1 \, \mathrm{N \, m^{-2}}$ or $1 \, \mathrm{kg \, m^{-1} \, s^{-2}}$. Next, Eq. (10.3) is solved for velocity in terms of f, and values for the quantities that are known so far are substituted:

$$U^2_{z, \, ave} = (2\tau_w)/(\rho f) = [(2)(7.35)]/[(1000)(f)] = 0.0147/f \, \mathrm{m^2 \, s^{-2}} \qquad \text{(iii)}$$

Examination of Fig. 10.3 shows that f is essentially constant at high N_{Re}. Thus, convergence will be hastened if this value of f is used to estimate the velocity. For the value of e/d_o in Eq. (i), the limiting value of f from Fig. 10.3 is 0.005. Inserting this number in Eq. (iii), the result is

$$U_{z, \, ave} = (0.0147/0.005)^{1/2} = 1.715 \, \mathrm{m \, s^{-1}} \qquad \text{(iv)}$$

The corresponding Reynolds number from Eq. (6.2) is

$$N_{Re} = d_o U_{z, \, ave} \rho/\mu = (0.06)(1.715)(1000)/(0.001) = 1.029 \times 10^5 \qquad \text{(v)}$$

Now Fig. 10.3 is used to estimate f at a Reynolds number of 1.029×10^5 and relative roughness of 0.000762. From Fig. 10.3:

$$f = 0.0054 \qquad \text{(vi)}$$

Use of Eq. (ii) yields a new $U_{z, \, ave}$:

$$U_{z, \, ave} = (0.0147/0.0054)^{1/2} = 1.650 \, \mathrm{m \, s^{-1}} \qquad \text{(vii)}$$

and the new Reynolds number is

$$N_{Re} = (0.06)(1.650)(1000)/(0.001) = 9.899 \times 10^4 \qquad \text{(viii)}$$

Consulting Fig. 10.3 at a Reynolds number of 9.899×10^4 and the relative roughness of 0.000 762, the new value of f will be 0.0053. Summarizing, the results of the second iteration are:

$$U_{z, \, ave} = 1.650 \, \mathrm{m \, s^{-1}}$$
$$N_{Re} = 9.899 \times 10^4 \qquad \text{(ix)}$$
$$f = 0.0053$$

Similarly, the results of a third iteration are

$$U_{z, \, ave} = 1.665 \, \mathrm{m \, s^{-1}}$$
$$N_{Re} = 9.992 \times 10^4 \qquad \text{(x)}$$
$$f = 0.0053$$

At this point, the value of f is deemed unchanged from the last iteration. Hence, the values above are the converged values. Note that the final answer is one of the conditions in Example 10.4, the case of N_{Re} equal to 10^5.

Example 10.6. Repeat Example 10.5 using the von Karman plot, Fig. 10.5.

Answer. The von Karman number is calculated from Eq. (10.13):

$$N_{VK} = N_{Re}(f)^{1/2} = (d_o\rho/\mu)\left[\frac{d_o(-\Delta p)}{2L\rho}\right]^{1/2}$$

$$= \frac{(0.06)(1000)}{10^{-3}}\left[\frac{-(0.06)(-1.47 \times 10^5)}{(2)(300)(1000)}\right]^{1/2}$$

$$\times \left[(m)(kg\ m^{-3})/(kg\ m^{-1}\ s^{-1})\right]\{[(m)(kg\ m^{-1}\ s^{-2})]/[(m)(kg\ m^{-3})]\}^{1/2}$$

$$= 7275\left[(s\ m^{-1})(m^2\ s^{-2})^{1/2}\right] = 7275 \tag{i}$$

From Fig. 10.5 at a von Karman number of 7275 and a relative roughness of 0.000 762, the friction factor is 0.0055. The Reynolds number can be computed by solving Eq. (10.13) for N_{Re}:

$$N_{Re} = N_{VK}/(f)^{1/2} = 7275/(0.0055)^{1/2} = 9.81 \times 10^4 \tag{ii}$$

From Eq. (6.2) the average velocity is

$$U_{z,\ ave} = N_{Re}[\mu/(d_o\rho)]$$

$$= [(9.81 \times 10^4)(10^{-3})]/[(0.06)(10^3)]\ [(kg\ m^{-1}\ s^{-1})(m^{-1})(kg^{-1}\ m^3)]$$

$$= 1.63\ m\ s^{-1} \tag{iii}$$

This answer differs from the velocity found in Example 10.4 by less than 2 percent, which exceeds the accuracy obtained with the graphs in Figs. 10.3 and 10.5.

10.2.4   Solutions of Large Molecules

The Reynolds number–friction factor correlations represented by Figs. 10.3 and 10.5 apply for ordinary fluids such as gases, water, and most organic materials. These figures also apply for many solutions such as sea water or gasoline or crude oil or sugar dissolved in water. Unfortunately, there are important exceptions, liquid solutions whose behavior deviates significantly from that predicted by Figs. 10.3 and 10.5. These fluids are called "non-Newtonian" because they either do not follow Newton's law of viscosity or they exhibit elastic properties, or both. Non-Newtonian transport phenomena are covered in Chapter 15.

Typical examples of non-Newtonian fluids include suspensions, dispersions, or solutions of polymers, soaps, surfactants, or solids. An important and interesting group of fluids exhibits a phenomenon called drag reduction [H1, H3, P1, V1]. If a small amount of a special high-molecular-weight polymer is added to a simple fluid such as water in turbulent flow, the pressure drop will actually decrease significantly. Figure 10.3 predicts an increase in pressure drop at constant flow, because the addition of polymer increases the viscosity and thus decreases the Reynolds number; from Fig. 10.3 it is seen that the friction factor increases if the Reynolds number decreases. For aqueous solutions, concentrations of a polymer in the parts-per-million range are sufficient to cause deviations. For nonaqueous solutions, minimum concentrations in the order of 0.1 percent are usually required. Polymer solutions of concentrations exceeding 1 percent are usually so viscous that it is impossible to achieve turbulent flow.

Some correlations are available for the simpler non-Newtonian materials and will be discussed in Chapter 15; however, data from the turbulent flow of drag-reducing solutions have not been correlated adequately. Up to now the dimensionless number approach to correlating friction factors has failed for these materials. The important variables for their analysis are yet to be fully identified. Design of such systems can always be based on the data for a particular solvent, with plenty of safety factors included to ensure satisfactory operation.

10.2.5   The Velocity Head Concept

The preceding example problems have shown that pressure drop calculations can be tedious. The concept of velocity head will be introduced to serve as a quick (and inexact) estimate of pressure drop. First, Eq. (10.3) is rearranged to the following

$$\frac{-\Delta p}{\rho} = 4f \frac{L}{d_o} \frac{U^2_{z,\,ave}}{2} \tag{10.14}$$

$$\frac{-\Delta p}{\rho} = N \frac{U^2_{z,\,ave}}{2} \tag{10.15}$$

with the number N of velocity heads being

$$N = 4f \frac{L}{d_o} \tag{10.16}$$

In this development, the magnitude of a velocity head equals $U^2_{z,\,ave}/2$. Equation (10.15) is exact as written, but usually an approximation is introduced through use of an average value of f. From Table 10.2, the absolute roughness for commercial steel pipe is 0.0018 in. Considering pipe diameters from $\frac{1}{2}$ in. to 18 in., and Reynolds numbers from 5×10^3 to 10^6, an average f of 0.0055 seems reasonable.

Equation (10.16) can be solved for the dimensionless length of pipe, L/d_o:

$$\frac{L}{d_o} = \frac{N}{4f} \tag{10.17}$$

For one velocity head ($N = 1$) and an average f (0.0055), an estimate for L/d_o of 45 can be computed from Eq. (10.17). Thus, as a crude approximation it takes 45 pipe diameters for the pressure drop to equal one velocity head $U^2_{z,\,ave}/2$. Hence, the number N of velocity heads is estimated by

$$N = \frac{(L/d_o)_{system}}{45} \tag{10.18}$$

where $(L/d_o)_{system}$ is the dimensionless length of the piping system for which a quick estimate of the pressure drop is to be made.

The accuracy of the velocity head approach is determined by the proximity of the true friction factor to 0.0055. The results may sometimes be off by a factor as large as 2, but never by a factor of 10 or more. Note also that N depends only on the piping system. Thus, for a given system, Eq. (10.15) predicts that the pressure drop is proportional to the square of the velocity (cf. Eq. (10.10) for rough pipes). The usefulness of the concept of velocity heads is clearly illustrated in the following example and in later sections.

Example 10.7. Using the velocity head concept, estimate the pressure drop in a 0.06-m ID commercial steel pipe at Reynolds numbers of 10^4 and 10^5. The fluid is water as in Example 10.4. The pipe length is 300 m.

Answer. Consider the Reynolds number of 10^4 first; the velocity was computed in Example 10.4 to be $(10/60)$ m s^{-1}. The velocity head is

$$U^2_{z, \text{ave}}/2 = (10/60)^2/2 = 0.01389 \text{ m}^2 \text{ s}^{-2} \tag{i}$$

The dimensionless length of the piping system, L/d_o, is

$$L/d_o = 300/0.06 = 5000 \tag{ii}$$

The number of velocity heads N is computed from Eq. (10.18):

$$N = (L/d_o)_{system}/45 = 5000/45 = 111.1 \tag{iii}$$

$$-\Delta p/\rho = N(U^2_{z, \text{ave}}/2) \tag{10.15}$$

$$-\Delta p = \rho N(U^2_{z, \text{ave}}/2) = (1000)(111.1)(0.01389) \left[(\text{kg m}^{-3})(\text{m}^2 \text{ s}^{-2})\right]$$

$$= 1543 \text{ kg m}^{-1} \text{ s}^{-2} = 1.543 \text{ kPa} = 0.224 \text{ psi} \tag{iv}$$

The calculations for a Reynolds number of 10^5 are summarized below:

$$U_{z, \text{ave}} = 100/60 \text{ m s}^{-1}$$

$$U^2_{z, \text{ave}}/2 = 1.389 \text{ m}^2 \text{ s}^{-2}$$

$$L/d_o = 5000$$

$$N = 111.1$$

$$-\Delta p = 1.543 \times 10^5 \text{ kg m}^{-1} \text{ s}^{-2} = 154.3 \text{ kPa} = 22.4 \text{ psi} \tag{v}$$

Comparisons of these estimates with the values in Table 10.3 for commercial steel pipe show errors of 31 percent and 5 percent for Reynolds numbers of 10^4 and 10^5, respectively. The Reynolds number of 10^4 is too low for a close estimate via the velocity head method. Note that N is the same for both flow rates, since it depends only on the equipment being used.

10.2.6 Curved Tubes

The pressure drop in curved tubes is larger than that predicted in the earlier sections for straight pipes of identical length. For rigid pipe, turns are accomplished by pipe fittings such as elbows; calculations for these will be presented in Section 10.2.8. Flow through curved tubes or helical coils occurs

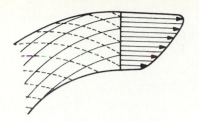

FIGURE 10.6
Flow in a curved pipe, after Prandtl
[P3]. (*From Schlichting, Boundary
Layer Theory, 7th ed., p. 626,
McGraw-Hill, New York, 1979. By
permission.*)

in a number of heat transfer applications. Usually such coils are immersed in a second fluid. The object is to be able to predict the pressure drop in the curved tube so that the required pump size can be designed. It is also possible to have flow in spiral coils [A1]. A thorough review is available elsewhere [S4].

In curved tubes, the momentum of the fluid rounding the curve causes the velocity profile to be distorted. The maximum velocity no longer occurs at the tube center line but nearer the wall at the outside of the coil bend, as shown in Fig. 10.6. Visual studies have indicated the presence of secondary flow patterns in which fluid flows outward from the center of the tube to the top of the bend and then around the outside in a pair of loops, as sketched to the right in Fig. 10.6 [P3]. The secondary flow pattern, often called the double-eddy or Dean effect, stabilizes laminar flow and increases the transition Reynolds number, $N_{Re, critical}$ [S4]:

$$N_{Re, critical} = (2100)[1 + (12)(d_o/d_c)^{1/2}] \qquad (10.19)$$

where d_o is the inside pipe diameter and d_c is the coil diameter.

The effect of coil curvature is substantially greater in laminar flow than in turbulent flow [S4]. For a gentle curvature, the pressure drop in laminar flow is essentially the same as that in a straight pipe, and Eqs. (6.124) and (10.4) apply. At the maximum curvature and just before the transition, a given length of coiled pipe or tubing may require five times the pressure drop of a straight length at the same flow rate. Thus, the correction for curved tubes can be highly significant. The following equation introduces the Dean number N_{Dn} (named in honor of an early worker in this field) and an empirical fit of White's data [W1] for laminar flow in coils:

$$\ln(f_{coil}/f_{straight}) = 2.8276 + 4.3719X - 0.8903X^2 \qquad X = \ln N_{Dn} \quad (10.20)$$
$$N_{Dn} = N_{Re}(d_o/d_c)^{1/2} = (d_o U_{z, ave}\rho/\mu)(d_o/d_c)^{1/2} \qquad 11.6 \le N_{Dn} \le 2000$$

Below a Dean number of 11.6, the ratio $f_{coil}/f_{straight}$ equals 1. Equation (10.20) predicts that at a Dean number of 2000 there will be five times the pressure drop during laminar flow in a coil as compared with that in a straight tube.

For turbulent flow in coiled tubes, the following correlation is offered [W2]:

$$f_{coil} = (0.08)(N_{Re})^{-1/4} + (0.012)(d_o/d_c)^{1/2} \qquad (10.21)$$
$$10 \le d_c/d_o \le 250$$
$$N_{Re, critical} \le N_{Re} \le 100\,000$$

The accuracy of Eq. (10.21) is probably only ±10 percent, especially for Reynolds numbers of less than 15 000, for which predictions of f_{coil} from Eq. (10.21) may be high. Notice the similarity of Eq. (10.21) to the Blasius correlation, Eq. (6.133), from which it originated.

10.2.7 Expansion and Contraction Losses

In any real piping layout, flow does not begin and end in a straight pipe. Instead, the fluid may originate in a tank or other large reservoir; often it proceeds through a short section of pipe into a pump or compressor where the pressure is raised significantly. From the pump the fluid flows through a number of pipe elbows to change directions, valves to control the flow rate, tees to split or combine streams, unions to connect sections of pipe, expansions to change pipe diameters, etc. Each of these expansions, contractions, fittings, valves, etc., contributes significantly to the pressure drop. This section deals with expansions and contractions in turbulent flow.

Sudden expansion. Consider first a sudden expansion, shown in Fig. 10.7, in which a fluid experiences an abrupt increase in flow area so that its velocity decreases. As the fluid enters the large pipe of cross sectional area S_3, a jet is formed as the fluid separates from the wall of the small tube. Because at location 2 there is no longer a pipe wall restraining the jet of fluid as it issues from the small pipe, the jet expands until it fills the entire area, shown between locations 2 and 3 in Fig. 10.7. Some fluid breaks away from the jet and circulates between the wall and the jet around location 2. The net effect of these eddies and of the fluid expansion coupled with the three changes in velocity profile, stable at location 1 in the small tube, relaxed (i.e., becoming more plug-like) at location 2, and re-established at location 3, is a significant drop in pressure and a resulting energy loss. This loss, called F_{loss}, may be expressed as

$$F_{loss} = k_e(U_1^2/2) \tag{10.22}$$

where k_e is the expansion loss coefficient (dimensionless), to be calculated later as Eq. (10.31). For brevity, the "z, ave" subscript has been dropped, and U_1 is the average upstream velocity at location 1 in the small tube in the z direction. The loss coefficient k_e is sometimes called the resistance coefficient.

In any problem in which the piping system is more complex than a single

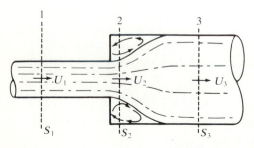

FIGURE 10.7
A sudden expansion.

length of pipe it is advisable to begin the problem with the mechanical energy balance, Eq. (7.61):

$$\frac{p_2 - p_1}{\rho} + g(z_2 - z_1) + \frac{1}{2}\left(\frac{U_{2,\,\text{ave}}^2}{\alpha_2} - \frac{U_{1,\,\text{ave}}^2}{\alpha_1}\right) + F' + W_s = 0 \qquad (7.61)$$

The term F_{loss} is identical to the F' term in Eq. (7.61), if Eq. (7.61) is applied to the expansion in Fig. 10.7. Equation (7.61) then becomes

$$\frac{p_3 - p_1}{\rho} + \tfrac{1}{2}(U_3^2 - U_1^2) + F_{\text{loss}} = 0 \qquad (10.23)$$

where α_1 and α_2 are assumed to be unity and the potential energy and shaft work terms are zero for this problem. Thus, the units of F_{loss} are ft lb$_f$ lb$_m^{-1}$ in English units or m^2 s^{-2} in SI units. In the English system, k_e must be divided by g_c to keep the units consistent in Eq. (10.23). Note also that Eq. (10.22) is in the form of the velocity head $U^2/2$ times number of heads k_e, as discussed in Section 10.2.5.

The expansion loss coefficient k_e is readily calculated through the mechanical energy balance, Eq. (10.23), and the integral momentum balance, Eq. (7.23). In Fig. 10.7, location 2 is chosen so that

$$U_2 = U_1 \qquad (10.24)$$

Again, the distance between location 1 and location 2 is very short, so there is no friction loss and $p_1 = p_2$.

The integral momentum balance equation, Eq. (7.23) for the x direction, is

$$\dot{P}_x = \frac{(U_1^2)_{\text{ave}}}{U_{1,\,\text{ave}}} w_1 \cos \alpha_1 - \frac{(U_2^2)_{\text{ave}}}{U_{2,\,\text{ave}}} w_2 \cos \alpha_2 + p_1 S_1 \cos \alpha_1$$
$$- p_2 S_2 \cos \alpha_2 - F_{x,\,\text{drag}} + F_{x,\,\text{ext}} \qquad (7.23)$$

where α_1 and α_2 are the angles between the velocity vector U and the horizontal unit vector (i) (both equal to 0° in Fig. 10.7). As discussed in Chapter 7, each term with $(U^2)_{\text{ave}}/U_{\text{ave}}$ is replaced with U_{ave}/β, and then β is assumed to be unity in turbulent flow. When Eq. (7.23) is applied to the sudden expansion in Fig. 10.7, it is convenient to choose locations 2 and 3; the usual assumptions are that both β_2 and β_3 are unity, and the losses are negligible:

$$U_2 w - U_3 w + p_2 S_3 - p_3 S_3 = 0 \qquad (10.25)$$

where w is the steady-state flow (units of kg s^{-1}) and S_3 is the cross sectional area at both locations. Note that location 2, which is defined solely by Eq. (10.24), is vital in the use of Eq. (7.23). If the integral momentum balance equations were to be applied between locations 1 and 3 in Fig. 10.7, there would be components in the y and z directions as well as the x direction, plus some other non-zero terms.

The mass flow rate w in Eq. (10.25) is replaced by using Eq. (7.10):

$$w = \rho U_3 S_3 \tag{10.26}$$

The velocity U_2 is replaced with U_1 [Eq. (10.24)], and Eq. (10.25) becomes

$$U_3(U_1 - U_3) - \frac{p_3 - p_1}{\rho} = 0 \tag{10.27}$$

since p_1 equals p_2 and the area S_3 may be factored out and cannot be equal to zero. Equation (10.27) is solved for the term $(p_3 - p_1)/\rho$, and the result is substituted into Eq. (10.23). After rearrangement, F_{loss} is

$$F_{\text{loss}} = \tfrac{1}{2}(U_1^2 - U_3^2) - (U_3)(U_1 - U_3) = \tfrac{1}{2}(U_1^2 - 2U_1 U_3 + U_3^2)$$
$$= \tfrac{1}{2}(U_1 - U_3)^2 \tag{10.28}$$

Equations (10.22) and (10.28) are combined to solve for k_e:

$$k_e = \frac{(U_1 - U_3)^2}{U_1^2} = \left(1 - \frac{U_3}{U_1}\right)^2 \tag{10.29}$$

Use of the integral mass balance, Eq. (7.13), at constant density yields the ratio of U_3 to U_1

$$\frac{U_3}{U_1} = \frac{S_1}{S_3} = \frac{d_1^2/4}{d_3^2/4} = \frac{d_1^2}{d_3^2} \tag{10.30}$$

where d_1 and d_3 are the inside diameters of the small and large sections, respectively, in Fig. 10.7. Thus, the final expression for the expansion loss coefficient k_e is

$$k_e = \left(1 - \frac{d_1^2}{d_2^2}\right)^2 \tag{10.31}$$

where d_1 is the diameter of the small section and d_2 is the diameter of the large section. The most restrictive assumption in the derivation of Eq. (10.31) is that both α and β (defined in Chapter 7) are unity; this assumption limits Eq. (10.31) to turbulent flow. For a typical turbulent flow, say a Reynolds number of 10^5 or 10^6, both α and β are very close to unity, and Eq. (10.31) is essentially rigorous, since the other assumptions are reasonable.

Sudden contraction. A sudden contraction (also called reduction) is shown in Fig. 10.8. The flow phenomena in the case of a contraction are quite different from those in an expansion. At location 1, the velocity profile is fully developed as the fluid flows in the large section. The sharp-edged contraction causes the fluid to accelerate as it enters the small section. The fluid actually contracts to an area smaller than the area of the small section. This well-known phenomenon is termed the "vena contracta", and is noted in any flow that abruptly enters a section of a smaller diameter, such as flow through an orifice. Determination of the loss due to a sudden contraction is accomplished by

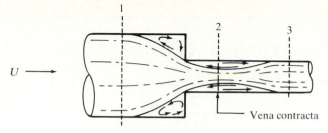

FIGURE 10.8
Vena contracta   A sudden contraction.

the introduction of a contraction loss coefficient k_c:

$$F_{loss} = k_c(U_3^2/2) \tag{10.32}$$

Note that in Eq. (10.32) the contraction loss coefficient is based on U_3, the velocity in the small section. Unfortunately, an exact determination of k_c for turbulent flow is not possible. Let us illustrate by attempting the analysis followed previously for the equations leading to Eq. (10.31). The first assumption is that the loss between locations 1 and 2 in Fig. 10.8 is zero. Then all the loss occurs between locations 2 and 3. Recall that the integral momentum balance must be applied to a pair of areas for which the velocity vector U has a non-zero component in one direction only. Examination of Fig. 10.8 shows that the only possibilities are locations 2 and 3. When the integral momentum balance, Eq. (7.23), is applied to locations 2 and 3 in Fig. 10.8, the resulting equation is

$$w(U_2 - U_3) + p_2 S_2 - p_3 S_3 = 0 \tag{10.33}$$

Unfortunately, Eq. (10.33) contains the vena contracta area S_2, which is unknown. Thus, it is impossible to factor out S_2 and/or S_3 from Eq. (10.33), as was done previously to obtain Eq. (10.27) for the case of a sudden expansion. The analysis stops at this point, and k_c is obtained from experimental data. The curves for both the expansion and the contraction loss coefficients are shown in Fig. 10.9. For turbulent flow, a suitable empirical equation for the curve in Fig. 10.9 is

$$k_c = 0.42\left(1 - \frac{d_2^2}{d_1^2}\right) \qquad d_2/d_1 \le 0.76 \tag{10.34}$$

where d_2 is the diameter of the smaller section in Fig. 10.8 and d_1 is the larger diameter. Note in Fig. 10.9 that the sudden contraction curve merges with the sudden enlargement curve above $d_2/d_1 = 0.76$. Hence Eq. (10.31) can be used above $d_2/d_1 = 0.76$ for the determination of k_c if the definitions of d_1 and d_2 are reversed. For laminar flow, k_c has been found to be less than 0.1 and therefore is negligible.

Sometimes a gradual transition is used to change a small-diameter pipe d_1 to a larger diameter d_2. Let θ be the total angle between the walls of transition, as shown in Fig. 10.10. For a sudden enlargement, θ equals 180°. Figure 10.10 presents k_e for such pipe transitions, usually called conical

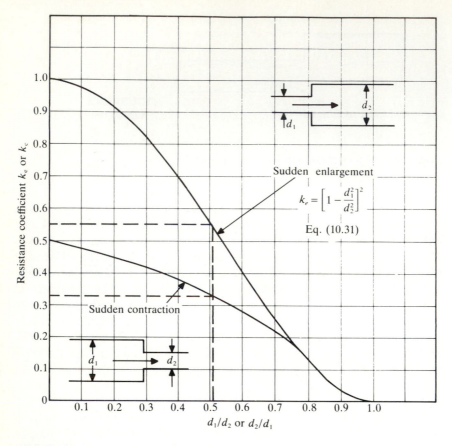

FIGURE 10.9
Resistance due to sudden enlargements and contractions. (*Reproduced from Tech. Paper 410, Flow of Fluids. Courtesy Crane Co.*)

expansions, conical diffusers, or uniformly diverging ducts. The curves pass through a minimum at an angle of 7°. Note also that above $\theta = 40$ to 60°, the loss coefficient k_e actually exceeds that for a sudden enlargement. In other words, a sudden enlargement is preferred to a fairly sharp-angled conical expansion.

A pipe transition that uniformly converges (flow from right to left in Fig. 10.10) has a very low loss coefficient. Figure 10.11 shows that a well-rounded pipe entrance (i.e., a contraction) has a k_c of 0.04. All loss coefficients such as those in Figs. 10.9, 10.10, and 10.11 apply in Eq. (10.22) or Eq. (10.32) for F_{loss}, just as do those from Fig. 10.9. Use of these loss coefficients is easy when the mechanical energy balance is combined with the velocity head concept.

Consider first the flow in a straight pipe of constant diameter. The mechanical energy balance [Eq. (7.61)] applies with all terms zero except the

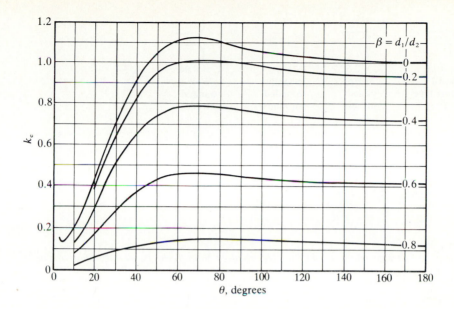

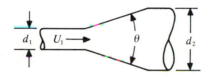

FIGURE 10.10
Loss coefficient for conical diffusers. (*Excerpted by special permission from Chemical Engineering (June 17, 1968), copyright © 1968 McGraw-Hill, New York.*)

two associated with pressure drop and losses:

$$(p_2 - p_1)/\rho = F' = F_{\text{pipe}} \tag{10.35}$$

where F_{pipe} is the frictional loss due to pressure drop in the pipe. The definition of friction factor was rearranged and solved for the term $(p_1 - p_2)/\rho$ previously in Eq. (10.14). Combining Eqs. (10.35) and (10.14) yields

$$(p_1 - p_2)/\rho = F_{\text{pipe}} = (4fL/d_o)(U_{z,\text{ave}}^2/2) \tag{10.36}$$

Again, Eq. (10.36) is restricted to a straight pipe of constant diameter and length L. The loss from expansions and contractions is found from the sum of Eqs. (10.22) and (10.32):

$$F_{\text{loss}} = (k_e + k_c)(U_{z,\text{ave}}^2/2) \tag{10.37}$$

These last two equations can be combined and included in Eq. (7.61), which may be solved for the pressure drop. The general design equation for piping

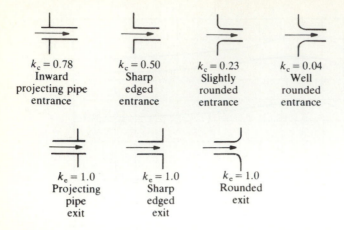

$k_c = 0.78$
Inward
projecting pipe
entrance

$k_c = 0.50$
Sharp
edged
entrance

$k_c = 0.23$
Slightly
rounded
entrance

$k_c = 0.04$
Well
rounded
entrance

$k_e = 1.0$
Projecting
pipe
exit

$k_e = 1.0$
Sharp
edged
exit

$k_e = 1.0$
Rounded
exit

FIGURE 10.11
Resistance due to pipe entrance and exit. (*Reproduced from Tech. Paper 410, Flow of Fluids. Courtesy Crane Co.*)

systems is Eq. (7.61) with F' expanded to include all possible losses. Complete details will be presented in the next section.

10.2.8 Pipe Fittings and Valves

In general, any time the velocity profile in a pipe is disturbed, there is an increase in the pressure loss, as compared to a straight pipe of equivalent length. This section deals with the pressure loss in pipe fittings and valves, the presence of which disturbs the velocity profile.

Equipment. In the United States, pipe and tubing are sized in English units. Complete tables of pipe and tubing data are in Table B.1 and B.2, respectively. For tubing, the nominal size is the actual outside diameter. Many homes have $\frac{1}{2}$-in. copper tubing in use as water supply lines. Such tubing has an outside diameter of 0.500 in.

Pipe tends to be thicker than tubing. Pipe and pipe fittings are interconnected by screw-type tapered threads, by flanges that bolt together with a gasket in between, or by flanges that are welded together. Pipe sizes are strictly nominal, as is evident in Table B.1. For example, $1\frac{1}{2}$-in. pipe has an outside diameter of 1.900 in. All $1\frac{1}{2}$-in. fittings, unions, elbows, tees, valves, bushings, etc., are sized to this diameter. The schedule number denotes the wall thickness, which is designed according to the allowable stress and the pressure to prevent bursting. For ordinary water service, galvanized pipe of thickness schedule 40 is adequate. Note that the inside diameter of $1\frac{1}{2}$-in. pipe, schedule 40, is 1.610 in. For higher pressures, schedule 80 $1\frac{1}{2}$-in. pipe, which has an inside diameter of 1.500 in., may be used. Table 10.4 compares pressure and schedule numbers.

TABLE 10.4

Comparison of schedule number and pressure rating for steel pipe*

Valve or fitting ASA pressure classification		Schedule No. of pipe thickness†
Steam rating	Cold rating	
250-pound and lower	500 psig	Schedule 40
300-pound to 600-pound	1440 psig	Schedule 80
900-pound	2160 psig	Schedule 120
1500-pound	3600 psig	Schedule 160
2500-pound: $\frac{1}{2}$–6 in.	6000 psig	xx (double extra strong)
8 in. and larger	3600 psig	Schedule 160

* Reproduced from Tech. Paper 410, Flow of Fluids. Courtesy Crane Co.
† These schedule numbers have been arbitrarily selected only for the purpose of identifying the various pressure classes of valves and fittings with specific pipe dimensions for the interpretation of flow test data; they should not be construed as a recommendation for installation purposes. Note that schedule numbers indicate the approximate values of the expression $(1000p/S_f)$, where p is the internal pressure (psi) and S_f is the allowable stress (psi).

Figures 10.12 and 10.13 show the common fittings and valves. Note that a nipple is simply a length of pipe threaded on either end. The pipe threads must be tapered in order for the nipple to snug up to the corresponding threads in the female end of the fitting. Usually some type of pipe dope is required for a tight seal.

Pressure loss. Valves or fittings increase the pressure drop in a pipe system in turbulent flow as compared with that predicted for a straight pipe without the valve or fittings. Even a coupling or union, which joins two long lengths of pipe, disturbs the velocity profile in turbulent flow sufficiently to increase the pressure drop by a small amount.

There are two standard procedures for determining the pressure loss in turbulent flow due to the presence of fittings. One procedure is to use a table of equivalent lengths; the second is to define a loss coefficient k for each type of fitting, which is to be used in an expanded form of Eq. (10.37). These factors are listed in Table 10.5. More complete lists are available from equipment manufacturers or from handbooks [C3, P2]. Either procedure is accurate to only ±30 percent. Any type of fitting that changes the direction of flow, such as a globe valve, causes a large loss. On the other hand, frictional losses in fittings such as couplings and unions are usually negligible, especially in view of the overall accuracy. A third procedure, not covered in this text, is especially recommended for design in large pipes [H2].

The equivalent-length procedure rates each fitting in terms of the equivalent length of straight pipe. For example, a common globe valve, fully

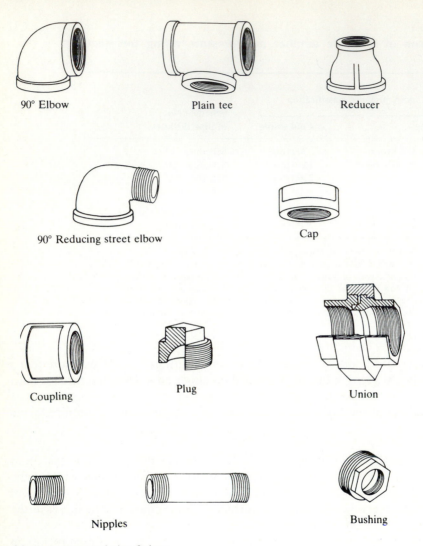

90° Elbow   Plain tee   Reducer

90° Reducing street elbow   Cap

Coupling   Plug   Union

Nipples   Bushing

(*a*) Typical screwed pipe fittings

FIGURE 10.12
Some typical pipe fittings. (*From Foust et al., Principles of Unit Operations, 2nd ed., pp. 550–551, Wiley, New York, 1980. By permission.*)

open, is rated at 340 equivalent lengths, as stated in Table 10.5. Thus, if the pipeline had an inside diameter of 0.02 m, the equivalent length of the open globe valve would be 6.8 m. The total length of the pipe system is considered to be 6.8 m longer as a result of flow through this fitting. The equation for total length L is

$$L = L_{\text{pipe}} + L_{\text{e, fittings}} + L_{\text{loss}} \tag{10.38}$$

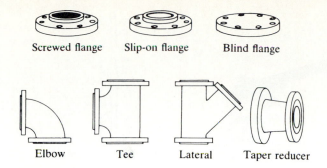

Screwed flange   Slip-on flange   Blind flange

Elbow   Tee   Lateral   Taper reducer

(b) Typical flanged pipe fittings

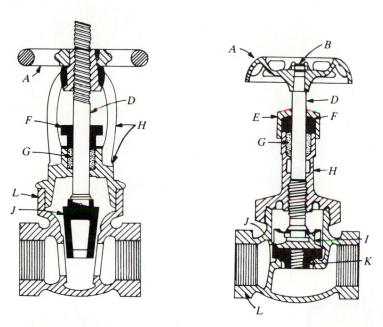

(c) Sectional view of gate valve (left) and globe valve (right). A—wheel; B—wheel nut; D—spindle; E—packing nut; F—gland; G—packing; H—bonnet; I—disk holder; J—disk; K—disk nut; L—body.

where $L_{e, \text{fittings}}$ is the sum of the equivalent lengths of all fittings, L_{loss} is for expansions and contractions, and L_{pipe} is the length of straight pipe. The total equivalent length [L from Eq. (10.38)] may be used in an equation similar to Eq. (10.36), which relates Δp to ρ, f, L, d_o, and $U_{z, \text{ave}}$.

Design and calculations with equivalent lengths are especially useful to the engineer who works only occasionally with Table 10.5. The equivalent length shows quickly the penalty associated with each fitting in easy-to-visualize terms. Also, it is easy to verify the equivalent length for a plant pipe system if it is possible to measure one pressure drop and one flow rate.

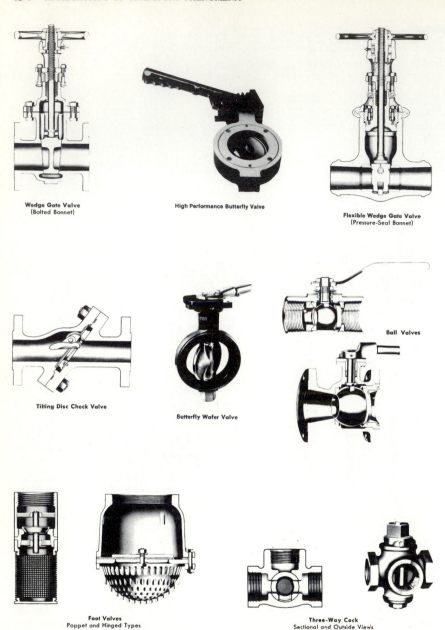

Wedge Gate Valve
(Bolted Bonnet)

High Performance Butterfly Valve

Flexible Wedge Gate Valve
(Pressure-Seal Bonnet)

Tilting Disc Check Valve

Butterfly Wafer Valve

Ball Valves

Foot Valves
Poppet and Hinged Types

Three-Way Cock
Sectional and Outside Views

FIGURE 10.13
Types of valves. (*Reproduced from Tech. Paper 410, Flow of Fluids. Courtesy Crane Co.*)

TABLE 10.5

Loss coefficient and equivalent length L/d_o for turbulent flow through valves and fittings*

Type of fitting or valve	Loss coefficient, k	Equivalent length, L/d_o
45° ell, standard[a,b,e,g,i]	0.35	16
45° ell, long radius[b]	0.2	—
90° ell, standard[a,b,d,g,i,m]	0.75	30
long radius[a,b,e,g]	0.45	20
square or miter[m]	1.3	57
180° bend, close return[a,b,g]	1.5	50
Tee, std, along run, branch blanked off[g]	0.4	20
used as ell, entering run[d,h]	1.0	60
used as ell, entering branch[b,d, h]	1.0	60
branch flowing[f,h,l]	1.0	—
Coupling[b,g]	0.04	0.1
Union[g]	0.04	0.1
Ball valve, orifice to d_o ratio 0.9, fully open	0.17	13
Gate valve, open[a,g,j]	0.17	13
$\frac{3}{4}$ open[p]	0.9	35
$\frac{1}{2}$ open[p]	4.5	160
$\frac{1}{4}$ open[p]	24.0	900
Diaphragm valve, open[n]	2.3	—
$\frac{1}{4}$ open[p]	2.6	—
$\frac{1}{2}$ open[p]	4.3	—
$\frac{1}{4}$ open[p]	21.0	—
Globe valve, bevel seat, open[g,j]	6.0	340
$\frac{1}{2}$ open[p]	9.5	—
Globe valve, composition seat, open	6.0	340
$\frac{1}{2}$ open[p]	8.5	—
Globe valve, plug disk, open	9.0	450
$\frac{3}{4}$ open[p]	13.0	—
$\frac{1}{2}$ open[p]	36.0	—
$\frac{1}{4}$ open[p]	112.0	—
Angle valve, open[a,g]	2.0	145
Y or blowoff valve, open[a,j]	3.0	175
Check valve, swing[a,g,j]	2.0[q]	135
disk check valve	10.0[q]	—
ball check valve	70.0[q]	—
Foot valve[g]	15.0	420

* This table was compiled from Lapple [L1]; *Chemical Engineers' Handbook* [P2]; and the Crane Co. [C3]. Excerpted by special permission from *Chemical Engineering* (May, 1949), copyright © 1968 by McGraw-Hill, New York; from *Perry's Chemical Engineers' Handbook,* 6th ed., Perry and Green (eds.), McGraw-Hill, New York, 1984; reproduced from *Tech. Paper 410, Flow of Fluids,* courtesy Crane Co.

[a] *Flow of Fluids through Valves, Fittings, and Pipe, Tech Paper* 410., Crane Co., 1969.

[b] Freeman: *Experiments upon the Flow of Water in Pipes and Pipe Fittings,* American Society of Mechanical Engineers, New York, 1941.

[c] Gibson: *Hydraulics and Its Applications,* 5th ed., Constable, London, 1952.

[d] Giesecke and Badgett: *Heating, Piping Air Conditioning* **4**(6): 443 (1932).

Table 10.5 (*footnotes continued*)

[e] Giesecke: *J. Am. Soc. Heat. Vent. Engrs.* **32**: 461 (1926).

[f] Gilman: *Heating, Piping Air Conditioning* **27**(4): 141 (1955).

[g] *Pipe Friction Manual*, 3rd ed., Hydraulic Institute, New York, 1961.

[h] Hoopes, Isakoff, Clarke, and Drew: *Chem. Eng. Progr.* **44**: 691 (1948).

[i] Ito: *J. Basic Eng.* **82**: 131 (1960).

[j] Lansford: *Loss of Head in Flows of Fluids through Various Types of* $1\frac{1}{2}$-*in. Valves*, Univ. Illinois Eng. Expt. Sta. Bull. Series 340, 1943.

[k] Lapple: *Chem. Eng.* **56**(5): 96 (1949). [General survey reference.]

[l] McNown: *Proc. Am. Soc. Civil Engrs.* **79**, Separate 258, 1–22 (1953); see discussion, *ibid.*, **80**, Separate 396, 19–45 (1954).

[m] Schoder and Dawson: *Hydraulics*, 2d ed., McGraw-Hill, New York, 1934, p. 213.

[n] Streeter: *Prod. Eng.* **18**(7): 89 (1947).

[o] This is pressure drop (including friction loss) between run and branch, based on velocity in the main stream before branching. Actual value depends on the flow split, ranging from 0.5 to 1.3 if main stream enters run and from 0.7 to 1.5 if main stream enters branch.

[p] The fraction open is directly proportional to stem travel or turns of hand wheel. Flow direction through some types of valves has a small effect on pressure drop (see Freeman, *op. cit.*). For practical purposes this effect may be neglected.

[q] Values apply only when check valve is fully open, which is generally the case for velocities more than $3\,\text{ft s}^{-1}$ for water.

[r] Values should be regarded as approximate because there is much variation in equipment of the same type from different manufacturers.

The loss coefficient calculation for pipe fittings is similar to that presented previously for losses in enlargements and contractions. Equation (7.61) is expanded to include specifically all losses—straight pipe, fittings, expansions, and contractions:

$$\frac{p_2 - p_1}{\rho} + g(z_2 - z_1) + \frac{1}{2}\left(\frac{U^2_{2,\,\text{ave}}}{\alpha_2} - \frac{U^2_{1,\,\text{ave}}}{\alpha_1}\right)$$
$$+ F_{\text{pipe}} + F_{\text{fittings}} + F_{\text{loss}} + W_s = 0 \qquad (10.39)$$

where F_{pipe} is from Eq. (10.36) and F_{loss} is the expansion and contraction losses, Eq. (10.37):

$$\frac{(p_1 - p_2)}{\rho} = F_{\text{pipe}} = \frac{4fL}{d_o}\frac{U^2_{z,\,\text{ave}}}{2} \qquad (10.36)$$

$$F_{\text{loss}} = (k_e + k_c)\frac{U^2_{z,\,\text{ave}}}{2} \qquad (10.37)$$

By analogy with Eq. (10.37), the term F_{fittings} may be expressed as

$$F_{\text{fittings}} = k_{\text{fittings}}\frac{U^2_{z,\,\text{ave}}}{2} \qquad (10.40)$$

with k_{fittings} being the sum of all loss coefficients (cf. Table 10.5). Equation (10.39) is the general design equation for piping systems. Equations (10.36) through (10.40) are supporting equations for the terms in Eq. (10.39). Use of Eqs. (10.36) through (10.40) for piping systems in which the diameter varies from section to section will require each section to be considered separately. There will be as many sets of F_{pipe}, $F_{fittings}$, and F_{loss} as there are diameters.

Sometimes it is useful to have available an equation relating the equivalent length $L_{e,\,fittings}$ to $k_{fittings}$. First, Eq. (10.36) is recast in terms of $F_{fittings}$ and $L_{e,\,fittings}$:

$$F_{fittings} = \frac{4fL_{e,\,fittings}}{d_o} \frac{U_{z,\,ave}^2}{2} \tag{10.41}$$

When Eqs. (10.40) and (10.41) are equated, the result is

$$\frac{L_{e,\,fittings}}{d_o} = \frac{k_{fittings}}{4f} \tag{10.42}$$

The sum of the loss coefficients $(k_e + k_c)$ may also be expressed in terms of an equivalent length $L_{e,\,loss}$. The derivation uses Eq. (10.37) and follows exactly that just given:

$$\frac{L_{e,\,loss}}{d_o} = \frac{k_e + k_c}{4f} \tag{10.43}$$

Thus, at high Reynolds numbers in rough pipe for which f is constant, the equivalent length is directly proportional to the sum of the loss coefficients. All losses may be converted to equivalent lengths via equations of the type of Eqs. (10.42) and (10.43). If the system consists of a single-size pipe, then Eq. (10.38) yields the total length due to pipe, fittings, expansions, and contractions. That total length is used in Eq. (10.36) to find F_{pipe}, which then includes all losses (straight pipe, fittings, enlargements, and contractions). If the system consists of several pipe sizes, then Eq. (10.39) must be used, and there is no point in converting losses into equivalent lengths. Instead, Eq. (10.39) must be expanded to include a set of F_{pipe}, $F_{fittings}$, and F_{losses} for each section of pipe. This calculation will be illustrated later in Example 10.11.

These two methods for determining the pressure loss in fittings are approximate to the point that fine details are more of theoretical interest than of practical interest. Nevertheless, it is noted that the dependence of pressure drop through fittings on changes in flow rate differs slightly in the two methods. In the case of the equivalent length method, pressure drop through fittings varies as the 1.8 power of the flow rate at low Reynolds numbers. But in rough pipe at high Reynolds numbers, pressure drop varies as the second power of the flow rate, since Fig. 10.3 shows that f becomes constant. Note that Eq. (10.38) shows that the loss coefficient approach also predicts second-power variation of pressure drop with flow rates.

Finally, careful measurements have discerned that the equivalent length or loss coefficient is sometimes a function of Reynolds number and roughness as well as diameter and geometry. Equipment manufacturers do not in general maintain geometric similarity between sizes; thus, a Reynolds number dependency is predicted theoretically. Figure 10.14 shows how k varies with diameter

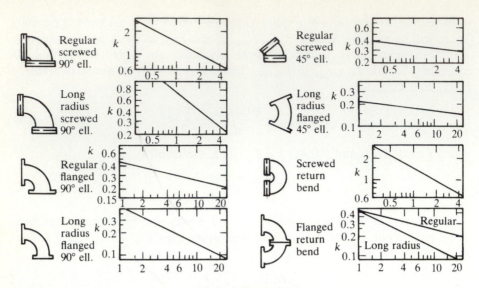

Nominal pipe diameter

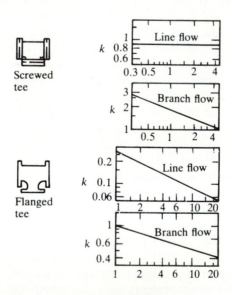

Nominal pipe diameter

FIGURE 10.14

Variation of the loss coefficient k with nominal pipe size. (*Excerpted by special permission from Chemical Engineering (June 17, 1968), copyright © 1968 by McGraw-Hill, New York.*)

for some common fittings (S3). In general, differences between screwed fittings, welded fittings, and flanged fittings are ignored for most fittings. At high Reynolds number, k and L_e are independent of the Reynolds number.

The data in Table 10.5, in which each type of fitting has a single k value or equivalent length, are reasonably reliable for 1-in. to 6-in. diameter commercial steel pipe. Even charts such as Fig. 10.14 extend the reliability range marginally. Hooper's method is recommended for large pipe and for Reynolds numbers under 10 000 [H2].

Laminar flow. It has already been mentioned that pipe roughness is not a factor in pressure loss in laminar flow. The data and methods for Table 10.5 greatly underestimate laminar head losses. The loss due to a fluid undergoing a sudden contraction is usually small. In precise work, such as viscometry, entrance effects are important, however [H1, M2]. Methods for laminar flow in fittings [H2] and correlations for expansion [P2] are available.

Example 10.8. Figure 10.15 shows a pipe flow system where air at pressure p_1 forces water from a large tank through a pipe of total length 137 ft that contains a series of valves and fittings. The discharge is at atmospheric pressure. All elements are on the same horizontal plane. The pipe and all components are $2\frac{1}{2}$-in. schedule 40. The Reynolds number in the pipe is 10^5. Compute p_1 by (a) the equivalent length method and (b) the loss coefficient method.

Answer. English units will be used. The properties of water as given in Example

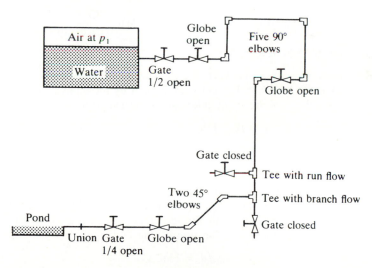

Note: All pipe and fittings are on the same
horizontal elevation

FIGURE 10.15
An example pipe flow system.

10.3 include viscosity of $6.72 \times 10^{-4}\,\text{lb}_\text{m}\,\text{ft}^{-1}\,\text{s}^{-1}$ and density of $62.4\,\text{lb}_\text{m}\,\text{ft}^{-3}$. The properties of steel pipe are given in Table B.1:

$$S \text{ (flow area)} = 0.03322\,\text{ft}^2$$

$$d_\text{o} = 2.469\,\text{in.} = 0.206\,\text{ft} \tag{i}$$

From Table 10.2, the absolute roughness for commercial steel pipe is $1.5 \times 10^{-4}\,\text{ft}$. Then the relative roughness is

$$e/d_\text{o} = 1.5 \times 10^{-4}/0.206 = 7.29 \times 10^{-4} \tag{ii}$$

The friction factor, as read from Fig. 10.3 at a Reynolds number of 10^5 and relative roughness 7.29×10^{-4}, is 0.0053.

The velocity is computed from the Reynolds number, Eq. (6.1):

$$\begin{aligned}
U_{z,\,\text{ave}} &= N_\text{Re}(\mu)/(\rho d_\text{o}) \\
&= [(10^5)(6.72 \times 10^{-4})]/[(62.4)(0.206)]\,[(\text{lb}_\text{m}\,\text{ft}^{-1}\,\text{s}^{-1})(\text{lb}_\text{m}^{-1}\,\text{ft}^3)(\text{ft}^{-1})] \\
&= 5.234\,\text{ft s}^{-1} \tag{iii}
\end{aligned}$$

The volume rate of flow is the velocity times the flow area:

$$\begin{aligned}
Q = U_{z,\,\text{ave}}S &= (5.234)(0.03322)\,[(\text{ft s}^{-1})(\text{ft}^2)] \\
&= 0.1739\,\text{ft}^3\,\text{s}^{-1} = 78.0\,\text{gal min}^{-1} \tag{iv}
\end{aligned}$$

where 7.48 gal equals 1.0 ft³.

Equivalent length method. Since the flow rate and friction factor are known, the pressure drop per foot can be computed from Eq. (10.3):

$$\begin{aligned}
-\Delta p/L &= (f)(4/d_\text{o})[\rho U_{z,\,\text{ave}}^2/(2g_\text{c})] \\
&= [(0.0053)(4/0.206)(62.4)(5.234)^2]/[(2)(32.174)]\left(\frac{(\text{lb}_\text{m}\,\text{ft}^{-3})(\text{ft}^2\,\text{s}^{-2})}{(\text{ft})(\text{lb}_\text{m}\,\text{lb}_\text{f}^{-1}\,\text{ft s}^{-2})}\right) \\
&= 2.74\,\text{lb}_\text{f}\,\text{ft}^{-3} = 0.0190\,\text{psi ft}^{-1} \tag{v}
\end{aligned}$$

Note the inclusion of g_c, which converts the pressure drop into force units. If the pressure drop per unit length in Eq. (v) is multiplied by the equivalent length L [Eq. (10.38)], then the pressure at the inlet can be calculated from the following:

$$L = L_\text{pipe} + L_{\text{e, fittings}} + L_\text{loss} \tag{10.38}$$

$$-\Delta p = (-\Delta p/L)(L) = 0.0190\,L \tag{vi}$$

$$p_1 = p_\text{atm} - \Delta p \tag{vii}$$

where $L_{\text{e, fittings}}$ is the sum of the equivalent lengths of all fittings, L_loss is for expansions and contractions, and L_pipe is the length of straight pipe (137 ft, as given). The equivalent lengths for all fittings in Fig. 10.15 are obtained from Table 10.5 and listed in Table 10.6. The sum of these is

$$L_{\text{e, fittings}}/d_\text{o} = 2342.1 \tag{viii}$$

Solving Eq. (viii) for the equivalent length of the fittings:

$$L_{\text{e, fittings}} = (L_{\text{e, fittings}}/d_\text{o})(d_\text{o}) = (2342.1)(0.206) = 481.9\,\text{ft} \tag{ix}$$

TABLE 10.6
Losses in valves and fittings for Example 10.8

Fitting	Equivalent length, L_e/d_o	Loss coefficient, k
Gate valve, $\frac{1}{2}$ open	160	4.5
Globe valve, open	340	6.0
90° standard ell	30	0.75
90° standard ell	30	0.75
90° standard ell	30	0.75
90° standard ell	30	0.75
Globe valve, open	340	6.0
90° standard ell	30	0.75
Tee, run flow	20	0.4
Tee, branch flow	60	1.0
45° standard ell	16	0.35
45° standard ell	16	0.35
Globe valve, open	340	6.0
Gate valve, $\frac{1}{4}$ open	900	24.0
Union	0.1	0.04
Total	2342.1	52.39

Examination of Fig. 10.15 reveals an entrance loss where the water at pressure p_1 enters the pipe; there is an exit loss where the water drains from the pipe into the pond. Since the problem does not specify the type of construction, sharp-edged connections will be assumed. From Fig. 10.11:

$$\text{Entrance (contraction):} \quad k_c = 0.50$$
$$\text{Exit (enlargement):} \quad k_e = 1.0 \tag{x}$$

Equation (10.43) is used to express these loss coefficients as an equivalent length:

$$L_{e,\,loss}/d_o = (k_e + k_c)/(4f) = (0.5 + 1.0)/[(4)(0.0053)] = 70.75 \tag{xi}$$

or

$$L_{e,\,loss} = (70.75)(0.206) = 14.56 \text{ ft} \tag{xii}$$

From Eq. (10.38) the total length for pressure drop is

$$L = L_{pipe} + L_{e,\,fittings} + L_{loss} = 137 + 481.9 + 14.6 = 633 \text{ ft} \tag{xiii}$$

Note that the fittings contribute 3.5 times the length of straight pipe in this example. The inlet pressure is computed by substituting the numbers into Eqs. (vi) through (viii):

$$-\Delta p = (-\Delta p/L)(L) = (0.0190)(633) = 12.0 \text{ psi} \tag{xiv}$$
$$p_1 = p_{atm} - \Delta p = 14.696 + 12.0 = 26.7 \text{ psia} \tag{xv}$$

Loss coefficient method. The loss coefficient method uses Eqs. (10.36), (10.37), and

(10.40) to find the terms needed for the general design equation, Eq. (10.39):

$$\frac{p_2 - p_1}{\rho} + g(z_2 - z_1) + \frac{1}{2}\left(\frac{U_{2,\,\text{ave}}^2}{\alpha_2} - \frac{U_{1,\,\text{ave}}^2}{\alpha_1}\right)$$

$$+ F_{\text{pipe}} + F_{\text{fittings}} + F_{\text{loss}} + W_s = 0 \tag{10.39}$$

$$\frac{p_1 - p_2}{\rho} = F_{\text{pipe}} = \frac{4fL}{d_o}\frac{U_{z,\,\text{ave}}^2}{2} \tag{10.36}$$

$$F_{\text{loss}} = (k_e + k_c)\frac{U_{z,\,\text{ave}}^2}{2} \tag{10.37}$$

$$F_{\text{fittings}} = k_{\text{fittings}}\frac{U_{z,\,\text{ave}}^2}{2} \tag{10.40}$$

The sum of the loss coefficients for all fittings in Fig. 10.15 is also in Table 10.6:

$$k_{\text{fittings}} = 52.39 \tag{xvi}$$

The sum of all the loss terms is found from Eqs. (10.36), (10.37), and (10.40). For F_{pipe}, the length was 137 ft and the friction factor 0.0053:

$$\sum F' = F_{\text{pipe}} + F_{\text{loss}} + F_{\text{fittings}} = [(4fL/d_o) + k_e + k_c + k_{\text{fittings}}][U_{z,\,\text{ave}}^2/(2g_c)]$$

$$= [(4)(0.0053)(137)/(0.206) + 1.0 + 0.5 + 52.39](5.234)^2/[(2)(32.174)]$$

$$\times [(\text{ft})(\text{ft}^{-1})(\text{ft}^2\,\text{s}^{-2})(\text{lb}_\text{m}^{-1}\,\text{lb}_\text{f}\,\text{ft}^{-1}\,\text{s}^2)]$$

$$= 28.95 \text{ ft lb}_\text{f}\,\text{lb}_\text{m}^{-1} \tag{xvii}$$

In Eq. (10.39), the kinetic energy term is negligible and the potential energy and shaft work terms zero. Inserting the numbers into the remaining terms, the pressure drop is

$$-\Delta p = \rho \sum F' = (62.4)(28.95)\,[(\text{lb}_\text{m}\,\text{ft}^{-3})(\text{ft lb}_\text{f}\,\text{lb}_\text{m}^{-1})]$$

$$= 1807 \text{ lb}_\text{f}\,\text{ft}^{-2} = 1807/144 = 12.5 \text{ psi} \tag{xviii}$$

The inlet pressure is atmospheric plus Δp, or 27.2 psia. Computation of the pressure drop by the loss coefficient method differs from that by the equivalent length method by less than 1 psia.

10.2.9 Gases

The methods described in this chapter are applicable to incompressible fluids that are Newtonian, as discussed earlier. The engineer must sometimes consider a piping system with a gas flow. Usually, changes in the density of such a gas are negligible, and the methods and charts presented previously can be used directly.

In fluid mechanics, the topic of "compressible flow" is important in aeronautical research, compressors, high-speed turbines, and the design of nozzles that operate at velocities near the speed of sound. The basic equations of compressible flow originate in the field of thermodynamics, and will not be covered here. Most of the general references cited at the end of this chapter treat compressible flow, and the reader is directed to those.

In piping systems, sonic flow will be achieved across any valve or other fitting that has a ratio of outlet to inlet pressure of 0.5 or less. In long pipe systems, it is possible to consider sections of short length in which an average density may be assumed with negligible error. If the flow is isothermal, then the volume and hence the velocity of the gas will increase as the pressure decreases. This consideration will lengthen the computation, but it presents no further complexities.

10.2.10 Complex Fluid Flow Systems

Many pipe systems are designed with different pipe diameters in different sections to achieve the most economical design. Similarly, branching pipe systems are often encountered in processing situations. These multiple systems are illustrated in Fig. 10.16. The principles needed to solve the systems in Fig. 10.16 have already been introduced. In the parallel case, Fig. 10.16(a), the pressure drop across each leg is the same. Hence it will be necessary to find the flow rate in each leg. For the series example, Fig. 10.16(b), the flow rate is the same in each diameter section. The intermediate pressures p_c and p_d are unknown. The solution to the series network will involve a system of equations that may be solved directly or by trial and error.

The following examples illustrate the approach. Note that the presence of valves and fittings may be included as equivalent length by using Eq. (10.38).

Example 10.9. A three-pipe system is connected according to Fig. 10.16(a). Pipe one is 50 m long and 0.04 m in diameter, pipe two is 150 m long and 0.06 m in diameter, and pipe three is 100 m long and 0.08 m in diameter. All the pipes are smooth. Assume all losses due to entry, exit, and pipe fittings are already included in the lengths given. The overall pressure drop is $1.47 \times 10^5 \, \text{N m}^{-2}$ (147 kPa). The properties of water were given in Example 10.3. Determine the total flow rate of water through the pipe system.

Answer. The pressure drop between a and b is given, but the flow rate in each branch is unknown. Let w_1 be the flow (kg s^{-1}) in line 1, etc. Then

$$w_{\text{total}} = w_1 + w_2 + w_3 = \rho U_1 S_1 + \rho U_2 S_2 + \rho U_3 S_3 \tag{i}$$

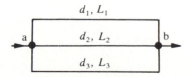

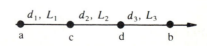

(*a*) Three pipes in parallel   (*b*) Three pipes in series

FIGURE 10.16
Complex fluid flow systems.

where once again, for brevity, U_1 is used for $U_{1,\,ave}$, etc. Equation (10.36) applies:

$$(p_1 - p_2)/\rho = F_{pipe} = (4fL/d_o)(U_{z,\,ave}^2/2) \tag{10.36}$$

Since the pressure drop across each line is the same and equal to 147 kPa $(1.47 \times 10^5 \text{ kg m}^{-1}\text{s}^{-2})$, this equation will be applied to each pipe to find the product of friction factor times velocity squared. Rearranging Eq. (10.36) for branch 1, the product is

$$f_1 U_1^2 = [(-\Delta p)/\rho](d_o/L)(2/4)$$

$$= (1.47 \times 10^5/1000)(0.04/50)(0.5) \left(\frac{(\text{kg m}^{-1}\text{s}^{-2})(\text{m})}{(\text{kg m}^{-3})(\text{m})}\right) = 0.0588 \text{ m}^2\text{ s}^{-2} \tag{ii}$$

The method of solution of Eq. (i) is given in Examples 10.5 and 10.6. From Eq. (10.13) the dimensionless von Karman number is

$$N_{VK} = N_{Re}(f)^{1/2} = (d_o\rho/\mu)[-(d_o\Delta p)/(2L\rho)]^{1/2}$$

$$= [(0.04)(1000)/(10^{-3})]\{[-(0.04)(-1.47 \times 10^5)]/[(2)(50)(1000)]\}^{1/2}$$

$$\times ([(\text{m})(\text{kg m}^{-3})/(\text{kg m}^{-1}\text{s}^{-1})]\{[(\text{m})(\text{kg m}^{-1}\text{s}^{-2})]/[(\text{m})(\text{kg m}^{-3})]\}^{1/2})$$

$$= 9699 \, [(\text{m}^{-1}\text{s})(\text{m}^2\text{s}^{-2})^{1/2}] = 9699 \tag{iii}$$

Either Fig. 10.5 or Eq. (6.132) can be used to find the friction factor:

$$1/(f)^{1/2} = 4.0 \log_{10} N_{VK} - 0.4 = 15.55 \tag{iv}$$

$$f = 0.00414 \tag{v}$$

The velocity is found from Eq. (ii):

$$U_1 = (0.0588/f_1)^{1/2} = 3.77 \text{ m s}^{-1} \tag{vi}$$

The mass flow from Eq. (7.10) is

$$w_1 = \rho U_1 S_1 = (1000)(3.77)[\pi(0.04)^2/(4)] \, [(\text{kg m}^{-3})(\text{m s}^{-1})(\text{m}^2)]$$

$$= 4.74 \text{ kg s}^{-1} \tag{vii}$$

Repeating the calculations for branch 2:

$$f_2 U_2^2 = (1.47 \times 10^5/1000)(0.06/150)(0.5) \left(\frac{(\text{kg m}^{-1}\text{s}^{-2})(\text{m})}{(\text{kg m}^{-3})(\text{m})}\right) = 0.0294 \text{ m}^2\text{ s}^{-2} \tag{viii}$$

$$N_{VK} = [(0.06)(1000)/(10^{-3})]\{[(0.06)(1.47 \times 10^5)]/[(2)(150)(1000)]\}^{1/2}$$

$$= 1.029 \times 10^4 \tag{ix}$$

$$f_2 = 1/[4.0 \log_{10} 1.029 \times 10^4 - 0.4]^2 = 0.00408 \tag{x}$$

$$U_2 = (0.0294/0.00408)^{1/2} = 2.68 \text{ m s}^{-1} \tag{xi}$$

$$w_2 = (1000)(2.68)[\pi(0.06)^2/(4)] = 7.59 \text{ kg s}^{-1} \tag{xii}$$

For branch 3:

$$f_3 U_3^2 = 0.0588 \qquad N_{VK} = 1.940 \times 10^4$$

$$f_3 = 0.00356 \qquad U_3 = 4.062 \text{ m s}^{-1}$$

$$w_3 = 20.42 \text{ kg s}^{-1} \tag{xiii}$$

The total flow from Eq. (i) is

$$w_{\text{total}} = 4.74 + 7.59 + 20.42 = 32.7 \text{ kg s}^{-1} \tag{xiv}$$

Example 10.10. Find the flow rate in Example 10.9 if the three sections of pipe are connected in series as shown in Fig. 10.16(b).

Answer. In this example, the flow rate in each section is the same:

$$w = w_1 = w_2 = w_3 = \rho U_1 S_1 = \rho U_2 S_2 = \rho U_3 S_3 \tag{i}$$

The areas of the pipes are

$$S_1 = \pi d_1^2/4 = \pi (0.04)^2/4 = 0.001\ 257 \text{ m}^2$$
$$S_2 = 0.002\ 827 \text{ m}^2 \tag{ii}$$
$$S_3 = 0.005\ 027 \text{ m}^2$$

The total pressure drop $(p_a - p_b)$ is the sum of the pressure drops per section:

$$-\Delta p = p_a - p_b = 1.47 \times 10^5 \text{ kPa} = (p_a - p_c) + (p_c - p_d) + (p_d - p_b)$$
$$(-\Delta p_1) + (-\Delta p_2) + (-\Delta p_3) = 1.47 \times 10^5 \text{ kPa} \tag{iii}$$

The pressure drop in each section is expressible in terms of the equivalent length L, velocity, density, diameter, and friction factor by any of Eqs. (10.3), (10.14), or (10.36):

$$-\frac{\Delta p}{\rho} = 4f \frac{L}{d_o} \frac{U_{z,\,\text{ave}}^2}{2} \tag{10.14}$$

Equation (10.14) is applied to each section, with the average velocity replaced by the mass flow rate w from Eq. (i):

$$-\Delta p_1 = [(4f_1)(L_1/d_1)][w^2/(2\rho S_1^2)]$$

$$= [(4)(f_1)(50/0.04)]\{(w_1^2)/[(2)(1000)(0.001\ 257)^2]\}\left(\frac{(\text{m})(\text{kg}^2\ \text{s}^{-2})}{(\text{m})(\text{kg m}^{-3})(\text{m}^2)}\right)$$

$$= 1.583 \times 10^6 (f_1 w^2) \tag{iv}$$
$$-\Delta p_2 = [(4f_2)(L_2/d_2)][w^2/(2\rho S_2^2)] = 6.254 \times 10^5 (f_2 w^2) \tag{v}$$
$$-\Delta p_3 = [(4f_3)(L_3/d_3)][w^2/(2\rho S_3^2)] = 9.895 \times 10^4 (f_3 w^2) \tag{vi}$$

Equations (iii) through (vi) constitute four equations in four unknowns, i.e., w, Δp_1, Δp_2, and Δp_3. To solve these nonlinear equations in their present form is a sophisticated task. However, a clever choice of the order of calculation yields a one-dimensional root-finding problem that can be solved by hand calculation or by a computer program.

The friction factors are functions of the Reynolds numbers [Eq. (6.2)], which may also be expressed in terms of w:

$$N_{\text{Re},1} = d_1 U_1 \rho/\mu = (d_1 w)/(S_1 \mu) = [(0.04)(w)]/[(0.001\ 257)(0.001)]$$
$$= 3.183 \times 10^4 w \tag{vii}$$
$$N_{\text{Re},2} = 2.122 \times 10^4 w \tag{viii}$$
$$N_{\text{Re},3} = 1.592 \times 10^4 w \tag{ix}$$

Equations (iii) through (vi) can be combined as follows:

$$(-\Delta p_1) + (-\Delta p_2) + (-\Delta p_3)$$
$$= (w^2)[(1.583 \times 10^6)(f_1) + (6.254 \times 10^5)(f_2) + (9.895 \times 10^4)(f_3)] = 1.47 \times 10^5 \quad (x)$$

Thus, the final answer to this problem will be the value of w that yields friction factors from Eq. (6.132) or Fig. 10.3, all of which satisfy Eq. (x). The method of successive substitution works well for this problem because the friction factors vary slowly with small changes in w (i.e., Reynolds number). The solution proceeds as follows:

1. Obtain a good initial guess for w. Let 0.0055 be the estimated value of f, as was used in deriving Eq. (10.18) in the velocity head approximation. Then Eq. (x) is solved for the initial guess:

$$(0.0055w^2)[1.583 \times 10^6 + 6.254 \times 10^5 + 9.895 \times 10^4] = 1.47 \times 10^5 \quad (xi)$$

From this equation, the value of w is 3.40 kg s^{-1}.

2. For the value of w at hand, compute the three Reynolds numbers from Eqs. (vii), (viii), and (ix).
3. From Eq. (6.132) or from Fig. 10.3 find the friction factor for each of the three sections.

TABLE 10.7
Summary of calculations for Example 10.10

Trial	Quantity	Fig. or Eq. Number	Value
0	w	Eq. (x)	3.40 kg s^{-1}
1	$N_{Re,1}$	Eq. (vii)	1.082×10^5
	$N_{Re,2}$	Eq. (viii)	7.215×10^4
	$N_{Re,3}$	Eq. (ix)	5.411×10^4
	f_1	Fig. 10.3	0.00445
	f_2	Fig. 10.3	0.00475
	f_3	Fig. 10.3	0.00513
	w	Eq. (x)	3.74 kg s^{-1}
2	$N_{Re,1}$	Eq. (vii)	1.190×10^5
	$N_{Re,2}$	Eq. (viii)	7.937×10^4
	$N_{Re,3}$	Eq. (ix)	5.952×10^4
	f_1	Fig. 10.3	0.00440
	f_2	Fig. 10.3	0.00470
	f_3	Fig. 10.3	0.00500
	w	Eq. (x)	3.76 kg s^{-1}
3	$N_{Re,1}$	Eq. (vii)	1.197×10^5
	$N_{Re,2}$	Eq. (viii)	7.980×10^4
	$N_{Re,3}$	Eq. (ix)	5.984×10^4
	f_1	Fig. 10.3	0.00440
	f_2	Fig. 10.3	0.00470
	f_3	Fig. 10.3	0.00500
	w	Eq. (x)	3.76 kg s^{-1}

4. Substitute the values of the friction factors into Eq. (x) and solve for the new estimate of w.

5. Test the new w for convergence. An appropriate test is

$$\left| \frac{w_{new} - w}{w} \right| < \text{EPS} \qquad \text{(xii)}$$

where EPS is an appropriate tolerance, commonly 0.5×10^{-5}.

6. If there is no convergence, then loop to step 2. If there is convergence, then calculate the flow rate.

The calculations using this procedure are given in Table 10.7. The pressure drops and velocities can be computed from the equations given previously if desired. The flow rate at convergence is $3.76 \, \text{kg s}^{-1}$, which is close to the initial guess. Naturally the parallel configuration of the previous example yielded a much higher flow rate for the same pressure drop.

The design equations presented so far in this text are by no means complete, in that many more equations are available for a wide variety of specific systems. For example, in Chapter 12 flow over immersed objects will be covered. The engineer often must design systems that involve more than just the material presented thus far. Thus, recourse to more specific references will often be necessary.

Figure 10.17 is an example of a complex process flow system for which it is desired to determine the overall pressure drop so that the type and size of pump and motor can be selected.

Example 10.11. A hydrocarbon of specific gravity 1.1 and viscosity 2 cP is introduced into a process through a complex flow system, which is shown in Fig. 10.17. This compound is unloaded from a tank car at 10°C and held in the storage tank at that temperature. When the storage tank is full, the level at point (a) is 15 ft. When the level at point (a) reaches 1 ft, the tank is refilled. The acceleration due to gravity is $32.1 \, \text{ft s}^{-2}$. For this preliminary design the properties of the hydrocarbon are to be assumed constant at the values shown, since the heating needed is modest. Determine the pump size necessary to maintain a spray velocity of $15 \, \text{ft s}^{-1}$ and a flow rate of 400 gpm if the pump is 60 percent efficient.

Answer. In this case all the information needed to estimate the pressure drop has already been given or can be found in the tables or graphs in this chapter or in the Appendix. The pump must operate under the most severe of the conditions given; thus, the inlet tank height will be taken at the minimum value of 1 ft. The pump will require slightly less power as the level at point (a) approaches its maximum value of 15 ft. The basic design equation is Eq. (10.39):

$$\frac{p_2 - p_1}{\rho} + g(z_2 - z_1) + \frac{1}{2}\left(\frac{U_{2,\,ave}^2}{\alpha_2} - \frac{U_{1,\,ave}^2}{\alpha_1}\right)$$
$$+ F_{pipe} + F_{fittings} + F_{loss} + W_s = 0 \qquad (10.39)$$

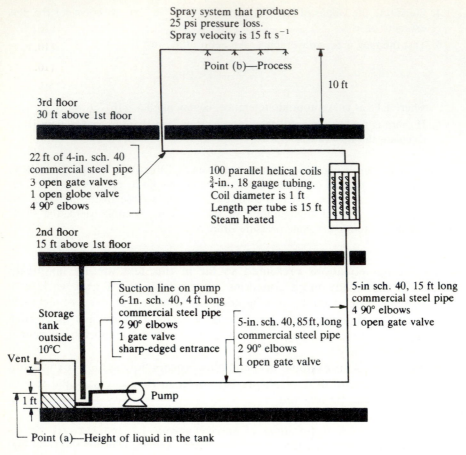

FIGURE 10.17
Process flow system for Example 10.11.

This equation is applied between the surface of the reservoir (a) and the spray point (b) with g_c included as needed for English units. With the assumption that α_a and α_b are unity, Eq. (10.39) becomes

$$\frac{p_b - p_a}{\rho} + \frac{U_b^2 - U_a^2}{2g_c} + \frac{g}{g_c}(z_b - z_a) + F_{\text{pipe}} + F_{\text{fittings}} + F_{\text{loss}} + W_s = 0 \qquad \text{(i)}$$

The velocity at the surface of the tank can be taken as zero, and the pressure at both points is the same, namely atmospheric. In this equation, each of the loss terms may contain several contributions; e.g., F_{pipe} consists of the sum of the losses in the three sections: 4-in., 5-in., and 6-in. Additional factors that must also be included are the losses in the helical coils, losses in the spray system, entrance losses from the outside storage tank, and expansion and contraction losses associated with the heater. Other equations besides Eq. (i) that will be used in this example are

$$(p_1 - p_2)/\rho = F_{\text{pipe}} = (4fL/d_o)(U^2_{z,\,\text{ave}}/2) \tag{10.36}$$

$$F_{\text{loss}} = (k_e + k_c)(U^2_{z,\,\text{ave}}/2) \tag{10.37}$$

$$L = L_{\text{pipe}} + L_{e,\,\text{fittings}} + L_{\text{loss}} \tag{10.38}$$

$$F_{\text{fittings}} = k_{\text{fittings}}(U^2_{z,\,\text{ave}}/2) \tag{10.40}$$

In these equations, there are some terms that can appear twice; here, F_{fittings} will be included in $L_{e,\,\text{fittings}}$, and L_{loss} will be in F_{loss}. Even though the flow is not isothermal, all properties will be assumed independent of temperature, since this design is preliminary. The temperature rise of 10°C through the steam coils will only serve to decrease the required horsepower. The properties of the hydrocarbon in English units are

$$\rho = (1.1)(62.4) = 68.64 \text{ lb}_m \text{ ft}^{-3} \tag{ii}$$

$$\mu = (2)(6.72 \times 10^{-4}) = 1.344 \times 10^{-3} \text{ lb}_m \text{ ft}^{-1} \text{ s}^{-1} \tag{iii}$$

The roughness e of steel pipe from Table 10.2 is 1.5×10^4 ft. From Table B.1, the diameter and velocity at 400 gpm can be found:

4-in. schedule 40 pipe

$$d_o = 4.026/12 = 0.3355 \text{ ft}$$

$$1 \text{ ft s}^{-1} = 39.6 \text{ gal min}^{-1} \text{ (gpm)}$$

$$U_4 = 400/39.6 = 10.10 \text{ ft s}^{-1} \tag{iv}$$

$$e/d_o = 1.5 \times 10^{-4}/0.3355 = 4.47 \times 10^{-4}$$

5-in. schedule 40 pipe

$$d_o = 5.047/12 = 0.4206 \text{ ft}$$

$$1 \text{ ft s}^{-1} = 62.3 \text{ gpm} \tag{v}$$

$$U_5 = 400/62.3 = 6.42 \text{ ft s}^{-1}$$

$$e/d_o = 1.5 \times 10^{-4}/0.4206 = 3.57 \times 10^{-4}$$

6-in. schedule 40 pipe

$$d_o = 6.065/12 = 0.5054 \text{ ft}$$

$$1 \text{ ft s}^{-1} = 90 \text{ gpm}$$

$$U_6 = 400/90 = 4.44 \text{ ft s}^{-1} \tag{vi}$$

$$e/d_o = 2.97 \times 10^{-4}$$

$\frac{3}{4}$-in. 18 gauge tube (100 in parallel)

$$d_o = 0.652/12 = 0.05433 \text{ ft}$$

$$0.962 \text{ ft s}^{-1} = 1 \text{ gpm}$$

$$U_{3/4} = (400)(0.962)/(100) = 3.848 \text{ ft s}^{-1} \tag{vii}$$

$$e/d_o = 0.0 \text{ (smooth tube assumed)}$$

where in the $\frac{3}{4}$-in. tube the flow rate in each tube is assumed to be $\frac{1}{100}$th of the total flow.

The two lines of 5-in. pipe will be considered together. The total length is 100 ft. From Table 10.5 the following equivalent lengths are found:

$$\begin{aligned} \text{5-in. gate valves:} \quad & (2)(13)(0.4206) = 10.94 \text{ ft} \\ \text{90° elbows:} \quad & (6)(30)(0.4206) = 75.71 \text{ ft} \end{aligned} \tag{viii}$$

The total equivalent length from Eq. (10.38) is

$$L = L_{\text{pipe}} + L_{\text{e, fittings}} + L_{\text{loss}} = 100 + 10.94 + 75.71 + 0.0 = 186.6 \text{ ft} \tag{ix}$$

Repeating for the 4-in. pipe and 6-in. pipe:

4-in. pipe

$$\begin{aligned} \text{gate valves: } & (3)(13)(0.3355) = 13.08 \text{ ft} \\ \text{globe valve: } & (1)(340)(0.3355) = 114.1 \text{ ft} \\ \text{90° elbows: } & (4)(30)(0.3355) = 40.26 \text{ ft} \\ L = 22 + 13.09 & + 114.04 + 40.25 + 0.0 = 189.4 \text{ ft} \end{aligned} \tag{x}$$

6-in. pipe

$$\begin{aligned} \text{gate valve: } & (1)(13)(0.5054) = 6.570 \text{ ft} \\ \text{90° elbows: } & (2)(30)(0.5054) = 30.36 \text{ ft} \\ L = 4.0 & + 6.57 + 30.36 + 0.0 = 40.91 \text{ ft} \end{aligned} \tag{xi}$$

The Reynolds numbers from Eq. (6.2), friction factors from Fig. 10.3, and the pipe frictional losses from Eq. (10.36) are

4-in. pipe

$$N_{\text{Re}} = d_o U_4 \rho / \mu = (0.3355)(10.10)(68.64)/(1.344 \times 10^{-3}) = 1.731 \times 10^5$$

$$\begin{aligned} F_{\text{pipe}} &= (4fL/d_o)(U_4^2)/(2g_c) \\ &= [(4)(0.00475)(189.4/0.3355)(10.10)^2]/[(2)(32.174)] \\ &= 17.00 \text{ ft lb}_f \text{ lb}_m^{-1} \end{aligned} \tag{xii}$$

5-in. pipe

$$N_{\text{Re}} = 1.379 \times 10^5$$
$$f = 0.00470$$
$$F_{\text{pipe}} = 5.34 \text{ ft lb}_f \text{ lb}_m^{-1} \tag{xiii}$$

6-in. pipe

$$N_{\text{Re}} = 1.147 \times 10^5$$
$$f = 0.00487$$
$$F_{\text{pipe}} = 0.484 \text{ ft lb}_f \text{ lb}_m^{-1} \tag{xiv}$$

It is always important to design the entrance leg to a pump with as low a pressure loss as possible. Otherwise, the pump will cavitate at high flow rates.

Cavitation occurs when the suction pressure from the pump becomes lower than the vapor pressure of the fluid, which will then boil and evaporate. Hence, the inlet pipe is usually at least one pipe size larger than the outlet from a pump. Furthermore, since the tank must be valved off from the pump, which may leak when shut down, a low-loss valve such as a ball valve or a gate valve is specified. The loss due to the sharp-edge entrance to the 6-in. pipe is found as in Example 10.8. From Fig. 10.11, k_e is 0.50. The frictional loss at the entrance is found from Eq. (10.37) as

$$F_{\text{loss, 6-in.}} = k_e[U_6^2/(2g_c)] = [0.50(4.44)^2]/[(2)(32.174)]$$
$$= 0.153 \text{ ft lb}_f \text{ lb}_m^{-1} \tag{xv}$$

Thus, the total frictional loss in the inlet leg to the pump will be the sum of the losses in the entrance and the losses in the 6-in. pipe plus fittings. At this point the pressure drop from tank to pump should be computed to check for possible cavitation. Equation (10.39) is applied for this section only, where the contributions of potential and kinetic energy are neglected and W_s is zero. Solving Eq. (10.39) for Δp gives

$$-\Delta p = \rho[F_{\text{pipe}} + F_{\text{fittings}} + F_{\text{loss}}] = (68.64)(0.484 + 0.0 + 0.153)$$
$$= 43.75 \text{ lb}_f \text{ ft}^{-2} = 0.304 \text{ psia} \tag{xvi}$$

A pressure drop of only 0.3 psia is very low and assures no cavitation in the pump. The 6-in. line is designed properly.

The calculation continues by considering the 5-in. line on the pump discharge. That line expands into a header before feeding the 100 parallel $\frac{3}{4}$-in. helical tubes (each carrying 4 gpm). The expansion into the header is best approximated as a sharp-edge expansion into a tank and similarly for the contraction into the 4-in. pipe and the entrance and exit of the $\frac{3}{4}$-in. tubes. From Fig. 10.11:

$$k_{\text{exit}} = 1.0$$
$$k_{\text{entrance}} = 0.5 \tag{xvii}$$

From Eq. (10.37) the loss for a single $\frac{3}{4}$-in. tube is

$$F_{\text{loss, 3/4-in.}} = (k_e + k_c)(U_{z,\text{ave}}^2/2) = [(1.0 + 0.5)(3.848)^2]/[(2)(32.174)]$$
$$= 0.3452 \text{ ft lb}_f \text{ lb}_m^{-1} \tag{xviii}$$

or for 100 tubes:

$$F_{\text{loss, 3/4-in.}} = (0.3452)(100) = 34.52 \text{ ft lb}_f \text{ lb}_m^{-1} \tag{xix}$$

Similarly for the 5-in. expansion and the 4-in. contraction:

$$F_{\text{loss, 5-in.}} = [(1.0 + 0.0)(6.42)^2]/[(2)(32.174)] = 0.641 \text{ ft lb}_f \text{ lb}_m^{-1} \tag{xx}$$
$$F_{\text{loss, 4-in.}} = [(0.0 + 0.5)(10.10)^2]/[(2)(32.174)] = 0.793 \text{ ft lb}_f \text{ lb}_m^{-1} \tag{xxi}$$

For the coils themselves, the Reynolds number at the laminar–turbulent transition is found from Eq. (10.19):

$$N_{\text{Re, critical}} = (2100)[1 + (12)(d_o/d_c)^{1/2}]$$
$$= (2100)[1 + (12)(0.05433/1.0)^{1/2}] = 7974 \tag{xxii}$$

The Reynolds number in the $\frac{3}{4}$-in. tube is

$$N_{Re} = d_o U_{3/4}\rho/\mu = (0.05433)(3.848)(68.64)/(1.344 \times 10^{-3}) = 1.068 \times 10^4 \quad \text{(xxiii)}$$

Clearly the flow is turbulent, and Eq. (10.20) yields the friction factor:

$$\begin{aligned}
f_{coil} &= (0.08)(N_{Re})^{-1/4} + (0.012)(d_o/d_c)^{1/2} \\
&= (0.08)(1.068 \times 10^4)^{-1/4} + (0.012)(0.05433)^{1/2} \\
&= 7.870 \times 10^{-3} + 2.797 \times 10^{-3} = 0.01067 \quad \text{(xxiv)}
\end{aligned}$$

Note that the correction for curvature in the above equation (2.797×10^{-3}) amounted to 26 percent in this problem.

The pressure drop across each coiled tube may be calculated by applying Eq. (10.36) to a single coil:

$$\begin{aligned}
-\Delta p &= (4\rho f L/d_o)[(U_{3/4}^2)/(2g_c)] \\
&= [(4)(68.64)(0.01067)(15/0.05433)(3.848)^2]/[(2)(32.174)] \\
&= 186.1 \text{ lb}_f \text{ ft}^{-2} = 186.1/144 = 1.292 \text{ psi} \quad \text{(xxv)}
\end{aligned}$$

The frictional loss for all tubes is also computed from a modification of Eq. (10.36), which is:

$$(p_1 - p_2)/\rho = F_{pipe} = (4fL/d_o)(U_{z, \text{ave}}^2/2) \quad \text{(10.36)}$$

This equation applies for the loss in a single tube for which f and the other variables are known. For N tubes, Eq. (10.36) becomes

$$\begin{aligned}
F'_{coil} &= (N)(4fL/d_o)[(U_{3/4}^2)/(2g_c)] \\
&= [(100)(4)(0.01067)(15/0.05433)(3.848)^2]/[(2)(32.174)] \\
&= 271.1 \text{ ft lb}_f \text{ lb}_m^{-1} \quad \text{(xxvi)}
\end{aligned}$$

The maximum potential energy occurs when the level in the tank is 1 ft above ground level; hence 39 ft is the approximate Δz, as seen in Fig. 10.17. Then the potential energy term in Eq. (i) is

$$(g/g_c)(z_b - z_a) = (32.1/32.174)(39)\left(\frac{(\text{ft s}^{-2})(\text{ft})}{(\text{lb}_m \text{ lb}_f^{-1} \text{ ft s}^{-2})}\right)$$

$$= 38.9 \text{ ft lb}_f \text{ lb}_m^{-1} \quad \text{(xxvii)}$$

The frictional losses in the spray system are computed from another modification of Eq. (10.36). The pressure drop in the spray nozzles is 25 psi, and the loss in the spray system is

$$\begin{aligned}
F_{spray system} &= (\Delta p)/\rho = 25/68.64 = 0.3642 \text{ lb}_f \text{ in.}^{-2} \text{ lb}_m^{-1} \text{ ft}^3 \\
&= (0.3642)(144) = 52.45 \text{ ft lb}_f \text{ lb}_m^{-1} \quad \text{(xxviii)}
\end{aligned}$$

The method of computing the frictional losses in the nozzles illustrates a useful procedure. Whenever a pressure drop is known, the frictional loss is easily found by dividing by density.

All frictional losses have now been computed and are listed in Table 10.8. The pressure drops are computed from Eq. (10.36) where appropriate. The pressure drop in the entrance and exit sections before and after the one hundred

TABLE 10.8
Summary of frictional losses for Example 10.11

Item	F, ft lb$_f$ lb$_m^{-1}$	Δp, psi
Entrance to 6-in. pipe	0.153	0.07
6-in. pipe, 40.87 ft equivalent	0.484	0.23
5-in. pipe, 186.6 ft equivalent	5.34	2.55
Entrance from 5-in. pipe to chamber of heater	0.641	0.31
Entrance and exit, 100 $\frac{3}{4}$-in. coils	34.52	0.38
$\frac{3}{4}$-in. coils, 100 in parallel	271.1	1.29
Exit from chamber of heater to 4-in. pipe	0.793	0.38
4-in. pipe, 189.4 ft equivalent	17.00	8.11
Spray system loss	52.45	25.0

Total 382.5 ft lb$_f$ lb$_m^{-1}$

$\frac{3}{4}$-in. coils is found by the following equation, obtained by inspection from Eqs. (10.36) and (10.37):

$$-\Delta p = [(\rho)(k_e + k_c)][U_{3/4}^2/(2g_c)]$$
$$= \frac{(68.64)(1.0 + 0.5)(3.848)^2}{(2)(32.174)(144)} = 0.1645 \text{ psi} \qquad \text{(xxix)}$$

To find the shaft work, Eq. (i) is solved for W_s:

$$-W_s = \frac{p_b - p_a}{\rho} + \frac{U_b^2 - U_a^2}{2g_c} + \frac{g}{g_c}(z_b - z_a) + F_{\text{pipe}} + F_{\text{fittings}} + F_{\text{loss}}$$
$$= 0 + [(15)^2 - 0]/[(2)(32.174)] + 38.9 + 382.5 = 424.9 \text{ ft lb}_f \text{ lb}_m^{-1} \qquad \text{(xxx)}$$

The mass flow rate can be calculated using Eq. (7.10) at any point in the system or from the density of hydrocarbon and the volume flow rate, 400 gpm:

$$w = Q\rho = (400)(68.64)/(7.48) [(\text{gal min}^{-1})(\text{lb}_m \text{ ft}^{-3})(\text{gal}^{-1} \text{ ft}^3)]$$
$$= 3671 \text{ lb}_m \text{ min}^{-1} \qquad \text{(xxxi)}$$

Thus, the horsepower that must be supplied to the fluid is

$$-W_s = (424.9)(3671)/(33\,000) [(\text{ft lb}_f \text{ lb}_m^{-1})(\text{lb}_m \text{ min}^{-1})(\text{hp}^{-1} \text{ min}^{-1} \text{ ft lb}_f)]$$
$$= 47.26 \text{ hp} \qquad \text{(xxxii)}$$

Since the pump efficiency is 60 percent, the power supplied to the pump is

$$(-W_s)_{\text{actual}} = (-W_{s,\text{fluid}})/\eta = 47.26/0.6 = 78.8 \text{ hp} \qquad \text{(xxxiii)}$$

Note in Table 10.8 the large loss in the heater and spray system. Nearly 80 percent of the energy being used in pumping is being consumed in the heater alone. A better design could be found, perhaps eliminating the helical coils in favor of a straight tube design.

Example 10.12. Estimate the power required in the previous problem by using the velocity head approximation.

Answer. The velocity head concept was introduced in Section 10.2.5. It is meant to be a rough field estimate of the pressure drop requirement. The basic equations are

$$(-\Delta p)/\rho = N(U^2_{z,\,ave}/2) \qquad (10.15)$$

$$N = (L/d_o)_{system}/45 \qquad (10.18)$$

The calculations are similar to those of the previous example. The 5-in. pipe is 100 ft long:

$$L_e/d_o = (100)(12)/5.047 = 238 \qquad (i)$$

Valves contribute 26 diameters, and six elbows contribute 30 diameters each. The total diameters (L_e/d_o) is the sum of these:

$$(L_e/d_o)_{5\text{-in.}} = 238 + 26 + (6)(30) = 444 \qquad (ii)$$

From Eq. (10.18), the corresponding number of velocity heads is

$$N = (L/d_o)_{system}/45 = 444/45 = 9.9 \qquad (iii)$$

From Eq. (xvii) of the previous example, k_{exit} and $k_{entrance}$ are 1.0 and 0.5, respectively. The sum of these is the velocity head contribution of contraction into and expansion from the 5-in. pipe. The value for total velocity heads is

$$N_{5\text{-in.}} = 9.9 + 1.0 + 0.5 = 11.4 \qquad (iv)$$

The calculations for the 4-in. pipe are summarized below:

$$\text{pipe: } L_e/d_o = (22)(12)/(4.026) = 66$$
$$\text{fittings: } L_e/d_o = (3)(13) + (1)(340) + (4)(30) = 500 \qquad (v)$$
$$N_{4\text{-in.}} = (66 + 500)/(45) + 0.0 + 0.5 = 13.1$$

For the 6-in. pipe:

$$\text{pipe: } L_e/d_o = (5)(12)/(6.065) = 9.9$$
$$\text{fittings: } L_e/d_o = (1)(13) + (2)(30) = 73 \qquad (vi)$$
$$N_{6\text{-in.}} = (9.9 + 73)/(45) + 0.0 + 0.5 = 2.3$$

For the 100 $\frac{3}{4}$-in. heater tubes, the Reynolds numbers calculations are repeated, and the friction factor is 0.01067, as found in Eq. (xxiv) from the previous example. The number of velocity heads per tube is found by solving Eq. (10.17) for N:

$$N = (4f)(L/d_o) = (4)(0.01067)(15/0.05433) = 11.78 \qquad (vii)$$

The entrance and exit velocity heads for the heater tubes are identical to those for the 5-in. pipe. Thus, for 100 tubes:

$$N_{total,\,3/4\text{-in.}} = 100(11.78 + 1.0 + 0.5) = 1328 \qquad (viii)$$

The next step is to convert the velocity heads into a frictional loss term that is needed by Eq. (i) in the previous example. The frictional losses term F_{pipe} is given in Eq. (10.36). Comparison of Eqs. (10.15) and (10.36) yields

$$F_{pipe} = (4fL/d_o)[U^2_{z,\,ave}/(2g_c)] = (N)[U^2_{z,\,ave}/(2g_c)] \qquad (ix)$$

This equation is essentially unchanged from Eq. (xxvi) in Example 10.11, in which F'_{coil} was computed to be $271.1 \, \text{ft} \, \text{lb}_f \, \text{lb}_m^{-1}$. Likewise, it is necessary to calculate the loss in the spray system by Eq. (xxviii) in the previous example. Equation (ix) is used for the three large pipes:

$$F_{6\text{-in.}} = [(2.3)(4.44)^2]/[(2)(32.174)] = 0.719 \, \text{ft} \, \text{lb}_f \, \text{lb}_m^{-1}$$

$$F_{5\text{-in.}} = [(11.4)(6.42)^2]/[(2)(32.174)] = 7.28 \, \text{ft} \, \text{lb}_f \, \text{lb}_m^{-1}$$

$$F_{4\text{-in.}} = [(13.1)(10.1)^2]/[(2)(32.174)] = 20.69 \, \text{ft} \, \text{lb}_f \, \text{lb}_m^{-1}$$

$$F_{\text{large pipes}} = 0.719 + 7.28 + 20.69 = 28.68 \, \text{ft} \, \text{lb}_f \, \text{lb}_m^{-1}$$

(x)

From this point on, the solution follows that in the previous example. Since the velocity head concept was not used for either of the pieces of equipment that cause the major pressure drop, naturally the final answer will be close to the previous answer. Comparing the sum of the losses in the three large pipes from Eq. (x) ($28.68 \, \text{ft} \, \text{lb}_f \, \text{lb}_m^{-1}$) with the numbers for the large pipes in Table 10.8 ($22.82 \, \text{ft} \, \text{lb}_f \, \text{lb}_m^{-1}$), the error is seen to be 25 percent if the velocity head concept is used.

In the preceding two problems an estimate was made of the pumping requirement for a specific flow system. More often than not, the pump selected is a centrifugal pump unless other circumstances dictate some other design. The selection is often dependent more on the material to be pumped than on the specific requirements of the flow system. The most economical approach is to order standard pump sizes. Extensive discussions elsewhere cover the details of pump selection [C1, P2].

10.3 NONCIRCULAR CONDUITS

Conduits with noncircular cross sections are extremely useful for many applications. It is granted that circular pipes have the lowest pressure drop and the greatest ratio of volume (which translates directly to throughput) to metal weight of any duct design. Nevertheless, many ducts commonly used in furnace and air conditioning systems are rectangular in cross section. A rectangular shape is the only practical duct to place in the stud space of a house in order to deliver air from a basement furnace to a second floor room. Also, most forced-air furnaces for homes require duct areas at the entrance or exit in the order of 200 in². A typical rectangular duct of this area would be 8 in. by 24 in., but a circular duct equivalent would be 15.6 inches in diameter and would reduce the ceiling-to-floor clearance as well as the attractiveness of the installation.

Secondary flow. Visual studies of the turbulent flow of water in ducts has revealed that secondary flows exist in triangular, trapezoidal, and rectangular ducts. Naturally, the primary flow is in the z direction down the length of the conduit. Superimposed on this longitudinal flow are secondary flow patterns in which eddies move toward the corners of the conduit and away from the sides, as shown in Fig. 10.18.

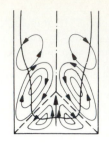

FIGURE 10.18
Secondary flows in ducts of triangular and rectangular cross section. (*From Schlichting, Boundary Layer Theory, 7th ed., p. 614, McGraw-Hill, New York, 1979. By permission.*)

Equivalent diameter. Introduction of the equivalent diameter d_e allows the previous smooth tube friction factor correlations for tube flow to be applied to turbulent flows in noncircular conduits. The equivalent diameter d_e is four times the hydraulic radius r_H:

$$d_e = 4r_H \tag{10.44}$$

$$r_H = S/L_p \tag{10.45}$$

where Eq. (10.45) defines the hydraulic radius, S is the cross sectional area of the flow, and L_p is the wetted perimeter. The equivalent diameter as defined above is based on applying Eq. (10.45) to a pipe running full:

$$r_H = \frac{\pi d_o^2/4}{\pi d_o} = \frac{d_o}{4} \tag{10.46}$$

Equation (10.46), when solved for d_o, yields Eq. (10.44) where d_o is renamed d_e, the equivalent diameter. Note also that the hydraulic radius has meaning in circular pipes that are not full, such as is usually the case for storm and sewer pipes leading away from one's home.

The procedure for determining pressure drop in partially filled conduits or conduits with noncircular cross sections is to determine the hydraulic radius from Eq. (10.45) and the equivalent diameter from Eq. (10.44). Then this diameter d_e is used in all the previous equations to solve the problem in a standard manner, as illustrated previously. Note that the hydraulic radius rule does not apply in laminar flow.

Equations for determining the hydraulic radius or various cross sections are available [P2]. For a circular tube that is completely full, as already indicated in Eq. (10.44), the hydraulic radius is $\frac{1}{4}$ the diameter. For a rectangular duct of size L_1 by L_2:

$$r_H = \frac{L_1 L_2}{2L_1 + 2L_2} \tag{10.47}$$

If the duct width is four times the height, then Eq. (10.47) shows r_H to be 0.4 times the height.

Relative roughness is also important in turbulent flow in channels, partially filled pipes, and other noncircular conduits. For these, the relative roughness is e/d_e, where e is the height of a protrusion and d_e is the equivalent diameter, Eq. (10.44). Schlichting [S2] reports that for geometrically similar roughness the following proportion holds:

$$f \propto (e/r_H)^{0.314} \tag{10.48}$$

The normal procedure is to measure pressure drop versus flow rate and determine the equivalent sand roughness from Fig. 10.3 or Fig. 10.5. Many experiments are on record in which the effective equivalent sand roughness varied by a large factor from actual measurements of e/d_e, which do not take into account the spacing, the pattern, and the shape of protrusions. In the absence of data, the engineer's only choice is to use the rough pipe correlation with the equivalent relative roughness.

Flow in annuli. An important flow problem is to determine the pressure drop of a fluid as it flows in the annular space between two concentric pipes. The hydraulic radius is

$$r_H = \frac{\pi d_o^2/4 - \pi d_i^2/4}{\pi d_o + \pi d_i} = \frac{d_o - d_i}{4} \tag{10.49}$$

where d_o is the inside diameter of the large pipe and d_i is the outside diameter of the small pipe. From this equation, the equivalent diameter can be calculated and used in all the previous equations. Also, there has been considerable experimental work on flow in annuli, and specific correlations are available [K1].

Open channel. Flow in open channels is extremely sensitive to the roughness factor of the walls and the slope of the bottom surface, which is responsible for maintaining the flow. A more complete discussion can be found elsewhere [C1, P2, S5, S6]. The flow velocity U in ft s^{-1} is

$$U = C[(r_H)(\text{SLOPE})]^{1/2} \tag{10.50}$$

where r_H is hydraulic radius in feet, SLOPE is the slope of the channel for small changes in flow depth, and C is the Chezy coefficient. The value of the Chezy coefficient in open channel flows is

$$C = 1.49(r_H)^{0.167}/n \tag{10.51}$$

where n is the roughness factor, r_H is in units of ft, and U is in units of ft s^{-1}. The roughness factor normally varies from 0.012 for a wood flume to 0.023 for an earth ditch to 0.07 for a weedy, natural stream. There are other formulas for C, depending on the application.

When Eqs. (10.50) and (10.51) are combined, the result is the widely-used Manning formula for incompressible, steady flow at constant depth in open channels:

$$U = (1.49/n)(R)^{2/3}(\text{SLOPE})^{1/2} \tag{10.52}$$

Note that the constant 1.49 becomes equal to 1.0 when Eqs. (10.51) and (10.52) are used in SI units.

Example 10.13. Determine the hydraulic radius for the following conduits: (a) square running full; (b) equilateral triangle running full; (c) equilateral triangle resting on its base and filled with running water to a depth of $\frac{1}{2}$ the height.

Answer. Equation (10.45) will be applied to each part:

$$r_H = S/L_p \tag{10.45}$$

Part (a). For a square, Eq. (10.45) reduces to Eq. (10.47) with $L_1 = L_2$, or

$$r_H = L/4 \tag{i}$$

where L is the length of one side.

Part (b). Since all angles of an equilateral triangle are 60°, the height is computed from

$$\sin 60° = h/L = (3)^{1/2}/2 \tag{ii}$$

Equation (ii) may be solved for h in terms of L, the length of a side:

$$h = L(3)^{1/2}/2 \tag{iii}$$

The flow area is the area of the triangle, $\frac{1}{2}h$ times L:

$$S = [\tfrac{1}{2}(L)(3)^{1/2}/2](L) = L^2(3)^{1/2}/4 \tag{iv}$$

The wetted perimeter of a completely filled equilateral triangle is simply $3L$:

$$r_H = S/L_p = [(L^2)(3)^{1/2}/4]/(3L) = L(3)^{1/2}/12 = L/[(4)(3)^{1/2}] \tag{v}$$

Part (c). Determination of S and L_p for a triangular duct filled to half the height is a simple problem in geometry. The flowing water actually occupies a trapezoidal-shaped area, whereas the vapor space above the water is triangular. A simple procedure is to subtract the vapor area from the total area, since the vapor area is triangular. The solution offered here will use the concept of similar triangles. The top of the water must bisect each of the top sides of the duct. Hence the wetted perimeter is the base plus the contributions from each side:

$$L_p = \tfrac{1}{2}L + L + \tfrac{1}{2}L = 2L \tag{vi}$$

Note that the top of the water contacting the vapor space does not contribute to L_p. The vapor space triangle is also equilateral; its base is of length $L/2$. The area of a trapezoid is the average of the top and bottom edges times the height of the trapezoid. For the case of a half-filled triangular duct, the height is half that in Eq. (iii), and the area of the water is

$$S = [(L + L/2)/2][(L)(3)^{1/2}/4] = L^2(3)(3)^{1/2}/(16) \tag{vii}$$

Thus, Eq. (10.45) yields the hydraulic radius:

$$r_H = \frac{L^2(3)(3)^{1/2}/(16)}{2L} = (3L)(3)^{1/2}/(32) = 0.1624L \tag{viii}$$

Example 10.14. Consider a triangular duct, 0.09238 m on a side, in which water is flowing turbulently at a depth of one-half the height, as in Example 10.13, part (c). The equivalent relative sand grain roughness is 0.0008. Determine the pressure drop over a length of 300 m if the flow velocity is 1.667 m s⁻¹.

Answer. The hydraulic radius is given by Eq. (viii) in Example 10.13:

$$r_H = 0.1624L = (0.1624)(0.09238) = 0.015 \text{ m} \tag{i}$$

From Eq. (10.44), the equivalent pipe diameter is

$$d_e = 4r_H = 0.06 \text{ m} \tag{ii}$$

The properties of water from Example 10.5 are

$$\rho = 1000 \text{ kg m}^{-3}$$
$$\mu = 10^{-3} \text{ kg m}^{-1} \text{s}^{-1} \tag{iii}$$

From Eq. (6.2), the Reynolds number is

$$N_{Re} = d_o U_{ave} \rho / \mu = (0.06)(1.667)(1000)/(10^{-3}) = 10^5 \tag{iv}$$

At $e/d_o = 0.0008$ and a Reynolds number of 10^5, the friction factor is 0.0053 from Fig. 10.3. Now the pressure drop can be found from Eq. (10.36):

$$-\Delta p = (4fL/d_o)(\rho U_{z,\,ave}^2/2) = (4)(0.0053)(300/0.06)(1000)(1.667)^2/(2)$$
$$= 1.473 \times 10^5 \text{ kg m}^{-1} \text{s}^{-2} = 1.473 \times 10^5 \text{ N m}^{-2} = 147.3 \text{ kPa} \tag{v}$$

The pressure drop (1.45 atm or 21.4 psia in English units) is sufficiently high to indicate that the problem as formulated is unreasonable. The height of the fluid will be much greater at the inlet to the duct, and hence the pressure drop per unit length will be correspondingly higher than at the discharge 300 m away. The exact solution to this problem is beyond the scope of this text.

10.4 MEASUREMENT OF FLUID FLOW

In any process the flow rate is one of the most important variables; therefore, it must often be precisely measured and must usually be controlled. Because of the need for fluid flow measurement, much effort has gone into the development and design of fluid meters. The methods range from direct weighing or volume measurement to those generating an analog or digital signal. The main measuring devices that will be discussed here are turbine flow meters, variable-head meters, and variable-area meters. These are summarized in Table 10.9. Other reviews are available [B1, B3, F2, M1, P2].

Measurements of temperature and concentration will be discussed briefly to round-out the material provided. Also, the reader should be aware of the vast amount of help that is available from specific equipment manufacturers of measuring devices. Indeed, the task of the design engineer is often the evaluation of competing proposals, where performance must be balanced against cost, both in initial investment and subsequent operation.

Several measuring devices for fluid flow have already been encountered in this text. In Example 7.11 and Fig. 7.11, a venturi metering device was considered for a trichloroethylene flow. The venturi was used to measure the overall flow rate. A simple engineering Bernoulli balance was used in the solution of this problem as will often be the case for such devices. Note that the pressure drop in a venturi meter is a measure of the overall flow, as

TABLE 10.9
Summary of flow measuring devices*

(A) Variable-head meters
    1. Venturi (Fig. 7.11)
    2. Orifice (Fig. 10.19)
    3. Pitot tube (Fig. 7.15)
        (a) point velocity (Fig. 7.15)
        (b) Prandtl tube [Fig. 7.15(c)]
        (c) Delta Pitot gauge (Fig. 10.26)
    4. Flow nozzle
        (a) standard nozzle (Fig. 10.22)
        (b) critical flow nozzle
(B) Positive displacement
    1. Reciprocating piston
    2. Nutating disc
    3. Rotary piston
    4. Rotary vane
(C) Mechanical
    1. Rotameter (Figs. 10.23 to 10.25)
    2. Turbine meter (electromagnetic) (Fig. 10.28)
(D) Acoustic
    1. Ultrasonic (travel time difference) (Fig. 10.29)
    2. Beam deflection
    3. Doppler method
(E) Electrically heated
    1. Hot-wire
    2. Hot-film (Fig. 6.4)

* From Cheremisinoff, *Fluid Flow: Pumps, Pipes and Channels*, copyright 1981, Ann Arbor Science Publishers. Used with permission of the author.

contrasted to the Pitot tube presented in Example 7.17 and Fig. 7.15. The Pitot tube measures the local velocity at the tip of the tube. Again, the engineering Bernoulli equation provided the relation between the pressure drop and the fluid velocity at the tip of the tube. These and other devices will now be treated in more detail.

10.4.1 Orifice Meter

An orifice meter is a widely used flow-measuring device. An orifice is a metal plate with a reasonably large hole carefully machined in the center. The orifice plate is inserted into a straight length of pipe. As fluid enters the orifice, it must accelerate because the flow area, as expressed by Eq. (7.10), is reduced. The Bernoulli balance predicts a corresponding pressure decrease, which may be measured and used to correlate the mass flow rate.

    A typical orifice meter is shown in Fig. 10.19. A pair of flanges (see Fig. 10.12) is welded or screwed onto the pipe, and a suitable gasket prevents leaks. There are five common designs for locating the pressure taps as listed in

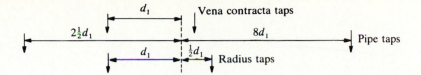

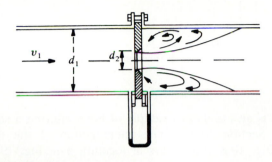

FIGURE 10.19
Sectional diagram of an orifice meter. Flange taps as shown are 1 inch from faces. Corner taps are as close as possible.

Table 10.10 and illustrated in Fig. 10.19. The shape of an orifice plate is usually square-edged, although less common designs such as rounded or beveled edges are in use. A truly sharp-edged orifice plate is machined with a complete bevel on the downstream side so that entering flow first encounters a knife edge. Such an orifice plate has the same coefficient as a square-edge plate except at very low Reynolds numbers; also the sharp-edged orifice plate will wear out rapidly, and therefore the opening will tend to enlarge as time passes.

TABLE 10.10
Orifice designs

Description	Location of upstream tap	Location of downstream tap	Remarks
Corner tap	in flange	in flange	widely used; most convenient design; taps built into flange
Radius tap	1.0 diameters	0.5 diameters	theoretically best
Pipe tap	2.5 diameters	8.0 diameters	measured Δp is low
Flange tap	1-in.	1-in.	also widely used; taps built into extra thick "orifice flange"
Vena contracta tap	0.5–2.0 diameters	0.3–0.8 diameters	inconvenient to use because location of vena contracta varies with flow rate and orifice size

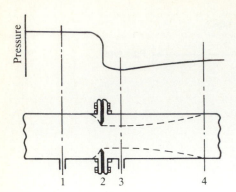

FIGURE 10.20

Pressure distribution in an orifice meter.

Flow through an orifice is an excellent example of flow entering a sharp contraction, as discussed in Section 10.2.7. The phenomenon of the vena contracta was illustrated in Fig. 10.8 and occurs at location 3 in Fig. 10.20. Since the vena contracta contains the highest velocity reached by the fluid as it passes through the orifice, the Bernoulli theorem indicates that this will be the point of minimum pressure, as shown in Fig. 10.20. In the vena contracta design, the downstream tap is at location 3 in order to provide the maximum Δp for the greatest accuracy in pressure measurement. The vena contracta usually occurs at 0.3 to 0.8 diameters downstream, depending on the flow conditions. The problem with vena contracta taps is that if the flow conditions are changed drastically or if the orifice size is changed, the location of the vena contracta will change. Then one has to relocate the downstream tap. The radius tap or corner tap configuration is probably the best compromise, especially since the radius tap and the corner tap have the advantage of the taps being an integral part of the flange that mounts the orifice. The corner tap is the easiest to install, since an orifice meter could be inserted at any point in the system where there is already a flange. The radius flanges would require the pipe to be shortened and rethreaded or welded. With these differences in mind, the following discussion concentrates on the design of the corner-tap, square-edge orifice meter.

Liquids. The mechanical engineering balance, Eq. (7.61) [or Eq. (10.39)], is the starting equation for analysis of flow through an orifice:

$$\frac{1}{2}\left(\frac{U_1^2}{\alpha_1} - \frac{U_3^2}{\alpha_3}\right) + \frac{p_1}{\rho} - \frac{p_3}{\rho} - F' = 0 \tag{10.53}$$

where the kinetic energy correction term has been included but the potential energy and shaft work terms are assumed to be zero. Equation (10.53) was applied between location 1 (upstream of the orifice) and the vena contracta (location 3) because it is impossible to measure the pressure in a commercial orifice at location 2. Also, Eq. (10.53) assumes isothermal flow. If the orifice is mounted at an angle with the horizontal, the pressure head may be included in p_1 and p_3.

Equation (7.13) can be used to relate the mass flow at locations 1 and 3:

$$w = \rho U_1 S_1 = \rho U_3 S_3 \tag{10.54}$$

For α_1 equal to α_3 and constant liquid density, Eq. (10.53) is solved for U_1, and U_3 is eliminated by using Eq. (10.54):

$$U_1^2 = 2\alpha \left(\frac{p_3 - p_1}{\rho} + F' \right) \Big/ \left(1 - \frac{S_1^2}{S_3^2} \right) \tag{10.55}$$

Note that both $p_3 - p_1$ and $1 - (S_1^2/S_3^2)$ are negative quantities. The pressure and frictional contribution can be expressed by

$$\alpha \left(\frac{p_3 - p_1}{\rho} + F' \right) = C_1^2 \left(\frac{p_3 - p_1}{\rho} \right) \tag{10.56}$$

where C_1 is obviously not a constant but a parameter that depends on the orifice tap design, the ratio of orifice diameter d_2 to pipe diameter d_1, and on the orifice Reynolds number $N_{Re,2}$:

$$N_{Re,2} = \frac{d_2 U_2 \rho}{\mu} = \frac{4w}{\pi d_2 \mu} \tag{10.57}$$

where U_2 is the average velocity through the orifice and w is the mass flow, Eq. (7.10) or Eq. (10.54).

Equation (10.56) is used to introduce C_1 into Eq. (10.55):

$$U_1^2 = 2C_1^2 \left(\frac{p_3 - p_1}{\rho} \right) \Big/ \left(1 - \frac{S_1^2}{S_3^2} \right) \tag{10.58}$$

The flow cross section at point 3 is unknown because of the contraction in the flow stream jet. Recall that this problem also occurred in Eq. (10.33) and prevented an exact solution to the flow through the sudden contraction in Fig. 10.8. At this juncture, it is useful to relate S_3 to the known area of the orifice S_2 by a second empirical constant C_2:

$$S_2 = C_2 S_3 \tag{10.59}$$

where C_2 is also a complex parameter. With this substitution, Eq. (10.58) becomes

$$U_1 = C_1 \left[2 \left(\frac{p_3 - p_1}{\rho} \right) \Big/ \left(1 - C_2^2 \frac{S_1^2}{S_2^2} \right) \right]^{1/2} \tag{10.60}$$

It is difficult to determine the two coefficients separately. Considering the problems associated with accuracy of calibration, accuracy of pressure measurement, wear on the orifice plate, etc., the calculation of both constants is not warranted. Thus, the following simplified formula is used:

$$U_1 = C_o\left[2\left(\frac{p_3 - p_1}{\rho}\right)\bigg/\left(1 - \frac{S_1^2}{S_2^2}\right)\right]^{1/2} \tag{10.61}$$

where C_o is the dimensionless orifice coefficient that must be correlated with $N_{Re,2}$. Let β be the ratio of orifice diameter to pipe diameter:

$$\beta = d_2/d_1 \qquad \text{or} \qquad \beta^2 = S_2/S_1 \tag{10.62}$$

If both sides of Eq. (10.61) are multiplied by ρS_1, then the design equation for orifice meters in terms of the mass flow rate w becomes

$$w = C_o S_2[(2\rho)(p_1 - p_3)/(1 - \beta^4)]^{1/2} = C_o \beta^2 S_1[(2\rho)(p_1 - p_3)/(1 - \beta^4)]^{1/2} \tag{10.63}$$

Equation (10.63) is the general design equation for the flow of liquids through an orifice. A check of units will show that for English units the quantity 2ρ will become $2\rho g_c$ in Eq. (10.63) and other similar equations. Equation (10.63) is a fourth-order equation in β:

$$\beta^4 = \frac{1}{1 + [(2\rho)(p_1 - p_3)](C_o S_1/w)^2} \tag{10.64}$$

This equation can be solved directly for β.

The orifice coefficient C_o has been determined for a wide variety of tap designs [F1]. For the corner tap, square-edge orifice, Fig. 10.21 shows how C_o varies with $N_{Re,2}$ and β. Above orifice Reynolds numbers of 30 000, the orifice constant is independent of flow rate and diameter ratio, that value being 0.61. In this region, the most consistent performance is obtained; note that Eq. (10.63) shows that the flow rate is directly proportional to the square root of the pressure drop across the orifice.

Figure 10.21 can also be used for radius and flange taps with errors of only a few percent, but the correlation deviates significantly from that for an orifice with pipe taps [P2]. Figure 10.21 does not apply for orifices with rounded edges. Finally, the location of the orifice with relation to other fittings in the system can be critical. A safe general recommendation is to have at least fifty pipe diameters as the distance from the upstream fitting to the orifice and ten pipe diameters as the distance from the orifice to the downstream fittings [F1]. If these distances are impossible for your specific configuration, flow straightening vanes can be used within the pipe. Careful fabrication of the orifice assembly is necessary for Fig. 10.21 to apply. The following are some guidelines: (1) the walls of the hole and the upstream surface of the plate must meet sharply at right angles; (2) the diameter of the opening must be precisely known; (3) the plate should not be thicker than $(d_1/30)$, $(d_2/8)$, or one-quarter of the distance from the pipe wall to the edge of the opening; and (4) the upstream face of the orifice plate should be smooth.

The orifice meter is extremely simple and inexpensive, in contrast to a

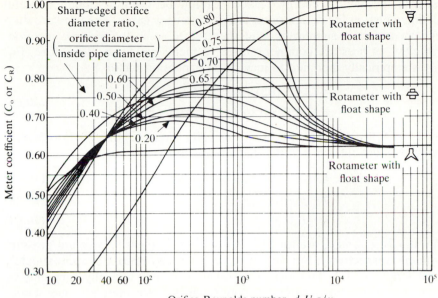

FIGURE 10.21
Orifice coefficients for circular, square-edged, corner tap orifice [T1] and rotameters. (*From Perry's Chemical Engineers' Handbook, 6th ed., p. 5-15, Perry and Green (eds.), McGraw-Hill, New York, 1984; Tuve and Sprenkle, Instruments, 6: 201 (1933); rotameter curves courtesy of Fischer and Porter Co.*)

venturi meter or other similar device that is classified under the general heading "variable-head meters" in Table 10.9. The principal disadvantage of the orifice meter is its large pressure loss; indeed, the basic design creates an excessive amount of turbulence, which results in a large, irrecoverable pressure drop. The permanent or overall fraction of the pressure differential developed by the orifice meter that is lost can be estimated as follows:

$$\frac{p_1 - p_4}{p_1 - p_3} = 1 - \beta^2 \qquad 0 \le \beta \le 0.9 \tag{10.65}$$

where p_1 is the upstream pressure, p_3 is the pressure at the downstream orifice tap, and p_4 is the fully-recovered pressure (4–8 pipe diameters downstream). Equation (10.65) applies to sharp-edged orifices. This pressure loss is permanent, i.e., friction that must be overcome by the pump. If the design Reynolds number is high enough to ensure that the orifice coefficient is kept equal to 0.61, the calibration will be constant even if there is variation of the flow from the design level. However, if the flow rate is increased far above the design level, the permanent pressure loss across the orifice may become excessive because the orifice diameter is too small.

Gases. The mechanical energy balance cannot be used to obtain a useful correlating equation for design of an orifice meter for gases. The pressure drop through an orifice is significant, and thererefore so is the volume increase. Nevertheless, orifices are commonly used to meter gas flows. Therefore, Eq. (10.63) is empirically modified to include an expansion factor Y:

$$w = C_o Y S_2 [(2\rho)(p_1 - p_3)/(1 - \beta^4)]^{1/2}$$
$$= C_o Y \beta^2 S_1 [(2\rho)(p_1 - p_3)/(1 - \beta^4)]^{1/2} \tag{10.66}$$

where Y is a function of the compressibility ratio k, the downstream to upstream pressure ratio r, and the diameter ratio β:

$$Y = 1 - (1 - r)(0.41 + 0.35\beta^4)/k \tag{10.67}$$

$$r = p_3/p_1 \tag{10.68}$$

$$k = c_p/c_v \tag{10.69}$$

In Eq. (10.69), c_p and c_v are the heat capacities of the gas at constant pressure and volume, respectively. For air, the compressibility ratio k is approximately 1.4, and for steam 1.3. The expansion function Y may typically vary only by 5–10 percent over a fairly extended flow range. Orifice meters in gas service produce modest pressure drops so r is nearly unity. Then Y as calculated from Eq. (10.67) approaches values of 0.95–1.0.

If the mass flow rate is increased to extremely high rates, the flow becomes sonic when r reaches the neighborhood of 0.5 [P2, S1]. Solution to sonic flow problems is in the realm of thermodynamics, because sonic flow is created in flow nozzles that are designed so that the entropy change of the gases is as close to zero as possible. Sonic flow nozzles are commonly used in industry for accurate metering, because the flow rate is proportional only to the upstream pressure when the downstream pressure is maintained at a value less than half the upstream pressure. Application of sonic nozzles is restricted to gas flows.

Example 10.15. Size a sharp-edged, corner-tap orifice meter for the 4-in. leg in Fig. 10.17 if the flow rate and fluid are unchanged from Example 10.11.

Answer. From Example 10.11, the following are available:

$$Q = 400 \text{ gpm} \tag{i}$$

$$\rho = (1.1)(62.4) = 68.64 \text{ lb}_m \text{ ft}^{-3} \tag{ii}$$

$$\mu = (2)(6.72 \times 10^{-4}) = 1.344 \times 10^{-3} \text{ lb}_m \text{ ft}^{-1} \text{ s}^{-1} \tag{iii}$$

The roughness e of steel pipe from Table 10.2 is 1.5×10^4 ft. From Table B.1, the diameter and velocity at 400 gpm can be found:

4-in. schedule 40 pipe

$$d_o = 4.026/12 = 0.3355 \text{ ft}$$

$$S_1 = \pi d_o^2/4 = 0.08840 \text{ ft}^2$$

$$1 \text{ ft s}^{-1} = 39.6 \text{ gal min}^{-1} \text{ (gpm)}$$

$$U_4 = 400/39.6 = 10.10 \text{ ft s}^{-1}$$

$$e/d_o = 1.5 \times 10^{-4}/0.3355 = 4.4 \times 10^{-4} \qquad \text{(iv)}$$

$$w = 3671 \text{ lb}_m \text{ min}^{-1} = 61.18 \text{ lb}_m \text{ s}^{-1} \qquad \text{(v)}$$

For convenience of reading, a liquid mercury manometer height of 30 in. (2.5 ft) is selected; this height is approximately equal to 1 atm for mercury whose specific gravity is 13.45:

$$\rho_m = \text{(specific gravity)(density of water)} = (13.45)(62.4) = 839.3 \text{ lb}_m \text{ ft}^{-3} \quad \text{(vi)}$$

The 30-in. reading on the mercury manometer establishes the pressure drop across the corner taps via the manometer equation, Eq. (7.71):

$$p_1 - p_2 = (g/g_c)(\rho_m - \rho_A)(\Delta z)$$

$$= (32.1/32.174)(839.28 - 68.64)(2.5) \left(\frac{(\text{ft s}^{-2})(\text{lb}_m \text{ ft}^{-3})(\text{ft})}{(\text{lb}_m \text{ lb}_f^{-1} \text{ ft s}^{-2})} \right)$$

$$= 1922 \text{ lb}_f \text{ ft}^{-2} = (1922)/(144) = 13.35 \text{ psi} \qquad \text{(vii)}$$

where g_c is inserted as needed for English units and ρ_A is the density of the process fluid in the manometer equation.

The design equation for liquid orifice meters is Eq. (10.63). Orifice meters are usually operated in the constant-C_o range, in which C_o is 0.61. The only unknown in Eq. (10.63) becomes β, the ratio of areas. Using Eq. (10.64), β is given by

$$\beta^4 = \frac{1}{1 + [(2\rho g_c)(p_1 - p_2)][(C_o S_1/w)^2}$$

$$= \frac{1}{1 + [(2)(68.64)(32.174)(1922)][(0.61)(0.08840)/(61.18)]^2}$$

$$\times [(\text{lb}_m \text{ ft}^{-3})(\text{lb}_m \text{ lb}_f^{-1} \text{ ft s}^{-2})(\text{lb}_f \text{ ft}^{-2})(\text{ft}^4)/(\text{lb}_m^2 \text{ s}^{-2})]$$

$$= 0.13163$$

$$\beta = 0.6023 \qquad \text{(viii)}$$

Thus, from Eq. (10.62) the orifice diameter d_2 is given by

$$d_2 = \beta d_1 = (0.6023)(0.3355) = 0.2021 \text{ ft} = 2.43 \text{ in.} \qquad \text{(ix)}$$

The Reynolds number through the orifice must be checked in order to ascertain whether the orifice coefficient of 0.61 is valid. From Eq. (10.57):

$$N_{\text{Re}, 2} = d_2 U_2 \rho / \mu = (4w)/(\pi d_2 \mu)$$

$$= [(4)(61.18)]/[(\pi)(0.2021)(1.344 \times 10^{-3})] \left(\frac{\text{lb}_m \text{ s}^{-1}}{(\text{ft})(\text{lb}_m \text{ ft}^{-1} \text{s}^{-1})} \right)$$

$$= 2.87 \times 10^5 \qquad \text{(x)}$$

The Reynolds number is high enough that further calculation is unnecessary. Furthermore, at the high Reynolds number, the square-edged orifice correlation in Fig. 10.21 is adequate for the sharp-edged orifice as specified in this problem.

For a square-edged orifice and orifice Reynolds number below 30 000, a trial and error computation would be necessary to match β with C_o and $N_{Re,2}$ in Fig. 10.21.

The permanent pressure loss through the orifice meter can be obtained from Eq. (10.65):

$$\frac{p_1 - p_4}{p_1 - p_3} = 1 - \beta^2 = 1 - (0.6024)^2 = 0.64 \tag{xi}$$

The permanent pressure loss is

$$(\Delta p)_{\text{loss}} = (0.64)(p_1 - p_3) = (0.64)(1922) = 1225 \ \text{lb}_f \ \text{ft}^{-2} = 8.51 \ \text{psi} \tag{xii}$$

The frictional loss corresponding to this pressure drop is calculated from a modification of Eq. (10.39) in the same manner as that used for the spray nozzles in a previous example [cf. Eq. (xxviii) in Example 10.11]:

$$F_{\text{orifice loss}} = (\Delta p)/\rho = 1224/68.64 \ [(\text{lb}_f \ \text{ft}^{-2})(\text{lb}_m^{-1} \ \text{ft}^3)]$$
$$= 17.84 \ \text{ft} \ \text{lb}_f \ \text{lb}_m^{-1} \tag{xiii}$$

The orifice loss times the flow rate equals the power required to pump this fluid through this orifice [cf. Eq. (7.61) or Eq. (10.39)]:

$$-W_s = wF_{\text{orifice loss}}$$
$$= (3671)(17.84)/(33\,000) \ [(\text{lb}_m \ \text{min}^{-1})(\text{ft} \ \text{lb}_f \ \text{lb}_m^{-1})(\text{hp} \ \text{min} \ \text{ft}^{-1} \ \text{lb}_f^{-1})]$$
$$= 1.98 \ \text{hp} \tag{xiv}$$

If electricity costs 7 cents per kilowatt-hour, then assuming 24-hour operation the cost of operating an orifice meter of this design is

$$\text{Cost} = (1.98/1.341)(365)(24)(0.07)$$
$$\times [(\text{hp})(\text{kW hp}^{-1})(\text{days yr}^{-1})(\text{h days}^{-1})][\$ \ (\text{kW h})^{-1}]$$
$$= \$908 \ \text{yr}^{-1} \tag{xv}$$

This result shows that orifices are often expensive to operate. The pertinent orifice details are

> orifice diameter = 2.43 in.
> corner taps, square edge
> orifice plate not over 0.134-in. thick, from the smallest of
> $(1/30)(4.026) = 0.134$ in.
> $(1/4)(2.013 - 1.21) = 0.20$ in.
> $(1/8)(2.42) = 0.30$ in.

If the upstream edge of the orifice plate were rounded, so as to minimize the permanent pressure loss, the orifice coefficient would approach unity. The pressure loss for a rounded orifice plate is quickly estimated from Eq. (10.63), which predicts that the flow rate through an orifice is proportional to the square root of the pressure drop and to the first power of the coefficient C_o. Then a rearrangement leads to the following relation:

$$C_o(\Delta p)^{1/2} = C_r(\Delta p)_r^{1/2} \tag{xvi}$$

where the subscript r denotes the rounded orifice. This equation can be solved for the pressure drop available for measurement:

$$(\Delta p)_r = (\Delta p)(C_o/C_r)^2 = (30)(0.61/1.0)^2 = 11.2 \text{ in. Hg} \qquad \text{(xvii)}$$

This pressure drop might be too low for accurate metering over the desired range of flow rates.

10.4.2 Venturi and Nozzle

Venturi meter. The venturi meter was considered previously in Example 7.11 and Fig. 7.11. Referring to Fig. 7.11 and the discussion in Section 10.2.7 (expansion and contraction losses), a venturi is designed to minimize the permanent pressure loss. The throat diameter d_2 is usually in the range of one-quarter to one-half of the pipe diameter d_1. The angle of the throat leading up to d_2 is usually 25–30° so that no vena contracta is formed. The expansion angle (in the section downstream of the throat) must be 5–7° to prevent separation of the boundary layer from the wall.

The general design equation is Eq. (10.63), which was presented previously for orifices. Note that this equation differs from those derived in Example 7.11 because of the orifice coefficient C_o and the fact that the throat velocity U_2 was used instead of U_1. If the Reynolds numbers in the pipe section is above 10^4, the value of C_o is 0.98 for a venturi installed in pipes of diameters of 8 inches or less; for larger units, C_o is 0.99. The permanent pressure loss in a venturi is usually about 10 percent of the total pressure drop across the unit.

Flow nozzles. A typical flow nozzle is shown in Fig. 10.22. The design of a flow nozzle is similar to the specifications for a venturi in the inlet section

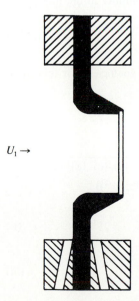

$U_1 \rightarrow$

FIGURE 10.22
Sectional diagram of a flow nozzle.

leading to the throat. Consequently, the coefficient C_o is nearly unity; the design engineer should consult the manufacturer or the literature [S5] for more exact values. The flow nozzle is more expensive than an orifice but less costly than a venturi and takes up less room in the piping system than a venturi. Its principal disadvantage is that the permanent pressure loss is about the same as that for an orifice, because the fluid separates from the solid boundary after it passes through the throat. The general design equation is Eq. (10.63), which was also used for orifices and venturis. The advantage of the venturi over the orifice and nozzle is that its use results in a considerably lower permanent pressure loss.

Gas design. For both nozzles and venturi meters, Eq. (10.66) applies with Y computed from

$$Y^2 = [(r^a)(1 - r^b)(1 - \beta^4)]/[(b)(1 - r)(1 - \beta^4 r^a)] \qquad (10.70)$$

$$a = 2/k \qquad (10.71)$$

$$b = 1 - 1/k \qquad (10.72)$$

$$k = c_p/c_v \qquad (10.69)$$

The expansion factor Y for nozzles and venturis is approximately double the value for orifices at the same value of $(1 - r)/k$. This observation results in the measured pressure drop $p_1 - p_2$ for venturis and nozzles being considerably less than that for a typical orifice at the same flow rate.

Example 10.16. Size a venturi meter for the application cited in Example 10.15.

Answer. First, it is necessary to compute the Reynolds number in the pipe:

$$N_{Re} = d_1 U_1 \rho / \mu = \frac{(0.3355)(10.10)(68.64)}{1.344 \times 10^{-3}} \left(\frac{(\text{ft})(\text{ft s}^{-1})(\text{lb}_m \text{ ft}^{-3})}{\text{lb}_m \text{ ft}^{-1} \text{s}^{-1}} \right) = 1.73 \times 10^5 \quad (i)$$

Since this Reynolds number far exceeds 10^4, the venturi coefficient for this liquid is 0.98. Using Eq. (10.64), the diameter ratio β is

$$\beta^4 = \frac{1}{1 + [(2\rho g_c)(p_1 - p_2)](C_o S_1/w)^2}$$

$$= \frac{1}{1 + [(2)(68.64)(32.174)(1922)][(0.98)(0.08840)/(61.18)]^2}$$
$$\times [(\text{lb}_m \text{ ft}^{-3})(\text{lb}_m \text{ lb}_f^{-1} \text{ ft s}^{-2})(\text{lb}_f \text{ ft}^{-2})(\text{ft}^4)/(\text{lb}_m^2 \text{ s}^{-2})]$$

$$= 0.05547$$

$$\beta = 0.4853 \qquad (ii)$$

From Eq. (10.62), the diameter of the venturi throat is

$$d_2 = \beta d_1 = 0.163 \text{ ft} = 1.95 \text{ in.} \qquad (iii)$$

The pertinent details of the venturi design are:

> Throat diameter = 1.95 in. (use nearest 1/8-in.)
> Approach angle 25°
> Divergence angle 7°

The permanent loss in the venturi is about 10 percent of total pressure drop across the unit. Actually, this is a poor venturi design—the pressure drop specified is too large for such an efficient device.

10.4.3 Rotameter

A rotameter consists of a float, free to move, within a tapered glass tube as shown in Figs. 10.23, 10.24, and 10.25. The position of the float is noted visually and correlated with the mass flow rate. Rotameters are classed as "variable area" meters because the area available to the fluid to pass around the float increases as the flow rate increases. The equilibrium position of the float indicates the flow rate; naturally, the rotameter must be mounted vertically. The actual position of the float depends upon the gravitational force acting downward, the change in kinetic energy of the fluid as it passes through the annular space between the float and the glass wall, and the frictional losses of the fluid passing around the float (also called form drag).

With proper design, the rotameter reading can be insensitive to the effect of viscosity variation over a wide range and to fluid density changes over a narrower range. Furthermore, the design of the tube and float can be such that a linear relation between position and flow rate is obtained. Many designs allow the interchanging of floats and tubes, or even the use of more than one float at a time. As a result, the rotameter can be used over wide ranges of the flow variables. In addition, it is insensitive to the nature of the approach stream, and, as a result, long lengths of straight pipe or straightening vanes are not necessary as in the case of the orifice or venturi meter. The only disadvantage is that the cost of the rotameter increases rapidly with the diameter. Consequently, it has generally been restricted to systems of a few inches in diameter or less, although much larger units are available.

For precise work, the rotameter is often calibrated with the working fluid by means of weighing for a given period of time. However, the flow rates through rotameters of modern design can be reasonably estimated with a knowledge of the meter coefficient, which is a function of the Reynolds number in the annular space. Usually such information and calibrations are obtained from the manufacturer.

Derivation of a useful equation for the performance of a rotameter begins with the mechanical energy balance [Eq. (7.61) or Eq. (10.39)]. The early steps follow those for the orifice until Eq. (10.61) is reached:

$$U_1 = C_o \left[2\left(\frac{p_1 - p_2}{\rho}\right) \middle/ \left(\frac{S_1^2}{S_2^2} - 1\right) \right]^{1/2} \tag{10.73}$$

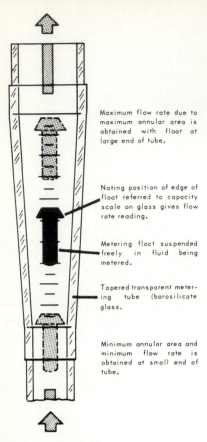

Maximum flow rate due to maximum annular area is obtained with float at large end of tube.

Noting position of edge of float referred to capacity scale on glass gives flow rate reading.

Metering float suspended freely in fluid being metered.

Tapered transparent metering tube (borosilicate glass.

Minimum annular area and minimum flow rate is obtained at small end of tube.

Fluid passes through this annular opening between periphery of float head and I.D. of tapered tube. Of course, flow rate varies directly as area of annular opening varies.

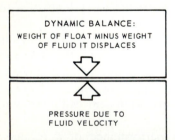

DYNAMIC BALANCE:
WEIGHT OF FLOAT MINUS WEIGHT OF FLUID IT DISPLACES

PRESSURE DUE TO FLUID VELOCITY

FIGURE 10.23
Sectional diagram of a rotameter float in a tapered tube. (*Courtesy of Fischer & Porter Co.*)

Outlet

Metering float

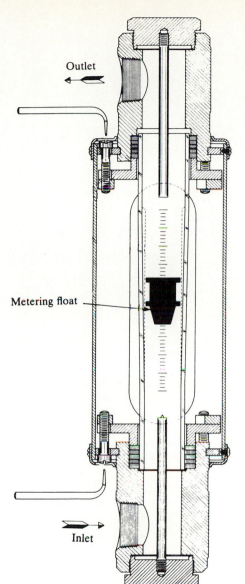

Inlet

FIGURE 10.24
Sectional drawing of a rotameter. (*Courtesy of Fischer & Porter Co.*)

where the subscripts have been changed to 1 (inlet) and 2 (minimum flow area between the float and the tapered tube). At steady-state, the rotameter float is stationary; hence, a force balance can be made to describe the equilibrium. A rotameter float is depicted in Figure 10.26 along with the forces of gravity (F_G), buoyancy (F_B), and drag (F_D) that act on that float:

$$F_G = m_f g = V_f \rho_f g \tag{10.74}$$

$$F_B = V_f \rho_A g \tag{10.75}$$

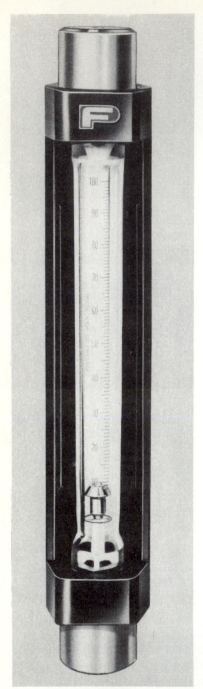

FIGURE 10.25
A commercial rotameter. (*Courtesy of Fischer & Porter Co.*)

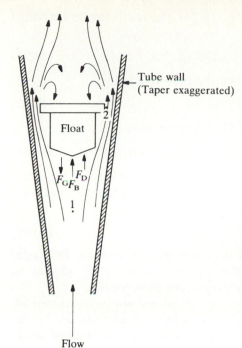

Tube wall
(Taper exaggerated)

Float

$F_G F_B$ F_D

Flow

FIGURE 10.26
Force balance on a rotameter float. (*From Foust, et al., Principles of Unit Operations, 2nd ed., p. 565, Wiley, New York, 1980. By permission.*)

where the subscripts f and A refer to the float and the process fluid, respectively. The difference between these forces equals the drag force:

$$F_D = F_G - F_B = (V_f g)(\rho_f - \rho_A) \tag{10.76}$$

In a rotameter, the drag force is assumed to be proportional to the pressure loss times the float area, or

$$F_D/S_f = C_1(-\Delta p)_{\text{loss}} \tag{10.77}$$

where C_1 is a constant. The pressure loss is not exactly equal to $p_1 - p_2$ because a small fraction is recovered downstream. Therefore, another constant must be introduced:

$$(-\Delta p)_{\text{loss}} = C_2(p_1 - p_2) \tag{10.78}$$

Equations (10.77) and (10.78) can be combined and the result used to replace pressure in Eq. (10.73):

$$p_1 - p_2 = C_3 F_D/S_f = C_3(V_f g)(\rho_f - \rho_A)/S_f \tag{10.79}$$

$$U_1 = C_o\{2[C_3(V_f g)(\rho_f - \rho_A)]/[(\rho_A S_f)(S_1^2/S_2^2 - 1)]\}^{1/2} \tag{10.80}$$

A rotameter tube can be tapered so that the following relation is true:

$$S_f = S_1 - S_2 \tag{10.81}$$

When this equation is substituted into Eq. (10.78), the result can be simplified to

$$U_1 = C_R(S_2/S_f)\{[(2V_fg)(\rho_f - \rho_A)]/[(\rho_A)(S_1 + S_2)]\}^{1/2} \qquad (10.82)$$

If the area S_2 is much smaller than S_1, then the following holds:

$$S_1^2 - S_2^2 \cong S_1^2 \qquad (10.83)$$

Equation (10.82) can be simplified with this approximation to

$$U_1 = C_R(S_2/S_1)\{[(2V_fg)(\rho_f - \rho_A)]/(\rho_A S_f)\}^{1/2} \qquad (10.84)$$

The rotameter constant C_R is also plotted in Fig. 10.21. In Eq. (10.84), for a fluid of constant density the terms within the brackets raised to the power $\frac{1}{2}$ are nearly constant so that Eq. (10.84) reduces to

$$U_1 \propto S_2 \qquad (10.85)$$

This equation shows that the flow area increases directly with the flow rate, i.e., a linear calibration instead of the square root relation alluded to previously in conjunction with orifices, venturis, and flow nozzles.

In practice, the design equations just presented will not be used; instead, calibration curves will be supplied by the rotameter manufacturer, or the rotameter will be calibrated by the user. One company makes units no larger than 200 gpm but can provide a by-pass design (where only a fixed part of the flow is measured) that can be used to measure much higher flows. Typical specifications include pipe diameter, the maximum flow rate of fluid to be handled, and the range of density and viscosity to be encountered.

10.4.4   Pitot Tube

The Pitot tube was introduced in Fig. 7.15. For pipe service, the Pitot tube is more commonly used as a research tool than as a commercial flow metering device. Sometimes a Pitot tube is used to measure air velocities in a duct when errors in the determination are tolerable. The appropriate equation was derived in Example 7.17 as Eq. (vii):

$$U^2 = 2(-\Delta p)/\rho \qquad (10.86)$$

Note that in this equation the velocity is proportional to the square root of pressure drop, just as predicted by Eq. (10.63) for orifices, venturis, and nozzles.

There are several ways in which the Pitot tube can be used to establish the average velocity across the pipe from measurements made at several radial locations. If the point of measurement is far enough downstream from any interference, then a single measurement at the center of the pipe will give the maximum velocity. Using the velocity profile equation of Pai, the average velocity in the pipe is related to the maximum velocity by Eq. (6.118). While this procedure seems simple enough, in practice it works out poorly. First, the experimental data from which Eq. (6.118) was derived show much scatter. Secondly, the Pitot tube must be perfectly aligned with the velocity vector, a condition that may be hard to meet in an industrial installation. Thirdly, the flow field must be undisturbed, and the velocity profile must be fully established. A final observation is that for liquid flows there is considerable capacitance in the probe itself and in the manometer lines. Depending on the type of pressure readout, equilibrium may be hard to obtain.

Use of Eq. (6.118) includes a trial and error calculation, since $U_{z, \text{max}}/U_{z, \text{ave}}$ is a function of Reynolds number and so are the constants in Eq. (6.118). The equation can be graphed as $U_{z, \text{max}}/U_{z, \text{ave}}$ versus N_{Re} to avoid the trial and error [P2].

The commercial device that is shown in Fig. 10.27 is an averaging Pitot tube system that has low pressure drop and the convenience of not needing the sensor to be moved to several positions. The Pitot tube is most useful in research applications when a velocity profile is desired. The velocity profile is obtained by measuring the velocity U_z with the Pitot tube probe at a series of radial locations. If desired, the average velocity can be computed graphically or numerically from the velocity profile via Eq. (7.8) or Eq. (7.9), but the experiments and calculations are tedious. It is even possible to divide the pipe cross section into equal annular areas to improve the statistical accuracy. For an even number of points, N, equal annular areas will be found from

$$r/r_o = [(2n - 1)/N]^{1/2} \qquad n = 1, 2, \ldots, (N/2) \qquad (10.87)$$

It is recommended that an additional point be taken at the pipe center line ($r = 0$), if possible. The usefulness of Eq. (10.87) is limited because a traversing Pitot tube probe will not be able to approach both $+r_o$ and $-r_o$.

Of more common use is the three-point traverse which is based upon the Gauss method of integration. The three points are located at the center and at $\pm 0.880 r_o$. The mean velocity is

$$U_{z, \text{ave}} = \tfrac{4}{9} U_{z, \text{max}} + \tfrac{5}{18}(U_{+0.880 r_o} + U_{-0.880 r_o}) \qquad (10.88)$$

Example 10.17. Use the results in Example 6.7 to estimate the velocity at $0.880 r_o$ by Pai's method. Then compute the average velocity by Eq. (10.88) and compare with the 2.778 ft s^{-1} as given.

Answer. In Example 6.7, the following values were computed for cyclohexane at a Reynolds number of 3.75×10^4 using Pai's equations:

$$U_{z, \text{max}} = 3.455 \text{ ft s}^{-1} \qquad \qquad \text{(i)}$$

$$m = 32 \qquad \qquad \text{(ii)}$$

$$a_1 = -0.3527 \qquad \qquad \text{(iii)}$$

$$a_2 = -0.6473 \qquad \qquad \text{(iv)}$$

Equation (6.118) was used to compute the value of $U_{z, \text{max}}$ in Eq. (i). The velocity

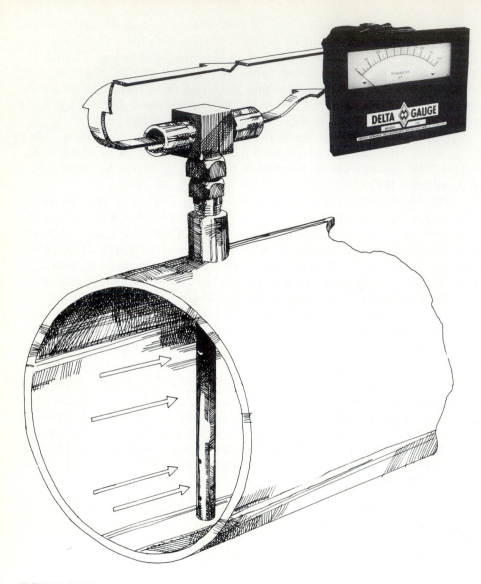

FIGURE 10.27
The Delta Pitot gauge. (*From Mid-West Instrument, Troy, MI. By permission.*)

at $0.880r_o$ is calculated from Eq. (6.114):

$$U_z/U_{z,\,max} = 1 + a_1(r/r_o)^2 + a_2(r/r_o)^{2m}$$
$$= 1 - (0.3527)(0.880)^2 - (0.6473)(0.880)^{64} = 0.7267 \qquad \text{(v)}$$

From this equation, U_z at $\pm 0.880r_o$ is

$$U_z = (U_{max})(0.7267) = (3.455)(0.7267) = 2.511 \text{ ft s}^{-1} \qquad \text{(vi)}$$

Note that the a_2 term is negligible because of the large value of the exponent $2m$.

   If these are indeed the velocities observed with a traversing Pitot tube probe, then Eq. (10.88) estimates the average velocity as follows

$$U_{z,\,\text{ave}} = \tfrac{4}{9}U_{\text{max}} + \tfrac{5}{18}(U_{+0.880r_o} + U_{-0.880r_o})$$
$$= \tfrac{4}{9}(3.455) + \tfrac{5}{18}(2.511 + 2.511) = 2.93 \text{ ft s}^{-1} \qquad \text{(vii)}$$

Thus, in this example there is an inherent error in Eq. (10.88) of 5.5 percent, even before any experimental errors are introduced.

10.4.5 Other Flow Metering Devices

The turbine flow meter, as shown in Fig. 10.28, features within the flow a propeller that is rotated by the flowing fluid. Mounted in the hub of the vane is a magnet that gives a pulse for each rotation as detected by an electrical coil. The output is digital and usually indicated by a frequency meter. Turbine flow meters are becoming increasing popular because the digital output is compatible with digital control computers.

   The permanent pressure loss in turbine flow meters is low, being from 2 to 10 psi for normally sized units. Their sizes and ranges are usually obtained from the manufacturer's specifications. The turbine flow meter and its associated digital electronics are expensive, however. To make a rough comparison, flow meters rank in the order of most expensive to least expensive as follows: turbine meter, Delta Pitot gauge, rotameter, venturi meter, and orifice meter.

   There are many other metering devices that are fundamentally similar to those previously discussed, as well as metering devices that are based on totally different principles. Several, like the Pitot tube probe, are designed for point measurements and are more often used in research. The most important of

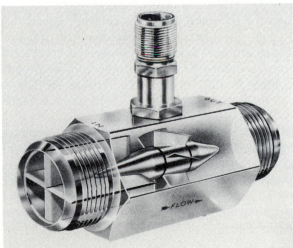

FIGURE 10.28
Turbine flow meter. (*Courtesy of Flow Technology, Inc., Tempe, AZ.*)

FIGURE 10.29
Ultrasonic flow meter. (*Courtesy of Controlotron Corp., Hauppauge, NY.*)

these are the hot-wire and hot-film anemometers and the laser Doppler anemometer (see Chapter 6). Such units are available commercially and can be very expensive, especially when one wants to measure all components of a velocity vector rather than just one component of that vector.

Ultrasonic flow meters are highly recommended for those applications that require no internally mounted components in the flow. In some designs, the time of flight of a sonic pulse is determined. From the known distance and time, the velocity of flow is obtained. In others, measurement of the Doppler shift in the sonic frequency is measured (similar in principle to the laser Doppler velocimeter). Some units can even be clamped onto a pipe without any internal connections, as shown in Fig. 10.29. Other designs include a complete unit to be inserted into the pipe. Again, design is with the assistance of the manufacturer.

Finally, there are other devices worthy of brief mention. The electromagnetic flow meter is often used for blood flows, since probe designs that do not require any internally mounted components are available. Other flow meters use the pressure drop across a short capillary or the variation in heat transfer (temperature) along a hot pipe as an indication of flow. Indeed, nearly any change effected by flow can be used as a flow indicator if the relation between flow and the variable can be established.

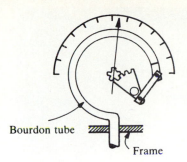

Bourdon tube

Frame

FIGURE 10.30
Bourdon pressure gauge.

10.5 MEASUREMENT OF PRESSURE

Pressure measurement is required in order to use many flow-measuring devices, as well as being important in general plant and laboratory operations. Figure 10.30 shows the internal mechanism of an inexpensive and low-accuracy Bourdon pressure gauge. For process work, such gauges are being replaced by modern pressure transducers that can be used for either analog or digital control. The modern pressure transducer has an electrical detection system that senses a change in some property as the pressure changes. One common design features a strain gauge. When a wire or other electrical conductor is

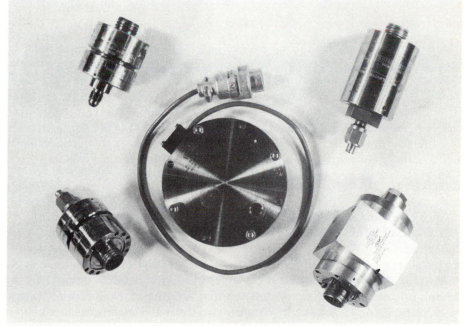

FIGURE 10.31
Pressure transducers. (*Photograph by M. B. Kukla.*)

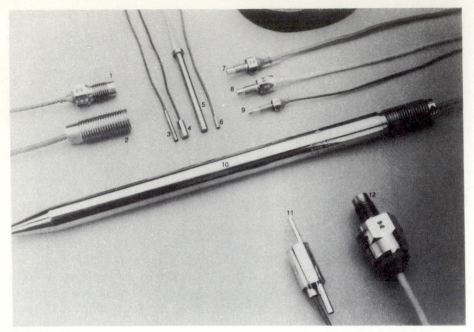

FIGURE 10.32
Piezoelectric pressure transducers. (*Courtesy of Endevco, San Juan Capistrano, CA.*)

stretched as a result of a pressure increase, the length increases and the diameter decreases. As a result, the resistance changes, and this change can be detected by a Wheatstone bridge or similar circuit. Other common designs operate on a principle of variable reluctance or a piezoelectric effect. More information is available from handbooks [P2] and manufacturers. Some typical strain gauges and piezoelectric transducers are shown in Figs 10.31 and 10.32.

Pressure transducers are purchased with a calibration curve included. For high accuracy the transducer usually must be calibrated against a manometer, which is the primary standard of pressure measurement (see Section 7.2).

10.6 MEASUREMENT OF TEMPERATURE AND CONCENTRATION

Temperature. Temperature is measured by detecting the change in some property as temperature changes. Temperature is measured industrially by utilizing one of the coupling phenomena that are often introduced in physics. An excellent example is a thermocouple. Two dissimilar metals, such as copper and constantan, an alloy composed of 60 percent copper and 40 percent nickel, when in contact will generate a small potential difference that is a function of temperature. This voltage is then detected and either displayed or converted to

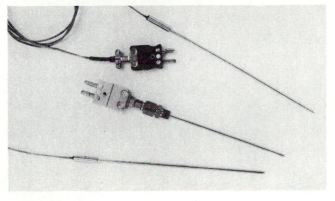

FIGURE 10.33
Typical thermocouples. (*Courtesy of Conax Corp., Buffalo, NY.*)

a more useful electric signal that can be transmitted elsewhere and recorded or detected. Figure 10.33 shows some commercially available thermocouples.

The resistance of a metal such as platinum is a reproducible function of temperature and can thus be utilized for temperature measurement. The same is true for certain glass and ceramic compositions which are given the special name of thermistors. For either device, its resistance is the basis for temperature measurement and is converted into an appropriate electrical voltage for output. Some of these devices are fairly expensive but can be extremely useful because of their portability and non-contacting nature. Several thermistors are shown in Fig. 10.34.

Concentration. Concentration measuring devices are more complex and specialized than the devices for flow metering, which use the equations of transport. For example, instruments are available for pH measurement. Also, the hot-wire anemometer can be used for concentration measurements if the differences in concentration produce differences in thermal conductivity that can be detected. Concentrations of gases are measured by the same principle that governs mass spectrometers, i.e., that molecules of differing molecular weights are deflected by varying amounts. Species of each molecular weight are separately collected and counted. Devices to measure concentrations do not in general involve transport phenomena and are beyond the scope of this text.

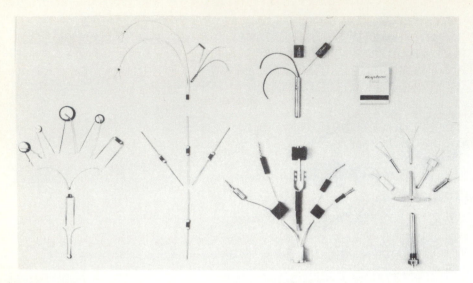

FIGURE 10.34
Typical thermistors. (*Courtesy Keystone Carbon Co., St. Mary, PA.*)

PROBLEMS[1]

10.1. The friction factor can be pictured as the combination of two other dimensionless numbers. Explain.

10.2. Describe the usefulness of the von Karman number N_{VK}, Eq. (10.13).

10.3. Compute the percentage error in the Blasius friction factor equation, Eq. (6.133), at a Reynolds number of 10^6 as compared with (a) smooth pipe; (b) rough pipe ($e/d_o = 0.001$).

10.4. What is the usefulness of the velocity head approximation?

10.5. Determine the pressure drop in psi and the horsepower required to pump the fluid in 100 ft of 2-in. schedule 40 cast iron pipe for the flow of:
(a) water at 295 K at 5 ft^3 min^{-1}
(b) air at 295 K and 1 atm at 500 ft^3 min^{-1}
(c) ethanol at 20°C at 5 ft^3 min^{-1}
(d) air at 295 K and 6 atm at 500 ft^3 min^{-1}
(e) mercury (specific gravity 13.59, viscosity 1.554 cP) at 5 ft^3 min^{-1}
(f) air at 295 K and 1 atm at 50 ft^3 min^{-1}
(g) air at 295 K and 1 atm at 5 ft^3 min^{-1}
(h) oil at 500 gpm (viscosity 4.0 cP, specific gravity 0.9)

10.6. Determine the flow rate in gpm and the horsepower required in 100 ft of 1-in.

---

[1] These problems are in English units. If practice is needed with SI units, the assignments may be solved in SI.

schedule 40 steel pipe if the pressure drop is

(a) 60 psi for the flow of water at 295 K

(b) 10 psi for the flow of air at 295 K and 1 atm

10.7. Determine the velocity in $ft\,s^{-1}$ at the beginning of the laminar-turbulent transition for the flow of water at 68°F in the following:

(a) a $\frac{3}{4}$-in. smooth tube, BWG 14

(b) a 1-in. smooth tube, BWG 14

(c) a 2-in. smooth tube, BWG 12

(d) a 1-in. cast iron pipe, schedule 40.

10.8. Repeat Problem 10.7 if the flow is air at 295 K and 1 atm.

10.9. Estimate for the assigned cases the total pressure drop (psi) and horsepower, if the pipe in Problem 10.5 is replaced with the same length of cast iron square pipe, 2.067-in. on a side.

10.10. Determine the pressure drop in psi, the loss in units of $ft\,lb_f\,lb_m^{-1}$, and the power requirement (hp) for the pump in an annulus between a $\frac{3}{4}$-in. schedule 40 pipe and a 6-in. schedule 40 pipe which is 100 ft long for:

(a) water at 295 K at 5 $ft^3\,min^{-1}$

(b) air at 295 K and 1 atm at 500 $ft^3\,min^{-1}$

(c) ethanol at 20°C at 5 $ft^3\,min^{-1}$

(d) air at 295 K and 6 atm at 500 $ft^3\,min^{-1}$

(e) mercury (specific gravity 13.59, viscosity 1.554 cP) at 5 $ft^3\,min^{-1}$

(f) air at 295 K and 1 atm at 50 $ft^3\,min^{-1}$

(g) air at 295 K and 1 atm at 5 $ft^3\,min^{-1}$

(h) oil at 500 gpm (viscosity 4.0 cP, specific gravity 0.9)

10.11. In Problem 10.10, determine for the assigned cases the correct size of round commercial pipe that will give the same pressure drop as the flow inside the annulus.

10.12. Determine the loss in $ft\,lb_f\,lb_m^{-1}$ in a sudden expansion from a 6-in. schedule 40 to a 12-in. schedule 40 pipe for a liquid (viscosity 1.171 cP and specific gravity 1.0) at 400 gpm. Then determine the loss if the flow is in the reverse direction, and compare results.

10.13. Determine the pressure drop in psi and the loss in $ft\,lb_f\,lb_m^{-1}$ in a gradual expansion of 20° from a 6-in. schedule 40 to a 12-in. schedule 40 pipe for water at 300 K at 400 gpm.

10.14. Calculate the percentage decrease in pressure drop if the sharp-edged contraction in Problem 10.12 is changed to a well-rounded contraction.

10.15. Calculate the equivalent length of the following system in feet:

200 ft of 4-in. schedule 40 pipe

2 open gate valves

1 open globe valve, bevel seat

4 90° standard elbows

2 standard tees, flow through run

1 standard tee, flow through branch

10.16. Determine the pressure drop in psi and the power requirement (hp) in 278 ft (equivalent) of 3-in. schedule 40 pipe for:

(a) 100 gpm water at 295 K

    (b) 100 gpm ethanol at 20°C (density 789.45 kg m^{-3},
        viscosity 1.18×10^{-3} N s m^{-2})
    (c) air at 295 K and 1 atm at 50 ft min^{-1}

10.17. Ethanol at 20°C (density 789.45 kg m^{-3}, viscosity 1.18×10^{-3} N s m^{-2}) flows at $U_{ave} = 3$ m s^{-1} through 100 m of 0.1-m diameter steel pipe. Compute: (a) the head loss (ft lb$_f$ lb$_m^{-1}$); (b) the wall shear stress (N m^{-2}); (c) the local velocity U_x (ft s^{-1}) at $r = 0.02$ m; (d) the horsepower required; and (e) the percentage increase in head loss due to the roughness of the tube.

10.18. Calculate the equivalent length of the following system in feet:
250 ft of 2-in. diameter wrought iron pipe, schedule 40, with screwed fittings
1 open globe valve
1 open gate valve, plug disk
3 regular radius elbows
1 tee, branch flow, the third end is plugged off

10.19. You are to design a pump to move 80 gpm of water from a pond at 20°C to a holding tank 328 ft higher than the pond. The acceleration due to gravity is 32.1 ft s^{-2}. There is negligible pressure loss in the suction pipe between pump and pond. The rest of the piping system is:
    4000 ft of 0.05-m cast iron pipe between pump and tank
    2 45° elbows
    4 90° long-radius elbows
    1 open globe valve, bevel seat
    sharp exit into tank
    (a) Find the power requirement in hp.
    (b) Find the pressure drop in the pipe from the pump discharge to the entrance to the tank.

10.20. Determine the flow rate in gpm of water at 295 K through a 0.02-m globe valve (plug disk construction) with upstream gauge pressure of 236 kPa and downstream pressure atmospheric when the valve is
    (a) open
    (b) $\frac{1}{4}$ closed
    (c) $\frac{1}{2}$ closed
    (d) $\frac{3}{4}$ closed

10.21. A tank contains oil (kinematic viscosity 1.2×10^{-4} ft^2 s^{-1}, density 118.6 lb$_m$ ft^{-3}). A pipe located 10 ft below the surface of the oil in the tank drains oil from the tank. The tank is at atmospheric pressure. The pipe outlet is located 20 ft below the surface of the oil in the tank, and the oil discharges from the pipe into the atmosphere. If $g = 32.0$ ft s^{-2}, determine the mass flow in lb$_m$ s^{-1}. The pipe system consists of:
12 000 ft of 6-in. diameter commercial steel pipe, schedule 40
14 000 ft of 3-in. diameter commercial steel pipe, schedule 40
1 6-in. ball valve, wide open
HINT: assume first that the flow is laminar and check the Reynolds number to verify this assumption. Losses in fittings are usually negligible in laminar flow.

10.22. Water at 295 K is to be withdrawn from a large main, in which the pressure is 35 psig, and carried through 175 ft (equivalent length) of pipe to discharge to the atmosphere at a point 22 ft above the main. Select the appropriate size of commercial steel pipe to assure a flow of 275 gpm. Let $g = 32.0$ ft s^{-2}.

10.23. Water at 20°C flows in a $\frac{5}{8}$-in. smooth tube, BWG 16, 20 ft long, between two reservoirs which differ in surface height by 20 ft. The existing pipe must be replaced with another design where the water will be flowing in the annular space whose inside diameter is 0.5 in. and outside diameter is 1.0 in. The roughness is the same as commercial steel pipe. Let $g = 32.0 \, \text{ft s}^{-2}$. Compute the flow rate in the new design in $\text{ft}^3 \, \text{s}^{-1}$ if the length is unchanged.

10.24. Water at 20°C flows through a 6-in. diameter pipe, schedule 40, of equivalent length 2000 ft with a head loss of 165 ft of water at a flow rate of 950 gpm. Let $g = 32.0 \, \text{ft s}^{-2}$.
(a) Estimate the pipe roughness in inches.
(b) If this roughness is doubled, find the percentage increase in head loss if the same flow rate is maintained.

10.25. A leaky pipe has allowed an oil tank to fill with water at 330 K to a depth of 20 ft. There is oil of specific gravity 0.8 floating on the surface of the water at a depth of 5 ft. At the bottom of the tank is located a drain line consisting of 3000 equivalent ft of 6-in. commercial steel pipe schedule 40. This line leads to a second tank at a pressure of 5 psig, but contains no pump. Find the air pressure (psig) necessary in the first tank to remove the water at a rate of 450 gpm. Let $g = 32.0 \, \text{ft s}^{-2}$.

10.26. A pipe system consists of a reservoir with a smooth tube attached to the bottom. The tube is 8 m long and 0.04 m in diameter. If the reservoir is filled with water at 20°C to a height of 1 m above the top of the tube, find the volume flow in gpm at the point in time being considered. Let $g = 32.05 \, \text{ft s}^{-2}$.

10.27. A tank holds water at 20°C and 100 psig. This tank empties into a second tank through a complex piping system as follows:
(1) 3000 equivalent ft of 8-in. diameter commercial steel pipe, schedule 40
(2) two pipes in parallel:
       1300 ft of 8-in. commercial steep pipe, schedule 40
       1300 ft of 6-in. commercial steel pipe, schedule 40
If the flow rate is 450 gpm, find the pressure in the second tank in psig.

10.28. Suppose that the 8-in. branch in Problem 10.27 is valved off so that the flow is only through the 3000 ft of 8-in. and 1300 ft of 6-in. pipe. If the flow is 450 gpm, find the pressure in the second tank in psig.

REFERENCES

A1. Ali, S., and C. V. Seshadri: *Ind. Eng. Chem. Process Des. Develop.* **10**(3): 328 (1971).
B1. Binder, R. C.: in *Handbook of Fluid Dynamics*, V. L. Streeter (ed.), McGraw-Hill, New York, 1961.
B2. Blasius, H.: *Mitt. Forschungsarbeit* **131:** 1 (1913).
B3. Brown, G. G., and associates: *Unit Operations*, Wiley, New York, 1950.
C1. Cheremisinoff, N. P.: *Fluid Flow*, Ann Arbor Sci., Ann Arbor, MI, 1981.
C2. Colebrook, C. F.: *J. Inst. Civil Engrs. London*, February, 1939.
C3. Crane Company: *Flow of Fluids through Valves, Fittings, and Pipe, Tech. Paper 410*, 1969.
F1. *Fluid Meters: Their Theory and Applications*, 6th ed., ASME, New York, 1971.
F2. Foust, A. S., L. A. Wenzel, C. W. Clump, L. Maus, and L. B. Andersen: *Principles of Unit Operations*, 2d ed., Wiley, New York, 1980.
H1. Hershey, H. C.: *Drag Reduction in Newtonian Polymer Solutions*, Ph.D. Dissertation, The University of Missouri at Rolla, 1965.

H2. Hooper, W. B.: *Chem. Eng.* **88**(17): 96 (August 24, 1981).

H3. Hoyt, J. W.: *J. Basic Eng.* **94**: 258 (June, 1972).

I1. *International Critical Tables,* **3**: 29, McGraw-Hill, New York, 1928.

K1. Knudsen, J. G., and D. L. Katz: *Fluid Dynamics and Heat Transfer,* McGraw-Hill, New York, 1958.

L1. Lapple, C. E.: *Chem. Eng.* **56**(5): 96 (1949).

M1. McCabe, W. L., J. C. Smith, and P. Harriott: *Unit Operations of Chemical Engineering,* 4th ed., McGraw-Hill, New York, 1985.

M2. Metzner, A. B.: in *Handbook of Fluid Dynamics,* V. L. Streeter (ed.), McGraw-Hill, New York, 1961.

M3. Moody, L. F.: *Trans. ASME* **66**: 671 (1944); *Mech. Eng.* **69**: 1005 (1947).

N1. Nikuradse, J.: *VDI-Forschungsheft* No. 361, 1933.

P1. Patterson, G. K., J. L. Zakin, and J. M. Rodriguez, *Ind. Eng. Chem.* **61**(1): 22 (1969).

P2. Perry, R. H., and D. W. Green: *Perry's Chemical Engineers' Handbook,* 6th ed., McGraw-Hill, New York, 1984.

P3. Prandtl, L.: in *Aerodynamic Theory* III, W. F. Durand (ed.), p. 142 (1935); see also *Z. VDI.* **77,** 105 (1933).

S1. Schlichting, H.: *NACA TM* 1218 (1949).

S2. Schlichting, H.: *Boundary-Layer Theory,* 7th ed., McGraw-Hill, New York, 1979.

S3. Simpson, L. L.: *Chem. Eng.* **75**(13): 192 (June 17, 1968).

S4. Srinivasan, P. S., S. S. Nandapurkar, and F. A. Holland: *Chem. Eng. (London)* **208**: CE113 (1968).

S5. Streeter, V. L., and E. B. Wylie: *Fluid Mechanics,* 7th ed., McGraw-Hill, New York, 1979.

S6. Streeter, V. L. (ed.): *Handbook of Fluid Dynamics,* McGraw-Hill, New York, 1961.

T1. Tuve, G. I., and R. E. Sprenkle: *Instruments* **6**: 201 (Nov. 1933); present title: *Instruments and Control.*

V1. Virk, P. S.: *AIChE J.* **21**: 625 (1975).

W1. White, C. M.: *Proc. Roy. Soc. (London)* **A123,** 645 (1929). [See also pp. 5–37 in [P2], 5th ed.].

W2. White, C. M.: *Trans. Inst. Chem. Eng.* **10**: 66 (1932).

CHAPTER 11

HEAT
AND MASS
TRANSFER
IN DUCT
FLOW

NOMENCLATURE

A	Area (m^2, ft^2); subscripts denote direction normal to coordinate, e.g., A_r is area normal to radius (area of a cylinder); A_i is heat transfer area of the inside surface of a pipe or tube $(2\pi r_i L)$; A_o is heat transfer area of the outside surface $(2\pi r_o L)$
A	Species A
A	Constant in Eq. (11.68)
a	Empirical constant, Eqs. (11.65), (11.68), and (11.69)
B	Empirical constant, Eqs. (11.65) and (11.68); also, B_1 and B_2 are used to simplify Eqs. (11.123) and (11.124)
b	Empirical constant, Eqs. (11.65), (11.68), and (11.69)
C	Concentration $(kmol\ m^{-3},\ lb\ mol\ ft^{-3})$; C_A is concentration of species A
c	Subscript denoting cold; ci and co are subscripts for entering cold fluid and exiting cold fluid respectively
c_p	Heat capacity at constant pressure $(kJ\ kg^{-1}\ K^{-1},\ Btu\ lb_m^{-1}\ °F^{-1})$; c_c is c_p of cold fluid; c_h is c_p of hot fluid; other subscripts defined as used
D	Diffusion coefficient (mass diffusivity) $(m^2\ s^{-1},\ ft^2\ s^{-1})$

d	Diameter (m, ft); d_i is inside diameter of a pipe
E	Eddy diffusivity ($m^2\,s^{-1}$, $ft^2\,s^{-1}$); E_τ, E_M, E_H are eddy diffusivities of momentum, mass, and heat, respectively
F	Correction factor for design of multipass heat exchangers, Eqs. (11.122) to (11.124)
f	Fanning friction factor, Eq. (6.89)
f	Subscript denoting fouling; cf. Eq. (11.96)
f	Subscript denoting film; when subscript f is applied to a dimensionless group (e.g., $N_{Pr,f}$), then all physical properties in the dimensionless group are to be evaluated at the film temperature T_f
H	Enthalpy (J, Btu); subscripts denote location
h	Subscript denoting hot fluid; hi and ho are subscripts for entering hot fluid and exiting hot fluid respectively
h	Heat transfer coefficient, defined by Eq. (6.86) or Eq. (11.3) ($W\,m^{-2}\,K^{-1}$, $Btu\,ft^{-2}\,h^{-1}\,°F^{-1}$); h_i and h_o are based in the inside area A_i and outside area A_o, respectively [cf. Eq. (11.24)]; $\bar{h}$ is the mean heat transfer coefficient, as averaged over a length L
i	Subscript denoting the inside surface of a pipe or tube
j	The Colburn j-factor; j_H is for heat, Eq. (11.79); j_M is for mass, Eq. (11.81)
k	Thermal conductivity ($W\,m^{-1}\,K^{-1}$ or $J\,m^{-1}\,K^{-1}\,s^{-1}$, $Btu\,ft^{-1}\,°R^{-1}\,s^{-1}$); k_m is mean thermal conductivity over the range of integration
$k_{L,\,ave}$	Liquid phase mass transfer coefficient in wetted wall column, Eq. (11.73) [$kmol\,m^{-2}\,s^{-1}\,(kmol\,m^{-3})^{-1}$, $lb\,mol\,ft^{-2}\,s^{-1}\,(lb\,mol\,ft^{-3})^{-1}$]
L	Length (m, ft)
LMTD	Log mean temperature difference (K, °R, °C, °F); see Eq. (11.115) for single pass; see Eq. (11.122) for multipass
lm	Subscript denoting log mean; cf., Eq. (11.115)
l	Prandtl mixing length, cf. Eq. (6.69)
mb	Subscript denoting mean bulk; when subscript mb is applied to a dimensionless group (e.g., $N_{Pr,mb}$), then all physical properties in the dimensionless group are to be evaluated at the mean bulk temperature T_{mb}
N_{Nu}	Nusselt number, hd_i/k, defined in general by Eq. (8.21) or Eq. (11.39); $N_{Nu,mb}$ is Nusselt number with properties evaluated at the mean bulk temperature T_{mb}; $N_{Nu,f}$ is Nusselt number with properties evaluated at the film temperature T_f
N_{Pr}	Prandtl number, $c_p\mu/k$, Eq. (8.4); in $N_{Pr,mb}$, all physical properties are evaluated at the mean bulk temperature T_{mb}; $N_{Pr,f}$ is Prandtl number with properties evaluated at the film temperature T_f; $N_{Pr,w}$ is Prandtl number with properties evaluated at the wall temperature T_w
N_{Re}	Reynolds number, $d_i U_{z,\,ave}\rho/\mu$ for pipe flow, Eq. (6.2); $N_{Re,mb}$ is Reynolds number with properties evaluated at the mean bulk

temperature T_{mb}; $N_{Re,f}$ is Reynolds number with properties evaluated at the film temperature T_f

N_{Sc} Schmidt number, v/D, Eq. (8.6)

N_{Sh} Sherwood number, $k_{L,ave}d_i/D$ for pipe flow, Eq. (11.73)

N_{St} Stanton number, defined as the Nusselt number divided by the product of the Reynolds number times the Prandtl number, Eq. (8.24); $N_{St,mb}$ is Stanton number with properties evaluated at the mean bulk temperature

$N_{St,mass}$ Stanton number for mass transfer, defined as the Sherwood number divided by the product of Reynolds number times Schmidt number, Eq. (11.81)

o   Subscript denoting the boundary between solid and fluid in convective heat transfer

q Energy (heat) flow vector ($J\,s^{-1}$, $Btu\,s^{-1}$); q_{rad} is heat transferred by radiation; subscripts denote components in coordinate directions

R Resistance to heat transfer, cf. Eq. (11.7)

R_f Fouling factor, cf. Eq. (11.97)

r Cylindrical coordinate

r Radius (m, ft); in fluid flow equations, r_o is value of r at the inside tube wall; in heat transfer, r_i is radius of inside tube wall, r_o is radius of outside tube wall; if the pipe is insulated, r_o is the radius of the pipe plus insulation

T Temperature (K, °R, °C, °F); T_1 and T_2 are temperatures at locations 1 and 2; T_w is temperature of the wall or surface; T_∞ is temperature in open channel; T_{ave} or T_b is bulk temperature, Eq. (11.31); T_f is film temperature, Eq. (11.32); T_{mb} is mean of two bulk temperatures, Eq. (11.34); T_{sat} is saturation temperature, temperature of condensing vapor; T_{hi}, T_{ho}, T_{ci}, T_{co} are temperatures in multipass shell-and-tube heat exchangers, as defined in Eq. (11.120)

t Time (s)

U Velocity vector ($m\,s^{-1}$, $ft\,s^{-1}$); U_z is component in z direction; $U_{z,ave}$ is mean velocity in z direction; $U_{z,max}$ is velocity at the center line; $\bar{U}_z$ is time-averaged velocity in z direction; U^* is friction velocity, Eq. (6.53)

U Overall heat transfer coefficient, Eq. (11.90) ($W\,m^{-2}\,K^{-1}$, $Btu\,ft^{-2}\,h^{-1}\,°F^{-1}$); U_i and U_o are based in the inside area A_i and outside area A_o, respectively [see Eqs. (11.90) and (11.91)]

w Mass flow rate ($kg\,s^{-1}$, $lb_m\,s^{-1}$); w_c and w_h are mass flow rates of cold and hot fluid, respectively

w   Subscript denoting wall; when subscript w is applied to a dimensionless group (e.g., $N_{Pr,w}$), then all physical properties in the dimensionless group are to be evaluated at the wall temperature T_w

x Rectangular (Cartesian) coordinate

y	Rectangular (Cartesian) coordinate
Z	Hourly heat capacity ratio, Eq. (11.118)
z	Rectangular (Cartesian) coordinate
α	Thermal diffusivity ($m^2 s^{-1}$, $ft^2 s^{-1}$)
Δ	Difference, state 2 minus state 1
δ	Generalized diffusivity ($m^2 s^{-1}$, $ft^2 s^{-1}$)
ε	Emissivity ($0 \leq \varepsilon \leq 1.0$)
η_H	Heating effectiveness, Eq. (11.119)
μ	Viscosity ($kg\, m^{-1} s^{-1}$ or $N\, m^{-2} s$, $lb_m\, ft^{-1} s^{-1}$, cP); μ_w is viscosity at T_w
ν	Kinematic viscosity (momentum diffusivity) ($m^2 s^{-1}$, $ft^2 s^{-1}$)
ξ	Generalized transport coefficients associated with h, f, k_c', Eq. (6.90)
π	Ratio of circumference of a circle to its diameter ($3.141\,592\,65\ldots$)
ρ	Density ($kg\, m^{-3}$, $lb_m\, ft^{-3}$); subscripts refer to species
σ	Stefan–Boltzmann constant, $5.670 \times 10^{-8}\, J\, s^{-1}\, m^{-2}\, K^{-4}$ ($W\, m^{-2}$ K^{-4}), $0.1714 \times 10^{-8}\, Btu\, h^{-1}\, ft^{-2}\, °R^{-4}$
$\boldsymbol{\Psi}$	Generalized flux vector (e.g., units for heat flux are $J\, m^{-2} s^{-1}$ or $W\, m^{-2}$, $Btu\, ft^{-2} s^{-1}$; see Tables 2.1 and 4.1 for more details); Ψ_x, Ψ_y, Ψ_z are components in directions x, y, z; $\Psi_{x,m}$ or $\boldsymbol{\Psi}_m$ is flux due to molecular transport; $\Psi_{x,c}$ or $\boldsymbol{\Psi}_c$ is flux due to convection
ψ	Generalized concentration of property (e.g., units for concentration of heat are $J\, m^{-3}$, $Btu\, ft^{-3}$; see Table 3.1 for complete listing)

This chapter is a continuation of the previous one, which covered fluid flow in ducts under steady-state conditions. Many of the most important examples of heat transfer are concerned with flow in ducts or other conduits. A common type of heat exchanger is a radiator in an automobile or freon coils in an air conditioner. A liquid flows through tubes, and heat is transferred from the liquid to the tubes. The tubes are attached to fins, and air flows in the spaces between the fins. In the heat exchanger just described, the momentum transfer must be understood first, and the reader may need to return to Chapter 10 periodically. It is similarly possible to have mass transfer in ducts; however, most mass transfer equipment does not involve transport in ducts. Some examples of mass transfer equipment in this text are the mixing tanks as discussed in Chapter 9 and packed beds as will be discussed in Chapter 12. In general, the rates of heat or mass transfer are significantly increased in the presence of flow; hence, these multi-transport problems are commonly encountered and must be mastered.

This text has emphasized the close analogy between the transport processes, and in particular between heat and mass transfer. In this chapter there will be further examples of this analogy, sometimes with physically different transports. These will be explained as encountered. This chapter begins with a review of molecular transport from Chapter 4 and transfer coefficients and analogies from Chapter 6. The molecular transport is recast into the resistance form, which is particularly suited to heat transfer with fluid flow in pipes and exchangers. Next, the heat or mass transfer during laminar pipe flow is covered, followed by turbulent flow.

11.1 REVIEW AND EXTENSIONS

The three modes of heat transfer: conduction, convection, and radiation, will be reviewed first. The resistance concept will be covered and then applied to problems with both conduction and convection.

11.1.1 Radiation

Energy may be transferred through a transparent fluid by electromagnetic radiation. The driving force is temperature. Radiation usually occurs from a solid surface, although emission may also originate from liquids or gases. Radiation is transferred by electromagnetic waves or photons that pass through a fluid or through a vacuum from one body to another according to the Stefan–Boltzmann law:

$$q_{rad} = A\sigma T^4 \tag{11.1}$$

where q is the amount of energy transferred per unit time ($J\,s^{-1}$ or W), A is the area surface, T is absolute temperature (K) and σ is the Stefan–Boltzmann constant ($5.670 \times 10^{-8}\,J\,s^{-1}\,m^{-2}\,K^{-4}$). A surface for which Eq. (11.1) applies is termed an ideal radiator or black body. A real surface emits radiation at a lower rate, and Eq. (11.1) is corrected by multiplying by the emissivity ε:

$$q_{rad} = \varepsilon A\sigma T^4 \qquad 0 \le \varepsilon \le 1.0 \tag{11.2}$$

The emissivity is an empirical constant. Treatment of the topic of radiation requires many other considerations, and the reader is directed elsewhere [F1, G2, H3, I1, M2, M3, P1].

11.1.2 Convection

Convection was introduced in Section 3.2.2 and further covered in Chapters 5, 6, and 10. Convection is defined as the bulk flow of a fluid induced by unequal molar mass transfer or by the external influence of a pressure difference or a force field such as gravity. The general balance equations of Chapter 5 can sometimes be solved approximately for cases of convective heat transfer, but more often the empirical heat transfer coefficient h is introduced and correlated. Equation (6.86) for heat transfer between a pipe wall and a fluid is

$$(q/A)_{r,w} = h(\bar{T}_w - T_{ave}) \tag{6.86}$$

where the units of h may be $J\,s^{-1}\,m^{-2}\,K^{-1}$ ($W\,m^{-2}\,K^{-1}$). Equation (6.86) in various forms is often called Newton's law of cooling, although engineering practice uses it for both heating and cooling. In the sequel, the overbar on T

will be dropped where it will be assumed that if turbulent flow is being considered the time-averaged temperature is used:

$$(q/A)_{r,w} = h(T_w - T_{ave}) \tag{11.3}$$

The concept of average temperature T_{ave} will be explained in Section 11.1.6. Furthermore, the overbar on all turbulent flow quantities will be dropped in order to simplify the notation.

11.1.3 Conduction

Conduction is the most easily understood of the three modes of heat transfer; our discussion of it began with Section 2.1.1 and Fourier's law:

$$(q/A)_x = -k(\partial T/\partial x) \tag{2.2}$$

where k is the thermal conductivity. The mechanism of conduction for fluids is explained by the collision of the more energetic molecules (at higher temperatures) with those at lower temperatures. The result is a net transfer of energy in the direction of the lower average temperature.

Simple conduction problems were introduced in Chapter 4, which covered molecular transport with no convection. Equation (4.2) began the discussion with the statement that the product of the flux Ψ times the transfer area A is constant when there is no accumulation or generation. The general flux equation for one-dimensional molecular transfer, which reduces to Eq. (2.2) for heat transfer, is Eq. (2.7) or Eq. (4.6). Either of these equations can be combined with Eq. (4.2) to yield Eq. (4.7), which can be integrated for constant area to

$$-(\Psi_m A)_x = \delta A_x(\Delta\psi/\Delta x) \tag{11.4}$$

This equation is the starting point for the discussion of the resistance concept, which is particularly useful for problems with both convection and conduction.

11.1.4 The Resistance Concept

Equation (11.4) can be rearranged into the form of the general rate equation:

$$(\text{RATE}) = (\text{DRIVING FORCE})/(\text{RESISTANCE}) \tag{2.1}$$

$$-(\Psi_m A)_x = \frac{\Delta\psi}{(\Delta x)/(\delta A_x)} \tag{11.5}$$

The resistance concept is widely applied to a variety of transfer problems. Heat transfer is by far the most common in this respect, and examples of heat conduction and convection in which the resistance concept is important are encountered daily around the home, as well as in industry.

A comparison of one-dimensional heat conduction with electrical circuits is useful at this point. In the study of electrical circuits, Ohm's law states that

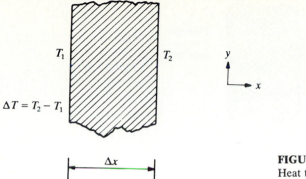

FIGURE 11.1
Heat transfer across a slab.

the rate of flow of electrons (current) equals the potential difference (voltage) divided by the resistance. In molecular transport under conditions of steady-state and no generation, the product $\Psi_m A$ is analogous to current; the difference $\Delta\psi$ is analogous to voltage. Hence, the remaining terms may be lumped together and termed resistance. Specifically, for the one-dimensional heat transfer case shown in Fig. 11.1, Eq. (11.5) becomes after substitution from Table 4.1:

$$-q_x = \frac{\rho c_p \, \Delta T}{\dfrac{\Delta x}{(kA_x)/(\rho c_p)}} = \frac{\Delta T}{\Delta x/(kA_x)} = \frac{\Delta T}{R} \tag{11.6}$$

where the resistance R is given by

$$R = \frac{\Delta x}{kA_x} \tag{11.7}$$

Equations (11.6) and (11.7) apply at steady-state. Also, they are useful only if the thermal conductivity is constant. For heat transfer, the driving force is the temperature difference ΔT:

$$\Delta T = T_2 - T_1 \tag{11.8}$$

Notice again that the minus sign in Fourier's law requires a positive heat flow for a negative temperature gradient. It is also possible for the quantity $\rho c_p \Delta T$ to be considered as the driving force, in which case the resistance R becomes $(\Delta x)/(\alpha A_x)$.

Suppose the slab in Fig. 11.1 represents a concrete wall. If this were the wall of a building, the owner might add fiber glass insulation and dry wall, as shown in Fig. 11.2(a). At steady-state, all the heat entering face 1 (the dry wall) passes through each section of the composite wall in Fig. 11.2(a):

$$q_x = q_{12} = q_{23} = q_{34} \tag{11.9}$$

Equation (11.6) can be applied to each resistance in Fig. 11.2(a); substituting

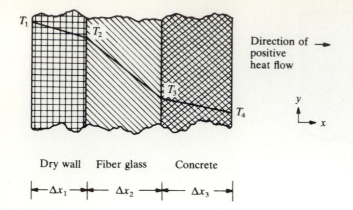

Dry wall   Fiber glass   Concrete

$\left|\leftarrow\Delta x_1\rightarrow\right|\leftarrow\Delta x_2\rightarrow\right|\leftarrow\Delta x_3\rightarrow\right|$

(*a*) Temperature profile

(*b*) Electrical analogy

FIGURE 11.2
Heat transfer through three resistances in series.

those into the constant heat flow equation, Eq. (11.9), the following is obtained:

$$-q_x = \frac{\rho_1 c_{p,1} \, \Delta T_1}{\Delta x_1} = \frac{\rho_2 c_{p,2} \, \Delta T_2}{\Delta x_2} = \frac{\rho_3 c_{p,3} \, \Delta T_3}{\Delta x_3} \qquad (11.10)$$
$$\frac{}{[k_1/(\rho_1 c_{p,1})](A_x)} \quad \frac{}{[k_2/(\rho_2 c_{p,2})](A_x)} \quad \frac{}{[k_3/(\rho_3 c_{p,3})](A_x)}$$

Equation (11.10) reduces to

$$-q_x = \frac{\Delta T_1}{\Delta x_1/(k_1 A_x)} = \frac{\Delta T_2}{\Delta x_2/(k_2 A_x)} = \frac{\Delta T_3}{\Delta x_3/(k_3 A_x)} \qquad (11.11)$$

From Eq. (11.11), the following resistances can be defined:

$$R_1 = \Delta x_1/(k_1 A_x) \qquad R_2 = \Delta x_2/(k_2 A_x) \qquad R_3 = \Delta x_3/(k_3 A_x) \qquad (11.12)$$

The overall temperature difference equals the sum of the differences across each resistance:

$$\Delta T = T_4 - T_1 = (T_2 - T_1) + (T_3 - T_2) + (T_4 - T_3) \qquad (11.13)$$

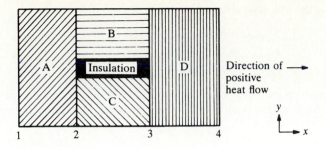

(a) Composite wall

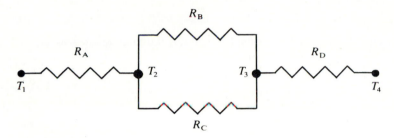

(b) Electrical analogy

FIGURE 11.3
Complex wall and electrical analogy.

If each part of Eq. (11.11) is solved for the respective ΔT and substituted into Eq. (11.13), one obtains

$$\Delta T = T_4 - T_1 = -q_x(R_1 + R_2 + R_3) \qquad (11.14)$$

or

$$-q_x = \frac{T_4 - T_1}{R_1 + R_2 + R_3} = \frac{\Delta T}{\Sigma R_i} \qquad (11.15)$$

In Fig. 11.2(b), the electrical analogy for the composite wall is shown. The electrical analogy is also valid for more complex systems, such as thermal resistances in parallel. A complex wall with parallel resistances is shown in Fig. 11.3. This wall is constructed from four materials, some of which are in parallel as well as in series. The electrical analogy is also shown. Note that, if the thermal conductivities of the materials in parallel differ significantly, it is possible that some two-dimensional heat transfer occurs. Analysis of these problems is covered elsewhere [H3, I1].

Example 11.1. Suppose that in Fig. 11.2 the dry wall is $\frac{1}{2}$-inch thick, the insulation is 3.625-inch thick, and the concrete wall is 0.5-ft thick. A check of handbooks shows the following data:

$$k_{\text{dry wall}} = 0.28 \text{ Btu h}^{-1} \text{ ft}^{-1} \, {}^{\circ}\text{F}^{-1}$$

$$k_{\text{fiber glass}} = 0.024 \text{ Btu h}^{-1} \text{ ft}^{-1} \, {}^{\circ}\text{F}^{-1} \tag{i}$$

$$k_{\text{concrete}} = 0.5 \text{ Btu h}^{-1} \text{ ft}^{-1} \, {}^{\circ}\text{F}^{-1}$$

Let the temperature on the inside of the dry wall be 65°F and the temperature on the outside of the concrete wall be 0°F. Compute and plot the temperature profile.

Answer. Assume that the construction was done in the United States, where English units are still used. In Fig. 11.2(a), T_1 is 65°F and T_4 is 0°F; Eq. (11.13) yields the driving force for heat transfer:

$$\Delta T = T_4 - T_1 = 0 - 65 = -65{}^{\circ}\text{F} \tag{ii}$$

Let us pick an area of 1 ft^2. Then using Eq. (11.12), the three resistances are

$$R_1 = \Delta x_1/(k_1 A_x)$$

$$= (0.5/12)/[(0.28)(1.0)]\left(\frac{\text{ft}}{(\text{Btu h}^{-1} \text{ ft}^{-1} \, {}^{\circ}\text{F}^{-1})(\text{ft}^2)}\right)$$

$$= 0.1488 \text{ h } {}^{\circ}\text{F Btu}^{-1} \tag{iii}$$

$$R_2 = (3.625/12)/[(0.024)(1.0)] = 12.59 \text{ h } {}^{\circ}\text{F Btu}^{-1} \tag{iv}$$

$$R_3 = (6/12)/[(0.5)(1.0)] = 1.00 \text{ h } {}^{\circ}\text{F Btu}^{-1} \tag{v}$$

Equation (11.15) is used to compute the heat flow:

$$-q_x = \frac{-65}{0.1488 + 12.59 + 1.00} = -4.73 \text{ Btu h}^{-1}$$

$$q_x = 4.73 \text{ Btu h}^{-1} \tag{vi}$$

Note that the overall resistance is completely dominated by the highest resistance, that of the insulation. Fourier's law, Eq. (2.2) or Eq. (11.11), is used to compute the intermediate temperatures:

$$-q_{12} = k_1 A_x (\Delta T_1/\Delta x_1) \tag{vii}$$

This equation is solved for ΔT_1 and the numbers for dry wall inserted:

$$\Delta T_1 = (-q_{12})(\Delta x_1)/(k_1 A_x) = [(-4.73)(0.5/12)]/[(0.28)(1.0)] = -0.70 \deg \text{F} \tag{viii}$$

where q_{12} equals q_x from Eqs. (11.9) and (vi). Therefore, the temperature at the dry wall–fiber glass interface is

$$T_2 = T_1 + \Delta T_1 = 65.0 - 0.70 = 64.30{}^{\circ}\text{F} \tag{ix}$$

The other intermediate temperatures are found similarly:

$$\Delta T_2 = (-q_{23})(\Delta x_2)/(k_2 A_x)$$

$$= [(-4.73)(3.625/12)]/[(0.024)(1.0)] = -59.56 \deg \text{F} \tag{x}$$

$$T_3 = T_2 + \Delta T_2 = 4.73{}^{\circ}\text{F} \tag{xi}$$

$$\Delta T_3 = (-q_{34})(\Delta x_3)/(k_3 A_x)$$

$$= [(-4.73)(6/12)]/[(0.5)(1.0)] = -4.73 \deg \text{F} \tag{xii}$$

Note that T_4 as computed from $T_3 + \Delta T_3$ is 0°F (within round-off error), the boundary condition given in the problem.

Fourier's law states that, for conduction with constant transfer area and constant physical properties, the temperature profile is linear with distance. Thus, the temperature gradient is found by plotting the interface temperatures and connecting them with straight lines. The temperature profile is plotted accordingly in Fig. 11.2(a), and one notes that essentially all the temperature drop is across the insulation.

In the foregoing example, the heat transfer area was constant throughout the composite wall (Fig. 11.2). Variable-area problems are often encountered, e.g., an insulated pipe, as shown in Fig. 11.4. Derivation of the thermal resistance to heat flowing through a cylinder wall begins with Eq. (4.23), which is Fourier's law for one-directional transfer in the r direction:

$$q_r \int_{r_1}^{r_2} \frac{dr}{A_r} = -\int_{T_1}^{T_2} k \, dT \tag{4.23}$$

The area of heat transfer in Fig. 4.1(b) is circumference times length:

$$A_r = 2\pi r L \tag{4.25}$$

If the heat flow q_r is constant, Eqs. (4.23) and (4.25) can be combined and integrated to yield

$$q_r \ln(r_2/r_1) = -(2\pi L k_m)(T_2 - T_1) \tag{4.27}$$

where k_m is the appropriate average value of thermal conductivity. Equation (4.27) can be rearranged into the resistance form:

$$-q_r = \frac{T_2 - T_1}{R} = \frac{T_2 - T_1}{[\ln(r_2/r_1)]/(2\pi L k_m)} \tag{11.16}$$

where L is the distance in the z direction in Fig. 4.1. The resistance R follows

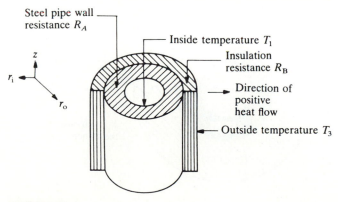

Steel pipe wall resistance R_A

Inside temperature T_1

Insulation resistance R_B

Direction of positive heat flow

Outside temperature T_3

FIGURE 11.4
Heat flow through an insulated pipe.

from Eq. (11.16):

$$R = [\ln(r_2/r_1)]/(2\pi L k_m) = [\ln(d_2/d_1)]/(2\pi L k_m) \tag{11.17}$$

For the insulated cylinder in Fig. 11.4, the equations are

$$-q_r = (T_2 - T_1)/R_A \tag{11.18}$$

$$-q_r = (T_3 - T_2)/R_B \tag{11.19}$$

$$R_A = [\ln(r_2/r_1)]/(2\pi L k_A) = [\ln(d_2/d_1)]/(2\pi L k_A) \tag{11.20}$$

$$R_B = [\ln(r_3/r_2)]/(2\pi L k_B) = [\ln(d_3/d_2)]/(2\pi L k_B) \tag{11.21}$$

These equations may be combined into

$$-q_r = (T_3 - T_1)/(R_A + R_B) \tag{11.22}$$

or in general form:

$$-q_r = \frac{\Delta T}{\sum R_i} \tag{11.23}$$

The derivations of Eqs. (11.22) and (11.23) follow exactly the derivation of Eq. (11.15).

Convection resistance. The thermal resistance approach is even more useful when modes of heat transfer are mixed. Suppose the pipe in Fig. 11.4 contains high-temperature steam and is located outdoors, where the temperature is low and a wind is blowing. Now there will be four resistances to be included in Eq. (11.23): two conduction resistances [Eqs. (11.20) and (11.21)] and two convection resistances, as shown in Fig. 11.5. The convection resistance is found by examination of Eqs. (11.3) and (2.1). From Eq. (11.3):

$$q_{r,o} = h_o A_o (T_{o,w} - T_{o,ave}) \qquad q_{r,i} = h_i A_i (T_{i,w} - T_{i,ave}) \tag{11.24}$$

where the subscript i stands for the inside and the subscript o stands for the

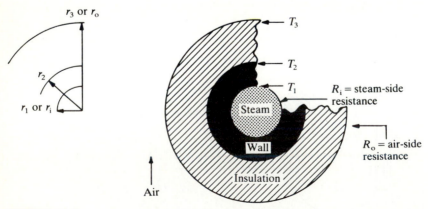

FIGURE 11.5
An insulated pipe with convection.

outside. The subscript w refers to the wall or actual surface conditions, i.e., $T_{o,w}$ means the outside wall surface temperature. The subscript ave means the average fluid temperature in contact with the wall, i.e., $T_{o,ave}$ means the average temperature of the fluid on the outside of the insulation. The outside fluid in Fig. 11.5 is the air. The average temperature will be defined precisely in Section 11.1.6.

Equation (11.24) in resistance form is

$$q_{r,o} = \frac{\Delta T_o}{1/(h_o A_o)} \qquad q_{r,i} = \frac{\Delta T_i}{1/(h_i A_i)} \tag{11.25}$$

Obviously, the convection resistances are of the form

$$R_o = \frac{1}{h_o A_o} \qquad R_i = \frac{1}{h_i A_i} \tag{11.26}$$

where the wall areas A_o and A_i are the areas through which the heat is being transferred. For a circular pipe, that area is circumference times length:

$$A_o = \pi d_o L \qquad A_i = \pi d_i L \tag{11.27}$$

For the problem in Fig. 11.5, the steam flowing on the inside with coefficient h_i and air flowing on the outside with coefficient h_o, the term $\sum R_i$ becomes

$$\sum R_i = \frac{1}{h_i A_i} + \frac{\ln(r_2/r_1)}{2\pi L k_A} + \frac{\ln(r_3/r_2)}{2\pi L k_B} + \frac{1}{h_o A_o} \tag{11.28}$$

The log-mean area, Eq. (4.29), can be used to form an alternate definition of the conduction resistance in the radial direction of a pipe or tube. Equations (11.17), (11.20), and (11.21) can be cast into the following, which is similar to Eq. (11.7):

$$R = \frac{\Delta r}{k A_{\text{lm}}} \tag{11.29}$$

where Δr is the appropriate difference in the radii, $r_2 - r_1$.

Example 11.2. In Example 4.2, the heat loss was calculated through the wall of a 2-in. schedule 40 pipe with inside temperature 10°C (50°F) and outside temperature 0°C (32°F). Let the pipe be lagged (insulated) with a 3-in. layer of 85 percent magnesia; the temperatures are unchanged. Find the heat loss and compute the temperature at the steel–magnesia interface. For steel and 85 percent magnesia, the thermal conductivities are 26 and 0.04 Btu h^{-1} ft^{-1} °F^{-1}, respectively.

Answer. Figure 11.4 applies as well as Eqs. (11.16) through (11.23). The dimensional data for the 2-in. pipe are in Example 4.1. The radii as defined in Fig. 11.5 are

$$r_1 = 2.067/2 = 1.0335 \text{ in.} = 0.086125 \text{ ft}$$

$$r_2 = 0.086125 + 0.154/12 = 0.09896 \text{ ft} \tag{i}$$

$$r_3 = 0.09896 + 3/12 = 0.34896 \text{ ft}$$

The small differences in some of the above numbers and other considerations require the retention of as many digits as possible in the intermediate results of this and many other problems. The resistances R_A of the pipe and R_B of the insulation will be computed from Eqs. (11.20) and (11.21) for unit length:

$$R_A = \ln(r_2/r_1)/(2\pi L k_A)$$

$$= \ln(0.09896/0.086125)/[(2)(\pi)(1.0)(26)] = 8.502 \times 10^{-4}\,\text{h °F Btu}^{-1} \qquad \text{(ii)}$$

$$R_B = \ln(0.34896/0.09896)/[(2)(\pi)(1.0)(0.04)] = 5.014\,\text{h °F Btu}^{-1} \qquad \text{(iii)}$$

The total resistance is the sum of these:

$$R = 8.502 \times 10^{-4} + 5.014 = 5.015\,\text{h °F Btu}^{-1} \qquad \text{(iv)}$$

Note that the pipe resistance is often negligible. The overall driving force is $-10°C$, which is equivalent to $-18°F$. Equation (11.23) yields the heat flow per foot of pipe:

$$-q_r = \Delta T / \sum R = (-18)/5.015 = -3.589\,\text{Btu h}^{-1}$$

$$q_r = 3.589\,\text{Btu h}^{-1} \qquad \text{(v)}$$

Note that in Example 4.2 the heat flow was 8080 Btu h^{-1}. The insulation reduced the heat loss from the pipe by 99.96 percent.

The intermediate temperature T_2 is found by considering either resistance individually. For the steel, the temperature change is

$$\Delta T_A = (-q_r)(R_A) = (-3.589)(8.504 \times 10^{-4}) = -3.052 \times 10^{-3}\,\text{deg F} \qquad \text{(vi)}$$

The interface temperature is

$$T_2 = T_1 + \Delta T_A = 50 - 3.052 \times 10^{-3} = 49.997\,°\text{F} \qquad \text{(vii)}$$

Example 11.3. Suppose a 2-in. schedule 40 pipe lagged with 3 inches of 85 percent magnesia insulation has steam flowing on the inside at 400°F with a heat transfer coefficient of 840 Btu h^{-1} ft^{-2} °F^{-1}. The outside temperature is 0°F. The wind is blowing, and $h_o = 25$ Btu h^{-1} ft^{-2} °F^{-1}. Estimate the heat loss for 500 ft of pipe.

Answer. In this problem, heat is transferred from the steam to the surrounding air by both conduction and convection mechanisms (cf. Fig. 11.5). There are a total of four resistances, and Eq. (11.28) applies. From Example 11.2 for a 1-ft length:

$$\text{pipe:} \qquad R_A = 8.502 \times 10^{-4}\,\text{h °F Btu}^{-1} \qquad \text{(i)}$$

$$\text{insulation:} \quad R_B = 5.014\,\text{h °F Btu}^{-1} \qquad \text{(ii)}$$

The diameters from Example 11.2 are

$$d_i = 2r_1 = (2)(0.086125) = 0.17225\,\text{ft}$$
$$d_o = 2r_3 = (2)(0.34896) = 0.6979\,\text{ft} \qquad \text{(iii)}$$

The convection resistances R_o and R_i are found from Eqs. (11.26) and (11.27).

Consider a 1-ft length:

$$R_o = 1/(h_o A_o) = 1/(h_o \pi d_o L)$$
$$= 1/[(25)(\pi)(0.6979)(1)] = 0.01824 \text{ h °F Btu}^{-1} \qquad \text{(iv)}$$
$$R_i = 1/(h_i A_i) = 1/(h_i \pi d_i L)$$
$$= 1/[(840)(\pi)(0.17225)(1)] = 0.002200 \text{ h °F Btu}^{-1} \qquad \text{(v)}$$

The total resistance is the sum of those in Eqs. (i), (ii), (iv), and (v):

$$R = 0.00220 + 8.504 \times 10^{-4} + 5.014 + 0.01824 = 5.036 \text{ h °F Btu}^{-1} \qquad \text{(vi)}$$

This value is substituted into Eq. (11.23), with the driving force equal to $-400°F$:

$$-q_r = \Delta T / \sum R = (-400.0)/5.035 = -79.43 \text{ Btu h}^{-1} \qquad \text{(vii)}$$

Equation (vii) presents the heat loss per foot. For 500 ft:

$$-q_r = \left(\Delta T / \sum R \right)(L) = (-79.43)(500) = -3.97 \times 10^4 \text{ Btu h}^{-1}$$
$$q_r = 3.97 \times 10^4 \text{ Btu h}^{-1} \qquad \text{(viii)}$$

Equation (vi) tells the engineer that the insulation accounts for more than 99 percent of the resistance to heat loss.

Example 11.4. Prove that it is possible to add a layer of material to an arbitrary cylinder of radius r_2 and length L and thereby increase the amount of heat lost. The "critical" thickness is the radius r_o where the heat transfer rate is a maximum. If the convection coefficient h_o is 7.0 W m^{-2} K^{-1}, determine the critical radius for 85 percent magnesia $(k = 0.07 \text{ W m}^{-1} \text{ K}^{-1})$ and for steel $(k = 45 \text{ W m}^{-1} \text{ K}^{-1})$.

Answer. Let us assume that Fig. 11.5 applies and that the temperature of the pipe–insulation interface T_2 is constant. A heat balance now contains only two resistances: the insulation resistance and the convection resistance between the outside area of the insulation A_o and the surrounding fluid. Under this restriction, Eq. (11.28) reduces to

$$\sum R = \frac{\ln(r_o/r_2)}{2\pi L k} + \frac{1}{h_o A_o} = \frac{\ln(r_o/r_2)}{2\pi L k} + \frac{1}{h_o(2\pi L r_o)} \qquad \text{(i)}$$

where k is the thermal conductivity of the insulation and r_o is the outside radius. The heat flow from Eq. (11.23) and Eq. (i) is

$$-q_r = \frac{\Delta T}{\sum R} = \frac{\Delta T}{\dfrac{\ln(r_o/r_2)}{2\pi L k} + \dfrac{1}{h_o(2\pi L r_o)}} = 2\pi L(\Delta T) \left(\frac{\ln(r_o/r_2)}{k} + \frac{1}{h_o r_o} \right)^{-1} \qquad \text{(ii)}$$

where ΔT is the driving force for heat transfer in the radial direction (the temperature of the fluid surrounding the outside surface of the insulation minus the temperature at r_2).

The next step is to form the derivative dq_r/dr_o and set that equal to zero in order to determine whether a maximum or a minimum exists:

$$\frac{dq_r}{dr_o} = 0 = (-1)(-2\pi L)(\Delta T)\left(\frac{\ln(r_o/r_2)}{k} + \frac{1}{h_o r_o}\right)^{-2}\left(\frac{1}{r_o k} - \frac{1}{h_o r_o^2}\right) \tag{iii}$$

Equation (iii) is zero only if the following term is zero:

$$\frac{1}{r_o k} - \frac{1}{h_o r_o^2} = 0 \tag{iv}$$

Equation (iv) can be solved for the critical radius:

$$(r_o)_{\text{critical}} = \frac{k}{h_o} \tag{v}$$

In order to determine if this value corresponds to a maximum or a minimum, it is necessary to obtain the second derivative $d^2 q_r/dr_o^2$ at the above point and determine its sign. The second derivative is negative, and therefore the critical radius in Eq. (v) corresponds to a maximum.

Under the assumptions of constant T_2 and constant k, the critical radius depends only on the thermal conductivity and the convection coefficient. For the two materials, the numerical values are

For 85 percent magnesia

$$(r_o)_{\text{critical}} = k/h_o = 0.07/7 = 0.01 \text{ m} = 1 \text{ cm} \tag{vi}$$

For steel

$$(r_o)_{\text{critical}} = 45/7 = 6.43 \text{ m} \tag{vii}$$

In conclusion, when insulation is added to a cylindrical solid such as a pipe or an electrically heated wire, the heat loss actually increases up to some "critical" radius $(r_o)_{\text{critical}}$. Beyond this radius, the heat loss decreases. For large pipe, adding insulation always decreases the heat flow, thereby saving energy. Also, insulation decreases the skin temperature and if designed properly will prevent burns upon contact. For small wires, adding a layer of electrically insulating material may actually help keep the wire cool by increasing the heat flow.

The calculation for steel proves that adding a high-conductivity solid increases the area available for convective transfer and therefore increases the heat transfer up to a large radius. Of course, it is not practical to fabricate a thick-walled steel pipe 6.43 m in diameter.

11.1.5   Slope at the Wall

If Newton's law of cooling, Eq. (11.24), is combined with Fourier's law of conduction, Eq. (2.2), the result expresses the heat transfer coefficient as a function of the temperature gradient in the solid $(\partial T/\partial x)_w$ and of the driving force in the fluid $(T_w - T_{\text{ave}})$:

$$h = \frac{-k(\partial T/\partial x)_w}{T_w - T_{\text{ave}}} \tag{11.30}$$

There are no assumptions in Eq. (11.30). This equation is useful in analytical or numerical solutions of heat transfer problems.

11.1.6 Bulk and Film Temperatures

In heat transfer with convection, the fluid properties such as viscosity and density affect the shape of the velocity profile, and hence the rate of heat transfer. Similarly, heat capacity and thermal conductivity are important. All these are functions of temperature, which varies from the value at the wall to the center line temperature. This section defines several "average" temperatures to be used in such problems.

Bulk temperature. The bulk temperature T_b is defined as the temperature reached when the fluid at a particular axial location is removed and allowed to come to equilibrium with no heat loss to the surroundings. A more descriptive definition of T_b is the "mixing cup" temperature, i.e., the temperature reached at equilibrium if the fluid removed were to be placed in an adiabatic mixing cup. Mathematically, the full expression for T_b is

$$T_b = T_{ave} = \frac{\int_0^{r_i} (\rho 2\pi r)(U_z c_p T)\, dr}{\int_0^{r_i} (\rho 2\pi r)(U_z c_p)\, dr} \tag{11.31}$$

The bulk temperature appeared previously in Eq. (11.3), which defined the heat transfer coefficient:

$$(q/A)_{r,w} = h(T_w - T_{ave}) \tag{11.3}$$

In the sequel, T_b will be used to replace T_{ave}. The numerator of Eq. (11.31) represents the total energy flow through the tube; the denominator is the product of mass flow and specific heat, integrated over the flow area. Equation (11.31) is rarely used in practice because both the velocity and temperature profile must be known. Instead, the average temperature T_b (or T_{ave}) is specified or computed at the location of interest, and the calculations proceed from that point. Note also that T_b (or T_{ave}) is the appropriate temperature to be used in heat or enthalpy balances.

Film temperature or concentration. The "film" temperature T_f attempts to average the properties of the fluid at the wall (at temperature T_w) with those in the free stream (at T_∞ or T_b). For pipe flow T_f is defined as

$$T_f = (T_w + T_b)/2 \tag{11.32}$$

A film concentration can be defined similarly:

$$C_{A,f} = (C_{A,w} + C_{A,\,ave})/2 \tag{11.33}$$

The word "film" originates from the old film theory, described in Section 6.3.4. As discussed previously, this model of transfer is incorrect, but the subscript f remains because many correlations use T_f.

Mean bulk temperature. The bulk temperature is not always a sufficient definition for heat transfer problems because both T_w and T_b vary with length down the tube and their difference is not constant or simply described. Hence, heat transfer correlations define the mean bulk temperature T_{mb} as

$$T_{mb} = (T_{b,1} + T_{b,2})/2 \tag{11.34}$$

where $T_{b,1}$ is the bulk temperature at location 1, etc. This temperature is also known as the arithmetic mean temperature.

11.2 LAMINAR PIPE FLOW

Momentum transport in laminar pipe flow was covered in Section 10.1.1. Examples 5.4 and 5.6 presented solutions for the temperature profile in a tube. For the pipe in Fig. 5.3, the energy equation from Table 5.6 simplified to

$$U_z \frac{\partial T}{\partial z} = \alpha \left[\frac{1}{r} \frac{\partial}{\partial r} \left(r \frac{\partial T}{\partial r} \right) + \frac{\partial^2 T}{\partial z^2} \right] \tag{11.35}$$

where α has been taken as a constant. This equation is identical to Eq. (i) in Example 5.6. Equation (11.35) is a partial differential equation that is very complex to solve; hence, a further simplification (the boundary layer assumption first introduced in Example 5.8) is required. When the conduction in the z direction $(\partial^2 T/\partial z^2)$ is assumed to be much less than that in the radial direction, Eq. (11.35) becomes

$$U_z \frac{\partial T}{\partial z} = \alpha \left[\frac{1}{r} \frac{\partial}{\partial r} \left(r \frac{\partial T}{\partial r} \right) \right] \tag{11.36}$$

Equation (11.36) is the basis for solutions of heat transfer in laminar flow. It applies when fluid at some temperature passes through a duct whose walls are at a different temperature.

11.2.1 Fully Developed Transfer

The term "fully developed profile" denotes that the profile (temperature, concentration, velocity) is fully established at the location in question; in other words, the profile does not change with tube length and is not a function of z. Let us consider Eq. (11.36) for a fully developed temperature profile; both U_z and $\partial T/\partial z$ are constant. Therefore, the following must hold:

$$\frac{\partial}{\partial r} \left(\frac{T_w - T}{T_w - T_b} \right)_{r=r_i} = -\left(\frac{\Delta T/\Delta r}{T_w - T_b} \right)_{r=r_i} = \text{constant} \tag{11.37}$$

Combining Eqs. (11.30) and (11.37) results in

$$h/k = \text{constant} \tag{11.38}$$

Equation (11.38) contains the group h/k, which is part of the Nusselt number, Eq. (8.21); N_{Nu} can be obtained by multiplying both sides of Eq. (11.38) by the tube diameter d_i:

$$N_{Nu} = hd_i/k = \text{constant} \tag{11.39}$$

Equation (11.39) states that for constant fluid properties, h is a constant, independent of z, the distance down the pipe. This prediction is approximately true for some applications in fully developed laminar flow.

It is useful to develop an equation for T_b as a function of z, the distance down the tube. Equation (7.48) is the energy balance on the fluid, and since the shaft work W_s is zero inside a heat exchanger tube, Eq. (7.48) becomes

$$\Delta H = q_w \tag{11.40}$$

where q_w is the heat flow at the wall. For an ideal gas or liquid (and heat capacity not a function of T):

$$\Delta H = wc_p \, \Delta T = q_w \tag{11.41}$$

where w is the mass flow rate (kg s^{-1}) and ΔT is the change in bulk temperature. Equations (11.3) and (11.41) can be written in differential form:

$$dq_w = h(T_w - T_b) \, dA \tag{11.42}$$

$$dq_w = wc_p \, dT_b \tag{11.43}$$

Since the radial area for heat transfer to or from a circular tube is the perimeter πd_i times length dz, Eqs. (11.42) and (11.43) yield

$$h(\pi d_i)(T_w - T_b) \, dz = wc_p \, dT_b \tag{11.44}$$

This equation can be rearranged into the following form:

$$\frac{h(\pi d_i)(\Delta T)}{wc_p} = \frac{dT_b}{dz} = -\frac{d(\Delta T)}{dz} \tag{11.45}$$

where the driving force ΔT is

$$\Delta T = T_w - T_b \tag{11.46}$$

Equation (11.45) is a very general equation with no assumptions save the form of the enthalpy in Eq. (11.41). There are two boundary conditions that are applied to Eqs. (11.35) and (11.45), constant wall temperature and constant heat rate (or flux):

Constant wall temperature

$$T(r = r_i) = T_w \qquad (L_1 \le z \le L_2) \tag{11.47}$$

Constant heat rate or flux

$$q_w = \text{constant} \qquad (L_1 \le z \le L_2) \tag{11.48}$$

These will be discussed in turn.

Constant wall temperature. This boundary condition, Eq. (11.47), is commonly encountered in such heat exchangers as condensers and evaporators, in which a phase change occurs on the outside of the tube. The wall temperature is also approximately constant when the product wc_p for one fluid greatly exceeds that for the second fluid. For the boundary condition of constant T_w, Eq. (11.45) becomes

$$\frac{\pi d_i h}{wc_p} dz = \frac{dT_b}{T_w - T_b} \tag{11.49}$$

Next, Eq. (11.49) is integrated with the following boundary conditions:

$$\begin{aligned}
T(z = 0) &= T_{b,1} \\
T(z = L) &= T_{b,2} \\
\Delta T(z = 0) &= \Delta T_1 \\
\Delta T(z = L) &= \Delta T_2
\end{aligned} \tag{11.50}$$

with the result

$$\frac{\Delta T_2}{\Delta T_1} = \frac{T_w - T_{b,2}}{T_w - T_{b,1}} = \exp\left(-\frac{\pi d_i \bar{h} L}{wc_p}\right) \tag{11.51}$$

where $\bar{h}$ is the average value of h between zero and the point L. Figure 11.6(a) shows the temperature predicted by Eq. (11.51). Note the exponential decay of ΔT as L increases.

A second important relation is the estimation of the Nusselt number for this boundary condition. The variation of T with radius has been expressed by the differential equation from the energy balance, Eq. (11.36). More importantly, it is useful to calculate $\bar{h}$ for fully developed laminar flow. For the boundary condition of constant wall temperature, a general solution to Eq.

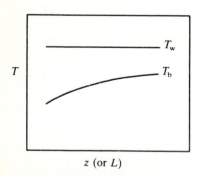

z (or L)

(a) Constant wall temperature

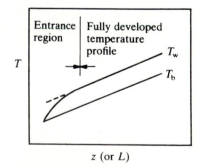

z (or L)

(b) Constant heat rate

FIGURE 11.6
Bulk temperature in laminar pipe flow for boundary conditions of constant wall temperature and constant heat rate.

(11.36) is possible only through the use of a successive approximation method [K1]. The procedure is to assume a velocity profile, Eq. (4.72), and then solve Eq. (11.36) iteratively by making successive approximations to $T(r)$. There is no simple algebraic expression for the profile, but N_{Nu} approaches the following limit [K1]:

$$N_{Nu} = \bar{h} d_i / k = 3.658 \qquad (T_w = \text{constant}) \tag{11.52}$$

where k is evaluated at T_{mb}.

Constant heat rate. This boundary condition, previously expressed in Eq. (11.48), is commonly found in electric resistance heating, radiant heating, nuclear heating, etc. It is also found in counterflow heat exchangers where the product wc_p is approximately the same for both fluids. If Eq. (11.48) applies, then Eq. (11.24) shows that if h (or $\bar{h}$) is constant, ΔT must be constant:

$$\Delta T = T_w - T_b = \text{constant} \tag{11.53}$$

Under this restriction, every term in Eq. (11.45) is constant:

$$\frac{h(\pi d_i)(\Delta T)}{wc_p} = \frac{dT_b}{dz} = -\frac{d(\Delta T)}{dz} = \text{constant} \tag{11.54}$$

The prediction from this equation is shown in Fig. 11.6(b) for flow in the fully developed region.

The Nusselt number will now be determined for this boundary condition. The variation of temperature with radius at a given z, with q_w constant, can be found using the energy equation. For constant q_w, the term $\Delta T/L$ is constant and Eq. (11.36) applies. The solution to Eq. (11.36) with the constant q_w boundary condition was presented in Example 5.6 [cf. Eq. (xviii)] and Fig. 5.4:

$$\frac{\frac{8}{3}(T_w - T)}{(U_{z,\,ave}/\alpha)(\Delta T/L)(r_i^2)} = 1 - \frac{4}{3}\frac{r^2}{r_i^2} + \frac{1}{3}\frac{r^4}{r_i^4} \tag{11.55}$$

$$q_w = \text{constant} \qquad \Delta T/L = \text{constant}$$
$$U_{z,\,ave} = \text{constant} \qquad \Delta p/L = \text{constant}$$

There are five assumptions listed underneath Eq. (xviii) that apply to Eq. (11.55), two of which are listed above.

Equation (11.39) showed that for fully developed transfer the Nusselt number is constant. To find this constant, the parabolic velocity profile, Eq. (4.74), is expressed in terms of $U_{z,\,ave}$:

$$U_z = U_{z,\,max}\left[1 - \left(\frac{r}{r_o}\right)^2\right] = 2U_{z,\,ave}\left[1 - \left(\frac{r}{r_o}\right)^2\right] \tag{11.56}$$

Equation (11.55) is solved for T, and that result and Eq. (11.56) are substituted into Eq. (11.31), the definition of T_b. After integration and simplification, T_b is

$$T_b = T_w - \frac{11}{48} \frac{U_{z,\text{ave}}}{\alpha} \frac{\Delta T}{L} r_i^2 \tag{11.57}$$

Equation (11.57) can be rearranged with the definition of ΔT and solved for the aveage velocity:

$$U_{z,\text{ave}} = \frac{48}{11} \frac{\alpha L}{r_i^2} = \frac{48}{11} \frac{kL}{\rho c_p r_i^2} \tag{11.58}$$

Equation (11.54) also applies, and the term $d(\Delta T)/dz$ equals $\Delta T/L$ after integration. The mass flow rate w is eliminated by using Eq. (7.10):

$$w = \rho U_{z,\text{ave}} S = \rho U_{z,\text{ave}} \pi r_i^2 \tag{11.59}$$

Then Eq. (11.54) can be solved for $U_{z,\text{ave}}$ and equated to Eq. (11.58):

$$U_{z,\text{ave}} = \frac{hd_i L}{r_i^2 \rho c_p} = \frac{48}{11} \left(\frac{kL}{r_i^2 \rho c_p} \right) \tag{11.60}$$

From this equation, the Nusselt number is

$$N_{\text{Nu}} = hd_i/k = 48/11 = 4.3636 \qquad (q_w = \text{constant}) \tag{11.61}$$

where k is evaluated at T_b. It is seen that the boundary condition of constant heat rate increases the Nusselt number and the heat transfer coefficient by 19 percent as compared with the boundary condition of constant wall temperature.

Correlations for heat transfer in the entry region will be discussed in the next section. Laminar flows in other geometries are covered elsewhere [K1, K5, S2].

11.2.2 Entry Region

Flow in the entry region of a pipe was discussed briefly in Section 10.2.7. Figure 11.7 shows the velocity profiles when fluid from a large tank enters a

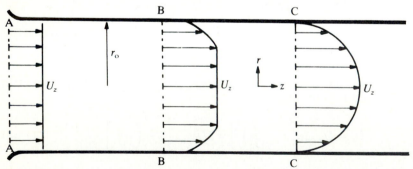

FIGURE 11.7
Development of the velocity profile in the entry region.

pipe. At location A–A, just outside the entrance, the velocity profile is essentially plug-like. At location B–B, the presence of the wall has led to the establishment of zero velocity at the wall and a gradient from the wall toward the center. At this point, the influence of the wall has not reached the fluid near the center. At location C–C, the velocity profile is completely established and follows Eq. (4.72).

Considerable work has been done on heat transfer in the entry region during laminar flow. Excellent summaries are available [K1, K5, M3, S2]. For engineering design, the Sieder–Tate equation [S4] is recommended [W1]:

$$N_{\text{Nu,mb}} = \frac{\bar{h}d_i}{k} = 1.86(N_{\text{Re,mb}})^{1/3}(N_{\text{Pr,mb}})^{1/3}\left(\frac{d_i}{L}\right)^{1/3}\left(\frac{\mu_{\text{mb}}}{\mu_{\text{w}}}\right)^{0.14}$$

$$= 1.86\left(\frac{4wc_p}{\pi k_{\text{mb}}L}\right)^{1/3}\left(\frac{\mu_{\text{mb}}}{\mu_{\text{w}}}\right)^{0.14} \tag{11.62}$$

$$T_{\text{w}} = \text{constant}$$

$$0.48 < N_{\text{Pr,mb}} < 16\,700$$

$$0.0044 < (\mu_{\text{mb}}/\mu_{\text{w}}) < 9.75$$

$$N_{\text{Nu,mb}}/1.86 \geq 2$$

In Eq. (11.62), the subscripts mb and w refer to the evaluation of properties at the mean bulk temperature T_{mb}, Eq. (11.34), and the wall temperature T_{w}. Also, $\bar{h}$ is the mean heat transfer coefficient from the entrance of the tube to the location L. The term $(\mu_{\text{mb}}/\mu_{\text{w}})^{0.14}$ is an empirical correction for the distortion of the velocity profile by a large ΔT [cf. Eq. (11.46)]. McAdams noted that experimental data sometimes deviate from Eq. (11.62) by several hundred percent, but that the deviations are such that heat exchanger design will be conservative [M3]. The reliability of any such laminar flow correlation is greatly reduced by the effects of natural convection, which is important in slowly moving fluids for which ΔT is large. If the value of the term $N_{\text{Nu,mb}}/1.86$ falls below 2, then it is likely that fully developed conditions exist throughout most of the tube radius. In this instance, the Nusselt number is constant and equal to 3.658 [I1, W1] [cf. Eq. (11.52) for constant wall temperature].

For the case of a long pipe with laminar flow, the discharge temperature $T_{\text{b,2}}$ approaches the wall temperature T_{w}. Then Eqs. (11.42) and (11.43) can be combined and integrated from the entrance to length L:

$$wc_p(T_{\text{b,2}} - T_{\text{b,1}}) = \int_0^L h(T_{\text{w}} - T_{\text{b}})\,dA = \bar{h}(T_{\text{b,2}} - T_{\text{b,1}})(\pi d_i L) \tag{11.63}$$

This equation can be rearranged into the following form:

$$N_{\text{Nu}} = \frac{\bar{h}d_i}{k} = 0.5N_{\text{Re}}N_{\text{Pr}}\frac{d_i}{L} \tag{11.64}$$

Note that the same dimensionless groups appear in Eq. (11.64) as in the Sieder–Tate equation, Eq. (11.62).

There are no mass transfer problems worthy of discussion for the case of laminar flow in ducts. There is an overwhelming amount of work published in the area of laminar forced-convection heat transfer [S2].

11.3 HEAT AND MASS TRANSFER DURING TURBULENT FLOW

Chapter 10 covered momentum transport of fluids in ducts. For turbulent flow, it was necessary to develop empirical correlation for design. In Section 11.2, empirical correlations were also necessary for laminar heat transfer in the entry region of pipes. Most process equipment involves turbulent flow, especially equipment designed for heat and/or mass transfer. Correlations for heat and mass transfer for turbulent flows are likewise empirical in nature and will be covered in this section.

11.3.1 Review of Turbulence Models

Models for heat, mass, and momentum transfer in turbulent flow were discussed in Section 6.3. Reviewing briefly, Boussinesq separated the total shear stress into the laminar contribution μ plus a turbulent contribution ε, which is called the eddy viscosity. This term was divided by density to obtain E_τ, which was defined as the eddy diffusivity of momentum. The resulting equation contains both v and E_τ:

$$\tau_{rz} = \rho \frac{r}{r_o}(U^*)^2 = -(v + E_\tau)\frac{d(\rho \bar{U}_z)}{dr} \tag{6.65}$$

Similar equations were written for heat and mass transfer. The Prandtl mixing length theory expressed the shear stress in terms of a laminar term as in Eq. (6.65) and a turbulent term, where E_τ was replaced by the mixing length l. The result was Eq. (6.72).

More modern theories, such as the penetration theory and stochastic models of turbulent diffusion, were also discussed in Section 6.3. None of these turbulence models is refined to the point of being fully satisfactory for design. Hence, an alternate approach is to propose analogies that model one transport based on a second transport process for which data are obtained more easily.

11.3.2 Correlations for Fully Developed Turbulent Flow

Heat and mass transfer coefficients have been successfully correlated for turbulent flow. These correlations are empirical, as were the fluid flow correlations in Chapter 10.

Heat transfer. The form of the heat transfer equation was derived through dimensional analysis in Example 8.3; the result can be expressed as

$$N_{Nu} = hd_i/k = B(N_{Re})^a(N_{Pr})^b \qquad (11.65)$$

where a, b and B are empirical constants. This equation is widely used for all fluids except liquid metals. Note that this equation does not take into account wall roughness conditions. The modern form [M3, S6] of the Dittus–Boelter correlation [D3], which is based on Eq. (11.65), is

$$N_{Nu,mb} = \bar{h}d_i/k_{mb} = 0.023(N_{Re,mb})^{0.8}(N_{Pr,mb})^n \qquad (11.66)$$

$$0.7 \le N_{Pr,mb} \le 100$$

$$10\,000 \le N_{Re,mb} \le 120\,000$$

$$L/d_i \ge 60 \quad \text{(smooth tubes)}$$

where n is 0.4 for heating $(T_w > T_b)$ and 0.3 for cooling. Note that the conditions listed below Eq. (11.66) are the range of data used in the correlation and applies only for smooth tubes. Equation (11.66) evaluates all properties at the mean bulk temperature T_{mb} [see Eq. (11.34)], which restricts its use to small ΔT [Eq. (11.46)].

For large ΔT, another equation by Sieder and Tate [S4] is recommended:[1]

$$N_{Nu,mb} = 0.027(N_{Re,mb})^{0.8}(N_{Pr,mb})^{1/3}(\mu_{mb}/\mu_w)^{0.14} \qquad (11.67)$$

$$0.7 < N_{Pr,mb} \le 160$$

$$N_{Re,mb} \ge 10\,000$$

$$L/d_i \ge 60 \quad \text{(smooth tubes)}$$

where all properties save μ_w are to be evaluated at T_{mb}.

Equations (11.66) and (11.67) are not valid for long lengths of pipe, for entry regions, or for very rough pipes [K4]. In general, the thermal profile in turbulent flow is quickly established, perhaps in 10 to 12 diameters and almost always by 50 diameters [M2]. These equations are used anyway, because that section is small compared to the total length and the predicted h is conservative, i.e., h in the entry region is substantially greater than the value at L/d_i of 60. Equations for the entry region are available [K5, M2]. Example 11.5 will demonstrate how to use Eqs. (11.66) and (11.67).

The correlations of Eqs. (11.66) and (11.67) were developed in the 1930s. They are still widely used and are especially recommended for hydrocarbons. Although Equations (11.66) and (11.67) are often applied to gases, they are less accurate, and better correlation methods are available, especially for gas

---

[1] Seider and Tate used 0.027. McAdams reported that 0.023 is better for air [M3]; Drexel and McAdams reported 0.021 for other air data [D4]. It is recommended that 0.027 be used for liquids and 0.023 for gases. The values of h are larger for rough pipes than for smooth pipes [K5].

applications with large ΔT [K3, P2, S6] and for water with large ΔT [H4]. The prediction of heat transfer coefficients is often improved by arbitrarily including an additive constant to the general equation, Eq. (11.65):

$$N_{Nu} = hd_i/k = A + B(N_{Re})^a(N_{Pr})^b \tag{11.68}$$

The form of Eq. (11.68) has also proved useful for liquid metals, for which the thermal conductivity is very large and the Prandtl numbers are small ($N_{Pr} < 0.1$).

The correlations for gases and liquids are generally divided into two categories: constant properties (for which the fluid properties change only a little) and variable properties. Petukhov prepared complex and accurate equations for both cases [P2]. A useful and simple equation is that of Sleicher and Rouse [N1, S6]:

Variable properties

$$N_{Nu,mb} = 5.0 + 0.015(N_{Re,f})^a(N_{Pr,w})^b \tag{11.69}$$
$$a = 0.88 - 0.24/(4.0 + N_{Pr,w})$$
$$b = 1/3 + 0.5\exp[(-0.6)(N_{Pr,w})]$$
$$10^4 \leq N_{Re,f} \leq 10^6 \qquad 0.1 \leq N_{Pr,w} \leq 10^5$$

This equation is recommended for use with liquids for both constant-property and variable-property design. For the constant-property case, all properties are evaluated at T_{mb}. For gases, the equation becomes

$$N_{Nu,mb} = 5.0 + 0.012(N_{Re,f})^{0.83}(N_{Pr,w} + 0.29) \tag{11.70}$$
$$10^4 \leq N_{Re,f} \leq 10^6 \qquad 0.6 \leq N_{Pr,w} \leq 0.9$$

Here, the Nusselt, Reynolds, and Prandtl numbers are evaluated as for Eq. (11.69). These two equations have been compared to others in the literature, as well as the best experimental data, and are sufficiently accurate for use [S6]. Again, both equations apply only for smooth tubes.

There are many correlations besides those presented here, both for smooth tubes as given, and for many other applications, such as annuli, noncircular tubes, etc. Some excellent references are available [K1, K3, K4, K5, M3, P1].

Liquid metals. Liquid metals find application in removing heat from nuclear reactors. Heat transfer in liquid metals poses a unique set of problems because the thermal conductivity is very high compared with that of other liquids. Hence, the Prandtl number of liquid metals is very low, ranging between 0.001 and 0.1. Molecular conduction is the dominant mechanism of transfer, even in turbulent flow [K1]. Excellent reviews of heat transfer in liquids metals are available [K5, S8].

In the 1950s, Seban and Shimazaki [S1] and Skupinski *et al.* [S5] developed correlations for liquid metals for constant wall and constant heat flow, respectively. More modern correlations have been proposed by Sleicher and Rouse [S6]:

Constant heat flow

$$N_{\text{Nu,mb}} = 6.3 + 0.0167(N_{\text{Re,f}})^{0.85}(N_{\text{Pr,w}})^{0.93} \qquad N_{\text{Pr,w}} \leqslant 0.1 \qquad (11.71)$$

Constant wall temperature

$$N_{\text{Nu,mb}} = 4.8 + 0.0156(N_{\text{Re,f}})^{0.85}(N_{\text{Pr,w}})^{0.93} \qquad N_{\text{Pr,w}} \leqslant 0.1 \qquad (11.72)$$

These equations are especially recommended for the variable-property case, in which the Nusselt number is evaluated at T_{mb}, the Reynolds number at T_{f}, and the Prandtl number at T_{w}. It is expected that these equations also hold for the constant property case, although they are presently untested [S6].

Mass transfer. There are essentially three experiments in which mass is transferred to or from a flowing fluid in a duct: the wetted-wall column (shown in Fig. 11.8), flow through soluble pipes, and diffusion of ions in a diffusion-controlled electrolytic system. None of these experiments has any important practical applications in industry. Therefore, the resulting correlations from these experiments are used primarily to gain understanding of the transfer mechanisms and to extend the range of data for correlations.

The earliest correlation was that of Gilliland and Sherwood [G1], who studied the evaporation of nine liquids in a wetted-wall column:

$$N_{\text{Sh}} = k_{\text{L, ave}} d_i / D = 0.023(N_{\text{Re}})^{0.83}(N_{\text{Sc}})^{0.44} \qquad (11.73)$$

$$2000 \leqslant N_{\text{Re}} \leqslant 35\,000 \qquad 0.6 \leqslant N_{\text{Sc}} \leqslant 2.26$$

$$N_{\text{Sc}} = v/D \qquad (8.6)$$

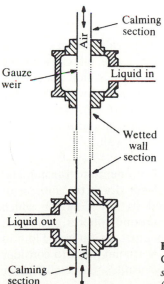

Calming section

Gauze weir

Liquid in

Air

Wetted wall section

Liquid out

Calming section

Air

FIGURE 11.8
Cross section of a wetted-wall column. (*Reprinted with permission from Gilliland and Sherwood, Ind. Eng. Chem.* **26:** *516 (1934). Copyright 1934 American Chemical Society.*)

where the Schmidt number N_{Sc} [Eq. (8.6)] is the kinematic viscosity divided by the diffusion coefficient, and the Sherwood number is based on the average liquid-phase mass transfer coefficient $k_{L, ave}$ [L1, S3, T2]. The data of Gilliland and Sherwood covered a pressure range of 0.1–3.0 atm. Later data extended the range of Eq. (11.73) and corrected some high-Schmidt-number results [L1, T1]. The most recent and the recommended correlation is that of Harriott and Hamilton [H1]:

$$N_{Sh} = 0.0096(N_{Re})^{0.913}(N_{Sc})^{0.346} \tag{11.74}$$

$$10\,000 \le N_{Re} \le 100\,000 \qquad 432 \le N_{Sc} \le 97\,600$$

The general similarity of the above equations, (11.73) and (11.74), to the corresponding equations for heat transfer [cf. Eqs. (11.66) and (11.67)] is noteworthy. It must be pointed out that the Sherwood number, defined in Eq. (11.73), is based on $k_{L, ave}$. This mass transfer coefficient is for a single component being transferred from a liquid to the bulk gas, as in the case of the wetted-wall column, or from a solid wall to the bulk liquid, in the case of a pipe manufactured from a solid that slowly dissolves as the liquid passes through it. It is possible to relate this coefficient to k'_c, as defined by Eq. (6.87) [T2].

11.3.3 The Analogies

The concept of a valid analogy among mass, heat, and momentum transport is that the basic mechanisms of transfer are essentially the same. The earliest analogy was that of Reynolds in 1874, which was presented in Chapter 6 in Eqs. (6.91) through (6.96). These can be summarized as follows:

$$\xi = \frac{h}{\rho c_p} = k'_c = \tfrac{1}{2} f U_{z, ave} \tag{11.75}$$

As stated after Eq. (6.96), this analogy is approximately valid for gas systems in which the Prandtl or Schmidt number is near unity. The influence of the fluid properties expressed in these dimensionless groups is not adequately accounted for in the Reynolds analogy, which was obtained by equating the generalized transport coefficients, as suggested by Eq. (6.94). This failure results from the fact that the Reynolds analogy considers conditions at the wall and neglects transfer of property through the fluid to the wall.

Momentum transfer analogy. The analogy between momentum transfer and heat or mass transfer is valid only if there is no form drag (the subject of Chapter 12). Thus, the analogy cannot be applied to any flow for which separation of the boundary layer occurs, e.g., flow around spheres, cylinders, and other "bluff" objects or flow perpendicular to pipes or tubing. Flow in ducts and flow over flat plates do qualify, however. A second point to consider is that heat or mass transfer may distort the velocity profiles, especially under large driving forces. The analogy does not hold if the velocity profile with momentum transfer alone differs from that with both momentum transfer and heat or mass transfer.

For any turbulent flow analogy to be valid, the mathematical statement of the boundary conditions used to solve all the applicable differential equations must be analogous (i.e., for momentum, heat, and mass). In practically all mass transfer equipment, mass transfer occurs between two fluid phases (a gas and a liquid or two immiscible liquids), while the momentum transfer occurs between the fluid phases and a solid (the duct wall, packing, etc.). In such equipment, the analogy is impossible.

For a mechanistic analogy between the transports to exist, the appropriate eddy diffusivities must be equal:

$$E_\tau = E_H = E_M \tag{6.84}$$

In practice, none of the three eddy diffusivities is usually known, and so the engineer must use his or her intuition as to whether or not Eq. (6.84) is a reasonable assumption.

Heat and mass transfer analogy. The analogy between heat and mass transfer is usually sounder than the momentum analogy discussed previously. Most of the restrictions in the previous section apply; additionally, some new restrictions may appear. The applicable restrictions to the analogy between heat and mass transfer are: (1) same velocity profile; (2) analogous mathematical boundary conditions; and (3) equal eddy diffusivities. The analogy between heat and mass transfer is often valid even if there is form drag. The analogy between heat and mass transfer will not be valid if there are additional mechanisms of transfer present in one transfer but not in the other. Examples in which analogies would not be applicable include: (1) viscous heating; (2) chemical reaction; (3) a source of heat generation (such as a nuclear source) within the flowing fluid; (4) absorption or emission of radiant energy; and (5) pressure or thermal mass diffusion.

The analogy between heat and mass transfer is obtained by substituting the analogous dimensionless groups. The Reynolds number appears unchanged in both heat and mass transfer equations. The Prandtl number in the heat transfer equations is replaced by the Schmidt number in the mass transfer equations. Similarly, the Nusselt number in heat transfer is analogous to the Sherwood number in mass transfer. A true analogy between heat and mass transfer would differ only in the substitution of the proper dimensionless group from these two pairs. This point will be illustrated in the following paragraphs on the Colburn and Friend–Metzner analogies.

Colburn analogy. The Colburn analogy [C2], or the Chilton–Colburn analogy [C1], has proved useful since its introduction in 1933 because it is based on empirical correlations, as previously introduced, and not on mechanistic assumptions that are only approximations. Thus, the Colburn analogy represents experimental data extremely well over the range in which the empirical correlations are valid. Of course, caution should be exercised in any extrapolation of an empirical equation. If extrapolation is required, then a sound mechanistic theory is necessary.

The starting point for the Colburn analogy is the Blasius relation between Reynolds number and friction factor in a smooth tube, given as Eq. (6.133). Equation (6.133) was determined in 1913, and McAdams [M3] presented constants based on more accurate data over a Reynolds number range of 5000 to 200 000. The resulting equation for turbulent flow in circular tubes is

$$f = 0.046(N_{Re})^{-0.2} \tag{11.76}$$

which, if divided by two on each side, becomes

$$f/2 = 0.023(N_{Re})^{-0.2} \tag{11.77}$$

Note that the constant 0.023 has already appeared in previous correlations, Eqs. (11.66) and (11.73).

The Dittus–Boelter turbulent correlation, Eq. (11.66), may be rearranged into the following form with n set arbitrarily to 1/3:

$$(N_{St})(N_{Pr})^{2/3} = 0.023(N_{Re})^{-0.2} \tag{11.78}$$

where the Stanton number for heat transfer N_{St} is related to the Reynolds, Nusselt, and Prandtl numbers by

$$N_{St} = \frac{N_{Nu}}{N_{Re}N_{Pr}} = \frac{h}{\rho c_p U_{z,\,ave}} \tag{8.24}$$

The Colburn analogy in its present form empirically defines a j-factor for heat transfer, j_H:

$$j_H = (N_{St,mb})(N_{Pr,f})^{2/3} \tag{11.79}$$

where the physical properties in N_{Pr} are evaluated at the film temperature T_f and the physical properties in N_{St} are evaluated at T_{mb}. Note that the Colburn analogy evaluates c_p at two different temperatures in the same correlation: at T_f in N_{Pr} and at T_{mb} in N_{St}. The Colburn analogy combines the two correlations, Eqs. (11.77) and (11.78); the j factor is equated to $f/2$ and the film Reynolds number substituted into Eq. (11.77) to account for nonisothermal flow:

$$j_H = f/2 = 0.023(N_{Re,f})^{-0.2} \tag{11.80}$$

where the physical properties in the Reynolds number are evaluated at the film temperature. The Colburn analogy is restricted to the same range and conditions as the Sieder–Tate correlation, Eq. (11.67). For extension to mass transfer, it is necessary to alter slightly the exponents in the Gilliland–Sherwood correlation, Eq. (11.73), in order to define the j-factor for mass transfer, j_M:

$$j_M = (N_{St,\,mass})(N_{Sc})^{2/3} = (N_{Sh})(N_{Re})^{-1}(N_{Sc})^{-1/3} \qquad (11.81)$$

$$N_{St,\,mass} = \frac{N_{Sh}}{N_{Re}N_{Sc}} = \frac{k_{L,\,ave}}{U_{z,\,ave}}$$

$$2000 \le N_{Re} \le 300\,000 \qquad 0.6 \le N_{Sc} \le 2500$$

where N_{Sc} is based on the fluid properties at T_f and the ranges are subject to considerable error [F1].

Colburn's analogy is based on the similarity of constants in the empirical equations that in his day were used to correlate heat, mass, and momentum transfer. The Colburn analogy may be summarized as

$$f/2 = j_H = j_M \qquad (11.82)$$

where f is the friction factor for smooth tubes.

Friend–Metzner analogy. The Friend–Metzner analogy uses an equation of substantially different form in order to correlate data over wide ranges of N_{Pr} and N_{Sc} [F3]. Their correlation for heat transfer is

$$N_{Nu,mb} = \frac{N_{Re,mb}N_{Pr,mb}(f/2)(\mu_{mb}/\mu_w)^{0.14}}{1.20 + (11.8)(f/2)^{1/2}(N_{Pr,mb} - 1)(N_{Pr,mb})^{-1/3}} \qquad (11.83)$$

$$0.5 \le N_{Pr,mb} \le 600 \qquad N_{Re,mb} \ge 10\,000$$

where f is the friction factor for smooth tubes. An important exclusion for the Friend–Metzner correlation is the region for liquid metals where the Prandtl number is much less than 0.5. Again, no correlation is valid at high heat transfer rates when the velocity profile is distorted and fluid properties vary significantly across the pipe radius. By analogy, the mass transfer correlation is

$$N_{St,\,mass} = \frac{f/2}{1.20 + (11.8)(f/2)^{1/2}(N_{Sc} - 1)(N_{Sc})^{-1/3}} \qquad (11.84)$$

$$N_{St,\,mass} = \frac{N_{Sh}}{N_{Re}N_{Sc}} = \frac{k_c'}{U_{z,\,ave}}$$

$$0.5 < N_{Sc} < 3000$$

Equation (11.84) is based on limited data, especially at high Schmidt numbers. The scatter and inherent error in mass transfer data are usually much larger than those in corresponding heat transfer data. Mass transfer data in gases (low Schmidt numbers) follow Eq. (11.84) or Eq. (11.81), since for gases the analogy between heat transfer and mass transfer has been shown experimentally to be valid. Application of Eq. (11.84) to liquid mass transfer coefficients (high Schmidt numbers) should be made with the realization that experimental data vary between investigators over a range as large as 35 percent [H1].

Summary. In view of the many conflicting correlations, a summary is warranted. The analogies are most useful for predicting or correlating mass transfer data. The analogies are less useful for heat transfer because accurate correlations exist. Also, the variation of temperature between T_w and T_b complicates the evaluation of the physical properties of the fluid. All the correlations in this chapter apply to smooth tubes, as are normally found in typical commercial heat exchange equipment. Roughness in air flows has been reviewed elsewhere [E1]. The Sleicher–Rouse equation, Eq. (11.69), is recommended for general usage; it is simple and can be adapted to both constant-property and variable-property design. For hydrocarbons, the Dittus–Boelter and Sieder–Tate equations, Eqs. (11.66) and (11.67) respectively, are still in use. The two best equations for predicting mass transfer coefficients in pipe flow are the Friend–Metzner analogy, Eq. (11.84), and the Harriott–Hamilton correlations, Eq. (11.74). At present one has no firm basis upon which to pick one over the other. Deviations up to 25 percent may be expected from either.

11.3.4 Other Methods

More complex analogies and similar methods of analysis have been proposed. Some of the well-known ones are by Von Karman [V1], Boelter *et al.* [B1], Martinelli [M1], Seban and Shimazaki [S1], Deissler [D1, D2], and Lyon [L2]. Some of these are based on constant heat rate and the rest on a constant wall temperature. Sleicher and Tribus studied heat transfer in a pipe with turbulent flow and arbitrary wall temperature distribution [S7]. These really do not offer significant improvement over the empirical equations presented earlier [H2]. However, they may allow prediction of the Nusselt number for geometries for which no data exist. Excellent reviews are available [E1, F1, H3, K5, M3].

If the velocity profile is known, then the temperature (or concentration) distribution throughout the fluid stream can be obtained by equating the eddy diffusivities, as in Eq. (6.84). In Example 6.6 the equation was derived, and in Example 6.8 the numerical solution for the temperature distribution was shown for a typical turbulent flow. Clearly, the turbulent flow problem can be treated as was the laminar flow problem just analyzed in Section 11.2. The procedure usually involves two integrations, one to obtain the temperature profile, as done in Example 6.8, and the second to obtain T_b by Eq. (11.31). Then the new value of T_b is used to repeat the two integrations until all equations and boundary conditions are satisfied.

An early attempt to bypass the simplifying (but unsatisfactory) assumptions in the analogies relaxed the assumption of equal eddy diffusivities and made the ratio of eddy diffusivities a unique function of Prandtl number [J1]. A single consistent theory and numerical computing procedure were used later by Kays and Leung [K2] to predict the Nusselt number over the entire range of N_{Pr} and N_{Re}. Their results are in Fig. 11.9. These authors indicate that the plot agrees very favorably with the experimental data over most of the Prandtl

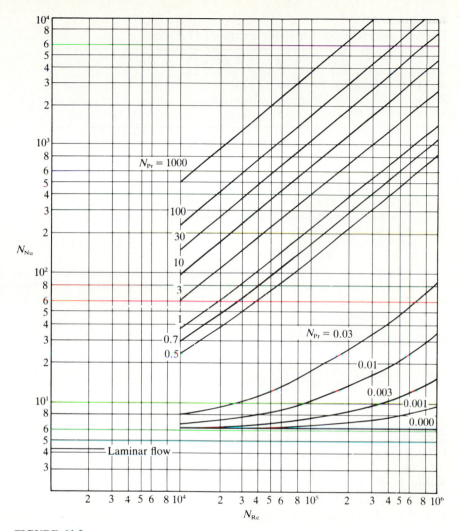

FIGURE 11.9
Nusselt number for turbulent flow, fully developed profiles, circular tube, constant heat rate. (*From Kays and Crawford, Convective Heat and Mass Transfer, 2d ed., p. 248, McGraw-Hill, New York, 1980. By permission.*)

number range, but that at low Prandtl numbers for liquid metals and at high Reynolds numbers deviations of up to 40 percent have been reported.

Example 11.5. Estimate the heat transfer coefficient when water at 20°C flows in a smooth pipe 0.04 m in diameter at a Reynolds number of 50 000, if the pipe wall is maintained at 40°C. Assume that a very short section of pipe is being considered so that 20°C is the mean bulk temperature.

TABLE 11.1
Physical properties of water for Example 11.5

T, K	T, °C	ρ, kg m^{-3}	μ, cP	k, W m^{-1} K^{-1}	c_p, J kg^{-1} K^{-1}	N_{Pr}
293.15	20	999.0	1.001	0.603	4182	6.94
303.15	30	996.0	0.800	0.618	4178	5.41
313.15	40	992.1	0.654	0.632	4179	4.32

Answer. The flow is fully turbulent. The physical properties of water will be needed at temperatures of 20°C, 30°C, and 40°C, in order to use the six methods of prediction covered in Section 11.3. Data in Table 11.1 were taken from Table A.1 in the Appendix; the liquid density is the reciprocal of the specific volume. Since the tube diameter is 0.04 m, the ratio k_{mb}/d_i is

$$k_{mb}/d_i = 0.603/0.04 = 15.08 \text{ W m}^{-2}\text{ K}^{-1} \tag{i}$$

Dittus–Boelter. This correction evaluates all properties at the mean bulk temperature, which is 20°C here. Equation (11.66) is used for the conditions given. This equation is solved for h below and the values for k_{mb}/d_i, N_{Re}, N_{Pr}, and n (0.4 for heating) are inserted:

$$h = (k_{mb}/d_i)(0.023)(N_{Re,mb})^{0.8}(N_{Pr,mb})^{0.4} = (15.08)(0.023)(5.0 \times 10^4)^{0.8}(6.94)^{0.4}$$

$$= 4322 \text{ W m}^{-2}\text{ K}^{-1} \tag{ii}$$

or in English units, using the conversion from Table C.10 in the Appendix:

$$h = (4322)(0.17611) = 761 \text{ Btu ft}^{-2}\text{ h}^{-1}\text{ °F}^{-1} \tag{iii}$$

Sieder–Tate. This correlation evaluates all properties save μ_w at the mean bulk temperature. Equation (11.67) is solved for h, using the definition of N_{Nu} in Eq. (11.65), and the appropriate substitutions are made:

$$h = (k_{mb}/d_i)(0.027)(N_{Re,mb})^{0.8}(N_{Pr,mb})^{1/3}(\mu_{mb}/\mu_w)^{0.14}$$

$$= (15.08)(0.027)(5.0 \times 10^4)^{0.8}(6.94)^{1/3}(1.001/0.654)^{0.14}$$

$$= 4733 \text{ W m}^{-2}\text{ K}^{-1} = 834 \text{ Btu ft}^{-2}\text{ h}^{-1}\text{ °F}^{-1} \tag{iv}$$

Sleicher–Rouse. The Sleicher–Rouse equation is

$$N_{Nu,mb} = 5.0 + 0.015(N_{Re,f})^a(N_{Pr,w})^b \tag{11.69}$$

$$a = 0.88 - 0.24/(4.0 + N_{Pr,w})$$

$$b = 1/3 + 0.5 \exp[(-0.6)(N_{Pr,w})]$$

The film temperature from Eq. (11.32) is:

$$T_f = (T_w + T_{mb})/2 = 30°C \tag{v}$$

The properties of water at the film temperature, 30°C, are in Table 11.1. The film Reynolds number is

$$N_{Re,f} = N_{Re,mb}(\mu_{20}/\mu_{30})(\rho_{30}/\rho_{20})$$

$$= (5.0 \times 10^4)(1.001/0.800)(996.0/999.0) = 6.24 \times 10^4 \tag{vi}$$

The Prandtl number at the wall temperature (40°C) from Table 11.1 is 4.32. The exponents a and b are

$$a = 0.88 - 0.24/(4.0 + N_{\text{Pr,w}}) = 0.88 - 0.24/(4.0 + 4.32) = 0.8512$$

$$b = 1/3 + 0.5 \exp[(-0.6)(N_{\text{Pr,w}})]$$

$$= 1/3 + 0.5 \exp[(-0.6)(4.32)] = 0.3708 \tag{vii}$$

The Nusselt number from Eq. (11.69) is

$$N_{\text{Nu,mb}} = 5.0 + 0.015(N_{\text{Re,f}})^a(N_{\text{Pr,w}})^b$$

$$= 5.0 + 0.015(6.24 \times 10^4)^{0.8511}(4.32)^{0.3708} = 316.2 \tag{viii}$$

The thermal conductivity in the Nusselt number is evaluated at 20°C, T_{mb}. The heat transfer coefficient is

$$h = (N_{\text{Nu,mb}})(k_{\text{mb}}/d_i) = (316.2)(0.603)/(0.04)$$

$$= 4766 \text{ W m}^{-2}\text{ K}^{-1} = 839 \text{ Btu ft}^{-2}\text{ h}^{-1}\text{ °F}^{-1} \tag{ix}$$

Colburn analogy. The j factor for heat transfer is calculated from Eq. (11.80) using the film Reynolds number from Eq. (vi):

$$j_{\text{H}} = f/2 = 0.023(N_{\text{Re,f}})^{-0.2} = (0.023)(6.26 \times 10^4)^{-0.2} = 2.528 \times 10^{-3} \tag{x}$$

The Stanton number from Eq. (11.79) is

$$N_{\text{St,mb}} = (j_{\text{H}})(N_{\text{Pr,f}})^{-2/3} = (2.528 \times 10^{-3})(5.41)^{-2/3} = 8.202 \times 10^{-4} \tag{xi}$$

where the Stanton number at T_{mb} is

$$N_{\text{St,mb}} = h/(\rho_{\text{mb}}c_{\text{p,mb}}U_{z,\text{ ave}}) \tag{xii}$$

In order to obtain h using Eq. (xii), the velocity in the pipe must first be calculated using the Reynolds number, Eq. (6.2). When the properties are evaluated at the mean bulk temperature T_{mb}, the Reynolds number is 50 000. Therefore, the velocity is

$$U_{z,\text{ ave}} = (N_{\text{Re}})(\mu)/(d_i\rho) = [(5.0 \times 10^4)(1.001)(10^{-3})]/[(0.04)(999.0)]$$

$$= 1.253 \text{ m s}^{-1} \tag{xiii}$$

Equation (xii) is solved for h and the correct values for the properties are substituted

$$h = (N_{\text{St,mb}})(\rho_{\text{mb}}c_{\text{p,mb}}U_{z,\text{ ave}}) = (8.202 \times 10^{-4})(999.0)(4182)(1.253)$$

$$= 4292 \text{ W m}^{-2}\text{ K}^{-1} = 756 \text{ Btu ft}^{-2}\text{ h}^{-1}\text{ °F}^{-1} \tag{xiv}$$

Friend–Metzner. The Friend–Metzner equation is

$$N_{\text{Nu,mb}} = \frac{N_{\text{Re,mb}}N_{\text{Pr,mb}}(f/2)(\mu_{\text{mb}}/\mu_{\text{w}})^{0.14}}{1.20 + (11.8)(f/2)^{1/2}(N_{\text{Pr,mb}} - 1)(N_{\text{Pr,mb}})^{-1/3}} \tag{11.83}$$

The friction factor f may be estimated from Eq. (11.76) or Eq. (6.132) for smooth tubes. Using Newton's method, as illustrated in Example 10.2, the friction factor from Eq. (6.132) is

$$f(N_{\text{Re}} = 50\ 000) = 0.005\ 227 \tag{xv}$$

TABLE 11.2

Comparison of h from various correlations

Method	h, W m^{-2} K^{-1}	h, Btu ft^{-2} h^{-1} °F^{-1}
Dittus–Boelter	4322	761
Seider–Tate	4733	834
Sleicher–Rouse	4766	839
Colburn analogy	4292	756
Friend–Metzner	4713	830
Numerical analysis	4824	850

Next, the appropriate numbers are inserted into Eq. (11.83):

$$N_{\text{Nu,mb}} = \frac{(5 \times 10^4)(6.94)(0.005\,227/2)(1.001/0.654)^{0.14}}{1.20 + (11.8)(0.005\,227/2)^{1/2}(6.94 - 1)(6.94)^{-1/3}} = 313 \qquad \text{(xvi)}$$

Equation (11.65) is solved for the heat transfer coefficient:

$$h = (N_{\text{Nu,mb}})(k_{\text{mb}}/d_i) = (313)(0.603)/(0.04)$$

$$= 4713 \text{ W m}^{-2}\text{ K}^{-1} = 830 \text{ Btu ft}^{-2}\text{ h}^{-1}\text{ °F}^{-1} \qquad \text{(xvii)}$$

Numerical analysis. From Fig. 11.9, the Nusselt number is about 320. The heat transfer coefficient is

$$h = N_{\text{Nu}}(k/d_i) = (320)(0.603)/(0.04)$$

$$= 4824 \text{ W m}^{-2}\text{ K}^{-1} = 850 \text{ Btu ft}^{-2}\text{ h}^{-1}\text{ °F}^{-1} \qquad \text{(xviii)}$$

Summary. Table 11.2 summarizes the various values of the heat transfer coefficients as calculated from all six methods. There is roughly a 10 percent spread among the values—certainly very reasonable in light of other problems such as tube fouling and corrosion. In general, the Colburn analogy is outdated. For small driving force ΔT, the Dittus–Boelter correlation is preferred; it is based on good experimental data. For large ΔT, such as in this problem, the Sleicher–Rouse correlation is preferred for water and gases. The Seider–Tate correlation is recommended for hydrocarbons, although the Sleicher–Rouse and Friend–Metzner equations are also satisfactory. The graph of Fig. 11.9 is excellent for a quick estimate of N_{Nu}, given N_{Re} and N_{Pr}, but it is inconvenient for computer-aided design.

This example was simplified by considering the mean bulk temperature to be constant and equal to 20°C. In a real heat exchanger, the fluid temperature is a strong function of length. The procedure is to divide the exchanger into small sections, perhaps 1 ft or 1 m in length. The mean bulk temperature is the average of that at the beginning and end [Eq. (11.34)]. The heat transfer through the wall must balance the enthalpy change [cf., Eq. (11.44)]. A trial and error calculation is required: the temperature at the end of the small section is guessed; the properties are calculated, the mean heat transfer coefficient h is estimated from a suitable correlation, and the heat through the wall is calculated [Eqs. (11.23) and (11.28)]; the temperature at the end of the wall is calculated from the enthalpy equation; finally, when the guess equals that temperature calculated from the enthalpy equation, convergence has been obtained for that length interval. This procedure is repeated until the entire length of the exchanger has been traversed.

Example 11.6. The liquid metal NaK is often used in nuclear reactors to transfer heat between the core and the boilers. Consider an NaK mixture of 45 percent Na that is flowing in a smooth tube (inside diameter 0.04 m) at a Reynolds number of 50 000. Find the Nusselt number if the fluid temperature is 640 K and the wall temperature is 680 K. Assume that a very short section of pipe is being considered so that 640 K is the mean bulk temperature.

Answer. The Sleicher–Rouse equations for liquid metals apply:

Constant heat flow

$$N_{\text{Nu,mb}} = 6.3 + 0.0167(N_{\text{Re,f}})^{0.85}(N_{\text{Pr,w}})^{0.93} \qquad N_{\text{Pr,w}} \leq 0.1 \qquad (11.71)$$

Constant wall temperature

$$N_{\text{Nu,mb}} = 4.8 + 0.0156(N_{\text{Re,f}})^{0.85}(N_{\text{Pr,w}})^{0.93} \qquad N_{\text{Pr,w}} \leq 0.1 \qquad (11.72)$$

These equations require physical properties at T_{mb} (640 K), T_{w} (680 K), and T_{f}, which from Eq. (11.32) is

$$T_{\text{f}} = (T_{\text{w}} + T_{\text{b}})/2 = (680 + 640)/2 = 660 \text{ K} \tag{i}$$

The physical properties needed for these equations are estimated in Table 11.3, which was prepared by a linear interpolation from data at 644 K and 977 K [I1]. The kinematic viscosity v is in the definition of Reynolds number:

$$N_{\text{Re}} = d_i U_{z,\text{ave}}/v \tag{ii}$$

Therefore, the film Reynolds number is

$$N_{\text{Re,f}} = N_{\text{Re}}(v_{\text{mb}}/v_{\text{f}}) = (50\,000)(2.88 \times 10^{-7})/(2.84 \times 10^{-7}) = 50\,700 \tag{iii}$$

From Table 11.3, the Prandtl number at the wall is 8.74×10^{-3}. The Nusselt numbers and heat transfer coefficients follow from Eqs. (11.71) and (11.72):

Constant heat flow

$$N_{\text{Nu,mb}} = 6.3 + 0.0167(N_{\text{Re,f}})^{0.85}(N_{\text{Pr,w}})^{0.93}$$

$$= 6.3 + (0.0167)(50\,700)^{0.85}(8.74 \times 10^{-3})^{0.93} = 8.33 \tag{iv}$$

$$h = (N_{\text{Nu,mb}})(k_{\text{mb}}/d_i) = (8.33)(27.48)/(0.04)$$

$$= 5723 \text{ W m}^{-2}\text{ K}^{-1} = 1010 \text{ Btu ft}^{-2}\text{ h}^{-1}\,^{\circ}\text{F}^{-1} \tag{v}$$

TABLE 11.3
Estimated physical properties of NaK for Example 11.6

T, K	v, m^2 s^{-1}	k, W m^{-1} K^{-1}	N_{Pr}
640	2.88×10^{-7}	27.48	9.14×10^{-3}
660	2.84×10^{-7}	27.57	8.94×10^{-3}
680	2.80×10^{-7}	27.65	8.74×10^{-3}

Constant wall temperature

$$N_{Nu,mb} = 4.8 + 0.0156(N_{Re,f})^{0.85}(N_{Pr,w})^{0.93}$$

$$= 4.8 + (0.0156)(50\,700)^{0.85}(8.74 \times 10^{-3})^{0.93} = 6.70 \qquad \text{(vi)}$$

$$h = (N_{Nu,mb})(k_{mb}/d_i) = (6.70)(27.48)/(0.04)$$

$$= 4600 \text{ W m}^{-2}\text{ K}^{-1} = 810 \text{ Btu ft}^{-2}\text{ h}^{-1}\,{}^{\circ}\text{F}^{-1} \qquad \text{(vii)}$$

The constant wall boundary condition is probably more apropos. Note that this example problem used the same pipe and the same Reynolds number as Example 11.5. For liquid metals, the Nusselt number was much lower, 6.70 as compared to over 300 for water, but the heat transfer coefficient was comparable as a result of the large thermal conductivity: 27.5, compared with 0.598 W m^{-1} K^{-1} for water at 20°C.

11.4 DOUBLE-PIPE HEAT EXCHANGER

A double-pipe heat exchanger is shown in Fig. 11.10. Among heat exchangers the double-pipe model is particularly simple and easy to understand. Double-pipe heat exchangers are fairly common, especially where the temperature driving force is large and the transfer area small, say 15 m^2 (150 ft^2) or less [M2].

In Fig. 11.10, fluid A is flowing in the annular space between the pipes, and fluid B enters from the opposite end and flows inside the smaller pipe or tube. This case is called counterflow, as depicted in Fig. 11.11(a). For cocurrent (parallel) operation, both fluids A and B enter the equipment at the same end, as shown in Fig. 11.11(b). A third case is that in which one fluid changes phase. Figure 11.11(c) presents the case of the hot fluid condensing as a result of heat exchange with a cold fluid. Note that the left-hand end of the exchanger is denoted as "1", and the other as "2". This convention allows the same equations to hold for all cases. Not shown and less common is the case in which the cold fluid boils. That temperature profile is the mirror image (vertically) of that in Fig. 11.11(c).

Temperature notation. The equations for the double-pipe heat exchanger are all expressed in terms of the mean bulk temperature, Eq. (11.31). The

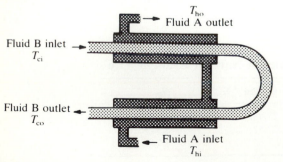

FIGURE 11.10
Double-pipe heat exchanger.

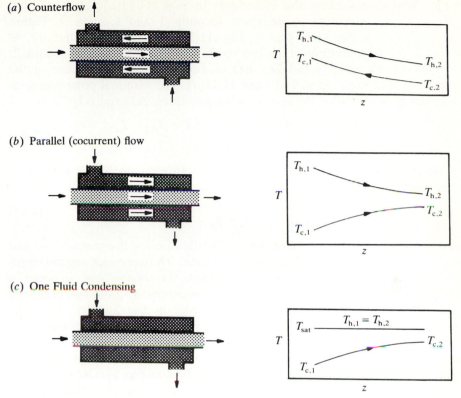

FIGURE 11.11
Flow configurations in the double-pipe heat exchanger.

subscript b is dropped for the sake of clarity, however. There are four bulk average temperatures in conjunction with Fig. 11.10. It is convenient to denote the two fluids as hot (h) and cold (c), rather than as A and B. It makes no difference in the following analysis whether fluid A (in the annular section) is hot or cold.

Two separate sets of notation are required in order to develop the design equations for heat exchangers. In Fig. 11.10, the inlet and outlet temperatures are denoted as follows:

$$T_{hi} = \text{inlet temperature, annular-side (or hot) fluid}$$
$$T_{ho} = \text{outlet temperature, annular-side (or hot) fluid}$$
$$T_{ci} = \text{inlet temperature, tube-side (or cold) fluid}$$
$$T_{co} = \text{outlet temperature, tube-side (or cold) fluid}$$

(11.85)

For utilization of the equations to be developed in this section, it makes no difference whether the cold fluid is on the tube side [cf. Eq. (11.85)] or on the outside. When considering the exchangers in Figs. 11.11(a), 11.11(b), and 11.11(c), it is convenient to designate location 1 and location 2. Figure 11.11(a), which is the same case as Fig. 11.10, indicates this notation. At location 1, the temperatures of the two streams are $T_{h,1}$ and $T_{c,1}$; at location 2, the temperatures are $T_{h,2}$ and $T_{c,2}$. Let us further consider the case of the counterflow exchanger, Figs. 11.10 and 11.11(a). The terminal point temperature differences are called the approach temperatures, ΔT_1 and ΔT_2:

$$\begin{aligned} \text{Approach at location 1:} &\quad \Delta T_1 = T_{h,1} - T_{c,1} \\ \text{Approach at location 2:} &\quad \Delta T_2 = T_{h,2} - T_{c,2} \end{aligned} \tag{11.86}$$

The range of each stream is the absolute difference between inlet and outlet temperatures:

$$\begin{aligned} \text{Hot fluid range:} &\quad \Delta T_h = T_{hi} - T_{ho} = |T_{h,1} - T_{h,2}| \\ \text{Cold fluid range:} &\quad \Delta T_c = T_{co} - T_{ci} = |T_{c,2} - T_{c,1}| \end{aligned} \tag{11.87}$$

Figure 11.11 also shows the temperature distribution for the counterflow and parallel cases where neither fluid changes phase. The approach temperatures for parallel flow are defined identically to those for counterflow, as noted in Figs. 11.11(a) and 11.11(b). Usually the counterflow operation is preferred since the driving force can become very small in the parallel case. The counterflow configuration allows the temperature of each exiting stream to approach that of the stream entering at the same end. Parallel operation has proven successful when the cold stream is heat-sensitive because the cold stream approaches a well-defined plateau, as shown in Fig. 11.11(b).

When the hot fluid is a condensing vapor, as in Fig. 11.11(c), the temperature of the hot fluid is essentially constant and equal to the saturation temperature T_{sat}. For a pure vapor, the saturation temperature is governed by the pressure in the annulus. The approach temperatures become

$$\begin{aligned} \text{Approach at location 1:} &\quad \Delta T_1 = T_{h,1} - T_{c,1} = T_{sat} - T_{c,1} \\ \text{Approach at location 2:} &\quad \Delta T_2 = T_{h,2} - T_{c,2} = T_{sat} - T_{c,2} \end{aligned} \tag{11.88}$$

The case of a hot fluid transferring heat to a cold fluid which is evaporating is less common in a double-pipe heat exchanger.

The notation ΔT is used to denote the driving force for heat transfer between hot and cold streams at a given point in the exchanger:

$$\Delta T = T_h - T_c \tag{11.89}$$

When for each fluid the products of heat capacity times mass flow rate differ, the driving force ΔT changes with length in the counterflow case.

11.4.1 The Overall Heat Transfer Coefficient

Design of heat exchange equipment is usually formulated in terms of the overall heat transfer coefficient U:

$$q = U_i A_i \, \Delta T = U_o A_o \, \Delta T \tag{11.90}$$

Equation (11.90) emphasizes that there are two overall heat transfer coefficients, U_i and U_o, but this equation has no use for design because both ΔT and U vary with length. The inside overall heat transfer coefficient U_i is based on the inside heat transfer area A_i of the inside pipe or tube in Fig. 11.10. Similarly, U_o is based on A_o. These areas were defined in Eq. (11.27). The existence of two heat transfer coefficients is admittedly confusing. Either is valid, however, and it is common to choose whichever corresponds to the largest resistance in Eq. (11.28) (cf. Fig. 11.5). Note that ΔT is defined in Eq. (11.89) as the driving force for the heat transfer, the bulk temperature of the hot fluid minus that of the cold. Also, U_i and U_o are related by

$$\frac{U_o}{U_i} = \frac{A_o}{A_i} = \frac{d_o}{d_i} \tag{11.91}$$

as is obvious from Eqs. (11.27) and (11.90).

Now let us consider the resistance to heat transfer in Fig. 11.10. At any cross section in the exchanger, there are three phases, fluid h, fluid c, and the pipe wall. Following the analysis in Section 11.1.4, there must be two convection resistances, as given by Eq. (11.26), and one conduction resistance as given by Eq. (11.17). Equation (11.23) still applies

$$-q_r = \frac{\Delta T}{\Sigma\, R_i} \tag{11.23}$$

where ΔT is from Eq. (11.89) and the sum of the resistances for the double-pipe heat exchanger is

$$R_i = \frac{1}{h_i A_i} + \frac{\ln(d_o/d_i)}{2\pi L k_m} + \frac{1}{h_o A_o} \tag{11.92}$$

Comparing Eqs. (11.23) and (11.92) with Eq. (11.90) yields for the overall heat transfer coefficients:

$$\frac{1}{U_o A_o} = \frac{1}{U_i A_i} = \frac{1}{h_i A_i} + \frac{\ln(d_o/d_i)}{2\pi L k_m} + \frac{1}{h_o A_o} \tag{11.93}$$

This equation may be solved for either U_i or U_o:

$$\frac{1}{U_i} = \frac{1}{h_i} + \frac{A_i \ln(d_o/d_i)}{2\pi L k_m} + \frac{A_i}{A_o h_o} \tag{11.94}$$

$$\frac{1}{U_o} = \frac{A_o}{A_i h_i} + \frac{A_o \ln(d_o/d_i)}{2\pi L K_m} + \frac{1}{h_o} \tag{11.95}$$

These important equations are used frequently in the design of heat exchangers.

It is possible to have more than the three resistances that are included in Eq. (11.92). One example is an outside steam pipe with insulation. In this case, there are two convection resistances and two conduction resistances. Contact resistance and fouling may require other resistances to be included, as

TABLE 11.4
Approximate magnitudes of heat transfer coefficients*

Application	Range of values	
	h, W m^{-2} K^{-1}	h, Btu ft^{-2} h^{-1} °F^{-1}
Steam (dropwise condensation)	3×10^4–1×10^5	5×10^3–2×10^4
Steam (film-type condensation)	5×10^3–2×10^4	1×10^3–3×10^3
Boiling water	2×10^3–5×10^4	300–9×10^4
Condensing organic vapors	1×10^3–2×10^3	200–400
Water (heating)	300–2×10^4	50–3×10^3
Oils (heating or cooling)	60–2×10^3	10–300
Steam (superheating)	30–100	5–20
Air (heating or cooling)	1–60	0.2–10

* From McAdams, *Heat Transmission*, 3d ed., p. 5, McGraw-Hill, New York, 1954. By permission.

will be discussed in the next section. Equation (11.95) contains two convection coefficients, h_i and h_o, which were defined in Eq. (11.3) and Eq. (11.26). Heat transfer coefficients may be defined by similar equations for a variety of heat transfer applications. Some common examples are boiling, condensation, radiation, and natural convection. Table 11.4 indicates some typical values of heat transfer coefficients; note that the variation is of the order of 10^5.

11.4.2   Contact Resistance and Fouling Factors

Previous discussion has neglected the fact that whenever two solids are in contact, there may be an additional resistance to heat transfer due to imperfect contact. One example occurs in the installation of insulation around a pipe. Insulation is often held in place by means of metal straps. Obviously the thermal expansion coefficients of the pipe, the insulation, and the straps are all different. Hence, the tightness of the fit will vary with temperature. In this case, the existence of an additional resistance between the pipe and the insulation will serve to increase the effectiveness of the insulation. Another common example is that of fins attached to tubes or to other surfaces in order to increase the area available for heat transfer. Common examples include finned-tube heat exchangers in car radiators and air conditioners, as well as fins on air-cooled engines such as used in lawn mowers. Whenever the fins are imperfectly joined to the solid object, an additional resistance will be needed in Eq. (11.23). The contact resistance may be due to a pair of rough surfaces that touch in some spots and have voids elsewhere. In this case, there is a conduction resistance in parallel with a convection resistance through the void spaces. The contact resistance may simply be due to a poor fit. Although some analysis is possible, in general contact resistances must be determined experimentally. A more complete discussion is available [F2].

Fouling factors. The heat exchange surfaces can become dirty during operation because of corrosion or deposition of contaminants on the heat exchange surfaces. The term fouling denotes that the heat transfer surfaces have been altered by such processes. Thus, when fouling occurs on both surfaces, there is a total of five resistances to heat transfer. Equations (11.92) through (11.95) require two additional resistances corresponding to the resistances to heat transfer on the inside and outside surfaces as a result of the fouling. If the fouling resistance is expressed in the form of two additional coefficients $h_{i,f}$ or $h_{o,f}$, Eq. (11.92) becomes

$$R_i = \frac{1}{h_{i,f}A_i} + \frac{1}{h_iA_i} + \frac{\ln(d_o/d_i)}{2\pi L k_m} + \frac{1}{h_oA_o} + \frac{1}{h_{o,f}A_o} \qquad (11.96)$$

where $h_{i,f}$ and $h_{o,f}$ are the inside and outside fouling film coefficients, respectively. Fouling film coefficients are usually in the range of 1700–5700 W m^{-2} K^{-1} [M2].

Practically all industrial heat exchangers undergo fouling after a period of time, especially exchangers using water or steam. This fouling represents lower overall coefficients and thus decreased performance. Fouling factors cannot be calculated from theory; they must be obtained experimentally. There are several ways to express fouling factors quantitatively besides Eq. (11.96). One way is to define a fouling factor R_f by determining values of U_o or U_i for both clean and dirty conditions [K4]:

$$\frac{1}{U_{\text{dirty}}} = R_f + \frac{1}{U_{\text{clean}}} \qquad (11.97)$$

where values of R_f are given in Table 11.5. Note that use of Eq. (11.97) and

TABLE 11.5
Typical values for fouling resistance*

Types of fluid	Fouling factor	
	h ft^2 °F Btu^{-1}	m^2 K W^{-1}
Sea water below 50°C	0.0005	0.00009
Sea water above 50°C	0.001	0.0002
Treated boiler feed water above 50°C	0.001	0.0002
Fuel oil	0.005	0.0009
Quenching oil	0.004	0.0007
Alcohol vapors	0.0005	0.00009
Steam, non-oil-bearing	0.0005	0.00009
Industrial air	0.002	0.0004
Refrigerating liquid	0.001	0.0002

*From Holman, *Heat Transfer,* 4th ed., p. 392, McGraw-Hill, New York, 1976, modified from the Tubular Exchangers Manufacturers Association [T1]. By permission.

Table 11.5 emphasizes only one fouling resistance. Better tabulations are avaialble [P1, T1].

There is a tremendous amount of uncertainty in choosing values for fouling resistances or fouling film coefficients. In dirty service, these resistances are continuously increasing with time. Nevertheless, it is possible to design so as to minimize fouling. In the first place, the fluid most likely to foul is placed on the inside of the tube. Secondly, heat exchanger tubes are carefully manufactured with extremely close tolerances on the inside diameter. This precision allows the tube to be cleaned easily by disassembling the heat exchanger and pushing out the build-up with a metal rod. In fact, this is a routine procedure, and many companies are available to perform this task. The design engineer should also keep in mind that many fluids, especially organic liquids, do not foul at all. Furthermore, fouling rates decrease with increasing fluid velocity. The rule of thumb is to attempt to design with velocities above 3 m s^{-1} [P1].

11.4.3   Design Equations

Enthalpy balance. Application of the first law of thermodynamics, Eq. (7.45), to a heat exchanger results in

$$\Delta_H = 0 = \Delta H_{\text{hot fluid}} + \Delta H_{\text{cold fluid}} \tag{11.98}$$

Since there is no pump or turbine in the exchanger, kinetic and potential energy changes are small, and the usual assumption is that the heat exchanger is insulated from its surroundings so that q is zero. Equation (11.98) is commonly called an enthalpy balance and states that the enthalpy change in the hot fluid plus the enthalpy change in the cold fluids adds algebraically to zero. If neither fluid changes phase, then in differential form Eq. (11.98) becomes

$$dH_h = w_h c_h \, dT_h$$
$$dH_c = w_c c_c \, dT_c \tag{11.99}$$

where the signs of dH_h and dH_c are governed by the signs of dT_h and dT_c, respectively. In Eq. (11.99) and subsequent equations, c_h and c_c refer to the heat capacities at constant pressure, and w_h and w_c are the mass flow rates of the hot and cold fluids, respectively. If the heat capacities are not functions of temperature, each part of Eq. (11.99) can be integrated at steady-state and included in Eq. (11.98):

$$w_h c_h (T_{ho} - T_{hi}) + w_c c_c (T_{co} - T_{ci}) = 0 \tag{11.100}$$

This equation must always be satisfied in a heat exchanger.

Next, a heat balance on a differential element in a counterflow exchanger will be considered, as shown in Fig. 11.12. At steady-state, the enthalpy decrease of the hot fluid is

$$dH_h = -dq = w_h c_h \, dT_h \tag{11.101}$$

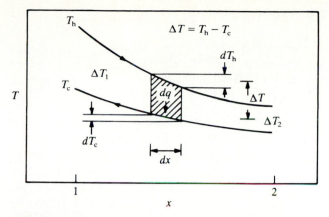

FIGURE 11.12
Balance on a differential element—counterflow exchanger.

where dT_h is negative as shown in Fig. 11.12. The cold fluid flows in the opposite direction. The enthalpy increase of the cold fluid is

$$dH_c = dq = w_c c_c \, dT_c \qquad (11.102)$$

An expression for dq is

$$dq = w_c c_c \, dT_c = -w_h c_h \, dT_h \qquad (11.103)$$

It is convenient to solve Eq. (11.103) for dT_c and dT_h:

$$dT_h = \frac{-dq}{w_h c_h}$$

$$dT_c = \frac{dq}{w_c c_c} \qquad (11.104)$$

From Fig. 11.12 and Eq. (11.104), it is seen that $d(\Delta T)$ is

$$d(\Delta T) = d(T_h - T_c) = dT_h - dT_c = (-dq)\left(\frac{1}{w_h c_h} + \frac{1}{w_c c_c}\right) \qquad (11.105)$$

Equation (11.90) can also be expressed in differential form:

$$dq = U_i(T_h - T_c) \, dA_i = U_o(T_h - T_c) \, dA_o \qquad (11.106)$$

Equation (11.106) is the general design equation for double-pipe heat exchangers. In many problems, both U and ΔT vary with position in the exchanger, sometimes nonlinearly. Hence, Eq. (11.106) is usually rearranged for integration according to the problem at hand, often in combination with Eq. (11.98), the enthalpy balance. Equation (11.106) will next be solved for some commonly encountered cases.

 If neither hot nor cold fluid changes phase, then it is useful to eliminate

dq by combining Eqs. (11.105) and (11.106):

$$\frac{d(\Delta T)}{\Delta T} = \frac{d(T_h - T_c)}{T_h - T_c} = -\left(\frac{1}{w_h c_h} + \frac{1}{w_c c_c}\right) U_i \, dA_i$$

$$= -\left(\frac{1}{w_h c_h} + \frac{1}{w_c c_c}\right) U_o \, dA_o \tag{11.107}$$

If the overall heat transfer coefficient varies with length in the exchanger, then a numerical or graphical solution will be required. The exact manner in which the equations in this section must be combined depends on what the design engineer is given and needs to find. For instance, if all temperatures, flow rates, physical properties and convection correlations are given, then the unknown is the size of the exchanger, i.e., the area. The solution begins by finding the total duty q_{total} of the exchanger from integration of Eq. (11.103) for either fluid:

$$q_{total} = \int_{T_{hi}}^{T_{ho}} w_h c_h \, dT_h = \int_{T_{ci}}^{T_{co}} w_c c_c \, dT_c \tag{11.108}$$

or if the heat capacity may be assumed constant:

$$q_{total} = w_h c_h (T_{ho} - T_{hi}) = w_c c_c (T_{co} - T_{ci}) \tag{11.109}$$

Either Eq. (11.105) or (11.106) must be integrated with the following boundary conditions:

	Location 1	Location 2	
z	0	L	(11.110)
q	0	q_{total}	
A	0	A_{total}	
ΔT	ΔT_1	ΔT_2	

where ΔT_1 and ΔT_2 are the approach temperatures defined earlier and ΔT is the driving force for heat transfer [cf. Eq. (11.89)]. One result is

$$q_{total} = \int_0^{A_{total,i}} U_i \, \Delta T \, dA_i = \int_0^{A_{total,o}} U_o \, \Delta T \, dA_o \tag{11.111}$$

A more useful set of equations for trial and error calculations, also based on Eq. (11.106), is

$$A_i = \int_0^{q_{total}} \frac{dq}{U_i \, \Delta T} \quad \text{or} \quad A_o = \int_0^{q_{total}} \frac{dq}{U_o \, \Delta t} \tag{11.112}$$

Equation (11.112) allows the length to be divided into a series of small increments when U varies strongly and nonlinearly throughout the exchanger. Generally, dq will be replaced with $w c_p \, dT$, where either the hot or cold fluid (whichever is more convenient) can be used:

$$A_i = \int_{T_1}^{T_2} \frac{w c_p \, dT}{U_i \, \Delta T} \quad \text{or} \quad A_o = \int_{T_1}^{T_2} \frac{w c_p \, dT}{U_o \, \Delta T} \tag{11.113}$$

Both the enthalpy balance, Eq. (11.108), and the transport equation, Eq. (11.112), must be satisfied. Equation (11.113) combines both into a useful equation. Next, some useful solutions to Eqs. (11.112) and (11.113) will be presented.

11.4.4 Simple Solutions

The simplest solution to the design of a double-pipe heat exchanger makes the following assumptions: (1) U is constant throughout; (2) fluid properties (c_h and c_c) are constant; (3) no heat losses from exchanger to surroundings; (4) steady-state; and (5) flow is either counterflow or parallel, as in Fig. 11.11(a, b, c). Then Eq. (11.107) is integrated according to the limits in Eq. (11.110):

$$\left(\ln \frac{T_{h,2} - T_{c,2}}{T_{h,1} - T_{c,1}}\right) \bigg/ \left(\frac{1}{w_h c_h} + \frac{1}{w_c c_c}\right) = U_o A_o = U_i A_i \tag{11.114}$$

Log-mean temperature difference. The log-mean form has been previously introduced, beginning in Chapter 4 with Eq. (4.29) for log-mean area. Equation (11.114) can be represented in another form by eliminating flow rates and heat capacities with the enthalpy balance, Eq. (11.109), which reintroduces q:

$$\frac{q_{\text{total}}}{U_o A_o} = \frac{q_{\text{total}}}{U_i A_i} = \frac{(T_{h,2} - T_{c,2}) - (T_{h,1} - T_{c,1})}{\ln[(T_{h,2} - T_{c,2})/(T_{h,1} - T_{c,1})]} = \frac{\Delta T_2 - \Delta T_1}{\ln(\Delta T_2/\Delta T_1)}$$

$$= \Delta T_{\text{lm}} = \text{LMTD} \tag{11.115}$$

Equation (11.115) defines the log-mean temperature difference ΔT_{lm}, which is commonly abbreviated LMTD. The assumptions used in Eq. (11.114) are fairly reasonable, except for assuming U to be constant. In practice, U may vary over a wide range.

Linear overall coefficient. A solution more accurate than Eq. (11.114) may be obtained by assuming that U varies linearly throughout the exchanger. Let U_1 and U_2 be the overall coefficients at the ends of the exchanger where the approach temperatures are ΔT_1 and ΔT_2 and ΔT is given by Eq. (11.89). Equation (11.109) can be solved once for $1/(w_h c_h)$ and once for $1/(w_c c_c)$. The sum of these can be substituted into Eq. (11.107) and the result rearranged to the following form:

$$\frac{q}{\Delta T_2 - \Delta T_1} \int_{\Delta T_1}^{\Delta T_2} \frac{d(\Delta T)}{U_i \, \Delta T} = \int_0^{A_i} dA_i \qquad \text{or} \qquad \frac{q}{\Delta T_2 - \Delta T_1} \int_{\Delta T_1}^{\Delta T_2} \frac{d(\Delta T)}{U_o \, \Delta T} = \int_0^{A_o} dA_o$$

$$\tag{11.116}$$

Beginning with this equation, Colburn [C3] derived the following:

$$q_{\text{total}} = A_{\text{total}} \left(\frac{U_2 \, \Delta T_1 - U_1 \, \Delta T_2}{\ln[(U_2 \, \Delta T_1)/(U_1 \, \Delta T_2)]}\right) \tag{11.117}$$

where A_{total}, U_1, and U_2 are all based on either the inside area or the outside area. Equation (11.117) is often useful when U varies substantially with temperature. The procedure is to divide the exchanger into a number of small increments, and assume that Eq. (11.117) applies across each increment. It can also be used as a rough but quick approximation to the performance of a heat exchanger.

Example 11.7. It is desired to heat 12 gpm of water from 50°F to 110°F. Saturated steam at 67 psia is available. Estimate (a) the duty of the exchanger, (b) the number of pounds per hour of steam required, and (c) the length of a double-pipe heat exchanger to perform this task. Use $\frac{3}{4}$-in. 16-BWG tubing with steam on the shell side and water on the tube side. For simplicity let the heat transfer coefficient of water and steam be constant and equal to 80 and 500 Btu h^{-1} ft^{-2} °F^{-1} respectively. Neglect fouling.

Answer. In this problem, the overall heat transfer coefficient is constant. Hence, the length of exchanger is found from Eq. (11.114) or Eq. (11.115). Table B.2 provides the following for $\frac{3}{4}$-in. tubing, 16-BWG thickness:

$$d_i = 0.620 \text{ in.} \qquad A_i = 0.1623 \text{ ft}^2 \text{ per ft}$$
$$d_o = 0.750 \text{ in.} \qquad A_o = 0.1963 \text{ ft}^2 \text{ per ft}$$
$$1 \text{ ft s}^{-1} = 0.9425 \text{ gpm} = 471.3 \text{ lb}_m \text{ h}^{-1} \tag{i}$$

An important design consideration is the flow rate of 67 psia steam required to heat the 12 gpm of cold water. The monetary value of the steam can be calculated from the flow rate by an economic analysis. The steam flow rate is found from an enthalpy balance around the exchanger. The usual practice is to find the enthalpy of steam in a "steam table" [P1]; the temperature of saturated steam at 67 psia is 300°F. Both the temperature and pressure of the steam will be assumed to be constant in the exchanger. The enthalpy of water vapor is 1179.7 Btu lb$_m^{-1}$, and the enthalpy of liquid water is 269.59 Btu lb$_m^{-1}$, both at 67 psia and 300°F. The mass flow of liquid water in the tube is

$$w_c = (12)(471.3)/(0.9425) \, [(\text{gal min}^{-1})(\text{lb}_m \text{ h}^{-1})/(\text{gal min}^{-1})]$$
$$= 6000 \text{ lb}_m \text{ h}^{-1} \tag{ii}$$

The duty is found from Eq. (11.108) with the heat capacity of water approximately 1.0 Btu lb$_m^{-1}$ °F^{-1}:

$$q_{total} = \int_{T_{ci}}^{T_{co}} w_c c_c \, dT_c = w_c c_c (T_{co} - T_{ci})$$
$$= (6000)(1.0)(110 - 50) \, [(\text{lb}_m \text{ h}^{-1})(\text{Btu lb}_m^{-1} \text{ °F}^{-1})(\text{°F})]$$
$$= 3.6 \times 10^5 \text{ Btu h}^{-1} \tag{iii}$$

The mass flow of steam is calculated starting from Eq. (11.98). The duty is the enthalpy increase of the cold stream, Eq. (iii), which equals the enthalpy decrease of the hot stream. Since the enthalpy change of the steam is its mass times its enthalpy of vaporization, the mass flow rate of steam is:

$$w_h = \frac{\Delta H_{cold \, water}}{\Delta H_{vaporization}} = \frac{3.6 \times 10^5}{1179.7 - 269.59} \left(\frac{\text{Btu h}^{-1}}{\text{Btu lb}_m^{-1}} \right) = 395.6 \text{ lb}_m \text{ h}^{-1} \tag{iv}$$

The areas for heat transfer are the table values (ft^2 per ft) times the length L:

$$A_i = 0.1623L \text{ ft}^2 \qquad A_o = 0.1963L \text{ ft}^2 \tag{v}$$

The inside overall heat transfer coefficient U_i will be selected, since the tube-side resistance is the highest. With the thermal conductivity of steel as $26 \text{ Btu h}^{-1} \text{ft}^{-1} \text{°F}^{-1}$, U_i is calculated from Eq. (11.94):

$$\frac{1}{U_i} = \frac{1}{h_i} + \frac{A_i \ln(d_o/d_i)}{2\pi L k_m} + \frac{A_i}{A_o h_o} = \frac{1}{80} + \frac{(0.1623)(L)[\ln(0.750/0.620)]}{(2\pi)(L)(26)}$$

$$+ \frac{(0.1623)(L)}{(0.1963)(L)(500)}$$

$$= 0.0125 + 1.891 \times 10^{-4} + 0.001654$$

$$= 1.434 \times 10^{-2} \text{ h ft}^2 \text{ °F Btu}^{-1} \tag{vi}$$

From Eq. (vi), U_i is the reciprocal of 1.434×10^{-2}, or $69.7 \text{ Btu h}^{-1} \text{ft}^{-2} \text{°F}^{-1}$.

Since U_i is assumed constant for this example, Eq. (11.115) can be used directly to find the area required to transfer $3.6 \times 10^5 \text{ Btu h}^{-1}$:

$$\frac{q_{total}}{U_o A_o} = \frac{q_{total}}{U_i A_i} = \frac{(T_{h,2} - T_{c,2}) - (T_{h,1} - T_{c,1})}{\ln[(T_{h,2} - T_{c,2})/(T_{h,1} - T_{c,1})]} = \frac{\Delta T_2 - \Delta T_1}{\ln(\Delta T_2/\Delta T_1)}$$

$$= \Delta T_{lm} = \text{LMTD} \tag{11.115}$$

The approach temperatures from Eq. (11.88) are

$$\Delta T_1 = T_{sat} - T_{c,1} = 300 - 50 = 250 \text{ deg F}$$
$$\Delta T_2 = T_{sat} - T_{c,2} = 300 - 110 = 190 \text{ deg F} \tag{vii}$$

First, the log-mean temperature difference is found from Eq. (11.115):

$$\text{LMTD} = \frac{\Delta T_2 - \Delta T_1}{\ln(\Delta T_2/\Delta T_1)} = \frac{190 - 250}{\ln(190/250)} = 218.6 \text{ deg F} \tag{viii}$$

Next, Eq. (11.115) is solved for the inside area:

$$A_i = \frac{q_{total}}{(U_i)(\text{LMTD})} = \frac{(3.6 \times 10^5)}{(69.7)(218.6)} = 23.63 \text{ ft}^2 \tag{ix}$$

The length of the exchanger comes from Eq. (v):

$$L = \frac{A_i}{0.1623} = 145.6 \text{ ft} \tag{x}$$

This answer indicates that a double-pipe heat exchanger is not practical because a length of 145.6 ft is too long. Better designs might increase the heat transfer coefficient on the tube side, since h_i is always greater than the largest U_i or U_o. Another possibility is to use a shell-and-tube or a multipass heat exchanger, which will be described in Section 11.5.

Example 11.8. Water enters a double-pipe heat exchanger at 50°F and 12 gpm. The inside tube is $\frac{3}{4}$-in., 16-BWG tubing stock, 30 ft long. Saturated steam at 67 psia is introduced in the shell side. Let the heat transfer coefficients of water and steam be 80 and 500 Btu h^{-1} ft^{-2} °F^{-1}, respectively. If fouling is negligible, estimate the outlet temperature of the water.

Answer. The physical dimensions of the tube are identical to those in Example 11.7. Hence for a 30 ft length:

$$A_i = (0.1623)(L) = (0.1623)(30) = 4.869 \text{ ft}^2 \tag{i}$$

Also, U_i is unchanged from the previous problem as are the properties of the hot fluid (steam) and the cold fluid flow rate.

The enthalpy balance is not useful immediately in this problem because neither the steam flow rate nor the cold water outlet temperature is known. The solution proceeds by equating the enthalpy change of the cold fluid, Eq. (11.103), with the heat transferred through the tube wall from the hot fluid to the cold fluid, Eq. (11.106):

$$dq = w_c c_c \, dT_c = U_i (T_h - T_c) \, dA_i \tag{ii}$$

The boundary conditions are

$$A_i(z = 0) = 0$$
$$A_i(z = L) = A_{\text{total}} = 4.869 \text{ ft}^2$$
$$T(z = 0) = T_{c,1} = 50°F \tag{iii}$$
$$T(z = L) = T_{c,2}$$

The variables in Eq. (ii) are separated:

$$\frac{dT_c}{T_h - T_c} = \frac{U_i}{w_c c_c} \, dA_i \tag{iv}$$

Next, this equation is integrated with the above boundary conditions:

$$-\ln \frac{T_{h,2} - T_{c,2}}{T_{h,1} - T_{c,1}} = -\ln \frac{T_{\text{sat}} - T_{c,2}}{T_{\text{sat}} - T_{c,1}} = \ln \frac{\Delta T_1}{\Delta T_2} = \frac{U_i A_i}{w_c c_c} \tag{v}$$

Equation (v) is solved for ΔT_2 and the numbers inserted:

$$\Delta T_2 = \Delta T_1 / \exp[(U_i A_i)/(w_c c_c)] = (300 - 50)/\exp\{[(69.7)(4.869)]/[(6000)(1.0)]\}$$
$$= (250)(0.9450) = 236.3 \text{ deg F} \tag{vi}$$

Therefore, the outlet temperature of the cold fluid is

$$T_{c,2} = T_{h,2} - \Delta T_2 = T_{\text{sat}} - \Delta T_2 = 300 - 236.3 = 63.7°F \tag{vii}$$

If desired, the duty of this exchanger and the steam flow rate can be found as in the previous example.

Example 11.9. Repeat Example 11.8 if the water side fouling factor is 0.002 h ft^2 °F Btu^{-1}.

Answer. Table 11.5 indicates that 0.002 is a reasonable value for a typical fouling factor. Equation (11.97) is solved for U_{dirty}:

$$U_{\text{dirty}} = \frac{1}{R_f + (1/U_{\text{clean}})} = \frac{1}{0.002 + (1/69.685)}$$
$$= 1/0.01635 = 61.16 \text{ Btu h}^{-1} \text{ ft}^{-2} \text{ °F}^{-1} \tag{i}$$

The derivations of Eqs. (iv), (v), and (vi) in Example 11.8 apply here, and ΔT_2 is found using U_{dirty} in place of U_i in Eq. (vi) from that example:

$$\Delta T_2 = \Delta T_1/\exp[(U_{dirty}A_i)/(w_c c_c)]$$

$$= (300 - 50)/\exp\{[(61.16)(4.869)]/[(6000)(1.0)]\} = 237.9 \text{ deg F} \qquad \text{(ii)}$$

The outlet temperature is

$$T_{c,2} = T_{h,2} - \Delta T_2 = 300 - 237.9 = 62.1°F \qquad \text{(iii)}$$

For this problem, fouling reduced the overall heat transfer coefficient by 12 percent, which reduced the range of the cold fluid by 13.5 percent. Sometimes, fouling reduces the amount of heat transferred by much greater amounts.

11.5 MULTIPASS HEAT EXCHANGERS

The double-pipe heat exchanger of Fig. 11.10 is very inefficient for most heat transfer applications. Long pipe lengths, such as the 145.6 ft found in Example 11.7, require high pressure drops, which in turn cause high pumping costs. If several double-pipe exchangers are placed in parallel, the weight of the heavy outer tubes quickly becomes excessive. A better design is to eliminate the outer pipe in favor of a single shell, as shown in Fig. 11.13. The shell-side fluid flows essentially perpendicularly to the inside tubes as a result of the baffles. The exchanger in Fig. 11.13 is called a 1–1 exchanger because it has one shell-side pass and one tube-side pass.

11.5.1 Equipment

Design of heat exchangers is highly developed because of their widespread use in both industry and homes. Often, selection of a piece of heat exchange equipment depends as much on considerations such as the space available as on other factors such as efficiency and cost. Various standards and codes, such as the Standards of the Tubular Exchange Manufacturers Association, abbreviated TEMA [T1], and the ASME-API Unfired Pressure Vessel Code [A1] are helpful in design work.

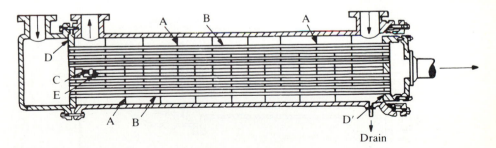

FIGURE 11.13
Single pass 1–1 counterflow heat exchanger. (A) baffles; (B) tubes; (C) guide rods; (D, D') tube sheets; (E) spacer tubes. (*From McCabe, Smith, and Harriott, Unit Operations of Chemical Engineering, 4th ed., p. 383, McGraw-Hill, New York, 1985. By permission.*)

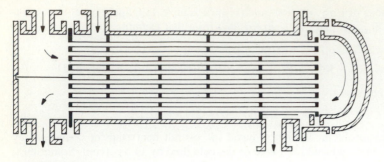

FIGURE 11.14
1–2 Parallel counterflow exchanger. (*From McCabe, Smith, and Harriott, Unit Operations of Chemical Engineering, 4th ed., p. 385, McGraw-Hill, New York, 1985. By permission.*)

The 1–1 exchanger is rarely used except when the shell-side fluid changes phase. The 1–2 or 2–4 heat exchangers, shown in Figs. 11.14 and 11.15, are usually cheaper and more efficient. More complex designs are also used [B2]. The 1–2 exchanger has two passes of fluid on the tube side and one pass on the shell side. Note that the number of passes on the tube side is always even, in order to save on construction costs.

The multipass exchangers of Figs. 11.14 and 11.15, when applied to a given process application, usually have short tubes and high velocities. The high velocities result in higher heat transfer coefficients and less fouling, but considerably higher pressure drops and higher pumping costs than designs having low velocities. Note also that the 1–2 exchanger has nearly parallel flow on the shell side, which is a disadvantage when trying to extract or add as much heat as possible from the shell-side fluid. The 2–4 exchanger in Fig. 11.15 is more counter current and in general can extract more heat from the hot fluid than the 1–2 exchanger. Of course, if one fluid is changing phase (usually on the shell side), then the 1–1 or the 1–2 exchanger may prove cheaper and quite satisfactory. There are many other configurations in

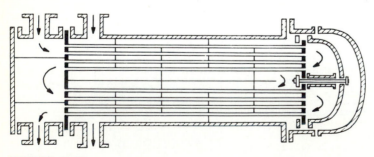

FIGURE 11.15
2–4 Shell-and-tube heat exchanger. (*From McCabe, Smith, and Harriott, Unit Operations of Chemical Engineering, 4th ed., p. 386, McGraw-Hill, 1985. By permission.*)

common use besides the few presented here. For example, for a condenser, a 1–4 exchanger might be most economical.

11.5.2 Design Equations

The log-mean temperature difference was introduced with the five assumptions in conjunction with Eqs. (11.114) and (11.115). In shell-and-tube heat exchangers, the outside flow is neither entirely counterflow nor parallel to the inside flow. The baffles shown in Figs. 11.13 through 11.15 cause cross flow, where the shell-fluid flow is perpendicular to the tubes.

No phase change. For heat exchangers in which the fluids do not change phase and which operate according to the assumptions listed for Eq. (11.114), the quantity LMTD is always less for parallel operation than for counterflow. In multipass exchangers, LMTD lies between these extremes. The differential equations in Section 11.4.3 were integrated by Bowman *et al.* [B2] with the following assumptions:

1. U is constant
2. fluid properties are constant
3. steady-state
4. no phase change for either fluid
5. no heat losses to ambient
6. equal heat transfer surface in each pass
7. no leakage of fluid around any baffles
8. the temperature of the shell-side fluid in any shell-side pass is uniform over any cross section

Bowman *et al.* [B2] introduced two dimensionless ratios:

$$Z = \frac{T_{hi} - T_{ho}}{T_{co} - T_{ci}} = \frac{w_c c_c}{w_h c_h} \tag{11.118}$$

$$\eta_H = \frac{T_{co} - T_{ci}}{T_{hi} - T_{ci}} \tag{11.119}$$

McAdams [M3] calls Z the "hourly heat-capacity ratio", equal to the temperature fall over rise, and η_H the "heating effectiveness". The nomenclature for the temperatures in the equations in this section is

$$\begin{aligned} T_{hi} &= \text{inlet temperature, shell-side (or hot) fluid} \\ T_{ho} &= \text{outlet temperature, shell-side (or hot) fluid} \\ T_{ci} &= \text{inlet temperature, tube-side (or cold) fluid} \\ T_{co} &= \text{outlet temperature, tube-side (or cold) fluid} \end{aligned} \tag{11.120}$$

This notation is very similar to that in Eq. (11.85) for the double-pipe exchanger. The notation selected is consistent with that in Eq. (11.85), and it is arbitrary as to whether the hot fluid is on the shell-side or the tube side. In any case, let the subscripts "hi" and "ho" refer to the fluid on the shell-side. Note that if the shell-side and tube-side temperature definitions are interchanged, the value of the design factor F (to be introduced subsequently) will be unchanged.

For multipass shell-and-tube heat exchangers, the following is the basic design equation:

$$q_{\text{total}} = (U_i A_i)(\text{LMTD}) = (U_o A_o)(\text{LMTD}) \tag{11.121}$$

In this equation, the true mean temperature difference LMTD is defined by

$$\Delta T_1 = T_{\text{hi}} - T_{\text{co}}$$
$$\Delta T_2 = T_{\text{ho}} - T_{\text{ci}} \tag{11.122}$$
$$\text{LMTD} = \frac{F(\Delta T_2 - \Delta T_1)}{\ln[(\Delta T_2)/(\Delta T_1)]}$$

where F is a geometric correction factor applied to the log-mean temperature difference for counterflow, Eq. (11.114). Comparison of the definitions in Eq. (11.122) with that of the approach temperatures, Eq. (11.86), as illustrated in Figs. 11.10 and 11.11(a), shows that ΔT_1 and ΔT_2 are defined as the approach temperatures for a counterflow heat exchanger. Graphs of F versus Z and η_H will be presented for some common designs of heat exchangers for the case of no phase change. Note that $F = 1$ for a 1–1 heat exchanger.

1–2 Heat exchanger. The following equation represents the value of the correction F for the 1–2 heat exchanger:

$$B_1 = (Z^2 + 1)^{0.5}$$

$$F_{1,2} = \left[\frac{B_1}{Z-1} \log_{10}\left(\frac{1-\eta_H}{1-\eta_H Z}\right)\right] \Big/ \left[\log_{10}\left(\frac{(2/\eta_H) - 1 - Z + B_1}{(2/\eta_H) - 1 - Z - B_1}\right)\right] \tag{11.123}$$

Figure 11.16(a) shows a plot of Eq. (11.123) as $F_{1,2}$ versus η_H, with lines of constant Z. Since F is a purely geometric factor, it is immaterial which is the hot or cold fluid; the direction of flow is also immaterial. When F is less than 0.75, the design is unacceptable because the exchanger configuration chosen is inefficient [P1], i.e., the driving force LMTD is reduced to an unacceptably small value.

2–4 Heat exchanger. The following equation represents the value of correction F in the 2–4 heat exchanger:

$$B_1 = (Z^2 + 1)^{0.5}$$
$$B_2 = (2/\eta_H) - 1 - Z + (2/\eta_H)[(1 - \eta_H)(1 - \eta_H Z)]^{0.5}$$
$$F_{2,4} = \left[\frac{B_1}{2(Z-1)} \log_{10}\left(\frac{1-\eta_H}{1-\eta_H Z}\right)\right] \Big/ \left[\log_{10}\left(\frac{B_2 + B_1}{B_2 - B_1}\right)\right] \tag{11.124}$$

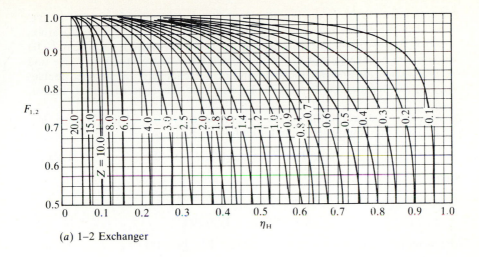

(a) 1–2 Exchanger

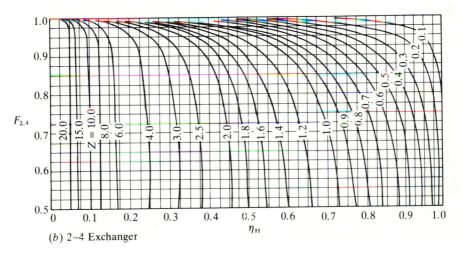

(b) 2–4 Exchanger

FIGURE 11.16
Correction of LMTD for multipass heat exchangers. (*From McCabe, Smith, and Harriott, Unit Operations of Chemical Engineering, 4th ed., p. 390, McGraw-Hill, New York, 1985; as modified from Bowman, Mueller, and Nagle, Trans. ASME* **62:** *283 (1940). By permission.*)

Figure 11.16(*b*) is a plot of Eq. (11.124). Similar plots are available for more complex exchangers [F1, G2, H3, I1, K1, K4, M2, M3, P1].

Phase change. If one fluid in a multipass exchanger changes phase, then Fig. 11.16 does not apply. In fact, if either or both fluids are at constant temperaure, as in a condenser or vaporizer, then the design follows that for a simple double-pipe exchanger, as detailed previously [F1].

Example 11.10. Water at the rate of 1.2 kg s^{-1} is to be heated from 15°C to 50°C by a hot hydrocarbon stream of specific heat 0.45 at 120°C. The hydrocarbon stream is to be cooled to 65°C. Let the overall heat transfer coefficient U_i be constant and equal to 325 W m^{-2} K^{-1}. Calculate the hydrocarbon flow rate and the heat exchanger area for the following heat exchangers: (a) parallel double-pipe; (b) counterflow double-pipe; (c) 1–2 shell-and-tube; and (d) 2–4 shell-tube.

Answer. The hydrocarbon flow rate is determined by the enthalpy balance, Eq. (11.100) and therefore is the same for all four exchangers:

$$w_h c_h (T_{ho} - T_{hi}) + w_c c_c (T_{co} - T_{ci}) = 0 \qquad (11.100)$$

where the temperatures are

$$\begin{aligned} T_{hi} &= 120°C & T_{ho} &= 65°C \\ T_{ci} &= 15°C & T_{co} &= 50°C \end{aligned} \qquad (i)$$

The heat capacity of water is 1.0 kcal kg^{-1} K^{-1} or 4184 J kg^{-1} K^{-1}; the heat capacity of the hydrocarbon is

$$c_h = (4184)(0.45) = 1883 \text{ J kg}^{-1} \text{ K}^{-1} \qquad (ii)$$

For the hydrocarbon flow rate, Eq. (11.100) is solved for w_h and the numbers are inserted:

$$\begin{aligned} w_h &= [(w_c c_c)(T_{co} - T_{ci})]/[(c_h)(T_{hi} - T_{ho})] \\ &= [(1.2)(4184)(50 - 15)]/[(1883)(120 - 65)] = 1.697 \text{ kg s}^{-1} \end{aligned} \qquad (iii)$$

The duty of the exchanger is also identical for all exchangers. From Eq. (11.109), the duty is

$$\begin{aligned} q_{total} &= w_c c_c (T_{co} - T_{ci}) \\ &= (1.2)(4184)(50 - 15) [(\text{kg s}^{-1})(\text{J kg}^{-1} \text{ K}^{-1})(\text{K})] \\ &= 1.757 \times 10^5 \text{ J s}^{-1} = 1.757 \times 10^5 \text{ W} \end{aligned} \qquad (iv)$$

Part (a)—Parallel double-pipe. For this exchanger, the factor F is unity. A summary of the temperature notation for the double-pipe exchanger in parallel flow follows:

$$\begin{aligned} T_{h,1} &= 120°C & T_{h,2} &= 65°C \\ T_{c,1} &= 15°C & T_{c,2} &= 50°C \end{aligned} \qquad (v)$$

Following Eq. (11.86), the approach temperatures are

$$\begin{aligned} \Delta T_1 &= T_{h,1} - T_{c,1} = 120 - 15 = 105 \text{ deg C} = 105 \text{ deg K} \\ \Delta T_2 &= T_{h,2} - T_{c,2} = 65 - 50 = 15 \text{ deg C} = 15 \text{ deg K} \end{aligned} \qquad (vi)$$

For parallel or counterflow double-pipe heat exchangers, Eq. (11.115) applies for the assumptions in this problem:

$$\frac{q_{total}}{U_o A_o} = \frac{q_{total}}{U_i A_i} = \frac{(T_{h,2} - T_{c,2}) - (T_{h,1} - T_{c,1})}{\ln[(T_{h,2} - T_{c,2})/(T_{h,1} - T_{c,1})]} = \frac{\Delta T_2 - \Delta T_1}{\ln(\Delta T_2/\Delta T_1)}$$

$$= \Delta T_{lm} = \text{LMTD} \qquad (11.115)$$

From this equation, the LMTD is

$$\text{LMTD} = \Delta T_{\text{lm}} = \frac{\Delta T_2 - \Delta T_1}{\ln(\Delta T_2/\Delta T_1)} = \frac{15 - 105}{\ln(15/105)} = 46.25 \text{ deg K} \tag{vii}$$

Equation (11.115) is solved for area and the numbers inserted:

$$A_{\text{i}} = q_{\text{total}}/[(U_{\text{i}})(\text{LMTD})]$$
$$= (1.757 \times 10^5)/[(325)(46.25)] \, [(W)(W^{-1} \, \text{m}^2 \, \text{K})(\text{K}^{-1})] = 11.69 \text{ m}^2 \tag{viii}$$

Part (b)—Counterflow double-pipe. For this case, all equations are unchanged from part (a). Again, the factor F is unity. From Fig. 11.11(*a*), the temperature notation for the double-pipe exchanger in counterflow is

$$\begin{aligned} T_{\text{h},1} &= 120°\text{C} & T_{\text{h},2} &= 65°\text{C} \\ T_{\text{c},1} &= 50°\text{C} & T_{\text{c},2} &= 15°\text{C} \end{aligned} \tag{ix}$$

The approach temperatures from Eq. (11.86) are

$$\begin{aligned} \Delta T_1 &= 120 - 50 = 70 \text{ deg C} = 70 \text{ deg K} \\ \Delta T_2 &= 65 - 15 = 50 \text{ deg C} = 50 \text{ deg K} \end{aligned} \tag{x}$$

The LMTD and area from Eq. (11.115) are:

$$\text{LMTD} = \Delta T_{\text{lm}} = \frac{\Delta T_2 - \Delta T_1}{\ln(\Delta T_2/\Delta T_1)} = \frac{50 - 70}{\ln(50/70)} = 59.44 \text{ deg K} \tag{xi}$$

$$A_{\text{i}} = q_{\text{total}}/[(U_{\text{i}})(\text{LMTD})]$$
$$= (1.757 \times 10^5)/[(325)(59.44)] \, [(W)(W^{-1} \, \text{m}^2 \, \text{K})(\text{K}^{-1})] = 9.10 \text{ m}^2 \tag{xii}$$

Part (c)—1-2 Shell-and-tube. If U_{i} is assumed constant, then the area does not depend on which fluid is in the tube side; usually, the water is in the tube side because of fouling considerations. The temperatures in Eq. (11.120) are

$$\begin{aligned} T_{\text{hi}} &= \text{inlet temperature, shell-side (or hot) fluid} = 120°\text{C} \\ T_{\text{ho}} &= \text{outlet temperature, shell-side (or hot) fluid} = 65°\text{C} \\ T_{\text{ci}} &= \text{inlet temperature, tube-side (or cold) fluid} = 15°\text{C} \\ T_{\text{co}} &= \text{outlet temperature, tube-side (or cold) fluid} = 50°\text{C} \end{aligned} \tag{xiii}$$

To evaluate F, the quantities Z and η_{H} are found using Eqs. (11.118) and (11.119):

$$Z = (T_{\text{hi}} - T_{\text{ho}})/(T_{\text{co}} - T_{\text{ci}}) = (w_c c_c)/(w_h c_h) = (120 - 65)/(50 - 15) = 1.57$$
$$\eta_{\text{H}} = (T_{\text{co}} - T_{\text{ci}})/(T_{\text{hi}} - T_{\text{ci}}) = (50 - 15)/(120 - 15) = 0.3333 \tag{xiv}$$

The quantity F can be evaluated from either Eq. (11.123) or Fig. 11.16(*a*), and the value is about 0.92. The LMTD from Eq. (11.122) is

$$\Delta T_1 = T_{\text{hi}} - T_{\text{co}} = 120 - 50 = 70 \text{ deg C} = 70 \text{ deg K}$$
$$\Delta T_2 = T_{\text{ho}} - T_{\text{ci}} = 65 - 15 = 50 \text{ deg C} = 50 \text{ deg K}$$
$$\text{LMTD} = \frac{F(\Delta T_2 - \Delta T_1)}{\ln[(\Delta T_2)/(\Delta T_1)]} = (0.92)(70 - 50)/[\ln(70/50)]$$
$$= (0.92)(59.44) = 54.69°\text{C} = 54.69 \text{ deg K} \tag{xv}$$

TABLE 11.6
Summary of calculated areas

Exchanger type	Required area, m²
(a) Parallel double-pipe	11.69
(b) Counterflow double-pipe	9.10
(c) 1–2 Shell-and-tube	9.89
(d) 2–4 Shell-and-tube	9.33

The approach temperatures calculated in Eq. (xv) are identical to those calculated in Eq. (x) for the counterflow double-pipe. Thus, the LMTD for multipass exchangers is the value for counterflow (59.44 K) times F. The area follows from Eq. (11.121):

$$A_i = q_{total}/[(U_i)(\text{LMTD})]$$
$$= (1.757 \times 10^5)/[(325)(54.68)] \, [(\text{W})(\text{W}^{-1} \, \text{m}^2 \, \text{K})(\text{K}^{-1})] = 9.89 \, \text{m}^2 \quad \text{(xvi)}$$

Part (d)—2–4 Shell-and-tube. The definitions of Eq. (xiii) are unchanged, as are the values of Z and η_H, Eq. (xiv). The quantity F can be evaluated from either Eq. (11.124) or Fig. 11.16(b), and the value is about 0.975. Therefore

$$\text{LMTD} = (0.975)(59.44) = 57.95 \, \text{K} \quad \text{(xvii)}$$
$$A_i = (1.757 \times 10^5)/[(325)(57.95)] \, [(\text{W})(\text{W}^{-1} \, \text{m}^2 \, \text{K})(\text{K}^{-1})] = 9.33 \, \text{m}^2 \quad \text{(xviii)}$$

Summary. Table 11.6 summarizes the results. The counterflow double-pipe exchanger always gives the lowest area when the problem is specified as in this example. However, it is usually not a practical design when the other factors are considered (such as size and weight of the exchanger, variation of U with fluid velocity, temperature-dependent fluid properties, and pressures losses).

11.6 OTHER TOPICS

This chapter has reviewed or presented perhaps all the undergraduate engineer needs to know about heat and mass transfer in duct flow. In addition, the topic of heat transfer by one-dimensional conduction and convection has been discussed, particularly as it relates to transport phenomena. This chapter has also introduced the design of heat transfer equipment that involves flow in ducts. Further texts and references cited as well as further course work can provide a much more in-depth discussion or further extension. For example, computer calculation for heat exchangers is now common; here, the assumptions of constant properties and constant heat transfer coefficients are relaxed, and a stepwise trial-and-error calculation is made along the length of the exchanger. No new principles are introduced in this more precise approach. More detailed discussion of the heat and mass transfer coefficients is possible, i.e., for boiling or condensing fluids, extended surfaces such as fins, and direct contact exchangers involving gas–liquid, liquid–liquid, or gas–liquid–liquid exchange.

PROBLEMS

11.1. A 4-in. schedule 40 pipe is maintained at a temperature of 400 K at the inside wall. The pipe is lagged with a 1-in. layer of 85 percent magnesia pipe covering. On top of the magnesia is a 2-in. layer of fiber glass (see Table 2.2). The outside temperature is 300 K. Compute the heat loss in W and in Btu h^{-1} per 100 ft of pipe. Convert all given data to SI.

11.2. For Problem 11.1:

(a) Compute the temperatures in kelvins at the steel-magnesia interface and the magnesia–fiber glass interface.

(b) Prepare a plot of temperature versus radius. Locate the inside and outside surfaces, the two interfaces, plus three other points inside each insulating material.

11.3. Heat transfer at steady-state in a hollow sphere is one-dimensional if the inside surface is at a constant temperature T_1 and the outside surface is at a constant T_2.

(a) Show that the heat flow is given by

$$-q_r = \frac{4\pi k(T_2 - T_1)}{1/r_1 - 1/r_2}$$

(b) Find the expression for the thermal resistance R.

11.4. The thermal conductivity of rock wool is approximately $0.025 + 0.00005T$ where T is in °F and k is in Btu h^{-1} ft^{-1} °F^{-1}. A 2-in. schedule 40 pipe, 18 ft long, is insulated with a 2-in. layer of rock wool. If the outside temperature of the rock wool is 50°F and the temperature at the pipe–wool interface is 200°F, find the heat loss in Btu h^{-1}.

11.5. Consider the composite wall in Fig. 11.3 where $k_A = 0.28$, $k_B = 0.12$, $k_C = 0.07$, and $k_D = 0.19$, all in W m^{-1} K^{-1}. Let the area of B be 1.5 times the area of C; the area of A is 1 m^2. Let $\Delta x_A = \Delta x_B = \Delta x_C = \Delta x_D = 1.0$ m; neglect the thickness of the insulation. If the overall temperature drop is 100 deg K, compute the heat flow in watts through the wall for unit area. Assume one-dimensional heat flow (i.e., that the boundary between B and C is insulated perfectly).

11.6. A furnace wall is constructed with fire brick ($k = 1.1$ W m^{-1} K^{-1}) of thickness 0.3 m. To reduce heat loss and to prevent burns, the outside of the wall is covered with 0.05 m of an insulating material ($k = 0.086$ W m^{-1} K^{-1}). If the inner wall temperature is 1200 K and the heat flux q/A is 930 W m^{-2}, determine the outside temperature of the insulation. Is the operation safe; if not, what corrections would you make?

11.7. A 3-in. schedule 80 steel pipe is covered with a layer of 85 percent magnesia that is 0.06 m thick. The ambient temperature is 25°C. The pipe contains steam that maintains the inside pipe wall at 550°C. Calculate the heat loss for a length of 1 m, and the temperature at the steel–magnesia interface. Repeat the calculation neglecting the thermal resistance of the steel and compute the percentage error.

11.8. Let the thermal conductivity of a certain solid be expressed as a linear function of temperature:

$$k = a + bT \tag{i}$$

(a) Find the expression for the heat flow if the geometry is a slab.

(b) Find the expression for the heat flow if the solid is in the shape of a pipe and the heat flow is in the radial direction only.

11.9. Suppose the wall in Fig. 11.2 is composed of $\frac{5}{8}$-in. thick drywall, 5.625-in. thick insulation (fiber glass), and 0.16-m thick concrete. Let the inside heat transfer coefficient be $8 \, \text{W} \, \text{m}^{-2} \, \text{K}^{-1}$, and let the outside heat transfer coefficient be $16 \, \text{W} \, \text{m}^{-2} \, \text{K}^{-1}$. When the inside temperature is 20°C and the outside temperature is −20°C, determine the heat flux and the surface temperatures, both inside and outside. Convert all quantities to SI units and work the problem entirely in SI.

11.10. In Problem 11.9, convert all quantities to English units and work the problem entirely in English units.

11.11. Find for Problem 11.9 in both SI and English units: (a) U_o; (b) U_i.

11.12. A thick-walled copper tube is insulated on the outside and is heated by an electric current. The inside diameter is 0.01 m. Air flows through the pipe and is heated. At a point far from the entrance, the air is at 200 kPa, 80°C, and velocity $1.2 \, \text{m} \, \text{s}^{-1}$. A thermocouple indicates that the wall temperature is 400 K. Assuming constant heat flux, estimate the rate of heat transfer ($\text{W} \, \text{m}^{-1}$) at this point.

11.13. Assuming a fully developed flow, determine the length (in meters) of capillary tubing required to raise the bulk temperature of water from 290 K to 330 K in a bath that maintains the wall temperature at 350 K. The capillary tubing is 0.0025 m inside diameter. The Reynolds number is 1800 at 330 K.

11.14. Estimate the Nusselt number and the heat transfer coefficient by (a) Dittus–Boelter, (b) Sieder–Tate, (c) Sleicher–Rouse, (d) Colburn analogy, (e) Friend–Metzner, (f) Figure 11.9, for the assigned cases below. In each case, the fluid is flowing in a 1-in. schedule 40 drawn pipe that is smooth on the inside and whose inside wall temperature is maintained at 55°C:

(1) water at $N_{\text{Re}} = 70\,000$ and 293.15 K

(2) water at $N_{\text{Re}} = 20\,000$ and 320 K

(3) air at $N_{\text{Re}} = 50\,000$, 1 atm, and 20°C

(4) air at $N_{\text{Re}} = 18\,000$, 1 atm, and 30°C

11.15. A heat exchanger has been in operation for a year and by now transfers 10 percent less heat. Assume that the operating conditions have been maintained the same and that there have been no geometry changes. Estimate the fouling factor in terms of the original design overall coefficient.

11.16. Your task is to design a heat exchanger to cool 150 gpm of water (measured at 30°C) from 45°C to 35°C. A cold water stream is available at 20°C, and its outlet temperature must be 26°C. The overall heat transfer coefficient may be assumed constant at $900 \, \text{W} \, \text{m}^{-2} \, \text{K}^{-1}$. Assume that the heat capacity of water is constant and equal to $4.18 \, \text{kJ} \, \text{kg}^{-1} \, \text{K}^{-1}$. Using SI units, find

(a) the area in m^2 required for a parallel flow double-pipe exchanger

(b) the area in m^2 required for a counterflow double-pipe exchanger

(c) the area in m^2 required for a 1–2 exchanger, the hot water being on the tube side

11.17. Your task is to design a heat exchanger to cool $1500 \, \text{kg} \, \text{h}^{-1}$ of kerosene (specific heat 0.5) from 100°C to 65°C. A cold water stream is available at 20°C, and its outlet temperature must be 35°C; let the heat capacity of water be 4.184 kJ kg^{-1} K^{-1} (independent of temperature). The overall heat transfer coefficient U_o may be assumed constant at 280 W m^{-2} K^{-1}. Using SI units, find

(a) the area A_o in m^2 required for a parallel flow double-pipe exchanger
(b) the area A_o in m^2 required for a counterflow double-pipe exchanger
(c) the area A_o in m^2 required for a 1–2 exchanger, the water being on the tube side
(d) the area A_o in m^2 required for a 2–4 exchanger, the water being on the tube side

REFERENCES

A1. American Society of Mechanical Engineers: *Rules for Construction of Unfired Pressure Vessels,* ASME, New York, 1983.
B1. Boelter, L. M. K., R. C. Martinelli, and F. Jonassen: *Trans. ASME* **63:** 447 (1941).
B2. Bowman, R. A., A. C. Mueller and W. M. Nagle: *Trans. ASME* **62:** 283 (1940).
C1. Chilton, T. H., and A. P. Colburn: *Ind. Eng. Chem.* **26:** 1183 (1934).
C2. Colburn, A. P.: *Trans. Am. Inst. Chem. Eng.* **29:** 174 (1933).
C3. Colburn, A. P., *Ind. Eng. Chem.* **25:** 873 (1933).
D1. Deissler, R. G.: *NACA TN* 3145, 1954.
D2. Deissler, R. G., and C. S. Eian: *NACA TN* 2629, 1952.
D3. Dittus, F. W., and L. M. K. Boelter: *Univ. Calif. (Berkeley) Publs. Eng.* **2:** 443 (1930).
D4. Drexel, R. E., and W. H. McAdams: *NACA WR-108* (formerly ARR 4F28, Feb., 1945).
E1. Eckert, E. R. G., and R. M. Drake: *Analysis of Heat and Mass Transfer,* McGraw-Hill, New York, 1972.
F1. Foust, A. S., L. A. Wenzel, C. W. Clump, L. Maus and L. B. Andersen: *Principles of Unit Operations,* 2d ed., Wiley, New York, 1980.
F2. Fried, E.: in *Thermal Conductivity,* vol. 2, R. P. Tye (ed.), Academic Press, London, 1969.
F3. Friend, W. L., and A. B. Metzner: *AIChE J.* **4:** 393 (1958).
G1. Gilliland, E. R., and T. K. Sherwood: *Ind. Eng. Chem.* **26:** 516 (1934).
G2. Geankoplis, C. J.: *Transport Processes and Unit Operations,* 2d ed., Allyn and Bacon, Boston, 1983.
H1. Harriott, P., and R. M. Hamilton: *Chem. Eng. Sci.* **20:** 1073 (1965).
H2. Hubbard, D. W., and E. N. Lightfoot: *Ind. Eng. Chem. Fundam.* **5:** 370 (1966).
H3. Holman, J. P.: *Heat Transfer,* 6th ed., McGraw-Hill, New York, 1986.
H4. Hufschmidt, W., E. Burck, and W. Riebold: *Int. J. Heat Mass Transfer* **9:** 539 (1966).
I1. Incropera, F. P., and D. P. DeWitt: *Fundamentals of Heat and Mass Transfer,* 2d ed., Wiley, New York, 1985.
J1. Jenkins, R.: *Heat Transfer and Fluid Mechanics Institute,* Stanford University Press, 1951, p. 147.
K1. Kays, W. M., and M. E. Crawford: *Convective Heat and Mass Transfer,* 2d ed., McGraw-Hill, New York, 1980.
K2. Kays, W. M., and E. Y. Leung: *Int. J. Heat Mass Transfer* **6:** 537 (1963).
K3. Kays, W. M., and H. C. Perkins: in *Handbook of Heat Transfer,.* 2d ed., W. M. Rohsenow, J. P. Hartnett, and E. N. Ganic (eds.), McGraw-Hill, New York, 1985.
K4. Kern, D. Q.: *Process Heat Transfer,* McGraw-Hill, New York, 1950.
K5. Knudsen, J. G., and D. L. Katz: *Fluid Dynamics and Heat Transfer,* McGraw-Hill, New York, 1958.
L1. Linton, W. H., and T. K. Sherwood: *Chem. Eng. Progr.* **46:** 258 (1950).
L2. Lyon, R. N.: *Chem. Eng. Progr.* **47:** 75 (1951).
M1. Martinelli, R. C.: *Trans. ASME* **69:** 947 (1947); Mech. Eng. **70:** 366 (1948).

M2. McCabe, W. L., J. C. Smith, and P. Harriott: *Unit Operations of Chemical Engineering,* 4th ed., McGraw-Hill, New York, 1985.

M3. McAdams, W. H.: *Heat Transmission,* 3d ed., McGraw-Hill, New York, 1954.

N1. Notter, R. H., and C. A. Sleicher: *Chem. Eng. Sci.* **27:** 2073 (1972).

P1. Perry, R. H., and D. W. Green: *Perry's Chemical Engineers' Handbook,* 6th ed., McGraw-Hill, New York, 1984.

P2. Petukhov, B. S.: in *Advances in Heat Transfer,* vol. 6, J. P. Hartnett and T. F. Irvine (eds.), Academic Press, New York, 1970.

S1. Seban, R. A., and T. T. Shimazaki: *Trans. ASME* **73:** 803 (1951).

S2. Shah, R. K., and A. L. London: *Laminar Flow Forced Convection in Ducts,* in *Advances in Heat Transfer, Supplement I,* T. F. Irvine and J. P. Hartnett (eds.), Academic Press, New York, 1978.

S3. Sherwood, T. K., R. L. Pigford, and C. R. Wilke, *Mass Transfer,* McGraw-Hill, New York, 1975.

S4. Sieder, E. N., and G. E. Tate: *Ind. Eng. Chem.* **28:** 1429 (1936).

S5. Skupinski, E., J. Tortel and L. Vautrey: *Int. J. Heat Mass Transfer* **8:** 937 (1965).

S6. Sleicher, C. A., and M. W. Rouse: *Int. J. Heat Mass Transfer* **18:** 677 (1975).

S7. Sleicher, C. A., and M. Tribus: in *Heat Transfer and Fluid Mechanics Institute,* Stanford Press, 1956, p. 59; *Trans. ASME* **79:** 789 (1957).

S8. Stein, R. P.: in *Advances in Heat Transfer,* vol. 3, T. F. Irvine and J. P. Hartnett (eds.), Academic Press, New York, 1966.

T1. Tubular Exchangers Manufacturers Association: *Standards of the TEMA,* 6th ed., TEMA, New York, 1978.

T2. Treybal, R. E.: *Mass Transfer Operations,* 3d ed., McGraw-Hill, New York, 1980.

V1. von Karman, T: *Trans. ASME* **61:** 705 (1939).

W1. Whitaker, S.: *AIChE J.* **18:** 361 (1972).

TRANSPORT PAST IMMERSED BODIES

NOMENCLATURE

A Area (m^2, ft^2); A is usually the heat transfer area, as opposed to S, the flow area; A_p is surface area of packing in a packed bed

A Species A; A$_1$ and A$_2$ are species A at locations 1 and 2

A Constant in Problems 12.11 and 12.13

a_s Surface area of particles divided by the volume of the bed, Eq. (12.104); in a packed bed, a_v is surface area of packing per unit volume, Eq. (12.140)

B Constant in Eq. (12.24) and Table 12.1

b Width of a flat plate (m, ft) (z direction)

C Concentration (kmol m^{-3}, lb mol ft^{-3}); C_A, C_B, C_i are concentrations of species A, B, i, respectively; $C_{A,\,ave}$ is average concentration of A in the fluid; $C_{A,\,sat}$ is concentration of A at saturation; $C_{A,w}$ and $C_{A,\infty}$ are concentrations at the wall and in the free stream approaching a flat plate or other bluff object, respectively

C Constant; $C_1 = 0.33206$ (in the solution of boundary layer equations); C_1 and C_2 are constants in Eq. (12.97)

C_D Drag coefficient defined by Eq. (12.15); $C_{D,x}$ is the local drag coefficient based on $N_{Re,x}$; other subscripts defined as used

c	Empirical constant used in Example 12.9
c	Subscript denoting start of the transition (critical)
c_p	Heat capacity at constant pressure $(kJ\,kg^{-1}\,K^{-1}$, $Btu\,lb_m^{-1}\,°F^{-1})$; other subscripts defined as used
D	Diffusion coefficient (mass diffusivity) $(m^2\,s^{-1}$, $ft^2\,s^{-1})$
D_{ax}	Axial dispersion coefficient in Eq. (12.110)
d	Diameter (m, ft); for fluidization, d_o is diameter of column; for pipe, d_o is inside diameter for flow area; d_p is diameter of sphere or particle; $\bar{d}_s$ is mean diameter of sphere having same surface area as the particle; d_e is equivalent diameter used in hydraulic radius based on area in banks of tubes [cf. Eq. (12.152)]; d_v is equivalent diameter based on volume; d_t is diameter of a cylinder
E	Constant in Eq. (12.161)
e	Constant in Eq. (12.161)
F	Total force or drag on one side of a flat plate (N, lb_f); F_B is buoyancy force, Eq. (12.70); F_p is drag force on a particle (or sphere), Eq. (12.66); F_W is gravity force, Eq. (12.71)
f	Dimensionless function, Eq. (12.8); f', f'', f''' are derivatives of f with respect to η
f	Fanning friction factor, Eq. (6.89)
$f(x)$	Function of x in root-finding problem, Example 12.16
f	Subscript indicating that the property is to be evaluated at the film temperature T_f, Eq. (12.146)
fb	Subscript denoting fluidization (or fluidized bed)
G_{max}	Mass flow rate in the minimum area in a heat exchanger $(kg\,m^{-2}\,s^{-1}$, $lb_m\,ft^{-2}\,s^{-1})$
g	Acceleration due to a gravitational field $(m\,s^{-2}$, $ft\,s^{-2})$; $\mathbf{g}$ is the gravitational vector, Eq. (4.49); g_ω is acceleration due to the angular velocity ω
g_c	Gravitational conversion constant $(32.174\,lb_m\,lb_f^{-1}\,ft\,s^{-2})$
h	Heat transfer coefficient, defined in a general manner by Eq. (6.86) $(W\,m^{-2}\,K^{-1}$, $Btu\,ft^{-2}\,h^{-1}\,°F^{-1})$; h_{lm} is based on the log mean driving force, cf. Eq. (12.139); h_m is integrated mean, Eq. (12.41); h_x is evaluated at the location x, cf. Eq. (12.39); h_w is the coefficient between the wall and the fluidized bed; h_θ is local heat transfer coefficient at location θ around the circumference of a cylinder (cf. Fig. 12.29)
j	The Colburn j-factor, cf. Eq. (12.47); j_H is for heat, cf. Eqs. (12.136) and (12.137); j_M is for mass, cf. Eqs. (12.89), (12.90), and (12.136)
K_{mb}	Constant in Eq. (12.99) for estimation of minimum bubbling velocity U_{mb}
k	Thermal conductivity $(W\,m^{-1}\,K^{-1}$ or $J\,m^{-1}\,K^{-1}\,s^{-1}$, $Btu\,ft^{-1}\,°R^{-1}\,s^{-1})$; k_m is mean thermal conductivity over the range of integration
k	Mass transfer coefficient $[kmol\,m^{-2}\,s^{-1}\,(kmol\,m^{-3})^{-1}$, $lb\,mol\,ft^{-2}\,s^{-1}$

(lb mol ft^{-3})$^{-1}$]; k_c' is equimolar coefficient, cf. Eq. (6.87); k_c is coefficient for a single component; k_{fb} is overall mass transfer coefficient for fluidization

k Subscript in fluidization indicating transition between slugging and turbulent fluidization

k_3 Fluidization constant, Eq. (12.123)

k_v Correction factor for hindered settling, Eqs. (12.82) through (12.84)

L Length (m, ft); L_e is pipe entry length, Eqs. (12.19) and (12.26); in fluidization, L_{fb} is height of a fluidized bed (also L_1 and L_2); L_{mf} is height of a fluidized bed at the velocity at which the onset of fluidization occurs

lm   Subscript denoting log-mean, cf. Eqs. (12.139) and (12.141)

m Mass (kg, lb$_m$)

m   Subscript denoting mean value

mf   Subscript denoting minimum for onset of fluidization

ms   Subscript denoting minumum for onset of slugging

N Number of rows in the flow direction in a heat exchanger

N Molar flow vector (kmol s^{-1}, lb mol s^{-1}); subscripts A or B are for species A or B, respectively; if written not as a vector, then N is subscripted for direction of transfer; w is wall subscript

N_{Ar} Archimedes (or Galileo) number, Eq. (12.96)

N_{Nu} Nusselt number, defined in general by Eq. (8.21), hL/k; subscripted for various characteristic lengths, for particular applications, and for temperature at which k is evaluated: $N_{Nu,x}$, cf. Eq. (12.40); $N_{Nu,L}$, cf. Eq. (12.43); $N_{Nu,p}$, cf. Eq. (12.85); $N_{Nu,pb}$, cf. Eq. (12.142); $N_{Nu,fb}$, cf. Eq. (12.102); $N_{Nu,t}$, cf. Eq. (12.147); $N_{Nu,\theta}$ is the local Nusselt number at location θ around the circumference of a cylinder, cf. Fig. 12.29; $N_{Nu,tb}$, cf. Eq. (12.161)

$N_{Pe,f}$ Peclet number with all properties evaluated at the film temperature, the product of N_{Re} and N_{Pr}, cf. Eq. (12.151)

N_{Pr} Prandtl number, $c_p\mu/k$, Eq. (8.4); $N_{Pr,f}$ evaluates μ and k at T_f; $N_{Pr,w}$ evaluates properties at the wall temperature

N_{Re} Reynolds number, charactersitic length times characteristic velocity divided by kinematic viscosity (μ/ρ); for a flat plate at location x, N_{Re} is $xU_\infty\rho/\mu$, cf. Eq. (6.3); $N_{Re,L}$, cf. Eq. (12.16); $N_{Re,c}$ is the flat plate Reynolds number evaluated with x_c; $N_{Re,p}$, cf. Eq. (12.68); $N_{Re,fb}$, cf. Eq. (12.94); $N_{Re,mf}$, cf. Eq. (12.95); N_{MRe}, cf. Eq. (12.113); $N_{Re,pb}$, cf. Eq. (12.130) $N_{Re,T}$, cf. Eq. (12.121); $N_{Re,t}$ is cylinder Reynolds number evaluated at T_f, Eq. (12.145); $N_{Re,v}$ is Reynolds number based on d_v, Eq. (12.156); $N_{Re,tb}$, Eq. (12.162)

N_{Sc} Schmidt number, v/D, Eq. (8.6)

N_{Sh} Sherwood number, defined generally in Eq. (8.22); $N_{Sh,y}$, Eq. (12.87); $N_{Sh,fb}$, Eq. (12.111); $N_{Sh,pb}$, Eq. (12.143)

n Number of spheres

n Exponent defined in Eqs. (12.109) and (12.161)

n	Exponent in Richardson–Zaki equation, Eq. (12.114), correlated by Eqs. (12.116) through (12.120)
p	Pressure (kPa, atm, $lb_f\,in.^{-2}$ or psi); p_A and p_B are pressures along a streamline at locations A and B in Figs. 12.18 and 12.19; $-\Delta p_{mf}$ is pressure drop at minimum fluidization
p	Subscript denoting particle or sphere
pb	Subscript denoting packed beds
q	Energy (heat) flow vector ($J\,s^{-1}$, $Btu\,s^{-1}$)
r	Cylindrical coordinate (m, ft)
r	Radius, (m, ft); r_p is radius of a sphere or particle; r_H is hydraulic radius, Eqs. (12.126) and (12.128)
S	Flow area, cf. Chapter 7; subscripts defined as used
S_L	Spacing of rows in a tube bundle in flow direction (m, ft)
S_T	Spacing of rows perpendicular to flow in a tube bundle (m, ft)
s	Subscript denoting solids in U_s
T	Temperature (K, °R, °C, °F); T_w is temperature of the wall or surface; T_∞ is temperature of the fluid approaching a flat plate or cylinder or other bluff object; T_{ave} or T_b is bulk temperature, Eq. (11.31); T_f is film temperature, Eq. (11.32) or (12.146); T_{mb} is mean of two bulk temperatures, Eq. (11.34); ΔT_{lm}, Eq. (12.141)
t	Time (s)
t	Subscript denoting cylinder; also, U_t is terminal (settling) velocity of a particle (sphere) settling in a fluid
tb	Subscript denoting tube bank
tr	Subscript denoting fast fluidization (entrainment)
U	Velocity vector ($m\,s^{-1}$, $ft\,s^{-1}$); U is magnitude of U; U_x, U_y, U_z, U_θ, U_r, U_ϕ are components in directions x, y, z, θ, r, ϕ; $U_{z,ave}$ or U_{ave} is mean velocity in z direction; U_∞ is velocity in open channel (free stream velocity); U_t is terminal (settling) velocity; in fluidization, U_o is superficial velocity, calculated on the basis of an empty column; U_{mf} is minimum superficial velocity for fluidization; U_{mb} is minimum superficial bubbling velocity [Eq. (12.99)]; U_{ms} is minimum superficial velocity for onset of slugging fluidization; U_k is minimum superficial velocity for onset of turbulent fluidization [Eq. (12.100)]; U_{tr} is minimum superficial velocity for pneumatic transport of solids by a gas or hydraulic transport of solids by a liquid; U_s is mean (superficial) solids velocity; U_i is superficial velocity for a void fraction equal to unity, from Eq. (12.115)
V	Volume (m^3, ft^3); V_p is volume of packing in a packed bed
v_f	Specific volume of liquid ($m^3\,kg^{-1}$); in this chapter, v_f is specific volume of water from Table A.1
v	Subscript denoting that d_v is based on volume; $N_{Re,v}$ is based on d_v
w	Mass flow rate ($kg\,s^{-1}$, $lb_m\,s^{-1}$); w_s is mass of solids in a fluidized bed
w	Subscript denoting wall
x	Rectangular (Cartesian) coordinate

x	Distance from the leading edge of a flat plate; x_c is location of the transition from laminar to turbulent flow
x	Subscript denoting that h_x or $N_{Re,x}$ or $N_{Nu,x}$ is based on the distance x (flat plate)
x	Unknown in root-finding problem, Example 12.16
x_s	Volume fraction of solids involved in mass transfer
y	Rectangular (Cartesian) coordinate; in the flat plate geometry, y is the distance normal to the plate
y	Mole fraction; y_{lm} is the log-mean mole fraction, Eq. (12.88)
Z_t	Distance between tube centers in a bundle of tubes
z	Rectangular (Cartesian) coordinate; in the flat plate geometry, z is the width of the plate
z_1	Variable in the decomposition of Eq. (12.11) in Example 12.1; also z_2
α	Thermal diffusivity, $k/(\rho c_p)$, cf. Eqs. (2.10) and (12.31) ($m^2\,s^{-1}$, $ft^2\,s^{-1}$)
Δ	Difference, state 2 minus state 1; e.g., $-\Delta p$ means $p_1 - p_2$
δ	Generalized diffusivity ($m^2\,s^{-1}$, $ft^2\,s^{-1}$)
δ	Thickness of boundary layer, usually the distance in the y direction where U_x equals or exceeds 99 percent of the free stream velocity U_∞ (m, ft); δ_H and δ_M are the thicknesses of the heat and mass boundary layers, respectively
ε	Void fraction (also called porosity or voidage), defined as the ratio of free volume to total volume, Eq. (12.81); ε_{mf} is minimum porosity or void fraction for the onset of fluidization; cf. Eq. (12.92)
η	Similarity variable, Eq. (12.5)
Θ	Dimensionless temperature, Eq. (12.29); Θ' is derivative with respect to η; Θ_M is dimensionless concentration, Eq. (12.48)
θ	Curvilinear coordinate
μ	Viscosity ($kg\,m^{-1}\,s^{-1}$ or $N\,m^{-2}\,s$, $lb_m\,ft^{-1}\,s^{-1}$, cP); μ_w is viscosity at wall; in fluidization, μ is viscosity of solids-free fluid
ν	Kinematic viscosity, μ/ρ (momentum diffusivity) ($m^2\,s^{-1}$, $ft^2\,s^{-1}$)
π	Ratio of circumference of a circle to its diameter (3.141 592 65...)
ρ	Density ($kg\,m^{-3}$, $lb_m\,ft^{-3}$); in fluidization equations, ρ is density of solids-free fluid; subscripts 1 and 2 refer to overall density of fluidized bed at heights L_1 and L_2; ρ_m is density of solid-fluid mixture; ρ_p is density of particle; ρ_s is solids density in Eq. (12.100)
ϕ	Velocity potential, defined by Eq. (12.53) ($m^2\,s^{-1}$, $ft^2\,s^{-1}$)
ϕ_s	Sphericity, defined by Eq. (12.105)
τ_w	Shear stress at the wall of a flat plate, Eq. (12.13) ($N\,m^{-2}$, $lb_f\,ft^{-2}$)
$\boldsymbol{\Psi}$	Generalized flux vector (e.g., units for heat flux are $J\,m^{-2}\,s^{-1}$ or $W\,m^{-2}$, $Btu\,ft^{-2}\,s^{-1}$; see Tables 2.1 and 4.1 for more details)
ψ	Stream function, defined in Eq. (12.6) ($m^2\,s^{-1}$, $ft^2\,s^{-1}$)
ψ	Generalized concentration of property (e.g., units for concentration of heat are $J\,m^{-3}$, $Btu\,ft^{-3}$; see Table 3.1 for complete listing) (see Table 4.2 for units; e.g., for heat, units are $J\,m^{-3}\,s^{-1}$, $Btu\,ft^{-2}\,s^{-1}$)

ω Angular velocity in Eq. (12.91) (rad^{-1})

∇ Vector operator del, defined by Eqs. (2.16) or (3.45); cf. Table 5.1 (m^{-1}, ft^{-1})

The laminar boundary layer concept as presented in Chapter 5, Section 5.1.7 can be considered as a flow over an immersed body (i.e., a flat plate). Only the basic equations were presented there. In this chapter, the analysis will be extended to indicate the nature of the solution, its limitation (separation), and the equations useful for design. The equations for heat and mass transfer in a boundary layer will be discussed, as well as the analogous equations for turbulent flow conditions. One of the most important aspects of the developing boundary layer is in the entry region of ducts, and a discussion for both laminar and turbulent flow is included.

The boundary layer on a flat plate is one aspect of flow over an immersed body. Practical applications of flow over immersed bodies abound; for instance, streamlining is applied to automobiles in order to reduce the drag forces and increase gas mileage. Streamlining is also important in airplanes, in missiles, and in the shields mounted on top of the cabs of tractor-trailer trucks (the so-called "semis").

In this chapter, considerable emphasis is placed on the flow of a fluid past a stationary sphere; note that this problem is identical to the movement of a sphere in a stationary fluid. Stokes' law applies to a fluid flowing at a very low rate past a stationary sphere. Flow at higher velocities generally requires an empirical solution. Applications include settling of smoke particles, collection of dust to prevent air pollution, settling of solids in liquids, flow in packed (fixed) beds, and flow in fluidized beds. Often the packed or fluidized beds contain catalyst particles, and a chemical reaction takes place along with heat and mass transfer [H2]; thus, correlations for these are needed also.

This chapter also covers flow over a stationary cylinder, as well as flow through a group of cylinders. An important application is in the design and operation of heat exchangers, in which both heat transfer and momentum transfer must be considered. Empirical correlations will be presented and discussed. Another application is in the operation of research equipment, such as the hot-wire anemometer.

In chemical engineering, the flow over individual objects is important, but more important is the flow over multiple bodies. Thus, this chapter will cover hindered settling, transport in packed beds, transport in fluidized beds, and flow across tube banks.

12.1 THE BOUNDARY LAYER AND THE ENTRY REGION

The boundary layer is considered to be the region of changing velocity when a viscous fluid flows past a solid boundary, such as a flat plate. In the boundary layer region, both fluid inertia (or momentum convection) and viscous effects are important. The no-slip condition of the fluid at the solid surface means that the velocity of the fluid is zero at the surface. The velocity then increases as distance from the surface increases, as illustrated in Figs. 5.6 and 6.2. In those figures, the fluid external to the boundary layer is shown with a uniform velocity U_∞. The boundary layer begins when the fluid passes over the plate, as shown by the dotted line, and includes the entire region in which the velocity is less than the free-stream velocity U_∞. In the case of the flat plate, the boundary layer continues to increase in thickness with increasing distance x. Eventually there will be a transition to turbulent flow. For pipe flow, flow in ducts, etc., the entry region is that region in which the velocity profile changes with the distance from the entrance until a fully developed profile is reached.

The next sections will cover the laminar boundary layer, the turbulent boundary layer, and then heat and mass transfer during boundary layer flow.

12.1.1 The Laminar Boundary Layer

The flat plate boundary layer is the classical problem to present, since only one surface need be considered. Again consult Fig. 5.6. Analysis of this problem begins with Example 5.8. The Navier–Stokes equations for fluids of constant density and viscosity from Table 5.7 are greatly simplified because most terms are zero, as shown in Example 5.8. All velocities and derivatives in the z direction are zero. After the usual boundary layer assumption was made, the following two equations were obtained in Example 5.8 [cf. Eqs. (iii) and (iv)]:

$$U_x \frac{\partial U_x}{\partial x} + U_y \frac{\partial U_x}{\partial y} = \nu \frac{\partial^2 U_x}{\partial y^2} \tag{12.1}$$

$$U_x \frac{\partial U_y}{\partial x} + U_y \frac{\partial U_y}{\partial y} = \nu \frac{\partial^2 U_y}{\partial y^2} \tag{12.2}$$

For this problem the continuity equation from Table 5.3 reduces to Eq. (vi) in Example 5.8:

$$\frac{\partial U_x}{\partial x} + \frac{\partial U_y}{\partial y} = 0 \tag{12.3}$$

Equations (12.1) and (12.3) adequately define the system. These two independent equations include the two unknowns U_x and U_y, and may be solved with appropriate boundary conditions. Equations (12.2) need not be used to obtain the solution for U_x and U_y. In essence, the problem is over-determined. An analysis of the orders of magnitude of the terms shows that those in Eqs. (12.1) or (12.3) are of first order, while those in Eq. (12.2) are of a much smaller order (of the boundary layer thickness). Thus, only the first-order equations are selected for the solution.

Equations (12.1) and (12.3) were derived for the following assumptions: (1) the approach velocity U_∞ is in the x direction only; (2) the fluid is incompressible and of constant viscosity; (3) the flow is at steady-state; (4)

there is no pressure gradient in the x direction because U_∞, the free stream velocity, is constant; (5) there are no external forces, such as gravity; and (6) $\partial^2 U_x / \partial x^2 \ll \partial^2 U_x / \partial y^2$ and thus $\partial^2 U_x / \partial x^2$ can be neglected [B2].

The appropriate boundary conditions are

At $y = 0$ for all x

$$U_x(y = 0) = 0 \qquad U_y(y = 0) = 0$$

At $y = \infty$
(12.4)

$$U_x(y = \infty) = U_\infty$$

Equations (12.1) and (12.3) are simultaneous partial differential equations that were first solved by Blasius [B1] in 1908. Blasius deduced that the velocity profiles at various points along the plate were similar. He was able to recast Eqs. (12.1) and (12.3) into a dimensionless form through use of a "similarity" variable η, where

$$\eta = y \left(\frac{U_\infty}{vx} \right)^{1/2}$$
(12.5)

A similarity transformation is defined mathematically as a transformation to reduce the number of independent variables [A1].

It is convenient to express the continuity equation, Eq. (12.3), in terms of a "stream function" ψ, which is defined as follows:

$$U_x = \frac{\partial \psi}{\partial y} \qquad \text{and} \qquad U_y = -\frac{\partial \psi}{\partial x}$$
(12.6)

where ψ is not to be confused with the general concentration of property from Chapter 2. The stream function ψ satisfies the continuity equation, because upon substitution of Eq. (12.6) into Eq. (12.3), the result is

$$\frac{\partial^2 \psi}{\partial x \, \partial y} - \frac{\partial^2 \psi}{\partial y \, \partial x} = 0$$
(12.7)

Next, a dimensionless function f is defined as

$$f = \frac{\psi}{(xvU_\infty)^{1/2}}$$
(12.8)

where f is a function of η only. Now, Eq. (12.1) with the aid of Eq. (12.6) becomes

$$\frac{\partial \psi}{\partial y} \frac{\partial^2 \psi}{\partial x \, \partial y} - \frac{\partial \psi}{\partial x} \frac{\partial^2 \psi}{\partial y^2} = v \frac{\partial^3 \psi}{\partial y^3}$$
(12.9)

After using Eqs. (12.5) and (12.8), Eq. (12.9) becomes

$$f \frac{\partial^2 f}{\partial \eta^2} + 2 \frac{\partial^3 f}{\partial \eta^3} = 0$$
(12.10)

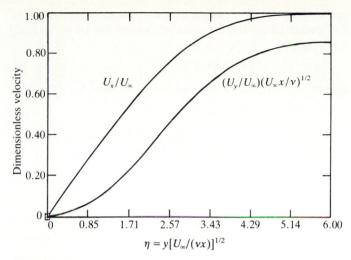

FIGURE 12.1
Boundary layer solution for flat plate problem.

or, using the common notations, f'' and f''' to indicate derivatives:

$$ff'' + 2f''' = 0 \qquad (12.11)$$

Since Eq. (12.3) was used in the definition of the stream function, Eq. (12.6), the introduction of the similarity variable η and the function f has resulted in the coupled set of partial differential equations being reduced to a single ordinary differential equation, Eq. (12.11), with transformed boundary conditions:

At the wall

$$f\,(\eta = 0) = 0 \qquad f'\,(\eta = 0) = 0$$

Far from the wall

$$f'\,(\eta = \infty) = 1 \qquad (12.12)$$

Equation (12.11) is nonlinear but can be solved (with the boundary conditions) in terms of a power series [H4]. A modern computation might use an analog computer or, better yet, a digital computer simulation of the analog formulation by numerical methods, as shown by Example 12.1. Figure 12.1 shows the solution to Eq. (12.11) in terms of the dimensionless variables η, U_x/U_∞, and $(U_y/U_\infty)(U_\infty x/v)^{1/2}$. Note that when η exceeds 6 the slopes of both curves approach zero.

Example 12.1. Set-up the boundary layer solution of Eqs. (12.11) and (12.12) for a digital computer.

Answer. Rather than a series solution (which involves finding many terms), a digital simulation that utilizes integration by numerical means will be performed. First, Eq. (12.11) is rewritten as

$$f''' + \tfrac{1}{2}ff'' = 0 \tag{i}$$

This problem is classified as a boundary value problem, since from Eq. (12.12)

$$f'\,(\eta = \infty) = 1 \tag{ii}$$

Hence, it will be necessary to guess values of $f''(0)$ until Eq. (ii) is satisfied. Equation (i) is decomposed into a coupled set of differential equations:

$$z_1 = \frac{df}{d\eta} = f' \qquad\qquad f(0) = 0 \tag{iii}$$

$$z_2 = \frac{d^2 f}{d\eta^2} = f'' \qquad\qquad f'(0) = 0 \tag{iv}$$

$$f''' = \frac{d^3 f}{d\eta^3} = -(f/2)z_2 \qquad f''(0) = C_1 \tag{v}$$

where the constant C_1 is varied until Eq. (ii) is satisfied.[1] Since infinity is not a viable option, the value of η must also be varied until the boundary condition of Eq. (ii) is satisfied. A value of η equal to 6 is satisfactory.

The solution to Eqs. (iii) through (v) in FORTRAN or BASIC using Runge–Kutta or some other method [P1, R1] is fairly involved, since the step size, the boundary condition $\eta = \infty$, and the constant C_1 must all be located properly by trial and error. Since systems of ordinary differential equations are commonly encountered, several excellent simulation languages, including CSMP[2] and ACSL,[3] have been developed. These are easy to use, and the reader should consult the appropriate manuals for detailed instructions.

Figure 12.2 illustrates the solution of Eqs. (iii) through (v) with ACSL. The ACSL program is 13 lines long, whereas an analogous FORTRAN program would be quite lengthy. First, application of algebra and calculus to the appropriate definitions yields a useful pair of equations:

$$U_x/U_\infty = f' \tag{vi}$$

$$(U_y/U_\infty)(U_\infty x/v)^{1/2} = \tfrac{1}{2}(\eta f' - f) \tag{vii}$$

In the ACSL program, line 2 defines constants that are the boundary conditions, Eq. (iii)—FIC; Eq. (iv)—FDIC; Eq. (v)—FDDIC; and the condition for $\eta = \infty$, which is ETAT. Line 4 contains ETA, or η, since ACSL always uses time as the independent variable. Line 5 solves Eq. (i) for f'''. Then lines 6, 7 and 8 integrate (by Runge–Kutta) the system of equations in Eqs. (iii) through (v). Lines 9 and 10 compute the quantities in Eqs. (vi) and (vii). Line 11 terminates the integration when η exceeds 6.

---

[1] C_1 is used in this text to avoid confusion; other authors use α.

[2] Trademark of IBM Corp., White Plains, NY 10604.

[3] Trademark of Mitchell and Gauthier, Assoc., Inc., Concord, MA 01742.

```
PROGRAM BOUNDARY LAYER              $ "LINE 1"
CONSTANT FIC=0.0,FDIC=0.0,FDDIC=0.33206,ETAT=6.
CONSTANT CINT=0.01
DERIVATIVE
ETA=T
FDDD=-0.5*F*FDD                     $ "LINE 5"
FDD=INTEG(FDDD,FDDIC)
FD=INTEG(FDD,FDIC)                  $ "LINE 7"
F=INTEG(FD,FIC)
U=FD                                $ "LINE 9"
V=0.5*(ETA*FD-F)
TERMT(ETA.GT.ETAT)                  $ "LINE 11"
END
END                                 $ "LINE 13"
```

FIGURE 12.2
Simulation program for boundary layer over a flat plate.

The program given in Fig. 12.2 was used to prepare Fig. 12.1, which presents the nondimensional velocity curves for the boundary layer flow over a flat plate. Note that in this simple program no provision is made for automatically varying C_1 so as to force Eq. (ii) to be correct. The constant C_1 or FDDIC in the program is changed by repeatedly editing and executing the program until Eq. (ii) is satisfied.

Boundary layer parameters. From the results of Example 12.1, certain parameters of the flow in a laminar boundary layer can be obtained. The shear stress at the wall at any position along the plate is given by

$$\tau_w = -\mu\left(\frac{dU_x}{dy}\right)_w = -(\mu U_\infty C_1)\left(\frac{U_\infty}{\nu x}\right)^{1/2} \tag{12.13}$$

where $C_1 = 0.33206$ from the numerical solution to the problem.

The total force or drag on one side of the plate is the shear stress integrated over the area of the plate:

$$F = (\mu U_\infty C_1 b)\left(\frac{U_\infty}{\nu}\right)^{1/2}\int_0^L \left(\frac{1}{x^{1/2}}\right) dx = (2C_1 U_\infty b)(\mu \rho L U_\infty)^{1/2} \tag{12.14}$$

where b is the width and L is the length of the plate. Note that the drag force F in Eq. (12.14) is represented as a scalar (without sign); F acts on the plate in the same direction as U_∞.

If the shear stress τ_w were constant over the area, then τ_w times the area bL would equal F. Since τ_w varies with x according to Eq. (12.13), it is often useful to introduce a dimensionless "drag coefficient" C_D, which is defined as

$$C_D = \frac{F}{\frac{1}{2}\rho U_\infty^2 A} \tag{12.15}$$

Note that C_D is similar in form to the Fanning friction factor previously defined in Eq. (6.89):

$$f = \frac{\tau_w}{\frac{1}{2}\rho U_{\text{ave}}^2} = \frac{F/A}{\frac{1}{2}\rho U_{\text{ave}}^2} = \frac{F}{\frac{1}{2}\rho U_{\text{ave}}^2 A}$$

After some algebra, C_D becomes

$$C_{D,\text{laminar}} = 4C_1\left(\frac{\mu}{LU_\infty\rho}\right)^{1/2} = 4C_1(N_{\text{Re},L})^{-1/2} \tag{12.16}$$

where the constant C_1 is 0.33206 as before. The Reynolds number is based on the length of the plate, and the subscript "laminar" is used to note the conditions. Some authors also define a "local" drag coefficient $C_{D,x}$:

$$C_{D,x} = \frac{\tau_w}{\frac{1}{2}\rho U_\infty^2} = 2C_1\left(\frac{xU_\infty}{\nu}\right)^{-1/2} = 2C_1(N_{\text{Re},x})^{-1/2} \tag{12.17}$$

This equation utilized Eq. (12.13) which is the expression for the "local" shear stress at the wall.

A precise mathematical definition of the laminar boundary layer thickness is arbitrary; in the solution to Example 12.1, the velocity approaches U_∞ but theoretically never reaches U_∞. If U_x/U_∞ is taken as 0.99, the boundary layer thickness δ can be found from the following equation:

$$\frac{\delta}{x} = 5.0\frac{(\nu x/U_\infty)^{1/2}}{x} = 5.0(N_{\text{Re},x})^{-1/2} \tag{12.18}$$

where $N_{\text{Re},x}$ is based on the distance x from the leading edge:

$$N_{\text{Re},x} = xU_\infty\rho/\mu \tag{6.3}$$

Note that Eq. (12.18) predicts that the boundary layer thickness δ is proportional to the square root of x.

Example 12.2. A wall in a wind tunnel is used as the test area for drag and other measurements. The forward edge of the test area is located 1 ft from the leading edge of the test wall. The test area is a square, 1 ft by 1 ft. The free-stream air velocity is $6\,\text{ft}\,\text{s}^{-1}$ ($1.829\,\text{m}\,\text{s}^{-1}$), and the temperature is 68°F. Estimate the boundary layer thickness and the local drag coefficient at the trailing edge of the test section. Also estimate the force (drag) on the test section.

Answer. This problem will be solved in English units to illustrate the use of g_c. The trailing edge of the test section is 2 ft (0.6096 m) from the leading edge of the test wall. The necessary conversions are in Tables C.5, C.6, and C.17; the properties of air at 68°F (20°C, 293 K) from Table A.2 are

$$\rho = (1.2047\,\text{kg}\,\text{m}^{-3})(0.06243\,\text{lb}_m\,\text{ft}^{-3}\,\text{kg}^{-1}\,\text{m}^3) = 0.07521\,\text{lb}_m\,\text{ft}^{-3}$$

$$\mu = (18.17 \times 10^{-6}\,\text{kg}\,\text{m}^{-1}\,\text{s}^{-1})(0.6720\,\text{lb}_m\,\text{ft}^{-1}\,\text{s}^{-1}\,\text{kg}^{-1}\,\text{s}\,\text{m})$$

$$= 1.221 \times 10^{-5}\,\text{lb}_m\,\text{ft}^{-1}\,\text{s}^{-1}$$

$$\nu = \mu/\rho = 18.17 \times 10^{-6}/1.2047 = 1.508 \times 10^{-5}\,\text{m}^2\,\text{s}^{-1} = 1.623 \times 10^{-4}\,\text{ft}^2\,\text{s}^{-1} \tag{i}$$

First it is necessary to determine whether the flow is laminar or turbulent. The local Reynolds number at 2 ft, from Eq. (6.3), is

$$N_{\text{Re},x} = xU_\infty/\nu = (2)(6)/(1.623 \times 10^{-4}) = 7.391 \times 10^4 \tag{ii}$$

This Reynolds number is well within the laminar region, since the Reynolds number at the transition to turbulence is usually around 5×10^5. See Fig. 6.2 and the discussion following that equation.

The boundary layer thickness δ is calculated from Eq. (12.18):

$$\delta = (5.0)(x)(N_{\mathrm{Re},x})^{-1/2} = (5)(2)(7.391 \times 10^4)^{-1/2} = 0.03678 \text{ ft} = 0.44 \text{ in.} \quad \text{(iii)}$$

In other words, if the y distance from the plate at two feet from the leading edge is 0.44 in. or greater, the air velocity is 6 ft s^{-1}. From Eq. (12.17), the local drag coefficient is

$$C_{\mathrm{D},x} = 2C_1(N_{\mathrm{Re},x})^{-1/2} = (2)(0.33206)(7.391 \times 10^4)^{-1/2} = 2.443 \times 10^{-3} \quad \text{(iv)}$$

Since Eq. (12.14) was integrated from the leading edge of the plate to L, the force or drag on the test section of 1 ft^2 must be calculated as the difference between the drag on the test wall from the leading edge to the end of the test area and the drag on the test wall up to the test area:

$$F_{1-2\,\mathrm{ft}} = F_{0-2\,\mathrm{ft}} - F_{0-1\,\mathrm{ft}} \quad \text{(v)}$$

From Eqs. (v) and (12.14), the force on the test section is

$$F_{1-2\,\mathrm{ft}} = (2C_1 U_\infty b)(\mu \rho U_\infty)^{1/2}[(L_2)^{1/2} - (L_1)^{1/2}] \quad \text{(vi)}$$

where the constant C_1 is 0.33206. After inserting the appropriate numbers, plus a width of 1 ft, into Eq. (vi), the force is

$$F = [(2)(0.33206)(6.0)(1)][(1.221 \times 10^{-5})(0.07521)(6.0)]^{1/2}[(2)^{1/2} - (1)^{1/2}]$$
$$\times \{(\text{ft s}^{-1})(\text{ft})[(\mathrm{lb_m\ ft^{-1}\ s^{-1}})(\mathrm{lb_m\ ft^{-3}})(\text{ft s}^{-1})]^{1/2}(\text{ft}^{1/2})\}$$
$$= 3.874 \times 10^{-3} \text{ lb}_\mathrm{m} \text{ ft s}^{-2} \quad \text{(vii)}$$

The value of F is properly expressed in force units, using g_c:

$$F = 3.874 \times 10^{-3}/32.174 \, [(\mathrm{lb_m\ ft\ s^{-2}})(\mathrm{lb_m^{-1}\ lb_f\ ft^{-1}\ s^2})]$$
$$= 1.204 \times 10^{-4} \text{ lb}_\mathrm{f} \quad \text{(viii)}$$

Entry region for a pipe. Solutions exist for other boundary layer problems such as the flow between parallel plates and the flow in the entry region of a pipe. For this latter case, Fig. 12.3 shows the nature of the flow to be expected. Of particular interest is the length of pipe necessary for the development of the

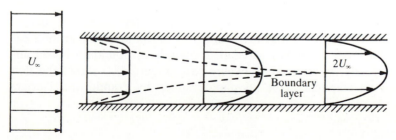

FIGURE 12.3
Boundary layer formation at the entrance to a pipe.

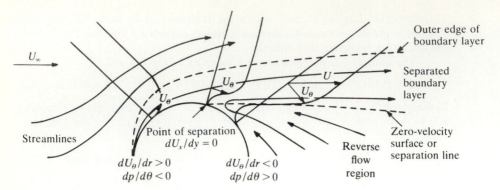

FIGURE 12.4
The boundary layer over a cylindrical object.

velocity profile. In any experimental study of velocity profiles in laminar flow, the length of pipe necessary for the complete development of that profile must be known. In addition, this length is necessary when calculating the additional pressure drop in the entry region of a capillary viscometer. Langhaar [L2] gives the entry length L_e in laminar flow as

$$L_e/d_o = 0.0567 N_{Re} \qquad (12.19)$$

where L_e is the point at which the center line velocity reaches a value of $[(1.98)(U_{z,\text{ave}})]$. For a flow with a Reynolds number of 2000, the entry length from Eq. (12.19) is a distance of 113 pipe diameters. The excess pressure drop experienced in the entrance region during the laminar flow can be computed from information given elsewhere [B2].

Separation. For flow over a flat plate and flow in the entry region of a pipe, the boundary conditions are in such a form that a mathematical solution is obtainable, as just discussed. Exact solutions are not obtainable if the boundary layer separates from the solid. A classic example of separation occurs when a fluid of uniform velocity U_∞ flows over a cylinder, as shown in Figure 12.4. Note the reverse flow region where the pressure gradient dp/dx becomes positive. When an adverse pressure gradient exists, i.e., if the pressure is increasing in the direction of flow (opposing the flow), the boundary layer can separate from its associate body. A flow over a cylinder, as shown in Fig. 12.4, is used to illustrate the problem, although separation can occur along a flat plate also. For a detailed analysis of boundary layers and separation, the reader is referred elsewhere [S1]. Figure 12.5 shows the flow separation over an elliptical shape[4] as photographed by Prandtl and Tietjens [P5].

---

[4] Film loops FM-12, FM-4, and FM-6 can be used to illustrate separation.

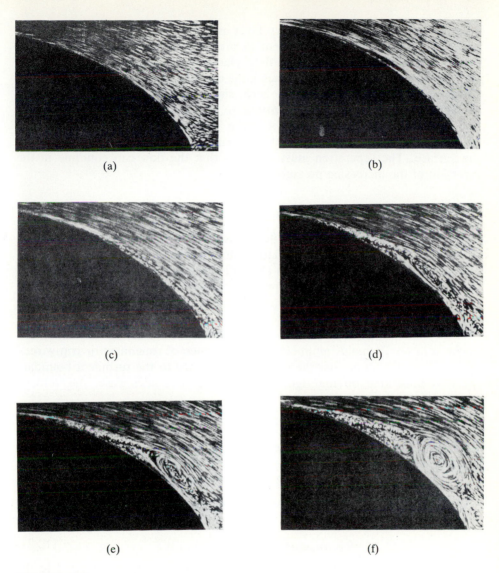

(a)

(b)

(c)

(d)

(e)

(f)

FIGURE 12.5
Boundary layer separation. (*From Prandtl and Tietjens, Applied Hydro- and Aeromechanics, Dover Publications, Inc., New York. Reprinted by permission of publisher.*)

The reason for separation can be analyzed in terms of the Bernoulli equation, Eq. (7.63), as follows: as the flow passes over the cylinder in Fig. 12.4 it must accelerate over the forward portion and decelerate over the rear part. Over the forward part, the increase in velocity is accompanied by a decrease in pressure ($dp/dx < 0$) or a favorable pressure gradient exists, as shown by Eq. (7.63). The opposite is true over the rearward part. Since the pressure drop across the boundary layer is negligible, this adverse gradient penetrates to the wall. The gradient in pressure, as well as the shear force, causes a rapid deceleration of the fluid elements in the immediate vicinity of the wall. The deceleration continues until the fluid elements come to rest, at which point the viscous forces are zero, since the velocity is zero. However, the adverse pressure effect will continue to act, and the fluid will reverse and flow backward. The point at which the reversal occurs is that at which $(dU_x/dy)_w$ is zero, and is the point of separation of the boundary layer from the surface. The separation must occur so that the flow can continue in the direction of the increasing pressure.

12.1.2   The Turbulent Boundary Layer

The boundary layer for laminar flow was presented in Section 12.1.1 as a solution to the Navier–Stokes equations for flow over a flat plate. However, laminar flow will only exist over a short distance before transition occurs and turbulence is introduced. The flow in the laminar and turbulent boundary layers was illustrated in Fig. 6.2.[5] Along the front part of the plate a laminar boundary layer forms. When the Reynolds number, Eq. (6.3), is in the range of 5×10^5 to 5×10^6, the transition to turbulent flow begins. The transition can begin at lower Reynolds numbers in the presence of roughness or trip wires.[5] Once the transition occurs, there is a rapid change to the turbulent boundary layer as illustrated on the right of the figure. For each case, the velocity distribution is shown.

Equations (12.13) through (12.16) presented the relations for the stress at the wall, the total drag, and the drag coefficients for laminar boundary layers. Equation (12.15), relating the force or drag on a plate to the drag coefficient C_D, still applies:

$$F = \tfrac{1}{2}(\rho U_\infty^2)(Lb)(C_D) \tag{12.20}$$

where the area A has been replaced by Lb. The drag coefficient C_D has been correlated empirically [S1]:

$$C_{D,\text{turbulent}} = 0.455[\log_{10}(N_{\text{Re},L})]^{-2.58} \tag{12.21}$$

where the subscript "turbulent" indicates that Eq. (12.21) is restricted to the portion of the boundary layer that is turbulent. Similarly, the local shear stress at the wall is

$$\tau_w = \tfrac{1}{2}(\rho U_\infty^2)[2\log_{10}(N_{\text{Re},x}) - 0.65]^{-2.3} \tag{12.22}$$

If the turbulent velocity profile is approximated by the 1/7th-power law, Eq. (6.110), then the boundary layer thickness is

$$\delta/x = 0.376(N_{\text{Re},x})^{-0.2} \tag{12.23}$$

---

[5] Film loop FM-5 illustrates the laminar and turbulent boundary layers and the tripping of a laminar layer.

TABLE 12.1
Variation of B with transition Reynolds number in Equation (12.24)

$N_{\text{Re},c}$	B
3×10^5	1050
5×10^5	1700
1×10^6	3300
3×10^6	8700

* Values taken from Knudsen and Katz, *Fluid Dynamics and Heat Transfer*, p. 277, McGraw-Hill, New York, 1958.

Since Eq. (12.23) is based on the Blasius equation, Eq. (6.133), both are subject to the same restrictions.

The correlation in Eq. (12.21) applies to fully turbulent flow. Equation (12.21) can be empirically modified to account for the transition region and the effect of the laminar initial length [S1]:

$$C_D = 0.455[\log_{10}(N_{\text{Re},L})]^{-2.58} - \frac{B}{N_{\text{Re},L}} \tag{12.24}$$

where B is a function of the transition Reynolds number $N_{\text{Re},c}$, as shown in Table 12.1. Here no subscript to denote conditions has been added since Eq. (12.24) applies over the entire region. If the point of transition is not known precisely, Eq. (12.24) will be approximate. The assumption of B equal to 1050 will be the most conservative, and a value of B equal to 1700 will be the most probable.

The total force obtained from Eqs. (12.20) and (12.21) assumes that the plate is subject to turbulent flow only. However, this condition is rarely encountered, and there is normally a laminar section preceding the turbulent region. Instead of using Eq. (12.24), an alternate procedure combines Eq. (12.14) for the force exerted in the laminar section and Eq. (12.20) for the force exerted in the turbulent section:

$$F_{\text{actual}} = F_{\text{laminar},0-x_c} + F_{\text{turbulent},0-L} - F_{\text{turbulent},0-x_c} \tag{12.25}$$

$F_{\text{laminar},0-x_c}$ evaluated from Eq. (12.14) from $x = 0$ to $x = x_c$ (at $N_{\text{Re},c}$)

$F_{\text{turbulent},0-L}$ evaluated from Eqs. (12.20) and (12.21) from $x = 0$ to $x = L$

$F_{\text{turbulent},0-x_c}$ evaluated from Eqs. (12.20) and (12.21) from $x = 0$ to $x = x_c$

Here, the subscript $0-L$ refers to the entire length of plate and $0-x_c$ refers to the leading edge of the plate to x_c, the location of $N_{\text{Re},c}$. Use of Eq. (12.25) will be illustrated in Example 12.3. Note that Eq. (12.24) included the laminar contribution when the parameter B was determined; thus Eqs. (12.24) and (12.25) cannot be used together.

Entry region for a pipe. For turbulent flow, the length in which the center line velocity reaches 99 percent of the maximum value is correlated by

$$L_e/d_o = 0.693(N_{Re})^{1/4} \qquad (12.26)$$

Equation (12.26) is satisfactory for most normal problems where vibrations and flow disturbances result in a transition Reynolds number of approximately 2100. As a rule, Eq. (12.26) will compute a much shorter length L_e than will Eq. (12.19), the corresponding equation for the laminar entry in a pipe:

$$L_e/d_o = 0.0567 N_{Re} \qquad (12.19)$$

Summary. The boundary layer equations of this and the previous section are summarized in Table 12.2.

TABLE 12.2
Summary of boundary layer equations

Description	Regime	Equation	
Boundary layer thickness	laminar	$\delta/x = 5.0(N_{Re,x})^{-1/2}$	(12.18)
	turbulent	$\delta/x = 0.376(N_{Re,x})^{-0.2}$	(12.23)
Wall shear stress	laminar	$\tau_w = -(\mu U_\infty C_1)[U_\infty/(vx)]^{1/2}$	(12.13)
	turbulent	$\tau_w = \frac{1}{2}(\rho U_\infty^2)[2\log_{10}(N_{Re,x}) - 0.65]^{-2.3}$	(12.22)
Total drag force	laminar	$F = (2C_1 U_\infty b)(\mu\rho L U_\infty)^{1/2}$	(12.14)
	turbulent	$F = \frac{1}{2}(\rho U_\infty^2)(Lb)(C_D)$	(12.20)
Local drag coefficient	laminar	$C_{D,x} = 2C_1(N_{Re,x})^{-1/2}$	(12.17)
Drag coefficient	laminar	$C_{D,\,laminar} = 4C_1(N_{Re,L})^{-1/2}$	(12.16)
	turbulent	$C_{D,\,turbulent} = 0.455[\log_{10}(N_{Re,L})]^{-2.58}$	(12.21)
	combined	$C_D = 0.455[\log_{10}(N_{Re,L})]^{-2.58} - B/(N_{Re,L})$	(12.24)
Pipe entry length	laminar	$L_e/d_o = 0.0567 N_{Re}$	(12.19)
	turbulent	$L_e/d_o = 0.693(N_{Re})^{1/4}$	(12.26)

Notes:

B	constant, cf. Table 12.1	L_e	entry length in a pipe
b	plate width	$N_{Re,x}$	equal to $xU_\infty\rho/\mu$
C_1	value of 0.33206	x	distance from leading edge
d_o	diameter of pipe	U_∞	free stream velocity
L	length of plate	δ	location at which $U_x/U_\infty = 0.99$

Example 12.3. Water flows over a flat plate at a velocity U_∞ of 3 m s^{-1}. Calculate the total drag on a section of the plate that is 1 m wide and 2 m long, the beginning of the section coinciding with the leading edge of the plate. Assume the transition occurs at a Reynolds number of 5×10^5. Also, calculate the shear stress at the wall (in units of N m^{-2}) at a distance of 1 m from the leading edge of the plate.

Answer. The first step is to calculate $N_{\text{Re},x}$ at distances of 1 m and 2 m from the leading edge. From Table A.1, the properties of water at room temperature (20°C or 293.15 K) are

$$\rho = \frac{1}{v_f} = \frac{1}{1.001 \times 10^{-3}} = 999 \text{ kg m}^{-3} \tag{i}$$

$$\mu = 1 \text{ cP} = 0.001 \text{ kg m}^{-1}\text{s}^{-1}$$

At $x = 1$ m and $x = 2$ m, the Reynolds numbers from Eq. (6.3) are

$$N_{\text{Re},x}(x = 1) = (1.0)(3.0)(999)/(0.001) = 2.997 \times 10^6$$

$$N_{\text{Re},L}(x = 2) = (2.0)(3.0)(999)/(0.001) = 5.994 \times 10^6 \tag{ii}$$

The flow is clearly turbulent at both locations. The shear stress at the wall is given by Eq. (12.22):

$$\tau_w = \tfrac{1}{2}(\rho U_\infty^2)[2 \log_{10}(N_{\text{Re},x}) - 0.65]^{-2.3}$$
$$= \tfrac{1}{2}(999)(3.0)^2[2 \log_{10}(2.997 \times 10^6) - 0.65]^{-2.3}$$
$$= 14.0 \, [(\text{kg m}^{-3})(\text{m}^2\text{s}^{-2})] = 14.0 \text{ kg m}^{-1}\text{s}^{-2} = 14.0 \text{ N m}^{-2} \tag{iii}$$

The easiest approach is to calculate C_D from Eq. (12.24). For this problem $B = 1700$ from Table 12.1:

$$C_D = 0.455[\log_{10}(N_{\text{Re},L})]^{-2.58} - B/(N_{\text{Re},L})$$
$$= 0.455[\log_{10}(5.994 \times 10^6)]^{-2.58} - (1700)/(5.994 \times 10^6) = 0.00298 \tag{iv}$$

From Eq. (12.20), the drag on the plate is

$$F = \tfrac{1}{2}(\rho U_\infty^2)(Lb)(C_D) = \tfrac{1}{2}(999)(3.0)^2(2.0)(0.00298)$$
$$= 26.8 \, [(\text{kg m}^{-3})(\text{m}^2\text{s}^{-2})(\text{m}^2)] = 26.8 \text{ kg m s}^{-2} = 26.8 \text{ N} \tag{v}$$

The drag force on the plate can alternatively be calculated from Eq. (12.25):

$$F_{\text{actual}} = F_{\text{laminar},0-x_c} + F_{\text{turbulent},0-L} - F_{\text{turbulent},0-x_c} \tag{12.25}$$

$F_{\text{laminar},0-x_c}$ evaluated from Eq. (12.14) from $x = 0$ to $x = x_c$ (at $N_{\text{Re},c}$)

$F_{\text{turbulent},0-L}$ evaluated from Eqs. (12.20) and (12.21) from $x = 0$ to $x = L$

$F_{\text{turbulent},0-x_c}$ evaluated from Eqs. (12.20) and (12.21) from $x = 0$ to $x = x_c$

The first step is to locate the point of transition x_c, which can be found from the definition of $N_{\text{Re},x}$, Eq. (6.3), where $N_{\text{Re},c}$ is 5×10^5:

$$x_c = (N_{\text{Re},c} \mu)/(U_\infty \rho) = [(5 \times 10^5)(0.001)]/[(3.0)(999)] = 0.167 \text{ m} \tag{vi}$$

In other words, the boundary layer is laminar for the first 16.7 cm, the point at which the transition to turbulence begins. Next, the laminar drag coefficient and the force on the plate are calculated from the leading edge ($x = 0$) to x_c (0.167 m). Equation (12.16), evaluated at x_c, yields

$$C_{D, \text{laminar}} = 4C_1(N_{\text{Re},x})^{-1/2} = (4)(0.33206)(5 \times 10^5)^{-1/2} = 0.00188 \qquad \text{(vii)}$$

This result is used in Eq. (12.15), which is solved for the drag force F:

$$\begin{aligned}
F_{\text{laminar},0-x_c} &= \tfrac{1}{2}(\rho U_\infty^2)(Lb)(C_{D, \text{laminar}}) \\
&= \tfrac{1}{2}(999)(3.0)^2(0.167)(1.0)(0.00188) \, [(\text{kg m}^{-3})(\text{m}^2 \, \text{s}^{-2})(\text{m})(\text{m})] \\
&= 1.411 \, \text{kg m s}^{-2} = 1.411 \, \text{N} \qquad \text{(viii)}
\end{aligned}$$

The last two terms in Eq. (12.25) are calculated from Eqs. (12.20) and (12.21) using the lengths indicated in the subscripts. The middle term is

$$\begin{aligned}
C_D &= 0.455[\log_{10}(N_{\text{Re},L})]^{-2.58} \\
&= 0.455[\log_{10}(5.994 \times 10^6)]^{-2.58} = 0.003\,264 \qquad \text{(ix)}
\end{aligned}$$

$$\begin{aligned}
F_{\text{turbulent},0-L} &= \tfrac{1}{2}(\rho U_\infty^2)(Lb)(C_D) \\
&= \tfrac{1}{2}(999)(3.0)^2(2.0)(1.0)(0.003\,264) = 29.35 \, \text{N} \qquad \text{(x)}
\end{aligned}$$

For the length $0-x_c$, the drag force is

$$C_D = 0.455[\log_{10}(N_{\text{Re},c})]^{-2.58} = 0.455[\log_{10}(5 \times 10^5)]^{-2.58} = 0.005\,106 \qquad \text{(xi)}$$

$$\begin{aligned}
F_{\text{turbulent},0-x_c} &= \tfrac{1}{2}(\rho U_\infty^2)(Lb)(C_D) \\
&= \tfrac{1}{2}(999)(3.0)^2(0.167)(1.0)(0.005\,106) = 3.833 \, \text{N} \qquad \text{(xii)}
\end{aligned}$$

Substitution of the results from Eqs. (viii), (x), and (xii) into Eq. (12.25) yields the total drag on the plate:

$$F_{\text{actual}} = 1.411 + 29.35 - 3.833 = 26.93 \, \text{N} \qquad \text{(xiii)}$$

This value agrees well with that obtained by the short procedure, Eq. (12.24), i.e., 26.8 N in Eq. (v).

Example 12.4. Calculate the entry lengths in pipe flow for 99 percent development of the velocity profile at turbulent Reynolds numbers of 2100, 4000, 10^4, and 10^5. Compare these to the laminar length that might be obtained under very

TABLE 12.3
Entry lengths for Example 12.4

Reynolds number $N_{\text{Re},x}$	L_e/d_o	
	Laminar $0.0567N_{\text{Re}}$	Turbulent $0.693(N_{\text{Re}})^{1/4}$
2100	119	4.7
4000	227	5.5
10^4	567	6.9
10^5	5670	12.3

unusual conditions where no instabilities exist to trigger the transition to turbulence.

Answer. At Reynolds numbers of 2100 and 4000, the flow in most equipment is really neither fully laminar nor fully turbulent. Therefore, the correct entry length is open to question. At Reynolds numbers of 10^4 and 10^5, the flow is almost always fully turbulent, and Eq. (12.26) applies.

The results from Eq. (12.19) for laminar entry and from Eq. (12.26) for turbulent entry are compared in Table 12.3. The entry lengths for turbulent flow are quite small.

12.1.3 Heat and Mass Transfer During Boundary Layer Flow Past a Flat Plate

Of particular interest are problems of mass and heat transfer in boundary layer flows past a flat plate [E1, S1]. The simplified momentum equations for steady-state laminar flow have already been given as Eqs. (12.1) and (12.3), which must now be coupled with an additional equation for either heat or mass transfer, or both. The appropriate simplifications of the general equations, Eq. (5.13) or Eq. (5.8), were detailed in Example 5.8. The results were

$$U_x \frac{\partial T}{\partial x} + U_y \frac{\partial T}{\partial y} = \alpha \frac{\partial^2 T}{\partial y^2} \tag{12.27}$$

$$U_x \frac{\partial C_A}{\partial x} + U_y \frac{\partial C_A}{\partial y} = D \frac{\partial^2 C_A}{\partial y^2} \tag{12.28}$$

These equations are similar to Eq. (12.1), the momentum equation:

$$U_x \frac{\partial U_x}{\partial x} + U_y \frac{\partial U_x}{\partial y} = v \frac{\partial^2 U_x}{\partial y^2} \tag{12.1}$$

Reviewing briefly, Figure 12.1 presented the solution to the coupled differential equations, Eq. (12.1) and Eq. (12.3), which were solved together through the introduction of a similarity transformation. If there is also heat transfer as well as momentum transfer, then Eqs. (12.1), (12.3), and (12.27) must all be solved together. If there is heat, mass, and momentum transfer all in the same problem, then Eqs. (12.1), (12.3), (12.27) and (12.28) form a "coupled set" and must be solved together.

Heat transfer. The simplest heat transfer problem is the case of fluid at U_∞ and T_∞ passing over a flat plate that is maintained at a constant and uniform temperature T_w. Even this problem is not solvable directly. The usual assumption is to "decouple" the partial differential equations by assuming that T_w differs only slightly from T_∞ so that the solution of Eqs. (12.1) and (12.3) in Fig. 12.1 remains valid. In actual practice, the presence of a temperature gradient alters the velocity profile.

The boundary conditions for this problem in terms of the dimensionless variable Θ are

At $y = 0$, for all x

$$\frac{U_x}{U_\infty} = 0 \qquad \Theta = \frac{T_w - T}{T_w - T_\infty} = 0 \tag{12.29}$$

At $y = y_\infty$ and at $x = 0$ for all y

$$\frac{U_x}{U_\infty} = 1 \qquad \Theta = \frac{T_w - T}{T_w - T_\infty} = 1 \tag{12.30}$$

The Prandtl number is

$$N_{Pr} = c_p \mu / k \tag{8.4}$$

The thermal diffusivity, Eq. (2.10), can be expressed in terms of the Prandtl number:

$$\alpha = \frac{k}{\rho c_p} = \frac{\nu}{N_{Pr}} \tag{12.31}$$

Equation (12.27) is converted into an ordinary differential equation by another similarity transformation:

$$\frac{d^2\Theta}{d\eta^2} + \frac{N_{Pr}f}{2}\frac{d\Theta}{d\eta} = 0 \tag{12.32}$$

where η is from Eq. (12.5), f (a function of η) is from Eq. (12.8), Θ is from Eq. (12.29), and α is replaced via Eq. (12.31). Equation (12.32) is an ordinary differential equation that can be integrated directly [K3]. This problem was solved by Pohlhausen [P4], and the results are shown in Fig. 12.6. For each

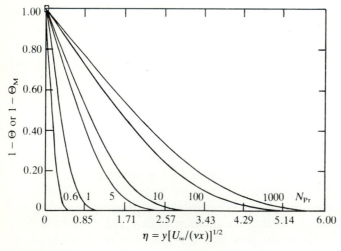

FIGURE 12.6
Dimensionless temperature distribution for flow over a flat plate.

Prandtl number, the slope of the temperature gradient at the wall, $\Theta'(0)$, necessary for the integration of Eq. (12.32), must be adjusted to give the dimensionless temperature Θ far from the wall as unity as specified in Eq. (12.30). This is analogous to the adjustment of the constant C_1 [equal to $f''(0)$] in Eq. (v) of Example 12.1 to give $f'(\eta = \infty) = 1$.

For fluids whose Prandtl numbers are unity, Eq. (12.27) reduces to Eq. (12.1). Then the ordinate in Fig. 12.1 can represent both the dimensionless velocity distribution U_x/U_∞ and the dimensionless temperature distribution Θ as well. Many gases and a few liquids, such as water at 350°F, have a Prandtl number of about unity. The condition of the momentum transfer equation being identical with the heat transfer equation is another statement of the Reynolds analogy, Eqs. (6.94) and (6.95).

The thermal boundary layer thickness δ_H is defined as the thickness (distance in y) at which $\Theta = 0.99$. Pohlhausen [P4] showed that for fluids whose Prandtl number exceeds 0.6:

$$\delta_H/x = 5.0(N_{\mathrm{Re},x})^{-1/2}(N_{\mathrm{Pr}})^{-1/3} \qquad (12.33)$$

Equation (12.18) can be divided by Eq. (12.33) to find the ratio of the momentum boundary layer thickness to the thermal boundary layer thickness:

$$\delta/\delta_H = (N_{\mathrm{Pr}})^{1/3} \qquad (12.34)$$

which applies for $N_{\mathrm{Pr}} > 0.6$. Equation (12.34) actually comes from the values of $\Theta'(0)$ that were necessary to satisfy the boundary condition of Eq. (12.30); i.e., the ratio δ/δ_H is approximately equal to the quantity $\Theta'(0)/C_1$. For liquid metals, the exponent $\frac{1}{3}$ becomes $\frac{1}{2}$ [C5].

The form of Eq. (12.33) suggests that for $N_{\mathrm{Pr}} > 0.6$ the dimensionless temperature Θ can be plotted against the product $\eta(N_{\mathrm{Pr}})^{1/3}$, which is

$$\eta(N_{\mathrm{Pr}})^{1/3} = \frac{y}{x}(N_{\mathrm{Re},x})^{1/2}(N_{\mathrm{Pr}})^{1/3} \qquad (12.35)$$

This plot is given in Fig. 12.7; the slope is 0.33206 at low abscissa values, i.e., the value of C_1. Both Figs. 12.6 and 12.7 may be generated by numerical integration of the appropriate equations, as illustrated in Example 12.1. For example, the ACSL program for Fig. 12.6 is listed in Fig. 12.8. The variables

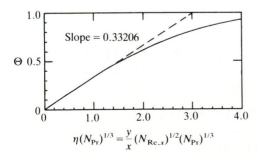

$$\eta(N_{\mathrm{Pr}})^{1/3} = \frac{y}{x}(N_{\mathrm{Re},x})^{1/2}(N_{\mathrm{Pr}})^{1/3}$$

FIGURE 12.7
Dimensionless temperature versus $[\eta(N_{\mathrm{Pr}})^{1/3}]$ for laminar flow past a flat plate ($N_{\mathrm{Pr}} > 0.6$).

```
PROGRAM POHLHAUSEN
INITIAL
ARRAY NPR(6),TDIC1(6)
INTEGER I
CONSTANT FIC=0.0,FDIC=0.0,FDDIC=0.33206,ETAT=6.
CONSTANT TIC=1.0,I=1,NPR=0.6,1.,5.,10.,100.,1000.
CONSTANT TDIC1=0.28007,0.33206,0.57626,0.7282,1.5735,3.39
CONSTANT CINT= 0.01
L1..CONTINUE
TDIC=-TDIC1(I)
END
DYNAMIC
DERIVATIVE
ETA=T
FDDD=-0.5*F*FDD
FDD=INTEG(FDDD,FDDIC)
FD=INTEG(FDD,FDIC)
F=INTEG(FD,FIC)
U=FD
V=0.5*(ETA*FD-F)
TDD=-0.5*NPR(I)*F*TD
TD=INTEG(TDD,TDIC)
TN=INTEG(TD,TIC)
THETA=1.0 - TN
END
TERMT(ETA.GT.ETAT)
END
TERMINAL
I=I+1
IF(I.GT.6)GO TO L2
GO TO L1
L2..CONTINUE
END
END
```

FIGURE 12.8
Program to generate Pohlhausen's solution.

TDIC1 and TN are $\Theta'(0)$ and $(1 - \Theta)$, respectively. The values listed for TDIC1 on line 7 in Fig. 12.8 are within 2 percent of those calculated from Eq. (12.34), expressed in terms of $\Theta'(0)/C_1$.

Heat transfer coefficient. Let us assume that there is a stagnant and very thin layer of fluid adjacent to the wall of the plate; heat is conducted through this layer from the plate at uniform temperature T_w into the boundary layer:

$$dq = -(k)(dA)(dT/dy)_{y=0} \tag{12.36}$$

The heat transferred by convection to this thin film is

$$dq = h_x(T_w - T_\infty) \, dA \tag{12.37}$$

where h_x is the local heat transfer coefficient at position x. The heat transfers represented by Eqs. (12.36) and (12.37) are equal. When these equations are combined, the result can be solved for h_x:

$$h_x = k(d\Theta/dy)_{y=0} = k\Theta'(0) \tag{12.38}$$

Equation (12.38) is an equivalent definition of the local heat transfer coefficient over a flat plate [cf. Eq. (11.30)].

The quantity $(d\Theta/dy)_{y=0}$ [i.e., $\Theta'(0)$] can be found from the slope in Fig. 12.7 at a zero value of the abscissa. Using Eq. (12.38), it can be shown that

$$h_x = \frac{0.33206k}{x}(N_{\mathrm{Re},x})^{1/2}(N_{\mathrm{Pr}})^{1/3} \tag{12.39}$$

where Eq. (12.39) is restricted to $N_{\mathrm{Pr}} > 0.6$. The group $h_x x/k$ contains the same variables as the Nusselt number, Eq. (8.21); thus, Eq. (12.39) may be rewritten as

$$N_{\mathrm{Nu},x} = \frac{h_x x}{k} = 0.33206(N_{\mathrm{Re},x})^{1/2}(N_{\mathrm{Pr}})^{1/3} \tag{12.40}$$

Equations (12.39) and (12.40) correlate the local heat transfer coefficient h_x. This quantity is often less useful than a mean coefficient h_m, which may be found from

$$h_{\mathrm{m}} = \frac{b}{A}\int_0^L h_x \, dx \tag{12.41}$$

where b is the width of the flat plate in the z direction and A is the area for heat transfer in the following expression for q, the total heat transferred:

$$q = h_{\mathrm{m}}A(T_{\mathrm{w}} - T_\infty) = (T_{\mathrm{w}} - T_\infty)b\int_0^L h_x \, dx \tag{12.42}$$

The mean Nusselt number is

$$N_{\mathrm{Nu},L} = \frac{h_{\mathrm{m}}L}{k} \tag{12.43}$$

Then Eq. (12.40) becomes

$$N_{\mathrm{Nu},L} = \frac{h_{\mathrm{m}}L}{k} = 0.664(N_{\mathrm{Re},L})^{1/2}(N_{\mathrm{Pr}})^{1/3} = (2N_{\mathrm{Nu},x})(N_{\mathrm{Re},L}/N_{\mathrm{Re},x})^{1/2} \tag{12.44}$$

Equation (12.44) applies in the laminar region ($N_{\mathrm{Re},L} < 5 \times 10^5$) for fluids whose Prandtl number is greater than 0.6. The primary exclusion of the Prandtl number constraint is heat transfer in liquid metals.

In laminar heat transfer, as x approaches zero, h must approach infinity, as shown by Eq. (12.39). Similarly, as x becomes very large, the temperature in the boundary layer approaches the plate wall temperature. From Eq. (12.39), it can be shown that h_x is proportional to $x^{-1/2}$; thus for large x, Eq. (12.39) predicts that h_x approaches zero.

For turbulent flow, the recommended equations for correlation of the local heat transfer coefficient h_x are [H3]

$$N_{\mathrm{Nu},x} = \frac{h_x x}{k} = 0.0296(N_{\mathrm{Re},x})^{0.8}(N_{\mathrm{Pr}})^{1/3} \qquad 5 \times 10^5 \le N_{\mathrm{Re},x} \le 10^7$$

$$\tag{12.45}$$

$$N_{\mathrm{Nu},x} = \frac{h_x x}{k} = 0.185(N_{\mathrm{Re},x})(N_{\mathrm{Pr}})^{1/3}[\log_{10}(N_{\mathrm{Re},x})]^{-2.584} \qquad 10^7 \le N_{\mathrm{Re},x} \le 10^9$$

The average Nusselt number over both the laminar and turbulent boundary layer (x goes from 0 to L) is [H3]

$$N_{\text{Nu},L} = \frac{h_m L}{k} = [0.037(N_{\text{Re},L})^{0.8} - 850](N_{\text{Pr}})^{1/3} \qquad 5 \times 10^5 \le N_{\text{Re},x} \le 10^7$$
(12.46)

This latter equation in terms of the Colburn j-factor becomes

$$j_H = j_M = f/2 = 0.037(N_{\text{Re},L})^{-0.2} \tag{12.47}$$

where the analogy has been indicated and the j-factors are as discussed in conjunction with Eqs. (11.79) to (11.82). Note the similarity of Eq. (12.47) to the corresponding pipe flow equation, Eq. (11.80). Also, Eq. (12.46) is quite similar to the heat transfer correlations for pipe flow, such as the Dittus–Boelter and the Sieder–Tate, Eqs. (11.66), and (11.67), where the Reynolds number exponent is identical and the Prandtl number exponent is similar or identical.

Methods of correlating turbulent boundary layer heat transfer are given by Churchill [C6].

Example 12.5. Water is flowing over a flat plate that is maintained at a constant 290 K. The free stream velocity is 3 m s^{-1}. The free stream temperature is 285 K. Find (a) the length of the laminar boundary layer, (b) the thickness of the momentum boundary layer and the thermal boundary layer at the transition point, (c) the local heat transfer coefficient at the transition point, and (d) the mean heat transfer coefficient between the leading edge of the plate and the transition point.

Answer. For this problem, all properties to be evaluated at 285 K will be assumed constant. From the Appendix, Table A.1, the properties of water in SI units are

$$\rho = 1/v_f = 1/(1 \times 10^{-3}) = 1000 \text{ kg m}^{-3}$$
$$\mu = 1225 \times 10^{-6} \text{ N s m}^{-2} = 1.225 \text{ cP} = 1.225 \times 10^{-3} \text{ kg m}^{-1} \text{s}^{-1} \tag{i}$$
$$k = 0.590 \text{ W m}^{-1} \text{K}^{-1}$$
$$N_{\text{Pr}} = 8.70$$

(a) Length. The transition will be assumed to occur at $N_{\text{Re},c}$ equal to 5×10^5 (for a typical flat plate), although this number can be lowered if a disturbance is introduced into the flow. Thus

$$x_c = (N_{\text{Re},c})[\mu/(\rho U_\infty)] = [(5 \times 10^5)(1.225 \times 10^{-3})]/[(1000)(3.0)] = 0.2042 \text{ m} \quad \text{(ii)}$$

(b) Thickness. The thickness of the momentum boundary layer is computed from Eq. (12.18):

$$\delta = (5.0)(x)(N_{\text{Re},x})^{-1/2} = (5.0)(0.2042)(5 \times 10^5)^{-1/2} = 1.444 \times 10^{-3} \text{ m} \quad \text{(iii)}$$

The thickness of the thermal boundary layer is computed from Eq. (12.33) or Eq. (12.34):

$$\delta_H = (\delta)(N_{\text{Pr}})^{-1/3} = (1.444 \times 10^{-3})(8.70)^{-1/3} = 7.019 \times 10^{-4} \text{ m} \quad \text{(iv)}$$

(c) Local heat transfer coefficient. The local heat transfer coefficient at x equal to 0.7 ft is computed from Eq. (12.39):

$$h_x = \left(\frac{0.33206k}{x}\right)(N_{\text{Re},x})^{1/2}(N_{\text{Pr}})^{1/3} = \left(\frac{(0.33206)(0.590)}{0.2042}\right)(5 \times 10^5)^{1/2}(8.70)^{1/3}$$

$$= 1396 \text{ W m}^{-2}\text{ K}^{-1} = (1396)(0.17611) = 246 \text{ Btu h}^{-1}\text{ ft}^{-2}\text{ °F}^{-1} \qquad \text{(v)}$$

where the conversion between SI and English units is from Table C.10.

(d) Mean heat transfer coefficient. The mean heat transfer coefficient between the leading edge $(x = 0)$ and the transition $(x = L = 0.2042 \text{ m})$ is found from Eq. (12.44). Since x equals L for this problem, the ratio $N_{\text{Re},L}/N_{\text{Re},x}$ is unity. Therefore, Eq. (12.44) reduces to

$$N_{\text{Nu},L} = 2N_{\text{Nu},x} \qquad \text{(vi)}$$

Since the ratio k/L equals k/x, the expression reduces to

$$h_m = 2h_x = (2)(1396) = 2791 \text{ W m}^{-2}\text{ K}^{-1} = 492 \text{ Btu h}^{-1}\text{ ft}^{-2}\text{ °F}^{-1} \qquad \text{(vii)}$$

Mass transfer. If the flat plate were porous, or perhaps soluble in the fluid passing over it, so that a constant concentration $C_{\text{A,w}}$ could be maintained at the surface, then there would be a mass boundary layer as a result of mass transfer from (or to) the plate. The basic equations are the coupled set formed by Eqs. (12.1), (12.3), and (12.28). The assumptions to be invoked were discussed in Example 5.8.

For the case of mass transfer from a flat plate in isothermal, constant density flow, the concentration is changed to dimensionless form so that the boundary conditions become

At $y = 0$, for all x

$$\frac{U_x}{U_\infty} = 0 \qquad \Theta_{\text{M}} = \frac{C_{\text{A,w}} - C_{\text{A}}}{C_{\text{A,w}} - C_{\text{A},\infty}} = 0 \qquad \text{(12.48)}$$

At $y = y_\infty$ and at $x = 0$ for all y

$$\frac{U_x}{U_\infty} = 1 \qquad \Theta_{\text{M}} = \frac{C_{\text{A,w}} - C_{\text{A}}}{C_{\text{A,w}} - C_{\text{A},\infty}} = 1 \qquad \text{(12.49)}$$

where $C_{\text{A,w}}$ is the concentration of A at the plate surface and is constant. The definition of the dimensionless mass concentration Θ_{M} is similar to that of the dimensionless temperature Θ [cf. Eq. (12.29)].

The method of solution of the coupled set of differential equations, Eq. (12.1), Eq. (12.3), and Eq. (12.28), for the boundary conditions of Eqs. (12.48) and (12.49) is analogous to the solution of the previous heat transfer problem:

$$\frac{d^2\Theta_{\text{M}}}{d\eta^2} + \frac{N_{\text{Sc}}f}{2}\frac{d\Theta_{\text{M}}}{d\eta} = 0 \qquad \text{(12.50)}$$

where f is the dimensionless function in Eq. (12.8), Θ_{M} is defined in Eqs.

(12.48) and (12.49), and N_{Sc} is the Schmidt number, Eq. (8.6):

$$N_{Sc} = \frac{\nu}{D} = \frac{\mu}{\rho D} \tag{8.6}$$

The Schmidt number is the ratio of the momentum diffusivity to the mass diffusivity, and is the dimensionless group in mass transfer that is analogous to N_{Pr} in heat transfer. If the Schmidt number is unity, then the dimensionless concentration profile is identical to the dimensionless velocity profile of Fig. 12.1.

For the general case, the dimensionless mass transfer solution is analogous to the dimensionless heat transfer solution of Fig. 12.6. The ordinate $(1 - \Theta)$ in Fig. 12.6 is replaced by the dimensionless concentration $(1 - \Theta_M)$, the abscissa is unchanged, and each curve corresponds to a particular value of N_{Sc} instead of N_{Pr}. Figure 12.7 can be similarly altered for the mass transfer case. The ratio of the momentum boundary layer thickness to the mass boundary layer thickness is

$$\delta / \delta_M = (N_{Sc})^{1/3} \tag{12.51}$$

for fluids whose Schmidt number is greater than 0.6, as expected from comparing with Eq. (12.34).

12.2 FLOW OVER CYLINDERS AND SPHERES

Flow over bluff bodies such as spheres and cylinders is a natural extension of the boundary layer flow concepts; indeed, the flow over a cylinder was depicted in Fig. 12.4 to illustrate boundary layer separation. In this section, the concepts of ideal and potential flow will be outlined to show one possible approximation for the flow over a cylinder. A more realistic approximation will then be outlined for the laminar flow over a sphere (called Stokes flow). Turbulent conditions will be treated next, and finally the necessary extensions for heat and mass transfer correlations will be discussed.

12.2.1 Ideal Flow (Nonviscous Fluids)

In many problems, viscous forces are negligible when compared with other forces that might be present and acting on the fluid. Such cases are termed "ideal flow"; the viscosity is assumed to be zero. This assumption reduces the order of the differential equation, and as a result all the boundary conditions cannot be satisfied. The no-slip condition at the wall cannot be maintained; thus, the concept of ideal flow might be valid where the field of interest is the main fluid stream and not the interactions of the stream with the boundaries.

When the assumption of ideal flow ($\nu = 0$) is made, the Navier–Stokes equation, Eq. (5.15), reduces to Euler's equation:

$$\frac{\partial U}{\partial t} + (U \cdot \nabla) = -\frac{1}{\rho}\nabla p + g \tag{12.52}$$

Equation (12.52) can be rewritten as three equations, one for each component of velocity; these plus the equation of continuity constitute a set of four equations, which can be solved in theory for the four unknowns. Even for steady-state, Eq. (12.52) is nonlinear and, in general, much too complicated to solve.

Potential and stream functions. Useful solutions to some important problems in fluid mechanics can be found through use of potential and stream functions. The stream function ψ was given previously as

$$U_x = \frac{\partial \psi}{\partial y} \qquad U_y = -\frac{\partial \psi}{\partial x} \tag{12.6}$$

where again ψ is not to be confused with the generalized concentration of property from Chapter 2. Note that Eq. (12.6) assumes no variation of velocity in the z direction (i.e., a two-dimensional flow field).

The velocity potential ϕ is defined so that the derivative of ϕ in any direction gives the velocity in that direction:

$$U_x = \frac{\partial \phi}{\partial x} \qquad U_y = \frac{\partial \phi}{\partial y} \qquad U_z = \frac{\partial \phi}{\partial z} \tag{12.53}$$

Equation (12.53) can be expressed in vector form:

$$U = \nabla \phi \tag{12.54}$$

where ∇ is the del operator, Eq. (2.16).

The velocity potential as defined in the above equations is a mathematical quantity that is picked more or less by trial and error so as both to satisfy Eq. (12.54) and to represent some practical flow situations. These will be illustrated later. For an incompressible fluid, the equation of continuity reduces to Eq. (3.74), which after substituting Eq. (12.54) gives the well-known Laplace equation:

$$(\nabla \cdot U) = (\nabla \cdot \nabla \phi) = \nabla^2 \phi = 0 \tag{12.55}$$

Thus, for a flow of an incompressible fluid for which a velocity potential exists, Eq. (12.55) shows that ϕ follows Laplace's equation. Furthermore, the term $\nabla^2 U$ can be expanded to show with the aid of Eq. (12.55):

$$\nabla^2 U = \nabla^2 (\nabla \phi) = \nabla(\nabla^2 \phi) = 0 \tag{12.56}$$

Therefore, the term $v(\nabla^2 U)$ in the Navier–Stokes equation [Eq. (5.15)] is zero. In ideal flow, the viscosity was assumed zero; in potential flow, the term

$\nabla^2 U$ is zero by the definition of the velocity potential for an incompressible fluid. Hence, it follows that solutions of Laplace's equation with appropriate potential functions and boundary conditions are legitimate solutions to the Euler equation, Eq. (12.52), under the condition just outlined.

Equation (12.55) can be expressed in any coordinate system by use of the del operator as given in Table 5.1. For two dimensions and rectangular coordinates, Eq. (12.55) reduces to

$$\frac{\partial^2 \phi}{\partial x^2} + \frac{\partial^2 \phi}{\partial y^2} = 0 \tag{12.57}$$

which is the two-dimensional form of the Laplace equation. Equation (12.57) is a linear partial differential equation of the second order. Furthermore, Eq. (12.55) with ϕ replaced by the appropriate variable applies for many different problems, such as steady-state conduction (heat transfer), electrical conduction, etc. Solutions of the Laplace equation are available for many boundary conditions [C1].

Equation (12.54) can be differentiated and the results used to show the assumption of a velocity potential ϕ requires that the flow be irrotational. In an irrotational flow, the angular velocity of the fluid elements about their center axis is zero. In other words, in potential flow, fluid elements may deform but not rotate. Note that the property of irrotation is a mathematical consequence of the introduction of ϕ [B2, L1], not an assumption.

The flow potential ϕ, which obeys Laplace's equation, Eq. (12.55), forms an orthogonal (right-angle) set of lines with the stream function ψ, Eq. (12.6). The lines of constant potential represent the lines of constant force during the flow, while the lines of constant stream function ψ represents the lines of the flow direction that result from the flow potential ϕ. The lines formed by constant values of ϕ and ψ form a "flow net". Such a system of lines can be very useful when, in addition, the functions obey the Cauchy–Riemann conditions, which are

$$\frac{\partial \phi}{\partial x} = \frac{\partial \psi}{\partial y} \qquad \frac{\partial \phi}{\partial y} = -\frac{\partial \psi}{\partial x} \tag{12.58}$$

The functions ϕ and ψ are said to be analytic when Eq. (12.58) applies and if ϕ and ψ are real, continuous, single-valued, and if all four derivatives in Eq. (12.58) are continuous. It can be shown that when ϕ and ψ are analytic functions, the stream function ψ must also obey Laplace's equation:

$$\nabla^2 \psi = \frac{\partial^2 \psi}{\partial x^2} + \frac{\partial^2 \psi}{\partial y^2} = 0 \tag{12.59}$$

The Cauchy–Riemann equations, Eq. (12.58), are used to relate the stream function ϕ to U_x and U_y. The result of combining Eqs. (12.53) and (12.58) is

$$U_x = \frac{\partial \phi}{\partial x} = \frac{\partial \psi}{\partial y} \qquad U_y = \frac{\partial \phi}{\partial y} = -\frac{\partial \psi}{\partial x} \tag{12.60}$$

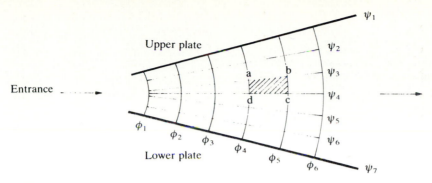

FIGURE 12.9
Ideal flow between nonparallel plates.

When equations are available to describe the potential ϕ, this set of equations can be integrated to find equations for the stream function ψ, if the flow is incompressible and irrotational.

Streamlines. Figure 12.9 shows the ideal flow between infinite nonparallel plates, which form a diverging duct. In this figure, the intervals between adjacent ϕ's and ψ's are constant. The area abcd is a typical mesh. Notice how the meshes become larger as the flow progresses through the diverging section. The lines of constant ψ are called streamlines. No element of fluid ever crosses a streamline. The separation of the streamlines is a measure of the relative velocity [recall that $\partial \psi / \partial y = U_x$, cf. Eq. (12.60)]. Notice how the streamlines are more closely spaced at the entrance than at the exit in Fig. 12.9. The streamlines display the velocity pattern, and by use of the Bernoulli equation, Eq. (7.63), the pressure pattern as well.

There are an infinite number of solutions to the Laplace equation, Eq. (12.57), each corresponding to a particular set of boundary conditions (four needed). Although most problems (turbulent flow, for example) are not solvable as ideal flow, many important examples of nonviscous, incompressible, irrotational flow abound, including flow through diverging (Fig. 12.9) and converging sections of large two-dimensional ducts, flow through sharp-edged orifices, flow over sharp-crested weirs, flow past Pitot tubes, and the discharge of fluids to or from large reservoirs through small inlets.

Example 12.6. A simple velocity potential known to be analytic is

$$\phi = U_\infty x \tag{i}$$

Determine the flow so described and the equation for the stream function. Prepare a graph of U_x and U_y as functions of x and y.

Answer. Since ϕ is an analytic function, the potential in Eq. (i) must obey Laplace's equation. Using Eq. (12.57), it is seen that $\nabla^2 \phi$ is zero, and the flow

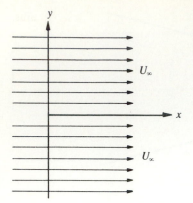

FIGURE 12.10
Uniform ideal flow in the x direction for $\phi = U_\infty x$.

therefore is incompressible by Eq. (12.55). As previously shown, for the same boundary conditions this incompressible, potential flow will be equivalent to an ideal (nonviscous), irrotational flow.

Equation (12.53), which defines the velocity potential, is used to evaluate U_x and U_y:

$$U_x = \frac{\partial \phi}{\partial x} \qquad U_y = \frac{\partial \phi}{\partial y} \qquad U_z = \frac{\partial \phi}{\partial z} \tag{12.53}$$

The derivatives of Eq. (i) yield

$$U_x = \frac{\partial \phi}{\partial x} = U_\infty \qquad U_y = \frac{\partial \phi}{\partial y} = 0 \qquad U_z = 0 \tag{ii}$$

This flow, shown in Fig. 12.10, is simply a flow in the x direction with the x velocity U_x equal to U_∞ for all values of y and z, since U_y and U_z are zero. The streamlines can be obtained from Eq. (12.60):

$$U_x = \frac{\partial \phi}{\partial x} = \frac{\partial \psi}{\partial y} \qquad U_y = \frac{\partial \phi}{\partial y} = -\frac{\partial \psi}{\partial x} \tag{12.60}$$

Each equation can be integrated in order to solve for the stream function ψ:

$$\psi = \int U_x \, dy = U_\infty y + C(x) \qquad \text{from } U_x = U_\infty = \partial \psi / \partial y \tag{iii}$$

$$\psi = C(y) \qquad \text{from } U_y = 0 = \partial \psi / \partial x \tag{iv}$$

There are really no boundary conditions for finding the two constants of integration, $C(x)$ and $C(y)$. However, the only way the second equation (iv) can be true is if $C(x) = 0$; therefore

$$\psi = U_\infty y \tag{v}$$

The veracity of Eq. (v) can be checked via Eq. (12.60). Indeed, $\partial \psi / \partial y$ does equal U_x and $-\partial \psi / \partial x$ equals U_y, which is zero.

Example 12.7. Repeat Example 12.6 for the analytic velocity potential:

$$\phi = U_\infty (x^2 - y^2) \tag{i}$$

Answer. Since ϕ is an analytic function, the potential in Eq. (i) must obey Laplace's equation, Eq. (12.57):

$$\nabla^2 \phi = 0 = 2U_\infty - 2U_\infty \tag{ii}$$

The flow therefore is incompressible by Eq. (12.55). As previously shown, for the same boundary conditions this incompressible, potential flow will be equivalent to an ideal (nonviscous), irrotational flow. From Eq. (12.53) and the derivative of Eq. (i):

$$U_x = \frac{\partial \phi}{\partial x} = 2U_\infty x, \qquad U_y = \frac{\partial \phi}{\partial y} = -2U_\infty y \qquad U_z = 0 \tag{iii}$$

The streamlines of flow can be obtained by integration with the Cauchy–Riemann conditions, Eq. (12.60):

$$\psi = 2U_\infty xy + C(x) \qquad \text{from} \quad 2U_\infty x = \partial \psi/\partial y$$
$$\psi = 2U_\infty xy + C(y) \qquad \text{from} \; -2U_\infty y = -\partial \psi/\partial x \tag{iv}$$

For these to be true:

$$\psi = 2U_\infty xy \tag{v}$$

The streamlines and potentials are shown in Fig. 12.11 for a negative U_∞ and a positive x. Both positive and negative values of ψ are shown. The flow can be pictured as occurring around the inside of a corner (upper quarter) or against a flat plate (entire picture). The actual velocities are obtained from Eq. (iii).

Example 12.8. Repeat Example 12.6 for the following analytic velocity potential in polar (cylindrical) coordinates.

$$\phi = U_\infty\left(r + \frac{1}{r}\right)(\cos \theta) \tag{i}$$

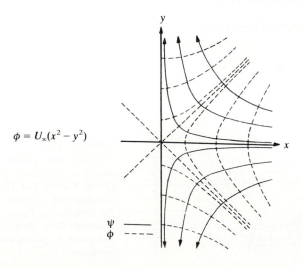

$\phi = U_x(x^2 - y^2)$

ψ ———
ϕ - - - -

FIGURE 12.11
Potential flow around the inside of a corner or against a plate.

Answer. The Laplace equation in cylindrical coordinates is given in Table 5.1:

$$\nabla^2 \phi = \frac{\partial^2 \phi}{\partial r^2} + \frac{1}{r}\frac{\partial \phi}{\partial r} + \frac{1}{r^2}\frac{\partial^2 \phi}{\partial \theta^2} = 0 \qquad (ii)$$

If the potential in Eq. (i) satisfies Eq. (ii), the flow is incompressible. Combining Eqs. (i) and (ii):

$$U_\infty(\cos \theta)(2r^{-3}) + (U_\infty/r)(\cos \theta)(1 - r^{-2}) + (U_\infty/r^2)[r + (1/r)](-\cos \theta) = 0 \quad (iii)$$

Equation (iii) can be simplified:

$$U_\infty(\cos \theta)(2r^{-3} + r^{-1} - r^{-3} - r^{-1} - r^{-3}) = U_\infty(\cos \theta)(0) = 0 \qquad (iv)$$

Thus, Laplace's equation is satisfied. For polar coordinates, the velocities are given by

$$U_r = \frac{\partial \phi}{\partial r} = \frac{1}{r}\frac{\partial \psi}{\partial \theta} = U_\infty\left(1 - \frac{1}{r^2}\right)\cos \theta \qquad (v)$$

$$U_\theta = \frac{1}{r}\frac{\partial \phi}{\partial \theta} = -\frac{\partial \psi}{\partial r} = -U_\infty\left(1 + \frac{1}{r^2}\right)\sin \theta \qquad (vi)$$

To obtain the streamlines:

$$\psi = U_\infty\left(r - \frac{1}{r}\right)\sin \theta + C(r) \qquad \text{from } U_r = \frac{1}{r}\frac{\partial \psi}{\partial \theta} \qquad (vii)$$

$$\psi = U_\infty\left(r - \frac{1}{r}\right)\sin \theta + C(\theta) \qquad \text{from } U_\theta = -\frac{\partial \psi}{\partial r} \qquad (viii)$$

Clearly

$$\psi = U_\infty\left(r - \frac{1}{r}\right)\sin \theta \qquad (ix)$$

The streamlines and potentials are shown in Fig. 12.12. They may be visualized as the flow outside a cylindrical shape ($r > 1$), or the flow inside a semicircle ($r < 1$).

Example 12.9. Find several representative streamlines for the potential given in Example 12.8:

$$\phi = U_\infty\left(r + \frac{1}{r}\right)\cos \theta \qquad (i)$$

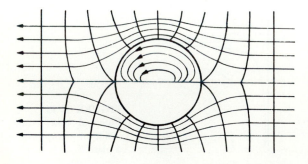

FIGURE 12.12
Potential flow outside and inside a cylindrical shape. (*From Prandtl and Tietjens, Fundamentals of Hydro- and Aeromechanics, Dover Publications, Inc., New York. Reprinted by permission of publisher.*)

Answer. The stream function ψ is Eq. (ix) in Example 12.8:

$$\psi = U_\infty\left(r - \frac{1}{r}\right)\sin\theta \tag{ii}$$

Equations (i) and (ii) are not in convenient form for plotting. The streamline $\psi = 0$ is located by realizing that Eq. (ii) can be zero two ways:

$$r - (1/r) = 0 \tag{iii}$$

$$\sin\theta = 0 \tag{iv}$$

Equation (iii) is the equation for a circle of unit radius and constitutes the cylinder in Fig. 12.12. Equation (iv) is the equation for the x axis.

The remaining streamlines follow easily if Eq. (ii) is parameterized through a constant c, where

$$\psi = cU_\infty \tag{v}$$

Equating Eqs. (ii) and (v), the result is

$$c = \left(r - \frac{1}{r}\right)\sin\theta \tag{vi}$$

This equation rearranges to the following quadratic:

$$r^2 - \frac{cr}{\sin\theta} - 1 = 0 \tag{vii}$$

Since r is the radius in polar coordinates, only the positive root of Eq. (vii) is meaningful. From the quadratic formula, the positive root is

$$r = \frac{c + (c^2 + 4\sin^2\theta)^{1/2}}{2\sin\theta} \tag{viii}$$

The graph of Fig. 12.12 can be plotted from Eq. (viii) by selecting a value for c (e.g., 1.0, 1.9, 2.0, etc.) and then calculating the corresponding values of r for

$$0° \leqslant \theta \leqslant 360° \tag{ix}$$

Some representative values for c of 1 are given in Table 12.4. The values for $\phi = U_x$ ($c = 1$) and $\phi = 0$ are plotted in Fig. 12.13. This calculation is repeated until Fig. 12.12 is complete.

TABLE 12.4
Values of r and θ for the stream function $\psi = U_\infty$

θ, degrees	$(1 + 4\sin^2\theta)^{1/2}$	r
0 or 180	1.000	0
15 or 165	1.128	−0.247 or 4.11
30 or 150	1.414	−0.414 or 2.415
50 or 130	1.82	−0.535 or 1.84
70 or 110	2.13	−0.602 or 1.66
90	2.24	−0.620 or 1.62

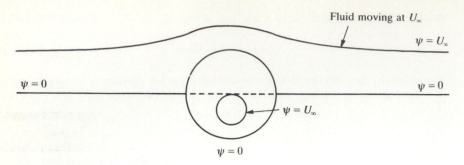

FIGURE 12.13
The streamlines of flow about a cylindrical shape.

Path and streamlines. There are three types of lines to be considered. First, there are the streamlines of flow just mentioned, which map out the velocity direction at every point in the field. Second, there are path lines, which describe the paths of separate fluid particles (a small fluid element) with time. Finally, there are streak lines, which at a given instant are the loci of all fluid elements that had previously passed through some specific point in the flow field. These lines are of experimental interest in flow visualization studies; for example, one obtains a streak line when smoke or dye is injected into a moving stream.

For steady-state motion, all three lines are identical. The streamlines are fixed in the flow field with time. At each point, the fluid particle moves in the direction of the velocity, but since this is fixed, each fluid particle that originates on a given streamline must remain on that streamline. Thus, for steady-state motion the fluid path is the same as the streamline. The streak line will coincide with the streamline and path line, since there is only one streamline at any specific point in the flow field, and each fluid element that has passed this point must have been on this streamline and must remain there. For steady-state, streak lines can give useful information about the streamlines of flow and paths of fluid elements.

For unsteady-state motions, the three lines do not coincide and are related in a complex manner. The path and streak lines can be obtained from a knowledge of the instantaneous streamlines.[6]

Since in electrical conduction the voltage distribution obeys the Laplace equation, an electrical analogy can be used to solve potential flow problems experimentally. The method involves the use of a conducting plate, a solution, or a conducting paper, in the manner suggested by Fig. 12.14. The voltages, or

---

[6] The movie *Flow Visualization* and film loops FM-47 and 48 illustrate these lines for both steady-state and unsteady-state.

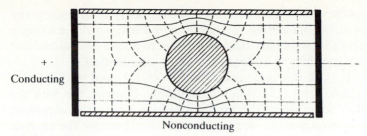

FIGURE 12.14
Electrical analogy to ideal flow.

potentials (dashed lines), are read using a probe, voltmeter, or a conducting paint. The streamlines (solid lines) can be obtained directly by exchanging the conducting elements for the nonconducting, including the center disk in the figure.

12.2.2 Stokes Flow Past a Sphere

The problem of a sphere moving very slowly through a stationary fluid was first solved by Stokes [S6] in 1851. Actually, there is a whole class of problems dealing with very slow motion (or creeping motion) of fluids past bodies of various shapes [L1]. Stokes' law is commonly encountered and is by far the most important of these.

Most practical applications of Stokes flow involve determination of the settling velocity, i.e., the velocity with which small solid or liquid particles fall through a fluid such as air or water. In flows where Stokes' law applies, viscous effects are paramount; the ideal flow solutions of the last section made the opposite assumption and are clearly inapplicable. Engineering applications of Stokes flow occur in problems of settling, viscosity determination, air pollution, aerosols, fluidization, and other two-phase flows with very low relative motion between fluid and particle.

Solution of the Stokes problem begins with the Navier–Stokes equation, Eq. (5.15), for steady flow. Since motion is very slow, the inertial term $(U \cdot \nabla)U$ is negligible, and Eq. (5.15) for an incompressible fluid reduces to

$$\nabla p = \mu(\nabla^2 U) \tag{12.61}$$

where the boundary conditions are

At $r = r_p$

$$U_x = U_y = U_z = 0 \tag{12.62}$$

At $r = r_\infty$

$$U_x = U_\infty \qquad U_y = U_z = 0 \tag{12.63}$$

Note that these boundary conditions assume that the sphere is stationary and the fluid moves past it. In engineering practice, the problem usually involves a sphere moving relative to a stationary fluid or relative to a fluid of constant and uniform velocity. The solutions to all three problems are identical.

Equation (12.61) is of the same order as Eq. (5.15), and all boundary conditions in Eqs. (12.62) and (12.63) can be satisfied. Contrast this with the ideal or potential flow solutions of the previous section where the important boundary condition of no-slip-at-the-wall was not satisfied because the analysis reduced the order of the differential equation. By further differentiation of Eq. (12.61), Stokes showed that Laplace's equation for pressure holds:

$$\nabla^2 p = 0 \tag{12.64}$$

The solution by Stokes to the sphere problem is approximate because it neglects the inertial term and assumes incompressibility. The mathematics involved is lengthy, and will not be reproduced here. Naturally, the velocities U_x, U_y, and U_z are all complex functions of position relative to the sphere. Equations for these are reproduced elsewhere [B2]. Figure 12.15 compares streamlines calculated from Stokes' equations with streamlines calculated by the potential flow assumption. Stokes' streamlines predict curvature around the sphere at distances much greater from the solid surface than does the potential flow prediction.

Stokes' law relates the force (or drag) on the sphere, exerted by the fluid, to viscosity, particle radius r_p, and free stream velocity U_∞:

$$F_p = 6\pi\mu r_p U_\infty \tag{12.65}$$

In this equation, the drag force F_p due to the fluid passing around the stationary sphere acts in the direction opposite to the direction of the velocity U_∞. Equation (12.65) is commonly expressed by means of Eq. (12.15) in terms of the drag coefficient C_D:

$$F_p = \tfrac{1}{2}(\rho U_\infty^2)(\pi r_p^2)(C_D) = 6\pi\mu r_p U_\infty \tag{12.66}$$

where the area used is the projected area of the sphere. This equation can be

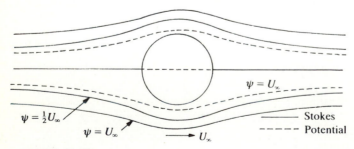

FIGURE 12.15
Streamlines for flow past a sphere.

rearranged as follows:

$$C_D = \frac{24}{(2r_p U_\infty \rho)/\mu} = \frac{24}{N_{Re,p}} \qquad (12.67)$$

where the particle Reynolds number $N_{Re,p}$ is based on the diameter of the sphere:

$$N_{Re,p} = \frac{d_p U_\infty \rho}{\mu} \qquad (12.68)$$

The free-settling velocity (also called "terminal velocity") of a small particle (at steady-state) can be obtained by a force balance using Newton's second law, Eq. (7.29). There are three forces acting on the sphere: the Stokes drag F_p, the buoyancy force F_B, and the weight F_W:

$$\sum F = F_p + F_B + F_W = ma = 0 \qquad (12.69)$$

where at steady-state the acceleration is zero. In the following derivation, it is customary to assume that the velocity in the direction of gravity is positive. Following the analysis in Section 7.3.2, the buoyancy force is obtained by applying Eq. (7.84) to a sphere submerged in a fluid of density ρ:

$$-F_B = \rho \Psi g = (\rho)(\tfrac{4}{3})(\pi r_p^3)(g) \qquad (12.70)$$

where the buoyancy force acts in the negative direction (upward). The gravity force (due to the weight of the sphere) F_W is

$$F_W = m_p g = (\rho_p)(\tfrac{4}{3})(\pi r_p^3)(g) \qquad (12.71)$$

where the weight acts in the positive direction. If the sphere is falling with positive velocity, the drag force acts oppositely. After the appropriate substitutions, Eq. (12.69) becomes

$$-6\pi\mu r_p U_t - (\rho)(\tfrac{4}{3})(\pi r_p^3)(g) + (\rho_p)(\tfrac{4}{3})(\pi r_p^3)(g) = 0 \qquad (12.72)$$

where U_t is the terminal velocity of the sphere relative to a medium of uniform velocity and replaces U_∞ (defined earlier as the velocity of the fluid relative to a stationary particle). Solving for the terminal velocity gives

$$U_t = \frac{(2gr_p^2)(\rho_p - \rho)}{9\mu} \qquad (12.73)$$

This equation is restricted to the region where Stokes' law applies. Note also that the sphere falls when ρ_p exceeds ρ.

The movement of particles in fluid systems is very important, and much work has been done to determine, both by theory and experiment, the range of application of Stokes' law. For example, the law is found to be accurate up to a Reynolds number of 0.5 (which, for drops of water in air, would be diameters less than 0.1 mm). At a Reynolds number of 1, predictions from the law are about 7 percent low. At Reynolds numbers above 8, vortex rings form that are stable up to a Reynolds number of 150; above this value, the rings become unstable and, from time to time, move off downstream. The flow at these higher Reynolds numbers will be discussed further in the next section.

Very small particles are subject to Brownian motion, whereby collisions between the particles and fluid molecules result in the particles following random paths. This effect is stronger than gravity for very small particles of $0.1\,\mu m$ (microns) or less in diameter. When Brownian motion is important, there is no settling by gravity. In fact, Brownian motion is often significant up to a particle size of $3\,\mu m$, depending on the relative density difference.

Example 12.10. Find the terminal velocity and drag force when a spherical water drop, $5\,\mu m$ in diameter, falls through air at 20°C. Let $g = 9.80\,\mathrm{m\,s^{-2}}$.

Answer. From the Appendix, Table A.1, the density of the water drop at 293.15 K is

$$\rho_p = \frac{1}{v_f} = \frac{1}{1.001 \times 10^{-3}} = 999.0\,\mathrm{kg\,m^{-3}} \tag{i}$$

From Table A.2, the properties of air are

$$\mu = 0.01817\,\mathrm{cP} = 1.817 \times 10^{-5}\,\mathrm{kg\,m^{-1}\,s^{-1}}$$
$$\rho = 0.001\,205\,\mathrm{g\,cm^{-3}} = 1.205\,\mathrm{kg\,m^{-3}} \tag{ii}$$

The particle diameter is $5\,\mu m$ or $5 \times 10^{-6}\,m$ (from Table C.11).

The terminal settling velocity is given by Eq. (12.73) in the Stokes' law region:

$$U_t = \frac{(2gr_p^2)(\rho_p - \rho)}{9\mu} \tag{12.73}$$

The procedure is to calculate the terminal settling velocity using Eq. (12.73), check to see if the Reynolds number is less than 0.5, and then find the force on the sphere. From Eq. (12.73), with r_p being half the diameter or $2.5 \times 10^{-6}\,m$, U_t is

$$U_t = (2)(9.80)(2.5 \times 10^{-6})^2(999.0 - 1.205)/[(9)(1.817 \times 10^{-5})]$$
$$\times [(\mathrm{m\,s^{-2}})(\mathrm{m^2})(\mathrm{kg\,m^{-3}})(\mathrm{kg^{-1}\,m\,s})]$$
$$= 7.474 \times 10^{-4}\,\mathrm{m\,s^{-1}} \tag{iii}$$

From Eq. (12.68), the particle Reynolds number is

$$N_{Re,p} = d_p U_\infty \rho/\mu = (5 \times 10^{-6})(7.474 \times 10^{-4})(1.205)/(1.817 \times 10^{-5}) = 2.478 \times 10^{-4} \tag{iv}$$

In the above equation, U_t can be used for U_∞, since it does not matter whether the particle is stationary and the fluid moves with velocity U_∞ or the fluid is stationary and the particle moves with velocity U_t. Clearly, the flow is in the Stokes' law region at this low Reynolds number; therefore, the drag force from

Eq. (12.65) is

$$F_p = 6\pi\mu r_p U_\infty = (6\pi)(1.817 \times 10^{-5})(2.5 \times 10^{-6})(7.474 \times 10^{-4})$$
$$\times [(\text{kg m}^{-1}\text{s}^{-1})(\text{m})(\text{m s}^{-1})]$$
$$= 6.40 \times 10^{-13} \text{ kg m s}^{-2} = 6.40 \times 10^{-13} \text{ N} \tag{v}$$

Example 12.11. Calculate the time for the drop of water in Example 12.10 to accelerate from an initial velocity of zero to $0.99U_t$.

Answer. The results of Example 12.10 show that Stokes' law applies. Newton's second law of motion, Eq. (7.29), is applied to the accelerating sphere. As in the derivations of Eqs. (12.70) through (12.73), let the y coordinate be positive in the direction of gravity. Newton's second law applies with the same three forces as in Eq. (12.69), except that in this problem the acceleration is not zero:

$$\sum F = F_p + F_B + F_W = m\frac{dU_y}{dt} \tag{i}$$

Using Eqs. (12.66), (12.70), and (12.71), Eq. (i) becomes

$$-6\pi\mu r_p U_y - (\rho)(\tfrac{4}{3})(\pi r_p^3)(g) + (\rho_p)(\tfrac{4}{3})(\pi r_p^3)(g) = m\frac{dU_y}{dt} = (\rho_p)(\tfrac{4}{3})(\pi r_p^3)\frac{dU_y}{dt} \tag{ii}$$

where U_y is the terminal velocity of the sphere relative to a medium of uniform velocity and replaces U_∞ and U_t. Equation (ii) is an ordinary differential equation whose variables are easily separated and integrated according to the boundary conditions:

$$U_y (t = 0) = 0 \qquad U_y (t = t) = 0.99U_t \tag{iii}$$

After integration of the equation, the form of which is $(a + bx)^{-1} dx$, the answer is

$$t = \frac{2r_p^2\rho_p}{9\mu}\left[\ln\left(1 - \frac{(9\mu)(0.99U_t)}{(2r_p^2)(g)(\rho_p - \rho)}\right)\right] \tag{iv}$$

Next, U_t is eliminated via Eq. (12.73) to yield the final equation

$$t = -\frac{2r_p^2\rho_p}{9\mu}[\ln(1 - 0.99)] \tag{v}$$

The numbers from Example 12.10 are substituted into Eq. (v)

$$t = -\left(\frac{(2)(2.5 \times 10^{-6})^2(999.0)}{(9)(1.817 \times 10^{-5})}\right)[\ln(0.01)] = 3.517 \times 10^{-4} \text{ s} \tag{vi}$$

In other words, the drop accelerates almost instantaneously to its terminal velocity.

12.2.3 Drag Coefficient Correlations

This section covers form drag and skin friction for a variety of bodies of revolution (spheres, cylinders, disks, etc.) over a wide range of flows. Also to be discussed are some miscellaneous topics such as hindered settling, separation by centrifugal force, stagnation pressure, and streamlining.

The drag coefficient, first introduced in Eq. (12.15), finds its most useful application in flows past bodies of revolution. For these bodies, the area A is the area of the object that is projected on a plane normal to the flow direction:

$$C_D = \frac{F_p}{\frac{1}{2}\rho U_\infty^2 A} \tag{12.74}$$

Equation (12.74) is a generalization of Eq. (12.66), in which the projected area of a sphere πr_p^2 is replaced by A.

There are no exact solutions for flow past a single sphere at high Reynolds numbers. Figure 12.16 [L3] presents the experimental data for a sphere in the form of a plot of C_D versus the particle Reynolds number:

$$N_{Re,p} = \frac{d_p U_\infty \rho}{\mu} \tag{12.68}$$

where U_∞ is the free stream velocity if the particle is at rest. More accurately, U_∞ represents the difference in velocity between the fluid and the particle. Clearly, if the particle is settling at its terminal velocity in a fluid at rest, U_∞ would be replaced by U_t.

Figure 12.16 shows that Eq. (12.67) from Stokes' law applies accurately up to a Reynolds number of 0.5. The curves for spheres is available in equation form [M3] by using three correlations. Stokes' law is usually applied in the region $0 \le N_{Re,p} \le 2$:

$$C_D = 24/N_{Re,p} \qquad 0 \le N_{Re,p} \le 2 \tag{12.67}$$
$$C_D = 18.5/(N_{Re,p})^{0.6} \qquad 2 \le N_{Re,p} < 500 \tag{12.75}$$
$$C_D = 0.44 \qquad 500 \le N_{Re,p} < 2 \times 10^5 \tag{12.76}$$

Equation (12.76) is commonly termed "Newton's law"; the Newton's law region ends at a critical Reynolds number of 2×10^5; above this number, the boundary layer over the sphere becomes fully turbulent, and $C_D = 0.2$.

The terminal velocity is given by a force balance similar to that used to obtain Eq. (12.72) except that the Stokes drag is replaced by F_p from Eq. (12.74):

$$F_p = \frac{1}{2}(\rho U_t^2)(\pi r_p^2)(C_D) \tag{12.77}$$

Retaining the earlier convention, the terminal velocity is positive in the direction of gravity, and the drag force acts in the direction opposite to the velocity. After substituting Eqs. (12.77), (12.70), and (12.71), Newton's second law [Eq. (12.69)] becomes

$$-\frac{1}{2}(\rho U_t^2)(\pi r_p^2)(C_D) - (\rho)(\tfrac{4}{3})(\pi r_p^3)(g) + (\rho_p)(\tfrac{4}{3})(\pi r_p^3)(g) = 0 \tag{12.78}$$

Equation (12.78) can be solved for the terminal velocity:

$$U_t^2 = \frac{8 r_p g(\rho_p - \rho)}{3\rho C_D} = \frac{4 d_p g(\rho_p - \rho)}{3\rho C_D} \tag{12.79}$$

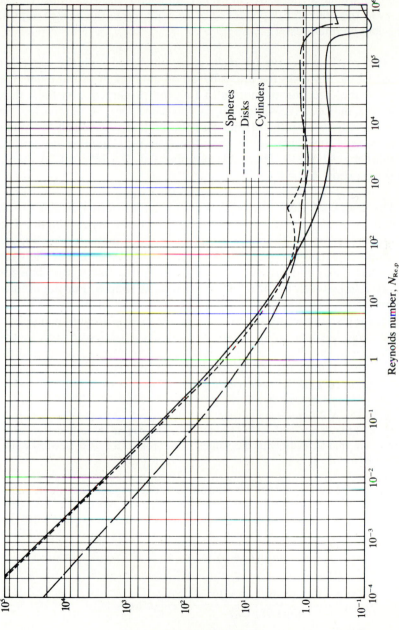

FIGURE 12.16

Drag coefficients for spheres, disks, and cylinders. For disks, the flat side is perpendicular to the direction of motion. For cylinders, the axis is perpendicular to the direction of motion (i.e., cross flow), and $L/d_t = \infty$. (*Reprinted with permission from Lapple and Shepherd, Ind. Eng. Chem.* **32**: *606 (1940). Copyright 1940 American Chemical Society.*)

Notice that above the Stokes region the terminal velocity depends on the square root of the density difference, as compared to Eq. (12.73) for the Stokes region in which the density difference and fluid viscosity were to the first power. Also the diameter dependence of U_t, squared in the Stokes region, is less in the above equations.

Disks. The drag coefficient curve for disks is also included with the curve for spheres in Fig. 12.16. For disks the line is based on data taken with the flat side perpendicular to the direction of motion. Thus, the projected area for a disk and for a sphere in Eq. (12.74) for C_D is the same, $\pi d_p^2/4$. Similarly, the Reynolds number is based on the diameter of the disk, d_p. Note that the curve for disks bears little resemblance to that for spheres. There is no critical Reynolds number. Above a Reynolds number of 2×10^4, all available experimental data show $C_D = 1.1$.

Cylinders. The drag coefficient for the flow of a cylinder perpendicular to the axis is defined in terms of the projected area, diameter times length. The Reynolds number in Fig. 12.16 is based on the cylinder diameter, d_t. Figure 12.16 shows only the line for cross flow over a cylinder of infinite length; Knudsen and Katz [K3] and Streeter and Wylie [S7] summarize the data for other values of L/d_t, as well as for ellipsoids and other shapes. For the infinite cylinder in cross flow, Newton's law regime shows $C_D = 1.0$ from $N_{Re} = 10^4$ up to a critical Reynolds number of 4×10^5. Above the critical Reynolds number, the boundary layer becomes fully turbulent and $C_D = 0.3$. Note that in the Newton's law region, the drag coefficient is a strong function of L/d_t, and up to a 50 percent reduction in C_D can be expected. In the fully turbulent region, C_D is not a function of L/d_t.

Example 12.12. A 2-mm diameter lead particle ($\rho_p = 1.13 \times 10^4 \text{ kg m}^{-3}$) falls in air ($\rho = 1.22 \text{ kg m}^{-3}$, $\mu = 1.81 \times 10^{-5} \text{ kg m}^{-1} \text{ s}^{-1}$). Determine its terminal velocity. Then compare that velocity with the values from Stokes' law and Newton's law. Let g be 9.80 m s^{-2}.

Answer. If the Reynolds number lies outside the Stokes region, then the terminal velocity must be found by trial and error. The terminal velocity of this heavy particle is probably outside the Stokes' law region. The diameter d_p is 2×10^{-3} m. From Eq. (12.79), the terminal velocity is

$$U_t^2 = \frac{8 r_p g (\rho_p - \rho)}{3 \rho C_D} = \frac{4 d_p g (\rho_p - \rho)}{3 \rho C_D}$$

$$= \frac{(4)(2 \times 10^{-3})(9.80)(1.13 \times 10^4 - 1.22)}{(3)(1.22)(C_D)} \left[(\text{m})(\text{m s}^{-2})\left(\frac{\text{kg m}^{-3}}{\text{kg m}^{-3}}\right) \right]$$

$$= \frac{242.0}{C_D} \tag{i}$$

where the units of U_t^2 are $\text{m}^2 \text{ s}^{-2}$. The drag coefficient C_D is a function of the

Reynolds number, Eq. (12.68):

$$N_{\text{Re,p}} = U_\infty d_p \rho / \mu = U_t(2 \times 10^{-3})(1.22)/(1.81 \times 10^{-5}) = 134.8 U_t \qquad \text{(ii)}$$

This problem will be solved by using Fig. 12.16. First, Newton's law, Eq. (12.76), will be tried. Let C_D be 0.44, and from Eqs. (i) and (ii):

$$U_t = (242.0/0.44)^{1/2} = 23.45 \text{ m s}^{-1} \qquad \text{(iii)}$$

$$N_{\text{Re}} = (134.8)(23.45) = 3162 \qquad \text{(iv)}$$

From Fig. 12.16, C_D is 0.4. Repeating:

$$U_t = (242.0/0.4)^{0.5} = 24.60 \text{ m s}^{-1} \qquad \text{(v)}$$

$$N_{\text{Re}} = (134.8)(24.60) = 3316 \qquad \text{(vi)}$$

Within the readability of the chart, C_D is unchanged, and 24.60 m s^{-1} is the final answer.

Note that Newton's law, Eq. (12.76), predicted 23.45 m s^{-1}, which is not significantly different from the correct answer. Stokes' law, Eq. (12.73), predicts

$$U_t = (2gr_p^2)(\rho_p - \rho)/(9\mu)$$
$$= (2)(9.80)(1 \times 10^{-3})^2(1.13 \times 10^4 - 1.22)/[(9)(1.81 \times 10^{-5})]$$
$$= 1.36 \times 10^3 \text{ m s}^{-1} = 4460 \text{ ft s}^{-1} \qquad \text{(vii)}$$

This answer is clearly unreasonable!

Example 12.13. A falling-ball viscometer for liquids generally consists of a tube similar to a graduated cylinder that is long enough and wide enough to eliminate side and end effects. A colored sphere, made from plastic (insoluble in the fluid of interest, density $58 \text{ lb}_m \text{ ft}^{-3}$), will be droppd into the liquid, which is carefully maintained at a constant temperature of 25°C. The rate of fall of the sphere is to be timed between two marks. The design criterion dictates that the sphere falls 1 inch in 1 minute. The test fluid is to be a moderately viscous polymer solution of density $50 \text{ lb}_m \text{ ft}^{-3}$ and approximate zero-shear viscosity of 2500 cP $(1.68 \text{ lb}_m \text{ ft}^{-1} \text{ s}^{-1})$. Determine the appropriate diameter of the sphere to achieve the design criteria, if $g = 32 \text{ ft s}^{-2}$. Is this a practical design?

Answer. The terminal velocity is easily computed from the statement of the problem:

$$U_t = \frac{\text{distance}}{\text{time}} = \frac{1/12}{60} = 1.389 \times 10^{-3} \text{ ft s}^{-1} \qquad \text{(i)}$$

Next, the particle radius is calculated from Eq. (12.73), assuming that the flow is in the Stokes' law region:

$$r_p = [(9\mu)(U_t)(2g)^{-1}(\rho_p - \rho)^{-1}]^{1/2}$$
$$= [(9)(1.68)(1.389 \times 10^{-3})(64)^{-1}(58 - 50)^{-1}]^{1/2}$$
$$\times [(\text{lb}_m \text{ ft}^{-1} \text{ s}^{-1})(\text{ft s}^{-1})(\text{ft}^{-1} \text{ s}^2)(\text{lb}_m^{-1} \text{ ft}^3)]^{1/2}$$
$$= 6.404 \times 10^{-3} \text{ ft} = 0.077 \text{ in.} \qquad \text{(ii)}$$

The required particle diameter would be about 0.15 in. (approximately $\frac{1}{6}$-in.), which is reasonable. The Reynolds number from Eq. (12.68) is

$$N_{Re,p} = d_p U_t \rho / \mu = (0.00640)(2)(1.389 \times 10^{-3})(50)/(1.68) = 5.29 \times 10^{-4} \quad \text{(iii)}$$

This Reynolds number is well within the Stokes' law region; thus, the design is reasonable.

Separation of boundary layer. The flow patterns associated with Eqs. (12.75) and (12.76) are complex. The previously-alluded-to vortex ring, stable at Reynolds numbers between 8 and 150, is shown in Fig. 12.17. This ring is a laminar flow phenomenon. The vortex increases in size as the free stream velocity U_∞ (and therefore the particle Reynolds number $N_{Re,p}$) increases; further increases in U_∞ result in the vortex being detached from the sphere (commonly referred to as being "shed").

Figure 12.18 shows the patterns during flow past a sphere. As the Reynolds number increases, the separation of the boundary layer from the solid surface is actually shifted towards the rear of the sphere. At first, the boundary layer and the circulation within the wake are both in laminar flow. The transition to turbulence begins in the wake, as $N_{Re,p}$ increases, and eventually moves to the 'front of the cylinder. The point B is called the 'stagnation point", which is the point of highest pressure around the body. That pressure may be estimated from the Bernoulli equation, Eq. (7.63), which simplifies to

$$\Delta p = p_{\text{stagnation}} - p_A = \rho U_\infty^2 / 2 \tag{12.80}$$

The description accompanying Fig. 12.18 is useful in explaining the experimental data in Fig. 12.16. In the transition region where Eq. (12.75) applies, the wake behind the sphere is changing from laminar to turbulent flow. The third region where Eq. (12.76) applies, sometimes called the Newton's law region, has a nearly constant drag coefficient that drops suddenly to a very low value, before rising to a nearly constant value at particle

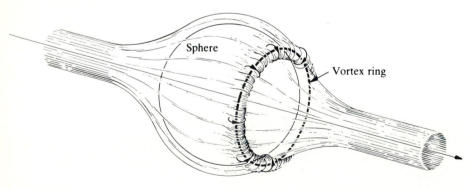

FIGURE 12.17
Vortex ring on a sphere.

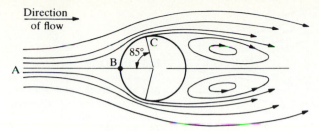

(*a*) Laminar flow in the boundary layer.

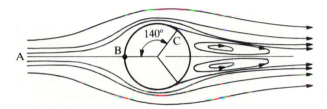

(*b*) Turbulent flow in the boundary layer.

FIGURE 12.18
Flow past a single sphere, showing separation and wake formation. (A) free stream velocity; (B) stagnation point; (C) separation point. (*From McCabe, Smith, and Harriott, Unit Operations of Chemical Engineering, 4th ed., p. 132, McGraw-Hill, New York, 1985. By permission.*)

Reynolds numbers exceeding 3×10^5. At this drop point, the boundary layer over the sphere becomes fully turbulent.

Form drag. The drag force on a body can be divided into two parts: that attributed to skin friction (sometimes called skin drag) and that attributed to form drag. Skin friction is the tangential friction associated with the fluid flowing over the surface. For pipe flow, all of the friction is skin friction. In flow over spheres or other bodies, a part of the total drag is attributed to the skin friction. The remainder, the form drag, is associated with the pressure difference which must exist in front of and behind the object. The fluid must accelerate to get around the body, and if the body is not perfectly symmetrical or if separation occurs, the streamlines and flow patterns in front of the body differ from those in back. Consequently, the velocities will be different, and by a Bernoulli balance the pressures will be different. The difference in pressure acting on the projected area is responsible for the form drag.

In Stokes flow around a sphere, there is no form drag because the pressure on the surface is everywhere the same, i.e. the flow is symmetrical in front and back of the body. However, there is form drag for the flow in Figs. 12.17 and 12.18, in which the boundary layer separates from the object. Bodies

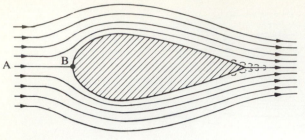

AB is the streamline to the stagnation point B

FIGURE 12.19
Streamline body. (*From McCabe, Smith, and Harriott, Unit Operations of Chemical Engineering, 4th ed., p. 133, McGraw-Hill, New York, 1985. By permission.*)

which cause boundary layer separation are called "bluff objects". Spheres are bluff objects at high flow rates, but not in the Stokes region.

Form drag can be minimized by streamlining, as is done with the design of an airfoil such as shown in Fig. 12.19. Note that the airfoil has a tail that tapers to a point, in order to minimize turbulence in the wake. However, it is impossible to reattach the top boundary layer to the bottom boundary layer so as to eliminate turbulence completely and hence eliminate form drag.

There has been additional work on the drag of objects other than spheres, cylinders, and disks. Corrections to Eqs. (12.67) and (12.75) for nonspherical particles are available [P1]; details are to be found elsewhere [K3, S1]. Liquid drops have also been studied [P1]. As the Reynolds number increases, the drag on the liquid drop can cause fluid motions within the drop itself and therefore changes the drag coefficient, as compared with that for a solid particle of the same diameter.

Hindered settling. If there is only one sphere in an infinitely large fluid, or if the particles are so far apart that the passage of one does not affect the rest, then "free settling" takes place. However, if there is more than one sphere (or particle of any shape) passing through a fluid, the frictional force may change as the wake of one particle interferes with the passage of adjacent particles. In this case "hindered settling" will take place. The usual criterion is that the void fraction or porosity ε is less than 0.999 [P1]. The void fraction is the ratio of the free volume to the total volume:

$$\varepsilon = \frac{V_{\text{total}} - V_{\text{p}}}{V_{\text{total}}} \tag{12.81}$$

where V_{p} is the total volume of all particles. Values of V_{p} may be either measured or calculated from the weight fraction of solids and the densities ρ_{p} and ρ. In other words, ε is unity minus the volume fraction of particles. Another example of hindered settling is the settling of particles near a wall or boundary. Details can be found elsewhere [P1].

For hindered settling in the Stokes' law region, spheres or cylinders only, a correction factor to the viscosity k_{v} has been proposed [S5]. Thus, the terminal velocity is

$$U_t = 2r_p^2 g(\rho_p - \rho_m)(\varepsilon k_v)/(9\mu) \tag{12.82}$$

where ρ_m is the density of the solid–fluid mixture and k_v is correlated with ε:

$$k_v = \exp[(-4.19)(1 - \varepsilon)] \tag{12.83}$$

Generally, Eqs. (12.82) and (12.83) are valid if the particle Reynolds number is 2 or less; this criterion can be recast into

$$0 \leqslant d_p[g\rho_m(\rho_p - \rho_m)(k_v/\mu)^2]^{1/3} \leqslant 3.3 \tag{12.84}$$

For nonspherical and angular particles, the effect of concentration is greater [G1]. For transitional and turbulent flow, there are no recommended generalized correlations for hindered settling, although an alternative approach has been suggested [M3]. In summary, hindered settling is a difficult area, and experimental data may be required for many applications.

Heat and mass transfer. There are correlations available for both heat and mass transfer between spheres and fluid. For heat transfer between the surface of a single sphere of size d_p, a simple equation is [R2]:

$$N_{Nu,p} = h_p d_p/k = 2 + 0.6(N_{Pr})^{1/3}(N_{Re,p})^{1/2} \tag{12.85}$$

where k and N_{Pr} [cf. Eq. (8.4)] are properties of the pure fluid and $N_{Nu,p}$ is the Nusselt number for the sphere. The particle Reynolds number $N_{Re,p}$ is given in Eq. (12.68). If the fluid surrounding the sphere is stagnant (i.e., $U_\infty = 0$ and $N_{Re,p} = 0$), Eq. (12.85) predicts that $N_{Nu,p} = 2$. This result is also obtainable by solving the one-dimensional conduction equation in spherical coordinates with the appropriate boundary conditions.

An improved correlation for heat transfer to a single sphere is [W2]:

$$N_{Nu,p} = 2 + [0.4(N_{Re,p})^{1/2} + 0.06(N_{Re,p})^{2/3}](N_{Pr})^{0.4}(\mu/\mu_w)^{0.14} \tag{12.86}$$

$$3.5 \leq N_{Re,p} \leq 7.6 \times 10^4$$

$$0.71 \leq N_{Pr} \leq 380$$

$$1.0 \leq (\mu/\mu_w) \leq 3.2$$

where the heat transfer coefficient is applied in conjunction with the area of the sphere, $4\pi d_p^2$. Equation (12.86) correlates the data to ±30 percent at the worst and much better most of the time [W2]. In Eq. (12.86), k, μ, ρ, and N_{Pr} are evaluated at the free stream temperature T_∞; μ_w is evaluated at the wall temperature.

The mass transfer equation [K4] is analogous to Eq. (12.85):

$$N_{Sh,y} = k_c d_p y_{lm}/D = N_{Sh,p} y_{lm} = 2 + 0.6(N_{Sc})^{1/3}(N_{Re,p})^{1/2} \tag{12.87}$$

where D and N_{Sc} [cf. Eq. (8.6)] are properties of the pure fluid. The Sherwood number is modified from that in Chapter 8 by multiplying by y_{lm}, which is the logarithmic mean mole fraction of the inert or nondiffusing component (usually close to unity):

$$y_{lm} = \frac{y_i - y}{\ln[(1 - y)/(1 - y_i)]} \tag{12.88}$$

where y_i is the concentration of the diffusing species at the surface of the sphere and y is the concentration in the bulk fluid.

Equation (12.87) is often recast in terms of the j-factor:

$$j_M = (k_c y_{lm}/U_\infty)(N_{Sc})^{2/3} \tag{12.89}$$

In terms of dimensionless groups, the j-factor is

$$j_M = N_{Sh,y}(N_{Re,p})^{-1}(N_{Sc})^{-1/3} \tag{12.90}$$

This equation is similar to Eq. (11.81), but the Sherwood number has been modified and the particle Reynolds number is appropriate.

Flow across a simple cylinder or a bank of cylinders is important and will be covered in Section 12.3.3. Also, flow across beds of spheres will be covered in Section 12.3.2 under the topic of packed beds.

Miscellaneous topics. There are many practical applications of centrifugal force being used to separate solids. Examples include cyclone separators for removal of solids from stack gases, centrifuges in the chemistry laboratory, and ultracentrifuges for separation of species of slightly differing molecular weights. The acceleration due to a circular motion is

$$g_\omega = r\omega^2 \tag{12.91}$$

where r is the radius of the particle path and ω is the angular velocity. The presence of ω overwhelms the acceleration due to gravity; hence, in such a case g_ω can be used to replace g in the equations for terminal velocity, Eqs. (12.73), (12.79), and (12.82).

For particles with nonspherical shapes, the drag coefficient may be estimated with the aid of Fig. 12.16. Usually d_p is replaced by an equivalent diameter, defined as the diameter of a sphere having the identical surface-to-volume ratio as the particle. The further the particle deviates from a sphere, the worse is the error. A correction factor for nonspheres is available [P3].

Flow through packed beds (towers), flow past banks of tubes as in heat exchangers, and fluidized beds are important enough to be covered in detail later in this chapter. In closing, it must be noted that Fig. 12.16 does not apply to needle-shaped particles or to short cylinders falling through a fluid. The particles must be somewhat spherical in shape.

12.3 FLOW PHENOMENA WITH SOLIDS

Operations such as slurry transport, flow through packed beds, flow outside of heat exchanger tubing, settling, fluidization, pneumatic transport, etc., often involve the relative movement of a solid phase with respect to a fluid phase. To begin, let us consider a 15-cm-diameter vertical pipe, filled with solids. Suppose the solids are very fine, like talcum (baby) powder. If air is introduced into the pipe at a high rate, the air will entrain the solids and carry them out of the pipe. This is called "pneumatic transport", because the air will transport the particles until all the particles are removed. A second case is a pipe filled with small ceramic cylinders, each a centimeter long and a centimeter in diameter. If air is passed through the pipe, the solids will not be entrained. This second case is an example of a packed bed, which is in common use in chemical engineering operations. Typical applications occur in absorption towers, drying of solids (e.g., grain), heat treating, and both catalytic and non-catalytic reactions.

An important phenomena, called fluidization, is intermediate between the extremes of pneumatic transport and flow through packed beds. Actually, pneumatic transport can include some types of fluidization, and this topic will be discussed later. The pneumatic transport of solids not involving a fluidized bed is outside the scope of this text. The interested reader should consult other references for details [B2, D1, H1, L4, P1].

12.3.1 Introduction to Fluidization

Fluidization is the process by which a bed of solids is changed to a fluid-like state by the passage of a gas or liquid through the bed. Let us replace the ceramic packing in the 15-cm pipe with granular particles whose sizes are of the order of 250 μm (250 microns, 50 mesh, or 0.01 in.). If the air velocity is initially very low, the bed behaves as a packed bed. If the air velocity continues to rise, then fluidization occurs. A gas-fluidized bed closely resembles a thin soup that is boiling vigorously. The solids appear to be in random motion, without being excessively entrained or being removed by the gas passing through the bed. There is a definite solid boundary at the top; hence, the term fluidized bed is appropriate.

Fluidization is best described by discussing the changes in the system of the pipe plus the 250-μm particles as the air velocity is increased. At very low velocities, there is no change in the physical appearance of the bed, as shown schematically in Fig. 12.20(*a*). As the velocity increases, friction produces an ever-increasing pressure drop until the force on each particle exceeds its weight. At this point, the bed expands. This expansion increases the space between particles, which reduces the velocity of fluid between particles and the pressure drop as well. Hence, the particles are not transported out of the pipe. Initially the bed simply expands slightly from its static or rest position. But as the air velocity continues to increase, the bed expands until the particles no longer touch. Figure 12.20(*b*) shows the particles at this point of incipient fluidization. At this point, the bed has become fluidized. The length of bed at the point of incipient fluidization is L_{mf}. The velocity at the point of incipient fluidization is the superficial velocity U_{mf}, which is calculated as the velocity of the fluid were it to pass through an empty column of the same diameter at the

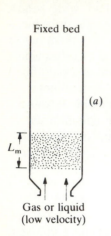

Fixed bed

(a)

L_m

Gas or liquid
(low velocity)

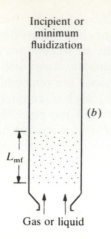

Incipient or
minimum
fluidization

(b)

L_{mf}

Gas or liquid

FIGURE 12.20
The fixed bed (a) and incipient fluidization (b). (*From Kunii and Levenspiel, Fluidization Engineering, p. 2, Wiley, New York, 1969. By permission.*)

same conditions. The superficial velocity is used because it is impossible to measure the actual velocity between particles. The air velocity can be increased at least three to five times U_{mf} for large particles and ten to twenty times U_{mf} for small particles before excessive entrainment occurs.

A fluidized bed resembles a boiling liquid in many ways. For instance, if the tube containing a fluidized bed is tilted to one side, the top surface remains horizontal. If an object more dense than the bed is thrown in from the top, it sinks to the bottom, and a lighter cork will float at the top interface. The bed can be drained from a valve in the side of the pipe.

Particulate fluidization. As the fluid velocity is increased above that required for incipient fluidization, the behavior of gas–solid fluidized beds differs substantially from the behavior of liquid–solid fluidized beds. Figure 12.21 details these differences [P2]. In particulate fluidization, the particles move individually and randomly throughout the bed without formation of voids (often called bubbles). This behavior is found especially in liquid–solid systems, although some gas–solid systems can exhibit particulate fluidization over a limited range of velocities [D1]. The bed is relatively homogeneous, so that large clumps or aggregates of particles do not form (see Fig. 12.21). For liquid–solid systems, the particulate fluidization is basically the only type observed, except for a few cases in which the density difference can be

---

FIGURE 12.21
Various contacting modes of solids in gas-solid and liquid-solid fluidization. (*Adapted from Peters and Fan, Design of Gas-Solid Catalytic Fluidized Bed Reactors, CACHE Corp. Module DES59i, 1983; and from Yerushalmi and Avidan in Fluidization, 2d ed., p. 226, Davidson, Clift, and Harrison (eds), Academic Press, New York, 1985. By permission.*)

U_k = superficial velocity at transition from slugging to turbulent
U_{mb} = superficial velocity at transition to bubbling bed fluidization

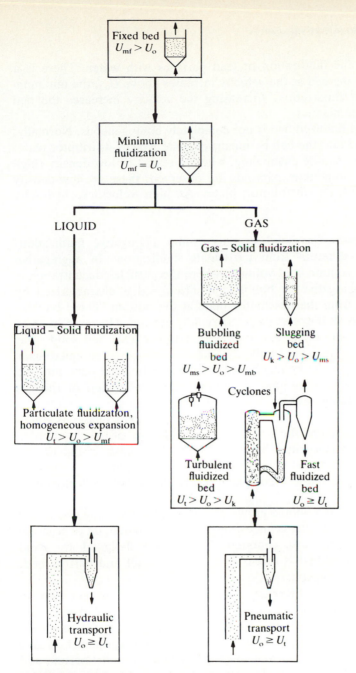

FIGURE 12.21
(*Continued*)

U_{mf} = superficial velocity at point of minimum fluidization
U_{ms} = superficial velocity at transition from bubbling to turbulent
U_o = superficial velocity (in general), based on empty column
U_t = terminal (settling) velocity of a single sphere in a fluid
U_{tr} = superficial velocity necessary for hydraulic or pneumatic transport

extreme, such as in the fluidization of lead particles with water. There is a smooth expansion of the bed as the velocity increases above U_{mf}, the minimum velocity for incipient fluidization. Increasing the velocity increases the bed height in a predictable manner.

The liquid–solid fluidized bed is not completely homogeneous. Normally, the fluid is introduced into the bed by means of some type of distributor plate. At this location, there can be channeling, where a region of low density (high void fraction) exists. Sometimes parvoids are observed; these are low-density strata that form near the distributor plate. At high velocities, hydraulic transport occurs.

Aggregative fluidization. Gas–solid systems exhibit aggregative fluidization, which is completely different from particulate fluidization. In aggregative fluidization, the beds contain void volumes where the particle concentration is almost zero. The aggregative or bubbling fluidized bed is characterized by bubbles of gas rising from the distributor plate at the bottom. These bubbles will not completely break down as they rise rapidly upward. However, the gas void does exchange some of its gas with the mixture of gas and solids that surround the bubble. When the bubbles break the surface, they eject solids above the free surface of the boiling bed; these solids often fall back into the bed or are recaptured in a cyclone separator. The total region of the gas bubbles is called the bubble phase; the rest of the bed, comprising solids plus gas, is called the emulsion phase. A third phase, the cloud phase, is found between the bubble phase and the emulsion phase. The size of the cloud phase depends on the relative velocities between the bubble phase (rising up the column) and the interstitial gas velocity (in the emulsion phase). A detailed description of the cloud phase is complex; the reader is referred elsewhere [B2].

Slugging occurs when a bubble grows until it is about the same size as the bed (or pipe) diameter. Slugging is undesirable from the standpoint of scale-up and modeling; therefore, most commercial units are designed to avoid slugging. A shallow, wide bed is often preferable to a tall and narrow bed, which tends to promote slugging.

In gas–solid fluidization, there are four separate regimes of operation (in contrast to the liquid–solid case, for which there is just one). As shown in Fig. 12.21, these are (1) bubbling fluidized bed, (2) slugging bed, (3) turbulent fluidized bed, and (4) fast fluidized bed. In addition, the spouted bed is a separate design. At extremely high velocities, pneumatic transport occurs, and the solids are entrained by the gas. In "fast fluidization", this entrainment is designed into a fluidized bed unit, as shown in Fig. 12.21. Here, the solids are entrained by the gas in the fluidized bed. At the top of the bed is located a cyclone separator, in which the solids are separated from the gas phase and are recycled. This regime of operation is common in industry. The first commercial fluid catalytic cracking plant, which converted crude oil into aromatics suitable for high-octane aviation gasoline, operated in the fast fluidization regime.

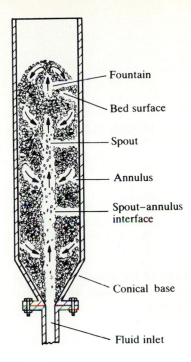

Fountain

Bed surface

Spout

Annulus

Spout–annulus
interface

Conical base

Fluid inlet

FIGURE 12.22
A spouted bed. Arrows indicate direction of movement
of solids. (*From Mathur and Epstein, Spouted Beds, p.
2, Academic Press, New York, 1974. By permission.*)

Spouted bed. The spouted bed, shown in Fig. 12.22, is a special type of
fluidized bed. Fluid is injected upward through a centrally located aperture in
the bottom of a bed of coarse solids. At high velocities, the fluid will stay in a
column for a long distance because the coarse solids act more or less as tube
walls. As the fluid progresses upward, more and more solids are entrained,
until finally the fluid velocity contains a significant radial component. If the bed
is filled with solids to an appropriate height, a fountain (or spout) occurs at the
top of the bed surface. Note the velocity vectors in Fig. 12.22. The gas core is
called the spout. The region where the solids are falling downward is called the
annulus. There is a systematic cyclic pattern of movement of solids, as shown
by the arrows in Fig. 12.22. Continuous operation is possible; solids may be
fed into the bed either at the top near the wall or with the entering gas. Solids
may be removed conveniently near the top by an appropriate pipe. The
spouted bed is not completely fluidized, yet some of its charactersitics resemble
the behavior of coarse particle fluidization. The spouted bed may operate with
either a gas or a liquid. However, particulate liquid fluidization is much
preferred; consequently, almost all applications of spouted beds are in
gas–solid systems. The reader is referred elsewhere for more details [D1, M1].

Fast fluidization. Fast fluidization was introduced in Fig. 12.21. The gas
velocity is sufficiently high so that the solids are transported out the top of the
reactor. The cyclone in Fig. 12.21 separates the solid catalyst from the gas; the

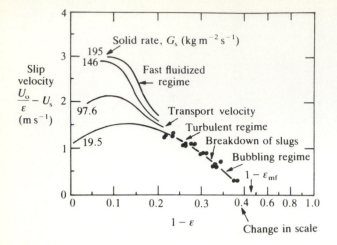

FIGURE 12.23
Slip velocity versus (1 − void fraction) for a fluid cracking catalyst. (*From Yerushalmi and Avidan, in Fluidization, 2nd ed., p. 226, Davidson, Clift, and Harrison (eds.), Academic Press, New York, 1985. By permission.*)

solids are then recycled via a standpipe to the bottom of the reactor [Y1]. Fast fluidization is characterized by a large concentration of solids and a high throughput of gas. The high velocity improves performance by overcoming particle agglomeration.

Yerushalmi and Avidan [Y2] present some fluidization data taken on a fluid cracking catalyst in a 15.2-cm column. They define a "slip velocity" as the difference in the superficial gas velocity divided by porosity U_o/ε and the mean solid velocity U_s. Figure 12.23 shows a comparison of fast fluidization with bubbling and turbulent fluidization. Over the bubbling and turbulent ranges, there exists a unique curve for various solids rates. However, in the fast fluidization range, a different curve is found for each solids rate.

There are few, if any, correlations for fast fluidization. Commercial processes are plentiful, but careful scale-up is required [Y2]. The region of fast fluidization (pneumatic transport) generally occurs at void fractions in the range 0.75–0.95, depending on U_o and the type of solids. There are no correlations available for U_{tr}, the minimum velocity for pneumatic or hydraulic transport. Certainly, large values of the particle diameter d_p and particle density ρ_p favor large values of U_{tr}. Based on present results, there are no valid correlations for pressure drop or for prediction of U_{tr} [G5, Y2].

12.3.2 Gas–Solid Fluidization

Gas–solid fluidization, as described previously, consists of five separate regimes; these are: (1) bubbling fluidized bed, (2) slugging bed, (3) turbulent fluidized bed, (4) fast fluidized bed, and (5) pneumatic transport. All of these are normally in the aggregate region. Lengthy reviews of aggregate fluidization can be found elsewhere [D1, H1, K4].

The void fraction or porosity ε, as defined in Eq. (12.81), is an important variable in fluidization. When the static bed of solids is introduced into the

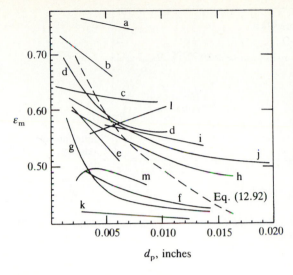

FIGURE 12.24
Typical values of minimum voidage for gas–solid fluidization near atmospheric pressure. (*From Leva, Fluidization, p. 21, McGraw-Hill, New York, 1959. By permission.*)
(a) soft brick; (b) absorption carbon; (c) broken Raschig rings; (d) coal and glass powder; (e) silicon carbide; (f) sand; (g) round sand, $\phi_s = 0.86$; (h) sharp sand, $\phi_s = 0.67$; (i) Fischer–Tropsch catalyst, $\phi_s = 0.58$; (j) anthracite coal, $\phi_s = 0.63$; (k) mixed round sand, $\phi_s = 0.86$; (l) coke; (m) silicon carbide.

15-cm pipe mentioned previously, the void fraction becomes a function of the method of loading. As air passes through the pipe, the void fraction reaches a predictable value, called the minimum porosity or void fraction for fluidization ε_{mf}, where the onset of fluidization occurs. Figure 12.24 shows some approximate values of ε_{mf} for some common particles at atmospheric pressure. Note that ε_{mf} does depend somewhat on the shape of the particles (a fact neglected in Fig. 12.24), as well as on d_p. Also, the sphericity ϕ_s, which is included in Fig. 12.24 for reference purposes, will be defined in Eq. (12.104).

For particles for which no data exist, the following equation has been proposed for gas–solid fluidization [L4]:

$$\varepsilon_{mf} = 1.0 - 0.356[\log_{10}(d_p) - 1] \tag{12.92}$$

where d_p is the particle diameter in μm (microns). Note that Eq. (12.92) is based on data near 1 atm total pressure. Equation (12.92) is plotted in Fig. 12.24 for reference.

The void fraction after fluidization can be calculated from ε_{mf}, L_{mf} (the height of the bed at ε_{mf}), and L_{fb} (the height of the bed after fluidization). In fact for any two heights, L_1 and L_2, ε_2 is related to ε_1 by

$$\frac{L_2}{L_1} = \frac{1 - \varepsilon_1}{1 - \varepsilon_2} = \frac{\rho_1}{\rho_2} \tag{12.93}$$

where ρ is the overall density. Equation (12.93) applies to both gas–solid and liquid–solid fluidized beds.

The appropriate Reynolds number for fluidization $N_{Re,fb}$ is defined as

$$N_{Re,fb} = d_p U_o \rho / \mu \tag{12.94}$$

where ρ and μ are properties of the pure fluid.

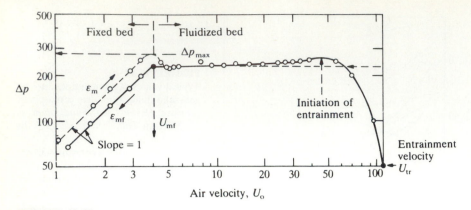

FIGURE 12.25
Pressure drop in fluidized beds. (*From Kunii and Levenspiel, Fluidization Engineering, p. 74, McGraw-Hill, New York, 1969. By permission.*)

The change in pressure drop with superficial velocity U_o is shown in Fig. 12.25. In the fixed (or static) bed region, $\log(-\Delta p)$ is linear with $\log N_{Re,fb}$, which increases as U_o increases (slope of -1 on the log–log plot). The pressure drop actually goes through a maximum [G5, K4, L4, W3] just before the onset of fluidization (at U_{mf}); one explanation of this phenomenon is that more energy is required to "unlock" the solid particles than to maintain a state of fluidization [L4]. The pressure drop at the onset of fluidization is approximately equal to the buoyancy force on the solid particles divided by the area [K4, L4].

When a column is initially filled with solids, the particles are oriented randomly; however, when the bed is fluidized for the first time, the particles no longer touch. Furthermore, the particles, which are irregularly shaped in most applications, tend to be oriented during fluidization by the flow of fluid on all sides. Thus, the hysteresis shown in Fig. 12.25 when the pressure drop is lowered after a bed has been fluidized is caused by the fact that on the downward curve the particles have been oriented, as compared to the upward curve for which the particles were packed randomly. If the bed were to be fluidized a second time, there would be no hysteresis. Therefore, the minimum voidage ε_{mf} is represented by the value for the downward curve in Fig. 12.25. The height L_{mf} represents the height of the bed upon reaching the superficial velocity U_{mf} in a bed of "oriented" particles.

When the velocity is increased above U_{mf}, the pressure drop increases only slightly as the velocity increases 10-fold. At even a higher velocity, entrainment is initiated. At U_{tr}, the void fraction approaches 1.0, and pneumatic transport occurs. The entrainment velocity U_{tr} exceeds by many times the minimum velocity for fluidization, U_{mf}, as seen in Fig. 12.25. Also, the entrainment velocity is much greater than the terminal settling velocity U_t. The solids in gas–solid fluidization form "clusters" of particles, even at void fractions approaching unity. The effective diameter of these clusters is much greater than that of any one particle; hence, it is observed that $U_{tr} \gg U_t$. In fact, a bed of fine solids can be maintained at gas velocities that are 10–20 times U_t [Y1]. Note that U_t (the calculation of which was discussed in Section 12.2.3 and Example 12.12) is the settling velocity of a single particle in an infinite fluid; this velocity is equivalent to a superficial velocity, since the void fraction is unity.

Estimation of velocities. The velocity for minimum fluidization (low pressure only) can be estimated from the following [G5]:

$$N_{\mathrm{Re,mf}} = d_p U_{mf} \rho / \mu \tag{12.95}$$

$$N_{\mathrm{Ar}} = \rho g d_p^3 (\rho_p - \rho) / \mu^2 \tag{12.96}$$

$$N_{\mathrm{Re,mf}} = (C_1^2 + C_2 N_{\mathrm{Ar}})^{1/2} - C_1 \quad \begin{cases} C_1 = 27.2 \\ C_2 = 0.0408 \end{cases} \tag{12.97}$$

Note that some researchers prefer $C_1 = 33.4$ [C3]. The term N_{Ar} is the Archimedes number (sometimes called the Galileo number), and ρ and μ are properties of the pure fluid.

The minimum pressure drop for fluidization $(-\Delta p_{mf})$ should equal the value predicted by the Bernoulli equation, i.e., the pressure drop necessary to support the bed weight plus the vertical fluid head:

$$-\Delta p_{mf} = (\rho_p - \rho)g(1 - \varepsilon_{mf})(L_{mf}) + \rho g L_{mf} \tag{12.98}$$

In practice, $-\Delta p_{mf}$ can be less than the value predicted by Eq. (12.98) because of channeling.

The simplest equation for minimum bubbling velocity U_{mb} is [G2, G3]

$$U_{mb} = K_{mb} \bar{d}_s \tag{12.99}$$

where $\bar{d}_s$ is the mean surface diameter of the powder. This simple equation works well for many cases, but more sophisticated equations are available for solids that contain a considerable mass fraction of "fines" [C2, G3]. To assist in evaluating solids with a wide range of sizes, the solids must be classified according to mean particle size and density range. Details can be found elsewhere [C1, G3].

The transition from bubbling or slugging to turbulent fluidization can be estimated by [Y1]

$$U_k = 7.0(\rho_s \bar{d}_s)^{1/2} - 0.77 \tag{12.100}$$

where U_k is the transition velocity (m s^{-1}) and $\rho_s \bar{d}_s$ is the solids density times mean diameter (kg m^{-2}). The transition from bubbling to slugging can also be predicted. These criteria include diverse factors, such as the stable bubble size and the aspect ratio of the column (height-to-diameter ratio), as well as U_{mf} [G5].

The transport velocity U_{tr} cannot be predicted with any reliability [G5]. It is advisable to perform careful scale-up in any case when designing fluidization equipment.

Heat transfer. Heat transfer in fluidized beds occurs as a result of several mechanisms, including conduction, convection, and often radiation. There is heat transfer from particle to particle and from the bed to surfaces (or the walls). The correlations in the literature are numerous [D1, H1, K4, L4]; more than 35 have been proposed to date. For aggregative fluidization, a simple correlation of h_w (heat transfer coefficient at the wall), for estimation only, is [K4]

$$N_{Nu,fb} = 0.6 N_{Pr}(N_{Re,fb})^{0.3} \qquad (12.101)$$

where

$$N_{Re,fb} = d_p U_o \rho / \mu \qquad (12.94)$$

$$N_{Nu,fb} = h_w d_p / k \qquad (12.102)$$

$$N_{Pr} = c_p \mu / k \qquad (8.4)$$

with k, c_p, and μ being properties of the pure fluid and h_w the heat transfer coefficient at the wall.

Heat transfer in gas–solid fluidization is relatively high; in fact, the attractiveness of fluidization lies in the favorable rates of heat transfer, the lack of "hot spots", and the thoroughness of mixing between the fluid and the solid phases. Typical values of heat transfer coefficients are in the range 200–500 W m^{-2} K^{-1}, as shown by the data for quartz sand in Fig. 12.26 [Z1]. This number is a factor of 100 greater than the coefficient for a corresponding flow of the same gas through an empty tube [G5].

Finally, note that Eq. (12.101) will not predict the maximum in h that is observed experimentally. Also, radiation effects must be included for high-temperature reactors.

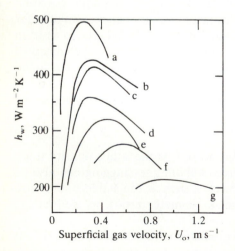

FIGURE 12.26
Bed-to-wall heat transfer coefficients for quartz sand particles. (*Modified from Zabrodsky, Hydrodynamics and Heat Transfer in Fluidized Beds, p. 272, MIT Press, Cambridge, MA, 1962. Permission purchased.*)

(a) 140 μm; (b) 198 μm; (c) 216 μm; (d) 428 μm; (e) 515 μm; (f) 650 μm; (g) 1100 μm.

Mass transfer. Knowledge of mass transfer coefficients in fluidized beds is important since mass transfer occurs in many of the common applications of fluidization, such as gas–solid reactions, drying, absorption, ion exchange, and dissolution (leaching). There are three modes of mass transfer in fluidized beds: fluid-to-solid, lean-to-dense, and bed-to-surface. In mass transfer between fluid and solid, a transferable species moves between the bulk fluid to the fluidized solid. Most often, the solid is a catalyst, and the reactants move to the solid and the products move away from the solid. In an aggregative fluidized bed, transfer occurs between the lean phase (large void fraction) and the dense phase (high concentration of solids). Lastly, bed-to-surface mass transfer is analogous to the corresponding heat transfer, just discussed. Of these, mass transfer between bed and surface is not important and has been reviewed elsewhere [W1].

Let us review mass transfer coefficients briefly. Mass transfer in the wetted-wall column of Section 11.5 is expressed in terms of the overall mass transfer coefficients k_c', where

$$(N_A/A)_{r,w} = k_c'(C_{A,w} - C_{A,\,ave}) \tag{6.87}$$

In this equation, the normal overbar on $\bar{C}_{A,w}$ has been dropped for convenience. For mass transfer between fluid and the fluidized particles, the flux $(N_A/A)_{r,w}$ is replaced by a bulk flow term that is taken as the superficial velocity U_o (assuming plug flow) times dC_A/dz, the rate of change of concentration with bed height [K4]. Note that the units agree, moles divided by the product of area times time. The term k_c' in Eq. (6.87) is replaced with the overall mass transfer coefficient for fluidization k_{fb} times the specific surface area of solids a_s:

$$U_o\frac{dC_A}{dz} = (k_{fb}a_s)(C_{A,\,sat} - C_A) \tag{12.103}$$

where $C_{A,\,sat}$ is the saturation concentration of solute A and C_A is the average concentration of A in the bulk gas. Additionally, for convenience the subscript "ave" has been dropped. The term a_s is a function of the diameter d_p and of the sphericity ϕ_s, which is defined as

$$a_s = \frac{\text{surface area particles}}{\text{volume bed}} = \frac{(6)(1 - \varepsilon)}{d_p\phi_s} \tag{12.104}$$

The sphericity ϕ_s is an important term in fixed and fluidized beds; its definition is

$$\phi_s = \left(\frac{\text{surface area sphere}}{\text{surface area particle}}\right)_{\text{both of the same volume}} \tag{12.105}$$

Thus, for a sphere the sphericity is 1; for particles of other shapes, the sphericity lies between 0 and 1. Note that d_p is the diameter of a sphere that has the same volume as the particle; also, the quantity $6/(d_p\phi_s)$ in Eq. (12.104)

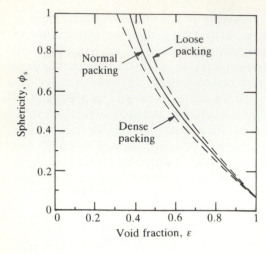

FIGURE 12.27
Correlation of sphericity versus void fraction for uniformly sized randomly packed beds. (*Adapted from Brownell, Dombrowski, and Dickey, Chem. Eng. Progr.* **46:** *415 (1950). By permission of AIChE.*)

is the ratio $(\pi d_p^2/\phi_s)/(\pi d_p^3/6)$, i.e. the surface area of the equivalent spherical particle divided by the volume of the particle. The sphericity correlates well with the void fraction in a packed bed [B3, B4], as shown in Fig. 12.27.

Equation (12.103) applies at any point in the bed. A more useful equation relates k_{fb} to the inlet and outlet concentrations $C_{A,in}$ and $C_{A,out}$. The usual assumptions are plug flow and k_{fb} independent of z; then the variables in Eq. (12.103) are separated and integrated with the obvious boundary conditions:

$$\int_{C_{A,in}}^{C_{A,out}} \frac{dC_A}{C_{A,sat} - C_A} = \frac{k_{fb}a_s}{U_o} \int_0^{L_{fb}} dz \tag{12.106}$$

After integration, Eq. (12.106) becomes

$$\ln \frac{C_{A,sat} - C_{A,out}}{C_{A,sat} - C_{A,in}} = \frac{k_{fb}a_s L_{fb}}{U_o} \tag{12.107}$$

Equation (12.107) points out that if either $C_{A,in}$ or $C_{A,out}$ approaches $C_{A,sat}$, the accuracy of determination of k_{fb} rapidly diminishes. Equation (12.107) rearranges to

$$C_{A,out} = (C_{A,in})(\exp n) + (C_{A,sat})(1 - \exp n) \tag{12.108}$$

with

$$n = -k_{fb}a_s L_{fb}/U_o \tag{12.109}$$

If the ratio of L_{fb} to bed diameter is less than 10, axial dispersion becomes important. Now the flux $(N_A/A)_{r,w}$ in Eq. (6.87), which was replaced with the bulk flow term $U_o(dC_A/dz)$ to give Eq. (12.103), now consists of two terms: the bulk flow term and Fick's law for the axial diffusion:

$$U_o \frac{dC_A}{dz} - D_{ax} \frac{d^2C_A}{dz^2} = (k_{fb}a_s)(C_{A,sat} - C_A) \tag{12.110}$$

where D_{ax} is an axial dispersion coefficient correlated by Chung and Wen [C3] for gas to particle mass transfer.

Mass transfer coefficients for gas to particle have been correlated reasonably well; the Sherwood number, Eq. (12.87), is a function of the Schmidt number [Eq. (8.6)], the fluidization Reynolds number [Eq. (12.94)], and the quantity $d_p/(x_s L_{fb})$, where x_s is the volume fraction of solids involved in the mass transfer ($x_s = 1$ when no inert solids are present).

The most recent correlations, as recommended by Wen and Fane [W1] for gas to particle fluidized beds, are:

$$N_{Sh,fb} = k_{fb} d_p y/D = 0.43(N_{MRe})^{0.97}(N_{Sc})^{0.33} \qquad 0.5 \le N_{MRe} \le 80 \qquad (12.111)$$

$$N_{Sh,fb} = k_{fb} d_p y/D = 12.5(N_{MRe})^{0.2}(N_{Sc})^{0.33} \qquad 80 \le N_{MRe} \le 10^3 \qquad (12.112)$$

where N_{MRe} is the empirically modified Reynolds number defined as

$$N_{MRe} = N_{Re,fb}\left(\frac{d_p}{x_s L_{fb}}\right)^{0.6} = \frac{d_p U_o \rho}{\mu}\left(\frac{d_p}{x_s L_{fb}}\right)^{0.6} \qquad 5 < N_{Re,fb} < 120$$

$$(12.113)$$

These equations work fairly well, except in the case of catalytic reaction systems, where k_{fb} is underestimated [W2].

The above correlations can be of use in heat transfer estimation by assuming that the Colburn analogy is valid; i.e., j_H equals j_M.

12.3.3 Liquid–Solid Fluidization

Liquid–solid fluidization is almost exclusively particulate fluidization—a mostly uniform bed where the solids circulate randomly and individually throughout the bed without significant bubble formation. The void fraction in particulate fluidization has been correlated by many investigators [C2]. The most widely used equation is that of Richardson and Zaki [R3, R4, R5]:

$$\varepsilon^n = U_o/U_i \qquad (12.114)$$

where U_o is the superficial velocity measured in the empty column and U_i is the superficial velocity for a void fraction equal to unity. Equation (12.114) is useful for both particle sedimentation and fluidization; for fluidization, U_i is

$$\log_{10} U_i = \log_{10} U_t - d_p/d_o \qquad (12.115)$$

with d_p being the particle diameter and d_o the column diameter, and U_t the terminal free-falling velocity (cf. Section 12.2.3). The empirical exponent n in the Richardson–Zaki equation for fluidization has been correlated as follows [C2]:

$$n = 4.65 + (20)(d_p/d_o) \qquad\qquad N_{Re,T} < 0.2 \qquad (12.116)$$

$$n = [4.4 + (18)(d_p/d_o)](N_{Re,T})^{-0.03} \qquad 0.2 < N_{Re,T} < 1 \qquad (12.117)$$

$$n = [4.4 + (18)(d_p/d_o)](N_{Re,T})^{-0.01} \qquad 1 < N_{Re,T} < 200 \qquad (12.118)$$

$$n = 4.4(N_{Re,T})^{-0.1} \qquad\qquad 200 < N_{Re,T} < 500 \qquad (12.119)$$

$$n = 2.4 \qquad\qquad N_{Re,T} > 500 \qquad (12.120)$$

where the Reynolds number $N_{Re,T}$[7] is based on the terminal velocity U_t and the viscosity and density of the fluid at zero solids concentration:

$$N_{Re,T} = d_o U_t \rho / \mu \tag{12.121}$$

Correlations for nonspherical particles and fluidization with a range of particle sizes have been reviewed elsewhere [C2, F1].

The expanded bed height L_{fb} is calculated from

$$L_{fb} = \frac{4w_s}{\pi \rho_s} d_o^2 (1 - \varepsilon) \tag{12.122}$$

The velocity for minimum fluidization can be estimated from Eqs. (12.116) through (12.120). Also, the Richardson–Zaki equation, Eq. (12.114), applies to gas–solid fluidization, although the experimentally observed values of n are significantly higher than those predicted by Eqs. (12.116) through (12.120). Likewise, Eq. (12.122) applies equally for gas–solid and liquid–solid fluidization.

The pressure drop between fluid and particles during particulate fluidization has not yet been correlated satisfactorily. The pressure drop is a complex function of the fluid properties as well as d_p, ρ_p, ε, the shape of the particles, $(\rho_p - \rho)$, and the flow patterns within the bed. This lack of correlation is not a serious problem, however, as the use of purely particulate beds is usually limited to liquid systems. A modification of the Ergun equation [E2] is widely used to correlate pressure drop; however, no generalization is recommended because the resulting equations are very sensitive to the values of ε_{mf} and to the sphericity [C2]. Figure 12.25 is based on gas–solid fluidization, but it applies equally to particulate fluidization. Since the pressure drop increases only slightly with a 3- to 5-fold velocity increase from U_{mf}, Eq. (12.98) can be used to calculate $-\Delta p_{mf}$, once ε_{mf} and the other variables have been determined. Note that the liquid head is often significant and must be included in $-\Delta p$.

Equations (12.95) through (12.97) for prediction of U_{mf} apply equally for liquid–solid fluidization, since the constants in Eq. (12.97) were obtained from both liquid and gas systems. In order to correlate the superficial velocity with pressure drop, it is recommended that several bed heights, L_{fb}, be measured experimentally for known U_o (and, better still, known $\Delta p/L$). Then from Eq. (12.93) and the following

$$U_o = \frac{k_3 \varepsilon^3}{1 - \varepsilon} = \frac{(-\Delta p) d_p^2 \varepsilon^3}{(150)(L_{fb}\mu)(1 - \varepsilon)^2} \tag{12.123}$$

the constant k_3 may be determined for the system of interest.

---

[7] The notation used in the literature is that $N_{Re,T}$ is the Reynolds number based on the terminal settling velocity, and $N_{Re,t}$ is the Reynolds number based on the diameter of a cylinder [cf. Eq. (12.145)].

Heat and mass transfer. Grace [G5] has reviewed the heat transfer correlations applicable to liquid–solid fluidization. It is evident that gas–solid heat transfer equations do not apply to liquid–solid systems. For mass transfer between particle and liquid, Wen and Fane [W1] recommend

Liquid fluidized beds

$$N_{Sh,fb} = k_{fb}d_p y/D = 2.0 + 1.5[(1 - \varepsilon)(N_{Re,fb})]^{0.5}(N_{Sc})^{0.33} \qquad (12.124)$$

Also, Shen *et al.* [S3] studied particle–liquid mass transfer in a fluidized bed using Reynolds numbers from 0.6 to 7.3.

Conclusion. Fluidized beds have several advantages over static beds. The small size of the particle used in fluidized beds results in a large surface area for a given quantity of solids, which in turn gives high rates of surface reaction, heat transfer, and mass transfer. Also, the small size reduces the resistance to mass diffusion within the particle. The rapid mixing of solids with fluid within a fluidized bed results in a uniform temperature within the bed and a high rate of heat transfer between the fluid and the walls. This increased heat transfer is especially important when highly exothermic or endothermic reactions are taking place in the bed. Another advantage lies in the ability to increase the velocity by varying the area so as to transport the solid particles into or out of the reactor. Fluid catalytic cracking of petroleum is a very important example of fluidization and pneumatic transport.

Of course, there are problems associated with fluidization. If the particles are the catalyst, which is so often the case, then the fluidization process will cause attrition (i.e., breakdown) of the solids. These "fines" are immediately entrained and must be removed after the fluid has exited the bed. The process by which the small particles are pneumatically transported out the top while the normally sized particles are fluidized in the bed is called elutriation. Over a period of time, the catalyst must be replaced because of the combined processes of attrition and elutriation.

At the present time, there is no satisfactory way to design a large-scale fluidization unit with bench-scale kinetic data alone. Scale-up is a serious problem in fluidization. Careful attention must also be given to the design of the fluid distributor plates that introduce the gas into the bed of solids.

Example 12.14. Anthracite coal, density 94 $lb_m\,ft^{-3}$ (1506 $kg\,m^{-3}$), is to be fluidized with air at 20 psia and 842°F in a vessel 10 ft in diameter. Fifteen tons of coal, ground to an average diameter of 200 μm, are placed in the vessel, which is filled to a height of 7 ft. The acceleration due to gravity is 9.78 $m\,s^{-2}$.

Compute (a) the static void fraction, (b) the minimum void fraction and bed height for fluidization, (c) the settling velocity for a single particle in a static fluid, (d) the minimum pressure drop for fluidization, (e) the minimum velocity for entrainment, and (f) the heat transfer coefficient at the wall for a superficial velocity 2.5 times U_{mf}.

For air at 842°F and 14.696 psia, the following are available:

$$\rho = 0.487 \times 10^{-3} \text{ g cm}^{-3} = 0.487 \text{ kg m}^{-3}$$
$$\mu = 3.431 \times 10^{-2} \text{ cP} = 3.431 \times 10^{-5} \text{ kg m}^{-1} \text{s}^{-1} \qquad \text{(i)}$$
$$k = 0.05379 \text{ W m}^{-1} \text{K}^{-1}$$
$$N_{Pr} = 0.7025$$

Answer. English units will be selected for this solution.

(a) Static void fraction. To find the void fraction, first the volume of coal and the total volume are calculated. The total volume of coal is the mass divided by density:

$$V_{coal} = (15)(2000)/94 \, [(\text{ton})(\text{lb}_m \text{ ton}^{-1})/(\text{lb}_m \text{ ft}^{-3})] = 319.1 \text{ ft}^3 \qquad \text{(ii)}$$

The total volume of the vessel at a height of 7 ft is

$$V_{total} = (\text{area})(\text{length}) = (\pi d^2/4)(L) = \pi(10)^2(7)/(4) = 549.8 \text{ ft}^3 \qquad \text{(iii)}$$

Using Eq. (12.81), the static void fraction is

$$\varepsilon = \frac{\text{volume air}}{\text{total volume}} = \frac{V_{total} - V_{coal}}{V_{total}} = \frac{549.8 - 319.1}{549.8} = 0.42 \qquad \text{(iv)}$$

(b) Minimum void fraction and bed height. The minimum void fraction for fluidization can be estimated from either Fig. 12.24 (for atmospheric pressure only) or Eq. (12.92). The particle diameter is 200 μm, or 0.00787 in. Figure 12.24 predicts ε_{mf} to be about 0.58. From Eq. (12.92):

$$\varepsilon_{mf} = 1.0 - 0.356[\log_{10}(d_p) - 1] = 1.0 - 0.356[\log_{10}(200) - 1] = 0.537 \qquad \text{(v)}$$

This value seems a little low, and 0.58 will be used. Note that the effect of pressure is to increase ε_{mf} slightly. The corresponding bed height from Eq. (12.93) is

$$L_{mf} = (L_1)(1 - \varepsilon_1)/(1 - \varepsilon_{mf}) = (7)(1 - 0.42)/(1 - 0.58)$$
$$= 9.675 \text{ ft} = 2.949 \text{ m} \qquad \text{(vi)}$$

(c) Minimum fluidization velocity. The minimum velocity for fluidization is estimated using the Archimedes number. Of the properties of air in Eq. (i), only the density changes appreciably with a small increase in pressure to 20 psia:

$$p_1/\rho_1 = p_2/\rho_2$$
$$\rho = (0.487)(20)/(14.696) = 0.663 \text{ kg m}^{-3} = 0.0414 \text{ lb}_m \text{ ft}^{-3} \qquad \text{(vii)}$$

From Eq. (12.96), the Archimedes number is

$$N_{Ar} = (\rho g d_p^3)(\rho_p - \rho)/\mu^2$$
$$= (0.663)(9.78)(200 \times 10^{-6})^3(1506 - 0.663)/(3.431 \times 10^{-5})^2$$
$$\times [(\text{kg m}^{-3})(\text{m s}^{-2})(\text{m}^3)(\text{kg m}^{-3})/(\text{kg m}^{-1}\text{s}^{-1})^2]$$
$$= 66.33 \qquad \text{(viii)}$$

From Eq. (12.97), the Reynolds number at minimum fluidization is

$$N_{Re,mf} = (C_1^2 + C_2 N_{Ar})^{1/2} - C_1$$
$$= [(27.2)^2 + (0.0408)(66.33)]^{1/2} - 27.2 = 0.04970 \qquad \text{(ix)}$$

Using the definition of $N_{\text{Re,mf}}$, Eq. (12.95), the velocity for minimum fluidization is

$$U_{\text{mf}} = (N_{\text{Re,mf}})(\mu)/(d_p\rho) = [(0.04970)(3.431 \times 10^{-5})]/[(200 \times 10^{-6})(0.663)]$$
$$= 0.01286 \text{ m s}^{-1} = 0.0422 \text{ ft s}^{-1} \tag{x}$$

This velocity seems low, but remember that U_{mf} is a superficial velocity, based on an empty chamber. The velocity in the gaps surrounding these very fine particles will be much higher.

(d) Minimum pressure drop. The minimum pressure drop for fluidization is calculated from Eq. (12.98):

$$-\Delta p_{\text{mf}} = (\rho_p - \rho)g(1 - \varepsilon_{\text{mf}})(L_{\text{mf}}) + \rho g L_{\text{mf}} \tag{12.98}$$
$$-\Delta p_{\text{mf}} = (1506 - 0.663)(9.78)(1 - 0.58)(2.949) + (0.663)(9.78)(2.949)$$
$$\times [(\text{kg m}^{-3})(\text{m s}^{-2})(\text{m})]$$
$$= 1.825 \times 10^{4} \text{ kg m}^{-1} \text{ s}^{-2} = 1.825 \times 10^{4} \text{ Pa} = 2.647 \text{ psi} \tag{xi}$$

(e) Particle settling velocity. Assuming no hindered settling, Eq. (12.79) will be used to find an expression for the terminal velocity:

$$U_t^2 = (8r_p g)(\rho_p - \rho)/(3\rho C_D) \tag{12.79}$$
$$U_t^2 = [(8)(200 \times 10^{-6}/2)(9.78)(1506 - 0.663)]/[(3)(0.663)(C_D)]$$
$$\times [(\text{m})(\text{m s}^{-2})(\text{kg m}^{-3})/(\text{kg m}^{-3})]$$
$$= 5.923/C_D \tag{xii}$$

where the units of U_t^2 are $\text{m}^2 \text{ s}^{-2}$. Following the procedure in Example 12.12, Newton's law, Eq. (12.76), will be tried ($C_D = 0.44$):

$$U_t = (5.923/0.44)^{1/2} = 3.669 \text{ m s}^{-1} = 12.04 \text{ ft s}^{-1} \tag{xiii}$$

The particle Reynolds number, Eq. (12.68), is

$$N_{\text{Re,p}} = U_t d_p \rho/\mu = (U_t)(200 \times 10^{-6})(0.663)/(3.431 \times 10^{-5}) = 3.865 U_t$$
$$= (3.865)(3.669) = 14.18 \tag{xiv}$$

Clearly, at the point of minimum velocity for fast fluidization, the terminal settling velocity is not in the range of Newton's law. Therefore, Eq. (12.75) for the transition region will be tried. Equation (12.75) is solved for C_D and then substituted into Eq. (xii):

$$U_t^2 = \frac{5.923}{C_D} = \frac{5.923}{18.5}(N_{\text{Re}})^{0.6} = \frac{5.923}{18.5}\left(\frac{d_p\rho}{\mu}\right)^{0.6}(U_t)^{0.6}$$
$$= \left(\frac{5.923}{18.5}\right)\left(\frac{(2 \times 10^{-4})(0.663)}{3.431 \times 10^{-5}}\right)^{0.6}(U_t)^{0.6} = (0.7205)(U_t)^{0.6} \tag{xv}$$

Equation (xv) is solved for the terminal velocity (the entrainment velocity):

$$U_t = (0.7205)^{1/(2-0.6)} = 0.7912 \text{ m s}^{-1} = 2.596 \text{ ft s}^{-1} \tag{xvi}$$

Checking the solution, from Eq. (xiv) the Reynolds number is 3.06; from Eq. (12.75), C_D is 9.46, and from Fig. 12.16 C_D is about 12. Since U_t is for a single particle, the void fraction is zero, and U_t is both a superficial velocity and the actual velocity.

The spread between the calculated values of U_{mf} and U_t is large:

$$U_t/U_{mf} = 0.7912/0.01286 = 61.5 \qquad \text{(xvii)}$$

(f) Bed to wall heat transfer coefficient. Equations (12.94), (12.101), and (12.102) are used to find the Nusselt number:

$$N_{Re,fb} = d_p U_o \rho / \mu \qquad \text{(12.94)}$$

$$N_{Nu,fb} = 0.6 N_{Pr}(N_{Re,fb})^{0.3} \qquad \text{(12.101)}$$

$$N_{Nu,fb} = h_w d_p / k \qquad \text{(12.102)}$$

From Eq. (12.94), the Reynolds number at superficial velocity 2.5 times U_{mf} is

$$\begin{aligned}
N_{Re,fb} &= d_p U_o \rho / \mu \\
&= (200 \times 10^{-6})(2.5)(0.01286)(0.663)/(3.431 \times 10^{-5}) \\
&\qquad \times [(m)(m\,s^{-1})(kg\,m^{-3})/(kg\,m^{-1}\,s^{-1})] \\
&= 0.1242 \qquad \text{(xviii)}
\end{aligned}$$

From Eq. (12.101), the Nusselt number is

$$N_{Nu,fb} = 0.6 N_{Pr}(N_{Re,fb})^{0.3} = (0.6)(0.7025)(0.1242)^{0.3} = 0.2254 \qquad \text{(xix)}$$

From Eq. (12.102), the heat transfer coefficient at the wall at a velocity of 2.5 times U_{mf} is

$$h_w = (N_{Nu,fb})(k/d_p) = (0.2254)(0.05379)/(200 \times 10^{-6}) = 60.6 \text{ W m}^{-2}\text{K}^{-1} \qquad \text{(xx)}$$

Comparison of this value with that from Fig. 12.26 shows that at the velocity of 0.032 m s^{-1} (i.e., $2.5U_{mf}$), the value of h_w is low for particles of size 200 μm. The velocity should be around 0.2 m s^{-1} for maximum heat transfer. Note also that Eq. (12.101) does not predict the maximum in Fig. 12.26.

Example 12.15. A bed of activated alumina catalyst of size 400 μm is to be fluidized in liquid of viscosity 10 cP $(6.72 \times 10^{-3} \text{ lb}_m \text{ ft}^{-1}\text{s}^{-1})$ and density 58 $\text{lb}_m \text{ ft}^{-3}$. The height and void volume of the static bed are 5 ft and 0.45, respectively. The density of the catalyst is 4 g cm^{-3} (249.6 $\text{lb}_m \text{ ft}^{-3}$). Calculate the pressure drop in psi and the superficial velocity (ft s^{-1}) at the point of incipient fluidization. Let $g = 32.174 \text{ ft s}^{-2}$.

Answer. Since 1 μm $= 3.937 \times 10^{-5}$ in., the diameter of the catalyst is 0.0157 in. (a relatively coarse catalyst). For this problem, in which coarse particles are fluidized by a liquid, ε_{mf} is probably not much greater than 0.45. The pressure drop at the minimum fluidization velocity from Eq. (12.98) is

$$\begin{aligned}
-\Delta p_{mf} &= (\rho_p - \rho)(g/g_c)(1 - \varepsilon_{mf})(L_{mf}) \\
&= (249.6 - 58)(1.0)(1 - 0.45)(5) [(\text{lb}_m \text{ ft}^{-3})(\text{lb}_f \text{ lb}_m^{-1})(\text{ft})] \\
&= 526.9 \text{ lb}_f \text{ ft}^{-2} = 3.66 \text{ lb}_f \text{ in.}^{-2} \qquad \text{(i)}
\end{aligned}$$

where g_c is added to Eq. (12.98) in order to introduce the unit of force. Equations (12.95) through (12.97) are used to find the minimum velocity for fluidization.

From Eq. (12.96), the Archimedes number is

$$N_{Ar} = (\rho g d_p^3)(\rho_p - \rho)/\mu^2$$
$$= (58)(32.174)(0.0157/12)^3(249.6 - 58)/(6.72 \times 10^{-3})^2$$
$$\times [(\text{lb}_m \text{ ft}^{-3})(\text{ft s}^{-2})(\text{ft}^3)(\text{lb}_m \text{ ft}^{-3})/(\text{lb}_m^2 \text{ ft}^{-2} \text{s}^{-2})]$$
$$= 17.73 \tag{ii}$$

A value of $N_{Ar} = 17.73$ is still in the small-particle range, and following the calculation in Eq. (ix) in Example 12.14:

$$N_{Re,mf} = d_p U_{mf} \rho/\mu = [(27.2)^2 + (0.0408)(17.73)]^{1/2} - 27.2 = 0.01330 \tag{iii}$$

Solving for U_{mf}, as done in Example 12.14, Eq. (x), gives

$$U_{mf} = (N_{Re,mf})[\mu/(d_p \rho)] = (0.01330)(6.72 \times 10^{-3})(0.0157/12)^{-1}(58)^{-1}$$
$$= 1.18 \times 10^{-3} \text{ ft s}^{-1} \tag{iv}$$

12.3.4 Packed Beds

Figure 12.20 illustrated flow through a bed of solids at superficial velocities below the minimum velocity for fluidization, i.e., $U_o < U_{mf}$. Equipment so designed is termed a packed or fixed bed. Important applications include drying operations, absorption or desorption of gas or liquids to or from solids, mass transfer through gases or liquids to catalyst particles, and mass transfer between gas and liquid promoted by increased contact provided by the solid surfaces.

Pressure drop. Pressure drop in packed beds is usually correlated in the form of friction factor versus a modified Reynolds number. In Chapter 10, the concept of hydraulic radius r_H [Eq. (10.45)] was used by relating r_H to an equivalent diameter d_e. Then the Reynolds number in Eq. (6.2) becomes

$$N_{Re} = U_{ave} d_e \rho/\mu = (U_{ave})(4r_H)(\rho/\mu) \tag{12.125}$$

where U_{ave} is the average velocity in the voids of the packed bed. The most convenient definition of hydraulic radius for a packed bed is on a volume to area basis:

$$r_H = \frac{\text{VOID VOLUME IN BED}}{\text{SURFACE AREA OF PARTICLES}} \tag{12.126}$$

Since the void (free) volume is the total volume minus the volume of solids, and ε [Eq. (12.81)] is the ratio of void volume to total volume, the following identities are true for n spheres, each of volume $\pi d_p^3/6$:

$$V_{void} = V_{total} - V_{solids} = \varepsilon V_{total} = \frac{V_{solids}}{1 - \varepsilon} - V_{solids}$$
$$= n \frac{\pi d_p^3}{6} \left(\frac{1}{1 - \varepsilon} - 1\right) \tag{12.127}$$

Equation (12.127) is inserted into Eq. (12.126) along with the surface area, $n\pi d_p^2$:

$$r_H = \frac{n(\pi d_p^3/6)[\varepsilon/(1-\varepsilon)]}{n\pi d_p^2} = \frac{d_p}{6}\left(\frac{\varepsilon}{1-\varepsilon}\right) \tag{12.128}$$

The velocity in Eq. (12.125) is simply related to the superficial velocity U_o (the velocity in the empty chamber) by

$$U_o = \varepsilon U_{ave} \tag{12.129}$$

which can be proved from Eq. (7.10) for constant flow w.

Equations (12.125), (12.128), and (12.129) can be combined to yield a modified Reynolds number for packed beds $N_{Re,pb}$:

$$N_{Re,pb} = \frac{d_p U_o \rho}{\mu(1-\varepsilon)} \tag{12.130}$$

where the factor $(2/3)$ that naturally arises is always dropped from Eq. (12.130), since $N_{Re,pb}$ will be used in empirical correlations.

The friction factor can be similarly cast into the previously introduced variables for the packed bed. Using Eqs. (12.128) and (12.129) with Eq. (6.89) gives

$$f = \frac{\tau_w}{\rho U_{ave}^2/2} = \frac{(d_e/4)(-\Delta p/L)}{\rho U_{ave}^2/2} = \frac{(-\Delta p/L)(\varepsilon^3 d_p)}{3\rho U_{ave}^2(1-\varepsilon)} \tag{12.131}$$

The packed bed friction factor f_{pb} is defined from Eq. (12.131) by omitting the factor of 3:

$$f_{pb} = \frac{\varepsilon^3}{1-\varepsilon}\frac{(d_p)(-\Delta p/L)}{\rho U_o^2} \tag{12.132}$$

For laminar flow, the variables $N_{Re,pb}$ and f_{pb} form the Kozeny–Carman equation [E2, K4]:

$$f_{pb} = \frac{150}{N_{Re,pb}} \qquad N_{Re,pb} < 20 \tag{12.133}$$

Equation (12.133) is similar to Eq. (12.67) for flow past a sphere. Note that Δp will usually include a static pressure head, since Δp will be small in laminar flow.

The Burke–Plummer equation [B5, K4] is

$$f_{pb} = 1.75 \qquad 10^3 < N_{Re,pb} < 10^4 \tag{12.134}$$

The Burke–Plummer equation applies only at very high Reynolds numbers. Again, Eq. (12.134) and Eq. (12.76) are very similar in form.

Ergun [E2] combined Eqs. (12.133) and (12.134) into a general equation for flow in packed beds:

$$f_{pb} = \frac{150}{N_{Re,pb}} + 1.75 \qquad 1 < N_{Re,pb} < 10^4 \tag{12.135}$$

Ergun's equation applies in the region of intermediate Reynolds numbers. Also, this equation can be used for gases by using the density of the gas as evaluated at the mean of the inlet and outlet pressures [G1]. Additional references are available [B3, E2, G1, K4, P1].

Often the pressure drop Δp and superficial velocity U_o are measured in order to calculate ε from Eq. (12.135), since ε is difficult to measure in industrial equipment. There may be substantial errors in predictions from Eq. (12.135), especially in view of uncertainties in ε and d_p for many types of packing.

Heat and mass transfer. Heat and mass transfer to a single sphere were given by Eqs. (12.85) or (12.86) and (12.87). For flow in a packed bed of spheres, Sen Gupta and Thodos [S2] showed that the analogy between heat and mass transfer is valid. The following is the most recent correlation [D2, G1]:

$$j_M = j_H = (0.4548/\varepsilon)(N_{Re,p})^{-0.4069} \qquad 10 \le N_{Re,p} \le 10^4 \qquad (12.136)$$

where j_M is from Eq. (12.89) and j_H is slightly modified from Eq. (11.79) (as is everything else in packed beds) to give

$$j_H = N_{St}(N_{Pr})^{2/3} = (h\rho c_p/U_o)(N_{Pr})^{2/3} \qquad (12.137)$$

with ρ, c_p, and N_{Pr} all being properties of the pure fluid; U_o is the superficial velocity.

For heat transfer only, the most accurate correlation is [W2]:

$$\frac{h_{lm}d_p}{k}\left(\frac{\varepsilon}{1-\varepsilon}\right)(N_{Pr})^{-1/3} = (0.5)\left(\frac{1}{1-\varepsilon}\right)^{1/2}(N_{Re,p})^{1/2} + (0.2)\left(\frac{1}{1-\varepsilon}\right)^{2/3}(N_{Re,p})^{2/3}$$

$$(12.138)$$

$$2.2 \le \left(N_{Re,p}\frac{1}{1-\varepsilon}\right) \le 8000$$

In Eq. (12.138), all properties are evaluated at the average fluid temperature in the bed. The heat transfer coefficient h_{lm} is the log-mean coefficient in the equation:

$$\frac{q}{a_v V} = h_{lm}\,\Delta T_{lm} \qquad (12.139)$$

In Eq. (12.139), V is the total volume of the fixed bed and a_v is the surface area of the packing per unit volume:

$$a_v = (A_p/V_p)(1-\varepsilon) \qquad (12.140)$$

where A_p and V_p are the surface area of the packing and the volume of the packing, respectively; ΔT_{lm} is the log-mean temperature difference:

$$\Delta T_{lm} = \frac{\Delta T_{out} - \Delta T_{in}}{\ln(\Delta T_{out}/\Delta T_{in})} \qquad (12.141)$$

Note that all data used to obtain Eq. (12.138) were taken with air, $N_{Pr} = 0.7$. Hence, the dependency of N_{Nu} on N_{Pr} is strictly a guess based on other boundary layer correlations.

Reference data for mass transfer are available at Reynolds numbers above 4000, but no equation exists. An excellent review is available [G1]. Also, other equations for packed beds may be found in the literature [G1, H3, M3]. For beds of coarse solids, the following can be used:

$$N_{Nu,pb} = 2.0 + 1.8(N_{Pr})^{1/3}(N_{Re,pb})^{1/2} \qquad N_{Re,pb} > 100 \qquad (12.142)$$

$$N_{Sh,pb} = 2.0 + 1.8(N_{Sc})^{1/3}(N_{Re,pb})^{1/2} \qquad N_{Re,pb} > 80 \qquad (12.143)$$

The mass transfer problem in fixed beds is more important than the heat transfer problem. Fluidized beds are more satisfactory than packed beds for applications in which appreciable heat transfer is likely. The mass transfer data for packed and fluidized beds are surprisingly good. Figure 12.28 summarizes the equations and data for mass transfer between solid particles and fluid. Looking at a constant $N_{Re,p}$, say 1000, it is seen that

$$k_{c,\text{sphere}} < k_{c,\text{fluidized}} < k_{c,\text{fixed}} \qquad (12.144)$$

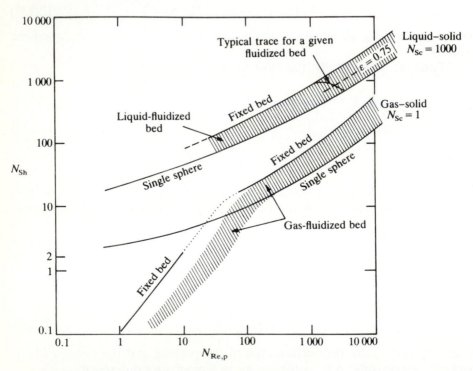

FIGURE 12.28
Sherwood number versus Reynolds number for mass transfer with spheres and beds of solids. (*Adapted from Kunii and Levenspiel, Fluidization Engineering, p. 196, Wiley, New York, 1969. By permission.*)

In Fig. 12.28, it is surprising to see mass transfer data for both fixed and fluidized beds below the prediction for single spheres, Eq. (12.87). At such low flows, it can be surmised that significant channeling occurs so that some parts of the bed see no fluid movement. Yet Eq. (12.87) predicts a Sherwood number of 2.0 for diffusion from a sphere into a stagnant fluid. At this point, there is no satisfactory explanation for this discrepancy.

In summary, this section has discussed the momentum, heat, and mass transfer in flow through packed (fixed) beds; these form the basis for solution to any problem in this subject. These solutions are detailed in books on unit operations and kinetics [G1, H2, M3, P1, S3, T1].

12.3.5 Single-Cylinder Heat Transfer

Prediction of the heat transfer coefficient from a cylinder to a flowing fluid is an important problem. In this section heat transfer to a single cylinder is covered, and in the next section heat transfer to a group of cylinders (a bank of tubes or tube bundle) is covered. The drag force on a single cylinder was discussed previously in conjunction with Fig. 12.16. There are no important mass transfer problems in this area.

Heat transfer from a cylinder in cross flow is shown in a plot of the local Nusselt number versus the angle θ from the stagnation point in Fig. 12.29 [G4]. The first minimum at $\theta = 90°$ is at a point where the turbulent boundary layer separates, as shown in Figs. 12.4 and 12.18. There are many correlations for heat transfer to a single cylinder over which the fluid is flowing in a normal direction with velocity U_∞. Only the most modern will be offered here. In the following correlations, the appropriate Reynolds number is $N_{Re,t}$:

$$N_{Re,t} = d_t U_\infty \rho_f / \mu_f \tag{12.145}$$

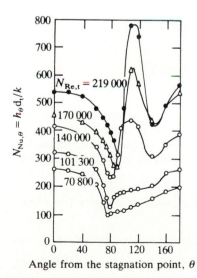

FIGURE 12.29
Local Nusselt number for heat transfer from a cylinder in cross flow. (*Adapted from Giedt, Trans. ASME* **71:** *375 (1949). By permission of ASME.*)

where d_t is the diameter of the cylinder and ρ_f and μ_f are evaluated at the film temperature T_f [cf. Eq. (11.32)]:

$$T_f = (T_\infty + T_w)/2 \tag{12.146}$$

The Nusselt number for flow past a single cylinder of diameter d_t is correlated by [C4]

$$N_{\text{Nu},t} = hd_t/k_f$$

$$= 0.3 + \left(\frac{(0.62)(N_{\text{Re},t})^{1/2}(N_{\text{Pr},f})^{1/3}}{[1 + (0.4/N_{\text{Pr},f})^{2/3}]^{1/4}}\right)\left[1 + \left(\frac{N_{\text{Re},t}}{2.82 \times 10^5}\right)^{5/8}\right]^{4/5} \tag{12.147}$$

$$100 \le N_{\text{Re},t} \le 10^7 \qquad N_{\text{Re},t}N_{\text{Pr},f} \ge 0.2$$

where all fluid properties are evaluated at the film temperature T_f. The correlation in Eq. (12.147) covers a wide range of Reynolds numbers; closer agreement with the experimental data for the midrange of Reynolds numbers is obtained from the following simplification of Eq. (12.147) [H3, L5]:

$$N_{\text{Nu},t} = 0.3 + \left(\frac{(0.62)(N_{\text{Re},t})^{1/2}(N_{\text{Pr},f})^{1/3}}{[1 + (0.4/N_{\text{Pr},f})^{2/3}]^{1/4}}\right)\left[1 + \left(\frac{N_{\text{Re},t}}{2.82 \times 10^5}\right)^{1/2}\right] \tag{12.148}$$

$$2 \times 10^4 \le N_{\text{Re},t} \le 4 \times 10^5 \qquad N_{\text{Re},t}N_{\text{Pr},f} \ge 0.2$$

Another correlation is [N1]

$$N_{\text{Nu},t} = [0.8237 - 0.5 \ln(N_{\text{Re},t}N_{\text{Pr},f})]^{-1} \tag{12.149}$$

$$N_{\text{Re},t}N_{\text{Pr},f} < 0.2$$

Again, all properties in the above three correlations are evaluated at T_f; the heat transfer coefficient h in Eqs. (12.147) through (12.149) is defined by

$$q = hA_{\text{cylinder}}(T_w - T_\infty) \tag{12.150}$$

Note that the product of the Reynolds number and the Prandtl number is the Peclet number [cf. Eq. (8.3)]:

$$N_{\text{Re},t}N_{\text{Pr},f} = U_\infty d_t \rho_f c_{p,f}/k_f = N_{\text{Pe},f} \tag{12.151}$$

Example 12.16. A new design of a hot-wire anemometer 24 μm in diameter is to be used to measure the velocity of air. The anemometer is operating at a constant temperature of 415 K, and the anemometer indicates that the power consumption is 0.1 W. The length of the wire is 250 diameters. If the air in the duct is at 385 K, estimate the velocity in m s^{-1}.

Answer. The area for heat transfer is the circumference of the wire (πd_t) times the length $250d_t$:

$$A_{\text{heat}} = (\pi d_t)(250d_t) = \pi(24 \times 10^{-6})^2(250) = 4.524 \times 10^{-7} \text{ m}^2 \tag{i}$$

From Eq. (12.146), the film temperature is the average of 385 K and 415 K, which is 400 K. The properties of air at 400 K are given in Table A.2:

$$\rho_f = 0.8825 \text{ kg m}^{-3}$$

$$\mu_f = 2.294 \times 10^{-2} \text{ cp} = 2.294 \times 10^{-5} \text{ kg m}^{-1} \text{s}^{-1}$$

$$c_{p,f} = 1013 \text{ J kg}^{-1} \text{K}^{-1}$$

$$k_f = 0.03305 \text{ W m}^{-1} \text{K}^{-1} \tag{ii}$$

$$N_{Pr,f} = 0.703 \tag{iii}$$

Since the velocity is unknown, the Reynolds number and the Peclet number are unknown. But the Nusselt number can be calculated from the information given and Eq. (12.150):

$$q = hA_{\text{cylinder}}(T_w - T_\infty) \tag{12.150}$$

$$h = q/[A_{\text{cylinder}}(T_w - T_\infty)]$$

$$= 0.1/[(4.524 \times 10^{-7})(415 - 385)] = 7.368 \times 10^3 \text{ J m}^{-2} \text{K}^{-1} \text{s}^{-1} \tag{iv}$$

From Eq. (12.147), the Nusselt number is

$$N_{Nu,t} = hd_t/k_f = (7.368 \times 10^3)(24 \times 10^{-6})/(0.03305) = 5.351 \tag{v}$$

The Reynolds number must be found by trial and error from whichever of Eq. (12.147) or (12.148) applies. In this problem, Eq. (12.147) will be tried first, since the Nusselt number appears to be low; the root of Eq. (12.147) is the value of $N_{Re,t}$ that makes the following zero:

$$f(N_{Re,t}) = 0 = N_{Nu,t} - 0.3 - \left[\frac{(0.62)(N_{Re,t})^{1/2}(N_{Pr,f})^{1/3}}{[1 + (0.4/N_{Pr,f})^{2/3}]^{1/4}}\right]\left[1 + \left(\frac{N_{Re,t}}{2.82 \times 10^5}\right)^{5/8}\right]^{4/5} \tag{vi}$$

Let x replace $N_{Re,t}$ for ease of notation in finding the root in Eq. (vi); after the appropriate substitutions:

$$f(x) = 0 = 5.351 - 0.3 - \left[\frac{(0.62)(x)^{1/2}(0.703)^{1/3}[1 + (x/2.82 \times 10^5)^{5/8}]^{4/5}}{[1 + (0.4/0.703)^{2/3}]^{1/4}}\right]$$

$$= 5.051 - 0.48375(x)^{1/2}[1.0 + (x/2.82 \times 10^5)^{5/8}]^{4/5} \tag{vii}$$

The standard root-finding techniques, such as Newton's method and the false position [P1, R1], are satisfactory for the solution of Eq. (vii). Alternatively, a short program to calculate $f(x)$ for each entry of x may be written in FORTRAN or BASIC or with a programmable calculator. Figure 12.30 presents a program in BASIC, written for a microcomputer. As a first guess, the term $(x/2.82 \times 10^5)$ is neglected. Then

$$x_1 = (5.051/0.48375)^2 = 109.0 \tag{viii}$$

The value of the function $f(x)$ for 109.0 is

$$f(x_1) = 5.051 - (0.48375)(109.0)^{1/2}[1.0 + (109.0/2.82 \times 10^5)^{5/8}]^{4/5}$$

$$= -2.957 \times 10^{-2} \tag{ix}$$

The value of x_1 selected should be too high, since inclusion of the term $x/282\,000$ will decrease x. Since Eq. (12.147) is recommended down to $N_{Re,t}$ equal to 100,

```
70 REM
80 REM
100 REM EXAMPLE 12-16 - HEAT TRANSFER FROM A TUNGSTEN WIRE
110 PI=3.141592654#
120 ONE=1!:E13=ONE/3!:E14=ONE/4!:E23=2!/3!:E58=5!/8!:E45=4!/5!
130 REM PROPERTIES OF AIR IN SI UNITS
140 RHO=.8825#:XMU=.00002294#:CP=1013!:XK=.03305
150 PR=.703
160 REM DIAMETER OF CYLINDER
170 DT=.000024
180 A=PI*DT*DT*250!
200 REM HEAT TRANSFER COEFFICIENT AND N-NUSSELT
210 Q=.1#:TD=415!-385!
220 H=Q/(A*TD)
230 XNU=H*DT/XK
240 PRINT"EXAMPLE 12-16":PRINT"     AREA = ";A:PRINT"     N-PR = ";PR
250 PRINT"     H = ";H:PRINT"     N-NU = ";XNU
260 C1=.62*PR^E13/(ONE+(.4/PR)^E23)^E14
270 PRINT"     C1 = ";C1
300 REM LOOP FOR TRIAL AND ERROR TO FIND THE ROOT F(X)
310 PRINT:INPUT"ENTER X";X
315 IF X=0 THEN GOTO 500
320 F=C1*SQR(X)*(ONE+(X/282000!)^E58)^E45
330 F=XNU - .3# - F
340 PRINT"     X = ";X
350 PRINT"     F = ";F
360 GOTO 310
500 PRINT:PRINT"END OF JOB":END
```

FIGURE 12.30
BASIC program to find the root of Eq. (vi) in Example 12.16.

let us try 100:

$$x_2 = 100 \qquad f(x_2) = 0.1862 \tag{x}$$

Now a bracket on the root has been located, i.e.

$$100.0 < x < 109.0 \tag{xi}$$

After several more trials, the following root is located:

$$x = N_{\text{Re},t} = 107.7 \qquad f(x) = 1.037 \times 10^{-3} \tag{xii}$$

Equation (12.145) is solved for velocity, and the result is

$$U_\infty = \frac{N_{\text{Re},t}\mu_f}{d_t\rho_f} = \frac{(107.7)(2.294 \times 10^{-5})}{(24 \times 10^{-6})(0.8825)}$$
$$= 116.6 \text{ m s}^{-1} = 382 \text{ ft s}^{-1} \tag{xiii}$$

In practice, the hot wire anemometer is primarily a research tool; in this application, the anemometer is carefully calibrated, rather than relying on correlations such as illustrated above. In fact Eqs. (12.147) and (12.148) follow the well-known King's law [K2]:

$$N_{\text{Nu}} \propto (N_{\text{Re}})^{1/2} \qquad h \propto (U_\infty)^{1/2} \tag{xiv}$$

However, a significant part of the King study was conducted at low flow rates where natural convection effects are important (i.e., buoyancy of the heated air).

12.3.6 Banks of Tubes

Flow across a bundle of tubes occurs in many heat exchangers. As a result, there are many excellent summaries of pressure drop [K3] and heat transfer

[G6, H3, I1, K3, W2, Z2] across banks of tubes. Most of the work was done over 30 years ago but is still valid. There is no practical mass transfer application here.

A number of new terms apply to flow across banks of tubes. Figure 12.31 shows the two possible configurations: in-line and staggered. From Fig. 12.31, the following are defined:

1. Spacing of rows perpendicular to flow: S_T
2. Spacing of rows in flow direction: S_L (both in-line and staggered)
3. Number of rows in flow direction: N
4. Effective flow length through tube bundle: L_{tb}
5. Equivalent diameter based on volume: d_v
6. Equivalent diameter based on area: d_e
7. Mass velocity through the minimum area perpendicular to the flow: G_{max}

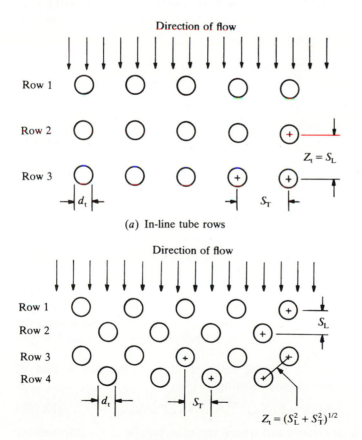

(a) In-line tube rows

(b) Staggered tube rows

FIGURE 12.31
Notation for in-line and staggered tube rows.

Expanding on the above:

$$L_{tb} = NS_L \tag{12.152}$$

$$d_e = (4)(\text{FREE CROSS SECTIONAL AREA})/(\text{WETTED PERIMETER})$$

$$= \frac{(4)(S_T S_L - \pi d_t^2/4)}{\pi d_t} \tag{12.153}$$

$$d_v = \frac{(4)(\text{FREE VOLUME IN TUBE BANK})}{\text{EXPOSED SURFACE AREA OF ALL TUBES}} \tag{12.154}$$

$$G_{max} = (\text{MASS FLOW RATE})/(\text{MINIMUM AREA}) \tag{12.155}$$

Note that d_e and d_v are essentially equal for large banks of tubes with no fins. The mass velocity has units of mass divided by area times time. The Reynolds number based on d_v is

$$N_{Re,v} = d_v G_{max}/\mu \tag{12.156}$$

Comparison of results between researchers is difficult because each favors a slightly different definition of the friction factor for use in heat exchangers. The friction factor of Gunter and Shaw [G7] is

$$f_{tb} = \frac{(-\Delta p)(2g_c \rho)}{G_{max}^2} \frac{d_v}{L_{tb}} \left(\frac{S_T}{d_v}\right)^{0.4} \left(\frac{S_T}{Z_t}\right)^{0.6} \tag{12.157}$$

where Z_t is the distance between tube centers in adjacent rows:

$$\begin{aligned} Z_t &= S_L & \text{(in-line)} \\ Z_t &= (S_L^2 + S_T^2)^{1/2} & \text{(staggered)} \end{aligned} \tag{12.158}$$

Figure 12.31 includes Z_t for these cases. For laminar flow:

$$f_{tb} = \frac{180}{N_{Re,v}} \tag{12.159}$$

For turbulent flow ($N_{Re,v} > 100$):

$$f_{tb} = 1.92(N_{Re,v})^{-0.145} \tag{12.160}$$

From Fig. 12.31, it is obvious that the first line of tubes that the fluid encounters is essentially isolated from the effects of adjacent tubes. This is in fact the case, and Eqs. (12.145) through (12.151) apply. The tubes behind the first row are subject to higher levels of turbulence, and the heat transfer coefficients are much higher.

The best correlation for Nusselt number in tube bundles is that of Zukauskas [Z2] who proposed the following:

$$N_{Nu,tb} = hd_t/k = E(N_{Pr})^{0.36}(N_{Pr}/N_{Pr,w})^n(N_{Re,tb})^e \tag{12.161}$$

where E, e, and n are constants and where the tube bundle Reynolds number is

$$N_{Re,tb} = d_t G_{max}/\mu = d_t U_{max}\rho/\mu \tag{12.162}$$

with G_{max} already defined in Eq. (12.155). Obviously, G_{max} equals the product of U_{max} and ρ, both of which depend on temperature. Therefore, it is best to find G_{max} directly; the velocity U_{max} is the velocity of the fluid as it passes through the minimum area along the flow path. In Eq. (12.161), $N_{Pr,w}$ is evaluated at the constant wall temperature T_w. All other properties are evaluated at the mean bulk temperature T_b:

$$T_b = (T_{in} + T_{out})/2 \tag{12.163}$$

The heat transfer coefficient in Eq. (12.161) is defined in a manner similar to that in Eq. (12.150) for single cylinders:

$$q = hA_{tubes}(T_w - T_\infty) \tag{12.164}$$

where A_{tubes} is the surface area of all the tubes.

The constants for Eq. (12.161) are given in Table 12.5. Note that n is zero for gases and 0.25 for liquids. Also, researchers have found that heat exchangers with the in-line configuration operate poorly if $S_T/S_L \geq 0.7$. Hence, no correlations in the range $0.7 \leq S_T/S_L \leq 2.0$ are recommended because no exchangers are manufactured with this design. The analysis of Grimison [G6, H3, I1, M3] includes correlations for various geometries; the optimum must be ascertained for each design.

Since the upstream rows of tubes have lower heat transfer coefficients than the "inner" ones, Eq. (12.161) was prepared using the inner rows of tubes only. Figure 12.32 corrects in an approximate way for this effect, if it is desired to compute an average h for bundles where N is smaller than 10. Details may

TABLE 12.5
Heat transfer correlation for tube bank in cross flow*

			Constants for Eq. (12.161)†					
			In-line			**Staggered**		
Range of Reynolds number applicability			**Range of**				**Range of**	
Lower	**Upper**	S_T/S_L	**E**	e	S_T/S_L	**E**		e
10	100	all	0.8	0.4	all	0.9		0.4
100	1000	all	‡	‡	all	‡		‡
1000	2×10^5	<0.7	0.27	0.63	≤ 2	$(0.35)\left(\dfrac{S_T}{S_L}\right)^{0.2}$		0.6
		>2.0	0.40	0.60				
2×10^5		all	0.021	0.84	all	§		0.84

* Compiled from Zukauskas [Z2] and Lienhard [L5], p. 333. The reference temperature for all properties is T_b, Eq. (12.163).
† The Prandtl number exponent n equals zero for gases and 0.25 for liquids.
‡ Equations (12.145) to (12.151) for isolated tubes apply in this range. Do not use Eq. (12.161).
§ For $N_{Pr} = 0.7$, the constant E equals 0.019; for $N_{Pr} \geq 1.0$, E equals 0.022.

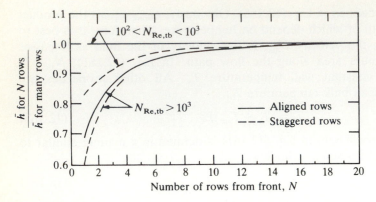

FIGURE 12.32
Correction to Eq. (12.161) for heat transfer in the front rows of a tube bundle. (*From Zukauskas, in Advances in Heat Transfer, vol. 8, p. 156, Hartnett and Irvine (eds.), Academic Press, New York, 1972. By permission.*)

be found in Example 12.17. Table 12.6 summarizes the data for the high-Reynolds-number region [K1]. Corrections are also available for cases in which the flow crosses the tube bundle at an angle [L5, Z2]. In Chapter 11, the flow patterns in the shell side of a heat exchanger were briefly discussed. A big problem in these designs is leakage of fluid through the baffles where the tubes pass from one section into another. This leakage greatly reduces the heat transfer coefficients, sometimes by as much as 60 percent.

Example 12.17. A heat exchanger consists of a bank of tubes, 12 rows high and 8 rows deep, arranged in-line. The surfaces of all tubes are maintained at 55°C (328.15 K). The tube diameter is 0.75 inches, and the length is 1 meter. The ratio S_T/d_t is 1.5, and S_L/D_t is 3.0. Air at 14.696 psia and 20°C (293.15 K) enters at a velocity of $7 \, \text{m s}^{-1}$. Calculate the exit temperature of the air if its properties can be estimated from the following correlations:

$$\rho \, [\text{kg m}^{-3}] = -0.208 \times 10^{-3} + 353.044/T$$

$$\mu \, [\text{kg m}^{-1} \, \text{s}^{-1}] = -9.810 \times 10^{-6} + 1.6347 \times 10^{-6}(T)^{1/2}$$

$$c_p \, [\text{J kg}^{-1} \, \text{K}^{-1}] = 989.85 + 0.05T$$

$$k \, [\text{J s}^{-1} \, \text{m}^{-1} \, \text{K}^{-1}] = 0.003\,975 + 7.378 \times 10^{-5}T$$

(i)

TABLE 12.6
Ratio of h for N tubes divided by h for 10 tubes ($N_{\text{Re,tb}} > 10^3$)*

N	1	2	3	4	5	6	7	8	9	10
In-line	0.68	0.80	0.87	0.90	0.92	0.94	0.96	0.98	0.99	1.0
Staggered	0.64	0.75	0.83	0.89	0.92	0.95	0.97	0.98	0.99	1.0

* From Kays and Lo, Stanford Univ. Tech. Rept. 15, Navy Contact N6-ONR-251 T.O.6, 1952. By permission.

where T is in K ($273 \le T \le 333$) and c_p, μ, k, and ρ are in SI units. Also, find the pressure drop through the bundle.

Answer. The calculations begin with the tube bundle. Referring to Fig. 12.31, the minimum flow area is the width ($L_w = 1$ m) times the area between tubes. The ratio of total area to minimum flow area is therefore

$$\frac{\text{TOTAL AREA}}{\text{MIN AREA}} = \frac{NS_T L_w}{(N)(S_T - d_t)(L_w)} = \frac{S_T}{S_T - d_t} \tag{ii}$$

The values of S_L and S_T are

$$S_T = 1.5 d_t = (1.5)(0.75) = 1.125 \text{ in}$$
$$S_L = 3 d_t = (3.0)(0.75) = 2.25 \text{ in} \tag{iii}$$
$$S_T/S_L = 1.125/2.25 = 0.5$$

In accordance with the recommendations for Eq. (12.161), the above numbers indicate a good geometric design. The total and minimum areas are also needed:

$$S_{\text{total area}} = NS_T L_w$$
$$= (12)(1.125/12)(0.3048)(1)\,[(\text{ft})(\text{m ft}^{-1})(\text{m})] = 0.3429 \text{ m}^2$$
$$S_{\text{min area}} = N(S_T - d_t)(L_w) \tag{iv}$$
$$= (12)[(1.125 - 0.75)/(12)](0.3048)(1) = 0.1143 \text{ m}^2$$

Here it is assumed that the free area is equal to 12 spaces between tubes, i.e., 11 spaces between the 12 tubes plus half a space $(S_T - d_t)L_w$ on the top and half a space on the bottom. The properties of air at 293.15 K from Eq. (i) are

$$\rho = 1.204 \text{ kg m}^{-3}$$
$$\mu = 1.818 \times 10^{-5} \text{ kg m}^{-1}\text{s}^{-1}$$
$$c_p = 1005 \text{ J kg}^{-1}\text{K}^{-1} \tag{v}$$
$$k = 0.02560 \text{ J s}^{-1}\text{m}^{-1}\text{K}^{-1}$$
$$N_{Pr} = c_p\mu/k = 0.7132$$

A mass balance [Eq. (7.13)] allows the calculation of the total mass flow and the maximum velocity $U_{\max}$:

$$w = \rho_1 U_{1,\text{ave}}S_1 = \rho_2 U_{2,\text{ave}}S_2 \tag{7.13}$$

Note the possible confusion regarding the nomenclature: in Eq. (7.13), S_1 and S_2 are the flow areas at locations 1 and 2, whereas S_T and S_L are dimensions. Hence, S_1 and S_2 will be abandoned in favor of $S_{\text{total area}}$ and $S_{\text{min area}}$. At constant density, Eq. (7.13) becomes

$$U_{\max} S_{\text{min area}} = U_\infty S_{\text{total area}} \tag{vi}$$

Combining Eqs. (ii) and (vi) results in

$$U_{\max} = U_\infty \frac{S_T}{S_T - d_t} = (7)\left(\frac{1.125}{1.125 - 0.75}\right) = 21.00 \text{ m s}^{-1} \tag{vii}$$

The total mass flow rate entering can be found using Eq. (7.13) above:

$$w = \rho U_{\max} S_{\text{min area}} = (1.204)(21.00)(0.1143) = 2.890 \text{ kg s}^{-1} \tag{viii}$$

The heat transferred from the bundle to the air is calculated from Eq. (12.164):

$$q = hA_{\text{tubes}}(T_w - T_\infty) \qquad (12.164)$$

The area for heat transfer is computed with the assistance of Table B.2, which gives the circumference for 0.75 in. tubing as $0.1963 \text{ ft}^2 \text{ ft}^{-1}$ or $0.05983 \text{ m}^2 \text{ m}^{-1}$. The total area for heat transfer is the circumference of each tube times its length L_w times the number of tubes, (12)(8):

$$A_{\text{tubes}} = (0.05983)(1.0)(96) = 5.744 \text{ m}^2 \qquad (\text{ix})$$

In Eq. (12.164), the heat q is the sensible heat that passes to the air, which raises the enthalpy of the air according to the following:

$$q = hA_{\text{tubes}}(T_w - T_\infty) = wc_p \Delta T \qquad (\text{x})$$

where ΔT is the temperature rise of the air:

$$\Delta T = T_{\text{out}} - T_{\text{in}} \qquad (\text{xi})$$

In Eq. (x), the heat transfer coefficient h is estimated from Eq. (12.161):

$$N_{\text{Nu,tb}} = hd_t/k = E(N_{\text{Pr}})^{0.36}(N_{\text{Pr}}/N_{\text{Pr,w}})^n(N_{\text{Re,tb}})^e \qquad (12.161)$$

where E, e, and n are constants in Table 12.5 and where

$$N_{\text{Re,tb}} = d_t G_{\text{max}}/\mu = d_t U_{\text{max}}\rho/\mu \qquad (12.162)$$

In Eqs. (12.161) and (12.162), all properties are evaluated at the mean bulk temperature T_b:

$$T_b = (T_{\text{in}} + T_{\text{out}})/2 \qquad (12.163)$$

Since the outlet temperature T_{out} is unknown, the calculation proceeds by trial and error. The usual starting assumption is to let T_b equal T_{in} (293.15 K). From Eq. (12.162), the Reynolds number is

$$d_t = (0.75)(0.0254) = 0.01905 \text{ m}$$

$$G_{\text{max}} = w/S_{\text{min area}} = U_{\text{max}}\rho = (2.890/0.1143) = 25.28 \text{ kg m}^{-2}\text{ s}^{-1} \qquad (\text{xii})$$

$$N_{\text{Re,tb}} = d_t G_{\text{max}}/\mu = (0.01905)(25.28)/(1.818 \times 10^{-5}) = 2.649 \times 10^4$$

Note that G_{max} is independent of the temperature of the air, whereas neither U_{max} nor ρ are. Therefore, G_{max} is used in Eq. (xii).

Next, Eq. (12.161) is applied to this problem. Table 12.5 states that $n = 0$ for gases; also, for $S_T/S_L < 0.7$, E and e are 0.27 and 0.63, respectively. Now Eq. (12.161) reduces to

$$N_{\text{Nu}} = hd_t/k = E(N_{\text{Pr}})^{0.36}(N_{\text{Re,tb}})^e = (0.27)(N_{\text{Pr}})^{0.36}(N_{\text{Re,tb}})^{0.63} \qquad (\text{xiii})$$

Equation (xiii) is solved for the heat transfer coefficient:

$$h = 0.27(k/d_t)(N_{\text{Pr}})^{0.36}(N_{\text{Re,tb}})^{0.63} \qquad (\text{xiv})$$

For the first guess ($T_{\text{out}} = T_{\text{in}} = 293.15$ K), the heat transfer coefficient is

$$h = (0.27)(0.02560/0.01905)(0.7132)^{0.36}(2.649 \times 10^4)^{0.63}$$

$$= 196.5 \text{ J m}^{-2}\text{ s}^{-1}\text{ K}^{-1} \qquad (\text{xv})$$

The value of h in the last equation is the mean heat transfer coefficient for all tubes in a large bundle. If the number of rows N is less than 10, a correction from Fig. 12.32 must be made. This figure is difficult to read, but the correct value from Table 12.6 is 0.98. Therefore

$$h_8 = (h_{10+})(0.98) = (196.5)(0.98) = 192.6 \text{ J m}^{-2}\text{s}^{-1}\text{K}^{-1} \tag{xvi}$$

Next, Eq. (x) is solved for ΔT:

$$\Delta T = \frac{hA_{\text{tubes}}}{wc_p}(T_w - T_\infty) = \frac{(192.6)(5.744)(328.15 - 293.15)}{(2.890)(1005)} = 13.33 \text{ K} \tag{xvii}$$

Thus, the exit temperature for the first trial is

$$T_{\text{out}} = T_{\text{in}} + \Delta T = 293.15 + 13.33 = 306.5 \text{ K} \tag{xviii}$$

The second trial begins by finding the local fluid bulk temperature. From Eq. (12.163):

$$T_b = (T_{\text{in}} + T_{\text{out}})/2 = (293.15 + 306.5)/2 = 299.8 \text{ K} \tag{xix}$$

The second iteration uses 299.8 K to find the fluid properties. The results are

$$
\begin{aligned}
&T_b = 299.8 \text{ K} && N_{\text{Pr}} = 0.7122 \\
&G_{\text{max}} = 24.72 \text{ kg m}^{-2}\text{s}^{-1} && N_{\text{Re}} = 2.547 \times 10^4 \\
&h_8 = 191.4 \text{ J m}^{-2}\text{s}^{-1}\text{K}^{-1} && \Delta T = 13.55 \text{ K} \\
&T_{\text{out}} = 306.7 \text{ K} && T_b = 299.9 \text{ K}
\end{aligned}
\tag{xx}
$$

The value of T_{out} from the second iteration has changed little from that obtained on the first. In fact, a third trial yields no change at all from the second.

Pressure drop. The correlations for pressure drop are based on isothermal flow. The usual procedure is to use T_b. At $T_b = 299.9$ K, the viscosity and density are

$$\mu = 1.850 \times 10^{-5} \text{ kg m}^{-1}\text{s}^{-1} \qquad \rho = 1.177 \text{ kg m}^{-3} \tag{xxi}$$

Next, the equivalent diameters d_v or d_e must be computed. Using Eq. (12.153) and assuming $d_v = d_e$:

$$d_v = d_e = 4(S_T S_L - \pi d_t^2/4)/(\pi d_t) = (4)[(1.125)(2.25) - \pi(0.75)^2/4]/[(\pi)(0.75)]$$
$$= 3.547 \text{ in.} = 0.09010 \text{ m} \tag{xxii}$$

From Eqs. (12.156) and (12.160) the Reynolds number and friction factor are

$$N_{\text{Re},v} = d_v G_{\text{max}}/\mu = (0.0901)(24.72)/(1.850 \times 10^{-5}) = 1.204 \times 10^5$$
$$f_{tb} = 1.92(N_{\text{Re},v})^{-0.145} = 0.3521 \tag{xxiii}$$

Notice that $N_{\text{Re},v}$ does not equal $N_{\text{Re,tb}}$. For in-line geometries, Eq. (12.158) applies

$$Z_t = S_L = 2.25 \text{ in.} \tag{xxiv}$$

Equation (12.157) is solved for $-\Delta p$, with the flow length L_{tb} from Eq. (12.152):

$$L_{tb} = NS_L = (8)(2.25) = 18 \text{ in.} = 0.4572 \text{ m} \tag{xxv}$$

$$f_{tb} = \frac{(-\Delta p)(2g_c\rho)}{G_{\text{max}}^2}\frac{d_v}{L_{tb}}\left(\frac{S_T}{d_v}\right)^{0.4}\left(\frac{S_T}{Z_t}\right)^{0.6} \tag{12.157}$$

$$-\Delta p = \frac{f_{tb} G_{max}^2}{2\rho \frac{d_v}{L_{tb}} \left(\frac{S_T}{d_v}\right)^{0.4} \left(\frac{S_T}{Z_t}\right)^{0.6}}$$

$$= \frac{(0.3521)(24.72)^2}{(2)(1.177)(3.547/18)(1.125/3.547)^{0.4}(1.125/2.25)^{0.6}}$$

$$\times [(kg^2\, m^{-4}\, s^{-2})(kg^{-1}\, m^3)(in.\, in.^{-1})(in.\, in.^{-1})^{0.4}(in.\, in.^{-1})^{0.6}]$$

$$= 1113\, kg\, m^{-1}\, s^{-2} = 1113\, N\, m^{-2} = 0.1614\, psia \qquad \text{(xxvi)}$$

The pressure drop across the tube bundle is extremely small. This example points out the advantages of baffling heat exchangers so as to increase velocity, increase h, and improve performance. For example, in this problem, two baffles would triple the velocity G_{max} or U_{max}. The cost in pressure-energy dissipated would increase but would still be small. The heat transfer coefficient in Eq. (12.161) predicts that h is proportional to $(G_{max})^{0.63}$. Thus, tripling G_{max} doubles h, which would double the performance of the exchanger, except for the possible inefficiencies discussed previously in this section and Chapter 11.

12.4 FLOW PHENOMENA WITH GAS–LIQUID AND LIQUID–LIQUID MIXTURES

Problems in transport phenomena with two-phase flow are considerably more difficult to analyze than their single-phase counterparts. First to be considered is a single flow, as in a pipe, of a gas–liquid (two-phase) or a gas–liquid–solid (three phase) mixture. The presence of two or three phases alters drastically the rate of transfer of heat, mass, and momentum. In spite of much work on the subject [B2, H1], there are no totally reliable and simple correlations for design methods.

Many of the important unit operations are carried out with gas–liquid mixtures—absorption, evaporation, and distillation, for instance. Design of equipment for these usually bypasses the transport phenomena approach. The flow patterns are too complex and poorly characterized. Besides, there are so many successful applications that design by comparison is a safe and easy alternative. Absorption is usually carried out in a three-phase system—a fixed bed of ceramic packing with large surface area, through which the gas rises and the liquid falls. Also, three-phase fluidized beds are important. A complete review by Muroyama and Fan [M4] is available.

Another important area is "free flow" [B2], i.e., motions of drops, jets, bubbles, etc., in which the boundary between solid and fluid plays only a minor role (if any) in the phenomena. Formation of liquid drops or gas bubbles constitutes an important consideration in the design of spray dryers, distillation columns, boilers, and condensers. Perhaps heat transfer in boilers and condensers is the most completely characterized topic in this area. The phenomenon is well-understood from both mechanistic and computational viewpoints. Excellent summaries are available [G1, H1, M2, M3, P1].

Transport in systems of two immiscible liquids is also important.

Liquid–liquid extraction involves at least a three-component system in which solute A is preferentially transferred from one liquid phase (the feed) to the second (the extract) [S4, T1]. The two phases must be brought into close contact, which can be accomplished in a packed column, a mixer, or a sieve plate. There may be flow of two immiscible fluids in a pipe as well.

Clearly, a detailed discussion of such transport phenomena is not warranted here, because current practices preclude the use of the basic equations presented in this text. The use of transport phenomena constitutes an active research area for many of the applications just cited.

PROBLEMS

12.1. Define entry length. Why is it desirable to know the entry length?

12.2. Define and discuss separation.

12.3. Make an equation by equation comparison between the laminar and turbulent boundary layers.

12.4. Compare the form of the drag coefficient over a sphere to the Fanning friction factor.

12.5. A baseball announcer says: "Because of the high humidity today, the baseball will not travel as far as it normally does on a dry day". Comment critically on the announcer's logic.

12.6. Air at 283 K and 1 atm is flowing at 10 m s^{-1} past a plate 2 m wide.
  (a) Find the thickness of the boundary layer 30 cm from the leading edge.
  (b) Calculate the drag force on the plate from the leading edge to $x = 30$ cm.
  (c) Find the direction and magnitude of the velocity vector at $x = 30$ cm and $y = \delta/8$.

12.7. Air at 300 K and 1 atm moves over a flat plate at a speed of 15 m s^{-1}. Find the boundary layer thickness and the shear stress 1 m from the front edge of the plate if turbulent flow is assumed in the boundary layer.

12.8. A smooth, flat plate 3 m wide and 30 m long is towed through still water at 20°C with a speed of 6 m s^{-1}.
  (a) Determine the drag force (in newtons) on one side of the plate.
  (b) Determine the location of the laminar–turbulent transition (in meters).
  (c) Determine the total drag force (in newtons) over the laminar portion of the boundary layer.

12.9. A laminar boundary layer of air is in some manner maintained over a 2-m long, 1-m wide, flat plate. The air is at 273 K and 1 atm; its velocity with respect to the plate is 3 m s^{-1}. Find the drag force in newtons.

12.10. A flat plate is located in a wind tunnel; the fluid is air at 283 K and 1 atm, with free stream velocity 2 m s^{-1}. An instrumented test area is located 1 m from the leading edge; this test area is 50 cm by 50 cm. Estimate the velocity components of the air at a distance 1.25 m from the leading edge and at $y = \delta/2$.

12.11. Find the equations for the streamlines of the flow described by the following potential functions:
  (a) $\phi = A(\ln r)$
  (b) $\phi = A\theta$

12.12. Find the equations for the streamlines of the flow described by the following potential functions:

$$\phi = 3x + \ln r$$

12.13. Find the equations for the streamlines of the flow described by the following potential function:

$$\phi = U_\infty\left(r + \frac{1}{r}\right)\cos\theta + A\theta$$

12.14. On a sheet of graph paper, plot lines of constant ψ and ϕ for the following potential:

$$\phi = 12(x^2 - y^2)$$

Include the following values only:

ϕ: 10, 20, 30
ψ: 10, 20, 30

12.15. A glass sphere (specific gravity 2.62) falls through carbon tetrachloride (specific gravity 1.595, viscosity 0.958 cP) at 20°C. The terminal velocity is $0.65\,\text{m s}^{-1}$. The gravitational acceleration is $9.78\,\text{m s}^{-2}$. Find the diameter of the sphere in meters.

12.16. Calculate the terminal velocity in m s^{-1} for a 0.001-in. diameter particle of density $160\,\text{kg m}^{-3}$, falling through a pressurized gas of density of $32\,\text{kg m}^{-3}$ and viscosity of 0.1 cP. The gravitational acceleration is $9.81\,\text{m s}^{-2}$. Work entirely in SI units.

12.17. Find the distance in km that a 5-μm smoke particle travels in 1 h if the wind blows at $8\,\text{km h}^{-1}$. The particle density is $1\,\text{g cm}^{-3}$. The gravitational acceleration is $9.80\,\text{m s}^{-2}$. The release height is a stack 100 ft high. Neglect turbulence. The air temperature is 300 K, at atmospheric pressure. Work entirely in SI units.

12.18. A particle 5 μm in diameter (specific gravity 2.5) is ejected horizontally with velocity $8\,\text{m s}^{-1}$ into still air at 300 K and 1 atm. Assuming that Stokes' law is valid, calculate the distance (in meters) traveled by the particle in the x direction between time zero and time infinity; assume that y space is infinite so that the particle never touches the ground.

12.19. Calculate the rise velocity in m s^{-1} of 0.01-cm air bubble (density $1.2\,\text{kg m}^{-3}$) rising in an oil of viscosity of 0.04 poise and density $900\,\text{kg m}^{-3}$. The gravitational acceleration is $9.80\,\text{m s}^{-2}$. Assume that the bubble remains spherical.

12.20. Estimate the normal force (in newtons) on a circular sign 8 ft in diameter during a hurricane whose winds are blowing at 120 mph. Assume that the temperature is 293 K and the pressure is 1 atm (although usually the barometer is much lower in hurricanes).

12.21. A jet aircraft discharges solid particles of matter (10 μm in diameter and of specific gravity 2.5) at the base of the stratosphere at 11 000 m. The gravitational acceleration is $9.79\,\text{m s}^{-2}$. Let the viscosity of air be expressed by

$$\mu = 1.74 \times 10^{-5} - 3.06 \times 10^{-10}y$$

where y is the elevation relative to sea level (in meters) and μ is in $\text{kg m}^{-1}\text{s}^{-1}$.

Estimate the time (in seconds and in hours) for these particles to reach sea level. Neglect air currents and wind effects.

12.22. A member of the university aviation club drops three objects from an airplane 5000 m from the earth. Each object has a mass of 12 kg, and is manufactured from a special light-weight composite of aluminum (specific gravity 2.017). For simplicity, assume that the air temperature is 20°C, and that the properties at 1 atm apply. Let $g = 9.81$ m s^{-2}. Estimate the time of descent for the following geometries:
  (a) sphere
  (b) disk, $L/d_p = 1.0$, falling with axis always perpendicular to the ground
  (c) cylinder, $L/d_t = 100$, falling with axis always parallel to the ground.

12.23. A particle 5 microns in diameter (specific gravity 3.0) is falling in still air at 300 K and 1 atm. Let the acceleration due to gravity be 9.82 m s^{-2}. Estimate the heat transfer coefficient in SI units.

12.24. A fluidization catalyst, specific gravity 1.75, is fluidized with air at 650 K and 1.8 atm. The catalyst may be assumed spherical, with diameter 175 μm. The gravitational acceleration is 9.8 m s^{-2}. The static void fraction is 0.55. The unfluidized bed height is 3 m. Find in SI units:
  (a) The minimum void fraction and the bed height for fluidization
  (b) The settling velocity for a single particle in a static fluid
  (c) The minimum pressure drop for fluidization
  (d) The minimum velocity for entrainment
  (e) The heat transfer coefficient at the wall for a superficial velocity 3.0 times U_{mf}.

12.25. A coarse catalyst of size 300 μm and density 4200 kg m^{-3} is to be fluidized in an oil (8 cP and specific gravity 0.8). The height and void volume of the static bed are 2 m and 0.48, respectively. The gravitational acceleration is 9.81 m s^{-2}. Find the pressure drop (N m^{-2}) and the superficial velocity (m s^{-1}) at that point of incipient fluidization.

12.26. A packed bed is composed of cylinders of diameter 0.03 m; the cylinder length is 1.5 times the diameter; each cylinder has a density of 1800 kg m^{-3}. The bulk density of the overall packed bed is 950 kg m^{-3}. Calculate the void fraction.

12.27. Show that $\varepsilon U_{z,\,ave} = U_o$ for a fluidized bed, where $U_{z,\,ave}$ is the actual average fluid velocity.

12.28. An electrically heated rod 0.01 m in diameter is immersed in a rapidly flowing air stream whose bulk temperature is 450 K. The surface temperature of the rod is maintained constant at 550 K. The rod is 350 diameters in length. Estimate the air velocity required to remove 2400 W.

12.29. Solve Example 12.17 if the 0.75-in. tubes are replaced with 1.00-in. tubes.

REFERENCES

A1. Ames, W. F.: *Ind. Eng. Chem. Fundam.* **8:** 522 (1969).
B1. Blasius, H.: *Z. Math. Physik.* **56:** 1 (1908); *NACA TM* 1256 translation.
B2. Brodkey, R. S.: *The Phenomena of Fluid Motions,* Addison Wesley, Reading, MA, 1967. [Fourth printing available from The Ohio State University Bookstores, Columbus, Ohio 43210.]

B3. Brown, G. G., and associates: *Unit Operations,* Wiley, New York, 1950.

B4. Brownell, L. E., H. S. Dombrowski, and C. A. Dickey: *Chem. Eng. Progr.* **46:** 415 (1950).

B5. Burke, S. P., and W. B. Plummer: *Ind. Eng. Chem.* **20:** 1196 (1928).

C1. Carslaw, H. S., and J. E. Jaeger: *Conduction of Heat in Solids,* 2d ed., Oxford University Press, New York, 1959.

C2. Couderc, J.-P.: in *Fluidization,* 2d ed., J. F. Davidson, R. Clift, and D. Harrison (eds.), Academic Press, New York, 1985.

C3. Chung, S. F., and C. Y. Wen: *AIChE J.* **14:** 857 (1968).

C4. Churchill, S. W., and M. Bernstein: *J. Heat Transfer, Trans. ASME, Ser. C,* **99:** 300 (1977).

C5. Churchill, S. W., and H. Ozoe: *AIChE J.* **19:** 177 (1973).

C6. Churchill, S. W.: *AIChE J.* **22:** 264 (1976).

D1. Davidson, J. F., R. Clift, and D. Harrison: *Fluidization,* 2d ed., Academic Press, New York, 1985.

D2. Dwivedi, P. N., and S. N. Upadhyay: *Ind. Eng. Chem. Process Des. Dev.* **16:** 157 (1977).

E1. Eckert, E. R. G., and R. M. Drake: *Analysis of Heat and Mass Transfer,* McGraw-Hill, New York, 1972.

E2. Ergun, S.: *Chem. Eng. Progr.* **48:** 89 (1952).

F1. Fouda, A. E., and C. E. Capes: *Can. J. Chem. Eng.* **55:** 386 (1977).

G1. Geankoplis, C. J.: *Transport Processes and Unit Operations,* 2d ed., Allyn and Bacon, Boston, 1983.

G2. Geldart, D.: *Proc. Int. Symp. Fluid.,* p. 171, 1967.

G3. Geldart, D.: *Powder Technol.* **7:** 285 (1973).

G4. Giedt, W. H.: *Trans. ASME* **71:** 375 (1949).

G5. Grace, J. R.: in *Handbook of Multiphase Systems,* G. Hetsroni (ed.), Hemisphere Publishing, Washington, DC, 1982.

G6. Grimison, E. D.: *Trans. ASME* **59:** 583 (1937).

G7. Gunter, A. Y., and W. A. Shaw: *Trans. ASME* **67:** 643 (1945).

H1. Hetsroni, G. (ed.): *Handbook of Multiphase Systems,* Hemisphere Publishing, Washington, DC, 1982.

H2. Hill, C. G., Jr.: *An Introduction to Chemical Engineering Kinetics & Reactor Design,* Wiley, New York, 1977.

H3. Holman, J. P.: *Heat Transfer,* 6th ed., McGraw-Hill, New York, 1986.

H4. Howarth, L.: *Proc. Roy. Soc. (London)* **A164,** 547 (1938).

I1. Incropera, F. P., and D. P. DeWitt: *Fundamentals of Heat and Mass Transfer,* 2d ed., Wiley, New York, 1985.

K1. Kays, W. M., and R. K. Lo: *Stanford University Technical Report 15,* Navy Contract N6-ONR-251 T.O.6, 1952.

K2. King, L. V.: *Phil. Trans. Roy. Soc. (London)* **A214:** 373 (1914).

K3. Knudsen, J. G., and D. L. Katz: *Fluid Dynamics and Heat Transfer,* McGraw-Hill, New York, 1958.

K4. Kunii, D., and O. Levenspiel: *Fluidization Engineering,* Wiley, New York, 1969.

L1. Lamb, H.: *Hydrodynamics* (reprint of the 1932 ed.), Dover Publications, New York, 1945.

L2. Langhaar, H. L.: *Trans. ASME* **A64:** 55 (1942).

L3. Lapple, C. E., and C. B. Shepherd: *Ind. Eng. Chem.* **32:** 605 (1940).

L4. Leva, M.: *Fluidization,* McGraw-Hill, New York, 1959.

L5. Lienhard, J. H.: *A Heat Transfer Textbook,* Prentice-Hall, Englewood Cliffs, NJ, 1981.

M1. Mathur, K. B., and N. Epstein: *Spouted Beds,* Academic Press, New York, 1974.

M2. McAdams, W. H.: *Heat Transmission,* 3d ed., McGraw-Hill, New York, 1954.

M3. McCabe, W. L., J. C. Smith, and P. Harriott: *Unit Operations of Chemical Engineering,* 4th ed., McGraw-Hill, New York, 1985.

M4. Muroyama, K., and L.-S. Fan: *AIChE J.* **31:** 1 (1985).

N1. Nakai, S., and T. Okazaki: *Int. J. Heat Mass Transfer* **18:** 387 (1975).

P1. Perry, R. H., and D. W. Green: *Perry's Chemical Engineers' Handbook,* 6th ed., McGraw-Hill, New York, 1984.

P2. Peters, M. H., and L.-S. Fan: *Design of Gas–Solid Catalytic Fluidized Bed Reactors,* Cache Corp. Module DES59i, 1983.

P3. Pettyjohn, E. S., and E. B. Christiansen: *Chem. Eng. Progr.* **44:** 157 (1948).

P4. Pohlhausen, E.: *Z. Angew. Math. Mech.* **1:** 115 (1921).

P5. Prandtl, L., and O. G. Tietjens: *Fundamentals of Hydro- and Aeromechanics* (reprint of the 1934 ed.), Dover Publications, New York, 1957.

R1. Ralston, A., and P. Rabinowitz: *A First Course in Numerical Analysis,* 2d ed., McGraw-Hill, New York, 1978.

R2. Ranz, W. E., and W. R. Marshall, Jr.: *Chem. Eng. Progr.* **48:** 141 (1952).

R3. Richardson, J. F.: in *Fluidization,* J. F. Davidson and D. Harrison (eds.), Academic Press, London, 1971.

R4. Richardson, J. F., and R. A. Meikle: *Trans. Inst. Chem. Eng.* **39:** 348 (1961).

R5. Richardson, J. F., and W. N. Zaki: *Trans. Inst. Chem. Eng.* **32:** 35 (1954).

S1. Schlichting, H.: *Boundary Layer Theory,* 7th ed., McGraw-Hill, New York, 1979.

S2. Sen Gupta, A., and G. Thodos: *Ind. Eng. Chem. Fundam.* **3:** 218 (1964).

S3. Shen, G. C., C. J. Geankoplis, and R. S. Brodkey: *Chem. Eng. Sci.* **40:** 1797 (1985).

S4. Sherwood, T. K., and R. L. Pigford: *Absorption and Extraction,* 2d ed., McGraw-Hill, New York, 1952.

S5. Steinour, H. H.: *Ind. Eng. Chem.* **36:** 618 (1944).

S6. Stokes, G. G.: *Trans. Cambridge Phil. Soc.* **9:** 8 (1851); *Math. and Phys. Pap.* **3:** 1.

S7. Streeter, V. L., and E. B. Wylie: *Fluid Mechanics,* 7th ed., McGraw-Hill, New York, 1979.

T1. Treybal, R. E.: *Mass-Transfer Operations,* 3d ed., McGraw-Hill, New York, 1980.

W1. Wen, C. Y., and A. G. Fane: in *Handbook of Multiphase Systems,* G. Hetsroni (ed.), Hemisphere Publishing, Washington, DC, 1982.

W2. Whitaker, S.: *AIChE J.* **18:** 361 (1972).

W3. Wilhelm, R. H., and M. Kwauk: *Chem. Eng. Progr.* **44:** 201 (1948).

Y1. Yerushalmi, J., and N. T. Cankurt: *Powder Technol.* **24:** 187 (1979).

Y2. Yerushalmi, J., and A. Avidan: in *Fluidization,* 2d ed., J. F. Davidson, R. Clift, and D. Harrison (eds.), Academic Press, New York, 1985.

Z1. Zabrodsky, S. S., Y. G. Epanov, and D. M. Galershtein: in *Fluidization,* J. F. Davidson and D. L. Keairns (eds.), Cambridge University Press, Cambridge, England, 1978, pp. 362–370.

Z2. Zukauskas, A.: in *Advances in Heat Transfer,* vol. 8, J. P. Hartnett and T. F. Irvine, Jr. (eds.), Academic Press, New York, 1972, pp. 93–160.

CHAPTER
13

UNSTEADY-STATE TRANSPORT

NOMENCLATURE

A	Area (m^2, ft^2)
A	Species A: A_1 and A_2 are species A at locations 1 and 2
A	Constant in Eq. (13.128)
a	Constant in Example 13.3
a_j	Constants in the general Fourier series, Eq. (13.38)
b	Radius of a cylinder (m, ft)
b_j	Constants in the general Fourier series, Eq. (13.38)
C	Concentration (kmol m^{-3}, lb mol ft^{-3}); C_A is concentration of species A; subscripts 1 and 2 refer to locations; $C_{A,0}$ is initial concentration (assumed constant); $C_{A,f}$ is concentration at slab boundary (constant); $C_{A,\infty}$ is concentration of species A in the free stream or surrounding fluid; $C_{A,c}$ is concentration at the center of a slab or cylinder
C	C_1, C_2, C_3 are integration constants, evaluated from given boundary conditions
c	Subscript denoting center; for a slab, c denotes the center plane, located a distance L from either face in the x direction; c denotes the line at a radius of zero in a long cylinder; also, c is a subscript denoting characteristic, e.g., L_c

640

c_p	Heat capacity at constant pressure (kJ kg^{-1} K^{-1}, Btu lb$_m^{-1}$ °F^{-1})
c_v	Heat capacity at constant volume (kJ kg^{-1} K^{-1}, Btu lb$_m^{-1}$ °F^{-1})
D	Diffusion coefficient (mass diffusivity) (m^2 s^{-1}, ft^2 s^{-1})
$D\psi/Dt$	Substantial derivative of ψ, defined by Eq. (5.52)
d	Diameter (m, ft); d_p is diameter of a particle or sphere
erf	Gauss error function, Eq. (13.14) and Table 13.1; erfc is the complementary error function, $1 - \mathrm{erf}$, Eq. (13.15)
f	$f(x)$ is a general function of x; $f(t)$ is a general function of t
g	The function $g(s)$ is the Laplace transform of the function $f(t)$; cf. Eq. (13.67)
h	Heat transfer coefficient, defined in a general manner by Eq. (6.86) (W m^{-2} K^{-1}, Btu ft^{-2} h^{-1} °F^{-1}); h_p is heat transfer coefficient to the surface of a particle or sphere
h	h is spacing in the x direction, cf., Eq. (13.89), as used in Fig. 13.24
i	Index in finite difference equations (distance)
j	Index in finite difference equations (time)
j	Index in summations; e.g., cf. general Fourier equation, Eq. (13.38)
k	Thermal conductivity (W m^{-1} K^{-1} or J m^{-1} K^{-1} s^{-1}, Btu ft^{-1} °R^{-1} s^{-1})
k_c'	Equimolar mass transfer coefficient, defined by Eq. (6.87) [kmol m^{-2} s^{-1} (kmol m^{-3})$^{-1}$, lb mol ft^{-2} s^{-1} (lb mol ft^{-3})$^{-1}$]
L	Length in the x direction; $2L$ is the length of slab, cf. Figs. 13.1 and 13.5; L_c is characteristic length (m, ft); other subscripts denote directions
$L(f)$	Laplace transform of the function f; $L^{-1}(g)$ is the inverse transform
m	Relative resistance in unsteady-state transport, used in the Heisler charts and defined in Table 13.3; for heat transfer, m is $k/(hL)$ (the reciprocal of the Biot number); for mass transfer, m is $D/(k_c L)$
N_{Bi}	Biot number, hL_c/k, Eq. (13.16); cf. Table 8.1
N_{Nu}	Nusselt number, defined in general by Eq. (8.21), hL/k; $N_{Nu,p}$ is Nusselt number for a particle or sphere, $h_p d_p/k$ [cf. Eqs. (12.85) and (12.130)]
N	Number of unknowns in a system of equations in Example 13.8
n	Number of moles (or the mass) of the system (kmol, lb mol)
n	Dimensionless distance (x/L), used in the Heisler charts
O	Denotes order, cf. Eqs. (13.91) and (13.92)
p	Pressure; $\bar{p}$ is partial pressure, defined in Eq. (2.38); $\bar{p}_A$ is partial pressure of A; subscripts 1 and 2 denote locations
p	Subscript denoting particular (i.e., steady-state) solution
Q	Heat added to the system in the first law (J, Btu); cf., Eq. (13.85); Q_0 is initial heat, Eq. (13.86)
q	Energy (heat) flow vector (J s^{-1}, Btu s^{-1}); subscripted for location
R	Gas constant; see Appendix, Table C.1 for values

r	Radius of a cylinder (m, ft); r_o is the distance from the center to the edge
s	Parameter that becomes the transformed independent variable in a Laplace transform (s^{-1}); cf. Eq. (13.67)
s	Subscript denoting surface; cf. T_s
T	Temperature (K, °R, °C, °F); T_1 and T_2 are temperatures at locations 1 and 2; T_∞ is the temperature of the free stream or surrounding fluid; T_0 is the initial temperature (assumed constant); T_f is the temperature at the slab boundary (a constant); T_c is temperature at the center of a slab, cylinder, or sphere
$\underline{T}$	A variable that is a general function of time (t) only; $\underline{T}'$ is the first derivative of $\underline{T}$ with respect to t
t	Time (s); Δt is spacing in time, cf., Eq. (13.90)
t	Independent variable in function $f(t)$ in Laplace transforms, cf. Eq. (13.67)
t	Subscript denoting steady-state solution
U	Internal energy of the system (J, Btu); subscripts denote location
U	Velocity vector (m s^{-1}, ft s^{-1}); U is magnitude of U; U_x, U_y, U_z are components in directions x, y, z
u	Argument in error function, erf(u), cf. Eq. (13.14)
V	Volume (m^3, ft^3)
v	Variable of integration in Eq. (13.14)
v	Variable in transformation in Eq. (13.131)
W	Total work done by the system in the first law (J, Btu)
X	Relative time, used in the Heisler charts and defined in Table 13.3 (dimensionless); for mass transfer, X is Dt/L^2; for heat transfer, X is $\alpha t/L^2$, which is the Fourier number, defined as N_{Fo} in Chapter 8; other subscripts denote directions
$\underline{X}$	A variable that is a general function of distance (x) only; $\underline{X}''$ is the second derivative of $\underline{X}$ with respect to x
x	Rectangular (Cartesian) coordinate
Y	Unaccomplished change, used in the Heisler charts and defined in Table 13.3 for heat or mass transfer; dimensionless; Y_c is change at center, cf., Eq. (13.83); other subscripts denote directions
y	Rectangular (Cartesian) coordinate
y	Mole fraction
Z	Dimensionless group in unsteady transport to a semi-infinite slab, $x/[2(\alpha t)^{1/2}]$ or $x/[2(Dt)^{1/2}]$
z	Rectangular (Cartesian) coordinate
α	Thermal diffusivity (m^2 s^{-1}, ft^2 s^{-1})
β	Constant in Fourier series solutions, introduced during the separation of variables [cf. Eq. (13.47)]
β	Dimensionless parameter in finite difference equations, Eqs. (13.95) and (13.104)
γ	Constant in Laplace transform solutions (m^{-1}, ft^{-1}); for heat transfer, $\gamma = (\alpha s)^{1/2}$, cf. Eq. (13.75)

Δ	Difference, state 2 minus state 1; e.g., ΔT means $T_2 - T_1$
δ	Generalized diffusivity ($\mathrm{m^2\,s^{-1}}$, $\mathrm{ft^2\,s^{-1}}$)
Θ	Transformed variable for analytic solutions of the heat equation (K, °R); for heat, Θ is $T - T_f$ [cf., Eq. (13.31)] and Θ_o is $T_o - T_f$; for mass, Θ_M is $C_A - C_{A,f}$ [cf., Eq. (13.36)]; Θ_{ss} is steady-state solution in Example 13.2; Θ_t is transient solution in Example 13.2
λ	Constant in integral formula in Example 13.2, $(j\pi)/(2L)$
η	Transformation variable, cf. Eq. (13.112)
μ	Viscosity ($\mathrm{kg\,m^{-1}\,s^{-1}}$ or $\mathrm{N\,m^{-2}\,s}$, $\mathrm{lb_m\,ft^{-1}\,s^{-1}}$, cP)
ν	Kinematic viscosity (momentum diffusivity) ($\mathrm{m^2\,s^{-1}}$, $\mathrm{ft^2\,s^{-1}}$)
π	Ratio of circumference of a circle to its diameter (3.141 592 65...)
ρ	Density ($\mathrm{kg\,m^{-3}}$, $\mathrm{lb_m\,ft^{-3}}$); subscripts refer to species
$\sum$	Summation
τ_t	Thermal time constant in lumped capacitance heat transfer (s), cf. Eq. (13.23)
$\boldsymbol{\tau}$	Momentum flux (or shear stress) tensor ($\mathrm{N\,m^{-2}}$, $\mathrm{lb_f\,ft^{-2}}$); τ_{xy}, τ_{yx}, etc. are components of the momentum flux tensor, where subscripts refer to direction of momentum transfer and direction of velocity
$\boldsymbol{\Psi}$	Generalized flux vector (e.g., units for heat flux are $\mathrm{J\,m^{-2}\,s^{-1}}$ or $\mathrm{W\,m^{-2}}$, $\mathrm{Btu\,ft^{-2}\,s^{-1}}$; see Table 2.1); Ψ_x, Ψ_y, Ψ_z are components in directions x, y, z; $\Psi_{x,m}$ or $\boldsymbol{\Psi}_m$ is flux due to molecular transport; $\Psi_{x,c}$ or $\boldsymbol{\Psi}_c$ is flux due to convection
ψ	Generalized concentration of property (e.g., units for concentration of heat are $\mathrm{J\,m^{-3}}$, $\mathrm{Btu\,ft^{-3}}$; see Table 3.1 for complete listing)
$\dot{\psi}_G$	Rate of generation of heat or mass or momentum in a unit volume (e.g., for heat, units are $\mathrm{J\,m^{-3}\,s^{-1}}$, $\mathrm{Btu\,ft^{-3}\,s^{-1}}$)
$\boldsymbol{\nabla}$	Vector operator del, defined by Eqs. (2.16) or (3.45) ($\mathrm{m^{-1}}$, $\mathrm{ft^{-1}}$)
∇^2	Laplacian operator, defined in Eq. (3.64) ($\mathrm{m^{-2}}$, $\mathrm{ft^{-2}}$)

The previous chapters have discussed steady-state transport. In unsteady-state (or transient) transport, the concentration of property ψ is a function of time as a result of a sudden change in the environment. Unsteady-state analysis may be used to describe conditions in the body of interest between the time of the sudden environmental changes and the time at which steady-state is again reached. In Chapter 3, the general property balance or conservation law was given as

$$\text{INPUT} + \text{GENERATION} = \text{OUTPUT} + \text{ACCUMULATION} \quad (3.1)$$

For an incompressible medium (constant density) and constant transport coefficient δ, the general equation is Eq. (3.78):

$$\frac{\partial \psi}{\partial t} + (\boldsymbol{U} \cdot \boldsymbol{\nabla})\psi = \dot{\psi}_G + \delta \nabla^2 \psi \quad (3.78)$$

where ∇^2 is the Laplacian operator, Eq. (3.64). Table 3.1 contains the appropriate values of δ and the concentration of property ψ for the three transports. In Eq. (3.78), the first term ($\partial \psi / \partial t$) is the accumulation term; the accumulation term is not zero under transient conditions:

$$\text{ACCUMULATION} = \frac{\partial \psi}{\partial t} \neq 0 \qquad (13.1)$$

As indicated in Chapter 5, Eq. (3.78) can be expressed in terms of the substantial derivative:

$$\frac{D\psi}{Dt} = \frac{\partial \psi}{\partial t} + (U \cdot \nabla)\psi \qquad (5.52)$$

The substantial derivative has the property of being zero for a steady-state, incompressible flow with no net velocity vector relative to the position of the observer. However, it is important to recall that steady-state means that the term $\partial \psi / \partial t$ is zero, not the substantial derivative $D\psi/Dt$.

Unsteady-state or, as it is often called, transient transport occurs commonly. In the kitchen, all cooking involves transient heat transfer. In the chemical industry, transient conditions exist whenever a unit or a piece of equipment begins operation, or whenever a change in process conditions is effected. Generally speaking, few problems in unsteady-state transport are solvable. Some of those that are solvable require advanced mathematical procedures, such as the use of Fourier series, Bessel functions, or Laplace transforms [W2]. There are also graphical and numerical solutions [D1, J1, S1]. All these will be covered here.

This chapter excludes flow problems of all types. Solutions that are available in unsteady laminar flow are mostly of limited practicality. In reality, turbulence is an inherently unsteady phenomenon, as discussed at length in Chapter 6. It was pointed out previously that no exact solutions to even the most simple problems in turbulence are known. Furthermore, when averages are taken, information is lost; thus, empirical methods are predominant in turbulence. As a result of these limitations, only problems in unsteady heat and mass diffusion will be discussed in this chapter.

13.1 BASIC EQUATIONS

In this chapter, transient problems in heat and mass transfer with no generation and no convection are considered. For the assumptions of constant density, constant transport coefficient, no generation, and no convection, Eq. (3.78) becomes

$$\frac{\partial \psi}{\partial t} = \delta \, \nabla^2 \, \psi \qquad (13.2)$$

This equation assumes many useful forms. The simplest case considers transient transport in the x direction in a solid, as shown in Fig. 13.1 for heat transfer and Fig. 13.2 for mass transfer. Equation (13.2) is classified as a parabolic partial differential equation, the solution of which requires three boundary conditions.

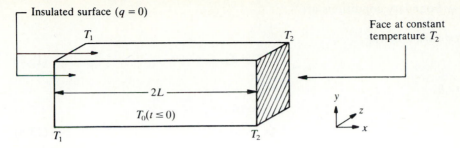

FIGURE 13.1
Transient heat transfer in the x direction.

13.1.1 Heat Transfer Equation

For heat transfer, Tables 2.1, 3.1, and 4.1 yield

$$\delta = \alpha = k/(\rho c_p) \tag{13.3}$$

$$\psi = \rho c_p T \tag{13.4}$$

Assuming constant physical properties, Eq. (13.2) becomes, after rearrangement:

$$\nabla^2 T = \frac{1}{\alpha}\frac{\partial T}{\partial t} \tag{13.5}$$

where the ∇^2 operator is presented in Table 5.1 for the various coordinate systems. If heat transfer is in the x direction only, as shown in Fig. 13.1, Eq. (13.5) reduces to

$$\frac{\partial^2 T}{\partial x^2} = \frac{1}{\alpha}\frac{\partial T}{\partial t} \tag{13.6}$$

In Fig. 13.1, T_0 is the initial temperature of the solid. In the most general case, T_0 may be a function of x. At time zero, the temperature T_1 is imposed instantaneously on the surface at the point $(x = 0)$, and the temperature T_2 is imposed instantaneously on the surface at the point $(x = x_2)$. Mathematically,

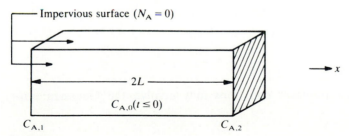

FIGURE 13.2
Transient mass diffusion in the x direction.

these boundary conditions are

At $t \leq 0$ and $0 \leq x \leq x_2$

$$T = T_0 \tag{13.7}$$

At $t > 0$

$$T (x = 0) = T_1$$
$$T (x = x_2) = T_2 \tag{13.8}$$

Exact solutions of Eq. (13.6) exist if the boundary conditions and the geometry are simple. Sometimes, simple boundary conditions are obtainable if the dependent variable (temperature) is transformed. These points will be illustrated in later sections.

13.1.2 Mass Transfer

Following the procedure just covered for heat transfer, the equations for mass transfer are

$$\delta = D \tag{13.9}$$

$$\psi = C_A \tag{13.10}$$

$$\nabla^2 C_A = \frac{1}{D} \frac{\partial C_A}{\partial t} \tag{13.11}$$

A typical problem in transient mass diffusion is shown in Fig. 13.2, in which a solid bar contains a concentration of species A equal to $C_{A,0}$. In the most general case, $C_{A,0}$ may be a function of x. At time zero, the concentrations at faces 1 and 2 are changed instantaneously to $C_{A,1}$ and $C_{A,2}$. These boundary conditions are

At $t \leq 0$ and $0 \leq x \leq x_2$

$$C_A = C_{A,0} \tag{13.12}$$

At $t > 0$

$$C_A (x = 0) = C_{A,1}$$
$$C_A (x = x_2) = C_{A,2} \tag{13.13}$$

13.1.3 Error Function

Exact solutions to the transient equations may involve the Gaussian error function:

$$\text{erf}(u) = \frac{2}{\pi^{1/2}} \int_0^u e^{-v^2} \, dv \tag{13.14}$$

TABLE 13.1
Short table of the error function

u	erf(u)	erfc(u)
0.0	0.00000	1.00000
0.1	0.11246	0.88754
0.2	0.22270	0.77730
0.3	0.32863	0.67137
0.4	0.42839	0.57161
0.5	0.52050	0.47950
0.6	0.60386	0.39614
0.7	0.67780	0.32220
0.8	0.74210	0.25790
0.9	0.79691	0.20309
1.0	0.84270	0.15730
1.1	0.88021	0.11979
1.2	0.91031	0.08969
1.3	0.93401	0.06599
1.4	0.95229	0.04771
1.5	0.96611	0.03389
2.0	0.99532	0.00468
∞	1.00000	0.00000

Also useful is the complementary error function:

$$\text{erfc}(u) = 1 - \text{erf}(u) \tag{13.15}$$

Table 13.1 shows a few typical values of the error function. Larger tables are included in most handbooks, although the reader must ascertain that exactly the same integral is tabulated. The error function is sometimes called the probability integral [P1]. Most large computer systems have the error function in their library of subroutines. Unfortunately, the error function is usually not available on small computers. Hence, Fig. 13.3 provides a useful pair of FORTRAN subroutines, plus the check program used to generate Table 13.1. The reader may easily convert the program provided into BASIC, PASCAL, or some other language, if desired.

13.1.4 Heat Transfer with Negligible Internal Resistance

When the internal resistance to heat transfer is small compared to the resistance due to convection at the surface, the solution to the transient heat problem is greatly simplified. The Biot number compares heat transfer due to convection with heat transfer due to conduction:

$$N_{\text{Bi}} = hL_c/k \tag{13.16}$$

where L_c is a characteristic length in the direction of conduction and h is the

```
C            FIGURE 13-3.  PROGRAM FOR TABLE OF ERF AND ERFC
             IMPLICIT REAL*8(A-H,O-Z)
             REAL*4 US
2            FORMAT(1H1,10X,'TABLE 13-1.')
3            FORMAT(F10.1,F11.5,F12.5)
4            FORMAT(1H0/1H0,7X,1HU,5X,6HERF(U),3X,7HERFC(U)/1H )
5            FORMAT(8X,2Hoo,F11.5,F12.5)
6            FORMAT(11H1END OF JOB)
             IO=6
             WRITE(IO,2)
             WRITE(IO,4)
             ONE=1.0D0
             ZERO=0.0D0
             WRITE(IO,3)ZERO,ZERO,ONE
             DU=0.1D0
             DO 20 I=1,15
             U=DU*DFLOAT(I)
             US=U
             U1=ERF(US)
             UC=ERFC(US)
20           WRITE(IO,3)U,U1,UC
             US=2.0
             U1=ERF(US)
             UC=ERFC(US)
             WRITE(IO,3)US,U1,UC
             WRITE(IO,5)ONE,ZERO
             WRITE(IO,6)
             STOP
             END
             FUNCTION ERF(X)
             DATA PI/3.141592654/
             DATA TOL/0.5E-07/
             DATA IN,IC/5,6/
2            FORMAT(A)
3            FORMAT('0*** ERROR IN FUNCTION ERF.'/
   1         1H0,5X,'ARGUMENT IS OUT OF BOUNDS: X =',E16.7/
   2         '0PRESS RETURN TO CONTINUE'/1H )
             IF(X)20,25,30
20           WRITE(IC,3)X
             READ(IN,2)I
25           ERF=0.0
             RETURN

30           IF(X-4.) 35,35,31
31           ERF=1.0
             RETURN
   35 X2=X*X
             S3=X
             T4=X
             I=0
40           I=I+1
             H3=S3
             T4=T4*X2*2.0/FLOAT(1+I+I)
             S3=T4+H3
             IF(T4-TOL*S3) 50,50,40
50           ERF=2.0*S3*EXP(-X2)/SQRT(PI)
             RETURN
             END
             FUNCTION ERFC(X)
             DATA PI/3.141592654/
             DATA TOL/0.5E-07/
             DATA IN,IC/5,6/
2            FORMAT(A)
3            FORMAT('0*** ERROR IN FUNCTION ERFC.'/
   1         1H0,5X,'ARGUMENT IS OUT OF BOUNDS: X =',E16.7/
   2         '0PRESS RETURN TO CONTINUE'/1H )
             IF(X)20,25,30
```

FIGURE 13.3
FORTRAN program for the error function.

```
20          WRITE(IC,3)X
            READ(IN,2)I
23          ERFC=0.
            RETURN
25          ERFC=1.0
            RETURN
30          IF(X-4.) 32,32,23
32          IF(X-1.5) 35,35,40
35          ERFC=1.0-ERF(X)
            RETURN
40          X2=X*X
            K=12
            V=0.5/X2
            U=1.+V*FLOAT(K+1)
            J=13
            DO 50 I=1,K
            J=J-1
            S3=1.0+V*FLOAT(J)/U
50          U=S3
            ERFC=EXP(-X2)/(X*S3*SQRT(PI))
            RETURN
            END
```

FIGURE 13.3
(*Continued*)

heat transfer coefficient from the surroundings to the solid. The Biot number determines the relative magnitudes of the conduction in the solid and the convective heat transfer to the solid. Note the similarity of the Biot number to the Nusselt number used in Eq. (12.85): $N_{Nu,p} = h_p d_p/k$. Here, the particle Nusselt number contains the thermal conductivity of the fluid, whereas the Biot number contains the thermal conductivity of the solid.

When the Biot number is less than 0.1, the conduction in a solid occurs at a much more rapid rate than the rate of transfer by convection. Figure 13.4 shows a simple problem that can be solved when N_{Bi} is less than 0.1. A solid, depicted as a sphere in Fig. 13.4 but of arbitrary shape, is initially at temperature T_0. Subsequently, the solid is submerged in a fluid of temperature T_∞. The mass of the fluid is assumed to be much larger than that of the solid so that T_∞ is constant. The solid may be assumed to be at a uniform temperature when the Biot number is small. Analysis of this problem is via the first law of thermodynamics:

$$\text{CHANGE IN TOTAL ENERGY OF SYSTEM} = Q - W \quad (7.33)$$

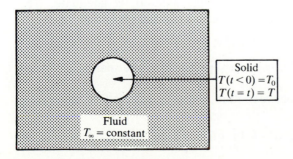

Solid
$T(t < 0) = T_0$
$T(t = t) = T$

Fluid
$T_\infty = \text{constant}$

FIGURE 13.4
Transient heat transfer to a solid at low Biot numbers.

The solution may proceed by assuming either constant volume or constant pressure, as the answer to either case is approximately the same. Let us assume that the volume of the system is approximately constant so that the work term W is zero. The system is taken as the solid. Then Q is the heat received by the solid due to convection, which on a differential basis is

$$dQ = hA(T_\infty - T) \, dt \tag{13.17}$$

where the temperature difference $(T_\infty - T)$ is positive when the fluid is warmer than the solid. The change in total energy of the system is $(\Delta U)_{\text{system}}$, which was previously given as Eq. (7.35):

$$(\Delta U)_{\text{constant volume}} = (U_2 - U_1)_V = n \int c_v \, dT \tag{7.35}$$

For a solid body, the heat capacities at constant volume and constant pressure are approximately equal. Since c_p is usually in mass units, the mass of the solid is density times volume; then Eq. (7.35) becomes

$$\Delta u = \rho V c_p \, dT \tag{13.18}$$

Combining Eqs. (7.33), (13.17), and (13.18) gives

$$hA(T_\infty - T) \, dt = \rho V c_p \, dT \tag{13.19}$$

The boundary conditions are

$$T \ (t = 0) = T_0 \qquad T \ (t = t) = T \tag{13.20}$$

The variables in Eq. (13.19) are separated:

$$\int_{T_0}^{T} \frac{dT}{T_\infty - T} = -\int_{T_0}^{T} \frac{dT}{T - T_\infty} = \frac{hA}{\rho V c_p} \Big|_0^t dt \tag{13.21}$$

Equation (13.21) is easily integrated and rearranged as follows:

$$\frac{T - T_\infty}{T_0 - T_\infty} = \exp[(-hAt)/(\rho V c_p)] \qquad N_{\text{Bi}} < 0.1 \tag{13.22}$$

In any transient heat transfer problem involving both convection and conduction, the Biot number should be calculated first. If N_{Bi} is less than 0.1, the simple analysis just given, which is also known as the lumped capacity method or the Newtonian cooling (or heating) method, is adequate. The quantity $(\rho V c_p)/(hA)$ may be interpreted as a thermal time constant τ_t:

$$\tau_t = \rho V c_p/(hA) \tag{13.23}$$

The thermal time constant can be used to represent the thermal decay by an electrical RC circuit [I1].

The total heat transferred between fluid and solid is found by integrating Eq. (13.17):

$$Q = \int_0^t q \, dt = hA \int_0^t (T_\infty - T) \, dt \tag{13.24}$$

Using Eq. (13.22) to replace $T_\infty - T$, the total heat is

$$Q = \rho V C_p (T_\infty - T_0)[1 - \exp(-t/\tau_t)] \tag{13.25}$$

If the solid is being quenched by a cold fluid, then Q is negative because the term $T_\infty - T_0$ is negative. As time approaches infinity, the temperature of the solid approaches the temperature of the surrounding fluid T_∞; also, the exponential term in Eq. (13.25) is zero, and the total heat transferred is

$$Q = \rho V c_p (T_\infty - T_0) \tag{13.26}$$

In the Biot number, the characteristic length L_c is obtained from the volume divided by the surface area for heat transfer:

$$L_c = V/A \tag{13.27}$$

In the following example, the characteristic length L_c is calculated and the Biot number for several geometries determined.

Example 13.1. The thermal conductivity of copper is $400 \text{ W m}^{-1}\text{K}^{-1}$. If the heat transfer coefficient is $12 \text{ W m}^{-2}\text{K}^{-1}$, find the Biot number for: (a) a copper sphere of radius 5 cm; (b) a copper cylinder of radius 5 cm and length 30 cm; and (c) a square copper rod of length 40 cm and cross sectional area the same as the cylinder of radius 5 cm.

Answer. The equations for Biot number and characteristic length are

$$N_{Bi} = hL_c/k \tag{13.16}$$

$$L_c = V/A \tag{13.27}$$

(a) For a sphere. Let r be the radius. Then Eq. (13.27) becomes

$$L_c = \frac{V}{A} = \frac{4\pi r^3/3}{4\pi r^2} = \frac{r}{3} \tag{i}$$

The Biot number is

$$N_{Bi} = hL_c/k = (12)(0.05/3)/(400) \, [(\text{W m}^{-2}\text{K}^{-1})(\text{m})/(\text{W m}^{-1}\text{K}^{-1})] = 5 \times 10^{-4} \tag{ii}$$

(b) For a cylinder. The circumference of a cylinder is $2\pi r$ and the heat transfer area $2\pi rL$, neglecting the areas at each end:

$$L_c = \frac{V}{A} = \frac{\pi r^2 L}{2\pi rL} = \frac{r}{2} \tag{iii}$$

$$N_{Bi} = hL_c/k = (12)(0.05/2)/(400) = 7.5 \times 10^{-4} \tag{iv}$$

Note that the Biot number is greater for a long cylinder than for a sphere of the same radius.

(c) For a long square rod. Let x be the length of one side of the square. From the area of the cylinder of radius 0.05 m, x is

$$x = (A)^{1/2} = (\pi r^2)^{1/2} = [\pi (0.05)^2]^{1/2} = 0.08862 \text{ m} \tag{v}$$

From Eqs. (13.16) and (13.27):

$$L_c = \frac{V}{A} = \frac{x^2 L}{4xL} = \frac{x}{4} \tag{vi}$$

$$N_{Bi} = hL_c/k = (12)(0.08862/4)/(400) = 6.647 \times 10^{-4} \tag{vii}$$

The Biot number for the square rod is 11.4 percent less than that for a circular rod of the same cross sectional area. The Biot numbers calculated in this example are all less than 0.1 because copper is an excellent conductor.

13.2 FINITE SLAB AND CYLINDER

In this section, one-directional heat transfer in a finite slab is considered; this problem is analogous to one-directional mass transfer as depicted in Fig. 13.2. Consider Fig. 13.5, which shows a slab of infinite extent in both the y and z directions. Let the initial temperature be T_0, as previously illustrated in Fig. 13.1. At time zero, the temperatures at either side are instantaneously changed to T_1 and T_2, as shown in Fig. 13.5. In this section, solutions will be offered for the cases illustrated in Figs. 13.1, 13.2, and 13.5. Heat transfer will be used to illustrate the solutions, and the mathematically analogous mass transfer will be discussed briefly. Heat transfer may also be restricted to one direction if insulation prevents heat transport in the other directions. Similarly, in Fig. 13.2 the surface of the bar is impervious to mass transfer; thus, mass transfer in that figure is in the x direction only.

The problem of transient heat transfer to a slab infinite in the y and z directions is the simplest case of unsteady transport. The equation for one-dimensional heat transport becomes

$$\frac{\partial^2 T}{\partial x^2} = \frac{1}{\alpha} \frac{\partial T}{\partial t} \tag{13.6}$$

The boundary conditions illustrated in Fig. 13.5 are

At $t \leq 0$ and $0 \leq x \leq 2L$

$$T = T_0 \tag{13.7}$$

At $t > 0$

$$T(x = 0) = T_1 \qquad T(x = 2L) = T_2 \tag{13.28}$$

where T_1 is the temperature at one edge of the slab and T_2 is the temperature at the other. Because the slab is infinite in the y and z directions, the transport

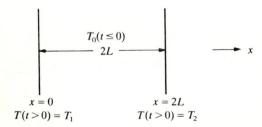

$T_0(t \leq 0)$

$2L$

x

$x = 0$
$T(t > 0) = T_1$

$x = 2L$
$T(t > 0) = T_2$

FIGURE 13.5
Transient heat transfer in a one-directional slab.

is one-dimensional. These simple boundary conditions are actually too complex for a direct analytical solution. However, a solution is possible through use of a superposition of solutions, as will be illustrated later in Example 13.2.

A simplified set of boundary conditions is

$$T_0 = \text{constant } [\neq f(x)] \qquad T_1 = T_2 = T_f = \text{constant } [\neq f(t)] \qquad (13.29)$$

where T_0 and T_f are constants and not functions of time. For this special case of the same temperature T_f being superimposed on each side of the slab, the temperature distribution is always symmetric about the center plane $(x = L)$, and the derivative at the center plane is zero:

$$T(x) = T(2L - x) \qquad \frac{dT}{dx}(x = L) = 0 \qquad (13.30)$$

The implications of Eq. (13.30) will prove useful in the solution of the transient transport equations by Fourier series and Laplace transforms.

For the finite slab, four methods of solution of the one-directional transient heat (or mass) transfer equation, Eq. (13.6) [or a simplified Eq. (13.11)], will be presented: Fourier series, Laplace transforms, graphical solutions, and numerical integration. The boundary conditions in Eq. (13.28) are too complex for the first two of these, and the restrictions in Eq. (13.29) are required.

In the case where T_0 and T_f are constants, a simple transformation is useful. In Chapter 12, a dimensionless temperature Θ was introduced to facilitate the presentation of the Pohlhausen solution for the temperature distribution for flow over a flat plate. In Eq. (12.29), Θ was the ratio between the temperature difference of the wall and the boundary layer fluid and the temperature difference of the wall and the free stream. For transient heat transfer, the variable Θ is defined as

$$\Theta = T - T_f \qquad (13.31)$$

where T is the temperature at any point in the slab and T_f is defined in Eq. (13.29). Note that Θ has dimensions of temperature (K, etc.). The transient heat transfer equation, Eq. (13.6), can be expressed in terms of Θ:

$$\frac{\partial^2 \Theta}{\partial x^2} = \frac{1}{\alpha} \frac{\partial \Theta}{\partial t} \qquad (13.32)$$

This transformation is useful only when the boundary conditions are not a function of temperature, i.e., Eq. (13.29) applies. The boundary conditions in terms of Θ are

At $t \leq 0$ and $0 \leq x \leq 2L$

$$\Theta = \Theta_0 = T_0 - T_f \qquad (13.33)$$

At $t > 0$

$$\Theta(x = 0) = 0 \qquad \Theta(x = 2L) = 0 \qquad (13.34)$$

It is common practice to abbreviate Eqs. (13.33) and (13.34) as

$$\Theta(x, 0) = \Theta_0$$
$$\Theta(0, t) = 0 \tag{13.35}$$
$$\Theta(2L, t) = 0$$

Similarly, it is desirable to transform the mass transfer equation, Eq. (13.11), using some convenient variable such as Θ_M:

$$\Theta_M = C_A - C_{A,f} \tag{13.36}$$

where again the transformation is useful only if the boundary conditions are not a function of time. For one-dimensional transient mass transfer, Eq. (13.11) becomes

$$\frac{\partial^2 \Theta_M}{\partial x^2} = \frac{1}{D} \frac{\partial \Theta_M}{\partial t} \tag{13.37}$$

The boundary conditions in terms of Θ_M are almost identical to those in Eq. (13.35); the variable Θ_M is simply substituted for Θ.

13.2.1 Fourier Series Solution

The solution of partial differential equations using Fourier series is usually given in an advanced mathematics course at most universities. Hence, in this section only a typical Fourier series solution to Eq. (13.32) will be given. The reader is referred to the several excellent texts devoted to a more complete treatment [C3, M1, M4, R1, W2].

A Fourier series may be defined as

$$f(x) = a_0 + \sum_{j=1}^{\infty} a_j \cos j\pi x + \sum_{j=1}^{\infty} b_j \sin j\pi x \qquad 0 \le x \le 2L \tag{13.38}$$

where the function $f(x)$ is represented in terms of two periodic infinite series, as shown in Eq. (13.38). If the function $f(x)$ is assumed to be periodic, with period[1] $2L$ as shown in Fig. 13.6, then it is easily shown that

$$a_0 = \frac{1}{L} \int_0^{2L} f(x)\, dx \tag{13.39}$$

$$a_j = \frac{1}{L} \int_0^{2L} f(x) \cos\frac{j\pi x}{L}\, dx \tag{13.40}$$

$$b_j = \frac{1}{L} \int_0^{2L} f(x) \sin\frac{j\pi x}{L}\, dx \tag{13.41}$$

---

[1] A function is periodic if $f(t + 2L) = f(t)$ for all t.

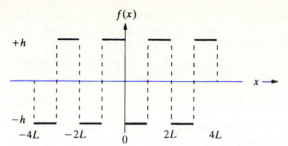

FIGURE 13.6
A simple periodic function.

The power of Fourier series arises from the fact that any function may be assumed periodic, even if it is not, by assuming that the length of the period is the region of interest. For clarification, let us consider the following boundary conditions:

$$\Theta(x, 0) = \Theta_0 \qquad \Theta(0, t) = 0 \qquad \Theta(2L, t) = 0 \qquad (13.35)$$

These are the simplest possible; since the transformed temperature is zero at either end, these boundary conditions are termed "homogeneous". Obviously, those are not in themselves periodic; yet they may be considered as a periodic function of period $2L$, as shown in Fig. 13.7. Physically the boundary conditions in Fig. 13.7 have no meaning for x less than zero or greater than $2L$, but the mathematical assumption of periodicity allows a Fourier series solution, as will be shown later.

Many functions likely to be encountered in our engineering problems can be expanded in a Fourier series. There are some mathematical restrictions, known as the Dirichlet conditions [M4], that cannot be violated. A function is Fourier expandable if in the interval $0 \le x \le 2L$ the following are true:

1. The function $f(x)$ is single-valued.
2. The function $f(x)$ never becomes infinite.
3. The function $f(x)$ has a finite number of maxima and minima.
4. The function $f(x)$ has a finite number of discontinuities.

A practical concern that does limit the utility of Fourier series solutions is that

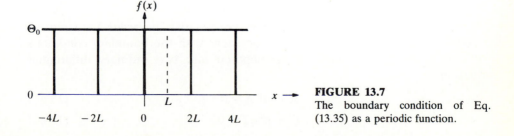

FIGURE 13.7
The boundary condition of Eq. (13.35) as a periodic function.

the integrals in Eqs. (13.39) to (13.41) must be analytic, since a_j and b_j are coefficients in an infinite series. Also, not all boundary conditions are amenable to Fourier series solution [C2, C3, C6, J2, M1, M4, R1, W2].

The first step in the Fourier series solution of a partial differential equation is to assume that the solution is a product of two quantities:

$$\Theta(x, t) = \underline{X}(x) \cdot \underline{T}(t) \tag{13.42}$$

where $\underline{X}$ is a function of x only and $\underline{T}$ is a function of t only. This assumption can be justified only in that it leads to a solution satisfying the partial differential equation and its boundary conditions. The assumed solution, Eq. (13.42) is substituted into the partial differential equation of interest, Eq. (13.32). Since $\underline{X}$ is a function of x only, it follows that

$$\frac{\partial^2 \Theta}{\partial x^2} = \underline{T}(t) \cdot \frac{\partial^2 \underline{X}(x)}{\partial x^2} = \underline{T} \cdot \underline{X}'' \tag{13.43}$$

Similarly

$$\frac{\partial \Theta}{\partial t} = \underline{X}(x) \cdot \frac{\partial \underline{T}(t)}{\partial t} = \underline{X} \cdot \underline{T}' \tag{13.44}$$

Substituting the above into Eq. (13.32), the result is

$$\underline{T}\underline{X}'' = \frac{1}{\alpha} \underline{X}\underline{T}' \tag{13.45}$$

The variables in Eq. (13.45) are separated as follows

$$\frac{\underline{X}''}{\underline{X}} = \frac{1}{\alpha} \frac{\underline{T}'}{\underline{T}} \tag{13.46}$$

It is argued that, if x is varied there is no effect on the term $\underline{T}'/(\alpha\underline{T})$ since $\underline{T}'/(\alpha\underline{T})$ is not a function of x. Thus, the term $\underline{T}'/(\alpha\underline{T})$ must be independent of x. A similar argument about varying t and its effect on the term $\underline{X}''/\underline{X}$ leads to the conclusion that each side of Eq. (13.46) must be equal to a constant. This constant shall be designated as $-\beta^2$ to facilitate later forms of the solution:

$$\frac{\underline{X}''}{\underline{X}} = \frac{1}{\alpha} \frac{\underline{T}'}{\underline{T}} = -\beta^2 \tag{13.47}$$

The constant $-\beta^2$ in Eq. (13.47) must be negative in order to avoid an exponential solution that would be inconsistent with the boundary conditions [R1]. Equation (13.47) may be decomposed into two ordinary differential equations:

$$\underline{X}'' + \beta^2 \underline{X} = 0 \tag{13.48}$$

$$\underline{T}' + \beta^2 \alpha \underline{T} = 0 \tag{13.49}$$

The solutions to Eqs. (13.48) and (13.49) are assumed to be

$$T = C_1 \exp(-\beta^2 \alpha t) \tag{13.50}$$

$$X = C_2 \cos \beta x + C_3 \sin \beta x \tag{13.51}$$

Appropriate boundary conditions for a direct Fourier series solution must be the simplest possible, i.e., homogeneous:

$$\Theta(x, 0) = \Theta_0$$

$$\Theta(0, t) = 0$$

$$\Theta(2L, t) = 0 \tag{13.35}$$

At this stage in the solution, there are four constants (C_1, C_2, C_3. and β) to be determined from the boundary conditions. Using the boundary condition at the point $x = 0$, Eq. (13.42) becomes

$$\Theta(0, t) = X(0) \cdot T(t) = 0 \tag{13.52}$$

Since for the nontrivial case $T(t)$ cannot be zero for all t, it follows that Eq. (13.52) is true only if

$$X(0) = 0 \tag{13.53}$$

Substituting the results of Eq. (13.53) into Eq. (13.51), Eq. (13.51) becomes

$$0 = C_2 \cos [(\beta)(0)] + C_3 \sin [(\beta)(0)] \tag{13.54}$$

Since the sine of zero is zero and the cosine of zero is one, then by Eq. (13.54), C_2 must be zero. Next, the boundary condition at the other end is applied, and by similar reasoning

$$X(2L) = 0 = C_3 \sin 2\beta L \tag{13.55}$$

Equation (13.55) equals zero only if C_3 is zero or if $\sin 2\beta L$ is zero or if both are zero. However, if C_3 is zero, then X is zero and our assumed solution, Eq. (13.42) is trivial. Therefore

$$\sin 2\beta L = 0 \tag{13.56}$$

The sine of an arbitrary angle α is zero if $\alpha = \pi$, 2π, 3π, etc. Hence

$$2\beta L = j\pi \qquad (j = 1, 2, 3, \ldots) \tag{13.57}$$

From Eq. (13.57), the constant β is found to be

$$\beta = \frac{j\pi}{2L} \tag{13.58}$$

The solution as determined so far is substituted from Eqs. (13.50), (13.55), and (13.58) into Eq. (13.42):

$$\Theta(x, t) = C_1 C_3 \left(\sin \frac{j\pi x}{2L} \right) \exp\left(-\left(\frac{j\pi}{2L} \right)^2 \alpha t \right) \tag{13.59}$$

where each and every j, as j goes from 1 to ∞, is a solution to the original partial differential equation, Eq. (13.32). Thus, the total solution is the sum over j of all possible solutions, since Eq. (13.32) is a linear partial differential equation:

$$\Theta(x, t) = \sum_{j=1}^{\infty} \left[b_j \sin\left(\frac{j\pi x}{2L}\right) \exp\left(-\left(\frac{j\pi}{2L}\right)^2 \alpha t\right) \right] \tag{13.60}$$

where the product $C_1 C_3$ has been replaced by b_j.

The remaining boundary condition at time zero, Eq. (13.33), is used to evaluate b_j. Applying that condition to Eq. (13.60):

$$\Theta(x, 0) = \Theta_0 = \sum_{j=1}^{\infty} \left[b_j \sin\left(\frac{j\pi x}{2L}\right) \exp\left(-\left(\frac{j\pi}{2L}\right)^2 \alpha(0)\right) \right] \tag{13.61}$$

Since the exponential of zero is one, Eq. (13.61) reduces to

$$\Theta_0 = \sum_{j=1}^{\infty} b_j \sin\left(\frac{j\pi x}{2L}\right) \tag{13.62}$$

A comparison of Eq. (13.62) with the Fourier series of Eq. (13.38) shows that a_j must be zero for all j and

$$b_j = \frac{1}{L} \int_0^{2L} \Theta_0 \sin\left(\frac{j\pi x}{2L}\right) dx \tag{13.63}$$

By substituting Eq. (13.63) into Eq. (13.60), a complete solution is now available. Note that a Fourier series solution is possible as long as the integration in Eq. (13.63) can be performed. For the case of constant Θ_0, integration of Eq. (13.63) yields

$$b_j = \frac{\Theta_0}{L} \int_0^{2L} \sin\left(\frac{j\pi x}{2L}\right) dx = \frac{\Theta_0}{L} \frac{-1}{j\pi/(2L)} \cos\left(\frac{j\pi x}{2L}\right) \Big|_0^{2L}$$

$$= \frac{2\Theta_0}{j\pi} [-\cos j\pi - (-\cos 0)] = \frac{4\Theta_0}{j\pi} \quad \text{[for odd } j] \tag{13.64}$$

The simplification of Eq. (13.64) resulted from the following reasoning. The cosine of zero is one. The cosine of $j\pi$ equals -1 for odd j and $+1$ for even j. Hence

$$-(\cos j\pi) + 1 = 0 \qquad \text{if } j \text{ is even}$$
$$-(\cos j\pi) + 1 = 2 \qquad \text{if } j \text{ is odd} \tag{13.65}$$

Note that a single value of b_j from Eq. (13.64) cannot possibly satisfy the boundary condition of Eq. (13.33). Hence, it is argued that only the sum from one to infinity of all possible b_j will satisfy the boundary condition, since Eq. (13.32) [or Eq. (13.37)] is a linear partial differential equation.

Combining results, the final solution to Eq. (13.32) as determined by the method of Fourier series is

$$\frac{\Theta}{\Theta_0} = \frac{T(x, t) - T_f}{T_0 - T_f} = \frac{4}{\pi} \sum_{j=1,3,5,\dots}^{\infty} \frac{1}{j} \left[\sin\left(\frac{j\pi x}{2L}\right) \exp\left(-\left(\frac{j\pi}{2L}\right)^2 \alpha t\right) \right] \quad (13.66)$$

Equation (13.66) expresses in terms of an infinite series the dimensionless temperature Θ/Θ_0 for any x and t when the boundary conditions of Eq. (13.35) are valid. However, the engineer will usually be interested in the temperature for a particular x and t or for a series of x and t combinations. In general a Fourier series such as Eq. (13.38) or Eq. (13.66) converges very slowly, especially for small t. Often thousands of terms are required in order to evaluate Θ to the required accuracy. In fact, evaluation of Eq. (13.66) on a digital computer requires almost as much effort as a direct numerical method (to be discussed subsequently), not including the lengthy steps required to get Eq. (13.66).

A mass transfer problem with nonhomogeneous boundary conditions is solved in Example 13.2.

Example 13.2. A 3-in. schedule 40 pipe is 3 ft long and contains helium at 26.03 atm and 317.2 K (44°C), as shown in Fig. 13.8. The ends of the pipe are initially capped by removable partitions. At time zero, the partitions are removed, and across each end of the pipe flows a stream of air plus helium at the same temperature and pressure. On the left end, the stream is 90 percent air and 10 percent He (by volume) and on the right 80 percent air and 20 percent He. It may be assumed that the flow effectively maintains the helium concentration constant at the ends. If isothermal conditions are maintained and there are no end effects associated with the air flowing past the pipe, calculate the composition profile (to four decimal places) after 1.2 h at space increments of 0.5 ft. Use Fourier series. The value of $D_{\text{He–air}}$ is $0.7652 \times 10^{-4} \, \text{m}^2 \, \text{s}^{-1}$ ($2.965 \, \text{ft}^2 \, \text{h}^{-1}$) [F2].

Answer. First, note that mass transfer in Fig. 13.8 occurs in the z direction only; there is no transport in either the r- or θ-directions. Since the previous equations (derived with heat transfer as the example) are in terms of the x direction, the solution to this problem will arbitrarily use the x direction as the direction of mass transfer.

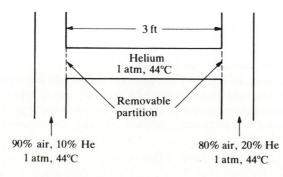

90% air, 10% He
1 atm, 44°C

80% air, 20% He
1 atm, 44°C

FIGURE 13.8
Transient diffusion of helium in a pipe.

Concentration is related to partial pressure by Eq. (2.37):

$$C_A = n/V = \bar{p}_A/(RT) \tag{2.37}$$

where R is the gas constant ($0.082057 \text{ atm m}^3 \text{ kmol}^{-1} \text{ K}^{-1}$ from Table C.1). The partial pressure of species A is defined by Eq. (2.38):

$$\bar{p}_A = y_A p_{total} \tag{2.38}$$

where y_A is the mole fraction of A and p_{total} is the total pressure.

Example 2.7 illustrated the method of converting partial pressures into concentrations. Initially, the partial pressure of helium in the tube equals the total pressure, 26.03 atm. When the partitions are removed, the partial pressures of helium at the ends of the pipe are

$$\bar{p}_1 = y_1 p_{total} = (0.1)(26.03) = 2.603 \text{ atm}$$
$$\bar{p}_2 = y_2 p_{total} = (0.2)(26.03) = 5.206 \text{ atm} \tag{i}$$

Inserting these into Eq. (2.37), the concentrations are

$$C_{A,0} = \bar{p}_0/(RT) = (26.03)/[(8.2057 \times 10^{-2})(317.2)] = 1.0 \text{ kmol m}^{-3}$$
$$C_{A,1} = \bar{p}_1/(RT) = (2.603)/[(8.2057 \times 10^{-2})(317.2)] = 0.1 \text{ kmol m}^{-3} \tag{ii}$$
$$C_{A,2} = \bar{p}_2/(RT) = (5.206)/[(8.2057 \times 10^{-2})(317.2)] = 0.2 \text{ kmol m}^{-3}$$

Following the nomenclature of Eq. (13.35), these are

$$C_{A,0}(x, 0) = 1.0 \text{ kmol m}^{-3}$$
$$C_{A,1}(0, t) = 0.1 \text{ kmol m}^{-3} \tag{iii}$$
$$C_{A,2}(2L, t) = 0.2 \text{ kmol m}^{-3}$$

where the total length of the pipe is $2L$, or 3 ft. Although $C_{A,1}$ does not equal $C_{A,2}$, it is still convenient to transform C_A to Θ_M:

$$\Theta_M = C_A - C_{A,1} \tag{iv}$$
$$\Theta_M(x, 0) = C_{A,0} - C_{A,1} = 0.9 = \Theta_0 \tag{v}$$
$$\Theta_M(0, t) = C_{A,1} - C_{A,1} = 0 \tag{vi}$$
$$\Theta_M(2L, t) = C_{A,2} - C_{A,1} = \Theta_2 = 0.1 \tag{vii}$$

where the definition of Θ_M is arbitrarily based on $C_{A,1}$; for ease of notation, Θ_0 and Θ_2 have also been introduced in the above equations. Using the above transformation, Eq. (13.37) still applies:

$$\frac{\partial^2 \Theta_M}{\partial x^2} = \frac{1}{D} \frac{\partial \Theta_M}{\partial t} \tag{13.37}$$

where the total length of the pipe is $2L$, or 3 ft.

The boundary conditions in Eqs. (iv) through (vii) do not allow a solution by Fourier series because the condition in Eq. (vii) does not equal zero. This limitation is easily circumvented by expressing the total solution as the sum of the unsteady-state (or transient or particular) solution Θ_t and the steady-state solution Θ_{ss} [R1]:

$$\Theta_M(x, t) = \Theta_{ss}(x) + \Theta_t(x, t) \tag{viii}$$

The steady-state solution Θ_{ss} is obtained from Fick's law, Eq. (2.4). For equimolar counter diffusion, it is easily shown that the ratio $\Delta\bar{p}_A/\Delta x$ must be constant at steady-state. If the ratio $\Delta\bar{p}_A/\Delta x$ is constant, then the ratio $\Delta C_A/\Delta x$ is also constant [cf. Eq. (2.37)]. Since two points uniquely determine the equation for a straight line, the equation for Θ_{ss} is

$$\Theta_{ss} = \Theta_M(0, \infty) + [\Theta_M(2L, \infty) - \Theta_M(0, \infty)][x/(2L)]$$
$$= 0 + (\Theta_2 - 0)[x/(2L)]$$
$$= \Theta_2[x/(2L)] = (0.1)(x/3) = x/30 \tag{ix}$$

The boundary conditions for the transient solution are found by combining the last two equations. First, Eq. (viii) is solved for $\Theta_t(x, t)$; then the conditions in Eqs. (v) through (vii) are inserted into the resulting equation:

$$\Theta_t(x, 0) = \Theta_M(x, 0) - \Theta_{ss}(x) = 0.9 - x/30 = \Theta_0 - \Theta_2[x/(2L)] \tag{x}$$
$$\Theta_t(0, t) = \Theta_M(0, t) - \Theta_{ss}(0) = 0 - 0 = 0 \tag{xi}$$
$$\Theta_t(2L, t) = \Theta_M(2L, t) - \Theta_{ss}(2L) = 0.1 - (0.1)(2L)/(2L) = 0 \tag{xii}$$

The solution to Eq. (13.37) subject to the above boundary conditions follows the derivation of Eq. (13.66) from the inception, Eq. (13.42), up through Eq. (13.60), which after replacing α with D is

$$\Theta_t(x, t) = \sum_{j=1}^{\infty} \left[b_j \sin\left(\frac{j\pi x}{2L}\right) \exp\left(-\left(\frac{j\pi}{2L}\right)^2 Dt \right) \right] \tag{xiii}$$

The boundary condition of Eq. (x) is used to evaluate the remaining constant, b_j:

$$\Theta_t(x, 0) = \Theta_0 - \Theta_2[x/(2L)] = 0.9 - x/30 = \sum_{j=1}^{\infty} \left[b_j \sin\left(\frac{j\pi x}{2L}\right) \exp\left(-\left(\frac{j\pi}{2L}\right)^2 (D)(0) \right) \right]$$
$$= \sum_{j=1}^{\infty} b_j \sin\left(\frac{j\pi x}{2L}\right) \tag{xiv}$$

A comparison of Eq. (xiv) with the Fourier series of Eq. (13.38) shows that a_j must be zero for all j and

$$b_j = \frac{1}{L} \int_0^{2L} \left(\Theta_0 - \Theta_2 \frac{x}{2L} \right) \sin\left(\frac{j\pi x}{2L}\right) dx \tag{xv}$$

Equation (xv) equals the sum of two integrals:

$$b_j = \frac{\Theta_0}{L} \int_0^{2L} \sin\left(\frac{j\pi x}{2L}\right) dx - \frac{\Theta_2}{2L^2} \int_0^{2L} x \sin\left(\frac{j\pi x}{2L}\right) dx \tag{xvi}$$

The first integral is identical to that in Eq. (13.64):

$$\frac{\Theta_0}{L} \int_0^{2L} \sin\left(\frac{j\pi x}{2L}\right) dx = \frac{4\Theta_0}{\pi j} \qquad \text{[for odd } j \text{]} \tag{xvii}$$

The second integral may be located in a standard table of integrals [P1]:

$$\int x \sin \lambda x \, dx = -\frac{x \cos \lambda x}{\lambda} + \frac{\sin \lambda x}{\lambda^2} \tag{xviii}$$

where λ equals $j\pi/(2L)$. Substituting, the second integral is

$$-\frac{\Theta_2}{2L^2}\int_0^{2L} x \sin\left(\frac{j\pi x}{2L}\right) dx = \frac{\Theta_2}{2L^2}\left(\frac{x\cos[(j\pi x)/(2L)]}{j\pi/(2L)} - \frac{\sin[(j\pi x)/(2L)]}{[j\pi/(2L)]^2}\right)\Big|_0^{2L} \quad \text{(xix)}$$

The first term in the above is

$$\frac{\Theta_2}{2L^2}\frac{2L}{j\pi}[2L(\cos j\pi) - (0)(\cos 0)] = \frac{2\Theta_2}{j\pi}\cos j\pi = \frac{2\Theta_2}{j\pi}(-1)^j \quad \text{(xx)}$$

since $\cos j\pi = +1$ for even values of j and -1 for odd values of j. The second term is zero since $\sin j\pi$ equals zero for all values of j:

$$\sin[(j\pi)(2L)/(2L)] - \sin 0 = \sin j\pi - 0 = 0 \quad \text{(xxi)}$$

The value of b_j is the combination of Eqs. (xvii) and (xx). The final expression is obtained by the summation of all b_j between 1 and infinity, which is then included in Eq. (xiii):

$$\Theta_t(x, t) = \frac{4\Theta_0}{\pi}\sum_{j=1,3,5,...}^{\infty}\frac{1}{j}\left[\sin\left(\frac{j\pi x}{2L}\right)\exp\left(-\left(\frac{j\pi}{2L}\right)^2 Dt\right)\right]$$
$$+ \frac{2\Theta_2}{\pi}\sum_{j=1,2,3,...}^{\infty}\frac{1}{j}(-1)^j\left[\sin\left(\frac{j\pi x}{2L}\right)\exp\left(-\left(\frac{j\pi}{2L}\right)^2 Dt\right)\right] \quad \text{(xxii)}$$

As a rule, these infinite series converge slowly; hence, it may be advantageous to combine the two infinite series:

$$\Theta_t(x, t) = \frac{2}{\pi}\sum_{j=1}^{\infty}\frac{1}{j}[\Theta_0 + (-1)^j(\Theta_2 - \Theta_0)]\left[\sin\left(\frac{j\pi x}{2L}\right)\exp\left(-\left(\frac{j\pi}{2L}\right)^2 Dt\right)\right] \quad \text{(xxiii)}$$

Note that if $\Theta_2 = 0$, Eq. (xxiii) reduces to Eq. (13.66). Inserting Eqs. (ix) and (xxiii) into Eq. (viii) yields the final expression for the concentration or for Θ_M as a function of time and distance:

$$\Theta_M(x, t) = \Theta_{ss}(x) + \Theta_t(x, t)$$
$$= \Theta_2\left(\frac{x}{2L}\right) + \frac{2}{\pi}\sum_{j=1}^{\infty}\frac{1}{j}[\Theta_0 + (-1)^j(\Theta_2 - \Theta_0)]\left[\sin\left(\frac{j\pi x}{2L}\right)\exp\left(-\left(\frac{j\pi}{2L}\right)^2 Dt\right)\right] \quad \text{(xxiv)}$$

where

$$\Theta_0 = 0.9 \qquad \Theta_2 = 0.1 \qquad 2L = 3 \text{ ft} \qquad D = 2.965 \text{ ft}^2 \text{ h}^{-1} \quad \text{(xxv)}$$

A computer program to evaluate Eq. (xxiv) at the t and z of interest is given in Fig. 13.9. Equation (xxiv) is a converging infinite series, in which the signs of the terms alternate in an irregular pattern. The best procedure is to combine all terms of like sign, then test the magnitude to see if that combination is less than the accuracy desired. In the case of a simple alternating converging series, the truncation error is smaller in absolute value than the first term neglected and is of the same sign. The results are given in Table 13.2. The last column is an indication of how many terms are required for the infinite series to converge.

```
C .......................EXAMPLE  13-2 ..........................
C
C FOURIER SERIES SOLUTION OF AN UNSTEADY-STATE MASS TRANSFER PROBLEM
C     WITH NONHOMOGENEOUS BOUNDARY CONDITIONS
C
      IMPLICIT REAL*8(A-H,O-Z)
      DIMENSION ZZ(5),TIME(8),ANS(5)
    2 FORMAT(1H0/113H0EXAMPLE  13-2  - FOURIER SERIES SOLUTION OF AN UNS
     1TEADY-STATE MASS TRANSFER PROBLEM WITH NONHOMOGENEOUS BOUNDARY/
     218X10HCONDITIONS)
    3 FORMAT(11H1END OF JOB)
    4 FORMAT(1H0/19H0THE TUBE LENGTH IS,F20.4/29H0THE DIFFUSIVITY(FT*FT/
     1HR) IS,F10.4/1H0/40H0THE BOUNDARY CONDITION FOR ZERO TIME IS,F11.4
     2/36H THE BOUNDARY CONDITION FOR Z = 0 IS,F15.4
     3/37H THE BOUNDARY CONDITION FOR Z = 2L IS,F14.4)
    5 FORMAT(1H0,20X,'CONCENTRATION CA AT DISTANCE (X/2L)',
     1  2X,'<KG M**-3>'/8H0TIME(S),5X,3H0.0,7X,3H1/6,7X,
     2  3H1/3,7X,3H1/2,7X,3H2/3,7X,3H5/6,7X,3H1.0,7X,'MAX TERMS'/1H )
    6 FORMAT(1H0/11H0END OF JOB)
    7 FORMAT(F7.1,7F10.4,I12)
      IN=5
      IO=7
C
C     ZZ IS X IN FT; D IS IN FT*FT/H; T IS S;TWOL IS IN FT
C     TWOL IS TOTAL THICKNESS OF SLAB
C
      TWOL=3.0D0
      D = 2.965D0
      PI=3.141592653589793D0
      NZ=5
      ZZ(1)=0.5D0
      ZZ(2)=1.0D0
      ZZ(3)=1.5D0
      ZZ(4)=2.0D0
      ZZ(5)=2.5D0
      TIME(1)=1.D0
      TIME(2)=10.D0
      TIME(3)=100.D0
      TIME(4)=600.D0
      TIME(5)=1000.D0
      TIME(6)=3600.D0
      TIME(7)=6000.D0
      TIME(8)=1.D10
      EPS=0.5D-05
      ZERO=0.D0
C
C     C0 IS CONCENTRATION AT T = 0
C     C1 IS CONCENTRATION AT Z = 0
C     C2 IS CONCENTRATION AT Z = TWOL
C
      C0=1.0D0
      C1=0.1D0
      C2=0.2D0
      WRITE(IO,2)
      WRITE(IO,4)TWOL,D,C0,C1,C2
C           THETA-M IS CA - C1
      TH0=C0-C1
      TH2=C2-C1
C           THE FOLLOWING ARE COMPUTED ONCE ONLY FOR EFFICIENCY
      A7=TH2/TWOL
      A8=2.D0/PI
C        A9 IS FOR ODD J ONLY; FOR EVEN J, USE TH2
      A9=TH0+TH0-TH2
      WRITE(IO,5)
      WRITE(IO,7)ZERO,(C0,I=1,7)
      DO 200 II=1,8
```

FIGURE 13.9

Program to evaluate Fourier series in Example 13.2.

```
C                T IS TIME IN H
        TSEC=TIME(II)
        T=TSEC/3600.D0
        DO 100 K=1,NZ
        J=1
        IALT=2
        JMAX=0
        A1=-D*T*(PI/TWOL)**2
        A6=PI*ZZ(K)/TWOL
        SUM=ZERO
        TERMJ1=FS(A1,A6,J)*A9
        SUMT=TERMJ1
        SLAST=ZERO
C
C         SUM - SUMMATION OF TERMS OF SERIES
C         TERMJ1 - CONTAINS 1ST TERM WITH SIGN
C         TERMJ - CALCULATIONS FOR J
C         SUMT - SUMMATION OF TERMS WITH SAME SIGN
C         SLAST - VALUE OF THE PREVIOUS SUMMATION
C
  40        J=J+1
        TERMJ=FS(A1,A6,J)
C              BYPASS IF TERMJ IS IDENTICALLY ZERO
        IF(TERMJ)41,45,41
  41 GO TO (42,43),IALT
C              FOR ODD J
  42 TERMJ=TERMJ*A9
        IALT=2
        GO TO 44
C              FOR EVEN J
  43 TERMJ=TERMJ*TH2
        IALT=1
  44 CONTINUE
        IF(DABS(TERMJ)+DABS(TERMJ1)-DABS(TERMJ+TERMJ1))55,55,45
C              DIFFERENT SIGN - TEST FOR CONVERGENCE
C                (WHEN THE SUM OF TERMS OF LIKE SIGN BECOMES LESS
C                   THAN EPS
  45        SUM=SUM+SLAST
        IF(DABS(SUMT)-EPS)60,50,50
C              NO CONVERGENCE
  50        SLAST=SUMT
        SUMT=TERMJ
        TERMJ1=TERMJ
        GO TO 40

C              SAME SIGN - ADD AND LOOP
  55        SUMT=SUMT+TERMJ
        GO TO 40
C              CONVERGENCE - BUILD THE SOLUTION
  60        THETA=ZZ(K)*A7+A8*SUM
        IF(J.GT.JMAX)JMAX=J
C              CHANGE FROM THETA-M TO CA
 100    ANS(K)=THETA+C1
        IF(TSEC.GT.9999.D0)TSEC=ZERO
        WRITE(IO,7)TSEC,C1,(ANS(I),I=1,5),C2,JMAX
 200    CONTINUE
        WRITE(IO,6)
        STOP
        END
        FUNCTION FS(A,B,J)
        REAL*8 FS,A,B,XJ
        XJ=DFLOAT(J)
        FS=DSIN(B*XJ)/XJ*DEXP(A*XJ*XJ)
        RETURN
        END
```

FIGURE 13.9

(*Continued*)

TABLE 13.2
Solution to Example 13.2—transient diffusion

Time, s	Concentration C_A at distance x							Max j
	0 ft	0.5 ft	1.0 ft	1.5 ft	2.0 ft	2.5 ft	3.0 ft	
0.0	1.0000	1.0000	1.0000	1.0000	1.0000	1.0000	1.0000	
1.0	0.1000	1.0000	1.0000	1.0000	1.0000	1.0000	0.2000	81
10.0	0.1000	0.9999	1.0000	1.0000	1.0000	0.9999	0.2000	29
100.0	0.1000	0.8038	0.9876	0.9996	0.9390	0.8256	0.2000	11
600.0	0.1000	0.4373	0.6816	0.7767	0.7087	0.4977	0.2000	5
1000.0	0.1000	0.3368	0.5139	0.5885	0.5458	0.4020	0.2000	5
3600.0	0.1000	0.1376	0.1696	0.1919	0.2030	0.2043	0.2000	3
6000.0	0.1000	0.1191	0.1375	0.1548	0.1708	0.1857	0.2000	3
∞	0.1000	0.1167	0.1333	0.1500	0.1667	0.1833	0.2000	2

13.2.2 Laplace Transform Solution

The Laplace transformation is one of the most important forms of operational calculus. In the field of chemical engineering, the most important application of the Laplace transform is in the area of process control. The Laplace transform can also be used to solve ordinary and partial differential equations [C1, C4, M1, M3, R1, W2].

The solution of partial differential equations by Laplace transforms comprises three steps: (1) the given partial differential equation is transformed into an ordinary differential equation; (2) the ordinary differential equation is solved by standard procedures; and (3) the solution is transformed back into the original variables such that it becomes the correct solution of the original problem.

Let $f(t)$ be a function defined for all positive t and let the following integral exist:

$$g(s) = \int [\exp(-st)][f(t)]\, dt \tag{13.67}$$

where s is a parameter that becomes the transformed independent variable in g. Then the function $g(s)$ is defined as the Laplace transform $L(f)$ of the original function $f(t)$:

$$L(f) = g(s) = \int_0^\infty [\exp(-st)][f(t)]\, dt \tag{13.68}$$

The inverse transform $L^{-1}(g)$ is defined as

$$f(t) = L^{-1}(g) \tag{13.69}$$

The Laplace transform possesses many useful properties that allow transforms of many seemingly complex functions to be computed simply.

Tables of Laplace transforms are available in many references [C1, C4, J2, M1, M3, R1, W2]. The following example problem illustrates two simple transformations.

Example 13.3. Find the Laplace transform of: (a) $f(t) = t$; and (b) $f(t) = \exp(at)$, where a is a constant.

Answer. For part (a), t must be nonnegative. Application of Eq. (13.68) to the function yields

$$L(f) = g(s) = \int_0^\infty [\exp(-st)][f(t)] \, dt = \int_0^\infty [\exp(-st)]t \, dt = \frac{e^{-st}}{s^2}(-st - 1)\bigg|_0^\infty$$

$$= \frac{e^{-\infty}}{s^2}(-\infty) - \frac{-1}{s^2} = \frac{1}{s^2} \qquad (s > 0) \tag{i}$$

For part (b), with the restriction of t nonnegative

$$L(e^{at}) = \int_0^\infty [\exp(-st)][\exp(at)] \, dt = \frac{1}{a-s} \exp[-(s-a)(t)]\bigg|_0^\infty$$

$$= \frac{1}{s-a} \qquad (s-a) > 0 \tag{ii}$$

The Laplace transform can also be applied to derivatives [J2]. If the derivative of the function $f(t)$ is $f'(t)$, then the Laplace transform of this derivative is

$$L[f'(t)] = \int_0^\infty [f'(t)][\exp(-st)] \, dt$$

$$= [f(t)][\exp(-st)]\bigg|_0^\infty - s\int_0^\infty [f(t)][\exp(-st)] \, dt = sL[f(t)] - f(0) \tag{13.70}$$

The Laplace transform involves integrating from zero to infinity. The above equation can be extended to show how a derivative may be removed from a partial differential equation. The method of Laplace transforms can be used to reduce a partial differential equation to an ordinary differential equation if all variables except one have an open range.[2] The Laplace transform is very useful in solving some problems in which one boundary condition is a function of time. A compendium of solutions is available for heat transfer problems [C2] and for mass transfer problems [B1, C6].

For purposes of illustration, let us reconsider the simple boundary

---

[2] In considering boundary conditions, the range of a variable is said to be open if the boundary conditions specify the value of that variable at the start of a range; in other words, the problem with respect to that variable is an "initial value" one.

conditions of Eq. (13.35):

$$\Theta(x, 0) = \Theta_0 \qquad \Theta(0, t) = 0 \qquad \Theta(2L, t) = 0 \qquad (13.35)$$

These cannot be used directly for Laplace transforms because the last two are both boundary value boundary conditions. However, as mentioned previously, these boundary conditions result in a symmetric temperature distribution about the center plane. When the above boundary conditions apply, the derivative of Θ with respect to distance must be zero at the center plane. In the Laplace transform solution using the above, it is convenient to translate the x axis so that the origin in Figs. 13.5 through 13.7 is now at L. After translation, the slab extends from $-L$ to L. Then the following boundary conditions describe the physical problem:

$$\Theta(x, 0) = \Theta_0 \qquad \Theta(L, t) = 0 \qquad \frac{\partial \Theta}{\partial x}(0, t) = 0 \qquad (13.71)$$

The boundary conditions of Eqs. (13.35) and (13.71) are compared in Fig. 13.10. The temperature profiles in Figs. 13.10(a) and 13.10(b) are identical in the region $0 \le x \le L$. Hence, the Laplace transform solution using Eq. (13.71) must yield the same numerical result as the Fourier series solution using Eq. (13.35). This comparison will be illustrated in Example 13.4.

The boundary conditions of Eq. (13.71) will now be applied to Eq. (13.32):

$$\frac{\partial^2 \Theta}{\partial x^2} = \frac{1}{\alpha} \frac{\partial \Theta}{\partial t} \qquad (13.32)$$

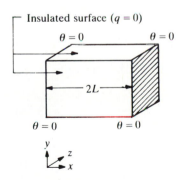

(a) Fourier problem

$$\Theta(x, 0) = \Theta_0$$
$$\Theta(-L, t) = 0$$
$$\Theta(+L, t) = 0$$

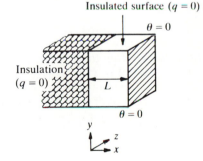

(b) Laplace transform problem

$$\Theta(x, 0) = \Theta_0$$
$$\Theta(+L, t) = 0$$
$$\frac{d\Theta}{dx}(0, t) = 0$$

FIGURE 13.10
Comparison of boundary conditions for one-dimensional unsteady-state transport.

The first step in the Laplace transform solution of Eq. (13.32) is to transform Eq. (13.32) along with the boundary conditions, which for illustration are Eq. (13.71). The details of this transformation are lengthy; since ample discussion is elsewhere [C1, C2, C4, J2, M1], the results will be summarized here. Recalling that $g(s)$ is the Laplace transform of the original function $f(t)$, Eq. (13.32) becomes

$$\frac{d^2g}{dx^2} = \frac{1}{\alpha}(sg - \Theta_0) \qquad (13.72)$$

The transformed boundary conditions [from Eq. (13.71)] become

$$g(x = \pm L) = 0 \qquad \frac{dg}{dx}(x = 0) = 0 \qquad (13.73)$$

Note that Eq. (13.32), the partial differential equation, has been transformed into Eq. (13.72), which is an ordinary differential equation, the solution of which is [C4, R1]

$$g = \Theta_0/s + C_1 \sinh(\gamma x) + C_2 \cosh(\gamma x) \qquad (13.74)$$

where

$$\gamma = (\alpha s)^{1/2} \qquad (13.75)$$

The boundary conditions of Eq. (13.73) are used to evaluate C_1 and C_2 in Eq. (13.74). Using the derivative of g:

$$\frac{dg}{dx} = 0 = \gamma C_1 \cosh(0) + \gamma C_2 \sinh(0) \qquad (13.76)$$

The following is true:

$$\sinh(0) = 0 \qquad \cosh(0) = 1 \qquad (13.77)$$

Comparing the last two equations, obviously Eq. (13.76) is true only if the constant C_1 is zero. Then Eq. (13.74) reduces to

$$g = \theta_0/s + C_2 \cosh(\gamma x) \qquad (13.78)$$

Using the other boundary condition, Eq. (13.78) becomes

$$g = \theta_0/s + C_2 \cosh(\gamma L) = 0 \qquad (13.79)$$

or

$$C_2 = \frac{-\Theta_0/s}{\cosh(\gamma L)} \qquad (13.80)$$

After substituting the above expression for C_2 into Eq. (13.78), the result is

$$g = \frac{\Theta_0}{s} - \frac{\Theta_0}{s}\left(\frac{\cosh(\gamma x)}{\cosh(\gamma L)}\right) \qquad (13.81)$$

The last step in the solution by Laplace transforms is to find the inverse transform of Eq. (13.81). Equation (13.81) is converted to exponentials, and after simplification an inverse transformation is obtainable. The answer is [C4]

$$\frac{\Theta}{\Theta_0} = \frac{T(x, t) - T_f}{T_0 - T_f}$$

$$= 1 - \sum_{j=0}^{\infty} [-1]^j \left[\text{erfc}\left(\frac{(2j + 1)(L) - x}{(2)(\alpha t)^{1/2}}\right) + \text{erfc}\left(\frac{(2j + 1)(L) + x}{(2)(\alpha t)^{1/2}}\right) \right]$$

$$(13.82)$$

An example problem using this equation is presented in the next section. Obviously, Eq. (13.82) is mathematically equivalent to Eq. (13.66), since each is a solution to the same physical problem. Note, however, that the independent variable x is defined differently in Eq. (13.66), as compared with Eq. (13.82) (cf. Fig. 13.10).

13.2.3 Generalized Chart Solutions

Generalized charts for unsteady-state heat transfer were originally prepared by Gurney and Lurie [G4], who presented the mathematical solutions to useful heat transfer problems in graphical form. Their charts avoided the tedious evaluation of the many terms of the infinite series that often comprise the solutions. In the solutions presented in Sections 13.2.1 and 13.2.2, the boundary conditions were fairly simple; however, the charts allow for convective heat or mass transfer to solids of various shapes, such as slabs, cylinders, and spheres.

The charts prepared by Heisler [H1] are more accurate than those of Gurney and Lurie. Heisler prepared graphs for the temperature history at the center of the slab (or other body), the temperature of which is hereafter called T_c. Other graphs correlated T_c with the temperature T at any position. Figures 13.11 and 13.12 are the graphs of T_c and T for the slab or flat plate, as discussed in the last two sections (cf. Figs. 13.1, 13.5, and 13.10). Table 13.3 presents the necessary nomenclature for use of the charts. Figure 13.11 was prepared using a dimensionless temperature which McAdams [M2] termed "unaccomplished change". For heat transfer, the unaccomplished change at the center Y_c is

$$Y_c = \frac{T_\infty - T_c}{T_\infty - T_0} \qquad (13.83)$$

where T_c is the temperature at the center plane of the slab, T_∞ is the temperature of the surrounding fluid, and T_0 is the initial temperature of the slab at time zero. The Heisler charts were prepared using m, which in heat transfer is the reciprocal of the Biot number:

$$m = N_{Bi}^{-1} = \frac{k}{hL} \qquad (13.84)$$

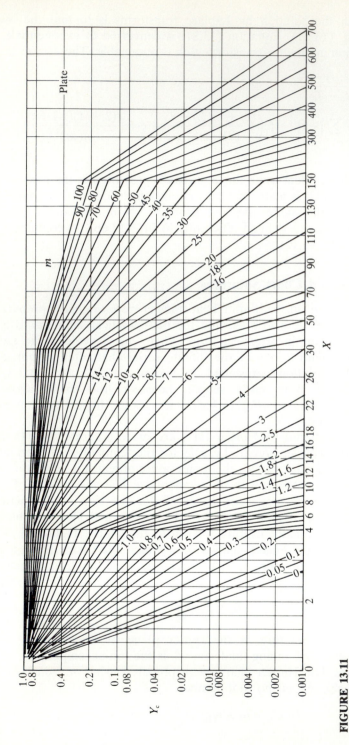

FIGURE 13.11

Temperature or concentration at the center plane of a large flat plate of thickness 2L. (*From Heisler, Trans. ASME* **69:** *227 (1947). By permission of ASME.*)

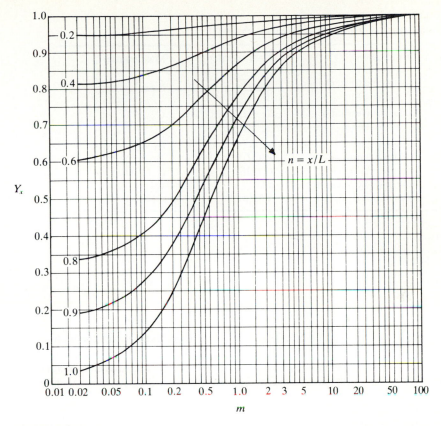

FIGURE 13.12
Position-correction chart for Figure 13.11 (flat plate). (*From Heisler, Trans. ASME 69: 227 (1947). By permission of ASME.*)

where L is half the thickness of the slab as before. To find the temperature at some specified location x, the variables m and X are calculated; then Y_c is determined from Fig. 13.11; T_c is calculated from Eq. (13.83); Y_x is determined from Fig. 13.12; and finally T_x is calculated from the definition of Y_x, as given in Table 13.3.

The charts just presented apply to the case of the boundary conditions of Eq. (13.29):

$$T_0 = \text{constant} \quad [\neq f(x)]$$
$$T_1 = T_2 = T_f = \text{constant} \quad [\neq f(t)]$$

(13.29)

These boundary conditions are equivalent to a Biot number of infinity, or a value of m equal to zero. The line of $m = 0$ is included in the preceding figures.

Example 13.4. A sheet of extruded polystyrene (rigid) is 8 ft long, 4 ft wide, and 2 in. thick. Initially, its temperature is 253 K. If the temperature at each face is

TABLE 13.3

Nomenclature for transient transport charts

Symbol	Description	Heat transfer	Mass transfer
Y_c	unaccomplished change at the center	$\dfrac{T_\infty - T_c}{T_\infty - T_0}$	$\dfrac{C_{A,\infty} - C_{A,c}}{C_{A,\infty} - C_{A,0}}$
Y_x	dimensionless ratio at location x	$\dfrac{T_\infty - T_x}{T_\infty - T_c}$	$\dfrac{C_{A,\infty} - C_{A,x}}{C_{A,\infty} - C_{A,c}}$
X	relative time	$\alpha t/L^2$	Dt/L^2
m	relative resistance	$k/(hL)$	$D/(k_cL)$
m_∞	relative resistance	$(h/k)(\alpha t)^{1/2}$	$(k_c/D)(Dt)^{1/2}$
n	dimensionless distance	x/L	x/L
Z	dimensionless distance	$x/[2(\alpha t)^{1/2}]$	$x/[2(Dt)^{1/2}]$

Subscripts

∞, fluid surrounding the solid
0, value at time zero
c, value at the center of the body
x, value at position x (or r)

instantaneously increased to 303 K, find the temperature at the center line after 640 s by three methods: (a) Fourier series; (b) Laplace transform; (c) Heisler charts. For this plastic, the density is 55 kg m^{-3}, the thermal conductivity 0.027 W m^{-1} K^{-1}, the heat capacity 1.21 kJ kg^{-1} K^{-1}, and the thermal diffusivity 4.057×10^{-7} m^2 s^{-1}.

Answer. The sheet of polystyrene is large enough so that end effects may be neglected. Therefore, there is negligible error in the assumption that all heat transfer occurs in the x direction, i.e.. the coordinate corresponding to the thickness, which in SI units is

$$2L = (2)(0.0254)\,[(\text{in.})(\text{m in.}^{-1})] = 0.0508 \text{ m} \tag{i}$$

$$L = 0.0254 \text{ m} \tag{ii}$$

The boundary conditions as given correspond to those of Eq. (13.29):

$$T_0 = 253 \text{ K} = \text{constant}$$
$$T_1 = T_2 = T_f = 303 \text{ K} = \text{constant} \tag{iii}$$

The above boundary conditions and the governing transient heat equation, Eq. (13.6), are easily transformed into the variable Θ using Eq. (13.31):

$$\Theta = T - T_f = T - 303 \tag{iv}$$

The applicable partial differential equation is Eq. (13.32):

$$\frac{\partial^2 \Theta}{\partial x^2} = \frac{1}{\alpha}\frac{\partial \Theta}{\partial t} \tag{13.32}$$

The boundary conditions in terms of Θ are in the form of Eq. (13.35):

$$\Theta(x, 0) = \Theta_0 = T_0 - T_f = 253 - 303 = -50$$

$$\Theta(0, t) = 0 \qquad \Theta(2L, t) = 0 \tag{v}$$

(a) Fourier series. The Fourier series solution to Eq. (13.32) was presented previously:

$$\frac{\Theta}{\Theta_0} = \frac{T(x, t) - T_f}{T_0 - T_f} = \frac{4}{\pi} \sum_{j=1,3,5,\dots}^{\infty} \frac{1}{j} \left[\sin\left(\frac{j\pi x}{2L}\right) \exp\left(-\left(\frac{j\pi}{2L}\right)^2 \alpha t\right) \right] \tag{13.66}$$

For this problem, the ratio $x/(2L)$ is $1/2$. Then

$$\sin(j\pi/2) = (-1)^j \tag{vi}$$

$$\left(\frac{j\pi}{2L}\right)^2 (\alpha t) = \left(\frac{j\pi}{0.0508}\right)^2 (4.057 \times 10^{-7})(t) = 1.522 \times 10^{-3} j^2 t \tag{vii}$$

Equation (13.66) for this problem becomes

$$T(L, t) = 303 + \frac{(4)(-50)}{\pi} \sum_{j=1,3,5,\dots}^{\infty} \left(\frac{1}{j}\right)(-1)^j (\exp[(-1.522 \times 10^{-3}) j^2 t]) \tag{viii}$$

The program for Example 13.2 in Fig. 13.9 is easily modified to compute the answer in Eq. (viii); the result is in Fig. 13.13.

```
C
C ................EXAMPLE   13-4 ..........................
C
C FOURIER SERIES AND LAPLACE SOLUTION OF AN UNSTEADY-STATE HEAT TRANSFER
C      PROBLEM WITH HOMOGENEOUS BOUNDARY CONDITIONS
C
       IMPLICIT REAL*8(A-H,O-Z)
       DIMENSION ZZ(5),ANS(5),ANSL(5)
     2 FORMAT(1H0/'0EXAMPLE 13-4 - FOURIER SERIES AND LAPLACE TRANSFORM '
     1 ' SOLUTION OF AN UNSTEADY-STATE HEAT TRANSFER PROBLEM'/
     2 '       WITH HOMOGENEOUS BOUNDARY CONDITIONS')
     3 FORMAT(11H1END OF JOB)
     4 FORMAT(1H0/'0THE SLAB THICKNESS (2L, IN M) IS',F20.4/
     1 '0THE THERMAL DIFFUSIVITY (M*M/S) IS',D16.4/
     2 '0THE VARIABLE THETA IS THE TRANSFORMED TEMP, T - TF'/
     3 40H0THE BOUNDARY CONDITION FOR ZERO TIME IS,F11.4
     4 /36H THE BOUNDARY CONDITION FOR Z - 0 IS,F15.4
     5 /37H THE BOUNDARY CONDITION FOR Z - 2L IS,F14.4)
     5 FORMAT(1H0,20X,'THETA (K) AT DISTANCE (X/2L)',
     1 /8H0TIME(S),5X,3H0.0,7X,3H1/6,7X,
     2 3H1/3,7X,3H1/2,7X,3H2/3,7X,3H5/6,7X,3H1.0,7X,'MAX TERMS'/1H )
     6 FORMAT(1H0/11H0END OF JOB)
     7 FORMAT(F7.1,7F10.4,I12)
     8 FORMAT(1H )
     9 FORMAT('0THE TEMPERATURE TF (K) IS ',F10.2)
       IN=5
       IO=6
C
C      ZZ IS X IN M; ALPHA IS IN MT*M/S; T IS S;TWOL IS IN M
C      TWOL IS TOTAL THICKNESS OF SLAB
```

FIGURE 13.13
FORTRAN program for Example 13.4.

```
C
         TWOL=0.0508D0
         XL=TWOL/2.0D0
         ALPHA=4.057D-07
         PI=3.141592653589793D0
         NZ=3
         DO I=1,NZ
         ZZ(I)=TWOL/6.0D0*DFLOAT(I)
         ENDDO
         EPS=0.5D-05
         ZERO=0.D0
         ONE=1.0D0
C
C        THETA IS T(K) - TF  WHERE TF IS TEMP AT FACES AT T > 0
C        TH0 IS THETA AT T = 0
C        TH1 IS THETA AT Z = 0
C        TH2 IS THETA AT T = TWOL
C
         TH0=-50.0D0
         TH1=ZERO
         TH2=ZERO
         TF=303.D0
         WRITE(IO,2)
         WRITE(IO,4)TWOL,ALPHA,TH0,TH1,TH2
         WRITE(IO,9)TF


C             THE FOLLOWING ARE COMPUTED ONCE ONLY FOR EFFICIENCY
         A8=4.D0*TH0/PI
         WRITE(IO,5)
         WRITE(IO,7)ZERO,(TH0,I=1,7)
          DO 200 II=1,10
          TSEC=DFLOAT(II*64)
         DO 100 K=1,NZ
C                 FOURIER SERIES SOLUTION
         J=1
         JMAX=0
         IZERO=0
         KOUNT=0
         A1=-ALPHA*TSEC*(PI/TWOL)**2
         A6=PI*ZZ(K)/TWOL
         SUM=ZERO
         TERMJ1=FS(A1,A6,J)
         SUMT=TERMJ1
         SLAST=ZERO
C
C     SUM - SUMMATION OF TERMS OF SERIES
C     TERMJ1 - CONTINS 1ST TERM WITH SIGN
C     TERMJ - CALCULATIONS FOR J
C     SUMT - SUMMATION OF TERMS WITH SAME SIGN
C     SLAST - VALUE OF THE PREVIOUS SUMMATION
C
  40       J=J+2
         IF(J.GT.10000)GO TO 60
         TERMJ=FS(A1,A6,J)
         KOUNT=KOUNT+1
         IF(TERMJ)43,52,43
     43 IF(DABS(TERMJ)+DABS(TERMJ1)-DABS(TERMJ+TERMJ1))55,55,45
C            DIFFERENT SIGN - TEST FOR CONVERGENCE
C                (WHEN THE SUM OF TERMS OF LIKE SIGN BECOMES LESS
C                THAN EPS
  45       SUM=SUM+SLAST
         IF(DABS(SUMT)-EPS)60,50,50
C            NO CONVERGENCE
  50       SLAST=SUMT
         SUMT=TERMJ
         TERMJ1=TERMJ
         GO TO 40
```

FIGURE 13.13
(*Continued*)

```
C             TERMJ MAY BE ZERO THREE TIMES ONLY
   52 IZERO=IZERO+1
      IF(IZERO-3)43,45,45
C             SAME SIGN - ADD AND LOOP
   55    SUMT=SUMT+TERMJ
      IZERO=0
      GO TO 40
C             CONVERGENCE - BUILD THE SOLUTION
   60    THETA=A8*SUM
      TFOUR=THETA+TF
      IF(JMAX.LT.J)JMAX=J
C
C     LAPLACE TRANSFORM SOLUTION
C
      JMAX1=0
      DENOM=2.0D0*DSQRT(ALPHA*TSEC)
      Z=XL*DFLOAT(3-K)/3.D0
      ISIGN=1
C             J=0 TERM
      SUM=DERFC((XL-Z)/DENOM)+DERFC((XL+Z)/DENOM)
      J=0
   70 J=J+1
      X2J=DFLOAT(J+J)+ONE
      TERM=DERFC((X2J*XL-Z)/DENOM)+DERFC((X2J*XL+Z)/DENOM)
      IF(DABS(TERM)-EPS)90,75,75
C     IF(K.GT.50)GO TO 90
C             NO CONVERGENCE
   75 GO TO (80,85),ISIGN
C             SUBTRACT FOR ODD J
   80 SUM=SUM-TERM
      ISIGN=2
      GO TO 70
   85 SUM=SUM+TERM
      ISIGN=1
      GO TO 70

C             CONVERGENCE - THOTHO IS THETA DIVIDED BY THETA ZERO
   90 THOTHO=ONE-SUM
      TLAPL=TF+TH0*THOTHO
      IF(JMAX1.LT.J)JMAX1=J
      ANS(K)=THETA
      ANSL(K)=TH0*THOTHO
  100 CONTINUE
      ANS(4)=ANS(2)
      ANS(5)=ANS(1)
      ANSL(4)=ANSL(2)
      ANSL(5)=ANSL(1)
      WRITE(IO,7)TSEC,TH1,(ANS(I),I=1,5),TH2,JMAX
      WRITE(IO,7)TSEC,TH1,(ANSL(I),I=1,5),TH2,JMAX1
      WRITE(IO,8)
  200 CONTINUE
      WRITE(IO,6)
      STOP
      END
      FUNCTION FS(A,B,J)
      REAL*8 FS,A,B,XJ
      XJ=DFLOAT(J)
      FS=DSIN(B*XJ)/XJ*DEXP(A*XJ*XJ)
      RETURN
      END
      FUNCTION DERFC(X)
      IMPLICIT REAL*8(A-H,O-Z)
      DATA PI/3.1415926535897930/
      DATA TOL/0.5D-07/
      DATA IN,IC/5,6/
      DATA ZERO,ONE/0.0D0,1.0D0/
```

FIGURE 13.13
(*Continued*)

```
2         FORMAT(A)
3         FORMAT('0*** ERROR IN FUNCTION DERFC.'/
      1    1H0,5X,'ARGUMENT IS OUT OF BOUNDS: X =',E16.7/
      2    '0PRESS RETURN TO CONTINUE'/1H )

          IF(X)20,25,30
20        WRITE(IC,3)X
          READ(IN,2)I
23        DERFC=ZERO
          RETURN
25        DERFC=ONE
          RETURN
30        IF(X-4.) 32,32,23
32        IF(X-1.5) 35,35,40
35        DERFC=ONE-DERF(X)
          RETURN
40        X2=X*X
          K=12
          V=0.50/X2
          U=ONE+V*DFLOAT(K+1)
          J=13
          DO 50 I=1,K
          J=J-1
          S3=ONE+V*DFLOAT(J)/U
50        U=S3
          DERFC=DEXP(-X2)/(X*S3*DSQRT(PI))
          RETURN
          END
          FUNCTION DERF(X)
          IMPLICIT REAL*8(A-H,O-Z)
          DATA PI/3.1415926535897930/
          DATA TOL/0.5D-07/
          DATA IN,IC/5,6/
          DATA ZERO,ONE/0.0D0,1.0D0/
2         FORMAT(A)
3         FORMAT('0*** ERROR IN FUNCTION DERF.'/
      1    1H0,5X,'ARGUMENT IS OUT OF BOUNDS: X =',E16.7/
      2    '0PRESS RETURN TO CONTINUE'/1H )
          IF(X)20,25,30
20        WRITE(IC,3)X
          READ(IN,2)I
25        DERF=ZERO
          RETURN
30        IF(X-4.) 35,35,31
31        DERF=ONE
          RETURN
35        X2=X*X
          S3=X
          T4=X
          I=0
40        I=I+1
          H3=S3
          T4=T4*X2*2.0D0/DFLOAT(1+I+I)
          S3=T4+H3
          IF(T4-TOL*S3) 50,50,40
50        DERF=2.0D0*S3*DEXP(-X2)/DSQRT(PI)
          RETURN
          END
```

FIGURE 13.13
(*Continued*)

(b) Laplace transform. As indicated in Fig. 13.10, the boundary conditions in the form of Eq. (13.71) are required:

$$\Theta(x, 0) = \Theta_0 = -50 \text{ K} \qquad \Theta(L, t) = 0 \text{ K} \qquad \frac{\partial \Theta}{\partial x}(0, t) = 0 \qquad \text{(ix)}$$

The Laplace transform solution given in Eq. (13.82) applies:

$$\frac{\Theta}{\Theta_0} = \frac{T(x, t) - T_f}{T_0 - T_f}$$

$$= 1 - \sum_{j=0}^{\infty} (-1)^j \left[\text{erfc}\left(\frac{(2j+1)L - x}{2(\alpha t)^{1/2}}\right) + \text{erfc}\left(\frac{(2j+1)L + x}{2(\alpha t)^{1/2}}\right) \right] \qquad \text{(13.82)}$$

where x is now zero at the center of the slab (cf. Fig. 13.10). The computer program in Fig. 13.13 also computes the answer to this equation for this problem.

(c) Generalized chart. Using the definitions in Table 13.3, the following dimensionless groups are calculated:

$$X = \alpha t / L^2 = (4.057 \times 10^{-7})(640)/(0.0254)^2 = 0.04025$$
$$m = k/(hL) = 0 \qquad n = x/L = 1 \qquad \text{(x)}$$

From Fig. 13.11, the value of Y_c at the above values is 0.45. The temperature at the center plane is obtained using the definition of Y_c, Eq. (13.83):

$$Y_c = 0.45 = \frac{T_\infty - T_c}{T_\infty - T_0} = \frac{303 - T_c}{303 - 253} \qquad \text{(xi)}$$

$$T_c = 303 - (0.45)(50) = 280.5 \text{ K} \qquad \text{(xii)}$$

The answers from the computer program in Fig. 13.13 are

$$T_c \text{ (Fourier)} = 279.5 \text{ K} \qquad T_c \text{ (Laplace)} = 279.5 \text{ K} \qquad \text{(xiii)}$$

These compare well with the graphical solution.

Example 13.5. A jacketed agitation vessel is depicted in Fig. 9.1. Consider such a vessel of inside diameter 1.3 m, the outside of which is well insulated. The jacket wall is 1.3 cm thick and is made of steel with the following properties: density 7800 kg m^{-3}, heat capacity 435 J kg^{-1} K^{-1}, thermal conductivity 84 W m^{-1} K^{-1}, and thermal diffusivity 2.476×10^{-5} m^2 s^{-1}. The initial temperature of the steel is 300 K. At time zero,, hot oil at 400 K is pumped through the jacket. If the heat transfer coefficient is 600 W m^{-2} K^{-1}, calculate the time for the temperature at the steel–insulation interface to reach 380 K.

Answer. The Heisler charts will be used to solve this problem. The thickness of the jacket wall is 1.3 cm (0.013 m). Since the diameter of the jacket wall in the r direction exceeds 1.3 m, the ratio of these two numbers exceeds 100. Obviously, with such a thin wall it can be assumed that the cylindrical-shaped jacket wall can be approximated as a plane wall. In Table 13.3 and the accompanying figures, L is half the thickness of the slab when the same temperature is imposed on each face in the x direction of the slab. When one face is insulated, then L becomes

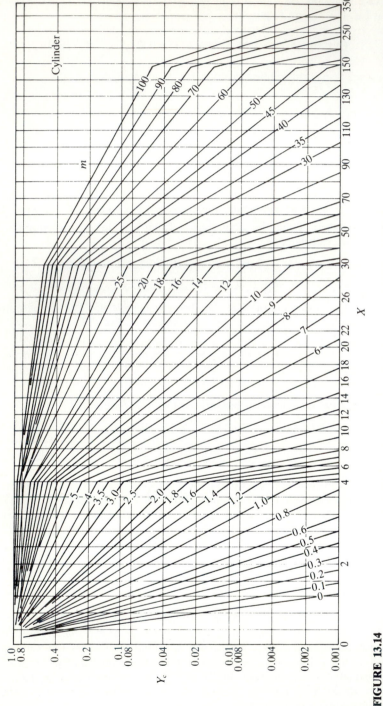

FIGURE 13.14

Temperature or concentration at the center axis of a long cylinder of radius L (or r_o). [*From Heisler, Trans. ASME* **69**: *227 (1947). By permission of ASME.*]

the thickness, as discussed previously:

$$L = 0.013 \text{ m} \tag{i}$$

Using the definitions in Table 13.3, the following dimensionless groups are calculated:

$$Y_c = \frac{T_\infty - T_c}{T_\infty - T_0} = \frac{400 - 380}{400 - 300} = 0.2 \tag{ii}$$

$$m = k/(hL) = (64)/[(600)(0.013)] = 8.205 \tag{iii}$$

$$n = x/L = 1 \tag{iv}$$

From Fig. 13.11 the value of X is 14.3. With the definition of the Fourier number, the time is

$$t = XL^2/\alpha = (14.3)(0.013)^2/(2.476 \times 10^{-5}) = 97.6 \text{ s} \tag{v}$$

Cylinders and spheres. Graphs are also available for solids with other geometries, such as cylinders and spheres [G4, H1]. Figures 13.14 and 13.15

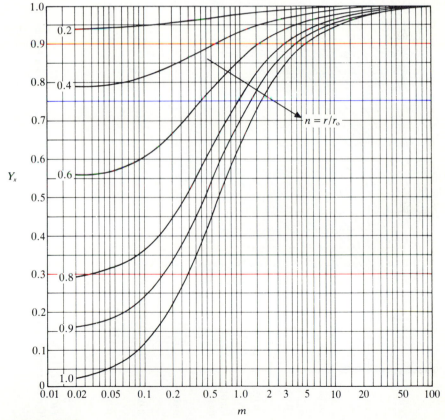

FIGURE 13.15

Position-correction chart for Figure 13.14 (cylinder). [*From Heisler, Trans. ASME* **69**: *227 (1947).
By permission of ASME.*]

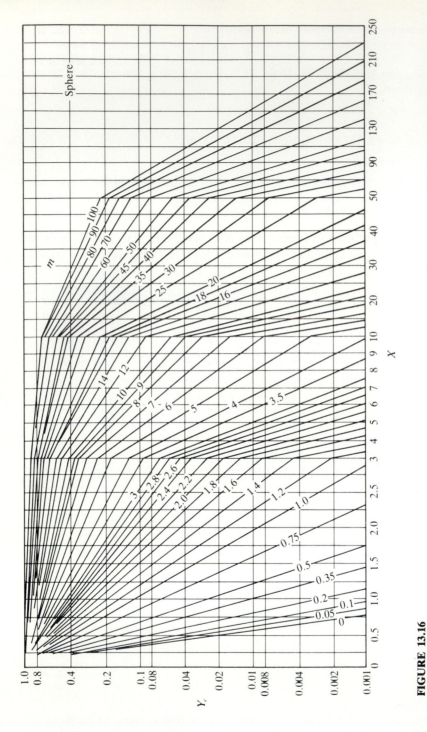

FIGURE 13.16

Temperature or concentration at the center of a sphere of radius r_0. [*From Heisler, Trans. ASME* **69:** *227 (1947). By permission of ASME.*]

are the corresponding figures for transient heat or mass transfer to (or from) a long cylinder. Here, it is assumed that the length in the z direction is large so that all heat transfer is in the r direction only. The characteristic length of such a cylinder is its radius, r_o; the value of r_o is used in place of L in the variables in Table 13.3. Figures 13.16 and 13.17 are for transient heat or mass transfer to (or from) a sphere.

Total heat transferred. If a mathematical expression, such as in Eq. (13.66), Eq. (xxiii) in Example 13.2, and Eq. (13.82), is available to relate T to x, then the instantaneous rate of heat transfer (at any time) can be calculated directly with Fourier's law:

$$(q/A)_x = -k(\partial T/\partial x) \tag{2.4}$$

where the partial derivative is evaluated analytically. The total heat Q is then

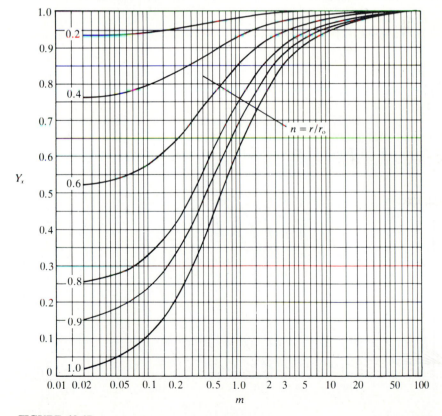

FIGURE 13.17
Position-correction chart for Figure 13.16 (sphere). [*From Heisler, Trans. ASME* **69**: *227 (1947).* *By permission of ASME.*]

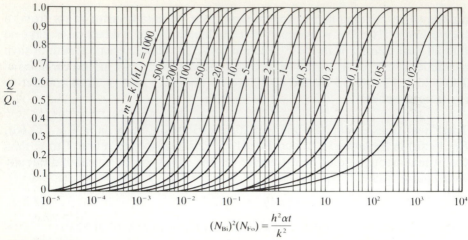

FIGURE 13.18
Dimensionless heat transfer for a slab of thickness 2L. (*From Grober, Erk, and Grigull, Fundamentals of Heat Transfer, p. 52, McGraw-Hill, New York, 1961. By permission.*)

found by integrating Eq. (2.4):

$$Q = \int_0^t q \, dt \tag{13.85}$$

These integrals are in the literature [C2, S1] for some simple boundary conditions.

Grober *et al.* [G3] prepared charts for the dimensionless heat transfer between solid and fluid for the cases in Figs. 13.11, 13.14, and 13.16. The charts are shown in Figs. 13.18 through 13.20, respectively. In these figures,

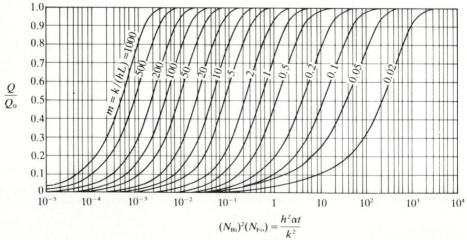

FIGURE 13.19
Dimensionless heat transfer for a long cylinder of radius L (or r_o). (*From Grober, Erk, and Grigull, Fundamentals of Heat Transfer, p. 56, McGraw-Hill, New York, 1961. By permission.*)

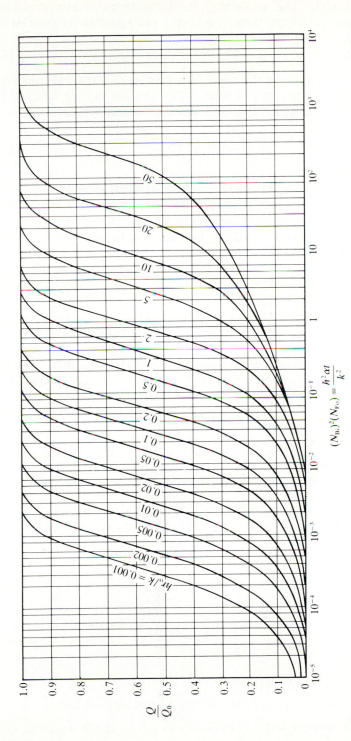

FIGURE 13.20

Dimensionless heat transfer for a sphere of radius r_o. Note $h r_o / k = 1/m$. (From Grober, Erk, and Grigull, *Fundamentals of Heat Transfer*, p. 60, McGraw-Hill, New York, 1961. By permission.)

the ordinate is Q/Q_0. The quantity Q_0 is the quantity of heat that can be transferred when the driving force is constant and equal to its greatest (i.e., initial) value:

$$Q_0 = \rho c_p V (T_0 - T_\infty) \qquad (13.86)$$

where V is the total volume of the solid. The quantity Q is the total quantity of heat transferred from time zero to time t. The abscissa in Figs. 13.18, 13.19, and 13.20 is the product of the Biot number squared times the Fourier number:

$$\frac{h^2 \alpha t}{k^2} = (N_{\text{Bi}})^2 (N_{\text{Fo}}) \qquad (13.87)$$

Unsteady-state transport in two- and three-dimensional systems. There are a few exact solutions to unsteady transport in multidimensional systems, as well as for geometries and boundary conditions more complex than have been discussed here [C2, C6, H3, I1, M2]. It is interesting to note that it is possible to solve some multidimensional problems by combining solutions from the preceding graphs or equations. The principle of superposition of solutions allows combination of one-dimensional solutions [N1]. This topic will be illustrated by the following example.

Example 13.6. A piece of banana 1.2 inches long and 1.0 inch in diameter is initially at room temperature, 295 K. The banana is placed in a convection oven that has been preheated to 400 K. Calculate the temperature at the center after 1.2 s if the heat transfer coefficient is $20 \text{ W m}^{-2} \text{K}^{-1}$. The following data for banana are available [I1]: density 980 kg m^{-3}, thermal conductivity $0.481 \text{ W m}^{-1} \text{K}^{-1}$, heat capacity $3.35 \text{ J kg}^{-1} \text{K}^{-1}$, and thermal diffusivity $1.465 \times 10^{-4} \text{ m}^2 \text{s}^{-1}$.

Answer. This cylindrically-shaped object is much too short to assume that heat transfer is in either the radial or the axial direction exclusively. It is more likely that each direction contributes more or less equally to the heating of the center. Therefore, it is necessary to use superposition.

Let the subscript r be introduced to designate transient heat transfer in the r direction, while the subscript z hereafter refers to the axial direction. Using the definitions in Table 13.3:

$$L_r = d_o/2 = 0.5 \text{ in.} = 0.0127 \text{ m}$$
$$L_z = 1.2/2 = 0.6 \text{ in.} = 0.01524 \text{ m}$$
$$m_r = k/(hL_r) = (0.481)/[(20)(0.0127)] = 1.894$$
$$m_z = k/(hL_z) = (0.481)/[(20)(0.01524)] = 1.578 \qquad \text{(i)}$$
$$n_r = r/L_r = 1$$
$$n_z = x/L_z = 1$$
$$X_r = \alpha t/L_r^2 = (1.454 \times 10^{-4})(1.2)/(0.0127)^2 = 1.090$$
$$X_z = \alpha t/L_z^2 = (1.454 \times 10^{-4})(1.2)/(0.01524)^2 = 0.7569$$

The value (hereafter called $Y_{c,r}$) for the above m_r, n_r, and X_r using Fig. 13.14 is

0.42. Similarly, the value for $Y_{c,z}$ from Fig. 13.11 is 0.70. Note that the charts are hard to read accurately. According to the principle of superposition, the value of Y_c is given by

$$Y_c = Y_{c,r} Y_{c,z} = (0.42)(0.75) = 0.294 \qquad \text{(ii)}$$

Using the definition of Y_c from Eq. (13.83), the temperature at the center is

$$T_c = T_\infty - Y_c(T_\infty - T_0) = 400 - (0.294)(400 - 295) = 369 \text{ K} \qquad \text{(iii)}$$

13.2.4 Numerical Solution

The solution to unsteady transport phenomena by the previous methods is limited to those problems in which the boundary conditions are relatively simple. In this section, the modern approach will be presented, i.e., numerical solutions using a digital computer.

The approach is to approximate the partial differential equation by finite differences. The slope is related to the derivative as follows:

$$\text{SLOPE} = \frac{\text{RISE}}{\text{RUN}} = \frac{dT}{dx} \qquad (13.88)$$

Let the "RUN" in the x direction be Δx and in the t-direction be Δt:

$$\Delta x = x_{i+1} - x_i \qquad (13.89)$$
$$\Delta t = t_{j+1} - t_j \qquad (13.90)$$

The transient heat equation for one direction is

$$\frac{\partial^2 T}{\partial x^2} = \frac{1}{\alpha} \frac{\partial T}{\partial t} \qquad (13.6)$$

Let the quantity $T(x_i, t_j)$ be the temperature at location x_i and time t_j.

Explicit method. Experience has shown that the best choice for a second-order differential is the central difference formula

$$\left. \frac{\partial^2 T}{\partial x^2} \right|_{x=x_i, \, t=t_j} = \frac{T(x_{i+1}, t_j) - 2T(x_i, t_j) + T(x_{i-1}, t_j)}{\Delta x^2} + O(\Delta x^2) \qquad (13.91)$$

where the term $O(\Delta x^2)$ denotes that the truncation error is of the order of the square of Δx. A simple choice for the first-order derivative is the forward difference equation:

$$\left. \frac{\partial T}{\partial t} \right|_{x=x_i, \, t=t_j} = \frac{T(x_i, t_{j+1}) - T(x_i, t_j)}{\Delta t} + O(\Delta t) \qquad (13.92)$$

where the truncation error is of the order of Δt. Equations (13.91) and (13.92) can be used to approximate the derivatives in Eq. (13.6):

$$\frac{T(x_{i+1}, t_j) - 2T(x_i, t_j) + T(x_{i-1}, t_j)}{\Delta x^2} = \frac{1}{\alpha} \frac{T(x_i, t_{j+1}) - T(x_i, t_j)}{\Delta t} \qquad (13.93)$$

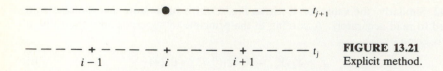

FIGURE 13.21
Explicit method.

Thus, the partial differential equation has been replaced with a finite difference equation, Eq. (13.93), which may be solved for $T(x_i, t_{j+1})$:

$$T(x_i, t_{j+1}) = \beta T(x_{i+1}, t_j) + (1 - 2\beta)T(x_i, t_j) + \beta T(x_{i-1}, t_j) \qquad (13.94)$$

where the quantity β is given by

$$\beta = \alpha \, \Delta t/(\Delta x)^2 \qquad (13.95)$$

The quantity β is related to X, used in the charts, and to the Fourier number, given in Table 8.1.

This method of computation, as performed using Eqs. (13.94) and (13.95), is called the "explicit" method, because each unknown point $T(x_i, t_{j+1})$ is computed directly from the three adjacent points in the t_j row, as shown in Fig. 13.21. Sometimes, each interior point $T(x_j, t_{j+1})$ is called an "interior node". It is easy to apply the explicit method to any set of boundary conditions. However, for certain values of β, the finite difference solution may become unstable, i.e., the solution may oscillate or even become unreasonable and not converge to the true solution. The criterion of stability is [K1, R2]

$$\beta \le 0.5 \qquad (13.96)$$

In practice, this equation constitutes a serious limitation of the explicit method. Usually, a value of Δx is chosen from geometrical or other practical considerations. Then Eq. (13.96) is used to compute the maximum value of Δt so that Eq. (13.96) is satisfied.

Insulated boundary. Consider the boundary conditions illustrated in Fig. 13.10(b):

$$\Theta(x, 0) = \Theta_0 \qquad \Theta(L, t) = 0 \qquad \frac{\partial \Theta}{\partial x}(0, t) = 0 \qquad (13.71)$$

It is possible to transform these boundary conditions to those of Eq. (13.35) [cf. Fig. 13.10(a)], but that would effectively double the amount of calculation required. A better approach is to force the derivative of Θ with respect to x to be zero at the insulated boundary through use of the central finite difference formula:

$$\left. \frac{\partial T}{\partial x} \right|_{x=x_N, \, t=t_j} = \frac{T(x_{N+1}, t_j) - T(x_{N-1}, t_j)}{\Delta x} \qquad (13.97)$$

where the insulated boundary is assumed to be at the node $(i = N)$. The

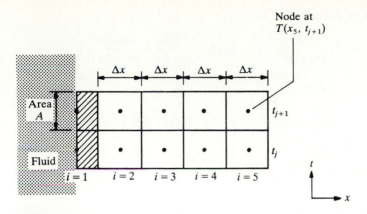

FIGURE 13.22
Surface node for a convection boundary condition.

derivative $\partial T/\partial x$ is zero if

$$T(x_{N+1}) = T(x_{N-1}) \tag{13.98}$$

This result is used in Eq. (13.94) to compute the temperature at the insulated boundary:

$$T(x_i, t_{j+1}) = 2\beta T(x_{N-1}, t_j) + (1 - 2\beta)T(x_N, t_j) \tag{13.99}$$

Convection boundary condition. Consider a solid body of which one or both faces are subjected to a fluid with heat transfer coefficient h, as shown in Fig. 13.22. Let the temperature at the boundary correspond to the location x_1, since some computing languages do not allow a zero subscript. The convection boundary condition is introduced into the finite difference solution by making an energy balance on the node at the surface. Let the thickness of this node be $(\Delta x/2)$ and the area A; thus, the volume becomes $(A\Delta x/2)$. Energy enters this node by convection, leaves by conduction, and is also accumulated:

$$\text{INPUT} = hA[T_\infty - T(x_1, t_j)]$$

$$\text{OUTPUT} = -kA\,\frac{T(x_2, t_j) - T(x_1, t_j)}{\Delta x}$$

$$\text{ACCUMULATION} = \rho c_p A\,\frac{\Delta x}{2}\,\frac{T(x_1, t_{j+1}) - T(x_1, t_j)}{\Delta t} \tag{13.100}$$

These terms are combined according to the law of the conservation of energy [cf. Eq. (3.1)]:

$$hA[T_\infty - T(x_1, t_j)]$$
$$= -kA\,\frac{T(x_2, t_j) - T(x_1, t_j)}{\Delta x} + \rho c_p A\left(\frac{\Delta x}{2}\right)\frac{T(x_1, t_{j+1}) - T(x_1, t_j)}{\Delta t} \tag{13.101}$$

This expression can be solved for $T(x_1, t_{j+1})$:

$$T(x_1, t_{j+1}) = T_\infty \frac{2h\,\Delta t}{\rho c_p\,\Delta x} + T(x_1, t_j)\left(1 - \frac{2h\,\Delta t}{\rho c_p\,\Delta x} - \frac{2k\,\Delta t}{\rho c_p(\Delta x)^2}\right)$$

$$+ T(x_2, t_j)\frac{2k\,\Delta t}{\rho c_p\,(\Delta x)^2} \tag{13.102}$$

Equation (13.102) is incorporated into the finite difference solution as required.

Mass transfer. The mass transfer equation for an impervious boundary follows from Eq. (13.99):

$$C_A(x_i, t_{j+1}) = 2\beta C_A(x_{N-1}, t_j) + (1 - 2\beta)C_A(x_N, t_j) \tag{13.103}$$

$$\beta = D\,\Delta t/(\Delta x)^2 \tag{13.104}$$

For a convection boundary condition, the mass balance terms are

$$\text{INPUT} = k_c A[C_{A,\infty} - C_A(x_1, t_j)]$$

$$\text{OUTPUT} = -DA\,\frac{C_A(x_2, t_j) - C_A(x_1, t_j)}{\Delta x} \tag{13.105}$$

$$\text{ACCUMULATION} = \frac{A\,\Delta x}{2}\frac{C_A(x_1, t_{j+1}) - C_A(x_1, t_j)}{\Delta t}$$

These are combined according to Eq. (3.1):

$$C_A(x_1, t_{j+1}) = C_{A,\infty}\frac{2k_c\,\Delta t}{\Delta x} + C_A(x_1, t_j)\left(1 - \frac{2k_c\,\Delta t}{\Delta x} - \frac{2D\,\Delta t}{(\Delta x)^2}\right)$$

$$+ C_A(x_2, t_j)\frac{2D\,\Delta t}{(\Delta x)^2} \tag{13.106}$$

The following example illustrates the explicit method for a heat transfer problem. The mass transfer problem is exactly analogous.

Example 13.7. Consider the agitation vessel in Example 13.5. Divide the thickness into 10 increments and perform two iterations of the explicit method.

Answer. From Example 13.5, the following are obtained:

$$T(x, 0) = 300 \text{ K}$$
$$T_\infty = 400 \text{ K}$$
$$L = 0.013 \text{ m} \tag{i}$$
$$\alpha = 2.476 \times 10^{-5}\,\text{m}^2\,\text{s}^{-1}$$
$$h = 600\,\text{W m}^{-2}\,\text{K}^{-1}$$
$$\rho c_p = (7800)(435) = 3.393 \times 10^6\,\text{J m}^{-3}\,\text{K}^{-1}$$

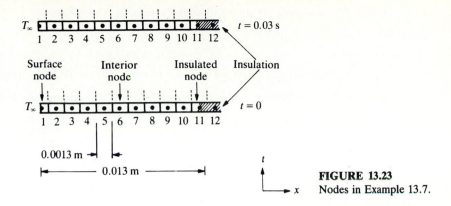

FIGURE 13.23
Nodes in Example 13.7.

Figure 13.23 shows the tank wall with the fluid located at $x = 0$ and the insulation at $x = L$, in order for the notation in Eq. (13.102) to apply. The problem statement specifies Δx:

$$\Delta x = L/10 = 0.0013 \text{ m} \tag{ii}$$

The time increment Δt is calculated with the aid of the criterion of Eq. (13.96), i.e., β must be less than $\frac{1}{2}$. Equation (13.95) yields, for $\beta = 0.5$:

$$\Delta t = \beta (\Delta x)^2 / \alpha = (0.5)(0.0013)^2 / (2.476 \times 10^{-5}) = 0.03413 \text{ s} \tag{iii}$$

To be sure that the solution is stable, it is customary to truncate this number:

$$\Delta t = 0.03 \text{ s} \tag{iv}$$

With the temperature increment thus reduced, the actual value of β to be used is

$$\beta = \alpha \, \Delta t / (\Delta x)^2 = (2.476 \times 10^{-5})(0.03)/(0.0013)^2 \, [(\text{m}^2 \text{ s}^{-1})(\text{s})/(\text{m}^2)] = 0.4395 \tag{v}$$

Note that a total of 12 nodes, including the half-node at the convection boundary are required, as shown in Fig. 13.23. The surface node (labeled 1) is calculated using Eq. (13.102):

$$T(x_1, t_{j+1}) = T_\infty \frac{2h \, \Delta t}{\rho c_p \, \Delta x} + T(x_1, t_j)\left(1 - \frac{2h \, \Delta t}{\rho c_p \, \Delta x} - \frac{2k \, \Delta t}{\rho c_p (\Delta x)^2}\right)$$

$$+ T(x_2, t_j) \frac{2k \, \Delta t}{\rho c_p (\Delta x)^2} \tag{13.102}$$

where

$$\frac{2h \, \Delta t}{\rho c_p \, \Delta x} = \frac{(2)(600)(0.03)}{(3.393 \times 10^6)(0.0013)} \left(\frac{(\text{J s}^{-1} \text{ m}^{-2} \text{ K}^{-1})(\text{s})}{(\text{J m}^{-3} \text{ K}^{-1})(\text{m})}\right) = 0.08162 \tag{vi}$$

$$\frac{2k \, \Delta t}{\rho c_p (\Delta x)^2} = \frac{(2)(2.476 \times 10^{-5})(0.03)}{(0.0013)^2} \left(\frac{(\text{m}^2 \text{ s}^{-1})(\text{s})}{\text{m}^2}\right) = 0.8791 \tag{vii}$$

A computer program for the explicit method requires only two dimensioned variables, TOLD(12) and TNEW(12). At time zero, all values of TOLD in this problem are equal to the initial temperature, 300 K. The value of T_∞ plus

Eqs. (13.102), (vi), and (vii) are used to find the values for TNEW(1):

$$TNEW(1) = (400)(0.08162) + TOLD(1)(1 - 0.08162 - 0.8791)$$
$$+ TOLD(2)(0.8791)$$
$$= (400)(0.08162) + (300)(0.03933) + (300)(0.8791) = 308.16 \text{ K} \quad \text{(viii)}$$

The temperatures at the interior nodes (2 through 10) are computed using Eq. (13.94):

$$T(x_i, t_{j+1}) = \beta T(x_{i+1}, t_j) + (1 - 2\beta)T(x_i, t_j) + \beta T(x_{i-1}, t_j) \quad (13.94)$$

In terms of TOLD and TNEW, this equation becomes

$$TNEW(I) = \beta TOLD(I + 1) + (1 - 2\beta)TOLD(I) + \beta TOLD(I - 1) \quad 2 \le I \le 10$$
$$\text{(ix)}$$

A consideration of Eq. (ix) demonstrates a serious deficiency of the explicit method. Since all values of TOLD(I) in the range $(2 \le I \le 10)$ are initially the same and equal to 300 K, the values of TNEW(I) calculated from Eq. (ix) are also 300 K; in other words, only TNEW(1) has changed value on the first time increment.

The node at the boundary of the insulation is calculated using Eq. (13.98), which in terms of TOLD is

$$TOLD(N + 1) = TOLD(N - 1) \quad \text{(x)}$$

where N in this example equals 11. Using Eq. (x), Eq. (ix) becomes

$$TNEW(N) = (2\beta)TOLD(N - 1) + (1 - 2\beta)TOLD(N)$$
$$TNEW(11) = (2\beta)TOLD(10) = (1 - 2\beta)TOLD(11)$$
$$\text{(xi)}$$

Since both TOLD(10) and TOLD(11) equal 300 K for the first time step, TNEW(11) also equals 300 K. In summary, the first time step in the explicit method changes only the temperature next to any uninsulated boundary.

For the second time step, a computer program transfers all the newly computed values of TNEW(I) to TOLD(I) and then repeats the above calculation:

$$TNEW(1) = (400)(0.08162) + TOLD(1)(1 - 0.08162 - 0.8791)$$
$$+ TOLD(2)(0.8791)$$
$$= (400)(0.08162) + (308.16)(0.03933) + (300)(0.8791) = 308.48 \text{ K} \quad \text{(xii)}$$

From Eq. (ix), the interior nodes are

$$TNEW(2) = \beta TOLD(3) + (1 - 2\beta)TOLD(2) + \beta TOLD(1)$$
$$= (0.4395)(300 + 308.16) + [1 - (2)(0.4395)](300) = 303.59 \text{ K} \quad \text{(xiii)}$$
$$TNEW(I) = \beta TOLD(I + 1) + (1 - 2\beta)TOLD(I) + \beta TOLD(I - 1) = 300 \text{ K}$$
$$3 \le I \le 10$$

From Eq. (xi) the insulated boundary node is

$$TNEW(11) = (2\beta)TOLD(10) = (1 - 2\beta)TOLD(11) = 300 \text{ K} \quad \text{(xiv)}$$

A complete computer program to perform this calculation for an arbitrary set of time and space increments is very easy and is left as a homework problem.

Crank–Nicolson method. The shortcomings of the explicit method were obvious in the previous example. Changes in the interior nodes come only after many steps in time; information at the boundary at t_{j+1} is not used to calculate any of the points at time t_{j+1}. A better numerical method involves using a second derivative that is spaced half-way between t_j and t_{j+1}. The Crank–Nicolson method [C5] computes the space derivative as the mean of the derivative at t_j and that at t_{j+1}. After completing the algebra, the finite difference equation becomes

$$(\beta/2)T(x_{i-1}, t_{j+1}) - (\beta + 1)T(x_i, t_{j+1}) + (\beta/2)T(x_{i+1}, t_{j+1})$$
$$= (\beta/2)T(x_{i-1}, t_j) - (\beta + 1)t(x_i, t_j) + (\beta/2)t(x_{i+1}, t_j) \quad (13.107)$$

This equation for the Crank–Nicolson scheme is to be compared with Eq. (13.94) for the explicit method. Equation (13.94) expresses a single node at time t_{j+1} in terms of three closely located nodes at t_j, whereas Eq. (13.107) expresses three nodes at time t_{j+1} in terms of three nodes at t_j. Hence, the use of Eq. (13.107) requires that a system of equations be solved at every time step. The choice of the intervals Δx and Δt is restricted for stability [K1, R2] by

$$\beta \le 1 \quad (13.108)$$

Note that this criterion allows increments in time twice as large for fixed α and Δx as does the explicit method. The ability to use twice the time interval enables the Crank–Nicolson method to execute a solution more rapidly than the explicit method. The programming of Crank–Nicolson requires more steps, but is still very simple. The approximation of the derivative $\partial^2 T/\partial x^2$ in the Crank–Nicolson method results in the lowest truncation error possible [F1]. The following example problem illustrates the ease of computation of the Crank–Nicolson scheme. Note that the system of equations formed by Eq. (13.107) is tridiagonal in nature and hence easily solved by standard numerical algorithms [W1]. The convection and insulated boundary conditions are handled just as in the explicit case.

Example 13.8. Find the temperature distribution in a bar of iron (insulated on all surfaces except both ends) after 50 h if the initial temperature distribution is given by

$$T(x, 0) = 500 - 4x - 4x^2 \quad (i)$$

where T is in K and x is in m. Let the bar be 4 m long. After the temperature distribution has been fully established, the temperature at each exposed face is instantaneously lowered to 400 K and maintained constant at that value. For iron, $\rho = 7870 \text{ kg m}^{-3}$, $c_p = 447 \text{ J kg}^{-1}\text{K}^{-1}$, $k = 80 \text{ W m}^{-1}\text{K}^{-1}$, and $\alpha = 2.274 \times 10^{-5} \text{ m}^2\text{s}^{-1}$.

Answer. Let the space increment Δx be 0.1 m. If the time increment is arbitrarily selected to be 120 s, then β is

$$\beta = \alpha \, \Delta t / (\Delta x)^2 = (2.274 \times 10^{-5})(120)/(0.1)^2 = 0.2729 \qquad \text{(ii)}$$

This value is well within the stability limit imposed by Eq. (13.108).

The first step in the solution of this problem is to form the tridiagonal system of equations. Let a one-dimensioned variable in a computer program be called a vector. The following notation will be used to avoid any two-dimensioned computer variables: the vector U contains the temperatures at time t_{j+1} (unknown, except at the boundary); the vector T contains the temperatures at time t_j (all known); the vector R contains the main diagonal; the vector C contains the upper diagonal; the vector A contains the lower diagonal; the vector D contains the constants; and N is the number of unknowns and the number of simultaneous equations to be solved. For illustration, suppose that N equals 5, and the unknowns are U(1) through U(5). Then the tridiagonal system of equations is

$$R(1)U(1) + C(1)U(2) + 0 + 0 + 0 = D(1)$$
$$A(2)U(1) + R(2)U(2) + C(2)U(3) + 0 + 0 = D(2)$$
$$0 + A(3)U(2) + R(3)U(3) + C(3)U(4) + 0 = D(3) \qquad \text{(iii)}$$
$$0 + 0 + A(4)U(3) + R(4)U(4) + C(4)U(5) = D(4)$$
$$0 + 0 + 0 + A(5)U(4) + R(5)U(5) = D(5)$$

The tridiagonal nature of the above system of equations is evident. When N is large, the representation of Eq. (iii) by four vectors eliminates the need to store all the zero elements that are present.

In Eq. (13.107), the t_j temperatures are all known at each step in time. There are N unknown temperatures at time t_{j+1}, plus the two known boundary conditions:

$$U(1) = U(N + 2) = 400 \text{ K} \qquad \text{(iv)}$$
$$N = (\text{LENGTH OF BAR})/(\Delta x) - 1 = 4.0/0.1 - 1 = 39 \qquad \text{(v)}$$
$$N1 = N + 1 \qquad \text{(vi)}$$
$$N2 = N + 2 \qquad \text{(vii)}$$
$$T(1) = T(N2) = 400 \text{ K} \qquad \text{(viii)}$$

The vector U now consists of the N unknown temperatures, plus the two above boundary conditions (total length N2). For the first time step ($J = 1$), and in all subsequent time steps, U(1) and U(N2) are considered to be equal to 400 K. Let the index I go from 2 to (N2). Then the first unknown is U(2). The Crank–Nicolson formula is Eq. (13.107):

$$(\beta/2)T(x_{i-1}, t_{j+1}) - (\beta + 1)T(x_i, t_{j+1}) + (\beta/2)T(x_{i+1}, t_{j+1})$$
$$= (\beta/2)T(x_{i-1}, t_j) - (\beta + 1)T(x_i, t_j) + (\beta/2)T(x_{i+1}, t_j) \quad \text{(13.107)}$$

which in terms of the computer variables T and U is

$$[\beta/2][U(I - 1)] - [\beta + 1][U(I)] + [\beta/2][U(I + 1)]$$
$$= [\beta/2][T(I - 1)] - [\beta + 1][T(I)] + [\beta/2][T(I + 1)] \quad \text{(ix)}$$

For I = 2, Eq. (ix) becomes

$$-[\beta + 1][U(2)] + [\beta/2][U(3)] = [\beta/2][T(1)] - [\beta + 1][T(2)]$$
$$+ [\beta/2][T(3)] - [\beta/2][U(1)] \qquad \text{(x)}$$

In terms of the vectors U, R, C, and D, Eq. (x) is

$$R(1)U(2) + C(1)U(3) = D(1) \qquad \text{(xi)}$$

For I = 3, Eq. (ix) becomes

$$[\beta/2][U(2)] - [\beta + 1][U(3)] + [\beta/2][U(4)]$$
$$= [\beta/2][T(2)] - [\beta + 1][T(3)] + [\beta/2][T(4)] \quad \text{(xii)}$$

This equation in terms of the computer variables is

$$A(2)U(2) + R(2)U(3) + C(2)U(4) = D(2) \qquad \text{(xiii)}$$

Equation (xiii) is easily generalized for the range $3 \le I \le N$:

$$A(I-1)U(I) + R(I-1)U(I+1) + C(I-1)U(I+2) = D(I-1) \qquad (3 \le I \le N)$$
$$\text{(xiv)}$$

The last equation is for I = N1:

$$[\beta/2][U(N1-1)] - [\beta + 1][U(N1)] = [\beta/2][T(N1-1)] - [\beta + 1][T(N1)]$$
$$+ [\beta/2][T(N2)] - [\beta/2][U(N2)] \quad \text{(xv)}$$

or in terms of the computer variables:

$$A(N)U(N1-1) + R(N)U(N1) = D(N) \qquad \text{(xvi)}$$

The system of equations is now complete; the notation now allows a concise formulation of the solution:

$$\begin{aligned} A(I) &= \beta/2 & (2 \le I \le N) \\ R(I) &= -(\beta + 1) & (1 \le I \le N) \qquad \text{(xvii)} \\ C(I) &= \beta/2 & (1 \le I \le N1) \end{aligned}$$

Note that the values of A(I), R(I), and C(I) do not change with each time step. An efficient computer program takes advantage of this fact. The values of D(I) do change, however:

$$\begin{aligned} D(1) &= [\beta/2][T(1) + T(3) - U(1)] - [\beta + 1][T(2)] \\ D(N) &= [\beta/2][T(N1-1) + T(N2) - U(N2)] - [\beta + 1][T(N1)] \qquad \text{(xviii)} \\ D(I) &= [\beta/2][T(I) + T(I+2)] - [\beta + 1][T(I+1)] \qquad (3 \le I \le N-1) \end{aligned}$$

The final program using these equations is shown in Fig. 13.24. The subroutine TRIDG2 is used to solve the system of N equations at each time step. Since TRIDG2 does not alter the numbers stored in A, R, and C, it is necessary to compute these only once. After 50 hours, the temperature at the center of the bar has dropped from its initial value of 476 K to 407.4 K. Figure 13.25 shows the temperature of the center of the bar as a function of time.

```
C
C    SOLUTION OF UNSTEADY-STATE HEAT TRANSFER PROBLEM BY FINITE
C      DIFFERENCES USING THE CRANK-NICHOLSON METHOD
C
     IMPLICIT REAL*8(A-H,O-Z)
     DIMENSION U(41),A(39),R(39),C(38),D(39),XL(41)
   2 FORMAT('0EXAMPLE 13-8 - SOLUTION OF AN UNSTEADY-STATE HEAT'
   1 ' HEAT TRANSFER PROBLEM USING THE CRANK-NICHOLSON APPROACH')
   3 FORMAT(11H1END OF JOB)
   4 FORMAT(40H0THE NUMBER OF UNKNOWNS ALONG THE BAR IS,I10)
   5 FORMAT(40H0THE NUMBER OF TIME STEPS TO BE TAKEN IS,I10)
   6 FORMAT('0THE THERMAL DIFFUSIVITY(SQ M/S) IS',E18.8)
   7 FORMAT(21H0THE VALUE OF BETA IS,E18.8,10X41HBETA MUST BE LESS THAN
   1 ONE FOR STABILITY.)
   8 FORMAT(1H0/10H0AT TIME =,F6.1,' HOURS, THE TEMPERATURE DISTRI',
   1 'BUTION IS'/1H0,10X,9HLENGTH(M),11X,14HTEMPERATURE(K))
   9 FORMAT(F19.5,F23.3)
  10 FORMAT('0THE SPACE INCREMENT (DELTA X) IN M, EQ. (13-89), IS'
   1 ,E18.8/
   2 '0THE TIME INCREMENT (DELTA T) IN S, EQ. (13-90), IS',E18.8)
C
C    H     - SPACE INCREMENT (DELTA X) IN M, EQ. (13-89)
C    XK    - TIME INCREMENT (DELTA T) IN S, EQ. (13-90)
C    ALPHA - THERMAL DIFFUSIVITY IN SQ M/S
C    BAR   - LENGTH OF BAR IN M
C    FIN   - LENGTH OF TIME TO BE COMPUTED IN S
C    N     - NUMBER OF UNKNOWN TEMPERATURES ALONG THE BAR
C    NT    - NUMBER OF TIME STEPS
C    BETA  - EQ. (13-95)
C
     IO=7
     ZERO=0.0D0
     ONE=1.0D0
     H=0.1D0
     XK=120.D0
     ALPHA=2.274D-05
     BAR=4.D0
     FIN=50.0D0*3600.D0
     TIME=ZERO
     TBOUND=400.D0
     N=(BAR/H)*1.0001
     N=N-1
     NT=(FIN/XK)*1.0001
     WRITE(IO,2)
     WRITE(IO,10)H,XK
     WRITE(IO,4)N
     WRITE(IO,5)NT
     WRITE(IO,6)ALPHA
     BETA=ALPHA*XK/(H*H)
     WRITE(IO,7)BETA
     A1=BETA*0.5D0
     A2=-BETA-ONE
     A3=BETA-ONE
     N1=N+1
     N2=N+2

     IPRNT=N1/4
     JPRNT=60
C
C    THE BOUNDARY CONDITIONS AT X=0 AND X=L FOR ALL TIME
C
     U(1)=TBOUND
     XL(1)=ZERO
     U(N2)=TBOUND
     WRITE(IO,8)TIME
C
C    BOUNDARY CONDITIONS AT TIME EQUAL ZERO
```

FIGURE 13.24
FORTRAN program using the Crank–Nicolson method—Example 13.8.

```
C
         DO 20 I=2,N1
         XL(I)=H*FLOAT(I-1)
      20 U(I)=500.D0-4.D0*XL(I)*(ONE+XL(I))
         XL(N2)=BAR
         WRITE(IO,9)(XL(I),U(I),I=1,N2,IPRNT)
C
C        SET UP THE THREE DIAGONALS FOR SUBROUTINE TRIDG2
C
         R(1)=A2
         C(1)=A1
         DO 26 I=2,N
         A(I)=A1
         C(I)=A1
      26 R(I)=A2
C
C        THE D VECTOR. FIRST THE J-TH ROW ELEMENTS
C
         DO 30 I=1,N
      30 D(I)=A3*U(I+1)-A1*(U(I)+U(I+2))
         ISTEP=0
         IMOD=1
      38 ISTEP=ISTEP+1
C
C        THE FINAL D VECTOR REQUIRES TWO TERMS FROM J+1 ROW. THESE ARE
C           SHOWN FOR COMPLETENESS EVEN THOUGH THEY ARE ZERO FOR THIS
C           PARTICULAR PROBLEM.
C
         D(1)=D(1)-A1*U(1)
         D(N)=D(N)-A1*U(N2)
         CALL TRIDG2(A,R,C,D,U,N)
         IF(IMOD-JPRNT) 45,42,42
      42 IMOD=0
         THOUR=TIME+XK*DFLOAT(ISTEP)/3600.D0
         WRITE(IO,8)THOUR
         DO 44 I=1,N2,IPRNT
      44 WRITE(IO,9)XL(I),U(I)
      45 IMOD=IMOD+1
         IF(ISTEP-NT)46,50,50
C
C        REINITIALIZE D VECTOR FOR NEXT TIME STEP. NOTE THAT A,R, AND C ARE
C           NOT ALTERED BY TRIDG2 AND THUS DO NOT NEED TO BE RESET.
C
      46 DO 47 I=1,N
      47 D(I)=A3*U(I+1)-A1*(U(I)+U(I+2))
         GO TO 38
      50 CONTINUE
         WRITE(IO,3)
         CALL EXIT
         END
C ......................SUBROUTINE TRIDG2......................
C
C DESCRIPTION - FINDS THE SOLUTION OF A SYSTEM OF LINEAR EQUATIONS BY=D
C               WHOSE COEFFICIENT MATRIX B IS TRIDIAGONAL
C               THE NOMENCLATURE IS EXPLAINED IN EXAMPLE 13-8
C
C CALLING PARAMETERS
C   A      - VECTOR CONTAINING N-1 ELEMENTS OF THE BAND BELOW THE MAIN
C               DIAGONAL. A(1) IS NOT USED, AS THE BAND IS STORED IN A(2)
C               TO A(N). THE CONTENTS OF A ARE UNCHANGED BY TRIDG2.
C   R      - VECTOR CONTAINING MAIN DIAGONAL IN R(1) TO R(N). THE
C               CONTENTS OF R ARE UNCHANGED BY  0jTRIDG2.
C   C      - VECTOR CONTAINING N-1 ELEMENTS OF THE BAND ABOVE THE MAIN
C               DIAGONAL. THE BAND IS STORED IN C(1) TO C(N-1). THE CONTENTS
C               OF C ARE UNCHANGED BY TRIDG2.
C   D      - VECTOR REPRESENTING THE PRODUCT OF B TIMES Y. THE CONTENTS
C               OF D ARE DESTROYED BY TRIDG2.
```

FIGURE 13.24
(*Continued*)

```
C    Y       - SOLUTION VECTOR.
C
      SUBROUTINE TRIDG2 (A,R,C,D,Y,N)
      IMPLICIT REAL*8(A-H,O-Z)
      DIMENSION A(1),R(1),C(1),D(1),Y(1)
      DATA ONE/1.0D0/
      NC=N+1
      NA=NC-2
      Y(2)=D(1)/R(1)
      D(1)=-C(1)/R(1)
      DO 9042 I=2,NA
      AA=ONE/(R(I)+A(I)*D(I-1))
      Y(I+1)=(D(I)-A(I)*Y(I))*AA
      D(I)=-C(I)*AA
 9042 CONTINUE
      Y(NC)=(D(N)-A(N)*Y(N))/(R(N)+A(N)*D(NA))
      DO 9046 I=1,NA
      IJ=NC-I
 9046 Y(IJ)=D(IJ-1)*Y(IJ+1)+Y(IJ)
      RETURN
      END
```

FIGURE 13.24
(*Continued*)

13.3 OTHER GEOMETRIES

Other geometries, such as the cylinder and the sphere, have been briefly mentioned previously in Section 13.2, where it was convenient to present the various charts together. Remember that those charts are based on actual solutions of Eq. (13.2) for the specific geometry and boundary conditions as specified. In this section, some additional comments will be made on some of these alternate geometries.

13.3.1 Infinite Slab

A solution to the unsteady-state transport equations is obtainable for the infinite slab geomery. A simple example of transient heat transfer is an experiment in which two identical solids are contacted at time zero along a

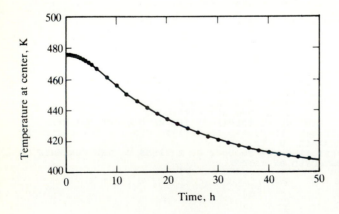

FIGURE 13.25
Temperature at the center of iron bar—Example 13.8.

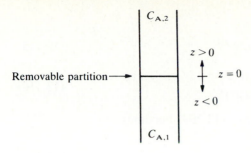

FIGURE 13.26

Time = 0 — Schematic of the free diffusion cell.

common plane face. Suppose one solid is at T_1 initially and the other at T_2. If the solids are instantaneously joined at a common surface, then the heat transfer will follow the solutions for an infinite slab until there is appreciable temperature change at the boundaries removed from the contact surfaces. Heat transfer applications are discussed by Carslaw and Jaeger [C2]. Since these are less important than the mass transfer applications, this section will discuss mass transfer.

Transient diffusion in an infinite slab is the theoretical basis for determining diffusion coefficients in liquids by the free diffusion method. Figure 13.26 shows a schematic diagram of a free diffusion cell. Since mass transport is in the z direction only, Eq. (13.11) reduces to

$$D\frac{\partial^2 C}{\partial z^2} = \frac{\partial C}{\partial t} \tag{13.109}$$

where C_A has been replaced by C for simplification of notation. The four boundary conditions for the experiment in Fig. 13.26 are

At time zero

$$C\,(z<0) = C_1 \qquad C\,(z>0) = C_2 \tag{13.110}$$

At time t

$$C\,(z\rightarrow -\infty) = C_1 \qquad C\,(z\rightarrow +\infty) = C_2 \tag{13.111}$$

Boltzmann's similarity transform [B2] is

$$\eta = z/(t)^{1/2} \tag{13.112}$$

Note that this transform is similar to that used in the boundary layer analysis [cf. Eq. (12.5)], but naturally involves the time derivative, since Eq. (13.109) is substantially different from Eqs. (12.1) through (12.3). The chain rule states

$$\frac{\partial C}{\partial z} = \frac{\partial C}{\partial \eta}\frac{\partial \eta}{\partial z} \tag{13.113}$$

$$\frac{\partial C}{\partial t} = \frac{\partial C}{\partial \eta}\frac{\partial \eta}{\partial t} \tag{13.114}$$

From Eq. (13.112):

$$\frac{\partial \eta}{\partial z} = (t)^{-1/2} \tag{13.115}$$

$$\frac{\partial \eta}{\partial t} = \frac{-z}{(2)(t)^{3/2}} \tag{13.116}$$

Using Eqs. (13.113) through (13.116), Eq. (13.109) becomes

$$- D \frac{d^2 C}{d\eta^2} = \frac{\eta}{2} \frac{dC}{d\eta} \tag{13.117}$$

Equation (13.117) is an ordinary differential equation whose solution is well-documented in the literature [G2]. There are two useful solutions, the first of which relates the concentration gradient $\partial C / \partial z$ to the diffusion coefficient D and to the independent variables z and t; the second predicts the actual concentration as a function of D, z, and t:

$$\frac{dC}{dz} = \frac{|C_1 - C_2|}{2(\pi D t)^{1/2}} \exp\left(\frac{-z^2}{4Dt}\right) \tag{13.118}$$

$$C(z, t) = \tfrac{1}{2}(C_1 + C_2) + \tfrac{1}{2} |C_1 - C_2| \operatorname{erf}\left(\frac{z}{2(Dt)^{1/2}}\right) \tag{13.119}$$

where $|C_1 - C_2|$ is the absolute value of the concentration differences at the distances $z = \pm\infty$.

In the free diffusion cells, the refractive index is used as a measure of concentration. Since the refractive index is often directly proportional to concentration, it is easy to show that Eq. (13.118) and Eq. (13.119) are changed only in that the refractive index replaces concentration [G2, J3]. In practice, the cell is loaded with liquids of two concentrations, C_1 and C_2; the loading time is short compared to the time of diffusion. Then the refractive index or the refractive index gradient is measured as a function of time and position. The value of D may be obtained from either Eq. (13.118) or (13.119) by a relatively simple trial-and-error solution.

13.3.2 Semi-Infinite Slab

A semi-infinite slab is characterized by a single face in the yz plane on which the boundary conditions are imposed. At this face, x is zero and extends positively to infinity so that heat transfer or mass transfer is in the x direction only. This geometry also leads to a plethora of exact solutions to the unsteady transport equations, both for heat transfer [C2] and for mass transfer [B1, C6, J3]. These solutions are well-documented and follow the procedures outlined for the infinite slab in the preceding section.

The boundary conditions for this geometry are

$$T(x, 0) = T(\infty, t) = T_0 \tag{13.120}$$

The simplest surface condition is for the yz plane at the location $x = 0$ to be held constant:

$$T(0, t) = T_s \tag{13.121}$$

$$\frac{T(x, t) - T_s}{T_0 - T_s} = \mathrm{erf}\left(\frac{x}{2(\alpha t)^{1/2}}\right) \tag{13.122}$$

$$q_{x=0} = -k\left.\frac{\partial T}{\partial x}\right|_{x=0} = \frac{k(T_s - T_0)}{(\pi \alpha t)^{1/2}} \tag{13.123}$$

Another important solution is the case of surface convection:

$$q_{x=0} = hA[T_\infty - T(0, t)] \tag{13.124}$$

$$\frac{T(x, t) - T_0}{T_\infty - T_0} = \mathrm{erfc}\left(\frac{x}{2(\alpha t)^{1/2}}\right)$$

$$- \left[\exp\left(\frac{hx}{k} + \frac{h^2 \alpha t}{k^2}\right)\mathrm{erfc}\left(\frac{x}{2(\alpha t)^{1/2}} + \frac{h(\alpha t)^{1/2}}{k}\right)\right] \tag{13.125}$$

Lastly, if the surface flux ($x = 0$) is maintained constant:

$$q_{x=0,t} = \text{constant} = q_0 \tag{13.126}$$

$$T(x, t) = T_0 + \left(\frac{(2q_0)(\alpha t/\pi)^{1/2}}{k}\right)\exp\left(\frac{-x^2}{4\alpha t}\right) - \frac{q_0 x}{k}\mathrm{erfc}\left(\frac{x}{2(\alpha t)^{1/2}}\right) \tag{13.127}$$

Of these, Eq. (13.125) is most often encountered and is shown in Fig. 13.27.

A Fourier series solution in the form of an infinite series exists for this problem also [M3]. There are many other solutions in the literature for transfer in a semi-infinite plate with various boundary conditions. For example, exact solutions exist for the temperature at the surface ($x = 0$) being a harmonic function of time:

$$T(0, t) = A \cos(\omega t - \varepsilon) \tag{13.128}$$

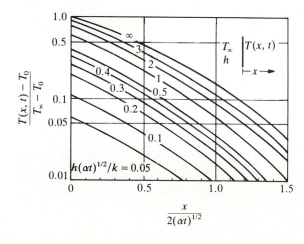

FIGURE 13.27
Distribution in a semi-infinite solid. (*From Schneider, Conduction Heat Transfer, p. 266, Addison–Wesley, Reading, MA, 1956. Adapted with permission.*)

where ω and ε are constants. Carslaw and Jaeger [C2] compiled many other solutions, including those with generation, periodic surface temperature, and radiation. The exact solutions have proved to be useful for a variety of applications; for fluid mechanics, the physical picture is one of a flat plate immersed in an infinite fluid. At the initial time, a constant velocity U_0 is imposed on the plate. Thus, the velocity field as a function of time and space can be determined. The semi-infinite solid has also served as a model for explaining the mechanism of turbulent flow. Higbie [H2] proposed that Eq. (6.101) be used to model the absorption of a slightly soluble gas in packed towers. His model formed the basis for more sophisticated treatments of the mechanisms of mass transfer in turbulent flow.

Example 13.9. It is desired to estimate the depth to which the ground freezes in a northern town. Assume that the ground reaches 20°C by early autumn, and that the air temperature can average -20°C. Estimate the depth that corresponds to a temperature of -5°C if it is assumed that the period of time is 4 months.

Answer. Obviously, an exact solution to this problem is very complex. The ground temperature is not uniform at early autumn, and the air temperature cycles continuously between day and night, sun and shade, etc. Furthermore, there is not a "step change" at time equal to zero. Additionally, the properties of the soil are likely to be highly variable, depending on factors such as soil type and moisture received during the spring and summer. However, a reasonable estimate may be made by assuming an infinite heat transfer coefficient and the following boundary conditions:

$$T(x, 0) = T(\infty, t) = 20°C \qquad T(0, t) = -20°C \tag{i}$$

The properties of soil are [I1]

$$\rho = 2050 \text{ kg m}^{-3} \qquad c_p = 1840 \text{ J kg}^{-1} \text{K}^{-1}$$
$$k = 0.52 \text{ W m}^{-1} \text{K}^{-1} \qquad \alpha = 0.138 \times 10^{-6} \text{ m}^2 \text{ s}^{-1} \tag{ii}$$

The number of seconds in 4 months is

$$t = (4)(30)(24)(3600) \, [(\text{month})(\text{day month}^{-1})(\text{h day}^{-1})(\text{s h}^{-1})] = 1.037 \times 10^7 \text{ s} \tag{iii}$$

The unaccomplished change is

$$Y_{x,\infty} = \frac{T_x - T_0}{T_\infty - T_0} = \frac{-5 - 20}{-20 - 20} = 0.625 \tag{iv}$$

The relative resistance is

$$m_\infty = (h/k)(\alpha t)^{1/2} = \infty \tag{v}$$

From Fig. 13.24, the dimensionless distance is 0.46. Then the depth is

$$x = 2(\alpha t)^{1/2}(Z) = (2)[(0.138 \times 10^{-6})(1.037 \times 10^7)](0.46) = 1.10 \text{ m} = 3.6 \text{ ft} \tag{vi}$$

In many northern cities in the USA, water pipes must be buried much deeper than the above depth. Of course, when water flows in the buried pipes, the temperature of the surrounding soil must be much colder than -5°C in order to freeze the water inside the pipes.

13.3.3 Cylinder

In this section, the problem of unsteady-state transfer in the radial direction (r direction) is considered. Either the cylinder is infinite along the z axis or the end faces are insulated or impervious so that there is no transfer along the z axis or in the θ direction. Then the transport is in one direction only.

Let us use mass transfer as the example. For transfer in the radial direction only, Eq. (13.11) reduces to

$$\frac{D}{r}\frac{\partial}{\partial r}\left(r\frac{\partial C}{\partial r}\right) = \frac{\partial C}{\partial t} \tag{13.129}$$

where the concentration C_A has been abbreviated to C and Table 5.1 has been used to express $\nabla^2 C_A$ in cylindrical coordinates. The boundary conditions are

$$C(r, 0) = C_0 \qquad C(b, t) = 0 \tag{13.130}$$

where b is the radius of the cylinder. The following transformation is proposed:

$$C = v \exp[(-Dt)(\beta)^2] \tag{13.131}$$

where β is a parameter to be determined from the boundary conditions. This transformation reduces Eq. (13.129) to an ordinary differential equation with v as the dependent variable:

$$r^2\frac{d^2v}{dr^2} + r\frac{dv}{dr} + \beta^2 r^2 v = 0 \tag{13.132}$$

Equation (13.132), a special case of an ordinary differential equation that appears repeatedly in practical problems, is known as Bessel's equation. The general form of Bessel's equation is

$$x^2\frac{d^2y}{dx^2} + x\frac{dy}{dx} + (x^2 - k^2)y = 0 \tag{13.133}$$

Equation (13.133) is known as Bessel's equation of order k. A comparison of Eq. (13.132) with Eq. (13.133) shows that Eq. (13.132) is Bessel's equation of order zero. Because Bessel's equation appears so often, its solutions have been widely discussed and tabulated in terms of coefficients called Bessel functions [C2, J2, M3, M4]. The solution of Eq. (13.132), even with the aid of Bessel functions, is tedious and still requires evaluation of an infinite series in terms of Bessel functions. However, Figs. 13.14 and 13.15 can be used to solve many problems.

> **Example 13.10.** A cylindrical porous plug of diameter 1 cm is saturated with a 10.0 kg m^{-3} KCl solution. The plug is then washed by a high-velocity stream of water passing over the outer surface. If the diffusion coefficient is 2×10^{-9} m^2 s^{-1}, find the concentration of KCl at the center after 60 min. Assume that the plug is covered on both top and bottom so that all mass transfer is in the radial direction.

Answer. Figure 13.14 will be used for this example. The radius is 0.005 m, and the parameter L in Table 13.3 is the radius of the cylinder. The resistance parameter m is zero because the mass transfer coefficient is very large:

$$m = D/(k_c b) = 0 \tag{i}$$

Using Table 13.3, the relative time is

$$X = Dt/b^2 = (2 \times 10^{-9})(60)(60)/(0.005)^2\,[(m^2\,s^{-1})(\min)(s\,\min^{-1})(m^{-2})] = 0.288 \tag{ii}$$

From Fig. 13.14, the ordinate is about 0.7. Note that the readability of Fig. 13.14 is poor in this region; a better chart for the case $(m = 0)$ is to be found in Crank [C6]. From the definition of the unaccomplished change:

$$Y_c = \frac{C_{A,\infty} - C_{A,c}}{C_{A,\infty} - C_{A,0}} = 0.7 \tag{iii}$$

$$C_{A,c} = C_{A,\infty} - Y_c(C_{A,\infty} - C_{A,0}) = 0.0 - (0.7)(0.0 - 10.0) = 7.0\ \text{kg m}^{-3} \tag{iv}$$

13.3.4 Sphere

Both heat transfer and mass transfer to spheres are commonly encountered, as discussed in Chapter 12. This section will illustrate the equations for mass transfer, which are similar in form to those for the cylinder. For the case of unsteady-state equimolar mass transfer in a sphere, Eq. (13.11) becomes

$$D\left(\frac{\partial^2 C}{\partial r^2} + \frac{2}{r}\frac{\partial C}{\partial r}\right) = \frac{\partial C}{\partial t} \tag{13.134}$$

Equation (13.134) is simplified by the following transformation:

$$\eta = Cr \tag{13.135}$$

Substitution of Eq. (13.135) into Eq. (13.134) after taking the first derivatives of η with respect to t and the second derivative of η with respect to r yields

$$D\frac{\partial^2 \eta}{\partial r^2} = \frac{\partial \eta}{\partial t} \tag{13.136}$$

Equation (13.136) is the same equation as for unsteady-state transfer in a slab [cf. Eqs. (13.6), (13.32), and (13.37)]. Hence, the solutions presented here and in the literature for the slab geometry apply to the unsteady-state transport in a sphere when the boundary conditions are transformed by Eq. (13.135). Many texts contain generalized charts for unsteady-state transport in a sphere [C2, C6, G1, G4, H1, H3, I1, M2], as well as Figs. 13.16, 13.17, and 13.20, presented earlier.

Example 13.11. The inside surface of a hollow spherical shell is maintained at a concentration of C_1. The inside radius of the sphere is r_1, and the outside radius is r_2. The outside surface of the sphere is maintained at C_2. If the initial concentration at time zero is given by

$$C(r, 0) = C_0/r \qquad \text{(i)}$$

Derive the equation for the concentration as a function of r and t.

Answer. One boundary condition was given as Eq. (i). The other two boundary conditions are

$$C(r_1, t) = C_1 \qquad C(r_2, t) = C_2 \qquad \text{(ii)}$$

The solution proceeds by transforming the boundary conditions with Eq. (13.135):

$$\eta(r, 0) = C_0 \qquad \eta(r_1, t) = r_1 C_1 \qquad \eta(r_2, t) = r_2 C_2 \qquad \text{(iii)}$$

where the products $r_1 C_1$ and $r_2 C_2$ are constants. This problem was solved in Example 13.2. The computer program in Fig. 13.9 could be used, or the problem could be solved by numerical methods, as discussed earlier.

PROBLEMS

13.1. A steel ball of diameter 0.3 m is at a temperature of 273 K. It is suddenly plunged into a large water bath whose temperature is 350 K. The heat transfer coefficient may be assumed constant and equal to $10 \text{ W m}^{-2} \text{K}^{-1}$. For this steel ball, the following physical properties may be used:

$$k = 43 \text{ W m}^{-1} \text{K}^{-1} \qquad \rho = 7850 \text{ kg m}^{-3} \qquad c_p = 460 \text{ J kg}^{-1} \text{K}^{-1}$$

(a) Find the Biot number.
(b) Find the temperature and the heat transferred after 50 s.
(c) Find the time required for the temperature to reach 349.9 K.
(d) Find the heat transferred between time zero and steady-state.

13.2. A large slab of steel is 4 m thick. Initially, the temperature is uniform and at 500 K. Suddenly, both faces are reduced to, and maintained at, 300 K. Using Fourier series, compute the temperature at midplane after 1 h. Properties of steel are

$$k = 60 \text{ W m}^{-1} \text{K}^{-1} \qquad \rho = 7850 \text{ kg m}^{-3} \qquad c_p = 434 \text{ J kg}^{-1} \text{K}^{-1}$$

13.3. Consider a steel bar, with properties as given in Problem 13.2, that is insulated on the sides. The bar is 0.1 m long. First, one end is maintained at 350 K while the other is at 400 K, until steady-state is achieved. Then suddenly the temperature at the 350 K end is raised to 390 K, while the temperature at the 400 K end is lowered to 340 K. Using Fourier series, compute the temperature at midplane after 1 h.

13.4. Consider a silver bar 1.0 m long. Initially, the bar is maintained at a uniform temperature of 400 K. Suddenly, the ends of the bar are raised to temperatures of 500 K and 600 K, respectively. Assume that the sides of the bar are insulated so that heat transfer is in one direction only. Using Fourier series, find the temperature at midplane after 15 s. For silver:

$$k = 430 \text{ W m}^{-1} \text{K}^{-1} \qquad \rho = 1.05 \times 10^4 \text{ kg m}^{-3} \qquad c_p = 235 \text{ J kg}^{-1} \text{K}^{-1}$$

13.5. Two copper blocks, each cubic in shape and 40 cm on a side, are insulated on five sides. One block is allowed to reach 800 K throughout, and the other 300 K. Then the blocks are brought together so that the uninsulated sides touch in thermal contact; let $h_c = 25\,000\ \text{W m}^{-2}\,\text{K}^{-1}$. Assuming the lumped-capacity method of analysis, plot the temperature of each block as a function of time. For copper:

$$k = 380\ \text{W m}^{-1}\,\text{K}^{-1} \qquad \rho = 8930\ \text{kg m}^{-3} \qquad c_p = 385\ \text{J kg}^{-1}\,\text{K}^{-1}$$

13.6. Two blocks, each cubic in shape and 40 cm on a side, are insulated on five sides. One block, which is steel, is allowed to reach 800 K throughout; the other, which is copper, is allowed to reach 300 K. The blocks are brought together so that the uninsulated sides touch in thermal contact; let $h_c = 25\,000\ \text{W m}^{-2}\,\text{K}^{-1}$. Assuming the lumped-capacity method of analysis, plot the temperature of each block as a function of time. Use the properties given in Problems 13.2 and 13.5.

13.7. A polymer solid is saturated with a salt solution such that the initial concentration of salt is constant and equal to $0.1\ \text{kmol m}^{-3}$. The solid is in the shape of a slab, 1 cm thick. At zero time, both sides of the slab are washed with pure water of sufficient velocity that the mass transfer coefficient may be assumed infinite. The diffusion coefficient of salt in the polymer is equal to $2 \times 10^{-10}\ \text{m}^2\,\text{s}^{-1}$. Find the concentration of salt at three equispaced locations in the slab after 10 h.

13.8. Repeat Problem 13.7 if the mass transfer coefficient equals $8 \times 10^{-8}\ \text{kmol m}^{-2}\,\text{s}^{-1}\,(\text{kmol m}^{-3})^{-1}$.

13.9. A polymer solid is saturated with a salt solution such that the initial concentration of salt is constant and equal to $0.1\ \text{kmol m}^{-3}$. The solid is in the shape of a cube, 10 cm on a side. The diffusion coefficient of salt in the polymer is equal to $2 \times 10^{-10}\ \text{m}^2\,\text{s}^{-1}$. At zero time, four sides of the cube are washed with pure water of sufficient velocity that the mass transfer coefficient may be assumed infinite. The two sides not contacted with water are kept dry; these sides are located at the planes $z = 0$ and $z = 10$. Find the time in hours for the concentration in the middle of the solid to drop to 10 percent of the original concentration.

13.10. A polymer solid is saturated with a salt solution such that the initial concentration of salt is constant and equal to $0.1\ \text{kmol m}^{-3}$. The solid is in the shape of a cylinder 1 cm in diameter and 1.2 cm in length. The ends of the cylinder are capped so that no mass transfer is allowed. At zero time, the curved surface of the cylinder is washed with pure water of sufficient velocity that the mass transfer coefficient may be assumed infinite. The diffusion coefficient of salt in the polymer is equal to $2 \times 10^{-10}\ \text{m}^2\,\text{s}^{-1}$. Find the concentration of salt at the center of the cylinder after 10 h.

13.11. A polymer solid is saturated with a salt solution such that the initial concentration of salt is constant and equal to $0.2\ \text{kmol m}^{-3}$. The solid is in the shape of a cylinder 1 cm in diameter and 1.2 cm long. At zero time, all surfaces of the cylinder are washed with pure water of sufficient velocity that the mass transfer coefficient may be assumed infinite. The diffusion coefficient of salt in the polymer is equal to $2 \times 10^{-10}\ \text{m}^2\,\text{s}^{-1}$. Find the concentration of salt at the center of the cylinder after 10 h.

13.12. A polymer solid is saturated with a salt solution such that the initial concentration of salt is constant and equal to $0.2\,\text{kmol m}^{-3}$. The solid is in the shape of a sphere 1 cm in diameter. At zero time, the surface of the sphere is washed with pure water of sufficient velocity that the mass transfer coefficient may be assumed infinite. The diffusion coefficient of salt in the polymer is equal to $2 \times 10^{-10}\,\text{m}^2\,\text{s}^{-1}$. Find the concentration of salt at the center of the sphere after 10 h.

13.13. A slab of meat served by a fast-food restaurant is rectangular in shape, with dimensions 0.08 cm, 10 cm, and 5 cm. The uncooked meat is kept in a refrigerator at 275 K. It is then dropped into a vat of cooking oil at 400 K. Calculate the time for the center of the meat to reach 350 K if the heat transfer coefficient is $120\,\text{W m}^{-2}\,\text{K}^{-1}$. The properties of the meat are

$$k = 0.5\,\text{W m}^{-1}\,\text{K}^{-1} \qquad \rho = 900\,\text{kg m}^{-3} \qquad c_p = 3500\,\text{J kg}^{-1}\,\text{K}^{-1}$$

13.14. A piece of meat served by a fast-food restaurant is spherical in shape, with diameter 2 cm. The uncooked meat is kept in a refrigerator at 275 K. It is then dropped into a vat of cooking oil at 400 K. Calculate the time for the center of the meat to reach 350 K if the heat transfer coefficient is $120\,\text{W m}^{-2}\,\text{K}^{-1}$. The properties of the meat are

$$k = 0.5\,\text{W m}^{-1}\,\text{K}^{-1} \qquad \rho = 900\,\text{kg m}^{-3} \qquad c_p = 3500\,\text{J kg}^{-1}\,\text{K}^{-1}$$

13.15. In the USA, butter is generally sold by the pound, with four sticks per pound, and each stick being 11.45 cm in length. If each stick is in the shape of a rectangle with square cross section, find the dimensions of each stick in SI units. For butter:

$$k = 0.2\,\text{W m}^{-1}\,\text{K}^{-1} \qquad \rho = 998\,\text{kg m}^{-3} \qquad c_p = 2300\,\text{J kg}^{-1}\,\text{K}^{-1}$$

Suppose that a stick of butter is kept for a week at 280 K. Then it is placed in surroundings at room temperature (293 K) so that all six sides are exposed to air with convective coefficient $8\,\text{W m}^{-2}\,\text{K}^{-1}$. Find the temperature at the center after 1 h.

13.16. Write a computer program to solve Problem 13.3. Use the explicit method. Print out the temperatures at 1-cm intervals and 10-s intervals, up to 100 s.

13.17. Write a computer program to solve Problem 13.3 with the following changes: initially, one end is at 450 K and the other at 300 K; finally, the 450 K end is maintained at 375 K, and the other at 400 K. Use the Crank–Nicolson method. Print out the temperatures at 1-cm intervals and 10-s intervals, up to 100 s.

13.18. A semi-infinite slab of silver is initially at 500 K. Suppose that the slab is exposed to a constant heat flux at the surface of $10^5\,\text{W m}^{-2}$. Use the properties of silver in Problem 13.4.
(a) Find the surface temperature after 1000 s.
(b) Find the temperature 4 cm from the surface after 1000 s.

13.19. A large piece of steel at 300 K has one plane surface. Suppose the surface temperature is suddenly changed from 300 K to 400 K. Find the time for the temperature 5 cm from the surface to reach 350 K. Use the properties in Problem 13.2.

13.20. In Columbus, Ohio, the temperature changed from 10°F to 72°F in 30 h. It is desired to estimate the influence of this temperature change on the soil temperature. Assuming that the soil temperature was uniformly 32°F, calculate the soil temperature 2 cm from the air–soil interface after 10 h. Assume that initially the temperature of the soil is 0°C, that at time zero the air temperature instantaneously becomes 22°C, and that the convective heat transfer coefficient is 12 W m^{-2} K^{-1}. For this soil:

$$k = 0.5 \text{ W m}^{-2}\text{ K}^{-1} \qquad \rho = 2000 \text{ kg m}^{-3} \qquad c_p = 1600 \text{ J kg}^{-1}\text{ K}^{-1}$$

Do all work in SI units.

REFERENCES

B1. Barrer, R. M.: *Diffusion in and through Solids,* Cambridge University Press, Cambridge, 1951.

B2. Boltzmann, L.: *Ann. Physik* **[3]**. **53:** 959 (1894).

C1. Carslaw, H. S., and J. C. Jaeger: *Operational Methods in Applied Mathematics,* 2d ed., Clarendon Press, Oxford, 1948. [Also available from Dover Publications, New York, 1963.]

C2. Carslaw, H. S., and J. C. Jaeger: *Conduction of Heat in Solids,* 2d ed., Clarendon Press, Oxford, 1959.

C3. Churchill, R. V., and J. W. Brown: *Fourier Series and Boundary Value Problems,* 3d ed., McGraw-Hill, New York, 1978.

C4. Churchill, R. V.: *Operational Mathematics,* 3d ed., McGraw-Hill, New York, 1972.

C5. Crank, J., and P. Nicolson: *Proc. Cambridge Phil. Soc.* **43:** 50 (1947).

C6. Crank, J.: *The Mathematics of Diffusion,* 2d ed., Oxford University Press, London, 1975.

D1. Dusinberre, G. M.: *Numerical Analysis of Heat Flow,* McGraw-Hill, New York, 1949.

F1. Fox, L.: *Numerical Solution of Ordinary and Partial Differential Equations,* Pergamon Press, London, Addison-Wesley, Reading, MA, 1962.

F2. Fuller, E. N., P. D. Schettler, and J. C. Giddings: *Ind. Eng. Chem.* **58**(5): 18 (1966); **58**(8): 81 (1966).

G1. Geankoplis, C. J.: *Mass Transport Phenomena,* Geankoplis, Minneapolis, MN, 1972.

G2. Gosting, L. J.: *Adv. Protein Chem.* **11:** 429 (1956).

G3. Grober, H., S. Erk, and U. Grigull: *Fundamentals of Heat Transfer,* 3d ed., McGraw-Hill, New York, 1961.

G4. Gurney, H. P., and J. Lurie: *Ind. Eng. Chem.* **15:** 1170 (1923).

H1. Heisler, M. P.: *Trans. ASME* **69:** 227 (1947).

H2. Higbie, R.: *Trans. AIChE* **31:** 365 (1935).

H3. Holman, J. P.: *Heat Transfer,* 6th ed., McGraw-Hill, New York, 1986.

I1. Incropera, F. P., and D. P. DeWitt: *Fundamentals of Heat and Mass Transfer,* 2d ed., Wiley, New York, 1985.

J1. Jacob, M.: *Heat Transfer,* vol. I, Wiley, New York, 1949, p. 451.

J2. Jenson, V. G., and G. V. Jeffreys: *Mathematical Methods in Chemical Engineering,* Academic Press, New York, 1963.

J3. Jost, W.: *Diffusion in Solids, Liquids, Gases,* Academic Press, New York, 1960, 3d printing with addendum.

K1. Keller, H. B.: in *Mathematical Methods for Digital Computers,* A. Ralston and H. S. Wilf (eds.), Wiley, New York, 1960.

M1. Marshall, W. R., Jr., and R. L. Pigford: *The Application of Differential Equations to Chemical Engineering Problems,* University of Delaware Press, Newark, DE, 1947.

M2. McAdams, W. H.: *Heat Transmission,* 3d ed., McGraw-Hill, New York, 1954.

M3. Mickley, H. S., T. K. Sherwood, and C. E. Reed: *Applied Mathematics in Chemical Engineering,* 2d ed., McGraw-Hill, New York, 1957.

M4. Miller, K. S.: *Partial Differential Equations in Engineering Problems,* Prentice-Hall, Englewood Cliffs, NJ, 1953.

N1. Newman, A. B.: *Ind. Eng. Chem.* **28:** 545 (1936).

P1. Peirce, B. O., and R. M. Foster: *A Short Table of Integrals,* 4th ed., Blaisdell Publishing Co., New York, 1956.

R1. Reddick, H. W., and F. H. Miller: *Advanced Mathematics for Engineers,* 3d ed., Wiley, New York, 1957.

R2. Richtmyer, R. D., and K. W. Morton: *Difference Methods for Initial-Value Problems,* 2d ed., Wiley-Interscience, New York, 1967.

S1. Schneider, P. J.: *Conduction Heat Transfer,* Addison-Wesley, Cambridge, MA, 1955.

W1. Wachspress, E. L.: in *Mathematical Methods for Digital Computers,* A. Ralston and H. S. Wilf (eds.), Wiley, New York, 1960.

W2. Wylie, C. R., and L. C. Barrett: *Advanced Engineering Mathematics,* 5th ed., McGraw-Hill, New York, 1982.

PART
III

TRANSPORT
PROPERTIES

CHAPTER
14

ESTIMATION
OF TRANSPORT
COEFFICIENTS

NOMENCLATURE

A   Species A

A Constant in Eq. (2.52)

B   Species B

B Constant in Eq. (2.52)

b   Subscript referring to boiling point

C Concentration (kmol m^{-3}); C_m is molecular concentration or total molecules per volume, cf. Eq. (14.4); C_T is total molar concentration

c_p, c_v Heat capacity $(\text{kJ kg}^{-1}\,\text{K}^{-1})$; c_p or c_v is heat capacity at constant pressure or constant volume; c_{pb} is constant pressure heat capacity at the boiling point; $c_{v,tr}$ is translational contribution [cf. Eq. (14.45)]

D Diffusion coefficient $(\text{m}^2\,\text{s}^{-1})$; D_{AB} is diffusion coefficient of species A diffusing through a mixture of A plus B; D_{AA} is self-diffusion coefficient, Eq. (14.26) ff.; D_o is the diffusion coefficient at the reference temperature T_o and reference pressure p_o in Eq. (2.50); D_{AB}^* is tracer diffusion coefficient of labeled A within the mixture of A and B; D_{AB}^o is mutual diffusion coefficient at infinite dilution, i.e., a single molecule of A diffusing in pure B

d Diameter (m) of gas molecule in kinetic theory (assumed to be a smooth, rigid, elastic sphere)

711

E_D	Activation energy of diffusion, defined by Eq. (14.79)
e	Base of natural logarithms (also called exp) (2.718 281 8. . .)
F_p	Force (N); in Stokes' law, F_p is the drag force on a particle (or sphere) as given in Eq. (12.66) or Eq. (14.76)
f_1	Frictional resistance defined in Eq. (14.76)
G^*	Molar free energy of activation (J mol^{-1})
h	Planck's constant, 6.625×10^{-34} J s molecule^{-1}
J_A/A	Molar flux vector of species A (kmol m^{-2} s^{-1})
k	Thermal conductivity (W m^{-1} K^{-1} or J m^{-1} K^{-1} s^{-1}); k_{tr} is the translational conductivity
k	Specific rate constant where the subscripts f, r, and 0 refer to forward, reverse, and equilibrium, respectively; cf. Eqs. (14.55), (14.56), (14.58), and (14.59)
k_B	The Boltzmann constant, defined as R/N
L	Length (m)
m	Mass of a single molecule (kg molecule^{-1})
M	Molecular weight (kg kmol^{-1}); subscripts refer to species
N	Avogadro's number, $6.022\ 143\ 8 \times 10^{23}$ molecules per mole
n	Number of moles
n	Power in Eq. (2.50)
p	Pressure (kPa, atm); p_o is pressure at reference conditions; p_c is critical pressure (atm); in Eq. (14.48) the units of p are Pa; in Eq. (14.49) p_{atm} is in atm
R	Gas constant; see Appendix Table C.1 for values
r	Cylindrical coordinate (m)
r	Radius (m); r_p is the particle radius
T	Temperature (K, °C); T_b is the boiling point; T_c is the critical temperature (K); T^* is dimensionless temperature in the Chapman–Enskog theory, Eq. (14.38), for viscosity or thermal conductivity and Eq. (14.50) for mutual diffusion coefficient; T_o is reference temperature, Eq. (2.50)
t	Time; the time interval in kinetic theory of gases (s)
U	Instantaneous velocity vector (m s^{-1}); U is magnitude of $\boldsymbol{U}$; U_x, U_y, U_z, U_θ, U_r, U_ϕ are components in directions x, y, z, θ, r, ϕ; U_λ is a net velocity given by Eq. (14.55); U_∞ is velocity of the fluid in Stokes' law; U_s is velocity of sound in a liquid
U	Molecular speed in the kinetic theory (m s^{-1}); $\bar{U}$ is the mean speed of a gas molecule in kinetic theory
V	Volume (m^3); V_o is the molar volume of a liquid at its normal boiling point; V_A and V_B are molar volumes of A and B at the normal boiling point; V' is atomic diffusion volume increment in Table 14.3; $(\Sigma V')_A$ and $(\Sigma V')_B$ are atomic diffusion volumes, calculated from data in Table 14.3
x	Rectangular (Cartesian) coordinate
y	Rectangular (Cartesian) coordinate
z	Rectangular (Cartesian) coordinate

α Thermal diffusivity ($m^2 s^{-1}$)

α Parameter in the Eyring rate approach, Eq. (14.60)

β Constants in equation for a straight line; see Example 14.7

γ Ratio of heat capacities, c_p/c_v; cf. Eq. (14.32)

Δ Difference, state 2 minus state 1; e.g., Δp means $p_2 - p_1$

ε Characteristic energy of interaction used in the Lennard-Jones potential, Eq. (14.37); subscripts A for component A, etc., AB for an averaged value defined by Eq. (14.52)

Θ Collision frequency per molecule (s^{-1}), i.e., the number of collisions divided by the time interval

κ Transmission coefficient used in Eq. (14.54)

λ Mean-free-path (m)

λ In the Eyring rate approach, λ is the distance of two equilibrium positions of the molecule (or a cluster of molecules); λ_1 is the distance between sets of parallel shear layers; λ_2 is the distance between neighboring molecules (or clusters) in the direction of λ; λ_3 is the distance between neighboring molecules in the moving layer in a direction at right angles to the shear

μ Viscosity ($kg\, m^{-1} s^{-1}$ or $N\, m^{-2} s$)

ν Kinematic viscosity ($m^2 s^{-1}$)

π Ratio of circumference of a circle to its diameter (3.141 592 65. . .)

ρ Mass density ($kg\, m^{-3}$); ρ_b is the density at the boiling point

σ Characteristic diameter used with the Lennard-Jones potential, Eq. (14.37); subscript A is for component A, etc.; AB is for an averaged value defined by Eq. (14.51)

τ Momentum flux (or shear stress) tensor ($N\, m^{-2}$, $lb_f\, ft^{-2}$); τ_{xy}, τ_{yx}, etc. are components of the momentum flux tensor, where subscripts refer to direction of momentum transfer and direction of velocity; τ_λ is the shearing force per unit area in Eq. (14.57)

ϕ Association parameter in Wilke–Chang correlation, Eq. (14.80)

Ψ Generalized flux vector (e.g., units for heat flux are $J\, m^{-2} s^{-1}$ or $W\, m^{-2}$, $Btu\, ft^{-2} s^{-1}$; see Table 2.1 for more details); Ψ_x, Ψ_y, Ψ_z are components in directions x, y, z; Ψ_A is flux of component A

ψ Generalized concentration of property (e.g., units for concentration of heat are $J\, m^{-3}$ or $Btu\, ft^{-3}$; see Table 2.1 for more details); ψ_m is molecules per unit volume

Ω Collision integral, subscript μ is for viscosity and D is for diffusion

ω Acentric factor, defined as minus $\log_{10}$ (vapor pressure at a reduced temperature of 0.7 divided by critical pressure) minus 1.0

The proportionality constants in the transport equations are thermal conductivity k or thermal diffusivity α, diffusion coefficient or mass diffusivity D, and viscosity μ or momentum diffusivity (kinematic viscosity) ν. Since these coefficients appear in the design equations for equipment that involves transport phenomena, they must be determined, either from experimental tabulations or by using suitable estimation methods. For the most part, the physical properties have been measured, and tables are available in the literature [C3, F1, G7, J3, L1, L6, P2, R1, T4–T7, V3], as was indicated in Section 2.5. In order to reduce the bulk of tabular material, research workers have been striving to provide compact correlations for the physical properties of materials. Ideally, one would like to have a thorough understanding of the basic molecular processes occurring so that the properties could be estimated from first principles. Some progress has been made in this regard, but, unfortunately, the task is far from complete. Nevertheless, because of their importance, some of the accomplishments along these lines will be reviewed.

This chapter introduces sufficient information for the estimation of transport properties for most materials. A short section on measurements is also included. In this chapter, the viscosity is treated as a function of pressure and temperature, but not of the shear rate or stress level; i.e., the materials are considered Newtonian in nature. The next chapter is devoted to non-Newtonian fluids.

Most of the progress on theoretical prediction of the transport properties has been for gas systems, and is based on the kinetic theory of gases. The theoretical approaches for liquids and solids are not as well developed because of the complexities in these denser systems.

14.1 GASES

This section considers the simple "mean-free-path" kinetic theory, which is the starting point for more realistic approaches.

14.1.1 Kinetic Theory of Gases

The kinetic theory of gases attempts to explain and correlate the basic physical properties of gases and gaseous phenomena on the basis that the molecule is the smallest quantity of a substance that retains its chemical properties. This theory is commonly used in several areas besides transport phenomena, especially physical chemistry [M4] and physics [P3]. The kinetic theory provides estimates of the transport properties k, D, and μ from molecular considerations. Furthermore, the theory predicts variations of these with temperature and pressure, as well as ways to compute one from the others. Many excellent references are available, including Chapman and Cowling [C2], Hirschfelder, Curtiss, and Bird [H5], Jeans [J1], Kennard [K2], and Present [P3].

The kinetic theory of gases require many assumptions. This text will present only the most elementary treatment. The most important general assumptions are:

1. The molecule is the appropriate quantity of a substance to be treated.
2. The conservation laws of classical mechanics are valid: namely, the

conservation of momentum and the conservation of energy in regard to collisions between molecules and to collisions between molecules and container walls.

3. The behavior of the gas is described by the average behavior of the molecules (i.e., statistical averages can be used and the laws of probability are valid).

4. The molecules can be idealized as smooth, rigid, elastic spheres of diameter d. The assumption of a smooth surface precludes any rotation effects. The assumption of elasticity allows all collisions to follow the "billiard ball" model, in which all collisions are sudden and result in a sharply defined change in direction.

5. The presence of long-range forces can be neglected.

Mean-free-path. The mean-free-path is defined as the average distance a molecule travels before it collides with a surface or with another molecule. The collision frequency per molecule, Θ, is defined as the average number of collisions per unit time. The mean speed $\bar{U}$ is the time-averaged velocity of a single molecule; $\bar{U}$ is assumed to be also the statistical average over the velocity distribution, the velocity distribution being caused by the temperature distribution present in a sample of gas molecules existing in an appropriate container at some average temperature and pressure.

In order to define the mean-free-path, let us picture a molecule over a long time period t, during which it would travel on the average a distance L:

$$L = \bar{U}t \tag{14.1}$$

The number of collisions is frequency times time, i.e., Θt collisions. The mean-free-path λ is the average distance between collisions; therefore, the distance L is also the product of the average distance between collisions and the number of collisions:

$$L = \bar{U}t = \lambda\Theta t \tag{14.2}$$

This equation is solved for the mean-free-path:

$$\lambda = \bar{U}/\Theta \tag{14.3}$$

Thus, the mean-free-path is the mean speed $\bar{U}$ (m s^{-1}) divided by the collision frequency Θ (s^{-1}).

Let the molecular concentration be C_m (molecules per m^3), where C_m is the total number of gas molecules present divided by the total volume; C_m is related to the total molar concentration C_T by Avodagro's number N:

$$C_m = C_T N = \frac{\rho}{m} = \frac{\rho N}{M} \tag{14.4}$$

where ρ is the mass density (kg m^{-3}), m is the mass of a single molecule (kg molecule^{-1}), and M is molecular weight (kg kmol^{-1}). For an ideal gas [Eq.

(1.1)], the total molar concentration C_T is the number of moles n divided by volume V [cf., Eq. (2.37)]:

$$C_m = C_T N = \frac{nN}{V} = \frac{pN}{RT} = \frac{p}{(R/N)T} = \frac{p}{k_B T} \tag{14.5}$$

where k_B is the Boltzmann constant:

$$k_B = \frac{R}{N} \tag{14.6}$$

A collision occurs between two rigid, elastic spheres of diameter d when the centers of the two spheres are separated by the distance d. Let us picture ourselves as moving with one sphere through the other spheres. The speed of our sphere is denoted by U. Our sphere traces out a cylinder of length U and a cross sectional area $\pi d^2/4$ in a given unit of time. Any molecules whose edge is located within the cylindrical trace will be hit by our moving molecule. An equivalent expression is that any sphere whose center lies within a larger sphere of influence of diameter $2d$ will be hit by our moving molecule. The cross sectional area of this larger cylinder of influence is πd^2; i.e., the cross sectional area of a diameter of $2d$. The number of molecules struck per unit time (i.e., the collision frequency, Θ) is

$$\Theta = \pi d^2 U C_m \tag{14.7}$$

where $\pi d^2 U$ is simply the larger volume of influence of the cylinder traced out.

Actually, the average relative speed $\bar{U}$, not the absolute speed U, between our molecule and the others in the volume is important. This relative speed must lie between zero and twice the mean speed; i.e., for a grazing collision, the relative speed is zero, and for a head-on collision the relative speed is twice the mean speed when the molecules are assumed to be moving at the same speed. A simple picture of the collision process is that the average collision (between the grazing and head-on extremes) is a collision at 90°. The vectors form a right triangle and the relative speed is $2^{1/2}\bar{U}$. Thus

$$\Theta = 2^{1/2}\pi d^2 \bar{U} C_m \tag{14.8}$$

When Eqs. (14.3) and (14.8) are combined, the mean-free-path becomes

$$\lambda = \frac{\bar{U}}{\Theta} = \frac{1}{2^{1/2}\pi d^2 C_m} = \frac{k_B T}{2^{1/2}\pi d^2 p} \tag{14.9}$$

The mean-free-path is inversely proportional to the molecular density, which for constant temperature means that it is inversely proportional to the cross sectional area of the sphere of the molecule.

The preceding results can be obtained by a rigorous integration of a Maxwellian distribution of velocities [P3]. It can also be shown that the mean relative speed is

$$\bar{U} = \left(\frac{8k_B T}{\pi m}\right)^{1/2} \tag{14.10}$$

where m is the mass of the molecule or sphere.

Transport balance. The treatment that follows is similar to that found in several of the books already cited. Let ψ_m denote the concentration of property for a single gas molecule; ψ is defined in Table 4.1, as are the various fluxes Ψ. Over the range of a few mean-free-paths, let us assume that the variation in the concentration of property is uniform in the arbitrary direction x. Consider now the flux Ψ_A across the plane located at $x = 0$. The average number of molecules that will cross the plane in a unit area and time will be proportional to $\frac{1}{6}C_m \bar{U}$, since the plane is one side of a cube and represents one-sixth of the direction. The molecules that cross the plane carry the property ψ_m, which is characteristic of the region from which the molecule originated. The region or source in the x direction will be denoted by Δx; thus the volume of interest is of length Δx and area unity. The length Δx is of the same order of magnitude as the mean-free-path. The transport from the region on the negative side of the plane (at $x = 0$) is

$$\text{Transport from the negative side} = \tfrac{1}{6}C_m \bar{U}\psi_{m1}(\Delta x) \tag{14.11}$$

where ψ_{m1} is for side 1 or the negative side of the plane. The property entering the volume of interest across the plane at $x = \Delta x$ is

$$\psi_{m2} = \psi_{m1} + \frac{d\psi_m}{dx}(2\Delta x) \tag{14.12}$$

The factor of 2 comes from the fact that molecules enter the volume of interest across two planes (at $x = 0$ and $x = \Delta x$). The transport on the positive side is

$$\text{Transport (positive side)} = \tfrac{1}{6}C_m \bar{U}\psi_{m2}(\Delta x) \tag{14.13}$$

The net amount of the property transported across a unit area and unit time is found by subtracting Eqs. (14.11) from (14.13):

$$\Psi_A = \tfrac{1}{6}C_m \bar{U}(\Delta x)(\psi_{m1} - \psi_{m2}) = \frac{1}{6}C_m \bar{U}(\Delta x)\left(-\frac{d\psi_m}{dx}\right)(2\Delta x)$$

$$= -\frac{1}{3}C_m \bar{U}(\Delta x)\frac{d\psi_m}{dx} \tag{14.14}$$

Assuming the region is of the size of the mean-free-path; i.e., Δx equals λ, the flux of A becomes

$$\Psi_A = -\frac{1}{3}C_m \bar{U}\lambda \frac{d\psi_m}{dx} \tag{14.15}$$

In this simple model, the transport rate is proportional to the mean-speed, the mean-free-path, and the density. By Eq. (14.9), the mean-free-path varies inversely with the molecular density so that the transport rate is independent of the pressure and density of the gas. The similarity of this equation to the empirical transport equations of Chapter 2 should be noted.

Heat transport. The energy exchanged in a collision between a smooth, rigid sphere (or molecule) of mass m is translational energy:

$$\psi_m = \frac{m\overline{U^2}}{2} \qquad (14.16)$$

where $\overline{U^2}$ is the mean-square-speed. Equation (14.16) can be related to the temperature. It can be shown that the pressure exerted by gas molecules is [K2, P3]

$$p = \tfrac{1}{3}C_m m\overline{U^2} \qquad (14.17)$$

This equation can be multiplied on both sides by the volume of the gas; the resultant is then equated to the product pV that can be found from Eq. (14.5):

$$pV = \frac{2C_m V}{(3)(2)}m\overline{U^2} = \frac{2}{3}nN\frac{m\overline{U^2}}{2} = \frac{2}{3}nN\frac{RT}{N} \qquad (14.18)$$

or, in terms of the Boltzmann constant:

$$\frac{m\overline{U^2}}{2} = \frac{3RT}{2N} = \frac{3k_B T}{2} \qquad (14.19)$$

where $m\overline{U^2}/2$ is the kinetic energy of a gas molecule. Equations (14.16) and (14.19) define ψ_m in terms of temperature:

$$\psi_m = 3k_B T/2 \qquad (14.20)$$

From Table 4.1, the flux Ψ_A in Eq. (14.15) becomes $(q/A)_x$; this result plus Eq. (14.20) yields

$$(q/A)_x = -\frac{C_m \overline{U}\lambda k_B}{2}\frac{dT}{dx} \qquad (14.21)$$

Comparison of Eq. (14.21) with Fourier's law, Eq. (2.2), results in the definition of the thermal conductivity based on the kinetic theory of gases:

$$k = C_m \overline{U}\lambda k_B/2 \qquad (14.22)$$

Equation (14.22), which is derived for a monatomic gas, can be further modified by the introduction of the heat capacity of the gas. In Eq. (14.19), $m\overline{U^2}/2$ is the translational energy, which can be shown [M4] to be equal to $mc_v T$, where c_v (kJ kg^{-1} K^{-1}) is the heat capacity at constant volume; thus, by use of Eq. (14.19):

$$mc_v = 3k_B/2 \qquad (14.23)$$

Now, the thermal conductivity becomes

$$k = \tfrac{1}{3}mC_m \bar{U}\lambda c_v = \tfrac{1}{3}\rho \bar{U}\lambda c_v \tag{14.24}$$

since the mass density ρ equals mC_m [cf. Eq. (14.4)]. If k from Eq. (14.24) is introduced into Fourier's law, the quantity $\rho c_v T$ is formed, which is similar to the definition of ψ for heat transfer in Chapter 2, i.e., $\rho c_p T$.

Mass transport. The kinetic theory of gases can be applied to "self-diffusion", i.e., the case of a molecule diffusing through identical molecules.[1] Let D_{AA} be the self-diffusion coefficient of species A diffusing through pure A. For self-diffusion, the property being transferred is $C_{m,A}/C_m$. The flux in the x direction is denoted by $(J_A/A)_x$. Substituting in the general flux equation, Eq. (14.15), gives

$$(J_A/A)_x = -\frac{1}{3}C_m \bar{U}\lambda \frac{d(C_{m,A}/C_m)}{dx} = -\frac{1}{3}\bar{U}\lambda \frac{d(C_{m,A})}{dx} \tag{14.25}$$

where, at constant temperature and pressure, the total concentration of molecules C_m is constant if there is no chemical reaction. Comparison of Eq. (14.25) with Fick's law, Eq. (2.4), yields

$$D_{AA} = \tfrac{1}{3}\bar{U}\lambda \tag{14.26}$$

where D_{AA} is the self-diffusion coefficient. The double subscript on the diffusion coefficient is used to emphasize that it is the diffusion of a marked molecule (or sphere in this analysis) through otherwise identical molecules.

While the kinetic theory estimates D_{AA} for a simple spherical molecule reasonably well, the mean-free-path method of treatment gives a very poor approximation to D_{AB}, the diffusion coefficient of species A diffusing through a mixture of A plus B [K2, P3].

Momentum transport. In momentum transport, the concentration of property ψ is momentum $\rho \bar{U}$, or, on the basis of a single molecule, $m\bar{U}$. The flux Ψ_A is τ_{yx}; now Eq. (14.15) becomes

$$\tau_{yx} = -\tfrac{1}{3}mC_m \bar{U}\lambda \frac{d\bar{U}}{dx} \tag{14.27}$$

This equation can be compared with Newton's law of viscosity, Eq. (2.7):

$$\mu = \tfrac{1}{3}mC_m \bar{U}\lambda = \tfrac{1}{3}\rho \bar{U}\lambda \tag{14.28}$$

Finally, Eqs. (14.9) and (14.10) are used to eliminate λ and $\bar{U}$, respectively:

$$\mu = \frac{2}{3(\pi)^{3/2}}\frac{(mk_B T)^{1/2}}{d^2} \tag{14.29}$$

---

[1] Self-diffusion coefficients are contrasted with tracer and mutual diffusion coefficients in Section 14.2.3.

Equation (14.29) relates viscosity to the square root of temperature and to the zero power of pressure. This prediction is only qualitatively satisfactory, as discussed in Section 2.5.3. The observed temperature dependency ranges from 0.6 to almost 1.0. The viscosity is essentially independent of pressure up to ten times atmospheric pressure, a result in agreement with Eq. (14.29).

Since Eq. (14.15) is the starting point for estimating all three transport coefficients, naturally an interdependency is predicted. From Eqs. (14.24), (14.26), and (14.28), the following is predicted:

$$\frac{k}{\rho c_\mathrm{v}} = v = \frac{\mu}{\rho} = D_\mathrm{AA} = \tfrac{1}{3}\bar{U}\lambda \tag{14.30}$$

or, in terms of the thermal diffusivity α:

$$\alpha = \frac{k}{\rho c_\mathrm{p}} = \frac{kc_\mathrm{v}}{\rho c_\mathrm{v}c_\mathrm{p}} = \frac{D_\mathrm{AA}}{\gamma} = \frac{\bar{U}\lambda}{3\gamma} \tag{14.31}$$

where the heat capacity ratio γ is

$$\gamma = c_\mathrm{p}/c_\mathrm{v} \tag{14.32}$$

The above equations are restricted to dilute monatomic gases that act as rigid spheres; these equations are usually not valid for real materials under most normal conditions. Note the relationship between the transport coefficients:

$$k = c_\mathrm{v}\mu = \rho c_\mathrm{v}D_\mathrm{AA} \tag{14.33}$$

$$D_\mathrm{AA} = \frac{\mu}{\rho} = v = \alpha\gamma \tag{14.34}$$

where v is the kinematic viscosity. The mean-free-path development has predicted equality among the transport coefficients.

Equation (14.30) can be used with Eq. (14.29) to determine estimates of the temperature and pressure dependency of k and D_AA. For an ideal, monatomic gas (called the perfect gas in many chemical engineering texts), the heat capacity c_v is equal to the following constant, independent of temperature and pressure:

$$c_\mathrm{v} = \frac{3}{2}\frac{R}{M} \tag{14.35}$$

where R is the gas constant. In the case of D_AA, the density may be substituted through use of the ideal gas law:

$$\rho = \frac{nM}{V} = \frac{pM}{RT} \tag{14.36}$$

The reliability of the predictions for thermal conductivity or self-diffusion coefficient is about the same as for viscosity.

14.1.2 Non-Uniform Gas Theory

The mathematical theory of non-uniform gases (developed about the time of World War I by Chapman [C1] and Enskog [E2]) allows a much more rigorous and realistic treatment of the problem of estimating transport coefficients from molecular properties. Its development requires four important assumptions:

1. The gas is "dilute" in that only binary collisions occur.
2. The motion of the molecules during the binary collision can be described by classical mechanics.
3. All collisions are elastic.
4. The intermolecular forces act only between fixed centers of the molecules; i.e., the forces at any radius r are identical for all angles.

The Chapman–Enskog theory itself is too lengthy to treat in detail and is available elsewhere [C2, H5]. The "dilute" gas assumptions must always be satisfied. The theory is often successfully applied to viscosity and diffusion coefficients of polyatomic gases (in fact, no better theory has been developed), but in the case of thermal conductivity, significant corrections are necessary.

The Lennard-Jones 12–6 potential [L5] is commonly used to describe the potential energy, $u(r)$, of the interaction of two spherical, nonpolar molecules as a function of distance:

$$u(r) = 4\varepsilon\left[\left(\frac{\sigma}{r}\right)^{12} - \left(\frac{\sigma}{r}\right)^{6}\right] \tag{14.37}$$

where ε is the minimum value of $u(r)$ and is called the characteristic energy of interaction and σ is a characteristic diameter of the collision and is of the same order as d from the mean-free-path kinetic theory. The Lennard-Jones 12–6 potential, plotted in Fig. 14.1, contains two characteristic parameters (σ and ε); these are determined from viscosity data when estimating transport coefficients. Table A.3 contains these constants, which are to be used to evaluate a certain integral in the Chapman–Enskog theory called the collision integral: Ω_μ for viscosity or thermal conductivity and Ω_D for diffusion. The collision integral has a value of unity for collisions between rigid spheres. For real gas molecules, the collision integrals have been worked out [C2, H5, R1]. Convenient equations for both Ω_μ and Ω_D (nonpolar and polar molecules) are

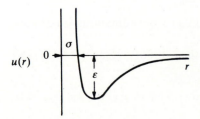

FIGURE 14.1
Lennard–Jones 12–6 potential for the interaction of two spherical, nonpolar molecules.

in Appendix A, Section A.2. The collision integral is a function of the dimensionless (also called reduced) temperature T^*:

$$T^* = \frac{T}{\varepsilon/k_B} \tag{14.38}$$

When the Lennard-Jones parameters are not known, it is possible to estimate them from thermodynamic data [B4, H5]. The recommended equations for estimation are [T1]

$$\sigma\left(\frac{p_c}{T_c}\right)^{1/3} = (10^{-10})(2.3551 - 0.087\omega) \tag{14.39}$$

$$\frac{\varepsilon/k_B}{T_c} = 0.7915 + 0.1693\omega \tag{14.40}$$

where p_c is the critical pressure (atm), T_c is the critical temperature (K), ω is the acentric factor,[2] and the parameter σ is in meters. Substantial errors may result when σ and ε/k_B are estimated by Eqs. (14.39) and (14.40) or by other equations listed in Appendix A. Note that because $\log \Omega_\mu$ is almost a linear function of $\log T^*$, the set of Lennard-Jones parameters for a given compound cannot be unique [R1]. Therefore, it is very important to use a consistent set of Lennard-Jones parameters, without worrying about disagreement in values from different investigators.

Viscosity. For viscosity, the Chapman–Enskog theory predicts

$$\mu = 2.6693 \times 10^{-26}\left(\frac{(MT)^{1/2}}{\sigma^2 \Omega_\mu}\right) \tag{14.41}$$

where M is the molecular weight, T is the absolute temperature in K, μ is the viscosity in SI units (kg m^{-1} s^{-1} or Pa s^{-1}), and the parameter σ is in meters. Use of Eq. (14.41) and the associated Appendix material will be illustrated in Example 14.1.

Thermal conductivity. For thermal conductivity, the Chapman–Enskog theory predicts

$$k = 8.3224 \times 10^{-22}\left(\frac{(T/M)^{1/2}}{\sigma^2 \Omega_\mu}\right) \tag{14.42}$$

where the units of k are W m^{-1} K^{-1}, and the units of the remaining quantities are the same as for Eq. (14.41).

The predictions from the Chapman–Enskog theory [Eqs. (14.41) and

---

[2] Extensive tabulations of p_c, T_c, and ω are in many standard references [e.g. R1] and all modern thermodynamics texts.

(14.42)] can be combined [H5]:

$$k = \frac{15}{4}\frac{R}{M}\mu = \tfrac{5}{2}c_v\mu \tag{14.43}$$

where c_v for an ideal, monatomic gas is given in Eq. (14.35). Note that Eq. (14.43) predicts k to be 2.5 times larger (for the same $c_v\mu$) as that from the mean-free-path approach, Eq. (14.33).

Equation (14.43) applies to gases that are composed of spherically symmetric molecules having only translational energy. For such systems, one can see from Eq. (14.43) that the prediction of temperature and pressure dependence for thermal conductivity is the same as for viscosity. Equation (14.43) can be rearranged into dimensionless form:

$$\frac{k}{\mu c_v} = \frac{5}{2} \tag{14.44}$$

where the group $k/(\mu c_v)$ is called the Eucken factor [E3, R1]. The constant 5/2 is confirmed to within experimental error by data for monoatomic gases, but the Eucken factor for even the simplest polyatomic gases, such as hydrogen, is much lower [R1]. Note the similarity between the dimensionless Eucken factor and dimensionless Prandtl number, Eq. (8.3).

Polyatomic gases. Equations (14.42) to (14.44) are valid only for noble or monatomic gases. In the theory presented in Section 14.1.1, only translational energy was considered [see comments following Eq. (14.22)]. For polyatomic gases, the problem becomes more complicated. Inelastic collisions and molecule orientation become important factors and contribute to internal energy changes.

The perfect gas used to obtain Eq. (14.43) is capable only of translational energy. Therefore, let us denote k_{tr} as the translational contribution; then from Eq. (15.43):

$$k_{tr} = \frac{15}{4}\frac{R}{M}\mu = \tfrac{5}{2}c_{v,tr}\mu \tag{14.45}$$

where the subscript "tr" denotes the translational contribution only. The thermal conductivity and heat capacity of a polyatomic molecule contains potential and kinetic energy contributions from vibrational and rotational modes of motion. Eucken [E3] proposed that these internal-energy contributions be added to those from Eq. (14.45). His simplistic analysis yields the Eucken correlation for polyatomic gases:

$$\frac{k}{\mu} = c_v\left(\frac{9\gamma - 5}{4}\right) = c_p + \frac{5}{4}\frac{R}{M} = c_v + \frac{9}{4}\frac{R}{M} \tag{14.46}$$

where γ is the ratio of heat capacities, Eq. (14.32). Later analyses yielded the modified Eucken correlation [R1]:

$$\frac{k}{\mu} = 1.32c_v + \frac{1.4728 \times 10^4}{M} = 1.32\frac{c_p}{\gamma} + \frac{1.4728 \times 10^4}{M}$$

$$= c_v\left(\frac{7.032\gamma - 1.720}{4}\right) \tag{14.47}$$

where k is in $\text{W m}^{-1}\text{K}^{-1}$, μ is in $\text{kg m}^{-1}\text{s}^{-1}$, and c_v (or c_p) is in $\text{J kg}^{-1}\text{K}^{-1}$.

The modified Eucken correlation, Eq. (14.47), predicts larger values of k than the original correlation, Eq. (14.46); both reduce to Eq. (14.43) for the perfect gas. According to Reid, Prausnitz, and Sherwood [R1], experimental values of k lie between values calculated by the two Eucken correlations, except for polar gases, for which both predict k values that are too high.

Diffusion coefficient. The Chapman–Enskog equation for the diffusion coefficient in a binary mixture is

$$D = D_{AB} = D_{BA} = 1.8829 \times 10^{-22}\frac{\{T^3[(1/M_A) + (1/M_B)]\}^{1/2}}{p\sigma_{AB}^2\Omega_D} \tag{14.48}$$

where D_{AB} is in m^2s^{-1}, p is pressure (N m^{-2} or Pa), and T is in K. A useful form of Eq. (14.48) has the pressure in units of atm:

$$D_{AB} = 1.8583 \times 10^{-27}\frac{\{T^3[(1/M_A) + (1/M_B)]\}^{1/2}}{p_{\text{atm}}\sigma_{AB}^2\Omega_D} \tag{14.49}$$

The collision integral Ω_D differs markedly from that determined from viscosity data. Appropriate correlating equations for nonpolar and polar gas pairs are in Appendix A, Section A.2. The appropriate dimensionless temperature for mixtures is

$$T^* = \frac{T}{\varepsilon_{AB}/k_B} \tag{14.50}$$

Experience has shown that the following combining rules are often adequate to determine σ_{AB} and ε_{AB} [R1]:

$$\sigma_{AB} = \tfrac{1}{2}(\sigma_A + \sigma_B) \tag{14.51}$$

$$\varepsilon_{AB} = (\varepsilon_A\varepsilon_B)^{1/2} \tag{14.52}$$

Inspection of the symmetry of the subscripts A and B demonstrate the equality of the diffusion coefficients as noted in Eq. (14.48). Note that D_{AB} is often called the mutual diffusion coefficient. Equation (14.48) also applies to self-diffusion, i.e., D_{AA}.

Summary. The mean-free-path treatment is instructive in explaining some of the basic principles and mechanisms that take place in transport phenomena. That theory leads to the more rigorous and successful Chapman–Enskog theory, which can be used to predict transport coefficients. The Chapman–Enskog theory is particularly satisfactory in predicting viscosities of nonpolar gases and gas mixtures at low density, since the Lennard-Jones parameters were determined from such data. Accuracies in the order of 1 percent or less are common [R1]; when σ and ε/k_B must be estimated from Eqs. (14.39) and (14.40), the errors may be 3 percent [R1].

For thermal conductivity, the modified Eucken correlation, Eq. (14.47), predicts larger values of k than the original, Eq. (14.46). Bird, Stewart, and Lightfoot [B4] compared the experimental Prandtl number with that from the original equation and found good agreement for monatomic and diatomic molecules and poor agreement for more complex gases. Usually, the experimental values of k lie between the values calculated from Eqs. (14.46) and (14.47), except for polar gases whose thermal conductivities are less than those from the equations [R1].

Prediction of the mutual diffusion coefficient D_{AB} from Eq. (14.48) or Eq. (14.49) is usually within 6 percent for nonpolar gas pairs at low density, if the collision constants are available from viscosity data [B2, B4, F1]. If the Lennard-Jones parameters must be estimated from Eqs. (14.39) and (14.40), the errors increase to about 10 percent.

A deficiency of the Chapman–Enskog theory is that it fails to predict a variation in the diffusion coefficient with concentration. For example, diffusion coefficients in some binary gas systems such as chloroform–air may vary as much as 9 percent with concentration, whereas in other systems such as methanol–air the diffusion coefficient is independent of concentration, at least within the experimental accuracy, usually 3 percent [M5].

The Chapman–Enskog equations for the transport coefficients are valid for the range 200–1000 K. Below 200 K, quantum effects become important [H5], and above 1000 K the Lennard-Jones potential function is no longer applicable. However, if the force constants are derived from diffusion data (instead of the usual viscosity data), the equations may be extended to 1200 K or so. Above 1200 K the force constants must be evaluated from molecular beam scattering experiments.

The transport property equations that have been presented were developed for dilute gases composed of nonpolar, spherical, monatomic molecules. Empirical functions and correlations (the Lennard-Jones potential) must be used, with the net result that the equations are remarkable for their ability to predict transport coefficients for many gas systems. The pressure and temperature limitations have already been discussed. Agreement in nonpolar gas systems is excellent, even for polyatomic molecules. For a polar–nonpolar gas system the same equations are used with different combining laws, which must be modified slightly [H5, R1]. For polar–polar gas pairs, the changes are more severe [R1], and there have been very few experimental investigations to support the proposed methods. Brokaw [B6] shows how to estimate transport properties of polar–polar systems; more details are in Example 14.5 and Appendix A, Section A.2.

Example 14.1. Estimate the viscosity of air at 40°C (313.15 K) and atmospheric pressure; compare the answer with the value of 19.11×10^{-6} N s m^{-2} (0.01911 cP) given in Table A.2.

Answer. Equation (14.41), which is based on the Chapman–Enskog theory, is used to estimate the viscosity:

$$\mu = 2.6693 \times 10^{-26} \left(\frac{(MT)^{1/2}}{\sigma^2 \Omega_\mu} \right) \tag{14.41}$$

From Table A.3, the Lennard-Jones parameters for air are

$$\sigma = 3.711 \times 10^{-10} \, \text{m} \qquad \varepsilon/k_B = 78.6 \, \text{K} \tag{i}$$

The collision integral is calculated from Eq. (A.1):

$$\Omega_{\mu, \text{nonpolar}} = \frac{A}{(T^*)^B} + \frac{C}{\exp(DT^*)} + \frac{E}{\exp(FT^*)} \tag{A.1}$$

where the constants in Eq. (A.1) are

$$A = 1.16145 \qquad B = 0.14874 \qquad C = 0.52487$$
$$D = 0.77320 \qquad E = 2.16178 \qquad F = 2.43787 \tag{A.2}$$
$$0.3 \leq T^* \leq 100$$

The dimensionless temperature T^* from Eq. (14.38) is

$$T^* = \frac{T}{\varepsilon/k_B} = \frac{313.15}{78.6} = 3.984 \tag{ii}$$

Substituting the above numbers into Eq. (A.1), the collision integral is

$$\Omega_\mu = 0.96984 \tag{iii}$$

The molecular weight of air (Table A.2) is 28.966 kg kmol^{-1}. From Eq. (14.41), the viscosity of air is

$$\mu = 2.6693 \times 10^{-26} \left(\frac{(MT)^{1/2}}{\sigma^2 \Omega_\mu} \right) = 2.6693 \times 10^{-26} \left(\frac{[(28.966)(313.15)]^{1/2}}{(3.711 \times 10^{-10})^2 (0.96984)} \right)$$

$$= 19.03 \times 10^{-6} \, \text{N s m}^{-2} = 0.01903 \, \text{cP} \tag{iv}$$

The excellent agreement of about 0.4 percent is expected, since the Lennard-Jones constants were determined from viscosity data.

Example 14.2. Calculate the thermal conductivity of air and of argon at 40°C and 1 atm using the Chapman–Enskog equation.

Answer. The Lennard-Jones parameters and collision integral for air are in Eqs. (i) and (iii) in Example 14.1. Using Eq. (14.42), the estimate of k is

$$k = 8.3224 \times 10^{-22} \left(\frac{(T/M)^{1/2}}{\sigma^2 \Omega_\mu} \right) = 8.3224 \times 10^{-22} \left(\frac{[(313.15)/(28.966)]^{1/2}}{(3.711 \times 10^{-10})^2 (0.96984)} \right)$$

$$= 0.02049 \, \text{W m}^{-1} \text{K}^{-1} \tag{i}$$

Agreement between this value and that from Table A.2 (0.02709) is poor; the Chapman–Enskog theory is in error when applied to the thermal conductivity of polyatomic gases.

For argon (molecular weight 39.948), the Lennard-Jones parameters from Table A.3 are

$$\sigma = 3.542 \times 10^{-10} \text{ m} \qquad \varepsilon/k_B = 93.3 \text{ K} \qquad \text{(ii)}$$

Proceeding as in Example 14.1 for air:

$$T^* = \frac{T}{\varepsilon/k_B} = \frac{313.15}{93.3} = 3.356 \qquad \Omega_\mu = 1.010 \qquad \text{(iii)}$$

Using Eq. (14.42), the estimate of k is

$$k = 8.3224 \times 10^{-22} \left(\frac{(T/M)^{1/2}}{\sigma^2 \Omega_\mu} \right) = 8.3224 \times 10^{-22} \left(\frac{[(313.15)/(39.948)]^{1/2}}{(3.542 \times 10^{-10})^2 (1.010)} \right)$$

$$= 0.01839 \text{ W m}^{-1} \text{ K}^{-1} \qquad \text{(iv)}$$

The thermal conductivity from the Chapman–Enskog theory agrees closely with the experimental value of 0.0185; note that argon is a monatomic gas.

Example 14.3. Calculate the thermal conductivity of air at 40°C and 1 atm, given that the heat capacity c_p is 1005 J kg^{-1} K^{-1}.

Answer. The Eucken formulas require the heat capacity ratio γ. For an ideal gas, it can be shown that

$$c_v = c_p - R/M \qquad \text{(i)}$$

where from Table C.1 the value of R is 8.3143×10^3 J kmol^{-1} K^{-1}. Then

$$c_v = 1005 - 8314.3/28.966 = 718 \text{ J kg}^{-1} \text{ K}^{-1} \qquad \text{(ii)}$$

$$\gamma = c_p/c_v = 1005/718 = 1.400 \qquad \text{(iii)}$$

From Table A.2, the viscosity of air is 19.11×10^{-6} kg m^{-1} s^{-1}. Using the original Eucken correlation, Eq. (14.46), k is

$$k = \mu \left(c_p + \frac{5}{4} \frac{R}{M} \right) = (19.11 \times 10^{-6}) \left(1005 + \frac{(5)(8.3143 \times 10^3)}{(4)(28.966)} \right)$$

$$= 0.02606 \, [(\text{kg m}^{-1} \text{ s}^{-1})(\text{J kg}^{-1} \text{ K}^{-1})]$$

$$= 0.02606 \text{ J s}^{-1} \text{ m}^{-1} \text{ K}^{-1} = 0.02606 \text{ W m}^{-1} \text{ K}^{-1} \qquad \text{(iv)}$$

The modified Eucken correlation, Eq. (14.47), yields

$$k = \mu \left(1.32 \frac{c_p}{\gamma} + \frac{1.4728 \times 10^4}{M} \right) = (19.11 \times 10^{-6}) \left(\frac{(1.32)(1005)}{1.400} + \frac{1.4728 \times 10^4}{28.966} \right)$$

$$= 0.02782 \text{ W m}^{-1} \text{ K}^{-1} \qquad \text{(v)}$$

As discussed, the value from the modified Eucken equation is higher than the experimental value (0.02709), and the value predicted by the original Eucken equation is lower than the experimental value, each being about 3 percent different, in this case.

TABLE 14.1
Comparison of results for Example 14.4

T, K	T*	Ω_D	Diffusion coefficient, $D_{AB} \times 10^4$, m² s⁻¹ Part (a) Eq. (14.49)	Part (b) Eq. (viii)	Part (c) Eq. (2.50)	Experimental*
323	11.96	0.7205	0.794	—	—	0.766
413	15.29	0.6929	1.194	1.152	1.178	1.20
600	22.21	0.6535	2.216	2.138	2.264	2.40
900	33.32	0.6134	4.336	4.185	4.603	4.76
1200	44.42	0.5865	6.983	6.738	7.615	7.74

* From Seager, Geertson, and Giddings, *J. Chem. Eng. Data* **8:** 168 (1963).

Example 14.4. The diffusion coefficient of the helium–nitrogen system is 7.66×10^{-5} m² s⁻¹ at 323 K and 1 atm [S5].
(a) Use the Chapman–Enskog equation to find the diffusion coefficient at 413 K, 600 K, 900 K, and 1200 K.
(b) Use the experimental diffusion coefficient and the Chapman–Enskog equation to estimate the diffusion coefficients in part (a).
(c) Use Eq. (2.50).
(d) Compare all answers with experimental results [S5].

Answer. A sample calculation for 413 K will be given for each of parts (a), (b), and (c). The complete results will be summarized in Table 14.1.

Part (a). The Chapman–Enskog equation, Eq. (14.49), applies:

$$D_{AB} = 1.8583 \times 10^{-27} \frac{\{T^3[(1/M_A) + (1/M_B)]\}^{1/2}}{p_{atm}\sigma_{AB}^2\Omega_D} \tag{14.49}$$

For helium, the molecular weight [P2] and Lennard-Jones parameters (Table A.2) are

$$M_A = 4.0026 \qquad \sigma_A = 2.551 \times 10^{-10} \text{ m} \qquad \varepsilon_A/k_B = 10.22 \text{ K} \tag{i}$$

For nitrogen, the molecular weight [P2] and Lennard-Jones parameters (Table A.2) are

$$M_B = 28.0134 \qquad \sigma_B = 3.798 \times 10^{-10} \text{ m} \qquad \varepsilon_B/k_B = 71.4 \text{ K} \tag{ii}$$

The combining rules, Eqs. (14.51) and (14.52), yield

$$\sigma_{AB} = \tfrac{1}{2}(\sigma_A + \sigma_B) = \tfrac{1}{2}(2.551 \times 10^{-10} + 3.798 \times 10^{-10}) = 3.1745 \times 10^{-10} \text{ m} \tag{iii}$$

$$\varepsilon_{AB}/k_B = \frac{(\varepsilon_A\varepsilon_B)^{1/2}}{k_B} = [(10.22)(71.4)]^{1/2} = 27.01 \text{ K} \tag{iv}$$

The dimensionless temperature from Eq. (14.50) is

$$T^* = \frac{T}{\varepsilon_{AB}/k_B} = \frac{413.0}{27.01} = 15.29 \tag{v}$$

This temperature, plus the constants in Eq. (A.15) in Appendix A, are used in Eq. (A.14) to find the collision integral for diffusion:

$$\Omega_D = 0.6929 \tag{vi}$$

Equation (14.49) is used to find the mutual diffusion coefficient:

$$D_{AB} = 1.8583 \times 10^{-27} \frac{\{T^3[(1/M_A) + (1/M_B)]\}^{1/2}}{p_{atm}\sigma_{AB}^2\Omega_D}$$

$$= 1.8583 \times 10^{-27} \frac{\{(413)^3[(1/4.0026) + (1/28.016)]\}^{1/2}}{(1.0)(3.1745 \times 10^{-10})^2(0.6929)} = 1.194 \times 10^{-4} \, \text{m}^2 \, \text{s}^{-1} \tag{vii}$$

Part (b). In this calculation, Eq. (14.49) will be used to establish the ratio of D_{AB} evaluated at the four unknown temperatures, divided by D_{AB} at 323 K (D_{323}). Let us call D_{AB} at the unknown temperatures D_T. All terms cancel except temperature and collision integral:

$$D_T/D_{323} = (T/323)^{3/2}(\Omega_{D,323}/\Omega_{D,T}) \tag{viii}$$

Following the procedure in part (a), the dimensionless temperature and collision integral are

$$T^* = \frac{T}{\varepsilon_{AB}/k_B} = \frac{323.0}{27.01} = 11.96 \tag{ix}$$

$$\Omega_{D,323} = 0.7205 \tag{x}$$

For 413 K, the collision integral $\Omega_{D,413}$ was found in Eq. (vi). Equation (viii) is solved for D_{413}:

$$D_{413} = D_{323}\left(\frac{413}{323}\right)^{3/2}\left(\frac{\Omega_{D,323}}{\Omega_{D,413}}\right) = (7.66 \times 10^{-5})\left(\frac{413}{323}\right)^{3/2}\left(\frac{0.7205}{0.6929}\right)$$

$$= 1.152 \times 10^{-4} \, \text{m}^2 \, \text{s}^{-1} \tag{xi}$$

Part (c). Equation (2.50) is

$$D = D_0 \frac{p_0}{p}\left(\frac{T}{T_0}\right)^n \tag{2.50}$$

where the exponent n varies from 1.75 to 2.0. For this example, let n be equal to 1.75:

$$D_{413} = D_{323}\left(\frac{413}{323}\right)^{1.75} = (7.66 \times 10^{-5})\left(\frac{413}{323}\right)^{1.75} = 1.178 \times 10^{-4} \, \text{m}^2 \, \text{s}^{-1} \tag{xii}$$

Note that this answer agrees closely with that from part (a).

Part (d). Table 14.1 summarizes the results at all temperatures. Note that Eq. (14.49) is within 10 percent at 1200 K and within 1 percent at 413 K; however, the temperature dependence is clearly erroneous, as seen by the results of part (b). The exponent 1.75 is closer to the experimentally observed exponent (which can be easily calculated from Table 14.1 to be 1.74) than is the predicted temperature dependence of Eq. (14.49). Therefore, if one or more experimental points are available, Eq. (2.50) is preferable.

TABLE 14.2
Data for Example 14.5*

	Methyl chloride	Sulfur dioxide
Dipole moment, debyes	1.9	1.6
Normal boiling point, K	249	263
Liquid molar volume at T_b, $m^3 \, kmol^{-1}$	5.06×10^{-2}	4.38×10^{-2}
Molecular weight M_A, $kg \, kmol^{-1}$	50.48806	64.0628

* From Reid, Prausnitz, and Sherwood, *Properties of Gases and Liquids*, 3d ed., p. 552. McGraw-Hill, New York, 1977.

Example 14.5. The diffusion coefficient of the methyl chloride–sulfur dioxide system is $7.7 \times 10^{-6} \, m^2 \, s^{-1}$ at 1 atm and 323 K [R1]. Compare this result with that predicted by the Chapman–Enskog theory. Table 14.2 contains some pertinent information.

Answer. The solution to this problem differs from that in Example 14.4 in that the Stockmayer potential replaces the Lennard-Jones for estimating diffusion coefficients in polar gas systems. Let species A and B be methyl chloride and sulfur dioxide, respectively. Following Appendix A, Section A.2, the Stockmayer parameters and the dimensionless dipole moment are calculated from Eqs. (A.8), (A.9), and (A.10):

$$\delta_A = \frac{(1.94)(DPM)^2}{V_b T_b} = \frac{(1.94)(1.9)^2}{(5.06 \times 10^{-2})(249)} = 0.5559 \tag{i}$$

$$\delta_B = \frac{(1.94)(1.6)^2}{(4.38 \times 10^{-2})(263)} = 0.4311 \tag{ii}$$

$$\sigma_A = 1.166 \times 10^{-9} \left(\frac{V_b}{1 + 1.3\delta^2} \right)^{1/3} = 1.166 \times 10^{-9} \left(\frac{5.06 \times 10^{-2}}{1 + (1.3)(0.5559)^2} \right)^{1/3}$$

$$= 3.854 \times 10^{-10} \, m \tag{iii}$$

$$\sigma_B = 1.166 \times 10^{-9} \left(\frac{4.38 \times 10^{-2}}{1 + (1.3)(0.4311)^2} \right)^{1/3} = 3.824 \times 10^{-10} \, m \tag{iv}$$

$$\varepsilon_A / k_B = (1.18)(1 + 1.3\delta^2)(T_b) = (1.18)[1 + (1.3)(0.5559)^2](249) = 411.9 \, K \tag{v}$$

$$\varepsilon_B / k_B = (1.18)[1 + (1.3)(0.4311)^2](263) = 385.3 \, K \tag{vi}$$

Using the combining rules of Eqs. (14.51), (14.52), and (A.17):

$$\sigma_{AB} = \tfrac{1}{2}(\sigma_A + \sigma_B) = \tfrac{1}{2}(3.854 \times 10^{-10} + 3.824 \times 10^{-10}) = 3.839 \times 10^{-10} \, m \tag{vii}$$

$$\varepsilon_{AB} / k_B = \frac{(\varepsilon_A \varepsilon_B)^{1/2}}{k_B} = [(411.9)(385.3)]^{1/2} = 398.4 \, K \tag{viii}$$

$$\delta_{AB} = (\delta_A \delta_B)^{1/2} = [(0.5559)(0.4311)]^{1/2} = 0.4895 \tag{ix}$$

The dimensionless temperature from Eq. (14.50) is

$$T^* = \frac{T}{\varepsilon_{AB}/k_B} = \frac{323.0}{398.4} = 0.8108 \tag{x}$$

This temperature, plus the constants in Eq. (A.15) in Appendix A, is used in Eq. (A.14) to find the nonpolar collision integral for diffusion:

$$\Omega_{D,\,nonpolar} = 1.602 \tag{xi}$$

Next, the polar diffusion integral is found via Eq. (A.16):

$$\Omega_{D,\,polar} = \Omega_{D,\,nonpolar} + (0.19\delta_{AB}^2)/T^* = 1.602 + \frac{(0.19)(0.4895)^2}{0.8108} = 1.658 \tag{xii}$$

Finally, Eq. (14.49) is used to find the mutual diffusion coefficient:

$$D_{AB} = 1.8583 \times 10^{-27} \frac{\{T^3[(1/M_A) + (1/M_B)]\}^{1/2}}{p_{atm}\sigma_{AB}^2\Omega_D}$$

$$= 1.8583 \times 10^{-27} \frac{\{(323)^3[(1/50.488) + (1/64.063)]\}^{1/2}}{(1.0)(3.839 \times 10^{-10})^2(1.658)}$$

$$= 8.308 \times 10^{-6}\,\mathrm{m^2\,s^{-1}} \tag{xiii}$$

The Chapman–Enskog prediction is about 8 percent high.

14.1.3 Empirical Correlations for Gases

Viscosity. Inasmuch as the Chapman–Enskog equation is often as accurate as 1 percent, no empirical equations are recommended. Estimation of the viscosity of mixtures is covered in Appendix A.

Thermal conductivity. The Eucken equations are recommended in spite of their simplicity. Reid, Prausnitz, and Sherwood [R1] discuss other correlations that may be somewhat more accurate. There is significant disagreement between investigators in determining k for gases, and these uncertainties carry over into the empirical correlations. Small errors in k for gas systems are not usually of significance in engineering design.

Diffusion coefficient. The experimental uncertainty in the mutual diffusion coefficient D_{AB} is larger than that for either μ or k. Naturally, this uncertainty affects the accuracy of any correlation. The Chapman–Enskog theory is reasonably accurate, as illustrated in Examples 14.4 and 14.5.

The early correlations of D_{AB} were based on data of questionable accuracy [S4]. An excellent correlation, proposed by Fuller, Schettler, and Giddings [F1], considered only the most modern and reliable data. In the FSG correlation, use was made of high-temperature data taken by techniques not

TABLE 14.3

Atomic diffusion volumes for the correlation of Fuller, Schettler, and Giddings, Eq. (14.53)

Atomic structural diffusion volume increments, V'			
C	16.5	(Cl)*	19.5
H	1.98	(S)	17.0
O	5.48	Aromatic ring	−20.2
(N)	5.69	Heterocyclic ring	−20.2

Diffusion volumes for simple molecules, $(\Sigma V')_A$			
H_2	7.07	CO	18.9
D_2	6.70	CO_2	26.9
He	2.88	N_2O	35.9
N_2	17.9	NH_3	14.9
O_2	16.6	H_2O	12.7
Air	20.1	(CCl_2F_2)	114.8
Ar	16.1	(SF_6)	69.7
Kr	22.8	(Cl_2)	37.7
(Xe)	37.9	(Br_2)	67.2
Ne	5.59	(SO_2)	41.1

* Parentheses indicate that the value listed is based on only a few data points.

available when the earlier correlations were made:

$$D_{AB} = 10^{-7} \frac{T^{1.75}[(1/M_A) + (1/M_B)]^{1/2}}{p_{atm}[(\Sigma V')_A^{1/3} + (\Sigma V')_B^{1/3}]^2} \tag{14.53}$$

where D is in $m^2 s^{-1}$, T is in K, and p_{atm} is the pressure in atm. For each species, the term $\Sigma V'$ is found by summing the atomic diffusion volumes given in Table 14.3. Example 14.6 illustrates this calculation.

The FSG correlation, Eq. (14.53), although strictly empirical, requires less supplementary information than the Chapman–Enskog equation, Eq. (14.49), and therefore is recommended for general use. Equation (14.49) is more rigorous and gives comparable results when the force constants are available from Table A.3. Otherwise, the FSG correlation, Eq. (14.53), is recommended.

Dense gases. There are very few experimentally determined diffusion coefficients for dense gases. Theoretical treatments of dense gases are usually valid for liquids as well, as has been treated elsewhere [B3, C2, H5]. They are of little use to engineers in their present state of development.

Example 14.6. Find the diffusion coefficient of the helium–1-propanol system at 423.2 K and 5 atm using the FSG correlation. The molecular weights are 4.0026 and 60.09121, respectively. Compare your answer with the experimental value of $1.352 \times 10^{-5} \, \text{m}^2 \, \text{s}^{-1}$ [S5].

Answer. Equation (14.53) will be used to obtain the diffusion coefficient. For 1-propanol (chemical formula $CH_3CH_2CH_2OH$), the atomic diffusion volumes for carbon, hydrogen, and oxygen are found in Table 14.3 and used in the following:

$$(\Sigma V')_A = 3V'_C + 8V'_H + V'_O = (3)(16.5) + (8)(1.98) + (1)(5.48) = 70.82 \quad \text{(i)}$$

For helium, the atomic diffusion volume is 2.88. Substituting in Eq. (14.53), the mutual diffusion coefficient for the helium–1-propanol system is

$$D_{AB} = 10^{-7} \frac{T^{1.75}[(1/M_A) + (1/M_B)]^{1/2}}{p_{\text{atm}}[(\Sigma V')_A^{1/3} + (\Sigma V')_B^{1/3}]^2}$$

$$= 10^{-7} \left[\frac{(423.2)^{1.75}[(1/4.0026) + (1/60.091)]^{1/2}}{(5)[(70.82)^{1/3} + (2.88)^{1/3}]^2} \right]$$

$$= 1.32 \times 10^{-5} \, \text{m}^2 \, \text{s}^{-1} \quad \text{(ii)}$$

The FSG correlation agrees to about 2 percent with the experimental value.

14.2 LIQUIDS

While estimation of transport properties in gas systems is on a sound theoretical basis, in liquid systems the high densities, and therefore short separation distances between molecules, result in a strong influence of the intermolecular force fields. Our present knowledge of intermolecular forces is insufficient to allow direct calculation of liquid transport properties. Of most importance to the engineer are the extensive tabulations and empirical correlations available for the liquid state.

Theories of the liquid state may be separated according to their basic premises, which differ substantially, to say the least. Various models treat liquids as dense gases, as disordered solids, from a hydrodynamic view, or as kinetic systems.

14.2.1 Viscosity

The kinetic approach[3] of Eyring and coworkers [G4, H5] is based on the theory of rate processes applied to relaxation processes that may be important in determining the nature of the flow. Eyring's rate theory postulates the existence of an intermediate and unstable "activated complex" that is first formed from the reactants and later decomposes into the products. The decomposition of the complex is assumed to be the rate-controlling step, with an associated activation energy. The form of the specific rate constant k for the

---

[3] The discussion on the kinetic approach is adapted from Brodkey [B5].

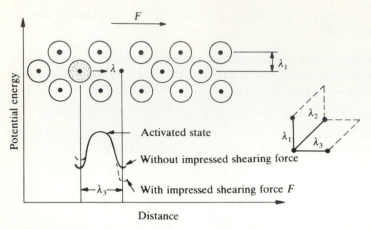

FIGURE 14.2
Model for the relaxation theory of liquids. (*Adapted from Hirschfelder, Curtiss, and Bird, Molecular Theory of Gases and Liquids, p. 626, Wiley, New York, 1954. By permission.*)

decomposition reaction is

$$k = (\kappa)(k_B T/h)\exp[(-\Delta G^*)/(RT)] \tag{14.54}$$

where k_B is the Boltzmann constant, h is Planck's constant, ΔG^* is the change in the molar free energy of activation, and κ is a transmission coefficient used to correct for the fact that not all molecules arriving at the activated state continue to complete the reaction.

The application of Eq. (14.54) to the relaxation theory of liquids is suggested by the model given in Fig. 14.2, which is a cross section of an idealized liquid. The flow is pictured as taking place by a unimolecular process [E5]; when a shearing force is applied to the fluid, the shaded molecule in Fig. 14.2 squeezes past the neighboring particles and moves into an unoccupied hole. The distance traveled by the particle is denoted by λ, which is shown as the forward direction in Fig. 14.2. The distance λ is the distance between two equilibrium positions of the molecule (or a cluster of molecules). The movement from one equilibrium position to another is termed a "jump". Shown also in Fig. 14.2 are the molecular distances λ_1, λ_2, and λ_3, which are defined as follows [E5]:

λ_1 The distance between sets of parallel shear layers

λ_2 The distance between neighboring in the moving layer in a direction at right angles to the shear

λ_3 The distance between neighboring molecules (or clusters) in the direction of λ

The net velocity of flow is the net number of jumps times the distance per jump:

$$U_\lambda = \lambda(k_f - k_r) \tag{14.55}$$

where U_λ is the net velocity and k_f and k_r are the specific jumping rates in the forward and reverse directions, respectively. If no force is acting, the forward and reverse rates will be equal, and from Eq. (14.54):

$$k_f = k_r = k_0 = (\kappa)(k_B T/h)\exp[(-\Delta G^*)/(RT)] \qquad (14.56)$$

where k_0 is the specific rate for the flow process (the jumping process of a molecule from an equilibrium position into the neighboring vacant site at zero stress). If the force is acting in the positive (forward) direction, then the forward process is increased and the reverse decreased. The amount of change per mole is the stress (force per unit area, τ_λ) times the area, acting over a distance $\frac{1}{2}\lambda$ times Avogadro's number N:

$$\text{Change in free energy} = (\tau_\lambda)(\lambda_2\lambda_3)(\tfrac{1}{2}\lambda)(N) \qquad (14.57)$$

where the area $\lambda_2\lambda_3$ is shown in Fig. 14.2. Using the Boltzmann constant as given in Eq. (14.6), the forward and reverse specific rates become

$$k_f = k_0 e^{\alpha F} \qquad (14.58)$$

$$k_r = k_0 e^{-\alpha F} \qquad (14.59)$$

where α is constant at a given temperature:

$$\alpha = \frac{\lambda\lambda_2\lambda_3}{2k_B T} \qquad (14.60)$$

Equation (14.55) becomes

$$U_\lambda = \lambda k_0 (e^{\alpha F} - e^{-\alpha F}) = 2\lambda k_0 \sinh(\alpha\tau_\lambda) \qquad (14.61)$$

Viscosity is defined by Newton's law, Eq. (2.5). The velocity U_λ is introduced into Newton's law via the shear rate, which in terms of U_λ is

$$\frac{dU_x}{dy} = \frac{U_x}{y} = \frac{U_\lambda}{\lambda_1} \qquad (14.62)$$

This result, plus Eqs. (14.60) and (14.61), is substituted into Eq. (2.5):

$$\mu = -\frac{\tau_{yx}}{dU_x/dy} = -\frac{\tau_{yx}}{U_\lambda/\lambda_1} = \frac{-\tau_{yx}\lambda_1}{2\lambda k_0 \sinh(-\alpha\tau_{yx})} \qquad (14.63)$$

The shear stress τ_λ in Eq. (14.61) was replaced by the negative of the shear stress in Eq. (14.63). For small external forces, the sinh term can be expanded in a Taylor's series. If only the first term in the expansion is retained, Eq. (14.63) becomes

$$\mu = \frac{\lambda_1 k_B T}{k_0 \lambda^2 \lambda_2 \lambda_3} \qquad (14.64)$$

Equations (14.56) and (14.64) can be combined and rearranged:

$$\mu = \frac{h\lambda_1}{\kappa\lambda^2\lambda_2\lambda_3} \exp\left(\frac{\Delta G^*}{RT}\right) \qquad (14.65)$$

Equation (14.65) is more simply expressed as

$$\mu = Ae^{B/(RT)} \qquad (2.52)$$

This equation is often called an "Arrhenius" equation. Equation (2.52) was used in Example 2.12 to determine μ for water at 326.15 K by interpolation of data at 300 K and 373.15 K. Equation (2.52) should not be used for extrapolation, as illustrated in Example 14.7.

> **Example 14.7.** Prepare a plot of viscosity of water between 273 K and 373 K; use Eq. (2.52) to extrapolate to 420 K. Compare the answer with $0.185 \times 10^{-3}\,\text{N s m}^{-2}$ (0.185 cP), given in Table A.1.
>
> **Answer.** Equation (2.52) is
>
> $$\mu = Ae^{B/(RT)} \qquad (2.52)$$
>
> Equation (2.52) is transformed as follows:
>
> $$y = \ln \mu \qquad \text{(i)}$$
> $$x = 1/T \qquad \text{(ii)}$$
> $$\beta_0 = \ln A \qquad \text{(iii)}$$
> $$\beta_1 = B/R \qquad \text{(iv)}$$
> $$y = \beta_0 + \beta_1 x \qquad \text{(v)}$$
>
> Equation (v) is the equation of a straight line. The 22 data points in Table A.1 for the viscosity of water between 273.15 K and 373.15 K can be fitted by least-squares, using standard techniques [P2]. With viscosity in cP, the constants are:
>
> $$\beta_0 = -6.301\,289 \qquad \beta_1 = 1853.374 \qquad \text{(vi)}$$
>
> At 420 K:
>
> $$\mu = \exp(\beta_0 + \beta_1 x) = \exp(-6.301\,289 + 1853.374/420) = 0.151\ \text{cP} \qquad \text{(vii)}$$
>
> When Eq. (v) is extrapolated to 420 K, the error is seen to be 18 percent. At midrange (320 K), Eq. (v) is approximately 4 percent in error.
>   Figure 14.3 is a plot of the data, plus Eq. (v) and the Table A.1 value at 420 K. Note the pronounced curvature of the data. Equation (2.52) is clearly inadequate over this temperature range. If Eq. (2.52) were to be used to interpolate, then only the adjacent points should be used to evaluate β_0 and β_1, not the 22 points used to compute the constants in Eq. (vi).

14.2.2 Thermal Conductivity

The semi-theoretical approach of Sakiadis and Coates [S1] considers a molecule that travels the intermolecular distance λ at the velocity of sound U_s. Upon collision, this molecule transfers an amount of heat ρc_p per unit temperature gradient. This analysis yields

$$k = \rho c_p U_s \lambda \qquad (14.66)$$

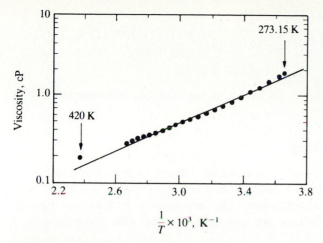

FIGURE 14.3
Temperature variation of the viscosity of water.

While all the quantities in Eq. (14.66) can be estimated or measured, this equation is not particularly convenient to use. Presently, there is no theory available to predict k from fundamental information alone, such as from critical properties, or from molecular models such as Lennard-Jones.

Many empirical equations have been proposed to estimate k; these are reviewed elsewhere [R1]. For a quick, approximate value of k for organic liquids, the method of Sato [R1] is recommended:

$$k = \frac{1.105}{M^{1/2}} \frac{c_p}{c_{pb}} \left(\frac{\rho}{\rho_b}\right)^{4/3} \frac{T_b}{T} \tag{14.67}$$

where the subscript b refers to the boiling point, T is in K, and M is the molecular weight. The units of k are $W\,m^{-1}\,K^{-1}$. Note that for the thermal conductivity at the normal boiling point, the equation simplifies because the last three ratios are unity.

Example 14.8. Estimate the thermal conductivity of tetrachloromethane (carbon tetrachloride) at its boiling point (349.90 K) and 20°C (293.15 K). The heat capacities at the two temperatures are 0.9205 and 0.8368 $kJ\,kg^{-1}\,K^{-1}$, respectively. The corresponding densities are 1480 and 1590 $kg\,m^{-3}$. The molecular weight of CCl_4 is 153.82.

Answer. Equation (14.67) is used to estimate k. At the normal boiling point, Eq. (14.67) reduces to

$$k = \frac{1.105}{M^{1/2}} \frac{c_p}{c_{pb}} \left(\frac{\rho}{\rho_b}\right)^{4/3} \frac{T_b}{T} = \frac{1.105}{M^{1/2}} \tag{i}$$

Thus, at the boiling point of 349.90 K, the estimated thermal conductivity is

$$k_b = 1.105/(153.82)^{1/2} = 0.08910\ W\,m^{-1}\,s^{-1} \tag{ii}$$

At 293.15 K (20°C), Eq. (14.67) yields

$$k = \frac{1.105}{M^{1/2}} \frac{c_p}{c_{pb}} \left(\frac{\rho}{\rho_b}\right)^{4/3} \frac{T_b}{T} = (0.08910)\left(\frac{0.8368}{0.9205}\right)\left(\frac{1590}{1480}\right)^{4/3}\left(\frac{349.90}{293.15}\right)$$

$$= 0.1064 \text{ W m}^{-1} \text{ K}^{-1} \tag{iii}$$

The estimate in Eq. (iii) is 3.4 percent higher than the experimental value of $0.1029 \text{ W m}^{-1} \text{ K}^{-1}$ [R1].

14.2.3   Diffusion Coefficient

Diffusion in liquids is complicated by nonideal effects, such as the variation in D_{AB} with concentration. In gas systems, it is usually possible to assume that D_{AB} is independent of concentration. This assumption is poor for liquids. Present theories or correlations are not able to deal with these nonlinear effects.

In this text, two diffusion coefficients have been introduced; D_{AA} is the self-diffusion coefficient for the case of species A diffusing through pure A, and D_{AB} is the mutual or binary diffusion coefficient for the case of species A diffusing through a mixture of A and B. There are two others that are of interest in liquid systems: D_{AB}^* is the tracer (or intradiffusion) diffusion coefficient for the diffusion of a labeled component within a homogeneous mixture [R1], and D_{AB}° is the mutual diffusion coefficient at infinite dilution, i.e., a single molecule of A diffusing in pure B.

Self-diffusion is the measure of mobility of a species in itself.[4] To perform the measurement, a small concentration of tagged molecules is followed. Tagging the molecule presumably does not measurably alter its properties or diffusion coefficient. The solution of tagged A in A is thus ideal, and there are no actual gradients "forcing" or "driving" the diffusion. Thus, the progress of the tagged A is purely statistical in nature. Self-diffusion measurements are of significant theoretical use in understanding the mechanisms of diffusion. Also, in theory, the mutual diffusion coefficient D_{AB} might be predicted from the pure-component self-diffusion coefficients D_{AA} and D_{BB}.

Tracer diffusion is similar to self-diffusion in that a small sample of tagged molecules is added; the difference is that tracer diffusion is the diffusion of tagged A in a mixture of A and B. Hence, tracer diffusion is often strongly concentration-dependent [V1], whereas self-diffusion is not. Another similarity is that no concentration gradient for diffusion exists in tracer diffusion experiments. Nevertheless, measurements can be important in providing insight into the nature of diffusion, as well as order-of-magnitude estimates of D_{AB}. Note that as the mole fraction of A approaches unity, D_{AB}^* approaches D_{AA}.

---

[4] Adapted from Kayser, J. C., and Knaebel, K. S., *Diffusion Coefficient Estimation*, Oct. 10, 1985. Unpublished course material. Department of Chemical Engineering, The Ohio State University, Columbus, OH 43210 [K1].

Some progress has been made in the theory of diffusion in liquids in that the theory at least predicts what variables to correlate. Again, none of the liquid theories has been developed to the point of engineering usefulness. There have been three approaches to the theory of diffusion in liquids: hydrodynamic, thermodynamic, and kinetic [B4, G6, H5, J3, J4, R1, T7]. Each of these will be discussed briefly in the next sections.

Hydrodynamic theory. In the formulation of the laws of Brownian motion, Sutherland [S9] and Einstein [E1] independently derived an equation for the diffusion coefficient by regarding the diffusion flow as a balance between a driving force and a flow resistance. These are usually called hydrodynamic theories. Sutherland and Einstein originally used the gradient of osmotic pressure as the driving force, but more modern developments use chemical potential.

Let us consider diffusion by Brownian motion in one dimension only; the following are assumed:

1. The solute particle concentration is sufficiently dilute so that all particles move independently under the influence of Brownian motion.
2. Each particle moves the same distance s in a given time Δt.
3. Half of the particles move in the $+x$ direction and the rest move in the $-x$ direction.

Figure 14.4 depicts a shape whose cross sectional area S is 1 m^2. Let us consider the flow across the plane QQ in the time Δt. First, by assumption (2), particles outside the planes PP and RR are not considered because they cannot cross the plane QQ in the time Δt. Let the average concentration in the PPQQ region be C_1 and the concentration in the QQRR region be C_2 where C_2 is greater than C_1. Under the influence of the concentration difference $C_2 - C_1$ there will be a net transfer of particles from right to left across the plane PP as

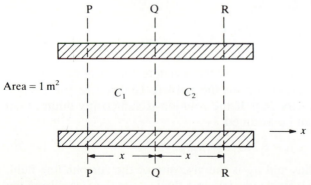

FIGURE 14.4
Movement of molecules due to Brownian motion.

follows:

$$\text{Particles per second in QQRR moving to the left} = \left(\frac{1}{2}\frac{x}{\Delta t}C_2\right)(1 \text{ m}^2) \quad (14.68)$$

$$\text{Particles per second in PPQQ moving to the right} = \left(\frac{1}{2}\frac{x}{\Delta t}C_1\right)(1 \text{ m}^2) \quad (14.69)$$

$$\text{Net transfer across QQ} = -\left(\frac{1}{2}\frac{x}{\Delta t}\right)(C_2 - C_1) \text{ (particles m}^{-2}\text{ s}^{-1}) \quad (14.70)$$

In Eq. (14.70), the minus sign signifies that transfer occurs from right to left, in the $-x$ direction. If the distance between planes PP and RR is small, then the concentration gradient is

$$\frac{dC}{dx} = \frac{C_2 - C_1}{x} \quad (14.71)$$

or

$$C_2 - C_1 = x\frac{dC}{dx} \quad (14.72)$$

Combining Eq. (14.70) with Eq. (14.72) gives the net transfer across QQ:

$$\text{Particles m}^{-2}\text{ s}^{-1} = -\left(\frac{1}{2}\frac{x^2}{\Delta t}\right)\frac{dC}{dx} \quad (14.73)$$

The quantity (particles $\text{m}^{-2}\text{ s}^{-1}$) is a diffusion flux, based on particles (or molecules). Therefore, Eq. (14.73) is seen to be in the form of Fick's law, Eq. (2.4). As discussed previously, the diffusion coefficient is the proportionality constant in Fick's law that relates the flux to the concentration gradient. Thus the diffusion coefficient is

$$D = \frac{1}{2}\frac{x^2}{\Delta t} \quad (14.74)$$

Einstein showed that the mean-square displacement in the x direction due to Brownian movement is [E1, G3, G6]

$$\overline{x^2} = \frac{2k_B T}{f_1}\Delta T \quad (14.75)$$

where k_B is the Boltzmann constant, T is the absolute temperature, and f_1 is the frictional resistance of the liquid on the particle (defined as the friction force F_p divided by the velocity U_∞). If the solution is sufficiently dilute, then Stokes' law [Eq. (12.65)] can be assumed:

$$f_1 = F_p/U_\infty = 6\pi\mu_B r_p \quad (14.76)$$

where r_p is the particle radius and μ_B is the viscosity of the surrounding fluid. Since Stokes' law considers a single particle in a fluid, μ_B is the viscosity of the solvent. From Eqs. (14.74) through (14.76), the Stokes–Einstein equation is obtained:

$$D = k_B T/(6\pi\mu_B r_p) \tag{14.77}$$

The Stokes–Einstein equation predicts

$$D\mu_B/T = \text{constant} \tag{14.78}$$

Equation (14.78) is reasonably valid for liquids over small changes in viscosity and temperature. Equation (14.78) has been widely used as a basis for interpreting experimental data in liquids, both for the diffusion of electrolytes and for nonelectrolytes.

Thermodynamic theory. From the thermodynamics of irreversible processes, as originally formulated by Onsager [O2], a formalized approach to the evaluation of diffusion coefficients has been developed. In spite of considerable effort, irreversible thermodynamics offers little to the engineer interested in predicting diffusion coefficients in liquid systems.

Kinetic theory. Two types of kinetic theories have been developed for liquids. The first is based on statistical mechanics as was the Chapman–Enskog theory for dilute gases. However, the liquid theory has not evolved to the same point as the dilute gas theory. The more successful kinetic theory was originally formulated by Eyring to explain chemical reaction rates [E4, G4], and was considered earlier in regard to the temperature dependence of viscosity. The Eyring approach to liquid diffusion predicts that the diffusion coefficient times the solvent viscosity divided by the temperature is a constant [i.e., the identical result to that reported in Eq. (14.78)]. The Eyring constant is a function of the distances between molecules in the lattice structure. From the Eyring theory, the dependence of diffusion coefficient on temperature is

$$D_{AB} = A e^{-E_D/(RT)} \tag{14.79}$$

where A is a constant and E_D is the activation energy of diffusion. Equation (14.79) suggests that diffusion data plotted as the log D versus $1/T$ should be a straight line, and such is the case over a limited temperature range. The temperature dependence in Eq. (14.79) has been used as a basis for correlations by several investigators [L7, R1].

Correlations. Since the theories of diffusion in liquids are still incomplete from the standpoint of being able to predict the transport coefficient D_{AB}, empirical correlations and direct laboratory measurements are the only recourse. The large variation in diffusion coefficient with changes in concentration cannot be predicted theoretically or empirically with consistency. The concentration effects are reviewed elsewhere [H4, R1, T7]. Even the most modern correlations are often in considerable error. Again, there is substantial disagreement between different experimentalists studying the same system.

TABLE 14.4
Correlations for liquid phase diffusion coefficients*

Type of system	Correlation	reference
Binary		
Electrolytes	1. Nernst–Haskell (1888)	[N1]
	2. Gordon (1937)	[G5]
Nonelectrolytes		
Self-diffusion coefficients	1. Hildebrand (1971)	[H3]
	2. Dullien (1972)	[D3]
Dilute A through solvent B		
Macromolecules	1. Stokes–Einstein (1905)	[E1]
Viscous solvents	1. Hiss–Cussler (1973)	[H6]
Gases in liquids	1. Sridhar–Potter (1977)	[S7]
	2. Wilke–Chang (1955)	[W2]
Diffusion in water (B)	1. Wilke–Chang (1955)	[W2]
	2. Hayduk–Laudie (1974)†	[H1]
Diffusion of water (A)	1. Sitaraman et al. (1963)	[S6]
	2. Olander (1961)	[O1]
	3. Wilke–Chang (1955)	[W2]
Normal paraffins	1. Hayduk–Minhas (1982)	[H2]
Organic (A) in organic (B)	1. Scheibel (1954)	[S3]
Concentrated	1. Bearman (1961); Darken (1948)	[B1, D1]
	2. Vignes (1966)	[V4]
	3. Leffler–Cullinan (1970)	[L3]
	4. Cussler (1980)	[C5]
	5. Duda et al. (1982)	[D2]
Multicomponent		
	1. Perkins–Geankoplis (1969)	[P1]
	2. Cullinan–Cusick (1967)	[C4]
	3. Leffler–Cullinan (1970)	[L3]
	4. Akita (1981)	[A1]

* Adapted from Kayser, J. C., and Knaebel, K. S., *Diffusion Coefficient Estimation,* Oct. 10, 1985. Unpublished course material. Department of Chemical Engineering, The Ohio State University, Columbus, OH 43210 [K1].

† The proposed equation in this article, as cited in references [H1, R1], has an incorrect exponent for viscosity; the correct exponent is 1.14 [H2].

    Correlations for liquid diffusion coefficients usually apply only to specific systems, such as nonelectrolyte or electrolyte solutions, dilute or concentrated solutions, and even aqueous or nonaqueous systems. Table 14.4 presents a summary of the available (and recommended) correlations for these categories.

Wilke–Chang correlation. Equation (14.78) forms the basis for the Wilke–Chang correlation. Although not the most modern correlation for dilute solutions of nonelectrolytes, the Wilke–Chang [W2] is the most general correlation proposed to date:

$$D_{AB} = \frac{1.17 \times 10^{-16}(T)(\phi M_B)^{1/2}}{\mu_B V_A^{0.6}} \tag{14.80}$$

where D_{AB} is the diffusion coefficient of solute A in solvent B ($m^2 s^{-1}$), M_B is the molecular weight of the solvent, T is the temperature in K, μ_B is the viscosity of the solvent in $kg\,m^{-1}\,s^{-1}$ ($N\,s\,m^{-2}$ or Pa s), and V_A is the molal volume of the solute at its normal boiling point in ($m^3\,kmol^{-1}$). The subscripts are used on D_{AB}, since Eq. (14.80) is clearly not symmetric (see discussion in Chapter 2). The term ϕ is the Wilke–Chang "association parameter" with the following values: water, 2.6 (a value of 2.26 appears better [R1]); methanol, 1.9; ethanol, 1.5; other unassociated solvents (such as benzene, ether, heptane), 1.0. The molal volume V_A of the solute is obtained by the Le Bas method [L2, R1], using the volumes or the volume increments in Table A.4, Appendix A. To find V_A, the number of each atom appearing in a molecule of species A times its increment is summed for every atom in the molecule. The additive volume method is illustrated in Example 14.9. Note that Eq. (14.80) is an empirical equation whose constant has units.

The Wilke–Chang correlation is usually accurate to within 10–15 percent [R1] in the temperature range 10–30°C; most of the data used by these authors were in this range. The Wilke–Chang correlation was proposed for both aqueous and nonaqueous systems. Later, studies have shown that the Eq. (14.80) is satisfactory for most cases of an organic solute diffusing in water. In the opposite case, water diffusing through an organic solvent, a study by Reid, Prausnitz, and Sherwood [R1] showed that both the Wilke–Chang and the Olander modification [O1] fail for many systems. The correlation of Sitaraman, Ibrahim, and Kuloor [S6] requires latent heats of vaporization; if these must be estimated, then the uncertainty increases.

In summary, most of the correlations proposed for liquid systems are valid only for a particular subset of solutes and solvents. The Wilke–Chang is the most general and requires a minimum of supplementary data. Because diffusion coefficients in liquids are so low ($10^{-9}\,m^2\,s^{-1}$), they are difficult to measure accurately. Careful investigations at different laboratories often yield results that differ from one another by 50 percent [J3]. The concentration dependence of D_{AB} is difficult to predict accurately.

Example 14.9. Compare the diffusion coefficient of water diffusing through 1-propanol (chemical formula $CH_3CH_2CH_2OH$) with that of 1-propanol diffusing through water, each at infinite dilution, at 288 K. For 1-propanol, the viscosity at 288 K and the molecular weight are 2.6 cP ($2.6 \times 10^{-3}\,kg\,m^{-1}\,s^{-1}$) and 60.09 kg kmol^{-1}. For water, the viscosity at 288 K and the molecular weight are 1.14 cP ($1.14 \times 10^{-3}\,kg\,m^{-1}\,s^{-1}$) and 18.015 kg kmol^{-1}.

Answer. The Wilke–Chang correlation will be used to find D_{AB} in each case. First, the Le Bas method of calculating the molal volumes of solute and solvent will be used. From Table A.4, Appendix A, the increments for carbon, hydrogen, and oxygen are 14.8×10^{-3}, 3.7×10^{-3}, 7.4×10^{-3} m^3 $kmol^{-1}$, respectively. For water, the Le Bas volume is 18.9×10^{-3} m^3 $kmol^{-1}$. The Le Bas volume for 1-propanol is

$$V_p = [(3)(14.8) + (8)(3.7) + (1)(7.4)] \times 10^{-3} = 0.0814 \text{ m}^3 \text{ kmol}^{-1} \qquad \text{(i)}$$

For the diffusion of 1-propanol (A) through water (B), the association factor is 2.26. Equation (14.80) yields

$$D_{AB} = \frac{1.17 \times 10^{-16}(T)(\phi M_B)^{1/2}}{\mu_B V_A^{0.6}} = \frac{(1.17 \times 10^{-16})(288)[(2.26)(18.015)]^{1/2}}{(1.14 \times 10^{-3})(0.0814)^{0.6}}$$

$$= 8.52 \times 10^{-10} \text{ m}^2 \text{ s}^{-1} \qquad \text{(ii)}$$

For water (A) diffusing through 1-propanol, the association factor for 1-propanol is unknown. It is possible to use the value for ethanol; alternatively, since ϕ is 1.9 for methanol and 1.5 for ethanol, an arbitrary choice might be 1.2. Let us choose 1.5:

$$D_{AB} = \frac{(1.17 \times 10^{-16})(288)[(1.5)(60.09)]^{1/2}}{(2.6 \times 10^{-3})(0.0189)^{0.6}} = 1.33 \times 10^{-9} \text{ m}^2 \text{ s}^{-1} \qquad \text{(iii)}$$

Literature comparison. The diffusion coefficient in the 1-propanol–water system changes by a factor of almost 10 over the full concentration range [J3]. Further, the diffusion coefficient changes most rapidly with concentration in the dilute region, whether the solvent is water or 1-propanol. Thus, a risky extrapolation is necessary to obtain the diffusion coefficient at infinite dilution. The following data are available:

Dilute 1-propanol (A) through water (B)—literature

$$D_{AB} = 7.7 \times 10^{-10} \text{ m}^2 \text{ s}^{-1} \qquad \text{at 284 K [L4]} \qquad \text{(iv)}$$

$$D_{AB} = 8.7 \times 10^{-10} \text{ m}^2 \text{ s}^{-1} \qquad \text{at 288 K [T1]}[5] \qquad \text{(v)}$$

$$D_{AB} = 4.4 \times 10^{-10} \text{ m}^2 \text{ s}^{-1} \qquad \text{at 293 K [G2]}[6] \qquad \text{(vi)}$$

Note that these data do not form a consistent set with regard to temperature dependence, owing to experimental error. The Wilke–Chang correlation estimate of D_{AB} for the data at 288 K is about 2 percent in error, obviously much better than the experimental error. The Hayduk–Laudie correlation [H1], also recommended in Table 14.4, is about 2.3 percent in error for this system [R1].

For water as the dilute species, the correlations are not satisfactory:

Dilute water (A) through 1-propanol (B)—literature

$$D_{AB} = 4.7 \times 10^{-10} \text{ m}^2 \text{ s}^{-1} \qquad \text{at 284 K [L4]} \qquad \text{(vii)}$$

$$D_{AB} = 6.1 \times 10^{-10} \text{ m}^2 \text{ s}^{-1} \qquad \text{at 288 K}[7] \qquad \text{(viii)}$$

$$D_{AB} = 7.2 \times 10^{-10} \text{ m}^2 \text{ s}^{-1} \qquad \text{at 283 K [G1]} \qquad \text{(ix)}$$

---

[5] Corrected to 288 K by Thovert [T2]. This value has been misquoted in ref. [G2] as being for water through 1-propanol.

[6] Probably erroneous.

[7] Quoted in Johnson and Babb [J3]; source unknown.

While these values are at least consistent, they are far from the prediction of 13.3×10^{-10} from the Wilke–Chang correlation.

14.3 SOLIDS

The most important transport property for solids is the thermal conductivity. It is fortunate that the thermal conductivity of a solid can be easily and accurately measured, since the theories proposed to date are of limited value. Diffusion in solids was covered in Section 5.3.5. As discussed previously, diffusion in solids may occur by several mechanisms. The variation of the diffusion coefficient shown in Table 2.10 for diffusion in silicon indicates that there is little hope for a general correlation.

14.4 MEASUREMENT OF THE TRANSPORT PROPERTIES

This section provides a brief, qualitative overview of the type of equipment required to measure the transport coefficients. Actually, a detailed study of such equipment provides excellent examples of the use of the equations developed in this text.

14.4.1 Viscosity Measurements[8]

"Viscometry" is defined as the measurement of the shear stress and the shear rate such that the viscosity of a fluid can then be determined from Newton's law, Eq. (2.5). It is often necessary to distinguish viscometry from "rheogoniometry", which is the measurement of all the stresses [Eq. (2.43)] within the material [J2]. Naturally, rheogoniometry encompasses viscometry and is far more difficult [M2, S2]. In this section, some measuring equipment will be considered.

The reader will rarely have to measure the viscosity of gases. The success of the Chapman–Enskog equation, documented in Section 14.1.2, makes such measurements more of a scientific interest, rather than an engineering necessity. Hence, most viscosity experiments deal with liquids. For materials that follow Newton's law, commercial equipment is readily available. The simplest viscometers are glass. For example, the Ostwald viscometer and its many modifications [V2] are of the gravitational type and are single-point instruments (i.e., they measure μ at a single shear rate). Other commercial viscometers are rotational in nature, but likewise easy to use.

The most interesting problem in viscosity measurement is the study of non-Newtonian materials. These materials do not follow Newton's law of viscosity, in that the viscosity is a function of the shear rate (or shear stress). Hence, to characterize a non-Newtonian fluid, it is necessary to make shear

---

[8] Adapted from Brodkey [B5].

stress–shear rate determinations at many points, often over a range of 10^4 in shear rate. This topic is the subject of Chapter 15.

There are two major types of viscometers that are capable of determining the viscosity as a function of the shear rate: the capillary tube viscometer and the rotational instrument. There are many variations of these. In the capillary tube viscometer, the flow can either be induced by gravity or by imposed pressure, although for non-Newtonian fluids adequate characterization can be made only with imposed pressure. This instrument is capable of very high shear rates. The rotational viscometer is usually of the concentric cylinder type (in which either cylinder can be rotated) or of a plate-and-cone design. Van Wazer *et al.* [V2] have compiled an extensive list of the commercially available units. They have presented detailed descriptions, advantages and disadvantages, possible modifications, and recommended experimental procedures. Rotational, capillary, and miscellaneous commercial viscometers are covered, and there is a chapter on viscoelastic systems.

Of considerable interest in any measurement system are the various problems that can introduce unexpected complications [T3]. Among these are: the existence of plug flow, wall slip, temperature heating effects, end effects, laminar instability, and turbulence. In most cases the effect can be eliminated or corrections can be made.

14.4.2 Thermal Conductivity

Measurement of the thermal conductivity of gases and liquids is inherently inaccurate because of the ease with which convection currents are established in the fluid. The lack of agreement between investigators has already been discussed.

The thermal conductivity can be measured by placing the unknown sample between two parallel plates of known separation and measuring the resulting temperature difference for some given impressed heat flux. To minimize convection effects, the heat is transferred downward so that the upper plate is at a higher temperature than the lower one. The amount of heat input lost to the surroundings must be minimized in order to make accurate measurements. At low temperatures, transfer by radiation is not important; at high temperatures, appropriate instruments have been designed to obtain reasonably accurate measurements [M3]. A concentric cylinder design can also be used. As in viscometry, the cylinder gap is kept as small as possible, and the unit is operated vertically.

14.4.3 Diffusion Coefficient Measurements

Marrero and Mason [M1] provide an excellent review of measurement techniques for gas-phase diffusion coefficients. Summarizing briefly, the Stefan method [S8] for the measurement of the diffusion coefficient in gases uses the rate of evaporation of a liquid in a narrow tube. The first component must be a liquid, while the second gas is passed across the top of the tube. The inside capillary diameter is known, and from the evaporation rate the diffusion coefficient can be determined. Precision is poor at high or low vapor pressures, and so the range of temperatures for a given system is restricted.

In the Loschmidt method [L7], two gaseous components are placed in a tube that is divided into two sections by a removable partition. The partition is removed for a time and the gases are allowed to diffuse under unsteady-state conditions. The partition is reinserted and the contents of each chamber are analyzed. From this, the diffusion coefficient can be calculated. The method often yields diffusion coefficients that are in error because of convection currents. If the gases have different densities, then there may be appreciable mass transfer by natural convection currents. The apparatus is also very sensitive to variations in temperature during the course of the experiment.

The point source method for gases, developed by Walker and Westenberg [W1], has been used to measure diffusion coefficients at temperatures up to 1200 K with a precision of about 1 percent. The point source method injects a trace sample of one gas into the laminar flow of a second gas stream. In a flow system it is relatively easy to control the temperature by adding a constant amount of heat to a constant flow of gas. In the region of the injection probe, the total pressure may be assumed constant, and the injected species diffuses along the direction of flow as well as in a radial direction. The concentration of the injected gas is measured by a special sampling technique in which the gas sample is continually withdrawn and passed through a thermal conductivity cell. The point source technique appears to be the most satisfactory technique developed so far for measurements of diffusion coefficients over wide ranges of temperature and pressure. The Stefan method was severely limited by the requirement that one component be a liquid with vapor pressure neither too high or too low, and the Loschmidt method, while capable of high temperature measurements, is relatively imprecise even with the best available constant-temperature equipment.

Diffusion coefficients in liquids are of interest not only to engineers designing mass transfer equipment but also to physical chemists and others studying the properties of proteins and other high molecular weight polymer and colloid solutions. This interest has resulted in a proliferation of experimental methods. The details of these methods have been reviewed elsewhere [G1, G3, J3, J4, N2, T7].

PROBLEMS

14.1. The kinetic theory can predict all three transport coefficients. Discuss the error in using this theory for engineering calculations and illustrate with experimental data from Table 2-10 or another source.

14.2. Describe the concept of self-diffusion and outline an experiment to estimate a self-diffusion coefficient.

14.3. Compare the temperature dependency of viscosity, thermal conductivity, and diffusion coefficient for both gases and liquids.

14.4. The molecular diameter of nitrogen is 3.16×10^{-10} m (M4). Using the kinetic theory of gases at 1 atm and 300 K
   (a) Find all diffusivities in $m^2 s^{-1}$.
   (b) Estimate k in $W m^{-1} s^{-1}$, given $c_p = 29.16$ kJ $kmol^{-1} K^{-1}$.

14.5. The Lennard-Jones parameters for ethyl acetate are in Table A.3.
   (a) Compare the table values with those estimated from the Tee–Gotoh–Stewart equations; obtain the necessary thermodynamic data from a handbook.
   (b) Compare the table values with those estimated from Eqs. (A.1) through (A.4).

14.6. Estimate the error of prediction of the Chapman–Enskog theory for the viscosity of air at 1 atm and temperatures of 300 K, 400 K, 1000 K, and 2000 K.

14.7. Estimate the error of prediction of the Chapman–Enskog theory for the viscosity of saturated water vapor at temperatures of 300 K, 400 K, 500 K, 600 K, and 640 K.

14.8. Compare the estimation of k from both Eucken equations with published data for saturated water vapor at 1 atm and temperatures of 295 K, 400 K, and 640 K.

14.9. Compare the estimation of k from both Eucken equations with published data for air at 1 atm and temperatures of 293 K, 1000 K, and 2000 K.

14.10. Find an equation to relate the thermal conductivity of liquid water as a function of temperature between 283 K and 303 K.

14.11. Freon-12 (CCl_2F_2, molecular weight 120.92 kg $kmol^{-1}$) boils at 245 K, at which temperature $c_p = 0.898$ kJ $kmol^{-1} K^{-1}$ and $\rho = 1.484 \times 10^3$ kg m^{-3}.
   (a) Estimate the thermal conductivity at T_b; compare with the published value of 0.0695 $W m^{-1} K^{-1}$ [I1].
   (b) Using the above value of k, estimate k at 300 K if $c_p = 0.9781$ kJ $kmol^{-1} K^{-1}$ and $\rho = 1.3058$ kg m^{-3}; compare with the published value of 0.072 $W m^{-1} K^{-1}$ [I1].

14.12. Prove the following:

$$\frac{D_{AA}}{\mu_A} = 1.20 \frac{RT}{Mp} \frac{\Omega_\mu}{\Omega_D}$$

14.13. Using the function in Problem 14.12:
   (a) Graph D_{AA}/μ_A versus T for air at 1 atm between 200 K and 600 K.
   (b) Draw any possible conclusions about the temperature variation of the Schmidt number with temperature.

14.14. Find the mutual diffusion coefficient of oxygen diffusing through water vapor at atmospheric pressure and 352.3 K; compare with the experimental value of $0.352 \times 10^{-4} m^2 s^{-1}$ [R1].
   (a) Use the Chapman–Enskog theory with the Lennard-Jones potential.
   (b) Use the FSG correlation.

14.15. Find the mutual diffusion coefficient of hydrogen diffusing through sulfur dioxide at atmospheric pressure and 285.5 K; compare with the experimental value of $0.525 \times 10^{-4} m^2 s^{-1}$ [R1].

(a) Use the Chapman–Enskog theory with the Lennard-Jones potential.

(b) Use the FSG correlation.

14.16. The diffusion coefficient of fluorine in air is $6.26 \times 10^{-6} \, m^2 \, s^{-1}$ at 300°F and 5 atm.

(a) Compare this value with that predicted by the Chapman–Enskog theory.

(b) From this one point, estimate the special diffusion volume of molecular fluorine (F_2) in the FSG correlation.

14.17. The diffusion coefficient of ethanol in aqueous solutions has been measured at infinite dilution for three temperatures [R1]:

D_{AB}, m² s⁻¹	T, K
0.84×10^{-9}	283
1.00×10^{-9}	288
1.24×10^{-9}	298

(a) Estimate the diffusion coefficient of ethanol in aqueous solution at infinite dilution at 40°C from the above data.

(b) Find an equation to correlate D_{AB} with temperature.

(c) Estimate the diffusion coefficient of ethanol in water at 298 K; determine the error as compared with the value given above.

14.18. Estimate the error of prediction of the Wilke–Chang equation for:

(a) dilute benzene in chloroform at 313 K; observed: $3.35 \times 10^{-9} \, m^2 \, s^{-1}$ [R1]

(b) dilute water in ethanol at 298 K; observed: $1.24 \times 10^{-9} \, m^2 \, s^{-1}$ [R1]

(c) oxygen in water at 298 K; observed: $2.41 \times 10^{-9} \, m^2 \, s^{-1}$ [R1]

(d) benzene in water at 293 K; observed: $1.02 \times 10^{-9} \, m^2 \, s^{-1}$ [R1]

(e) dilute methanol in benzene at 298 K; observed: $3.30 \times 10^{-9} \, m^2 \, s^{-1}$ [J3]

REFERENCES

A1. Akita, K.: *Ind. Eng. Chem. Fundam.* **20:** 89 (1981).

B1. Bearman, R. J.: *J. Chem. Phys.* **32:** 1308 (1960).

B2. Bird, R. B., J. O. Hirschfelder, and C. F. Curtiss: *Trans. ASME* **76:** 1011 (1954).

B3. Bird, R. B.: in *Advances in Chemical Engineering*, vol. 1, T. B. Drew and J. W. Hoopes (eds.), Academic Press, New York, 1956.

B4. Bird, R. B., W. E. Stewart, and E. N. Lightfoot: *Transport Phenomena*, Wiley, New York, 1960.

B5. Brodkey, R. S.: *The Phenomena of Fluid Motions*, Addison-Wesley, Reading MA, 1967. [Fourth printing available from The Ohio State University Bookstores, Columbus, Ohio 43210.]

B6. Brokaw, R. S.: *Ind. Eng. Chem. Process Des. Dev.* **8:** 240 (1969).

C1. Chapman, S.: *Philos. Trans. Roy. Soc. (London)* **A217:** 115 (1918).

C2. Chapman, S., and T. G. Cowling: *The Mathematical Theory of Non-Uniform Gases*, 3d ed., Cambridge University Press, Cambridge, 1970.

C3. *CRC Handbook of Chemistry and Physics*, 64th ed., CRC Press, Boca Raton FL, 1984.

C4. Cullinan, H. T., and M. R. Cusick: *Ind. Eng. Chem. Fundam.* **6:** 72, 616 (1967); *AIChE J.* **13:** 1171 (1967).

C5. Cussler, E. L.: *AIChE J.* **26:** 43 (1980).

D1. Darken, L. S.: *Trans. Am. Inst. Mining Metall. Eng.* **175:** 184 (1948).

D2. Duda, J. L., J. S. Vrentas, S. T. Ju, and H. T. Liu: *AIChE J.* **28:** 279 (1982).

D3. Dullien, F. A. L.: *AIChE J.* **18:** 62 (1972).

E1. Einstein, A.: *Ann. Physik* **[4] 17:** 549 (1905); **[4] 19:** 371 (1906); *Z. Elektrochem.* **14:** 235 (1908).

E2. Enskog, D.: *Kinetische Theorie der Vorgänge in mässig verdünnten Gasen,* Inaugural Dissertation, Uppsala, 1917.

E3. Eucken, A.: *Physik. Z.* **14:** 324 (1913).

E4. Eyring, H.: *J. Chem. Phys.* **3:** 107 (1935); Powell, R. E., W. E. Roseveare, and H. Eyring: *Ind. Eng. Chem.* **33:** 430 (1941); Kincaid, J. F., H. Eyring, and A. E. Stearn: *Chem. Rev.* **28:** 301 (1941).

E5. Eyring, H.: *J. Chem. Phys.* **4:** 283 (1936); see also Ree, T., and H. Eyring in *Rheology,* vol. 2, F. R. Eirich (ed.), Academic Press, New York, 1958.

F1. Fuller, E. N., P. D. Schettler, and J. C. Giddings: *Ind. Eng. Chem.* **58**(5): 18 (1966); **58**(8): 81 (1966).

G1. Geddes, A. L., and R. B. Pontius: in *Technique of Organic Chemistry,* A. Weissberger (ed.), vol. 1 (Part 2), Interscience, New York, 1960.

G2. Gerlach, B.: *Ann. Physik* **[5] 10:** 437 (1931).

G3. Glasstone, S.: *Textbook of Physical Chemistry,* 2d ed., D. Van Nostrand, Princeton, NJ, 1946.

G4. Glasstone, S., K. J. Laidler, and H. Eyring: *The Theory of Rate Processes,* McGraw-Hill, New York, 1941.

G5. Gordon, A. R.: *J. Chem. Phys.* **5:** 522 (1937).

G6. Gosting, L. J.: *Adv. Protein Chem.* **11:** 429 (1956).

G7. Gray, D. E.: *American Institute of Physics Handbook,* 3d ed., McGraw-Hill, New York, 1972.

H1. Hayduk, W., and H. Laudie: *AIChE J.* **20:** 611 (1974); corrected equation cited in [H2].

H2. Hayduk, W., and B. S. Minhas: *Can. J. Chem. Eng.* **60:** 295 (1982).

H3. Hildebrand, J. H.: *Science* **174:** 490 (1971).

H4. Hines, A. L., and R. N. Maddox: *Mass Transfer,* Prentice-Hall, Englewood Cliffs NJ, 1985.

H5. Hirschfelder, J. O., C. F. Curtiss, and R. B. Bird: *Molecular Theory of Gases and Liquids,* fourth printing April 1967, Wiley, New York, 1954.

H6. Hiss, T. G., and E. L. Cussler: *AIChE J.* **19:** 698 (1973).

I1. Incropera, F. P., and D. P. DeWitt: *Fundamentals of Heat and Mass Transfer,* 2d ed., Wiley, New York, 1985.

J1. Jeans, J. H.: *An Introduction to the Kinetic Theory of Gases,* Cambridge University Press, Cambridge, 1948.

J2. Jobling, A., and J. E. Roberts: *Rheology,* vol. 2, F. R. Eirich (ed.), Academic Press, New York, 1958; *J. Polymer Sci.* **36:** 433 (1959).

J3. Johnson, P. A., and A. L. Babb: *Chem. Rev.* **56:** 387 (1956).

J4. Jost, W.: *Diffusion in Solids, Liquids, Gases,* Academic Press, New York, 1960, 3d printing with addendum

K1. Kayser, J. C., and K. S. Knaebel: *Diffusion Coefficient Estimation,* Oct. 10, 1985. Unpublished course material. Department of Chemical Engineering, The Ohio State University, Columbus OH 43210.

K2. Kennard, E. H.: *Kinetic Theory of Gases,* McGraw-Hill, New York, 1938.

L1. Lange, N. A.: *Lange's Handbook of Chemistry,* 13th ed., J. A. Dean (ed.), McGraw-Hill, New York, 1985.

L2. Le Bas, G.: *The Molecular Volumes of Liquid Chemical Compounds,* Longmans, Green, London, 1915.

L3. Leffler, J., and H. T. Cullinan: *Ind. Eng. Chem. Fundam.* **9:** 84, 88 (1970);

L4. Lemonde, H.: *Ann. Phys.* **[11] 9:** 539 (1938).

L5. Lennard-Jones, J. E.: *Proc. Roy. Soc.* (*London*) **A106:** 463, 709 (1924); **A107:** 157 (1925); **A109:** 476, 584 (1925); **A112:** 214, 230 (1926).

L6. Liley, P. E.: in *Handbook of Heat Transfer Fundamentals,* 2d ed., W. M. Rohsenow, J. P. Hartnett, and E. N. Ganic (eds.), McGraw-Hill, New York, 1985.

L7. Loschmidt, J.: *Sitzungsber. Akad. Wiss. Wien* **[II] 61:** 367, 468 (1870).

M1. Marrero, T. R., and E. A. Mason: *J. Phys. Chem. Ref. Data* **1:** 3 (1972).

M2. Markovitz, H.: *Trans. Soc. Rheol.* **1:** 37 (1957).

M3. Michels, A., J. V. Sengers, and P. S. Van Der Gulik: *Physica* **28:** 1201, 1216 (1962).

M4. Moore, W. J.: *Physical Chemistry,* 4th ed., Prentice-Hall, Englewood Cliffs NJ, 1972.

M5. Mrazek, R. V., C. E. Wicks, and K. N. S. Prabhu: *J. Chem. Eng. Data* **13:** 508 (1968).

N1. Nernst, W.: *Z. Physik. Chem.* **2:** 613 (1888).

N2. Nienow, A. W.: *Br. Chem. Eng.* **10:** 827 (1965).

O1. Olander, D. R.: *AIChE J.* **7:** 175 (1961).

O2. Onsager, L.: *Phys. Rev.* **37:** 405 (1931); **38:** 2265 (1931).

P1. Perkins, L. R., and C. J. Geankoplis: *Chem. Eng. Sci.* **24:** 1035 (1969).

P2. Perry, R. H., and D. W. Green: *Perry's Chemical Engineers' Handbook,* 6th ed., McGraw-Hill, New York, 1984.

P3. Present, R. D.: *Kinetic Theory of Gases,* McGraw-Hill, New York, 1958.

R1. Reid, R. C., J. M. Prausnitz, and T. K. Sherwood: *The Properties of Gases and Liquids,* 3d ed., McGraw-Hill, New York, 1977.

S1. Sakiadis, B. C., and J. Coates: *AIChE J.* **1:** 275 (1955); **3:** 121 (1957).

S2. Savins, J. G.: *J. Appl. Polymer Sci.* **6:** S67 (1962); *AIChE J.* **11:** 673 (1965).

S3. Scheibel, E. G.: *Ind. Eng. Chem.* **46:** 2007 (1954).

S4. Scott, D. S.: *Ind. Eng. Chem. Fundam.* **3:** 278 (1964).

S5. Seager, S. L., L. R. Geertson, and J. C. Giddings: *J. Chem. Eng. Data* **8:** 168 (1963).

S6. Sitaraman, R., S. H. Ibrahim, and N. R. Kuloor: *J. Chem. Eng. Data* **8:** 198 (1963).

S7. Sridhar, T., and O. E. Potter: *AIChE J.* **23:** 590 (1977).

S8. Stefan, J.: *Wien. Ber.* **[II] 68:** 385 (1873); *Wien. Ber.* **[II] 98:** 473 (1889); *Ann. Physik* **[3] 41:** 725 (1890).

S9. Sutherland, W.: *Philos. Mag.* **9,** 781 (1905).

T1. Tee, L. S., S. Gotoh, and W. E. Stewart: *Ind. Eng. Chem. Fundam.* **5:** 356 (1966); **5:** 363 (1966).

T2. Thovert, J.: *Ann. Phys.* **[9] 2:** 369 (1914).

T3. Toms, B. A.: *Rheology,* vol. 2, F. R. Eirich (ed.), Academic Press, New York, 1958.

T4. Touloukian, Y. S. (ed.): *Thermophysical Properties Research Literature Retrieval Guide,* 2d ed., Plenum, New York, 1967.

T5. Touloukian, Y. S. (ed.): *Thermophysical Properties of High Temperature Solid Materials,* Macmillan, New York, 1967.

T6. Touloukian, Y. S. and C. Y. Ho (eds.): *Purdue University Thermophysical Properties Research Center. Thermophysical Properties of Matter,* IFI/Plenum, New York, 1970. [There are 13 volumes, beginning with vol. 1 in 1970 plus a master index volume.]

T7. Tyrrell, H. J. V., and K. R. Harris: *Diffusion in Liquids,* Butterworths, London, 1984.

V1. Van Geet, A. L., and A. W. Adamson: *J. Phys. Chem.* **68:** 238 (1964).

V2. Van Wazer, J. R., J. W. Lyons, K. Y. Kim, and R. E. Colwell: *Applied Rheology-Viscometers and Their Use,* Interscience, New York, 1963.

V3. Vargaftik, N. B.: *Handbook of Physical Properties of Liquids and Gases,* 2d ed., Hemisphere, Washington, DC, 1983.

V4. Vignes, A.: *Ind. Eng. Chem. Fundam.* **5:** 189 (1966).

W1. Walker, R. E., and A. A. Westenberg: *J. Chem. Phys.* **29:** 1139, 1147 (1958).

W2. Wilke, C. R., and P. Chang: *AIChE J.* **1:** 264 (1955).

CHAPTER
15

NON-NEWTONIAN PHENOMENA[1]

NOMENCLATURE

A	Parameter in the Reiner–Philippoff model, Eq. (15.9)
A	Species A
A	Area upon which shear stress acts (m^2, ft^2)
a_T	Shift factor defined by Eq. (15.20), dimensionless
C	Concentration in Eq. (15.19) $(kmol\,m^{-3}, lb\,mol\,ft^{-3})$
C_1	Constant in Eq. (15.19)
D	Diffusion coefficient $(m^2\,s^{-1})$
D_R	Drag ratio, Eq. (15.31)
d	Diameter (m, ft); d_o is inside diameter of pipe, as used in fluid flow
E	Constant in Eq. (15.35)
e	Base of natural logarithms (also called exp) $(2.718\,281\,8\ldots)$
F	Force (N, lb_f)
f	Fanning friction factor, Eq. (6.89)
G	Shear modulus in Eq. (15.11) $(kg\,m^{-1}\,s^{-1}$ or $N\,m^{-2}\,s$, $lb_m\,ft^{-1}\,s^{-1})$
g_c	Gravitational conversion constant $(32.174\,lb_m\,lb_f^{-1}\,ft\,s^{-2})$

---

[1] Adapted from Chapter 15 in Brodkey [B7] *The Phenomena of Fluid Motions.*

h	Heat transfer coefficient, defined by Eq. (6.86) $(\mathrm{W\,m^{-2}\,K^{-1}},$ $\mathrm{Btu\,ft^{-2}\,h^{-1}\,{}^\circ F^{-1}})$
i	Unit vector in the x direction
K	Empirical constant in the power law, Eq. (15.6); K_e is constant in Ellis model, Eq. (15.7); K_s is constant in Sisko model, Eq. (15.8)
K'	Empirical constant in non-Newtonian viscosity equation, Eq. (10.5)
k	Thermal conductivity $(\mathrm{W\,m^{-1}\,K^{-1}}$ or $\mathrm{J\,m^{-1}\,K^{-1}\,s^{-1}},$ $\mathrm{Btu\,ft^{-1}}$ ${}^\circ\mathrm{R^{-1}\,s^{-1}})$
k	k_s is constant in agitation equation, Eq. (15.33); k_σ is a constant in the temperature-dependent form of the power law, Eq. (15.34)
k'_c	Equimolar mass transfer coefficient, defined by Eq. (6.87) $[\mathrm{kmol\,m^{-2}\,s^{-1}\,(kmol\,m^{-3})^{-1}},\ \mathrm{lb\,mol\,ft^{-2}\,s^{-1}\,(lb\,mol\,ft^{-3})^{-1}}]$
L	Length (m, ft)
M	Molecular weight (molecular mass) $(\mathrm{kg\,kmol^{-1}},\ \mathrm{lb_m\,lb\,mol^{-1}})$
N	Rotational impeller speed, Eq. (15.33)
N_{De}	Deborah number, Eq. (15.18), defined as the characteristic time of the viscoelastic material divided by the characteristic time of the experiment
$N_{\mathrm{Nu, mb}}$	Mean bulk Nusselt number defined in Eq. (11.66)
$N_{\mathrm{Pr, mb}}$	Prandlt number, defined in Eq. (8.4); all properties are evaluated at the mean bulk temperature
N_{Re}	Reynolds number, Eq. (6.1) or Eq. (6.2), $d_oU_{z,\,\mathrm{ave}}\rho/\mu$ for pipe flow; $N_{\mathrm{Re,s}}$ is solvent Reynolds number with ρ and μ based on solvent properties, Eq. (15.32); N'_{Re} is the Metzner–Reed Reynolds number, Eq. (15.28); $N_{\mathrm{Re,mb}}$ is the mean bulk Reynolds number, Eq. (11.62)
n	Empirical constant in the power law, Eq. (15.6); exponent in Eqs. (15.10) and (15.34)
n'	Empirical constant in non-Newtonian viscosity equation, Eq. (10.5), defined in Eq. (15.25)
p	Pressure $(\mathrm{kPa},\ \mathrm{atm},\ \mathrm{lb_f\,in.^{-2}})$
Q	Volume rate of flow $(\mathrm{m^3\,s^{-1}},\ \mathrm{ft^3\,s^{-1}})$
q	Energy (heat) flow vector $(\mathrm{J\,s^{-1}},\ \mathrm{Btu\,s^{-1}})$; subscripts denote components in coordinate directions
R	Gas constant; see the Appendix, Table C.1, for values
r	Cylindrical coordinate (m, ft)
r	Radius (m, ft); r_o is value of r at the tube wall
S	Area of a pipe or tube that is perpendicular to the z direction (i.e., the flow or cross sectional area) $(\mathrm{m^2},\ \mathrm{ft^2})$; cf. Eq. (7.10)
S_r	Reduced shear rate for heat transfer in laminar flow; cf. Eq. (15.35)
T	Instantaneous temperature (K, °R); T_o is reference temperature for shift factor a_T
T	Superscript meaning transpose of a tensor

t	Time (s); t_M is Maxwell relaxation time, Eq. (15.14); t_K is retardation time in Kelvin model, Eq. (15.17); t_m is a material time constant given in Eq. (15.19)
U	Instantaneous velocity vector (m s^{-1}, ft s^{-1}); U is magnitude of U; U_x, U_y, U_z, U_θ, U_r, U_ϕ are components in directions x, y, z, θ, r, ϕ; $U_{z,\,ave}$ is mean velocity in z direction
w	Mass rate of flow (kg s^{-1}, lb$_m$ s^{-1}); cf. Eqs. (7.10) and (15.29)
w	Subscript denoting wall
x	Rectangular (Cartesian) coordinate
y	Rectangular (Cartesian) coordinate
z	Rectangular (Cartesian) coordinate
α	Thermal diffusivity (m^2 s^{-1})
α	α_e is constant in Ellis model, Eq. (15.7); α_s is constant in Sisko model, Eq. (15.8)
β	Constants in equation for a straight line; see Eq. (i), Example 15.1
$\dot{\gamma}$	The rate-of-strain tensor; for one-dimensional flow, the rate of strain $\dot{\gamma}$ is the derivative of velocity with respect to the distance perpendicular to the flow direction, cf. Eq. (15.1); $\dot{\gamma}_c$ is constant in Cross model, Eq. (15.10)
Δ	Difference, state 2 minus state 1; e.g., Δp means $p_2 - p_1$
μ	Viscosity (kg m^{-1} s^{-1} or N m^{-2} s, lb$_m$ ft^{-1} s^{-1}, cP); μ_w is viscosity at wall; μ_a is apparent viscosity, Eq. (15.4), often a function of shear rate and tube diameter for non-Newtonian fluids; μ_B is viscosity in Bingham model, Eq. (15.5); μ_0 is limiting viscosity of a pseudoplastic fluid at very low shear rates; μ_∞ is limiting viscosity of a pseudoplastic fluid at very high shear rates; μ_s is viscosity of the solvent
π	Ratio of circumference of a circle to its diameter (3.141 592 65...)
ρ	Density (kg m^{-3}, lb$_m$ ft^{-3})
τ	Momentum flux (or shear stress) tensor (N m^{-2}, lb$_f$ ft^{-2}); τ_{xy}, τ_{yx}, etc., are components of the momentum flux tensor, where subscripts refer to direction of momentum transfer and direction of velocity; note that in this chapter, the subscripts are usually omitted to simplify the notation; τ_w is shear stress at the wall; τ_0 is yield stress in Bingham model, Eq. (15.5); τ_{eq} is shear stress at infinite time at constant shear rate, cf. Fig. 15.7
∇	Vector operator del, defined by Eq. (2.16) (m^{-1}, ft^{-1})
∇U	Shear rate tensor, defined by Eq. (2.41) (s^{-1})
$(\nabla U)^{T}$	Transpose of shear rate tensor, defined by Eq. (2.42) (s^{-1})

The three material properties (k, D, and μ) introduced in Chapter 2 may vary with the conditions of the transport. For example, the thermal conductivity is a weak function of temperature, and the diffusion coefficient may vary with changes in concentration. Similarly, for many fluids, Newton's law of viscosity is valid only at a single point. Newton's law is

$$F/A = \tau_{yx} = -\mu \frac{\partial U_x}{\partial y} \tag{2.5}$$

where τ_{yx} is the momentum flux and $\partial U_x/\partial y$ is the shear rate, also noted as $\dot{\gamma}$. A Newtonian fluid is a gas or liquid for which Eq. (2.5) is valid. Examples of Newtonian fluids are pure gases, mixtures of gases, pure liquids of low molecular weight (i.e., nonpolymeric), and solutions of these liquids in which the solute is also of low molecular weight. In some cases, fluids may be Newtonian at commonly encountered shear rates but deviate from Newton's law under extreme conditions.

For "non-Newtonian" materials, the viscosity is a strong function of the shear rate. In other words, for a non-Newtonian fluid, the viscosity in Eq. (2.5) is not constant over the range of shear stresses and shear rates encountered, but may vary by a factor of 100 or more. Rheology is the science of the deformation and flow of matter. The field of rheology concentrates on non-Newtonian fluids, as well as on the solids that deform and flow under an applied shear stress.

Non-Newtonian fluids often have both solid-like (i.e., elastic) behavior and viscous behavior. Such fluids are called "viscoelastic"; examples are molten high-molecular-weight polymers like polyethylene, solutions of high-molecular-weight polymers, and colloidal suspensions. Non-Newtonian fluids are commonly encountered in chemical processes. Examples mentioned in Chapter 2 include multigrade motor oils, greases, elastomers, many emulsions, clay suspensions, concrete mixes, toothpaste, foodstuffs (such as milk shakes, ketchup, and mayonnaise), and fluids including high-molecular-weight polymers (either molten or in solution). Naturally, liquids (as opposed to gases) comprise practically all examples of non-Newtonian materials, with materials that are often considered solids (like aluminum) being capable of deformation and/or flow as well. This chapter will introduce the topic of non-Newtonian phenomena, which are often important in the application of the principles of transport phenomena to practical problems.

The correlations for Newtonian heat transfer, mass transfer, and pressure drop are significantly different from those for non-Newtonian fluids. Thus, this chapter will include a brief discussion of non-Newtonian transport.

15.1 RHEOLOGICAL CHARACTERISTICS OF MATERIALS

In Chapter 2, Newton's law was seen to be a one-dimensional simplification of a tensor equation as given in Eq. (2.42):

$$\boldsymbol{\tau} = -\mu[\nabla U + (\nabla U)^{\mathrm{T}}] \tag{2.40}$$

or

$$\boldsymbol{\tau} = -\mu \dot{\boldsymbol{\gamma}} \tag{15.1}$$

where $\dot{\gamma}$ is the rate of strain tensor that equals the sum of ∇U and $(\nabla U)^T$. The symbol τ is commonly used for either shear stress or momentum flux. The momentum flux and rate of strain will always be of opposite sign. When τ is used as a shear stress, it is customary to use the first quadrant (0–90°) for plotting τ versus $\dot{\gamma}$ (or $\dot{\gamma}$ versus τ) and disregarding any sign difference between τ and $\dot{\gamma}$. Just as the tensor τ contains nine terms, so does $\dot{\gamma}$. In Eq. (2.5), which applies to simple, one-dimensional flows, most components in the stress tensors τ and the rate of strain tensor $\dot{\gamma}$ are zero, and the rate-of-strain tensor reduces to simply the shear rate $\dot{\gamma}_{yx}$:

$$\dot{\gamma}_{yx} = \frac{\partial U_x}{\partial y} \tag{15.2}$$

Under such conditions, Newton's law becomes

$$\tau_{yx} = -\mu \dot{\gamma}_{yx} \tag{15.3}$$

The literature abounds with many other symbols used for the shear rate and/or the rate of strain tensor. For simplicity, the subscripts yx will be discarded in the sequel in favor of τ and $\dot{\gamma}$.

The variables in Eq. (15.3) can be determined by a variety of experiments. Design of some representative apparatuses will be covered in Section 15.2. A plot of τ versus $\dot{\gamma}$ is called "the basic shear diagram". If a log–log plot of τ versus $\dot{\gamma}$ is linear with slope unity, then Newton's law is obeyed. The basic shear diagram is used to describe the various types of non-Newtonian behavior.

Non-Newtonian materials can be classified as shear-thinning or shear-thickening. In addition, they can be classified by their time-dependence, viscoelasticity, and the extent to which they exhibit the effects of normal stress. There has been much confusion in the literature over the classification of non-Newtonian materials; the reader is referred elsewhere for a more complete account [B7].

An apparent viscosity, which will not be constant for a non-Newtonian fluid, can be defined as follows:

$$\tau = -\mu_a \dot{\gamma} \tag{15.4}$$

The apparent viscosity is useful in understanding the physics of non-Newtonian behavior, as will be illustrated next.

15.1.1   Time-Independent Behavior

Figure 15.1 shows the basic shear diagram for several materials, plotted both as a linear plot, Fig. 15.1(a), and a log–log plot, Fig. 15.1(b). Pseudoplastic fluids, also called shear-thinning, show a decrease in viscosity with increasing shear rate; the slope in Fig. 15.1(b) is less than 1. Shear-thickening fluids, also called dilatant fluids, show a viscosity increase with increasing shear rate; the slope in Fig. 15.1(b) exceeds 1. The Bingham plastic is a fluid with a constant

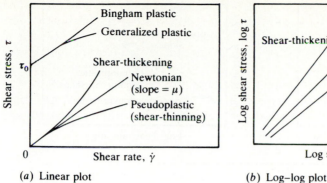

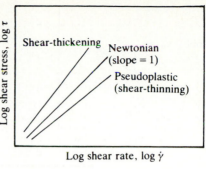

(a) Linear plot   (b) Log–log plot

FIGURE 15.1
Basic shear diagram illustrating typical behavior of real fluids.

plastic viscosity μ_B and a yield stress τ_0:

$$\tau - \tau_0 = -\mu_B\dot{\gamma} \qquad (15.5)$$

Note that μ_B is not a real viscosity, but a viscosity defined after the τ axis is shifted by τ_0; thus, the term plastic viscosity is used. A Bingham plastic fluid does not flow until the shear stress exceeds the yield value τ_0. In practice, Eq. (15.5) represents an ideal material; experimental observations confirm that the plastic viscosity μ_B is usually not constant over an appreciable range of shear rates. Hence, in Fig. 15.1 the curve marked "generalized plastic" is more representative of actual behavior. Examples of fluids with yield stresses include many suspensions, mayonnaise, ketchup, paints, printing inks, toothpaste, and drilling muds.

Pseudoplastic fluid. Of the four non-Newtonian fluids identified in Fig. 15.1, the most commonly encountered is the pseudoplastic fluid (or shear-thinning fluid). The term "pseudoplastic" was introduced to distinguish this material from the Bingham material, which possesses a yield stress at low rates of shear. Examples of pseudoplasticity include solutions and melts of most high-molecular-weight polymers, emulsions, and colloidal solutions. Ostwald [O5] pointed out that the curve of the pseudoplastic fluid in Fig. 15.1 is incomplete.[2] The complete pseudoplastic (or Ostwald) curve under laminar flow conditions is depicted in Fig. 15.2. When a complete basic shear diagram is determined,

---

[2] The so-called "pseudoplastic" or shear-thinning fluid is more correctly called the Ostwald fluid, since the early investigators relegated the term "pseudoplastic" to describe fluids that deviated from Bingham's "plastic" fluid (cf., Fig. 15.1). However, usage of the term "pseudoplastic" is more common and will be continued here.

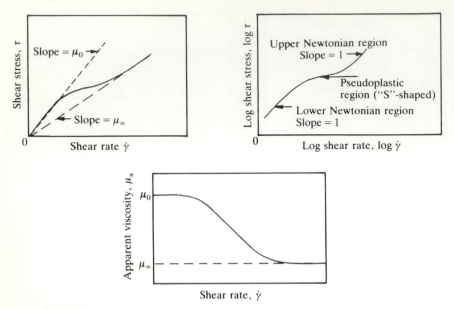

FIGURE 15.2
Complete basic shear diagram for a pseudoplastic fluid.

the pseudoplastic material exhibits three distinct regions: (1) the lower Newtonian, (2) the variable viscosity, and (3) the upper Newtonian. The viscosity in the lower Newtonian region is μ_0; the viscosity in the upper Newtonian region is μ_∞. Naturally, this curvature over widely varying ranges of shear rates makes mathematical modeling of the flow curve difficult. However, in the central region of the curve, the Ostwald–de Waele equation [O6], commonly called the power law, is often used to correlate the shear stress and the shear rate:

$$\tau = K(-\dot{\gamma})^n \tag{15.6}$$

The power law equation, Eq. (15.6), applies to variations of shear rates over one to three decades. Other empirical laws more complicated than Eq. (15.6) have been suggested to extend this region of fit. Clearly, to describe a pseudoplastic solution adequately, equations with more parameters are required. One solution is to use the Ellis model [B7] at low shear rates and the Sisko model [S4] at high shear rates:

$$\text{Ellis:} \quad \dot{\gamma} = -\tau_{yx}\left(\frac{1}{\mu_0} + K_e \left| \tau_{yx} \right|^{\alpha_e - 1}\right) \tag{15.7}$$

$$\text{Sisko:} \quad \tau_{yx} = -\dot{\gamma}(\mu_\infty + K_s \left| \tau_{yx} \right|^{\alpha_s - 1}) \tag{15.8}$$

where K_e, K_s, α_e, and α_s are parameters to be determined experimentally. Both of these equations contain three adjustable parameters in contrast to two for the power law. The Ellis model is extremely flexible, containing Newton's

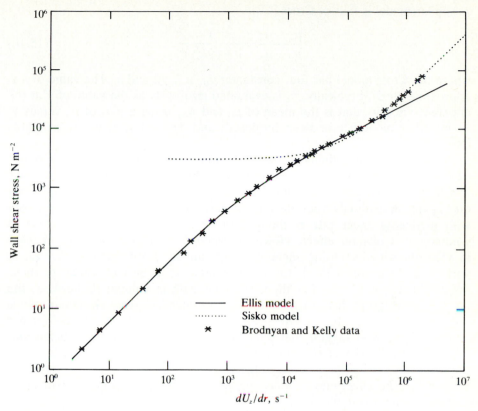

FIGURE 15.3
Data fitted with the Ellis and Sisko models.

law and the power law (with α_e equal to $1/n$) as limiting forms. The Sisko model has similar limiting forms, and was originally proposed to describe greases at high shear rates [S4]. For a pseudoplastic fluid ($n < 1$ and $\alpha_e > 1$), the Ellis model approaches the limiting lower Newtonian range as the shear rate approaches zero; the model fails as the shear rate becomes large, because the model cannot predict the curve above the inflection point in Fig. 15.2. Similarly, the Sisko model approaches the upper Newtonian range as the shear rate approaches infinity; however, the Sisko model fails as the shear rate becomes small. Figure 15.3 shows how Eqs. (15.7) and (15.8) may be combined to approximate the basic shear diagram for a pseudoplastic fluid. The parameters for the data [B8] are given elsewhere [B7].

Several equations that have three or more constants can be used to fit the entire Ostwald curve. For example, the Reiner–Philippoff model [P3] contains three parameters: μ_0, μ_∞, and A:

$$\tau = -\left(\mu_\infty + \frac{\mu_0 - \mu_\infty}{1 + (\tau^2/A)}\right)\dot{\gamma} \tag{15.9}$$

A similar model is that of Cross [C7]:

$$\frac{\mu_a - \mu_\infty}{\mu_0 - \mu_\infty} = \frac{1}{1 + (\dot{\gamma}/\dot{\gamma}_c)^n} \qquad (15.10)$$

where the Cross model has four constants: μ_0, μ_∞, $\dot{\gamma}_c$, and n. The value of n is approximately 2/3; typically, $\dot{\gamma}_c$ is evaluated rigorously as the value of $\dot{\gamma}$ at the apparent viscosity that is the mean of μ_0 and μ_∞, using a plot of μ_a versus $\dot{\gamma}$. Many other models have been proposed, and detailed reviews are available [B7, S3].

Shear-thickening fluids are less commonly encountered than pseudoplastic fluids. One example of a shear-thickening fluid is a dilatant fluid; dilatancy is a term introduced by Reynolds [R5] to describe an increase in rigidity that takes place in materials when they are closely packed. The increase in viscosity with increasing shear rate is thought to be associated with an increase in volume, or a dilatant effect. However, since fluids may exhibit an increase in viscosity with increasing shear rate without an accompanying increase in volume and vice versa [M9], the term "dilatancy" is best restricted to those fluids where it is known that there is an increase in volume. Otherwise, the more general term "shear-thickening" is recommended, since all dilatant fluids are shear-thickening, but not all shear-thickening fluids are dilatant. Metzner and Whitlock [M9] suggest that dilatancy occurs in concentrated suspensions when the breakdown of structure, which causes shear thinning, just balances the increase in rigidity as a result of the volume's dilating. Over some ranges of shear rates, this effect may produce dilatancy when it predominates over other effects causing pseudoplasticity.

Example 15.1. Table 15.1 contains data for the basic shear diagram for a molten polymeric material. Determine whether this fluid is a pseudoplastic. If so, find the power law parameters.

Answer. The data as given are first plotted on log–log paper to determine

TABLE 15.1
Basic shear data for a molten polymeric material

$\dot{\gamma}$, s^{-1}	τ, N m^{-2} × 10^{-4}
10	2.2
20	3.1
50	4.4
100	5.8
200	7.4
400	9.8
600	11.1
1000	13.9
2000	17.0

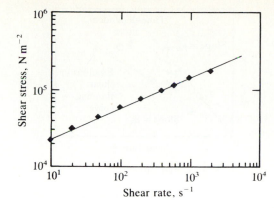

FIGURE 15.4
Basic shear diagram for the fluid in Example 15.1.

whether they obey the power law, Eq. (15.6):

$$\tau = K(-\dot{\gamma})^n \tag{15.6}$$

The data fall on a nearly-straight line; thus, Eq. (15.6) is satisfactory as long as no extrapolations are attempted. The constants n and K can be determined graphically or by a least-squares analysis for a straight line [P2]. Equation (15.6) is transformed as follows:

$$y = \beta_0 + \beta_1 x \tag{i}$$

$$y = \ln(\tau) \tag{ii}$$

$$x = \ln |\dot{\gamma}| \tag{iii}$$

From least-squares:

$$\beta_0 = \ln(K) = 9.17046 \quad \text{or} \quad K = 0.9609 \times 10^4 \, \text{N m}^{-2} \tag{iv}$$

$$\beta_1 = n = 0.3841 \tag{v}$$

This fluid is a pseudoplastic, since the slope n is less than 1. Figure 15.4 shows the log–log plot, and the line represented by the power law.

15.1.2 Time-Dependent Behavior

There are several types of time-dependent behavior [B7], the most important of which is thixotropy. The terminology used for describing time-dependent behavior is very confusing. Thus, thixotropic behavior is best explained by describing the results of a simple experiment. Let a fixed shear rate be applied to the thixotropic material in a rotational viscometer. The observed stress first increases rapidly to a maximum, depending on the measuring instrument's response; the stress then decreases until eventually an equilibrium stress is reached, as shown in Fig. 15.5(a). If the fluid is then allowed to rest (shear stress equal to zero) for an appropriate period of time, the material recovers its initial viscosity, and the curve in Fig. 15.5(a) can be duplicated.

A thixotropic material can be pictured as a material that undergoes a slow reaction from some unbroken structure to its equilibrium state. A more

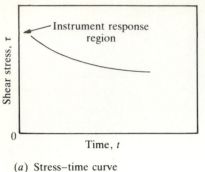

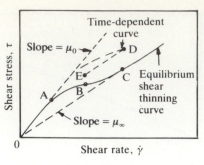

(a) Stress–time curve   (b) Stress–strain curve

FIGURE 15.5
Ostwald curve for a pseudoplastic fluid including thinning with time.

complete flow curve for a thixotropic fluid is shown in Fig. 15.5(*b*). The equilibrium shear-thinning curve is denoted by OABC. For an experiment in which the shear rate is first increased and then decreased, a thixotropic material will exhibit a loop as shown by curve OADE. To obtain such a loop, the material must have been at rest for an extended period of time. The viscometer is turned on; the shear rate is slowly increased, and readings of the shear stress form the curve OAD. When the shear rate reaches the value at point D, the shear stress will follow the curve DE if the shear rate is decreased to the value at point E. If the shear rate is reduced to zero, then the material structure will slowly return, and the entire curve can be repeated. If the shear rate is maintained constant at the value of point D, the structure in the fluid will break down, and the equilibrium shear stress at point C will be obtained after a period of time. Note that the results of this loop experiment are instrument-dependent, as the time for the shear rate to change differs from instrument to instrument.

    Thixotropic behavior is of importance in the paint and coatings industry, in the polymer industry, and in the food industry. Fluids whose viscosities increase with time are less important. A more complete review of time-dependent behavior is to be found elsewhere [B7, M4].

15.1.3 Viscoelastic Behavior

Some non-Newtonian fluids exhibit both fluid-like (viscous) behavior and solid-like (elastic) behavior; these are termed viscoelastic. The experimental manifestations of viscoelasticity are strong indeed. For example, when a rotating shaft is placed in a viscoelastic fluid, the fluid actually climbs the shaft. Naturally, this phenomenon (called the Weissenberg effect [R3, W1, W2] and shown in Fig. 15.6) leads to considerable difficulty in agitation. In Fig. 15.7(*a*),

(*a*) mixer

(*b*) purely viscous

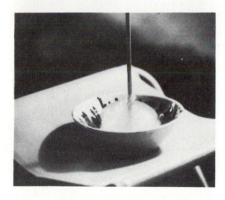

(*c*) viscoelastic

FIGURE 15.6
The Weissenberg effect in a viscoelastic liquid.

a Newtonian fluid issues from a tube as a jet; in Fig. 15.7(*b*) is a similar photograph for a viscoelastic fluid. Instead of the normal contraction, the latter fluid shows a swelling or expansion, which is a result of normal stress effects associated with the viscoelastic properties [M5]. If the transient experiment, shown in Fig. 15.5(*a*) for a purely viscous non-Newtonian fluid, is repeated for a viscoelastic fluid, the viscoelastic material often exhibits "stress overshoot"; stress overshoot can be observed only by an instrument whose response time is much faster than the time scale of viscosity changes. Figure 15.8 shows a set of typical curves for stress overshoot [C4]. The solution is 35 percent by weight

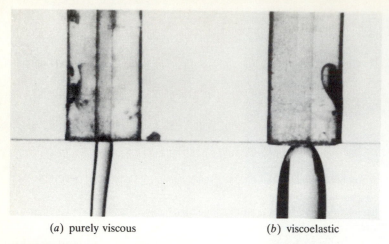

(*a*) purely viscous   (*b*) viscoelastic

FIGURE 15.7
Flow from a jet. (*From Lodge, Elastic Liquids, p. 242, Academic Press, New York, 1964. By permission.*)

poly(methyl methacrylate) (PMMA) in diethyl phthalate (DEP) at 20°C. At a shear rate of $0.54 \, \text{s}^{-1}$, there is no stress overshoot. However, at shear rates of 1.67 and $4.25 \, \text{s}^{-1}$, the phenomenon appears. Data for Fig. 15.8 were obtained by fixing the shear rate and measuring the shear stress as a function of time. In Fig. 15.8, the stress is normalized with τ_{eq}, the equilibrium value of the shear stress (reached after the transient effects have decayed to zero).

There are many other manifestations of viscoelastic behavior. The reader is directed elsewhere for more details [B3, B7, F3, L2, M10].

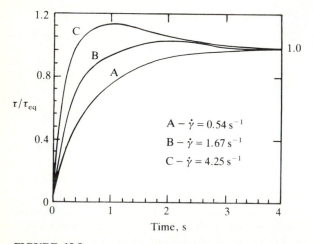

FIGURE 15.8
Stress overshoot: 35 percent PMMA in DEP at 20°C. (*From Chung, PhD Dissertation, The Ohio State University, Columbus, Ohio, 1985.*)

Hooke's law. Elastic behavior is normally associated with solids; however, non-Newtonian fluids may also exhibit elasticity. An ideal elastic material possesses neither time-dependent nor viscous effects during deformation and obeys the classic Hooke's law, which states that the applied stress is proportional to the deformation. Hooke's law has several forms, all of which are analogous to Newton's law of viscosity. Hooke's law is

$$\tau = -G\gamma \tag{15.11}$$

where G is the shear rigidity modulus and γ is the shear deformation divided by the shear thickness.

Many common materials, such as cross-linked plastics and even some hard metals, depart from ideal elastic behavior in physical situations of interest. Usually, the larger the deformation, the more nonideal is the behavior. Rubber is a common example of a cross-linked polymer. Rubber and rubber-like materials have two remarkable characteristics. They are capable of sustaining large deformations without rupture; many rubbers can elongate to five or ten times their unstretched length without breaking. The second characteristic of rubber is that the material returns very nearly to the initial dimensions after the deforming stress has been removed; in other words, no appreciable fraction of the deformation remains after removal of the stress. Note that rubber-like materials resemble liquids in their deformability without rupture; they resemble solids in their capacity to recover from a deformation [F2].

Mechanical and constitutive models. Massless mechanical models have been successful in depicting rheological behavior of viscoelastic materials. If the total deformation under a shear stress is the sum of contributions from a Hookean spring in series with a Newtonian dashpot,[3] then a Maxwell model results (Fig. 15.9). The fundamental differential equation for the Maxwell model is obtained by differentiating Eq. (15.11) with respect to time and adding the shear rate to that in Newton's law:

$$\frac{d\gamma}{dt} = \dot{\gamma} = -\frac{\tau}{\mu} - \frac{1}{G}\frac{d\tau}{dt} \tag{15.12}$$

Note again that minus signs have been used to maintain consistency with the concepts of momentum transfer. For any specific application in rheology, one must carefully determine the correct sign to be used.

If a constant strain γ is imposed on the Maxwell model, then the shear rate $\dot{\gamma}$ is zero, and the solution to Eq. (15.12), for constant G/μ, is

$$\tau = \tau_0 \exp(-Gt/\mu) \tag{15.13}$$

---

[3] A dashpot is similar to a fluid shock absorber on an automobile. A cylinder filled with fluid contains a frictionless piston with a rod extending from the top. The viscosity of the fluid resists movement of the rod.

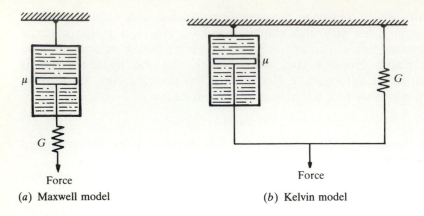

(a) Maxwell model (b) Kelvin model

FIGURE 15.9
Mechanical models for viscoelastic behavior.

The relaxation time of a Maxwell element t_M is

$$t_M = \mu/G \tag{15.14}$$

When a constant deformation γ is applied for a time equal to t_M, Eq. (15.13) predicts that the stress has decayed to $1/e$ of its initial value.

Another useful model is the Kelvin (or Voigt) model, also shown in Fig. 15.9. The Kelvin model assumes that the total shear stress under a constant strain is the sum of contributions from a Hookean spring in parallel with a Newtonian dashpot. The fundamental equation for this model is the sum of Newton's law and Eq. (15.11):

$$\tau = -\mu\dot{\gamma} - G\gamma \tag{15.15}$$

If the Kelvin model is subjected to a constant stress τ_0, then the solution to Eq. (15.15), for constant G and μ, is

$$\gamma = (\tau_0/G)[1 - \exp(-Gt/\mu)] \tag{15.16}$$

$$t_K = \mu/G \tag{15.17}$$

where t_K is the retardation time of the material. When the constant stress has been applied to a time equal to t_K, the strain will have reached $1 - (1/e)$ of its ultimate value, τ_0/G.

The Maxwell model is used to depict stress–relaxation behavior, particularly of liquids such as polymer solutions. In general, several Maxwell models in parallel are found to approximate experimental data more closely. Similarly, a "generalized" model of several Kelvin models in series is often useful, particularly in creep experiments.

The fundamental relationships among elastic, viscous, and viscoelastic materials may be illustrated by consideration of the simple Maxwell model, Eq. (15.12). If the material is such that $(G \, \partial t) \gg \mu$ (where ∂t is the characteristic time scale of the deformation), then the last term in Eq. (15.12) becomes negligible, and the material behaves in a viscous manner. For purely viscous liquids, the Maxwellian G approaches infinity. Conversely, if the material is such that $(G \, \partial t) \ll \mu$, the last term in Eq. (15.12) dominates, and the material behaves in an elastic manner.

The preceding analysis leads to a useful definition of a viscoelastic fluid. A viscoelastic material can be defined as one in which the viscosity and the term $G \, \partial t$ are of the same order of magnitude. It may be seen that in the most general case, all materials are viscoelastic, since all have some viscous and some elastic response. A dimensionless group, the Deborah number N_{De} [C2, R4], quantifies this definition. The Deborah number represents the ratio of the duration of the fluid memory to the duration of the deformation process, and is often used as a measure of the degree of viscoelasticity. For any fluid, the Deborah number is

$$N_{\text{De}} = \frac{t_{\text{fluid}}}{t_{\text{process}}} \tag{15.18}$$

where t_{fluid} is a characteristic time for the fluid. For a material whose behavior follows the Maxwell model, t_{fluid} is t_{M}, the relaxation time defined in Eq. (15.14). The characteristic time of the process t_{process} is less specifically defined. For a Maxwell material, this time is ∂t, the characteristic time scale of the deformation, as before.

It has been proposed that the behavior of generalized mechanical models is analogous to the behavior of real materials. This suggestion has led to continuum models or the linear theory of viscoelasticity for small strains. Other theories, such as those of Oldroyd [O2, O3], Rivlin and Ericksen [R6], and Coleman and Noll [C5] have attempted to describe nonlinear viscoelasticity as well as shear dependence of viscosity.

Through the use of such models, a coupling between the time aspects of viscoelasticity and steady-state behavior can be made. Viscoelastic materials under apparently steady-state conditions can be anything but steady-state to an individual fluid element of material progressing through the flow. For example, a fluid element leaves a container and enters a pipe, passes through the pipe, and exits into the atmosphere. The element undergoes a contraction and is stretched in the entry. It flows through the tube and then expands upon exiting from the pipe. Clearly, if one moves with a fluid element, one sees that the element undergoes a time rate of change at both the entry and at the exit. Under these conditions, the finite normal stresses (τ_{xx}, τ_{yy}, and τ_{zz}) for non-Newtonian liquids are found by experiment to differ appreciably. These normal stresses can be related to the viscoelastic time constants of the specific model under consideration.

Molecular models. An alternate approach to viscoelasticity involves formulation of models based on molecular theories. The best known of these are the theories of Rouse [R7] and Bueche [B9], which apply to the linear viscoelastic properties of solutions of free-draining monodisperse polymer molecules. Discrete values of relaxation times were obtained from each theory, with those from Rouse being half those from Bueche. Also, Zimm [Z1] developed a theory which includes hydrodynamic interaction and treats both the free-draining and non-free-draining case. The theories of Rouse, Bueche, and Zimm predict a steady flow viscosity independent of the shear rate. Pao [P1] found that if Rouse's theory is extended to include perturbations from all shear rate components, then the viscosity becomes dependent on the shear rate. Pao also developed continuum theories on the flow of polymer solutions. Bueche [B9] later extended his theory to account for the distribution of forces that can exist along a polymer molecule. This theory also resulted in a non-Newtonian shear-thinning viscosity. Common to all of these theories is a relaxation time parameter that has the general form

$$t_m = \frac{C_1(\mu_0 - \mu_s)M}{\pi^2 CRT} \tag{15.19}$$

where C_1 is a constant that depends on the theory, μ_0 is the zero-shear viscosity, μ_s is the solvent viscosity, M is the molecular weight, and C is the concentration of the polymer. Furthermore, Bueche's theory predicts that the dimensionless viscosity term $(\mu - \mu_s)/(\mu_0 - \mu_s)$ is a unique function of the product $(t_m \dot{\gamma})$. This product can be used to define shift conditions, and in particular a shift temperature [M10], as will be described next.

Superposition. In the aforementioned theories, the time constant t_m contains the effects of temperature, concentration, and molecular weight. Thus, a shift factor a_T can be defined by taking the ratio of Eq. (15.19) at the specific temperature under consideration to that at a reference temperature:

$$a_T = \frac{(\mu_0 - \mu_s)_T}{(\mu_0 - \mu_s)_{T_0}} \frac{T_0}{T} \tag{15.20}$$

where T_0 is an arbitrary (or convenient) reference temperature (in units of K). According to Bueche's theory, a plot of the dimensionless viscosity term $(\mu - \mu_s)/(\mu_0 - \mu_s)$ versus the quantity $a_T \dot{\gamma}$ should be universal for any and all temperatures. This point is illustrated in Figs. 15.10 and 15.11 for the molten polyethylene data of Philippoff and Gaskins [P4]. Figure 15.10 shows viscosity versus shear rate for six temperatures. In Fig. 15.11, a master curve is found by computing a_T via Eq. (15.20), using 112°C as the reference temperature; however, the data at 250°C do not superimpose with the rest. Figure 15.11 shows that principle of superposition can be used to estimate the flow curve at any temperature from data obtained over a range of temperatures. Note that this method is based on an inexact theory, and therefore the results are not

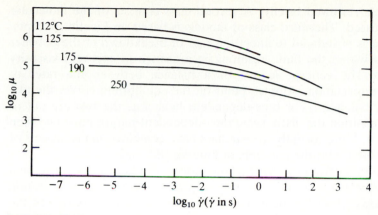

FIGURE 15.10
Viscosity–shear rate curves for molten polyethylene at various temperatures. (*From Philippoff and Gaskins, J. Polymer Sci.* **21**: *205 (1956). By permission. Adapted from Middleman, The Flow of High Polymers, p. 150, Wiley, New York, 1968. By permission.*)

exact; thus, the data at 250°C do not superimpose. Note also that for a pure material the solvent viscosity μ_s is arbitrarily dropped; in fact, in most polymer–solvent data at higher concentrations, μ_s is negligible.

A shift factor similar to a_T can be formulated for the other variables in Eq. (15.19), i.e., concentration and molecular weight. The field of rheology includes many other applications of superposition. Among the most successful of these is the Williams–Landel–Ferry (WLF) equation for viscoelastic effects [B2, W3].

Kinetic models. Three classes of models for non-Newtonian behavior may be identified. The first of these is based on observations of the fluid response on a macroscopic scale, e.g., the Bingham ideal plastic law of Eq. (15.5), the other empirical laws such as Reiner–Philippoff, Cross, etc., and the mechanical and

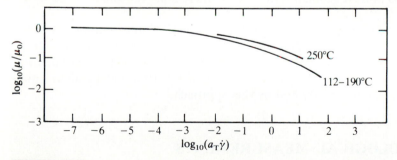

FIGURE 15.11
Data of Fig. 15.10, "shifted" to 112°C using a_T. (*From Philippoff and Gaskins, J. Polymer Sci.* **21**: *205 (1956). By permission. Adapted from Middleman, The Flow of High Polymers, p. 150, Wiley, New York, 1968. By permission.*)

continuum models reviewed briefly. A second class consists of the molecular models just discussed. The third class of models is based on kinetic concepts. The rate of shear is postulated to affect the rate of breakdown of the polymer structure formed within the fluid, resulting in a change in apparent viscosity with shear rate. The concept is one of a balance between the rates of breakdown and reformation. At each point on the equilibrium curve, the two rates are exactly balanced. For time-dependent behavior, the two are out of balance, and in addition the viscoelastic time-dependent nature must be taken into consideration. More recently, researchers have combined many aspects of the molecular models with the concepts of kinetics [B4, B5].

The change that occurs during the flow process can be considered to be a result of several mechanisms. For example, a preferred molecular orientation occurs during flow. This alignment in the direction of flow increases as the shear rate increases, and may lead to non-Newtonian behavior. A second mechanism that has been suggested is the possible rotation of a large polymer molecule or a mass of aggregates in the flow field. Steric and other hindrances may lead to non-Newtonian effects because the polymer molecular cannot respond instantaneously to the deforming stress. When the time for rotation of the molecule is less than the relaxation time of the coil, then the molcule can respond less effectively to the applied stress by expansion and contraction as the shear rate increases. The molecule demonstrates elastic behavior, and energy is stored to be released at a later time, thus causing less viscous loss.

In Chapter 14 there was presented a theory of liquid behavior that showed that the viscosity can be a function of shear rate [see Eq. (14.63)]. Ree and Eyring introduced a mathematical treatment of thixotropic substances [R2] based on this development. Their analysis applied the theory of rate processes to the molecular relaxations that are fundamental to the nature of flow. Although this theory is formulated in terms of various molecular distances and the specific rate for molecular jumps from equilibrium positions into neighboring vacant sites, these parameters are not known in general and must be determined from experimental data. In final form, the model of Ree and Eyring consists of a Newtonian term plus as many non-Newtonian terms as are needed.

Brodkey and coworkers developed a kinetic interpretation of time-dependent non-Newtonian flow [J1, K1]. They assumed that the non-Newtonian characteristics of flow are associated with a structural breakdown, to which reaction kinetics can be applied. Time-independent non-Newtonianism can also be treated by this approach.

15.2 RHEOLOGICAL MEASUREMENTS

Equation (2.5), Newton's law, is a laminar flow equation. Naturally, all viscosity determinations are conducted under conditions of laminar flow. Four common experiments to determine viscosity are: flow in a capillary viscometer,[4] laminar flow between parallel plates, laminar flow in a Couette (or plate-and-cone) viscometer,[5] and a falling-ball viscometer.[6] The falling-ball viscometer measures viscosity at very low shear rates and can be used to find μ_0, the viscosity at zero shear. In the other experiments, the rate of shear is easily varied. Therefore, the capillary and/or rotational experiments are used to determine the viscosity as a function of the shear rate.

15.2.1 Capillary Viscometer

In the capillary viscometer, the flow rate is varied by varying the pressure. Usually, tubes of differing diameters are used, along with a range of pressures, in order to obtain the widest possible range of shear rates. The tubes are carefully chosen to ensure that the inside is as smooth as possible in order to maintain perfectly laminar flow. It is common to determine the tube diameters by actual calibration using one or more fluids of known viscosity.

The equations for laminar flow are summarized in Table 4.5. For laminar flow of a Newtonian fluid, the Hagen–Poiseuille equation applies:

$$Q = \frac{-\Delta p}{8\mu L} \pi r_o^4 \tag{4.76}$$

Equation (4.76) can be rearranged into an equivalent form given by Eq. (4.83):

$$\tau_w = \frac{(r_o)(-\Delta p)}{2L} = \mu \frac{4U_{z,\,ave}}{r_o} = \mu \frac{8U_{z,\,ave}}{d_o} = \mu \frac{4Q}{\pi r_o^3} \tag{4.83}$$

As indicated in Eq. (4.84), the term $(4Q)/(\pi r_o^3)$ has several equivalent forms:

$$\left(\frac{\partial U_z}{\partial r}\right)_{wall} = \frac{4Q}{\pi r_o^3} = \frac{4U_{z,\,ave}}{r_o} = \frac{8U_{z,\,ave}}{d_o} \tag{4.84}$$

In the notation being used here, the shear rate at the wall $\dot\gamma_w$ is the velocity gradient at the wall, which for tube flow is

$$\dot\gamma_w = \left(\frac{dU_z}{dr}\right)_{wall} = \left(\frac{dU_z}{dr}\right)_w \tag{15.21}$$

Example 4.7 illustrated the use of the above relations to determine the viscosity of a Newtonian material. For a non-Newtonian material, the wall shear stress from the force balance [Eq. (4.79) and shown above in Eq. (4.83)]

---

[4] A horizontal capillary viscometer is depicted in Fig. 4.9; most units are vertical, however, as was used in Example 10.1. Examples 4.7 and 10.1 illustrate the analysis of data.

[5] A Couette flow is shown in Fig. 5.5. Equation (xxv) in Example 5.7 is the relation used to find the viscosity from the measurements available in the Couette experiment.

[6] A falling ball viscometer is a simple device in which a sphere settles in the fluid of interest in the Stokes' law region. The terminal settling velocity is determined by timing the descent over a known distance. Examples 12.10 and 12.11 illustrate some of the calculations.

is still valid, no matter what the nature of the fluid, as long as it is homogeneous. From the definition of the flow rate, Q in terms of the velocity U_z, and the definition of the velocity in terms of the velocity gradient dU_z/dr, the following rigorous relation can be obtained [B7, O2]:

$$\frac{4Q}{\pi r_o^3} = \frac{8U_{z,\,ave}}{d_o} = \frac{4}{\tau_w^3} \int_0^{\tau_w} \tau^2(-\dot{\gamma})\, d\tau \tag{15.22}$$

Equation (4.83) can be obtained by substituting Newton's law for $-\dot{\gamma}$ [Eq. (15.3)] into Eq. (15.22) and integrating. A simple relation for the shear rate in laminar flow through round tubes, as first derived independently by Weissenberg and Rabinowitsch [R1] and Mooney [M12], is obtained by differentiating Eq. 15.22 twice [B7]:

$$-\dot{\gamma}_w = -\left(\frac{dU_z}{dr}\right)_w = \frac{3}{4}\left(\frac{8U_{z,\,ave}}{d_o}\right) + \frac{\tau_w}{4}\left(\frac{d(8U_{z,\,ave}/d_o)}{d\tau_w}\right) \tag{15.23}$$

Equation (15.23) is a general equation for all fluids in tube flow, the only assumption being no slip at the wall. This equation is used extensively to obtain the variables in the basic shear diagram from capillary viscometric data. Equation (15.23) can be rearranged to [M8]

$$-\dot{\gamma}_w = -\left(\frac{dU_z}{dr}\right)_w = \frac{3n'+1}{4n'}\left(\frac{8U_{z,\,ave}}{d_o}\right) \tag{15.24}$$

where

$$n' = \frac{d(\ln \tau_w)}{d[\ln(8U_{z,\,ave}/d_o)]} \tag{15.25}$$

Equation (15.25) is actually a definition of n' as given in Eq. (10.5):

$$\tau_w = K'\left(\frac{8U_{z,\,ave}}{d_o}\right)^{n'} \tag{10.5}$$

where K' and n' are material parameters (not necessarily constant for non-Newtonian fluids) and τ_w is given by Eq. (4.83) above. The only assumptions in Eqs. (15.23) and (15.24) are no slip at the wall and purely viscous behavior; there are no assumptions about fluid behavior or about the constancy of K' and n'. Naturally, for a Newtonian fluid the exponent n' is unity, and the constant K' equals μ. The constants K' and n' are evaluated from a plot of $\ln \tau_w$ versus $\ln(8U_{z,\,ave}/d_o)$; this plot is termed the capillary shear diagram.

The power law, Eq. (15.6), is perhaps the best known empirical model for non-Newtonian fluids. This equation is often adequate to describe non-Newtonian behavior over a considerable range (10 to 100-fold) of shear rates [M4]. If K and n are both constant, then the following can be shown:

$$n' = n \qquad K' = K\left(\frac{3n+1}{4n}\right)^n \tag{15.26}$$

Non-Newtonian Reynolds number. The Hagen–Poiseuille equation for a Newtonian fluid can be cast into the form of a friction factor:

$$f = 16/(d_o U_{z,\,ave}\rho/\mu) = 16/N_{Re} \qquad N_{Re} \le 2100 \qquad (6.124)$$

where the Fanning friction factor f is

$$f = \frac{\tau_w}{\frac{1}{2}\rho U_{z,\,ave}^2} = \frac{(d_o/4)(-\Delta p/L)}{\frac{1}{2}\rho U_{z,\,ave}^2} \qquad (10.1)$$

Note that Eq. (10.1) contains the expression for the wall shear stress in tube flow that had been given previously in Eqs. (4.80) and (4.83).

Equations (10.5) and (6.124) can be used to define N'_{Re}, the non-Newtonian Reynolds number of Metzner and Reed [M8]. After some algebraic rearrangement, Eq. (10.5) can be cast into the same form as Eq. (6.124):

$$f = 16/N'_{Re} \qquad (15.27)$$

where the Reynolds number N'_{Re} is

$$N'_{Re} = \frac{d_o^{n'} U_{z,\,ave}^{2-n'}\rho}{K' 8^{n'-1}} \qquad (15.28)$$

Equation (15.27) must always be valid for laminar flow ($N'_{Re} < 2000$), since it is merely a rearrangement of Eq. (10.5).

As discussed in Chapter 4, the shear stress τ_{rz} is zero at the pipe center line and a maximum at the wall. Equation (4.81) shows that τ_{rz} varies linearly with radius:

$$\frac{\tau_{rz}}{\tau_w} = \frac{r}{r_o} \qquad (4.81)$$

This equation applies equally to Newtonian and non-Newtonian materials and to laminar and turbulent flows.

Measurements. In the capillary viscometer, the pressure drop and the flow rate are measured; the velocity is computed from the flow rate through the use of Eq. (7.10):

$$w = \rho U_{z,\,ave} S = \rho Q \qquad (15.29)$$

where S is the inside area of the capillary in the direction perpendicular to the flow. Hence, by measuring Δp and w, the quantities τ_w and $8U_{z,\,ave}/d_o$ are computed. As previously indicated, the material constants K' and n' are determined from a log–log plot and Eq. (10.5); K' and n' are often constant over the shear rate range of interest.

In Example 15.2, the parameters K' and n' [Eq. (10.5)] are found from a typical set of viscometric data taken with a capillary instrument. In Example 15.3, the power law parameters are found from the same set of data. In Example 15.4, the basic shear diagram is determined from capillary data for which the slope n' varies.

TABLE 15.2

Flow data for polyisobutylene L-80 in cyclohexane at 25°C

$8U_{z,\,ave}/d_o,\,s^{-1}$	$\tau_w,\,N\,m^{-2}$	$8U_{z,\,ave}/d_o,\,s^{-1}$	$\tau_w,\,N\,m^{-2}$
651	3.71	7575	35.21
1361	7.49	11140	46.25
2086	11.41	19270	77.50
5089	24.08	25030	96.68

Example 15.2. Hershey [H1] measured the flow of a 1 percent solution of polyisobutylene L-80 (viscosity-average molecular weight approximately 700 000) in cyclohexane at 25.0°C. Use the eight points given in Table 15.2 to find the parameters in Eq. (10.5). The literature value of n' using 25 points is 0.887 [H1].

Answer. The capillary shear diagram for the data in Table 15.2 is found in Fig. 15.12. The data appear linear, and this result is confirmed by a statistical analysis [H1]. Equation (10.5) can be linearized as follows:

$$\ln \tau_w = \ln K' + n'(8U_{z,\,ave}/d_o) \tag{i}$$

Equation (i) is in the form of a straight line:

$$y = \beta_0 + \beta_1 x \tag{ii}$$

where

$$y = \ln \tau_w$$

$$x = \ln(8U_{z,\,ave}/d_o)$$

$$\beta_0 = \ln K' \qquad \beta_1 = n' \tag{iii}$$

Next, natural logarithms are taken for both ordinate and abscissa in Table 15.2; those numbers are used to calculate the linear least-squares line by the standard technique [P2]. The results are

$$\beta_0 = -4.3790514 \qquad \text{or} \qquad K' = 0.01254\,N\,m^{-2}$$

$$\beta_1 = n' = 0.8851 \tag{iv}$$

The final rheological model is

$$\tau_w = (0.01254)(8U_{z,\,ave}/d_o)^{0.8851} \tag{v}$$

Equation (v) is also plotted in Fig. 15.12.

Example 15.3. Find the power-law parameters for the data of Example 15.2 (Table 15.2).

Answer. The parameters K' and n', computed in Example 15.2, will be used to find K and n in the power law, Eq. (15.6). Using Eq. (15.26), the answers are

$$n = n' = 0.8851 \tag{i}$$

$$K = \frac{K'}{[(3n+1)/4n]^n} = \frac{0.01254}{1.029} = 0.01219\,N\,m^{-2} \tag{ii}$$

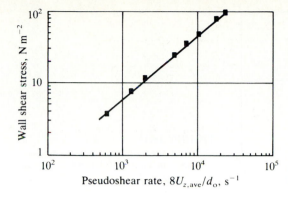

FIGURE 15.12
Capillary shear diagram for polyiso-butylene L-80 in cyclohexane.

Example 15.4. The data given in Table 15.3 (a commercial polyethylene melt at 190°C) were obtained on a capillary unit [M3]; the appropriate end corrections were also made. Obtain the basic shear diagram.

Answer. The basic shear diagram is a plot of the wall shear stress τ_w versus the actual wall shear rate $\dot{\gamma}_w$. The wall shear stress is measured directly in the capillary experiment; the actual wall shear rate must be calculated from the pseudoshear rate as follows:

$$-\dot{\gamma}_w = -\left(\frac{dU_z}{dr}\right)_w = \frac{3n'+1}{4n'}\left(\frac{8U_{z,\,\text{ave}}}{d_o}\right) \qquad (15.24)$$

The data as given in Table 15.3 are first plotted as $\log \tau_w$ versus $\log(8U_{z,\,\text{ave}}/d_o)$ in Fig. 15.13; from this plot the slope n' can be evaluated at each point by drawing a tangent and dividing the actual vertical distance (in inches or centimeters) by the horizontal distance.

At first glance, the data in Fig. 15.13 may appear linear; however, the slope n' varies significantly. The best procedure to determine the slope is to fit these data with the lowest order polynomial that adequately represents the observed

TABLE 15.3
Flow data for a commercial polyethylene melt at 190°C

$8U_{z,\,\text{ave}}/d_o$, s^{-1}	$\tau_w \times 10^{-4}$, N m^{-2}
10	2.24
20	3.10
50	4.35
100	5.77
200	7.50
400	9.73
600	11.00
1000	13.52
2000	16.40

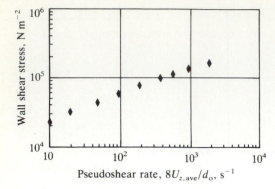

FIGURE 15.13
Capillary shear diagram for a commercial polyethylene melt at 190°C. (Data from Table 15.3.)

variation [H3]. Such a calculation finds that a second-order polynomial is optimal:

$$y = \beta_0 + \beta_1 x + \beta_2 x^2 \tag{i}$$

where, as in Example 15-2:

$$y = \ln \tau_w \tag{ii}$$

$$x = \ln(8U_{z,\,ave}/d_o) \tag{iii}$$

Note that Eqs. (ii) and (iii) can be defined alternately in terms of $\log_{10}$, since the slope n' will be identical in either case. A least-squares regression [P2] of the above data yields

$$\beta_0 = 8.966\,94 \qquad \beta_1 = 0.484\,525\,20 \qquad \beta_2 = -0.010\,923\,041 \tag{iv}$$

The slope n' is found by differentiating Eq. (i):

$$n' = \beta_1 + 2\beta_2 x \tag{v}$$

The nine values of x are used along with the constants in Eq. (iv) to find n' at each point. The answers are given in Table 15.4. Next, Eq. (15.24) is used to calculate the actual wall shear rate $\dot{\gamma}_w$; these values are also given in Table 15.4, along with the correction factor $(3n' + 1)/(4n')$. The correction factor is appreciable, ranging from 33 percent to 53 percent.

TABLE 15.4
Calculations for Example 15.4

$8U_{z,\,ave}/d_o$, s^{-1}	n'	$(3n'+1)/(4n')$	$\dot{\gamma}_w$, s^{-1}	μ_a, poise
10	0.434	1.33	13.3	16 900
20	0.419	1.35	26.9	11 500
50	0.399	1.38	68.8	6 320
100	0.384	1.40	140	4 120
200	0.369	1.43	285	2 630
400	0.354	1.46	583	1 670
600	0.345	1.48	885	1 240
1000	0.334	1.50	1500	902
2000	0.318	1.53	3070	534

Table 15.4 also includes the apparent viscosity at the wall conditions, which is found from Eq. (15.4):

$$\tau = -\mu_a \dot\gamma \tag{15.4}$$

Note the dramatic variation of the apparent viscosity, and thus the need to consider some materials as non-Newtonian.

15.2.2 Rotational Viscometers

Two additional designs in common use for viscometric measurements are the Couette (concentric cylinders) and the plate-and-cone. These can be designed to give a rate of shear that is essentially constant in the gap. The two systems are shown in Fig. 15.14. For the Couette viscometer, the best design includes a fixed inside cylinder, with the outside cylinder rotating at variable angular velocities. This scheme minimizes the formation of Taylor vortices (mentioned briefly in Chapter 6); however, the opposite design is more common.

In the plate-and-cone design, the top plate is stationary and is usually equipped with instrumentation to measure the torque T_Q exerted by the fluid. Also, the total force exerted by the fluid on the plate can be measured and then used to calculate the normal stresses. In practice, the cone is usually located on top, so that the material under test will not tend to flow down-hill and out of the system. Note that careful design is necessary for both instruments in order to ensure that the shear rate is constant in the gap. The equations required to analyze rotational viscometers are summarized elsewhere [B7, O1].

Since rotational viscometers can be designed with constant shear rate $\dot\gamma$,

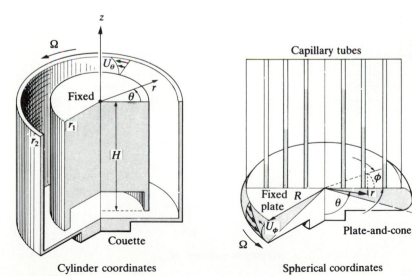

FIGURE 15.14
Rotational Couette system and plate-and-cone system.

and since the shear stress τ is directly measured, rotational viscometers are especially suitable for determination of constants in rheological laws. A modern rotational viscometer can be used to determine the basic shear diagram over the lower ranges of shear rates. However, in order to determine the entire curve for a pseudoplastic fluid (cf. Fig. 15.2), a capillary viscometer is usually required to obtain data in the laminar flow regime at high shear rates.

15.3 TURBULENT FLOW

In Chapter 6, it was shown that the Fanning friction factor was correlated for Newtonian fluids by the Reynolds number; both the friction factor and the Reynolds number are, of course, dimensionless. Naturally, early investigators tried to extend the same techniques to flow problems involving non-Newtonian materials. The most successful (and most widely quoted) correlation is that of Dodge and Metzner [D1]:

$$1/(f)^{1/2} = \frac{4.00}{(n')^{0.75}} \log_{10}[N'_{\text{Re}}(f)^{(1-n')/2}] - \frac{0.40}{(n')^{1.2}} \tag{15.30}$$

Figure 15.15 is a plot of this equation plus Eq. (15.27) for the laminar region.

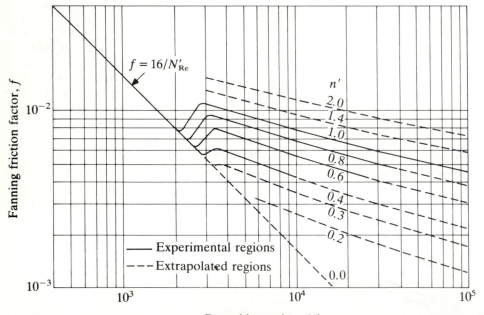

FIGURE 15.15
Fanning friction factor for shear-thinning materials. (*From Dodge and Metzner, AIChE J.* **5:** *198 (1959). By permission.*)

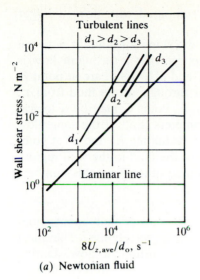

(a) Newtonian fluid

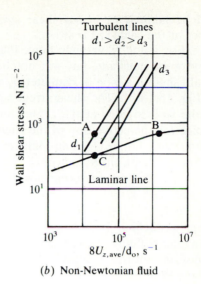

(b) Non-Newtonian fluid

FIGURE 15.16
Laminar and turbulent flow on a capillary shear diagram.

Equation (15.30) is a generalization of the von Karman equation, Eq. (6.132). The generality of Figure 15.15 is open to question, since it is based on several concentrations of only two fluids, aqueous solutions of carbopol (a polymer) and attagel (a clay suspension). Many fluids do not follow the Dodge–Metzner correlation; these will be discussed shortly under the subtopic of "drag reduction". Nevertheless, Eq. (15.30) is appealing in its logical construction.

The Reynolds number in Eq. (15.30) is that of Reed and Metzner [Eq. (15.28)]. Evaluation of this Reynolds number is straightforward in those cases where K' and n' are constant. When K' and n' vary, Dodge and Metzner recommend that these parameters be evaluated from the capillary shear diagram at the same wall shear stress. This recommendation is strictly empirical and is based on the fact that the best correlation is obtained in this manner.

Actually, selection of an appropriate Reynolds number for the turbulent flow of non-Newtonian fluids is arbitrary. For Newtonian fluids, the viscosity in the definition of Reynolds number is based on laminar flow conditions. The value of the viscosity is independent of either shear rate or shear stress. Figure 15.16(a) is a log–log plot of the wall shear stress versus the pseudoshear rate $8U_{z,\,ave}/d_o$ for a typical Newtonian fluid; three turbulent flow curves [calculated from Eq. (6.133)] are plotted along with the laminar line representing the Hagen–Poiseuille equation. The slope of the laminar Newtonian line n' is of course unity. The viscosity of the fluid is K'. In small-diameter tubes, the flow will be laminar at higher shear stresses when compared with flow in larger tubes at the same shear stress.

For a non-Newtonian fluid, Fig. 15.16(b), the slope for laminar flow can vary or be constant, but will not be unity. Suppose that a turbulent flow is established in a pipe of diameter d_1 such that τ_w and $8U_{z,\,ave}/d_o$ are at point A in Fig. 15.16(b). The shear stress actually varies throughout the fluid from τ_w at the wall to zero at the center line [Eq. (4.81)]. Point C may be a logical choice for the estimation of the rheological parameters (i.e., at the same flow conditions), but Dodge and Metzner recommend evaluating K' and n' at point B; their value is more indicative of the viscosity of the fluid in the wall region. A review of the many other possibilities for defining other Reynolds numbers is available [B7].

Drag reduction. Experimental observations have shown that many non-Newtonian fluids do not obey the Dodge–Metzner correlation. The most important of these fluids exhibit drag reduction in turbulent flow. During World War II, Agoston and associates [A1] investigated the turbulent flow of both gasoline and gasoline thickened with an aluminum disoap additive. The aluminum disoap–gasoline mixture forms napalm, which has a gel-like structure. They found that the pressure drop of the napalm in a $\frac{1}{8}$-in. tube was as much as 70 percent less than that of gasoline alone at a flow rate of roughly 11 gallons per minute. In 1949, Mysels received a patent on this type of friction-reducing additive [M13]. About the same time, Toms published data on the laminar and turbulent flow of poly(methyl methacrylate) in monochlorobenzene [T1]. From Toms' plots of his data, it was obvious that in considering any one flow rate the effect of increasing the concentration of polymer was to lower the pressure drop until a minimum was reached. Further increase in concentration increased the pressure drop gradually, until the pressure drop exceeded that of the original solvent.

Savins was the first to describe this phenomenon as drag reduction [S1]. His drag ratio D_R is the ratio of the observed pressure gradient for the solution in question to the observed pressure gradient for the solvent under the same flow conditions [S2]:

$$D_R = \frac{(\Delta p)_{\text{fluid}}}{(\Delta p)_{\text{solvent}}} \tag{15.31}$$

From Eq. (15.31), it follows that any fluid whose drag ratio is less than unity is a drag-reducing fluid.

Figure 15.17 shows a typical plot of the drag ratio D_R versus the pseudoshear rate $8U_{z,\,ave}/d_o$; these particular data are for 0.8 percent aluminum monohydroxide distearate in toluene at 25°C in an 0.165-cm tube [H4, M2]. In Fig. 15.17, the drag ratio exceeds unity in the laminar region and is below unity in the turbulent region. A similar plot for a solution of sugar in water never crosses below the line of incipient drag reduction ($D_R = 1$) because no drag reduction exists in the sugar–water system. The presence of sugar

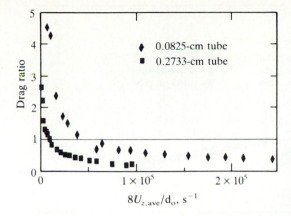

FIGURE 15.17
Drag ratio versus flow rate for 0.8 percent aluminum monohydroxide distearate in toluene at 25°C in a 0.165-cm tube. (*From McMillan, Ph.D. Dissertation, The Ohio State University, 1970.*)

increases the viscosity of the solution; hence, the drag ratio in sugar solutions exceeds unity in both the laminar and the turbulent regions.

Drag reduction in solutions may be separated into two categories: solution drag reduction and suspension drag reduction. It is likely that each category has a different mechanism. The mechanism of drag reduction has been a topic of much speculation ever since the discovery of the phenomenon. Yet the exact mechanism has remained elusive. It was noted early that drag-reducing solutions were also viscoelastic. However, that observation has not led to any general and successful correlations, in spite of numerous attempts.

Solution drag reduction has been studied extensively using both polymers and micellar solutes such as surfactants and aluminum disoaps. Typical experimental data plots of friction factor versus Reynolds number show a large diameter effect. This diameter effect is present regardless of which Reynolds number is plotted. Hence, a useful approach is to define a "solvent Reynolds number" as

$$N_{\mathrm{Re,\,s}} = d_o U_{z,\,\mathrm{ave}} \rho / \mu_s \qquad (15.32)$$

where ρ and μ_s are the density and viscosity of pure solvent. A plot of $N_{\mathrm{Re,\,s}}$ versus f will clearly show the presence or absence of drag reduction. Drag reduction is occurring whenever the experimental points fall below the line of the von Karman equations [Eq. (6.132)].

Figure 15.18 shows friction factor versus solvent Reynolds number for a solution of 0.1 percent polyisobutylene in cyclohexane [H1]. There is turbulent flow in several pipe sizes, ranging in diameter from 0.032 in. to 0.999 in., and the diameter effect is striking. Note the presence of the critical solvent Reynolds number [H2], shown best in the 0.509 in. tube. At low flow rates, the friction factors for this tube are clearly in the turbulent region; yet they lie above the von Karman line [Eq. (6.132)], as would be expected from the viscosity increase alone in Eq. (6.132). At a solvent Reynolds number of approximately 61 000 (i.e., the critical solvent Reynolds number), the onset of

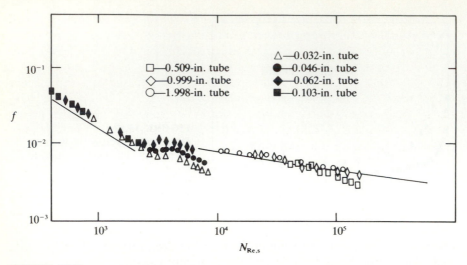

FIGURE 15.18
Friction factor versus solvent Reynolds number (0.1 percent polyisobutylene in cyclohexane at 25°C). (*From Hershey and Zakin, Ind. Eng. Chem. Fundam.* **6:** *381 (1967).*)

drag reduction occurs. Further increases in flow rate result in increasing amounts of drag reduction. For the 0.032 in. tube, Fig. 15.18 shows that the drag reduction begins almost immediately as the flow becomes turbulent; note the small transition between laminar and turbulent flow at a solvent Reynolds number of 2500. The data points for the 0.999 in. tube are barely in the drag reduction region in Fig. 15.18. At this point, the maximum flow rate of the pump has been reached; no data at higher flow rates were obtainable. Note that in the 1.998-in. tube the solvent Reynolds number was not sufficiently high to observe drag reduction.

Numerous effects affecting drag reduction, in addition to the diameter effect, have been investigated. For example, there exists a minimum concentration below which drag reduction will not occur [H1]. Each tube diameter has its point of maximum drag reduction at a given flow rate at a different concentration. The phenomenon of drag reduction is a strong function of the molecular weight of the additive [F1, H2]. The higher the molecular weight, the more drag reduction is observed. However, the problem of degradation has limited the applications of the drag-reduction phenomenon. When polymer drag-reducing additives are introduced into a piping system, they quickly degrade mechanically when passing through a pump (i.e., the molecular weight decreases as a result of cleavage of the long polymer chains), and drag reduction is quickly reduced to zero. The type of solvent strongly affects the amount of drag reduction. The conformation of the polymer molecule in solution (i.e., whether the polymer molecule is expanded or contracted) is a crucial consideration in the presence or absence of drag reduction [H2]. Also, experimental studies have shown that solutions of some polymers are drag reducing, while others are not; possibly, if sufficiently high-molecular-weight polymer were available, drag reduction might be found. Studies have shown that the most effective coiled polymer additives are those with flexible chains [L1]. Significant drag reduction has been reported at concentrations of only a few parts per million for some polymers, primarily in aqueous solutions. Other additives such as aluminum disoaps, surfactants, and fibers can be very successful in causing drag reduction, although higher concentrations may be required. Presently, it is difficult to predict the behavior of a new polymer–solvent combination in the absence of experimental data, although some guidance is available [L1].

There are no useful and general correlations for drag-reducing fluids. Dodge and Metzner showed that Fig. 15.15 did not apply to drag-reducing fluids [D1]. Basically, any precise design of a piping system must rely on an empirical [B6] or semi-empirical [G2] method and experimental data. The diameter effect is especially troublesome. Also, the design must allow for the degradation of molecular weight that always occurs.

The most successful application of drag reduction is the pipeline transport of crude oil. In the trans-Alaska (Alyeska) pipeline, drag reducing additives are injected to reduce pumping costs and to increase flow rates by 10 to 20 percent [B10]. In oil wells, drag-reducing additives have been used to increase water flow rates and reduce pressure losses during fracturing operations, thus increasing the effectiveness of the project. In offshore oil production, drag-reducing additives enable pipe of smaller diameter to be used, thus reducing capital costs and increasing production through existing pipe networks [B1]. Other applications include storm sewers, hydroelectric plants, hydraulic machines, biomedical applications, marine performance, heating systems, and fire-fighting [G1].

15.4 AGITATION OF NON-NEWTONIAN FLUIDS

Design of agitation equipment with non-Newtonian fluids requires considerable experience. First, if the fluid is barely non-Newtonian, then the methods introduced in Chapter 9 are probably satisfactory. Secondly, if the fluid is highly non-Newtonian, in the sense that n or n' are much less than unity, the mixing may occur in the laminar regime where correlation is more certain. If neither of these cases applies, then unpredictable behavior, as well as difficulties in correlating results, may be expected.

Early investigators in agitation of non-Newtonian liquids assumed that an average shear rate $(dU/dr)_A$ must exist in an agitated vessel. The apparent viscosity μ_A corresponding to this average shear rate was assumed to be equal to the viscosity of a Newtonian fluid showing exactly the same power consumption under the same conditions in the laminar region. Metzner and Otto [M7] assumed that this average shear rate is linearly related to the rotational speed N of the impeller:

$$\left(\frac{dU}{dr}\right)_A = k_s N \tag{15.33}$$

The constant k_s is determined in a pilot plant by measuring the power number N_{po}, Eq. (9.10), and using Fig. 9.7 to estimate the Reynolds number for agitation N_{Re}, Eq. (9.9). The equivalent apparent viscosity μ_A is calculated from N_{Re}, and then $(dU/dr)_A$ is determined from the flow curve. Note that dilatant materials are difficult to handle, because their viscosity increases with increasing shear [C1]. Skelland compiled a list of values of k_s [S3].

Most companies that sell agitation equipment are experienced in assisting with problems involving non-Newtonian fluids. Skelland [S3] and Giesekus *et al.* [G1] reviewed the agitation literature. Ulbrecht and Carreau [U1] presented a thorough survey of agitation in non-Newtonian liquids, particularly emphasizing the strong influence of elasticity. Oldshue [O4] pointed out that the scale-up methods of Chapter 9 (geometric similarity, etc.) are often inadequate in tough scale-up problems, such as those with viscoelastic, non-Newtonian fluids. Also, the considerable work in heat and mass transfer in agitated vessels has been summarized [G1].

15.5 HEAT TRANSFER IN PIPE FLOW

Laminar flow. Many solutions to laminar flow heat transfer have been proposed. The most useful of these have been reviewed by Skelland [S3]. In general, the heat transfer equations for a particular geometry are solved in terms of a reasonable model.

For pipe flow, a general solution for the constant wall temperature case is available. Christiansen and Craig [C3] introduced a temperature-dependent form of the power law:

$$\tau_{rz} = k_\sigma S_r^n \tag{15.34}$$

with S_r being the "reduced shear rate":

$$S_r = -\left(\frac{dU}{dr}\right)\exp\frac{E}{RT} \tag{15.35}$$

where R is the gas constant; k_σ, E, and n are constants which are independent of temperature. These equations can be combined with the energy equation:

$$\frac{\partial T}{\partial x} = \alpha\left(\frac{\partial^2 T}{\partial r^2} + \frac{1}{r}\frac{\partial T}{\partial r}\right) \tag{15.36}$$

The resulting equation has been integrated numerically with the aid of some simplifying assumptions by Christiansen and Craig [C3]. The results appear to apply to many solutions, both drag-reducing and non-drag-reducing.

Turbulent flow. Many non-Newtonian fluids are inherently so viscous that heat transfer occurs in the laminar regime. On the other hand, the early investigators such as Winding, Dittman, and Kranich [W4] and Miller [M11] found that the Dittus–Boelter equation using μ_∞ gave a reasonable prediction of the heat transfer under turbulent conditions. Another popular equation is the Friend–Metzner analogy [F4]:

$$N_{\text{Nu, mb}} = \frac{N_{\text{Re, mb}} N_{\text{Pr, mb}}(f/2)(\mu_{\text{mb}}/\mu_{\text{w}})^{0.14}}{1.20 + (11.8)(f/2)^{1/2}(N_{\text{Pr, mb}} - 1)(N_{\text{Pr, mb}})^{-1/3}} \quad (11.83)$$

$$0.5 \le N_{\text{Pr, mb}} \le 600 \qquad N_{\text{Re, mb}} \ge 10\,000$$

where for non-Newtonian fluids the Prandtl number is evaluated using the apparent viscosity at the wall shear stress. Metzner and Friend [M6] showed that Eq. (11.83) is applicable when

$$\frac{N_{\text{Pr, mb}} N'_{\text{Re, mb}}}{(n')^{0.25}} \left(\frac{f}{2}\right)^{0.5} \ge 5000 \quad (15.37)$$

The Friend–Metzner correlation was developed and tested using some 80 data points, none of which was drag-reducing in nature. It is therefore not recommended for drag-reducing fluids.

Studies of heat transfer to drag-reducing fluids [C2, C6, G3, M1] showed that the heat transfer rate is reduced significantly in these fluids. Figure 15.19 summarizes the data of Corman [C6] for five concentrations of guar gum in water in a 0.62-in. pipe. The order of magnitude of the decrease in heat transfer is approximately the same as that for the decrease in pressure drop. All these investigators correlated their data by various means, but none of these correlations appears to be sufficiently general to be used without experimental data.

One important difference between heat transfer with Newtonian and

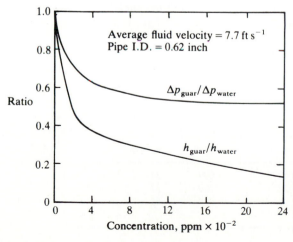

FIGURE 15.19
Heat transfer data for guar gum. (*From Corman, Ind. Eng. Chem. Process Des. Dev.* **9**: 254 (1970). *By permission.*)

non-Newtonian fluids is that the entry length for heat transfer with non-Newtonian fluids is far greater, i.e., 400–500 diameters [C2]. Also, it has been shown that there is no direct analogy between momentum, heat, and mass transfer phenomena for drag-reducing viscoelastic fluids in turbulent pipe flows [C2]. A lengthy review by Cho and Hartnett [C2] covers all three phenomena in non-Newtonian fluids.

15.6 SUMMARY

Non-Newtonian fluids occur in many practical chemical engineering applications. Their anomalous behavior has long been recognized. A careful analysis of the literature reveals progress in characterizing the laminar behavior, but precious little progress in general turbulent correlations for engineering design.

PROBLEMS

15.1. Clarify the following terms:

shear-thinning	shear-thickening	thixotropy
thinning with time	thickening with time	rheopectic
pseudoplastic	dilatant	antithixotropic

Why do you think materials exhibit non-Newtonian characteristics in general?

15.2. Discuss the origin of thixotropy and why a particular material might be thixotropic. Explain what effect, if any, thixotropy has on behavior in pipe flow (laminar and turbulent). Lastly, discuss the meaning of a basic shear diagram for such a material.

15.3. The power law, Eq. (15.6), has only two constants; yet, it is still very useful. Describe three major drawbacks and two major advantages, explaining each in detail.

15.4. For Fig. 15.3, the Ellis parameters are:

$$\mu_0 = 6.25 \text{ P} \qquad K_e = 1.35 \times 10^{-5} \qquad \alpha_e - 1 = 1$$

where the shear stress is in units of dyne cm^{-2} and the shear rate is in s^{-1}. Find the constants in SI and find the shear stress (N m^{-2}) for a shear rate of 2.224×10^4 s^{-1}.

15.5. A clay–silica material is to be produced by your company. The data shown in Table 15.5 (with all corrections properly made) were obtained in the laboratory.

TABLE 15.5
Data for Problem 15.5

$\dot{\gamma}, s^{-1}$	$\tau, N m^{-2}$	$\dot{\gamma}, s^{-1}$	$\tau, N m^{-2}$	$\dot{\gamma}, s^{-1}$	$\tau, N m^{-2}$
5	5.8	200	18	600	34
25	7.4	300	22	700	37
50	9.0	400	26	800	41
100	12.5	500	29		

TABLE 15.6
Raw viscometric data for Problem 15.6

Tube diameter, cm	Tube length, cm	Volume flow rate, $cm^3 s^{-1}$	Pressure drop, $lb_f in.^{-2}$
0.271	94.4	0.591	20.0
		2.95	39.3
		8.32	59.5
		21.0	85.8
0.271	67.4	0.733	15.0
		1.26	20.0
		7.06	39.5
		17.6	58.0
		35.1	79.5
0.182	63.4	0.192	20.5
		0.477	28.0
		0.801	37.5
		2.58	59.0
		5.56	79.5
		9.34	100.3
0.182	45.2	0.067	9.0
		0.350	20.5
		0.972	31.0
		2.72	45.0
		5.75	59.5
		9.84	75.0
0.0856	29.7	0.0906	41.0
		0.581	81.0
		1.00	100.0
		1.74	126.5
		2.66	154.0
0.0856	20.95	0.108	31.3
		0.506	55.0
		0.974	70.0
		1.81	91.5
		3.20	113.5
		3.85	134.0

TABLE 15.7
Basic shear data for a gel: Problem 15.7

$\dot{\gamma}, s^{-1}$	$\tau, N m^{-2}$	$\dot{\gamma}, s^{-1}$	$\tau, N m^{-2}$	$\dot{\gamma}, s^{-1}$	$\tau, N m^{-2}$
0.003525	0.125	0.28	1.48	27.8	3.69
0.00881	0.270	0.881	1.48	88.1	6.95
0.0280	0.775	2.80	1.83	280	15.5
0.0881	1.35	8.81	2.33	881	41.0
				1762	76.0

You are asked to describe this material to the company management at a technical committee meeting for the "R&D" department. Prepare a brief written description for this meeting.

15.6. Prepare a plot of the basic shear diagram (in SI units), given the data [B7, B8] in Table 15.6.

15.7. Your company is planning to produce a thixotropic material that forms a complex gel. Table 15.7 contains data for the basic shear diagram at steady-state. Prepare a brief report describing the nature of this material.

15.8. Prove that the constant $\dot{\gamma}_c$ in the Cross model, Eq. (15.10), equals the shear rate evaluated at the mean of μ_0 and μ_∞.

REFERENCES

A1.   Agoston, G. A., W. H. Harte, H. C. Hottel, W. A. Klemm, K. J. Mysels, H. H. Pomeroy, and J. M. Thompson: *Ind. Eng. Chem.* **46:** 1017 (1954).

B1.   Beatty, W. R., G. R. Wheeler, R. L. Johnstone, R. L. Kramer, L. G. Warnock: paper F.1 in "Drag Reduction: Papers Presented at the Third International Conference on Drag Reduction", R. H. J. Sellin and R. T. Moses (eds.), University of Bristol, 1984.

B2.   Billmeyer, F. W.: *Textbook of Polymer Science,* 3d ed., Wiley-Interscience, New York, 1984.

B3.   Bird, R. B., and C. F. Curtiss: *Physics Today* **37**(1): 36 (1984).

B4.   Bird, R. B., R. C. Armstrong, and O. Hassager: *Dynamics of Polymeric Liquids: Volume 1 Fluid Mechanics,* Wiley, New York, 1977.

B5.   Bird, R. B., O. Hassager, R. C. Armstrong, and C. F. Curtiss: *Dynamics of Polymeric Liquids: Volume 2 Kinetic Theory,* Wiley, New York, 1977.

B6.   Bowen, R. L.: *Chem. Eng.* **68**(12): 243 (1961); **68**(13): 127 (1961); **68**(14): 147 (1961); **68**(15): 143 (1961); **68**(16): 129 (1961); **68**(17): 119 (1961); **68**(18): 131 (1961).

B7.   Brodkey, R. S.: *The Phenomena of Fluid Motions,* Addison-Wesley, Reading MA, 1967. [Fourth printing available from the Ohio State University Bookstores, Columbus, Ohio 43210.]

B8.   Brodnyan, J. G., and E. L. Kelley: *Trans. Soc. Rheol.* **5:** 205 (1961).

B9.   Bueche, F.: *J. Chem. Phys.* **22:** 603, 1570 (1954).

B10. Burger, E. D., L. G. Chorn, and T. K. Perkins: *J. Rheol.* **24:** 603 (1980).

C1.   Calderbank, P. H., and M. B. Moo-Young: *Trans. Instn. Chem. Engrs.* (*London*) **39:** 337 (1961). For corrigenda, see Skelland [S3].

C2.   Cho, Y. I., and J. P. Hartnett: in *Advances in Heat Transfer,* Vol. 15, J. P. Hartnett and T. F. Irvine (eds.), Academic Press, New York, 1982.

C3.   Christiansen, E. B., and S. E. Craig: *AIChE J.* **8:** 154 (1962).

C4.   Chung, P. C.: *Time-Dependent Rheology of Polymer Solutions,* PhD Dissertation, The Ohio State University, 1985.

C5.   Coleman, B. D., and W. Noll: *Arch. Rat'l. Mech. Anal.* **3:** 289 (1959); see also Coleman, B. D., H. Markovitz, and W. Noll: *Viscometric Flows of Non-Newtonian Fluids,* Springer-Verlag, Berlin, 1966.

C6.   Corman, J. C.: *Ind. Eng. Chem. Process Des. Dev.* **9:** 254 (1970).

C7.   Cross, M. M.: *J. Colloid Sci.* **20:** 417 (1965).

D1.   Dodge, D. W., and A. B. Metzner: *AIChE J.* **5:** 189 (1959).

F1.   Fabula, A. G., *Proc. Fourth Int. Congr. on Rheology* (E. H. Lee, ed.), Part 3, p. 455, Interscience, New York, 1965.

F2.   Flory, P. J.: *Principles of Polymer Chemistry,* Cornell University Press, Ithaca NY, 1953.

F3.   Fredrickson, A. G.: *Principles and Applications of Rheology,* Prentice-Hall, Englewood Cliffs NJ, 1964.

F4.   Friend, W. L., and A. B. Metzner: *AIChE J.* **4:** 393 (1958).

G1.   Giesekus, H., H. Bewersdorff, B. Frings, M. Hibberd, K. Kleinecke, M. Kwade, D. Möller, R. Schröder: *Rheology* **23:** 3 (1985).

G2.   Granville, P. S.: *Scaling-up of Pipe Flow Frictional Data for Drag Reducing Polymer Solutions,* 2d International Conference on Drag Reduction, Cambridge (1977), paper B1. See also *A Method for Predicting Additive Drag Reduction from Small-Diameter Pipe Flows,* DTNSRDC/SPD-1142-01 (March, 1985).

G3.   Gupta, M. K., A. B. Metzner, and J. P. Hartnett: *Int. J. Heat Mass Transfer* **10:** 1211 (1967).

H1.   Hershey, H. C.: *Drag Reduction in Newtonian Polymer Solutions,* PhD Dissertation, The University of Missouri at Rolla, 1965.

H2.   Hershey, H. C., and J. L. Zakin: *Ind. Eng. Chem. Fundam.* **6:** 381 (1967).

H3.   Hershey, H. C., J. L. Zakin, and R. Simha: *Ind. Eng. Chem. Fundam.* **6:** 413 (1967); corrigenda available from authors.

H4.   Hershey, H. C., J. T. Kuo, and M. L. McMillan: *Ind. Eng. Chem. Prod. Res. Dev.* **14:** 192 (1975).

J1.   Jachimiak, P. D., Y.-S. Song., and R. S. Brodkey: *Rheol. Acta.* **13:** 745 (1974).

K1.   Kim, H. T., and R. S. Brodkey: *AIChE J.* **14:** 61 (1968).

L1.   Liaw, G. C., J. L. Zakin, and G. K. Patterson: *AIChE J.* **17:** 391 (1971).

L2.   Lodge, A. S.: *Elastic Liquids,* Academic Press, New York, 1964.

M1.   Marrucci, G., and G. Astarita: *Ind. Eng. Chem. Fundam.* **6:** 470 (1967).

M2.   McMillan, M. L.: *Drag Reduction and Light Scattering Studies of Aluminum Disoaps in Toluene,* PhD Dissertation, The Ohio State University, 1970.

M3.   Metzger, A. P. and R. S. Brodkey: *J. Appl. Polymer Sci.* **7:** 399 (1963).

M4.   Metzner, A. B.: in *Advances in Chemical Engineering,* vol. 1, T. B. Drew and J. W. Hoopes (eds.), Academic Press, New York, 1956.

M5.   Metzner, A. B., E. L. Carley, and I. K. Park: *Mod. Plastics* **37**(7): 133 (July 1960).

M6.   Metzner, A. B., and P. S. Friend: *Ind. Eng. Chem.* **51:** 879 (1959).

M7.   Metzner, A. B., and R. E. Otto: *AIChE J.* **3:** 3 (1957).

M8.   Metzner, A. B., and J. C. Reed: *AIChE J.* **1:** 434 (1955).

M9.   Metzner, A. B., and M. Whitlock: *Trans. Soc. Rheol.* **2:** 239 (1958).

M10. Middleman, S.: *The Flow of High Polymers,* Interscience, New York, 1968.

M11. Miller, A. P.: PhD Thesis in Chemical Engineering, University of Washington, Seattle, 1953.

M12. Mooney, M.: *J. Rheol.* **2:** 210 (1931).

M13. Mysels, K. J.: U.S. Patent 2 492 173 (1949).

O1.   Oka, S.: in *Rheology, Theory and Applications,* vol. 3, F. R. Eirich (ed.), Academic Press, New York, 1960.

O2.   Oldroyd, J. G.: *Proc. Roy. Soc.* (*London*) **A200:** 523 (1950).

O3.   Oldroyd, J. G.: *Proc. Roy. Soc.* (*London*) **A245:** 278 (1958).

O4.   Oldshue, J. Y.: in *Mixing of Liquids by Mechanical Agitation,* J. J. Ulbrecht and G. K. Patterson (eds.), Gordon and Breach, New York, 1985.

O5.   Ostwald, W.: *Z. Phys. Chem.* **A111:** 62 (1924); *Kolloid-Zeit.* **36:** 99 (1925).

O6.   Ostwald, W., and R. Auerbach: *Kolloid-Zeit.* **38:** 261 (1926).

P1.   Pao, Y.-H.: *J. Chem. Phys.* **25:** 1294 (1956).

P2.   Perry, R. H., and D. W. Green: *Perry's Chemical Engineers' Handbook,* 6th ed., McGraw-Hill, New York, 1984.

P3.   Philippoff, W.: *Kolloid-Zeit.* **71:** 1 (1935).

P4.   Philippoff, W., and F. H. Gaskins: *J. Polym. Sci.* **21:** 205 (1956).

R1.   Rabinowitsch, B.: *Z. Phys. Chem.* **A145:** 1 (1929).

R2.   Ree, T., and H. Eyring: in *Rheology,* Vol. 2, F. R. Eirich (ed.), Academic Press, New York, 1958.

R3.   Reiner, M.: *Am. J. Math.* **67:** 350 (1945).
R4.   Reiner, M.: *Phys. Today* **17**(1): 62 (1964).
R5.   Reynolds, O.: *Phil. Mag.* **20:** 46 (1885).
R6.   Rivlin, R. S., and J. L. Ericksen: *J. Rat'l Mech. Anal.* **4:** 323 (1955).
R7.   Rouse, P. E., Jr.: *J. Chem. Phys.* **21:** 1272 (1953).
S1.   Savins, J. G.: *J. Inst. Petr.* **47:** 329 (1961).
S2.   Savins, J. G.: *Soc. Petr. Eng. J.* **4:** 203 (1964).
S3.   Skelland, A. H. P.: *Non-Newtonian Flow and Heat Transfer,* Wiley, New York, 1967.
S4.   Sisko, A. W.: *Ind. Eng. Chem.* **50:** 1789 (1958).
T1.   Toms, B. A.: in *Proceedings of the (First) International Conference on Rheology,* North Holland, Amsterdam, 1949, p. II-135.
U1.   Ulbrecht, J. J., and P. Carreau: in *Mixing of Liquids by Mechanical Agitation,* J. J. Ulbrecht, and G. K. Patterson (eds.), Gordon and Breach, New York, 1985.
W1.   Weissenberg, K.: *Nature* **159:** 310 (1947).
W2.   Weissenberg, K.: in *Proceedings of the (First) International Congress on Rheology,* North Holland, Amsterdam, 1949, p. I–29.
W3.   Williams, M. L., R. F. Landel, and J. D. Ferry: *J. Am. Chem. Soc.* **77:** 3701 (1955).
W4.   Winding, C. C., F. W. Dittman, and W. L. Kranich: *Thermal Properties of Synthetic Rubber Latices,* Report to Rubber Reserve Company, Cornell University, Ithaca, NY, 1944.
Z1.   Zimm, B. H.: *J. Chem. Phys.* **24:** 269 (1956).

PROPERTIES
OF MATERIALS

A.1 PROPERTIES OF WATER AND AIR

Table A.1 contains the properties of saturated water, as taken from Liley
[I1, L1]. The methods introduced in Chapter 14 were used to expand the
temperatures to include five-degree-Celsius intervals in the neighborhood of
room temperature and to correct some entries.

Table A.2 contains the properties of (dry) air at 1 atm (101.325 kPa), as
compiled from data published by Kays and Crawford [K1], who compiled their
table from the three volumes of *Thermophysical Properties of Matter*,
published by the Thermophysical Properties Research Center (TPRC) at
Purdue University [T1, T2, T3]. The table entries for density ρ, viscosity μ,
and kinematic viscosity v are from the National Bureau of Standards Circular
564 [H1]. The data above 1000 K are from reference [P1].

H1. Hilsenrath, J., C. W. Beckett, W. S. Benedict, L. Fano, H. J. Hoge, J. F. Masi, R. L.
   Nuttall, Y. S. Touloukian and H. W. Woolley: *Tables of Thermal Properties of Gases*, NBS
   Circular 564, Washington, DC, 1955.
I1. Incropera, F. P., and D. P. DeWitt: *Fundamentals of Heat and Mass Transfer*, 2d ed., Wiley,
   New York, 1985, pp. 774–775.
K1. Kays, W. M., and M. E. Crawford: *Convective Heat and Mass Transfer*, 2d ed.,
   McGraw-Hill, New York, 1980.

TABLE A.1
Thermophysical properties of saturated water ($M = 18.015$ kg kmol⁻¹)

Subscript f denotes liquid phase; subscript g denotes vapor phase

Temperature T K	Vapor pressure p^{sat} bar*	Volume $v_f \times 10^3$ m³ kg⁻¹	v_g	Heat of Vaporization h_{fg} kJ kg⁻¹	Heat capacity $c_{p,f}$ kJ kg⁻¹ K⁻¹	$c_{p,g}$ kJ kg⁻¹ K⁻¹	Viscosity $\mu_f \times 10^6$ kg m⁻¹ s⁻¹	$\mu_g \times 10^6$	Thermal conductivity $k_f \times 10^3$ W m⁻¹ K⁻¹	$k_g \times 10^3$	Prandtl number $N_{Pr,f}$	$N_{Pr,g}$	Surface tension $\sigma_f \times 10^3$ N m⁻¹	Expansion coefficient $\beta_f \times 10^6$ K⁻¹	Temperature T K
273.15	0.00611	1.000	206.3	2502	4.217	1.854	1750	8.02	569	18.2	12.99	0.815	75.5	−68.05	273.15
275	0.00697	1.000	181.7	2497	4.211	1.855	1652	8.09	574	18.3	12.22	0.817	75.3	−32.74	275
280	0.00990	1.000	130.4	2485	4.198	1.858	1422	8.29	582	18.6	10.26	0.825	74.8	46.04	280
285	0.01387	1.000	99.4	2473	4.189	1.861	1225	8.49	590	18.9	8.70	0.836	74.3	114.2	285
288.15	0.01703	1.001	79.79	2466	4.186	1.863	1131	8.61	595	19.1	7.95	0.842	74.1	152.5	288.15
290	0.01917	1.001	70.51	2461	4.184	1.864	1080	8.69	598	19.2	7.56	0.841	73.7	174.0	290
293.15	0.02336	1.001	57.57	2454	4.182	1.866	1001	8.82	603	19.4	6.94	0.850	73.1	208.3	293.15
295	0.02617	1.002	51.33	2449	4.181	1.868	959	8.89	606	19.5	6.62	0.849	72.7	227.5	295
298.15	0.03165	1.003	42.53	2442	4.180	1.870	892	9.02	610	19.7	6.11	0.858	72.1	258.7	298.15
300	0.03531	1.003	38.23	2438	4.179	1.872	855	9.09	613	19.8	5.83	0.857	71.7	276.1	300
303.15	0.04240	1.004	32.10	2430	4.178	1.875	800	9.22	618	20.0	5.41	0.866	71.2	304.6	303.15
305	0.04712	1.005	29.08	2426	4.178	1.877	769	9.29	620	20.1	5.20	0.865	70.9	320.6	305
308.15	0.05620	1.006	24.73	2418	4.178	1.880	721	9.42	625	20.3	4.82	0.874	70.3	346.9	308.15
310	0.06221	1.007	22.56	2414	4.178	1.882	695	9.49	628	20.4	4.62	0.873	70.0	361.9	310
313.15	0.07373	1.008	19.40	2407	4.179	1.886	654	9.61	632	20.6	4.32	0.881	69.5	386.4	313.15
315	0.08132	1.009	17.81	2402	4.179	1.888	631	9.69	634	20.7	4.16	0.883	69.2	400.4	315
320	0.1053	1.011	13.98	2390	4.180	1.895	577	9.89	640	21.0	3.77	0.894	68.3	436.7	320
325	0.1351	1.013	11.06	2378	4.182	1.903	528	10.09	645	21.3	3.42	0.901	67.5	471.2	325
330	0.1719	1.016	8.82	2366	4.184	1.911	489	10.29	650	21.7	3.15	0.908	66.6	504.0	330
335	0.2167	1.018	7.09	2354	4.186	1.920	453	10.49	656	22.0	2.88	0.916	65.8	535.5	335
340	0.2713	1.021	5.74	2342	4.188	1.930	420	10.69	660	22.3	2.66	0.925	64.9	566.0	340
345	0.3372	1.024	4.683	2329	4.191	1.941	389	10.89	664	22.6	2.45	0.933	64.1	595.4	345
350	0.4163	1.027	3.846	2317	4.195	1.954	365	11.09	668	23.0	2.29	0.942	63.2	624.2	350
355	0.5100	1.030	3.180	2304	4.199	1.968	343	11.29	671	23.3	2.14	0.951	62.3	652.3	355
360	0.6209	1.034	2.645	2291	4.203	1.983	324	11.49	674	23.7	2.02	0.960	61.4	697.9	360
365	0.7514	1.038	2.212	2278	4.209	1.999	306	11.69	677	24.1	1.91	0.969	60.5	707.1	365
370	0.9040	1.041	1.861	2265	4.214	2.017	289	11.89	679	24.5	1.80	0.978	59.5	728.7	370
373.15	1.0133	1.044	1.679	2257	4.217	2.029	279	12.02	680	24.8	1.76	0.984	58.9	750.1	373.15

375	1.0815	1.045	1.574	2252	4.220	2.036	274	12.09	681	24.9	1.70	0.987	58.6	761	375
380	1.2869	1.049	1.337	2239	4.226	2.057	260	12.29	683	25.4	1.61	0.999	57.6	788	380
385	1.5233	1.053	1.142	2225	4.232	2.080	248	12.49	685	25.8	1.53	1.004	56.6	814	385
390	1.794	1.058	0.980	2212	4.239	2.104	237	12.69	686	26.3	1.47	1.013	55.6	841	390
400	2.455	1.067	0.731	2183	4.256	2.158	217	13.05	688	27.2	1.34	1.033	53.6	896	400
410	3.302	1.077	0.553	2153	4.278	2.221	200	13.42	688	28.2	1.24	1.054	51.5	952	410
420	4.370	1.088	0.425	2123	4.302	2.291	185	13.79	688	29.8	1.16	1.075	49.4	1010	420
430	5.699	1.099	0.331	2091	4.331	2.369	173	14.14	685	30.4	1.09	1.10	47.2	—	430
440	7.333	1.110	0.261	2059	4.36	2.46	162	14.50	682	31.7	1.04	1.12	45.1	—	440
450	9.319	1.123	0.208	2024	4.40	2.56	152	14.85	678	33.1	0.99	1.14	42.9	—	450
460	11.71	1.137	0.167	1989	4.44	2.68	143	15.19	673	34.6	0.95	1.17	40.7	—	460
470	14.55	1.152	0.136	1951	4.48	2.79	136	15.54	667	36.3	0.92	1.20	38.5	—	470
480	17.90	1.167	0.111	1912	4.53	2.94	129	15.88	660	38.1	0.89	1.23	36.2	—	480
490	21.83	1.184	0.0922	1870	4.59	3.10	124	16.23	651	40.1	0.87	1.25	33.9	—	490
500	26.40	1.203	0.0766	1825	4.66	3.27	118	16.59	642	42.3	0.86	1.28	31.6	—	500
510	31.66	1.222	0.0631	1779	4.74	3.47	113	16.95	631	44.7	0.85	1.31	29.3	—	510
520	37.70	1.244	0.0525	1730	4.84	3.70	108	17.33	621	47.5	0.84	1.35	26.9	—	520
530	44.58	1.268	0.0445	1679	4.95	3.96	104	17.72	608	50.6	0.85	1.39	24.5	—	530
540	52.38	1.294	0.0375	1622	5.08	4.27	101	18.1	594	54.0	0.86	1.43	22.1	—	540
550	61.19	1.323	0.0317	1564	5.24	4.64	97	18.6	580	58.3	0.87	1.47	19.7	—	550
560	71.08	1.355	0.0269	1499	5.43	5.09	94	19.1	563	63.7	0.90	1.52	17.3	—	560
570	82.16	1.392	0.0228	1429	5.68	5.67	91	19.7	548	69.9	0.94	1.59	15.0	—	570
580	94.51	1.433	0.0193	1353	6.00	6.40	88	20.4	528	76.7	0.99	1.68	12.8	—	580
590	108.3	1.482	0.0163	1274	6.41	7.35	84	21.5	513	84.1	1.05	1.84	10.5	—	590
600	123.5	1.541	0.0137	1176	7.00	8.75	81	22.7	497	92.9	1.14	2.15	8.4	—	600
610	137.3	1.612	0.0115	1068	7.85	11.1	77	24.1	467	103	1.30	2.60	6.3	—	610
620	159.1	1.705	0.0094	941	9.35	15.4	72	25.9	444	114	1.52	3.46	4.5	—	620
625	169.1	1.778	0.0085	858	10.6	18.3	70	27.0	430	121	1.65	4.20	3.5	—	625
630	179.7	1.856	0.0075	781	12.6	22.1	67	28.0	412	130	2.0	4.8	2.6	—	630
635	190.9	1.935	0.0066	683	16.4	27.6	64	30.0	392	141	2.7	6.0	1.5	—	635
640	202.7	2.075	0.0057	560	26	42	59	32.0	367	155	4.2	9.6	0.8	—	640
645	215.2	2.351	0.0045	361	90	—	54	37.0	331	178	12	26	0.1	—	645
647.3†	221.2	3.170	0.0032	0	∞	∞	45	45.0	238	238	∞	∞	0.0	—	647.3†

* 1 bar = 10^5 N m^{-2}.

† Critical temperature.

TABLE A.2
Thermophysical properties of dry air ($M = 28.966$ kg kmol^{-1}) at 1 atm (101.325 kPa)

Temperature T, K	Density ρ, kg m^{-3}	Viscosity $\mu \times 10^6$, kg m^{-1} s^{-1}	Kinematic viscosity $\nu \times 10^6$, m^2 s^{-1}	Heat capacity c_p, kJ kg^{-1} K^{-1}	Thermal conductivity $k \times 10^3$, W m^{-1} K^{-1}	Prandtl number N_{Pr}
100	3.5985	7.060	1.962	1.028	9.220	0.787
150	2.3673	10.38	4.385	1.011	13.75	0.763
200	1.7690	13.36	7.552	1.006	18.10	0.743
250	1.4119	16.06	11.37	1.003	22.26	0.724
263	1.3421	16.70	12.44	1.003	23.28	0.720
273	1.2930	17.20	13.30	1.004	24.07	0.717
275	1.2836	17.30	13.48	1.004	24.26	0.716
280	1.2607	17.54	13.92	1.004	24.63	0.715
283	1.2473	17.69	14.18	1.004	24.86	0.714
285	1.2385	17.79	14.36	1.004	25.00	0.714
288	1.2256	17.93	14.63	1.004	25.22	0.714
290	1.2172	18.03	14.81	1.004	25.37	0.714
293	1.2047	18.17	15.08	1.004	25.63	0.712
295	1.1966	18.27	15.27	1.005	25.74	0.713
298	1.1845	18.41	15.54	1.005	25.96	0.712
300	1.1766	18.53	15.75	1.005	26.14	0.711
303	1.1650	18.64	16.00	1.005	26.37	0.710
305	1.1573	18.74	16.19	1.005	26.48	0.711
308	1.1460	18.88	16.47	1.005	26.70	0.711
310	1.1386	18.97	16.66	1.005	26.85	0.710
313	1.1277	19.11	16.95	1.005	27.09	0.709
315	1.1206	19.20	17.14	1.006	27.22	0.709
320	1.1031	19.43	17.62	1.006	27.58	0.709
323	1.0928	19.57	17.91	1.006	27.80	0.708
325	1.0861	19.66	18.10	1.006	27.95	0.708
330	1.0696	19.89	18.59	1.006	28.32	0.707
333	1.0600	20.02	18.89	1.007	28.51	0.707
343	1.0291	20.47	19.89	1.008	29.21	0.706

350	1.0085	20.81	20.63	1.008	29.70	0.706
353	1.0000	20.91	20.91	1.008	29.89	0.705
363	0.9724	21.34	21.95	1.009	30.58	0.704
373	0.9463	21.77	23.01	1.010	31.26	0.703
400	0.8825	22.94	26.00	1.013	33.05	0.703
450	0.7844	24.93	31.78	1.020	36.33	0.700
500	0.7060	26.82	37.99	1.029	39.51	0.699
550	0.6418	28.60	44.56	1.039	42.60	0.698
600	0.5883	30.30	51.50	1.051	45.60	0.699
650	0.5431	31.93	58.80	1.063	48.40	0.701
700	0.5043	33.49	66.41	1.075	51.30	0.702
750	0.4706	34.98	74.32	1.087	54.10	0.703
800	0.4412	36.43	82.56	1.099	56.90	0.703
850	0.4153	37.83	91.10	1.110	59.70	0.703
900	0.3922	39.18	99.90	1.121	62.50	0.702
950	0.3716	40.49	109.0	1.131	64.90	0.705
1000	0.3530	41.77	118.3	1.141	67.20	0.709
1100	0.3209	44.4	138	1.160	73.2	0.705
1200	0.2942	46.9	159	1.177	78.1	0.705
1300	0.2715	49.3	182	1.195	83.7	0.705
1400	0.2521	51.7	205	1.212	89.1	0.704
1500	0.2353	54.0	229	1.230	94.6	0.704
1600	0.2206	56.3	255	1.248	100	0.703
1700	0.2076	58.5	282	1.266	105	0.702
1800	0.1961	60.7	310	1.286	111	0.701
1900	0.1858	62.9	339	1.307	117	0.700
2000	0.1765	65.0	368	1.331	124	0.699
2100	0.1681	67.2	404	1.359	131	0.696
2200	0.1605	69.3	432	1.392	139	0.693
2300	0.1535	71.4	465	1.434	149	0.688
2400	0.1471	73.5	500	1.487	161	0.681
2500	0.1412	75.7	536	1.556	175	0.673

L1. Liley, P. E.: in *Handbook of Heat Transfer Fundamentals*, 2d ed., W. M. Rohsenow, J. P. Hartnett, and E. N. Ganic (eds.), McGraw-Hill, New York, 1985, chap. 3.

P1. Poferl, D. J., R. A. Svehla, and K. Lewandowski: *Thermodynamic and Transport Properties of Air and the Combustion Products of Natural Gas and of ASTM-A-1 Fuel with Air*, NASA Technical Note D-5452, Washington, DC, 1969.

T1. Touloukian, Y. S., P. E. Liley, and S. C. Saxena: *Thermophysical Properties of Matter*, vol. 3: *Thermal Conductivity, Nonmetallic Liquids and Gases*, IFI/Plenum, New York, 1970.

T2. Touloukian, Y. S., and T. Makita: *Thermophysical Properties of Matter*, vol. 6: *Specific Heat, Nonmetallic Liquids and Gases*, IFI/Plenum, New York, 1970.

T3. Touloukian, Y. S., S. C. Saxena, and P. Hestermans: *Thermophysical Properties of Matter*, vol. 11: *Viscosity*, IFI/Plenum, New York, 1975.

A.2 PREDICTION OF TRANSPORT PROPERTIES

The tables in this section supplement the material in Chapter 14 on the prediction of transport properties. Table A.3, taken from reference [R1],

TABLE A.3
Constants in the Lennard-Jones 12–6 potential as determined from viscosity data*

Molecule	Compound name	Collision diameter $\sigma \times 10^{10}$, m	Energy ratio ε_μ/k_B, K
A	Argon	3.542	93.3
He	Helium	2.551†	10.22
Kr	Krypton	3.655	178.9
Ne	Neon	2.820	32.8
Xe	Xenon	4.047	231.0
Air	Air	3.711	78.6
AsH_3	Arsine	4.145	259.8
BCl_3	Boron chloride	5.127	337.7
BF_3	Boron fluoride	4.198	186.3
$B(OCH_3)_3$	Methyl borate	5.503	396.7
Br_2	Bromine	4.296	507.9
CCl_4	Carbon tetrachloride	5.947	322.7
CF_4	Carbon tetrafluoride	4.662	134.0
$CHCl_3$	Chloroform	5.389	340.2
CH_2Cl_2	Methylene chloride	4.898	356.3
CH_3Br	Methyl bromide	4.118	449.2
CH_3Cl	Methyl chloride	4.182	350
CH_3OH	Methanol	3.626	481.8
CH_4	Methane	3.758	148.6
CO	Carbon monoxide	3.690	91.7
COS	Carbonyl sulfide	4.130	336.0
CO_2	Carbon dioxide	3.941	195.2
CS_2	Carbon disulfide	4.483	467
C_2H_2	Acetylene	4.033	231.8
C_2H_4	Ethylene	4.163	224.7
C_2H_6	Ethane	4.443	215.7
C_2H_5Cl	Ethyl chloride	4.898	300
C_2H_5OH	Ethanol	4.530	362.6
C_2N_2	Cyanogen	4.361	348.6

TABLE A.3
(*continued*)

Molecule	Compound name	Collision diameter $\sigma \times 10^{10}$, m	Energy ratio ε_μ / k_B, K
CH_3OCH_3	Methyl ether	4.307	395.0
CH_2CHCH_3	Propylene	4.678	298.9
CH_3CCH	Methylacetylene	4.761	251.8
C_3H_6	Cyclopropane	4.807	248.9
C_3H_8	Propane	5.118	237.1
$n\text{-}C_3H_7OH$	n-Propyl alcohol	4.549	576.7
CH_3COCH_3	Acetone	4.600	560.2
CH_3COOCH_3	Methyl acetate	4.936	469.8
$n\text{-}C_4H_{10}$	n-Butane	4.687	531.4
$iso\text{-}C_4H_{10}$	Isobutane	5.278	330.1
$C_2H_5OC_2H_5$	Ethyl ether	5.678	313.8
$CH_3COOC_2H_5$	Ethyl acetate	5.205	521.3
$n\text{-}C_5H_{12}$	n-Pentane	5.784	341.1
$C(CH_3)_4$	2,2-Dimethylpropane	6.464	193.4
C_6H_6	Benzene	5.349	412.3
C_6H_{12}	Cyclohexane	6.182	297.1
$n\text{-}C_6H_{14}$	n-Hexane	5.949	399.3
Cl_2	Chlorine	4.217	316.0
F_2	Fluorine	3.357	112.6
HBr	Hydrogen bromide	3.353	449
HCN	Hydrogen cyanide	3.630	569.1
HCl	Hydrogen chloride	3.339	344.7
HF	Hydrogen fluoride	3.148	330
HI	Hydrogen iodide	4.211	288.7
H_2	Hydrogen	2.827	59.7
H_2O	Water	2.641	809.1
H_2O_2	Hydrogen peroxide	4.196	289.3
H_2S	Hydrogen sulfide	3.623	301.1
Hg	Mercury	2.969	750
$HgBr_2$	Mercuric bromide	5.080	686.2
$HgCl_2$	Mercuric chloride	4.550	750
HgI_2	Mercuric iodide	5.625	695.6
I_2	Iodine	5.160	474.2
NH_3	Ammonia	2.900	558.3
NO	Nitric oxide	3.492	116.7
NOCl	Nitrosyl chloride	4.112	395.3
N_2	Nitrogen	3.798	71.4
N_2O	Nitrous oxide	3.828	232.4
O_2	Oxygen	3.467	106.7
PH_3	Phosphine	3.981	251.5
SF_6	Sulfur hexafluoride	5.128	222.1
SO_2	Sulfur dioxide	4.112	335.4
SiF_4	Silicon tetrafluoride	4.880	171.9
SiH_4	Silicon hydride	4.084	207.6
$SnBr_4$	Stannic bromide	6.388	563.7
UF_6	Uranium hexafluoride	5.967	236.8

* From Svehla, *NASA Technical Report. R-132,* Lewis Research Center, Cleveland, OH, 1962. *Source*: Reid, Prausnitz, and Sherwood, *The Properties of Gases and Liquids,* 3d ed., McGraw-Hill, New York, 1977, pp. 678–679. By permission.

† The parameter σ was determined by quantum-mechanical formulas.

contains the collision diameter σ and the energy ratio ε/k_B, where ε is the characteristic (minimum) energy in the Lennard-Jones potential energy function [L3], and k_B is the Boltzmann constant. For compounds not included in Table A.3, Eqs. (14.39) and (14.40) are recommended; also satisfactory are the following equations [H2]:

$$\sigma = 1.18 \times 10^{-9}(V_b)^{1/3} \tag{A.1}$$

$$\varepsilon/k_B = 1.21 T_b \tag{A.2}$$

$$\varepsilon/k_B = 0.75 T_c \tag{A.3}$$

$$\varepsilon/k_B = 1.92 T_m \tag{A.4}$$

where σ is in meters, ε/k_B is in K, V_b is the molar volume ($m^3 \, kmol^{-1}$) at the normal boiling point T_b (K), T_m is the melting point temperature (K), and T_c is the critical temperature (K). Note that the Lennard-Jones constants must always be determined together, i.e., from the same set of data for a given compound; otherwise, serious errors may result.

The molar volume is estimated from Table A.4; if the compound is not given, then the volume increments published by Le Bas [L2], as given in Table A.4, are summed in order to estimate the molar volume at T_b. Example 14.9 illustrates this calculation.

Viscosity. The Chapman–Enskog theory [C1, H2] relates the viscosity μ of a gas at low pressure to the collision diameter σ, the molecular weight M, the temperature T, and the viscosity collision integral Ω_μ [see Eq. (14.41) and Example 14.1]. For nonpolar molecules, the collision integral (dimensionless) is conveniently available in equation form [N1]:

$$\Omega_{\mu, \text{nonpolar}} = \frac{A}{(T^*)^B} + \frac{C}{\exp(DT^*)} + \frac{E}{\exp(FT^*)} \tag{A.5}$$

where the constants in Eq. (A.5) are

$$
\begin{array}{lll}
A = 1.16145 & B = 0.14874 & C = 0.52487 \\
D = 0.77320 & E = 2.16178 & F = 2.43787 \\
& 0.3 \leq T^* \leq 100 &
\end{array} \tag{A.6}
$$

The dimensionless (also called reduced) temperature T^* is

$$T^* = \frac{T}{\varepsilon/k_B} \tag{14.38}$$

For quick estimates, Eq. (A.6) may be approximated by [K2]

$$\Omega_{\mu, \text{nonpolar}} = \frac{1.604}{(T^*)^{1/2}} \qquad 0.4 < T^* < 1.4 \tag{A.7}$$

Polar molecules. For polar molecules, the Lennard-Jones potential is not

TABLE A.4
Le Bas atomic and molar volumes at the normal boiling point*

Atom	Volume† $V_b \times 10^3$, m³ kmol⁻¹
Carbon	14.8
Hydrogen	3.7
Oxygen (except as noted below)	7.4
in methyl esters and ethers	9.1
in ethyl esters and ethers	9.9
in higher esters and ethers	11.0
in acids	12.0
joined to S, P, N	8.3
Nitrogen	
doubly bonded	15.6
in primary amines	10.5
in secondary amines	12.0
Bromine	27
Chlorine	24.6
Fluorine	8.7
Iodine	37
Sulfur	25.6
Ring, three-membered	−6.0
four-membered	−8.5
five-membered	−11.5
six-membered	−15.0
naphthalene	−30.0
anthracene	−47.5

* From Le Bas, *The Molecular Volumes of Liquid Chemical Compounds. Source:* Reid, Prausnitz, and Sherwood, *The Properties of Gases and Liquids,* 3d ed., McGraw-Hill, New York, 1977, p. 58. By permission.

† The additive-volume procedure should not be used for simple molecules. The following approximate values are employed in estimating diffusion coefficients by the methods of Chap. 14: H_2, 14.3; O_2, 25.6; N_2, 31.2; air, 29.9; CO, 30.7; CO_2, 34.0; SO_2, 44.8; NO, 23.6; N_2O, 36.4; NH_3, 25.8; H_2O, 18.9; H_2S, 32.9; COS, 51.5; Cl_2, 48.4; Br_2, 53.2; I_2, 71.5.

adequate. Brokaw [B1] determined the parameters in the Stockmayer potential [S1]; these are available elsewhere [R1], or can also be estimated by

$$\sigma = 1.166 \times 10^{-9}\left(\frac{V_b}{1 + 1.3\delta^2}\right)^{1/3} \tag{A.8}$$

$$\varepsilon/k_B = (1.18)(1 + 1.3\delta^2)(T_b) \tag{A.9}$$

where V_b (m³ kmol⁻¹) is the liquid molar volume at the normal boiling point T_b (K), ε/k_B is in K, and σ is in meters. The quantity δ is a dimensionless dipole moment, which Brokaw recommends be calculated by

$$\delta = \frac{(1.94)(DPM)^2}{V_b T_b} \tag{A.10}$$

In this equation (DPM) is the dipole moment in debyes (1 debye equals $3.162 \times 10^{-25} \, N^{1/2} \, m^2$), and the units of V_b and T_b are as before. Tables of dipole moments are available elsewhere [P2]. The collision integral for polar molecules is a modification of that for nonpolar:

$$\Omega_{\mu, \text{polar}} = \Omega_{\mu, \text{nonpolar}} + 0.2\delta^2/T^* \tag{A.11}$$

Mixtures. For gas mixtures, the following semiempirical equation is recommended (W1):

$$\mu_{\text{mix}} = \sum_{i=1}^{n} \frac{x_i \mu_i}{\sum_{j=1}^{n} x_j \phi_{ij}} \tag{A.12}$$

where

$$\phi_{ij} = \left(\frac{1}{8^{1/2}}\right)\left(1 + \frac{M_i}{M_j}\right)^{-1/2}\left[1 + \left(\frac{\mu_i}{\mu_j}\right)^{1/2}\left(\frac{M_i}{M_j}\right)^{1/4}\right]^2 \tag{A.13}$$

n = number of species in the mixture
x_i, x_j = mole fraction of species i, j
μ_i, μ_j = viscosity of pure i, j at the T and p of the mixture
M_i, M_j = molecular weights of species i, j

These equations are good to about 2 percent.

Thermal conductivity. The Chapman–Enskog theory is satisfactory only for estimating the thermal conductivity of noble or monatomic gases. For these, the viscosity collision integral is satisfactory.

Diffusion coefficient. The Chapman–Enskog theory for diffusion requires a unique collision integral, as discussed in conjunction with Eq. (14.48). Use of the necessary combining rules, etc., is illustrated in Example 14.4.

The diffusion collision integral for nonpolar gas molecules is [N1]

$$\Omega_{D, \text{nonpolar}} = \frac{A}{(T^*)^B} + \frac{C}{\exp(DT^*)} + \frac{E}{\exp(FT^*)} + \frac{G}{\exp(HT^*)} \tag{A.14}$$

with the following constants:

$$A = 1.06036 \qquad B = 0.15610 \qquad C = 0.19300$$
$$D = 0.47635 \qquad E = 1.03587 \qquad F = 1.52996$$
$$G = 1.76474 \qquad H = 3.89411 \tag{A.15}$$

The dimensionless temperature for mixtures is

$$T^* = \frac{T}{\varepsilon_{AB}/k_B} \tag{14.50}$$

The Lennard-Jones parameters in Table A.3 are also used for diffusion.

Polar molecules. For polar molecules, the equation proposed by Brokaw [B1] is recommended:

$$\Omega_{D, \text{polar}} = \Omega_{D, \text{nonpolar}} + 0.19\delta_{AB}^2/T^* \tag{A.16}$$

Again, the Stockmayer potential parameters must be used, not those in Table A.3; these are to be found elsewhere [R1] or may be estimated from Eqs. (A.8) and (A.9). The following combining rule is needed:

$$\delta_{AB} = (\delta_A \delta_B)^{1/2} \tag{A.17}$$

where δ_A and δ_B are found from Eq. (A.10). Example 14.5 illustrates the use of these equations.

B1. Brokaw, R. S.: *Ind. Eng. Chem. Process Des. Dev.* **8:** 240 (1969).
C1. Chapman, S., and T. G. Cowling: *The Mathematical Theory of Non-Uniform Gases,* 3d ed., Cambridge University Press, Cambridge, 1970.
H2. Hirschfelder, J. O., C. F. Curtiss, and R. B. Bird: *Molecular Theory of Gases and Liquids,* fourth printing April 1967, Wiley, New York, 1954.
K2. Kim, S. K., and J. Ross: *J. Chem. Phys.* **46:** 818 (1967).
L2. Le Bas, G.: *The Molecular Volumes of Liquid Chemical Compounds,* Longmans, Green, London, 1915.
L3. Lennard-Jones, J. E.: *Proc. Roy. Soc. (London)* **A106:** 463, 709 (1924); **A107:** 157 (1925); **A109:** 476, 584 (1925); **A112:** 214, 230 (1926).
N1. Neufeld, P. D., A. R. Janzen, and R. A. Aziz: *J. Chem. Phys.* **57:** 1100 (1972).
P2. Prausnitz, J. M., R. N. Lichtenthaler, and E. G. de Azevedo: *Molecular Thermodynamics of Fluid-Phase Equilibria,* 2d ed., Prentice-Hall, Englewood Cliffs, NJ, 1986.
R1. Reid, R. C., J. M. Prausnitz, and T. K. Sherwood: *Properties of Gases and Liquids,* 3d ed., McGraw-Hill, New York, 1977.
S1. Stockmayer, W. H.: *J. Chem. Phys.* **9:** 398, 863 (1941).
W1. Wilke, C. R.: *J. Chem. Phys.* **18:** 517 (1950); see also Buddenberg, J. W., and C. R. Wilke: *Ind. Eng. Chem.* **41:** 1345 (1949).

APPENDIX B

MECHANICAL CHARACTERISTICS OF PIPE AND TUBING

TABLE B.1
Standard steel pipe dimensions, capacities, and weights*

Nominal pipe size, in.	Outside diameter, in.	Schedule no.	Wall thickness, in.	I.D. in.	Cross-sectional area of metal, in.²	Inside sectional area, ft²	Circumference, ft, or surface, ft² ft⁻¹ of length Outside	Inside	Capacity at 1 ft s⁻¹ velocity U.S. gal min⁻¹	Water, lb_m h⁻¹	Pipe weight, lb_m ft⁻¹
$\frac{1}{8}$	0.405	40	0.068	0.269	0.072	0.00040	0.106	0.0705	0.179	89.5	0.24
		80	0.095	0.215	0.093	0.00025	0.106	0.0563	0.113	56.5	0.31
$\frac{1}{4}$	0.540	40	0.088	0.364	0.125	0.00072	0.141	0.095	0.323	161.5	0.42
		80	0.119	0.302	0.157	0.00050	0.141	0.079	0.224	112.0	0.54
$\frac{3}{8}$	0.675	40	0.091	0.493	0.167	0.00133	0.177	0.129	0.596	298.0	0.57
		80	0.126	0.423	0.217	0.00098	0.177	0.111	0.440	220.0	0.74
$\frac{1}{2}$	0.840	40	0.109	0.622	0.250	0.00211	0.220	0.163	0.945	472.0	0.85
		80	0.147	0.546	0.320	0.00163	0.220	0.143	0.730	365.0	1.09
$\frac{3}{4}$	1.050	40	0.113	0.824	0.333	0.00371	0.275	0.216	1.665	832.5	1.13
		80	0.154	0.742	0.433	0.00300	0.275	0.194	1.345	672.5	1.47
1	1.315	40	0.133	1.049	0.494	0.00600	0.344	0.275	2.690	1345	1.68
		80	0.179	0.957	0.639	0.00499	0.344	0.250	2.240	1120	2.17
$1\frac{1}{4}$	1.660	40	0.140	1.380	0.668	0.01040	0.435	0.361	4.57	2285	2.27
		80	0.191	1.278	0.881	0.00891	0.435	0.335	3.99	1995	3.00
$1\frac{1}{2}$	1.900	40	0.145	1.610	0.800	0.01414	0.497	0.421	6.34	3170	2.72
		80	0.200	1.500	1.069	0.01225	0.497	0.393	5.49	2745	3.63
2	2.375	40	0.154	2.067	1.075	0.02330	0.622	0.541	10.45	5225	3.65
		80	0.218	1.939	1.477	0.02050	0.622	0.508	9.20	4600	5.02
$2\frac{1}{2}$	2.875	40	0.203	2.469	1.704	0.03322	0.753	0.647	14.92	7460	5.79
		80	0.276	2.323	2.254	0.02942	0.753	0.608	13.20	6600	7.66

TABLE B.1
(*continued*)

Nominal pipe size, in.	Outside diameter, in.	Schedule no.	Wall thickness, in.	I.D. in.	Cross-sectional area of metal, in.²	Inside sectional area, ft²	Circumference, ft, or surface, ft² ft⁻¹ of length Outside	Inside	Capacity at 1 ft s⁻¹ velocity U.S. gal min⁻¹	Water, lbm h⁻¹	Pipe weight, lbm ft⁻¹
3	3.500	40	0.216	3.068	2.228	0.05130	0.916	0.803	23.00	11 500	7.58
		80	0.300	2.900	3.016	0.04587	0.916	0.759	20.55	10 275	10.25
3½	4.000	40	0.226	3.548	2.680	0.06870	1.047	0.929	30.80	15 400	9.11
		80	0.318	3.364	3.678	0.06170	1.047	0.881	27.70	13 850	12.51
4	4.500	40	0.237	4.026	3.17	0.08840	1.178	1.054	39.6	19 800	10.79
		80	0.337	3.826	4.41	0.07986	1.178	1.002	35.8	17 900	14.98
5	5.563	40	0.258	5.047	4.30	0.1390	1.456	1.321	62.3	31 150	14.62
		80	0.375	4.813	6.11	0.1263	1.456	1.260	57.7	28 850	20.78
6	6.625	40	0.280	6.065	5.58	0.2006	1.734	1.588	90.0	45 000	18.97
		80	0.432	5.761	8.40	0.1810	1.734	1.508	81.1	40 550	28.57
8	8.625	40	0.322	7.981	8.396	0.3474	2.258	2.089	155.7	77 850	28.55
		80	0.500	7.625	12.76	0.3171	2.258	1.996	142.3	71 150	43.39
10	10.75	40	0.365	10.020	11.91	0.5475	2.814	2.620	246.0	123 000	40.48
		80	0.594	9.562	18.95	0.4987	2.814	2.503	223.4	111 700	64.40
12	12.75	40	0.406	11.938	15.74	0.7773	3.338	3.13	349.0	174 500	53.56
		80	0.688	11.374	26.07	0.7056	3.338	2.98	316.7	158 350	88.57

*From McCabe, Smith, and Harriott, *Unit Operations of Chemical Engineering, 4th ed.*, McGraw-Hill, New York, 1985, p. 924; based on *ANSI B36.* 10-1959 by permission of ASME.

TABLE B.2
Condenser and heat-exchanger tube data*

O.D., in.	Wall thickness BWG no.	Wall thickness in.	I.D., in.	Cross-sectional area metal, in.²	Inside sectional area, ft²	Circumference, ft, or surface, ft² ft⁻¹ or length Outside	Inside	Velocity ft s⁻¹ for 1 U.S. gal min⁻¹	Capacity at 1 ft/s⁻¹ velocity U.S. gal min⁻¹	Water, lb_m h⁻¹	Weight, lb_m ft⁻¹†
$\frac{5}{8}$	12	0.109	0.407	0.177	0.000903	0.1636	0.1066	2.468	0.4053	202.7	0.602
	14	0.083	0.459	0.141	0.00115	0.1636	0.1202	1.938	0.5161	258.1	0.479
	16	0.065	0.495	0.114	0.00134	0.1636	0.1296	1.663	0.6014	300.7	0.388
	18	0.049	0.527	0.089	0.00151	0.1636	0.1380	1.476	0.6777	338.9	0.303
$\frac{3}{4}$	12	0.109	0.532	0.220	0.00154	0.1963	0.1393	1.447	0.6912	345.6	0.748
	14	0.083	0.584	0.174	0.00186	0.1963	0.1529	1.198	0.8348	417.4	0.592
	16	0.065	0.620	0.140	0.00210	0.1963	0.1623	1.061	0.9425	471.3	0.476
	18	0.049	0.652	0.108	0.00232	0.1963	0.1707	0.962	1.041	520.5	0.367
$\frac{7}{8}$	12	0.109	0.657	0.262	0.00235	0.2291	0.1720	0.948	1.055	527.5	0.891
	14	0.083	0.709	0.207	0.00274	0.2291	0.1856	0.813	1.230	615.0	0.704
	16	0.065	0.745	0.165	0.00303	0.2291	0.1950	0.735	1.350	680.0	0.561
	18	0.049	0.777	0.127	0.00329	0.2291	0.2034	0.678	1.477	738.5	0.432
1	10	0.134	0.732	0.364	0.00292	0.2618	0.1916	0.763	1.310	655.0	1.237
	12	0.109	0.782	0.305	0.00334	0.2618	0.2047	0.667	1.499	750.0	1.037
	14	0.083	0.834	0.239	0.00379	0.2618	0.2183	0.588	1.701	850.5	0.813
	16	0.065	0.870	0.191	0.00413	0.2618	0.2278	0.538	1.854	927.0	0.649
$1\frac{1}{4}$	10	0.134	0.982	0.470	0.00526	0.3272	0.2571	0.424	2.361	1181	1.598
	12	0.109	1.032	0.391	0.00581	0.3272	0.2702	0.384	2.608	1304	1.329
	14	0.083	1.084	0.304	0.00641	0.3272	0.2838	0.348	2.877	1439	1.033
	16	0.065	1.120	0.242	0.00684	0.3272	0.2932	0.326	3.070	1535	0.823
$1\frac{1}{2}$	10	0.134	1.232	0.575	0.00828	0.3927	0.3225	0.269	3.716	1858	1.955
	12	0.109	1.282	0.476	0.00896	0.3927	0.3356	0.249	4.021	2011	1.618
	14	0.083	1.334	0.370	0.00971	0.3927	0.3492	0.229	4.358	2176	1.258
2	10	0.134	1.732	0.7855	0.0164	0.5236	0.4534	0.136	7.360	3680	2.68
	12	0.109	1.782	0.6475	0.0173	0.5236	0.4665	0.129	7.764	3882	2.22

* From McCabe, Smith, and Harriott, *Unit Operations of Chemical Engineering*, 4th ed., McGraw-Hill, New York, 1985, p. 925; condensed from Perry and Green, *Perry's Chemical Engineers' Handbook*, McGraw-Hill, New York, 1984, pp. 6–42 to 6–44. By permission.

† For steel; for copper, multiply by 1.14; for brass, multiply by 1.06.

PHYSICAL
CONSTANTS,
UNITS AND
CONVERSION
TABLES

TABLE C.1
Physical constants

Gas Constant R in Ideal Gas Law [Eq. (1.1)]

$$R = 1.9872 \text{ cal mol}^{-1} \text{ K}^{-1} = 1.9872 \text{ Btu lb mol}^{-1} {}^\circ\text{R}^{-1}$$

$$= 82.057 \text{ atm cm}^3 \text{ mol}^{-1} \text{ K}^{-1} = 0.082\,057 \text{ atm m}^3 \text{ kmol}^{-1} \text{ K}^{-1}$$

$$= 8.3143 \text{ kJ kmol}^{-1} \text{ K}^{-1} = 8.3143 \text{ kPa m}^3 \text{ kmol}^{-1} \text{ K}^{-1}$$

$$= 0.7302 \text{ atm ft}^3 \text{ lb mol}^{-1} {}^\circ\text{R}^{-1}$$

$$= 10.731 \text{ lb}_f \text{ in.}^{-2} \text{ ft}^3 \text{ lb mol}^{-1} {}^\circ\text{R}^{-1}$$

$$= 1.5453 \times 10^3 \text{ ft lb}_f \text{ lb mol}^{-1} {}^\circ\text{R}^{-1}$$

Atmosphere (standard)

$$p = 1 \text{ atm} = 1.01325 \times 10^5 \text{ N m}^{-2}$$

Avogadro's number*

$$N_{av} = 6.022\,143\,8 \times 10^{23} \text{ molecules mol}^{-1}$$

Base of natural logarithms

$$e = 2.718\,281\,828\,5\ldots$$

Boltzmann's constant

$$k_B = R/N = 1.380 \times 10^{-23} \text{ J molecule}^{-1} \text{ K}^{-1}$$

TABLE C.1
(*continued*)

Gravitational acceleration (sea level)
$$g = 9.806\,65 \text{ m s}^{-2} = 32.1740 \text{ ft s}^{-2}$$

Joule's constant (mechanical equivalent of heat)
$$J_c = 4.184 \times 10^7 \text{ erg cal}^{-1} = 778.16 \text{ ft lb}_f \text{ Btu}^{-1}$$

Pi
$$\pi = 3.141\,592\,653\,6\ldots$$

Planck's constant
$$h = 6.625 \times 10^{-34} \text{ J s molecule}^{-1}$$

Speed of light in a vacuum
$$c = 2.998 \times 10^8 \text{ m s}^{-1}$$

Stefan–Boltzmann constant
$$\sigma = 5.670 \times 10^{-8} \text{ W m}^{-2} \text{ K}^{-4} = 0.1714 \times 10^{-8} \text{ Btu h}^{-1} \text{ ft}^{-2} \,^\circ\text{R}^{-4}$$

* Taylor, B. N., *J. Res. Natl. Bur. Stand.* **90:** 91 (1985).

TABLE C.2
SI base and supplementary quantities and units*

Quantity or "dimension"	SI unit	SI unit symbol ("abbreviation"); Use roman (upright) type
Base quantity or "dimension"		
length	meter	m
mass	kilogram	kg
time	second	s
electric current	ampere	A
thermodynamic temperature	kelvin	K
amount of substance	mole†	mol
luminous intensity	candela	cd
Supplementary quantity or "dimension"		
plane angle	radian	rad
solid angle	steradian	sr

* From Perry and Green, *Perry's Chemical Engineers' Handbook,* 6th ed., McGraw-Hill, New York, 1984, pp. 1–2. By permission.

† When the mole is used, the elementary entities must be specified; they may be atoms, molecules, ions, electrons, other particles, or specified groups of such particles.

TABLE C.3
Derived units of SI with special names*

Quantity	Unit	Symbol	Formula
Frequency (of a periodic phenomenon)	hertz	Hz	s^{-1}
Force	newton	N	$kg\,m\,s^{-2}$
Pressure, stress	pascal	Pa	$N\,m^{-2}$
Energy, work, quantity of heat	joule	J	$N\,m$
Power, radiant flux	watt	W	$J\,s^{-1}$
Quantity of electricity, electric charge	coulomb	C	$A\,s$
Electric potential, potential difference, electromotive force	volt	V	$W\,A^{-1}$
Capacitance	farad	F	$C\,V^{-1}$
Electric resistance	ohm	Ω	$V\,A^{-1}$
Conductance	siemens	S	$A\,V^{-1}$
Magnetic flux	weber	Wb	$V\,s$
Magnetic flux density	tesla	T	$Wb\,m^{-2}$
Inductance	henry	H	$Wb\,A^{-1}$
Luminous flux	lumen	lm	$cd\,sr$
Illuminance	lux	lx	$lm\,m^{-2}$
Activity (of radionuclides)	becquerel	Bq	s^{-1}
Absorbed dose	gray	Gy	$J\,kg^{-1}$

* From Perry and Green, *Perry's Chemical Engineers' Handbook,* 6th ed., McGraw-Hill, New York, 1984, pp. 1–2. By permission.

TABLE C.4
SI prefixes*

Multiplication factor	Prefix	Symbol
$1\,000\,000\,000\,000\,000\,000 = 10^{18}$	exa	E
$1\,000\,000\,000\,000\,000 = 10^{15}$	peta	P
$1\,000\,000\,000\,000 = 10^{12}$	tera	T
$1\,000\,000\,000 = 10^{9}$	giga	G
$1\,000\,000 = 10^{6}$	mega	M
$1\,000 = 10^{3}$	kilo	k
$100 = 10^{2}$	hecto†	h
$10 = 10^{1}$	deka†	da
$0.1 = 10^{-1}$	deci†	d
$0.01 = 10^{-2}$	centi	c
$0.001 = 10^{-3}$	milli	m
$0.000\,001 = 10^{-6}$	micro	μ
$0.000\,000\,001 = 10^{-9}$	nano	n
$0.000\,000\,000\,001 = 10^{-12}$	pico	p
$0.000\,000\,000\,000\,001 = 10^{-15}$	femto	f
$0.000\,000\,000\,000\,000\,001 = 10^{-18}$	atto	a

* From Perry and Green, *Perry's Chemical Engineers' Handbook,* 6th ed., McGraw-Hill, New York, 1984, pp. 1–2. By permission.
† Generally to be avoided

TABLE C.5
Density (or specific volume)

$1 \text{ kg m}^{-3} = 10^{-3} \text{ g cm}^{-3} = 0.06243 \text{ lb}_m \text{ ft}^{-3}$

$1 \text{ g cm}^{-3} = 62.43 \text{ lb}_m \text{ ft}^{-3} = 1000 \text{ kg m}^{-3}$

$\qquad = 8.345 \text{ lb}_m \text{ gal(U.S.)}^{-1}$

$1 \text{ lb}_m \text{ ft}^{-3} = 16.0185 \text{ kg m}^{-3}$

TABLE C.6
Diffusivity

Momentum diffusivity v, thermal
diffusivity α, diffusion coefficient D

$1 \text{ m}^2 \text{ s}^{-1} = 3.875 \times 10^4 \text{ ft}^2 \text{ h}^{-1} = 10.764 \text{ ft}^2 \text{ s}^{-1}$

$\qquad = 10^6 \text{ centistokes (cSt)} = 10^4 \text{ cm s}^{-1}$

TABLE C.7
Force

$1 \text{ kg m s}^{-2} = 1 \text{ N} = 10^5 \text{ dyne (g cm s}^{-2})$

$\qquad = 7.2330 \text{ poundals (lb}_m \text{ ft s}^{-2})$

$\qquad = 0.22481 \text{ lb}_f$

$1 \text{ lb}_f = 4.4482 \text{ N}$

TABLE C.8
Gravitational conversion constant

$g_c = 32.1740 \text{ lb}_m \text{ lb}_f^{-1} \text{ ft s}^{-2}$

$\qquad = 9.80665 \text{ kg}_m \text{ kg}_f^{-1} \text{ m s}^{-1}$

TABLE C.9
Heat capacity (c_p)

$1 \text{ cal(IT) g}^{-1} {}^\circ\text{C}^{-1} = 1 \text{ cal(IT) g}^{-1} \text{ K}^{-1}$

$\qquad = 4.184 \text{ kJ kg}^{-1} \text{ K}^{-1} = 1 \text{ Btu lb}_m^{-1} {}^\circ\text{F}^{-1}$

$\qquad = 1 \text{ Btu lb}_m^{-1} {}^\circ\text{R}^{-1}$

$1 \text{ cal(IT) mol}^{-1} {}^\circ\text{C}^{-1} = 1 \text{ cal(IT) mol}^{-1} \text{ K}^{-1}$

$\qquad = 4.184 \text{ kJ kmol}^{-1} \text{ K}^{-1}$

$\qquad = 1 \text{ Btu lb mol}^{-1} {}^\circ\text{F}^{-1} = 1 \text{ Btu lb mol}^{-1} {}^\circ\text{R}^{-1}$

TABLE C.10
Heat transfer coefficient

$1\,\mathrm{W\,m^{-2}\,K^{-1}} = 1\,\mathrm{kg\,s^{-3}\,K^{-1}}$

$\quad = 0.17611\,\mathrm{Btu\,ft^{-2}\,h^{-1}\,°F^{-1}}$

$\quad = 0.17611\,\mathrm{Btu\,ft^{-2}\,h^{-1}\,°R^{-1}}$

$1\,\mathrm{Btu\,ft^{-2}\,h^{-1}\,°R^{-1}} = 5.6783\,\mathrm{W\,m^{-2}\,K^{-1}}$

$\quad = 5.6783 \times 10^{-4}\,\mathrm{W\,cm^{-2}\,K^{-1}}$

$\quad = 1.3571 \times 10^{-4}\,\mathrm{cal\,cm^{-2}\,s^{-1}\,°C^{-1}}$

TABLE C.11
Length

$1\,\mathrm{m} = 100\,\mathrm{cm} = 10^{6}\,\mathrm{\mu m} = 3.2808\,\mathrm{ft} = 39.37\,\mathrm{in.}$

$1\,\mathrm{\mu m} = 1\,\mathrm{micron}$

$1\,\mathrm{in.} = 2.540\,\mathrm{cm} = 0.02540\,\mathrm{m}$

$1\,\mathrm{\mathring{A}\ (Angstrom)} = 10^{-10}\,\mathrm{m} = 10\,\mathrm{nm}$

$1\,\mathrm{mile} = 5280\,\mathrm{ft}$

TABLE C.12
Mass

$1\,\mathrm{kg} = 1000\,\mathrm{g} = 2.2046\,\mathrm{lb_m}$

$1\,\mathrm{lb_m} = 16\,\mathrm{oz} = 7000\,\mathrm{grains} = 453.59\,\mathrm{g}$

$\quad = 0.45359\,\mathrm{kg}$

$1\,\mathrm{ton\ (short)} = 2000\,\mathrm{lb_m}$

$1\,\mathrm{ton\ (long)} = 2240\,\mathrm{lb_m}$

$1\,\mathrm{ton\ (metric)} = 1000\,\mathrm{kg}$

TABLE C.13
Mass transfer coefficient

$1\,\mathrm{kg\,m^{-2}\,s^{-1}} = 0.1\,\mathrm{g\,cm^{-2}\,s^{-1}}$

$\quad = 0.20482\,\mathrm{lb_m\,ft^{-2}\,s^{-1}}$

$\quad = 6.3659 \times 10^{-3}\,\mathrm{lb_f\,ft^{-3}\,s}$

$\quad = 737.34\,\mathrm{lb_m\,ft^{-2}\,h^{-1}}$

$1\,\mathrm{lb_m\,ft^{-2}\,h^{-1}} = 1.3562 \times 10^{-3}\,\mathrm{kg\,m^{-2}\,s^{-1}}$

$\quad = 2.7778 \times 10^{-4}\,\mathrm{lb_m\,ft^{-2}\,s^{-1}}$

TABLE C.14
Power

$1\,\text{W} = 1\,\text{J s}^{-1} = 0.23901\,\text{cal s}^{-1}$
$\qquad = 14.340\,\text{cal min}^{-1} = 3.4122\,\text{Btu h}^{-1}$
$1\,\text{hp} = 550\,\text{ft lb}_f\,\text{s}^{-1} = 745.70\,\text{W}$
$\qquad = 0.7068\,\text{Btu s}^{-1}$
$1\,\text{Btu h}^{-1} = 0.29307\,\text{W}$

TABLE C.15
Pressure or momentum flux or shear stress

$1 \times 10^5\,\text{N m}^{-2} = 1 \times 10^5\,\text{Pa (Pascal)} = 1\,\text{bar}$
$1\,\text{atm} = 1.01325 \times 10^5\,\text{N m}^{-2} = 101.325\,\text{kPa}$
$\qquad = 1.01325\,\text{bar} = 14.696\,\text{lb}_f\,\text{in.}^{-2}\,\text{(psi)}$
$\qquad = 760\,\text{Torr} = 760\,\text{mm Hg (0°C)}$
$\qquad = 29.921\,\text{in Hg (0°C)}$
$\qquad = 33.90\,\text{ft H}_2\text{O (4°C)}$
$1\,\text{N m}^{-2} = 1\,\text{kg m}^{-1}\,\text{s}^{-2}$
$\qquad = 10\,\text{dyne cm}^{-2}\,(\text{g cm}^{-1}\,\text{s}^{-2})$
$\qquad = 9.8692 \times 10^{-6}\,\text{atm}$

TABLE C.16
Thermal conductivity

$1\,\text{W m}^{-1}\,\text{K}^{-1} = 0.57779\,\text{Btu h}^{-1}\,\text{ft}^{-1}\,°\text{F}^{-1}$
$\qquad = 2.3901 \times 10^{-3}\,\text{cal s}^{-1}\,\text{cm}^{-1}\,\text{K}^{-1}$
$1\,\text{Btu h}^{-1}\,\text{ft}^{-1}\,°\text{F}^{-1} = 1.73073\,\text{W m}^{-1}\,\text{K}^{-1}$
$\qquad = 1.73073 \times 10^5\,\text{g cm s}^{-3}\,\text{K}^{-1}$
$\qquad\qquad (\text{erg s}^{-1}\,\text{cm}^{-1}\,\text{K}^{-1})$
$\qquad = 4.1365 \times 10^{-3}\,\text{cal s}^{-1}\,\text{cm}^{-1}\,°\text{C}^{-1}$
$\qquad = 6.9546\,\text{lb}_m\,\text{ft s}^{-3}\,°\text{F}^{-1}$
$\qquad = 0.21616\,\text{lb}_f\,\text{s}^{-1}\,°\text{F}^{-1}$

TABLE C.17
Viscosity

$$1 \text{ kg m}^{-1} \text{s}^{-1} = 1 \text{ N s m}^{-2} = 1 \text{ Pa s} = 1000 \text{ cP}$$
$$= 10 \text{ P (poise)} = 0.67197 \text{ lb}_m \text{ ft}^{-1} \text{s}^{-1}$$
$$1 \text{ cP} = 10^{-2} \text{ g cm}^{-1} \text{s}^{-1} \text{ (poise)}$$
$$= 10^{-3} \text{ kg m}^{-1} \text{s}^{-1} = 2.4191 \text{ lb}_m \text{ ft}^{-1} \text{h}^{-1}$$
$$= 6.7197 \times 10^{-4} \text{ lb}_m \text{ ft}^{-1} \text{s}^{-1}$$
$$= 2.0886 \times 10^{-5} \text{ lb}_f \text{ s ft}^{-2}$$
$$1 \text{ lb}_m \text{ ft}^{-1} \text{s}^{-1} = 14.882 \text{ P}$$
$$= 1.4882 \text{ kg m}^{-1} \text{s}^{-1} = 3.1081 \times 10^{-2} \text{ lb}_f \text{ s ft}^{-2}$$
$$= 1.4882 \times 10^3 \text{ cP} = 3600 \text{ lb}_m \text{ ft}^{-1} \text{h}^{-1}$$

TABLE C.18
Volume

$$1 \text{ m}^3 = 10^6 \text{ cm}^3 = 10^3 \text{ L (liter)}$$
$$= 264.17 \text{ gal(U.S.)} = 35.316 \text{ ft}^3$$
$$1 \text{ ft}^3 = 28.317 \text{ L} = 0.028317 \text{ m}^3$$
$$= 7.481 \text{ gal(U.S.)}$$
$$1 \text{ gal(U.S.)} = 4 \text{ qt} = 3.7854 \text{ L}$$
$$= 3.7854 \times 10^3 \text{ cm}^3 = 0.8327 \text{ gal(British)}$$

TABLE C.19
Work, energy, and torque

$$1 \text{ J} = 1 \text{ N m} = 1 \text{ kg m}^2 \text{s}^{-2} = 0.23901 \text{ cal}$$
$$= 10^7 \text{ g cm}^2 \text{s}^{-2} \text{ (erg)} = 23.730 \text{ lb}_m \text{ ft}^2 \text{s}^{-2}$$
$$= 0.73756 \text{ ft lb}_f = 9.4783 \times 10^{-4} \text{ Btu}$$
$$= 3.7251 \times 10^{-7} \text{ hp h} = 2.7778 \times 10^{-7} \text{ kW h}$$
$$1 \text{ Btu} = 1.05506 \text{ kJ}$$
$$= 252.16 \text{ cal (thermochemical)}$$
$$= 778.16 \text{ ft lb}_f$$
$$= 3.9301 \times 10^{-4} \text{ hp h}$$
$$= 2.9307 \times 10^{-4} \text{ kW h}$$
$$1 \text{ cal} = 4.1840 \text{ J} = 3.9657 \times 10^{-3} \text{ Btu}$$
$$= 1.1622 \times 10^{-6} \text{ kW h}$$
$$1 \text{ ft lb}_f = 1.3558 \text{ J} = 0.32405 \text{ cal}$$
$$= 1.2851 \times 10^{-3} \text{ Btu}$$
$$1 \text{ hp h} = 0.7457 \text{ kW h} = 2544.5 \text{ Btu}$$
$$= 6.4162 \times 10^5 \text{ cal}$$
$$= 1.9800 \times 10^6 \text{ ft lb}_f$$

TABLE C.20
Miscellaneous

---

1 ft lb_f lb_m^{-1} = 2.9890 J kg^{-1}

Molecular weight of air: 28.966 kg $kmol^{-1}$

Molecular weight of water: 18.01534 kg $kmol^{-1}$

100°C = 211.9°F

273.15 K = 0.0°C = 491.67°R = 32.00°F

0.0°F = 459.67°R = 255.37 K = −17.78°C

APPENDIX
D

VECTOR MATHEMATICS

This Appendix is adapted from Brodkey, *Phenomena of Fluid Motions,* Addison-Wesley, Reading, MA, 1967. (Fourth printing available from The Ohio State University Bookstores, Columbus, Ohio, 43210.) By permission.

D.1 INTRODUCTION

In the study of transport phenomena, the physical quantities to be considered, such as temperature, velocity, and shear stress, are scalar, vector, and tensor quantities, respectively. In dealing with these quantities the convenient shorthand vector and Cartesian tensor notation can be used to advantage. To ignore this tool would necessitate the use of a number of long, cumbersome equations in various coordinate systems when a single vector equation would suffice. For this reason, a summary of the necessary mathematics is provided here.

D.2 SCALAR QUANTITIES AND VECTORS

Scalar quantities are numbers which may be dimensional or dimensionless. They are physical quantities which do not require direction in space for their

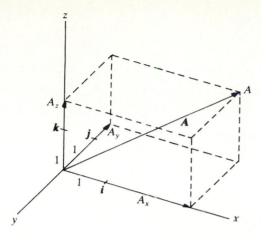

FIGURE D.1
Vector A in Cartesian coordinate space.

complete specification. Volume, density, viscosity, mass, and energy are examples of scalars.

Vector quantities need both magnitude and direction for their complete specification. Velocity and linear momentum are two good examples. *Speed* is the magnitude of the velocity vector and is a scalar quantity. Geometrically, a vector can be represented by a straight arrow in the direction of the vector, with its magnitude being shown by the length of the arrow compared to some chosen scale. Analytically, a vector can be represented by its projections on the coordinate axes (see Figs. D.1, D.2, and D.3). If i, j, and k are taken as unit vectors (magnitude unity) in the x, y, and z directions, then

$$A = iA_x + jA_y + kA_z \tag{D.1}$$

$$A = |A| = \sqrt{A_x^2 + A_y^2 + A_z^2} \tag{D.2}$$

The sum and difference of vectors can be obtained either geometrically or analytically. Geometrically, vectors are added by drawing the diagonal on a parallelogram constructed from the two vectors to be added. Analytically, the components of the vectors are added and the result is the new vector. One can

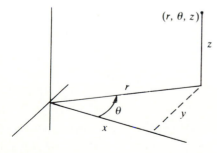

FIGURE D.2
Cylindrical coordinate system.

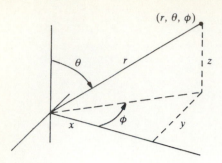

FIGURE D.3
Spherical coordinate system.

use the vector notation instead of a complicated coordinate notation for obtaining relations between variables.

D.3 TENSORS

When there is a change in the coordinate system, tensors must follow certain transformation laws. If an array obeys these transformation laws, then we may manipulate it by means of tensor algebra, which is simply a method of performing a number of proved operations (addition, differentiation, etc.) on the symbols used to represent the array. The use of tensor notation substitutes a symbol for the array; any operation on the symbol must be performed exactly as though we were performing an analogous operation on the array.

Scalars are tensors of zero order, and vectors are tensors of the first order. The second-order tensor is an array of nine components expressed as

$$\boldsymbol{\tau} = \begin{pmatrix} \tau_{xx} & \tau_{xy} & \tau_{xz} \\ \tau_{yx} & \tau_{yy} & \tau_{yz} \\ \tau_{zx} & \tau_{zy} & \tau_{zz} \end{pmatrix} = \tau_{ij}. \tag{D.3}$$

The rows are associated with the i's and the columns with the j's. The tensor array is an ordered set of numbers (but is not a determinant, which is a certain sum and products of the numbers). The diagonal terms are those in which the two subscripts are the same; all others are the nondiagonal terms. If $\tau_{xy} = \tau_{yz}$, $\tau_{xz} = \tau_{zx}$, and $\tau_{yz} = \tau_{zy}$, then the tensor is symmetrical.

The transposed tensor of τ is τ^{T} and is formed by exchanging the rows and columns.

APPENDIX
E

COMPUTER
PROGRAMS

TABLE E.1
Index of computer programs

AUTHOR
INDEX

818

SUBJECT INDEX

Citations of a generic nature are indexed only to the first and other major locations, not every time the name appears, e.g., Reynolds as in Reynolds number.